SOURCE BOOK AND BIBLIO-GRAPHICAL GUIDE FOR AMERICAN CHURCH HISTORY

BY

PETER G. MODE, A.M., Ph.D.

Assistant Professor of Church History in
The Divinity School of
The University of Chicago

Boston 20, Massachusetts 02120

J. S. CANNER & COMPANY INC.

1964

THE BAILEY PRESS
BOSTON, MASSACHUSETTS 02114

PREFACE

Through the publication of several source collections, much has been done to assist the student of American political, social and economic history. But no corresponding assistance has been given to such as are interested in the more specifically religious history of our nation. It is true of course, that for the colonial period, political history to a considerable degree resolves itself into the religious and that, therefore, the source books already published contain much material that is serviceable to the church historian. For the national period, however, with its multiplication of church organization, its controversies and divisions, its nation-wide revivals, and its missionary extension at home and abroad, no source material has been assembled for convenient access. Hence the publication of this volume, which within the briefest possible space embodies the most significant documents for the entire field of American church history.

The compiler wishes to state that the viewpoint from which he has approached the subject is that of regarding the church, not as the custodian of some divinely-revealed deposit of truth, nor as supernaturally detached from an environment that is ever affecting her inner life and organization. In his selection of material he has been guided by the principle of choosing only such documents as most significantly set forth the contribution that the church has made to the progress of American society, and the manner in which from time to time she has adjusted herself to her new and changing environment. Denominationalism, therefore, has been relegated to the background. Ardent denominationalists will find their respective bodies recognized only in so far as these have played a strategic part in the development of American Christianity as a whole. The only exception is that in the case of some small but significant groups, material has been inserted to remove prevailing ignorance or misconception.

In the matter of bibliography, it has seemed wise to supplement the information set forth in the compilations of Samuel M. Jackson and the several volumes of the American Church History Series. Not to emphasize the denominational horizon within which most of this bibliographical work was done, it is now almost a quarter of a century since even the latest appeared. Much has been published in the meantime which now calls for classification and appraisal. It will be noticed that the bibliographies are restricted to printed material, with a slight exception of a few dissertations inserted for the convenience of University of Chicago students, who may be pursuing historical work in the classes of the compiler. Newspaper material has had to be omitted. Its insertion, however valuable, would have made the. volume far too bulky for convenient handling. Bibliographical matter has been classified not alphabetically, nor in the order of importance, but chronologically. This method, while admittedly defective in some respects, has been adopted as the least objectionable. Painstaking labor has been taken to secure accuracy and comprehensiveness. It will not be surprising, however, if investigative experts in small sections of the field will find omissions. But it is hoped that the bibliographical apparatus will be of real service in speedily acquainting the student with the most significant literature bearing upon the subject under his investigation.

It only remains to express the hope that through its chapter analysis this work may prove suggestive to instructors in their class-room presentation of American religious history, and that its scientific spirit may have some part in stimulating the interdenominational co-operation that augurs so hopefully for the increasing efficiency of our American churches.

PETER G. MODE

Divinity School, University of Chicago,
  September 1st, 1920.

TABLE OF CONTENTS

CHAPTER I

Selected Bibliography of General Histories

CHAPTER II

Virginia in the Seventeenth Century

CHAPTER III

Maryland in the Seventeenth Century

CHAPTER VIII

NEW YORK IN THE COLONIAL PERIOD

CHAPTER XIII

EPISCOPALIANISM IN THE EIGHTEENTH CENTURY

CHAPTER XIV

PRESBYTERIANISM IN THE EIGHTEENTH CENTURY

CHAPTER XX

THE RISE OF UNITARIANISM AND UNIVERSALISM

CHAPTER XXVII
THE DISRUPTION OF THE CHURCHES

CHAPTER XXVIII
THE CHURCHES AND THE CIVIL WAR

CHAPTER XXIX

SINCE THE CIVIL WAR

CHAPTER I

SELECTED BIBLIOGRAPHY OF GENERAL HISTORIES

In entering upon a study of the church in American society, the investigator should early acquaint himself with the standard general histories. So frequently must these works be used to provide the necessary background for church history proper, that it seems wise in an introductory chapter to make mention of the most significant. In the bibliographies of all later chapters it will then be assumed that the student has this necessary acquaintance with the general works, and repeated reference thereto will be regarded as superfluous.

One of the earliest workers was James Grahame, whose "History of the United States of North America, from the Plantation of the British Colonies till Their Assumption of National Independence", commenced in 1824 and completed after eleven years of assiduous research, although treated so indifferently by the reviewers of his time, has since passed into merited appreciation for its judicial impartiality and thoroughness. Regarding 'religion as the great business of life and the extension of its influence as one of the appropriate objects of history,' his work shows a sympathy for issues deeper than the political and economic. With a perseverance surpassing Grahame, George Bancroft after fifty-two years of labor upon the field of colonial history, published his last revised "History of the United States of America, from the Discovery of the Continent" (VI vols. 1883-5), a work that altho biased and antiquated, for graceful diction and exhaustive information, established standards of which all American scholars have been justly proud. Meanwhile Richard Hildreth, beginning about the middle of the century, had produced "The History of the United States of America" (VI vols. 1849-1856, revised edition 1882), an accurate study covering the field 1497-1789 in the first three volumes, which he issued as a completed set, later supplementing these with vols. IV–VI, which cover the field to 1821. A contemporaneous worker was Rev. Edward D. Neill who in "The English Colonization of America during the Seventeenth Century" (1870) stressed the religious aspects of colonization and called attention to minor inaccuracies in the work of Bancroft. Five years later

1

appeared "The Constitutional and Political History of the United States" by Dr. Hermann von Holst (translated from the German by J. J. Lalor and A. B. Mason), whose substantial work represents the detachment of a foreigner with the intimate knowledge of a five year residence in America. His investigations cover the field 1750-1861, and convey much information to the student of church history.

In the next decade a monumental work appeared under the editorship of Justin Winsor, entitled a "Narrative and Critical History of America" (VIII vols, 1884-1889). Prepared by a corps of wide-awake scholars, this history presented the conclusions of latest research, an exhaustive bibliographical apparatus, and withal an interesting narrative of events. It remains to this day one of the most reliable guides to the diligent student. It was about the same time that James Schouler began (1880) to publish his thoughtful and independent studies upon the national period terminated (1913) in a VII-volume "History of the United States of America Under the Constitution" which covers the period 1783-1877. A contemporary "History of the People of the United States, from the Revolution to the Civil War" (VIII vols. 1882-1913) by John Bach McMaster, provides an intensive study with considerable emphasis on the social and economic, of the period from 1784 to 1861. The "English Colonies in America" (V vols. 1882-1907) by John A. Doyle, altho marred by occasional inaccuracies, is an invaluable interpretation of the colonial period, especially in its social and political aspects. "The American Colonies in the Seventeenth Century" (III vols. 1904-1907) by Herbert L. Osgood as an 'introduction to American institutional history . . . to illustrate the principles of British colonization,' is important for the church historian, although subordinate to Doyle's work. "A Short History of the English Colonies in America" (1881, revised ed. 1902) by H. C. Lodge gives a good account of the colonies on the eve of the Revolution. A "History of the United States" (II vols. 1894) by E. Benjamin Andrews, seeks in abbreviated form to give the 'political evolution of our country on the one hand, and the social culture, habits and life of the people on the other'. Its clear arrangement and fine sense of proportion make it a useful short history of America. "A History of the American People" (V vols. 1902) by Woodrow Wilson is a gracefully written and popular presentation of the subject. The next work is the notable "The American Nation, A History from Original Sources by Associated Scholars" edited by Albert Bushnell Hart, advised by various historical societies, (XXVII vols. 1904-1908). Thoroughly abreast of the latest results of critical investigation, interestingly written, with copious bibliographical essays, this work is indispensable to the church historian. Although a few volumes have more political details than are needed by the student of the church, this work as a whole should never be overlooked for all periods of the field. "The American People. A Study in National Psychology" (II vols. 1909-1911) by A. Maurice Low is a work of marked originality with a number of interpretations that cannot be taken seriously. "A History of the United States" (IV vols. 1905-1917, Vol. V, 1921) by Edward Channing, for conciseness, proportion, matured conclusions, and completeness of bibliographical apparatus, is a model history and undoubtedly the best of the shorter histories. A succinct scholarly restatement has recently appeared in "The Riverside History of the United States" (IV vols. 1915) edited and written in part by William E. Dodd, associated with Carl Becker, Allen Johnson, and Fred L. Paxson.

Turning to church histories, the earliest survey was "A Narrative of the Visit to the American Churches by the Deputation from the Congregational Union of England and Wales" (II vols. 1835) by Andrew Reed and James Matheson. A corresponding work, with emphasis upon Baptist activities, was "The Baptists in America; A Narrative of the Deputation from the Baptist Union in England to the United States and Canada" (1836) by the Rev. F. A. Cox and Rev. J. Hobey. Although both of these works are denominational in their sympathies and represent observations based on short residences in America, they contain a considerable amount of useful general information. The next worker was Robert Baird who while resident in Europe had been requested by his European friends to write a description of things in America. In response, he published (1842) his "Religion in America; or, an Account of The Origin, Relation to the State, and Present Condition of the Evangelical Churches in the United States, with Notices of the Unevangelical Denominations." The revised edition (1856) has a large amount of supplementary material. The work as a whole is valuable especially its treatment of the voluntary system and of the relations between the various governments and the churches The last part of the book stresses the missionary activities of American christianity. A shorter work entitled "State and Prospects of Religion in America" (1855) by the same writer, is a Report given at the Evangelical Alliance conference, Paris, August 25, 1855, of the American church at that date. Somewhat earlier (1844) "An Original History of the Religious Denominations at present existing in the United States, containing authentic accounts of their Rise, Progress, Statistics and

Doctrines, Written Expressly by Theological Professors, Ministers and Lay Members of the Respective Denominations" projected, compiled and arranged by I. Daniel Rupp was published. This work is a jungle of ill-arranged material, and serves little purpose.

The centennial of the Union was marked by considerable retrospection on the part of the various denominations, and consequently the leading religious periodicals such as "The Baptist Quarterly," "The New Englander," "The Methodist Quarterly Review," and "The Presbyterian Quarterly and Princeton Review," published notable articles reviewing the centennial achievements of their respective denominations. These articles have considerable historical material. There next appeared "Christianity in the United States, from the First Settlement down to the Present Time" (1887) by Daniel Dorchester. In point of massive information this volume is important. Its arrangement, however, is so hopelessly bad that its use is a continual strain on the good nature of the reader.

The great dearth of good church histories at last being recognized by American scholars, led to the production of the "American Church History Series" (XIII Vols. 1892 f.) published under the auspices of the American Society of Church History. With few exceptions these volumes maintain a high standard of scholarship. In the nature of the case they have suffered considerably from necessary condensation. Sectarianism has been fairly well eliminated. Good bibliographies appear in most of the volumes. The XIIIth volume, by Leonard W. Bacon, entitled "A History of American Christianity" is by far the best general work in existence. It should be read as an introduction to the study of American church history.

Two other monographs, while not to be technically classed as church history, serve an important place as introductory studies—"Church and State in the United States, or, The American Idea of Religious Liberty and its Practical Effects, with Official Documents" by Philip Schaff, D.D. ("Papers of the American Historical Association," Vol. II, No. IV), and "The Rise of Religious Liberty in America—A History" (1902) by Sanford H. Cobb. A brief survey is "The Movement and Mission of American Christianity" ("American Journal of Theology;" January 1912) by David S. Schaff.

CHAPTER II

VIRGINIA IN THE SEVENTEENTH CENTURY

Bibliography

The motives underlying Virginian colonization are to be seen in Robert Thorne's "Declaration" (1527—Hakluyt "Principal Navigations" extra series, Vol. II p. 159 f.); George Peckham's "The Western Planting" (1583—*ibid.* Vol. VIII, p. 89 f.); Christopher Carlile's "Discourse" (1583—*ibid.* Vol. VIII, p. 133 f.); such sermons as Robert Johnson's "Nova Britannia" (1609—Force, "Tracts and Papers," Vol. I, Tract VI) and William Symond's "Virginea Britannia" (1609–partial reprint, Brown's "Genesis of the United States" Vol. I p. 283 f.); "A True and Sincere Declaration of the Purpose and Ends of the Plantation begun in Virginia . . . " (1609—*ibid.* Vol. I, p. 339 f.); and Alexander Whitaker's "Good Newes From Virginia, . . ." (1613—for extracts see Neill's "History of the Virginia Company of London," p. 78 f.)

Two notable studies on Virginian colonization are "British Convicts Shipped to American Colonies" by James D. Butler, ("Amer. Hist. Rev." Vol. II, No. 1), and "Some English Conditions Surrounding the Settlement of Virginia" by Edward P. Cheyney (*ibid.* Vol. XII, No. 3).

The early fortunes of the Jamestown group have been set forth by Captain Smith in a "True Relation, . . . " (1608); "A Map of Virginia, . . . " (1612); a "Description of New England, . . . " (1616); "New England's Trials" (1620-22), and "The General History of Virginia" (1624). These may be found in No. 16 of the English Scholar's Library, under the title, "Captain John Smith's Works,"(1889), edited by Edward Arber. This volume also contains Percy's "Discourse on the Plantation of the Southern Colony in Virginia, . . . " (1607); Wingfield's "Discourse of Virginia" (1608, see also "Tran. & Coll. Amer. Antiq. Soc., Vol. IV, p. 69 f.); and Spelman's "Relation of Virginea" (1613?). John Rolf's "Relation of the State of Virginia, . . . " (later than 1616) is accessible in "The Virginia Historical Register," Vol. I, No. III

Narratives that throw light upon later periods of the century are: "A Perfect Description of Virginia" (1648--Force, "Tracts and Papers,"

Vol. II, Tract VIII); "A Voyage to Virginia" by Colonel Norwood (1649—*ibid.*, Vol. III, Tract X); John Hammond's "Leah and Rachel, or the Two Fruitful Sisters of Virginia and Maryland" (1656—*ibid.* Vol. III, Tract XIV); "Virginia's Cure, . . . " by R. G. (1662—*ibid.*, Vol. III, Tract XV); Sir William Berkeley's "Discourse and View of Virginia" (1663—Sabin's "Dictionary" Vol. II p. 4889); "The History of Bacon's and Ingram's Rebellion," (1676c., author unknown); "A True Narrative of the Late Rebellion in Virginia by the Royal Commissioners, 1677" (both reprinted in "Narratives of the Insurrections 1675-1690" edited 1915 by C. M. Andrews in "Original Narratives of Early American History"); "The Beginning, Progress and Conclusion of Bacon's Rebellion in Virginia in the Years 1675 and 1676" by T. M. (Force, "Tracts and Papers," Vol. I, Tract VIII; also Andrews as above).

Of Virginian histories there are several. Robert Beverley's pioneer "History and Present State of Virginia" (1705) is brief and informing, but partisan. It was followed by Sir William Keith's "History of Virginia" (1738) which shows little originality. Nine years later Rev. William Stith published his incomplete (to 1624) and inelegant yet broadly philosophic "History of the Present Discovery and Settlement of Virginia." John Buck followed with a tediously lengthy four volume "History of Virginia" (1804-1816). Next appeared Howison's "History of Virginia" (Vol. I, 1846, coming to 1763; Vol. II to 1847), a work rhetorical, and not always trustworthy. Charles Campbell's "History of the Colony and Ancient Dominion of Virginia" (1860) though faulty in arrangement is a work of intrinsic value. "Virginia and her Neighbors" (1897) written in the fascinating style characteristic of John Fiske does not materially supplement the information of earlier writers.

Besides histories there are several notable monographs. "The History of the Virginia Company of London" (1869) by Rev. E. D. Neill is valuable for its source material, as also the same author's "Virginia Carolorum" (1888) which treats of the later period 1625-1688. His "English Colonization of America during the Seventeenth Century" (1870) has considerable data bearing upon ecclesiastical affairs. In Alexander Brown's "Genesis of the United States" (1890) there is a large amount of documentary material for the church historian. His "First Republic in America" (1897) continuing the narrative from 1616 to 1627 has fewer source quotations. In "Local Institutions of Virginia" (J. H. U. Studies, Series III, Sect. II-III) Edward Ingle describes the

English parish regime as applied to Virginia. Within recent years work of an exceedingly high order has been done by Philip A. Bruce. His "Economic History of Virginia in the Seventeenth Century" (II vols. 1896), "Social Life of Virginia in the Seventeenth Century" (1907), and notably his "Institutional History of Virginia in the Seventeenth Century" (II vols. 1910) are indispensable to a grasp of Virginian church history. "Virginia Under the Stuarts, 1607–1688" (1914) by T. J. Wertenbaker and "Colonial Virginia: Its People and Customs" (1917) by May Stanard throw light upon the social background.

William and Mary College has been treated by Lyon G. Tyler in "The History of the College of William and Mary . . . from its Foundation, 1660, to 1874." Miscellaneous information appears in the "William and Mary College Quarterly." The Henrico experiment is discussed by John S. Flory in "The University of Henrico" ("Pub. South. Hist. Assoc.," Vol. VIII, pp. 40-56). The documents are in the "Abstract of the Proceedings of the Virginia Company of London 1619-1624" ("Coll. Virg. Hist. Soc.," New Series, Vol. VII). "Education in Colonial Virginia" by L. G. Tyler (IV Parts, "William and Mary Quarterly," April 1897 to January 1898) meets an important need as a study of the cultural side of Virginian life.

In the field of church history proper, the Rev. F. L. Hawks has the honor of being the "First Historiographer of the American Church." Vol. I of his "Contributions to the Ecclesiastical History of the United States of America" (1836-1839) has much material relating to Virginia. Bishop Samuel Wilberforce's "History of the Protestant Church in America" (1844, third edition 1856) betrays the lack of sympathy of one who never visited or lived in America. "The History of the Church of England in the Colonies" (III vols. 1848, second edition 1856) by Canon J. S. M. Anderson, though erudite is uncritical and antiquated. A work of genuine scholarship excellently written is that of Rev. W. S. Perry, "The History of the American Episcopal Church 1587-1883" (II vols. 1885). The "History of the American Episcopal Church' from the Planting of the Colonies to the end of the Civil War," (1890) by Rev. S. D. McConnell though brilliantly written, scarcely maintains the high standard of its immediate predecessor. In his contribution to the "American Church History Series" (Vol. VII, 2nd edition 1900) Prof. C. C. Tiffany has written "A History of the Protestant Episcopal Church in the United States of America," which in small compass and with considerable interest presents the salient features of Anglicanism.

For the Quakers one should consult the "Journals" of John Fox and Edmundson, also the standard histories of Quakerism (see page 154f).

For investigative purposes, documentary material for the period 1650 and later is to be found in "Historical Collections Relating to the American Colonial Church" (Vol. I, 1870) by Rev. W. S. Perry. Clergy lists, Proceedings, etc. appear in the "Digest of the Proceedings of the Conventions and Councils in the Diocese of Virginia" (1883) by T. D. Dashiell, D.D. Virginian statutes and charter material are accessible in W. W. Hening's "Statutes at Large" (1812). Assembly Proceedings are set forth in "Journals of the House of Burgesses in Virginia," Vol. I, 1619-1658/9, Vol. II, 1659-60 to 1693, edited (1914-1915) by H. R. McIlwaine. "An Abstract of the Proceedings of the Virginia Company of London, 1619-1624" is reprinted in the "Coll. Virg. Hist. Soc.," New Series, Vol. VII. "The Records of the Virginia Company of London" (Vol. I, 1619-1622; Vol. II, 1622-1624) have recently (1906) been edited with introduction and bibliography by Susan M. Kingsbury. Important data may be gleaned from the "Aspinwall Papers" ("Coll. Mass. Hist. Soc.," Series, IV, Vols. IX and X); "The Calendar of State Papers, Colonial Series" (1860-1916) and the "Reports of the Historical Commission," especially the third and eighth.

In certain lines of investigation the student will be well repaid by consulting the parish registers and vestry books—St. Mark's, Culpepper County; St. Peter's, New Kent County; Henrico; Christ Church, Middlesex County; Bristol; and others. County records are more abundant—Elizabeth City, Essex, Henrico, Isle of Wight, Lancaster, Lower Norfolk, Middlesex, Norfolk, Northampton, Northumberland, Rappanhannock, Richmond, Surry, Westmoreland, and York. Particularly rich is the "Lower Norfolk County Virginia Antiquary" (V vols. 1897-1906). "The Virginia Magazine of History" (1893 f.) is a mine that rarely disappoints a careful worker. The "Publications of the Southern History Association" (1897-1907) have some material relating to the church. The "William and Mary College Quarterly" (1892 f.) ofttimes supplies valuable ecclesiastical data, also the "Collections of the Virginia Historical Society." Miscellaneous information may be picked up in Rev. W. Meade's "Old Churches, Ministers, and Families of Virginia" (1857); Rev. E. D. Neill's "Notes on the Virginia Colonial Clergy" (1877); also his "Memoir of Rev. Patrick Copland" (1871); Rev. L. W. Burton's "Annals of Henrico Parish, 1611-1884" (1904), and the "New England Historical and Genealogical Register."

Documents

I. *CONSTITUTIONAL PROVISION FOR RELIGION*

The following appears among "Articles, Instructions and Orders" dated Nov. 20, 1606:

. . . And wee doe specially ordaine, charge, and require, the said presidents and councells, and the ministers of the said several colonies respectively, within their several limits and precincts, that they, with all diligence, care, and respect, doe provide, that the true word, and service of God and Christian faith be preached, planted, and used, not only within every of the said several colonies, and plantations, but alsoe as much as they may amongst the salvage people, which doe or shall adjoine unto them, or border upon them, according to the doctrine, rights, and religion now professed and established within our realme of England. . . . Furthermore, our will, and pleasure is, and wee doe hereby determine and ordaine, that every person and persons being our subjects of every the said collonies and plantations shall from time to time well entreate those salvages in those parts, and use all good meanes to draw the salvages and heathen people of the said several places, and of the territories and countries adjoining to the true service and knowledge of God, and that all just, kind and charitable courses, shall be holden with such of them as shall conforme themselves to any good and sociable traffique and dealing with the subjects of us, our heires and successors, which shall be planted there, whereby they may be the sooner drawne to the true knowledge of God, and the obedience of us, our heires, and successors, under such severe paines and punishments, as shall be inflicted by the same several presidents and councells of the said several colonies, or the most part of them within their several limits and precincts, on such as shall offend therein, or doe the contrary. . . .

Text—Hening: *Statutes at Large*, Vol. I, pp. 67-75.

II. *THE MOTIVE IN COLONIZATION*

*"A True and Sincere Declaration of the Purpose and Ends of the
Plantation begun in Virginia."*

This document appeared in London, December 14, 1609, by authority of the Governor and Councillors of Virginia.

The Principal and *Maine Endes* (out of which are easily derived to any meane understanding infinitnesse, and yet great ones) were *first* to preach and baptize into *Christian Religion*, and by propagation of the *Gospell*, to recover out of the armes of the Divell, a number of poore and miserable soules, wrapt up unto death, in almost invincible *ignorance;* to endeavour the fulfilling, and accomplishment of the number of the elect, which shall be gathered from out all corners of the earth; and to add our myte to the Treasury of Heaven, that as we pray for the coming of the Kingdome of Glory, so to expresse in our actions, the same desire, if God, have pleased, to use so weak instruments, to the ripening and consummation thereof.

Secondly, to provide and build up for the publike *Honour* and *Safety* of our *gratious King* and his *Estates* (by the favor of our Superiors even in that care) some small

Rampier of our owne, in this opportune and general summer of peace, by transplanting the rancknesse·and multitude of increase in our people; of which there is left no vent, but age; and evident danger that the number and infinitenesse of them, will outgrow the matter, whereon to worke for their life and sustention, and shall one infest and become a burthen to another. . . .

Lastly, the appearance and assurance of *Private commodity* to the *particular undertakers,* by recovering and possessing to themselves a fruitfull land, whence they may furnish and provide this Kingdome, with all such necessities and defects under which we labour, and are now enforced to buy, and receive at the curtesie of other Princes, under the burthen of great Customs, and heavy impositions, and at so high rates in trafique, by reason of the great waste of them from whence they are now derived, which threatens almost an impossibility long to recover them, or at least such losse in exchange, as both the Kingdome and Merchant, will be weary of the deerenesse and peril.

Text—Brown: *The Genesis of the United States,* Vol. I, pp. 339-40.

III. *BEGINNINGS OF WORSHIP AT JAMESTOWN*

Captain Smith in *"Advertisements For the Unexperienced Planters of New England or anywhere,"* written October 1630, thus recalls the early days:

"When I went first to Virginia, I well remember wee did hang an awning (which is an old saile) to three or foure trees to shadow us from the Sunne, our walles were rales of wood, our seats unhewed trees till we cut plankes, our Pulpit a bar of wood nailed to two neighbouring trees. In foule weather we shifted into an old rotten tent; for we had few better, and this came by the way of adventure for new. This was our Church, till wee built a homely thing like a barne, set upon Cratchets, covered with rafts, sedge, and earth; so was also the walls: the best of our houses [were] of the like curiosity; but the most part farre much worse workmanship, that could neither well defend [from] wind nor raine.

Yet wee had daily Common Prayer morning and evening, every Sunday two Sermons, and every three moneths the holy Communion, till our Minister died: but our Prayers daily, with an Homily on Sundaies, we continued two or three years after till more Preachers came: and surely God did most mercifully heare us, till the continuall inundations of mistaking directions, factions, and numbers of unprovided Libertines neere consumed us all, as the Israelites in the wildernesse."

Text—*Captain John Smith's Works,* Arber edition, pp. 957-8.

Articles, Lawes, and Orders, Divine, Politique and Martiall for the Celony in Virginia: etc., 1610

Established by Gates in 1610, these laws assumed their full martial form under Dale, who, having served in the wars of the Low Countries, had apportunity there of observing statutes of severe character. It does not appear, however, that they were ever rigidly enforced.

The clauses that concern religion are as follows:

1. First since we owe our highest and supreme duty, our greatest, and all our allegeance to him, from whom all power and authoritie is derived, and flowes as from the first, and onely fountaine, and being especiall souldiers emprest in this sacred cause, we must alone expect our successe from him, who is onely the blesser of all good attempts, the King of kings, the commaunder of commaunders, and Lord of Hostes, I do strictly commaund and charge all Captaines and Officers, of what qualitie or nature soever, whether commanders in the field, or in towne, or townes, forts or fortresses, to have a care that the Almightie God bee duly and daily served, and that they call upon their people to heare Sermons, as that also they diligently frequent Morning and Evening praier themselves by their owne exemplar and daily life, and dutie herein, encouraging others thereunto, and that such, who shall often and wilfully absent themselves, be duly punished according to the martiall law in that case provided.

2. That no man speake impiously or maliciously, against the holy and blessed Trinitie, or any of the three persons, that is to say, against God the Father, God the Son, and God the holy Ghost, or against the knowne Articles of the Christian faith, upon paine of death.

3. That no man blaspheme Gods holy name upon paine of death, or use unlawful oathes, taking the name of God in vaine, curse, or bunne, upon paine of severe punishment for the first offence so committed, and for the second, to have a bodkin thrust through his tongue, and if he continue the blaspheming of Gods holy name, for the third time so offending, he shall be brought to a martiall court, and there receive censure of death for his offence.

4. No man shall use any traiterous words against his Maiesties Person, or royall authority upon paine of death.

5. No man shall speake any word, or do any act, which may tend to the derision, or despight of Gods holy word upon paine of death: Nor shall any man unworthily demeane himselfe unto any Preacher, or Minister of the same, but generally hold them in all reverent regard, and dutiful intreatie, otherwise he the offender shall openly be whipt three times, and ask publike forgivenesse in the assembly of the congregation three several Saboth daies.

6. Everie man and woman duly twice a day upon the first towling of the Bell shall upon the working daies repaire unto the Church, to hear Divine Service upon pain of losing his or her dayes allowance for the first omission, for the second to be whipt, and for the third to be condemned to the Gallies for six Moneths. Likewise no man or woman shall dare to violate or breake the Sabboth by any gaming, publique, or private abroad, or at home, but duly sanctifie and observe the same, both himselfe and his familie, by preparing themselves at home with private prayer, that they may be the better fitted for the publique, according to the commandements of God, and the orders of our Church, as also every man and woman shall repaire in the morning to the divine service, and Sermons preached upon the Saboth day, and in the afternoon to divine service, and Catechising, upon paine for the first fault to lose their provision, and allowance for the whole weeke following, for the second to lose the said allowance, and also to be whipt, and for the third to suffer death.

7. All Preachers or Ministers within this our Colonie, or Colonies, shall in the Forts, where they are resident, after divine Service, duly preach every Sabbath day in

the forenoone, and Catechise in the afternoone, and weekely say the divine service, twice every day, and preach every Wednesday, likewise every Minister where he is resident, within the same Fort, or Fortresse, Townes or Towne, shall chuse unto him, foure of the most religious and better disposed as well to informe of the abuses and neglects of the people in their duties, and service to God, as also to the due reparation, and keeping of the Church handsome, and fitted with all reverent observances thereunto belonging: likewise every Minister shall keepe a faithful and true Record, or Church Booke, of all Christnings, Marriages, and deaths of such our people, as shall heppen within their Fort, or Fortresses, Townes or Towne at any time, upon the burthen of a neglectfull conscience, and upon paine of losing their Entertainement.

8. He that upon pretended malice, shall murther or take away the life of any man shall bee punished with death.

9. No man shal commit the horrible, and detestable sins of Sodomie upon pain of death; & he or she that can be lawfully convict of Adultery shall be punished with death.   No man shall ravish or force any womā, maid or Indian, or other, upon pain of death, and know ye that he or shee, that shall commit fornication, and evident proofe made thereof, for their first fault shall be whipt, for their second they shall be whipt, and for their third they shall be whipt three times a weeke for one month, and aske publique forgivenesse in the Assembly of the Congregation.

10. No man shall bee found guilty of Sacriledge, which is a Trespasse as well committed in violating and abusing any sacred ministry, duty or office of the Church, irreverently, or prophanely, as by beeing a Church robber, or filch, steale or carry away any thing out of the Church appertaining thereunto, or unto any holy, and consecrated place, to the divine Service of God, which no man should doe upon paine of death. . . .

33. There is not one man nor woman in this Colonie now present, or hereafter to arrive, but shall give up an account of his and their faith, and religion, and repaire unto the Minister, that by his conference with them, hee may understand, and gather, whether heretofore they have beene sufficiently instructed, and catechised in the principles and grounds of Religion, whose weaknesse and ignorance herein, the Minister finding, and advising them in all love and charitie, to repaire often unto him, to receive therein a greater measure of knowledge, if they shal refuse so to repaire unto him, and he the Minister give notice thereof unto the Governour, or that chiefe officer of that towne or fort, wherein he or she, the parties so offending shall remaine, the Governour shall cause the offender for his first time of refusall to be whipt, for the second time to be whipt twice, and to acknowledge his fault upon the Saboth day, in the assembly of the congregation, and for the third time to be whipt every day until he hath made the same acknowledgment, and asked forgivenesse for the same, and shall repaire unto the Minister, to be further instructed as aforesaid: and upon the Saboth when the Minister shall catechise, and of him demaund any question concerning his faith and knowledge, he shall not refuse to make answere upon the same perill.

Text—Force: *Historical Tracts*, Vol. III, Tract II.

IV. *SOME FEATURES OF THE PARISH*

The Church Wardens

Act XIII of Assembly, March 1661-2.

That the churchwardens shall twice every yeare (viz.) in December court and Aprill court deliver a true presentment in writing of such misdemeanors as to their

knowledge, or by comon fame have beene comitted whilst they have beene church-
wardens, namely swearing, profaneing Gods holy name, or sabbath abuseing or con-
temning his holy word or sacraments, or absenting themselves from the exercise thereof,
As alsoe of those foule and abominable sins of drunkennesse fornication, and adultery,
and of all malitious and envious slandering and backbiting for the better manifestation whereof the said churchwardens are impowered to cause all such persons upon
whose reports they ground their presentments to appeare at the next county courts to
which the presentments are made to give their evidences concerning the same.

Text—Hening: *Statutes at Large*, Vol. II, pp. 51-52.

The Maintenance of the Clergy

Act I of Assembly, March 1642-3, consolidating and unifying earlier
enactments.

Be it also enacted and confirmed That there be tenn pounds of tob'o. per poll &
a bushell of corne per poll paid to the ministers within the severall parishes of the
collony for all tithable persons, that is to say, as well for all youths of sixteen years of
age as upwards, as also for all negro women at the age of sixteen years, And it is further
ordered for the better convenience & ease of the ministers that upon the twentieth of
November if it be not Sunday, & then upon the day following (notice being first given
by the churchwardens a week before,) That the parishoners shall bring in the duties
of tenn pounds of tob'o. for the ministers unto a place appointed by the churchwardens
in that plantation, And that the ministers be warned to be there, or appoint some
others to receive the same, The said churchwardens to give the aforesaid warneing,
And it is likewise ordered that the duties of a bushel of corne to be brought in upon
the 19th of December to a place appinted by the churchwardens in that plantation by the minister (notice being given as aforesaid,) The payment to be made by
two bushells of ears for one bushell of shelled corne, & so rateably, And it is further
ordered that If any planter or parishoner do neglect the bringing of tho corn or tob'o.
as aforesaid, he or they for such default shall forfeit double the quantity of tob'o. or
corne to be leavied by distresse by the authority of the commander.

Text—Hening: *Statutes at Large*, Vol. I, pp. 242-243.

The Duties of the Clergy

Acts of Assembly February 1631–2.
Act VII.

Every mynister in this colony haveing cure of soules shall preache one sermon
every sunday in the yeare, having no lawful impediment, and yf the mynisters shall
neglect theire charge by unnecessarie absence or otherwise the church wardens are to
present it.   But because in this colony the places of their cure are in many places ffar
distant, It is thought fitt that the mynisters doe soe divide theire turnes as by joynt
agreement of the parishoners they should be desired.

Act VIII.

It is also thought fitt, That upon every Sunday the mynister shall halfe an hower
or more before evenenge prayer examine, catechise, and instruct the youth and ignorant
persons of his parrish, in the ten commandments the articles of the beliefe and in the

Lord's prayer; and shall diligentlie heere, instruct and teach them the catechisme, sett forth in the booke of common prayer. And all fathers, mothers, maysters and mistrisses shall cause theire children, servants or apprentizes which have not learned the catechisme to come to the church at the tyme appoynted, obedientlie to heare, and to be ordered by the mynister untill they have learned the same: And yf any of the sayd fathers, mothers, maysters and mistrisses, children, servants or apprentises, shall neglect theire duties as the one sorte in not causinge them to come and the other in refusinge to learne as aforesayd, they shall be censured by the corts in those places holden. And this act to take beginninge at Easter next.

Text—Hening: *Statutes at Large*, Vol. I, p. 157.

The Appointment of the Clergy

Act I of Assembly, March 1642-3.

It is also enacted and confirmed, by the authority aforesaid that the vestrie of evrie parish with the allowance of the commander & com'rs. of the county living & resideing within the said parish, or the vestrie alone in case of their non residence shall from henceforward have power, to elect and make choyce of their ministers, And he or they so elected by the commander and comr's. or by the vestrie in case of non residence as aforesaid to be recommended and presented to the said comander and com'rs. or vestrie alone, to the Governour & so by him admitted, Provided that it shall be lawfull for the Gov'r. for the time being to elect and admit such a minister as he shall allow of in James-Citty parish, And in any parish where the Governour & his successors shall have a plantation provided he or they enjoy not that priviledge but in one parish where he or they have such a plantation, And upon the neglect or misbecomeing behaviour of the ministers or any of them, compl't. thereof being made by the vestrie, the Governour & Council are requested so to proceed against such minister or Ministers by suspension or other punishment as they shall think fitt & the offence requirc. Removeall of such ministers to be left to the Grand Assembly.

Text—Hening: *Statutes at Large*, Vol. I, p. 242.

V. CONFORMITY AND DISSENT

The Quakers

Act I of Assembly, September 1663.   Supplementing the earlier acts of March 1659-60 and March 1661-62.

Whereas it is evident of late time that certaine persons under the names of Quakers and other names of separation have taken up and maintained sundry dangerous opinions and tenets, and whereas the said persons under pretext of religious worship doe often assemble themselves in greate numbers in several parts of this colony to the greate endangering its publique peace and safety and to the terror of the people by maintayning a secrett and strict correspondency among themselves, and in the meane time separating and dividing themselves from the rest of his majesties good and loyall subjects, and from the publique congregations and usuall places of divine service, for redressing whereof and for better preventing the many mischiefs and dangers that may and doe arise by such dangerous tenets and such unlawful assemblyes, Be it enacted by this present grand assembly and the authority thereof that if any person or persons commonly called Quakers, or any other separatists whatsoever in this colony shall at any time after the publishing of this act in the severall respective counties departe from the place of their severall habitations and assemble themselves to the number of five or more of the age of sixteene yeares or upwards at any one tyme in any place under pretense of joyning in a religious worship not authorized by the laws of England nor this country that then in all and every such cases the party soe offending being thereof lawfully convict by the verdict of twelve men, or by his owne confession, or by notorious evidence of the fact, shall for the first offence fforfeite and pay two hundred pounds of tobacco, and if any such person or persons being once convicted shall againe offend therein, and shall in forme aforesaid be thereof lawfully convicted shall for the second offence forfeite and pay five hundred pounds of tobacco to be levyed by distresse and sale of the goods of the party soe convicted, by warrant from any one of the justices before whome they shal be soe convicted rendering the overplus to the owners (if any be), and for want of such distresse or for want of ability of any person among them to pay the said fine or fines then it shalbe lawfull to levy and recover the same from the rest of the Quakers or other seperatists or any one of them then present, that are of greater ability to pay the said fine or fines, and if any person after he or she in forme aforesaid hath bin twice convicted of any of the said offences shall offend the third time and be thereof lawfully convicted, that then every person soe offending and convict as aforesaid shall for his or her third offence be banished this colony of Virginia to the places the governor and councell shall appoint.

And be it further enacted by the power and authority aforesaid, that each master of ship or vessell that shall import and bring in any Quaker into this colony to reside after the first day of July next, unles by virtue of an act of Parliament made in England the nineteenth day of May in the fourteenth yeare of the raigne of our soveraigne Lord the King, shalbe fined five thousand pounds of tobacco to be levyed by distresse and sale of the masters goods by warrant from any justice of peace in the county where such person or persons shall arrive, the same being proved by suffitient evidence, and further shalbe enjoyned to carry him or them out of the country againe when his ship returnes and to take especiall care to secure him, her or them soe brought in as afore-said from spreading any seditious tenets whilst he she or they remaine in the country.

And be it further enacted that any person or persons inhabitants of this country that shall entertaine any Quakers in or neare their houses, that is, to teach or preach shall likewise be fined five thousand pounds of tobacco for each time they do entertayne them, to be levyed by distresse and sale of the persons goods by order of the justices of peace in the next county court held for that county where the fact was committed before whome the same shalbe by evidence proved.

And be it further enacted that for prevention of neglects in the due execution of this act by any majestrate or majestrates officer or officers of this colony that in case any justice of the peace or any other officer shall neglect the performance of their duty in prosecuting this act or shall directly or indirectly connive at any breeches thereof he or they for every such offence shalbe fined two thousand pounds of tobacco to be levyed by distresse and sale of the goods of the party soe offending, he being thereof lawfully convicted by the verdict of twelve men or by his owne confession or evidence of the fact.

Text— Hening: *Statutes at Large*, Vol. II, pp. 180-2.

VI. *TRIALS AND PROBLEMS OF THE VIRGINIA CHURCH*

Virginia's Cure

Presented to the Lord Bishop of London in 1661 by G. R., to set forth the unhappiness and "only true remedy" of the churches, this narrative shows the inherent difficulties of religious work in Virginia.

That part of *Virginia* which hath at present craved your Lordships Assistance to preserve the Christian Religion, and to promote the Building Gods Church among them, by supplying them with sufficient Ministers of the Gospel . . . contains above half as much land as *England*; it is divided into several Counties, and those Counties contain in all about Fifty Parishes, the Families whereof are dispersedly and scatteringly seated upon the sides of Rivers; some of which running very far into the Country bear the *English* Plantations above a hundred Miles, and being very broad, cause the Inhabitants of either side to be listed in several Parishes. Every such Parish is extended many Miles in length upon the Rivers side, and usually not above a Mile in Breadth backward from the River, which is the common stated breadth of every Plantation belonging to each particular Proprietor, of which Plantations, some extend themselves half a mile, some a mile, some two miles, some three miles, and upward upon the sides of those Rivers, many of them are parted from each other by small Rivers and Creeks, which small Rivers and Creeks are seated after the manner of the great Rivers. The Families of such Parishes being seated after this manner, at such distances from each other, many of them are very remote from the House of God, though placed in the middest of them. Many Parishes as yet want both Churches and Gleabes, and I think not above a fifth part of them are supplyed with Ministers, where there are Ministers the People meet together Weekly, but once upon the Lords day, and sometimes not at all, being hir.dered by Extremities of Wind and Weather: and divers of the more remote Families being discouraged, by the length or tediousnesse of the way, through extremities of heat in Summer, frost and Snow in Winter, and tempestuous weather in both, do very seldome repair thither.

By which brief Description of their manner of seating themselves in that Wildernesse, Your Lordship may easily apprehend that their very manner of Planting themselves, hath caused them hitherto to rob God in a great measure of that publick Worship and Service, which as a Homage due to his great name, he requires to be constantly paid to him, at the times appointed for it, in the publick Congregations of his people in his House of Prayer.

. . . .

But long experience hath ascertained, and the before described manner of their Planting makes it evident, that whilest our Planters in *Virginia* continue as at this day, dispersedly and remotely planted from the House of God, they will continue to rob God in a very great measure of his publick Worship and Service in his House of Prayer. Which is the same Sin the Jews were Cursed for, and must needs put them under the same Curse of God.

But though this be the saddest Consequent of their dispersed manner of Planting themselves (for what Misery can be greater than to live under the Curse of God?) yet this hath a very sad Train of Attendants which are likewise consequents of their scater'd planting. For, hence is the great want of Christian Neighborhood, or brotherly admonition, of holy Examples of religious Persons, of the Comfort of theirs, and their Ministers Administrations in Sicknesse, and Distresses, of the Benefit of Christian and Civil Conference and Commerce.

And hence it is, that the most faithfull and vigilant Pastors, assisted by the most carefull Church-wardens, cannot possibly take notice of the Vices that reign in their Families, of the Spiritual defects in their Conversations, or if they have notice of them, and provide Spiritual Remedies in their publick Ministery, it is a hazard if they that are most concerned in them be present at the application of them: and if they should spend time in visiting their remote and far distant habitations, they would have little or none left for their necessary Studies, and to provide necessary spiritual food for the rest of their Flocks. And hence it is that through the licentious lives of many of them, the Christian Religion is like still to be dishonoured, and the Name of God to be blasphemed among the Heathen, who are near them, and oft among them, and consequently their Conversion hindred.

Lastly, their almost general want of Schooles, for the education of their Children, is another consequent of their scattered planting, of most sad consideration, most of all bewailed of Parents there, and therefore the arguments drawn from thence, most likely to prevail with them chearfully to embrace the Remedy. This want of Schooles, as it renders a very numerous generation of Christian Children born in *Virginia* (who naturally are of beautifull and comely Persons, and generally of more ingenious Spirits then these in England) unserviceable for any great Employments either in Church or State, so likewise it obstructs the hopefullest way they have, for the Conversion of the Heathen, which is, by winning the Heathen to bring in their Children to be taught and instructed in our Schooles, together with the Children of the Christians.

. . . .

What way soever they determine to be best, I shall humbly in obedience to your Lordships command endevour to contribute towards the compassing this Remedy by propounding,

1. That your Lordship would be pleased to acquaint the King with the necessity of promoting the building Towns in each County of *Virginia*, upon the consideration of the fore-mentioned sad Consequents of their present manner of living there.

2. That your Lordship upon the fore-going consideration, be pleased to move the pitiful, and charitable heart of His gracious Majesty (considering the Poverty and needs of *Virginia*) for a Collection to be made in all the Churches of his three Kingdomes (there being considerable numbers of each Kingdome) for the promoting a work of so great Charity to the Souls of many thousands of his Loyal Subjects, their Children, and the Generations after them, and of numberlesse poor Heathen; and that the Ministers of each Congregation be enjoyned with more then ordinary care, and pains to stirre up the people to a free and liberal Contribution towards it; or if this way be not thought sufficient, that some other way be taken to do it. . . .

Fourthly, That those Planters who have such a considerable number of Servants, . . . may by his Majesties Authority be enjoyned, to contribute the Assistance that shall be thought meet for them, to build themselves houses in the Towns nearest to them, and to inhabit them, for they having horses enough in that Country, may be convenienc'd as their occasions require, to visit their Plantations. And the Masters who shall inhabit the Towns, having Families of Servants upon remote Plantations, may be ordered to take care, that upon Saturdays Afternoon (when by the Custome of *Virginia*, Servants are freed from their ordinary labour) their Servants (except one or two, left by turns to secure their Plantations) may repair to their Houses in the Towns, and there remain with their Masters, until the publick Worship and Service of the Lords Day be ended.

Fifthly, That for a continual supply of able Ministers for their Churches, after a set term of years. Your Lordship would please to endeavour the procuring an Act of Parliament, whereby a certain number of Fellowships, as they happen to be next proportionably vacant in both the Universit ies, may bear the name of *Virginia* Fellowships, so long as the Needs of that Church shall require it; and none be admitted to them, but such as shall engage by promise to hold them seven years and no longer; and at the expiration of those seven years, transport themselves to *Virginia*, and serve that Church in the Office of the Ministery seven years more, (the Church there providing for them) which being expired, they shall be left to their own Liberty to return or not: and if they perform not the Conditions of their Admittance, then to be uncapable of any Preferment.

. . . .

For encouragement therefore of Minsters to adventure thither to help them, I humbly propound,

First, That your Lordship be pleased to procure, that the next grand Assembly in *Virginia* may enact. That what *Tobacco* any Parish agrees to pay their Minister, shall be payed of the best *Tobacco* of every Mans own Crop, and with Cask, otherwise experience hath shewed, that a Ministers livelyhood there will be very uncertain.

Secondly, That at the same Assembly it be Enacted, that every Parish chuse a Vestry (in case they have not one already chosen) and the Vestry of each Parish be enjoyned to subscribe what quantity of Corn and Tobacco of the best of their own Crops, with Cask, they will allow a sufficient Minister yearly.

Thirdly, That in the next and every Assembly, the Act for paying 15 lb. of Tobacco *per annum*, for every Tythable person, in every Parish destitute of a Minister (which Act was made at an Assembly *March* 27, 1656) be carefully executed, and strict Enquiry made, whether the Tobacco due by that Act, be duely collected, and employed to the ends express'd in that Act, viz. Building Churches, purchasing Gleabes, and stocks of Cattel to belong to them. And if any Parish hath imployed any part of such Arrears to any other use, that they be enjoyned to make them good again.

Fourthly, That the Act made in the same Assembly concerning disposing intestate estates to publick uses, (in case no Administratour of Kin to the diseased Proprietour appears) may serve in the first place the needs of the Church, for furnishing each Parish with Gleabes, and the Gleabes with Stocks of Cattel, before any part of such estates be employed to any other use.

Fifthly, that there being divers persons already in the Colony fit to serve the Church in the office of Deacon, a Bishop be sent over, so soon as there shall be a City for his See, as for other Needs of that Church, so also, that after due Probation and Examination, such persons may be ordained Deacons, and their duty and Service be appointed by the Bishop.

Sixthly, That the Ministers that go thither, be not hired by the year, as is now usual, but firmly instituted and inducted into Livings of stated value by the Subscriptions of their Vestries, according to the second Proposition.

Seventhly, That all Ministers desirous to go to *Virginia*, and not able to transport themselves, be acquainted with an Act of Assembly of that Country, whereby it is provided, that whatsoever sufficient Minister, shall not be able to pay for his transportation, any Merchant that shall defray the charge of it (if such Minister agree not with him upon other conditions) shall receive 20 l. *Sterling* for his passage, from the Parish that entertains him, or two Thousand pounds of Tobacco, who shall also repay any Sums of money disburs'd for his accomodation, and the Minister to be free to choose his Parish, which shall make such disbursements for him.

Text—Force: *Historical Tracts*, Vol. III, Tract XV.

VII. GEORGE FOX'S VISIT, 1672

"Our horses having rested, we set forward for Virginia again, travelling through the woods and bogs as far as we could well reach that day, and at night lay by a fire in the woods.   Next day we had a tedious journey through bogs and swamps, and were exceeding wet and dirty all the day, but dried ourselves at night by a fire.   We got that night to Sommertown.   When we came near the house, the woman of the house seeing us spoke to her son to keep up their dogs, for both in Virginia and Carolina they generally keep great dogs to guard their houses, living lonely in the woods, but the son said, 'He need not, for their dogs did not use to meddle with these people.'   Whereupon, when we were come into the house, she told us, 'We were like the children of Israel, whom the dogs did not move their tongues against.'   Here we lay in our clothes by the fire, as we had done many a night before.   Next day we had a meeting; for the people, having been informed of us, had a great desire to hear us; and a very good meeting we had among them, where we never had one before; praise be the Lord for ever!   After the meeting we hasted away.   When we had rid about twenty miles, calling at a house to enquire the way, the people desired us to tarry all night with them; which we did.   Next day we came among friends, after we had travelled about an hundred miles from Carolina into Virginia; in which time we observed great variety of climates, having passed in a few days from a very cold to a warm and spring-like country.   But the power of the Lord is the same in all; is over all, and doth reach the good in all; praised be the Lord for ever!

We spent about three weeks in travelling through Virginia, mostly amongst friends, having large and precious meetings in several parts of the country; as at the widow Wright's, where many of the magistrates, officers, and other high people came. A most heavenly meeting we had; wherein the power of the Lord was so great, that it struck a dread upon the assembly, chained all down, and brought reverence upon the people's minds.   Among the officers was a major, kinsman to the priest, who told me, 'The priest threatened to come and oppose us.'   But the Lord's power was too strong for him, and stopped him, and we were quiet and peaceable.   The people were wonderfully affected with the testimony of truth; blessed be the Lord for ever!   Another very good meeting we had at Crickatrough, at which many considerable people were, who had never heard a friend before; and they were greatly satisfied, praised be the Lord!   We had also a very good and serviceable meeting at John Porter's, which consisted mostly of other people, in which the power of the Lord was gloriously seen and felt and it brought the truth over all the bad walkers and talkers; blessed be the Lord!   Divers other meetings we had, and many opportunities of service for the Lord amongst the people where we came.   The last week that we staid we spent some time and pains among friends, sweeping away that which was to be swept out, and working down a bad spirit that was got up in some; and blessed for ever be the name of the Lord!   he it is that gives victory over all."

Text—*Journal of George Fox*, Philadelphia edition, pp. 459-460.

VIII. *WILLIAM AND MARY COLLEGE*
The following gives the history to 1727:

In the year 1691, Colonel *Nicholson* being Lieutenant Governor, the General Assembly considering the bad Circumstances of the Country for want of Education for their Youth, went upon a Proposition of a College, to which they gave the Name of *William* and *Mary*. They propos'd that in this College there should be three Schools, *viz.* A Grammar School, for teaching the *Latin* and *Greek* Tongues: A Philosophical School, for Philosophy and Mathematicks: and A Divinity School, for the Oriental Tongues and Divinity; for it was one part of their Design that this College should be a Seminary for the breeding of good Ministers, with which they were but very indifferently supply'd from abroad: They appointed what Masters should be in each of these Schools, and what Salaries they should have. For the Government and Visitation of this College, they appointed a College-Senate, which should consist of 18, or any other Number not exceeding 20, who were then the Lieutenant-Governor, four Gentlemen of the Council, four of the Clergy, and the rest nam'd out of the House of Burgesses, with Power to them to continue themselves by Election of a Successor in the room of any one that should dye, or remove out of the Country. They petition'd the King that he would make these Men Trustees for founding and building this College, and governing it by such Rules and Statutes, as they, or the major Part of them, should from Time to Time appoint. Accordingly, the King pass'd his Charter under the Great Seal of *England* for such a College, and contributed very bountifully, both to the Building and Endowment of it. Toward the Building he gave near 2000 *l.* in ready Cash, out of the Bank of Quit-Rents, in which Governor *Nicholson* left at that Time about 4500 *l.* And towards the Endowment the King gave the neat Produce of the Penny *per* Pound in *Virginia* and *Maryland*, worth 200 *l. per Annum*, (mention'd *pag.* 60) and the Surveyor General's Place, worth about 50 *l. per Annum*, and the Choice of 10000 Acres of Land in *Panmuckey Neck*, and 10000 more on the South-side of the *Black-water swamp*, which were Tracts of Land till that Time prohibited to be taken up. The General Assembly also gave the College·a Duty on Skins and Furrs, worth better than 100 *l.* A Year, and they got Subscriptions in *Virginia* in Governor *Nicholson's* Time for about 2500 *l.* towards the Building. With these Beginnings the Trustees of the College went to work, but their good Governor, who had been the greatest Encourager in that Country of this Design, (on which he has laid out 350 *l.* of his own Money) being at that time remov'd from them, and another put in his Place that was of a quite different Spirit and Temper, they found their Business go on very heavily, and such Difficulties in every thing, that presently upon change of the Governor, they had as many Enemies as ever they had had Friends; such an universal Influence and Sway has a Person of that Character in all affairs of that Country. The Gentlemen of the Council, who had been the forwardest to subscribe, were the backwardest to pay; then every one was for finding Shifts to evade and elude their Subscriptions; and the meaner People were so influenc'd by their Countenance and Example, (Men being easily perswaded to keep their Money) that there was not one Penny got of new Subscriptions, nor paid of the old 2500 *l.* but about 500 *l.* Nor durst they put the Matter to the Hazard of a Law-Suit, where this new Governor and his Favourites were to be their Judges. Thus it was with the Funds for Building: And they fared little better with the Funds for Endowments; for notwithstanding the first Choice they are to have of the Land by the Charter, Patents were granted to others for vast Tracts of Land, and every one was ready to oppose the College in taking up the Land; their Survey was violently stop'd, their Chain broke, and to this Day they can never get to the Possession of the Land.   But the Trustees of the College being encourag'd with a Gracious Letter the King writ to the Governor to encourage the College, and to remove all the Obstructions of it, went to work, and carry'd up one Half of the design'd Quadrangle of the Building, advancing Money out of their own Pockets, where the Donations fell short.   They founded their Grammar-School, which is in a very thriving Way; and having the clear Right and Title to the Land, would not be baffled in that Point, but have struggled with the greatest Man in the Government, next the Governor, *i.e.* Mr. Secretary *Wormley*, who pretends to have a Grant *in furturo* for no less than 13000 Acres of the best Land in *Panmuckey Neck*.   The Cause is not yet decided, only Mr. Secretary has again stop'd the Chain, which it is not likely he would do, if he did not know that he should be supported in it.   The Collectors of the Penny *per* Pound likewise are very remiss in laying their Accompts before the Governors of the College, according to the Instructions of the Commissioners of the Customs, so that illegal Trade is carry'd on, and some of these Gentlemen refuse to give any Account upon Oath.   This is the present State of the College.

Text—Hartwell, Blair, and Chilton: *The Present State of Virginia, and the College,* pp. 67-71.

CHAPTER III

MARYLAND IN THE SEVENTEENTH CENTURY

Bibliography

The beginnings of Maryland history are to be found in "A Relation of the Successful Beginnings of the Lord Baltimore's Plantation in Maryland" (May 27, 1634—in, Shea's "Early Southern Tracts" No. I, and "The Historical Magazine," October, 1865); in the more extensive "Relation of Maryland" (September 8, 1635), edited (1865) by Francis L. Hawks, D.D.; and in the "Relatio Itineris in Marylandiam" written (April, 1634) by Father White to the General of his Order (Maryland Hist. Soc., Fund Publ.," No. 7, and Force, "Tracts and Papers," Vol. IV, Tract XII). To the last are added letters from missionaries covering the period 1635-1677.

Political controversies of the Commonwealth era are given in "The Lord Baltimore's Case concerning the Province of Maryland," (1653), and a reply to this pamphlet, "Virginia and Maryland or the Lord Baltimore's printed case uncased and answered" (1655—Force, "Tracts and Papers" Vol. II, Tract IX). Several pamphlets belonging to this period are so distorted with the heat of controversy as to be scarcely worth mentioning (For list see Winsor, "Narr. & Crit. Hist. of America," Vol. III, p. 554). John Hammond's "Leah and Rachel or the Two Fruitful Sisters, Virginia and Maryland, . . . " (1656—Force, Vol. III, Tract XIV) is more restrained. Ten years later there appeared George Alsop's "A Character of the Province of Maryland" ("Maryland Hist. Soc. Fund Publ." No. 15), which quaintly sets forth social conditions of the colony. Another document of similar character is the "Journal of a Voyage to New York and a Tour in Several of the American Colonies in 1679-80" by Jasper Dankers and Peter Sluyter ("Memoirs of the Long Island Hist. Soc." Vol. I; also in "Original Narratives of Early American History" edited (1913) by B. B. James and J. F. Jameson).

The earliest historian of Maryland was George Chalmers, whose "Political Annals of the present United Colonies" (1780) is reasonably accurate. The first volume of a "Historical View of the Government of Maryland from its Colonization to the Present Day" (1831) by J. V.

L. McMahon sketches the history of the province to the Revolution, and concerns itself more largely with legal issues. John Leeds Bozman's "History of Maryland from its first settlement in 1633 to the Restoration in 1660" (II vols. 1837) abounds in source quotations and has an appendix that contains valuable documentary material. This work is thorough, but lacks literary finish. James McSherry briefly narrated the leading events of Maryland in "The History of Maryland from its first Settlement in 1634 to the year 1848" (1849). "The History of Maryland" (III vols. 1879) by J. T. Scharf excels Bozman's in point of literary finish and fulness, being based upon supplementary state papers preserved in the English State Paper Office. "Maryland, The History of a Palatinate" (1884) by W. Hand Browne in the "American Commonwealths" series, though brief is an admirable piece of work. "Old Virginia and Her Neighbors" (1897) by John Fiske devotes several chapters to Maryland, but is lacking in accuracy. "Maryland as a Proprietary Province" (1901) by N.D. Mereness is a scholarly presentation of the transition in Maryland from proprietary to representative government. "The Lords Baltimore and the Maryland Palatinate" being six lectures delivered (1902) before Johns Hopkins University by C. C. Hall is exceedingly valuable. The following studies by Bernard C. Steiner are worthy of closest attention: "Beginnings of Maryland, 1631-1639 (J. H. U. Studies, Series XXI); "Maryland During the English Civil Wars" (*ibid.*, Part I Series XXIV, Part II Series XXV); "Maryland Under the Commonwealth" (*ibid.*, Series XXIX); "The Protestant Revolution in Maryland" ("Ann. Report Amer. Hist. Assoc.," 1897, Sec. XVII); "The Restoration of the Proprietary of Maryland and the Legislation against the Roman Catholics during the Governorship of Captain John Hart (1714-1720)" (Ibid., 1899. Vol. I, Sec. VIII).

Biographical works worthy of mention are Burnap's "Life of Leonard Calvert" (published in Sparks' "American Biography," new series, vol. IX); "The Lords Baltimore" by Rev. J. G. Morris ("Maryland Hist. Soc. Fund Publ." No. 8); "Sir George Calvert, Baron of Baltimore" by L. W. Wilhelm (*ibid.*, No. 20); and "George Calvert and Cecilius Calvert, Barons Baltimore" (1890) in the "Makers of America" by W. Hand Browne.

The church affiliations of the first settlers and notably of the legislators, have been discussed by G. L. Davis in "The Day-Star of American Freedom" (1855); Rev. E. Allen in "Who Were the Early Settlers of Maryland" (1865); B. F. Brown in "Early Religious History of Maryland, . . . " (1876); Rev. E. D. Neill in "Lord Baltimore and Toleration in Maryland" ("Contemp. Rev.," Sept., 1876); also "The Founders of Maryland, . . . " (1876).

On the related subject of religious toleration, J. P. Kennedy delivered (1845) a discourse before the Maryland Historical Society on the "Life and Character of the First Lord Baltimore." Ten years later Rev. E. Allen issued a pamphlet on "Maryland Toleration." In 1875 Maryland religious history was injected into the controversy between Gladstone and Manning, and more literature on the subject appeared. (See "Mr. Gladstone and Maryland Toleration" in "The Catholic World," December, 1875). Hence the article published (April 1874) in the "Presbyterian Quarterly and Princeton Review" entitled "Catholic Toleration in the State of Maryland." An illuminating discussion is that of Bradley T. Johnson in "The Foundation of Maryland and the Origin of the Act Concerning Religion of April 21, 1649" ("Maryland Hist. Soc. Fund Publ." No. 18).

The Jesuit propaganda is well set forth in "Old Catholic Maryland and its Early Jesuit Missionaries" (1890) by Rev. W. P. Treacy, and the "Calvert Papers" ("Maryland Hist. Soc. Fund Publ." No. 28). "Maryland, the Land of Sanctuary" (1905) by Monsignor Russell, "Religious Liberty in Maryland and Rhode Island" (1903) by Rev. Lucian Johnston and "Maryland: the Pioneer of Religious Liberty" (1917) by E. S. Riley are recent contributions written from the Roman Catholic standpoint.

Church history proper has been presented from the Episcopalian viewpoint by Rev. F. L. Hawks, by Canon J. S. M. Anderson, by Bishop Samuel Wilberforce, by Rev. W. S. Perry, by Rev. S. D. McConnell, and by Prof. C. C. Tiffany. For the titles, dates, and comparative merits of the above histories, see p. 7. In Vol. IV of Rev. W. S. Perry's "Historical Collections relating to the American Colonial Church" (1870) a small amount of documentary material may be found.

From the Roman Catholic standpoint there is "The Catholic Church in Colonial Days" (1886) by Rev. John Gilmary Shea embodied as Volume I in his comprehensive "History of the Catholic Church in the United States" (1892), and the less satisfactory work of Professor Thomas O'Gorman in the "American Church History Series" (Vol. IX—third edition, 1900). "The History of the Society of Jesus in North America, Colonial and Federal" (1908) by Thomas Hughes, S.J., has important documents (Part I, Sec. I and II), followed by a biased exposition of the Maryland Mission (Text, Vol. I, Chapters III–VI, also Vol. II). The literature of the subject is well reviewed in Chapters I and II. Henry

Foley's "Records of the English Province of the Society of Jesus" (1878), Vol. III, has some material, which in view of misleading omissions, must be handled with care.

On the Quakers, the Maryland Historical Society published (1862) "The Early Friends (or Quakers) in Maryland," by J. S. Norris; and "Wenlock Christison and the Early Friends in Talbot County, Maryland," by Samuel A. Harrison, M.D. ("Maryland Hist. Soc. Fund Publ." No. 12).

On the Labadists, in addition to Dankers "Journal" as above, "The Labadist Colony in Maryland" by Bartlett B. James ("J. H. U. Studies," Series XVII; and "Papers Am. Soc. Church History" Vol. VIII) is highly satisfactory. "The Labadists of Bohemia Manor" by Geo. A. Leakin ("Maryland Hist. Mag." Vol. I, pp. 337-345) has some details.

A valuable paper entitled "Early Christian Missions Among the Indians of Maryland" by R. U. Campbell appears in the "Maryland Historical Magazine" Vol. I, pp. 293-316. This magazine (Vol. II, pp. 163-171) has an article, "Maryland at the End of the Seventeenth Century" by H. F. Thompson which has some side lights upon church conditions, also (Vol. XI, pp. 1-41) "The First Sixty Years of the Church of England in Maryland, 1632-1692" by Lawrence C. Wroth. "Church Life in Colonial Maryland" (1885) by Rev. T. C. Gambrall, although concerned more with eighteenth century history has considerable data upon earlier ecclesiastical affairs. "Terra Marlae, or Threads of Maryland Colonial History" (1867) by Rev. E. D. Neill is scarcely worth consulting. Considerable data may be gleaned from "Old Kent, the Eastern Shore of Maryland" (1876) by G. A. Hanson; "Parish Institutions of Maryland" by E. Ingle (J. H. U. Studies," Series I); "The Puritan Colony at Annapolis, Maryland" by D. R. Randall (*ibid.*, Series IV); "Church and State in Maryland" by G. Petrie (*ibid.*, Series X); "Side Lights on Maryland History, . . . " (1913) by Hester D. Richardson; "History of Talbot County, Maryland, 1661-1861" (1915) by Oswold Tilghman; and "Maryland Records Colonial, Revolutionary, County and Church" (1915) by G. M. Brumbaugh.

The investigator should be reminded that complete statutory data is available in "The Laws of Maryland at Large" (1765) by T. Bacon; that in the "Archives of Maryland" edited by W. H. Browne, and in the "Streetor Papers" (Maryland Hist. Soc. Fund Publ." No. 9), he will find the Proceedings and Acts of Assembly, Council and Court; that State Papers appear in "Calendars of State Papers, Colonial Series" (1860-1916), edited by Sainsbury, Fortescue and Headlam; and that in pursuing any investigation he should keep in touch with the publications of the "Maryland Historical Society," the "Maryland Historical Magazine," the "Records of the Columbia Historical Society," the "American Catholic Quarterly Review," the "American Catholic Historical Researches," and the "Records of the American Catholic Historical Society."

DOCUMENTS

I. *PROPRIETARY PROVISIONS FOR RELIGION. THE CHARTER OF JUNE 20/30, 1632*

CHARLES, by the grace of God, of *England, Scotland, France,* and *Ireland,* KING, Defender of the Faith, &c. To all to whom these Presents shall come, Greeting:

II. Whereas our well beloved and right trusty Subject Caecilius Calvert, Baron of Baltimore, in our Kingdom of *Ireland,* son and Heir of George Calvert, Knight, late Baron of Baltimore, in our said Kingdom of *Ireland,* treading in the Steps of his Father, being animated with a laudable, and pious Zeal for extending the *Christian Religion* and also the Territories of our Empire, hath humbly besought leave of Us, that he may transport, by his own Industry, and Expence, a numerous Colony of the *English* Nation, to a certain Region, herein after described, in a Country hitherto uncultivated, in the Parts of *America,* and partly occupied by Savages, having no Knowledge of the Divine Being, and that all that Region, with some certain Privileges, and Jurisdictions, appertaining unto the wholesome Government, and State of his Colony and Region aforesaid, may by our Royal Highness be given, granted, and confirmed unto him, and his Heirs.

. . . .

IV. Also We do Grant, and likewise confirm unto the said Baron of Baltimore, . . . all Islands and Islets within the Limits aforesaid, all and singular the Islands and Islets, from the Eastern Shore of the aforesaid Region, towards the East, which have been, or shall be formed in the Sea, situate within Ten marine Leagues from the said Shore; . . . And furthermore the Patronages and Advowsons of all Churches which (with the increasing Worship and Religion of CHRIST) within the said Region . . . , hereafter shall happen to be built, together with Licence and Faculty of erecting and founding Churches, Chapels, and Places of Worship, in convenient and suitable places, within the Premises, and of causing the same to be dedicated and consecrated according to the Ecclesiastical Laws of our Kingdom of *England,* with all, and singular such, and as ample Rights, Jurisdictions, Privileges, Prerogatives, Royalties, Liberties, Immunities, and royal Rights, and temporal Franchises whatsoever, as well by Sea as by Land, within the Region . . . aforesaid, to be had, exercised, used, and enjoyed, as any Bishop of Durham, within the Bishoprick or County Palatine of Durham, in our Kingdom of *England,* ever heretofore hath had, held, used, or enjoyed, or of Right could, or ought to have, hold, use, or enjoy.

Text—Poore: *The Federal and State Constitutions, Colonial Charters*—(Latin), Part I, pp. 811-812.

II. *THE JESUIT PROPAGANDA*

A Narrative of the Voyage to Maryland, by Father Andrew White; and Sundry Reports, from Fathers Andrew White, John Altham, John Brock, and Other Jesuit Fathers of the Colony, to the Superior General at Rome

. . . .

On the day of the annunciation of the Holy Virgin Mary, on the 25th of March, in the year 1634, we offered in this island, for the first time, the sacrifice of the mass: in th's region of the world it had never been celebrated before. Sacrifice being ended, having taken upon our shoulders the great cross which we had hewn from a tree, and going in procession to the place that had been designated, the Governor, commissioners, and other catholics participating in the ceremony, we erected it as a trophy to Christ the Saviour, while the litany of the holy cross was chaunted humbly on our bended knees, with great emotion of soul.

. . . The kings, however, and principal men have, as it were, their private apartments and bed, four posts being driven into the earth and poles placed on them to receive the bed. One of these huts has been allotted to me and my companions, in which we are accommodated sufficiently well for the time being, until more commodious edifices shall be built. This is the first chapel in Maryland, which was built, however, by the Indians. The next voyage, if God prosper our undertaking, we shall not be destitute of the things which are found necessary in other houses.

. . . .

1638. Four priests and one coadjutor in temporal affairs, had care of this mission; and he indeed, after many labors for the whole period of five years, with the greatest patience, humility, and fervent charity, having been seized with a sickness then prevailing, happily exchanged this miserable life for one that is immortal. One of the priests soon followed him, a young man indeed, but evidently of great promise, on account of his remarkable endowments of mind. Scarcely had he passed two months in this mission, when by the prevailent sickness of the colony, which not one of the three other priests escaped, he was carried off, to the great regret of all. Nevertheless, we have not ceased in an active manner to exert our endeavors for our neighbors; and although it is not yet permitted us by the rules of the province to live among the barbarians, both on account of the prevailing sickness and the hostile acts which the barbarians commit against the English, as one man from the colony who was among them for the purpose of traffic was slain, and a conspiracy also made against the whole nation—nevertheless, we hope in a short time that we will obtain one station of our own among the barbarians. In the interim we are more earnestly intent on the English, and since there are protestants as well as catholics in the colony, we have labored with both, and God has blessed our labors. For of the protestants who came from England this year, 1638, almost all have been converted to the faith, besides many others, with four servants that we bought for necessary use in Virginia, another colony of our empire. And of five workmen whom we hired for a month, we have in the meantime gained two.

. . . .

So far as concerns the catholics here, their attendance on the sacraments is such, that there is no greater among Europeans in proportion to the number. On every Lord's day catechisings are had before reading, and catechetic lessons before expositions; but on holydays meeting is rare, except for the mass. By every aid this year we have assisted the sick and dying who truly were many and much scattered about; so that not even one, when about to die, was destitute of the sacraments. We have buried very many; we have baptized various persons. And although there are not wanting frequent cases of discord, nevertheless, none of any moment has happened for the past nine months, which we have not immediately allayed. By the kindness of God we have this comfort, that as yet no vices have sprung up among the new catholics, although places like this are not expected to be settled by the best kind of men.

The two catholics who had sold themselves into servitude in Virginia we have redeemed, nor was the money ill expended. Both of them have since deported themselves as good christians; but one excels ordinary people. The same work of charity some others have performed, buying thence catholic servants, of whom there is a plenty there; for it is said that to each person there, very many have sold themselves as servants, who, living among men of most profligate example, and destitute of all spiritual aid, for the most part, make shipwreck of their souls.

. . . .

To the hope of the Indian harvest, are to be added also no mean fruits reaped from the colony and its inhabitants, to whom, on the principal festival days of the year, sermons are preached and the catechetical expositions given on the Lord's day. Not only catholics come in crowds, but also very many heretics—not without the reward of our labors; for this year, twelve in all, wearied of former errors, have returned to favor with God and the church. Our people cease not daily to engage in their divine employment, and to dispense the sacraments to those that come, as often as circumstances demand. In fine, to those in health, to the sick, to the afflicted, and the dying, we strive to be in season for counsel, for relief, for assistance of every kind whatsoever.

. . . .

This is about the sum of the labor and fruit for this year; one thing, however, remains not altogether to be omitted, though to be touched upon lightly, to wit: this thing, that occasion of suffering has not been wanting from those from whom rather it was proper to expect aid and protection; who, too intent upon their own affairs, have not feared to violate the immunities of the church, by using their endeavors that laws of this kind formerly passed in England and unjustly observed there, may obtain like force here, to wit: that it shall not be lawful for any person or community, even ecclesiastical, in any wise, even by gift, to acquire or possess any land, unless the permission of the civil magistrate first be obtained. Which thing, when our people declared it to be repugnant to the laws of the church, two priests were sent from England who might teach the contrary. But the reverse of what was expected happened; for our reasons being heard, and the thing itself being more clearly understood, they easily fell in with our opinion, and the laity in like manner generally. . . .

1671. The Maryland mission has four companions, two priests and two temporal coadjutors. This mission succeeds prosperously, as we have learned from the last letters, and bears no mean harvest; and would yield greater, if more laborers would till it. Of those who were sent in former years very few remain, the others being removed by death, of which number this year were father William Pellam, and Thomas Sherbon, temporal coadjutor. In this mission fifty four have been brought to the catholic faith; and twenty general confessions have been received.

1672. Two priests have care of the Maryland mission, to whom as many co-adjutors have been added for the care of temporal and domestic affairs. From the last return made, it is counted—seventy brought over to the church, one hundred baptized, twenty general confessions received.

1673. This year, two priests and one temporal coadjutor are here. They bestow their principal labor in confirming catholics in the faith, and imbuing them with piety, but labor also as occasion serves with the heretics, and of these have brought into the fold of the church twenty-eight; but by sacred baptism have regenerated seventy infants to Christ. But two fathers of the order of St. Francis, sent from England the year before, have entered into a portion of the labors and harvest; between whom and us offices of kindness are mutually observed for the common prosperity of the catholic cause.

Text—Force: *Historical Tracts*, Vol. IV, Tract XII.

III. *COMMONWEALTH CHANGES*

The Governor's Oath, August 6, 1648.

The civil convulsions in England with the imminent fall of the Royal-ist cause suggested to Lord Baltimore the propriety of concessions to the Puritans, also of safeguards to protect his Catholic subjects from reactionary Puritan persecutions. In entering upon his governorship, William Stone, a Protestant, was required to subscribe to the following religious oath:

. . . and do further swear that I will not by myself, nor any person directly or in-directly, trouble, molest, or discountenance any person whatsoever in the said province professing to believe in Jesus Christ, and in particular no Roman Catholick, for or in respect of his or her religion, nor in his or her exercise thereof within the said province, so as they be not unfaithful to his said lordship, or molest or conspire against the civil government established here under him, nor will I make any difference of persons in conferring of offices, rewards, or favours proceeding from the authority which his said lordship hath conferred upon me as his lieutenant here, for or in respect of their said religion respectively, but merely as I shall find them faithful and well deserving of his said lordship, and to the best of my understanding endowed with moral virtues and abilities fitting for such rewards, offices, or favours, wherein my prime aim and end from time to time shall sincerely be the advancement of his said lordship's service here and the public unity and good of the province, without partiality to any or any other sinister end whatsoever, and if any other officer or person whatsoever shall, during the time of my being his said lordship's lieutenant here, without my consent or privity molest or disturb any person within this province professing to believe in Jesus Christ merely for or in respect of his or her religion or the free exercise thereof, upon notice or complaint thereof made unto me I will apply my power and authority to relieve and protect any person so molested or troubled, whereby he may have right done him for any damage which he shall suffer in that kind, and to the utmost of my power will cause all and every such person or persons as shall molest or trouble any other person or persons in that manner to be punished.

Text—Scharf: *History of Maryland*, Vol. I, p. 173.

The "Act Concerning Religion"—April, 1649

Submitted by Lord Baltimore to the Assembly convened April 2, 1649, this Act was passed by a group of legislators eleven of whom were Catholic and three Protestant.   Hence the defensive attitude of the former.

AN ACT CONCERNING RELIGION

 fforasmuch as in a well governed and Xpian Comon Weath matters concerning Religion and the honor of God ought in the first place to bee taken, into serious con-sideracon and endeavoured to bee settled.   Be it therefore ordered and enacted by the Right Ho^ble Cecilius Lord Baron of Baltemore absolute Lord and Proprietary of this Province with the advise and consent of this Generall Assembly.   That whatso-ever pson or psons within this Province and the Islands thereunto belonging shall from henceforth blaspheme God, that is Cursè him, or deny our Saviour Jesus Christ to bee the sonne of God, or shall deny the holy Trinity the ffather sonne and holy Ghost, or the Godhead of any of the said three psons of the Trinity or the Unity of the Godhead, or shall use or utter any reproachfull Speeches, words or language concerning the said Holy Trinity, or any of the said three psons thereof, shalbe punished with death and confiscaton or forfeiture of all his or her lands and goods to the Lord Proprietary and his heires, And bee it also Enacted by the Authority and with the advise and assent aforesaid.   That whatsoever pson or psons shall from henceforth use or utter any reproachfull words or Speeches concerning the blessed Virgin Mary the Mother of our Saviour or the holy Apostles or Evangelists or any of them shall in such case for the first offence forfeit to the said Lord Proprietary and his heirs Lords and Proprietaries of this Province the sume of ffive pound Sterling or the value thereof to be Levyed on the goods and chattells of every such pson soe offending, but in case such Offender or Offenders, shall not then have goods and chattells sufficient for the satisfyeing of such forfeiture, or that the same bee not otherwise speedily satisfyed that then such offender or Offenders shalbe publiquely whipt and be ymprisoned during the pleasure of the Lord Proprietary or the Leive^t or cheife Governor of this Province for the time being.   And that every such offender or Offenders for every second offence shall forfeit tenne pound sterling or the value thereof to bee levyed as aforesaid, or in case such offender or Offen-ders shall not then haue goods and chattells within this Province sufficient for that pur-pose then to bee publiquely and severely whipt and imprisoned as before is expressed. And that every pson or psons before mentioned offending herein the third time, shall for such third Offence forfeit all his lands and Goods and bee for ever banished and expelled out of this Province.   And be it also further Enacted by the same authority advise and assent that whatsoever pson or psons shall from henceforth vppon any occasion of Offence or otherwise in a reproachful manner or Way declare call or denominate any pson or psons whatsoever inhabiting residing traffiqueing trading or comerceing within this Province or within any the Ports, Harbors, Creeks or Havens to the same belonging an heritick, Scismatick, Idolator, puritan, Independant, Prespiterian popish prest, Jesuite, Jesuited papist, Lutheran, Calvenist, Anabaptist, Brownist, Antinomian, Barrowist, Roundhead, Sepatist, or any other name or terme in a reproachfull manner relating to matter of Religion shall for every such Offence forfeit and loose the some or tenne shillings sterling or the value thereof to bee levyed on the goods and chattells of every such Offender or Offenders, the one half thereof to be forfeited and paid unto the person and persons of whom such reproachfull words are or shalbe spoken or vttered, and the other half thereof to the Lord Proprietary and his heires Lords and Proprietaries of this Province, But if such pson or psons who shall at any time vtter or speake any such reproachfull words or Language shall not have Goods or Chattells sufficient and overt w'thin th's Province to bee taken to satisfie the penalty aforesaid or that the same bee not otherwise speed ly satisfyed, that then the pson or persons soe offending shalbe publickly whipt, and shall suffer imprisonmt without baile or mainepr'se vntill hee shee or they respectively shall satisfy the party soe offended or greived by such reproachfull Language by asking him or her respectively forgivenes publiquely for such his Offence before the Magistrate or cheife Officer or Officers of the Towne or place where such Offence shalbe given.   And be it further likewise Enacted by the Authority and consent aforesaid 'That every person and persons within this Province that shall at any time hereafter pphane the Sabbath or Lords day called Sunday by frequent swearing, drunkennes or by any uncivill or disorderly recreacon, or by working on that day when absolute necessity doth not require it shall for every such first offence forfeit 2s 6d or the value thereof, and for the second offence 5s sterling or the value thereof, and for the third offence and soe for every time he shall offend in like manner afterwards 10s sterling or the value thereof. And in case such offender and offenders shall not have sufficient goods or chattells within this Province to satisfy any of the said Penalties respectively hereby imposed for prophaning the Sabbath or Lords day called Sunday as aforesaid, That in Every such case the ptie soe offending shall for the first and second offence in that kinde be impr'soned till hee or shee shall publickly in open Court before the cheife Commander Judge or Magistrate, of that County Towne or precinct where such offence shalbe committed acknowledg the Scandall and offence he hath in that respect given against God and the good and civill Government of this Province   And for the third offence and for every time after shall also bee publickly whipt.   And whereas the inforceing of the conscience in matters of Religion hath frequently fallen out to be of dangerous Consequence in those commonwealthes where it hath been practised, And for the more quiett and peaceable governemt of this Province, and the better to pserve mutuall Love and amity amongst the Inhabitants thereof.   Be it Therefore also by the Lo: Proprietary with the advise and consent of this Assembly Ordeyned & enacted (except as in this psent Act is before Declared and sett forth) that noe person or psons whatsoever within this Province, or the Islands, Ports, Harbors, Creekes, or havens thereunto belonging professing to beleive in Jesus Christ, shall from henceforth bee any waies troubled, Molested or discountenanced for or in respect of his or her religion nor in the free exercise thereof within this Province or the Islands thereunto belonging nor any way compelled to the beleife or exercise of any other Religion against his or her consent, soe as they be not unfaithfull to the Lord Proprietary, or molest or conspire against the civill Governemt established or to bee established in this Province vnder him or his heires.   And that all & every pson and psons that shall presume Contrary to this Act and the true intent and meaning thereof directly or indirectly either in person or estate willfully to wrong disturbe trouble or molest any person whatsoever within this Province professing to beleive in Jesus Christ for or in respect of his or her religion or the free exercise thereof within this Province other than is provided for in this Act that such pson or psons soe offending, shalbe compelled to pay trebble damages to the party soe wronged or molested, and for every such offence shall also forfeit 20s sterling in money or the value thereof, half thereof for the vse of the Lo:

Proprietary, and his heires Lords and Proprietaries of this Province, and the other half for the vse of the party soe wronged or molested as aforesaid, Or if the ptie soe offending as aforesaid shall refuse or bee unable to recompense the party soe wronged, or to satisfy such ffyne or forfeiture, then such Offender shalbe severely punished by publick whipping & imprisonmt during the pleasure of the Lord Proprietary, or his Leivetenat or cheife Governor of this Province for the tyme being without baile or maineprise. And bee it further alsoe Enacted by the authority and consent aforesaid That the Sheriff or other Officer or Officers from time to time to bee appointed & authorized for that purpose, of the County Towne or precinct where every particular offence in this psent Act conteyned shall happen at any time to bee comitted and wherevppon there is hereby a fforfeiture ffyne or penalty imposed shall from time to time distraine and seise the goods and estate of every such pson soe offending as aforesaid against this psent Act or any pt thereof, and sell the same or any part thereof for the full satisfaccon of such forfeiture, ffine, or penalty as aforesaid, Restoring vnto the ptie soe offending the Remainder or overplus of the said goods or estate after such satisfaccon soe made as aforesaid

The ffreemen haue assented. Tho: Hatton

Enacted by the Governor Willm Stone

Text—*Archives of Maryland, Proceedings of the Assembly, 1637/8–1664*, pp. 244-247.

"An Act Concerning Religion"—October, 1654

Governor Stone, having surrendered his commission to Bennett and Clayborne, ten commissioners in the name of the Commonwealth proceeded to "summon an assembly for which all such should be disabled to give any vote or be elected members thereof, as have borne arms in wars against the Parliament, or do profess the Roman Catholic religion." Thus constituted, the Assembly enacted:

AN ACT CONCERNING RELIGION

It is Enacted and Declared in the Name of his Highness the Lord Protector with the Consent and by the Authority of the present Generall Assembly That none who profess and Exercise the Popish Religion Commonly known by the Name of the Roman Catholick Religion can be protected in this Province by the Lawes of England formerly Established and yet unrepealed nor by the Government of the Commonwealth of England Scotland and Ireland and the Dominions thereunto belonging Published by his Highness the Lord protector but are to be restrained from the Exercise thereof, Therefore all and Every person or persons Concerned in the Law aforesaid are required to take notice.

Such as profess faith in God by Jesus Christ (though Differing in Judgment from the Doctrine worship & Discipline publickly held forth shall not be restrained from but shall be protected in the profession of the faith) & Exercise of their Religion so as they abuse not this Liberty to the injury of others   The Disturbance of the publique peace on their part, Provided that this Liberty be not Extended to popery or prelacy not to such as under the profession of Christ hold forth and practice Licentiousness.

Text— *Archives of Maryland, Proceedings of the Assembly, 1637/8–1664*, p. 340.

The Claybourne Rebellion

John Hammond expelled from the Virginia Assembly in "Leah and Rachel" throws considerable light upon religious commotion in Maryland.

Having for 19. yeare served *Virginia* the elder sister, I casting my eye on Maryland the younger, grew in amoured on her beauty, resolving like Jacob when he had first served for Leah, to begin a fresh service for Rachell.

Two year and upward have I enjoyed her company with delight and profit, but was enforced by reason of her unnaturall disturbances to leave her weeping for her children & would not be comforted, because they were not; yet will I never totally forsake or be beaten off from her.

Twice hath she been deflowerd by her own Inhabitants, stript, shorne and made deformed; yet such a naturall fertility and comelinesse doth she retain that she cannot but be loved, but be pitied; and although she would ever have vailed to *Virginia* as her elder, yet had not these two fatall mischiefs hapened, she would ere long have spread her self as largly, and produced as much in every respect as *Virginia* does or could doe. . . .

It is to be understood that in the time of the late King; *Virginia* being whol for monarchy, and the last Country belonging to England that submitted to obedience of the Common-wealth of England. And there was in *Virginia* a certaine people congregated into a Church calling themselves Independents, which daily encreasing, severall consultations were had by the state of that Coloney, how to suppresse and extinguish them, which was daily put in execution, as first their Pastor was banished, next their other Teachers, then many by informatios clapt up in prison, then generally disarmed) wch was very harsh in such a country where the heathen live round about them) by one Colonel *Samuel Mathews* then a Counsellor in *Virginia* and since Agent for *Virginia* to the then parliament, and lastly in a condition of banishment, so that they knew not in those streights how to dispose of, themselves.

Mary-land (my present subject) was courted by them as a refuge, the Lord Proprietor and his Governor solicited to, and severall addresses and treaties made for their admittance & entertainment into that province, their conditions were pitied, their propositions were harkened to and agree on, which was that they should have convenient portions of land assigned them, libertie of conscience, and priviledge to choose their owne officers, and hold courts within themselves, all was granted them, they had a whole Country of the richest land in the province asigned them, & such as themselves made choyce of, the conditions of plantations (such as were common to all adventurers) were shewed and propounded to them, which they extreamly approved of, and nothing was in those conditions exacted from them, but appeales to the Provincial court, quit-rents, and an oath of fidelitie to the Proprietor: An assembly was called thoroughout the whole County after their comming over (consisting aswell of themselves as the rest) and because there were some few papists that first inhabited these themselves, and others of being different judgments, an act passed that all professing in Jesus Christ should have equall justice, priviledges and benefits in that province, and that none on penaltie (mentioned) should disturb each other in their several professions, nor give the urging termes, either of Round-heads, sectarie, Independent, Jesuit, Papist, &c. Intending an absolute peace and union; the Oath of Fidelitie (although none other then such as every Lord of a manner requires from his tenant) was over hauled, and this clause added to it (provided it infring not the libertie of the conscience.)

They sat downe joyfully, followed their vocations chearfully, trad increased in their province, and divers others were by this incouraged and invited over from *Virginia*.

But these people finding themselves in a capacitie not only to capitulate, but to oversway, those that had so received and relieved them.

Began to pick quarrells, first with the Papists, next with the oath, and lastly declared their aversness to all conformalitie, wholy ayming (as themselves since confessed) to deprive the Lord proprietor of all his interest in that country, and make it their own: with unworthinesse? What ingratitude? with unparalled inhumanitie was in these practices made obvious.

Amongst others that became tenants in this aforesaid distress was one *Richard Bennet* Merchant, who seated and settled amongst them, and so (not only owed obedience to that government, but) was obliged as a man received in his pretended distresse, to be a gratful benefactor upon the setting torth of a fleet intended for the reducement of *Virginia*, the said Bennet and one *Claiborne* (a pestilent enemie to the wel-faire of that province and the Lord Proprietor, although he had formerly submissively acknowledged he owed his forfeited life to the said proprietor, for dealing so favorably with him for his misdemeanors, as by his treacherous letters under h's hand (now in print) is manifest, and many other acts of grace conferred on him, having a commission directed to them and others (who miscarried by sea) to reduce *Virginia* (not *Mary-land*, for they were in obedience to the Commonwealth of England, and great assistance to the said fleet) although they knew *Mary-land* to be excluded and dasht out of their Commission yet because the commission mentioned the Bay of Chesapeack (in which *Mary-land* was (as well as *Virginia*) yet they were resolved to wreth and stretch their commission to the prejudice of *Mary-land* and becomming abbetters and confederats with those serpents that have been so taken in, presumed to alter the government, and take away the governours Commission, putting in others in their place, *viz.* a Papist in cheife, and one more, who misgoverning the Country, they were excluded, and the former governor restored with an addition of Commissioners of their owne creatures, and as taking power from them, untill further knowledge from England, driving herein at their own interest.

The governour (so restored) being truly informed that their proceedings were illegal; held Courts and proceeds as if no such alteration had been made, issues out Writs (according to order) In the name of the Lord proprietor, but they require and command them to do it in the name of the Keepers of the Liberties of England, according to act of Parliament to which answer sufficient was given that they never were in opposition to the present power, they had taken the Engagement, & for the tenure or form of writs, they were not compelled byvertue of that act to make them other wise then they always had done, for by Patent from the late K. they had power to issue out in the Proprietors name, and never had used the Kings name at all, therefore that act requiring all Writs formerly issuing out in the late Kings name, now to revolve to the Keepers of the Liberties of England, was no way binding to them who had never used the kings name at all.

But it was not religion, it was not punctilios they stood upon, it was that sweete, that rich, that large Country they aimed at; and therefore agrees amongst themselves to frame petitions,' complaints, and subscriptions from those bandetoes [bandits] to themselves (the said *Bennet* and *Claiborne*) to ease them of their pretended sufferings, and then come with arms, and againe make the Province their own, exalting them-selves in all places of trust and command, totally expulsing the Governer, and all the hospitable Proprietors, Officers out of their places.

But when his Highnesse (not acquainted with these matchinations) had owned and under his hand and signet acknowledged Cap. *Will. Stone* (the former governor) Governor for the Lord *Ba'tamore* of his Province of *Mary-land*, he again endeavored to reasume the government, and fetched away the records from those usurpers, pro-claimed peace to all not obstinate, and favorably received many submissives, who with seeming joy returned, bewailing their unworthy ingratitude & inhumanitie, blaming the unbridled ambition and base averice of those that had misled them.

The Province consists of foure Counties already inhabited, viz. St. *Maries*, *Calverton*, *An Arundal* and *Kent*. St. *Maries* and *Calverton* submitted, *An Arundall* and part of *Kent* opposed.

The Governor desirous to reclaim those opposing, takes a partie about 130. per sons with him, and sailes into those parts, one *Roger Heamans* who had a great ship under him, and who had promised to be instrumentall to the governor, to wind up those differences (being *Judas*-like, hired to joyn with those opposing Countries) and having the Governour and his vessells within reach of his Ordnance, perfidiously & contrary to his undertaking and ingagments, fires at them and enforces them to the first shore to prevent that mischief.

The next morning he sends messengers to those of *An Arundall* to treat, and messengers aboard that . . . *Heamans*, but all were detained; and on the 25. of *March* last (being the next day and the Lords day) about 170. and odd of *Kent* and *Anne Arundall* came marching against them, *Heaman* fires a pace at them, and a small vessel of *New England* under the command of one *John Cutts* comes neere the shore and seazes the boats, provision and amunition belonging to the Governour and his partie, and so in a nick, in a streight were they fallen upon.

The Governour being shot in many places yeilds on quarter, which was granted; but being in hold, was threatned (notwithstanding that quarter given) to be imediatly executed, unlesse he would writ to the rest to take quarter, which upon his request they did, twentie odd were killed in this skirmish, and all the rest prisoners on quarter, who were disarmed & taken into custodie.

But these formerly distressed supplicants for admittance, being now become High and Mighty States, and supposing their Conquest unquestionable, consult with them-selves (notwithstanding their quarter given) to make their Conquest more absolute, by cutting off the heads of the Province, *viz*. the Governor, the Counsel and Command-ers thereof: And so make themselves a Counsel of War, and condemn them to death: Foure were presently executed, scilicet, Mr. *William Elton-head*, one of the Councel; Capt. *William Lewis*, Mr. *John Legate* Gentleman, and *John Pedro*; the rest at the importunity of some women, and resolutions of some of their souldiers (who would not suffer their designe to take thorough effect, as being pricked in Conscience for their ingratitudes) were saved, but were Amerced, Fined and Plundred at their pleasures: And although this was prophetiquely foreseen by diverse eminent Merchants of *London*, who Petitioned his Highnesse for prevention, and that his Highnesse sent a gra-cious command to *Bennet*, and all others, not to disturb the Lord *Baltamores* Officers, nor People in *Mary-land*, but recalled all Power or pretence of Power from them; yet they still hold, and possesse (in defiance of so sacred a mandate) the said Province of *Mary-land*, and sent an impious Agent home to Parlie whilest they plundred; but he hath long since given up his account to the great avenger of all injuries: Although sticklers (somewhat more powerfull, but by many degrees more brazen fac't then his spirit could bare him forth to appear) now labour to justifie these inhumanities, disorders, contempts, and rebellions; so that I may say with the Prophet *Jeremiah*; How doth the Citty sit solitary that was full of people? How is she become as a widdow? She that was great amongst the Nations, and Princesse amongst the Provinces? How is she become tributary. Thus have they brought to desolation, one of the happiest Plantations that ever *Englishmen* set foot in, and such a Country (that if it were again made formall) might harbor in peace and plenty all such as *England* shall have occasion to disburthen, or desire to forsake *England*.

Text—Force: *Historical Tracts*, Vol. III., tract XIV.

IV. *GEORGE FOX'S VISIT, 1672-3*

". . . from whence, the third of the eighth month, we went to the general meeting for all Maryland friends.

This meeting held five days. The first three we had meetings for publick worship, to which people of all sorts came; the other two were spent in the men's and women's meetings. To those publick meetings came many Protestants of divers sorts, and some Papists; amongst whom were several magistrates and their wives, with other persons of chief account in the country. Of the common people, it was thought there were sometimes a thousand at one of those meetings; so that though they had enlarged their meeting-place, and made it as big again as it was before, it could not contain the people. I went by boat every day four or five miles to the meeting, and there were so many boats at that time passing upon the river, that it was almost like the Thames. The people said, 'There were never so many boats seen there together before'; and one of the justices said, 'He never saw so many people together in that country.' It was a very heavenly meeting, wherein the presence of the Lord was gloriously manifested, friends were sweetly refreshed, the people generally satisfied, and many convinced; for the blessed power of the Lord was over all: everlasting praises to his holy name for ever! After the publick meetings were over, the men's and women's began, and were held the other two days; for I had something to impart to them, which concerned the glory of God, the order of the gospel, and the government of Christ Jesus. When these meetings were over, we took our leave of friends in those parts, whom we left well established in the truth. . . .

After this we sailed about ten miles to James Frizby's, a justice of peace; where, the sixteenth of the eighth month, we had a very large meeting, at which, besides friends, were some hundreds of people, as it was supposed. Amongst them were several justices, captains, and the sheriff, with other persons of note. A blessed heavenly meeting this was; a powerful, thundering testimony for truth was borne therein; a great sense there was upon the people, and much brokenness and tenderness amongst them. We staid till about the eleventh hour in the night, that the tide turned for us; then taking boat, we passed that night and the next day about fifty miles to another friend's house. The two next days we made short journies, visiting friends. The twentieth we had a great meeting at a place called Severn, where there was a meeting-place, but not large enough to hold the people. Divers chief magistrates were at it, with many other considerable people, and it gave them generally great satisfaction. Two days after we had a meeting with some that walked disorderly, and had good service in it. Then spending a day or two in visiting friends, we passed to the Western-shore, and the twenty-fifth had a large and precious meeting at William Coale's, where the speaker of their assembly, with his wife, a justice of peace, and several people of quality, were present. Next day we had a meeting, six or seven miles further, at Abraham Birkhead's, where many of the magistrates and upper sort were; and the speaker of the assembly for that country was convinced. A blessed meeting it was; praised be the Lord! We travelled next day; and the day following, the twenty-eighth, of the eighth month, had a large and very precious meeting at Peter Sharp's on the Clifts, between thirty and forty miles distant from the former. Many of the magistrates and upper rank of people were present and a heavenly meeting it was. One of the governor's council's wives was convinced; and her husband was very loving to friends. A justice of peace from Virginia was convinced, and hath a meeting since at his house. Some Papists were at this meeting, one of whom threatened, before he came, to dispute with me; but he was reached, and could not oppose. Blessed be the Lord, the truth reached into the hearts of people beyond words, and it is of a good savour amongst them!

. . . .

I went after the meeting to a friend's about four miles off, at the head of Anamessy River, where the day following the judge of the country and a justice with him came to me, and were very loving, and much satisfied with friends' order. The next day we had a large meeting at the justice's in his barn, for his house could not hold the company. There were several of the great folks of that country, and among the rest an opposer; but all were preserved quiet and well. A precious meeting it was; the people were much affected with the truth; blessed be the Lord! We went next day to see Captain Colburn, a justice of peace, and there we had some service. Then returning again, we had a very glorious meeting at the justice's where we met before, to which came many people of account in the world, magistrates, officers, and others. It was a large meeting, and the power of the Lord was much felt, so that the people were generally well satisfied and taken with the truth; and there being several merchants and masters of ships from New-England, the truth was spread abroad; blessed be the Lord!

. . . .

Of the Indians, was one called their emperor, an Indian king, and their speaker, who sat very attentive, and carried themselves very lovingly. An establishing, settling meeting it was. This was the twenty-third of the first month.

The twenty-fourth we went by water ten miles to the Indian town where this emperor dwelt; whom I had acquainted before with my coming, and desired to get their kings and councils together. In the morning the emperor came himself, and had me to the town; where they were generally come together, their speaker and other officers being with them, and the old empress sat among them. They sat very grave and sober, and were all very attentive, beyond many called Christians. I had some with me that could interpret to them. We had a very good meeting with them, and of considerable service it was; for it gave them a good esteem of truth and friends; blessed be the Lord!"

Text—*Journal of George Fox*, Philadelphia edition, pp. 456-7, 462-3.

V. ANGLICANISM ESTABLISHED.   THE ACT OF JUNE 2, 1692

An Act for the Service of Almighty God and the Establishment of the Protestant Religion within this Province

Foreasmuch as in a well Governed Commonwealth Matters of Religion and the Honour of God ought in the first place to be taken in serious consideration, and nothing being more acceptable to Almighty God, then the true and Sincere worship and Service of him according to his Holy Word   Bee it therefore Enacted by the King and Queens most Excellent Majestys by and wth the advice and consent of this present Generall Assembly and the Authority of the same That the Church of England within this Province shall have and Enjoy all her Rights Liberties and Franchises wholly inviolable as is now or shall be hereafter established by Law, . . .

Bee it Enacted by the King and Queens most Excellent Majestys and by and with the advice and consent aforesaid.   That from and after the publication of this Law no Person or Persons within this Province shall work or do any bodily Labour or Occupation upon any Lord's Day commonly called Sunday, nor shall command or wilfully suffer or permitt any of his or their children Servants or Slaves to work or labour as aforesaid (the absolute works of necessity and mercy allways Excepted) Nor shall suffer or permitt any of his her or their Children Servants or Slaves or any other under their Authority to abuse or Prophane the Lords Day by drunkenness, Swearing Gaming, fowling fishing, hunting or any other Sports Pastimes or Recreations whatsoever. And if any person or persons within this Province from and after the Publication hereof, shall offend in all or any the premisses, he she or they so offending, shall forfeit and pay for every offence one hundred pounds of Tobacco. . . .

And be it likewise Enacted by the Authority aforesaid that no ordinary keeper Master or Mistress of a family from and after the time aforesaid either directly or indirectly by any Colour or pretence whatsoever (unless in case of absolute necessity) shall or may uppon any Lords day as aforesaid sell any strong Liquor whatsoever to any person whatsoever or knowingly or wittingly suffer or permit in or about his her or their house or houses, any Tippleing Drunkeness or gameing Exercise or pastime whatsoever as aforesaid being convicted thereof by two Sufficient Witnesses under the penalty of two thousand pounds of Tobacco, . . .

Bee it Enacted by the Authority aforesaid that the severall Commissioners and Justices of each respective county within this Province shall . . . divide and lay out their severall and respective Counties into severall districts and Parishes so many as the conveniency of each respective county and the scituation of the same will afford and allow of, . . . (and that) each Parish do within some convenient time within two months as by the Justices of County Courts aforesaid shall be appointed, meet together at the most convenient place in the said Parish to be also appointed by the Justices aforesaid, and there make choice of six of the most able men of the said respective Parishes to be a Vestry for each respective Parish as aforesaid, who are hereby Authorized Impowered and required to take care of preserve and Imploy all such Tobaccos, Wares, goods and Merchandizes as by this Act or any other Act hereafter to be made, or by any other waies or means whatsoever shall be given or granted raised or allowed to the use of the Church or Ministry of the said Parish to which they belong . . . (and) That a Tax or assessment of forty pounds of Tobacco p pole be yearly and in every year raised and levyed upon every Taxable Person within each Parrish aforesaid, and to be collected and gathered by the Sherriff of the County in manner and form as the publick or County Levies hitherto have and still are collected and gathered which said Sheriff is to make punctuall payment of the said Tax or Assessment to the Vestrymen of each Parrish as aforesaid. . . .

Text—*Archives of Maryland, Proceedings and Acts of the Assembly of Maryland, 1684-1692,* pp. 425-430.

CHAPTER IV

PLYMOUTH COLONY IN THE SEVENTEENTH CENTURY

Bibliography

"Mourt's Relation" written in large part by Governor Bradford and Edward Winslow, printed in London in 1622, is a journal of the period September 6, 1620 to December 11, 1621. An excellent edition is that of Dr. H. M. Dexter (1865). "John Pory's Lost Description of Plymouth Colony in the Earliest Days of the Pilgrim Fathers . . . " edited (1918) by C. Burrage is a welcome supplement. Robert Cushman's "Sermon" of December 9, 1621, (Young's "Chronicles," p. 255 f.), and "New England's Trials" (1622) by Captain John Smith (Arber Edition, p. 249 f.), give supplementary details. Events from November 1621 to September 1623 are given in "Good Newes from New England" by Winslow (in part Young "Chronicles," p. 271 f., complete in "Pilgrim Notes and Queries," Vol. IV, No. 2—8 f.). In 1630 Governor Bradford began his "History of Plymouth Plantation" which, while somewhat cursory in its first six chapters, becomes more exhaustive at the point of the Pilgrims' departure from Leyden, carrying the narrative with lessening detail through to 1646. The manuscript of Bradford's great work, located (1855) in the Bishop's palace, Fulham, was issued first (1856) under the able editorship of Mr. Deane, and later (1908) in "Original Narratives of Early American History" edited by Wm. T. Davis.

In his "Brief Narration" (Young, "Chronicles" p. 379 f.) appended to "Hypocrisie Unmasked" (1646) Winslow has given the reasons for the Plymouth enterprise, Robinson's doctrinal views, and a report of his farewell address to the Pilgrims. "New England's Memorial . . . " (1669) by Nathaniel Morton, a nephew of Governor Bradford and secretary of the Colony from 1645, adds little to the content of his "much honored" uncle's history, but brings the narrative in calendar-like fashion down to 1668. Through access to Governor Bradford's manuscripts, Cotton Mather in his "Magnalia" (1702) was able to incorporate "A Life of Bradford" (Book II, Chapter I). These manuscripts enabled Rev. Thomas Prince in his "Chronological History of New England" (1736) to write a lifeless journal of the Plymouth colony.

40

"An Account of the Church of Christ in Plymouth, the First Church in New England, from its Establishment to the Present Day, By John Cotton, Esq., Member of Said Church," written in 1760 ("Coll. Mass. Hist. Soc.," Series I, Vol. IV) relies much upon Morton, but adds considerable ecclesiastical detail. In the "Summary of the Affairs of the Colony of New Plimouth" appended to Vol. II of Governor Hutchinson's "History of Massachusetts Bay" (1767), and Bradford's "Letter Book" found in 1794 ("Coll. Mass. Hist. Soc.," Series I, Vol. III), considerable light was thrown upon Bradford and other leaders of the colony. This material was brought to date in Dr. Jeremy Belknap's "American Biography" (Vo. II, 1798). Rev. William Hubbard's "General History of -New England from the Discovery to MDCLXXX" published in 1815 ("Coll. Mass. Hist. Soc." Series II, Vols. V & VI) in treating of Plymouth, drew only upon sources already known. "An Historical Memoir of the Colony of New Plymouth" (1830) by Hon. Francis Bayliss, and a "History of the Town of Plymouth" (1832) by Dr. James Thacher, marked an advance to higher standards of historical work which was well sustained by Rev. Alexander Young, who collected (1841) in "Chronicles of the Pilgrim Fathers from 1602 to 1625" several of the notable writings of the period illuminating them with extensive notes. This was followed by the publication of "The Works of John Robinson, Pastor of the Pilgrim Fathers" (III vols. 1851) by Rev. Robert Ashton. A "Memoir of Rev. John Robinson" by the same author ("Coll. Mass. Hist. Soc." Series IV, Vol. I) fills an important place.

Seven years later the first volume of Dr. John G. Palfrey's "History of New England" appeared. In scholarly and pleasing fashion this set forth all the then known data concerning Plymouth, and while in some respects it is now obsolete, yet in essentials it remains to the present a valuable presentation. Meanwhile, by order of the State Legislature, Dr. N. B. Shurtleff and Mr. David Pulsifer had entered upon the task of editing "Plymouth Colony Records" which, by 1861, was completed in a twelve volume edition, indispensable to all research in Plymouth affairs.

It was about this time that American students became interested in the birthplace and family history of the Pilgrims, the literary remains of which are embodied in "Collections Concerning the Early History of the Founders of New Plymouth" by Rev. Joseph Hunter (1852, "Coll. Mass. Hist. Soc." Series IV, Vol. I, also as separate publication, 1854); the "Pilgrim Fathers" (1853) by W. H. Bartlett; "A Visit to Scrooby" by Rev. H. M. Dexter ("The Congregationalist," August 8, 1851);

the same writer's "Recent Discoveries Concerning the Plymouth Pilgrims" ("Congregational Quarterly" January, 1862); his "Footprints of the Pilgrims in England" ("Sabbath at Home," March, 1867); Rev. Ashbel Steele's "Life of Elder Brewster" (1857); and Dr. John Waddington's "Track of the Hidden Church" (1863).

Congregational church history is the next subject to claim attention. In a "History of Congregationalism" by George Punchard (Vol. III, 1867), Plymouth comes under review, though not with much detail. Dr. Leonard Bacon's "The Genesis of the New England Churches" (1874) is an important work concerned with the contribution of the Plymouth fathers to New England congregationalism. Dr. John Waddington in a "Congregational History" (Vol. II, 1874) with unimportant variations covers the field of his predecessor Punchard. "The Congregationalism of the Last Three Hundred Years as Seen in its Literature" (1880) a lecture series delivered at Andover by Rev. H. M. Dexter, is a ponderous work of scholarship to be consulted by every serious student. An appended bibliography of congregationalism is exhaustive. Professor Williston Walker's "The Creeds and Platforms of Congregationalism" (1893), gives ready access to a large amount of material indispensable to the church historian. In the following year the same writer contributed "A History of the Congregational Church in the United States" to the "American Church History Series" (Vol. III). This is a succinct enlivened and very useful handbook. Popular, but scarcely worthy of a place among works of scholarship, is "Congregationalism in America" (1894) by Rev. A. E. Dunning and others. "The Pilgrim Church and Plymouth Colony" by Franklin B. Dexter in Winsor's "Narrative and Critical History of America" (Vol. III, chap. VIII), though brief, is too valuable to be overlooked.

Turning from church histories proper, an appreciative word should be recorded for J. A. Doyle's discriminatig treatment of this part of the subject in "The Puritan Colonies" (Vol. I, 1886). The older work of Rev. E. D. Neill, "The English Colonization of America in the Seventeenth Century" (1871) still has its claim. A "History of the Town of Plymouth, with a Sketch of the Origin and Growth of Separatism'ι (1885) by William T. Davis, is a work of genuine scholarship. His "Ancient Landmarks of Plymouth" (1883) deals largely with estates and genealogy. "The Pilgrim Republic" (1888) by John A. Goodwin is a substantial work rich in detailed information. "The Pilgrim Fathers of New England and their Puritan Successors" (1895) written by an Englishman Rev. John Brown, is interesting and fertile in suggestion.

"The Story of the Pilgrims" (1894) by Morton Dexter, though written for young people, is well worth reading by a wider constituency. "The Story of the Pilgrim Fathers, 1606-1623 A.D; as told by Themselves, their Friends and their Enemies" (1897) edited by Edward Arber, has a mass of source material dealing with Scrooby, Amsterdam, Leyden, the Voyage to America, Early Experiences in Plymouth, also the text of "Good Newes from New England." "The Puritan as a Colonist and Reformer" (1900) by Ezra H. Byington, contains an appreciative estimate of the Pilgrim group; also his older work, "The Puritan in England and New England" (1896). "John Robinson the Pilgrim Pastor" (1903) by Rev. Ozora S. Davis, with an introduction by Professor Williston Walker, is well written and embodies material otherwise difficult of access. Of secondary significance are the following: "Governor William Bradford and his Son, Major William Bradford" (1900) by James Shepard; "Ten New England Leaders" (1901—for Bradford) by Williston Walker; "William Brewster and the Independents" by Edwin D. Mead (in "Pioneers of Religious Liberty in America"—the Great and Thursday Lectures, Boston, 1903); "The Plymouth Settlement and Tisquantum" by Lincoln N. Kinnicutt ("Proceedings, Mass. Hist. Soc." Vol. XLVIII, pp. 103-118); "The Pilgrims in Holland and America" by Winslow Warren ("Pub. Col. Soc. Mass." Vol. XVIII, pp. 130-152). The identity of the master of the Mayflower in discussed by R. G. Marsden in "The Mayflower" ("The Eng. Hist. Rev. Oct. 1904. pp. 669-680.) "The England and Holland of the Pilgrims" (1904) by H. M. Dexter and his son Morton exhausitvely sets forth the English-Holland background of Plymouth history. A considerable portion has a purely academic interest. "The Pilgrim Fathers, Their Church and Colony" (1909) by Winnifred Cockshott is an interesting restatement of vital information. "New Facts Concerning John Robinson" (1910) by Champlin Burrage deals with fine critical points. The latest study (1918) by R. G. Usher entitled "The Pilgrims and their History" utilizes for the first time Plymouth Church records, and presents some new conclusions especially valuable from the social and economic standpoint.

For purposes of investigation the student should keep in touch with the "Plymouth Colony Records," the "Proceedings" and "Collections" of the Mass. Hist. Soc., and the "Publi. of the Col. Soc. of Mass." The "Mayflower Descendant" (1899 f.) has considerable data, especially Vols. XXII–XXIII which contain the First Church records. "Pilgrim Notes and Queries" (1913 f.) will repay attention.

DOCUMENTS

I. *THE DECLARATION OF FAITH AND CHURCH POLITY*

Seven Articles which the Church of Leyden sent to the Council of England to be considered of, in respect of Their Judgments: Occasioned about their going to Virginia.
(Date before November, 1617.)

To aid Carver and Cushman in their negotiations with the English Government for a patent, this declaration while yielding no essential points of difference, drew the Pilgrim group as closely as possible into conformity with the Church of England.

1. To the Confession of Faith published in the name of the Church of England, and to every *Article* thereof; we do (with the Reformed Churches where we live, and also elsewhere) assent wholly.

2. As we do acknowledge the Doctrine of Faith there taught; so do we, the fruits and effects of the same Doctrine, to the begetting of saving faith in thousands in the land, Conformists and Reformists, as they are called: with whom also, as with our brethren, we do desire to keep spiritual communion in peace; and will practice in our parts all lawful things.

3. The King's Majesty we acknowledge for Supreme Governor in his Dominions in all causes, and over all persons: and that none may decline or appeal from his authority or judgement in any cause whatsoever: but that in all things obedience is due unto him; either active, if the thing commanded be not against God's Word; or passive, if it be, except pardon can be obtained.

4. We judge it lawful for his Majesty to appoint Bishops Civil Overseers or Officers in authority under him in the several Provinces, Dioceses, Congregations, or Parishes, to oversee the Churches, and govern them civilly according to the laws of the land: unto whom, they are, in all things, to give an account; and by them, to be ordered according to godliness.

5. The authority of the present Bishops in the land, we do acknowledge so far forth as the same is indeed derived from His Majesty unto them; and as they proceed in his name: whom we will also therein honour in all things; and him, in them.

6. We believe that no Synod, Classes, Convocation, or Assembly of Ecclesiastical Officers hath any power or authority at all but as the same [is] by the Magistrate given unto them.

7. Lastly, we desire to give unto all Superiors due honour, to preserve the unity of the Spirit with all that fear GOD, to have peace with all men what in us lieth, and wherein we err to be instructed by any.

Subscribed per JOHN ROBINSON and WILLIAM BREWSTER.

Text—Arber: *Pilgrim Fathers*, pp. 280-281.

Robinson's Letter to Sir John Wolstenholme

With this letter (January 27, 1617) the briefs given below were enclosed, in the hope that "unjust insinuations" might be removed from the minds of certain members of the Privy Council. Sir John, after consulting his friends, was to use his judgment in submitting "the one more breefe and generall, which we think ye fitter to be presented; the other something more large, and in which we express some smale accidentall differences."

THE FIRST BREEFE NOTE WAS THIS

Touching the Ecclesiasticall ministrie, namly of pastores for teaching, elders for ruling, and deacons for distributing the churches contribution, as allso for the too Sacraments, baptisme, and the Lords supper, we doe wholy and in all points agree with the French reformed churches, according to their publick confession of faith.

The oath of Supremacie we shall willingly take if it be required of us, and that conveniente satisfaction be not given by our taking the oath of Alleagence.

John Rob:
William Brewster.

THE 2. WAS THIS

Touching the Ecclesiasticall ministrie, &c. as in the former, we agree in all things with the French reformed churches, according to their publick confession of faith; though some small differences be found in our practices, not at all in the substance of the things, but only in some accidentall circumstances.

1. As first, their ministers doe pray with their heads covered, ours uncovered.

2. We chose none for Governing Elders but such as are able to teach; which abilitie they doe not require.

3. Their elders and deacons are anuall, or at most for 2. or 3. years; our perpetuall.

4. Our elders doe administer their office in admonitions and excommunications for publick scandals, publickly and before the congregation; theirs more privately, and in their consistories.

5. We doe administer baptisme only to such infants as whereof the one parente, at the least, is of some church, which some of their churches doe not observe; though in it our practice accords with their publick confession and the judgmente of the most larned amongst them.

Other differences, worthy mentioning, we know none in these points. Then aboute the oath, as in the former.

Subscribed,
JOHN R.
W. B.

Text—Bradford: *History of Plymouth Plantation*, Davis edition, pp. 56-57.

II. *THE TEMPER OF THE PILGRIMS*

To strengthen the hands of Sir Edwin Sandys, Robinson and Brewster, deemed it wise to forward to him the following information:

. . . Notwithstanding, for your encouragemente in the worke, so farr as probabilities may leade, we will not forbeare to mention these instances of indusmente.

1. We veryly beleeve and trust the Lord is with us, unto whom and whose service we have given ourselves in many trialls; and that he will graciously prosper our indeavours according to the simplicitie of our harts therein.

2[ly] We are well weaned from the delicate milke of our mother countrie, and enured to the difficulties of a strange and hard land, which yet in a great parte we have by patience overcome.

3[ly] The people are for the body of them, industrious, and frugall, we thinke we may safly say, as any company of people in the world.

4[ly] We are knite togeather as a body in a most stricte and sacred bond and covenante of the Lord, of the violation whereof we make great conscience, and by vertue whereof we do hould our selves straitly tied to all care of each others good, and of the whole by every one and so mutually.

5. Lastly, it is not with us as with other men, whom small things can discourage, or small discontentments cause to wish them selves at home againe. We knowe our entertainmente in England, and in Holland; we shall much prejudice both our arts and means by removall; who, if we should be driven to returne, we should not hope to recover our present helps and comforts, neither indeed looke ever, for our selves, to attaine unto the like in any other place during our lives, which are now drawing towards their periods.

These motives we have been bould to tender unto you, which you in your wisdome may also imparte to any other our wor[PP] : freinds of the Counsell with you; of all whose godly dispossition and loving towards our despised persons, we are most glad, and shall not faile by all good means to continue and increase the same. We will not be further troublesome, but doe, with the renewed remembrance of our humble duties to your Wor[PP] : and (so farr as in modestie we may be bould) to any other of our wellwillers of the Counsell with you, we take our leaves, commiting your persons and counsels to the guidance and direction of the Almighty.

Yours much bounden in all duty,

Leyden, Desem: 15.   JOHN ROBINSON,
   An⁰: 1617.   WILLIAM BREWSTER.

Text—Bradford: *History of Plymouth Plantation*, Davis edition, pp. 54-55.

III. *THE LEAVE TAKING AT DELFSHAVEN*

So being ready to departe, they had a day of solleme humiliation, their pastor taking his texte from Ezra 8. 21. *And ther at the river, by Ahava, I proclaimed a fast, that we might humble ourselves before our God, and seeke of him a right way for us, and for our children, and for all our substance.* Upon which he spente a good parte of the day very profitably, and suitable to their presente occasion. The rest of the time was spente in powering our prairs to the Lord with great fervencie, mixed with abundance of tears. And the time being come that they must departe, they were accompanied with most of their brethren out of the citie, unto a towne sundrie miles of called Delfes-Haven, wher the ship lay ready to receive them. So they lefte that goodly and pleasante citie, which had been ther resting place near 12. years; but they knew they were pilgrimes, and looked not much on those things, but lift up their eyes to the heavens their dearest cuntrie, and quieted their spirits. When they came to the place they found the ship and all things ready; and shuch of their freinds as could not come with them followed after them, and sundrie also came from Amsterdame to see them shipte and to take their leave of them.   That night was spent with litle sleepe by the most, but with freindly entertainmente and christian discourse and other reall expressions of true christian love.   The next day, the wind being faire, they went aborde, and their freinds with them, where truly dolfull was the sight of that sade and mournfull parting; to see what sighs and sobbs and praires did sound amongst them, what teares did gush from every eye, and pithy speeches peirst each harte; that sundry of the Dutch strangers that stood on the key as spectators, could not refraine from tears.   Yet comfortable and sweete it was to see shuch lively and true expressions of dear and unfained love.   But the tide (which stays for no man) caling them away that were thus loath to departe, their Reverend pastor falling downe on his knees, (and they all with him,) with watrie cheeks commended them with most fervente praiers to the Lord and his blessing.   And then with mutuall imbrases and many tears, they tooke their leaves one of an other; which proved to be the last leave to many of them.

Text—Bradford: *History of Plymouth Plantation*. Davis edition, pp. 79, 80.

IV. *ROBINSON'S FAREWELL LETTER TO THE PILGRIMS*

Lovinge Christian friends, I doe hartile and in the Lord salute you all, as being they with whom I am presente in my best affection, and most ernest longings after you, though I be constrained for a while to be bodily absente from you.   I say constrained, God knowing how willingly, and much rather then otherwise, I would have borne my part with you in this first brunt, were I not by strong necessitie held back for the present.   Make accounte of me in the mean while, as of a man devided in my selfe with great paine, and as (naturall bonds set a side) having my better parte with you.   And though I doubt not but in your godly wisdoms, you both foresee and resolve upon that which concerneth your presente state and condition, both severally and joyntly, yet have I thought it but my duty to add some furder spurr of provocation unto them, who rune allready, if not because you need it, yet because I owe it in love and dutie.   And first, as we are daly to renew our repentance with our God, espetially for our sines known, and generally for our unknowne trespasses, so doth the Lord call us in a singuler maner upon occasions of shuch difficultie and danger as lieth upon you, to a both more narrow search and carefull reformation of your ways in his sight; least he, calling to remembrance our sines forgotten by us or unrepented of, take advantage against us, and in judgmente leave us for the same to be swalowed up in one danger or another; wheras, on the contrary, sine being taken away by ernest repentance and the pardon therof from the Lord sealed up unto a mans conscience by his spirite, great shall be his securitie and peace in all dangers, sweete his comforts in all distresses, with hapie deliverance from all evill, whether in life or in death.

Now next after this heavenly peace with God and our owne consciences, we are carefully to provide for peace with all men what in us lieth, espetially with our associats, and for that watchfullnes must be had, that we neither at all in our selves doe give, no nor easily take offence being given by others.   Woe be unto the world for offences, for though it be necessarie (considering the malice of Satan and mans corruption) that offences come, yet woe unto the man or woman either by whom the offence cometh, saith Christ, Mat. 18. 7.   And if offences in the unseasonable use of things in them selves indifferent, be more to be feared then death itselfe, as the Apostle teacheth,

I. Cor. 9. 15. how much more in things simply evill, in which neither honour of God nor love of man is thought worthy to be regarded. Neither yet is it sufficiente that we keepe our selves by the grace of God from giveing offence, exepte withall we be armed against the taking of them when they be given by others. For how unperfect and lame is the work of grace in that person, who wants charritie to cover a multitude of offences, as the scriptures speake. Neither are you to be exhorted to this grace only upon the commone grounds of Christianitie, which are, that persons ready to take offence, either wante charitie, to cover offences, or wisdome duly to waigh humane frailtie; or lastly, are grosse, though close hipocrites, as Christ our Lord teacheth, Mat. 7. 1, 2, 3, as indeed in my owne experience, few or none have bene found which sooner give offence, than shuch as easily take it; neither have they ever proved sound and profitable members in societies, which have nurished this touchey humor. But besids these, there are diverse motives provoking you above others to great care and conscience this way: As first, you are many of you strangers, as to the persons, so to the infirmities one of another, and so stand in neede of more watchfullnes this way, least when shuch things fall out in men and women as you suspected not, you be inordinatly affected with them; which doth require at your hands much wisdome and charitie for the covering and preventing of incident offences that way. And lastly, your intended course of civill comunitie will minister continuall occasion of offence, and will be as fuell for that fire, excepte you dilligently quench it with brotherly forbearance. And if taking of offence causlesly or easilie at mens doings be so carefully to be avoided, how much more heed is to be taken that we take not offence at God him selfe, which yet we certainly doe so ofte as we doe murmure at his providence in our crosses, or beare, impatiently shuch afflictions as wherwith he pleaseth to visite us. Store up therfore patience against the evil day, without which we take offence at the Lord him selfe in his holy and just works.

A 4. thing ther is carfully to be provided for, to witte, that with your commone imployments you joyne commone affections truly bente upon the generall good, avoyding as a deadly plague of your both commone and spetiall comfort all retirednes of minde for proper advantage, and all singularly affected any maner of way; let every man represe in him selfe and the whol body in each person, as so many rebels against the commone good, all private respects of mens selves, not sorting with the generall conveniencie. And as men are carfull not to have a new house shaken with any violence before it be well setled and the parts firmly knite, so be you, I beseech you, brethren, much more carfull, that the house of God which you are, and are to be, be not shaken with unnecessarie novelties or other oppositions at the first setling thereof.

Lastly, wheras you are become a body politik, using amongst your selves civill governmente, and are not furnished with any persons of spetiall eminencie above the rest, to be chosen by you into office of government, let your wisdome and godlines appeare, not only in chusing shuch persons as doe entirely love and will promote the comone good, but also in yeelding unto them all due honour and obedience in their lawfull administrations; not beholding in them the ordinarinesse of their persons, but Gods ordinance for your good, not being like the foolish multitud who more honour the gay coate, than either the vertuous minde of the man, or glorious ordinance of the Lord. But you know better things, and that the image of the Lords power and authoritie which the magistrate beareth, is honourable, in how meane persons soever. And this dutie you both may the more willingly and ought the more conscionably to performe, because you are at least for the present to have only them for your ordinarie governours, which your selves shall make choyse of for that worke.

Sundrie other things of importance I could put you in minde of, and of those before mentioned, in more words, but I will not so farr wrong your godly minds as to thinke you heedless of these things, ther being also diverce among you so well able to admonish both themselves and others of what concerneth them. These few things therfore, and the same in few words, I doe ernestly commend unto your care and conscience, joyning therwith my daily incessante prayers unto the Lord, that he who hath made the heavens and the earth, the sea and all rivers of waters, and whose providence is over all his workes, espetially over all his dear children for good, would so guide and gard you in your wayes, as inwardly by his Spirite, so outwardly by the hand of his power, as that both you and we also, for and with you, may have after matter of praising his name all the days of your and our lives. Fare you well in him in whom you trust, and in whom I rest.

An unfained well willer of your hapie
success in this hopefull voyage,
JOHN ROBINSON

Text—Bradford: *History of Plymouth Plantation*, Davis edition, pp. 84-86.

V. *THE MAYFLOWER COMPACT, NOVEMBER 11-21, 1620*

In the name of God, Amen. We whose names are under-written, the loyall subjects of our dread soveraigne Lord, King James, by the grace of God, of Great Britaine, Franc. and Ireland king, defender of the faith, etc., haveing undertaken, for the glorie of God, and advancemente of the Christian faith, and honour of our king and countrie, a voyage to plant the first colonie in the Northerne parts of Virginia, doe by these presents solemnly and mutualy in the presence of God, and one of another, covenant and combine our selves togeather into a civill body politick, for our better ordering and preservation and furtherance of the ends aforesaid; and by vertue hearof to enacte, constitute, and frame such just and equall lawes, ordinances, acts, constitutions, and offices, from time to time, as shall be thought most meete and convenient for the generall good of the Colonie, unto which we promise all due submission and obedience. In witnes wherof we have hereunder subscribed our names at Cap-Codd the 11. of November, in the year of the raigne of our soveraigne lord, King James, of England, France, and Ireland the eighteenth, and of Scotland the fiftie fourth. Anᵒ: Dom. 1620.

Text—Bradford: *History of Plymouth Plantation*, Davis edition, p. 107.

VI. *THE TESTING TIME*

Being thus arived in a good harbor, and brought safe to land, they fell upon their knees and blessed the God of heaven, who had brought them over the vast, and furious ocean, and delivered them from all the periles, and miseries therof againe to set their feete on the firme and stable earth, their proper elemente. And no marvell if they were thus Joyefull, seeing wise Seneca was so affected with sailing a few miles on the coast of his owne Italy; as he affirmed, that he had rather remaine twentie years on his way by land, then pass by sea to any place in a short time; so tedious, and dreadfull was the same unto him.

But hear I cannot but stay, and make a pause, and stand half amased at this poore peoples presente condition; and so I thinke will the reader too, when he well considers the same. Being thus passed the vast ocean, and a sea of troubles before in their preparation (as may be remembred by that which wente before) they had now no freinds to wellcome them, nor inns to entertaine, or refresh their weatherbeaten bodys, no houses, or much less townes to repaire too, to seeke for succoure. It is recorded in scripture as a mercie to the apostle and his shipwraked company, that the barbarians shewed them no smale kindnes in refreshing them, but these savage barbarians, when they mette with them (as after will appeare) were readier to fill their sids full of arrows then otherwise. And for the season it was winter, and they that know the winters of that cuntrie, know them to be sharp and violent, and subjecte to cruell and feirce stormes, deangerous to travill to known places, much more to serch an unknown coast. Besids what could they see, but a hidious and desolate wildernes, full of wild beasts, and willd men, and what multituds ther might be of them they knew not. Neither could they (as it were) goe up to the tope of Pisgah, to vew from this willdernes, a more goodly cuntrie to feed their hops; for which way so ever they turned their eys (save upward to the heavens) they could have litle solacè or content in respecte of any outward objects. For sumer being done, all things stand upon them with a wetherbeaten face; and the whole countrie full of woods and thickets represented a wild and savage heiw. If they looked behind them, ther was the mighty ocean which they had passed, and was now as a maine barr and goulfe to seperate them from all the civill parts of the world. If it be said they had a ship to sucour them, it is trew; but what heard they daly from the mr and company? but that with speede they should looke out a place with their shallop wher they would be, at some near distance; for the season was shuch, as he would not stirr from thence, till a safe harbor was discovered by them wher they would be, and he might goe without danger; and that victells consumed apace, but he must and would keepe sufficient for them selves, and their returne. Yea it was muttered by some, that if they gott not a place in time, they would turne them, and their goods a shore, and leave them. Let it be also considred what weake hopes of supply and succoure they left behinde them, that might bear up their minds in this sade condition and trialls they were under; and they could not but be very smale. It is true indeed, the affections and love of their brethren at Leyden was cordiall and entire towards them, but they had litle power to help them, or them selves; and how the case stode between them, and the marchants at their coming away, hath allready been declared. What could now sustaine them, but the spirite of God and his grace? May not, and ought not the children of these fathers rightly say: *our fathers were English men which came over this great ocean, and were ready to perish in this willderness; but they cried unto the Lord, and he heard their voyce, and looked on their aduersitie, etc. Let them therfore praise the Lord, because he is good and his mercies endure for ever. Yea, let them which have been redeemed of the Lord shew how he hath delivered them from the hand of the oppressour. When they wandered in the deserte willdernes out of the way, and found no citie to dwell in, both hungrie, and thirstie, their sowle was overwhelmed in them. Let them confess before the Lord his loving kindnes, and his wonderfull works before the sons of men.*

. . . After this they chose, or rather confirmed, Mr John Carver (a man godly and well approved amongst them) their Governour for that year. And after they had provided a place for their goods, or comone store, (which were long in unlading for want of boats, foulnes of the winter weather, and sickenes of diverce,) and begune some small cottages for their habitation as time would admitte, they mette and consulted of lawes, and orders, both for the civil and military Govermente, as the necessitie of their condition did require, still adding therunto as urgent occasion in severall times and as cases did require.

In these hard and difficulte beginnings they found some discontents and murmurings arise amongst some, and mutinous speeches and carriags in other; but they were soone quelled, and overcome by the wisdome, patience, and just and equall carrage of things, by the Govr and better part, which clave faithfully togeather in the maine. But that which was most sadd, and lamentable was, that in .2. or.3. moneths time halfe of their company dyed, espetialy in Jan : and February, being the depth of winter, and wanting houses and other comforts; being infected with the scurvie and other diseases, which this long vioage and their inacomodate condition had brought upon them; so as ther dyed some times 2. or 3. of a day, in the foresaid time; that of .100. and odd persons, scarce .50. remained. And of these in the time of most distres ther was but 6. or 7. sound persons, who, to their great comendations, be it spoken, spared no pains, night nor day, but with abundance of toyle and hazard of their owne health, fetched them wood, made them fires, drest them meat, made their beads, washed ther lothsome cloaths, cloathed and uncloathed them. . . . .

May 12. was the first mariage in this place, which according to the laudable custome of the Low-Cuntries, in which they had lived, was thought most requisite to be performed by the magestrate as being a civill thing, upon which many questions aboute inheritances doe depende, with other things most proper to their cogaizans, and most consonante to the Scripturs. Ruth. 4, and nowher found in the gospell to be layed on the ministers as a part of their office. "This decree or law ab ut mariage was publ'shed by the Stats of the Low-Cuntries Ano: 1590. That those of any religion, after lawfull and open publication, coming before the magistrats, in the Town or Stat-house, were to be orderly (by them) maried one to another." Petets Hist. fol: 1029. And this practiss hath continued amongst, not only them, but hath been followed by all the famous churches of Christ in these parts to this time.—Ano: 1646. . . . .

After the departure of this ship, (which stayed not above 14. days,) the Gover and his assistante haveing disposed these late commers into severall families, as they best could, tooke an exacte accounte of all their provissions in store, and proportioned the same to the number of persons, and found that it would not hould out above 6. months at halfe alowance, and hardly that. And they could not well give less this winter time till fish came in againe. So they were presently put to half alowance, one as well as an other, which begane to be hard, but they bore it patiently under hope of supply. . . . .

But this made them the more carefully to looke to them selves, so as they agreed to inclose their dwellings with a good strong pale, and make flankers in convenient places, with gates to shute, which were every night locked, and a watch kept and when neede required ther was also warding in the day time. And the company was by the Captaine and the Govr advise, devided into 4. squadrons, and every one had ther quarter apoynted them, unto which they were to repaire upon any suddane alarme. And if ther should be any crie of fire, a company were appointed for a gard, with muskets, whilst others quenchet the same, to prevent Indean treachery. This was accomplished very cherfully, and the towne impayled round by the begining of March, in which evry family had a pretty garden plote secured. And herewith I shall end this year. Only I shall remember one passage more, rather of mirth then of waight.   One the day called Chrismasday, the Govr caled them out to worke, (as was used) but the most of this new-company excused them selves and said it wente against their consciences to work on that day.   So the Govr tould them that if they made it mater of conscience, he would spare them till they were better informed.   So he led-away the rest and left them; but when they came home at noone from their worke, he found them in the streete at play openly; some pitching the barr, and some at stoole-ball, and shuch like sports.   So he went to them, and tooke away their implements, and tould them that was against his conscience, that they should play and others worke. If they made the keeping of it mater of devotion, let them kepe their houses, but ther should be no gameing, or revelling in the streets.   Since which time nothing hath been atempted that way, at least openly. . . .

All this whille no supply was heard of, neither knew they when they might expecte any.   So they begane to thinke how they might raise as much corne as they could, and obtaine a beter crope then they had done, that they might not still thus languish in miserie.   At length, after much debate of things, the Govr (with the advise of the cheefest amongest them) gave way that they should set corne every man for his owne perticuler, and in that regard trust to them selves; in all other things to goe on in the generall way as before.   And so assigned to every family a parcell of land, according to the proportion of their number for that end, only for present use (but made no devission for inheritance), and ranged all boys and youth under some familie.   This had very good success; for it made all hands very industrious, so as much more corne was planted then other waise would have bene by any means the Govr or any other could use, and saved him a great deall of trouble, and gave farr better contente.   The women now wente willingly into the feild, and tooke their litle-ons with them to set corne, which before would aledg weaknes and inabilitie; whom to have compelled would have bene thought great tiranie, and oppression. . . .

Text—Bradford: *History of the Plymouth Plantation,* Davis edition, pp. 95-97, 107-108, 116-117, 125-127, 146.

CHAPTER V

MASSACHUSETTS BAY IN THE SEVENTEENTH CENTURY

Bibliography

The history of settlement around Massachusetts Bay prior to the great emigration is to be gleaned from "Mourt's Relation"; Bradford's "History of the Plymouth Plantation" (for both see page 40); "A Brief Relation, . . . " by Sir Ferdinando Gorges (1622, edited by J. P. Baxter, A.M. in "Prince Society Publications," Vol. I, 1890); Winthrop's "Journal"; and Thomas Morton's "New English Canaan" (for both see below). A Paper on "Old Planters" by C. F. Adams is to be found in "Proc. Mass. Hist. Soc." Vol. XVI, pp. 194-206.

"The Planters Plea, . . . " (1630—Force, "Tracts and Papers," Vol. II, Tract III; in part, Young's "Chronicles of . . . Massachusetts Bay,") usually attributed to the Rev. John White, gives 'Ground of Plantations Examined, usual Objections answered, Together with a manifestation of the causes mooving such as have lately undertaken a Plantation in New England.' Higginson's Journal of the voyage of 1629 is embodied in "A True Relation of the Last Voyage to New England, . . . " (Young's "Chronicles"). The Company's letters of instructions to Endicott and his Council, the Instrument of Government for the Colony, the allotment of lands, oaths of office, and contract between the Company and the ministers, are all to be found among these "Chronicles"; also "New England's Plantation" (1630) by Higginson and "General Considerations or Conclusions" (1629), assigned by Savage to Governor Winthrop. Deputy Governor Dudley's letter to the Countess of Lincoln (ibid.) gives a fine insight into affairs up to date of writing, March, 1631. In his "Advertisements for the unexperienced Planters of New England or Anywhere" (1631) Captain Smith refers to the trying experiences of the Charleston-Salem settlers (Arber's edition of "Captain Smith's Works," and "Coll. Mass. Hist. Soc." Series III, Vol. III).

"New England's Prospects" (1634) by William Wood, descriptive of nature and natives in New England, is accessible in the "Prince

Society Publications," (1865). Thomas Morton, too pleasure loving to be appreciative of serious minded Puritans by whom he was twice banished, had his innings in his satire, "New English Canaan" (London, 1633—Force "Tracts and Papers," Vol. II Tract V) which despite its strictures, has real historical worth. Rev. Nathaniel Ward's "Body of Liberties" (1641) with critical introductory remarks by F. C. Gray, appears in "Coll. Mass. Hist. Soc." Series III, Vol. VIII, while John Cotton's "Abstract of the Laws of New England" (1641) may be found in "Coll. Mass. Hist. Soc." Series I, Vol. V. Thomas Lechford, resident in the Colony 1638-1641, having had hard times to make ends meet because of his being a lawyer, upon his return to England wrote "Plain Dealing" (1642) which is valuable both for its fullness and impartial spirit. J. H. Trumbull's edition (1867) is highly satisfactory. An older reprint appears in "Coll. Mass. Hist. Soc." Series III, Vol. III. The "Note Book" kept by Lechford June 27, 1638 to July 29, 1641, may be profitably consulted ("Transactions Amer. Antiq. Soc.," Vol. VII).

Within the limits of this abbreviated bibliography, detailed references to all the productions of John Cotton is impossible, and unnecessary inasmuch as many of them are too controversial to have real historical value. Two, however, should be mentioned—"Keys of the Kingdom of Heaven," showing Cotton's conception of church government, and "The Way of the Congregational Churches," which throws considerable light upon persons and affairs of the colony. "John Cotton's Farewell Sermon to Winthrop's Company at Southampton" by Edwin D. Mead ("Proc. Mass. Hist. Soc." Series III, Vol. I, pp. 101-114) has technical bibliographical data. For further information concerning Cotton, the reader is referred to the bibliography on Rhode Island (p. 111) and to the Appendix to Dexter's "Congregationalism of the Last Three Hundred Years, . . . ".

Around certain disturbers of the peace considerable literature developed. Roger Williams was the earliest. For his writings the reader is referred to the bibliography on Rhode Island (see p. 111). Ann Hutchinson, another of these disturbers, may be studied very satisfactorily in "Antinomianism in the Colony of Massachusetts Bay, 1636-1638" ("Prince Society Publications," 1893). This work, edited by C. F. Adams, contains "A Short Story" (1644), "The Examination of Mrs. Ann Hutchinson at the Court at Newtown," (November, 1637), and "A Report of the Trial of Mrs. Ann Hutchinson before the Church in Boston" (March, 1638). John Wheelwright is known through his "Fast Day Sermon" (Jan. 16, 1636), "The Mercurius Americanus"

(1645), and "His Will" (1679). These are accessible with a "Memoir" by C. H. Bell in the "Prince Society Publications" for 1876. Samuel Gorton, another agitator, was the author of "Simplicitie's Defence" (1646), a virulent pamphlet ("Coll. Rhode Island Hist. Soc.," Vol. II; and Force, "Tracts and Papers," Vol. IV, Tract VI) to which Edward Winslow replied in the same year in the "Hypocrisie Unmasked," now a very rare book. In the following year Winslow felt called upon in a tract entitled "New England's Salamander Discovered" ("Coll. Mass. Hist. Soc.," Series III, Vol. II), to reply to a Presbyterian group which, smarting under the loss of their franchise, had attacked the theocracy in a pamphlet called "New England's Jonas cast up at London" (1647). All this literature, altho controversial is worth consulting for side lights upon conditions in Massachusetts Bay.

The death (1649) of John Winthrop terminated the journal of events which, while itself not a history though so named by its author, supplied in a large measure the data from which the history of Massachusetts has been written. Obscured for many years, it was published in part by Noah Webster (1790) and complete (1825-6) by James Savage. It now appears among the "Original Narratives of Early American History" (II vols. 1908) edited by Dr. James K. Hosmer. The "Life and Letters of John Winthrop" (Vol. I, 1864, Vol. II, 1867) by R. C. Winthrop, are almost indispensable as companion volumes to the journal.

About this time interest in the evangelization of the Indian promoted by Winslow, Williams, Eliot, Mayhew and others, began to find expression in a series of tracts descriptive of missionary achievements among the natives—"New England's First Fruits" (1643), "The Daybreaking, if not the Sunrising of the Gospel with the Indians in New England" (1647), "The Clear Sunshine of the Gospel breaking forth upon the Indians, . . ." (1648), "The Glorious Progress of the Gospel Amongst the Indians in New England" (1649), "The Light appearing more and more towards the Perfect Day" (1651), "Strength out of Weakness" (1652), "Tears of Repentance" (1653). These and others are reprinted in "Coll. Mass. Hist. Soc.," Series III, Vol. IV. Bibliography of 1642-1646 (19 titles) is tabulated by W. C. Ford in a discussion of the authorship of "New England's First Fruits" ("Proc. Mass. Hist. Soc.," Series III, Vol. II, pp. 259-266).

To illustrate, 'The Goodness of God in the Settlement of These Colonies,' Edward Johnson wrote (1652) "Wonder-Working Providence of Sion's Saviour in New England" (Coll. Mass. Hist. Soc.," Series II, Vols. II, III, IV, VII, VIII; and "Original Narratives of Early American

History" edited by Dr. J. F. Jameson). This was based upon personal observations and is therefore valuable for details though from a literary standpoint it is not inviting.

Quaker history forms the next chapter in Massachusetts literature. Dr. John Clarke's arraignment of Massachusetts in "Ill Newes from New England" (1652—"Coll. Mass. Hist. Soc." Series IV, Vol. II), followed by harrowing accounts of Quaker sufferings such as "The Popish Inquisition Newly Erected in New England" (1659) and "A Call from Death to Life" (1660) culminated in "New England Judged" (Vol. I. 1661, Vol. II, 1667) by George Bishop.

Passing over the relatively unimportant literature of Philip's War (for details see Winsor, "Narrative and Critical History" Vol. III, p. 360 f.), the year 1681 brings us to "A General History of New England from the Discovery to MDCLXXX," by Rev. William Hubbard, transcribed by order of the Court, but not printed until 1815 by the Mass. Hist. Society ("Coll.," Series II, Vols. V and VI). Based upon Bradford's "History" and Winthrop's "Journal," this work in spite of some minor defects has substantial worth.

Much of the period (1647-76) covered by Hubbard was traversed by the "Diaries of John Hull," who well qualified by training and in his official capacity as director of the mint made discriminating observations upon the affairs of the colony ("Transactions and Coll. Amer. Antiq. Soc.," Vol. III). Another diary of intrinsic worth covering the last quarter of the century is that of Samuel Sewall ("Coll. Mass. Hist. Soc.," Series V, Vols. V-VII). His "Letter-Book" is reprinted in "Coll. Mass. Hist. Soc.," Series VI, Vols. I and II). A good study "Judge Samuel Sewall (1652-1730) a Typical Massachusetts Puritan" by Rev. John L. Ewell, appears in "Papers, Amer. Soc. Ch. Hist." Vol. VII, pp. 25-55. A third diary, exceptionally illuminating, covering the period 1674-1720 is that of Cotton Mather ("Coll. Mass. Hist. Soc.," Series VII, Vol. VII and VIII). "A Narrative of the Planting of the Massachusetts Colony Anno. 1628. . . . Published by Old Planters the Authors of the Old Men's Tears" (1694) usually cited as "Scottow's Narrative" ("Coll. Mass. Hist. Soc.," Series IV, Vol. IV) looks mournfully back to the "good old times" and must be interpreted with discrimination.

The eighteenth century opens (1702) with the "Magnalia" of Cotton Mather. Though devoid of all arrangement and lacking any index, this history is indispensable for its wealth of miscellaneous information. "The British Empire in America" (1708) by John Oldmixon, unoriginal and unreliable, is almost worthless. Rev. Daniel Neal's "History of

New England" (1720—republished and enlarged 1747) adds somewhat to the "Magnalia." "A Chronological History of New England, . . . " (Vol. I to 1630, in 1736; Vol. II to 1633, in 1755) by Rev. Thomas Prince is analytical, lifeless, poorly proportioned, yet accurate. "A Summary, Historical and Political . . . of the British Settlements of North America" (1747) by W. Douglass, M.D., left unfinished through the author's death, has considerable material relating to early New England, but bears the impress of haste and lack of assimilation. A work of standard value is Thomas Hutchinson's "History of Massachusetts Bay" (1767), two volumes of which bring the narrative down to 1749; a third (1828) posthumous, coming to 1774. "Original Papers" (1769) adds materially to the serviceableness of Vol. I. Only slightly inferior is John S. Barry's "History of Massachusetts" (III vols. 1855-57). "A History of New England" by John G. Palfrey (V vols., I-III 1858-64; IV, 1875) carrying the narrative to 1741, is a work both scholarly and lucid, by no means relegated to obsolescence by the more recent works.

Turning to the history of the church, an "Ecclesiastical History of Massachusetts" by Rev. John Eliot ("Coll. Mass. Hist. Soc.," Series I, Vols. IX and X; Series II, Vol. I), though antiquated, holds a place as written by one largely contemporaneous with the events under review. Of modern histories, the pioneer work is "The Ecclesiastical History of New England" (Vol. I, 1855; Vol. II, 1862) by Joseph P. Felt. Twenty years of investigation with unlimited access to source material, a scholarly mind, and a broad conception of church history, enabled this author to do work that, while supplemented (coming only to 1678) has by no means been displaced by more recent contributors.

Congregationalism finds its advocates in George Punchard, John Waddington, Leonard Bacon, Henry M. Dexter, and Williston Walker. For titles, dates, and estimates of these, see page 42. "The First Congregational Society in New Bedford" (1889) by Wm. J. Potter should not be overlooked, much less the "History of the Old South Church, Boston" (II Vols. 1889) by Hamilton A. Hills, illuminative of more than the history of this one church in Boston. The bibliography (Vol. II) will be prized by every investigator.

Anglicanism has been presented by Canon J. S. M. Anderson, Bishop Samuel Wilberforce, Rt. Rev. W. S. Perry, and Professor C. C. Tiffany. For titles, dates, and estimates, see page 7). The "Annals of King's Chapel" (Vol. I, 1881) by Henry W. Foote, is a scholarly and well documented work. "A History of King's Chapel in Boston, the First Episcopal Church in New England" (1833) by Francis W. Greenwood is not so thorough. Rev. W. S. Perry in his "Historical Collections Relating to the American Colonial Church" (Vol. III, 1870) has supplied some source material for the period subsequent to 1676.

The struggles of the Baptists may be studied in "A General History of the Baptist Denomination in America, . . . " (1813) by David Benedict, a work which though antiquated is informing. "A History of New England, With Particular Reference to the Denomination of Christians Called Baptists" (1777, 1784, 1796; 2nd edition, With Notes by David Weston, II Vols, 1871) by Isaac Backus is highly serviceable for its copious use of source material though somewhat lacking in literary quality. "A History of the Baptists Traced by Their Vital Principles" (1887) by Thomas Armitage is marred by its fulsome denominational enthusiasm. "A History of the Baptist Churches in America" by Professor A. H. Newman, ("Am. Ch. Hist. Series," Vol. II, 1893) gives the facts in attractive form. "A History of the Baptists in New England" (1894) by Henry S. Burrage, is a scholarly piece of work. "The History of the First Baptist Church of Boston 1665-1899" (1899) by Rev. Nathan E. Wood, and a "Historical Sketch of the First Baptist Church, Swansea, Mass. 1663-1863" (1863) by J. J. Thatcher, should be consulted.

The essential facts of Massachusetts Quakerism have been well set forth in a brief monograph, "The Quaker Invasion of Massachusetts" (1883) by Richard P. Hallowell. An appendix has valuable source material. "Quaker Protests, 1659-1675" (Proc. Mass Hist. Soc.," Series III, Vol. II, pp. 359-380) by W. C. Ford has considerable documentary material. For other standard histories of Quakerism, the reader is referred to the bibliography on Pennsylvania (page 154.)

On witchcraft much has been written of which the following is representative: "History of Witchcraft and Salem Village" (II Vols. 1867) by Charles W. Upham; "Witch Trials in Massachusetts" by Abner C. Goodell, Jr. ("Proc. Mass. Hist. Soc.," Vol. XX, pp. 280-326; also Series II, Vol. I, pp. 65-77); "Notes on the History of Witchcraft in Massachusetts; with Illustrative Documents" by George H. Moore ("Proc. Amer. Antiq. Soc.," New Series, Vol. II, pp. 162-192), and "Notes on the Bibliography of Witchcraft in Massachusetts" (Ibid. Vol. V, pp. 245-273); "Witchcraft in Salem Village in 1692, together with some account of other Witchcraft Persecutions in New England and Elsewhere" (1892) by Winfield S. Nevins; "The Literature of Witchcraft in New England" by Justin Winsor ("Proc. Amer. Antiq. Soc." New Series, Vol. X, pp. 351-373); "Notes on Witchcraft" by George L. Kittredge (*Ibid.* Vol. XVIII, pp. 148-212). The several studies on Puritanism (see below) have chapters devoted to witchcraft. One periodical article deserves notice—"Cotton Mather and Salem Witchcraft" ("The North American," April, 1869).

On Harvard University, "The History of Harvard University" (II Vols. 1840) by Josiah Quincy, and "A History of Harvard University from its Foundation in the Year 1636 to the Period of the American Revolution" (1831) by Benjamin Peirce are standard works enriched with much documentary material. "The Influence of the English Univversities in the Development of New England" by Franklin B. Dexter ("Proc. Mass. Hist. Soc." Vol. XVII, pp. 340-351) though brief is suggestive. Other valuable contributions are as follows: "The Lawes of Harvard Colledge agreed upon by the Overseers, President and fellows . . . 1655" by Samuel A. Green ("Proc. Mass. Hist. Soc.," Vol. XIV, pp. 206-215); "Subjects for Masters Degree in Harvard College from 1655 to 1791" by Edward J. Young (*Ibid.* Vol. XVIII, pp. 119-151); "The "Relations between Harvard College and the First Church in Cambridge" by Albert Bushnell Hart (*Ibid.* Series II, Vol. V, pp. 396-415); "Early Harvard Commencements" by Samual A. Green (*Ibid.* Series II, Vol. X, pp. 194-205); "Theses of Commencers at Harvard College in 1663" contributed by Henry H. Edes ("Pub. Col. Soc. of Mass." Vol. V, pp. 322-339); "Harvard College in 1671 as revealed in a letter Syned by thirteen" by Albert Matthews (*Ibid.* Vol. XI, pp. 336-340); "Harvard Commencement Days, 1642 1916" by the same writer (*Ibid.* Vol. XVIII, pp. 308-384).

On the related subject of Libraries there are four contributions: "Parochial Libraries in the Colonial Period" by Bishop John F. Hurst, D.D. ("Papers, Amer. Soc. of Church History" Vol. II, Part I, pp. 37-50); "Early Private Libraries in New England" by Franklin B. Dexter, ("Proc. Amer. Antiq. Soc.," New Series, Vol. XVIII, pp. 135-147); "The Libraries of the Mathers" by Julius H. Tuttle, (*Ibid.*, New Series, Vol. XX, pp. 269-356); also "Early Libraries in New England" by the same author ("Pub. Col. Soc. of Mass.," Vol. XIII, pp. 288-295).

"Early New England Catechisms" by Wilberforce Eames ("Proc. Amer. Antiq. Soc.," New Series, Vol. XII, pp. 76-182) will be useful to those interested in the religious education of New England; also "The New England Primer" with an historical introduction (1899) by Paul Leicester Ford, and "Religious Education in New England in the Colonial Era" (D. B. Dissertation, Univ. of Chicago, 1911) by E. LeRoy Dakin.

Puritanism in its several aspects, domestic, social, political and religious, has found reiterated exposition in the following: Hermann F. Uhden, "The New England Theocracy, A History of the Congregationalists in New England to the Revival of 1740" (n.d.); Thomas W. Coit, "Puritanism or a Churchman's Defence Against its Aspersion," (1845); Brooks Adams, "The Emancipation of Massachusetts," (1886); George E. Ellis, "The Puritan Age and Rule in the Colony of Massachusetts, 1629-1685" (1888); Paul E. Lauer, "Church and State in New England," ("J. H. U. Studies," Series X); Alice Morse Earle, "The Sabbath in Puritan New England" (7th ed., 1893); Ezra H. Byington, "The Puritan in England and New England" (1896) and "The Puritan as a Colonist and Reformer" (1900); Daniel W. Howe, "The Puritan Republic of the Massachusetts Bay in New England" (1899); W. De Loss Love, Jr., "The Fast and Thanksgiving Days of New England" (1895); William D. Northend, "The Bay Colony" (1896); Andrew McF. Davis, "John Harvard's Life in America, . . . " ("Pub. Col. Soc. of Mass.," Vol. XII); "The Early Homes of the Puritans" by T. F. Waters (Hist. Coll. Essex Institute. Vol. XXXIII—Parts I–VI, and "Literary Culture in Early New England . . . " by T. G. Wright (1920).

"Three Episodes of Massachusetts History" (II Vols. 1892) by Charles F. Adams, the fruit of long years of close study is fascinatingly written and one of the best books upon the subject. "Early New England Towns. A Comparative Study of their Development" by Anne B. Maclear ("Columbia Univ. Studies" Vol. XXIX—No. 1) and "Legal Development in Colonial Massachusetts 1630-1686" by C. J. Hilkey (ibid. Vol. XXXVII No. 2) touch many topics of ecclesiastical interest. "New England's Struggle for Religious Liberty" (1896) by David B. Ford is outclassed by "Church and State in Massachusetts, 1691-1740" (1914) by Susan M. Reed. The latter work has an excellent bibliography.

Of biographical studies there are the following: "Cotton Mather, the Puritan Priest" (1891) by Barrett Wendell; "The Life and Times of Cotton Mather, D.D., F.R.S." (1892) by Rev. Abijah T. Marvin; "The Services of the Mathers in New England Religious Development" by Williston Walker, ("Papers, Amer. Soc. Ch. Hist.," Vol. V, pp. 64-89); and "Cotton Mather and the Supernormal in New England History" by Josiah P. Quincy, ("Proc. Mass. Hist. Soc.," Series II, Vol. XX, pp. 439-453). On Higginson there is a "Life of Francis Higginson, . . . " ("Makers of America" Series, 1891) by Thomas W. Higginson; and "Rev. John Higginson of Salem" by Simeon E. Baldwin,

("Proc. Mass. Hist. Soc.," Series II, Vol. XVI, pp. 478-520). "Ten New England Leaders" (1901) by Williston Walker has studies on John Cotton, Richard Mather, John Eliot, and Increase Mather. "Samuel Sewall and the World he Lived In" (1897) by Rev. N. H. C. Chamberlain gives a vivid portraiture of the age.

In the "Organization of a Colonial Church" ("Pub. Col. Soc. of Mass.," Vol. XIII, pp. 82-95) and "Excommunication in Colonial Churches" (*Ibid.*, Vol. XII, pp. 321-332), Rev. Charles E. Park has given fresh presentations to familiar facts; also Rev. Edward H. Hall in "Relations between the First Church of Hartford and the First Church in Cambridge" ("Pub. Col. Soc. of Mass.," Vol. XIII, pp. 273-277).

Four related studies on church discipline and morality are as follows: "Some Phases of Sexual Morality and Church Discipline in Colonial New England" by Charles F. Adams ("Proc. Mass. Hist. Soc.," Series II, Vol. VI, pp. 477-516); "Domestic Relations in Colonial New England in the Seventeenth Century" (A. M. Dissertation, Univ. of Chicago, 1912) by Alfred P. James; "Moral Discipline in Early New England Churches" (D. B. Dissertation, Univ. of Chicago, 1915) by Harry W. Johnson; "The Moral Virtues and Vices of New England During the Seventeenth Century" (D. B. Dissertation, Univ. of Chicago, 1915) by Lewis A. Stark.

A large amount of ecclesiastical materal is to be found in church records, such as Cambridge, Dedham, First Church Dorchester and Beverly; also in town records as follows: Boxford, Baintree, Cambridge, Dedham, Groton, Ipswich, Lancaster, Rowley, Springfield, and Watertown. Local histories repay attention. The following list though lengthy is not presented as exhaustive: Abington, Andover, Amesbury, Attlebury, Beverly, Bradford, North Bridgewater, Brookline, Byfield, Charlestown, Chelsea, Concord, Cambridge, Dorchester, Dunstable, Hadley, Haver Hill, Ipswich, Hatfield, Malden, Marblehead, Mattapoisset, Medford, Newbury, Newton, Northampton, Reading, Reheboth, Roxbury, Salem, Wenham, and Worcester.

Legal documentary material is available in the "Records of Massachusetts" (1628-1686, V Vols.); "The Records of Court Assistants of the Colony of Massachusetts Bay" (II Vols.); "Records and Files of the Quarterly Court of Essex, Mass." (1636-1671, IV Vols.)

An investigator is likely to be rewarded by looking through the following: "Transactions and Collections of the American Antiquarian Society"; "Transactions and Proceedings of the Massachusetts Historical Society"; "The New England Historical and Genealogical Register"; "The Publications of the Colonial Society of Massachusetts"; "Historical Collections of The Essex Institute" (rich in church records) "The Granite Monthly"; the "Proceedings and Collections of the New Hampshire Historical Society;" "The Collections of the Maine Historical Society," and "The Collections of the Massachusetts Historical Society," especially "The Hinckley Papers" (Series IV, Vol. V), "The Mather Papers" (Series IV, Vol. VIII), "The Winthrop Papers" (Series III, Vol. IX and X; Series IV, Vols. VI and VII; Series V, Vols. I and VIII, and Series VI, Vols. III and V) and "Belknap Papers" (Series VI, Vol. IV).

DOCUMENTS

I. *THE PURITAN'S ATTITUDE TO SEPARATION*

The Humble Request of his Majestie's loyall Subjects, the Governour and (the) Company late gone for New-England; To the rest of their Brethren in and of the Church of England. For the obtaining of their Prayers, and the removall of suspitions and misconstructions of their Intentions.

REVEREND FATHERS AND BRETHREN:

The general rumor of this solemn enterprise, wherein ourselves with others, through the providence of the Almighty, are engaged, as it may spare us the labor of imparting our occasion unto you, so it gives us the more encouragement to strengthen ourselves by the procurement of the prayers and blessings of the Lord's faithful servants. For which end we are bold to have recourse unto you, as those whom God hath placed nearest his throne of mercy; which, as it affords you the more opportunity, so it imposeth the greater bond upon you to intercede for his people in all their straits. We beseech you, therefore, by the mercies of the Lord Jesus, to consider us as your brethren, standing in very great need of your help, and earnestly imploring it. And howsoever your charity may have met with some occasion of discouragement through the misreport of our intentions, or through the disaffection or indiscretion of some of us, or rather amonst us, (for we are not of those that dream of perfection in this world,) yet we desire you would be pleased to take notice of the principals and body of our Company, as those who esteem it our honor to call the Church of England, from whence we rise, our dear mother; and cannot part from our native country, where she specially resideth, without much sadness of heart and many tears in our eyes, ever acknowledging that such hope and part as we have obtained in the common salvation, we have received in her bosom, and sucked it from her breasts. We leave it not, therefore, as loathing that milk wherewith we were nourished there; but, blessing God for the parentage and education, as members of the same body, shall always rejoice in her good, and unfeignedly grieve for any sorrow that shall ever betide her, and while we have breath, sincerely desire and endeavor the continuance and abundance of her welfare, with the enlargement of her bounds in the Kingdom of Christ Jesus.

Be pleased, therefore, reverend fathers and brethren, to help forward this work now in hand; which, if it prosper, you shall be the more glorious, howsoever your judgment is with the Lord, and your reward with your God. It is a usual and laudable exercise of your charity to commend to the prayers of your congregations the necessities and straits of your private neighbors; do the like for a Church springing out of your own bowels. We conceive much hope that this remembrance of us, if it be frequent and fervent, will be a most prosperous gale in our sails, and provide such a passage and welcome for us from the God of the whole earth, as both we which shall find it, and yourselves, with the rest of our friends, who shall hear of it, shall be much enlarged to bring in such daily returns of thanksgivings, as the specialties of his providence and goodness may justly challenge at all our hands. You are not ignorant that the spirit of God stirred up the Apostle Paul to make continual mention of the Church of Philippi, which was a colony from Rome; let the same spirit, we beseech you, put you in mind, that are the Lord's remembrancers, to pray for us without ceasing, who are a weak colony from yourselves, making continual request for us to God in all your prayers.

What we intreat of you, that are the ministers of God, that we also crave at the hands of all the rest of our brethren, that they would at no time forget us in their private solicitations at the throne of grace.

If any there be who, through want of clear intelligence of our course, or tenderness of affection towards us, cannot conceive so well of our way as we could desire, we would intreat such not to despise us, nor to desert us in their prayers and affections, but to consider rather that they are so much the more bound to express the bowels of their compassion towards us, remembering always that both nature and grace doth ever bind us to relieve and rescue, with our utmost and speediest power, such as are dear unto us, when we conceive them to be running uncomfortable hazards.

What goodness you shall extend to us, in this or any other Christian kindness, we, your brethren in Christ Jesus, shall labor to repay in what duty we are or shall be able to perform, promising, so far as God shall enable us, to give him no rest on your behalfs, wishing our heads and hearts may be [as] fountains of tears for your everlasting welfare when we shall be in our poor cottages in the wilderness, overshadowed with the spirit of supplication, through the manifold necessities and tribulations which may not altogether unexpectedly, nor, we hope, unprofitably, befall us.

And so commending you to the grace of God in Christ, we shall ever rest

Your assured friends and brethren,

JOHN WINTHROPE, *Gov.*	RICHARD SALTONSTALL,
CHARLES FINES,	ISAAC JOHNSON,
	THOMAS DUDLEY,
GEORGE PHILLIPS,	WILLIAM CODDINGTON,
&c.	&c.

From Yarmouth, aboard the Arbella, April 7, 1630.

Text—Hubbard: *General History of New England. . .* Chapter XXIII: in Coll. Mass. Hist. Society, Series II, Vol. V, pp. 126-128.

II. *THE BEGINNING OF FELLOWSHIP BETWEEN PURITAN AND SEPARATIST*

Bradford thus describes the circumstances out of which the Puritans of Salem were led to look more charitably upon the church polity of the Separatist group at Plymouth.

It was before noted that sundry of those that came from Leyden, came over in the ships that came to Salem, wher Mr. Endecott had cheefe command; and by infection that grue amonge the passengers at sea, it spread also among them a shore, of which many dyed, some of the scurvie, other of an infectious feaoure, which continued some time amongst them (though our people, through Gods goodnes, escaped it). Upon which occasion he write hither for some help, understanding here was one that had some skill that way, and had cured diverse of the scurvie, and others of other diseases, by letting blood, and other means. Upon which his request the Govr hear sent him unto them, and also write to him, from whom he received an answere; the which, because it is breefe, and shows the beginning of their acquaintance, and closing in the truth and ways of God, I thought it not unmeete, nor without use, hear to inserte it: and an other showing the beginning of their fellowship and church estate ther.

Being as followeth:

Right worthy Sr:

It is a thing not usuall, that servants to one m^r and of the same household should be strangers; I assure you I desire it not, nay, to speake more plainly, I cannot be so to you. Gods people are all marked with one and the same marke, and sealed with one and the same seale, and have for the maine, one and the same harte, guided by one and same spirite of truth; and wher this is, ther can be no discorde, nay, here must needs be sweete harmonie. And the same request (with you) I make unto the Lord, that we may, as Christian breethren, be united by a heavenly and unfained love; bending all our harts and forces in furthering a worke beyond our strength, with reverence and fear, fastening our eyse allways on him that only is able to directe and prosper all our ways. I acknowledge my selfe much bound to you for your kind love and care in sending Mr. Fuller among us, and rejoyce much that I am by him satisfied touching your judgments of the outward forme of Gods worshipe. It is, as farr as I can yet gather, no other then is warrented by the evidence of truth, and the same which I have proffessed and maintained ever since the Lord in mercie revealed him selfe unto me; being farr from the commone reporte that hath been spread of you touching that perticuler. But Gods children must not looke for less here below, and it is the great mercie of God, that he strengthens them to goe through with it. I shall not neede at this time to be tedious unto you, for, God willing, I purpose to see your face shortly. In the mean time, I humbly take my leave of you, committing you to the Lords blessed protection, and rest,

Your assured loving friend,
Jo: Endecott.

Naumkeak, May 11. An^o. 1629.

Text—Bradford: *History of Plymouth Plantation*, Davis edition, pp. 259-261.

III. *THE CONGREGATIONALIZING OF PURITANISM*

The following letter addressed to Governor Bradford describes how the Puritans, influenced by the Pilgrims at Plymouth, passed to a polity congregational in character.

Sr: I make bould to trouble you with a few lines, for to certifie you how it hath pleased God to deale with us, since you heard from us. How, notwithstanding all opposition that hath been hear, and els wher, it hath pleased God to lay a foundation, the which I hope is agreeable to his word in every thing. The 20. of July, it pleased the Lord to move the hart of our Gov[r] to set it aparte for a solemne day of humlliation for the choyce of a pastor and teacher. The former parte of the day being spente in praier and teaching, the later parte aboute the election, which was after this maner. The persons thought on (who had been ministers in England) were demanded concerning their callings; they acknowledged ther was a towfould calling, the one an inward calling, when the Lord moved the harte of a man to take that calling upon him, and fitted him with guiftes for the same; the second was an outward calling, which was from the people, when a company of beleevers are joyned togither in covenante, to walke togither in all the ways of God, and every member (being men) are to have a free voyce in the choyce of their officers, etc. Now, we being persuaded that these 2. men were so quallified, as the apostle speaks to Timothy, wher he saith, A bishop must be blamles, sober, apte to teach, etc., I think I may say, as the eunuch said unto Philip, What should let from being baptised, seeing ther was water? and he beleeved. So these 2. servants of God, clearing all things by their answers, (and being thus fitted,) we saw noe reason but we might freely give our voyces for their election, after this triall. So Mr. Skelton was chosen pastor, and Mr. Higgison to be teacher; and they accepting the choyce, Mr. Higgison, with 3. or 4. of the gravest members of the church, laid their hands on Mr. Skelton, using prayer therwith. This being done, ther was imposission of hands on Mr. Higgison also. And since that time, Thursday (being, as I take it, the 6. of August) is appoynted for another day of humlliation, for the choyce of elders and deacons, and ordaining of them.

And now, good Sr, I hope that you and the rest of Gods people (who are acquainted with the ways of God) with you, will say that hear was a right foundation layed, and that these 2. blessed servants of the Lord came in at the dore, and not at the window. Thus I have made bould to trouble you with these few lines, desiring you to remember us, etc. And so rest,

At your service in what I may,
CHARLES GOTT.

Salem, July 30. 1629.

Text—Bradford: *History of Plymouth Plantation*, Davis edition, pp. 261, 262.

IV. *CHURCH POLITY*

The Organization of a Church

(Mo. 12. 1.) Mr. Shepherd, a godly minister, come lately out of England, and divers other good Christians, intending to raise a church body, came and acquainted the magistrates therewith, who gave their approbation. They also sent to all the neighboring churches for their elders to give their assistance, at a certain day, at Newtown, when they should constitute their body. Accordingly, at this day, there met a great assembly, where the proceeding was as followeth:

Mr. Shepherd and two others (who were after to be chosen to office) sate together in the elder's seat. Then the elder of them began with prayer. After this, Mr. Shepherd prayed with deep confession of sin, etc., and exercised out of Eph. v.—that he might make it to himself a holy, etc.; and also opened the cause of their meeting, etc. Then the elder desired to know of the churches assembled, what number were needful to make a church, and how they ought to proceed in this action. Whereupon some of the ancient ministers, conferring shortly together, gave answer: That the scripture did not set down any certain rule for the number. Three (they thought) were too few, because by Matt. xviii. an appeal was allowed from three; but that seven might be a fit number.   And for their proceeding, they advised, that such as were to join should make confession of their faith, and declare what work of grace the Lord had wrought in them; which accordingly they did, Mr. Shepherd first, then four others, then the elder, and one who was to be deacon, (who had also prayed), and another member.   Then the covenant was read, and they all gave a solemn assent to it.   Then the elder desired of the churches, that, if they did approve them to be a church, they would give them the right hand of fellowship.   Whereupon Mr. Cotton, (upon short speech with some others near them,) in the name of their churches, gave his hand to the elder, with a short speech of their assent, and desired the peace of the Lord Jesus to be with them. Then Mr. Shepherd made an exhortation to the rest of his body, about the nature of their covenant, and to stand firm to it, and commended them to the Lord in a most heavenly prayer.   Then the elder told the assembly, that they were intended to choose Mr. Shepherd for their pastor, (by the name of the brother who had exercised,) and desired the churches, that, if they had anything to except against him, they would impart it to them before the day of ordination.   Then he gave the churches thanks for their assistance, and so left them to the Lord.

Text—Winthrop: *History of New England*, Savage edition, Vol. I, pp. 214-215.

Election and Ordination

A fast was kept at Boston, and Mr. Leverett, an ancient, sincere professor, of Mr. Cotton's congregation in England, was chosen a ruling elder, and Mr. Firmin, a godly man, an apothecary of Sudbury in England, was chosen deacon, by imposition of hands; and Mr. Cotton was then chosen teacher of the congregation of Boston, and ordained by imposition of the hands of the presbytery, in this manner: First, he was chosen by all the congregation testifying their consent by erection of hands.   Then Mr. Wilson, the pastor, demanded of him, if he did accept of that call.   He paused, and then spake to this effect: that howsoever he knew himself unworthy and unsufficient for that place; yet, having observed all the passages of God's providence, (which he reckoned up in particular) in calling him to it, he could not but accept it.   Then the pastor and the two elders laid their hands upon his head, and the pastor prayed, and then, taking off their hands, laid them on again, and, speaking to him by his name, they did thenceforth design him to the said office, in the name of the Holy Ghost, and did give him the charge of the congregation, and did thereby (as by a sign from God) indue him with the gifts fit for his office; and lastly did bless him.   Then the neighboring ministers, which were present, did (at the pastor's motion) give him the right hands of fellowship, and the pastor made a stipulation between him and the congregation.

Text—Winthrop: *History of New England*, Savage edition, Vol. I, pp. 135-136.

We, of the congregation, kept a fast, and chose Mr. Wilson our teacher, and Mr. Nowell an elder, and Mr. Gager and Mr. Aspinwall, deacons.   We used imposition of hands, but with this protestation by all, that it was only as a sign of election and confirmation, not of any intent that Mr. Wilson should renouce his ministry he received in England.

Text—Winthrop: *History of New England*, Savage edition, Vol. I, p. 37.

The village at the end of Charlestown bounds was called Woburn, where they had gathered a church, and this day Mr. Carter was ordained their pastor, with the assistance of the elders of other churches. Some difference there was about his ordination; some advised, in regard they had no elder of their own, nor any members very fit to solemnize such an ordinance, they would desire some of the elders of the other churches to have performed it; but others supposing it might be an occasion of introducing a dependency of churches, etc., and so a presbytery, would not allow it. So it was performed by one of their own members, but not so well and orderly as it ought.

Text—Winthrop: *History of New England*, Savage edition, Vol. II, pp. 109-110. See also, "Congregationalizing of Puritanism." (page 64).

Settlement of Church Disputes

The congregat on at Watertown (whereof Mr. George Phillips was pastor) had chosen one Richard Brown for their elder, before named, who, persisting in his opinion of the truth of the Romish church, and maintaining other errors withal, and being a man of a very violent spirit, the court wrote a letter to the congregation, directed to the pastor and brethren, to advise them to take into consideration, whether Mr. Brown were fit to be continued their elder or not; to which, after some weeks, they returned answer to this effect: That if we would take the pains to prove such things as were objected against him, they would endeavour to redress them.

The said congregation being much divided about their elder, both parties repaired to the governour for assistance, etc.; whereupon he went to Watertown, with the deputy governour and Mr. Nowell, and the congregation being assembled, the governour told them, that being come to settle peace, etc., they might proceed in three distinct respects: 1. As the magistrates, (their assistance being desired). 2. As members of a neighbouring congregation. 3. Upon the answer which we received of our letter, which did no way satisfy us. But the pastor, Mr. Phillips, desired us to sit with them as members of a neighbouring congregation only, whereto the governour, etc., consented.

Then the one side, which had first complained, were moved to open their grievances; which they did to this effect: That they could not communicate with their elder, being guilty of errors, both in judgment and conversation. After much debate of these things, at length they were reconciled, and agreed to seek God in a day of humiliation, and so to have a solemn uniting; each party promising to reform what hath been amiss, etc.; and the pastor gave thanks to God, and the assembly brake up.

Text—Winthrop: *History of New England*, Savage edition, Vol. I, p. 81.

A woman of the church of Weymouth being cast out for some distempered speeches, by a major party, (the ruling elder and a minor party being unsatisfied therein,) her husband complained to the synod, which being then ready to break up, could do nothing in it, but only acquainted the pastor therewith privately. Whereupon complaint was made to the elders of the neighboring churches, and request made to them to come to Weymouth and to mediate a reconciliation. The elders acquainted their churches with it. Some scrupled the warrantableness of the course, seeing the major party of the church did not send to the churches for advice. It was answered, that it was not to be expected, that the major party would complain of their own act, and if the minor party, or the party grieved, should not be heard, then God should have left no means of redress in such a case, which could not be. Some of the churches approved their going; the rest permitted it. So they went, and the church of Weymouth, having notice before hand, gave them a meeting, and first demanded, whether they were sent by their churches or not. Being certified, as before, they objected this, that except they had been sent by their churches, they should never know when they had done, for others might come still, and require like satisfaction, etc. It was answered, the like objection would lie, if the churches had sent, for other churches might yet have required, etc., but they came not in way of authority, but only of brotherly communion, and therefore impose nothing upon them, but only to give their advice as occasion should require. This and some other scruples being removed, the church consented to have the cause heard, and opened from the beginning, whereupon some failing was found in both parties, the woman had not given so full satisfaction as she ought to have done, and the major party of the church had proceeded too hastily against a considerable party of the dissenting brethren, whereupon the woman who had offended was convinced of her failing, and bewailed it with many tears, the major party also acknowledged their error, and gave the elders thanks for their care and pains.

Text—Winthrop: *History of New England*, Savage edition, Vol. II, pp. 338-339.

Church Covenants

Salem—(Enlarged Form, 1636. Copy of John Fiske)

"Gathx my Sts. togethx unto me yos yt haue made a Covenant with me by sacrifice. Ps. 50. 5.

We whose names are hxunder written, members of ye pesent Church of X in Salem, haueing found by sad expience how dangerous it is to sit loose to ye Covenant we make with our god. And how apt we are to wander into bye pathes, yea, euen to ye loosing of our first aymes in entring Church Fellowship. . Doe therefore solemnly in ye pesence of ye eternall God, both for our own comforts & yos who shall or may be joyned unto us, renew yt Church Covenant, we find yis church bound unto at there jst beginning, viz: That we covenant with ye Lord, & one with another, & doe bynd ourselves in ye pesence of god to walke together in all his waies, according as he is pleased to reveale hims unto us in his Blessed word of truth, & doe more explicitely in ye name & feare of the Lord, pfesse and ptest to walke as followeth. thro ye helpe & poux of ye Lord Jeses.

1st. We Avow ye Lord to be our god, & ourselues.his people, in ye truth and simplicity of or Sp its.

2. We giue up or selues to ye Lord Jesus Christ, & ye word of his grace for ye teaching, ruling & sar ctifying of us in matters of worship & conversation, resoluing to cleaue to him alone for life & glory, & to oppose all Contrary wayes, cannons & 'stitutions of men in his worship.

3. We promise to walke with our brethren & sisters in yis Congregation, with all, watchfullness & tendernes, avoyding all Jealousies, suspitions, back bitings, censurings, provokings, secret risings of spit against them, but in all offences to follow ye rule of the Lord Jesus, & to beare & forbeare, giue & forgiue as he hath taught us.

4. In publick & private we will willingly doe nothing to ye offence of ye Church, but will be ready to take advice for or selues & ours, as occasion shal be pesented.

5. We will not, in ye Congregation, be forward, either to shew our owne gifts or parts in speaking or scrupuling, or there discouer ye fayling of or brethren or sisters,

but attend an orderly cale there untoo, knowing how much the Lord may bee dishonoured, and his gospel in ye p fession off it slighted by our distempers & weaknesses
in publick.

6. Wee bind our selues to study ye advancement of the gospel in all truth & peace,
both in regard of those yt are within or without, no waye sleighting our sister churches,
but useing there counsell as need shalbee, nor laying a stumbling block before any,
no, not ye Indians, whose good we desire to promote, & so to converse as we may avoyd
ye very appearance of euill.

7. We heereby promise to carry or selues in all lawfull obedience to those yt are
set our us in Church, & common wealth, knowing how well pleasing it wilbee to ye
Lord, yt they should haue encouragement in there places, by our not greiving theire
spirits through our Irregularities.

8. Wee resolue to approue or selues to ye Lord in or p ticular callings, shunning
idlenes as ye bane of any State, nor will we deale hardly or opp essingly with any
wherein we are the Lord's stewards, also promising to or best abilities to teach our
children & servants ye knowledge of ye Lord, & his will, that they may serue him also.

And all yis not by any strength of or owne, but by ye Lord Christ, whose bloud
we desire should be sprinckle. This or convenant made in his name."

Text—*Historical Collections of the Essex Institute*, Vol. I, No. 2, pp. 37-38.

Windsor (1647) "one of the earliest church creeds in New England."

1. We believe though God made man in an holy and blessed condition, yet by his
fall he hath plunged himself and all his posterity into a miseable state.—Rom. iii:23;
v:12.

2. Yet God hath provided a sufficient remedy in Christ for all broken hearted
sinners that are loosened from their sins and selves and world, and are enabled by faith
to look to Him in Christ, for mercy, inasmuch as Christ hath done and suffered for
such whatever His justice requires to atonement and life; and He doth accept his merits
and righteousness for them that believe in Him, and imputeth it to them to their
justification, as if they had satisfied and obeyed, themselves.—Heb. vii:25; Mat. xi:
28; xxii:24; v:4, 6; I Cor. i:30; Rom. vi:3, 5; v:19.

3. Yet we believe that there is no other name or means to be saved from the
guilt and power of sin.—John xiv:6; Acts iv:12.

4. We believe God hath made an everlasting covenant in Christ with all
penitent sinners that rest on Him in Christ, never to reject, or ceasc to do them good.—
Heb. viii:6; vii:22; I Sam. xii: 22; Jere. xxxii: 40.

5. We believe this covenant to be reciprocal, obliging us to be his people, to love,
fear, obey, cleave to him, and serve him with all our heart, mind, and soul; as him
to be our God, to love, choose, delight in us, and save and bless us in Christ: yea,
as his covenant binds us to love him and his Christ for his own sake, so to love our
brethren for his sake.—Deut. x:12; Hos. iii:3; ii:21; Deut. xxvi:17-19; John iv:21.

6. We believe that God's people, besides their general covenant with God, to
walk in subjection to him, and Christian love to all his people, ought also to join
themselves into a church covenant one with another, and to enter into a particular
combination together with some of his people to erect a particular ecclesiastical body,
and kingdom, and visible family and household of God, for the managing of discipline
and public ordinances of Christ in one place in a dutiful way, there to worship God and

Christ, as his visible kingdom and subjects, in that place waiting on Him for that blessing of his ordinances and promise of his covenant, by holding communion with him and his people in the doctrine and discipline of that visible kingdom, where it may be attained.—Rom. xii:4, 5, 6; I Cor. xii:27, 28; Eph. iv:11, 12; Acts ii:47; Exod. xii:43, 44, 45; Gen. xvii:13; Isa. xxiii:4.

7. We, for ourselves, in the sense of our misery by the fall and utter helplessness elsewhere, desire to renounce all other saviours but his Christ, and to rest on God in him alone, for all happiness, and salvation from all misery; and do here bind ourselves, in the presence of men and angels, by his grace assisting us, to choose the Lord, to serve him, and to walk in all his ways, and to keep all his commandments and ordinances, and his Christ to be our king, priest and prophet, and to receive his gospel alone for the rule of our faith and manners, and to (be) subject to the whole will of Christ so far as we shall understand it; and bind ourselves in special to all the members of this body, to walk in reverend subjection in the Lord to all our superiors, and in love, humility, wisdom, peaceableness, meekness, inoffensiveness, mercy, charity, spiritual helpfulness, watchfulness, chastity, justice, truth, self-denial, one to another, and to further the spiritual good one of another, by example, counsel, admonition, comfort, oversight, according to God, and submit, or[selves] subject unto all church administration in the Lord.

.FINIS.

Text—Walker: *The Creeds and Platforms of Congregationalism*, pp. 154-156.

V. *THE BODY OF LIBERTIES*

Only clauses biblical in character or ecclesiastical in their bearing have been inserted.

A Coppie of the Liberties of the Massachusets Collonie in New England

The free fruition of such liberties Immunities and priveledges as humanitie, Civilitie, and Christianitie call for as due to every man in his place and proportion; without impeachment and Infringement hath ever bene and ever will be the tranquillitie and Stabilitie of Churches and Commonwealths. And the deniall or deprivall thereof, the disturbance if not the ruine of both.

We hould it therefore our dutie and safetie whilst we are about the further establishing of this Government to collect and expresse all such freedomes as for present we foresee may concerne us, and our posteritie after us, And to ratify them with our sollemne consent.

Wee doe therefore this day religiously and unanimously decree and confirme these following Rites, liberties, and priveledges concerneing our Churches, and Civill State to be respectively impartiallie and inviolably enjoyed and observed throughout our Jurisdiction for ever.

1. No mans life shall be taken away, no mans honour or good name shall be stayned, no mans person shall be arested, restrayned, banished, dismembred, nor any wayes punished, no man shall be deprived of his wife or children, no mans goods or estaite shall be taken away from him, nor any way indammaged under Coulor of law, or Countenance of Authoritie, unlesse it be by vertue or equitie of some expresse law of the Country warranting the same, established by a generall Court and sufficiently published, or in case of the defect of a law in any partecular case by the word of god.

And in Capitall cases, or in cases concerning dismembring or banishment, according to that word to be judged by the Generall Court.

. . . .

Liberties more peculiarlie concerning the free men

58. Cilvill Authoritie hath power and libertie to see the peace, ordinances and Rules of Christ observed in every church according to his word, so it be done in a Civill and not in an Ecclesiasticall way.

59. Civill Authoritie hath power and libertie to deale with any church member in a way of Civill Justice, notwithstanding any Church relation, office, or interest.

60. No church censure shall degrade or depose any man from any Civill dignitie, office, or Authoritie he shall have in the Commonwealth.

61. No Magestrate, Juror, Officer, or other man shall be bound to informe present or reveale any private crim or offence, wherein there is no perill or danger to this plantation or any member thereof, when any necessaritye of conscience binds him to secresie grounded upon the word of god, unless it be in case of testimony lawfully required.

65. No custome or prescription shall ever prevaile amongst us in any morall cause, our meaneing is maintaine anythinge that can be proved to bee morrallie sinfull by the word of god.

. . . .

75. It is and shall be the libertie of any member or members of any Court, Councell or Civill Asembly in cases of makeing or executing any order or law, that properlie concerne religion, or any cause capitall, or warres, or Subscription to any publique Articles or Remonstrance, in case they cannot in Judgment and conscience consent to that way the Major vote or suffrage goes, to make their contra Remonstrance or protestation in speech or writeing, and upon request to have their dissent recorded in the Rolles of that Court. So it be done Christianlie and respectively for the manner. And their dissent onely be entered without the reasons thereof, for the avoiding of tediousness.

. . . .

Liberties of Forreiners and Strangers

89. If any people of other Nations professing the true Christian Religion shall flee to us from the Tiranny or oppression of their persecutors, or from famyne, warres or the like necessary and compulsarie cause, They shall be entertayned and succoured amongst us, according to that power and prudence god shall give us.

. . . .

91. There shall never be any bond slaverie villinage or Captivitie amongst us, unles it be lawfull Captives taken in just warres, and such strangers as willingly selle themselves or are sold to us. And these shall have all the liberties and Christian usages which the law of god established in Israell concerning such persons doeth morally require. This exempts none from servitude who shall be Judged thereto by Authoritie.

. . . .

94. Capitall Laws.

1

Dut. 13.6.10   If any man after legall conviction shall have or worship any
Dut. 17. 2. 6   other god, but the lord god, he shall be put to death.
Ex. 22.20

2.

Ex. 22.18
Lev. 20.27
Dut. 18.10

If any man or woeman be a witch, (that is hath or consulteth with a familiar spirit,) They shall be put to death.

3.

Lev. 24.15.16

If any person shall Blaspheme the name of god, the father, Sonne or Holie ghost, with direct, expresse, presumptuous or high handed blasphemie, or shall curse god in the like manner, he shall be put to death.

4.

Ex. 21.12
Numb. 35.13.14.
30.31

If any person committ any wilfull murther, which is man-slaughter, committed upon premeditated mallice, hatred, or Crueltie, not in a mans necessarie and just defence, nor by meere casualtie against his will, he shall be put to death.

5.

Numb. 25.20.21.
Lev. 24.17

If any person slayeth an other suddainely in his anger or Crueltie of passion, he shall be put to death.

6.

Ex. 21.14

If any person shall slay an other through guile, either by poysoning or other such divelish practice, he shall be put to death.

. . . .

10.

Ex. 21.16.

If any man stealeth a man or mankinde, he shall surely be put to death.

11.

Dut. 19.16.18.19.

If any man rise up by false witnes, wittingly and of purpose to take away any man's life, he shall be put to death.

12.

If any man shall conspire and attempt any invasion, insurrection, or publique rebellion against our commonwealth, or shall indeavour to surprize any Towne or Townes, fort or forts therein, or shall treacherously and perfediouslie attempt the alteration and subversion of our frame of politie or Government fundamentallie, he shall be put to death.

95. *A declaration of the Liberties the Lord Jesus hath given to the Churches.*

1. All the people of god within this Jurisdiction who are not in a church way, and be orthodox in Judgment, and not scandalous in life, shall have full libertie to gather themselves into a Church Estaite.   Provided they doe it in a Christian way, with due observation of the rules of Christ revealed in his word.

2. Every Church hath full libertie to exercise all the ordinances of god, according to the rules of Scripture.

3. Every Church hath free libertie of Election and ordination of all their officers from time to time, provided they be able, pious and orthodox.

4. Every Church hath free libertie of Admission, Recommendation, Dismission, and Expulsion, or deposall of their officers, and members, upon due cause, with free exercise of the Discipline and Censures of Christ according to the rules of his word.

5. No Injunctions are to be put upon any Church, Church Officers or member in point of Doctrine, worship or Discipline, whether for substance or cercumstance besides the Institutions of the lord.

6. Every Church of Christ hath freedome to celebrate dayes of fasting and prayer, and of thanksgiveing according to the word of god.

7. The Elders of Churches have free libertie to meete monthly, Quarterly, or otherwise, in convenient numbers and places, for conferences, and consultations about Christian and Church questions and occasions.

8. All Churches have libertie to deale with any of their members in a church way that are in the hand of Justice. So it be not to retard or hinder the course thereof.

9. Every Church hath libertie to deale with any magestrate, Deputie of Court, or other officer what soe ever that is a member in a church way in case of apparent and just offence given in their places. So it be done with due observance and respect.

10. Wee allowe private meetings for edification in religion amongst Christians of all sortes of people. So it be without just offence both for number, time, place, and other cercumstances.

11. For the preventing and removeing of errour and offence that may grow and spread in any of the Churches in this Jurisdiction. And for the preserveing of trueith and peace in the several churches within them selves, and for the maintenance and exercise of brotherly communion, amongst all the churches in the Countrie, It is allowed and ratified, by the Authoritie of this Generall Court as a lawfull libertie of the Churches of Christ. That once in every month of the yeare (when the season will beare it) It shall be lawfull for the minesters and Elders, of the Churches neere adjoyneing together, with any other of the breetheren with the consent of the churches to assemble by course in each severall Church one after an other. To the intent after the preaching of the word by such a minister as shall be requested thereto by the Elders of the church where the Assembly is held, The rest of the day may be spent in publique Christian Conference about the discussing and resolveing of any such doubts and cases of conscience concerning matter of doctrine or worship or government of the church as shall be propounded by any of the Breetheren of that church, with leave also to any other Brother to propound his objections or answeres for further satisfaction according to the word of god. Provided that the whole action be guided and moderated by the Elders of the Church where the Assemblie is helde, or by such others as they shall appoint. And that no thing be concluded and imposed by way of Authoritie from one or more Churches upon an other, but onely by way of Brotherly conference and consultations. That the trueth may be searched out to the satisfying of every man's conscience in the sight of god according to his worde. And because such an Assembly and the worke their of can not be duely attended to if other lectures be held in the same weeke. It is therefore agreed with the consent of the Churches. That in that weeke when such an Assembly is held. All the lectures in all the neighbouring Churches for that week shall be forborne. That so the publique service of Christ in this more solemne Assembly may be transacted with greater deligence and attention.

Text—*Coll. Mass. Hist. Soc., Series III*, Vols. VII-VIII, pp. 216-237.

VI. *HARVARD IN ITS EARLY DAYS* (1641)

1. After God had carried us safe to *New-England*, and wee had builded our houses, provided necessaries for our liveli-hood, rear'd convenient places for Gods worship,

and setled the Civill Government: One of the next things we longed for, and looked after was to advance *Learning* and perpetuate it to Posterity; dreading to leave an illiterate Ministery to the Churches, when our present Ministers shall lie in the Dust. And as wee were thinking and consulting how to effect this great Work; it pleased God to stir up the heart of one Mr. *Harvard* (a godly Gentleman and a lover of Learning, there living amongst us) to give the one halfe of his Estate (it being in all about 1700. l.) towards the erecting of a Colledge, and all his Library: after him another gave 300. l. others after them cast in more, and the publique hand of the State added the rest: the Colledge was, by common consent, appointed to be at *Cambridge*, (a place very pleasant and accommodate and is called (according to the name of the first founder) *Harvard Colledge*.

The Edifice is very faire and comely within and without, having in it a spacious Hall; (where they daily meet at Common Lectures) Exercises, [Commons, Lectures, and Exércises] and a large Library with some Bookes to it, the gifts of diverse of our friends, their Chambers and studies also, fitted for, and possessed by the Students, and all other roomes of Office necessary and convenient, with all needfull Offices thereto belonging: And by the side of the Colledge a faire *Grammar* Schoole, for the training up of young Schollars, and fitting of them for *Academicall Learning*, that still as they are judged ripe, they may be received into the Colledge of this Schoole: Master *Corlet* is the Mr. who hath very well approved himselfe for his abilities, dexterity and painfulnesse, in teaching and education of the youth under him.

Over the Colledge is master *Dunster* placed, as President, a learned conscionable and industrious man, who hath so trained up his Pupills in the tongues and Arts, and so seasoned them with the principles of Divinity and Christianity, that we have to our great comfort, (and in truth) beyond our hopes, beheld their progresse in Learning and godlinesse also; the former of these hath appeared in their publique declamations in *Latine* and *Greeke*, and Disputations Logicall and Philosophicall, which they have beene wonted (besides their ordinary Exercises in the Colledge-Hall) in the audience of the Magistrates, Ministers, and other Schollars, for the probation of their growth in Learning, upon set dayes, constantly once every moneth to make and uphold: The latter hath been manifested in sundry of them, by the savoury breathings of their Spirits in their godly conversation. Insomuch that we are confident, if these early blossomes may be cherished and warmed with the influence of the friends of Learning, and lovers of this pious worke, they will by the help of God. come to happy maturity in a short time.

Over the Colledge are twelve Overseers chosen by the generall Court, six of them are of the Magistrates, the other six of the Ministers, who are to promote the best good of it, and (having a power of influence into all persons in it) are to see that every one be diligent and proficient in his proper place.

Rules, and Precepts that are observed in the College

1. When any Schollar is able to understand *Tully*, or such like classicall Latine Author *extempore*, and make and speake true Latine in Verse and Prose, *suo ut aiunt Marte*; And decline perfectly the Paradigim's of *Nounes* and *Verbes* in the *Greek* tongue: Let him then and not before be capable of admission into the Colledge.

2. Let every Student be plainly instructed; and earnestly pressed to consider well the maine end of his life and studies is, *to know God and Jesus Christ which is eternall*

life, Joh. 17. 3. and therefore to lay *Christ* in the bottome, as the only foundation of all sound knowledge and Learning.

And seeing the Lord only giveth wisedome, Let every one seriously set himselfe by prayer in secret to seeke it of him *Prov* 2, 3.

3. Every one shall so exercise himselfe in reading the Scriptures twice a day, that he shall be ready to give such an account of his proficiency therein, both in *Theoreticall* observations of the Language, and *Logick*, and in *Practicall* and spirituall truths, as his Tutor shall require, according to his ability; seeing *the entrance of the word giveth light, it giveth understanding to the simple*, Psalm, 119. 130.

4. That they eshewing all profanation of Gods Name, Attributes, Word, Ordinances, and times of Worship, doe studie with good conscience, carefully to retaine God, and the love of his truth in their mindes, else let them know, that (notwithstanding their Learning) God may give them up *to strong delusions*, and in the end *to a reprobate minde*, 2 Thes. 2. 11, 12. Rom. 1, 28.

5. That they studiously redeeme the time; observe the generall houres appointed for all the Students, and the speciall houres for their owne *Classis*: and then diligently attend the Lectures, without any disturbance by word or gesture. And if in any thing they doubt, they shall enquire, as of their fellowes, so (in case of *Non satisfaction*) modestly of their Tutors.

6. None shall under any pretence whatsoever, frequent the company and society of such men as lead an unfit, and dissolute life.

Nor shall any without his Tutors leave, or (in his absence) the call of Parents or Guardians, goe abroad to other Townes.

7. Every Schollar shall be present in his Tutors chamber at the 7th. houre in the morning, immediately after the sound of the Bell, at his opening the Scripture and prayer, so also at the 5th. houre at night, and then give account of his owne private reading, as aforesaid in Particular the third, and constantly attend Lectures in the Hall at the houres appointed? But if any (without neccessary impediment) shall absent himself from prayer or Lectures, he shall bee lyable to Admonition, if he offend above once a weeke.

8. If any Schollar shall be found to transgresse any of the Lawes of God, or the Schoole, after twice Admonition, he shall be lyable, if not *adultus*, to correction, if *adultus*, his name shall be given up to the Overseers of the Colledge, that he may bee admonished at the publick monethly Act.

Text—*New Englands First Fruits.*

VII. *THE CAMBRIDGE PLATFORM, AUGUST 15, 1648*

The ominous outbreak in some quarters of Baptist sentiments, the growing discussion respecting conditions of church membership, and the fear of an imposition by the English Parliament of a Presbyterian creed and ecclesiastical order, impelled the General Court to summon (May 15, 1646) a Synod of the churches. It was only after lengthy argument that the churches at Boston and Salem consented to participate in an assembly convened by legislative authority. The first session did little other than appoint a committee to draft a "model of church government." Reassembled in June of the following year, it was speedily adjourned because of an epidemic.   Meanwhile, the General Court had commissioned seven Massachusetts ministers to proceed to the preparation of a creed to be submitted to the Synod at its next assembly, in the event that the Westminster Confession of Faith, completed but not as yet ratified by Parliament, should prove unacceptable.   The Synod that met August 13, 1648, having received at least two suggested "Models" accepted with modification that of Rev. Richard Mather. Thus amended, the draft became known as the "Cambridge Platform." For a confession of faith the Synod adopted in substance the Westminster Confession.   Hubbard thus gives the sum of the principles of the Congregational discipline as embodied in the Platform:

1. Ecclesiastical polity, church government, or church discipline, is nothing else but that form and order that is to be observed in the church of Christ upon earth, both for the constitution of it and all the administrations that are therein to be performed, the parts of which are all of them exactly described in the word of God, and is not left in the power of any to alter, add, or diminish any thing therein; the necessary circumstances of which, as time and place, etc. are left to men, to be ordered unto edification, and not otherwise.

2. There is a Catholic church visible, viz. the company of those that profess the Christian faith, whether in church order or not; but there is no political Catholic church, the state of the members of the visible church, since the coming of Christ, being only Congregational.

3. A Congregational church, by the institution of Christ, is a part of the visible church, consisting of a company of Saints by calling, united into one body, by an holy covenant, for the public worship of God, and the mutual edification one of another, in the fellowship of the Lord Jesus, the matter of which, as to its qualification, ought to be such as have attained the knowledge of the principles of religion, free from gross scandals, and, with the profession of their faith and repentance, walk in blameless obedience to the word of God.   As to its quantity, it ought not to be of greater number than may ordinarily meet together conveniently in one place, nor fewer than may conveniently carry on church work.   The form of such a church is an agreement, consent, or visible covenant, whereby they give up themselves unto the Lord, to the observing the ordinances of Christ together in the same society.

4. The fraternity or brotherhood of such a church is the first subject of all ordinary church power, which is either a power of office or of privilege.   But the power of privilege is in the brethren, formally and immediately; the other is in them no otherwise than in that they design the persons unto office, who only are to act and exercise that power.

5. The ordinary officers of the church are such as concern their spiritual and moral, temporal and natural good; of the first sort, are pastors, teachers, ruling elders, I Tim. v. 17, in which latter sort most of the churches in New England, as many of the Congregational churches elsewhere, are not so well satisfied as formerly, accounting ruling elders should be able to teach.

6. It is in the power of the churches to call their own officers and remove them from their office again, if there fall out just cause, yet so as the advice of neighbor churches,

where it may conveniently be done, be first had, and they who are to officiate ought to be tried and proved before they be elected. I Tim. v. 22.

7. Elders are to be ordained by imposition of hands, which is to be performed by the elders of the same church if it be furnished with any, or those of neighbor churches and may be done by some of the brethren deputed thereunto; which latter also is not disapproved by Dr. Hornbeck, the learned Professor of Divinity at Leyden, from Numb. viii. 10.

8. The power of government in a Congregational church ought to proceed after the manner of a mixt administration, for in an organic church no act can be consummate without the consent both of the elders and the brethren; so as the power of government or rule in the elders prejudice not the power of privilege in the brethren, nor the power of privilege in them prejudice the power of rule seated in the elders, seeing both may sweetly agree together.

9. For the maintenance of the ministers of the church, all that are taught are to communicate to him that teacheth in all good things: and in case of neglect, the magistrate ought to see that the ministry be duly provided for.

10. For the admission of members, those that have the weakest measure of faith, it ought to be accepted in them that desire admission, either by a personal relation in public, or by the elders acquainting the church with what satisfaction they have received from the persons in private. The things wherein satisfaction is required are faith and repentance, which ought to be found in all church members.

11. Where members of churches are called to remove from one church to another, it is convenient, for order's sake, that it be done by letters of recommendation or of dismission.

12. The censures of the church, which are for the preventing, removing, or healing of offences, are excommunication or admonition, wherein the church ought to proceed according to the rule of Matthew xviii. 15, 16, 17, wherein the offence is to be brought to the church by the mouth of the elders.

13. Particular churches, although they are distinct, and so have not one power over another, yet because they are united unto Christ, not only as a mystical but as a political head, they ought to have communion one with another, by way of mutual care, consultation, admonition, and participation in the same ordinances.

14. Synods orderly assembled, and rightly proceeding according to the pattern of Acts xv., are the ordinance of Christ, and if not absolutely necessary to the being, yet necessary to the well-being of churches, for the establishment of truth and peace therein. And many churches may so assemble together by their messengers and elders, and their directions and determinations, so far as consonant to the Word of God, are to be received with reverence and submission, not only for their agreement therewith, (without which they bind not at all,) but also for the power whereby they are made, as an ordinance of God, appointed thereunto in his Word.

15. Church government and civil government may very well stand together, it being the duty of the magistrates to take care of matters of religion, and to improve his civil authority, for observing the duties commanded in the first, as well as in the second table, seeing the end of their office is not only the quiet and peaceable life of the subject in matters of righteousness and honesty, but also in matters of godliness. I Tim. ii, 1, 2.

Text—Hubbard: *General History of New England*, Chapter LVIII, *Coll., Mass. Hist. Soc.* Series II, Vols. V-VI, pp. 537-540.

VIII. *A TIRADE AGAINST TOLERANCE*

Rev. Nathaniel Ward, minister of Ipswich, a victim of Archbishop Laud's persecution, and discontented at the domination of Boston, under the title "The Simple Cobbler of Agawam" wrote (1647)

. . . First, such as have given or taken any unfriendly reports of us *New-English*, should doe well to recollect themselves. Wee have beene reputed a Colluvies of wild Opinionists, swarmed into a remote wildernes to find elbow-roome for our phanatick Doctrines and practises: I trust our diligence past, and constant sedulity agains such persons and courses, will plead better things for us. I dare take upon me, to bee the Herauld of *New-England* so farre, as to proclaime to the world, in the name of our Colony, that all Familists, Antinomians, Anabaptists, and other Enthusiasts shall have free Liberty to keepe away from us, and such as will come to be gone as fast as they can, the sooner the better.

Secondly, I dare averre, that God doth no where in his word tolerate Christian States, to give Tolerations to such adversaries of his Truth, if they have power in their hands to suppresse them. . . .

Not to tolerate things meerly indifferent to weak consciences, argues a conscience too strong: pressed uniformity in these, causes much disunity: To tolerate more then indifferents, is not to deale indifferently with God: He that doth it, takes his Scepter out of his hand, and bids him stand by. Who hath to doe to institute Religion but God. The power of all Religion and Ordinances, lies in their purity: their purity in their simplicity: then are mixtures pernicious. I lived in a City, where a Papist preached in one Church, a Lutheran in another, a Calvinist in a third; a Lutheran one part of the day, a Calvinist the other, in the same Pulpit: the Religion of that place was but motly and meagre, their affections Leopard-like. . . .

That State is wise, that will improve all paines and patience rather to compose, then tolerate differences in Religion. There is no divine Truth, but hath much Cœlestiall fire in it from the Spirit of Truth: nor no irreligious untruth, without its proportion of Antifire from the spirit of Error to contradict it: the zeale of the one, the virulency of the other, must necessarily kindle Combustions. Fiery diseases seated in the spirit, imbroile the whole frame of the body: others more externall and coole, are lesse dangerous. They which divide in Religion, divide in God; they who divide in him, divide beyond *Genus Generalissimum*, where there is no reconciliation, without atonement; that is, without uniting in him, who is One, and in his Truth, which is also one.

Wise are those men who will be perswaded rather to live within the pale of Truth where they may bee quiet, than in the purlieves, where they are sure to be hunted ever & anon, do Authority what it can. Every singular Opinion, hath a singular opinion of it self; and he that holds it a singular opinion of himself, & a simple opinion of all contra sentients: he that confutes them, must confute at three at once, or else he does nothing; which will not be done without more stir than the peace of the State or Church can indure.

And prudent are those Christians, that will rather give what may be given, then hazard all by yeelding nothing. To sell all peace of Country, to buy some peace of conscience unseasonably, is more avarice than thrift, imprudence than patience: they deal not equally, that set any Truth of God at such a rate; but they deal wisely that will stay till the Market is fallen.

My prognosticks deceive me not a little, if once within three seaven years, peace prove not such a penny-worth at most Marts in Christendome, that hee that would not lay down his money, his lust, his opinion, his will, I had almost said the best flower of his Crowne for it, while he might have had it; will tell his own heart, he plaid the very ill husband.

Concerning Tolerations I may further assert.

That Persecution of true Religion, and Toleration of false, are the *Jannes* and *Jambres* to the Kingdome of Christ, whereof the last is farre the worse. *Augustines* tongue had not owed his mouth one penny-rent though he had never spake word more in it, but this, *Nullum malum pejus libertate errandi.*

Frederick Duke of *Saxon*, spake not one foote beyond the mark when he said. He had rather the Earth should swallow him up quick, then he should give a toleration to any opinion against any truth of God.

He that is willing to tolerate any Religion, or discrepant way of Religion, besides his own, unlesse it be in matters meerly indifferent, either doubts of his own, or is not sincere in it.

He that is willing to tolerate any unsound Opinion, that his own may also be tolerated, though never so sound, will for a need hang Gods Bible at the Devills girdle.

Every Toleration of false Religions, or Opinions hath as many Errours and sins in it, as all the false Religions and Opinions it tolerate, and one sound one more.

That State that will give Liberty of Conscience in matters of Religion, must give Liberty of Conscience and Conversation in their Morall Laws, or else the Fiddle will be out of tune, and some of the strings crack.

He that will rather make an irreligious quarell with other Religions then try the Truth of his own by valuable Arguments, and peaceable Sufferings; either his Religion, or himselfe is irreligious.

Experience will teach Churches and Christians, that it is farre better to live in a State united, though a little Corrupt, then in a State, whereof some Part is incorrupt, and all the rest divided.

I am not altogether ignorant of the eight Rules given by Orthodox divines about giving Tolerations, yet with their favour I dare affirme,

That there is no Rule given by God for any State to give an affirmative Toleration to any false Religion, or Opinion whatsoever; they must connive in some Cases, but may not concede in any.

That the State of *England* (so farre as my Intelligence serves) might in time have prevented with ease and may yet without any great difficultie deny both Toleration, and irregular connivences *salva Republica.*

That if the State of *England* shall either willingly Tolerate, or weakly connive at such Courses, the Church of that Kingdome will sooner become the Devils dancing-Schoole, then Gods Temple: The Civill State a Beare-garden, then an Exchange: The whole Realme a Pais base then an *England*. And what pity it is, that that Country which hath been the Staple of Truth to all Christendome, should now become the Aviary of Errors to the whole world, let every fearing heart judge.

I take Liberty of Conscience to be nothing but a freedome from sinne, and error. *Conscientia in tantum libera, in quntum ab errore liberata.* And Liberty of Errour nothing but a Prison for Conscience. Then small will be the kindnesse of a State to build such Prisons for their Subjects.

The Scripture saith, there is nothing makes free but Truth, and Truth faith, there is no Truth but one: If the States of the World would make it their summ-operous Care to preserve this One Truth in its purity and Authority it would ease you of all other Politicall cares.   I am sure Satan makes it his grand, if not only taske, to adulterate Truth; Falsehood is his sole Scepter, whereby he first ruffled, and ever since ruined the World.

If Truth be but One, me thinks all the Opinionists in *England* should not be all in that One Truth, some of them I doubt are out.   He that can extract an unity out of such a disparity, or contract such a disparity into an unity; had need be a better Artist, then ever was *Drebell*.

If two Centers (as we may suppose) be in one Circle, and lines drawn from both to all the points of the Compasse, they will certainly crosse one another, and probably cut through the Centers themselves.

There is talk of an universall Toleration, I would talke as loud as I could against it, did I know what more apt and reasonable Sacrifice *England* could offer to God for his late performing all his heavenly Truths then an universall Toleration of all hellish Errors, or how they shall make an universall Reformation, but by making Christs Academy the Divills University, where any man may commence Heretique *per saltum;* where he that is *filius Diabolicus,* or *simpliciter pessimus,* may have his grace to goe to Hell *cum Publico Privilegio;* and carry as many after him, as he can. . . .

It is said, Though a man have light enough himselfe to see the Truth, yet if he hath not enough to enlighten others, he is bound to tolerate them, I will engage my self, that all the Devills in *Britanie* shall sell themselves to their shirts, to purchase a Lease of this Position for three of their Lives, under the Seale of the Parliament.

It is said, That Men ought to have Liberty of their Conscience, and that it is persecution to debarre them of it: I can rather stand amazed then reply to this: it is an astonishment to think that the braines of men should be parboyl'd in such impious ignorance; Let all the wits under the Heavens lay their heads together and finde an Assertion worse then this (one excepted) I will petition to be chosen the universall Ideot of the world.

It is said, That Civill Magistrates ought not to meddle with Ecclesiasticall matters.

I would answer to this so well as I could, did I not know that some papers lately brought out of *New-England,* are going to the Presse, wherein the Opinions of the Elders there in a late Synod, concerning this point are manifested, which I suppose will give clearer satisfaction then I can.

The true English of all this their false Latine, is nothing but a generall Toleration of all Opinions; which motion if it be like to take, it were very requisite, that the City would repair *Pauls* with all the speed they can, for an English *Pantheon,* and bestow it upon the Sectaries, freely to assemble in, then there may be some hope that *London* will be quiet in time. . . .

Text—*The Simple Cobler of Aggavvamm in America,* Reprinted in Force, *Tracts and Papers,* Vol. III. Tract VIII.

IX. *THE QUAKERS*

Letter from the Commissioners of the United Colonies to Rhode Island concerning the Quakers (1657). See page 116-117.

The Trial of Wenlock Christison (1661)

Anno 1661.   At the said next General-Court, *Wenlock Christison* was again brought to the Bar.

The Governour asked him, *What he had to say for himself, why he should not die?*

Wenlock. I have done nothing worthy of Death; if I had, I refuse not to die.

Governour. *Thou art come in among us in Rebellion, which is as the Sin of Witchcraft, and ought to be punished.*

Wenlock. I came not in among you in Rebellion, but in Obedience to the God of Heaven; not in Contempt to any of you, but in Love to your Souls and Bodies; and that you shall know one Day, when you and all Men must give an Account of your Deeds done in the Body. Take heed, for you cannot escape the righteous Judgments of God.

Major-Meneral *Adderton.* *You pronounce Woes and Judgments, and those that are gone before you pronounced Woes and Judgments; but the Judgments of the Lord God are not come upon us yet.*

Wenlock. Be not proud, neither let your Spirits be lifted up; God doth but wait till the Measure of your Iniquity be filled up, and that you have seen your ungodly Race, then will the Wrath of God come upon you to the uttermost; And as for thy part, it hangs over thy Head, and is near to be poured down upon thee, and shall come as a Thief in the Night suddenly, when thou thinkest not of it. By what Law will ye put me to Death?

Court. *We have a Law, and by our Law you are to die.*

Wenlock. So said the Jews of Christ, *We have a Law, and by our Law he ought to die.* Who empowered you to make that Law?

Court. *We have a* Patent, *and are* Patentees, *judge whether we have not Power to make Laws?*

Wenlock. How! Have you Power to make Laws repugnant to the Laws of *England?*

Governour. *Nay.*

Wenlock. Then you are gone beyond your Bounds, and have forfeited your *Patont,* and this is more than you can answer. Are you Subjects to the King, yea, or nay?

Secretary *Rawson.* *What will you infer from that, what Good will that do you?*

Wenlock. If you are, say so; for in your Petition to the King, you desire that he will protect you, and that you may be worthy to kneel among his loyal Subjects.

Court. *Yes.*

Wenlock. So am I, and for any thing I know, am as good as you, if not better; for if the King did but know your Hearts, as God knows them, he would see, that your Hearts are as rotten towards him, as they are towards God. Therefore seeing that you and I are Subjects to the King, I demand to be tried by the Laws of my own Nation.

Court. *You shall be tried by a Bench and a Jury.*

Wenlock. That is not the Law, but the Manner of it; for if you will be as good as your Word, you must set me at Liberty, for I never heard or read of any Law that was in *England* to hang *Quakers.*

Governour. *There is a Law to hang* Jesuits.

Wenlock. If you put me to Death, it is not because I go under the name of a *Jesuit,* but a *Quaker,* therefore I do appeal to the Laws of my own Nation.

Court. *You are in our Hand, and have broken our Laws, and we will try you.*

Wenlock. Your Will is your Law, and what you have Power to do, that you will do: And seeing that the Jury must go forth on my Life, this I have to say to you in the Fear of the Living God: Jury, take heed what you do, for you swear by the Living God, *That you will true Trial make, and just Verdict give, according to the Evidence.* Jury, look for your Evidence: What have I done to deserve Death? Keep your Hands out of innocent Blood.

A Juryman. *It is good Counsel.*

The Jury went out, but having received their Lesson, soon returned, and brought in their Verdict *Guilty.*

Wenlock. I deny all Guilt, for my Conscience is clear in the Sight of God.

Governour. The Jury hath condemned thee.

Wenlock. The Lord doth justify me, who are thou that condemnest?

Then the Court proceeded to vote as to the Sentence of Death, to which several of them, *viz. Richard Russel* and others, would not consent, the Innocence and Stedfastness of the Man having prevailed upon them in his Favour. There happened also a Circumstance during this Trial, which could not but affect Men of any Tenderness or Consideration, which was, that a Letter was sent to the Court from *Edward Wharton,* signifying, *That whereas they had banished him on pain of Death, yet he was at Home in his own House in* Salem, and therefore proposing, *That they would take off their wicked Sentence from him, that he might go about his Occasions out of their Jurisdiction.* This Circumstance, however affecting to others, did only enrage *Endicot* the Governour, who was very much displeased, and in much Anger cried out, *I could find in my Heart to go Home.*

Wenlock. It were better for thee to be at Home than here, for thou art about a bloody piece of Work.

Governour. *You that will not consent, record it. I thank God, I am not afraid to give Judgment.* Wenlock Christison, *Hearken to your Sentence: You must return unto the Place from whence you came, and from thence to the Place of Execution, and there you must be hanged until you be* dead, dead, dead, *upon the* 13*th Day of* June, *being the Fifth-day of the Week.*

Wenlock. The Will of the Lord be done: In whose Will I came amongst you, and in his Counsel I stand, feeling his Eternal Power, that will uphold me unto the last Gasp, I do not question it. Known be it unto you all, That if you have Power to take my Life from me, my Soul shall enter into Everlasting Rest and Peace with God, where you yourselves shall never come: And if you have Power to take my Life from me, the which I do question, I believe you shall never more take *Quakers* Lives from them: [Note my Words] Do not think to weary out the Living God by taking away the Lives of his Servants: What do you gain by it? For the last Man you put to Death, here are *five* come in his Room. And if you have Power to take my Life from me, God can raise up the same Principle of Life in *ten* of his Servants, and send them among you in my Room, that you may have Torment upon Torment, which is your Portion: *For there is no Peace to the Wicked,* saith my God.

Governour. *Take him away. . . .*

Text—Joseph Besse: *A Collection of the Sufferings of the People called Quakers* Vol. II, pp. 222-223.

X. *THE HALF-WAY COVENANT AND CHURCH CONSOCIATION—SYNOD OF BOSTON, 1662*

While insisting that only adult persons of Christian experience should be admitted to the covenant fellowship of the church, the fathers of

New England had conceded the same privilege to the immediate offspring of the baptized. But with the declining zeal and piety of the second generation, the propriety of this inherited standing of their children became a subject of debate. The summons of the Massachusetts Court to the Cambridge Synod mentioned "baptisme & ye p'sons to be received thereto" as a topic for discussion. A lack of unanimity at Cambridge left the issue in abeyance until at a meeting in Boston June 4, 1657, attended by eleven from Massachusetts and Connecticut, though not from Plymouth or New Haven, the following answer was given to one of a series of connected questions:

"That it is the duty of infants, who confederate in their parents, when grown up unto years of discretion, tho' not yet fit, for the Lord's Supper, to own the covenant, they made with their parents, by entering thereinto, in their own persons; and it is the duty of the church, to call upon them for the performance thereof; and, if being called upon, they shall refuse the performance of this great duty, or otherwise do continue scandalous, they are liable to be censured for the same, by the church. And in case they understand the grounds of religion, and are not scandalous, and solemnly own the covenant, in their own persons, wherein they give up both themselves and their children unto the Lord, and desire baptism for them, we see not sufficient cause to deny baptism unto their children."

But this ministerial deliverance did not terminate the controversy. The Massachusetts legislature therefore felt called upon to summon a Synod March 11, 1662. The questions proposed were:

1. Who are the subjects of baptism?

2. Whether, according to the word of God, there ought to be a "consociation of churches."

After a heated debate, in which President Chauncey and Increase Mather led the minority, it was declared and subsequently ordered by the General Court:

Question I.—Who are the subjects of baptism?

1. They that, according to scripture, are members of the visible church, are the subjects of baptism.

2. The members of the visible church, according to scripture, are confederate visible believers, in particular churches, and their infant seed, i.e. children in minority, whose next parents, one or both, are in covenant.

3. The infant seed of confederate visible believers, are members of the same church with their parents, and when grown up are personally under the watch, discipline, and government of that church.

4. These adult persons, are not therefore to be admitted to full communion, merely because they are, and continue members, without such further qualifications as the word of God requireth thereunto.

5. Church members who were admitted in minority, understanding the doctrine of faith, and publickly professing their assent thereto, not scandalous in life, and solemnly owning the covenant before the church, wherein they give up themselves and their children to the Lord, and subject themselves to the government of Christ in the Church, their children are to be baptised.

6. Such church-members, who either by death, or some other extraordinary providence, have been inevitably hindred from publick acting as aforesaid, yet have given the church cause in judgment of charity, to look at them as so qualified, and such as had they been called thereunto, would have so acted, their children are to be baptised.

7. The members of orthodox churches, being sound in the faith, and not scandalous in life, and presenting due testimony thereof; these occasionally coming from one church to another may have their children baptised in the church, whither they come, by virtue of communion of churches: But if they remove their habitation, they ought orderly to covenant and subject themselves to the government of Christ in the church where they settle their abode, and so their children to be baptised. It being the churche's duty to receive such into communion, so far, as they are regularly fit for the same.

Question II.—Whether according to the word of God there ought to be a consociation of churches, and what should be the manner of it.

1. Every church or particular congregation of visible saints in gospel-order, being furnished with a presbytery, at least with a teaching elder, and walking together in truth and peace, hath received from the Lord Jesus full power and authority ecclesiastical within it self, regularly to administer all the ordinances of Christ, and is not under any other ecclesiastical jurisdiction whatsoever. . . . Hence it follows that consociation of churches is not to hinder the exercise of this power; but by counsel from the word of God to direct, and strengthen the same upon all just occasions.

2. The churches of Christ do stand in a sisterly relation each to other, being united in the same faith and order, to walk by the same rule, in the exercise of the same ordinances for the same end, under one and the same political head, the Lord Jesus Christ, which union infers a communion suitable thereunto.

3. Communion of churches is the faithful improvement of the gifts of Christ bestowed upon them, for his service and glory, and their mutual good and edification, according to capacity and opportunity. . . .

4. Acts of communion of churches are such as these.

   1. Hearty care and prayer one for another. . . .

   2. To afford relief by communication of their gifts in temporal or spiritual necessities. . . .

   3. To maintain unity and peace, by giving an account one to another of their publick actions, when it is orderly desired . . . and to strenghen one another in their regular administrations; as in special by a concurrent testimony against persons justly censured. . . .

   4. To seek and accept help from, and give help unto each other.

      1. In case of divisions and contentions whereby the peace of any church is disturbed. . . .

      2. In matters of more than ordinary importance, . . . as ordination translation and deposition of elders and such like . . .

      3. In doubtful and difficult questions and controversies, doctrinal or practical that may arise. . .

4. For the rectifying of male-administrations, and healing of errors and scandals, that are unhealed among themselves . . . Churches now have need of help in like cases, as well as churches then; Christ's care is still for whole churches, as well as for particular persons; and apostles being now ceased there remains the duty of brotherly love and mutual care, and helpfulness incumbent upon churches, especially elders for that end.

5. In love and faithfulness to take notice of the troubles and difficulties, errors and scandals of another church, and to administer help, (when the case necessarily calls for it) tho' they should so neglect their own good and duty, as not to seek it . . .

6. To admonish one another, when there is need and cause for it, and after due means with patience used, to withdraw from such a church, or peccant party therein, obstinately persisting in error or scandal; as in the platform of discipline is more at large declared. . . .

5. Consociation of churches is their mutual and solemn agreement to exercise communion in such acts, as aforesaid, amongst themselves, with special reference to those churches, which by Providence are planted in a convenient vicinity, though with liberty reserved without offence, to make use of others, as the nature of the case, or the advantage of opportunity may lead thereunto.

6. The churches of Christ in this country having so good opportunity for it, it is meet to be commended to them, as their duty thus to consociate. . . . There has constantly been in these churches a possession of communion, in giving the right hand of fellowship in the gathering of churches, and ordination of elders; which importeth a consociation, and obligeth to the practice thereof. Without which we should also want an expedient, and sufficient cure for emergent church difficulties and differences: with the want whereof our way is charged, but unjustly, if this part of the doctrine thereof were duly practiced.

7. The manner of the church's agreement herein, or entring into this consociation, may be by each church's open consenting unto the things, here, declared in answer to the second question, as also to what is said thereabout, in chap. 15 and 16. of the platform of discipline, with reference to other churches in this colony and countrey, as in propos. 5. is before expressed.

8. The manner of exercising and practising that communion, which this consent or agreement specially tendeth unto, may be, by making use occasionally of elders or able brethren of other churches; or by the more solemn meetings of both elders and messengers in lesser or greater councils, as the matter shall require.

Text—Mather: *Magnalia*, Book V, Third Part. (Scriptural notations and italics omitted.)

XI. *THE REFORMING COUNCIL OF 1679*

The following document addressed to the General Court, Sept. 10, 1679, in order to arouse the Governors to their responsibility in the matter of initiating reform, gives insight into prevailing conditions, and illustrates the "Puritan mind."

QUEST. I

(1) What are the evils that have provoked the Lord to bring his Judgements on New-England? . . .

I. There is a great and visible decay of the power of Godliness amongst many Professors in these .Churches. It may be feared, that there is in too many spiritual and heart Apostacy from God, whence Communion with him in the wayes of his Worship, especially in Secret, is much neglected, and whereby men cease to know and fear, and love and trust him; but take up their contentment and satisfaction in something else. . . .

II. The Pride that doth abound in New-England testifies against us. Hos. 5.5. Ezek. 7.10. Both spiritual Pride, Zeph. 3.11. Whence two great Evils and Provocations have proceeded and prevailed amongst us.

1. A refusing to be subject to Order according to divine appointment, Numb, 16.3. I Pet 5.5.

2. Contention. Prov. 13.10. An evil that is most eminently against the solemn Charge of the Lord Jesus, Joh, 13. 34, 35. And that for which God hath by severe Judgements punished his People, both in former and latter Ages. This Malady hath been very general in the Country: We have therefore cause to fear that the Wolves which God in holy Providence hath let loose upon us, have been sent to chastise his Sheep for their dividings and strayings one from another; and that the Warrs and Fightings, which have proceeded from the Lust of pride in special, have been punished with the Sword. Jam. 4. 1. Job. 19. 29.

Yea, and Pride in respect to Apparel hath greatly abounded. (3) Servants, and the poorer sort of People are notoriously guilty in this matter, who(too generally) goe above their estates and degrees, thereby transgressing the Laws both of God and man, Math. 11. 8. Yea, it is a Sin that even the light of nature, and Laws of civil Nations have condemned. I Cor. 11, 14. Also, many, not of the meaner sort, have offended God by strange Apparel, not becoming serious Christians, especially in these dayes of affliction and misery, wherein the Lord calls upon men to put off their Ornaments, Exod. 33. 5. Jer. 4 30.

III. Church Fellowship, and other divine Institutions are greatly neglected. Many of the Rising Generation are not mindfull of that which their Baptism doth engage them unto, viz. to use utmost endeavours that they may be fit for, and so partake in, all the holy Ordinances of the Lord Jesus. Mat. 28. 20. There are too many that with profane Esau slight spiritual priviledges. Nor is there so much of the Discipline, extended toward the Children of the Covenant, as we are generally agreed ought to be done. On the other hand, humane Inventions, and Will-worship have been set up even in Jerusalem. Men have set up their Thresholds by Gods Threshold, and their Posts by his Post. Quakers are false worshippers: and such Anabaptists as have risen up amongst us, in opposition to the Churches of the Lord Jesus, receiving into their society those that have been for scandal delivered unto Satan, yea, and improving those as Administrators of holy Things, who have been (as doth appear) *Justly* under Church Censures, do no better then set up an Altar against the Lords Altar. . . . . .

IIII. The Holy and Glorious Name of God hath been polluted and profaned amongst us. More especially.

(4) 1. By Oathes, and Imprecations in ordinary Discourse; Yea, and it is too common a thing for men in a more solemn way to Swear unnecessary Oaths. . . . .

2. There is great profaness, in respect of irreverent behaviour in the solemn Worship of God. It is a frequent thing for men (though not necessitated thereunto by any infirmity) to sit in prayer time, and some with their heads almost covered, and to

give way to their own sloth and sleepiness, when they should be serving God with attention and intention, under the solemn dispensation of his Ordinances. We read of but one man in the Scripture that slept at a Sermon, and that sin hath like to have cost him his life. Act. 20.9.

V. There is much Sabbath-breaking; Since there are multitudes that do profanely absent themselves or theirs from the publick worship of God, on his Holy day, especially in the most populous places in the Land; and many under the pretence of differing apprehensions about the beginning of the Sabbath, do not keep a seventh part of the Time Holy unto the Lord, as the fourth Commandment requireth, Walking abroad, and Travelling (not meerly on account of worshipping God in the solemn assemblyes of his people, or to attend to works of necessity or mercy) being a common practice on the Sabbath day, which is contrary unto that Rest enjoyned by the Commandment. Yea some that attend their particular servile callings and employments after the Sabbath is begun, or before it is ended. Worldly, unsuitable discourses are very common upon the Lords day, contrary to the Scripture which requireth that men should not on Holy Times find their own pleasure, nor speak their own words, Isai 58.13. Many that do not take care so to despatch their worldly businesses, that they may be free & fit for the dutyes of the Sabbath, and that do (if not wholly neglect) after a careless, heartless manner perform the dutyes that concern the sanctification of the Sabbath. This brings wrath, Fires and other Judgements upon a professing People. Neh. 3.17, 18. Jer. 17.27.

VI. As to what concerns Familyes and the Government thereof, (5) there is much amiss. There are many Familyes that doe not pray to God constantly morning and evening, and many more wherein the Scriptures are not daily read, that so the word of Christ might dwell richly with them. Some (and too many) Houses that are full of Ignorance and Profaness, and these not duely inspected; for which cause Wrath may come upon others round about them, as well as upon themselves. . . . And many Householders who profess Religion, doe not cause all that are within their gates to become subject to good order as ought to be. Ex. 20.10. Nay, children & Servants that are not kept in due subjection; their Masters, and Parents especially, being sinfully indulgent towards them. In this respect, Christians in this Land, have become too like unto the Indians, and we need not wonder if the Lord hath afflicted us by them. Sometimes a Sin is discerned by the Instrument that Providence doth punish with. Most of the Evils that abound amongst us, proceed from defects as to Family Government.

VII. Inordinate Passions. Sinful Heats and Hatreds, and that amongst Church Members themselves, who abound with evil Surmisings, uncharitable and unrighteous Censures, Back-bitings, hearing and telling Tales, few that remember and duely observe the Rule, with an angry countenance to drive away the Tale-bearer: Reproachfull and reviling Expressions, sometimes to or of one another. Hence Law suits are frequent, Brother going to Law with Brother, and provoking and abusing one another n publick Courts of Judicature, to the scandal of their Holy Profession. . . .

VIII. There is much Intemperance. The heathenish and Idolatrous practice of Health-drinking is too frequent. That shamefull iniquity of sinfull Drinking is become too general a Provocation. Dayes of Training, and other publick Solemnityes, have been abused in this respect: And not only English but Indians have been debauched, by those that call themselves Christians, who have put their (6) bottles to hem, and made them drunk also. This is a crying Sin, and the more aggravated in that the first Planters of this Colony did (as in the Patent expressed) come into this Land with a design to convert the Heathen unto Christ, but if instead of that, they be taught Wickedness, which before they were never guilty of, the Lord may well punish us by them.   Moreover, the Sword, Sickness, Poverty, and almost all the Judgements which have been upon New England,.are mentioned in the Scripture as the woeful fruit of *That Sin.* . . .   There are more Temptations and occasions unto *That Sin,* publickly allowed of, then any necessity doth require; the proper end of Taverns &c. being for the entertainment of Strangers which if they were improved to that end only, a far less number would suffice: But it is a common practice for Town-dwellers, yea, and Church-members, to frequent publick Houses, and there to misspend precious Time, unto the dishonour of the Gospel, and the scandalizing of others, who are by such examples induced to sin against God.   In which respect, for Church-members to be unnecessarily in such Houses, is sinfull, scandalous, and provoking to God. . . .

And there are other hainous breaches of the seventh Commandment.   Temptations thereunto become too common, viz. such as immodest Apparel, Prov. 7.10. Laying out of hair, Borders, naked Necks and Arms, or, which is more abominable, naked Breasts, and mixed Dancings, light behaviour and expressions, sinful Company-keeping with light and vain persons, unlawfull Gaming, an abundance of Idleness, which brought ruinating Judgement upon Sodom, and much more upon Jerusalem. Ezek. 16.49. and doth sorely threaten New-England, unless effectual Remedyes be throughly and timously applyed.

IX.   There is much want of Truth amongst men.   Promise-breaking is a common sin, for which New-England doth hear ill abroad in the world. . . .

X. Inordinate affections to the world. . . There hath been in many professors an insatiable desire after Land, and worldly Accomodations, yea, so as to forsake Churches and Ordinances, and to live like Heathen, only that so they might have Elbow-room enough in the world.   Farms and merchandising have been preferred before the things of God.   In this respect, the Interest of New-England seemeth to be changed.   We differ from other out-goings of our Nation, in that it was not any worldly consideration that brought our Fathers into this wilderness, but Religion, even that so they might build a sanctuary to the Lords Name, Whenas now, Religion is made subservient unto worldly Interests. . . .   Wherefore, we cannot but solemnly bear witness against that practice of setling Plantations without any Ministry, amongst them, which is to prefer the world before the Gospel. . . . .   Moreover, that many are under the prevailing power of the sin of worldliness is evident.

1. From that oppression which the Land groaneth under.   There are some Traders who sell their goods at excessive Rates, Day-labourers and Mechanicks are unreasonable in their demands; Yea, there have been those that have dealt deceitfully and oppressively toward the Heathen amongst whom we live, whereby they have been scandalized and prejudiced against the Name of Christ. . . .

2. It is also evident that men are under the prevailing power of a worldly Spirit, by their strait-handedness, as to publick concernments.   God by a continued series of providence, for many years one after another, hath been blasting the fruits of the Earth, in a great measure; and this year more abundantly; Now if we search the Scriptures, we shall find, that when the Lord hath been provoked to destroy the fruits of the Earth, either by noxious Creatures, or by his own immediate hand in blastings or droughts, or excessive Rains (all which Judgements we have experience of) it hath

been mostly for the sin of strait-handedness with reference unto publick and pious concerns, Hag. 1.9. . . .

XI. There hath been opposition unto the work of the Reformation. Although the Lord hath been calling upon us, not only by the voice of his Servants, but by awfull judgements, that we should return unto him, who hath been smiting us. . . and notwithstanding all the good Laws that are established for the suppression of growing evils, yet men *will not* return everyone fron his evil way. . . . .

XII. A publick Spirit is greatly wanting in the most of men. Few that are of Nehemiah's Spirit, Neh. 5.15. All seek their own, not the things that are Jesus Christs; Serving themselves upon Christ and his holy Ordinances. Matters appertaining to the Kingdome of God, are either not at all regarded, or not in the first place. Hence Schools of learning and other publick concerns are in a languishing state. Hence also are unreasonable complaints and murmurings because of publick charges, which is a great sin; and a private self-seeking Spirit, is one of those evils that renders the last Times perilous. 2 Tim. 3.1-

QUEST. II

WHAT is to be done that so these Evils may be Reformed?

Answ. I. It would tend much to promote the interest of Reformation, if all that are in place above others, do as to themselves and Familyes, become every way exemplary. Moses being to reform others began with what concerned himself and his.

. . . .

III. It is requisite that persons be not admitted into Communion in the Lords Supper without making a personal and publick profession of their Faith and Repentance, either orally, or in some other way, so as shall be to the just satisfaction of the Church; and that therefore the Elders and Churches be duely watchfull and circumspect in this matter. I Cor. 11.28, 29. Act. 2. 41, 42. Ezek. 44. 7, 8, 9.

IIII. In order to Reformation, it is necessary that the Discipline of Christ in the power of it should be upheld in the Churches. . . Discipline is Christs Ordinance, both for the prevention of Apostacy in Churches and to recover them when collapsed. And these New English Churches, are under peculiar engagements to be faithfull unto Christ, and unto his Truth in this matter, by virtue of the Church Covenant, as also in the management of Discipline according to the Scriptures, was the special design of our Fathers in coming into this wilderness. The degeneracy of the Rising Generation (so much complained of) is in a great measure to be attributed unto neglects of this nature. . . . .

V. It is requisite that utmost endeavours should be used, in order unto a full supply of Officers in the Churches, according to Christs Institution. The defect of these Churches on this account is very lamentable, there being in most of the Churches, only one Teaching Officer, for the burden of the whole Congregation to lye upon. The Lord Christ would not have instituted Pastors, Teachers, Ruling Elders (nor the Apostles have ordained Elders in every Church) Act. (11) 14.23. Tit. 1.5.) if he had not seen there was need of them for the good of his People; and therefore for men to think they can do well enough without them, is both to break the second Commandment, and to reflect upon the wisdome of Christ, as if he did appoint unnecessary Officers in his Church. . . .

VI. It is incumbent on the Magistrate, to take care that these Officers have due encouragement, and maintenance afforded to them. It is high injustice and oppres sion, yea, a Sin that cryes in the Lords ear for judgement, when wages is with he'd from faithful and diligent Labourers. . . . If therefore People be unwilling to doe that which justice and reason calls for, the Magistrate is to see them doe their duty in this matter.   Wherefore, Magistrates, and that in Scriptures referring to the dayes of the New Testament, are said to be the Churches nursing Fathers. Isa. 49.23. For that it concerns them to take care that the Churches be fed with the bread and water of Life. The Magistrate is to be a keeper of both Tables, which as a Magistrate he cannot be, if he does not promove the interest of Religion, by all whose means which are of the Lords appointment. . . .

VII. Due care and faithfullness with respect unto the establishment and execution of wholsome Laws, would very much promote the interest of Reformation. . .in particular, those Laws which respect the Regulation of Houses for publick entertainment, that the number of such Houses doe not exceed what is necessary, nor any so entrusted but persons of known approved piety and Fidelity, and that inhabitants be prohibited drinking in such Houses, and those that shall without License from Authority sell any sort of strong drink, be exemplarily punished.   And if withal, inferiur Officers, Constables, and Tithing men, be chosen constantly of the ablest and most prudent in the place, Authorized and Sworn to a faithful discharge of their respective Trusts, and duely encouraged in their just informations against any that shall transgress the Laws so established, we may hope that much of that prophaneness which doth threaten the ruine of the uprising Generation will be prevented.

VIII. Solemn and explicit Renewal of the Covenant is a Scripture expedient for Reformation.   We seldome read of any solemn Reformation but it was accomplished in this way, as the Scripture doth abundantly declare and testify. . . .

X. It seems to be most conducive unto Edification and Reformation, that in Renewing Covenant, such things as are clear and indisputable be expressed, that so all the Churches may agree in Covenanting to promote the Interest of holiness, and close walking with God.

XI. As an expedient for Reformation, it is good that effectual care should be taken, respecting Schools of Learning.   The interest of Religion and good Literature have been wont to rise and fall together.   We read in the Scriptures of Masters and Scholars, and of Schools and Colledges., I Chron. 25.8.   Mal. 2.12.   Act. 19.9. and 22.3.   And the most eminent Reformers among the Lords People of old, thought it their concern to erect and uphold them.   Was not Samuel (that great Reformer) President of the Colledge at Najoth, I Sam. 19.18, 19. and is thought to be one of the first Founders of Colledges. . . And we have all cause to bless God that put it into the hearts of our Fathers to take care concerning this matter.   For these Churches had been in a state most deplorable, if the Lord had not blessed the Colledge, so as from thence to supply most of the Churches, as at this day.   When New-England was poor, and we were but few in number comparatively, there was a Spirit to encourage Learning and the Colledge was full of Students, whom God hath made blessings, not only in this, but in other Lands; but it is deeply to be lamented, that now, when we are become many, and more able then at the beginnings, that Society and other inferior Schools are in such low and languishing State.   Wherefore, as we desire that Reformation and Religion should flourish, it concerns us to endeavour, that both the Colledge and all other Schools of Learning in every place, be duely inspected and encouraged.

Text—Walker: *The Creeds and Platforms of Congregationalism,* pp. 426-437.

XII. *BOSTON AND CAMBRIDGE IN 1680*

Jasper Danckaerts and Peter Sluyter have left the following diary records of a visit to Boston and vicinity.

1680 . . . 28*th, Friday.* One of the best ministers in the place being very sick, a day of fasting and prayer was observed in a church near by our house. We went into the church where, in the first place, a minister made a prayer in the pulpit, of full two hours in length; after which an old minister delivered a sermon an hour long, and after that a prayer was made, and some verses sung out of the psalms. In the afternoon, three or four hours were consumed with nothing except prayers, three ministers relieving each other alternately; when one was tired, another went up into the pulpit. There was no more devotion than in other churches, and even less than at New York; no respect, no reverence; in a word, nothing but the name of independents; and that was all. . . .

7th, Sunday. We heard preaching in three churches, by persons who seemed to possess zeal, but no just knowledge of Christianity. The auditors were very worldly and inattentive. The best of the ministers whom we have yet heard, s a very old man, named John Eliot, who has charge of the instruction of the Indians in the Christian religion. . . .

8th, Monday. We went accordingly, about eight o'clock in the morning, to Roxbury, which is three-quarters of an hour from the city, . . . We found it justly called *Rocksbury,* for it was very rocky, and had hills entirely of rocks. Returning to his house we spoke to him [Mr. Eliot], and he received us politely. Although he could speak neither Dutch nor French, and we spoke but little English, and were unable to express ourselves in it always, we managed, by means of Latin and English, to understand each other. He was seventy-seven years old, and had been forty-eight years in these parts. He had learned very well the language of the Indians, who lived about there. We asked him for an Indian Bible. He said in the late Indian war, all the Bibles and Testaments were carried away, and burnt or destroyed, so that he had not been able to save any for himself, but a new edition was in press, which he hoped would be much better than the first one, though that was not to be despised. We inquired whether any part of the old or new edition could be obtained by purchese, and whether there was any grammar of that language in English. Thereupon he went and brought us the Old Testament, and also the New Testament, made up with some sheets of the new edition, so that we had the Old and New Testaments complete. He also brought us two or three small specimens of the grammar. We asked him what we should pay him for them; but he desired nothing. We presented him our *Declaration* in Latin, and informed him about the persons and conditions of the church, whose declaration it was, and about Madam Schurman and others, with which he was delighted, and could not restrain himself from praising God, the Lord, that had raised up men, and reformers, and begun the reformation in Holland. He deplored the decline of the church in New England, and especially in Boston, so that he did not know what would be the final result. . . .

9th, Tuesday. We started out to go to Cambridge, lying to the northeast of Boston, in order to see their college, and printing office. We left about six o'clock in the morning, and were set across the river at Charlestown. We followed a road which we supposed was the right one, but went full half an hour out of the way, and would have gone still further, had not a negro who met us, and of whom we inquired, disabused us of our mistake. We went back to the right road, which is a very pleasant one. We reached Cambridge, about eight o'clock. It is not a large village, and the houses stand very much apart. The college building is the most conspicuous among them. We went to it, expecting to see something curious, as it is the only college, or would-be academy of the Protestants in all America, but we found ourselves mistaken. In approaching the house, we neither heard nor saw any thing mentionable; but, going to the other side of the building, we heard noise enough in an upper room, to lead my comrade to suppose they were engaged in disputation. We entered, and went up stairs, when a person met us, and requested us to walk in, which we did. We found there, eight or ten young fellows, sitting around, smoking tobacco, with the smoke of which the room was so full, that you could hardly see; and the whole house smelt so strong of it, that when I was going up stairs, I said, this is certainly a tavern. We excused ourselves, that we could speak English only a little, but understood Dutch or French, which they did not. However, we spoke as well as we could. We required how many professors' there were, and they replied not one, that there was no money to support one. We asked how many students there were. They said at first, thirty, and then came down to twenty; I afterwards understood there are probably not ten. They could hardly speak a word of Latin, so that my comrade could not converse with them. They took us to the library where there was nothing particular. We looked over it a little. They presented us with a glass of wine. This is all we ascertained there. The minister of the place goes there morning and evening to make prayer, and has charge over them. The students have tutors or masters. Our visit was soon over, and we left them to go and look at the land about there. We found the place beautifully situated on a large plain, more than eight miles square, with a fine stream in the middle of it, capable of bearing heavily laden vessels. As regards the fertility of the soil, we consider the poorest in New York, superior to the best here. As we were tired, we took a mouthful to eat, and left. We passed by the printing office, but there was nobody in it; the paper sash however being broken, we looked in; and saw two presses with six or eight cases of type. There is not much work done there. Our printing office is well worth two of it, and even more. We went back to Charlestown, where, after waiting a little, we crossed over about three o'clock. We found our skipper, John Foy, at the house, and gave him our names, and the money for our passage, six pounds each. He wished to give us a bill of it, but we told him it was unnecessary, as we were people of good confidence. I spoke to my comrade, and we went out with him, and presented him with a glass of wine. His mate came to him there, who looked more like a merchant than a seaman, a young man and no sailor. We inquired how long our departure would be delayed, and, as we understood him, it would be the last of the coming week. That was annoying to us. Indeed, we have found the English the same everywhere, doing nothing but lying and cheating, when it serves their interest. . . .

12th, Friday. We went in the afternoon to Mr. John Taylor's, to ascertain whether he had any good wine, and to purchase some for our voyage, and also some brandy. On arriving at his house, we found him a little cool; indeed, not as he was formerly. We inquired for what we wanted, and he said he had good Madeira wine, but he believed he had no brandy, though he thought he could assist us in procuring it. We also inquired how we could obtain the history and laws of this place. At ast it came out. He said we must be pleased to excuse him if he did not give us admission to his house; he durst not do it, in consequence of there being a certain evil report in the city concerning us; they had been to warn him not to have too much communication with us, if he wished to avoid censure; they said we certainly were Jesuits, who had come here for no good, for we were quiet and modest, and an entirely different sort of people from themselves; that we could speak several languages, were cunning and subtle of mind and judgment, had come there without carrying on any traffic or any other business, except only to see the place and country; that this seemed fabulous as it was unusual in these parts; certainly it could be for no good purpose. As regards the voyage to Europe, we could have made it as well from New York as from Boston, as opportunities were offered there. This suspicion seemed to have gained more strength because the fire at Boston over a year ago was caused by a Frenchman. Although he had been arrested, they could not prove it against him; but in the course of the investigation, they discovered he had been counterfeiting coin and had profited thereby, which was a crime as infamous as the other. He had no trade or profession; he was condemned; both of his ears were cut off; and he was ordered to leave the country. . . .

23d, *Thursday.* . . . They are all *Independents* in matters of religion, if it can be called religion, many of them perhaps more for the purposes of enjoying the benefit of its privileges than for any regard to truth and godliness. I observed that while the English flag or color has a red ground with a small white field in the uppermost corner where there is a red cross, they have here dispensed with this cross in their colors, and preserved the rest. They baptize no children except those of the members of the congregation. All their religion consists in observing Sunday, by not working or going into the taverns on that day; but the houses are worse than the taverns. No stranger or traveler can therefore be entertained on a Sunday, which begins at sunset on Saturday, and continues until the same time on Sunday. At these two hours you see all their countenances change. Saturday evening the constable goes round into all the taverns of the city for the purpose of stopping all noise and debauchery, which frequently causes him to stop his search, before his search causes the debauchery to stop. There is a penalty for cursing and swearing, such as they please to impose, the witnesses thereof being at liberty to insist upon it. Nevertheless, you discover little difference between this and other places. Drinking and fighting occur there not less than elsewhere; and as to truth and true godliness, you must not expect more of them than of others. When we were there, four ministers' sons were learning the silversmith's trade. . . .

Text—*Journal of a Voyage to New York to 1679-80, Memoirs Long Island Hist. Soc.*, Vol. I, pp. 377-395.

CHAPTER VI

CONNECTICUT IN THE SEVENTEENTH AND EARLY EIGHTEENTH CENTURIES

Bibliography

In Bradford's "History" and Winthrop's "Journal," considerable data will be found bearing upon the early stages of Connecticut. The "Colonial Records of Connecticut" (XV Vols. to 1776) edited by J. Hammond Trumbull and Charles J. Hoadly supply constitutions, laws, court orders, and related material. The "New Haven Colonial Records" (II Vols. 1638-1665) edited by Charles J. Hoadly give corresponding data for New Haven.

A "General History of Connecticut" (1781) by Rev. Samuel Peters is fearless and not entirely reliable. The "History of the Colony of New Haven before and after the Union with Connecticut. . . " (1838) by E. R. Lambert is quite antiquated. "The History of Connecticut from the First Settlement of the Colony" (II Vols. 1835, enlarged in 1857) by G. H. Hollister, may be profitably consulted though in point of accuracy it is not to be classed with "A Complete History of Connecticut, Civil and Ecclesiastical, . . . " (II Vols. 1818) by Dr. Benjamin Trumbull which for detailed information, ample source quotations, and dignified style, remains the standard work on Connecticut. Palfrey's "History of New England" (1858-75) will be found useful. "A History of the Colony of New Haven to its Absorption into Connecticut" (1880) by Edward E. Atwater is thorough and luminous. Some important documents are embodied in the appendix. To the same class belongs C. H. Livermore's "The Republic of New Haven" (1886). "Connecticut, A Study of a Commonwealth-Democracy" (1887) by Alexander Johnson is a hand book, of interest primarily to the constitutional historian. "The River Towns of Connecticut" ("J. H. U. Studies," Series VII) by C. M. Andrews gives a good account of the first settlements. "Connecticut as a Colony and as a State . . . " (IV Vols. 1904) by Forrest Morgan (editor-in-chief) is a well written embodiment of all important information to date.

94

Local histories with which the student of church history should keep in touch are as follows: "History of New London, . . . " (1852, 2nd edition, enlarged, 1866), by Frances M. Caulkins; also her "History of Norwich" (1845, latest enlargement, 1874); "The History of Waterbury" (1857) by Henry Bronson; "The History of Ancient Windsor" (II Vols. 1859-63) by H. R. Stiles; "The History of Stamford, . . . " (1868) by Rev. E. B. Huntington; "Ancient Woodbury" (1854-1879) by W. Cothren; "The History of the Old Town of Derby" (1880) by S. Orcutt and A. Beardsley; "History of Guildford, . . . " (1877) by R. D. Smith; "History of Guildford and Madison" (1897) by Bernard C. Steiner; "The History of Enfield" (III Vols. 1900) by F. O. Allen (editor); "Town Records of Derby, 1655-1710" (1901) by Nancy O. Phillips, (editor); "Colonial History of Hartford" (1914) by Rev. W. D. Love.

On Thomas Hooker there is a scholarly paper by Edwin D. Mead on "Thomas Hooker's Farewell Sermon in England," ("Proc. Mass. Hist. Soc.," Vol. XLVI, pp. 253-274) and an excellent portraiture by George L. Walker entitled, "Thomas Hooker Preacher, Founder, Democrat" ("Makers of America" series, 1891). A bibliography of Hooker's published writings by J. Hammond Trumbull makes a useful appendix. In "Pioneers of Religious Liberty in America" ("Great and Thursday Lectures" delivered in Boston, 1903) Williston Walker has an illuminating section on "Thomas Hooker and the Principle of Congregational Independency."

"Roger Ludlow, the Colonial Law-Maker" (1900) by John M. Thayer is well written, though unnecessarily padded with the testimony of authorities.

The "Papers of the New Haven Colony Historical Society" have the following suggestive contributions: "History of Trinity Church, New Haven" by Fred Croswell (Vol. I, pp. 47-74); "Bishop Berkeley's Gifts to Yale College," by Daniel C. Gilman (Vol. I, pp. 147-170); "Sketch of the Life and Writings of John Davenport" by Franklin B. Dexter (Vol. II, pp. 205-238); "The Founding of Yale College" by the same writer (Vol. III, pp. 1-30); "The Ecclesiastical Constitution of Yale College" by Simeon E. Baldwin (Vol. III, pp. 405-442); "Mrs. Eaton's Trial (1644) from the Records of the First Church of New Haven" by Rev. Newman Smyth, D.D. (Vol. V, pp. 133-148); "Theophilus Eaton, First Governor of the Colony of New Haven" by Simeon E. Baldwin (Vol. VII, pp. 1-33); "The Founding of Yale College" by Charles H. Smith (Vol. VII, pp. 34-64); "Saybrook in the Early Days" by Rev. Samuel Hart (Vol. VII, pp. 120-140); "Rev. William Hooke, 1601-1678" by Rev. Charles R. Palmer (Vol. VIII, pp. 56-81); "The Fundamental Orders and the Charter" by Rev. Samuel Hart (Vol. VIII, pp. 238-254).

"Documents relating to the Early History of Yale University" contributed by Henry H. Edes, are to be found in the "Pub. Col. Soc. Mass.," Vol. VI, pp. 173-210. These should be supplemented by the exhaustive material embodied in the "Documentary History of Yale University . . . 1701-1745" (1916) edited by Franklin B. Dexter. Older histories of Yale are as follows: "The Annals or History of Yale-College . . . 1700-1766" by Thomas Clapp, (1766); "Annals of Yale College, from its Foundation, to the year 1831" (1831) by Ebenezer Baldwin; "Yale College: a Sketch of its History, with Notices of its several Departments, . . . " (II Vols. 1879) edited by W. L. Kingsley. "The Life of Ezra Stiles, D.D., LL.D., . . . President of Yale College" (1798) by Abiel Holmes throws considerable light upon the college.

A "History of the First Church in Hartford" (1884) by George L. Walker supplies an important place in Connecticut ecclesiastical history. "The Rogerenes . . . " (1904) by John R. Bolles (Part I) and Anna B. Williams (Part II) sets forth in thoroughgoing fashion a much misunderstood group. A more satisfactory study appears (Vol. II, pp. 1261-1302) among the "Papers in Commemoration of the One Hundredth Anniversary of the Organization of the Seventh-Day Baptist General Conference" (1909) by C. F. Randolph.

On the Separates there are two studies: "The Congregationalist Separates of the Eighteenth Century in Connecticut," by Rev. Edwin P. Parker ("Papers, New Haven Col. Hist. Soc." Vol. VIII, pp. 151-162); and "The Separates, or Strict Congregationalists of New England" (1902) by Rev. S. L. Blake, with introduction by Williston Walker. The latter is a painstaking sympathetic treatment with bibliographical directions.

To the literature cited in connection with Massachusetts, much of which is pertinent to Connecticut, it is necessary to add the following: "The Blue Laws of Connecticut" ("American Catholic Quarterly Review," July, 1877); "Witchcraft in Connecticut" ("New England and Yale Review," November, 1886); "The Development of Religious Liberty in Connecticut" (1905) by M. Louise Greene; and "The Contrast in Ecclesiastical Legislation between Colonial Massachusetts and Connecticut" (D. B. Dissertation, Univ. of Chicago, 1904) by A. H. Shattuck.

DOCUMENTS

I. *THE FUNDAMENTAL ORDERS OF CONNECTICUT—JANUARY 14, 1638*

Forasmuch as it hath pleased the Allmighty God by the wise disposition of his diuyne pᴿuidence so to Order and dispose of things that we the Inhabitants and Residents of Windsor, Harteford and Wethersfield are now cohabiting and dwelling in and vppon the River of Conectecotte and the Lands thereunto adioyneing; And well knowing where a people are gathered togather the word of God requires that to mayntayne the peace and union of such a people there should be an orderly and decent Gouerment established according to God, to order the dispose of the affayres of the people at all seasons as occation shall require; doe therefore assotiate and conioyne our selues to be as one Publike State or Comonwelth; and doe, for our selues and our Successors and such as shall be adioyned to vs att any tyme hereafter enter into Combination and Confedcration togather, to mayntayne and pᴿsearue the liberty and purity of the gospell of our Lord Jesus wᶜʰ we now pᴿfesse, as also the disciplyne of the Churches, wᶜʰ according to the truth of the said gospell is now practised amongst vs; As also in oᴿ Ciuell Affaires to be guided and gouerned according to such Lawes, Rules, Orders and decrees as shall be made, ordered & decreed, as followeth:—

1. It is Ordered, sentenced, and decreed, that there shall be yerely two generall Assemblies or Courts, the on the second thursday in Aprill, the other the second thursday in September, following; the first shall be called the Courte of Election, wherein shall be yerely Chosen from tyme to tyme soe many Magestrats and other Publike Officers as shall be found requisitte: Whereof one to be chosen Gouernour for the yeare ensueing and vntill another be chosen, and noe other Magestrate to be chosen for more then one yeare; pᴿuided allwayes there be six chosen besids the Gouernour; wᶜʰ being chosen and sworne according to an Oath recorded for that purpose shall haue power to administer iustice according to the Lawes here established, and for want thereof according to the rule of the word of God; wᶜʰ choise shall be made by all that arc admitted freemen and haue taken the Oath of Fidellity, and doe cohabitte wᵗʰin this Jurisdiction, (hauing beene admitted Inhabitants by the maior pᴿte of the Towne wherein they liue,) or the maior pᴿte of such as shall be then pᴿsent.

. . . .

4. It is Ordered, Sentenced and decreed that noe pᴿson be chosen Gouernor aboue once in two yeares, and that the Gouernor be alwayes a member of some approved congregation, and formerly of the Magestracy wᵗʰin this Jurisdiction; and all the Magestrats Freemen of this Comonwelth: and that no Magestrate or other publike officer shall execute any pᴿte of his or their Office before they are seuerally sworne, wᶜʰ shall be done in the face of the Courte if they be pᴿsent, and in case of Absence by some deputed for that purpose.

. . . .

10. It is Ordered, sentenced and decreed, that euery Generall Courte, except such as through neglecte of the Gouᴿnor and the greatest pᴿte of Magestrats the Freemen themselves doe call, shall consist of the Gouernor, or some one chosen to moderate the Court, and 4 other Magestrats at lest, wᵗʰ the mayor pᴿte of the deputyes of the seuerall Townes legally chosen; and in case the Freemen or mayor pᴿte of them, through neglect or refusall of the Gouernor and mayor pᴿte of the magestrats, shall call a

Courte, y^t shall consist of the mayor p^rte of Freemen that are p^rsent or their deputyes, wth a Moderator chosen by them: In wch said Generall Courts shall consist the supreme power of the Comonwelth, and they only shall haue power to make lawes or repeale them, to graunt leuyes, to admitt of Freemen, dispose of lands vndisposed of, to seuerall Townes or p^rsons, and also shall haue power to call ether Courte or Magestrate or any other p^rson whatsoeuer into question for any misdemeanour, and may for just causes displace or deale otherwise according to the nature of the offence, and also may deale in any other matter that concerns the good of this comon welth, excepte election of Magestrats, wch shall be done by the whole boddy of Freemen.

. . . .

The Oath of the Gou^rnor, for the (p^rsent)

I, N. W. being now chosen to be Gou^rnor wth in this Jurisdiction, for the yeare ensueing, and vntil a new be chosen, doe sweare by the greate and dreadfull name of the everliueing God, to p^rmore the publike good and peace of the same, according to the best of my skill; as also will mayntayne all lawfull priuiledges of this Comonwealth; as also that all wholsome lawes that are or shall be made by lawfull authority here established, be duly executed; and will further the execution of Justice, according to the rule of Gods word; so helpe me God, in the name of the Lo: Jesus Christ.

Text—Hoadly: *Colonial Records of Connecticut*, Vol. I. pp. 20-26.

II. *THE FUNDAMENTAL ARTICLES OF NEW HAVEN— JUNE 4, 1639*

The 4th day of the 4th moneth called June 1639, all the free planters assembled together in a general meetinge to consult about settling civill Government according to God, and about the nomination of persons thatt might be founde by consent of all fittest in all respects for the foundation worke of a church which was intended to be gathered in Quinipieck. After solemne invocation of the name of God in prayer for the presence and help of his speritt, and grace in those weighty businesses, they were reminded of the business whereabout they mett viz for the establishment of such civill order as might be most pleasing unto God, and for the chuseing the fittest men for the foundation worke of a church to be gathered. For the better inableing them to discerne the minde of God and to agree accordingly concerning the establishment of civill order, Mr. John Davenport propounded divers quaeres to them publiquely praying them to consider seriously in the presence and feare of God the weight of the busines they met about, and nott to be rash or sleight in giveing their votes to things they understooke nott, butt to digest fully and throughly whatt should be propounded to them, and without respect to men as they should be satisfied and perswaded in their owne mindes to give their answers in such sort as they would be willing they should stand upon recorde for posterity.

This being earnestly pressed by Mr. Davenport, Mr. Robt. Newman was intreated to write in carracters and to read distinctly and audibly in the hearing of all the people whatt was propounded and accorded on that itt might appeare thatt all consented to matters propounded according to words written by him.

Quaer. 1. Whether the Scriptures doe holde forth a perfect rule for the direction and government of all men in all dueties which they are to performe to God and men as well in the government of famylyes and commonwealths as in matters of the chur.

This was assented unto by all, no man dissenting as was expressed by holding up of hands. Afterward itt was read over to them thatt they might see in whatt words their vote was expressed: They againe expressed their consent thereto by holdeing up their hands, no man dissenting.

Quaer. 2. Whereas there was a covenant solemnly made by the whole assembly of free-planters of this plantation the first day of extraordenary humiliation which wee had after wee came together, thatt as in matters thatt concerne the gathering and ordering of a chur. so likewise in all publique offices which concerne civill order, as choyce of magistrates and officers, makeing and repealing of lawes, devideing allottments of inheritance and all things of like nature we would all of us be ordered by those rules which the scripture holds forth to us. This covenant was called a plantation covenant to distinguish itt from a chur. covenant which could nott att thatt time be made, a chur. nott being then gathered, butt was deferred till a chur. might be gathered according to God: It was demaunded whether all the free planters doe holde themselves bound by thatt covenant in all businesses of thatt nature which are expressed in the covenant to submitt themselves to be ordered by the rules held forth in the scripture.

This also was assented unto by all, and no man gainesaid itt, and they did testefie the same by holdcing up their hands both when itt was first propounded, and confirmed the same by holdelng up their hands when itt was read unto them in publique. . . .

Quaer. 3. Those who have desired to be received as free planters, and are settled in the plantation with a purpose, resolution and desire thatt they may be admitted into chur. fellowship according to Christ as soone as God shall fitt them thereunto: were desired to express itt by holdeing up of hands: Accordingly all did expresse this to be their desire and purpose by holdeing up their hands twice, viz both att the proposall of itt, and after when these written words were read unto them.

Quaer. 4. All the free planters were called upon to expresse whether they held themselves bound to establish such civill order as might best canduce to the secureing of the purity and peace of the ordinances to themselves and their posterity according to God. In answer hereunto they expressed by holding up their hands twice as before, thatt they held them selves bound to establish such civil order as might best conduce to the ends aforesaid.

Then Mr. Davenport declared unto them by the scripture whatt kinde of persons might best be trusted with matters of government, and by sundry arguments from scripture proved that such men as were discribed in Exod. 18.2., Deut. 1.13, with Deut. 17.15, and I Cor. 6:1 to 7, ought to be intrusted by them, seeing they were free to cast themselves into thatt mould and forme of common wealth which appeareth best for them in referrence to the secureing of the pure and peaceable injoyment of all Christ his ordinances in the church according to God, whereunto they have bound themselves as hath beene acknowledged. Having thus said he satt downe, praying the company freely to consider whether they would have it voted att this time or nott: After some space of silence Mr. Theophilus Eaton answered itt might be voted, and some others allso spake to the same purpose, none att all opposeing itt. Thenn itt was propounded to vote.

Quaer. 5. Whether Free Burgesses shalbe chosen out of chur. members they thatt are in the foundation worke of the church being actually free burgesses, and to chuse to themselves out of the like estate of church fellowship and the power of chuseing magistrates and officers from among themselves and the power off makeing and repealing lawes according to the worde, and the devideing of inheritances and decideing of differences thatt may arise, and all the buisnesses of like nature are to be transacted by those free burgesses.

This was putt to vote and agreed unto by the lifting up of hands twice as in the former itt was done.   Then one man stood up after the vote was past, and expressing his dissenting from the rest in part yett grantinge 1. That magistrates should be men fearing God.   2.   Thatt the church is the company whence ordenaryly such men may be expected.   3.   Thatt they that chuse them ought to be men fearing God: onely att this he stuck, That free planters ought nott to give this power out of their hands: Another stood up and answered that in this case nothing was done but with their consent.   The former answered thatt all the free planters ought to resume this power into their owne hands againe if things were not orderly carryed.   Mr. Theophilus Eaton answered thatt in all places they chuse coommittyes, in like manner the companyes of London chuse the liveryes by whom the publique magistrates are chosen. In this the rest are not wronged because they expect in time to be of the livery themselves, and to have the same power.   Some others intreated the former to givè his arguments and reasons whereupon he dissented.   He refused to doe itt and said they might nott rationally demaund itt, seeing he lett the vote passe on freely and did nott speake till after itt was past, because he would not hinder whatt they agreed upon. Then Mr. Davenport, after a short relation of some former passages betweene them two about this quest. prayed the Company thatt nothing might be concluded by them in this weighty quest. butt whatt themselves were perswaded to be agreeing with the minde of God and they had heard whatt had beene said since the voteing, intreated them againe to consider of itt, and putt itt againe to vote as before.—Againe all of them by holding up their hands did shew their consent as before, And some of them professed thatt whereas they did waver before they came to the assembly they were now fully convinced thatt itt is the minde of God.   One of them said that in the morning, before he came, reading Deut. 17. 15. he was convinced att home, another said thatt he came doubting to the assembly butt he blessed God by whatt had beene saide he was now fully satisfied thatt the choyce of burgesses out of chur. members, and to intrust those with the power before spoken off is according to the minde of God revealed in the scriptures.   All haveing spoken their apprehensions, itt was agreed upon, and Mr. Robert Newman was desired to write itt as an order whereunto every one thatt hereafter should be admitted here as planters should submitt and testefie the same by subscribeing their names to the order, namely, that church members only shall be free burgesses, and thatt they onely shall chuse magistrates & officers among themselves to have the power of transacting all the publique civill affayres of this Plantation, of makeing and repealing lawes, devideing of inheritances, decideing of differences thatt may arise and doeing all things or businesses of like nature.

This being thus settled as a foundamentall agreement concerning civill government. Mr. Davenport proceeded to propound some things to consideration aboute the gathering of a chur.   And to prevent the blemishing of the first beginnings of the chur. worke, Mr. Davenport advised thatt the names of such as were to be admitted might be publiquely propounded, to the end thatt they who were most approved might be chosen, for the towne being cast into severall private meetings wherein they thatt dwelt nearest together gave their accounts one to another of Gods gracious worke upon them, and prayed together and conferred to their mutuall edification, sundry of them had knowledg one of another, and in every meeting some one was

25064

more approved of all then any other. For this reason, and to prevent scandalls, the whole company was intreated to consider whom they found fittest to nominate for this worke.

Quae. 6. Whether are you all willing and doe agree in this thatt twelve men be chosen thatt their fitness for the foundation worke may be tried, however there may be more named yett itt may be in their power who are chosen to reduce them to twelve, and itt be in the power of those twelve to chuse out of themselves seaven that shall be most approved of the major part to begin the church.

This was agreed upon by consent of all as was expressed by holdeing up of hands, and thatt so many as should be thought fitt for the foundation worke of the church shall be propounded by the plantation, and written downe and passe without exception unlesse they had given publique scandall or offence, yett so as in case of publique scandall or offence, every one should have liberty to propound their exception att thatt time publiquely against any man that should be nominated when all their names should be writt downe, butt if the offence were private, thatt mens names might be tendered, so many as were offended were intreated to deale with the offender privately, and if he gave nott satisfaction, to bring the matter to the twelve thatt they might consider of itt impartially and in the feare of God.   The names of the persons nominated and agreed upon were Mr. Theoph. Eaton, Mr. John Davenport, Mr. Robert Newman, Mr. Math. Gilbert, Mr. Richard Malbon, Mr. Nath: Turner, Eze: Chevers, Thomas Fugill, John Ponderson, William Andrewes, and Jer. Dixon. Noe exception was brought against any of those in publique, except one about takeing an excessive rate for meale which he sould to one of Pequanack in his need, which he confessed with griefe and declared thatt haveing beene smitten in heart and troubled in his conscience, he restored such a part of the price back againe with confession of his sin to the party as he thought himselfe bound to doe.   And itt being feared thatt the report of the sin was heard farther than the report of his satistaction, a course was concluded on to make the satisfaction known to as many as heard of the sinn. Itt was also agreed upon att the said meeting thatt if the persons above named did finde themselves straitened in the number of fitt men for the seaven, thatt itt should be free for them to take into tryal of fitnes such other as they should thinke meete, provided thatt itt should be signified to the towne upon the Lords day who they so take in, thatt every man may be satisfied of them according to the course formerly taken.

Text—Hoadly: *New Haven Colonial Records*, 1638-1649, pp. 11-17.

III. *THE GOVERNMENT OF NEW HAVEN—OCTOBER 27, 1643*

Settlements at Guilford, Milford, Stamford, and Southold, uniting with New Haven, agreed upon a constitution of which the following religious sections formed a part:

Itt was agreed and concluded as a foundamentall order nott to be disputed or questioned hereafter, thatt none shall be admitted to be free burgesses in any of the plantations wthin this Jurisdictio for the future, butt such planters as are members of some or other of the approved churches in New England, nor shall any butt such tree burgesses have any vote in any electio, (the six present freemen att Milforde enjoying the liberty wᵗh the cautions agreed,) nor shall any power or trust in the ordering of any civill affayres, be att any time putt into the hands of any other then such church members, though as free planters, all have right to their inherritance & to comerce, according to such grants, orders and lawes as shall be made concerning the same.

2. All such free burgesses shall have power in each towne or plantation w^th^in this jurisdictio to chuse fitt and able men, from amongst themselves, being church members as before, to be the ordinary judges, to heare and determine all inferio^r^ causes, w^t^her civill or criminall, provided that no civill cause to be tryed in any of these plantatio Courts in value exceed 20^l^, and thatt the punishment in such criminalls, according to the minde of God, revealed in his word, touching such offences, doe nott exceed stocking and whipping, or if the fine be pecuniary, thatt itt exceed nott five pounds. In w^c^h court the magistrate or magistrates, if any be chosen by the free burgesses of the jurisdictio for thatt plantatio, shall sitt and assist w^t^h due respect to their place, and sentence shall pass according to the vote of the major part of each such Court, onely if the partyes, or any of them, be nott satisfyed w^t^h the justice of such sentences or executions, appeales or complaints may be made from and against these Courts to the court of Magistrates for the whole jurisdictio.

3. All such free burgesses through the whole jurisdictio, shall have vote in the electio of all magistrates, whether Governo^r^, Deputy Governo^r^, or other magistrates, w^t^h a Treasurer, a Secretary and a Marshall, &c. for the jurisdictio. And for the ease of those free burgesses, especially in the more remote plantatios, they may by proxi vote in these elections, though absent, their votes being sealed vp in the p^r^sence of the free burgesses themselves, thatt their severall libertyes may be preserved, and their votes directed according to their owne perticular light, and these free burgesses may, att every electio, chuse so many magistrates for each plantatio, as the weight of affayres may require, and as they shall finde fitt men for thatt trust. Butt it is provided and agreed, thatt no plantatio shall att any electio be left destitute of a magistrate if they desire one to be chosen out of those in church fellowship with them.

. . . .

5. Besides the Plantatio Courts and Court of Magistrates, their shall be a gen^r^ll Co^rt^ for the Jurisdictio, . . . w^c^h Gen^r^ll Court shall, w^t^h all care and dilligence provide for the maintenance of the purity of religion, and shall suppress the contrary, according to their best light from the worde of God, and all wholsome and sovnd advice w^c^h shall be given by the elders and churches in the jurisdictio, so farr as may concerne their civill power to deale therein.

. . . .

6ly, (they shall have power) to heare and determine all causes, whether civill or criminall, w^c^h by appeale or complaint shall be orderly brought vnto them from any of the other Courts, or from any of the other plantatio. In all w^c^h, w^t^h whatsoever else shall fall w^t^hin their cognisance or judicature, they shall proceed according to the scriptures, w^c^h is the rule of all rightous lawes and sentences, and nothing shall pass as an act of the Gen^r^ll Court butt by the consent of the majo^r^ part of magistrates, and the greater part of Deputyes.

Text—Hoadly: *New Haven Colonial Records*, 1638-1649, pp. 112-116.

IV. *THE BLUE LAWS OF CONNECTICUT*

In general the Connecticut code resembled that of Massachusetts. A few characteristic sections are given as they appear in the genuine code of 1672.

CAPITAL LAWS

If any Man or Woman after legal conviction shall Have or Worship any other God but the Lord God, he shal be put to death. *Deu.* 13.6. 17, 21. *Ex.* 22. 2.

2. If any person within this Colony shall Blaspheme the Name of God the Father, Son or Holy Ghost, with direct, express, presumptuous or high-handed Blasphemy, or shall Curse in the like manner, he shall be put to death, *Levit.* 24. 15, 16.

3. If any Man or Woman be a Witch, that is, hath or consulteth with a Familiar Spirit, they shall be put to death, *Exo.* 22. 18. *Lev.* 20. 27. *Deu.* 18. 10. 11.

4. If any person shall commit any wilful Murther, committed upon Malice, Hatred or Cruelty, not in a mans just and necessary defence, nor by casualty against his will, he shall be put to death. *Exod.* 21, 12, 13, 14. *Numb.* 35. 30, 31.

5. If any person shall slay another through guile, either by Poysoning, or other such Devilish practises, he shall be put to death, *Exod.* 21. 14. . . .

10. If any Man stealeth a Man or Man kinde, and selleth him, or if he be found in his hand, he shall be put to death, *Exod.* 21. 16.

11. If any person rise up by False Witness wittingly and of purpose to take away any mans life, he or she shall be put to death, *Deut.* 19. 16, 18, 19 . . .

14. If any Childe or Children above *sixteen years old*, and of sufficient understanding, shall Curse or Smite their natural Father or Mother, he or they shall be put to death, unless it can be sufficiently testified, that the Parents have been very unchristianly negligent in the education of such Children, or so provoked them by extream and cruel correction, that they have been forced thereunto to preserve themselves from death or maiming. *Exod.* 21. 17. *Levit*, 20. 9. Exod, 21. 15.

15. If any man have a stubborn or rebellious Son, of sufficient understanding and years, *viz. sixteen years of age*, which will not obey the voice of his Father, or the voice of his Mother, and that when they have chastened him, he will not hearken unto them; then may his Father or Mother, being his natural Parents lay hold on him, and bring him to the Magistrates assembled in Court, and testifie unto them, that their Son is Stubborn and Rebellious, and will not obey their voice and chastisement, but lives in sundry notorious Crimes, such a Son shall be put to death. *Deut.* 21. 20. 21. . .

CHILDREN

Forasmuch as the good Education of Children is of singular behoof and benefit to any Colony, and whereas many Parents and Masters are too indulgent and negligent of their duty in that kinde;

It is therefore Ordered by the Authority of this Court; That the Selectmen of every Town in this Jurisdiction, in their several precincts and quarters shall have a vigilant eye over their Brethren and Neighbours, to see that none of them shall suffer so much Barbarisme in any of their Families, as not to endeavour by themselves, or others, to teach their Children and Apprentices so much learning as may enable them perfectly to reade the English Tongue, and knowledge of the Capital Laws, upon penalty of *twenty shillings* neglect therein: Also that all Masters of Families do once a week at least, Catechise their Children and Servants in the Grounds and Principles of Religion; and if any be unable to do so much, that then at the least they procure such Children and Apprentices to learn some short Orthodox Catechisme without book, that they may be able to answer to the Questions that shall be propounded to them out of such Catechisme, by their Parents or Masters, or any of the Select-men, when they shall call them to an accompt of what they have learned in that kinde. . . .

ECCLESIASTICAL

. . . It is therefore Ordered by the Authority of this Court, That if any Christian so called, within this Colony, shall contemptuously behave himself towards the Word preached, or the messengers thereof, called to Dispense the same in any Congregation, when he doth Faithfully execute his service and Office therein, according to the Will and Word of God; either by Interrupting him in his Preaching, or by charging him falsly with an Errour, which he hath not taught, in the open face of the Church; or like a Son of *Korah* cast upon his true Doctrine or himself, any reproach to the dishonour of the Lord Jesus who hath sent him, and to the disparagement of that his holy Ordinance and makeing Gods wayes contemptible and rediculous: That every such person or persons(whatsoever Censure the Church may pass) shall for the first scandall be convented and reproved openly by the Magistrate in some publick Assembly, and bound to their good behaviour. And if a Second time they break forth into the like contemptuous carriages, they shall either pay *five pounds* to the publick, or stand two hours openly upon a block or stool four foot high upon a publick meeting day, with a paper fixed on his Breast written with Capital Letters, AN OPEN AND OBSTINATE CONTEMNER OF GODS HOLY ORDINANCES, that others may fear and be ashamed of breaking out into the like wickedness.

It is further Ordered; That wheresoever the Ministry of the Word is established according to the order of the Gospel throughout this Colony, every person shall duely resort and attend thereunto respectively upon the Lords day, and upon such publick Fast dayes, and dayes of thanksgiving, as are to be generally kept by the appointment of Authority. And if any person within this Jurisdiction, shall without just and necessary cause, withdraw himself from hearing the publick Ministry of the Word, after due means of conviction used, he shall forfeit for his absence from every such meeting *five shillings*; all such offences to be heard and determined by any one Magistrate or more from time to time; provided all breaches of this Law be complained of, and prosecuted to effect within one moneth after the same. . . .

HERETICKS

This Court being sensible of the danger persons are in of being poysoned in their Judgements and Principles by Hereticks, whether Quakers, Ranters, Adamites, or such like:

Do see cause to Order; That no persons in this Colony shall give any unnecessary entertainment unto any Quaker, Ranter, Adamite, or other notorious Heretick, upon penalty of *five pounds* for every such persons entertainment, to be paid by him that shall so entertain them: And *five pounds per Week* shall be paid by each Town that shall suffer their entertainment as aforesaid.

It is also Ordered by the Authority of this Court, That it shall be in the power of the Governour, Deputy Governour or Assistants to order, that all such Hereticks as aforesaid be committed to Prison, or sent out of this Colony, and no person shall unnecessarily fall into discourse with any such Heretick, upon the penalty of *twenty shillings*.

And it is further Ordered; That no person within this Colony shall keep any Quaker-books or Manuscripts containing their Errours (except the Governour, Magistrates and Elders) upon penalty of *ten shillings per time* for every person that shall keep any such Books after the publication hereof, and shall not deliver such Books to the Magistrate or Minister. . . .

Prophanation of the Sabbath

Whereas the Sanctification of the Sabbath is a matter of great concernment to the Weal of a People, and the Prophanation thereof is that as brings down the judgements of God upon that Place or People that suffer the same;

It is therefore Ordered by this Court; That if any person shall Prophane the Sabbath, by unnecessary Travail, or Playing thereon in the time of publick Worship, or before or after, or shall keep out of the Meeting house during the time of publick Worship unneccessarily, there being convenient room in the House he shall Pay *five shillings* for every such offence, or sit in the Stocks one hour, any one Assistant or Commissioner to hear and determine any such case; And the Constables in the several Plantations are hereby required to make search after all Offenders against this Law, and to make return of those they shall finde transgressing to the next Assistant or Commissioner. . . .

SCHOOLS

It being one chief Project of Satan to keep men from the knowledge of the Scriptures, as in former times, keeping them in an unknown Tongue, so in these latter times, by persuading them from the use of Tongues, so that at least the true sense and meaning of the Original might be clouded with false Glosses of Saint seeming deceivers; and that Learning might not be buried in the Graves of our fore-fathers in Church and Colony, the Lord assisting our endeavours:

It is therefore Ordered by this Court and the Authority thereof; That every Township within this Jurisdiction, after the Lord hath increased them to the number of *Fifty* Householders, shall then forthwith appoint one within their Town to teach all such Children as shall resort to him, to Write and Reade, whose Wages shall be paid either by the Parents or Masters of such Children, or by the Inhabitants in General by way of supply, as the major part of those who Order the Prudentials of the Town shall appoint: Provided that those who send their Children, be not oppressed by paying much more then they can have them taught for in other Towns.

And it is further Ordered; That in every County Town there shall be set up and kept a Grammar School, for the use of the County, the Master thereof being able to instruct Youths so far as they may be fitted for the Colledge. . . .

Text—*The Laws of Connecticut*, George Brinley edition, pp. 1-63.

V. *THE SAYBROOK PLATFORM*

To assure representative attendance at periodic associations which since 1662 were merely voluntary, countenanced by no ecclesiastical institution, attended only by such ministers in one place and another as were willing to associate, and thereby to protect the churches from unworthy and ill prepared ministerial candidates, and also to provide them with accredited mediators for the settlement of their internal factions, the legislature in May 1708 enacted as under:

This assembly, from their own observation, and the complaint of many others, being made sensible of the defects of the discipline of the churches of this government, arising from the want of a more explicit asserting of the rules given for that end in the holy scriptures; from which would arise a permanent establishment among ourselves, a good and regular issue in cases subject to ecclesiastical discipline, glory to Christ, our head, and edification to his members; hath seen fit to ordain and require, and it is by the authority of the same ordained and required, that the ministers of the several counties in this government shall meet together, at their respective county towns, with such messengers, as the churches to which they belong shall see cause to send with them, on the last Monday in June next; there to consider and agree upon those methods and rules for the management of ecclesiastical discipline, which by them shall be judged agreeable and conformable to the word of God, and shall, at the same meeting, appoint two or more of their number to be their delegates, who shall all meet together at Saybrook, at the next commencement to be held there; where they shall compare the results of the ministers of the several counties, and out of and from them, to draw a form of ecclesiastical discipline, which, by two or more persons delegated by them, shall be offered to this court, at their session at New-Haven, in October next, to be considered and confirmed by them: And the expense of the above mentioned meetings shall be defrayed out of the public treasury of this colony.

In compliance therewith, delegates convened at Saybrook, September 9, 1708, when the subjointed 'platform of discipline' was adopted, though not with unanimity. In October the General Court legalized the platform by ordaining "that all the churches within this government, that are, or shall be, thus united in doctrine, worship, and discipline, be, and for the future shall be owned and acknowledged established by law; provided always, that nothing herein shall be intended or construed to hinder or prevent any society or church, that is or shall be allowed by the laws of this government, who soberly differ or dissent from the united churches hereby established, from exercising worship and discipline, in their own way, according to their consciences."

In compliance with an order of the general assembly, May 13th, 1708, after humble addresses to the throne of grace for the divine presence, assistance, and blessing upon us, having our eyes upon the word of God and the constitution of our churches, We agree that the confession of faith owned and assented unto by the elders and messengers assembled at Boston, in New-England May 12th, 1680, being the second session of that synod, be recommended to the honourable general assembly of this colony, at the next session, for their public testimony thereunto, as the Faith of the churches of this colony.

We agree also that the heads of agreement assented to by the united ministers, formerly called presbyterian and congregational, be observed by the churches throughout this colony.

And for the better regulation of the administration of church discipline, in relation to all cases ecclesiastical, both in particular churches and councils, to the full determining and executing the rules in all such cases, it is agreed,

I. That the elder, or elders of a particular church, with the consent of the brethren of the same, have power, and ought to exercise church discipline, according to the ru e of God's word, in relation to all scandals that fall out within the same. And it may be meet, in all cases of difficulty, for the respective pastors of particular churches, to take advice of the elders of the churches in the neighbourhood, before they proceed to censure in such cases.

II. That the churches which are neighbouring to each other, shall consociate, for mutual affording to each other such assistance as may be requisite, upon all occasions ecclesiastical. And that the particular pastors and churches, within the respective counties in this government, shall be one consociation, (or more, if they shall judge meet,) for the end aforesaid.

III. That all cases of scandal, that fall out within the circuit of any of the aforesaid consociations, shall be brought to a council of the elders, and also messengers of the churches within the said circuit, i.e. the churches of one consociation, if they see cause to send messengers, when there shall be need of a council for the determination of them.

IV. That, according to the common practice of our churches, nothing shall be deemed an act or judgment of any council, which hath not the act of the major part of the elders present concurring, and such a number of the messengers present, as makes the majority of the council: provided that if any such church shall not see cause to send any messengers to the council, or the persons chosen by them shall not attend, neither of these shall be any obstruction to the proceedings of the council, or invalidate any of their acts.

V. That when any case is orderly brought before any council of the churches, it shall there be heard and determined, which, (unless orderly removed from thence,) shall be a final issue; and all parties therein concerned shall sit down and be determined thereby. And the council so hearing, and giving the result or final issue, in the said case, as aforesaid, shall see their determination, or judgment, duly executed and attended, in such way or manner, as shall, in their judgment, be most suitable and agreeable to the word of God.

VI. That if any pastor and church doth obstinately refuse a due attendance and conformity to the determination of the council, that hath the cognizance of the case, and determineth it as above, after due patience used, they shall be reputed guilty of scandalous contempt, and dealt with as the rule of God's word in such case doth provide, and the sentence of non-communion shall be declared against such pastor and church. And the churches are to approve the said sentence, by withdrawing from the communion of the pastor and church, which so refused to be healed.

VII. That, in case any difficulties shall arise in any of the churches in this colony, which cannot be issued without considerable disquiet, that church, in which they arise, (or that minister or member aggrieved with them,) shall apply themselves to the council of the consociated churches of the circuit, to which the said church belongs; who, if they see cause, shall thereupon convene, hear, and determine such cases of difficulty, unless the matter brought before them, shall be judged so great in the nature of it, or so doubtful in the issue, or of such general concern, that the said council shall judge best that it be referred to a fuller council, consisting of the churches of the other consociation within the same county, (or of the next adjoining consociation of another county, if there be not two consociations in the county where the difficulty ariseth,) who, together with themselves, shall, hear, judge, determine, and finally issue such case, according to the word of God.

VIII. That a particular church, in which any difficulty doth arise, may, if they see cause, call a council of the consociated churches of the circuit to which the church belongs, before they proceed to sentence therein; but there is not the same liberty to an offending brother, to call the council, before the church to which he belongs proceed to excommunication in the said case, unless with the consent of the church.

IX. That all the churches of the respective consociations shall choose, if they see cause, one or two members of each church, to represent them in the councils of the said churches, as occasion may call for them, who shall stand in that capacity till new be chosen for the same service, unless any church shall incline to choose their messengers anew, upon the convening of such councils.

X. That the minister or ministers of the county towns, or where there are no ministers in such towns, the two next ministers to the said town, shall, as soon as conveniently may be, appoint time and place for the meeting of the elders and messengers of the churches in said county, in order to their forming themselves into one or more consociations, and notify the time and place to the elders and churches of that county who shall attend at the same, the elders in their persons, and the churches by their messengers, if they see cause to send them. Which elders and messengers, so assembled in council, as also any other council hereby allowed of, shall have power to adjourn themselves, as need shall be, for the space of one year, after the beginning or first session of the said council, and no longer. And that minister who was chosen at the last session of any council, to be moderator, shall, with the advice and consent of two more elders, (or, in case of the moderator's death, any two elders of the same consociation,) call another council within the circuit, when they shall judge there is need thereof. And all councils may prescribe rules, as occasion may require, and whatever they judge needful within their circuit, for the well performing and orderly managing of the several acts, to be attended by them, or matters that come under their cognizance.

XI. That if any person or persons, orderly complained of to a council, or that are witnesses to such complaints, (having regular notification to appear,) shall refuse, or neglect so to do, in the place, and at the time specified in the warning given, except they or he give some satisfying reason thereof to the said council, they shall be judged guilty of scandalous contempt.

. . . .

XIII. That the said associated pastors shall take notice of any among themselves that may be accused of scandal or heresy, unto or cognizable by them, examine the matter carefully, and if they find just occasion shall direct to the calling of the council, where such offenders shall be duly proceeded against.

XIV. That the associated pastors shall also be consulted by bereaved churches, belonging to their association, and recommend to such churches such persons, as may be fit to be called and settled in the work of the gospel ministry among them. And if such bereaved churches shall not seasonably call and settle a minister among them, the said associated pastors shall lay the state of such bereaved church before the general assembly of this colony, that they may take order concerning them, as shall be found necessary for their peace and edification.

XV. That it be recommended as expedient, that all the associations in this colony do meet in a general association, by their respective delegates, one or more out of each association, once a year, the first meeting to be at Hartford, at the general election next ensuing the date hereof, and so annually in all the counties successively, at such time and place, as they the said delegates shall in their annual meetings appoint.

Text—Trumbull: *History of Connecticut*, Vol. I, pp. 409-413.

VI. *YALE—ITS PURPOSE AND SPIRIT*

The following appears in the Proceedings of the Trustees (Nov. 11, 1701):

Present the Rev^d	Whereas it was the glorious publick design of our now blessed
Israel Chauncey	fathers in their Removal from Europe into these parts of
Thomas Buckingham	America, both to plant, and under ye Divine blessing to propa-
Abraham Pierson	gate in this Wilderness, the blessed Reformed, Protestant
Samuel Andrew	Religion, in ye purity of its Order, and Worship, not onely to
James Pierpont	their posterity, but also to ye barbarous Natives: In which
Noadiah Russell	great Enterprize they wanted not the Royal Commands, & fa-
Joseph Webb	vour of his Majtie. Charles ye Second to Authorize, & in-
	vigorate them.

We their unworthy posterity lamenting our past neglects of this Grand errand, & Sensible of our equal Obligations better to prosecute ye Same end, are desirous in our Generation to be Serviceable thereunto—Whereunto the Liberal, & Relligious Education of Suitable youth is under ye blessing of God, a chief, & most probable expedient. Therefore that we might not be wanting in cherishing the present observable, pious disposition of many wellminded people to Dedicate their Children, & Substance unto God in such a good service, and being our selves wth Sundry other Revd Elders not only desired by our godly people to undertake as Trustees for Erecting, forming, Ordering, & Regulating a Collegiate School, for ye advancement of such Education; But having also obtained of our present Religious Government, both full Liberty, & Asistance by their Donations to such an use, tokens likewise that particular persons will not be wanting in their benificence, Do in duty to God & the weal of our Countrey undertake in ye aforesd design.   And being now met according to the liberties, & Aids granted to us for ye use afores^d.   Do Order & Appoint that there shal, & hereby is Erected and formed a Collegiate School, Wherein shal be taught ye Liberal Arts, & Languages in such place, or places in Conecticut as the s^d Trustees, with their Asso- ciates, & Successors, do, or shal from time to time see cause to Order.   For the more Orderly, & effectual management of this Affair we agree to, & hereby appoint & Con- firm these following Rules. . . .

. . . .

1: The s^d. Rector shall take Especial Care as of the moral Behaviour of the Students at all Times so with industry to Instruct and Ground Them well in Theoretical devinity and to that End Shall neither By Himself nor by any other person Else whomsoever allow them to be Instructed and Grounded in any other Systems or Synopses of Divin- ity than such as the s^d Trustees do order and appoint But shall take Effectual Care that the s^d students be weekly in such seasons as he shall see Cause to appoint Caused memoriter To recite the Assemblies Catechism in Latin and Ames's Theological Theses of which as also Ames's Cases, He shall make or Cause to Be made from time to time such Explanations as may be (through the Blessing of God) most Conducive to their Establishment in the Principles of the Christian protestant Religion.

2: That the s^d Rector shall also Cause the Scriptures Daily (Except the Sabbath) morning and Evening to be read by the Students at the times of prayer in the School according to the Laudable orders and usages in Harvard College making Expositions upon the same, and upon the Sabbath Shall Either Expound practical Theology or Cause the Students non Graduated, to Repeat Sermons, and in all other ways according to his Best Discretion shall at all times studiously Indeavor in the Education of s^d students to promote the power and the Purity of Religion and Best Edification and peace of these New England Churches.

3:. The s^d Rector with Himself and Either the Tutor or tutors when there shall Be such shall have the power to punish the non Graduated Students According to their faults Either by Imposing Extraordinary School Exercises or by Degrading them in their Several Classes without the Benefit of appeal for the Delinquents.

4: That the Rector or Tutors until the Trustees Do otherwise farther provide Shall make use of the orders and institutions of Harvard College for the instructing and Ruling of the Collegiate School so far as he or they shall Judge them suitable and wherein we have not at this present meeting made provision.

. . . .

6: Each undergraduate or non Licensed Student shall By His parent or Guardian pay to the Rector or Tutor for his tuition 30 Shillings per annum In Country pay at price Currant in the Country And Each Graduate During His Residence under the Benefit of s^d School Shall pay 10s Per annum in Like pay and price.

7: That undergraduates Shall at the Discretion of the Rector have the Benefit of the Collegiate Library for their assistance in their Studies.

8: That at the Expiration of 4 years Continuance in their Studies and under the orderance of the Collegiate School Any person not Culpable and Convicted of Gross Ignorance or Scandalous Immoralities Shall on His Desire and at his Charge receive a Diploma or License for the Degree of Batchelors, And from thence at the Expiration of 3 years more so as in all to Compleat the number of 7 years shall receive upon his Desire and Charge a Diploma or License for Magister, But for the Especial Encouragement of Students in Their industry and good Literature as well as for the Ease of their parents Charges we not onely Disallow of Publick Commencements and forbid the same at all times But agree y^t. If the Students any of them shall demand Their Diploma or License at the Expiration of 3 years and from thence of 2 full years, they shall and hereby we order and appoint that they do receive the same provided they shall stand and be accepted upon such probation of their Qualifications as the s^d Trustees shall institute or Conclude upon.

Text—Dexter: *Documentary History of Yale University*, pp. 27-34.

CHAPTER VII

Rhode Island in the Seventeenth Century

Bibliography

Bradford's "History," Winthrop's "Journal," and John Cotton's controversial treatises (see bibliography on Massachusetts Bay, p. 54) should be consulted for the earlier Massachusetts experiences of Roger Williams. In the "Publications of the Narragansett Club" there is the following from Williams' pen:—"Key into the Language of America" (Vol. I, 1866, edited by J. Hammond Trumbull); "Mr. Cotton's Letter Examined and Answered" (Vol. I, edited by Reuben A. Guild,) with "John Cotton's Answer to Roger Williams" (Vol. II, 1867, edited by Rev. J. Lewis Diman); "Queries of Highest Consideration" (Vol. II, edited by R. A. Guild) "The Bloudy Tenent of Persecution" (Vol. III, 1867, edited by S. L. Caldwell); "The Bloudy Tenent Yet More Bloody" (Vol. IV, 1870, edited by S. L. Caldwell); "George Fox Digg'd out of his Burrowes" (Vol. V, 1872, edited by Rev. J. L. Diman); "The Letters of Roger Williams, 1632-1682" (Vol. VI, 1874, edited by J. R. Bartlett). A scholarly biographical introduction by Reuben Guild and excellent service rendered by the editors, make these publications of primary significance to every student of Roger Williams. Several letters of Williams may be found in "Pub. R. I. Hist. Soc." New Series, Vol. VIII; also in "Coll. Mass. Hist. Soc." Series III, Vol. I.

Of biographies of Williams, the earliest is a "Memoir of Roger Williams, . . . " (1834) by James D. Knowles, thorough, but unduly commendatory of Williams in his dealings with Massachusetts Bay. William Gammell in a "Life of Roger Williams" (1845) followed in the footsteps of Knowles. "A Life of Roger Williams" (1853) by Romeo Elton, has material lacking in the two earlier biographies. The biogaphical introduction to Vol. I of the "Narragansett Publications" by Reuben A. Guild, though brief is highly satisfactory. "Roger Williams, the Pioneer of Religious Liberty" (1894) by Oscar S. Straus, is a well written dispassionate study. In "Roger Williams, a Study of the Life, Times, and Character of a Political Pioneer," (1909) Edmund J. Carpenter has

111

approached his hero from a political and personal rather than a religious point of view, and has thereby been able to place upon Williams an estimate free from the extremes of earlier writers.

On the banishment of Williams, the following may be mentioned: "The Treatment of Intruders and Dissentients by the Founders of Massachusetts" by George E. Ellis (Lowell Lectures, Boston, 1869); "As to Roger Williams and His Banishment from the Massachusetts Plantation" (1876) by H. M. Dexter; "The Case of Roger Williams" ("Unitarian Review," January, 1891); "Why Was Roger Williams Banished" (1901) by H. S. Burrage; and J. Lewis Diman's preface (1867) to Vol. II, "Narragansett Publications." An exhaustive bibliography on Roger Williams by Clarence S. Brigham appears in the appendix to Vol. III of "State of Rhode Island . . . " edited (1902) by Edward Field.

From John Clarke, another victim of Massachusetts severity, there emanated (1652) "Ill Newes from New England" ("Coll. Mass. Hist. Soc.," Series IV, Vol. II). Although designed to give a picture of Massachusetts rigour, it incidentally refers to events in Providence and Rhode Island. The best biographical study of Clarke is that of J. C. C. Clarke, "John Clarke, the Pioneer Baptist Statesman" ("Baptist Quarterly," Vol. X, p. 180 f.; 257 f.).

The "Simplicitie's Defence" by Samuel Gorton (1646, "Coll. R. I. Hist. Soc." Vol. II; Force, "Tracts and Papers" Vol. IV, Tract VI), and "Hypocrisie Unmasked" by Edward Winslow, have sidelights upon the Rhode Island situation. Samuel Gorton's defence of himself may be read in his letter to Nathaniel Morton (Force, "Tracts and Papers," Vol. IV, Tract VII). Two studies on Gorton are, "A Life of S. Gorton" by J. M. Mackie (1848, Sparks, "American Biography Series, II, Vol. V), and "A defence of Samuel Gorton, . . . " (1883) by G. A. Brayton ("R. I. Hist. Tracts," No. 17).

Historical work upon Rhode Island began with "A Historical Discourse by John Callander, a minister of Newport (with notes by Romeo Elton, "Coll. R. I. Hist. Soc.," Vol. IV). In the "Providence Gazette" (January to March, 1765) there appeared a series of papers entitled "An Historical Account of the Planting and Growth of Providence" from the pen of Governor Stephen Hopkins ("Coll. Mass. Hist. Soc.," Series II, Vol. IX). Not to mention a newspaper contribution of Henry Bull entitled "Memoirs of Rhode Island" (1832) and a "Discourse, . . . " (1838) by Rev. A. A. Ross of Newport, Rev. Edward Peterson followed (1853) with a "History of Rhode Island." His inaccurate and incoherent work was soon completely outclassed by that of Samuel G. Greene, whose "History of the State of Rhode Island and Providence Plantations" (II Vols. 1859-60) holds its place to this day. Contemporary, but quite different in its interpretation of men and events, is the "History of New England" 1858 f.) by Samuel G. Palfrey, another work of abiding worth. George W. Greene's "Short History of Rhode Island" (1877) is a handly manual but nothing more. "The Beginnings of New England, or the Puritan Theocracy in its Relation to Civil and Religious Liberty" (6th edition, 1890) by John Fiske, is fair in its interpretations and reasonably full in details. Charles S. Brigham's political sketch in Vol. I of "State of Rhode Island and Providence Plantations at the End of the Century" (editor-in-chief, Edward Field, 1902) is well written, but necessarily brief. Two recent works by Irving B. Richman, "Rhode Island, Its Making and Its Meaning" (1902) and "Rhode Island, A Study in Separatism" (1905) are particularly worthy of careful study.

The social and economic are stressed in the following contributions by Charles B. Weeden: "Economic and Social History of New England, 1620-1789" (II Vols. 1890); "Early Rhode Island, A Social History of the People" (in "Grafton Historical Series," 1910); "Early Oriental Commerce in Providence" ("Proc. Mass. Hist. Soc.," Series III, Vol. I, pp. 236-278).

"Three Commonwealths, Massachusetts, Connecticut, Rhode Island: Their Early Development" ("Proc. Amer. Antiq. Soc.," New Series, Vol. XV, pp. 130-164) by the same author, sets forth the significance for individual liberty of Rhode Island. The latest work, (1916) by Howard M. Chapin, Librarian of the R. I. Hist. Society, entitled "Documentary History of Rhode Island" weaves into narrative form the source material dealing with Providence and Warwick to 1649.

"The Early History of Narragansett" by Elisha R. Potter ("Coll. R. I. Hist. Soc.," Vol. III) is well written and possesses a documentary appendix. "The Planting and Growth of Providence" by Henry C. Dorr ("R. I. Hist. Tracts," No. 15) though lacking in its citation of authorities is reliable. His treatment of "The Proprietors of Providence and Their Controversies with the Freeholders" ("Pub. R. I. Hist. Soc.," New Series, Vols. III and IV) is thoroughgoing.

A complete list of town histories may be consulted in "State of Rhode Island and Providence Plantations at the End of the Century" edited by Edward Field, Vol. III, pp. 670-676.

The "Rhode Island Colonial Records" (III Vols. 1856 f.) edited by John Russell Bartlett, fill an important place in Rhode Island historical apparatus; also the "Early Records of the Town of Providence" (XX Vols. 1892 f.) edited by Horatio Rogers and others, and "The Early Records of the Town of Portsmouth" (1901) edited by C. S. Brigham.

On the ecclesiastical side a general work is "The Ecclesiastical History of New England" (Vol. I, 1855, Vol. II, 1862) by Joseph B. Felt. Next come the several histories of the Baptists. Probably the best is "A History of New England, With Particular Reference to the Denomination of Christians Called Baptists" (III Vols. 1777, 1784, 1796) by Isaac Backus. The second edition (II Vols. 1871) with notes by D. Weston should be used. Benedict's "History of the Baptist Denomination in America, ... " (1813) is especially satisfactory in its treatment of Rhode Island. Rev. Morgan Edwards has done good work in putting together "Materials for a history of the Baptists in Rhode Island" ("Coll. R. I. Hist. Soc.," Vol. VI, pp. 302-370). A number of discourses and anniversary addresses dealing with local churches have appeared from time to time, some of which may be found in the "Pub. R. I. Hist. Soc." Others have been issued under separate cover (see "State of Rhode Island and Providence Plantations at the End of the Century," Ed. Field, editor, Vol. III, pp. 667-668).

For Quaker history the reader is referred to the standard Quaker histories (see page 154f), and to "The Narragansett Friends' Meeting in the Eighteenth Century, 1657-1784" (1899) by C. Hazard.

"The Huguenot Influence in Rhode Island" ("Proc. R. I. Hist. Soc.," 1885-86, pp. 46-74) by Esther B. Carpenter goes fully into the connection with Rhode Island of Gabriel Bernon.

On the Roman Catholics, an interesting article by R. H. Clarke entitled, "Rhode Island and Maryland; Which Established Religious Liberty First?" may be consulted in the "American Catholic Quarterly," Vol. XX, pp. 289-312. See also Maryland bibliography (page 24). "An Inquiry concerning the Origin of the Clause in the Laws of Rhode Island (1719-1783) disfranchising Roman Catholics" by S. S. Rider appears in the "Rhode Island Hist. Tracts," Series II, No. 1.

DOCUMENTS

I. *THE EARLIER COMPACT*

Although never formally adopted, this compact was respected and therefore may be regarded as the first constitution of the Rhode Island group.

We, whose names are hereunder written, late inhabitants of the Massachusetts (upon occasion of some difference of conscience) being permitted [?] to depart from the limits of that Patent under which we came over into these parts, and being cast by the God of Heaven remote from others of our countrymen amongst the barbarians in this town of New Providence, do with free and joint consent promise each unto other that, for our common peace and welfare (until we hear further of the King's royal pleasure concerning ourselves), we will from time to time subject ourselves, in active or passive obedience, to such orders and agreements as shall be made by the greater number of the present householders, and such as shall hereafter be admitted by their consent into the same privilege and covenant in our ordinary meeting.

Text—Richman: *Rhode Island, Its Making and its Meaning*, Vol. I, p. 95.

II. *THE FORMAL COMPACT*

Dated probably August 20, 1637, this instrument had thirteen signatures. The phrase "only in civil things" did not appear in Williams' original draft.

We whose names are here under-written, being desirous to inhabit in the town of Providence, do promise to submit ourselves, in active or passive obedience, to all such orders or agreements as shall be made for public good of the body, in an orderly way, by the major consent of the present inhabitants, masters of families, incorporated together into a township, and such others whom they shall admit unto the same, only in civil things.

Text—*Collections of the Rhode Island Historical Society*, Vol. IV, p. 207.

III. *DEED OF ROGER WILLIAMS TO HIS TWELVE ORIGINAL ASSOCIATES*

Providence, 8th of the 8th month, 1638,
(so called,)

Memorandum, that I, Roger Williams, having formerly purchased of Caunannicus and Miantinomu, this our situation, or plantation, of New-Providence, viz. the two fresh rivers, Wanasquatuckett and Mooshausick, and the ground and meadows thereupon, in consideration of thirty pounds received from the inhabitants of said place, do freely and fully pass, grant and make over equal right and power of enjoying and disposing of the same grounds and lands unto my loving friends and neighbors, Stukely Wescott, William Arnold, Thomas James, Robert Cole, John Greene, John Throckmorton, William Harris, William Carpenter, Thomas Olney, Francis Weston, Richard Waterman, Ezekiel Holliman, and such others as the major part of us shall admit into the same fellowship of vote with us:—As also I do freely make and pass over equal right and power of enjoying and disposing of the lands and grounds reaching from the aforesaid rivers unto the great river Pautuxett, with the grass and meadows thereupon, which was so lately given and granted by the aforesaid sachems to me. Witness my hand,

ROGER WILLIAMS.
(Providence Records).

Text—*Collections of the Rhode Island Historical Society*, Vol. IV, pp. 206-7.

IV. *THE PATENT OF MARCH 14-24, 1643*

Secured through Williams from the Parliamentary Commission of which Cromwell, Vane, Pym and others were members, this patent made no reference whatever to religious liberty, an issue hotly debated at that moment around Westminster.

And wheras divers well affected and industrious English inhabitants of the Towns of Providence, Portsmouth, and Newport in the tract aforesaid, have adventured to make a nearer neighborhood and Society with the great Body of the Narragansets, which may in Time by the blessing of God upon their Endeavours, lay a sure Foundation of Happiness to all America.   And have also purchased, and are purchasing of and amongst the said Natives, some other Places, which may be convenient both for Plantations, and also for building of Ships, Supply of Pipe Staves and other Merchandise.   And whereas the said English, have represented their Desire to the said Earl, and Commissioners, to have their hopeful Beginnings approved and confirmed, by granting unto them a Free Charter of Civil Incorporation and Government; that they may order and govern their Plantation in such a Manner as to maintain Justice and peace, both among themselves, and towards all Men with whom they shall have to do.   In due Consideration of the said Premises, the said Robert Earl of Warwick, Governor in Chief, and Lord High Admiral of the said Plantations, and the greater Number of the said Commissioners, whose Names and Seals are here underwritten and subjoined, out of a Desire to encourage the good Beginnings of the said Planters, Do, by the Authority of the aforesaid Ordinance of the Lords and Commons, give, grant, and confirm, to the aforesaid Inhabitants of the Towns of Providence, Portsmouth, and Newport, a free and absolute Charter of Incorporation, to be known by the Name of the Incorporation of Providence Plantations, in the Narraganset-Bay, in New England.—Together with full Power and Authority to rule themselves, and such others as shall hereafter inhabit within any Part of the said Tract of land, by such a Form of Civil Government, as by voluntary consent of all, or the greater Part of them, they shall find most suitable to their Estate and Condition. . . .

Text—Bartlett: *Records of the Colony of Rhode Island and Providence Plantations*, Vol. I, pp. 144-145.

V. *THE QUAKERS*

Letter from the Commissioners of the United Colonies to Rhode Island, concerning the Quakers.

The Commissioners being informed that divers Quakers are arrived this summer at Rode Island, and entertained there, which may prove dangerous to the Collonies, thought meet to manifest theire minds to the Governor there, as followeth:

Gent:

We suppose you have understood that the last yeare a companie of Quakers arived at Boston vpon noe other account than to disperse theire pernicious opinions had they not been prevented by the prudent care of that Government, whoe by that experience they had of them, being sencable of the danger that might befale the Christion religion heer professed, by suffering such to bee received or continued in the country, presented the same unto the Commissioners att theire meeting at Plymouth, whoe upon that occasion comended it to the Generall Courts of the United Collonies, that all Quakers, Ranters, and such notorious heretiques might bee prohibited coming among vs; and that if such should arise from amongst ourselves, syeedy care might bee taken to remove them (and as we are informed), the severall jurisdictions have made provision accordingly; but it is by experience found that meanes will fall short without further care by reason of your admission and receiveing of such from whence they may have opportunitie to creep in amongst us, or meanes to infuse and spread theire accursed tenates to the great trouble of the collonies, if not to the subversion of the [lawes] professed in them. Notwithstanding any care that hath been hitherto taken to prevent the same whereof wee cannot but bee very sensible, and thinke noe care too great to preserve us from such a pest, the contagion whereof (if received) within youer Collonie were dangerous, &c., to be defused to the other by meanes of the intercourse especially to the place of trade amongst us. Wee therefore make it our request that you, as well as the rest of the Collonies, take such order herein that youre naighbours may be freed from that danger; that you remove those Quakers that have been receaved, and for the future prohibite theire cominge amongst you, whereunto the rule of charitie to yourselves and vs (wee conceave), doth oblidge you wherein if you should, wee hope you will not be wantinge; yett wee could not but signifie this oure desire; and further declare that wee apprehend that it will bee our duty seriously to consider what further provision God may call us to make to prevent the aforesaid mischiefe; and for our further guidance and direction herein, wee desire you to imparte youer mind and resolution to the Generall Court of the Massachusetts, which assembleth the 14th October next; wee have not further to trouble you att present, but to assure you wee desire to continew your loveinge frinds and naighbours, the comissioners of the United Collonie.

> SIMON BRADSTREET *President.*
> Daniel Denison,
> Etc."

Boston, September 12, 1657.

Letter from the government of the Colony of Rhode Island, in reply to the letter from the Commissioners of the United Colonies, concerning the Quakers.

Much Honored Gentlemen:

Please you to understand, that there hath come to our view a letter subscribed by the honour'd gentlemen commissioners of the United Coloneys, the contents whereof are a request concerning certayne people called Quakers, come among us lately, &c.

Our desires are, in all things possible, to pursue after and keepe fayre and loveing correspondence and entercourse with all the collonys, and with all our countreymen in New England, and to that purpose we have endeavoured (and shall still endeavour), to answer the desires and requests from all parts of the countrey, coming unto us, in all just and equall returnes, to which end the coloney have made seasonable provision to preserve a just and equal entercourse between the coloneys and us, by giving justice to any that demand it among us, and by returneing such as make escapes from you, or from the other colonys, being such as fly from the hands of justice, for matters of crime done or committed amongst you, &c. And as concerning these quakers (so called), which are now among us, we have no law among us, whereby to punish any for only declaring by words, &c., theire mindes and understandings concerning the things and ways of God, as to salvation and an eternal condition. And we, moreover, finde, that in those places where these people aforesaid, in this coloney, are most of all suffered to declare themselves freely, and are only opposed by arguments in discourse, there they least of all desire to come, and we are informed that they begin to loath this place, for that they are not opposed by the civill authority, but with all patience and meeknes are suffered to say over their pretended revelations and admonitions, nor are they like or able to gain many here to their way; surely we find that they delight to be persecuted by civill powers, and when they are soe, they are like to gain more adherents by the conseyte of their patient sufferings, than by consent to their pernicious sayings. And yet we conceive, that theire doctrines tend to very absolute cutting downe and overturninge relations and civill government among men, if generally received. But as to the dammage that may in likelyhood accrue to the neighbour colloneys by theire being here entertained, we conceive it will not prove so dangerous (as else it might), in regard of the course taken by you to send them away out of the countrey, as they come among you. But, however, at present, we judge it requisitt (and do intend) to commend the consideration of their extravagant out-goinges unto the Generall Assembly of our colloney in March next, where we hope there will be such order taken, as may, in all honest and contientious manner, prevent the bad effects of theire doctrines and endeavours; and soe, in all courtious and loveing respects, and with desire of all honest and fayre commerce with you, and the rest of our honoured and beloved countreymen, we rest,

> Yours, in all loving respects to serve you,
> BENEDICT ARNOLD, *President,*

Providence, Oct 13th 1657.   William Baultson,—etc.

Text—Bartlett: *Records of the Colony of Rhode Island and Providence Plantations,* Vol. I: pp. 374-378.

VI. *WILLIAMS ON THE LIMITATIONS OF LIBERTY*

"To the Town of Providence.

[Providence, January, 1654-5]

That ever I should speak or write a tittle, that tends to such an infinite liberty of conscience, is a mistake, and which I have ever disclaimed and abhorred. To prevent such mistakes, I shall at present only propose this case: There goes many a ship to sea, with many hundred souls in one ship, whose weal and woe is common, and is a true picture of a commonwealth, or a human combination or society. It hath fallen out sometimes, that both papists and protestants, Jews and Turks, may be embarked in one ship; upon which supposal I affirm, that all the liberty of conscience, that ever I pleaded for, turns upon these two hinges—that none of the papists, protestants, Jews, or Turks, be forced to come to the ship's prayers or worship, nor compelled from their own particular prayers or worship, if they practice any. I further add, that I never denied, that notwithstanding this liberty, the commander of this ship ought to command the ship's course, yea, and also command that justice, peace and sobriety, be kept and practiced, both among the seamen and all the passengers. If any of the seaman refuse to perform their services, or passengers to pay their freight; if any refuse to help, in person or purse, toward the common charges of defense; if any refuse to obey the common laws and orders of the ship, concerning their common peace or preservation; if any shall mutiny and rise up against their commanders and officers, if any should preach or write that there ought to be no commanders or officers, because all are equal in Christ, therefore no masters nor officers, no laws nor orders, nor corrections nor punishments;—I say, I never denied, but in such cases, whatever is pretented, the commander or commanders may judge, resist, compel and punish such transgressors, according to their deserts and merits. This if seriously and honestly minded, may, if it so please the Father of lights, let in some light to such as willingly shut not their eyes.

I remain studious of your common peace and liberty.

ROGER WILLIAMS."

Text—*Publications of the Narragansett Club*, Vol. VI, pp. 278-279.

VII. *THE CHARTER OF JULY 8/18, 1663*

Charles the Second, (&c.) . . . : WHEREAS *wee* have been informed, by the humble petition of our trustie and well beloved subject, John Clarke, on the behalfe of Benjamine Arnold, William Brenton, William Codington, . . . and the rest of the purchasers and ffree inhabitants of our island, called Rhode-Island, and the rest of the colonie of Providence Plantations, in the Narragansett Bay, in New-England, in America, that they, pursueing, with peaceable and loyall mindes, their sober, serious and religious intentions, of godlie edifieing themselves, and one another, in the holie Christian ffaith and worshipp as they were perswaded: together with the gaineing over and conversione of the poore ignorant Indian natives, in those partes of America, to the sincere professione and obedienc of the same ffaith and worship, did, not onlie by the consent and good encouragement of our royall progenitors, transport themselves out of this kingdome of England into America, but alsoe, since their arrivall there, after their first settlement amongst other our subjects in those parts, ffor the avoideing of discorde, and those manie evills which were likely to ensue upon some of those oure subjects not beinge able to beare, in these remote partes, theire different apprehensiones in religious concernments, and in pursueance of the afforesayd ends, did once againe leave theire desireable stationes and habitationes, and with excessive labor and travell, hazard and charge, did transplant themselves into the middest of the Indian natives, who, as wee are infformed, are the most potent princes and people of all that country; where, by the good Providence of God, from whome the Plantationes have taken their name, upon theire labour and industrie, they have not onlie byn preserved to admiration, but have increased and prospered. . . . *And* WHEREAS, in theire humble addresse, they have ffreely declared, that it is much on their hearts (if they may be permitted), to hold forth a livelie experiment, that a most flourishing civill state may stand and best bee maintained, and that among our English subjects, with a full libertie in religious concernements, and that true pietye rightly grounded upon gospell principles, will give the best and greatest security to sovereignetye, and will lay in the hearts of men the strongest obligations to true loyaltye: *Now know yee*, that wee beinge willinge to encourage the hopefull undertakeinge of our sayd loyall and loveinge subjects, and to secure them in the free exercise and enjoyment of all theire civill and religious rights, appertaining to them, as our loveing subjects; and to preserve unto them that libertye, in the true Christian ffaith and worshipp of God, which they have sought with soe much travaill, and with peaceable myndes, and loyall subjectione to our royall progenitors and ourselves, to enjoye; and because some of the people and inhabitants of the same colonie cannot, in theire private opinions, conforme to the publique exercise of religion, according to the litturgy, formes and ceremonyes of the Church of England, or take or subscribe the oaths and articles made and established in that behalfe; and for that the same, by reason of the remote distances of those places, will (as wee hope) bee noe breach of the unitie and unifformitie established in this nation: . . . doe hereby . . . declare, That our royall will and pleasure is, that noe person within the sayd colonye, at any tyme hereafter, shall bee any wise molested, punished, disquieted, or called in question, for any differences in opinions in matters of religion, and doe not actually disturb the civill peace of our sayd colony; but that all and everye person and persons may, from tyme to tyme, and at all tymes hereafter, freelye and fullye have and enjoye his and theire owne judgments and consciences, in matters of religious concernments, throughout the tract of lande hereafter mentioned; they behaving themselves peaceablie and quietlie, and not useing this libertie to lycentiousnesse and profanenesse, nor to the civill injurye or outward disturbeance of others; any lawe, statute, or clause, therein contayned, or to bee contayned, usage or custome of this realme, to the contrary hereof, in any wise, not withstanding. And that they may bee in the better capacity to defend themselves, in theire just rights and libertyes against all the enemies of the Christian ffaith, and others, in all respects, wee . . . further . . . declare, That they shall have and enjoye the benefitt of our late act of indempnity and ffree pardon, as the rest of our subjects in other our dominions and territoryes have; and to create and make them a bodye politique or corporate, with the powers and priviledges hereinafter mentioned. . . . Neverthelesse, our will and pleasure is, and wee doe hereby declare to the rest of oure Collonies in New-England, that itt shall not bee lawfull ffor this our sayd Collony . . . to invade the natives inhabiting within the boundes and limitts of theire sayd Collonies without the knowledge and consent of the sayd other Collonies. And itt is hereby declared, that itt shall not bee lawfull to or ffor the rest of the Collonies to invade or molest the native Indians, or any other inhabitants, inhabiting within the bounds and lymitts hereafter mentioned (they having subjected themselves unto us, and being by us taken into our speciall protection), without the knowledge and consent of the Governour and Company of our Collony of Rhode-Island and Providence Plantations. . . . *And further*, our will and pleasure is, that in all matters of publique controversy which may fall out betweene our Collony of Providence Plantations, and the rest of our Collonies in New-England, itt shall and may bee lawfull to and for the Governour and Company . . . to make their appeales therein to us. . . for redresse in such cases, within this our realme of England: and that itt shall be lawfull to and for the inhabitants of the sayd Collony . . . without let or molestation, to passe and repasse with freedome, into and through the rest of the English Collonies, upon their lawfull and civill occasions, and to converse, and hold commerce and trade, with such of the inhabitants of our other English Collonies as shall bee willing to admitt them thereunto, they behaveing themselves peaceably among them . . . "

Text—Bartlett: *Records of the Colony of Rhode Island and Providence Plantations,* Vol. II, pp. 3-20.

VIII. *GEORGE FOX'S VISIT, 1672*

"As soon as the wind served we set sail, and arrived in Rhode-Island the thirtieth of the third month; where we were gladly received by friends. We went to Nicholas Eaton's, who was governor of the Island; where we lay, being weary with travelling. On first-day following we had a large meeting; to which the deputy governor and several justices came, and were mightily affected with the truth. The week following, the yearly meeting for friends of New-England, and other colonies adjacent, was held in this island; to which, besides many friends who lived in those parts, came John Stubbs from Barbadoes, and James Lancaster and John Cartwright from another way. This meeting lasted six days. The first four were spent in general publick meetings for worship; to which abundance of other people came. For having no priests in the island, and no restriction to any particular way of worship; and the governor and deputy-governor, with several justices of the peace, daily frequenting meetings; it so encouraged the people that they flocked in from all parts of the island. Very good service we had amongst them, and truth had good reception. I have rarely observed a people, in the state wherein they stood, to hear with more attention, diligence, and affection, then generally they did, during the four days; which was also taken notice of by other friends. These publick meetings over, the men's meeting began, which was large, precious, and weighty. The day following was the women's meeting, which also was large and very solemn. These two meetings being for ordering the affairs of the church, many weighty things were opened, and communicated to them, by way of advice, information, and instruction in the services relating thereunto; that all might be kept clean, sweet, and savoury amongst them. In these, several men's and women's meetings for other parts were agreed and settled, to take care of the poor, and other affairs of the church, and to see that all who profess truth walk according to the glorious gospel of God. When this great general meeting was ended, it was somewhat hard for friends to part; for the glorious power of the Lord, which was over all, and his blessed truth and life flowing amongst them, had so knit and united them together, that they spent two days in taking leave one of another, and of the friends of the island; and then, being mightily filled with the presence and power of the Lord, they went away with joyful hearts to their several habitations, in the several colonies where they lived.

. . . .

After this I had a great travail in spirit concerning the Ranters in those parts who had been rude at a meeting which I was not at. Wherefore I appointed a meeting amongst them, believing the Lord would give me power over them; which he did, to his praise and glory, blessed be his name for ever! There were at this meeting many friends, and divers other people; some of whom were justices of the peace, and officers, who were generally well affected with the truth. One, who had been a justice twenty years, was convinced, spoke highly of the truth, and more highly of me than is fit for me to make mention or take notice of.

. . . .

After this we went to Narraganset, about twenty miles from Rhode-Island; and the governor went with us. We had a meeting at a justice's, where friends never had any before. The meeting was very large, for the country generally came in; and people from Connecticut, and other parts round about. There were four justices of peace. Most of these people were such as had never heard friends before; but they were mightily affected, and a great desire there is after the truth amongst them. So that meeting was of very good service; blessed be the Lord for ever! The justice, at whose house it was, and another justice of that country, invited me to come again; but I was then clear of those parts, and was going towards Shelter-island. . . . At another place, I heard some of the magistrates said among themselves, 'If they had money enough, they would hire me to be their minister.' This was, where they did not well understand us, and our principles: but when I heard of it, I said, 'It was time for me to be gone; for if their eye was so much to me, or any of us, they would not come to their own teacher.' For this thing (hiring ministers) had spoiled many, by hindering them from improving their own talents; whereas our labour is, to bring every one to their own teacher in themselves."

Text—*George Fox's Journal*, Philadelphia edition, pp. 450-452.

CHAPTER VIII

New York in the Colonial Period

Bibliography

"The Voyages and Journal of Henry Hudson" (1607-1611) are reprinted in part in the "Collections of the New York Historical Society," Vol. I. Extracts from the histories of Meteren (1599 f.) and Wassenaer (1622 f.) appear in "Narratives of New Netherland" (1909) edited by by J. Franklin Jameson. A description of New Netherland is the "New World, or a Description of the West Indies" (1624 f.) by John DeLaet who although never resident in the colony had access to the journals of the Dutch voyagers (translation in part, "Coll. New York Hist. Soc.," Second Series, Vol. I; and " Narratives of New Netherland." "The Short History and Notes of a Journey Kept During Several Voyages" (1632-1644) by D. P. DeVries is to be found translated in the "Coll. N. Y. Hist. Soc." Second Series, Vol. III, Part I; and "Narratives of New Netherland," Another "Description of the New Netherlands" more detailed in character is that of Adrian Van der Donck (second edition, 1656, partially translated, "Coll. N. Y. Hist. Soc.," Second Series, Vol. I). Among the papers of Father Jogues, a Jesuit missionary captured by the Mohawk Indians, there appears a sketch of New Netherland as he saw it in 1643, ("Coll. N. Y. Hist. Soc.," Second Series, Vol. III, Part I).

Aitzemas' "Affairs of Church and Church, . . . 1621-1669" (1657-1671) is accessible in "Coll. N. Y. Hist. Soc." Second Series, Vol. II. "The Broad Advice, . . . " (1649) of unknown authorship but one of the most important of early histories, appears in part in "Coll. N. Y. Hist. Soc.," Second Series, Vol. III; also in O'Callaghan's "Documentary History," Vol. IV. "An Account of Two Voyages to New England" (1638-39 and 1663-71) valuable though crude, by John Josselyn, has been reprinted in "Coll. Mass. Hist. Soc.," Series III, Vol. III. "The Journal of Jasper Danckaerts 1679-80" ("Original Narratives of Early American History" edited (1913) by B. B. James and J. F. Jameson) gives a picture of New York as seen by Danckaerts and his fellow traveler, Sluyter. The letters of Michaelius, Megapolensis, Bogardus, and others, with a chronologically arranged digest of all documents for the period are to be found in the "Ecclesiastical Records of the State of New York" (Hugh Hastings, supervisor) Vols. I-VI.

A comprehensive set of Dutch documents taken from the archives at the Hague by John M. Brodhead covering the period 1608-1678, and translated by E. B. O'Callaghan, M.D. forms Vols. I and II of "Documents Relative to the Colonial History of the State of New York" (1856-58). Vols. III and IV (edited by J. M. Brodhead, 1853-54) contain transcripts of documents (1614-1706) lying in the State Paper Office, London, the office of the Privy Council, the British Museum, and the Library of the Archbishop of Canterbury. Vol. IX of the same work (1855) contains transcripts of documents (1631-1744) in the archives of the Ministers of War and Colonies, and the Royal Library, Paris, translated by E. B. O'Callaghan. In addition to this indispensable work, there are "The Records of New Amsterdam from 1653 to 1674, . . . " (VII Vols., 1897) edited by Berthold Fernow. These give the minutes in full of the Court of Burgomasters and Schepens. "The Documentary History of New York" (IV Vols. 1849-51) by E. B. O'Callaghan, M.D., in reality not a history but a compendium of documents, has a rich store of important material. Vol. III in particular throws light upon seventeenth century conditions, though none of the others should be overlooked.

Eliminating the contemporary histories above mentioned, the earliest attempt at a history of New Netherlands was that of N. C. Lambrechtsen (1818). Brief and limited in range, its value is insignificant (translation, "Coll. N. Y. Hist. Soc.," New Series, Vol. I). The task of writing a comprehensive history of New York was first undertaken by William Smith, whose "History of the Province of New York from the first Discovery to the year MDCCXXXII, . . . " (1756; American Edition, 1792, 1814), with its continuation to 1762 left in manuscript at his decease (since published in the "Coll. N. Y. Hist. Soc.," Vol. IV), is now universally pronounced to be incomplete in its earlier sections, and partisan in its posthumous chapters. The second attempt was that of James Macauley in his "Natural, Statistical and Civil History of the State of New York" (III Vols. 1829) a work descriptive of the physical features of the country but not in any detailed degree of its political or religious fortunes. The "History of the New Netherlands, . . . " (II Vols. 1839-40) by James Dunlap, an antiquarian rather than a historian, improved slightly if at all upon the work of its predecessors. The

"History of New Netherland" (II Vols. 1846-50) by E. B. O'Callaghan, M.D. was a long step in advance, both for its fulness of detail and its scientific handling of the sources. A "History of the State of New York" (first period 1609-1664, second period 1664-1691; II Vols. 1853-1871) by John Romeyn Brodhead, completely outclassed all earlier works. With a slight tendency to the legal rather than the judicial type of mind, and sympathies undisguisedly pro-Holland, his work is exhaustive and a monument of literary industry and careful execution. The "Influence of the Netherlands in the Making of the English Commonwealth and the American Republic" (1891) by William E. Griffis represents a different interpretation. John Fiske's "Dutch and Quaker Colonies in America" (II Vols. 1899) written with characteristic grace, is marred by too many unjust strictures upon the New Netherland government authorities. "The Puritan in Holland, England, and America" (II Vols. 1892) by Douglas Campbell is a suggestive work that should be seriously though discriminatingly used. It may profitably be compared with "The Dutch Element in American History" by H. T. Colenbrander, also by Ruth Putnam (An. Report. Amer. Hist. Ass. 1909, sections XII and XIII. Thomas A. Janvier's "Dutch Founding of New York" covering the period 1609-1664, (1903) while on the whole satisfactory, should be handled with reserve.

For the relative dearth of standard comprehensive histories there has been a compensation in monographs dealing with localities. Of these the following are worthy of mention: "The History of the Town of Flatbush" (1842) by T. M. Strong; "Annals of Newtown" (1852) by J. Riker; "History of the City of New York" (1853) by D. T. Valentine; also a later work (1909) with same title by Mrs. Schuyler Van Rensselaer; "Flushing, Past and Present" (1860) by H. G. Mandeville; "History of Brooklyn, . . . " (III Vols. 1867) by H. R. Stiles; "Early Hempstead" (1870) by C. B. Moore; "Antiquities of Long Island, . . . " (1875) by Gabriel Furman; "Memorial History of the City of New York" (IV Vols. 1891-93) edited by J. G. Wilson (particularly good); "Early Long Island" (1896) by Martha Flint; "History of the Town of Flushing, L. I." (1889) by H. D. Waller; "The Revised History of Harlem" (1904) by James Riker.

The Swedish settlements on the South River may be studied in "A History of the Original Settlements on the Delaware" (1846) by B. Ferris; "The Dutch and Swedish Colonies on the Delaware" by G. B. Keen (1902, "Pub. Delaware County Hist. Soc.," Vol. I; and Winsor

"Nar. & Crit. Hist." Vol. IV); "The Dutch and Swedish Settlements on the Delaware" by H. L. Carson, (1909, "Pa. Mag. of Hist. and Biog." Vol. XXXIII, pp. 1-21) and "Scandinavian Immigrants in New York 1630-1674" (1915) by J. O. Evjen.

As an introduction to the ecclesiastical field, two good studies are "New Amsterdam and its People" (1902) by J. H. Innes, and "Dutch New York" (1908) by Esther Singleton. An excellent general survey of the ecclesiastical situation will be found in "Religion in New Netherland; A History of the Development of the Religious Conditions in the Province of New Netherlands, 1623-1664" (1910) by Frederick J. Zwierlein. An exhaustive bibliography is appended. A valuable article of a general character ("Papers Amer. Soc. Ch. Hist.," Series II, Vol. III pp. 79-117) is that entitled, "The Ecclesiastical Condition of New York at the Opening of the Eighteenth Century" by E. T. Corwin.

The history of the Dutch Reformed Church has been treated by Jacob Brinkerhoff in a "History of the True Reformed Dutch Church" (1873); by E. T. Corwin in a "Manual of the Reformed Church in America" (4th edition, 1902) which has a bibliography; more notably though briefly by D. D. Demarest in "The Reformed Church in America, Its Origin, Development and Characteristics" (1889); and by E. T. Corwin in a "History of the Reformed Church, Dutch" (Vol. VIII of the "American Church History Series," 1894), a very satisfactory monograph though necessarily condensed. "Pictures of Early Church Life in New York City" (1893) by Daniel Van Pelt is illuminating, also the older work (1865) by Gabriel P. Disosway entitled "The Earliest Churches of New York and its Vicinity." A. J. Beekman's "History of the Reformed Dutch Church of the Town of Brooklyn" (1886) is useful, also Henry Whittemore's "History of the First Reformed Protestant Dutch Church of Breuekelen" (1896).

A "Preliminary Sketch of the old Dutch Church at Kingston, New York and of some of its Ministers" by R. R. Hoes ("Proc. N. Y. State Hist. Assoc.," Vol. XI, pp. 186-230) is popularly written. A "History of Long Island including also a Particular Account of the Different Churches and Ministers" (III Vols. 1843) by B. J. Thompson is the most comprehensive account of Long Island. Much ecclesiastical data is packed into a "History of Long Island" (1845) by N. S. Prime. "Antiquities of the Church of Jamaica" (1880) and especially, "Antiquities of the Parish Church of Hempstead, . . . " (1880) by H. Onderdonck have much information.

"A History of the School of the Reformed Protestant Dutch Church in New York" (1853) by Henry W. Dunshee will interest students of religious education; also the more satisfactory study" "The Dutch Schools of New Netherland and Colonial New York" (1912) by William Heard Kilpatrick.

The history of the Episcopalians has been presented by Canon J. S. M. Anderson, Bishop S. Wilberforce, Rev. W. S. Perry, Rev. S. D. McConnell and Professor C. C. Tiffany. For titles, dates and estimates see page 7. A scholarly chapter by Rev. Morgan Dix on "History of Trinity Parish" appears in Vol. IV of the "Memorial History of the City of New York."

The pioneer history of the Lutheran Church is a "Description of the Former and Present State of the Swedish Churches in the so-called New Sweden" (1759) by Israel Acrelius (translated in full by W. D. Reynolds in "Memoirs of the Hist. Soc. of Pennsylvania" Vol. XI; in part in "Narratives of Early Pennsylvania, . . . 1630-1707" (1912) edited by Albert C. Myers). Other standard works are C. W. Schaeffer's "Early History of the Lutheran Church in America" (new edition, 1868) and "A History of the Evangelical Lutheran Church in the United States" by Professor H. E. Jacobs (Vol. IV, "American Church History Series," 4th edition, 1902). An instructive paper by John Nicum entitled "The Beginnings of the Lutheran Church on Manhattan Island" will be found among the "Papers of the American Society of Church History" Second Series, Vol. II, pp. 84-101.

The work of the Jesuits in upper New York state is exhaustively set forth in "The Jesuit Relations and Allied Documents" edited by R. G. Thwaites (LXXIII Vols. 1896-1901). Vols. XXIII to XLVII should be consulted for the Five Nation Missions. O'Callaghan "Documents" and "Documentary History" and "the Ecclesiastical Records" (as above) are serviceable. W. Harper Bennett's "Catholic Footsteps in Old New York" (1909) gives a good account for its restricted area." For more extensive bibliography, see pp. 296f.

Quakerism has been discussed in H. Onderdonck's " . . . Rise and Growth of the Society of Friends on Long Island, and in New York, 1657-1826" in "The Annals of Hempstead, 1643-1842" (1878). The standard Quaker histories should be consulted (see page 154f)

On early Jewish settlements see bibliography on Jews p. 508.

For investigative purposes there are the "Documents Relative to the History of the State of New York" by E. B. O'Callaghan; his "Documentary History of New York" of which Vols. III and IV are particularly serviceable; his "Laws and Ordinances of New Netherland, 1638 to 1674" (1868); "Records of New Amsterdam from 1653 to 1674, . . . " edited by Berthold Fernow; also his "Minutes of the Orphan Master's Court in New Amsterdam, 1655 to 1663, . . . " (II Vols. 1907); "The Annals of Albany" (X Vols. 1850 f.) by Noel Munsell; "Town Records of Southampton" (VI Vols. 1874) edited by H. P. Hedges and others; "Town Records of Southold" (II Vols. 1882) edited by J. W. Case; "Town Records of Huntington" (III Vols. 1887) edited by C. R. Street; "Town Records of East Hampton" (1887) edited by J. T. Gardner; "Town Records of Hempstead" (VIII Vols. 1896) edited by B. J. Hicks; "Records of the Town of Jamaica, Long Island 1656-1751" (III Vols. 1914) edited by J. C. Frost. Finally, and of indispensable worth, there are the "Ecclesiastical Records of the State of New York" (VI Vols. 1901 f.), published under the supervision of Hugh Hastings, State Historian, through the services of Rev. E. T. Corwin.

DOCUMENTS

I. STATUTORY PROVISION FOR RELIGION

*Proposed Articles for the Colonization and Trade of New Netherlands,
September 2, 1638.*

The Patroon scheme not having proved a success, and the scant population of New Netherlands showing only a decrease, an attempt was made to put immigration upon a more popular basis. Religious worship therefore was provided for as under:

2. And inasmuch as it is of the highest importance, that, in the first commencement and settlement of this population, proper arrangement be made for Divine worship, according to the practice established by the government of this country, Religion shall be taught and preached there according to the Confession and formularies of union here publicly accepted in the respective churches, with which every one shall be satisfied and content, without, however, it being inferred from this, that any person shall be hereby in any wise constrained or aggrieved in his conscience, but every man shall be free to live up to his own in peace and decorum; provided he avoid frequenting any forbidden assemblies or conventicles, much less collect or get up any such; and further abstain trom all public scandals and offences, which the magistrate is charged to prevent by all fitting reproofs and admonitions, and if necesary, to advise the Company, from time to time, of what may occur herein, so that confusions and misunderstandings may be timely obviated and prevented.

. . . .

8. Each householder and inhabitant shall bear such tax and public charge as shall hereafter be considered proper for the maintenance of Clergymen, comforters of the sick, schoolmasters and such like necessary officers; and the Director and Council

there shall be written to touching the form hereof, in order, on receiving further information hereupon, it be rendered the least onerous and vexatious.

. . . .

All those who will be inclined to go thither, to inhabit the country or to trade, shall severally declare under their signatures, that they will voluntarily submit to these regulations, and to the orders of the Company, and shall allow all questions and differences there arising to be decided by the ordinary courts of justice, which shall be established in that country, and freely suffer there the execution of the sentences and verdicts, without any further opposition. And shall pay, for passage and board in the state room, one guilder, in the cabin (hutte), twelve stivers, and between decks eight stivers, per diem.

Text—O'Callaghan: *Documents relating to the Colonial History of the State of New York*, Vol. I, pp. 110-114.

II. *THE REFORMED CHURCH AT WORK IN MANHATTAN*

Rev. John Michaelius, first minister of Manhattan, in a letter to Rev. Adrian Smoutius of Amsterdam, writes (Aug. 11, 1628) of his work:

Reverend Sir, Well Beloved Brother in Christ, Kind Friend!

. . . .

Our coming here was agreeable to all, and I hope, by the grace of the Lord, that my service will not be unfruitful. The people, for the most part, are rather rough, and unrestrained, but I find in most all of them both love and respect towards me; two things with which hitherto the Lord has everywhere graciously blessed my labors, and which in our calling, as your Reverence well knows and finds, are especially desirable, in order to make (our ministry) fruitful.

From the beginning we established the form of a church; and as Brother Bastiaen Crol very seldom comes down from Fort Orange, because the Directorship of that fort and the trade there is committed to him, it has been thought best to choose two elders for my assistance and for the proper consideration of all such ecclesiastical matters as might occur, intending the coming year, if the Lord permit, to let one of them retire, and to choose another in his place from a double number first lawfully proposed to the congregation. One of those whom we have now chosen is the Honorable Director himself, and the other is the storekeeper of the Company, Jan Huyghens, his brother-in-law, persons of very good character, as far as I have been able to learn, having both been formerly in office in the Church, the one as deacon, and the other as elder in the Dutch and French churches, respectively, at Wesel.

At the first administration of the Lord's Supper which was observed, not without great joy and comfort to many, we had fully fifty communicants—Walloons and Dutch; of whom, a portion made their first confession of faith before us, and others exhibited their church certificates. Others had forgotten to bring their certificates with them not thinking that a church would be formed and established here; and some who brought them, had lost them unfortunately in a general conflagration, but they were admitted upon the satisfactory testimony of others to whom they were known, and also upon their daily good deportment, since we cannot observe strictly all the usual formalities in making a beginning under such circumstances.

We administer the Holy Sacraments of the Lord once in four months, provisionally, until a larger number of people shall otherwise require.   The Walloons and
French have no service on Sundays, otherwise than in the Dutch language, for those
who understand no Dutch are very few.   A portion of the Walloons are going back to
the Fatherland, either because their years here are expired, or else because some are
not very serviceable to the company.   Some of them live far away and could not well
come in time of heavy rain and storm, so that it is not advisable to appoint any special
service in French for so small a number, and that upon an uncertainty.   Nevertheless
the Lord's Supper was administered to them in the French language, and according
to the French mode, with a discourse preceding, which I had before me in writing, as
I could not trust myself extemporaneously.   If in this and in other matters your
Reverence and the Honorable Brethren of the Consistory, (at Amsterdam) who have
special superintendence over us here, deem it necessary to administer to us any correction, instruction or good advice, it will be agreeable to us and we will thank your
Reverence therefor; since we must have no other object than the glory of God in the
building up of his kingdom and the salvation of many souls.   I keep myself as far as
practicable within the pale of my calling, wherein I find myself sufficiently occupied.
And although our small Consistory embraces at the most—when Brother Crol is down
here—not more than four persons, all of whom, myself alone excepted, have also
public business to attend to, I still hope to separate carefully the ecclesiastical from the
civil matters which occur, so that each one will be occupied with his own subject.

. . . .

As to the natives of this country, I find them entirely savage and wild, strangers
to all decency, yea, uncivil and stupid as garden poles, proficient in all wickedness and
godlessness; devilish men, who serve nobody but the devil, that is, the spirit, which, in
their language, they call Menetto; . . .   How these people can best be led to the
true knowledge of God and of the Mediator Christ, is hard to say.   I cannot myself
wonder enough who it is that has imposed so much upon your Reverence and many
others in the Fatherland, concerning the docility of these people and their good nature,
the proper *principia religionis* and *vestigia legis naturae* which should be among them;
in whom I have as yet been able to discover hardly a single good point, except that they
do not speak so jeeringly and so scoffingly of the godlike and glorious majesty of their
Creator as the Africans dare to do.

. . . .

It would be well then to leave the parents as they are, and begin with the children
who are still young.   So be it.   But they ought in youth to be separated from their
parents; yea, from their whole nation.   For, without, this, they would forthwith be as
much accustomed as their parents to heathenish tricks and deviltries, which are
kneaded naturally into their hearts by themselves through a just judgment of God;
so that having once, by habit, obtained deep root, they would with great difficulty
be emancipated therefrom.   But this separation is hard to effect, for the parents have
a strong affection for their children, and are very loth to part with them; and, when
they are separated from them, as we have already had proof, the parents are never
contented, but take them away stealthily, or induce them to run away.   Nevertheless,
although it would be attended with some expense, we ought, by means of presents, and
promises to obtain the children, with the gratitude and consent of their parents; in
order to place them under the instruction of some experienced and godly schoolmaster,
where they may be instructed not only to speak, read, and write in our language, but

also especially in the fundamentals of our Christian religion; and where, besides, they will see nothing but the good example of virtuous living; but they must sometimes speak their native tongue among themselves, in order not to forget it, as being evidently a principal means of spreading the knowledge of religion through the whole nation.   In the meantime we should not forget to beseech the Lord, with ardent and continual prayers, for his blessing. . . .   I hope to keep a watchful eye over these people, and to learn as much of their language as will be practicable, and to seek better opportunities for their instruction than hitherto it has been possible to find.

As to what concerns myself and my household: I find myself by the loss of my good and helpful partner very much hindered and distressed—for my two little daughters are yet small; maid servants are not here to be had, at least none whom they advise me to take; and the Angola (female) slaves are thievish, lazy, and useless trash.   The young man whom I took with me, I discharged after Whitsuntide, for the reason that I could not employ him out-of-doors at any working of the land, and in-doors he was a burden to me instead of an assistance.   He is now elsewhere at service among the farmers.

The promise which the Honorable Directors of the Company had made me of some acres of surveyed lands for me to make myself a home, instead of a free table which otherwise belonged to me, is void and useless.   For their Honors well knew that there are no horses, cows, or laborers to be obtained here for money.   Every one is short in these particulars and wants more.   I should not mind the expense if the opportunity only offered, for the sake of our own comfort, although there were no profit in it (the Honorable Directors nevertheless remaining indebted to me for as much as the value of a free table), for refreshment of butter, milk, etc., cannot be here obtained; though some is indeed sold at a very high price, for those who bring it in or bespeak it are jealous of each other.   So I shall be compelled to pass through the winter without butter and other necessities, which the ships do not bring with them to be sold here.   The rations, which are given out and charged for high enough, are all hard stale food, as they are used to on board ship, and frequently not very good, and even so one cannot obtain as much as he desires.   I began to get considerable strength by the grace (favor) of the Lord, but in consequence of this hard fare of beans and gray peas, which are hard enough, barley, stockfish, etc., without much change I cannot fully recuperate as I otherwise would.   The summer yields something, but what of that for any one who has no strength?   The savages also bring some things, but one who has no wares, such as knives, beads, and the like, or seewan, cannot come to any terms with them.   Though the people trade such things for proper wares, I know not whether it is permitted by the laws of the Company.   I have now ordered from Holland most all necessaries; but I expect to pass through the winter with hard and scanty food. . . .

Text—(original and in translation) Hastings: *Ecclesiastical Records of the State of New York*, Vol. I, pp. 49-63.

III. *THE REFORMED CHURCH AND THE SECTS*

In early years New Netherland, imitating the Fatherland, while recognizing a National Reformed Church, adopted a policy of tolerance toward various sects which drifted to Manhattan for asylum.   It was not until 1652 when the Lutherans began to press for their rights of worship that the Reformed preachers began an agitation against conventicles, which four years later was effectively crystallized in the ordinance below. Though frowned upon by the Amsterdam Company, through the persistency of the New Netherland clergy this law remained upon the Statute Book, becoming the basis for a policy of persecution in which Baptists and Quakers suffered.

The Director General and Council have been credibly informed that not only conventicles and meetings have been held here and there in this Province, but also that unqualified persons presume in such meetings to act as teachers, in interpreting and expounding God's Holy Word, without ecclesiastical or secular authority. This is contrary to the general rules, political and ecclesiastical of our Fatherland; and besides, such gatherings lead to trouble, heresies and schisms.

Therefore, to prevent this, the Director General and Council strictly forbid all such public or private conventicles and meetings, except the usual and authorized ones, where God's Word, according to the Reformed and established custom, is preached and taught in meetings held for the religious service of the Reformed Church, conformably to the Synod of Dort, which is to be followed here, as in the Fatherland, and in the other Reformed Churches of Europe; under a fine of one hundred pounds Flemish ($240.), to be paid by all who, in such public or private meetings, except at the usual authorized gatherings on Sundays or other days, presume to exercise, without due qualification, the duties of a preacher, reader, or chorister; and each man or woman, married or unmarried, who is found at such a meeting, shall pay a fine of twenty five pounds Flemish ($60.).

The Director General and Council, however, do not hereby intend to force the consciences of any, to the prejudice of formerly given patents, or to forbid the preaching of God's Holy Word, the use of Family Prayers, and divine services in the family; but only all public and private conventicles and gatherings, be they in public or private houses, except the already mentioned usual, and authorized religious services of the Reformed. And that this order may be the better observed, and nobody plead ignorance thereof, the Director General and Council direct and charge their Fiscal, and the inferior Magistrates and Schouts, to publish the same everywhere in this Province, and to prosecute transgressors; inasmuch as we have so decreed this, for the honor of God, the advancement of the Reformed services, and the quiet, unity and welfare of the country generally.

Thus done, etc., February 1, 1656.

Text—Hastings: *Ecclesiastical Records of the State of New York*, Vol. I, pp. 343-344.

IV. *ARTICLES OF CAPITULATION ON THE REDUCTION OF NEW NETHERLAND, AUGUST 27, 1664*

2. All public houses shall continue for the uses which they are now for.
. . . .

6. The Dutch here shall enjoy the liberty of their consciences in Divine Worship and church discipline.
. . . .

12. All publique writings and records which concern the inheritances of any people, or the reglement of the church,, or poor, or orphans, shall be carefully kept by those in whose hands they are, and such writings as particularly concern the States-General, may, at any time, be sent to them.

Text—O'Callaghan: *Documents Relating to the Colonial History of the State of New York*, Vol. II, pp. 250-253.

V. *THE DUKE'S LAWS, FEBRUARY 28, 1665*

The Duke of York being a Roman Catholic, and the king his brother at least sympathetic towards Romanism, it was natural that their ordinances on religion should breathe a measure of tolerance. The following clauses relate to religion:

Whereas the public worship of God is much discredited for want of painful and able ministers to instruct the people in the true religion, and for want of convenient places capable to receive any number or assembly of people, in a decent manner, for celebrating God's holy ordinances, these ensuing laws are to be observed in every parish, viz.:

1. That in each parish within this government a church be built in the most convenient part thereof, capable to receive and accomodate two hundred persons.

2. That for the making and proportioning the levies and assessments for building and repairing the churches, provision for the poor, maintenance for the minister, as well as for the more orderly managing of all parochial affairs in other cases expressed; eight of the most able men of each parish be, by the major part of the householders of the said parish, chosen, to be overseers; out of which number the constable and the aforesaid eight overseers shall yearly make choice of two of the said number to be church-wardens, and in case of the death of any of the said overseers and church-wardens, or his or their departure out of the parish, the said constable and overseers shall make choice of another to supply his room.

3. Every overseer is to take the oath of allegiance at the time of his admittance into his office, in the presence of the minister, overseer, and constable of the parish, besides the oath of his office.

4. To prevent scandalous and ignorant pretenders to the ministry from intruding themselves as teachers, no minister shall be permitted to officiate within the government but such as shall produce testimonials to the governor that he hath received ordination either from some Protestant bishop or minister, within some part of his Majesty's dominions, or the dominions of any foreign prince of the Reformed religion; upon which testimony the governor shall induce the said minister into the parish that shall make presentation of him as duly elected by the major part of the inhabitants (being) householders.

5. That the minister of every parish shall preach constantly every Sunday, and shall also pray for the King, Queen, Duke of York, and the royal family. And every person affronting or disturbing any congregation on the Lord's day, and on such public days of fast and thanksgiving as are appointed to be observed, after the presentments thereof by the church-wardens to the sessions, and due conviction thereof, shall be punished by fine or imprisonment, according to the merit and nature of the offense. And every minister shall also publicly administer the sacrament of the Lord's Supper

once every year, at the least, in his parish church, not denying the private benefit thereof to persons that for want of health shall require the same in their houses, under the penalty of loss of preferment, unless the minister be restrained in point of conscience.

6. No minister shall refuse the sacrament of baptism to the children of Christian parents, when they shall be tendered, under penalty of loss of preferment.

7. Ministers are to marry persons after legal publication or sufficient license.

8. Legal publication shall be so esteemed, when the persons so to be married are three several days asked in the church, or have a special license.

9. Sundays are not to be profaned by travelers, laborers, or vicious persons.

10. That no congregations shall be disturbed in their private meetings, in the time of prayer, preaching, or other divine service; nor shall any person be molested, fined, or imprisoned, for differing in judgment in matters of religion, who professes Christianity.

11. No person of scandalous or vicious life shall be admitted to the holy sacrament, who hath not given satisfaction therein to the minister.

Public Charges

Every inhabitant shall contribute to all charges, both in church and state, whereof he doth or may receive benefit, according to the equal proportion of his estate.

Text—Hastings: *Ecclesiastical Records of the State of New York*, Vol. I, pp. 570-572.

VI. IMPRESSIONS OF NEW YORK IN 1679

Jasper Danckaerts and Peter Sluyter arriving in New York Sept 23, 1679, to select a site for a Labadist colony, had occasion to look around the city and to record as under:

24th. Sunday. We rested well through the night. I was surprised on waking up to find my comrade had already dressed himself and breakfasted upon peaches. We walked out awhile in the fine, pure morning air, along the margin of the clear running water of the sea, which is driven up this river at every tide. As it was Sunday, in order to avoid scandal and for other reasons, we did not wish to absent ourselves from church. We therefore went, and found there truly a wild worldly world. I say wild, not only because the people are wild, as they call it in Europe, but because most all the people who go there to live, or who are born there, partake somewhat of the nature of the country, that is, peculiar to the land where they live. We heard a minister preach, who had come from the up-river country, from fort Orange, where his residence is, an old man, named Domine Schaats, of Amsterdam. . . .

This Schaats, then, preached. He had a defect in the left eye, and used such strange gestures and language that I think I never in all my life have heard any thing more miserable; indeed, I can compare him with no one better than with one Do. Van Ecke, lately the minister at Armuyden, in Zeeland, more in life, conversation and gestures than in person. As it is not strange in these countries to have men as ministers who drink, we could imagine nothing else than that he had been drinking a little this morning. His text was, *Come unto me all ye, &c.*, but he was so rough that even the roughest and most godless of our sailors were astonished.

The church being in the fort, we had an opportunity to look through the latter, as we had come too early for preaching. It is not large, it has four points or batteries;

it has no moat outside, but is enclosed with a double row of palisades. It is built from the foundation with quarry stone. The parapet is of earth. It is well provided with cannon, for the most part of iron, though there were some small brass pieces, all bearing the mark or arms of the Netherlanders. The garrison is small. There is a well of fine water dug in the fort by the English, contrary to the opinion of the Dutch, who supposed the fort was built upon rock, and had therefore never attempted any such thing. . . . It has only one gate, and that is on the land slide, opening upon a broad plain or street called the Broadway or Beaverway. Over this gate are the arms of the Duke of York. During the time of the Dutch there were two gates, namely, another on the water side; but the English have closed it, and made a battery there, with a false gate. In front of the church is inscribed the name of Governor *Kyft*, who caused the same to be built in the year 1642. It has a shingled roof, and upon the gable towards the water there is a small wooden tower, with a bell in it, but no clock. There is a sun-dial on three sides. The front of the fort stretches east and west, and consequently the sides run north and south. . . .

. . . On my return home, the son of our old people asked me if I would not go to their usual catechizing, which they held once a week at the house of *Abraham Lanoy*, schoolmaster, and brother of the commissary in the custom house. I accompanied him there, and found a company of about twenty-five persons, male and female, but mostly young people. It looked like a school, as indeed it was, more than an assembly of persons who were seeking after true godliness; where the schoolmaster, who instructed them, handled the subject more like a schoolmaster in the midst of his scholars than a person who knew and loved God, and sought to make him known and loved. They sung some verses from the psalms, made a prayer, and questioned from the catechism, at the conclusion of which they prayed and sung some verses from the psalms again. It was all performed without respect or reverence, very literally, and mixed up with much obscurity and error. He played, however, the part of a learned and pious man, *enfin le suffisant et le petit precheur*. After their departure, I had an opportunity of speaking to him and telling him what I thought was good for him. He acknowledged that I convinced him of several things; and thus leaving him I returned home. . . .

We went from the city, following the Broadway, over the *valey*, or the fresh water. Upon both sides of this way were many habitations of negroes, mullattoes and whites. These negroes were formerly the proper slaves of the (West India) company, but, in consequence of the frequent changes and conquests of the country, they have obtained their freedom and settled themselves down where they have thought proper, and thus on this road, where they have ground enough to live on with their families. We left the village, called the *Bouwerij*, lying on the right hand, and went through the woods to New Harlem, a tolerably large village situated on the south side of the island, directly opposite the place where the northeast creek and the East river come together, situated about three hours journey from New Amsterdam, . . .

11th, Wednesday. We embarked early this morning in his boat and rowed over to Staten island, where we arrived about eight o'clock. . . . There are now about a hundred families on the island, of which the English constitute the least portion, and the Dutch and French divide between them about equally the greater portion. They have neither church nor minister, and live rather far from each other, and inconveniently to meet together. The English are less disposed to religion, and inquire little after it, but in case there were a minister, would contribute to his support. The French and Dutch are very desirous and eager for one, for they spoke of it wherever we went, and said, in the event ot not obtaining Domine Tessemaker, they would send, or had sent, to France for another.   The French are good Reformed churchmen, and some of them are Walloons.   The Dutch are also from different quarters. `. . .`

When we arrived at Gouanes, we heard a great noise, shouting and singing in the huts of the Indians, who as we mentioned before, were living there.   They were all lustily drunk, raving, striking, shouting, jumping, fighting each other, and foaming at the mouth like raging wild beasts.   Some who did not participate with them, had fled with their wives and children to Simon's house, where the drunken brutes followed, bawling in the house and before the door, which we finally closed.   And this was caused by Christians.   It makes me blush to call by that holy name those who live ten times worse than these most barbarous Indians and heathen, not only in the eyes of those who can discriminate, but according to the testimony of these poor Indians themselves. What do I say, the testimony of the Indians!   Yes, I have not conversed with an European or a native born, the most godless and the best, who has not fully and round- ly acknowledged it, but they have not acknowledged it salutarily, and much less de- sisted, disregarding all convictions external and internal, notwithstanding all the injury which springs therefrom, not only among the Indians, but others, as we will show in its proper place.   How will they escape the terrible judgment of God; how evade the wrath and anger of the Lord and King, Jesus, whom they have so dishonored and defamed, and caused to be defamed among the heathen?   Just judgment is their damnation.   But I must restrain myself, giving God all judgment and wrath, and keeping only what he causes us to feel therefor.   Such are the fruits of the cursed cupidity of those who call themselves Christians for the very little that these poor naked people have.

Text—*Journal of a Voyage to New York in 1679-80*, in *Memoirs Long Island Historical Society*, Vol. I, pp. 109-274.

VII. *INSTRUCTIONS TO GOVERNOR DONGAN, MAY 29, 1686*

. . . .

12. And whereas wee have been presented with a Bill or Charter passed in ye late Assembly of New York, containing several ffranchises, privileges & Immunitys men- tioned to be granted to the Inhabitants of our sd province,   You are to Declare Our Will & pleasure that ye said Bill or Charter of Franchises bee forthwith repealed & disallowed, as ye same is hereby Repealed, determined & made void.   But you are nevertheless with our said Council to continue the Dutys & Impositions therein men- tioned to bee raised untill you shall with the consent of the Council settle such Taxes and Impositions as shall be sufficient for ye support of our Governmt of New York.

. . . .

31. You shall take especiall care that God Almighty bee devoutly and duely served throughout yor Government: the Book of Common Prayer, as it is now es- tablisht, read each Sunday and Holyday, and the Blessed Sacrament administred according to the Rites of the Church of England.   You shall be careful that the Churches already built there shall bee well and orderly kept and more built as ye Colony shall, by God's blessing, bee improved.   And that besides a competent main- tenance to bee assigned to ye Minister of each Church, a convenient House bee built

at the Comon charge for each Minister, and a competent Proportion of Land assigned him for a Glebe and exercise of his Industry.

32. And you are to take care that the Parishes bee so limited & setled as you shall find most convenient for ye accomplishing this good work.

33. Our will and pleasure is that noe minister bee preferred by you to any Ecclesiastical Benefice in that Our Province, without a Certificat from ye most Reverend the Lord Archbishop of Canterbury of his being conformable to ye Doctrine and Discipline of the Church of England, and of a good life, & conversation.

34. And if any person preferred already to a Benefice shall appear to you to give scandal either by his Doctrin or Manners, you are to use the best means for ye removal of him; and to supply the vacancy in such manner as wee have directed. And alsoe our pleasure is that, in the direction of all Church Affairs, the Minister bee admitted into the respective vestrys.

35. And to th' end the Ecclesiastical Jurisdiction of the said Archbishop of Canterbury may take place in that Our Province as farr as conveniently may bee. Wee doe think fitt that you give all countenance and encouragement in ye exercise of the same; excepting only the Collating to Benefices, granting licenses for Marriage, and Probat of Wills, which wee have reserved to you our Govr & to ye Commander in cheif for the time being.

36. And you are to take especial care, that a Table of marriages established by ye Canons of the Church of England, bee hung up in all Orthodox Churches and duly observed.

37. And you are to take care that Books of Homilys & Books of the 39 Articles of ye Church of England bee disposed of to every of ye said Churches, & that they bee only kept and used therein.

38. And wee doe further direct that noe Schoolmaster bee henceforth permitted to come from England & to keep school within Our Province of New York, without the license of the said Archbishop of Canterbury; And that noe other person now there or that shall come from other parts, bee admitted to keep school without your license first had.

39. You are to take care that Drunkeness and Debauchery, Swearing and blasphemy bee severely punisht; And that none bee admitted to publick trust & Imploymt whose ill fame & conversation may bring scandal thereupon.

. . . .

42. You shall permit all persons of what Religion soever quietly to inhabit wihin yor Government without giving them any disturbance or disquiet whatsoever for or by reason of their differing Opinions in matters of Religion Provided they give noe disturbance to ye publick peace, nor doe molest or disquiet others in ye free Exercise of their Religion.

Text—O'Callaghan: *Documents relating to the Colonial History of the State of New York*, Vol. III, pp. 369-373.

VIII. *THE MINISTRY ACT*

Limited in application to certain parishes, and entirely unsectarian, this Act passed September 22, 1693 and confirmed May 11, 1697, was the utmost that the stout anglican Governor Fletcher, after remonstrance and prorogation, could extort from an Assembly overwhelmingly Dutch, set in their determination not to establish a Church of England.

Whereas, Profaneness and Licentiousness hath of late overspread this province, for Want of a settled Ministry throughout the same: to the End the same may be removed, and the Ordinances of God duly administered;

I. Be it enacted *by the Governor*, and *Council, and Representatives convened in General Assembly, and by the Authority of the same*, That in each of the respective Cities and Counties hereafter mentioned and expressed, there shall be called, inducted and establish; a good sufficient Protestant Minister, to officiate, and have the Care of Souls, within one Year next, and after the Publication hereof, *that is to say;* In the City of *New York*, One; in the county of *Richmond*, One; in the county of *Westchester*, Two;—One to *have* the Care of *Westchester, Eastchester, Yonkers*, and the Manor of *Pelham;* the Other to have the Care of *Rye, Mamarenock*, and *Bedford;* in *Queen's* County, Two; One to have the Care of *Jamaica*, and the adjacent Towns and Farms; the Other to have the Care of *Hamstead*, and the next adjacent Towns and Farms.

II. And for their respective Encouragement, Be it further enacted, *by the authority aforesaid*, That there shall be annually, and once in every Year, in every of the respective Cities and Counties aforesaid, assessed, levied, collected, and paid, for the Maintenance of each of their respective Ministers, the respective Sums hereafter mentioned, . . .

III. And for the more orderly Raising the respective Maintenances for the Ministers aforesaid, Be it further enacted, *by the authority aforesaid*, That the respective Justices of every City and County aforesaid, or any Two of them, shall every Year, issue out their Warrants to the Constables, to summons the Freeholders of every City, County and Precinct aforesaid, together, on the second Tuesday of *January*, for the chusing of Ten Vestry-Men, and two Church Wardens; and the said Justices and Vestry-Men, or major Part of them, are hereby impowered, within Ten Days after the, the said Day, or any Day after, as to them shall seem convenient, to lay a reasonable Tax on the said respective Cities, Counties, Parish, or Precincts for the Maintenance of the Minister and Poor of their respective Places, . . .

. . . .

VI. Always provided, and be it further Enacted, *by the Authority aforesaid*, that all and every of the respective Ministers, that shall be settled in the respective Cities, Counties, and Precincts aforesaid, shall be called to officiate in their respective Precincts, by the respective Vestry-Men, and Church-Wardens aforesaid. And, *Always Provided*, That all the former Agreements, made with Ministers throughout this Province, shall continue and remain in their full Force and Virtue, anything contained herein to the contrary hereof, in any wise notwithstanding.

Text—Corwin: *A History of the Reformed Church, Dutch*, (Amer. Ch. Hist. Sec. Vol. VIII.) pp. 100-103.

IX. *THE LANGUAGE PROBLEM IN THE REFORMED DUTCH CHURCHES*

William Livingstone in *The Independent Reflector* (January 1754) analyses the denominational situation as follows:

The visible decay to which those churches, no less venerable for their purity of doctrine, discipline and worship, than their antiquity in this province, were subject, raised the most commiserating sentiments in the breast of every lover of virtue and true religion. Their once crowded assemblies now scarcely existed, save in the sad remembrance of their primitive glory. Their youth, forgetting the religion of their ancestors, wandered in search of new persuasions; and the most diligent labors of those who were set over them, proved ineffectual to attach them to the profession in which they were educated. These, indeed, were circumstances woeful and distressing!

Nor unknown was the cause of this melancholy declension. In all the British colonies, as the knowledge of the English tongue must necessarily endure, and instead of declining, will naturally become more perfect and improved; so every foreign language, however generally practised and understood for a time, must, at length, be neglected and forgotten. Thus it is with the Dutch tongue, which, though once the common dialect of this province, is now scarcely understood, except by its more ancient inhabitants. It has also been observed that the churches have kept exact pace with the language in its retragrade state, so that there is no room to doubt (that) the decay of the former was caused by the disuse of the latter; and that the one and the other will in process of time sink into perfect oblivion. To retain the use of the Dutch language, the greatest pains have not been wanting. They have had well-regulated free-schools, richly supported by their churches, and yet maugre their utmost efforts, parents have found it in a degree impossible to transmit it to their children. Whence it is generally feared that the very next generation will scarce furnish one person in this city, except their clergy, well acquainted with the tongue. To prevent, therefore, the ruin of the Dutch churches, common sense pointed out the absolute necessity of disuniting them from the language, by translating their public Acts of devotion and worship into English, or the speedy introduction of the present translations now used by several of their churches in Holland, nothing being more certain than that the celebration of divine service in an unknown tongue, would, in a Protestant country, prove as disgustful as it would be unprofitable.

I should have imagined that nothing could be objected to the immediate execution of so necessary and obvious an expedient. No sooner, however, was it proposed, than the sticklers for high-church raised a general cry upon the occasion. Mean and ungenerous were the arts used by them to discredit the proposal. Recourse was had to their old practice of reviling and calumniating the Presbyterians, who were charged with a design no less wicked than false and impossible, of seizing the Dutch churches and converting them and their congregations to their own use. Nay, so fashionable was the practice of falsifying for the church, that with an assurance unparallelled, the Dutch were told to their faces that they were not Presbyterians. The effrontery with which the assertion was repeated, pressed conviction on the ignorant. Whence it is common to hear the more illiterate members of the Dutch congregation disown themselves to be Presbyterians, and even insist on their being Episcopalians. These artifices were ingeniously detected by *Philo Reflector*, whose remarks on this subject compelled those high-flyers to play a different game.

Ashamed to persist any longer in obtruding so flagrant a falsehood, and bent upon supporting a wall of partition between the English and Dutch Presbyterians, they as confidently denied the former to be such, as they have for thirty years past imprudently abused them under that name. Not to dwell upon the shocking wickedness and absurdity of such conduct, who cannot see that the grand design was to prevent the introduction of the English tongue into the Dutch churches lest the discriminating badge with the vulgar, the difference of language, being removed, a coalition might ensue, and Presbyterianism by that means be strengthened and supported, while the augmentation of the *English,* by proselytes from the Dutch Church, would be in a great degree interrupted.   How inconsistent this, with the Gospel dispensation! How much estranged from the practice of Christian charity are those, who instead of promoting a harmony between sister churches, would endeavor to prevent it, even at the expense of the final destruction of one!   Had they no sinister views, far would they be from endeavoring the ruin of a Christian Church, sound in the faith, edifying in its worship, and well policied in its government.   But so determined are they on advancing the interest of their own party, that to accomplish the downfall of the Dutch congregation, it would to them be a trifling peccadille, could they by that means secure the grand object of their wishes.

. . . But is it not easy to observe that a greater stress is laid upon the importance of continuing the use of the Dutch language than any language can possibly deserve? Would the profession of the Dutch Church be less orthodox, their worship less edifying, and their discipline less sound, were their service performed in English?   Or can the same thoughts which, delivered in one language, are acceptable to the Almighty, displease him when expressed in another?   The truth is, those who oppose the introduction of the English tongue into one of the Dutch churches are convinced that the different languages are the only criteria to distinguish them from each other; and this is evident from their fear that the use of the same tongue will naturally produce an union.   Yet surely it cannot be so destructive of the interests of the Dutch churches to coalesce with a sect with whom they perfectly agree in doctrine, worship and government, as to follow the advice of those who, by endeavoring to dissuade them from introducing the English language evidently meditate their dissolution. . . . ."

Text—Hastings: *Ecclesiastical Records of the State of New York,* Vol. V, pp. 3459-60.

X. *THE COETUS*

"Circular Letter of the Consistory of New York, to all the Dutch Reformed Churches in New York and New Jersey, May 27, 1737

Respected Friends:—The Consistory of New York, anxious for the general welfare of all Dutch Reformed churches, especially in these provinces, has deliberated whether an Ecclesiastical Assembly of ministers and elders delegated from all the churches, organized on a proper basis, and held at least once a year, at such time and place as might be agreed on, might not be very useful.

In such an Ecclesiastical Assembly only ecclesiastical matters ought to be considered, agreeably to God's Word and our Formulas of Unity, and in subordination to the Classis of Amsterdam; and these subjects should be such as are presented by the respective Consistories, for the settlement of differences, the promotion and establishment of peace and harmony, and the general edification of the churches; yet in this Assembly, all the churches shall preserve their individual liberty agreeably to the Synod of Dort, but in subordination to the Classis of Amsterdam.   No Fundamental Articles shall be in force in this Coetus, until they have been ratified by the churches which unite in forming it, and until approved by the Classis of Amsterdam.   And this Assembly shall annually send a general letter to said Classis, giving a brief account of the condition of the churches in this land.

The Great Consistory of the Church of New York believed that a Coetus, established on a proper basis, would be highly useful; that not only the Classis, but others who are interested in our welfare, would thus obtain a true view of the condition of our churches, which is now not well known to them. Conflicting accounts are now sent to them, and they declare that they hear of nothing but complaints and defences; of false doctrines and private feuds; so that ministers and candidates are deterred from coming over; that dissensions are not healed, but are daily becoming worse; that offences multiply, to our reproach, before them who are without. Now a Coetus would be useful to guard against prevailing errors, to provide wisely against offences, and more quickly to restore peace to the churches. Surely no one would oppose such a Plan, on the plea that he is under no obligations to others; for we all confess that we are members of the same Body, and should therefore watch over each other's welfare

For these reasons has the Consistory of New York deemed it necessary to communicate their views on this subject to all the Consistories in these regions, and request them to take the subject into serious consideration; and if, as is earnestly hoped, they agree with the Consistory of New York, that the formation of a Coetus in this country, on a proper basis, would be useful and salutary; then they are urgently and affectionately requested by the Consistory of New York, to send their minister to New York, which is the most central place and most convenient, that a friendly conference may be held, to consult on what should constitute the Fundamental Articles of such an annual Assembly or Coetus of Ministers and Elders. These Articles are then to be laid before their respective Consistories, for approbation or amendment, as, according to their deliberate judgment, shall be for the best interest of all the congregations in this country.

In order, therefore that we may join hands, in true love and in common endeavor, after that which shall serve for the glory of God, the general welfare of all the churches, and the extension of Christ's kingdom in this land, we address this friendly and fraternal letter to you, with the urgent request that you will give it your favorable regard. And if you agree therewith, please signify the same to us, and delegate at least one of your ministers to attend a meeting in New York on September 5th (1737) for the attainment of this object; namely, that we may, in a fraternal manner, adopt Articles for the Constitution of such an annual Assembly, to be submitted to the judgment of the churches, that general agreement may be attained.

Having laid before you this subject, we remain, with fervent prayers for all temporal and spiritual blessings upon yourselves and your churches,

Respected Brethren,

Your obedient servants in Jesus Christ,

In the Name of the Consistory,

G. Du Bois, p. t. Praeses."

Text—Hastings: *Ecclesiastical Records of the State of New York*, Vol. IV, pp. 2683-84.

"*Convention in the Church of New York Concerning the Formation of a Coetus in this County. September 7, 1737. 4 p.m.*

. . . .

II. As to the business to be transacted in the Coetus.

1. In the Coetus nothing but ecclesiastical business shall be transacted, agreeably to the Word of God and our Formulas of Unity, and all in subordination to the Classis of Amsterdam.

2. No matters of dispute shall be considered in the Coetus, except such as are presented in a regular manner, according to the Rules of the Synod of Dort; and then, only for the removal of differences, the promotion and establishment of mutual peace and harmony, and for the general edification of the congregations.

3. Whoever feels himself aggrieved by the action of the Coetus shall have the right to appeal to the Classis of Amsterdam.

4. If the Coetus by a majority or unanimity of votes, judges any matter brought before it to be of too great importance for their own immediate action, they may request the advice and judgment of the Classis of Amsterdam.

5. Whoever appeals to the said Classis, or whose case is submitted to the Classis for advice and judgment, shall, as well as the Coetus itself, submit themselves to such advice and decision.

6. But every church shall preserve its own liberty of action, in the management of its own affairs, according to the Constitution of our Church, as established in the Synod of Dort.

7. For the greater advantage of the congregations, and according to the freedom and constitution of the Church-Order, the congregations belonging to the Coetus shall be divided into suitable Circles; so that if conditions occur which cannot be adjusted by the congregation itself, and which admit of no delay, they may be brought before the neighboring ministers composing that Circle, and be treated by them in love and wisdom; and thus prevent the necessity of their being brought before the Coetus.

8. No minister or Consistory shall allow anyone to preach in their church, unless he produces satisfactory evidences that he has received lawful ordination to the ministry of the Reformed Church. Therefore no Consistory, when their church is vacant, shall allow any preacher or candidate to officate until he shall first have submitted his testimonials to two neighboring ministers.

9. As to calls, either from Holland or from other churches in this country, they shall be made according to the Church Order of the Synod of Dort, and the circumstances of the churches in this country; with the proviso that henceforth it shall be expressly stipulated in all calls, that the minister shall belong to the Coetus, being received as a member, on the exhibition of a lawful call. And the congregations, which have calls outstanding, are hereby requested, to urge their ministers, when they arrive, to join the Coetus.

10. The churches shall, by their commissioners in the Coetus, consult together and decide for the greater advantage and edification of the churches, yet as subordinate to the Classis of Amsterdam.

11. As the liberty of the churches, as formerly defined and expressed, is neither increased or diminished by the Coetus, the commissioners to the Coetus shall, yearly, in the name of their congregations, send a common letter to the Classis of Amsterdam, stating concisely the condition of the churches in these provinces; thus also manifesting their subordination, as at present existing and inviolable, to the Classis; agreeably to the Constitution of the Dutch Reformed Churches in this country, and the 36th Article of the Church Order. And for the greater unity of our church to that of the Fatherland, we request the Classis to send us from year to year, copies of the Acta Synodi, in order that we may regulate better our own ecclesiastical affairs, to the advantage and edification of our churches.

12. If a Coetus be established upon such a proper basis as this, and held yearly at New York, or at such other place as may be designated from time to time, on the

first Monday in September, we, the undersigned, believe it would be with much profit and promote the welfare of the churches.

13. Therefore, the proposed Plan is sent down to the several churches by this friendly meeting, with the request that they carefully consider it, in the fear of the Lord, and with a spirit of impartiality, and a sincere desire for the welfare of God's Church. They are requested then to send their ministers, and with each, an elder, to meet on the last Monday of April next, 1738, in New York.

. . . .

Done at our friendly conference in the Consistory Chamber of our Dutch Reformed Church at New York this 12th day of September, 1737, and subscribed by us ministers:

GERARD HAEGHOORT, *Pres.* G. DU BOIS. B. FREEMAN. C. VAN SANTVOORD. A. CURTENIUS."

Text—Hastings: *Ecclesiastical Records of the State of New York*, Vol. IV, pp. 2686-89.

XI. *KINGS COLLEGE*

See pp. 244-250.

XII. *THE MISSION TO THE FIVE NATIONS*

See pp. 305-309.

XIII. *THE CLASSIS ISSUE*

The American Church in its Relation to Amsterdam

'The Coetus of New York to the Rev. Classis of Amsterdam, October 13, 1764. *To the Right Rev. Classis of Amsterdam, Right Rev. Sirs and Much Beloved Brethren:*—

The letter of your Revs. of January 11, and of October 3rd, 1763, reached us safely. According to the request of the Rev. Conferentie which followed (upon your letters) the Rev. Coetus attended a General Meeting (of the two Bodies) held in New York, June 19, 1764. The result of that Meeting may be seen in Document number One.

In the present condition of affairs we do not feel disposed to answer the above mentioned letters! for we can plainly foresee where the matter in dispute so apparent in them, will end, if it be followed up in debate. We would rather make still another attempt, with all indulgence possible, to settle these disputes by some accommodation.

. . . .

We therefore make this friendly and brotherly request that the following objections receive your careful deliberation.

1. We cannot at present content ourselves with the reasons given for the subordination (to the Classis) demanded of us. We believe that any subordination to a Church, which is destitute of all power (being under another civil government) is plainly contrary to the Netherlands Church Constitution. . . . The reasons given in support of subordination, and in advocacy of the demand, appear, more or less evidently, to be as follows:

(1) From the right of having planted these churches (in America). But that this does not confer the least right or power, nor deprive those who are planted of all

power, is, in our opinion, confirmed by the renowned Professor, Gysbert Voetius, *Pol. Eccl.*, Vol. I, Part 1, pages 104-108.

(2) But to be more direct, let me speak of the membership of our ministers in your Rev. Classis. This is taken for granted; but in all your letters, you do not give one conclusive reason to establish it. Nevertheless, this (the fact of such membership) appears to be the basis upon which all your reasons for the support of such subordination rest. But it seems to us as clear as day light, that we were never such real members of your Rev. Classis, as you claim.

. . . .

If we are really members of your Rev. Classis, and on an equal footing, in this respect, with the twenty-nine ministers of Amsterdam, are we not then also capable of being members of that Rev. Synod? But if, in reality, we are not at all members of your Rev. Classis, as, indeed, we are not, what force then, can your Revs.' arguments have, to convince our consciences? for your arguments are based upon this supposition, (that we are members of Classis).

However, the dispute over here is not concerning the historical account of an affair that is past; but concerning the possession or non-possession of the right and the power in regard to our own affairs. The Rev. Coetus does not promote (ordain) in quality as members of the Rev. Classis of Amsterdam, but as a company of neighboring ministers, to whom the pastoral office, with all that belongs to it, is entrusted. Now the power to promote (ordain) is an essential part of this office.

. . . .

Besides, it is to be borne in mind that your Revs.' arguments will have just as much weight a hundred years hence, as now; and according to a moderate calculation, the Dutch (in America) will then, (1864) by a proportionate growth, consist of a thousand congregations; and will need, accordingly, at least five or six hundred ministers. Let such circumstances declare what your arguments would be worth under such conditions. . . .

II. If in this land the opportunity is not given and further developed to provide ministers for the Dutch Church, we cannot fail to foresee that that Church will soon go to ruin. Passing by other weighty reasons, take only in proof the situation of these Colonies and the opportunities. For example: It is much more to the prejudice of our (American) Church, than it is of any of the other Churches of the Netherlands Colonies, (East Indies, Cape of Good Hope, West India Islands), to be obliged to obtain her ministers from Holland. This may be indisputably demonstrated by the following facts:

1. Everybody knows that nearly all the denominations around us prepare their ministers in this land and thus send them forth. They have, then, the opportunity to preach and establish congregations among the scattered people of this land, because they are ever ready to admit a sufficient number to the Holy Office. But the few (Dutch) ministers who are here have their hands more than full to serve the wants of the already established, but vacant congregations. For, on account of the dangers difficulties and heavy expenses, it is impossible to secure a sufficient number of young men for the Holy Office, if they must first go to the Netherlands (for ordination). Many of the established congregations do not dare to run the risk of sending (their young men) to the Netherlands; while those who are scattered here and there among the English cannot afford to do this. Under such circumstances hundreds are allured away to other denominations, since they cannot be provided with ministers as they

should be. But could not this deadly evil be effectually remedied, by admitting ministers to this holy service here in this country, even as do other denominations.

2. What has been said becomes still more evident if we compare the English Episcopalians and the Presbyterian Churches in this land with each other. The former is the "State Church" of England. Its adherents have the civil government chiefly in their hands. In short, in regard to all political rights, this Church has all the privileges imaginable above other denominations; yet the Presbyterians have established ten congregations in these two Provinces, to the Episcopalians one. Now what can be the reason of this? Only this: that those churches, being governed by Bishops must receive their ministers from Europe; while the Presbyterians, through the advice and help of the Church of Scotland, have been provided, from their first settlement, with the privileges of admitting their young men to this Holy Office,

Men and Brethren, do your Revs. not clearly see that if your Revs. had acted in regard to the Dutch Church as the Scotch have done in regard to the Presbyterian Church, the present number of our congregations would have been more than double? And both the Episcopalians (Bischoppelyken) and the Presbyterians have built up their churches on the ruin of ours.

3.. In the midst of us and all around us, the Seminaries of the Independents, of the Episcopalians and of the Presbyterians have already become seven or eight in number. And what will be the effect of all this? The Hollanders must either necessarily deny their children a free education, and thus relinquish all these advantages to others; or else send them to one of these schools. The inevitable result of this would be the alienation of their hearts from the Netherland doctrine and discipline. Only just imagine that our Church continues to receive, from time to time all her ministers from Holland; but, on the other hand, that the rising youth, who will soon hold the government and influence in both Church and State, receive their education in the Seminaries of these different denominations. By such a course, will not the (Dutch) Church finally go down altogether, unobserved.

4. Every one must understand, that since the political government and the entire business of the land are conducted in the English language, English schools are necessary, and Dutch schools are already passing away. The Dutch language will also certainly fall into disuse, and the English will everywhere take its place. Must then the religion (of the Dutch Church) go down with the language? Or how can this danger be remedied? It is simply impracticable to receive a sufficient number (of ministers) from Holland, especially such as would be able to perform service in the English tongue. To send a sufficient number (of our young men) from America to Holland to attend the Academies of your Revs., is impossible, even as has been said before. Who, then, does not see that the Church must go down, unless we have our own ecclesiastical Assemblies and Schools over here.

III. We send enclosed in this letter, a copy of an oath, (marked number 2), which some of us have taken in due form, and others, when required, are bound to take, under such penalty as is mentioned in the copy. Now who can, in good conscience, take such an oath, and then submit himself to subordination (of, to us, a Church in another nation) as proclaimed and demanded.

. . . .

The Rev. Coetus has explained to the Rev. Conferentie, as she now does also to your Revs., that on these conditions she is willing, according to the advice of the Synod, to hold herself in *a proper subordination* to the Rev. Classis of Amsterdam. This *proper subordination*, or rather "Church Relationship" (Combination) she wants thus explained and understood.   It must include the power to erect Seminaries, to ordain, and henceforth to do all those things that an Assembly of neighboring Church officers in the Netherlands may do.   As her presupposed right, she desires, however, to enjoy the privilege to bring said "Relationship" under the following regulations:

1. The Coetus shall yearly communicate her Acts to the Rev. Classis by means of correspondence.

2. That when any important matter arises concerning which the Rev. (Coetus) Assembly needs special light, she shall lay such matter before the Rev. Classis and abide by her advice.

3. That in case of differences among us concerning doctrine or manner of life, which we cannot settle correctly or bring to a satisfactory termination, after regular process, that we may then present such a case, prepared in an orderly manner by the Rev. (Coetus) Assembly, before the Rev. Classis of Amsterdam, or, if necessary, before the High Rev. Synod.   That the Rev. (Coetus) Assembly binds itself, to allow the advice thus given, according to the circumstances of the dispute, to have the strength of a decisive verdict among us, so far as the laws of our said (British) kingdom permit. . . ."

Text—Hastings: *Ecclesiastical Records of the State of New York*, Vol. VI, pp. 3963-66.

Articles of Union, October, 1771

PRELIMINARIES

Whereas certain misconceptions concerning the bond of union between the churches in this country and those in Holland, have been the unhappy causes of the past troubles: In order, therefore, to prevent these in future, and in consequence of the advice and direction of the Rev. Classis of Amsterdam, in their last letter to us, we unite ourselves in one body, and we agree with each other to regulate our church government, and union with the mother church in Holland, in the following manner:

Article I.—Adherence to the Constitution of the Church

We adhere, in all things, to the constitution of the Netherland Reformed Church, as the same was established in the church orders of the Synod of Dordrecht, in the years 1618 and 1619.

Article II.—Consistories

The consistories shall always be appointed, and their business conducted agreeably to the constitution of the Netherland churches.

Article III.—Organization of the superior Church Judicatories

In addition to the above, we organize or establish according to the counsel and advice of the Rev. Classis of Amsterdam, approved in the Synod of North Holland, such ecclesiastical assemblies as are consistent with the government of the Netherland Church, and our relation to the same; which judicatories shall be distinguished by such names as shall hereafter be determined.

. . . .

Article XX.—Examinations, Preparation and Peremptions

For this general assembly, with the approbation of the Rev. Synod of North Holland and the Rev. Classis of Amsterdam, we assume the long wished for right of examining candidates for licensure and for the ministry, and also further to qualify those who are lawfully called, as the same is practised in the Netherlands.

. . . .

Article XXII.—Union with the Church of Holland

To preserve, in the best possible manner, the bond of union with our highly esteemed mother church (which we greatly desire,) there shall, first, be sent every year a complete copy of all the acts of our general assembly, signed by the Praeses and Scriba for the time being, to the Classis of Amsterdam, as duly named by the Synod of North Holland for that purpose.

Article XXIII.—Appeals concerning Doctrines

Secondly, Whenever differences may arise on important doctrines among the brethren, whether ministers or communicants, a decision on which might be matter of grievance to some, the case in difference shall be left to the judgment of the Rev. Classis, or if need be to the Rev. Synod of North Holland, according to whose decision the general assembly, as well as the condemned party, shall conform or act.

Article XXIV.—Depositions

In case a minister, on account of doctrine or life, shall be deposed and conceive himself aggrieved by such deposition, he shall have the liberty of laying his case before the Rev. Classis of Amsterdam, or through it before the Rev. Synod, for their judgment whether he may be called again, or not; and the general Assembly, with the deposed minister, shall be bound to submit to the judgment of the Reverend Classis. In the meantime, however, in consequence of the length of time required for deciding an unhoped for case, the congregation of the deposed minister, if they request it, shall be furnished with another pastor.

. . . .

Article XXVIII.—Professorate

Concerning the Professorate, we will act according to the advice of the Rev. Classis of Amsterdam. We will provisionally choose one or two professors to teach didactic, eleutic, exegetic, etc. theology, according to the received doctrines of our Low Dutch Reformed Church, to which office we, according to the judgment of the classis, will choose, on favorable terms, such divines from the Netherlands as are of acknowledged learning, piety, and orthodoxy, and immutably attached to the Netherland formulas of union, said Classis having promised to recommend suitable characters.

Article XXIX.—Further regulations respecting the Professorate

The professor or professors above mentioned, as soon as the wished for reconciliation in this country is obtained and finally established, shall be chosen and called on a sufficient salary, though not without the approbation of the general assembly, with this provision, that such professors shall not stand in any connection with English academies, but shall give lectures in their own dwellings, to such students only who can produce testimony that they have studied two or three years at a college or academy under approved teachers, and improved themselves in preparatory studies, such as the languages, philosophy, etc. Such professor or professors shall also preach once every month or fortnight, in Dutch or English, as well to assist the minister of the place where he or they reside as to afford the student a good model of preaching, in consequence of which the Rev. professor or professors shall be subject to the particular and general assemblies in the same manner as is already specified particularly of the ministers.

. . . .

Article XXX.—*Provisional Exception*

Nevertheless, since we, according to the condition stipulated by the Classis, can cherish no hopes of reaping the fruits of the above mentioned professorate for a long time to come, we are of opinion, as there are now a number of students with one or other minister, who probably will in a short time be fitted for the exam. prepar., that these students ought, in consequence of the great need of the churches, to be provisionally examined at the next meeting of our general assembly.

Article XXI.—*Schools under the care of Churches*

Finally, the respective congregations shall hereafter make it their business to establish public or private schools, in which under the direction of Consistories, instructions shall be given as well in the languages as in the fundamental principles or doctrines of the Reformed Dutch Church as the same are taught in our Low Dutch Churches.

. . . .

CONCLUDING ARTICLES

. . . .

Article XI

After giving each other the right hand of fellowship, the committee, as also the Rev. Consistory of New York, were openly and formally thanked for their friendly and brotherly services, and after fervent thanksgiving to God for this unexpected blessing, accompanied by ardent supplications to the throne of grace, for a further completion of this holy union work, as also for the prosperity and well-being of the church, they parted in peace, and love and joy.

Done at New York, Oct. 1771."

Text—Hastings: *Ecclesiastical Records of the State of New York*, Vol. VI, pp. 4212-4218.

CHAPTER IX

Bibliography

In "Some Account of the Province of Pennsylvania in America, . . . " (1681, reprint largely in Hazard "Register of Pennsylvania" Vol. 1, No. 20) William Penn outlined his thoughts on colonies and described the territory recently ceded to him for purposes of settlement. In the following year he gave additional information in "A Brief Account, . . . ". Of the same date is William Loddington's "Plantation Work the Work of this Generation, . . . " containing the Markham letters descriptive of the province as Markham saw it on his arrival (for these letters see "Pa. Mag. Hist. & Biog." Vol. VI, p. 175 f.). "Information and Direction to such Persons as are Inclined to America" prepared under the direction if not written (1682) by Penn may be consulted in "Pa. Mag. Hist. & Biog." Vol. IV, p. 329 f. The policy by which the "Free Society of Traders" proposed to colonize their tract may be seen in "The Articles . . . of Traders in Pennsylvania" (1682 "Pa. Mag. of Hist. & Biog." Vol. V, p. 37f. and Vol. XI, p. 175f.) "A Vindication of William Penn" (1683) by Philip Ford contains abstracts of some of Penn's earliest letters from the colony ("Pa. Mag. of Hist. & Biog." Vol. VI, p. 174 f.). Another important letter of Penn's (1683) giving his personal impressions of his proprietary may be consulted in Hazard's "Register" Vol. I, p. 433. "A Further Account" (1685) by William Penn is among the most important of the early tracts. "The Planter's Speech, . . . " (1684) of unknown authorship, and "Good Order Established in Pennsilvania and New Jersey" by Thomas Budd, (1685) outline the moral and educational ideals of the Quaker group (reprint, 1902, with introduction and notes by F. J. Shepard). "A Letter from Doctor More, . . . " (1687, "Pa. Mag. Hist. & Biog." Vol. IV, p. 447 f.), and "Some Letters, . . . " (1691, *ibid.*, IV, p. 189) show the growth of the colony at these dates. An Account of Pennsylvania and West New Jersey" (1698) by Gabriel Thomas (reprint, 1903, by C. T. Brady, with introduction) polemical though not misleading, and a "Beschreibung der Provintz

Pennsylvaniae " (1700) by F. D. Pastorius, an early German settler, have informing narratives written from entirely different viewpoints.

Historical work upon Pennsylvania began with Samuel Smith in "The History of the Colonies of New Jersey and Pennsylvania in America . . . to 1721." Undertaken at the request of the Quakers, this work shows breadth of interest and fair mindedness (for Pennsylvania section, see Hazard, "Register of Pennsylvania" Vols. VI and VII). "The History of Pennsylvania in North America from . . . 1681 till after the year 1742 with an Introduction respecting the Life of William Penn . . . " (1760-1770) by Robert Proud, possesses to this day a deservedly high reputation for its careful execution and rich documentary· material. A later (V vols. 1793-99) "Erdbeschreibung und Geschichte von America" by Professor Ebeling is to be rated among the standard histories (translation in part, "Register of Pennsylvania," Vol. I). A "History of Pennsylvania" (1829) by T. F. Gordon, strongly antagonistic to Penn, and lifeless in its style, has never been popular. To a serious student, "Historical Collections, . . . " (1846) by S. Day, and an "Illustrated History of the Commonwealth of Pennsylvania" (1876) by W. H. Egle, M. D. will not be found profitable. A "History of Pennsylvania" (1876) by W. M. Cornell is a mere compilation not always based on reliable sources. A "History of Proprietary Government in Pennsylvania" by W. R. Shepherd, ("Columbia Univ. Studies in History and Economics" Vol. VI, 1896) is a most satisfactory treatment. "Pennsylvania, Colonial and Federal" (1906) by H. M. Jenkins, editor-in-chief although highly popular embodies some documentary material. "Pennsylvania in American History" (1910) by S. W. Pennypacker has a few chapters worth consulting. "The Relations of Pennsylvania with the British Government, 1696-1765" (1911) by Winfred T. Root, is indispensable. An excellent bibliography is appended. "Chronicles of Pennsylvania—1688-1748" (II Vols. 1917) by Charles P. Keith is attractively written, and has several chapters dealing with ecclesiastical history.

From a large list of local histories the following are recommended as especially worthy of notice: "Annals of Philadelphia, . . . " (1842) by J. F. Watson; "History of Lancaster County" (1844) by I. D. Rupp, also (1869) by J. I. Mombert; "History of Northampton, Lehigh, Munroe . . . Schuylkill Counties" (1845) by I. D. Rupp; "History of Delaware County" (1862) by George Smith; "Chester and its Vicinity" (1877) by John H. Martin, also (1881) by J. S. Futhey and G. Cope; "History of Philadelphia" (III Vols. 1884) by J. Scharf and T Westcott.

On the peopling of Pennsylvania by European immigration, an extensive literature has developed within recent years. Of this the following is notable: "The Lutheran Movement in England" (revised edition, 1894) by H. E. Jacobs; "The Story of the Palatines" (1899) by S. H. Cobb; "The German and Swiss Settlements of Colonial Pennsylvania; A Study of the So-Called Pennsylvania Dutch" (1901) by Oscar Kuhns; "German Emigration to the American Colonies, its Cause, and the Distribution of the Emigrants" by A. D. Mellick Jr. ("Pa. Mag. Hist. & Biog." Vol. X, pp. 241-250, 375-391); "The Settlement of Germantown and the Causes which led to it" by S. W. Pennypacker (*ibid.*, Vol. IV, pp. 1-42); the same author's "Settlement of Pennsylvania . . . " ("Proc. & Addr. Pa.-German. Soc." Vol. IX, pp. 51-345); "Daniel Falckner's Curieuse Nachricht from Pennsylvania," the book that stimulated the great German immigration to Pennsylvania in the early years of the eighteenth century (translated and annotated by J. F. Sachse, *ibid.*, Vol. XIV, pp. 1-256); The "German Exodus to England in 1709" by F. R. Diffenderffer (*ibid.*, Vol. VII, pp. 257-414); "Religious Causes Inducive to German Emigration" by J. F. Sachse (*ibid.*, Vol. VII, pp. 115-198); the "German Immigration into Pennsylvania through the Port of Philadelphia and 'the Redemptioners' " by F. R. Diffenderffer (*ibid.*, Vol. X,. pp. 7-314); "German Emigration to America, 1709-1740" by H. E. Jacobs (*ibid.*, Vol. VIII, pp. 29-150); "The German Emigration from New York Province into Pennsylvania" by M. H. Richards (*ibid.*, Vol. IX, pp. 351-447); "The Swedish Settlements on the Delaware . . . 1638-1664" (II Vols. 1911) by Amandus Johnson, Ph. D.; "Immigration of the Irish Quakers into Pennsylvania, 1682-1750" with bibliography (1902) by Albert C. Meyers, M.D.; "The Early Welsh Quakers and their Emigration to Pennsylvania" by J. J. Levick ("Pa. Mag. Hist. & Biog." Vol. XVII, pp. 385-413); "Welsh Settlement of Pennsylvania" (1912) by C. H. Browning; "The Mennonite Emigration to Pennsylvania" by Dr. J. G. DeHoop Scheffer (translated with notes by S. W. Pennypacker, "Pa. Mag. Hist. & Biog." Vol. II, pp. 117-138;) "The Moravian Immigration to Pennsylvania 1734-1765" by J. W. Jordan (*ibid.*, Vol. XXXIII, pp. 228-248); "The German Moravian Settlements in Pennsylvania, 1735-1800" by Rev. Paul de Schweinitz (Proc. & Addr. Pa.-German. Soc." Vol. IV, pp. 53-73); "Swiss Emigration to the American Colonies in the Eighteenth Century" by A. B. Faust (Amer. Hist. Rev. Vol. XXII, No. 1).

The social and religious atmosphere in which the several religious groups had to conduct their work is presented in the following: "The

Domestic Life and Characteristics of the Pennsylvania German Pioneer" by F. J. Schantz ("Proc. & Addr. Pa.-German. Soc "Vol. X, pp. 5-97); "Lutheran Landmarks and Pioneers in America," a series of sketches of colonial times, (1913) by W. J. Finck; "German Religious Life in Colonial Times" (1906) by Lucy F. Bittinger (a good chapter on Moravians and Methodists).

As an introductory study of Lutheranism "The Founding of the German Churches in Pennsylvania" by J. H. Dubbs ("Pa. Mag. Hist. & Biog." Vol. XVII, pp. 241-262) is to be commended. On Swedish Lutheranism the standard work is that of Israel Acrelius entitled, "The History of New Sweden" (1759, translated by W. M. Reynolds, 1874). Then follow the works of E. L. Hazelius,"History of the American Lutheran Church from its Commencement in 1685 to the year 1742" (1846); C. W. Schaeffer, "Early History of the Lutheran Church in America" (New edition, 1868); E. J. Wolf, "The Lutherans in America" (1889) a translation of which into German by John Nicum (1891) has important supplementary material; A. L. Gräbner, "Geschichte der Lutherischen Kircke in America" (Vol. I to 1820, 1892, particularly valuable); H. E. Jacobs, "A History of the Evangelical Lutheran Church in the United States" ("Amer. Ch. Hist. Ser.," Vol. IV, 1893); Rev. T. E. Schmauk, "The Lutheran Church in Pennsylvania, 1638-1800" ("Proc. & Addr. Pa.-German. Soc." Vol. XI, pp. 15-355, also Vol. XII, pp. 357-576, with extensive bibliography).

"The Life and Times of H. M. Muhlenberg" (1856) by M. L. Stoever; also (1887) by W. J. Mann fill an important place.

Local studies that should not be overlooked are: "The Early History of the Tulpehocken Churches" by Rev. B. M. Schmucker ("Luth. Ch. Rev. Vol. I); "A Documentary History of the Old Red (Zion) Church . . . " by Rev. H. A. Weller ("Pubs. Hist. Soc Schuylkill County" Vol. II pp. 187-267); "The Lutheran Church in New Hanover (Falckner Swamp), Montgomery County" by Rev. J. J. Kline ("Proc. & Addr. Pa.-German. Soc." Vol. XX, pp. 7-444).

The educational work of this denomination is discussed in "A History of Education in Pennsylvania" (1866) by J. P. Wickersham; "The Charity School Movement in Colonial Pennsylvania" (1905) by S. E. Weber; "The Educational Work of the German Reformed and Lutheran Churches in Pennsylvania during the Colonial Period" (A. M. Dissertation, Univ. of Chicago, 1916) by I. S. Nowlan.

Source material is found in the "Nachrichten von den vereinigten . . . " (II Vols. 1750-1787, republished with notes, Vol. I, 1886 by Mann,

Schmucker and Germann, translated in part (1882) by C. W. Schaeffer); "The Hallische Nachrichten Series," (translations, 1881 by J. Oswald); and a "Documentary History of the Evangelical Lutheran Ministerium of Pennsylvania and Adjacent States—Proceedings of the Annual Conventions from 1748 to 1821" compiled and translated from records and archives (1898) by a Committee.

Further bibliographical directions may be found in "Sources for the History of the Lutheran Church in America" by J. G. Morris ("Luth. Ch. Rev. Vol. XIV).

On the German Reformed Church the salient facts are given by J. H. Dubbs in "A History of the Reformed Church, German" ("Amer. Ch. Hist. Ser." Vol. VIII, 1895). Four years later a "History of the Reformed Church in the United States, 1725-1792" by James I. Good sought to embody, though not always with accuracy, material then recently discovered. A subsequent work (1902) by Dubbs, "The Reformed Church in Pennsylvania" ("Proc. & Addr. Pa.-German. Soc." Vol. XI, pp. 1-349; also issued under separate cover) made revisions in harmony with the researches of Professors Dotterer and Hinke. It will be found highly satisfactory. The "Early History of the Reformed Church in Pennsylvania" (1906) by Daniel Miller, although especially adapted for untrained readers, is thoroughly abreast of the results of latest research. "Early Attempts at Church Union in America" by James I. Good (Papers Amer. Soc. Ch. History, Series II, Vol. II, pp. 105-114) deals with an otherwise neglected chapter in Pa. & New York history.

Biographical sketches of value are as follows. "The Life of Michael Schlatter" (1857) by Henry Harbaugh; "The Fathers of the German Reformed Church in Europe and America" (V Vols. 1857 f.) by Henry Harbaugh and D. Y. Heisler; "The Life of Conrad Weiser" (1876) by C. Z. Weiser; "Life and Times of Henry Antes" (1886) by E. McMinn; "Rev. John Philip Boehm" (1890) by H. S. Dotterer and more notably his "Life and Letters" edited (1916) by W. J. Hinke.

Considerable information is to be found in several local histories, notably "History of the Reformed Church in Philadelphia" (1776) by David Van Horne; "History of Berks and Lebanon Counties" (1844) by I. D. Rupp; "History of the Reformed Churches in Chester County" (1892) by J. L. Fluck; "The Early History of the First Reformed Church of Philadelphia, Pa. 1727-1734" by W. J. Hinke, ("Jour. Pres. Hist. Soc." Vol. II, pp. 292-313); "History of the Falckner Swamp Reformed Church . . . " (1904) by Rev. G. W. Roth; "The Early History of Wentz's Reformed Church, Montgomery County, Pa." by W. J. Hinke, ("Jour. Pres. Hist. Soc." Vol. III, pp. 332-346).

For investigative purposes the following are accessible: "Report of Rev. Jacob Lischy to Bishop Augustus G. Spangenberg" edited by W. J. Hinke ("Ref. Ch. Rev." Vols. IX and X); "Diary of Lischy's and Rausch's Journey Among the Reformed Congregations in Pennsylvania" edited by W. J. Hinke (*ibid.*, Vol. XI); "Letters of the Classis of Amsterdam to John Philip Boehm" ("Ecclesiastical Records of the State of New York" Vols. III and IV); "Letters and Reports of Rev. J. P. Boehm" edited by W. J. Hinke ("Jour. Pres. Hist. Soc." Vols. VI and VII); "Diary of the Rev. Michael Schlatter" June 1 to September 15, 1746, edited by W. J. Hinke ("Jour. Pres. Hist. Soc. Vol. III); "Minutes and Letters of the Coetus of the German Reformed Congregations in Pennsylvania 1747-1797, together with Three Preliminary Reports of Rev. John Philip Boehm, 1734-1744" (1903) edited by W. J. Hinke and others; and the "Hallische Nachrichten" (as above)

More detailed bibliographical information may be found in "Proc. & Addr. Pa. German. Soc." Vol. XI, p. 342 f.

On Quakerism one should begin with the accomplished early Quaker writer, Robert Barclay, whose most important work "Apology for the Church and People of God called in derision Quakers, . . ." (1676) gives a good exposition of Quaker beliefs. The history proper of Quakerism began with George Fox in "A Journal or Historical Account of His Life, Travels, Sufferings, ..."(1694) in several editions, of which that of Norman Penney, with introduction by T. Harvey (1911) is the most satisfactory both for its text and copious notes. Another good "Journal" (1713) comes from W. Edmundson who frequently visited America, and once accompanied Fox. The "Collections of the Sufferings of the People Called Quakers . . . " (II Vols. 1753) by Joseph Besse, although undisguisedly Quaker in its sympathies, is unbiassed. "The History of the Rise, Increase and Progress of the Christian People Called Quakers . . . " by William Sewel, a native of Amsterdam, designed to correct misrepresentations of the Quakers, is a work of primary importance. Written in Dutch (1717) it was soon after (1722) translated by the author into English. The "Portraiture of Quakerism" (III Vols. 1806) by Thomas Clarkson is concerned not so much with fortunes of Quakerism, as with its customs and religious practices. Compared with earlier works, the "History of the People Called Quakers" by John Gough has no particular merit except that it carries the narrative to a later date (1790). A student seeking to hurriedly possess himself of the salient features of Quakerism may profitably turn to the compact and interesting work of Charles Evans, M. D. "Friends in the Seventeenth Century"

(1875).   A more exhaustive and essentially reliable treatment is that of
Samuel M. Janney (IV Vols 2nd edition, 1867), "History of the Religious
Society of Friends from the Rise to the Year 1828"   "The History of
the Society of Friends in America" (II Vols. 1850-54) by James Bowden,
who had access to important manuscript material in Devonshire House,
contains several significant documents.   Well written and trustworthy,
this work is almost indispensable.   In the "American Church History
Series" (Vol. XII, 1894) also issued independently, (4th edition, 1905)
A. C. and R. T. Thomas have presented a brief well documented and
interesting narrative with an excellent bibliography.   "A Quaker Experiment in Government" (1898) by Isaac Sharpless gives a fairminded view
of the religious and political principles of the Quakers.   A recent history
superior in many respects to all the other short historics, is "The Quakers
in the American Colonies" (1911) by Rufus M. Jones, Isaac Sharpless, and
Amelia Gummere.   "The Quakers in Great Britain and America"(1913)
by Charles F. Holder has a few suggestive chapters dealing with the colonial period.   To one desirous of getting information as to Quaker church
organization, conduct of worship, and religious customs, "Quaker Strong-
holds" (1890) by Caroline E. Stephens will be found useful.

In addition to histories, there are several "Journals" that should be
kept in mind: "Journal of the Life of Thomas Story" (1747); "A Journal or Historical Account of the Life, Travels, and Christian Experiences
of . . . Thomas Chalkley" (2nd edition, 1761); "An Account of the
Life and Travels of John Fothergill" (1753); "An Account of the Life
Travels, . . . of Samuel Bownas" (2nd edition, 1795).

Of biographies of William Penn the earliest is a sketch attached to an
edition of his works appearing in 1726.   Usually attributed to Joseph
Besse, it has formed the basis for the more exhaustive later biographies.
"The Memoirs of the Private and Public Life of William Penn" (II
Vols. 1813) by Thomas Clarkson, a standard work though in small details
somewhat inaccurate, is concerned not so much with Pennsylvania as
with the larger Quaker interests of Penn.   Another standard biography
is that of S. M. Janney, "The Life of William Penn, with Selections from
his Correspondence and Autobiography."   Enriched with many of
Penn's letters, reprinted complete, it laid under contribution all the data
available at the time (1851).   A contemporary work by W. H. Dixon,
entitled "William Penn, an Historical Biography" is fascinatingly written, but in point of interpretation will not stand the closest scrutiny.
"William Penn, the Founder of Pennsylvania" (1882) by John Stough-
ton, gives some material not to be found in earlier biographies.

"Quaker and Courtier, the Life and Work of William Penn" (1907) by Mrs. Colquhoun Grant, and "William Penn, Founder of Pennsylvania" (1917) by J. W. Graham are popular recitals of facts already known. "The Penn and Logan Correspondence" (1700–1750, in "Memoirs, Hist. Soc. Pa." Vols. IX and X), and the "Penn Papers" form a vast repository for political affairs, as also for an intimate knowledge of Penn himself. Aspects of Penn's life are seen in "Memorials of the Life and Times of Sir William Penn" (II Vols. 1833) by Granville Penn; "The Private Life and Domestic Habits of William Penn" by J. F. Fisher (1836, "Memoirs, Hist. Soc. of Pa." Vol. III, Part II); and "William Penn's Travels in Holland and Germany" (1877) by Oswald Seidensticker ("Pa. Mag. Hist. & Biog." Vol. II, pp. 237–282).

"A Collection of the Works of William Penn" first appeared in 1726, and has been re-issued 1771, 1782, 1825. The "Brief Account of the Rise and Progress of the People Called Quakers, . . . " originally appeared in the preface to George Fox's "Journal." It has since appeared in several separate editions. Many of Penn's letters relating to Pennsylvania affairs may be located through consulting "Pa. Mag. of Hist. & Biog." Vol VI, p. 368.

A few miscellaneous studies of interest may be added: "The Attitude of the Quakers in the Provincial Wars" by Charles J. Stillé ("Pa. Mag. Hist. & Biog."Vol. X pp. 283-315); "Religious Tests in Provincial Pennsylvania" by the same author(*ibid.*,Vol. IX, pp. 365-406); "Some Account of the Conduct of the Religious Society of Friends towards the Indian Tribes, . . . " (1844).

For investigative purposes there is "The Friend" (1827 f.); the "Friends Miscellany" (1831f.); the "Friends Library" (1837, XIV vols.); the "Friends Review" (1847 f.); the "Minutes of the Yearly Meetings; the "Disciplines"; "Proceedings of the Conferences;" and "The Journal of the Friends Historical Society" (1903 f.).

Moravianism has been set forth by Rev. L. T. Reichel in the old but in no wise antiquated " . . . Early History of the Church of the United Brethren in North America, A.D. 1734-1748" ("Trans. of the Moravian Hist. Soc." Vol. III). "The History of the Church known as the Unitas Fratrum" (2nd edition, 1901) by Edmund de Schweinitz is a reliable work. In "A History of the Unitas Fratrum . . . " ("Amer. Ch. Hist. Series," Vol. VIII, 1895) Prof. J. T. Hamilton has compressed the essential facts into the compass of 77 pages. The same author's " . . . History of the Church known as the Moravian Church . . . during the Eighteenth and Nineteenth Centuries" (1900) is more exhaustive and meets every requirement. "A History of Bethlehem, Pennsylvania, 1741-1892, with Some Account of its Founders and Their Early Activity in America" (1903) by J. M. Levering is an excellent piece of work and almost serves the purpose of a history of Moravianism. The "Leben des Herrn Nicholaus Ludwig, Grafen und Herrn von Zinzendorf . . " (1772-1775) by A. G. Spangenberg (trans. by Samuel Jackson, with introductory preface by Rev. P. Latrobe, 1838) and the "Memorials of the Life of Peter Böhler, Bishop of the Church of the United Brethren" (1868) by Rev. J. P. Lockwood are important biographical monographs. A local study of interest is that of Abraham Ritter, "History of the Moravian Church in Philadelphia from its Foundation in 1742, to the Present Time. . . " (1857). The "Sketch of the Early History of Lititz, 1742-1775" by H. A. Brickenstein ("Trans. Mor. Hist. Soc." Vol. II, pp. 343-374) gives an interesting church diary. Sketches of several of the Fathers of the American Moravian church by Rev. E. de Schweinitz appear in the "Trans. Mor. Hist. Soc." Vol. II, pp. 145-269.

For the literature on Moravian missions among the Indians, see page 534f.

Source material is to be found in "Memorials of the Moravian Church" (1870) by W. C. Reichel, who cites documents of the period 1742-1757; Zinzendorf's "Die Büdingische Sammlung einiger in die Kirchen Historie einschlagender sonderlich neuen Schriften"; also his "Pennsylvanische Nachrichten von dem Reiche Christi"; "Transactions of the Moravian Historical Society, 1859-1892"; Fresenius, "Herrnhutische Nachrichten" Vol. I-XVI (1748-1753); and the "Journals of the Provincial Synods of the American Moravian Church North" 1847 f.

For Otterbein the "Life of Rev. Philip William Otterbein" (1884) by A. W. Drury is very satisfactory. The history of the United Brethren in Christ, organized in 1789, has been written by W. Hanby "History of the Church of the United Brethren in Christ from 1825 to 1850" (1851); J. Lawrence "History of the Church of the United Brethren in Christ" (II Vols. 1860-61, I Vol. 1888); and D. Berger "History of the Church of the United Brethren in Christ" ("Amer. Ch. Hist. Series," Vol. XII, 1894).

The Mennonites have received treatment in the following studies: "History of the Mennonites" (1887) by Daniel K. Cassel; "Mennonites of America" (Doctoral Dissertation, 1909) by C. Henry Smith; "Social Attitudes among the Mennonites" (A. M. Dissertation, Univ. of Chicago, 1915) by J. W. Hoover.

In "The German Pietists of Provincial Pennsylvania" (1895) by Julius F. Sachse, there is an interesting and exhaustive study of "The Woman in the Wilderness" (Part I) and "The Hermits on the Wissahichon" (Part II). "Justus Falckner, Mystic and Scholar" (1903) by the same author is a fine interpretation. In "The German Sectarians of Pennsylvania" (Vol. I, 1708-1742, 1899; Vol. II, 1742-1800, 1900) the same writer has given a thorough treatment to the Ephrata Cloister and the Dunkers. On the latter there is a noteworthy contribution by George N. Falkenstein, "The German Baptist Brethren or Dunkers" ("Proc. & Addr. Pa.-German. Soc." Vol. X, pp. 5-147). Other studies on the Dunkers are as follows: "A History of the German Baptist Brethren in Europe and America" (1899) by Martin G. Brumbaugh; "History of the Tunkers and the Brethren Church" (embracing the Church of the Brethren, Seventh Day German Baptists, the German Baptists, the Old German Baptists, and the Brethren Church, 1901) by H R. Holsinger; "The Dunkers, A Sociological Interpretation" (1906) by John L. Gillin.

On the Seventh Day German Baptists, besides the work of Sachse there is a good study by C. F Randolph in the "Seventh Day Baptists in Europe and America . . Historical Papers . " (1902) Vol. II, pp. 936-1257. The "history of Lancaster County" by Mombert, and also by Rupp (see above) have sections that deal with this sect. Short articles are as follows: "A Colonial Monastery" by Oswald W. Seidensticker ("Century Mag." Dec. 1881); "A Peculiar People" by Howard Pyle ("Harpers Mag." Oct. 1889); "The Old Cloister of Ephrata" by R. D. Vol Neida ("Farm and Fireside" March, 1906).

"The Chronicon Ephratense . . . " to which all investigators make frequent reference, may be consulted in a translation by J. M. Hark, D.D. (1889).

On the Schwenkfelders, a thorough piece of work has been done by Howard W. Kriebel entitled "The Schwenkfelders in Pennsylvania" ("Proc. & Addr.-Pa. German Soc.," Vol XIII, pp 1-225). A good bibliography is added.

For the Episcopalians, Presbyterians, Baptists, and Roman Catholics, bibliographical suggestions will be found in chapters XIII, XIV, XV and XVI respectively.

DOCUMENTS

I *THE FUNDAMENTALL CONSTITUTIONS OF PENN-SYLVANIA AS THEY WERE DRAWN UP SETTLED AND SIGNED BY WILLIAM PENN PROPRIEATY AND GOVER-*

*NOUR, AND CONSENTED TO AND SUBSCRIBED BY ALL
THE FIRST ADVENTURERS AND FREE HOLDERS OF THAT
PROVINCE AS THE GROUND AND RULE OF ALL FUTURE
GOVERNMENT*

As an early, if not the earliest attempt of Penn at constitution making,
this document reflects the ideal to which the Proprietor steadfastly adhered.

Only religious clauses are inserted.

The Preamble or Introduction

When it pleased Almighty God, the Creator and upholder of all things, to make
man his great Governour of the World, he did not only endue him with excellent knowledge but an upright mind, so that his power over the Creation was ballanc'd by an
inward uprightness, that he might use it Justly: then was ye Law of light and truth
writt in his heart, and that was ye Guide and keeper of his Innocency, there was
not need of any Externall precepts to direct or terrify him; but when he leant his
ear to an other voice, and followed his lust, and did the thing he was forbidden of God,
the law was added, that is, the externall law came to awe and terrify such as would not
do the thing that was just according to the righteous law within themselves; thus transgression introduced and occasioned the outward law, and that, Govern^t, and both
Magistracy, that thos that would not answer the righteous law within, might be compelled by an Impartiall Execution ot the righteous law without: wherefore the Apostle
made it the end of Magistracy, to be a terror to evill doers, and a praise to them
that do well.

Good Government then, is a Constitution of Just laws wisely sett together for the
well ordering of men in society, to prevent all Corruption or Justly to Correct it, wherein it is most evident That the Governours and Governed have but one interest by the
Constitution: to witt preserving of right to all, and punishing corruption in all, which
is the end of Government, and Consequently of Governours so that if any Governours
shall sett up another Interest to themselves then that which tends to preserving right
to all and punishing evill in all; the Contradict the Constitution, and instead of serving
Government, makes Government only serve to their avarice or Ambition this is that
Corruption in man kind which Government is by Consent of all establish to Prevent.
If then Government it selfe be subservient to an higher end, to witt the generall good,
much more is it reasonable to beleive that all Instruments and Forms of Government
are to be subjected to that end, to which government it selfe is but a means.

. . . .

I. *Constitution*

Considering that it is impossible that any People or Government should ever prosper, where men render not unto God, that which is Gods, as well as to Caesar that
which is Caesers; and also perseiveing the disorders and Mischeifs that attend those
places where force in matters of faith and worship, and seriously reflecting upon the
tenure of the new and Spirituall Government, and that both Christ did not use force
and that he did expressly forbidd it in his holy Religion, as also that the Testimony of
his blessed Messengers was, that the weapons of the Christian warfare were not Carnall
but Spirituall; And further weighing that this unpeopled Country can never be planted

if there be not due encouragement given to sober people of all sorts to plant, & that they will not esteem any thing a sufficient encouragement where they are not assured but that after all the Hazards of the sea, and the troubles Of a Wilderness, the Labour of their hands and sweet of their browes may be made the forfeit of their Conscience, and they and their wives and Children ruin'd because they worship god in some different way from that which may be more generally owned. Therefore, In reverence to God the Father of lights and Spirits the Author as well as object of all divine knowledge, faith and worship I do hereby declare for me and myn and establish it for the first fundamentall of the Government of my Country, that every Person that does or shall reside therein shall have and enjoy the Free Prossession of his or her faith and exersise of worsip towards God, in such way and manner As every Person shall in Conscience beleive is most acceptable to God and so long as every such Person useth not this Christian liberty to Licentiousness, that is to say to speak loosly and prophainly of God Christ or Religion, or to Committ any evill in their Conversation, he or she shall be protected in the enjoyment of the aforesaid Christian liberty by yᵉ civill Magistrate.

II. *Constitution*

Because Corruption of manners and remissness in Magistrates to punish Euill doers, by which means virtue often falls in the streetes, have ever provoked Gods heavy displeasure against both Governours and People and that I cannot hope it should prosper better with me and myn and the People that doe or shall Inhabit this Country if an effectuall Care be not taken to prevent or appeas the wrath of God by an impartiall Execution of Justice upon every evill doer according to the law provided in such Cases; Therefore I for me and myn declare and Es[tablish] For the second Fundamentall of the Government of this Country, that all thos laws which relate to prevention or Correction of vice and injustice be impartially and vigorously executed, and that those Magistrates that doe not in their respective Charges vigilantly and impartially execute all such laws to the terror of evill doers, and praise of those that doe well; *shall be reputed and Marked as breakers of the Fundamentall Constitutions of the Country, and therein as well publique enemys to God as the people, and never to bare office till they had given good Testimonj of their repentance.*

. . . .

XV. *Constitution*

Since the due Proportion of Rewards and Punishmᵗˢ the wisdom and Justice of Government and that the example be of Gods law as well as the reason of the thing, guide all men to beleive that to shed mans blood and take away his life for Worldly goods, is a very hard thing; especially considering the tenderness of the holy Mercifull Christian Law, and Considering the little reformation this severity brings, and that it tempts the theif to be a murderer, when the Punishment is the same, to kill whom he robbs that so he may not discover or Prosecute him that Robbs him, which insteed of makeing theivs afraid may Constrain them to destroy good men therefore I do for me and my hereby Declare and establish for the 15th Fundamentall of the Government of this Province, that no Person committing Felony within the limitts thereof shall dye for the same. . .

. . . .

XIX. *Constitution*

Because all may be usefull and beneficiall in evidence to the Publique after the example of thos Countrys that Comply with the tenderness of their Conciences that

cant take any Oath, and yet are often the only Persons   to prove either theift murder, Titles of land wills &c: and having reflected . . . . .
. . . . that shutting out Oaths there would be the best way to shutt all loos and vain swearing, out of the Country, I do for me and myn hereby declare and Establish for the nineteenth Fundamentall of the Government of this Province that all evidence shall be by subscribsion upon record after this forme.

I A B do from the very bottom of my heart hereby engage and Promise in the Presence of God and the Coart to declare the whole truth, and nothing but the truth, in y matter I am to be inquired upon wittness my hand this——— of —————— in y year A.B.

. . . .

Text—*Pennsylvania Magazine of History*, Vol. XX, pp. 284-297.

II. *PENN'S PROPOSALS TO ADVENTURERS*

"Colonies, then, are the seeds of nations begun and nourished by the care of wise and populous countries, as conceiving them best for the increase of human stock, and beneficial for commerce.

"Some of the wisest men in history have justly taken their fame from this design and service. We read of the reputation given on this account to Moses, Joshua, and Caleb, in Scripture records; and what renown the Greek story yields to Lycurgus, Theseus, and those Greeks that planted many parts of Asia; nor is the Roman account wanting of instances to the credit of that people. . .

"Nor did any of these ever dream it was the way of decreasing their people or wealth, for the cause of the decay of any of those states or empires was not their plantations, but their luxury and corruption of manners; for when they grew to neglect their ancient discipline, that maintained and rewarded virtue and industry, and addicted themselves to pleasure and effeminacy, they debased their spirits and debauched their morals, from whence ruin did never fail to follow to any people. With justice, therefore, I deny the vulgar opinion against plantations, that they weaken England; they have manifestly enriched, and so strengthened her, which I briefly evidence thus:

"1st. Those that go into a foreign plantation, their industry there is worth more than if they stayed at home, the product of their labour being in commodities of a superior nature to those of their country. For instance, what is an improved acre in Jamaica or Barbadoes worth to an improved acre in England? We know it is three times the value, and the product of it comes for England, and is usually paid for in English growth and manufacture. . .

"2d. More being produced and imported than we can spend here, we export it to other countries in Europe, which brings in money, or the growth of those countries, which is the same thing; and this is the advantage of the English merchants and seamen.

"3d. Such as could not only not marry here, but hardly live and allow themselves clothes, do marry there, and bestow thrice more in all necessaries and conveniences, (and not a little in ornamental things too,) for themselves, their wives and children, both as to apparel and household stuff, which coming out of England, I say it is impossible that England should not be a considerable gainer.

"4th. But let it be considered that the plantations employ many hundreds of shipping, and many thousands of seamen, which must be, in divers respects, an advantage to England, being an island, and by nature fitted for navigation above any country in Europe. This is followed by other depending trades, as shipwrights, carpenters, sawyers, hewers, trunnelmakers, joiners, slop sellers, drysalters, iron-workers, the Eastland merchants, timber sellers, and victuallers, with many more trades which hang upon navigation; . . . But it is further said, they injure England, in that they draw away too many of the people, for we are not so populous in the countries as formerly. I say there are other reasons for that,

". . . These and the like evils are the true grounds of the decay of our people in the country, to say nothing of plague and wars; towns and cities cannot complain of the decay of people, being more replenished than ever, especially London, which, with reason, helps the countryman to this objection. And though some do go to the plantations, yet, numbering the parishes in England, and computing how many live more than die, and are born than buried, there goes not over to all the plantations a fourth part of the yearly increase of the people, and when they are there, they are not (as I said before) lost to England, since they furnish them with much clothes, household stuff, tools, and the like necessaries, and that in greater quantities than here their condition could have needed, or they could have bought, being there well to pass, that were but low here, if not poor; and now masters of families too, when here they had none, and could hardly keep themselves; and very often it happens that some of them, after their industry and success there have made them wealthy, they return and empty their riches into England, one in this capacity being able to buy out twenty of what he was when he went over.

. . . .

"To conclude, I desire all my dear country folks, who may be inclined to go into those parts, to consider seriously the premises, as well the present inconveniences, as future ease and plenty, that so none may move rashly, or from a fickle, but solid mind, having, above all things an eye to the providence of God, in the disposal of themselves. And I would further advise all such at least to have the permission, if not the good liking of their near relations, for that is both natural, and a duty incumbent upon all, and by this means will natural affection be preserved, and a friendly and profitable correspondence be maintained between them. In all which I beseech Almighty God to direct us, that his blessing may attend our honest endeavour, and then the consequence of all our undertaking will turn to the glory of his great name, and the true happiness of us and our posterity. Amen. "William Penn."

Text—Hazard: *Annals of Pennsylvania, 1609-1682*, pp. 505-513.

III. *THE GREAT LAW, DECEMBER 10/17, 1682*

In accordance with the Frame of Government drawn up by Penn and his associates in England, an Assembly convened at Chester, December 1682, and adopted a code of laws known as the Great Law. The following clauses relating to religion and morals may be profitably studied beside corresponding codes of the other colonies.

Whereas the glory of Almighty God, and the good of mankind, is the reason and end of government, and therefore government, in itself, is a venerable ordinance of God; and forasmuch as it is principally desired and intended by the proprietary and governor, and the freemen of the province of Pennsylvania, and territories thereunto belonging, to make and establish such laws as shall best preserve true Christians and civil liberty, in opposition to all unchristian, licentious, and unjust practices, whereby God may have his due, Caesar his due, and the people their due, from tyranny and oppression of the one side, and insolency and licentiousness of the other, so that the best and firmest foundation may be laid for the present and future happiness of both the governor and people of this province and territories aforesaid, and their posterity.—Be it therefore enacted, by William Penn, proprietary and governor, by and with the advice and consent of the deputies of the freemen of this province, and counties aforesaid, in assembly met, and by the authority of the same, that these following chapters and paragraphs shall be the laws of Pennsylvania and the territories thereof.

1. "Almighty God being only Lord of conscience, father of lights and spirits, and the author as well as object of all divine knowledge faith, and worship, who only can enlighten the mind, and persuade and convince the understanding of people, in due reverence to his sovereignty over the souls of mankind. It is enacted by the authority aforesaid, that no person now or at any time hereafter living in this province, who shall confess and acknowledge one Almighty God to be the creator, upholder, and ruler of the world, and that professeth him or herself obliged in conscience to live peaceably and justly under the civil government, shall in anywise be molested or prejudiced for his or her conscientious persuasion or practice, nor shall he or she at any time be compelled to frequent or maintain any religious worship, place, or ministry whatever, contrary to his or her mind, but shall freely and fully enjoy his or her Christian liberty in that respect, without any interruption or reflection; and if any person shall abuse or deride any other for his or her different persuasion and practice in matter of religion, such shall be looked upon as a disturber of the peace, and be punished accordingly. But to the end that looseness, irreligion, and atheism may not creep in under pretence of conscience, in this province, be it further enacted by the authority aforesaid, that according to the good example of the primitive Christians, and for the ease of the creation, every first day of the week, called the Lord's Day, people shall abstain from their common toil and labour, that whether masters, parents, children, or servants, they may the better dispose themselves to read the Scriptures of truth at home, or to frequent such meetings of religious worship abroad as may best suit their respective persuasions.

2. "And be it further enacted, by the authority aforesaid, that all officers and persons commissionated and employed in the service of the government of this province, and all members and deputies elected to serve in assembly thereof, and all that have right to elect such deputies, shall be such as profess and declare they believe in Jesus Christ to be the Son of God, and Saviour of the world, and that are not convicted of ill-fame, or unsober and dishonest conversation, and that are of one and twenty years of age at least. And be it further enacted, by the authority aforesaid, that whosoever shall swear, in their conversation, by the name of God, or Christ, or Jesus, being legally convicted thereof, shall pay for every such offence five shillings, or suffer five days' imprisonment in the house of correction, at hard labour, to the behoof of the public, and be fed with bread and water only, during that time.

3. "And be it further enacted, by the authority aforesaid, that whosoever shall swear by any other thing or name, and is legally convicted thereof, shall, for every such offence, pay half a crown, or suffer three days' imprisonment in the house of correction, at hard labour, having only bread and water for their sustenance.

4. "And be it further enacted, by the authority aforesaid, for the better preventing of corrupt communication, that whosoever shall speak loosely and profanely of Almighty God, Christ Jesus, the Holy Spirit, or the Scriptures of truth, and is legally convicted thereof, shall, for every such offence, pay five shillings, or suffer five days' imprisonment in the house of correction, at hard labour, to the behoof of the public, and be fed with bread and water only, during that time.

5. "And be it further enacted, by the authority aforesaid, that whosoever shall, in their conversation at any time, curse himself or another, or any thing belonging to himself or any other, and is legally convicted thereof, shall pay for every such offence five shillings, or suffer five days' imprisonment, as aforesaid.

6. "And be it further enacted, by the authority aforesaid, that if any person shall, with malice or premeditation, kill, or be accessory to the death of another person, man, woman, or child, being legally convicted thereof, shall, according to the law of God and all nations, suffer death; and that the estates of all capital offenders shall go one-half to the next of kin of the sufferer, and the remainder to the next kin of the criminal.

7. "And be it further enacted, by the authority aforesaid, that all persons guilty of manslaughter, or chance-medley, shall be punished according to the nature and circumstance of the offence.

8. "And be it further enacted, by the authority aforesaid, that whosoever defileth the marriage-bed, by lying with another woman or man than their own wife or husband, being legally convicted thereof, shall, for the first offence, be publicly whipped, and suffer one whole year's imprisonment in the house of correction, at hard labour, to the behoof of the public, and longer, if the magistrate see meet; and both he and the woman to be liable to a bill of divorcement, if required by the grieved husband or wife, within the said term of one whole year after conviction; and for the second offence, imprisonment in manner aforesaid during life; and if the party with whom the husband or wife shall defile their beds, be unmarried, for the first offence they shall suffer half a year's imprisonment, in the manner aforesaid; and for the second offence, imprisonment for life.

. . . .

13. "And be it further enacted, by the authority aforesaid, that whosoever shall be convicted of having two wives, or two husbands, shall be imprisoned all their lifetime in the house of correction, at hard labour, to the behoof of his former wife or children, or her former husband or children; and if a man or woman, being unmarried, do knowingly marry the husband or wife of another person, he or she shall be punished after the same manner aforesaid.

. . . .

40. "And be it further enacted, by the authority aforesaid, that the days of the week, and the months of the year, shall be called as in Scripture, and not by heathen names, (as are vulgarly used) as, the first, second, and third days of the week; and first, second, and third months of the year, &c., beginning with the day called Sunday, and the month called March.

Text—Hazard: *Annals of Pennsylvania, 1609-1682*, pp. 619-628.

IV. *THE CHARTER OF PRIVILEGES, OCTOBER 28, NOVEMBER 8, 1701*

Upon his return to Pennsylvania in 1699 to quiet dissensions, Penn consented to the appointment of a committee of the Council to draw up

ι new charter for the colony.   This charter, with the religious clauses as
ınder, remained in force until 1776.

First,

Because no People can be truly happy, tho' under the greatest Enjoyment of
ivil Liberties, if abridged of the Freedom of their Consciences, as to their Religous
'rofession and Worship: And Almighty God being the only Lord of Conscience,
'ather of Lights and Spirits; and the Author as well as Object of all divine Knowleidge,
'aith and Worship, who only doth enlighten the Minds, and persuade and convince
he Understandings of People, I do hereby grant and declare, That no Ferson or Per-
ons, inhabiting in this Province or Territories, who shall confess and acknowledge One
lmighty God, the Creator, Upholder and Ruler of the World; and profess him, or
hemselves, obliged to live quietly under the civil Government, shall be in any Case
iolested or perjudiced, in his or their Person or Estate, because of his or their con-
cientious Perswasion or Practice, nor be compelled to frequent or maintain any religous Worship, Place or Ministry, contrary to his or their Mind, or to do or suffer any
ther Act or Thing, contrary to their religious Perswasion.

AND that all Persons who also profess to believe in *Jesus Christ*, the Saviour of the
Vorld, shall be capable (notwithstanding their other Perswasions and Practices in
'oint of Conscience and Religion to) serve this Government in any Capacity, both
egislatively and executively, he or they solemnly promising, when lawfully required,
llegiance to the King as Sovereign, and Fidelity to the Proprietary and Governor,
nd taking the Attests as now established by the Law made at Newcastle, in the Year
'ne *Thousand* and *Seven Hundred*, intituled, *An Act directing the Attests of several
fficers and Ministers, as now amended and confirmed this present Assembly.*

.   .   .   .

AND no Act, Law or Ordinance whatsoever shall, at any Time hereafter, be made
r done, to alter, change or diminish the Form or Effect of this Charter, or of any
'art or Clause therein, contrary to the true Intent and Meaning thereof, without the
'onsent of the Governor for the Time being, and Six Parts of Seven of the Assembly
iet.

BUT because the Happiness of Mankind depends so much upon the Enjoying of
iberty of their Consciences as aforesaid, I do hereby solemnly declare, promise and
rant, for me, my Heirs and Assigns, That the first Article of this Charter relating to
iberty of Conscince, and every Part and Clause therein, according to the true Intent
nd Meaning thereof, shall be kept and remain, without any Alteration, inviolably for
ver.

Text—*Votes and Proceedings of the House of Representatives of Pennsylvania*, I,
'art II; pp. 1-111.

V. *THE CONFESSION OF THE SOCIETY OF FRIENDS, COMMONLY CALLED QUAKERS.* A.D. *1675.*

*To the Clergy, of what sort soever, unto whose hands these may come;
But more particularly*

'o *the Doctors, Professors, and Students of Divinity in the Universities and Schools
of Great Britain, whether Prelatical, Presbyterian, or any other;*

Robert Barclay, a Servant of the Lord God, and one of those who in derision are called Quakers, wisheth unfeigned repentance, unto the acknowledgment of the Truth.

"*Friends*,—Unto you these following propositions are offered; in which, they being read and considered in the fear of the Lord, you may perceive that simple, naked truth, which man by his wisdom hath rendered so obscure and mysterious that the world is even burthened with the great and voluminous tractates which are made about it, and by their vain jangling and commentaries, by which it is rendered a hundred-fold more dark and intricate than of itself it is: which great learning, so accounted of to wit, your school divinity, which takcth up almost a man's whole lifetime to learn, brings not a whit nearer to God, neither makes any man less wicked, or more righteous than he was. Therefore hath God laid aside the wise and learned, and the disputers of this world, and hath chosen a few despicable and unlearned instruments, as to letter-learning, as he did fishermen of old, to publish his pure and naked truth, and to free it of those mists and fogs wherewith the clergy hath clouded it, that the people might admire and maintain them. And among several others, whom God hath chosen to make known these things—seeing I also have received, in measure, grace to be a dispenser of the same gospel—it seemed good unto me, according to my duty, to offer unto you these propositions; which, though short, yet are weighty, comprehending much and declaring what the true ground of knowledge is, even of that knowledge which leads to Life Eternal; which is here witnessed of, and the testimony thereof left unto the Light of Christ in all your consciences.

Farewell,

R. B.

. . . .

The Second Proposition

Concerning Immediate Revelation

. . . which revelations of God by the Spirit, whether by outward voices and appearances, dreams, or inward objective manifestations in the heart, were of old the formal object of their faith, and remain yet so to be; since the object of the saints faith is the same in all ages, though set forth under divers administrations. More over, these divine inward revelations, which we make absolutely necessary for the building up of true faith, neither do nor can ever contradict the outward testimony of the Scriptures, or right and sound reason. Yet from hence it will not follow tha these divine revelations are to be subjected to the examination, either of the outward testimony of the Scriptures or of the natural reason of man, as to a more noble or cer tain rule or touchstone; for this divine revelation and inward illumination is tha which is evident and clear of itself, forcing, by its own evidence and clearness, the well disposed understanding to assent, irresistibly moving the same thereunto. . . .

The Third Proposition

Concerning the Scriptures

From these revelations of the Spirit of God to the saints have proceeded th Scriptures of truth, which contain: 1. A faithful historical account of the actings c God's people in divers ages, with many singular and remarkable providences attendin them. 2. A prophetical account of several things, whereof some are already past and some yet to come. 3. A full and ample account of all the chief principles of th doctrine of Christ, held forth in divers precious declarations, exhortations, and sentences, which, by the moving of God's Spirit, were at several times, and upon sundry occasions, spoken and written unto some churches and their pastors: nevertheless, because they are only a declaration of the fountain, and not the fountain itself, therefore they are not to be esteemed the principal ground of all truth and knowledge, nor yet the adequate primary rule of faith and manners. Nevertheless, as that which giveth a true and faithful testimony of the first foundation, they are and may be esteemed a secondary rule, subordinate to the Spirit, from which they have all their excellency and certainty. . . .

. . . .

The Sixth and Tenth Propositions

According to which principle (or hypothesis), all the objections against the universality of Christ's death are easily solved, neither is it needful to recur to the ministry of angels, and those other miraculous means which, they say, God makes use of, to manifest the doctrine and history of Christ's passion unto such, who, living in those places of the world where the outward preaching of the gospel is unknown, have well improved the first and common grace; for hence it well follows, that as some of the old philosophers might have been saved, so also may now some—who by providence are cast into those remote parts of the world where the knowledge of the history is wanting be made partakers of the divine mystery, if they receive and resist not that grace, a manifestation whereof is given to every man to profit withal.' This certain doctrine then being received, to wit, that there is an evangelical and saving light and grace in all, the universality of the love and mercy of God towards mankind—both in the death of his beloved Son, the Lord Jesus Christ, and in the manifestation of the light in the heart—is established and confirmed against all the objections of such as deny it. . . .

As by this gift, or light of God all true knowledge in things spiritual is received and revealed; so by the same, as it is manifested and received in the heart, by the strength and power thereof, every true minister of the gospel is ordained, prepared, and supplied in the work of the ministry; and by the leading, moving, and drawing thereof ought every evangelist and Christian pastor to be led and ordered in his labor and work of the gospel, both as to the place where, as to the persons to whom, and as to the times when he is to minister. Moreover, those who have this authority may and ought to preach the gospel, though without human commission or literature; as, on the other hand, those who want the authority of this divine gift, however learned or authorized by the commissions of men and churches, are to be esteemed but as deceivers, and not true ministers of the gospel. Also, who have received this holy and unspotted gift, 'as they have freely received, so are they freely to give,' without hire or bargaining, far less to use it as a trade to get money by it: yet if God hath called any from their employments or trades, by which they acquire their livelihood, it may be lawful for such, according to the liberty which they feel given them in the Lord, to receive such temporals—to wit, what may be needful to them for meat and clothing —as are freely given them by those to whom they have communicated spirituals.

The Eleventh Proposition
Concerning Worship

All true and acceptable worship to God is offered in the inward and immediate moving and drawing of his own Spirit, which is neither limited to places, times, or persons; for though we be to worship him always, in that we are to fear before him, yet as to the outward signification thereof in prayers, praises, or preachings, we ought not to do it where and when we will, but where and when we are moved thereunto by the secret inspirations of his Spirit in our hearts, which God heareth and accepteth of, and is never wanting to move us thereunto, when need is, of which he himself is the alone proper judge. All other worship then, both praises, prayers, and preachings, which man sets about in his own will, and at his own appointment, which he can both begin and end at his pleasure, do or leave undone, as himself sees meet, whether they be a prescribed form, as a liturgy, or prayers conceived extemporarily, by the natural strength and faculty of the mind, they are all but superstitions, will-worship, and abominable idolatry in the sight of God; which are to be denied, rejected ,and separated from, in this day of his spiritual arising; however it might have pleased him— who winked at the times of ignorance, with respect to the simplicity and integrity of some, and of his own innocent seed, which lay as it were buried in the hearts of men, under the mass of superstition—to blow upon the dead and dry bones, and to raise some breathings, and answer them, and that until the day should more clearly dawn and break forth.

The Twelfth Proposition
Concerning Baptism

As there is one Lord and one faith, so there is 'one baptism, which is not the putting away the filth of the flesh, but the answer of a good conscience before God, by the resurrection of Jesus Christ.' And this baptism is a pure and spiritual thing, to wit, the baptism of the Spirit and Fire, by which we are buried with him, that, being washed and purged from our sins, we may 'walk in newness of life;' of which the baptism of John was a figure, which was commanded for a time, and not to continue forever.

As to the baptism of infants, it is a mere human tradition, for which neither precept nor practice is to be found in all the Scripture.

The Thirteenth Proposition
Concerning the Communion, or Participation of
the Body and Blood of Christ

The communion of the body and blood of Christ is inward and spiritual, which is the participation of his flesh and blood, by which the inward man is daily nourished in the hearts of those in whom Christ dwells, of which things the breaking of bread by Christ with his disciples was a figure, which they even used in the Church for a time, who had received the substance, for the cause of the weak; even as 'abstaining from things strangled, and from blood;' the washing one another's feet, and the anointing of the sick with oil; all which are commanded with no less authority and solemnity than the former; yet seeing they are but the shadows of better things, they cease in such as have obtained the substance.

The Fourteenth Proposition
Concerning the Power of the Civil Magistrate, in Matters
Purely Religious, and Pertaining to the Conscience

Since God hath assumed to himself the power and dominion of the conscience who alone can rightly instruct and govern it, therefore it is not lawful for any whatsoever, by virtue of any authority or principality they bear in the government of this world, to force the consciences of others, and therefore all killing, banishing, fining, imprisoning, and other such things, which men are afflicted with, for the alone exercise of their conscience, or difference in worship or opinion, proceedeth from the spirit of Cain, the murderer, and is contrary to the truth; provided always that no man, under the pretense of conscience, prejudice his neighbor in his life or estate, or do any thing destructive to, or inconsistent with, human society; in which case the law is for the transgressor, and justice to be administered upon all, without respect of person.

The Fifteenth Proposition
Concerning Salutations and Recreations, etc.

Seeing the chief end of all religion is to redeem man from the spirit and vain conversation of this world, and to lead into inward communion with God, before whom, if we fear always, we are accounted happy, therefore all the vain customs and habits thereof, both in word and deed, are to be rejected and forsaken by those who come to this fear; such as the taking off the hat to a man, the bowings and cringings of the body, and such other salutations of that kind, with all the foolish and superstitious formalities attending them; all which man has invented in his degenerate state, to feed his pride in the vain pomp and glory of this world; as also the unprofitable plays, frivolous recreations, sportings, and gamings which are invented to pass away the precious time, and divert the mind from the witness of God in the heart, and from the living sense of his fear, and from that evangelical Spirit wherewith Christians ought to be leavened, and which leads into sobriety, gravity, and godly fear; in which, as we abide, the blessing of the Lord is felt to attend us in those actions in which we are necessarily engaged in order to the taking care for the sustenance of the outward man.

Text—Schaff: *The Creeds of Christendom* . . . Vol. III, pp. 789-798.

VI. *THE MENNONITES—ARTICLES OF FAITH*

1. Of God, of the Creation of all Things, and of Man.

. . . .

II. Of the Fall of Man.

. . . .

III. Of the Restoration of Man by the Promise of Christ's Coming.

. . . .

IV. Of the Coming of Christ and the Cause of his Coming.

. . . .

V. Of the Law of Christ, the Gospel of the New Testament.

. . . .

VI. Of Repentance and Reformation.

. . . .

VII. Of Baptism.—As regards Baptism, we confess that all penitent believers, who by faith, regeneration and renewing of the Holy Ghost are made one with God and written in heaven, must, upon their Scriptural confession of faith and reformation of life, be baptized with water, in the name of the Father, and of the Son, and of the Holy Ghost, agreeably to the doctrine and command of Christ and the usage of his Apostles to the burying of their sins, and thus be received into fellowship with the saints, whereupon they must learn to observe all things which the Son of God taught, left to and commanded his disciples.

VIII. Of the Church of Christ.

. . . .

IX. Of the Election and Office of Teachers, Deacons and Deaconesses in the Church.

. . . .

XI. Of Washing the Saint's Feet.—We also confess the washing of the saints' feet, which the Lord not only instituted and commanded, but He actually washed His Apostles' feet, although He was their Lord and Master, and gave them an example that they should wash one another's feet, and do as He had done unto them; they, as a matter of course, taught the believers to observe this as a sign of true humility, and particularly as directing the mind by *feet-washing* to that right washing, by which we are washed in His blood and have our souls made pure.

XII. Of Matrimony, or State of Marriage.—We confess that there is in the Church an honorable marriage between two believers, as God ordained it in the beginning in paradise, and instituted it between Adam and Eve; as also the Lord Jesus Christ opposed and did away the abuses of marriage which had crept in, and restored it to its primitive institution.

In this manner the Apostle Paul also taught *marriage* in the Church, and left it free for every one, according to its primitive institution, to be married in the Lord to any one who may consent; by the phrase, *in the Lord*, we think it ought to be understood, that as the patriarchs had to marry among their own kindred or relatives, so likewise the believers of the New Testament are not at liberty to marry except among the chosen generation and the spiritual kindred or relatives of Christ, namely, such and no others as have been united to the Church as one heart and soul, having received baptism and stand in the same communion, faith, doctrine and conversation before they became united in marriage. Such are then joined together according to the original ordinance of God in His Church, and this is called *marrying in the Lord*.

XIII. Of the Magistracy.—We believe and confess that God instituted and appointed authority and a magistracy for the punishing of the evildoers and to protect the good; as also to govern the world, and preserve the good order of cities and countries; hence, we dare not despise, gainsay or resist the same, but we must acknowledge the magistracy as the minister of God, be subject and obedient thereunto in all good works, especially in all things not repugnant to God's law, will and commandment; also faithfully pay tribute and tax, and render that which is due, even as the Son of God taught and practiced and commanded His disciples to do; that it is our duty constantly and earnestly to pray to the Lord for the government, its prosperity and the welfare of the country, that we may live under its protection, gain a livelihood, and lead a quiet, peaceable life in all godliness and sobriety. And further, that the Lord may reward them in time and eternity for all the favors, benefits and the liberty we here enjoy under their praiseworthy administration.

XIV. Of Defense or Revenge.—As regards revenge or defense, in which men resist their enemies with the sword, we believe and confess that the Lord Jesus Christ forbade His disciples, His followers, all revenge and defense, and commanded them, besides, not to render evil for evil, nor railing for railing, but to sheath their swords, or, in the words of the prophet, "to beat them into ploughshares."

Hence it is evident, according to His example and doctrine, that we should not provoke or do violence to any man, but we are to promote the welfare and happiness of all men; even, when necessary, to flee for the Lord's sake from one country to another and take patiently the spoiling of our goods, but to do violence to no man; when we are smitten on one cheek to turn the other, rather than take revenge or resent evil. . . . .

XV. Of Oaths or Swearing.—Respecting judicial oaths, we believe and confess that Christ our Lord did forbid His disciples the use of them and commanded them that they should not swear at all, but that yea should be yea, and nay, nay.   Hence we infer that all oaths, greater and minor, are prohibited; and that we must, instead of oaths, confirm all our promises and assertions, nay, all our declarations or testimonies in every case, with the word yea in that which is yea, and with nay in that which is nay; hence we should always and in all cases perform, keep, follow and live up to our word or engagement, as fully as if we had confirmed and established it by an oath.   And we do this, we have the confidence that no man, not even the magistrate, will have just reason to lay a more grievous burden on our mind and conscience.

XVI. Of Ecclesiastical Excommunication or Separation from the Church.—We also believe and profess a ban, excommunication, or separation and Christian correction in the Church, for amendment and not for destruction, whereby the clean or pure may be separated from the unclean or defiled.   Namely, if anyone, after having been enlightened and has attained to the knowledge of the truth and has been received into the fellowship of the saints, sins either voluntarily or presumptuously against God, or unto death, and falls into the unfruitful works of darkness, by which he separates himself from God and is debarred His kingdom; such a person, we believe, when the deed is manifest and the Church has sufficient evidence, ought not to remain in the congregation of the righteous, but shall and must be separated as an offending member and an open sinner, be excommunicated and reproved in the presence of all and purged out as leaven; and this is to be done for his own amendment and as an example and terror to others, that the Church be kept pure from such foul spots; lest, in default of this, the name of the Lord be blasphemed, the Church dishonored and a stumbling block and cause of offense be given to them that are without; in fine, that the sinner may not be damned with the world, but become convicted, repent and reform. . . . .

XVII. Of Shunning or Avoiding the Separated or Excommunicated.—Touching the avoiding of the separated, we believe and confess that if any one has so far fallen off, either by a wicked life or perverted doctrine, that he is separated from God, and, consequently, is justly separated from and corrected or punished by the Church, such a person must be shunned, according to the doctrine of Christ and His Apostles, and avoided without partiality by all the members of the Church, especially by those to whom it is known, whether in eating or drinking, or other similar temporal matters, and they shall have no dealings with him; to the end that they may not be contaminated by intercourse with him, nor made partakers of his sins; but that the sinner may be made ashamed, be convicted, and again led to repentance.

That there be used, as well in the avoidance as in the separation, such moderation and Christian charity as may have a tendency not to promote his destruction, but to insure his reformation; for if he is poor, hungry, thirsty, naked, sick or in distress, we are in duty bound, according to necessity and agreeably to love and to the doctrine of Christ and His Apostles, to render him aid and assistance; otherwise, in such cases, the avoidance might tend more to his ruin than to his reformation.

Hence we must not consider excommunicated members as enemies, but admonish them as brethren, in order to bring them knowledge, repentance and sorrow for their sins, that they may be reconciled with God and His Church, and, of course, be received again into the Church, and so may continue in love toward him as his case demands.

XVIII. Of the Resurrection of the Dead and the Last Judgment.

. . . .

Done and finished in our United Churches, in the city of Dortrecht, April 21st, A.D. 1632. Subscribed:

ISSAC DE KONING.
et al.

Text—Cassel: *History of the Mennonites*, pp. 25-40.

VII. *MENNONITES AND QUAKERS IN POLITICS*

The following is a letter of Samuel Purviance to Colonel Bird (1765)

"I went lately up to Bucks Court, in order to concert measures for their (i.e. some friends) election, in pursuance of which we have appointed a considerable meeting of Germans, Baptists and Presbyterians, to be held next Monday at Neshaminy, where some of us, some Germans and Baptists of this place have appointed to attend, in order to attempt a general confederacy of the three societies in opposition to the ruling party. We have sent up emissaries among the Germans, which I hope will bring them into this measure, and if it can be effected, will give us a great chance for carrying matters in that county. Could that be carried, it would infallibly secure our friends a majority in the House, and consequently enable them to recal our dangerous enemy, Franklin, with his petitions, which is the great object we have in view, and which should engage the endeavors of all our friends at the approaching election to make a spirited push for a majority in the Assembly, without which all our struggles here will prove of little service to the public interest. . . . If you knew thoroughly the methods Mr. Franklin is taking at home to blacken and stigmatize our society, you would perhaps judge with me that you never had more reason to exert yourselves in order to overset him, which we can only do by commanding a majority in the Assembly. I have seen a letter lately from a person of character, that advises us of his wicked designs against us. The little hopes of success, as well as the difficulty of engaging proper persons for the purpose, has discouraged me from attempting a project recommended by some friends, of sending up some Germans to work upon their countrymen. But that no probable means may fail, I have sent up some copies of a piece lately printed by Sowers of Germantown, to be dispersed, and which may possibly have some effect.

. . . .

"As I understand the Mennonites have certainly resolved to turn out one Isaac Saunders this year, though the only good member your county has, I would beg leave to offer you and other friends the following scheme, as the only probable chance, I think, you have to carry the election and keep Mr. Saunders. If the scheme is properly executed and can be conducted without danger of a riot, I think you could infallibly carry your ticket by it.

"Don't attempt to change any of your members save Webb. If you can run Dr. Kuhn, or any other popular German, and can keep Mr. Saunders, you will do great things. As soon as your ticket is agreed on, let it be spread through the country, that your party intend to come well armed to the election, and that you intend, if there's the least partiality in either sheriff, inspectors, or managers of the election, that you will thrash the sheriff, every inspector, Quaker and Mennonist to a jelly; and further I would report it, that not a Mennonist nor German should be admitted to give in a ticket without being sworn that he is naturalized and worth 50 pounds and that he has not voted already; and further, that if you discovered any person attempting to give in a vote without being naturalized, or voting twice, you would that moment deliver him up to the mob to chastise him. Let this report be industriously spread before the election, which will certainly keep great numbers of the Mennonists at home. I would at the same time have all our friends warned to put on a bold face, to be every man provided with a shillelah, as if determined to put their threats in execution, though at the same time let them be solemnly charged to keep the greatest order and peace. Let our friends choose about two dozen of the most reputable men, magistrates, etc., who shall attend the inspectors, sheriffs and clerks during the whole election, to mount guard half at a time, and relieve one another at spells, to prevent all cheating and administer the oath to every suspicious person, and to commit to immediate punishment every one who offers to vote twice. I'll engage, if you conduct the election in that manner, and our people turn out with spirit, you can't fail of carrying every man on your ticket, I am as well assured not a third of the Mennonists are naturalized. I would submit this to your consideration. If it's well thought of, take your measures immediately. I beg no mention may be made of the author of this. I see no danger in the scheme but that of a riot, which would require great prudence to avoid."

Text Thomas Balch: *Letters and Papers Relating Chiefly to the Provincial History of Pennsylvania*, pp. 209-212.

VIII. *THE EPHRATA COMMUNITY*

"At that time the Brethren still dwelt scattered here and there in the Settlement, while each one was allowed a small possession in land, because it was not considered right to constrain anyone to self-denial against his will. Among the Brethren there were four who lived together in a house. . . . Their house was built half against the hill, and therefore was called the Hill House. . . .

As now so many wooers of the Virgin continually announced themselves at the Settlement, the Superintendent was at a loss what should be done with these numerous young people, and whether it were not better to teach them to renounce their self-will in convents under Spiritual authority, than to let them raise up their own altars of selfhood in corners; in this matter a certain concurrence brought him to a decision. At that time a very rich young Swiss had himself received in the Settlement, Benedict Yuchly by name, from Kilchery-turnen in the district of Berne. Inflamed by the love to God he resolved to devote his fortune to the erection of a convent; which was accepted as coming by divine direction, and his proposition granted. There was in the Settlement a pleasant elevation from which one had a beautiful view of the fertile valley and the mountains lying opposite; of this height the Brethren in the Hill House at that time held possession. When now it came to the selection of a site, the most held that the valley along the Cocalico creek was the most desirable, on account of the water; the Superintendent, however, went up the hill until he came within the limits of the property of the Brethren of the Hill House, and there was the site chosen. . . . This hill was called Zion, and from it the society afterwards went by the name of the Zionitic Brotherhood, which name clung to them in all their doings. At this time, too, the name Ephrata was given to the Settlement by the Superintendent, of which he said, that here his Rachel, for whom he had served so many year, was buried, after she had borne to him Benoni, the child of anguish; whereby he pointed to the history of the patriarch Jacob

Work on this great house went forward rapidly. Its frame was erected in May, 1738, and in the following October the first Brethren moved into it; they were, with a few exceptions, all novices, and had but little experience in the spiritual life. . . . .

. . . .
Hitherto divine service had been held in the chapel of the Sisters; but now the fathers of the two mentioned Brethren, named Nägele and Funck, offered in the name of their sons to build a prayer and school house, which it was granted them to do. . . . This house of prayer was a large and sightly structure. Below was a large room furnished with chairs, and adorned with texts in Gothic letters, for the congregation. Here the Superintendent had his seat; behind him a choir-gallery was built, in the lower part of which sat the Solitary Brethren, and in the upper, the Sisters. In the second story there was another large hall, furnished with everything needed for holding the Agapae. In the third story were dwelling rooms for eight Solitary persons. In this house many wonders of God were manifested forth, so that its future fate was much lamented.

. . . .
Now they began to order their life in every respect in monastic wise. First of all, property was declared sinful, and everything was brought together in common, in support of a fund, out of which everything needed for the sustenance of the Brethren was bought; the same was also done in the Sisters' Convent. It was therefore a great reproach for anyone to be accused of ownership. This lasted many years, namely, that no one owned anything, until at last necessity forced a return to ownership; although to this day everything in the main work is held in common. And in order that no one who had contributed anything might even in the future claim it, as for example, if he should leave the convent, it was resolved that anyone who should leave it, should forfeit whatever he had contributed, to which all agreed without any objections. When, owing to an absurd separation which then was mutually observed, the Sisters had been obliged to cut their own fire-wood, there was afterwards a contract made with them, agreed to by the Superintendent, that the Brethren should supply the Settlement with wood, while the Sisters, on their part, should look after the Brethren's wash. A common table was also introduced in both convents, during the first hour of the evening. Now they also began to tear down the separate hermit houses in the Settlement, out of which several work-shops were built.

On the 21st of September of this year the two societies separated from each other in divine worship, and the Brethren held their first midnight prayer meeting in their new house of prayer. As at this time a bell was sent as a present to one of the Brethren in the convent by his father in Germany, the Brethren prevailed upon the Superintendent, after much begging, to let them hang it in their prayer-house. When this was rung at midnight, not only did all the Settlement arise, but as one could hear it for four English miles around the Settlement, all the families also rose and held their home worship at the same time; for in those days the fires of the first love still burned everywhere. The Brethren attended their services clothed in the garb of the Order, wearing in addition also a mantle with a hood like that of the Capuchins. . . . . .
. . . .
In this year, too, the ordinary Tonsure, or head-shearing, was introduced in the convents, which deserves to be mentioned here, as it contributed not a little to the

vicissitudes of the Settlement. Two Brethren engaged in an intimate conversation with the Superintendent with reference to their spiritual course, and confided to him that something was still wanting in their consecration; they were indeed baptized in the name of Christ, but they could still marry and have intercourse with the world; there was still wanting some special pledge for their particular estate, otherwise there was no difference between them and the domestic households. On this they were agreed; but they could come to no decision as to the nature of the covenant desired, until at last they unanimously chose the Virgin Mary as the Patroness of their Order. After they had arrived at this conclusion they sought to propagate the same secretly, for they supposed that it would cause a great stir in the Settlement. But the Brethren discovered their secret, and consulted one of their private counsellors, who opposed their project for three hours. They, however, did not care for this, but the Superintendent ordered the Prior to kneel down, and after the latter had made a vow of perpetual chastity, he cut a large bald spot on his head; after which he and the other Brethren had the same done to themselves by the Prior. Thereupon a day was ordained as a festival on which the Order of the Solitary should take their vows of perpetual chastity. And notwithstanding that secretly many objections were made to it, because the Scriptures expressly forbid the shaving of the head, and because it was nothing but the warming up again of a custom that had originated in the Popish church, yet at the time set, in holy obedience, the entire Brotherhood appeared in its chapel; for they knew that the Superintendent stood under God; and that whoever opposed him struck at the very apple of God's eye. After the pledges were openly read, one Brother after the other kneeled down, and had his hair cut and afterwards his crown shorn. Then the Superintendent went over to the Sisters, who were awaiting him in their chapel, and after their hair had been cut, after the manner of virgins in the primitive church, they all took the vow, and then had their crowns likewise shorn. . . .

. . . .

The domestic households at that time still had a high regard for the work of God in the Settlement. Their daily offerings were the main sustenance of the Solitary; yes, they brought tithes of their crops into the Settlement, although these were not placed upon the altar according to their sense of it, but were used in trade, on which account no one wanted to make any more offerings. Meanwhile God's work went forward rightly in the two convents of Zion and Sharon (which was the name of the Sisters' convent), which caused a great stir in the land; for the people again fell into the old suspicion that there must be Jesuits from Mexico concerned in the matter. The simplicity which the Brethren in Zion had learned from their spiritual father prevailed among them for quite a time. They drew their cart themselves; and were their own horses; when they travelled, they went heavily laden like camels, and sometimes the whole Brotherhood might be seen trooping around the hill of Zion. The communal life was now formally instituted, and all private ownership was declared to be an Ananias-sin; this was a matter which the Prior was continually impressing upon the Brethren, from which it was apparent that it was artificial rather than inspired by the Spirit. . . .

After the number of the Brethren increased, it was asked how so many young people should be kept employed, outside of the work of divine worship, and preserved from idleness. Circumstances, too, demanded this, for the convent was poor, because the good Brethren cared for others more than for themselves. And since at this time also the offerings did not come in very plentifully any more, the Prior was seized with unbelief, and sank into purely temporal prospects. . . . Through this much of the primitive simplicity was lost; wherein God had manifested his wonders; and in its stead was opened a wide outlook into the world, for the Brethren, whose intelligence had been widened at their conversion, set up various mechanical trades, which brought in great profits, and which they handed over to the Prior, so that in a short time the treasury became so rich that money began to be loaned out; yes, it is likely that if God had not destroyed this economy, the Brethren would by this time have ships upon the sea.

. . . Soon after this the Brethren purchased a mill near by, where they afterward set up the seat of their worldly realm. Sad it is that so many otherwise earnest Brethren fortified their calling there. For market was held there every day, and everybody wished to deal with these pious people, not only because of their honesty, but because there was erected an altar for a spurious atonement. This was the reason, too, that whenever his quarters became too narrow for a Brother at the Settlement, he betook himself to the mill, for there he could live according to his natural inclinations.

The garb of the Order of the Brotherhood was designed with particular care in the council, and was intended to represent a spiritual man. It consisted of a *Thaler* (surplice) reaching down to the feet; over this was a garment having an apron in front and a veil behind which covered the back, and to which was fastened a pointed monk's hood, which could be put on or allowed to hang down the back as one pleased; the whole was provided with a girdle around the waist. During services they wore a cloak besides, reaching down to the girdle, to which also a hood was fastened. Upon contemplating this garb it was found that they who had designed it for the order had, without knowing it, borrowed the style from the Order of Capuchins; and as said Order prided itself that its habit had been the dress of the first Christians, the Solitary at Ephrata felt flattered that they should have the honor to dip water from the same well with so venerable, famous and ancient an Order. This costume of the Order all the Solitary Brethren at that time adopted without any objections, and have kept it this long time; nor did they permit it to be worn either by a widower who might be among them, nor by a novice until after the close of his year of trial.

Soon afterwards the Sisters undertook a similar work in their convent, with the cooperation of the Superintendent. Their costume, like that of the Brethren, was designed so that but little was visible of that humiliating image revealed by sin. They wore hoods like the Brethren, but rounded instead of pointed, which while they were at work hung down the back; whenever they noticed anyone coming, however, they drew the same up over the head and face, so that one could see little of the latter. The distinguishing mark of their spiritual betrothal, however, was a large veil, which covered them entirely in front, and down to the girdle behind; of this members of Roman Catholic Orders, who saw it, said that it was known among them as the *Scapula*. This costume of the Order the Sisterhood has retained with particular care in its establishment, called Sharon, for now nigh unto fifty years.

. . . .

Now we will again return to the Solitary. Thus far they had sought self-sacrifice in hard labor; but now the Superintendent was urged by his Guide to establish higher schools, of which the singing-school was the beginning. This science belongs more to the angelic world than to ours. The principles of it are not only the same all over the world but the angels themselves, when they sang at the birth of Christ, had to make use of our rules. The whole art consists of seven notes, which form two thirds and one octave, which are always sung in such a way that you do not hear the tone which stands between the notes, thus occasioning a sweet dissonance, which renders the art a great wonder. It is also remarkable, that, although so great confusion of languages arose, the singing remained untouched. But as everything encessary in the Settlement had to be stolen from the world-spirit, so also in respect to singing. The Superintendent did not know anything about it, except some notes which he had learned on the violin. But a certain house-father, by the name of Ludwig Blum, was a master-singer, and was also versed in composition; he once brought some artistic pieces to the Superintendent, which induced him to make use of the Brother in his church building.

Now those of the Solitary, of whom about seventy of both sexes were in the Settlement, were selected who had talent for singing, and the above mentioned Ludwig Blum together with the Superintendent, arranged a singing-school in the Settlement, and everything prospered for a time. . . .

. . . .

. . . The singing-schools began with the Sisters, lasted four hours, and ended at midnight. Both master and scholars appeared in white habits, which made a singular procession, on which account people of quality frequently visited the school. The Superintendent, animated by the spirit of eternity, kept the school in great strictness, and every fault was sharply censured. The whole neighborhood, however, was touched by the sound of this heavenly music, a prelude of a new world and a wonder to the neighbors. . . "

Text—*Chronicon Ephratense,* translated by J. M. Hark, pp. 106-8; 119-26; 138-40; 160-162.

IX. *THE PROBLEM OF MINISTERS FOR LUTHERAN CHURCHES*

The following documents throw light upon the difficulties that retarded the progress of early Lutheran churches.

For as much as the delegate of the Evangelical Lutheran congregations at Philadelphia, New Hanover and Providence in Pennsylvania, Mr. Daniel Weisiger has represented to us the condition of the said congregations, adding that they propose to erect churches and school houses such as are demanded in the several localities; as also, that they ardently hope to obtain from Germany some true and faithful pastors and preachers of the Evangelical faith, and competent teachers for their schools, therefore we, in this city, are ready and willing, with the Divine help, to cooperate in this work according to our ability, and to take pains that these congregations may be supplied with one or more well qualified pastors and instructors as far as their wishes can be met in this place. Our desire is to secure such men as will heartily do their utmost, with all diligence and fidelity, in laboring for the spiritual good and the salvation of the churches and the youth committed to their charge.

In this matter the following conditions must be maintained:

1. Those persons who may be appointed as regular pastors and preachers must be ordained before leaving this country; and as a regular call to the work will be required, we shall expect that a plenipotentiary document to that effect, according to a certain

form which we have arranged, will be prepared and signed by all the elders of the congregations concerned, and then transmitted to us, and that this document shall be so framed as that it may be used for the same purpose whenever occasion may require.

. . . .

3. It is enjoined, with equal earnestness, upon the said elders and congregations to give good heed to furnish the necessary means of subsistence to the pastors and teachers who may be sent to them, to declare beforehand, the amount of the yearly salary, and to pay it in full, according to promise, so that the remuneration of those who serve them in the churches and schools may not be diminished, as has been the case in other places, by including contributions. of tobacco or other articles of produce, by which these persons might be led to involve themselves in business operations not suited to their station; but that it be always paid in money, honestly and without delay, and that all the necessary arrangements be made to that effect.

A declaration to the foregoing effect subscribed also by the aforesaid officers of the congregations is expected by us; and upon our receiving such declaration we shall not fail to help them in their good work, by the Grace of God, to the utmost of our power. To all which may the Lord graciously add His blessing, sending prosperity from above, and directing all for the Glory of His Name and the extension of His Kingdom for the sake of Christ our Lord.

Given at Halle, May 31, 1734.

Extract of a letter addressed to the Rev Court Chaplain, Dr. Ziegenhagen, dated Philadelphia, Dec. 6th, 1736.

In conclusion, it surprises us not a little, that as we have several times already explained to your Reverence the great poverty of our congregations, and based upon it our plea for assistance, you yet do nothing more than simply insist upon our placing a regular call in the hands of Prof. Francke, a thing which it is not in our power to do under the conditions prescribed by Mr. D. Gerdes and Prof. Francke. First of all, our congregations are located far apart. New Hanover is 40 miles from Philadelphia, and Providence 30 miles. Besides, the people of each of these congregations are scattered over more than 20 miles of the surrounding country, are mixed up amongst Quakers, Mennonites and other sects, and worst of all, those of them who profess to be Lutherans are not willing to enter into any obligations, although they promise to do their part as soon as they find that some regular order has been established, which, however, under the disturbances attending the present collections, cannot be done.

But if the fidelity and competency of a pastor is made to depend upon a large salary, or if they who come to teach us have more concern about their wages and the fleece than about feeding the flock, then, indeed, we have but little to hope for. Such a man may well be described as a hireling who teaches for his own advantage alone. This, however, would be of little benefit to us. In view of the conditions annexed to the call, as they have been sent to us by Prof. Francke and especially by Mr. D. Gerdes, it seems very strange to us that men who consider such a call to be a Divine act should show such respect to the idols of this world as first to demand the assurance that they shall have a sufficient supply of them before they will consent to accept a call, thus putting confidence in God in quite a subordinate position. This looks very much as if money were the inward principle impelling them to labor in the Kingdom of God; whereas, a bishop should not be given to covetousness, which also the Lord Himself has signified, commanding his disciples not to carry a purse.

Of course, we do not propose to let our pastors suffer want, but much rather to support them according to our ability.   On the other hand, we desire as our pastor not a covetous man, nor one ruled by temporal motives, but a man who out of a sincere heart and out of love to God is constrained to come to our help and to enter into the pastoral office amongst us.   We live in a land in which a pastor cannot expect to enjoy himself in an imposing parsonage, in a life of luxury and with large revenues, but for a faithful pastor who is a true Apostle of Christ, and has the Spirit of the Lord in him, measures will certainly be taken to secure him an adequate support.

In order that your Reverence may thoroughly understand our views, we have now to state clearly and candidly that we cannot bind ourselves either to raise a salary of 50 pounds sterling per year, or to advance to you any large sum to meet travelling expenses, or to defray the expense of going back to Germany incurred by those who having come to us are not willing to remain, which conditions Mr. D. Gerdes has laid down to us, as also, in a measure, has Prof. Francke himself.   On the other hand we do humbly propose that your Reverence, in connection with Prof. Francke whom we have addressed in the same terms, may send to us some good man, one who is grieved for the affliction of Joseph; pay his travelling and incidental expenses and his salary for one year out of the funds that have been collected for us in Europe, give him full authority to investigate everything here thoroughly, and permit him to return to Europe in case he should not be willing to remain with us, in order that he may give you an extended verbal report of everything.   It is impossible for us to send you the money for the expenses of the journey, because most people refuse to contribute to such a fund, fearing lest, as has happened already in New York, we might receive a teacher who would occasion more harm and offence than benefit and edification to the Church as Preacher Schultz himself has done.   No person could expect that one or two individuals should advance the whole of this sum themselves, for by so doing they might soon lose everything they have.

In addition to this it is our opinion that besides expending the money that has been collected in the building of churches and schoolhouses, it should be used also in the purchase of land, the revenue from which may be devoted forever to the support of one or more pastors and schoolmasters according as circumstances may require, this support being increased by the addition of certain perquisites and adequate contributions to be agreed upon by the members of the congregations.   We desire, however, first to be informed how much money we may expect and specially to be assured that it shall be transmitted to us, for it would be disastrous to make a purchase without being certain that we could make payment and whence the payment was to come.   At all events, it would be well to put the money out at interest, and to devote the interest forever towards helping to raise the salary of the pastor.

In short, in due time, we hope to be able to make good, practical arrangements for the support of one or more pastors; although at first, only one faithful teacher, relying upon God and His Favor, should be sent to us.   Such a man may help us to put matters into good order; for, we have no doubt that many who have separated themselves from the Church may be brought back again, and the wounds inflicted by Preacher Schultz may be healed.

We therefore beg your Reverence to take all these things into consideration; and if you should use a portion of the money that has been collected for us, in sending over to us some one whose high aim is to extend the Kingdom of Christ, we doubt not, that God would add His blessing to it.   We shall, at all times, be ready to do in favor of the work, everything that we possibly can.   But if none of our propositions should be accepted, than we can do nothing else than patiently wait for the salvation of God; commit ourselves to the Great Shepherd and Bishop of souls, Christ Jesus, and pray that Heaven may grant the richest rewards to all those who have kindly contributed on our behalf, although our congregations may derive no benefit from what they may have done. . . .

The Wardens of the Evangelical Lutheran Congregations at Philadelphia, New Hanover and Providence.

Letter of the three congregations in Pennsylvania, addressed to the Rev. Court Chaplain, Ziegenhagen, in London, Oct. 15th, 1739:

Most Reverend, Most Honored Chaplain.
Your letter of Sept. 26th, 1738, was duly delivered by Preacher Klug, and has been read with sincere respect. . . .   It looks as if money had more power than any spiritual principle has, to urge you to labor for the spreading of the Kingdom of God; although a bishop ought not to be covetous, and Christ commanded his disciples not to carry a purse.   It is not, at all, our purpose to let our pastor starve or suffer want; but we desire a man who will come to us not with covetous views, or ruled by other carnal principles.   We live in a country where a teacher or preacher cannot expect to have a showy parsonage, or a large salary, or an easy, comfortable life; and it is not possible for us to promise him these things.   But due arrangements shall be made to secure an adequate support for a faithful pastor who has the spirit of Christ dwelling in him.

We, the wardens and elders of the congregations, though giving great labor and diligence, have not been able to send out to you such a call for a pastor as you have wished us to send, Dr. Gerdes and Prof. Francke having furnished a formula, according to which the call should be drawn up, by the congregations.   We could not do what you demanded; and the first reason is this: Our people here are scattered so far around and are mixed up with so many sects, that no warden can tell who are members of his congregation until they come together to hear a sermon, or to have the Lord's Supper; and in respect to these matters, things are in a miserable state.   If any of the schoolmasters who have come from Germany undertakes to give a sermon, in such places, hardly half of the people come together; because many have an abhorrence of such preachers, since they even, at times, take upon themselves to give the Lord's Supper, though they are not regularly called servants of Christ; and therefore such a ministry does not belong to them.   The reason why some people have asked them to do this is the fact that, at the present time, there is not one German Lutheran preacher in the whole land except Caspar Stoever, who is now 60 English miles distant from Philadelphia.   Besides, they see that they have no reason to hope for the assistance of your Reverence in securing a pastor, unless they first give you certain satisfactory assurances; although every man, according to his ability, would willingly contribute to the support of a pastor, if only one man whose trust is in God could be induced to come to us.

Our last reason is this: No one is willing to subscribe to the support of a clergyman, as you require us to do, until we first see what kind of a man we are to get, and know that he is worthy of confidence; so that we may not be burdened with great expenses out of which no good can come.   Also, that we may not get another hireling like as preacher Schultz was, or like the specimen that was in a place called Raritan, which is connected with the New York congregation. . .

If your Reverence and Prof. Francke also could see with your own eyes the sad condition of the many poor people who are coming to this country every year and are put out to service among other sects; poor people who would be so glad to go, on Sunday, to a church of their own confession, so that they might not attend the meetings of other sects and thus be misled at last, as many indeed have already been, . . . then you would understand that in case you continue to hold back and delay any longer, you will surely have a great responsibility upon you in the presence of God, on that great Day of Judgment, because you have not so much as permitted the collected funds to be applied to the objects to which benevolent hearts have given them, that is the building of our churches and schools.

Text—Mann, Schmucker and Germann: *Hallische Nachrichten*, translated by Schaeffer, pp. 81-104.

X. THE CONSTITUTION OF FUNDAMENTAL PRINCIPLES OF THE SCHWENKFELDER CHURCH, AS ADOPTED IN 1782

After almost half a century of unorganized activity centered in home instruction and informal house to house conference worship, the Schwenkfelders felt the necessity of something more churchly. Hence the Constitution as under, framed by Christopher Schultz, and embodied in the several revisions of the Constitution and By-Laws of the Schwenkfelder Church.

"1. Every person desiring to be a member of this Church should concern himself about a proper and approved ideal upon which the members are to be established in all things, and in accordance with which they are to form their union.

2. All those who would be in this religious association should place this foundation and ideal before their eyes as an aim set before them for which they are to strive with becoming zeal and energy.

3. In God's nature one beholds love primarily as that excellent outflowing virtue which binds together God and man. All those who wish to take sure steps for the realization of said ideal must, first of all, form and maintain their unity by this bond of perfection among themselves.

4. Built on this fundamental principle of the divine nature—namely, love—their single, immovable aim must and will be to glorify God and promote the general welfare of each member.

5. In compliance with such object, their first care in their common affairs must be directed to a proper arrangement of public worship flowing from said foundation and agreeing with said ideal.

6. The gospel or word of God is the treasure which the Lord Jesus gave his apostles, and by which, as He commanded, the nations were to be called to faith and gathered, to be nurtured and ruled. It is the chief element in public worship and the rule of all its exercises.

7. It follows that they not only ought to possess this treasure, but they must also, with care, see to it that the gospel and the word of God are preserved and practiced by them in purity and simplicity, without which they cannot be nor remain a Christian people.

8. It follows, also, that they must have persons among themselves who know, live, and teach the doctrine; otherwise it would be a dead letter, and could not bring about the good referred to in 6; hence proper plans must be devised in this respect.

9. There follow also the unceasing effort and care for the instruction of youth, both in what may be learned in schools as also in what should be taught in the study of the word of God or Christian doctrine, without which their aim referred to in 4 cannot be maintained nor the doctrine be upheld.

10. The repeated voluntary gathering for public worship with appointment of time and place for the same belongs also to the common care and concern.

11. Besides the appointment of public worship and the practice of God's word, a religious society, if it would at all attain its object, must strive to uphold a proper discipline among themselves, in order that through the same a guard and restraint may be set against the attacks and hindrances of the evil one, and that his work may be destroyed where it has taken root; that a good and useful deportment may be maintained in intercourse and conduct; that the hand of mutual help may be offered under all occurrences, and that virtue and good morals may be promoted.

12. They must have fixed rules and regulations among themselves by which they may know who belong to their society or not; they must also use diligence to keep correct records of all that is enacted by them and upon which they have mutually agreed in matters relating to discipline, in order that no one may take ignorance as a excuse, but that all may conform thereto.

13. Since good rules are necessary in the exercise of commendable discipline, the revealed will of God contained in the Ten Commandments in their full and perfect sense will be to them the best and most adequate rule for the promotion of good conduct or morals, for defense against the evil, for discriminating between the good and the evil.

14. In conformity to their aim and rules, they will, besides this, also consider useful and proper regulations, so that commendable decorum may be preserved under the diverse circumstances, as marriage, training of children, family life, death, burials and the like.

15. The practice and maintenance of such discipline and regulations will always have their temptations, since we all carry these by nature in our own bosoms; it will, therefore, likewise be necessary to have faithful persons who will see to it that discipline and good order are not neglected, but maintained and promoted by each member.

16. In order, however, that such service may not be made too difficult, but be possible and endurable for such persons, each and every member, by proper regulations, must take part in said exercises and supervision, whereby at the first notice of the outbreak of an offence its progress may at once be checked, and the deacon not be troubled by it.

17. Certain conferences should also be appointed as time may occasion or the circumstances of the general welfare may demand, at which the condition of the Church, for weal or woe, may be considered, doubtful or questionable matters decided,

and the general welfare and useful arrangements and institutions in general may be cared for."

Text—*The Pennsylvania German Society, Proceedings and Addresses*, vol. XIII pp. 74-76.

XI. THE MORAVIANS

An Exposition of their Fundamental Views

The following is taken from a report of the Synod that met at Marienborn, July 1st, 1674.

"This synod was one of the most important assemblies, held by the church of the Brethren ever since its renewal; and it was the first since the decease of the late ordinary.

"Eleven bishops and co-bishops, seven civil seniors and conseniors, fifteen presbyters, twenty-four deacons of the church of the Brethren; in all, ninety-four persons were present at this synod, among whom were above thirty deputies from the congregations.

. . . .

"The whole work of God, which he, in our days, had committed to his Unity of the Brethren, among Christians and Heathens, in all its branches, in every country, in the congregation-places, the colonies, and on posts among the Heathen, was taken into consideration before the Lord, the state of each carefully weighed, and his *Thoughts of Peace* concerning them searched after.

"It was unanimously determined anew, that the *Doctrine of the Merits of the Life and Sufferings of Jesus*, shall be our only chief and fundamental knowledge, so, as it is revealed to us in the *Holy Scriptures of the Old and New Testament*, boldly avowed by the Protestant confessors in the *Augustan Confession*, experienced through his grace, and enjoyed in the remission of sins, by us, as well as many thousand other souls.

"The *Doctrinal Articles of the Augustan Confession* were read at the synod, and heard by the whole assembly with assent of our hearts, and with an emotion of spirit, like that of the ancient confessors; and our adherence to it was again confirmed. . . .

The fundamental thoughts of his heart concerning our household of grace, both in and out of our congregation-places, were renewed with clearness. I will communicate some of them, to the joy of my dear Brother.

A congregation of Jesus Christ is an assembly, consisting of living members of his body, of which he himself is the Head, which the Holy Ghost has gathered together, in which he himself governs, ordains, and appoints his servants, and where every thing aims at each member's being prepared once to be *presented faultless before the presence of his glory with exceeding joy*. (Jude, verse 24.)

This does not exclude its being a school and an hospital of his patients, where atience is to be exercised towards many who must be saved by compassion.

God has, in our time, formed for himself a people, which is to withstand the spirit that is gone forth into the world, to turn the doctrine of the atonement of Jesus into a fable; and they are called to show his death, till he come. (1 Cor. xi. 26.)

Should this doctrine (which God forbid!) be every where extinguished; it must be preserved in a congregation of Jesus, as a precious jewel; so, as formerly the holy scriptures were among the Jews. (Rom. iii. 2.)

By this it is perceived, whether a person really *is of us*, if the death of Jesus have taken root in his heart.

From hence also arises the call of a congregation of Jesus, to preach the gospel not only to Christians but to all men, with a view of leading them to our Saviour.

An essential point in a congregation of Jesus is likewise, to have it solidly at heart, that they may execute *His Testament, John* xvii: *That they all may be one*; endeavouring to establish and preserve *love* and *unity* among all the children of God upon the face of the earth, to avoid all religious disputes, and to love all that love Jesus.

A congregation of Christ is also honoured by its Master, with suffering reproach for the sake of his name, being and remaining a church under the cross.

He has, more particularly, opened to the congregations of the Brethren in our days, that part of the gospel, which directs them to derive the *sanctification* of spirit, soul and body, from the merits of his holy humanity, life, sufferings, and death, to understand it, and put it in practice. The separation of the sexes, according to the respective choirs, and the special care they enjoy, conduce greatly to promote this chief end of the Christian doctrine.

When the Holy Ghost, through the gospel, calls and units souls out of our congregations, in order to prepare them to be a joy to our Saviour; we rejoice, and look upon them as a congregation of Jesus.

With respect to the heart, the uninterrupted enjoyment of salvation in the wounds of Jesus, and all things that pertain unto life and godliness, there ought to be no difference between such little flocks and our congregations.

They, as well as we, ought to preserve their souls and bodies for him; and, for that purpose, also carefully to avoid all unnecessary intercourse between the two sexes; not as though we thought there was a particular holiness in it, but from a consciousness of human corruption and sinfulness.

As to the outward *Constitution*, and the regulations, which our Saviour has given to the Brethren, for the particular purpose of their dwelling together in congregation-places by themselves; it is our fixed principle to give no occasion to the societies, united with us in the religions, to imitate them; but we exhort them to abide in their church-constitution, and be faithful to their religion.

A *Directory* was chosen and appointed, to have the care of the whole Unity of the Brethren in inward and outward matters; a *Board of Wardens*, to have the inspection of the outward affairs of all the congregations; and a *Board of Syndics*, to see to it, that *all things be done decently and in order*, so, as the constitution and the good of the country, in which we live, require; and to stand forth, in all necessary cases, in behalf of the congregations.

The office of *Advocate of the Brethren* was again supplied in the person of count *Henry* XXVIII. *Reuss*, who was before deputy advocate.

Deacons were nominated, to have the care of the *Heathen-missions;* and, in like manner, other *Deacons*, to provide for the *Education of the Youth* in the œconomies of the Unity, who, in childlike dependence upon the hand of our heavenly Father, should receive, and expend with all faithfulness, for the service of these works of God, the contributions of our Brethren and Friends who gladly lend their assistance towards them.

All care and consideration was taken in supplying the offices in every congregation with proper persons.

Text—Crantz: *The Ancient and Modern History of the Brethren* . . ." La Trobe's translation, pp. 555-559.

The Society for the Furtherance of the Gospel

The following articles are the constitution of the earliest missionary society in America. It was organized Nov 28, 1745, continued energetic operations for about fifteen years, and a nominal existence until about 1770.

"1st. *The Society is founded* on the Exhortation of St. John in his 3d Epistle, & on our present Circumstances.

"2d. Everything therein shall be *freely transacted* & we do not desire that any Person shod bind himself to give a certain Sum, but that each may do according to his Ability and Pleasure.

"3d. Yet shall all be transacted in good Order, that *Accounts* may be *rendered* both to God & Man whenever it shall be required.

"4th. In this respect we will be careful in the *admitting of new Members*, & whoever thro' his Example may give Offence to Others, such will we entreat not to become Members of the Society.

"5th. We will appoint a *Committee* of four [six later] Persons, skilful and prudent Men who shall Weekly consider of what the Circumstances of the Society may require and dispose of the Contributions of such kind Friends as shall willingly give, according to the Mind of the Society.

"6th. A *Secretary* shall also be appointed to keep a Journal of their Proceedings & also their Accounts to keep in good Order; wch may be laid before the Society, as often as they meet together.

"7th. The Society shall also have a *regular Servant* to make known what shall be necessary for the Messengers of the Gospel, both on their going out & coming in & to take Care that the same may be provided.

"8th. Since a great deal depends on the keeping a *regular Correspondence* & that the Expense thereof might be too heavy for one Person to bear, *the Charges* may be defrayed out of the Monies belonging to the Society.

"9th. When either of the Members of the *Committee*, or the *Secretary* or *Servant* shall go away, the remaining members may propose a Person to supply his Place & in case the Society have nothing to object, when the same shall be proposed in their Meeting such *new Member* may be continued.

"10th. *The Meeting of the Society* may be as often as the Synod is held & then Matters may be concluded on, provided that one half of the Members at least be present.

"11th. If any Person will *contribute* thereunto *without becoming a Member* of the Society, he may deliver or send his Contribution either to one of the Members of the Committee, to the Secretary or the Servant, who are directly to deliver the same to the Cashier.

"12th. The Committee have *Power to propose* to the Society whatever may be for the Service thereof, & when such Proposals are agreed to by the majority of the Societies Votes, they shall be Valid.

"13th. Should *anything* in the foregoing Regulations be necessary to be *altered* it may not be done by any one Person, but by the *majority of the Votes* of the Society."

Text—*Transactions of the Moravian Historical Society*, Vol. V, pp. 330-331.

CHAPTER X

The Carolinas in the Colonial Period

Bibliography

An early description (1664) of the country, with a statement of the Proposals of the Lord Proprietor for settlers, is that of William Hilton entitled, "A Relation of a Discovery Lately Made on the Coast of Florida, . . . " (Force, "Tracts and Papers," Vol. IV, Tract II). Shortly after (1666) appeared, "A Brief Description of the Province of Carolina, . . . " (Carroll, "Historical Collections of South Carolina," Vol. II). The Royal Charters of 1663 and 1665; "A Declaration and Proposal to All that will Plant in Carolina" (1663); the "Articles and Concessions" (1665); "The Port Royal Discovery, . . . " (1666) by Robert Sandford, and "The Fundamental Constitutions of Carolina" (1669) are accessible in "Colonial Records of North Carolina" Vol. I (1886), edited by W. L. Saunders. The earliest account of the Port Royal Settlement, "Carolina, or a Description of the Present State of that Country" (1682) by Thomas Ash, may be consulted in Carroll, "Historical Collections," Vol. II. This volume also contains Samuel Wilson's anonymous, " . . . Account of the Province of Carolina, . . ." (1682). Omitting military literature of the opening years of the eighteenth century, the next production is that of Governor John Archdale who (1707) in his "New Description of that Fertile and Pleasant Province of Carolina" (Carroll, "Historical Collections," Vol. II) gives an account, interesting and impartial, though somewhat confused and rambling. John Lawson, who as Surveyor-General had occasion to travel extensively throughout North Carolina, has left his observations notably on Indian life in "A Voyage to Carolina, . . . " (1709, reprinted with some changes under another author's name, in "The Natural History of North Carolina" (1737) by John Brickell, M. D.). The Carey rebellion and the Indian wars of 1711 may be studied in the "Spotswood Letters" ("Coll. Va. Hist. Soc.," New Series, Vols. I and II). "An Account of the Breaking out of the Yamassee War in South Carolina," extracted from the "Boston News" June 13, 1715, is accessible in Carroll's "Historical Collections," Vol. II.   The contest leading to the renunciation of proprietary rule has been described by Francis Yonge in a "Narrative of the Proceedings of the People of South Carolina in the Year 1719, . . . " (1726, Carroll, "Historical Collections," Vol. II; and Force, "Tracts and Papers" Vol. II, Tract X).   "A Description of the Province of South Carolina.   Drawn up at Charles Town, September, 1731" by Jean Pierre Purry is reprinted (translation) in Carroll, "Historical Collections," Vol. II, and Force, "Tracts and Papers," Vol. II, Tract XI.

Historical work began with Alexander Hewatt in "An Historical Account of the Rise and Progress of the Colonies of South Carolina and Georgia" (II Vols. 1779).   This work well worth consulting though antiquated and inaccurate for the early periods, forms the main portion of Carroll's "Historical Collections," Vol. I.   In the following year (1780) there appeared the first volume (to 1688) of George Chalmers' "Political Annals of the Present United States from their Settlement to the Peace of 1763."   His strong anti-revolutionary sentiments seem to have disturbed his historical poise.   He must therefore be read with caution.   (For South Carolina section, see Carroll's "Historical Collections," Vol. II).   A later (II Vols. 1808) "History of South Carolina" by David Ramsay, M.D., shows a disposition to follow slavishly in the footsteps of Hewatt.   A "History of North Carolina" (II Vols. 1812) by Hugh Williamson is generally regarded as unpardonably inaccurate.   A "History of North Carolina" (II Vols. 1829) by Francois Xavier Martin, while free from Williamson's inaccuracies, is defective in point of perspective.   Seven years later, B. R. Carroll rendered a distinct service in publishing with notes and introduction his "Historical Collections of South Carolina. . . . ".   The South Carolina Historical Society, organized in 1855, has continued a similar service in its "Collections," several volumes of which have been published.   "Historical Sketches of North Carolina from 1584 to 1851" (1851) by John H. Wheeler is scarcely a work of history, but an ill-arranged compilation of data not always chosen with a due sense of proportion.   "A Sketch of the History of South Carolina to the Close of the Proprietary Government, 1719" (1856) and "A Chapter in the Early History of South Carolina" (1874) by W. G. Rivers are sections of what gave promise of becoming a high class completed history of South Carolina, unfortunately made impossible by the Civil War.   The colonial period however, is covered in "The Carolinas" (Winsor, "Narr. & Crit. Hist." Vol. V).   The "History of North Carolina" (1856) by Francis Lester Hawks, the second volume of which covers the period 1663-1729, holds a place as a standard work prepared largely from original manuscript material and embodying many documents. At several points, however, Hawks shows sectarian bias, and in some particulars recent discoveries have made his conclusions worthless.   John W. Moore's "History of North Carolina from the Earliest Discoveries to the Present Time" (II Vols. 1880) lacks the abundant source material of Hawks' work though it gains thereby in its attractiveness as a literary work. Two recent works by Edward Mc-Crady will be found highly satisfactory in point of interest and accuracy— "The History of South Carolina under the Proprietary Government" (1897), and "The History of South Carolina under the Royal Government, 1719-1776" (1899). "South Carolina as a Royal Province, 1719-1776" (1903) by W. Roy Smith, traces the struggles of the Province as they led to the American Revolution.

In the ecclesiastical field, good introductory studies are "The Religious Development in the Province of North Carolina" by S. B. Weeks (J.H.U. Studies, Series X, Sec. V and VI), and the same author's "Church and State in North Carolina" (ibid., Series XI, Sec. V and VI). David Humphrey's " . . . Historical Account of the Society for the Propagation of the Gospel in Foreign Parts" (1730, reprint 1853) will be found serviceable, especially its map showing parish churches and Indian settlements.   A chapter of this work has been embodied in Carroll's "Historical Collections," Vol. II.   Important correspondence of the S. P. G. missionaries is incorporated in "The South Carolina Historical and Genealogical Magazine", Vols. IV and V.   "The Society for the Propagation of the Gospel in the Province of North Carolina" ("James Sprunt Historical Publications—N. Car. Hist. Soc.," Vol. IX) by D. O. Oliver is a brief restatement. Frederick Dalcho's " . . . Historical Account of the Protestant Episcopal Church in South Carolina, From the First Settlement of the Province to the War of the Revolution, With Notices of the Present State of the Church in Each Parish . . . " (1820) has continued to hold a deservedly high place among students. "Sketches of Church History in North Carolina" (1892) by William L. de Rosset, Jr., and "An Historic Sketch of the Parish Church of St. Michael, 1752-1886" (1887) by George S. Holmes, furnish local details. Registers of the Independent or Congregationalist (Circular) Church (1732-1738) and of Saint Andrew's Parish, Berkeley County (1719-1774) appear in "The South Carolina Hist. & Geneal. Mag." Vols. XII-XV. Comprehensive surveys of Episcopalianism will be found in "Historical Notices of the Missions of the Church of England . . . " (1845) by Ernest Hawkins; also in the standard works of Anderson, Wilberforce, Perry, McConnell and Tiffany. (See page 7). Several documents relating to the relations of the Episcopalians and the dissenters may be consulted in the "Case of Protestant Dissenters in Carolina" (1706—note, appendix).

On Quakerism, George Fox's "Journal" (1694) and the "Journal of the Life, Travels, . . . of William Edmundson" (1715) are of special value. The "Journal of the Life of Thomas Story" (1747) is illuminating. Then follow the standard works of William Sewel, Joseph Besse, John Gough, Charles Evans, Samuel M. Janney, James Bowden, Allen C. and Richard Thomas, and Rufus M. Jones. For a critical estimate of the above see page 154 f.

The history of the Lutheran church may be approached through "The German Exodus to England in 1709" by Frank R. Diffenderffer ("Proc. & Addr. Pa. Ger. Soc." Vol. VII, pp. 257-413), and "German Emigration to America 1709-1740" by Rev. H. E. Jacobs, (ibid. Vol. VIII, pp. 29-150). A "History of the German Settlements and of the Lutheran Church in North and South Carolina" (1872) by Rev. G. D. Bernheim will be found useful, although it should not always be implicitly followed. Carolinan Lutheranism finds a place also in the comprehensive Lutheran histories of C. W. Schaeffer, Rev. E. J. Wolf, A. L. Gräbner, and H. E. Jacobs. See page 152.

On the Reformed Lutheran church a scholarly contribution by Professor W. J. Hinke entitled "The Origin of the Reformed Church in South Carolina" appears in the "Journal of the Presbyterian Historical Society," Vol. III, No. 8, pp. 367-389. "A Historic Sketch of the Reformed Church in North Carolina" (1908) by a Board of Editors under the Classis of North Carolina, is indefinitely general for the earliest period. More detailed is "A Historical Sketch of the Classis of North Carolina" (1895) by George W. Welker, D.D., and his "Early German Reformed Settlers in North Carolina" ("Col. Rec. North Carolina" edited by Saunders, Vol. VIII, pp. 727-757). See also the literature cited in connection with Pennsylvania, p. 153.

Moravianism has been studied by Rev. Levin T. Reichel in "The Moravians in North Carolina; an Authentic History" (1857). With less detail the same author has discussed Carolina in his "Early History of the Church of the United Brethren in North America, A.D. 1734-1748" ("Trans. Moravian Hist. Soc.," Vol. III). Rev. John Holmes' "History of the Protestant Church of the United Brethren" (II Vols. 1825-1830) though antiquated will repay attention. "Memorials of

the Life of Peter Böhler, Bishop of the Church of the United Brethren"
(1868) by Rev. J. P. Lockwood; a "History of the Unitas Fratrum,
. . . . " by Professor J. Taylor Hamilton ("Amer. Ch. Hist. Ser." Vol.
VIII, 1894) and his "History of the Unitas Fratrum during the Eighteenth and Nineteenth Centuries" (1900) have brief references to the
evanescent phase of Moravianism in Carolina. A "History of Wachovia
in North Carolina, The Unitas Fratrum or Moravian Church in North
Carolina during a Century and a Half . . . 1752-1902" (1902) by John
Henry Clewell, is a well written treatise based on the original manuscripts and records of the Wachovia archives.

On the Swiss a scholarly contribution has been made by Albert B.
Faust in "Swiss Emigration to the American Colonies in the Eighteenth
Century," ("Amer. Hist. Rev." Vol. XXII. Number 1.)

"Pioneers of France in the New World" (1865—later editions)
by Francis Parkman has an informing account of Huguenot fortunes
in South Carolina. "Names of the Huguenot Refugees who Emigrated
to South Carolina" appear in "Proc. Huguenot Soc. of America" Vol.
I, No. 1. "The French Protestant Church of Charleston, South Carolina. . . . " (1853) sketches Huguenot settlements in South Carolina.
"The French Protestants of Abbeville District, S. C. 1761-1765" is
discussed in "Coll. S. Car. Hist. Soc.," Vol. II. "The Huguenots of
South Carolina and their Churches" by C. S. Vedder is notably informing (Proc. Hug. Soc. Amer." Vol. I, No. I). The older works by W. H.
Foote, "The Huguenots" (1870) and Charles W. Baird, "The Huguenot Emigration to America" (1885) should be consulted. "The French
Blood in America" (1906) by Lucian J. Fosdick aims at popularity and
indulges too freely in panegyric. Considerable data bearing on immigration and early church affairs appears in "Trans Hug. Soc. South Car."
(1849 f.); also in "Proc. Hug. Soc. America." A doctoral dissertation
(Univ. of Chicago 1915) by Arthur H. Hirsch entitled "The Huguenots in South Carolina" supercedes all other studies.

"A History of the Presbyterian Church in South Carolina" (Vol. I
to 1800, 1870; Vol. II, 1883) by George Howe is an excellent treatise
save that its arrangement is confusing. An older work that contains a
vast amount of information is that of Rev. W. H. Foote, "Sketches of
North Carolina, Historical and Biographical; . . . " (1846). The
standard works on Presbyterianism by E. H. Gillett, Charles A. Briggs,
(the appendix to which contains several important documents) and
R. E. Thompson are valuable. For titles, and estimates see page 260f.
An article "The Early Presbyterian Immigration into South Carolina"

appears in "The Southern Presbyterian Review," January, 1859. Additional literature bearing on Carolina Presbyterianism is cited on page 261.

For Baptist beginnings, see p. 283.

DOCUMENTS

I. *CONSTITUTIONAL PROVISION FOR RELIGION*

The Royal Charter of March 24, 1663

"Charles the Second, by the grace of God, king of England, Scotland, France and Ireland, Defender of the Faith, &c., To all to whom these prents shall come: Greeting:

1st. WHEREAS our right trusty, and right well beloved cousins and counsellors, Edward Earl of Clarendon, our high chancellor of England, and George Duke of Albemarle, . . . being excited with a laudable and pious zeal for the propagation of the Christian faith, and the enlargement of our empire and dominions, have humbly besought leave of us, by their industry and charge, to transport and make an ample colony of our subjects, natives of our kingdom of England, and elsewhere within our dominions, unto a certain country hereafter described, in the parts of America not yet cultivated or planted, and only inhabited by some barbarous people who have no knowledge of Almighty God.

2d. . . . : Know ye, therefore, that we, favouring the pious and noble purpose of the said Edward Earl of Clarendon, . . . have given, granted and confirmed, and by this our present charter, for us, our heirs and successors, do give, grant and confirm to the said Edward Earl of Clarendon, . . . all that territory or tract of ground, situate, lying and being within our dominions of America, extending from. . . .

3d. And furthermore, the patronage and advowsons of all the churches and chappels, which as Christian religion shall increase within the country, isles, islets and and limits aforesaid, shall happen hereafter to be erected, together with license and power to build and found churches, chappels and oratories, in convenient and fit places, within the said bounds and limits, and to cause them to be dedicated and consecrated according to the ecclesiastical laws of our kingdom of England, together with all and singular the like, and as ample rights, jurisdictions, priviledges, prerogatives, royalties, liberties, immunities and franchises of what kind soever, within the countries, isles, islets and limits aforesaid.

. . . .

18th. And because it may happen that some of the people and inhabitants of the said province, cannot in their private opinions, conform to the publick exercise of religion, according to the liturgy, form and ceremonies of the church of England, or take and subscribe the oaths and articles, made and established in that behalf, and for that the same, by reason of the remote distances of these places, will, we hope be no breach of the unity and uniformity established in this nation, our will and pleasure therefore is and we do by these presents, for us, our heirs and successors, give and grant unto the said Edward . . . full and free license, liberty and authority, by such legal ways and means as they shall think fit, to give and grant unto such person or persons, inhabiting and being within the said province, or any part thereof, who really in their judgments, and for conscience sake, cannot or shall not conform to the said liturgy and ceremonies, and take and subscribe the oaths and articles aforesaid, or any of them, such indulgencies and dispensations in that behalf, for and during such time and times, and with such limitations as they, . . . shall in their discretion think fit and reasonable; and with this express proviso, and limitation also, that such person and persons, to whom such indulgencies and dispensations shall be granted as aforesaid, do and shall from time to time declare and continue, all fideltity, loyalty and obedience to us, our heirs and successors, and be subject and obedient to all other the laws, ordinances, and constitutions of the said province, in all matters whatsoever, as well ecclesiastical as civil, and do not in any wise disturb the peace and safety thereof, or scandalize or reproach the said liturgy, forms and ceremonies, or anything relating thereunto, or any person or persons whatsoever, for or in respect of his or their use or exercise thereof, or his or their obedience and conformity thereunto.

Text—Saunders: *The Colonial Records of North Carolina*, Vol. I, p. 20 f.

The Concessions and Agreements of January 7, 1665

8. Item That noe person or persons quallifyed as aforesaid within the Province or all or any of the Countyes before exprest at any time shalbe anywayes molested punished disquieted or called in question for any differences in opinion or practice in matters of religious concernment whoe doe not actually disturbe the civill peace of the said Province or Countyes but that all and every such person and persons may from time to time and at all times freely and fully have and enjoye his and their judgments and contiences in matters of religion throughout all the said Province they behaving themselves peaceably and quietly and not using this liberty to Lycentiousness nor to the Civill Injury or outward disturbance of others, any Law statute or clause conteyned or to be conteyned usage or custom of this realme of England to the contrary hereof in anywise notwithstanding.

9. Item That noe pretence may be taken by us our heires or assignes for or by reason of our right of patronage and power of advowson graunted unto us by his Majesties Letters pattents aforesaid to infringe thereby ye Generall clause of Liberty of Contience aforemenconed We doe hereby graunt unto the Generall assemblyes of ye severall Countyes power by act to constitute and appoint such and soe many Ministers or preachers as they shall thinke fitt, and to establish their maintenance Giving Liberty besides to any person or persons to keepe and mainteyne what preachers or Ministers they please.

. . . .

5. Item We doe alsoe graunt convenient proporcons of land for highways and for streetes not exceeding one hundred foote in bredth in Cittyes Townes Villages for churches Forts wharfs Keys Harbours and for publicke houses and to each parish for ye use of there Ministers one hundred Acres in such places as ye Generall Assembly shall appoynt; . . .

Text—Saunders: *The Colonial Records of North Carolina*, Vol. I, pp. 80, 81, 92.

The Fundamental Constitutions of Carolina, March 1, 1669

Never put into operation though honored in spirit by the Instructions sent periodically to the Governors and Council of Albemarle, these Constitutions have particular interest because of their association with the name of Locke.

The religious clauses enacted:

"95th. No man shall be permitted to be a freeman of Carolina, or to have any estate or habitation within it, that doth not acknowledge a God, and that God is publicly and solemnly to be worshipped.

96th. (As the country comes to be sufficiently planted, and distributed into fit divisions, it shall belong to the parliament to take care for the building of churches and the public maintenance of divines, to be employed in the exercise of religion, according to the church of England; which being the only true and orthodox, and the national religion of all the king's dominions, is so also of Carolina, and therefore it alone shall be allowed to receive public maintenance by grant of parliament.)

97th. But since the natives of that place, who will be concerned in our plantation, are utterly strangers to Christianity, whose idolatry, ignorance or mistake, gives us no right to expel or use them ill; and those who remove from other parts to plant there, will unavoidably be of different opinions, concerning matters of religion, the liberty whereof they will expect to have allowed them, and it will not be reasonable for us on this account to keep them out; that civil peace may be obtained amidst diversity of opinions, and our agreement and compact with all men, may be duly and faithfully observed, the violation whereof, upon what pretence soever, cannot be without great offence to Almighty God, and great scandal to the true religion which we profess; and also that Jews, Heathens and other dissenters from the purity of the Christian religion, may not be scared and kept at a distance from it, but by having an opportunity of acquainting themselves with the truth and reasonableness of its doctrines, and the peaceableness and inoffensiveness of its professors, may by good usage and persuasion, and all those convincing methods of gentleness and meekness, suitable to the rules and design of the gospel, be won over to embrace, and unfeignedly receive the truth; therefore any seven or more persons agreeing in any religion, shall constitute a church or profession, to which they shall give some name, to distinguish it from others.

98th. The terms of admittance and communion with any church or profession shall be written in a book, and therein be subscribed by all the members of the said church or profession; which book shall be kept by the public Register of the Precinct wherein they reside.

99th. The time of every one's subscription and admittance, shall be dated in the said book or religious record.

100th. In the terms of communion of every church or profession, these following shall be three, without which no agreement or assembly of men, upon pretence of religion, shall be accounted a church or profession within these rules.

1st. "That there is a God."

2d. "That God is publickly to be worshipped."

3d. "That it is lawful and the duty of every man, being thereunto called by those that govern, to bear witness to truth; and that every church or profession shall in their terms of communion, set down the eternal way whereby they witness a truth as in the presence of God, whether it be by laying hands on or kissing the bible, as in the church of England, or by holding up the hand, or any other sensible way."

101st. No person above seventeen years of age, shall have any benefit or protection of the law, or be capable of any place of profit or honor, who is not a member of some church or profession, having his name recorded in some one, and but one religious record, at once.

102d. No person of any other church or profession shall disturb or molest any religious assembly.

103d. No person whatsoever, shall speak anything in their religious assembly irreverently or seditiously of the government or governors, or of state matters.

104th. Any person subscribing the terms of communion, in the record of the said church or profession, before the precinct register and any five members of the said church or profession, shall be thereby made a member of the said church or profession.

105th. Any person, striking his own name out of any religious record, or his name being struck out by any officer thereunto authorized by such church or profession respectively, shall cease to be a member of that church or profession.

106th. No man shall use any reproachful, reviling, or abusive language against any religion of any church or profession; that being the certain way of disturbing the peace, and of hindering the conversion of any to the truth, by engaging them in quarrels and animosities, to the hatred of the professors and that profession which otherwise they might be brought to assent to.

107th. Since charity obliges us to wish well to the souls of all men, and religion ought to alter nothing in any man's civil estate or right, it shall be lawful for slaves as well as others, to enter themselves and be of what church or profession any of them shall think best, and thereof be as fully members as any freeman. But yet no slave shall hereby be exempted from that civil dominion his master hath over him, but be in all things in the same state and condition he was in before.

108th. Assemblies upon what pretence soever of religion, not observing and performing the above said rules, shall not be esteemed as churches, but unlawful meetings, and be punished as other riots.

109th. No person whatsoever shall disturb, molest, or persecute another, for his speculative opinions in religion, or his way of worship.

110th. Every freeman of Carolina, shall have absolute power and authority over his negro slaves, of what opinion or religion soever."

Text—Saunders: *The Colonial Records of North Carolina*, Vol. I, pp. 202-4.

II. *QUAKER PIONEERING*

William Edmundson, a Quaker, 'the first minister of Christ to preach in North America' has left the following account of his visit, April, 1672.

"Afterwards, it being upon me, I travelled to Carolina, and two Friends accompanied me, it being all wilderness and no English inhabitants or path-ways, but some marked trees to guide people. The first day's journey we did pretty well, and lay that night in the woods, as we often used to do in those parts. The next day being wet weather we were sorely foiled in swamps and rivers, and one of the two who were with me for a guide, was at a stand to know which way the place lay we were to go to. I perceiving that he was at a loss, turned my mind to the Lord, and as he led me, I led the way. So we travelled in many difficulties until about sun-set; then they told me they could travel no farther; for they both fainted, being weak-spirited men. I bid them stay there, and kindle a fire, and I would ride a little farther, for I saw a bright horizon appear through the woods, which travellers take as a mark of some plantation. I rode on to it, and found it was only tall timber trees without underwood.

But I perceived a small path, which I followed until it was very dark, and rained violently; then I alighted and set my back to a tree, until the rain abated. It being dark, and the woods thick, I walked all night between two trees; and though very weary, I durst not lie down on the ground, for my clothes were wet to my skin. I had eaten little or nothing that day, neither had I anything to refresh me but the Lord. In the morning I returned to seek my two companions and found them lying by a great fire of wood. I told them how I had fared; and he that should have been the guide, would have persuaded me that we were gone past the place where we intended; but my mind drew to the path which I had found the night before. So I led the way, and that path brought us to the place where we intended, viz: Henry Phillip's house by Albermarle river.

"He and his wife had been convinced of the truth in New England, and came here to live; and not having seen a Friend for seven years before, they wept for joy to see us. It being on a first-day morning when we got there, although I was weary and faint and my clothes wet, I desired them to send to the people thereaway to come to a meeting about the middle of the day, and I would lie down upon a bed, and if I slept too long, that they should awake me. Now about the hour appointed many people came, but they had little or no religion, for they came and sat down in the meeting smoking their pipes. In a little time the Lord's testimony arose in the authority of His power, and their hearts being reached by it, several of them were tendered and received the testimony. After meeting they desired me to stay with them, and let them have more meetings.

"One Tems, a justice of the peace, and his wife were at the meeting, who received the truth with gladness, and desired to have the next meeting at their house, about three miles off, on the other side of the water; so we had a meeting there the next day and a blessed time it was; for several were tendered with a sense of the power of God, received the truth, and abode in it.

"1672. I could stay no longer with them at that time, for I had appointed a man's meeting in Virginia, to be on the fifth-day of that week; things being much out of order among them. I therefore took my leave of them in the love of God, and began my journey on third-day morning, with my two fellow travellers."

Text—Saunders: *The Colonial Records of North Carolina*, Vol. I, pp. 215-16.

III. *THE EPISCOPALIAN CHURCH AT WORK*

The reading below is taken from Samuel Thomas' "Memorial relating to the State of the Church of England in the Province of South Carolina offered humbly to the consideration of the Hon. Society for Propagating the Gospel in Foreign Parts." December-January, 1705-6.

"The first and chief Parish in South Carolina is Charles Town which is a large Parish and hath a very honourable maintenance for the Minister, but it being at present under the pastoral care of M^r. Martson who hath been there for five years, I forbear to say anything of its inhabitants or their sentiments, as to religion.

The next Parish to Charles Town is Goose Creek, one of the most populous of our Country Parishes containing (as near as I can guess) about 120 familys in which Parish live many persons of considerable note for figure and Estate in the Country, many of which are concerned in the Government as Members of the Council and

Assembly, most of these Inhabitants are of the profession of the Church of England, excepting about five familys of French Protestants who are Calvinists and 3. Familys of Presbyterians and two Anabaptists.

Here is a small Church for some years erected by some few of the Chief Inhabitants in which they had divine service and sermons & sacraments as often as they could procure a Minister to officiate. I officiated there constantly once a quarter at which times I always administered the Blessed Sacrament of the Lords Supper, the number of Communicants were about 30. of which one was a Christian Negro man.

The Church of Goosecreek was very well frequented as often as any of our Ministers officiated there. The number of Heathen Slaves in this Parish I suppose to be about 200. twenty of which I observe to come constantly to church, and these and several others of them well understand the English tongue and can read.

The next Parish to Goose Creek is that upon the western branch of Cooper River, in this Parish there are two general Settlements, one called by the name of Watboe and the other called Wampee; this parish contains about seaventy families, there was no church in this Parish during my stay in Carolina, but there is a church now building in this and every other Parish by order of the Government, who have by an Act of Assembly appropriated several sums for this end, In this Parish I officiated one Lord's day in the month & one week day in the month, in some of the Planters houses or in the summer under some green tree in some airy place made convenient for Minister and people.

There are in this Parish about forty families of the profession of the Church of England, and 30. Families who dissent from the Church, these are more generally Anabaptists, and they have a preacher of that sort among them, one Lord's day in three; my congregation here consisted of about 80. persons and sometimes near 100. the Dissenters frequently making a very considerable part thereof, they coming to our Churches when their own Ministers did not preach. The number of communicants with the church of England were 20. the number of heathen slaves in this Parish are about 180. three only of wch are christians. The next Parish to this is situated upon the eastern branch of Cooper river which Parish I by order of the Honble Governor had the care of and did constantly officiate in 3. Lord's days in 4 throughout the year and two week days in a month, the number of Inhabitants in this Parish are about 100. families 80. of which are of the profession of the Church of England & about 20. Dissenters from the Church, 17. of which Presbyterians, 2. Anabaptists, and 1. Quaker.

The number of those who attended constantly upon the Lord's day service were generally 100. and upon those days on which the Lord's Supper was administered 140. The number of Comunicants in this Parish 45, the number of heathen slaves 200. of which 20. have by my encouragement learned to read and I hope by God's grace will with many others be fitted for Baptism and the Lord's Supper upon my return. Here is one church already erected (since my arrival) by the peculiar direction and religious care of Sir. Nathaniel Johnson and at the charge of the Parish. The next Parish to this is situated upon a river called Wandoe, and contains about 100. families, 60. of which are of the profession of the Church of England and about 40. Dissenters from the Church which are Presbyterians; here has been a small church for sometime erected, but the People has never had a constant Minister, The congregation when there is a Minister to officiate consists of about 70. The Lord's Supper has never been administered: the number of slaves may be about 100. not one of them Christian or preparing for it.

The next Parish to this is situated upon Ashly river and contains about 100. families, in this Parish there never hath been a Minister settled, so that at present but few of the People are in the interest of the Church of England; here are in this Parish many Presbyterians and Anabaptists, and but about 30. families of the profession of the Church of England. Here has been no church nor has the Lord's Supper ever been administered here: the number of slaves may be about 150. but one of them a Christian which I instructed and baptized.

The last Parish in Carolina is situated upon a river called Stono, it is very large and extensive being the only Parish in that County, which we call Colleton County, in the Southern parts of this Parish are settled about 60 families of Dissenters, Presbyterians and Anabaptists, but in the northern part thereof near Charles Town are about 40. families who profess themselves of the church of England, here is no church nor Minister, the Lord's Supper hath never been administered here: In this Parish are about 150 slaves not any of them Christians.

I crave leave further to acquaint this Honble Society that the Province of S. Carolina is but very lately divided into Parishes by Act of Assembly procured by the religious care of our present excellent Governor Sir Nathaniel Johnson, and that it is entirely owing to him and the present Members of the Council and Assembly that there are any salaries settled upon Ministers of the Church of England, for there being so many Dissenters in the Province (many of which have always been in the Government) it was a work of no small difficulty to get an Act to pass in favour of the Church of England clergy, especially for their having a publick salary, which those who dissent from us violently oppose in those parts of the world.

. . . .

I now beg leave to offer some brief remarks upon this account of the state of the Church in South Carolina to the consideration of this honorable Society.

First, By this account it is sadly evident how destitute our Brethren of the Church of England in South Carolina are of spiritual guides and Publick Ordinances, and in how much danger they are of famishing in grace for want of the word and sacraments or to be led aside to error while destitute of the public ministry to confirm them in the truth, for as circumstances are at present in this our Province not one person in 20 among those who profess themselves of the Church of England can have ordinarily, the benefit of the word and sacraments from a church of England minister, the Dissenters have at present 4 ministers among them besides one Anabaptist Preacher lately gone in to Carolina from Biddiford in the West of England, and I am informed that 3. or 4. more dissenting Ministers are going for Carolina in the Spring, all which (I humbly conceive) makes it very needful that our church of England members be provided with pious and painful divines such as will live exemplarily and preach practically and constantly, and catechise frequently that so their people may not be tempted to put themselves under the conduct of those who differ from us, as we have great reason to believe they will if they see themselves neglected.

. . . .

I further remark to this Honble Society who I well know delight in doing good and will rejoice to hear that the Church and Kingdom of Christ are enlarged that from the account that hath been given there seems to be a prospect of bringing many of the Indian and Negroe slaves to the knowledge and practice of Christianity, I have here presumed to give an account of 1000. slaves belonging to our English in Carolina, many of which are well affected to Christianity so far as they know of it, and are desirous of Christian knowledge and seem to be willing to prepare themselves for it in learning to read for which they redeem time from their labour, many of them can read in the Bible distinctly and great numbers of them were learning when I left the Province, and that which I have often reflected upon with pleasure is, that among many of our ignorant slaves there is a great freedom from immorality, so that in some Plantations of fifty and sixty slaves we find not a drunkard, nor a profane swearer among them, which aversion to vice, I hope may be some preparation for Christian virtues, when they shall know their duty and obligations thereunto and the means of attaining them, now if every one of these Parishes be so happy as to have a prudent, pious and zealous minister settled in it, they might very easily redeem time from their studies for the instruction of these poor slaves and I verily believe and hope by God's blessing many of these might be brought into the folds of Christ, were we so happy as to have men of true piety, zeal and prudence sent upon this evangelical design. . . ."

Text—*South Carolina Historical and Genealogical Magazine*, Vol. V, pp. 31-37.

IV. THE EPISCOPALIANS AND THE QUAKERS

The following selections appear in Rev. William Gordon's letter to the Secretary of the S. P. G., May 13, 1709.

"Sir:—

. . . .

There are few or no dissenters in this government but Quakers, who have been always the greatest sticklers against, and constant opposers of, the Church, and that with no small success; it will not, therefore, be improper to trace their rise with the privileges and immunities they still plead and contend for at the present day, to the great disturbance of the peace of that province, and the hinderance of good laws and other proper endeavors for its improval.

From the first settlement, I find for some years they were few in number, and had little or no interest in the government, until John Archdale, proprietor and Quaker, went over, by whose means some were made councillors; and ther being then no ministers in the place, they began to increase and grow powerful; for the council granting all commissions, in a short time they had Quaker members in most of their courts; nay, in some, the majority were such, who still, pushing at the government, were very diligent at the election of members of the Assembly, so that, what by themselves, the assistance of several unthinking people, and the carelessness of others, they carried all in that meeting likewise; so far that no encouragement could be obtained for ministers, notwithstanding some endeavors which were used to procure them a very small and inconsiderable allowance.

At last, after many attempts, the Churchmen carried an act, but by one or two votes, called "The Vestry Act," by which twelve vestrymen are to be chosen in every precinct, who have power to build a church in each, and to raise money from the inhabitants for that purpose, with a sum not exceeding thirty pounds for a minister; whom they have likewise (by that act) power, not only to disapprove, but displace, if they see cause. I took a copy of it and some other papers, but my servant and trunk being left behind by an accident, they are not yet come to my hand.

The Church party thought they had now made a good step, and therefore designed to improve it to the advantage of religion, and setting such a regular Church discipline as the lords proprietors were obliged by their charter to countenance and encourage; but herein they met with constant opposition from the Quakers, who, being still powerful in the council, numerous in the Assembly, and restless in their endeavors, spared neither pains not expense to have this act repealed or altered; and, by their mutual cavils and disputes, lengthened out the time of the Assembly's sitting, to their great trouble and charge.

In the year 1704, the law made in the first year of her present majesty, entitled "An act to declare the oath coming in place of the abrogated oaths," etc., reached Carolina, which the Quakers refusing to take, they were dismissed the council, Assembly, and courts of justice, and a law was made that none should bear any office or place of trust without taking the said oaths.

Some time after, the Quakers sent complaints against Colonel Daniel, then governor, deputed by Sir Nathaniel Johnston, in South Carolina. They prevail: Sir Nathaniel removes him, and sends one Colonel Cary in his room.

The Quakers then began their old game, and strive to get into the courts and Assembly again. This governor thereupon tenders them the oaths, which they refusing to take, are again dismissed, and an act made, that whoever would promote his own election, or sit and act, not qualifying himself first by taking the oaths, should forfeit five pounds. This so nettled the Quakers that, in the year 1706, they sent one Mr. John Porter to England, with fresh grievances and new complaints to the lords proprietors, who, by his cunning management, and the help of Mr. Archdale, a Quaker proprietor, obtained a new commission, by virtue whereof Sir Nathaniel Johnston's power in that province was suspended, Col. Cary removed, and several new deputations sent by the proprietors, with power to choose a president among themselves. Thus Porter, having procured a deputation for himself and some other Quakers, arrived in Carolina October 1707, about five months before we reached Virginia.

And here, sir, I could give you a large account of this man's management, and the use he made of his new commission, with his many tricks to advance the interest of the Quakers, and the confusion and disturbance of which he was the chief or only occasion,—but this would be as tedious as his actions are in themselves unwarrantable."

Text—Hawks: *History of North Carolina*, Vol. II, 302-4.

CHAPTER XI

GEORGIA IN THE COLONIAL PERIOD

Bibliography

The unfruitful attempt of Sir Robert Mountgomery (1717) to establish a colony in the area later deeded to the Georgia trustees is set forth in his "Discourse concerning the design'd Establishment of a New Colony to the South of Carolina in the most delightful Country of the Universe" (Force, "Tracts and Papers," Vol. I, Tract I). The mission of Sir Alexander Cuming (1730) to the Cherokees to establish trade connections and friendship forms the basis of a paper by Samuel G. Drake, entitled, "Early History of Georgia and Sir Alexander Cuming's Embassy to the Cherokees" ("New England Hist. & Gen. Register," Vol. XXVI, pp. 260-271).

The life story of Oglethorpe has been told by Thomas Spalding in a "Sketch of the Life of General James Oglethorpe" (1840, "Coll. Georgia Hist. Soc.," Vol. I); by Thaddeus Mason Harris, D.D., in "Biographical Memorials of James Oglethorpe, Founder of the Colony of Georgia in North America (1841); by William B. O. Peabody in a "Life of James Oglethorpe, the Founder of Georgia" (1847, "Library of American Biography," Series II, Vol. II); and best by Robert Wright in "A Memoir of General James Oglethorpe, One of the Earliest Reformers of Prison Discipline in England, and the Founder of Georgia in America" (1867). A recent condensed and well proportioned biography is "James Oglethorpe, The Founder of Georgia" (1904, "Historic Lives" Series) by Harriet C. Cooper. The Oglethorpe correspondence inserted in "The Colonial Records of the State of Georgia" (edited by A. D. Candler, 1910-1915 Vols. XXI-XXV inclusive) will be found highly valuable in throwing added light upon this extraordinary philanthropist.

The Charter issued to the trustees for establishing the colony appears in Vol. I of "The Colonial Records of the State of Georgia." A tract prepared by Oglethorpe, entitled, "A New and Accurate Account of the Provinces of South Carolina and Georgia" (1732, "Coll. Ga. Hist. Soc.," Vol. I) sets forth the economic motives that underlay this colonial

201

enterprise. Another tract, written by B. Martyn, Secretary of the Board, "Reasons for establishing the Colony of Georgia, . . . " (1733, "Coll. Ga. Hist. Soc.," Vol. I) throws supplementary light upon the economic advantages expected from colonial expansion, with detailed information as to how the trustees proposed to conduct their enterprise. Francis Moore's "Voyage to Georgia begun in the year 1735, . . . " (1744, "Coll. Ga. Hist. Soc.," Vol. I) gives a fine picture of the settlement as then founded. It also has the "Rules and Orders" made by the trustees for their immigrants. An anonymous tract, "An Impartial Enquiry into the State and Utility of the Province of Georgia" (1741, "Coll. Ga. Hist. Soc.," Vol. I) seeks to remove prevailing misconceptions of the colony—its climate, soil, land tenures, and negro policy. "An Account showing the Progress of the Colony of Georgia in America from its First Establishment" (1741) drawn up by Benjamin Martyn upon order of the trustees, is a document of prime importance with minute information chronologically arranged, ("Col. Rec. State of Ga." Vol. III; Force, "Tracts and Papers" Vol. I, Tract V). "A State of the Province of Georgia Attested upon Oath in the Court of Savannah, Nov. 10, 1740" by William Stephens, Secretary of the colony ("Coll. Ga. Hist. Soc.," Vol. II, and Force, "Tracts and Papers" Vol. I, Tract III) and "A Brief Account of the Causes that have retarded the Progress of the Colony of Georgia in America, Attested upon Oath, . . . " (1743, "Coll. Ga. Hist. Soc.," Vol. II) are controversial documents which, interpreted with discrimination, help the student to visualize the real experiences of the first settlers. "A True and Historical Narrative of the Colony of Georgia in America, . . . " (1741, "Coll. Ga. Hist. Soc.," Vol. II; Force, "Tracts and Papers" Vol. I, Tract IV) by Patric Tailfer, M.D. and others 'as a polemic is one of the most expert pieces of writing to be met with in our early literature', yet as history must be handled with great critical reserve. A "Journal of the Proceedings in Georgia beginning October 20, 1737" by William Stephens, ("The Col. Rec. State of Ga.," Vol. IV and Suppl. Vol.) although colored by the author's peculiar political and religious ideas, is informing in its accurate details. Almost as much may be said for the "Journal of the Earl of Egmont," first President of the Board of Trustees, 1738-1744. This has recently been made accessible in the "Col. Rec. of the State of Ga.," Vol. V.

Omitting references to the literature of Oglethorpe's military expeditions, the histories of Georgia next engage attention. "An Historical Account of the Rise and Progress of the Colonies of South Carolina and Georgia" (II Vols. 1779, see Carroll's "Hist. Coll.," Vol I) by Rev. Alexander Hewatt, a loyalist Presbyterian minister of Charleston, gives Georgia history accurately although subordinte to its main interest in the affairs of South Carolina. "A View of the Constitution of the British Colonies in North America and the West Indies at the time the Civil War broke out on the Continent of America" (1783) reflects the almost exclusively judicial interest of its author, Anthony Stokes, Chief Justice of Georgia. The "History of Georgia" (Vol. I, 1811, Vol. II, 1816) by Hugh McCall, although copious in its treatment of the Revolution, adds little to Hewatt, from whom without acknowledgment the author made large borrowings. "A History of Georgia from its First Discovery by Europeans to the Adoption of the Present Constitution in MDCCXCVIII" by Rev. William B. Stevens, M.D. (Vol. I, 1847, Vol. II, 1859) is fair minded, reasonably exhaustive, and dignified in its style. "Statistics of the State of Georgia, . . . " (1849) by Rev. George White, is much more informing than its uninviting title indicates. The "Historical Collections of Georgia, . . . " (3rd edition 1855) by the same author has an abundance of useful information. "The History of Georgia, . . . " by T. S. Arthur and W. H. Carpenter (1854) is a mere handbook scarcely worthy of serious notice. "The History of Georgia" (II Vols. 1883), by Charles C. Jones, Jr., gracefully written in an impartial spirit, with generous source quotations but usually lacking in documentary reference is quite indispensable. A "History of Georgia" (1898) by L. B. Evans aims only to meet the needs of boys and girls. "The Story of Georgia and the Georgia People" (1900) by George G. Smith, is a popular presentation, not so serviceable to thorough students as the work of Jones.

In the ecclesiastical field proper, no serious work for Episcopalianism appears prior to that of William Stevens Perry, D.D., who, in his "History of the American Church, 1587-1883" (1885) has devoted one chapter to setting forth Wesley's and Whitefields' experiences in Georgia. Rev. S. D. McConnell, and Prof. Tiffany review the salient facts. See page 7.

On Wesley's connection with Georgia, one does well to consult Rev. Luke Tyerman's " . . . Life and Times of the Rev. John Wesley" (III Vols. 1870-73); "John Wesley, His Life and His Work" (1871) by Rev. Matthew Leliévre, D.D.; and "The Life of John Wesley" (new ed. 1899) by Rev. John Telford. Wesley's "Journal" (Vol. I) will always be suggestive for religious conditions in Georgia in its early days. For full Wesley bibliography see page 314 f.

Whitefield's activities in Georgia may be studied in his "Journal of a Voyage from London to Savannah in Georgia" (edited by James Hutton, 1738, enlarged by A. C. Seymour, 1811), and a "Continuation of Rev. Mr. Whitefield's Journal from his Arrival at Savannah . . . " (1740); "The Works of the Reverend George Whitefield, A. M. . . . containing all his Sermons and Tracts . . . with a select Collection of Letters . . . " (VI Vols. 1771); "Memoirs of The Life and Character of the Rev. George Whitefield, A.M. . . . " by Rev. John Gillies, D.D., revised and corrected with sermons and letters appended (1845); and "The Life of Rev. George Whitefield, A.B. . . . " (II Vols. 1876) by Rev. L. Tyerman. The Bethesda orphanage receives frequent mention in Whitefield's Letters, a few of which are addressed to the orphans. "Early Methodist Philanthropy" (1915) by Eric M. North also throws light upon this institution.

On both Wesley and Whitefield the investigator should keep in touch with the "Colonial Records of the State of Georgia" (Vols. IV, V, XX —XXV incl.) where good indexes may direct him to much desired material.

In the "General Account of all Monies and Effects Received and Expended by the Trustees for Establishing the Colony of Georgia in America, . . . " ("Col. Rec. State of Ga.," Vol. III) there appears a suggestive reflection of the philanthropic and religious purpose that underlay the Georgia enterprise and the exact steps taken by the trustees to compass their end. Sermons preached before the trustees from time to time (for list see Perry, "History of the American Episcopal Church, . . . , Vol. I, pp. 368-71) also set forth the religious aims of the Colony.

On the Salzburgers, the work of Rev. P. A. Stroebel, entitled, "The Salzburgers and their Descendants, . . . " despite its age (1855) will still be found very useful. Their European experiences are described by E. B. Speirs in "The Salzburgers" ("The Eng. Hist. Rev. Oct. 1890, pp. 665-699. "The Colonial Records of the State of Georgia" (Vols. XXI-XXV incl.) contain scores of documents relating to these folk. Minute details of their settlements are accessible in Samuel Urlsperger's "Ausführliche Nachricht von den Salzburgischen Emigranten die sich in America, neidergelassen haben" (1735-1746) and "Americanisches Ackerwerk Gottes, oder Zuverlässige Nachrichten . . . Ebenezer in Georgia betreffend" (1754).

The story of the short lived colony of Moravians has been set forth in "The Moravians in Georgia" (1904) by Adelaide L. Fries, who has succeeded in embodying in her modest monograph all the relevant material contained in the standard works of Reichel, de Schweinitz, Hamilton, and others (see p. 156 f).

The Congregational experiment at Midway has been described by Rev. James Stacy in "History of the Midway Congregational Church" (1903). The same writer has set forth the beginnings of Presbyterianism in "A History of the Presbyterian Church in Georgia" (n.d.)

DOCUMENTS

I. *THE MOTIVES AND CONDUCT OF THE ENTERPRISE*

The following paragraphs are taken from a prospectus by Benjamin Martyn, secretary of the Board, entitled "Reasons for Establishing the Colony of Georgia with regard to the Trade of Great Britain" (1733).

"To show the disadvantage under which we purchase some of the products of other countries, I shall begin with the Italian trade, the balance of which is every year above three hundred thousand pounds against us, as appears by accounts taken from the custom-house books. And this balance is occasioned by the large importation of silk, bought there with our ready money, though we can raise raw silk of equal goodness in Georgia, and are now enabled to work it up here in as great perfection as the Italians themselves.

That we can raise it, we have sufficient proof by an importation of it from Carolina for several years, though for want of hands to carry it on, the quantity imported has been too small for any thing more than trials. With many navigable rivers for the convenience of its trade, the country is extremely rich and fruitful. It produces white mulberry-trees wild, and in great abundance. The air, as it is healthy for man (the latitude about thirty-two,) is also proper for the silk worms, and as care is the principal thing requisite in nourishing and feeding these, every person from childhood to old age can be of use.

. . . .

By raising raw silk in Georgia, and gaining it at so easy a rate for manufacturing here, we shall save not only the large sum paid annually to the Italians, but we shall likewise prevent a very large sum going every year into France for her wrought ones.

. . . .

It is well known, that with the same ease with which we can raise silk in Georgia, we can supply ourselves with flax, hemp and potashes.

. . . .

Though these articles are so very considerable, and enough to justify the settling such a colony as Georgia; they are not the only ones in which she will be advantageous to us. She can supply us with indigo, cochineal, olives, dying woods, and drugs of various kind, and many others which are needless to enumerate.

. . . .

If it should be asked here, How will these people, who cannot work at the plough at home, be able to go through the same labor abroad? The answer is obvious. Their fatigue, unless at first, will not be so great, as the climate is so much kinder, and the soil so much more fruitful. Besides, though a man, who has not been inured to the labor of the country, and has a family, will not go to the plough for so poor a support of them, as a laborer's hire, and even this likewise precarious; yet he will not repine at any fatigue, when it is on an estate of his own, and his gains from this estate will rise in proportion to his labor. Add to this, the high value of the commodities to be raised there, and the low prices of provisions will make it easy to conceive, that the man, who cannot do half the work of an able man here, may earn a sufficient provision for himself and family in Georgia, especially when he pays neither rent nor taxes for his lands.

If these people are of no benefit to the community, what are all those who are thrown into prison for debt? I believe the calculation will not be thought immodest, if I estimate these at four thousand every year; and that above one third part of the debts is never recovered hereby. If then half of these, or only five hundred of them were to be sent every year into Georgia, to be incorporated with those foreign protestants, who are expelled their own countries for religion, what great improvements might not be expected in our trade, when those, as well as the foreigners, would be so many new subjects gained by England? For while they are in prison, they are absolutely lost, the public loses their labor, and their knowledge. If they take the benefit of the act of parliament, that allows them liberty on the delivery of their all to their creditors, they come naked into the world again; as they have no money, and little credit, they find it almost impossible to get into business, especially when our trades are overstocked; they therefore by contracting new debts, must return again into prison, or, how honest soever their dispositions may be, by idleness and necessity will be forced into bad courses, such as begging, cheating, or robbing. These then likewise are useless to the state, not only so, but dangerous. But these (it will be said) may be serviceable by their labor in the country. To force them to it, I am afraid, is impracticable; to suppose they will voluntarily do it, I am sure is unlikely. The colony of Georgia will be a proper asylum for these. This will make the act of parliament of more effect. Here they will have the best motive for industry, a possession of their own and no possibility of subsisting without it.

. . . .
If what I have said here does not answer the second objection, the conduct of the Trustees for establishing the colony of Georgia will, I hope, and doubt not, satisfy those that make it. They have, and constantly do, (as I am credibly informed) use the utmost care, by a strict examination of those who desire to go over, and by their inquiries otherwise, to send none, who are in any respect useful at home. They admit no sailors, no husbandmen, or laborers from the country. They confine the Charity to such only as fall into misfortunes of trade, and even admit none of these, who can get a subsistence, how narrow soever it may be. They suffer none to go, who would leave their wives and families without a support; none who have the character of lazy and immoral men; and none, who are in debt, and would go without the consent of their creditors. To prevent which, they have resolved (I see by the newspapers,) to publish the names of such as shall be chosen at least a fortnight before embarkation; so that the honest creditor can suffer nothing hereby, nay he can be a gainer, as well as the public. For the poor artificer and tradesman, when he finds a decay in his trade, and that he cannot support it much longer, instead of holding it, till he increases his debts, and is thrown into a dungeon, by which they usually become irrecoverable: or, instead of running into a foreign country, in dread of a goal, by which the debts are lost, and his labor and increase are also lost by the public, and by which he imparts the knowledge of some useful manufactury, to the detriment of his country; he may

now make a dividend of what he has among his creditors, he may go with his wife and children, who will all be useful, into an easy, a sufficient, and pleasant support; where he will have no reason to be ashamed of his fortune, as he will see no inequality; or the labor of cultivating his lands, as they will be his own possession.

.   .   .   .

The poor, who are sent to Georgia on the Charity, have all the expenses of their passage defrayed, have likewise all conveniences allowed them in their passage: and great care is, (as I hear) and will be taken not to crowd too many of them in a ship for fear of illness.   When they are set down in Georgia, the Trustees supply them with arms for their defence, working-tools for their industry, seeds of all kinds for their lands, and provisions for a year, or until the land can yield a support.

.   .   .   .

Civil liberty is to be established there in its full extent.   No appearance of slavery, not even in negroes; by which means, the people being obliged to labor themselves for their support, will be, like the old Romans, more active and useful for the defence of their government.

That the people may not be long without public worship, the Trustees, (as I am informed,) have already fixed on a clergyman, who is well recommended, is to embark very soon, and is to be allowed by the Society for Propagating the Gospel in foreign parts, as good a salary, as they give any of their other missionaries.

As liberty of conscience will be granted, it cannot be doubted, but a well-regulated government in a country so temperate, so pleasant, and so fruitful, will draw thither many of the distressed Saltzburghers, and other persecuted Protestants; and by giving refuge to these, the power and wealth of Great Britain, as a reward for her hospitality, will be increased by the addition of so many religious and industrious subjects.

Since I have mentioned the foreign protestants, it may not be improper to consider their present situation, and to show how prudent it is to establish such a colony as Georgia, if only on their account.   As men, as fellow Christians, and as persecuted Christians, they have, as well as our own poor a claim on our humanity, notwithstanding the narrow opinions, and mistaken policies of some, who think their charity should begin, continue, and end at home.

.   .   .   .

At a time when the Protestants are so persecuted, how much will it be for our honor, that the crown of England, which in Queen Elizabeth's reign, and at some times since has been looked on as the head of the Protestant interest in Europe, should still preserve the same title?   And at this time, when his Majesty as elector of Hanover, when Holland, and Prussia have offered relief to so many of them, how much is our honor concerned, that England should not be the last to open her arms to receive her unhappy brethren, grant them a support, and allow them the valuable privilege of worshipping their Great Creator, in the way which they think will best secure their interests in eternity?"

Text—*Collections of the Georgia Historical Society*, Vol. I, pp. 205-229.

II. *PROVISIONS FOR RELIGION*

The Royal Charter of June 9, 1732

"Also we do, for ourselves and successors, declare, by these presents, that all and every the persons which shall happen to be born within the said province, and every of their children and posterity, shall have and enjoy all liberties, franchises and immunities of free denizens and natural born subjects, within any of our dominions, to all intents and purposes, as if abiding and born within this our kingdom of Great Britain, or any other dominion. And for the greater ease and encouragement of our loving subjects, and such others as shall come to inhabit in our said colony, we do, by these presents, for us, our heirs and successors, grant, establish and ordain, that forever, hereafter, there shall be a liberty of conscience allowed in the worship of God, to all persons inhabiting, or which shall inhabit or be resident within our said province, and that all such persons, except papists, shall have a free exercise of religion; so they be contented with the quiet and peaceable enjoyment of the same, not giving offence or scandal to the government."

Text—Chandler: *The Colonial Records of Georgia*, Vol. I, p. 21.

III. *JOHN WESLEY'S EXPERIENCE*

The far reaching significance for Methodism of Wesley's bitter disappointment over his Georgia missionary labors justifies the insertion of the selections as under.

Sun. 7. (March, 1736)— I entered upon my ministry at Savannah by preaching on the Epistle for the day, being the thirteenth of the first of Corinthians.

Sun. 14.—Having before given notice of my design to do so, every Sunday and holiday, according to the rules of our Church, I administered the holy communion to eighteen persons. Which of these will endure to the end?

Sat. 17 . . . Not finding, as yet, any door open for the pursuing our main design, we considered in what manner we might be most useful to the little flock at Savannah. And we agreed, I. To advise the more serious among them to form themselves into a sort of little society, and to meet once or twice a week, in order to reprove, instruct, and exhort one another. 2. To select out of these a smaller number for a more intimate union with each other, which might be forwarded, partly by our conversing singly with each, and partly by inviting them all together to our house; and this, accordingly, we determined to do every Sunday in the afternoon.

Sun. May 9.—I began dividing the public prayers, according to the original appointment of the Church: (still observed in a few places in England:) the morning service began at five; the Communion Office, (with the sermon,) at eleven; the evening service, about three; and this day I began reading prayers in the court-house,—a large and convenient place.

Mon. 10.—I began visiting my parishioners in order, from house to house; for which I set apart (the time when they cannot work, because of the heat, viz.) from twelve till three in the afternoon.

. . . .

Tues. June 22.—Observing much coldness in Mr. —'s behaviour, I asked him the reason of it. He answered, "I like nothing you do. All your sermons are satires upon particular persons, therefore I will never hear you more; and all the people people are of my mind, for we won't hear ourselves abused.

"Beside, they say, they are Protestants. But as for you, they cannot tell what religion you are of. They never heard of such a religion before. They do not know what to make of it. And then your private behaviour: all the quarrels that have been here since you came, have been 'long of you. Indeed there is neither man nor woman in the town, who minds a word you say. And so you may preach long enough, but nobody will come to hear you."

He was too warm for hearing an answer. So I had nothing to do but to thank him for his openness, and walk away.

. . . .

Wed. July 30.—I hoped a door was opened for going up immediately to the Choctaws, the least polished, that is, the least corrupted, of all the Indian nations. But upon my informing Mr. Oglethorpe of our design, he objected, not only the danger of being intercepted or killed by the French there; but much more, the inexpediency of leaving Savannah destitute of a Minister. These objections I related to our brethren in the evening, who were all of opinion, "We ought not to go yet."

Sat. 31.—We came to Charlestown. The church is of brick, but plastered over like stone. I believe it would contain three or four thousand persons. About three hundred were present at the morning service the next day; (when Mr. Garden desired me to preach;) about fifty at the holy communion. I was glad to see several negroes at church; one of whom told me, she was there constantly; and that her old mistress (now dead) had many times instructed her in the Christian religion. I asked her, what religion was. She said, she could not tell. I asked, if she knew what a soul was. She answered, "No." I said, "Do not you know there is something in you different from your body? something you cannot see or feel?" She replied "I never heard so much before." I added, "Do you think, then, a man dies altogether as a horse dies?" She said, "Yes, to be sure." O God, where are thy tender mercies? Are they not over all they works? When shall the Sun of Righteousness arise on these outcasts of men, with healing in his wings!

Mon. 18.—Finding there were several Germans at Frederica, who, not understanding the English tongue, could not join in our public service, I desired them to meet me at my house; which they did every day at noon from thence forward. We first sung a German hymn; then I read a chapter in the New Testament; then explained it to them as well as I could. After another hymn, we concluded with prayer.

. . . .

Sun. July 3, 1737.—Immediately after the holy communion, I mentioned to Mrs. Williamson (Mr. Causton's niece) some things which I thought reprovable in her behaviour. At this she appeared extremely angry; said, she did not expect such usage from me; and at the turn of the street, through which we were walking home, went abruptly away. The next day Mrs. Causton endeavoured to excuse her, told me she was exceedingly grieved for what had passed the day before, and desired me to tell her in writing what I disliked; which I accordingly did the day following.

But first, I sent Mr Causton the following note:—

"Sir,

"To this hour you have shown yourself my friend. I ever have and ever shall acknowledge it. And it is my earnest desire, that He who hath hitherto given me this blessing, would continue it still.

"But this cannot be, unless you will allow me one request, which is not so easy an one as it appears: *do not condemn me for doing, in the execution of my office, what I think it my duty to do.*

"If you can prevail upon yourself to allow me this, even when I act without respect of persons, I am persuaded there will never be, at least not long, any misunder-

standin between us. For even those who seek it shall, I trust, find no occasion against me, 'except it be concerning the law of my God.'
July 5, 1737. "   I am, &c.

Wed. 6.—Mr. Causton came to my house, with Mr. Bailiff Parker, and Mr. Recorder, and warmly asked, "How could you possibly think I should condemn you for executing any part of your office?" I said short, "Sir, what if I should think it the duty of my office to repel one of your family from the holy communion?" He replied, "If you repel me or my wife, I shall require a legal reason. But I shall trouble myself about none else. Let them look to themselves."

. . . .

Wed. 27.—I rejoiced to meet once more with that good soldier of Jesus Christ, August. Spangenberg, with whom, on Monday, August 1, I began my long-intended journey to Ebenezer. In the way, I told him, the calm we had so long enjoyed was now drawing to an end, that I hoped he would shortly see I was not (as some had told him) a respecter of persons; but was determined (God being my helper) to behave indifferently to all, rich or poor, friends or enemies. I then asked his advice as to the difficulty I foresaw, and resolved, by God's grace, to follow it.

In the evening, we came to New-Ebenezer, where the poor Saltzburghers are settled. The industry of this people is quite surprising. Their sixty huts are neatly and regularly built, and all the little spots of ground between them improved to the best advantage. One side of the town is a field of Indian corn; on the other are the plantations of several private persons; all which together one would scarce think it possible for a handful of people to have done in one year.

Wed. Aug. 3.—We returned to Savannah. Sunday, 7, I repelled Mrs. Williamson from the holy communion. And Monday, 8, Mr. Recorder, of Savannah, issued out the warrant following:—

. . . .

On *Thursday* or *Friday* was delivered out a list of twenty-six men, who were to meet, as a grand jury, on Monday, the 22d. But this list was called in the next day, and twenty-four names added to it. Of this grand jury, (fourty-four of whom only met,)one was a Frenchman, who did not understand English, one a Papist, one a professed infidel, three Baptists, sixteen or seventeen others Dissenters; and several others who had personal quarrels against me, and had openly vowed revenge.

. . . .

. . . . "A list of grevances, presented by the grand jury for Savannah, this   day of August, 1737."

. . . .

Herein they asserted, upon oath, "That John Wesley, Clerk, had broken the laws of the realm, contrary to the peace of our Sovereign Lord the King, his crown and dignity.

"1. By speaking and writing to Mrs. Williamson, against her husband's consent.
"2. By repelling her from the holy communion.
"3. By not declaring his adherence to the Church of England.
"4. By dividing the morning service on Sundays.
"5. By refusing to baptize Mr. Parker's child, otherwise than by dipping, except the parents would certify it was weak, and not able to bear it.
"6. By repelling William Gough from the holy communion.
"7. By refusing to read the burial service over the body of Nathaniel Polhill.

"8. By calling himself Ordinary of Savannah.

"9. By refusing to receive William Aglionby as a godfather, only because he was not a communicant.

"10. By refusing Jacob Matthews for the same reason, and baptizing an Indian trader's child with only two sponsors." (This, I own, was wrong; for I ought, at all hazards, to have refused baptizing it till he had procured a third.)

Fri. 2.—Was the third court at which I appeared since my being carried before Mr. P. and the Recorder.

I now moved for an immediate hearing on the first bill, being the only one of a civil nature: but it was refused. I made the same motion in the afternoon; but was put off till the next court-day.

On the next court-day I appeared again; as also at the two courts following: but could not be heard, because (the Judge said) Mr. Williamson was gone out of town.

The sense of the minority of the grand jurors themselves (for they were by no means unanimous) concerning these presentments, may appear from the following paper, which they transmitted to the Trustees:—

To the Honourable the Trustees for Georgia

"Whereas two presentments have been made, the one of August 23, the other of August 31, by the grand jury for the town and county of Savannah, in Georgia, against John Wesley, Clerk.

"We, whose names are underwritten, being members of the said grand jury, do humbly beg leave to signify our dislike of the said presentments; being, by many and divers circumstances, thoroughly persuaded in ourselves, that the whole charge against Mr. Wesley is an artifice of Mr. Causton's designed rather to blacken the character of Mr. Wesley, than to free the colony from religious tyranny, as he was pleased, in his charge to us, to term it. But as these circumstances will be too tedious to trouble your Honours with, we shall only beg leave to give the reasons of our dissent from the particular bills. . . . "

. . . .

It is now two years and almost four months since I left my native country, in order to teach the Georgian Indians· the nature of Christianity: but what have I learned myself in the mean time? Why, (what I the least of all suspected,) that I who went to America to convert others, was never myself converted to God. "I am not mad," though I thus speak, but "I speak the words of truth and soberness", if haply some of those who still dream may awake, and see, that as I am, so are they."

Text—*The Journal of the Rev. John Wesley*, London edition, (1903), Vol. I, pp. 26-71.

CHAPTER XII

THE GREAT AWAKENING

Bibliography

The phenomena of this movement have been described by Jonathan Edwards in a "Narrative of the Surprising Work of God, . . . " (1736; New York edition of Edwards' Works, Vol. III; also issued separately); George Gillespie in "A Letter to the Reverend Brethren of the Presbytery of New York. . . . As Also Some of the Causes of the Great Decay of Vital Religion and Practical Holiness in our Presbyterial Church. With Proofs of God's Remarkable Appearance for the Good of Many Souls" (1740); George Whitefield in "A Continuation of the Rev. Mr. Whitefield's Journal From a Few Days After his Arrival at Georgia to his Second Return Thither from Pennsylvania" (1740); Samuel Finley in a "Letter To a Friend Concerning Mr. Whitfield, Messrs. Tennents, and Their Opposers" (1740); Jonathan Dickinson in "A Display of God's Special Grace in . . . the Conviction and Conversion of Sinners so Remarkably of late Begun and Going on in these American Parts" (1742); Samuel Blair in "A Short and Faithful Narrative of the Late Remarkable Revival of Religion in the Congregation of New Londonderry and Other Parts of Pennsylvania" (1744); Thomas Prince in "The Christian History containing Accounts of the Revival and Propagation of Religion in Great Britain and America in 1743, 1744" (II Vols. 1744-45); John Rowland in "A Narrative of the Revival and Progress of Religion in the Towns of Hopewell, Amwell, and Maidenhead, in New Jersey, and New Providence, in Pennsylvania" (1745); Jonathan Edwards in "Memoirs of the Rev. David Brainerd, Missionary to the Indians on the Borders of New York, New Jersey, and Pennsylvania; Chiefly Takes from his own Diary" (1747, new edition by Sereno Edwards Dwight, "including his Journal, now for the First Time Incorporated with the Rest of his Diary in a Regular Chronological Order" 1822). Whitefield's correspondence is highly descriptive of his revival experiences. This is accessible in "The Works of Rev. George Whitefield, A.M. . . . with a Select Collection of Letters" (VI Vols. 1771).

Interpretations of this awakening are to be found in "Thoughts on the Revival of Religion in New England, A. D. 1740, and the Way in which It Ought to be Acknowledged and Promoted" (1740; New York edition, Vol. III) by Jonathan Edwards; also "Seasonable Thoughts on the State of Religion, . . . " (1743) by W. C. Chauncy. A substantial work embodying masses of documentary material drawn from Prince's history, is that of Joseph Tracy, "The Great Awakening; A History of the Revival of Religion in the Time of Edwards and Whitefield" (1842). Trumbull's "History of Connecticut" (1818) discourses quite freely of the revival and presents some important source material. In "A History of New England, With Particular Reference to the Denomination of Christians Called Baptists, . . ." (2nd ed., with notes by D. Weston, II Vols. 1871) by Isaac Backus, there are many references to this movement particularly in its relation to Baptist development, and to the Separates, (See also p. 96). "The Great Awakening of 1740" (1903) by Rev. F. L. Chapell is a popular presentation of the subject, but adds nothing to the knowledge of the movement. In a "History of American Revivals" (1913), F. G. Beardsley describes rather than interprets the movement. "The Great Awakening in the Middle Colonies" by Thomas Stacy Capers ("Jour. Pres. Hist. Soc." Vol. VIII, pp. 296-315) discusses the revival in its relation to the Presbyterian schism that followed. Psychological studies are "Primitive Traits in Religious Revivals" (1905) by F. M. Davenport, and "Primitive Elements in the Great Awakening" (D.B. Dissertation, Univ. of Chicago, 1907) by W. D. Wilcox. "Great Revivals and the Great Republic" (1904) by Warren A. Candler is a suggestive interpretation of the national significance of the awakening. "The Great Awakening in the Middle Colonies" (1920) by C. H. Maxson has much interpretative value.

Periodical literature is as follows: "The Great Awakening" ("Christian Review" September 1844); "President Wheelock and the Great Revival" ("Amer. Pres. Rev." July 1869); "The Great Awakening of 1740" ("Pres. Quar. and Princeton Rev." October 1876); "Revival Experiences during the Great Awakening in 1741-1744" ("New Englander," November 1883). For additional literature see p. 264.

DOCUMENTS

I. *REVIVAL PHENOMENA*

Such uniformity characterized the phenomena of the Awakening in the various regions affected, that it will suffice to single out representative points such as Northampton, where the revival began, New Londonderry and Boston.

Northampton

Jonathan Edwards, an eye witness of the revival in his own parish, thus described it in his "Narrative of Surprising Conversions," 1735.

The town of Northampton is of about eighty-two years standing, and has now about two hundred families; which mostly dwell more compactly together than any town of such size in these parts of the country; which probably has been an occasion that both our corruptions and reformations have been from time to time the more swiftly propagated from one to another through the town. Take the town in general, and so far as I can judge, they are as rational and intelligent a people as most I have been acquainted with: many of them have been noted for religion, and particularly have been remarkable for their distinct knowledge in things that relate to heart religion, and christian experience, and their great regards thereto.

. . . .

Just after my grandfather's death it seemed to be a time of extraordinary dulness in religion; licentiousness for some years greatly prevailed among the youths of the town; they were many of them very much addicted to night walking, and frequenting the tavern, and lewd practices, wherein some by their example exceedingly corrupted others. It was their manner very frequently to get together in assemblies of both sexes, for mirth and jollity, which they called frolics; and they would often spend the greater part of the night in them, without any regard to order in the families they belonged to: and indeed family government did too much fail in the town. It was become very customary with many of our young people to be indecent in their carriage at meeting, which doubtless would not have prevailed to such a degree, had it not been that my grandfather, through his great age, (though he retained his powers surprisingly to the last,) was not so able to observe them. There had also long prevailed in the town a spirit of contention between two parties, into which they had for many years been divided, by which was maintained a jealousy one of the other, and they were prepared to oppose one another in all public affairs.

. . . .

At the latter end of the year 1733 there appeared a very unusual flexibleness and yielding to advice in our young people. It had been too long their manner to make the evening after the Sabbath, and after our public lecture, to be especially the times of their mirth and company keeping. But a sermon was now preached on the Sabbath before the lecture, to show the evil tendency of the practice, and to persuade them to reform it; and it was urged on heads of families, that it should be a thing agreed upon among them, to govern their families and keep their children at home at these times; and withal it was more privately proposed that they should meet together the next day, in their several neighborhoods, to know each other's minds: which was accordingly done, and the suggestion complied with throughout the town. But parents found little or no occasion for the exercise of government in the case; the young people declared themselves convinced by what they had heard from the pulpit, and were willing of themselves to comply with the counsel that had been given: and it was immediately, and, I suppose, almost universally complied with; and there was

a thorough reformation of these disorders thence forward, which has continued ever
since.

Presently after this, there began to appear a remarkable religious concern at a
little village belonging to the congregation, called Pasommuck, where a few families
were settled, at about three miles distance from the main body of the town. At this
place a number of persons seemed to be savingly wrought upon. In the April following,
anno 1734, there happened a very sudden and awful death of a young man in the bloom
of his youth; who being violently seized with a pleurisy, and taken immediately very
delirious, died in about two days; which (together with what was preached publicly
on that occasion) much affected many young people. This was followed with another
death of a young married woman, who had been considerably exercised in mind about
the salvation of her soul before she was ill, and was in great distress in the beginning
of her illness; but seemed to have satisfying evidences of God's saving mercy to her
before her death; so that she died very full of comfort, in a most earnest and moving
manner warning and counselling others. This seemed much to contribute to the
solemnizing of the spirits of many young persons; and there began evidently to appear
more of a religious concern on people's minds.

In the fall of the year I proposed to the young people that they should agree among
themselves to spend the evenings after lectures in social religion, and to that end to
divide themselves into several companies to meet in various parts of the town; which
was accordingly done, and those meetings have been since continued, and the example
imitated by elder people. This was followed by the death of an elderly person, which
was attended with many unusual circumstances, by which many were much moved
and affected.

. . . And then it was, in the latter part of December, that the Spirit of God
began extraordinarily to set in, and wonderfully to work among us; and there were,
very suddenly, one after another, five or six persons, who were, to all appearance,
savingly converted, and some of them wrought upon in a very remarkable manner.

. . . .

Presently upon this a great and earnest concern about the great things of religion
and the eternal world became universal in all parts of the town, and among persons of
all degrees and all ages; the noise among the dry bones waxed louder and louder; all
other talk but about spiritual and eternal things was soon thrown by; all the conversation in all companies, and upon all occasions, was upon these things only, unless
so much as was necessary for people carrying on their ordinary secular business. Other
discourse than of the things of religion would scarcely be tolerated in any company.
The minds of people were wonderfully taken off from the world; it was treated among
us as a thing of very little consequence; they seemed to follow their worldly business
more as a part of their duty than from any disposition they had to it; the temptation
now seemed to lie on the other hand to neglect worldly affairs too much, and to spend
too much time in the immediate exercises of religion, which thing was exceedingly
misrepresented by reports that were spread in distant parts of the land, as though
the people here had wholly thrown by all worldly business, and betaken themselves
entirely to reading and praying, and such like religious exercises.

But though the people did not ordinarily neglect their worldly business, yet there
then was the reverse of what commonly is: religion was with all classes the great con
cern, and the world was a thing only by the by. The only thing in their view was to
get the kingdom of heaven, and every one appeared pressing into it: the engagedness

of their hearts in this great concern could not be hid; it appeared in their very countenances. It then was a dreadful thing amongst us to lie out of Christ, in danger every day of dropping into hell; and what persons' minds were intent upon was to escape for their lives, and to fly from the wrath to come. All would eagerly lay hold of opportunities for their souls; and were wont very often to meet together in private houses for religious purposes: and such meetings, when appointed, were wont greatly to be thronged.

There was scarcely a single person in the town, either old or young, that was left unconcerned about the great things of the eternal world. Those that were wont to be the vainest and loosest, and those that had been most disposed to think and speak slightly of vital and experimental religion, were now generally subject to great awakenings. And the work of conversion was carried on in a most astonishing manner, and increased more and more; souls did, as it were, come by flocks to Jesus Christ. From day to day, for many months together, might be seen evident instances of sinners brought out of darkness into marvellous light, and delivered out of a horrible pit, and from the miry clay and set upon a rock, with a new song of praise to God in their mouths.

This work of God, as it was carried on, and the number of true saints multiplied, soon made a glorious alteration in the town; so that in the spring and summer following, anno 1735, the town seemed to be full of the presence of God: it never was so full of love, nor so full of joy, and yet so full of distress as it was then. There were remarkable tokens of God's presence in almost every house. It was a time of joy in families on account of salvation being brought to them; parents rejoicing over their children as new born, and husbands over their wives, and wives over their husbands. The goings of God were then seen in his sanctuary, God's day was a delight, and his tabernacles were amiable. Our public assemblies were then beautiful; the congregation was alive in God's service, every one earnestly intent on the public worship, every hearer eager to drink in the words of the minister as they came from his mouth; the assembly in general were, from time to time, in tears while the word was preached; some weeping with sorrow and distress, others with joy and love, others with pity and concern for the souls of their neighbors.

. . . .

This seems to have been a very extraordinary dispensation of Providence: God has, in many respects, gone out of, and much beyond his usual and ordinary way. The work in this town, and some others about us, has been extraordinary on account of the universality of it, affecting all classes, sober and vicous, high and low, rich and poor, wise and unwise; it reached the most considerable families and persons to all appearance as much as others. In the former awakenings the bulk of the young people have been greatly affected; but old men and little children have been so now.

. . . .

This dispensation has also appeared extraordinary in the numbers of those on whom we have reason to hope it has had a saving effect: we have about six hundred and twenty communicants, which include almost all our adult persons. The church was very large before; but persons never thronged into it as they did in the late extraordinary time. Our seasons of celebrating the Lord's Supper were eight weeks asunder, and I received into our communion about a hundred before one sacrament, and fourscore of them at one time, whose appearance, when they presented themselves together to make an open, explicit profession of christianity, was very affecting to the congregation: I took in near sixty before the next sacrament day: and I had very sufficient evidence of the conversion of their souls, through divine grace, though it is not the custom here (as it is in many other churches in this country) to make a credible relation of their inward experiences the ground of admission to the Lord's Supper.

I am far from pretending to be able to determine how many have lately been the subjects of such mercy; but if I may be allowed to declare any thing that appears to me probable in a thing of this nature, I hope that more than three hundred souls were savingly brought home to Christ in this town, in the space of half a year.

. . . .

This has also appeared to be a very extraordinary dispensation, in that the Spirit of God has so much extended not only his awakening but regenerating influences, both to elderly persons and also to those that are very young. It has been a thing heretofore rarely heard of that any were converted past middle age: but now we have the same ground to think that many such have in this time been savingly changed, as that others have been so in more early years. I suppose there were upwards of fifty persons converted in this town above forty years of age; and more than twenty of them above fifty, and about ten of them above sixty, and two of them above seventy years of age.

It has heretofore been looked on as a strange thing when any have seemed to be savingly wrought upon, and remarkably changed in their childhood; but now, I suppose, near thirty were to appearance so wrought upon between ten and fourteen years of age, and two between nine and ten, and one about four years of age; and because, I suppose, this last will be with most difficulty believed, I shall hereafter give a particular account of it. The influences of God's Spirit have also been very remarkable on children in some other places, particularly at Sunderland and South Hadley, and the west part of Suffield.

Text—*The Works of President Edwards*, New York edition, Vol. III, pp. 231-276.

New Londonderry, Pennsylvania, 1744.

Rev. Samuel Blair thus presents the experience through which his church passed:

. . . .

In the beginning of March I took a journey into East Jersey, and was abroad for two or three Sabbaths. A neighbouring minister, who seemed to be earnest for the awakening and conversion of secure sinners, and whom I had obtained to preach a Sabbath to my people in my absence, preached to them, I think, on the first Sabbath after I left home. His subject was, the dangerous and awful case of such as continue unregenerate and unfruitful under the means of grace. The text was Luke xiii. 7. 'Then said he to the dresser of his vineyard; behold these three years I come seeking fruit on this fig-tree, and find none; cut it down, why cumbereth it the ground?' Under that sermon there was a visible appearance of much soul-concern among the hearers; so that some burst out with an audible noise into bitter crying (a thing not known in these parts before.) After I had come home, there came a young man to my house under deep trouble about the state of his soul, whom I had looked upon as a pretty light, merry sort of a youth. He told me that he was not any thing concerned about himself in the time of hearing the above-mentioned sermon, nor afterwards, till the next day that he went to his labor, which was grubbing in order to clear some new ground. The first grub he set about was a pretty large one with a high top, and when he had cut the roots, as it fell down, these words came instantly to his remembrance, and as a spear into his heart, 'Cut it down, why cumbereth it the ground?' 'So, thought he, 'must I be cut down by the justice of God for the burning of hell, unless I get into another state than I am now in.' He thus came into very great and abiding distress, which, to all appearance, has had a happy issue; his conversation being to this day as becomes the Gospel of Christ.

The news of this very public appearance of deep soul-concern among my own people met me an hundred miles from home: I was very joyful to hear of it, in hopes that God was about to carry on an extensive work of converting grace amongst them. And the first sermon I preached after my return to them, was from Matthew vi. 33. 'Seek ye first the kingdom of God, and his righteousness.' After opening up and explaining the parts of the text, when, in the improvement, I came to press the injunction in the text upon the unconverted and ungodly, and offered this as one reason among others, why they should now henceforth first of all seek the kingdom and righteousness of God, viz., that they had neglected too long to do so already, this consideration seemed to come and cut like a sword upon several in the congregation; so that while I was speaking upon it, they could no longer contain, but burst out in the most bitter mourning. I desired them, as much as possible to restrain themselves from making any noise that would hinder themselves or others from hearing what was spoken, and often afterwards I had occasion to repeat the same counsel. I still advised people to endeavor to moderate and bound their passions, but not so as to resist or stifle their convictions. The number of the awakened increased very fast. Frequently under sermons there were some newly convicted, and brought into deep distress of soul about their perishing estate. Our Sabbath assemblies soon became vastly large; many people from almost all parts around inclining very much to come where there was such appearance of the divine power and presence. I think there was scarcely a sermon or lecture preached here through that whole summer, but there were manifest evidences of impressions on the hearers; and many times the impressions were very great and general. Several would be overcome and fainting; others deeply sobbing, hardly able to contain; others crying in a most dolorous manner; many others more silently weeping; and a solemn concern appearing in the countenances of many others. And sometimes the soul-exercises of some (though comparatively but very few) would so far affect their bodies as to occasion some strange unusual bodily motions.

. . . .

There were likewise many up and down the land brought under deep distressing convictions that summer, who had lived very loose lives, regardless of the very externals of religion. In this congregation, I believe there were very few that were not stirred up to some solemn thoughtfulness and concern more than usual about their souls. The general carriage and behavior of people was very soon visibly altered. Those awakened were much given to reading in the Holy Scriptures and other good books. Excellent books that had lain by much neglected, were then much perused, and lent from one to another; and it was a peculiar satisfaction to people to find how exactly the doctrines they heard daily preached, harmonized with the doctrines contained and taught by great and godly men in other parts and former times. The subjects of discourse almost always, when any of them were together, were the matters of religion and great concerns of their souls. All unsuitable, worldly, vain discourse on the Lord's day seemed to be laid aside among them. Indeed, for anything that appeared, there seemed to be almost a universal reformation in this respect, in our public assemblies on the Lord's day.

. . . .

There was an earnest desire in people after opportunities for public worship and hearing the word. I appointed in the spring to preach every Friday through the summer when I was at home, and those meetings were well attended; and at several of them the power of the Lord was remarkably with us.

. . . .

Thus I have given a very brief account of the state and progress of religion here through that first summer after the remarkable revival of it among us. Towards the end of that summer, there seemed to be a stop put to the further progress of the work as to the conviction and awakening of sinners, and ever since there have been very few instances of persons convinced.

Text—*"Christian History,"* Vol. II, p. 242, reprinted in Tracy, *"The Great Awakening,"* pp. 25-33).

Boston, 1740

Rev. Thomas Prince, assistant pastor of the Old South Church writes:

"Upon Mr. Whitefield's leaving us, great numbers in this town were so happily concerned about their souls, as we had never seen any thing like it before, except at the time of the general earthquake. And their desires were excited to hear ministers more than ever; so that our assemblies, both on lectures and Sabbaths, were surprisingly increased. . . . .

Upon the Rev. Mr. Gilbert Tennent's coming and preaching here, the people appeared to be yet much more awakened about their souls than before. He came, I think, on Saturday, December 13th, this year; preached at the New North on both the parts of the following day; as also on Monday in the afternoon, when I first heard him, and there was a great assembly

. . . .

I do not remember any crying out, or falling down, or fainting, either under Mr. Whitefield's or Mr. Tennent's ministry, all the while they were here; though many, both women and men, both those who had been vicious, and those who had been moral, yea, some religious and learned, as well as unlearned, were in great concern of soul.

As to Mr. Tennent's preaching: It was frequently both terrible and searching. It was often for matter justly terrible, as he, according to the inspired oracles, exhibited the dreadful holiness, justice, law, threatenings, truth, power, majesty of God; and his anger with rebellious, impenitent, unbelieving and Christless sinners; the awful danger they were every moment in of being struck down to hell, and being damned for ever; with the amazing miseries of that place of torment. But his exhibitions, both for matter and manner, fell inconceivably below the reality: And though this terrible preaching may strongly work on the animal passions and frighten the hearers, rouse the soul, and prepare the way for terrible convictions; yet those mere animal terrors and these convictions are quite different things.

Such were the convictions wrought in many hundreds in this town by Mr. Tennent's searching ministry: and such was the case of those many scores of several other congregations as well as mine, who came to me and others for direction under them. And indeed by all their converse I found, it was not so much the terror as the searching nature of his ministry, that was the principal means of their conviction. It was not merely, nor so much, his laying open the terrors of the law and wrath of God, or damnation of hell; (for this they could pretty well bear, as long as they hoped these belonged not to them, or they could easily avoid them;) as his laying open their many vain and secret shifts and refuges, counterfeit resemblances of grace, delusive and damning hopes, their utter impotence, and impending danger of destruction; whereby they found all their hopes and refuges of lies to fail them, and themselves exposed to eternal ruin, unable to help themselves, and in a lost condition. This searching preaching was both the suitable and principal means of their conviction.

On Monday, March 2, 1741, Mr. Tennent preached his farewell sermon to the people of Boston, from Acts xi. 23, to an auditory extremely crowded, very attentive and much affected, in Dr. Colman's house of worship. It was an affectionate parting, and as great numbers of all conditions and ages appeared awakened by him, there seemed to be a general sadness at his going away.

Though it was natural for them to resort abundantly to him by whom it pleased the sovereign God chiefly to awaken them, for advice in their soul concerns; yet while he was here, many repaired to their ministers also, and many more and oftener when he was gone. Mr. Tennent's ministry, with the various cases of those resorting to us, excited us to treat more largely of the workings of the Spirit of grace, as a spirit of conviction and conversion, consolation and edification in the souls of men, agreeable to the Holy Scriptures, and the common experiences of true believers.

And now was such a time as we never knew. The Rev. Mr. Cooper was wont to say, that more came to him in one week in deep concern about their souls, than in the whole twenty-four years of his preceding ministry. I can also say the same as to the numbers who repaired to me. By Mr. Cooper's letter to his friend in Scotland, it appears, he has had about six hundred different persons in three months' time; and Mr. Webb informs me, he has had in the same space above a thousand.

Agreeable to the numerous bills of the awakened put up in public, sometimes rising to the number of sixty at once, there repaired to us both boys and girls, young men and women, Indians and Negroes, heads of families, aged persons; those who had been in full communion and going on in a course of religion many years. And their cases represented were; a blind mind, a vile and hard heart, and some under a deep sense thereof; some under great temptations; some in great concern for their souls; some in great distress of mind for fear of being unconverted; others for fear they had been all along building on a righteousness of their own, and were still in the gall of bitterness and bond of iniquity. Some under flighty, others under strong convictions of their sins and sinfulness, guilt and condemnation, the wrath and curse of God upon them, their impotence and misery; some for a long time, even for several months under these convictions: some fearing least the Holy Spirit should withdraw; others having quenched his operations were in great distress lest he should leave them for ever: persons far advanced in years, afraid of being left behind, while others were hastening to the great Redeemer.

. . . .

The people seemed to love to hear us more than ever. The weekly Tuesday evening lectures at the church in Brattle street were much crowded and not sufficient. April 17, 1741, another lecture was therefore opened every Friday evening at the South Church; and soon after, another lecture every Tuesday and Friday evening was opened at the New North, three of the most capacious houses of public worship in town, the least of which I suppose will hold three thousand people; besides the ancient lecture every Thursday noon at the Old Church, and other lectures in other churches.

Nor were the people satisfied with all these lectures: But as private societies for religious exercises, both of younger and elder persons, both of males and females by themselves, in several parts of the town, now increased to a much greater number than ever, viz., to near the number of thirty, meeting on Lord's day, Monday, Wednesday and Thursday evenings; so the people were constantly employing the ministers to pray and preach at those societies, as also at many private houses where no formed society met: and such numbers flocked to hear us as greatly crowded them, as well as much than usually filled our houses of public worship both on Lord's days and lectures, especially evening lectures, for about a twelve month after.

Some of our ministers, to oblige the people, have sometimes preached in public and private at one house or another, even every evening, except after Saturday, for a week together; and the more we prayed and preached, the more enlarged were our hearts, and the more delightful the employment. And O, how many, how serious and attentive were our hearers! How many awakened and hopefully converted by their ministers! And how many of such added soon to our churches, as we hope will be saved eternally! Scarce a sermon seemed to be preached without some good impressions.

. . . .

In this year 1741, the very face of the town seemed to be strangely altered. Some, who had not been here since the fall before, have told me their great surprise at the change in the general look and carriage of people, as soon as they landed. Even the negroes and boys in the streets surprisingly left their usual rudeness. I knew many of these had been greatly affected, and now were formed into religious societies. And one of our worthy gentlemen expressing his wonder at the remarkable change, informed me, that whereas he used with others on Saturday evenings to visit the taverns, in order to clear them of town inhabitants, they were wont to find many there, and meet with trouble to get them away; but now, having gone at those seasons again, he found them empty of all but lodgers.

And thus successfully did this divine work, as above described, go on in town, without any lisp, as I remember, of a separation, either in this town or province, for above a year and a half after Mr. Whitefield left us."

Text—Tracy: *The Great Awakening*, pp. 114-120.

II. *CONTROVERSY AND SCHISM*

It was to be expected that in certain quarters criticism would be launched against the irregularities of this campaign. The following "Testimony," although adopted by a bare majority after prolonged and heated debate, seems to indicate the lines along which controversy at first, and cleavage later proceeded.

The TESTIMONY *of the Pastors of the Churches in the Province of Massachusetts Bay, in New England, at their Annual Convention in Boston, May 25, 1743, against several Errors in Doctrine and Disorders in Practice, which have of late obtained in various Parts of the Land; as drawn up by a Committee chosen by the said Pastors, read and accepted, paragraph by paragraph, and voted to be signed by the Moderator in their name, and printed.*

We, the pastors of the churches of Christ in the province of Massachusetts Bay, in New England, at our Annual Convention, May 25, 1743, taking into consideration several errors in doctrine and disorders in practice that have of late obtained in various parts of the land, look upon ourselves bound, in duty to our great Lord and Master, Jesus Christ, and in concern for the purity and welfare of these churches, in the most public manner to bear our testimony against them.

I. As to errors in doctrine; we observe that some in our land look upon what are called secret impulses upon their minds without due regard to the written word, the rule of their conduct, that none are converted but such as know they are converted, and the time when; that assurance is of the essence of saving faith; that sanctification is no evidence of justification; with other Antinomian and Familiastical errors which flow from these; all which, as we judge, are contrary to the pure doctrines of the Gospel, and testified against and confuted in the Acts of the Synod of August, 1637; as printed in a book entitled 'The Rise, and Reign, and Ruin, of Antinominaism, &c., in New England.'

II. As to disorders in practice, we judge,

1. The itinerancy, as it is called, by which either ordained ministers or young candidates go from place to place, and without the knowledge, or contrary to the leave of the stated pastors in such places, assemble their people to hear themselves preach— arising, we fear, from too great an opinion of themselves, and an uncharitable opinion of those pastors, and a want of faith in the great Head of the churches, is a breach of order, and contrary to the Scriptures, I Pet. 4:15; 2 Cor. 10:12, to the end and the sentiments of our fathers expressed in their Platform of Church Discipline, Chap. 9, sect. 6.

2. Private persons of no education and but low attainments in knowledge and in the great doctrines of the gospel, without any regular call, under a pretence of exhorting, taking upon themselves to be preachers of the word of God, we judge to be a heinous invasion of the ministerial office, offensive to God, and destructive to these churches; contrary to Scripture, Numb. 16: 1 Cor. 28, 29, and testified against in a "Faithful Advice to the Churches of New England" by several of our venerable fathers.

3. The ordaining or separating of any persons to the work of the evangelical ministry at large, and without any relation to a particular charge, which some of late have unhappily gone into, we look upon as contrary to the Scriptures, and directly opposite to our Platform, chap. 6. sect. 3, and the practice of the Protestant churches; as may be seen in "The Order of the Churches Vindicated," by the very Reverend Dr. Increase Mather.

4. The spirit and practice of separation from the particular flocks to which persons belong, to join themselves with, and support lay exhorters or itinerants, is very subversive of the Churches of Christ, opposite to the rule of the gospel, Gal. 5:19, 20; Jude 19; 1 Cor. 12:25; 1 Cor. 3:3, and utterly condemned by our Platform, chap. 13, sect. 1, 5, and contrary to their covenant engagements.

5. Persons assuming to themselves the prerogatives of God, to look into and judge the hearts of their neighbours, censure and condemn their brethren, especially their ministers, as Pharisees, Arminians, blind and unconverted, &c., when their doctrines are agreeable to the gospel and their lives to their Christian profession, is, we think, most contrary to the spirit and precepts of the gospel, and the example of Christ, and highly unbecoming the character of those who call themselves the disciples of the meek and lowly Jesus.   John 13:34, 35; 1 Sam. 16:7; Mat. 7:1; Rom. 14:10.

6. Though we deny not that the human mind, under the operations of the Divine Spirit, may be overborne with terrors and joys; yet the many confusions that have appeared in some places, from the vanity of mind and ungoverned passions of people, either in the excess of sorrow or joy, with the disorderly tumults and indecent behaviour of persons, we judge to be so far from an indication of the special presence of God with those preachers that have industriously excited and countenanced them, or in the assemblies where they prevail, that they are a plain evidence of the weakness of human nature; as the history of the enthusiasms that have appeared in the world, in several ages, manifests.   Also, 1 Cor. 14: 23, 40.   At the same time, we bear our testimony against the impious spirit of those that from hence take occasion to reproach the work of the Divine Spirit in the hearts of the children of God.

Upon the whole, we earnestly recommend the churches of this country to the gracious care and conduct of the great Shepherd of the sheep, with our thankful acknowledgments for his merciful regard to them in supplying them with faithful pastors, and protecting them from the designs of their enemies, and advancing his spiritual kingdom in the souls of so many, from the foundation of this country to this day; and where there is any special revival of pure religion in any parts of our land at this time, we would give unto God all the glory.   And we earnestly advise all our brethren in the ministry carefully to endeavour to preserve their churches pure in their doctrine, discipline and manners, and guard them against the intrusion of itinerants and exhorters, to uphold a spirit of love towards one another, and all men; which, together with their fervent prayers, will be the most likely means, under God, to promote the true religion of the holy Jesus, and hand it, uncorrupt, to succeeding generations.

Signed,   NATHANIEL EELLS, Moderator,
in the name and by order of the Convention.

Text—Tracy: *The Great Awakening*, pp. 287, 288.

III. *YALE'S REACTION*

In the Governor's speech (May 13, 1742) there appeared the following: "The unhappy Circumstances of our Colledge which for want of supporting due Order and Regulation has dispersed ye Students at an unusual Season should be rectifyed before ye Return least it suffer a fatal Dissolution." A Committee appointed to take under advisement this reference reported as under:

The Comt^ee. appoynted to take into consideration that paragraph in his Honours Speech (made to this Assembly) relateing to the unhapie ciercomstances of the Colege, pursuant to the order of this assembly, have made Inqueiery of the Reuer^d Rector of s^d Coledge, and of others likelie to Inform us respecting the State thereof, and after deliberation, take leaue to report to your Honour, & to this Honourable Assembly, as followeth.

That Sundry of the Students of s^d Colege, haue as the reuer^d Rector Informeth us by the Instigation perswation & example of others, fallen into Seueral Errors in principal and disorders in practice, which may be uerry hurtfull to Relegion, and Some of them Inconsistant with the good order, & gouerment of that Societie.

Perticulerly, Some of the Students haue fallen into the practice of Rash Judgeing & censureing others, euen Some of the Gouernours, teachers & Instructors of the Colege, as being unconuerted, unexperienced & unskillfull guids, in matters of Relegion, and haue thereupon contemtuously refused to submit to theire authoritie, and to attend upon & harken to theire Religious Exercises & Instructions, but rather to attend upon the Instructions & directions of those to whome the care of Instructing ye Students is not committed.

Some under-Graduate Students haue made it theire practice by day & night, & Some times for Seueral days together, to go about in the Town of Newhauen, as well as in other Towns, and before greate Numbers of people, to teach & Exhort, much after the same maner, that ministers of the Gospel do, in theire publick preaching.

That much pains hath been taken, to prejudice the minds of the Students, against our Eclesiastical constitution and to perswade them to dissent & withdraw from the way of Worship & ministry Established by the Laws of this Gouerment, and to attend on priuate & Seperate meetings and that Sundry of the Students haue so don, in contempt of the Laws & authoretie of the Coledge.

that these things haue occationed greate expence of precious time, by disputs among the Scholers, and Neglect of theire Studies & exercises at Colege, and haue been a hinderance to the florishing of Relegion & uital pietie in that Societie, and if Tolerated, may defeat the good ends & designs of it's Institution.

Your Com^tee. thereupon are humbly of opinion, that it is of greate Importance, both to our Ciuil & Ecclesiastical State that the true principals of Relegion & good order be maintained in that Seminary of Learning.

and that it be Recommended to the Reuer^d. Rector, Trustees & others concerned in the Gouerment & Instruction of the Colege, to be uerry carfull to Instruct the Students in the true principals of Relegion, according to our confession of faith & Eclesiastical constitution; and to keep them from all Such errors as they may be in danger of Imbibeing from Strangers & foraigners, and to use all proper measurs, as are in theire power, to preuent theire being under the Influence & Instruction of Such as would prejudice theire minds against the way of worship & Ministry Established by the Laws of this Gouerment, and that order & authorety be duly maintained in that Societie; and that those should not Injoy the preueledges of it, who contumatiously refuse to submit to the Laws, orders & Rules thereof, which haue been made, or shall be made, according to the powers & Instructions giuen in theire Charter, but we thinke it highly reasonable, that all proper meanes be first used with such Scholers, that they may be reclaimed & redused to order, before they be dismissed the Colege as Incorageable.

Your Com^tee. are also Informed, that at a late meeting of the Trustees, they concluded, that in order to the remoueing the diffeculties of the Colege, it was proper that Some experienced Graue Devins repayer to Newhauen, and there to Instruct the Scholers by theire Sermons, that may be by them prepared for that end; and forasmuch as such devines must be taken from other pulpits, and the Trustees not haveing money in theire Treasury, suffetient to hire a person, to suply such pulpit or pulpits; we therefore recommend it to this assembly to Grant to the Trustees a suffetient sum, to enable them to hire a meet person to suply such pulpit or pulpit.

All which is Submitted by your humble Seru^{ts}

> James Wadsworth
> Jos. Whiting
> Jer. Miller
> E. Williams
> Sam^{ll}. Hill
> Jonth, Hait
> Jn⁰. Griswold
> Even^r Gray

Text—Dexter: *Documentary History of Yale University*, pp. 356-58.

IV. *THE ACT FOR REGULATING ABUSES AND CORRECTING DISORDERS IN ECCLESIASTICAL AFFAIRS*

The ministers of Connecticut, determined to avert the disorders of the revival, were able to secure from the Assembly in May 1742 the following act.

1. *Be it enacted by the Governor, Council and Representatives, in General Court assembled, and by the authority of the same,* That if any ordained minister, or other person licensed as aforesaid to preach, shall enter into any parish not immediately under his charge, and shall there preach or exhort the people, shall be denied and secluded the benefit of any law of this Colony made for the support and encouragement of the gospel ministry, except such ordained minister or licensed person shall be expressly invited and desired so to enter into such other parish and there to preach and exhort the people, either by the settled minister and the major part of the church of said parish, or, in case there be no settled minister, then by the church or society within such parish.

2. *And it is further enacted by the authority aforesaid,* That if any association of ministers shall undertake to examine or license any candidate for the gospel ministry, or assume to themselves the decision of any controversy, or as an association to counsel and advise in any affair that by the platform or agreement above mentioned, made at Saybrook aforesaid, is properly within the province and jurisdiction of any other aasociation, then and in such case, every member that shall be present in such association so licencing, deciding or counselling, shall be, each and every of them, denied and secluded the benefit of any law in this Colony made for the support and encouragement of the gospel ministry.

3. *And it is further enacted by the authority aforesaid,* That if any minister or ministers, contrary to the true intent and meaning of this act, shall presume to preach in any parish not under his immediate care and charge, the minister of the parish where he shall so offend, or the civil authority, or any two of the committee of such parish, shall give information thereof in writing, under their hands, to the clerk of the parish or society where such offending minister doth belong, which clerk shall receive such information, and lodge and keep the same on file in his office; and no assistant or justice of the peace in this Colony shall sign any warrant for the collecting any mini-

ster's rate, without first receiving a certificate from the clerk of the society or parish where such rate is to be collected, that no such information as is above mentioned hath been received by him or lodged in his office.

4. *And it is further enacted by the authority aforesaid,* That if any person whatsoever, that is not a settled and ordained minister, shall go into any parish and (without the express desire and invitation of the settled minister of such parish (if any there be) and the major part of the church, or if there be no such settled minister, without the express desire of the church or congregation within such parish,) publicly preach and exhort the people, shall for every such offence, upon complaint made thereof to any assistant or justice of the peace be bound to his peaceable and good behaviour until the next county court in that county where the offence shall be committed, by said assistant or justice of the peace, in the penal sum of one hundred pounds lawful money, that he or they will not again offend in the like kind; and the said county court may, if they see meet, further bind the person or persons offending as aforesaid to their peaceable and good behaviour during the pleasure of said court.

5. *And it is further enacted by the authority aforesaid,* That if any foreigner, or stranger that is not an inhabitant within this Colony, including as well such persons that have no ecclesiastical character or licence to preach as such as have received ordination or license to preach by any association or presbytery, shall presume to preach, teach or publickly to exhort, in any town or society within this Colony, without the desire and licence of the settled minister and the major part of the church of such town or society, or at the call and desire of the church and inhabitants of such town or society, provided that it so happen that there is no settled minister there, that every such preacher, teacher or exhorter, shall be sent (as a vagrant person) by warrant from any one assistant or justice of the peace, from constable to constable, out of the bounds of this Colony.

Text—Hoadly: *Colonial Records of Connecticut,* 1735-1743, p. 455-457.

V. *THE SEPARATES*

Unhappy among the conservative Congregationalists and not quite at home among the Baptists, a church organized at Mansfield 1745, with the Confession of Faith in part as under, may be taken as typical of the Separates. See also *Separates and Baptists,* p. 288.

Article 15. We believe we are of that number who were elected of God to eternal life, and that Christ did live on earth, die and rise again for us in particular; that he doth now, in virtue of his own merits and satisfaction, make intercession to God for us, and that we are now justified in the sight of God for the sake of Christ, and shall be owned by him at the great and general judgment;—which God hath made us to believe by sending according to his promise, (John 16,) the Holy Ghost into our souls, who hath made particular application of the above articles.

18. That all doubting in a believer is sinful, being contrary to the command of God, and hurtful to the soul, and an hindrance to the performance of duty.

20. We believe, by the testimony of Scripture and by our own experience, that true believers, by virtue of their union to Christ by faith, have communion with God, and by the same faith are in Christ united to one another; which is the unity of the

Spirit, whereby they are made partakers of each other's gifts and graces, without which, union there can be no communion with God, nor with the saints.

21. That whoever presumes to administer or partake of the seals of the covenant of grace without saving faith, are guilty of sacrilege, and are in danger of sealing their own damnation.

22. (This relates to the church, and has, among others, these particulars:—

3. That true believers, and they only, have a right to give up their children to God in baptism.

7. That at all times the doors of the church should be carefully kept against such as cannot give a satisfying evidence of the work of God upon their souls, whereby they are united to Christ

9. That a number of true believers, being thus essentially and visibly united together, have power to choose and ordain such officers as Christ has appointed in his church, such as bishops, elders and deacons; and by the same power, to depose such officers as evidently appear to walk contrary to the Gospel, or fall into any heresy. Yet we believe, in such cases, it is convenient to take advice of neighbouring churches of the same constitution.

12. We believe that all the gifts and graces that are bestowed upon any of the members, are to be improved by them for the good of the whole; in order to which there ought to be such a gospel freedom, whereby the church may know where every particular gift is, that it may be improved in its proper place and to its right end, for the glory of God and the good of the church.

13. That every brother that is qualified by God for the same, has a right to preach according to the measure of faith, and that the essential qualification for preaching is wrought by the Spirit of God; and that the knowledge of the tongues and liberal sciences are not absolutely necessary; yet they are convenient, and will doubtless be profitable if rightly used; but if brought in to supply the want of the Spirit of God, they prove a snare to those that use them and all that follow them.

Text—Tracy: *The Great Awakening*, pp. 317-318.

VI. *THE CONCERT OF PRAYER*

The following Memorial recommended by Jonathan Edwards to the christian constituency of America had an important place in the development of missionary interest.

MEMORIAL

From Several Ministers in Scotland, to Their Brethren in Different Places, on Continuing a Concert for Prayer, First Entered Into in the Year 1744

WHEREAS it was the chief scope of this Concert, to promote more abundant application to a duty that is perpetually binding, *prayer that our Lord's kingdom may come,* joined with *praises*: and it contained some circumstantial expedients, apprehended to be very subservient to that design, relating to stated times for such exercises, so far as this would not interfere with other duties; particularly a part of Saturday evening, and Sabbath morning, every week; and more solemnly of some one of the first days of each of the four great divisions of the year, that is, of each quarter; as the first Tuesday, or first convenient day after: and the concert, as to this circumstance, was extended only to two years; it being intended, that before these expired, persons engaged in the concert should reciprocally communicate their sentiments and inclinations, as to the prolonging of the time, with or without alteration, as to the circumstance mentioned: and it was intended by the first promoters, that others at a distance should propose such circumstantial amendments or improvements, as they should find proper: it is hereby earnestly entreated, that such would communicate their sentiments accordingly, now that the time first proposed is near expiring.

II. To induce those already engaged to adhere, and others to accede to this concert; it seems of importance to observe, that declarations of concurrence, the communicating and spreading of which are so evidently useful, are to be understood in such a latitude, as to keep at the greatest distance from entangling men's minds: not as binding men to set apart any stated days from secular affairs, or even to fix on any part of such and such precise days, whether it be convenient or not; nor as absolute promises in any respect: but as friendly, harmonious resolutions, with liberty to alter circumstances as shall be found expedient.   On account of all which latitude, and that the circumstantial part extends only to a few years, it is apprehended, the concert cannot be liable to the objections against periodical religious times of human appointment.

III. It is also humbly offered to the consideration of ministers, and others furnished with gifts for the most public instructions, whether it might not be of great use, by the blessing of God, if short and nervous scriptural *persuasives* and *directions to the duty in view, were composed and published* (either by particular authors, or several joining together; which last way might sometimes have peculiar advantages), *and that from time to time,* without too great intervals; the better to keep alive on men's minds a just sense of the obligations to a duty so important in itself, and in which many may be in danger to faint and turn remiss, without such repeated incitements: and *whether it would not also be of great use, if ministers would be pleased to preach frequently on the importance and necessity of prayer for the coming of our Lord's kingdom*; particularly near the quarterly days, or on these days themselves, where there is public worship at that time.

IV. They who have found it incumbent on them to publish this memorial at this time, having peculiar advantages for spreading it, do entreat that the desire of concurrence and assistance contained in it, may by no means be understood as restricted to any particular denomination or party, or to those who are of such or such opinions about any former instances of remarkable religious concern; but to be extended to all, who shall vouchsafe any attention to this paper, and have at heart the interest of vital Christianity, and the power of Godliness; and who, however differing about other things, are convinced of the importance of fervent prayer, to promote that common interest, and Scripture persuasives to promote such prayer.

V. As the first printed account of this concert was not a proposal of it, as a thing then to begin, but a narration of it, as a design already set on foot, which had been brought about with much harmony, by means of private letters; so the farther continuance, and, it is hoped, the farther spreading of it seems in a promising way of being promoted by the same means; as importunate desires of the renewing the concert have been transmitted already from a very distant corner abroad, where the regard to it has of late increased: but notwithstanding of what may be done by private letters, it is humbly expected, that a memorial spread in this manner, may, by God's blessing, farther promote the good ends in view, as it may be usefully referred to in letters, and may reach where they will not.

VI. WHEREAS in a valuable letter, from the corner just now mentioned as a place where regard to the concert has lately increased, it is proposed, that it should be continued for seven years, or at least for a much longer time than what was specified in the first agreement; those concerned in this memorial, who would wish rather to receive and spread directions and proposals on this head, than to be the first authors of any, apprehend no inconvenience, for their part, in agreeing to the seven years, with the latitude above described, which reserves liberty to make such circumstantial alterations, as may be hereafter found expedient: on the contrary it seems of importance, that the labor of spreading a concert, which has already extended to so distant parts and may, it is hoped, extend farther, may not need to be renewed sooner, at least much sooner; as it is uncertain but that may endanger the dropping of it; and it seems probable, there will be less zeal in spreading of it, if the time proposed for its continuance be too inconsiderable.   Meantime declarations of concurrence for a less number of years may greatly promote the good ends in view: though it seems very expedient, that it should exceed what was first agreed on; seeing it is found on trial, that that time, instead of being too long, was much too short.

VII. If persons who formerly agreed to this concert, should now discontinue it; would it not look too like that fainting in prayer, against which we are so expressly warned in Scripture?   And would not this be the more unsuitable at this time, in any within the British dominions, when they have the united calls of such public chastisements and deliverances, to more concern than ever about public reformation, and consequently about that which is the source of all thorough reformation, the regenerating and sanctifying influence of the Almighty Spirit of God?   August 26, 1746.

Text—*The Works of President Edwards* . . . New York edition Vol. III, pp. 437-439.

CHAPTER XIII

EPISCOPALIANISM IN THE EIGHTEENTH CENTURY

Bibliography

As an introductory study, "The Anglican Outlook on the American Colonies in the Early Eighteenth Century" by E B Green ("Amer. Hist. Rev." Vol. XX, No. 1) is valuable. An acquaintance with the facts of the field in general may be secured from "The History of the Church of England in the Colonies" (1848, 2nd edition 1856) by Canon J. S. M. Anderson; "The History of the American Episcopal Church, 1587-1883" (1885) by Rev. W. S. Perry; "History of the American Episcopal Church from the Planting of the Colonies to the End of the Civil War" (1890) by Rev. S. D. McConnell; and "A History of the Protestant Episcopal Church in the United States of America" ("Amer. Ch. Series," Vol. VII, 2nd edition 1900) by Prof. C. C. Tiffany. The last work is somewhat sketchy until it comes to the period of the Revolution and the organization of Episcopalianism where it is very satisfactory. All in all, Perry's history will be found the most serviceable.

Certain local church histories give detailed information for their areas: "An Historical Account of the Protestant Episcopal Church n South Carolina, from the First Settlement of the Province to the War of the Revolution" (1820) by Frederick Dalcho; "Contributions to the Ecclesiastical History of the United States of America (II Vols., I, Virginia; II Maryland, 1836-39) by Rev. F. L. Hawks; "Documentary History of the Protestant Episcopal Church in the United States of America. Connecticut" (II Vols. 1863-64) by Rev. F. L. Hawks and Rev. W. S. Perry, (very valuable); and "History of the Episcopal Church in Connecticut from the Settlement of the Colony to the Death of Bishop Seabury" (II Vols. 1865-68) by Rev. E. E. Beardsley.

The following documents show the condition of Episcopalianism for the periods indicated: "A Memorial Representing the Present State of Religion on the Continent of North America" (1700) by Thomas Bray; also the same author's "A Memorial representing the present Case of the Church in Maryland with relation to its establishment by

Law" (c. 1700, both in "Maryland Hist. Soc. Fund Pub.," No. 37); "A Journal of Travels from New Hampshire to Caratuck on the Continent of North America" (1706) by George Keith, (covers period 1702-1704; "Coll. Prot. Epis. Hist. Soc.," 1851, Vol. I); "A Short Memorial of the present State of the Church and Clergy in His Majesty's Province of South Carolina in America" by William Tredwell Bull (1723, Perry's "History of the American Episcopal Church," Vol. I, p. 390 f.); "List of the Several Parishes or Places where Divine Service is performed, according to the rites of the Church of England . . . July 1st, 1724" ("Coll. Prot. Epis. Hist. Soc.," Vol. I, p. 121 f.); "A Memorial . . . Representing the present State of Religion in the several Provinces on the Continent of North America . . . " (1730-1740) by Thomas Bray, (*Ibid.*, Vol. I, p. 99 f.); "List of Persons licensed to the Plantations by the Bishops of London from the year 1745 inclusive" (*Ibid.*, Vol. I, p. 107 f.); "Thoughts upon the Present State of the Church of England in America," (1764, *Ibid.*, Vol. I, p. 159 f.) writer not specified.

Concerning Dr. Bray, who played an important part in the founding of Episcopal churches during the opening years of the eighteenth century, much information is to be obtained from the "Maryland Hist. Soc. Fund Pub.," No. 37, which contains a number of his writings edited by Bernard C. Steiner, prefaced by a succinct account of his career by Rev. Richard Rawlinson. An important phase of Bray's work is discussed in "Rev. Thomas Bray and his American Libraries" ("Amer. Hist. Rev." Vol. II, No. 1) by Bernard C. Steiner.

The operations of "The Society for the Propagation of the Gospel" are well outlined in the correspondence between its missionaries and the home office. This in part is accessible in Perry's "Historical Collections relating to the American Colonial Church" (IV Vols. 1870); "The South Carolina Hist. and Geneal. Mag.," (Vols. IV and V); "The Ecclesiastical Records of the State of New York" edited under supervision of Hugh Hastings (Vols. III, IV, and V); and the "Keith and Talbot Correspondence" ("Coll. Prot. Epis. Hist. Soc.," Vol. I, pp. 1-55). Further information may be derived from "Abstracts of the Proceedings of the Society for Propagating the Gospel, appended to the Sermon preached at the annual meetings held in the parish church of St. Mary-le-Bow." (1701-1783, passim); "An Account of the Society for Propagating the Gospel," (1706, no author specified); a "Classified Digest of the Records of the Society for Propagating the Gospel" (1701-1892) compiled by C. F. Pascoe (3rd ed. 1893); and "The Results of 180 Years Work of the Society for Propagating the

Gospel" (1882). A good history of this Society does not exist. David Humphreys' " . . . Historical Account of the Society for the Propagation of the Gospel in Foreign Parts" (1730, reprinted 1853) will be found useful; also "Historical Notices of the Missions of the Church of England in the North American Colonies, . . . from Documents of the S P. G." (1845) by Ernest Hawkins. "Two Hundred Years of the S. P. G., An Historical Account of the Society for the Propagation of the Gospel in Foreign Parts, 1701-1900 (based on a digest of the Society's records)," by C. F. Pascoe, (1902) contains a large amount of information but the arrangement is so poor that the volume is very cumbersome. "Sketches of Church Life in Colonial Connecticut" (1902) edited by Lucy C. Jarvis has some data respecting the S. P. G. in Connecticut; also "A Biographical Sketch of the Rev. Thomas Allen, Missionary of the S. P. G. in Several of the Towns of Litchfield County, Conn. 1761-1766" by a Minister of the Country. "The Educational Work of the Church of England in the American Colonies 1700-1776." (A. M. Dissertation, Univ. of Chicago, 1916) by Ray A. Eusden, makes reference to this Society while giving a general history of educational effort.

The relation of the churches in the colonies to the mother church in England has been presented by Simeon E. Baldwin, in "The American Jurisdiction of the Bishop of London in Colonial Times" ("Proc. Amer. Antiq. Soc., New Series" Vol. XIII, 1900); also by Arthur Lyon Cross, in "The Anglican Episcopate and the American Colonies" (1902).

The various documents bearing upon the agitation for a bishop in America, prior to the Revolution, will be found in "The American Whig. A Collection of Tracts from the Late Newspapers . . . "(II Vols. 1768-9); Perry's "Historical Collections"; O'Callaghan's "Documents Relating to the Colonial History of the State of New York" (Vols. II, III, V, VII, and VIII), and Hastings' "Ecclesiastical Records of the State of New York" (Vol. III). Important documentary material is inserted in the appendix to Cross' "The Anglican Episcopate . . ." The pamphlets of the later phases of this agitation are as follows: "Considerations on the Character and Conduct of the Society for the Propagation of the Gospel" (1763) by East Apthorp; "Observations on the Charter and Conduct of the Society for the Propagation of the Gospel" (1763) by Jonathan Mayhew; "A Candid Examination of Dr. Mayhew's Observations concerning the Character and Conduct of the Society for the Propagation of the Gospel" (1763) by Henry Caner; "Remarks on Dr. Mayhew's Incidental Reflections relative to the Church of England as contained in his Observations. . . . By a Son of the

Church of England," (1763) by Arthur Browne; "An answer to Dr. Mayhew's Observtions on the Charter and Conduct of the Society" (1764) by Thomas Secker; "Defence of the Character and Conduct, . . . against a Candid Examination of Dr. Mayhew's Observations, . . . and against a Letter to a Friend" (1763) by Jonathan Mayhew; "Remarks on an Anonymous Tract, entitled an Answer to Dr. Mayhew's Observations, . . . " (1764) by Jonathan Mayhew; "A Review of Dr. Mayhew's Remarks on the Answer to his Observations," (1765) by East Apthorp; "A Letter to a Friend . . . before the Society for the Propagation of the Gospel, 1767 . . . " (1767) by Charles Chauncy; "A Letter to John, Bishop of Llandaff, occasioned by his Sermon, . . . in which the American Colonies are loaded with Reproach" (1768) by William Livingstone; "A Vindication of the Bishop of Llandaff's Sermon" (1768) by Charles Inglis; "An Appeal to the Public Answered, in behalf of the Non episcopal Churches in America," (1768) by Charles Chauncy;" An Appeal defended; or, The Proposed Episcopate Vindicated" (1769) by Thomas B. Chandler; "A Reply to Dr. Chandler's Appeal Defended" (1770) by Charles Chauncy; "An Appeal farther defended, in Answer to the Farther Misrepresentations of Dr. Chauncy" (1771) by Thomas B. Chandler; "A Critical Commentary on Archbishop Secker's Letter to Horatio Walpole" (1770) by Francis Blackburne; "A Free Examination of the Critical Commentary on Archbishop Secker's Letter to Mr. Walpole . . . " (1774) by Thomas B. Chandler. Through all this literature, Cross has carefully worked his way giving the reader a fair-minded view of its content.

The story of the struggle for a bishop has been told by F. Hawks in "Efforts to obtain the Episcopate before the Revolution" (1831, "Coll. Prot. Epis. Hist. Soc.," Vol. I); H. D. Evans (editor) in an "Essay on the Episcopate of the Protestant Episcopal Church in the United States of America" (1855); W. S. Perry in his "History of the American Episcopal Church" (1885) and notably by Cross.

Aside from controversial literature, the following should be consulted: "Minutes of a Convention of Delegates from the Synods of New York and Philadelphia and from the Associations of Connecticut, held annually, 1766-1775" (1843); "An Address from the Clergy of New York and New Jersey to the Episcopalians in Virginia" (1771); "A Letter to the Clergy of New York and New Jersey, occasioned by an Address to the Episcopalians in Virginia" (1772) by Thomas Gwatkin. The "Life and Correspondence of Samuel Johnson, D.D., Missionary of the Church of England in Connecticut, and First President of King's College" (new ed. 1881) by Rev. E. E. Beardsley, is illuminating; also "The Life of Samuel Johnson, the First President of King's College in New York" (1805) by Thomas B. Chandler. The "Memoirs of the Protestant Episcopal Church in the United States" (1880) by Rev. W. White, has important data. The "Life and Character of the late Reverend Dr. Benjamin Coleman" (1749) by Ebenezer Turell is useful in presenting the background of the controversy.

The course of events connected with the establishment of the American episcopate and the subsequent organization of the church, is to be found in the following: "Journals of the General Convention of the Protestant Episcopal Church in the United States of America, from 1785 to 1853 inclusive" (1861) by Hawks and Perry; "Documentary History of the Protestant Episcopal Church in the United States of America." (II Vols. 1863-4) by Hawks and Perry; "A Half Century of Legislation: Journals of the General Convention of the Protestant Episcopal Church in the United States, 1785-1835, With Historical Notes and Documents" (III Vols. 1874) by Perry; "Memoirs of the Protestant Episcopal Church in the United States" (1880) by Rev. Wm. White; "Life and Correspondence of the Right Reverend Samuel Seabury . . . " (2nd edition 1881) by Rev. E. E. Beardsley; "Life and Correspondence of Rev. William Smith, D.D., First Provost of the College of Philadelphia," (II Vols. 1880) by H. W. Smith; "Memoirs of the Life of Right Reverend William White, D.D." (1839) by Rev. Bird Wilson; "The Life and Times of Bishop White" (1892) by Julius H. Ward.

On the defection of Cutler and his friends in connection with Yale, the literature is as follows: "Documentary History of the Protestant Episcopal Church in the United States of America," (II Vols.1863-4) by Hawks and Perry; "Some Original Papers respecting the episcopal controversy in Connecticut, 1722" ("Coll. Mass. Hist. Soc.," Series II, Vol. II); Beardsleys' "Life and Correspondence of Samuel Johnson, D.D., . . . " (1881); Trumbull's "History of Connecticut" (1818); and Foote's "Annals of King's Chapel" (II Vols. 1882-1896).

The rise of King's College may be studied in "The Life of Samuel Johnson, the First President of King's College in New York" (1805) by T. B. Chandler; "A Memoir of William Livingstone" (1833) by T. Sedgwick; Beardsley's "Life and Correspondence of Samuel Johnson, . . . "; "Life and Correspondence of Rev. William Smith, D.D." (II Vols. 1880) by H. W. Smith; "History of Columbia College" (1884) by N. F. Moore; and "A Memoir of the Rev. William Smith, D.D." . . . (1869) by Charles J. Stillé. Many of the documents are available in

"The Ecclesiastical Records of the State of New York," Vols. V and VI.

The attitude of the episcopal clergy to the Revolution is discussed in "The Position of the Clergy at the Opening of the War of Independence" by Rev. W. S. Perry, in his "History of the American Episcopal Church . . . " Vol. II, ch. 24; "The Sentiment of Independence, its Growth and Consummation" by Dr. George E. Ellis in Winsor's."Narrative and Critical History" Vol. VI, ch. 3; "Life and Epoch of Alexander Hamilton, A Historical Study" (1880) by the Honorable George Shea; "The Influence of the Clergy and of Religious and Sectarian Forces in the American Revolution" by C. H. Van Tyne, ("Amer. Hist. Rev." Vol. XIX No. 1); "Religious Controversy as Effecting the American Revolution of 1776" by Samuel L. Levin ("Americana" Vol. VIII, May number); and "The Ecclesiastical Situation in New England Prior to the Revolution" by J. H. Allen ("Papers, Amer. Soc. Church Hist." Vol. VIII, pp. 67-77).

Two lesser points of interest are the Checkley controversy, and the struggle of the Episcopalians against church rates in New England. On the former, the books to be consulted are "Annals of King's Chapel" (II Vols. 1882-1896) by H. W. Foote, and "John Checkley or the Evolution of Religious Tolerance in Massachusetts Bay" by E. F. Slafter ("Prince Soc. Pub." II Vols. 1897). On the latter, Foote's "Annals" will be found sufficient.

In conclusion a few local histories may be itemized: "An Historical Account of Philadelphia, Pa., 1695-1841" (1841) by Benjamin Dorr; "A History of the Episcopal Church in Narragansett, R. I. . . . " (1847) by W. Updike (2nd edition 1907, enlarged and corrected by D. Goodwin); "History of the Protestant Episcopal Church in Westchester County, New York, from its Foundation (1693) to 1853" (1855) by Robert Bolton; "History of St. John's Church, Elizabethtown, N. J., from 1703 to the Present time" (1857) by Samuel A. Clark; "Sketch of the Protestant Episcopal Church in Portland, Maine, from 1763 to the Present Time" (1864) by W. S. Perry; "Annals of St. James's Church, New London, Conn., for One Hundred and Fifty Years" (1873) by Robert A. Hallam; "History of the Church in Burlington, New Jersey" (1876) by G. M. Hills; "An Historic Sketch of the Parish Church of St. Michael, 1752-1887" (1887) by George S. Holmes; "Record of Holy Trinity (Old Swedes') Church, Wilmington, Delaware." (1890) edited by Horace Burr; "The Protestant Episcopal Church in New York" (1893) by H. C. Potter; "History of Trinity Parish Church, New York" (1893) by Morgan Dix; "The Founding of the Episcopal Church in

Dutchess County, New York, 1755-1895" (1895) by H. O. Ladd; "The Rise of the Protestant Episcopal Church in the District of Columbia" by Arthur S. Browne (1905, "Records Columbia Hist. Soc.," Vol. IX, pp. 63-87); "History of St. Mark's Church New Britain, Conn. and of its predecessor Christ Church Wethersfield . . . " (1907) by James Shepard; "The Records of Christ Church, Poughkeepsie, New York," edited (1911) by Helen W. Reynolds.

DOCUMENTS

I. *THE SITUATION IN 1700*

A Memorial Representing the Present State of Religion on the Continent of North America

This Memorial to the clergy of England, issued (1700) by Dr. Bray, presents not only information upon religious conditions in the Colonies, but reveals the clearly defined Anglican propaganda out of which, a few months after, the S. P. G. was founded.

. . . And it is to represent to You, the present State of Religion in Mary-land, Pennsylvania, the East and West-Jerseys, New-York, Road-Island, Long-Island, North and South-Carolina, Bermudas, and Newfound-Land. And this in order to the Propagation of the true Christian Religion in those Parts, at a Crisis, when, as many Thousands are in a happy Disposition to embrace it, so Infidelity and Heresie seem to make their utmost Efforts to withdraw, and to fix those People at the greatest distance from it.

I. And to begin where I am more immediately concerned, with Mary-Land. . . . The Papists in this Province appear to me not to be above a twelfth Part of the Inhabitants; but their Priests are very numerous; whereof more have been sent in this last Year, than was ever known. And tho' the Quakers brag so much of their Numbers and Riches, with which Considerations they would incline the Government to favour them with such unpresidented Privileges, as to be free from paying their Dues to the Established Church, or rather, would fain overthrow its Establishment; yet they are not above a 12th Part in number, and bear not, that proportion, they would be thought to do, with those of the Church, in Wealth and Trade.

II. As for Pensylvania, . . . there pass'd Letters betwixt my self, and that Church, full of the greatest Respects on their sides: And by such Notices as I have receiv'd from some of the Principal Persons of that Country, I am fully made to understand the State of Religion there; where, I think, if in any part of the Christian World, a very good proportion of the People are excellently dispos'd to receive the Truth.

The Keithites, which are computed to be a Third Part, are truly such; and so very well affected are they to the Interest of our Church, that, in the late Election of Assembly-Men, even since Mr. Penn came into his Government, they had almost carried it for the Church-men, to their great Surprize; so as to let them see, they had been only wanting to themselves in not timely applying.

There are in Pensylvania two Congregations of Lutherans, being Swedes, whose Churches are finely built, and their two Ministers lately sent in, nobly furnished with 300 worth of Books by the Swedish King: And they live in very good Accord with our Minister, and his Church.

There is but one Church of England Minister as yet there, and he at Philadelphia, well esteem'd and respected by his People: And they do most importunately solicit both from thence, and from other Parts of that Province for more, where, I am assured, there are at least six wanting.

There are some Independents, but neither many, nor much bigotted.

III. Adjoyning to this, are the two Colonies of East and West-Jerseys, where they have some pretty Towns, and well-peopled; but are wholly left to themselves, without Priest, or Altar. The Quakers are very numerous in the Jerseys. The Keithians, who are many there, are a like affected to us, as in Pensylvania. And I think there would be a Reception for six Ministers in both the Jerseys.

IV. From New-York, I have an Account that a Church of England Clergy are much wanted there: And there will be room for at least two Ministers, besides one which they have already; the one to assist at New-York, th' other to be plac'd at Albany; where, besides the Inhabitants of the Town, which are many, we have two Companies of Soldiers in Garrison, but all without a Preacher.

I shall not here speak of the Number of Missionaries requisite to be sent to Convert the Native Indians, lying on the back of this, and all our other Colonies on the Continent. Now that the French of Canada do, by their Priests, draw over so many of these Indians, both to their Religion, and their Interests, in the Opinion of many wise Persons, who understand the active and inveterate Spirit of Popery, the Nature of the Indians, and the Scituation of those Parts, the Civil Government has very great Reason to take Umbrage, so as to think it of the highest consequence to the Preservation of our Plantations, to have those Indians, which border upon us, brought over to our Religion, in order to hold them in a stricter Alliance with us. This, I hope, may facilitate another Memorial relating to that particular Case, so as to obtain from the Publick such a Fund, as may maintain at least Twenty such Persons, as will learn their Language, live with them, and preach the Gospel amongst them. But the Reasons for making Provision for the Support of Religion within the Colonies, being not, as commonly apprehended, of so National a Concern; it is from particular Persons, and such only as are more than ordinarily zealous for the Honour of God, and the Good of Souls, that we can with much Assurance promise our selves a necessary Assistance towards Promoting in these so good a Work. And therefore shall address, in relation to them, in another way of Proposal. To proceed them.

V. In Long-Island there are Nine Churches, but no Church of England Minister, tho' much desired; and there ought to be at least Two sent to that Colony.

VI. In Road-Island, for want of a Clergy, many of the Inhabitants are said to be sunk downright into Atheism. The New Generation, being the Off-spring of Quakers, whose Children, for want of an Outward Teaching, which those Enthusiasts at first denied, being meer Ranters; as indeed the Sons of Quakers are found to be such in most Places, and equally to deny all Religion. However through the Noble Assistance of Colonel Nicholson, Governor of Virginia, there is a Church rais'd in that Colony, and something subscribed towards a Maintenance of one Minister. But there will be Work enough for Two substantial Divines at least.

VII. North-Carolina lies betwixt Virginia and South-Carolina: It has two Settlements; th' one called Roanoak, the other Pamplico, 100 Miles distant from each other. And as there will be Occasion for at least Two Missionaries to be sent amongst them; so the Governor, who is now going over to that Colony, being a very worthy Gentleman, I dare promise will give the best Countenance and Encouragement which shall be in his Power.

VIII. South-Carolina is the last Province that I shall now speak of, on the Continent, a very thriving Colony, and so large, as to want at least Three Missionaries, besides one lately sent there.

. . . .

It is no part of my Province to speak to Virginia, it being under the Jurisdiction of a very worthy Person, Mr. Commissary Blaire; whose Abilities, as they fit him for great Designs, so his Industry has been for some Years exercised in doing uncommon Services to that Church.

. . . .

Nor do I think my self oblig'd to speak here of New-England, where Independency seems to be the Religion of the Country. My Design is not to intermeddle, where Christianity under any Form has obtained Possession; but to represent rather the deplorable State of the English Colonies, where they have been in a manner abandoned to Atheism; or, which is much at one, to Quakerism, for want of a Clergy settled among them.

. . . .

. . . , so, upon the whole, it appears, that there are at present wanting no less than Forty Protestant Missionaries to be sent into all these Colonies. And the Necessity that there should be both so many, and those singularly well qualif'd for the purpose, I am next to shew you. And that there should be at least that Number sent into each of these Colonies, as I have now mentioned, appears from hence, That even then their Business will lie extreamly wide; but chiefly for this Reason, that there is so great an Inclination to embrace Christianity amongst many Quakers, all over those Parts where Mr. Keith has been, that it will be fatal Neglect, if our Church should not close with that Providence, which offers so many Proselytes into her Bosom. And the Plantations growing now into populous and powerful Provinces, with all Submission, in my Opinion, ought not to be so neglected, as that it should be indifferent to us, whether they be made Christians, or abandoned to Infidelity.

Nor is the Necessity less that these Missionaries should be singularly well qualify'd, than that they should be at all sent. And indeed, in order to make the better Choice, agreeable to what I have observed of the State, the Temper, and Constitution of the Country and People, is one great Reason that hath perswaded me so soon back. And the Persons which alone can do good there, as I conceive, must,

In the First place, be of such nice Morals, as to abstain from all Appearance of Evil; there being not such a calumniating people in the World, as the Quakers are every where found to be. And it is the worst Fault of the Plantations, that they give their Tongues too much liberty that way, especially if they can find the least Flaw.

Secondly, They must be Men of good Prudence, and an exact Conduct, or otherwise they will unavoidably fall into Contempt, with a people so well vers'd in Business, as every the meanest Planter seems to be.

Thirdly, They ought to be well experienced in the Pastoral Care, having a greater Variety, both of Sects and Humours, to deal with in those Parts, than are at home; and therefore it would be well, if we could be provided with such as have been Curates here for some time.

Fourthly, More especially they ought to be of a true Missionary Spirit, having an ardent Zeal for God's Glory, and the Salvation of Mens Souls.

Fifthly, Of a very active Spirit, and consequently, not so grown into Years, as to be uncapable of Labour and Fatigue, no more than very Young, upon which account they will be more liable to be despised.

And, Lastly, They ought to be good, substantial, well-studied Divines, very ready in the Holy Scriptures, able with sound Judgment to explicate and prove the great Doctrines of Christianity, to state the Nature and Extent of the Christian Duties, and with the most moving Considerations to enforce their Practice, and to defend the Truth against all its Adversaries: To which purpose, it will be therefore absolutely requisite to provide each of them with a Library of necessary Books, to be fix'd in those places to which they shall be sent, for the Use of them, and their Successors for ever: This to be a perpetual Encouragement to good and able Divines, always to go over, and to render them useful when they are there: A Design of whose Usefulness, of whose Necessity, I am now so fully perswaded, since I have been in, and know the Wants of those parts, that I am resolved to have no hand in sending, or taking over any one, the best Missionary, who shall not be so provided.

. . . .

And as neither the Clergy's Condition can be comfortable, nor can it properly be call'd a Settlement, till they shall be in Houses, and on Glebes of their own; so now is the time to endeavour both, or it will be too late hereafter to think of obtaining either. For as yet Land may be taken up, or had upon easie Terms; but should the Plantations continue to increase, as they have done of late, within Seven Years Land will not be purchased at treble the value, as now.

Text—*Maryland Historical Society, Fund Publication*, No. 37, pp. 159-171.

II. *THE SOCIETY FOR THE PROPAGATION OF THE GOSPEL*

Instructions for the Clergy employed by the Society for the Propagation of the Gospel in Foreign Parts

In 1706 the following instructions for the clergy and the schoolmasters were issued:

Upon their Arrival in the Country whither they shall be sent.

First, *With Respect to themselves .*

I. That they always keep in their View the great Design of their Undertaking, viz. To promote the Glory of Almighty God, and the Salvation of Men, by Propagating the Gospel of our Lord and Saviour.

II. That they often consider the Qualifications requisite for those who would effectually promote this Design, viz. A sound Knowledge and hearty Belief of the Christian Religion; an Apostolical Zeal, tempered with Prudence, Humility, Meekness, and Patience; a fervent Charity towards the Souls of Men; and finally, that Temperance, Fortitude, and Constancy, which become good Soldiers of Jesus Christ.

III. That in order to the obtaining and preserving the said Qualifications, they do very frequently in their Retirements offer up fervent Prayers to Almighty God for his Direction and Assistance; converse much with the Holy Scriptures; seriously reflect upon their Ordination Vows; and consider the Accounts which they are to render to the Great Shepherd and Bishop of our Souls at the Last Day.

IV. That they acquaint themselves thoroughly with the Doctrine of the Church of England, as contained in the Articles and Homilies, its Worship and Discipline, and Rules for Behaviour of the Clergy, as contained in the Liturgy and Canons; and that they approve themselves accordingly, as genuine Missionaries from this Church.

V. That they endeavour to make themselves Masters in those Controversies which are necessary to be understood, in order to the Preserving their Flock from the Attempts of such Gainsayers as are mixed among them.

VI. That in their outward Behaviour they be circumspect and unblameable, giving no Offence either in Word or Deed; that their ordinary Discourse be grave and edifying; their Apparel decent, and proper for Clergymen; and that in their whole Conversation they be Instances and Patterns of the Christian Life.

VII. That they do not board in, or frequent Publick-houses, or lodge in Families of evil Fame; that they wholly abstain from Gaming, and all such Pastimes; and converse not familiarly with lewd or prophane Persons, otherwise than in order to reprove, admonish, and reclaim them.

. . . .

IX. That they be not nice about Meats and Drinks, nor immoderately careful about their Entertainment in the Places where they shall sojourn; but contented with what Health requires, and the Place easily affords.

X. That as they be frugal, in Opposition to Luxury, so they avoid all Appearance of Covetousness. and recommend themselves, according to their Abilities, by the prudent Exercise of Liberality and Charity.

XI. That they take special Care to give no Offence to the Civil Government, by intermeddling in Affairs not relating to their own Calling and Function.

XII. That, avoiding all Names of Distinction, they endeavour to preserve a Christian Agreement and Union one with another, as a Body of Brethren of one and the same Church, united under the Superior Episcopal Order, and all engaged in the same great Design of Propagating the Gospel; and to this End, keeping up a Brotherly Correspondence, by meeting together at certain Times, as shall be most convenient, fos mutual Advice and Assistance.

Secondly, *With Respect to their Parochial Cure*

I. That they conscientiously observe the Rules of our Liturgy, in the Performance of all the Offices of their Ministry.

II. That, besides the stated Service appointed for Sundays and Holidays, they do, as far as they shall find it practicable, publickly read the daily Morning and Evening Service, and decline no fair Opportunity of Preaching to such as may be occasionally met together from remote and distant Parts.

III. That they perform every Part of Divine Service with that Seriousness and Decency, that may recommend their Ministrations to their Flock, and excite a Spirit of Devotion in them.

IV. That the chief Subjects of their Sermons be the great Fundamental Principles of Christianity, and the Duties of a sober, righteous, and godly Life, as resulting from those Principles.

V. That they particularly preach against those Vices which they shall observe to be most predominant in the Places of their Residence.

VI. That they carefully instruct the People concerning the Nature and Use of the Sacraments of Baptism and the Lord's Supper, as the peculiar Institutions of Christ, Pledges of Communion with Him, and Means of deriving Grace from Him.

VII. That they duly consider the Qualifications of those adult Persons to whom they administer Baptism; and of those likewise whom they admit to the Lord's Supper, according to the Directions of the Rubricks in our Liturgy.

VIII. That they take special Care to lay a good Foundation for all their other Ministrations, by Catechizing those under their Care, whether Children or other ignorant Persons, explaining the Catechism to them in the most easy and familiar Manner.

IX. That in their instructing *Heathens* and *Infidels*, they begin with the Principles of Natural Religion, appealing to their Reason and Conscience, and thence proceed to shew them the Necessity of Revelation, and the Certainty of that contained in the Holy Scriptures, by the plainest and most obvious Arguments.

X. That they frequently visit their respective Parishioners; those of our own Communion, to keep them steady in the Profession and Practice of Religion, as taught in the Church of *England*; those that oppose us, or dissent from us, to convince and reclaim them with a Spirit of Meekness and Gentleness.

XI. That those, whose Parishes shall be of large Extent, shall, as they have Opportunity and Convenience, officiate in the several Parts thereof, so that all the Inhabitants may by Turns partake of their Ministrations; and that such as shall be appointed to officiate in several Places shall reside sometimes at one, sometimes at another of those Places, as the Necessities of the People shall require.

XII. That they shall, to the best of their Judgments, distribute those small Tracts given them by the Society for that Purpose, amongst such of their Parishioners as shall want them most, and appear likely to make the best Use of them; and that such useful Books, of which they have not a sufficient Number to give, they be ready to lend to those who will be most careful in reading and restoring them.

XIII. That they encourage the setting up of Schools for the teaching of Children; and particularly by the Widows of such Clergymen as shall die in those Countries, if they be found capable of that Employment.

XIV. That each of them keep a Register of his Parishioners' Names, Profession of Religion, Baptism, &c. according to the Scheme annexed, No. I. for his own Satisfaction, and the Benefit of the People.

Thirdly, *With respect to the Society*

I. That each of them keep a constant and regular Correspondence with the Society, by their Secretary.

II. That they send every six Months an Account of the State of their respective Parishes, according to the Scheme annexed, No. II.

III. That they communicate what shall be done at the Meetings of the Clergy, when settled, and whatsoever else may concern the Society.

Text—Pascoe: *Two Hundred Years of the S. P. G., 1701-1900*, pp. 837-839.

III. *THE DEFECTION OF CUTLER AND HIS FRIENDS*

Very Reverend Sirs,

We have taken it, that yourselves were consulted upon the first erecting a collegiate school in our colony, nor can we account it improper, that yourselves and our reverend fraternity in the principal town of our country be apprized of the dark cloud drawn over our collegiate affairs, a representation whereof may already have been made by some of our reverend brethren trustees: But if not, and the case being of general concern, we are willing to make our mournful report, how it hath been matter of surprize to us (as we conclude it hath been or surely will be to you) to find how great a change a few years have made appear among us, and how our fountain, hoped to have been and continued the repositiory of truth, and the reserve of pure and sound principles, doctrine and education, in case of a change in our mother Harvard, shews itself in so little a time so corrupt. How is the gold become dim! and the silver become dross! and the wine mixed with water! Our school gloried and flourished under its first rector, the Rev. Mr. Pierson, a pattern of piety, a man of modest behaviour, of solid learning, and sound principles, free from the least Arminian or Episcopal taint: But it suffered decay for some years because of the want of a resident rector. But who could have conjectured, that its name being raised to Collegium Yalense from an Gymnasium Saybrookense, it should groan out Ichabod in about three years and a half under its second rector, so unlike the first, by an unhappy election set over it, into whose election or confirmation, or any act relating to him, the senior subscriber hereof (though not for some reason, through malice or mistake bruited) never came. Upon the management of our college three years and an half, how strangely altered is the aspect thereof! that its regents, sc. rector and tutor are become such capable masters of Episcopal leaven, and in such a time so able to cause how many to partake of it! . . .

Upon our commencement, Sept. 12, the rector distinguished his performance by the closing words of his prayer, which were these, viz. *and let all the people say, amen.*

On the evening of said day, it was rumored there, that on the next day the gentlemen become Episcopal, designed to propound to the trustees three questions.

. . . .

But the day following the commencement after dinner, these gentlemen appeared in the library before the trustees, where many other ministers were present, and first declared themselves viva voce, but after that, on the direction of the trustees, declared themselves in writing, a copy whereof is not with us. But the substance thereof is this, sc.

Some of us doubting the validity of Presbyterial ordination in opposition to Episcopal ordination, and others of us fully persuaded of the invalidity of said ordination, shall be thankful to God or man helping us if in error. Signed, Timothy Cutler, John Hart, Samuel Whittlesey, Jared Eliot, James Wetmore, Samuel Johnson, Daniel Brown. The persons doubting were Mr. Hart and Mr. Whittlesey.

Consequent to this declaration, the trustees advised that the doubters continue in the administration of the word and sacraments, but that the fully persuaded forbear sacramental ministration, until the meeting of the trustees, which was appointed on Tuesday evening at New Haven, following the opening of our General Assembly there, the said Tuesday being the 16th of the next month. The trustees also advised, that the said ministers would freely declare themselves to their respective congregations.

It may be added, that Mr. C. then declared to the trustees, that he had for many years been of this persuasion, (his wife is reported to have said that to her knowledge he had for eleven or twelve years been so persuaded) and that therefore he was the more uneasy in performing the acts of his ministry at Stratford, and the more readily accepted the call to a college improvement at N. Haven.

But then if he knew the college was erected for the education of such as dissented from the Church of England (and how could he not know it) and knew himself not one: with what good faith could he accept said call and the considerable encouragement he had, and the rather if he disseminated his persuasion so contrary to the very design of its erection, and the confidence of those that called him. Indeed he hath said, that he hath laboured only with one to be of his persuasion: Were it so, there would, in one instance, be a foul frustration of the confidence reposed in him, but what a number above one of the students may have been leavened by him, who can be assured, but coming time may discover the unhappy instances of it. . . .

. . . .

It must be acknowledged to the divine goodness, that all the trustees then present (and of the whole number wanted only three, sc. of Lime, N. London, Stamford) shewed themselves constant to your principles, and affected to the trust committed to them: yet desirous that the meeting of the trustees might (if possible) be fuller, and also their doings might be in the face of the colony, represented in General Assembly, they took care, that Mr. C. might have the use of the house they had hired for him until the Wednesday next after the opening of the General Court, viz. October 17. . . .

We subscribe ourselves, Reverend Sirs,
Your unworthy fellow-partners
in the ministry of the gospel,

The very Reverend,
INCREASE MATHER, D.D.
COTTON MATHER, D. D.
JOHN DAVENPORT,
S. BUCKINGHAM.

Stamford, Sept. 25, 1722.

Text—*Coll. Mass. Hist. Soc., Series* II, Vol. IV, pp. 297-301.

Proceedings of the Trustees, Oct. 22, 1722

. . . .

16.   By Vote agreed that all such Persons as may hereafter be elected to the Office of Rector or Tutor in Yale College shall before thay are accepted thereinto before the Trustees declare their Assent to the Confession of Faith owned & consented to by the Elders & messengers of the Churches in ye Colony of Connecticut in New England assembled by delagacion at Saybrook Septr 9th, 1718, & confirmed by Act of General Assembly and shall particularly give Satisfaction to them of the Soundness of their Faith in opposition to Armenian & prelatical Corruptions or any other of Dangerous Consequence to the Purity & Peace of our Churches but if it cannot be before the Trustees it be in ye Power of any two Trustees with the Recr to examine a Tutor with respect to the Confession & soundness of Faith in Opposition to sd Corruptions.

17. By Vote agreed that upon just Ground of Suspicion of the Rectors or Tutors Inclination to Armenian Principles or Prelatical, A meeting of the Trustees shall be called as soon as may be by any two of them to examine into the Case.

18. By Vote agreed that if any other Officer or member of this College shall give just Ground of Suspicion of their being corrupted with Armenian or prelatical Principles or any other of dangerous Consequence to the Purity & Peace of our Churches the Rector & Tutor or Tutors shall call them upon examination according to the Articles of said Confession that are contrary to the said Principles & in Case they either refuse to submit thereunto or do not give a satisfying Account of their Incorruptness they shall suspend them to the next meeting of the Trustees.

Text—Dexter: *Documentary History of Yale University*, p. 233.

. . . .

IV. *KING'S COLLEGE*

The following by William Livingstone appeared in the *Independent Reflector*, March 29, 1753.

Evils of a Sectarian College supported by public funds.

" . . .I shall now proceed to offer a few arguments, which I submit to the Consideration of my Countrymen, to evince the necessity and importance of constituting *our* College upon a Basis the most catholic, generous and free.

It is in the first place observable, that unless its Constitution and Government, be such as will admit Persons of all protestant Denominations, upon a perfect Parity as to Privileges, it will itself be greatly prejudiced, and prove a Nursery of Animosity, Dissension and Disorder. . . . Should our College, therefore, unhappily thro' our own bad Policy, fall into the Hands of any one religious Sect in the Province: Should that Sect, which is more than probable, establish its religion in the College, show favour to its votaries, and cast Contempt upon others; 'tis easy to foresee, that Christians of all Denominations amongst us, instead of encouraging its prosperity, will, from the same Principles, rather conspire to oppose and oppress it.   Besides *English and Dutch Presbyterians*, which perhaps exceed all our other religious Professions put together; we have Episcopalians, Anabaptists, Lutherans, Quakers, and a growing Church of Moravians, all equally zealous for their discriminating Tenents: Whichsoever of these has the sole Government of the College, will kindle the jealousy of the rest, not only against the persuasion so preferred, but the College itself. . . .

In such a state of things, we must not expect the Children of any, but of that sect which prevails in the Academy, will ever be sent to it: For should they, the established Tenets must either be implicitly received, or a perpetual religious War necessarily maintained.

. . . .

Another Argument against so pernicious a Scheme is, that it will be dangerous to Society. The extensive Influence of such a Seminary, I have already shown in my last Paper. And have we not reason to fear the worst Effects of it, where none but the Principles of one Persuasion are taught, and all others depressed and discountenanced? Where, instead of Reason and Argument, of which the Minds of the Youth are not capable, they are early imbued with the Doctrines of a Party, inforced by the Authority of a Professor's Chair, and the combining aids of the President and all the other Officers of the College? That religious Worship should be constantly maintained there, I am so far from opposing, that I strongly recommend it, and do not believe any such Kind of Society, can be kept under a regular and due Discipline without it. But instructing the youth in any particular Systems of Divinity, or recommending and establishing any single Method of Worship or Church Government, I am convinced would be both useless and hurtful. Useless, because not one in a Hundred of the Pupils is capable of making a just Examination, and reasonable Choice. Hurtful, because receiving Impressions blindly on Authority, will corrupt their Understanding, and fetter them with Prejudices which may everlastingly prevent a Judicious Freedom of Thought, and infect them all their Lives, with a contracted turn of Mind.

A Party-College, in less than half a Century, will put a new face upon the Religion, and in Consequence thereof, affect the Politics of the Country. Let us suppose what may, if the College should be entirely managed by one Sect, probably be supposed. Would not all possible Care be bestowed in tincturing the Minds of the Students with the Doctrines and Sentiments of that Sect? Would not the students of the College, after the Course of their Education, exclusive of any others, fill all the Offices of the Government? Is it not highly reasonable to think, that in the Execution of those Offices, the Spirit of the College would have a most prevailing Influence, especially as that Party would perpetually receive new Strength, become more fashionable and numerous? Can it be imagined that all other Christians wou d continue peaceable under, and unenvious of, the Power of that Church which was rising to so exalted a Pre-eminence above them? Would they not on the Contrary, like all other Parties, reflect upon, reluct at, and vilify such an odious Ascendency? Would not the Church which had that Ascendency be thereby irritated to repeated Acts of Domination, and stretch their ecclesiastical Rule to unwarrantable and unreasonable Lengths? Whatever others may in their Lethargy and Supineness think of the Project of a Party-College, I am convinced, that under the Management of any Particular Persuasion, it will necessarily prove destructive to the civil and religious Rights of the People: And should any future House of Representatives become generally infected with the Maxims of the College, nothing less can be expected than an Establishment of one Denomination above all others, who may, perhaps, at the good pleasure of their Superiors, be most graciously favoured with a bare Liberty of Conscience, while they faithfully continue their annual Contributions, their Tythes and their Peter-Pence.

A Third Argument against suffering the College to fall into the hands of a Party, may be deduced from the Design of its Erection, and Support by the Public.

The Legislature to whom it owes its Origin, and under whose Care the Affair has hitherto been conducted, could never have intended it as an Engine to be exercised for the Purpose of a Party. Such an Insinuation, would be false and scandalous. It would therefore be the Height of Indolence in any to pervert it to such mean, partial and little Designs. No, it was set on Foot, and I hope will be constituted for general Use, for the public Benefit, for the Education of all who can afford such Education: And to suppose it intended for any other less public-spirited Uses, is ungratefully to reflect upon all who have hitherto, had any Agency in an Undertaking so glorious to the Province, so necessary, so important and beneficial.

At present, it is but in Embrio, yet the Money hitherto collected is public Money; and till it is able to support itself, the Aids given to it will be public Aids. When the Community is taxed, it ought to be for the Defence, or Emolument of the Whole: Can it, therefore, be supposed, that all shall contribute for the Uses, the ignominious Uses of a few? Nay, what is worse to that which will be prejudicial, to a vast Majority! Shall the whole Province be made to support what will raise and spread desperate Feuds, Discontent and ill-Blood thro' the greatest Part of the Province? Shall the Government of the College be delivered out of the Hands of the Public to a Party! They who wish it, are Enemies to their Country: They who ask it, have, besides this *Anti-Patriotism*, a Degree of Impudence, Arrogance and Assurance unparalleled. And all such as are active in so iniquitous a Scheme, deserve to be stigmatized with Marks of everlasting Ignominy and Disgrace. Let it, therefore, ever remain where it is, I mean under the Power of the Legislature: The Influence, whether good or bad, we shall all of us feel, and are, therefore, all interested in it. It is, for that Reason, highly fit, that the People should always share in the Power to inlarge or restrain it: That Power they will have by their Representatives in Assembly; and no man who is a friend to Liberty, his Country and Religion, will ever rejoice to see it wrested from them.

It is further to be remarked, that a public Academy is, or ought to be a mere civil Institution, and cannot with any tolerable Propriety be monopolized by any religious Sect. The Design of such Seminaries, hath been sufficiently shown in my last Paper, to be entirely political, and calculated for the Benefit of Society, as a Society, without any Intention to teach Religion, which is the Province of the Pulpit: Tho' it must, at the same time, be confessed, that a judicious Choice of our Principles, chiefly depends on a free Education.

Again, the Instruction of our Youth, is not the only Advantage we ought to propose by our College. If it be properly regulated and conducted, we may expect a considerable Number of Students from the neighboring Colonies, which must, necessarily, prove a great Accession to our Wealth and Emolument. For such is our Capacity of endowing an Academy; that if it be founded on the Plan of a general Toleration, it must, naturally, eclipse any other on the Continent, and draw many Pupils from those Provinces, the Constitution of whose Colleges is partial and contracted: From *New England*, where the *Presbyterians* are the prevailing Party, we shall, undoubtedly, be furnished with great Numbers, who, averse to the Sect in vogue among them, will, unquestionably prefer the free Constitution, for which I argue, to that of their Colleges in which they cannot enjoy an equal Latitude, not to mention that such an Increase by foreign Students, will vastly augment the Grandeur of our Academy.

Add to all this, that in a new Country as ours, it is inconsistent with good Policy, to give any religious Profession the Ascendancy over others. The rising Prosperity of *Pennsylvania*, is the Admiration of the Continent, and tho' disagreeing from them, I should always, for political Reasons, exclude *Papists* from the common and equal Benefits of Society; Yet, I leave it to the Reflection of my judicious Readers, whether the impartial Aspect of their Laws upon all Professions, has not, in a great Degree, conduced to their vast Importation of religious Refugees, to their Strength and their Riches: And whether a like Liberty among us, to all Protestants whatsoever, without any Marks of distinction, would not be more commendable, advantageous, and politic."

Text—Hastings: *Ecclesiastical Records of the State of New York*, Vol. V, pp. 3339-41.

The Royal Charter of October 31, 1754

Only clauses having ecclesiastical significance are given.

"GEORGE THE SECOND, by the grace of God, of Great Britain, France, and Ireland, King, Defender of the Faith, etc. *To all to whom* these presents shall come, Greeting:

Moneys raised for Founding a College

Whereas, by several acts of the Governour, Council, and General assembly of our Province of New York, divers sums of money have been raised by Public Lotteries, and appropriated for the founding, erecting, and establishing a College in our said Government, for the Education and Instruction of Youth in the Liberal Arts and Sciences:

Land Given by Trinity Church

And Whereas, the Rector and inhabitants of the City of New York, in Communion of the Church of England, as by Law Established, for the encouraging and promoting of the same good design, have sett apart a parcell of ground for that purpose, of upwards of Three Thousand Pounds value, belonging to the said Corporation, on the west side of the broadway, in the west ward of our City of New York, fronting easterly to Church street, . . . And have declared that they are ready and desirous to Convey the said Land in Fee, to and for the use of a College, intended and proposed to be Erected and Established in our said Province, upon the terms in their said declaration mentioned.

. . . .

Religion of the President, Corporate Name of the Institution; . . .

And that in Consideration of such Grant, to be made by the Rector and Inhabitants of the City of New York, in Communion of the Church of England, as by Law Established, the President of the said College, for the time being, shall forever hereafter be a member of, and in Communion with the Church of England, as by Law established;

. . . .

Oaths of Office

And we do by these presents will, ordain, and direct, that the said Governors of the said College (Except always the Lord Archbishop of Canterbury for the time being, and our first Lord Commissioner for Trade and Plantations) do, at their first meeting, after the receipt of these our Letters patents, and before they proceed to any business of and concerning the said College, take the oaths appointed to be taken by an act passed in the first year of our Late Royal Father's Reign, Entituled, (an Act for the further security of his Majesty's Person and Government, and the Succession of the Crown, in the Heirs of the Late Princess Sophia, being protestants, and for extinguishing the Hopes of the pretended Prince of Wales, and his open and Secret abettors), and make and subscribe the declaration mentioned in An Act of Parliament made in the twenty fifth year of the Reign of King Charles the second, Entituled, (an act for preventing Dangers which may happen from popish Recusants;) as also, an oath, faithfully to execute the trust Reposed in them, as members of the said Corporation, which Oaths we authorize and Impower the Justices of our Supreme Court of Judicature, for our said Province of New York for the time being, any or either of them to administer; and that when, and as often as any person or persons, either by his office or place in our said Government, or Elsewhere, (Except always the Lord Archbishop of Canterbury for the time being, and our first Lord Commissioner for Trade and Plantations for the time being,) or by Choice of the said Governors of the said College, shall become, or be

Chosen, a Member or members of the said Corporation, they shall, before they are admitted, or enter into the said office or Trust, take the said Oaths, and Subscribe the said Declaration to be administered to them in the manner above directed.

. . . .

Appointment of Professors and Tutors

. . . Wee do for us, our heirs, and Successors, Give and Grant unto the said Governors of the said College of the Province of New York, . . . full power and authority to Elect, nominate, and appoint any person to be president of the said College in a Vacancy of the said Presidentship for and during his Good Behaviour; provided, always, such President Elect or to be elected by them, be a member of, and in Communion with the Church of England, as by Law Established;

And, also, to elect one or more Fellow or Fellows, Professor or Professors, Tutor or Tutors, to assist the President of the said College in the Education and Government of the Students belonging to the said College, which Fellow or Fellows, Professor or Professors, Tutor or Tutors, and every of them, shall hold and Enjoy their said office or place, either at the will and pleasure of the Governors of the said Corporation or during his or their Good Behaviour, according as shall be agreed upon Between such Fellow, or Fellows, Professor or Professors, Tutor ot Tutors, and the said Governors of the said College, *Provided, always,* such Fellow or Fellows, Professor or Professors, Tutor or Tutors, before they or either of them enter into or Take upon themselves such office, do take the Oaths and subscribe the declaration herein before directed, to be taken and subscribed by the Governors of the said College before they enter upon their said Respective offices, . . .

. . . .

Text-books, Rules, Discipline

And we do further, of our Especial Grace, Certain Knowledge, and meer motion, Give and Grant unto the said Governors of the said College, that they and their Successors, or the major part ot any fifteen or more of them Convened and met Together in manner aforesaid, shall and may direct and appoint what Books shall be publickly read and taught in the said College, by the President, Fellows, Professors, and Tutors:

And shall and may, under their Common seal, make and set down and they are hereby fully Impowered, from time to time, to make and set down in writing, such Laws, ordinances, and orders, for the Better Government of the said College, and Students, and Ministers thereof, as they shall think best for the General Good of the same, so that they are not Repugnant to the Laws and statutes of that part of our Kingdom of Great Britain called England, or of our said Province of New York, and do not extend to exclude any person ot any Religious Denomination whatever from Equal Liberty and advantage of Education, or from any the Degrees, Liberties, Privileges, Benefits, or Immunities of the said College, on account of his particular Tenets in matters of Religion, *And* such laws, Ordinances, and orders, which shall be so made as aforesaid, we do by these Presents, for us, our heirs, and Successors, Ratify, Confirm, and allow, as Good and Effectual to bind and oblige all and every the Students and Officers and Ministers of the said College;

. . . .

Public Worship. Visitation by Governors

And we do further will, ordain, and direct, that there shall be forever hereafter Publick morning and evening service Constantly performed in the said College, morning and evening forever, by the President, Fellows, Professors, or Tutors, of the said College, or one of them, according to the Liturgy of the Church of England as by Law Established, or such a Collection of prayers out of the said Liturgy, with a Collect peculiar for the said College, as shall be approved of from time to time by the Governors of the said College, or the major part of any fifteen or more of them Convened as aforesaid:

. . . .

Conferring of Degrees

And we do further, of our Especial Grace, Certain Knowledge, and meer motion, will, Give, and Grant, unto the said Governors of the said College, that for the Encouragement of the Students of the said College to Diligence and Industry in their Studies, that they and their Successors, and the major part of any fifteen or more of them Convened and mett together as aforesaid, do, by the President of the said College, or any other person or persons by them authorized and appointed, Give and Grant any such degree and degrees to any the students of the said College, or any other person or persons by them thought worthy thereof, as are usually Granted by any or either of our universities or Colleges in that part of our Kingdom of Great Britain called England, and that the President, or such other persons to be appointed for that purpose as aforesaid, do sign and seal Diplomas or Certificates of such Degree or Degrees, to be kept by the Graduates as a Testimonial thereof.

. . . .

Text—Hastings: *Ecclesiastical Records of the State of New York*, Vol. V, pp. 3506-13.

Advertisement, May 31, 1754

"To such Parents as have now (or expect to have) Children prepared to be educated in the College of New York.

I. As the Gentlemen who are appointed by the Assembly, to the Trustees of the intended Seminary or College of New York, have thought fit to appoint me to take the Charge of it, and have concluded to set up a Course of Tuition in the learned Languages, and in the Liberal Arts and Sciences: They have judged it advisible that I should publish this *Advertisement*, to inform such as have Children ready for a College Education, that it is proposed to begin Tuition upon the first Day of *July* next, at the *Vestry Room* in the new *School-House*, adjoining to *Trinity Church* in *New York*, which the Gentlemen of the Vestry are so good as to favour them with the Use of it in the Interim, till a convenient Place may be built.

II. The lowest Qualifications they have judged requisite in order to Admission into the said College, are as follows, *viz.* That they be able to read well, and write a good legible Hand; and that they be well versed in the Five first Rules in *Arithmetic*, i.e., as as far as *Division* and *Reduction*; And as to *Latin* and *Greek*, That they have a good Knowledge of the *Grammars*, and be able to make grammatical *Latin*, and both in construing and parsing, to give a good Account of two or three of the first select Orations of *Tully* and of the first Books of *Virgil's Aeneid*, and some of the first Chapter of the *Gospel of St. John*, in *Greek*. In these Books therefore they may expect to be examined; but higher Qualifications must hereafter be expected: and if there be any of the higher Classes in any College, or under private Instruction, that incline to come hither, they may expect Admission to proportionately higher Classes here.

III. And that People may be better satisfied in sending their Children for Education to this College, it is to be understood that as to Religion, there is no Intention to impose on the Scholars, the peculiar Tenets of any particular Sect of Christians; but to inculcate upon their tender Minds, the great Principles of Christianity and Morality, in which true Christians of each Denomination are generally agreed. And as to the daily Worship in the College Morning and Evening, it is proposed that it should, ordinarily, consist of such a Collection of Lessons, Prayers and Praises of the Liturgy of the Church, as are, for the most Part, taken out of the Holy Scriptures, and such as are agreed on by the Trustees, to be in the best Manner expressive of our common Christianity; and as to any peculiar Tenets, everyone is left to judge freely for himself, and to be required only to attend constantly at such Places of Worship, on the Lord's Day, as their Parents or Guardians shall think fit to order or permit.

IV. The chief Thing that is aimed at in this College is, to teach and engage the Children to *know God in Jesus Christ*, and to love and serve him, in all *Sobriety*, *Godliness*, and *Righteousness* of Life, with a *perfect Heart, and a willing Mind;* and to train them up in all virtuous Habits, and all such useful Knowledge as may render them creditable to their Families and Friends, Ornaments to their Country and useful to the public Weal in their Generations. To which good Purposes, it is earnestly desired, that their Parents, Guardians and Masters, would train them up from their Cradles, under strict Government, and in all Seriousness, Virtue and Industry, that they may be qualified to make orderly and tractable Members of this Society;—and above all, that in order hereunto, they be very careful themselves, to set them good Examples of true Piety and Virtue in their own Conduct. For as Examples have a very powerful Influence over young Minds, and especially those of their Parents, in vain are they solicitous for a good Education for their Children, if they themselves set before them Examples of Impiety and Profaneness, or of any sort of Vice whatsoever.

V. And, *lastly*, a serious, *virtuous*, and *industrious* Course of Live, being first provided for, it is further the Design of this College, to instruct and perfect the Youth in the Learned Languages, and in the Arts of *reasoning* exactly, of *writing* correctly, and *speaking* eloquently, and in the Arts of *numbering* and *measuring*; of *Surveying* and *Navigation*, of *Geography* and *History*, of *Husbandry, Commerce* and *Government*, and in the Knowledge of *all Nature* in the *Heavens* above us, and in the *Air, Water* and *Earth* around us, and the various kinds of *Meteors, Stones, Mines* and *Minerals, Plants* and *Animals*, and of every Thing *useful* for the Comfort, the Convenience and Elegance of Live, in the chief *Manufactures* relating to any of these Things: And, finally, to lead them from the Study of Nature to the Knowledge of themselves, and of the God of Nature, and their Duty to him, themselves, and one another, and every Thing that can contribute to their true Happiness, both here and hereafter.

Thus much, *Gentlemen*, it was thought proper to advertise you of, concerning the Nature and Design of this College: And I pray God, it may be attended with all the Success you can wish, for the best Good of the rising Generations; to which, (while I continue here), I shall willingly contribute my Endeavours to the Utmost of my Power.

Who am, Gentlemen, your Friend And most humble Servant.

SAMUEL JOHNSON

N.P. The Charge of the Tuition is established by the Trustees to be only 25s. for each Quarter."

Text—*A History of Columbia University, 1754-1904*, pp. 443-445.

V. *THE ANGLICAN EPISCOPATE*

Bishop Sherlock's Report

The following document written Feb. 1759, is one of the best condensed statements of the issue as seen from the Episcopalian standpoint:

"Bishop Sherlock's Report on the State of the Church of England in the Colonies, February, 1759.

To the King in Council:
Some considerations humbly offered by Thomas Bishop of London relating to Ecclesiastical Government in His Majestys Dominions in America."

After reviewing the status of the Bishop of London in Virginia and Jamaica from 1606, the writer proceeds:

In the year 1725 Bp. Gibson desirous of having a more explicit authority and direction from the Crown, for the exercise of the said Jurisdiction, applied to the King in Council for that purpose. The Petition was referred to the Attorney and Solicitor General & by their report their opinion appears to be that the authority by wch the Bps. of London had acted in ye Plantacons was insufficient, and that the Ecclial Jurisdiction in America did belong neither *to the Bishop of London*, nor *to any Bp. in England* but was solely in the Crown by virtue of the *Supremacy*, and that the most proper way of granting to any person the exercise of such jurisdiction, was by Patent under the Broad Seal. Accordingly, a Patent was granted to Dr Gibson late Bp. of London, but it was granted to him *Personally* & not to him as Bp. of London and his successors, so that the Patent expired with him and the Jurisdiction is now solely in His Majesty.

By the grant to Dr Gibson his exercise of the Jurisdiction was subjected to certain limitations and restraints, and 'tis not clear what powers he had in virtue of the s^d grant. The Patent gives him authority by himself or Commissaries (1) To *visit* all Churches in which the Rites & Liturgy of the Church of England were used. (2) To *Cite* all Rectors Curates and Incumbents and all Priests and Deacons *in Church of England Orders, et non alias quascumque personas*, cum omni et om nimodo jurisdictione potestate et coercione ecclesiastica, in premissis requisit. and to enquire *by Witnesses duly sworn* into the morals &^c with power to *Administer* Oaths in the Ecclesiastical Court, and to Correct & Punish the said Rectors &^c by suspension excommunication &^c (3) A power to appoint Commissaries for the exercise of this Jurisdiction and to remove them at pleasure. (4) An appeal is given, to all who shall find themselves aggrieved by any sentence, before the Great Officers of State in England.

Observations on this Patent

1. A power is given to *visit all churches*, but he has no power to *cite* the Churchwardens or any of the Parishioners to appear; and should any of them appear voluntarily he has no right to give them any orders relating to the Church or Church affairs; his whole power and jurisdiction being confined to the Clergy only.

2. He has power to cite all Priests and Deacons & to examine into their conduct *provided they have Church of England Orders*; but if a man should counterfeit Episcopal Orders and administer the Sacraments, he has no power to proceed ag^{st} him.

3. He has power to examine into the Conduct of the Clergy, upon the *Oath of Witnesses*, and power to *administer Oaths* for the purpose; but he has no power to *cite* any man, at least no *Layman* to give testimony before him; yet the Laymen may be many times necessary witnesses as in such cases; and they see daily how their Curate behaves, which other Clergymen, who serve distant parishes can give no account of.

4. The Bishop has power to appoint Commissaries to exercise such jurisdiction as is granted him by the Patent, and as the Bp. of London cannot be supposed to reside in America, he can do nothing by himself, as soon as he has appointed Commissaries, the Bishop can neither direct, nor correct, their judgment.   No appeal lyes to the Bp. nor indeed can there; for in judgment of Law, the Commissary's Sentence is the Bp's sentence, and the Appeal must go to a higher Court.

But this shows at the same time how very improper it is to give such power to a Bp. of England, which he cannot execute, but must be obliged to give it over to somebody else, as soon as he has it.   So that the Bp. receiving with the one hand what he must necessarily give away with the other, remains himself a Cypher without any authority power or influence.

If these observations are well founded the Bishop's jurisdiction, as under the Patent, seems to be defective.

But the Episcopal Churches in America suffer greater harships still, by being under a Bishop who never can reside among them.   There are some things necessary to such Churches wch the Bp. only can do himself.   Such for instance are *Confirmation* and *Ordination*, which are not acts of jurisdiction or transferable to Commissaries, but are acts peculiar to the Episcopal Order and the Episcopal Churches abroad are *totally* deprived of *Confirmation*.   As to Orders, since the Bp. *only* can give them, there is not in this vast tract of land, one who can ordain Ministers for the Church of England. In which respect the Dissenters of all kinds, upon the mere foot of Toleration, are in a better case: for they all appoint Ministers in their own way, and were the Dissenters in New England and elsewhere in America, to send all their Ministers to be ordained by their Brethren in England, they wo^d think it a great hardship and inconsistent with the rights they claim by Toleration.

From these considerations it appears that several Colonies abroad where the Church of England is established, are, with respect to their religious principles, put under great difficulties.   They are absolutely deprived of confirmation for all their youth and children, and they are oftentimes ill supply'd with Ministers to perform other duties of religion among them; for as the families settled in the country and which are able to provide otherwise for their children, will not send their Children at a great expence and hazard to the ordain'd in England, where they often (as by experience has been found) catch the Small Fox, a distemper more fatal to them than to others, and several who have come over hither for Orders have dyed here of this disease.   In consequence of this the Plantations are furnished with such Ministers from hence, as can be prevail'd upon to go among them, or such as are forced through necessity to seek a maintenance in a foreign country.   And they are chiefly *Scotch & Irish* who offer themselves for this service; and there is reason to apprehend that the Scotch Episcopal Clergy who cannot be employed at home, may think of settling in the Plantations; which may be attended with bad consequences in regard to the government.

The Churches abroad of the Episcopal Communion have been under a necessity of submitting to these difficulties; for as Protestants they cannot apply to Popish Bishops for Confirmation or Orders; and as Episcopal Churches they could resort for Orders only to English or Irish Bishops. But since the Moravians have been recognized by Parliament to be a Protestant Episcopal Church and have liberty to settle in His Majesty's American Dominions, should the Churches abroad admit ot Ordination by Moravian Bps. it may be attended by consequences not easily foreseen, but easily prevented by suffering the Episcopal Churches of England in America to have one or more Suffragan Bishops residing among them.

As the Dissenters at home and abroad may possibly think themselves concern'd in this question; it is necessary to observe that Bps. abroad are not desired in behalf of an *inconsiderable* party there, and that the Independents and other Dissenters do by no means (as the case is sometimes mistaken to be) make the body of the Inhabitants in His Majesty's Dominions. But previously to stating how the fact is at present, it is proper to recollect how the law stands with respect to the establishment of the Church of England in America, according to the royal Charters and Instructions given to the King's Governors abroad herein before mentioned.

For the Church of England being establish'd in America, the Independents and other Dissenters who went to settle in New England, co^d only have a Toleration and in fact they had no more, as appears by their several Charters, and more particularly in Rhode Island Charter, granted in the 14th year of Chas IInd.

Thus stands the right of the Church of England in America. And in fact, at least one half of the Plantations are of the established Church, and have built Churches and Minister's houses and have by *laws of their respective Assemblies* (confirm'd by the Crown) provided maintenance for Church of England Clergy, & no others are capable of having benefices among them.

This is the case of S^o Carolina, N^o Carolina, Virginia, Maryland, Jamaica, Barbadoes, Antegoa, Nevis, and the rest of the Caribee Islands.

On the other side—Pennsylvania is in the hands and under the governm^t of the Quakers, and New England and the adjoining Colonies are in the hands of the Independents. But in some of them are great numbers of Churchmen.

It is sometimes said that it wo^d be hard to send Bps. among the Dissenters in America; many of whom left their own Country to get from under their power.

If Bps. were proposed to be established in Pensilvania and New England, with *Coercive Powers*, there wo^d be some colour in the complaint. But as it never has been propos'd to settle Bps. in those Colonies, nor in any other Colonies, with *Coercive* powers, there is no ground for it. And whatever prejudices the Independents of New England may have to Bps. themselves, surely it can never be thought reasonable that because the Northern end of America is possessed chiefly by the Independents, therefore the Southern and Midland parts and the Islands, who profess the Established Religion of England and are Episcopal Churches, sho^d be denied the benefit of Episcopal administration, which according to their religious principles they think necessary to them.

If the Supremacy of the Crown be (as it has been often styled) a rich jewel in the Crown of England, it should be considered that the Supremacy is maintained and obeyed by the *Establish'd Church only*. Dissenters of all kinds are discharged from all regard to it, and are at full liberty to act for themselves in religious affairs, without taking the consent or even advice of the Crown: and therefore they make what Ministers they please. But the Episcopal Churches of England in America want their first and most necessary Member, a Bp. to reside with them; and have waited with patience for the consent of the Crown; and their bretheren at home, the Bps. of England

and the Society for Propagating the Gospel, have often been intercessors to the Crown on their behalf.

The objections to settling Bishops in the Plantations are chiefly these two.

1. It is doubted whether it will be agreeable to the people there.

2. It is doubted whether any maintenance can be had for such Bishops.

. . . .

By these Acts of Assembly it is plain that they have no objection agst Bishops, in the religious view, so far from it, that they admit no Minister to serve in the Churches supported by Publick Maintenance, but such as are Episcopally ordained. And it cannot be supposed that they wo^d be unwilling a Bp. should *reside* among them, where his authority & influence might be of great use in the due governm^t & direction of the Clergy; provided that a Bp. *residing* with them had power to do no more than they are now desirous sho^d be done by a Bishop at a distance.

But the difficulty arises from the 2nd view; and the question is, how far they will be contented to admit the jurisdiction wch the Bps. in England have in many cases, by and under the Crown.

As the first planters in America were members of the Church of England, and carried over with them a regard to the government and discipline of their Mother Church; there is no doubt to be made but that they would very willingly have continued under the same Ecclesiastical Government & Discipline in America, under which they had been bred in England, had they had any Bps. among them at their first settlement abroad. But being destitute of Bps. and for some years deprived of *Publick Church Communion* for want of Ministers regularly ordain'd; it is more to be wondered at that they have adhered so steadily to the Communion of the Church of England with respect to Episcopal Ordination and the established Liturgy, than that they have some prejudice against Ecclesiastical Courts and Jurisdictions of Bps. of which they have seen and known so little for many years. Many things which are under the care and authority of Bps. in England, are things necessary to be done by somebody, and where there are no Bps. they must be done by some other authority. Such are the repairs of Churches and the providing books and other necessaries for the service, the Instituting and inducting Incumbents, the repairs of Glebe Houses, the Probate of Wills, Licence for Marriage, examining and approving Clergymen, and Schoolmasters, and the correction of vice and immorality by coercive power. As the Colonies had no Bps. to discharge these duties they were necessitated to provide for them otherwise. And therefore these powers are placed by several Acts of Assembly, partly in the Churchwardens, partly in Justices of the Peace, and partly in the Governors of the respective Provinces.

That these provisions were made for *want* of a Bp. among them, and not out of dislike to *Episcopal Authority* appears from the Act of Assembly of the Leeward Islands before mentioned, by which the Governor is empowered to suspend Clergymen, but it passed under an obligation of giving notice to the Bp. of London, and of taking his directions. Had there been a Bp. among them, can it be supposed they would not have referr'd the matter *directly* to him?

The present generation of men in the Colonies being born and bred under this Constitution, it is natural to suppose that they are attached to the custom of their country, and would be alarm'd at the apprehension of having their power remov'd out of their hands, in wch the law of their country had plac'd them, and put into the hands of a Bp. with whose power in these cases they are unacquainted: and therefore these powers exercis'd in the Consistory Courts in England are not desired for Bps. residing in America.

But these Colonies however unaccustomed to *Episcopal Jurisdiction* have always been brought up in an opinion that their Clergy must be *Episcopally* Ordained. And it is not to be supposed that they had rather have their Children come to England for Orders than to have a Bp. among them to Ordain them at home, and as they are members of the Church of England, and have received it's liturgy, they cannot look into it without seeing that for want of a Bp. among them they and their Children are debarr'd from Confirmation.

. . . .

There have been Commissaries acting under the Bp. of London, ever since Bp. Compton's time, and no complaint has been made of their power being too great or any ways burdensome to the Country; and if Suffragan Bishops with the same Ecclesiastical Powers that the Commissaries have had, were settled in the Plantations,it could make no alteration with respect to the Civil Governm^t or to the people, but it will enable the Church of England there to do what all Churches of all denominations have thought necessary to their very being, to provide a succession for the Ministry among themselves: a right which the Established Church of England in the Plantations has been long deprived of, and wch as far as I can judge, no other Christian Church in the world ever wanted. Every sect of Christians, under the Toleration, claims it as their right, and exercises it; and it seems but reasonable to hope that an Established Church should enjoy the rights of a Church in equal degree at least with tolerated societies of Dissenters.

The other objection is—How shall Bishops in America be maintained? Not by *Tax* or imposition on the *People* certainly. If Bps. were to be sent them, and the country laid under contribution, Bishops would be received as *Excise Men* and *Tax-gath[er]s*; and this apprehension in the people abroad, of being burden'd with the maintenance of Bishops, would be the readiest way to raise an opposition in the Colonies to the settlement of the Bps. among them.

Nor ought the Crown to be burdened with the maintenance of such Bps., or put to more expence that what already lyes upon the Crown in providing Clergy for the Plantations. And yet there will not want means to provide a decent support for them by annexing some preferments abroad to these Bishopricks and by giving the Bp. a capacity of receiving Benefactions from such as will be ready to promote so good a design.

But as the care to maintain them will be premature till His Majesty's pleasure is known as to the appointing them it may wait His Majesty's determination.

As the Bp. of London is generally supposed to be the Bp. principally if not only concern'd in the Plantations: He desires to say one word for himself, and to assure Your Majesty that however necessary to the state of Religion & the Churches abroad, he apprehends the settlem^t of Bps. in America to be, and however sensible he is that with the Authority granted to the late Bishop of London, he co^d by no means answer the good purposes intended by Your Majesty; yet he submits himself to your Royal Pleasure, and whatever part you in your royal wisdom shall think fit to allot to him, he will discharge it to the best of his ability."

Text—O'Callaghan: *Documents Relating to the Colonial History of the State of New York*, Vol. VII, pp. 360-369.

VI. *ORGANIZATION OF THE AMERICAN EPISCOPAL CHURCH*

A General Ecclesiastical Constitution of the Protestant Episcopal Church in the United States of America

Adopted Oct 4, 1785 and amended slightly in sections ix-xi, June 23, 1786.

WHEREAS, in the course of Divine Providence, the Protestant Episcopal Church in the United States of America is become independent of all foreign authority, civil and ecclesiastical:

And WHEREAS, at a meeting of Clerical and Lay Deputies of the said Church in sundry of the said states, viz. in the states of Massachusetts, Rhode-Island, Connecticut, New York, New Jersey, Pennsylvania, Delaware, and Maryland, held in the city of New York, on the 6th and 7th days of October, in the year of our Lord, 1784, it was recommended to this Church in the said states represented as aforesaid, and proposed to this Church in the States not represented, that they should send Deputies to a Convention to be held in the city of Philadelphia, on the Tuesday before the feast of St. Michael in this present year, in order to unite in a Constitution of Ecclesiastical government, agreeably to certain fundamental principles, expressed in the said recommendation and proposal:

And WHEREAS, in consequence of the said recommendation and proposal, Clerical and Lay Deputies have been duly appointed from the said Church in the States of New York, New Jersey, Pennsylvania, Delaware, Maryland, Virginia, and South Carolina:

The said deputies being now assembled, and taking into consideration the importance of maintaining uniformity in doctrine, discipline, and worship in the said Church, do hereby determine and declare:

1. That there shall be a general Convention of the Protestant Episcopal Church in the United States of America, which shall be held in the city of Philadelphia on the third Tuesday in June, in the year of our Lord 1786, and for ever after once in three years, on the third Tuesday of June, in such place as shall be determined by the Convention; and special meetings may be held at such other times and in such place as shall be hereafter provided for; and this Church, in a majority of the States aforesaid, shall be represented before they shall proceed to business; except that the representation of this Church from two States shall be sufficient to adjourn; and in all business of the Convention freedom of debate shall be allowed.

II. There shall be a representation of both Clergy and Laity of the Church in each State, which shall consist of one or more Deputies, not exceeding four, of each Order; and in all questions, the said Church in each State shall have one vote; and a majority of suffrages shall be conclusive.

III. In the said Church in every State represented in this Convention, there shall be a Convention consisting of the Clergy and Lay Deputies of the congregation.

IV. "The Book of Common Prayer, and Administration of the Sacraments, and other Rites and Ceremonies of the Church, according to the use of the Church of England," shall be continued to be used by this Church, as the same is altered by this Convention, in a certain instrument of writing passed by their authority, intituled Alterations of the Liturgy of the Protestant Episcopal Church in the United States of America, in order to render the same conformable to the American revolution and the constitutions of the respective States."

V. In every State where there shall be a Bishop duly consecrated and settled, and who shall have acceded to the articles of this General Ecclesiastical Constitution, he shall be considered as a member of the Convention *ex officio*.

VI. The Bishop or Bishops in every State shall be chosen agreeably to such rules as shall be fixed by the respective Conventions; and every Bishop of this Church shall confine the exercise of his Episcopal office to his proper jurisdiction, unless requested to ordain or confirm by any church destitute of a Bishop.

VII. A Protestant Episcopal Church in any of the United States not now represented, may at any time hereafter be admitted, on acceding to the articles of this union.

VIII. Every Clergyman, whether bishop or presbyter or deacon, shall be amenable to the authority of the Convention in the State to which he belongs, so far as relates to suspension or removal from office, and the Convention in each State shall institute rules for their conduct, and an equitable mode of trial.

IX. And whereas it is represented to this Convention to be the desire of the Protestant Episcopal Church in these States, that there may be further alterations of the Liturgy than such as are made necessary by the American revolution; therefore the "Book of Common Prayer, and Administration of the Sacraments and other Rites and Ceremonies of the Church, according to the use of the Church of England," as altered by an instrument of writing, passed under the authority of this Convention, intituled "Alterations in the Book of Common Prayer, and Administration of the Sacraments and other rites and Ceremonies of the Church, according to the use of the Church of England, proposed and recommended to the Protestant Episcopal Church in the United States of America," shall be used in this Church, when the same shall have been ratified by the Conventions which have respectively sent Deputies to this General Convention.

X. No person shall be ordained or permitted to officiate as a Minister in this Church, until he shall have subscribed the following declaration, "I do believe the Holy Scriptures of the Old and New Testament to be the word of God, and to contain all things necessary to salvation; and I do solemnly engage to conform to the doctrines and worship of the Protestant Episcopal Church, as settled and determined in the Book of Common Prayer, and Administration of the Sacraments, set forth by the General Convention of the Protestant Episcopal Church in these United States."

XI. This general Ecclesiastical Constitution, when ratified by the Church in the different states, shall be considered as fundamental; and shall be unalterable by the Convention of the Church in any state.

The Hon. Mr. Duane, from the Committee for revising, &c, reported, that they had, according to order, prepared a plan for obtaining the consecration of Bishops, and a draft of an address to the most Reverend the Archbishops and the Right Reverend the Bishops of the Church of England, and were ready to report the same.

Text—*Journals of the General Conventions of the Protestant Episcopal Church, 1784-1814, pp. 8-10.*

Petition for Episcopal Consecration

To the Most Reverend and Right Reverend the Archbishops of Canterbury and York, and the Bishops of the Church of England.

We the Clerical and Lay Deputies of the Protestant Episcopal Church in sundry of the United States of America, think it our duty to address your Lordships on a subject deeply interesting, not only to ourselves and those whom we represent, but, as we conceive, to the common cause of Christianity.

Our forefathers, when they left the land of their nativity, did not leave the bosom of that Church over which your Lordships now preside; but, as well from a veneration for Episcopal government, as from an attachment to the admirable services of our Liturgy, continued in willing connection with their ecclesiastical superiors in England, and were subjected to many local inconveniences, rather than break the unity of the Church to which they belonged.

When it pleased the Supreme Ruler of the universe, that this part of the British empire should be free, sovereign, and independent, it became the most important concern of the members of our Communion to provide for its continuance. And while, in accomplishing of this, they kept in view that wise and liberal part of the system of the Church of England which excludes as well the claiming as the acknowledging of such spiritual subjection as may be inconsistent with the civil duties of her children; it was nevertheless their earnest desire and resolution to retain the venerable form of Episcopal government handed down to them, as they conceive, from the time of the Apostles, and endeared to them by the remembrance of the holy Bishops of the primitive Church, of the blessed Martyrs who reformed the doctrine and worship of the Church of England, and of the many great and pious Prelates who have adorned that Church in every succeeding age. But however general the desire of compleating the Orders of our Ministry, so diffused and unconnected were the members of our Communion over this extensive country, that much time and negociation were necessary for the forming a representative body of the greater number of Episcopalians in these States; and owing to the same causes, it was not until this Convention that sufficient powers could be procured for the addressing your Lordships on this subject.

The petition which we offer to your Venerable Body is,—that from a tender regard to the religious interests of thousands in this rising empire, professing the same religious principles with the Church of England, you will be pleased to confer the Episcopal character on such persons as shall be recommended by this Church in the several States here represented—full satisfaction being given of the sufficiency of the persons recommended, and of its being the intention of the general body of the Episcopalians in the said States respectively, to receive them in the quality of Bishops.

Whether this our request will meet with insurmountable impediments, from the political regulations of the kingdom in which your Lordships fill such distinguished stations, it is not for us to foresee. We have not been ascertained that any such will exist; and are humbly of opinion, that as citizens of these States, interested in their prosperity, and religiously regarding the allegiance which we owe them, it is to an ecclesiastical source only we can apply in the present exigency.

It may be of consequence to observe, that in these States there is a separation between the concerns of policy and those of religion; that, accordingly, our civil rulers cannot officially join in the present application; that, however, we are far from apprehending the opposition or even displeasure of any of those honorable personages; and finally, that in this business we are justified by the Constitutions of the States, which are the foundations and controul of all our laws. On this point we beg leave to refer to the enclosed extracts from the Constitutions of the respective States of which we are citizens, and we flatter ourselves that they must be satisfactory.

Thus, we have stated to your Lordships the nature and the grounds of our application; which we have thought it most respectful and most suitable to the magnitude of the object, to address to your Lordships for your deliberation before any person is sent over to carry them into effect. Whatever may be the event, no time will efface the remembrance of the past services of your Lordships and your predecessors. The Archbishops of Canterbury were not prevented, even by the weighty concerns of their high stations, from attending to the interests of this distant branch of the Church under their care. The Bishops of London were our Diocesans; and the uninterrupted although voluntary submission of our congregations, will remain a perpetual proof of their mild and paternal government. All the Bishops of England, with other distinguished characters, as well ecclesiastical as civil, have concurred in forming and carrying on the benevolent views of the Society for Propagating the Gospel in Foreign Parts: a Society to whom, under God, the prosperity of our Church is in an eminent degree to be ascribed. It is our earnest wish to be permitted to make, through your Lordships, this just acknowledgment to that venerable Society; a tribute of gratitude which we the rather take this opportunity of paying, as while they thought it necessary to withdraw their pecuniary assistance from our Ministers, they have endeared their past favors by a benevolent declaration, that it is far from their thoughts to alienate their affection from their brethren now under another government—with the pious wish, that their former exertions may still continue to bring forth the fruits they aimed at of pure religion and virtue. Our hearts are penetrated with the most lively gratitude by these generous sentiments; the long succession of former benefits passes in review before us; we pray that our Church may be a lasting monument of the usefulness of so worthy a body; and that her sons may never cease to be kindly affectioned to the members of that Church, the Fathers of which have so tenderly watched over her infancy.

For your Lordships in particular, we most sincerely wish and pray, that you may long continue the ornaments of the Church of England, and at last receive the reward of the righteous from the great Shepherd and Bishop of souls.

We are, with all the respect which is due to your exalted and venerable characters and stations,

Your Lordships
Most obedient and
Most humble Servants,
SIGNED BY THE CLERICAL AND LAY DEPUTIES
OF THE CONVENTION.

IN CONVENTION:
Christ Church, Philadelphia
October 5th, 1785.

Text—*Journals of the General Conventions of the Protestant Episcopal Church*, 1784-1814, pp. 12-15.

CHAPTER XIV

PRESBYTERIANISM IN THE EIGHTEENTH CENTURY

Bibliography

The first fruits of the project initiated by the General Assembly in May, 1791, "to devise measures for the collecting of materials necessary for a history of the Presbyterian Church in North America" was the publication in the "Christian Advocate" (1825 and 1830) by Dr. Green of two chapters designed to form the opening sections of a subsequent completed history of Presbyterianism. The first chapter was entitled "The Origin of the Presbyterian Church in the United States of America," the second, "The History of the Presbyterian Church from its Origin to A. D. 1716" (on all see "Jour. Pres. Hist. Soc.," Vol. II pp. 267-271). These studies with all the records that had been brought together by the Historical Committee of the General Assembly during its forty years of service were turned over to Dr. Charles Hodge, who shortly after (1839-40) published the scholarly and graceful "Constitutional history of the Presbyterian Church in the United States of America, Parts I and II, 1705-1788." Almost contemporary with Hodge's history, but distinctly inferior, were William Hill's "A History of the Rise, Progress, and Character of American Presbyterianism, together with a Review of 'The Constitutional History of the Presbyterian Church in the United States of America,'" (1839), and Irving Spence's "Letters on the Early History of the Presbyterian Church in America. With a Sketch of the Life of the Author" (1838). Next came Richard Webster with "A History of the Presbyterian Church in America From Its Origin Till the Year 1760. With Biographical Sketches of its Early Ministers. With a Memoir of its Author, by the Rev. C. van Rensselaer, D.D., and an Historical Introduction by the Rev. William Blackwood, D.D." (1858). Webster's work was followed by that of Ezra Hall Gillett, "History of the Presbyterian Church in the United States of America" (II Vols. 1864). Thus far the historians of Presbyterianism had been basing their investigations solely upon sources accessible in America. It remained for Charles Augustus Briggs,

D. D., upon the basis of documents stored in the libraries and museums of Great Britain to give a much more complete account in his "American Presbyterianism: Its Origin and Early History. Together with an Appendix of Letters and Documents, many of which have Recently Been Discovered" (1885). An abundance of unimportant detail has not enhanced the value or interest of this work. The appended documents however, are of first rate significance. The recent "History of the Presbyterian Churches in the United States" by Robert Ellis Thompson, ("Amer. Ch. Hist. Ser." Vol. VI, 3rd ed. 1902) in its brief compass of 69 pages gives only elementary generalities. "A Short History of American Presbyterianism from its Foundation to the Reunion of 1869" (1903) by A. T. McGill, and S. M. Hopkins, contains concise illuminating surveys. Hopkins is especially happy in his treatment of the "Presbyterian Church and the American Revolution." "The Scotch-Irish in America" (1915) by Henry J. Ford is virtually a history of Presbyterianism and represents high standards of interesting and accurate scholarship. Documentation unfortunately is almost entirely lacking.

Of histories confined to colonial areas, there are the following: "History of the Presbyterian Church in the State of Kentucky, with a Preliminary Sketch of the Churches in the Valley of Virginia" (1847) by Rev. Robert Davidson; "Sketches of North Carolina, . . . " (1846), and "Sketches of Virginia, . . . " (1st series 1850, 2nd series 1855) by Rev. W. H. Foote, which though antiquated contain rich stores of information; "Old Redstone, or Historical Sketches of Western Presbyterianism, its Early Ministers, . . . and its First Records" (1854) by Joseph Smith; "The Early Presbyterian Immigration into South Carolina" (1858, a Discourse) by George Howe; "The Early Presbyterian Immigration into South Carolina" ("The Southern Pres. Review" January, 1859); "History of the Presbyterian Church in South Carolina" (1870) by George Howe; "An Outline History of the Presbyterian Church in West or South Jersey from 1700 to 1865" (1869) by A. H. Brown; "Pioneer Presbyterianism in Tennessee," Centennial Addresses, October, 1897; "A History of the Development of the Presbyterian Church in North Carolina, and of Synodical Home Missions, . . . " (1907) by James I. Vance and others (3 chapters sketch the period to 1875); "Early Presbyterianism in Maryland" by J. W. McIlwain ("J. H. U. Studies" Series VIII, Suppl. to Chap. V-VI); also "Some Relics of Early Presbyterianism in Maryland" ("Papers, Amer. Soc. Ch. Hist." Vol. II, Part I, pp. 93-99); "The Beginnings of the Presbyterian Church in the District of Columbia" by W. B. Bryan ("Records of Columbia Hist. Soc." Vol. VIII, pp. 43-66); "The Planting of the Presbyterian Church in Northern Virginia prior to the Organization of Winchester Presbytery, December 4, 1794" (1904) by James R. Graham; "A History of the Presbyterian Church in Georgia" (n.d.) by Rev. James Stacy.

Studies more local are as follows: "Early Presbyterianism East of the Hudson" (1868) by John Johnson; "A History of Presbyterianism in New England; Its Introduction, . . . " (1881) by Alexander Blaikie; "History of the Presbytery of Carlisle" (II Vols. 1889) by George Norcross; "Presbyterianism in Perth Amboy, New Jersey" (1903) by Harlan G. Mendenhall; "History of the Presbytery of Carlisle" by Robert Davidson, ("Jour. Pres. Hist. Soc." Vol. III, No. VIII); "A Sketch of Abingdon Presbytery" by Rev. John B. Herndon (*ibid.* Vol. III, No. VIII); "History of the Presbytery of Albany," reprint of original manuscript (*ibid.*, Vol. III, No. V); "History of the Presbytery of Baltimore," reprint of original manuscript (*ibid.* Vol. VII, No. II); "The Erection of the Presbytery of New Brunswick, Together With Some Account of the Beginnings of Organized Presbyterianism in the American Colonies," by George H. Ingram (*ibid.*, Vol. VI, No. VI); "The New England Churches and the First Presbytery" by William H. Roberts, (*ibid.* Vol. V, No. VI); "The Beginnings of Presbyterianism in Albany" by V. H. Paltsits (*ibid.* Vol. V, No. IV and V).

On individual churches there are the following accounts: "Historical Account of the First Presbyterian Church of Princeton, New Jersey" (1851) by W. E. Schenck; "Churches of the Valley" (Cumberland and Franklin Counties, Pennsylvania, 1852) by Alfred Nevin; "Historical Sketch of the First Presbyterian Church in the City of New Brunswick" (1852) by Robert Davidson; "A History of the Old Presbyterian Congregation of 'The People of Maidenhead and Hopewell,' " (1856) by George Hale; "History of the Presbyterian Church in Trenton, New Jersey . . . " (1859) by John Hall; "The Mountain Society; a History of the First Presbyterian Church of Orange, New Jersey, Organized about 1719" (1860) by J. Hoyt; "Two Centuries in the History of the Presbyterian Church, Jamaica, Long Island" (1863) by J. M. Macdonald; "Earliest Churches of New York and its Vicinity" (1865) by G. P. Disosway; "The First Presbyterian Church of Cranbury, Trenton" (1869) by J. G. Symmes; "The Presbyterian Church in Basking Ridge, N. J." (1872) by J. G. Rankin; "One Hundred Years of the Presbyterian Church of Frankford" (1872) by Thomas Murphy; "History of Neshaminy Presbyterian Church of Warwick . . . Bucks Co.

Pa. 1726-1876" (1876) by D. R. Turner; "The Old and the New, 1743-1876; The Second Presbyterian Church of Philadelphia; its Beginning and Increase" (1876) by E. R. Beadle; "A History of the First Presbyterian Church of Carlisle" (1877) by C. P. Wing; "History of the First Presbyterian Church of Auburn, New York" (1876) by Charles Hawley; "History of the First Presbyterian Church of Albany" (1877) by C. B. Blayney; "Historical Sketch of Presbyterianism within the Bounds of the Synod of Central New York" (1877) by P. H. Fowler, and J. W. Mears; "History of the Presbyterian Church in the Forks of Brandywine, Chester County, Pa." (1885) by James McClune; "History of the Presbyterian Church of New Berne, N. C., with a Résumé of Early Ecclesiastical Affairs in Eastern North Carolina . . . " (1886) by L. C. Vass; "A Brief History of the First Presbyterian Church of Newtown, Long Island, . . . " (1902) by Wm. H. Hendrickson; "Historical Sketch of the First United Presbyterian Church of Philadelphia" (a sermon, 1902) by W. J. Edgar; "History of the Old Tennent Church" (2nd. ed. 1904) by F. R. Symmes, "A History of Old Pine Street" (1905) by H. O. Gibbons; "History of the Manokin Presbyterian Church, Princess Anne, Md." (1910) by Harry P. Ford; "The Early History of the First Presbyterian Church in Philadelphia" by John Edmands, D.D. ("Jour. Pres. Hist. Soc.," Vol. V, No. V); "History of the Presbyterian Church in Trenton, New Jersey, from the First Settlement of the Town" (1911) by John Hall; "The History of the First English Presbyterian Church in Amwell" (1912) by J. B. Kugler; "Historical Sketch of the Ewing Presbyterian Church" by W. M. Lanning ("Jour. Pres. Hist. Soc.," Vol. VI, No. V); and "Historcial Notes of the Presbyterian Church of Shrewsbury, N. J." by R. Taylor, (ibid., Vol. VII, No. 11). References to other histories and anniversary sermons will be found in Thompson's "Bibliography" (A. C. H. Series Vol. VI) and in the section "Records of New Publications Relating to Presbyterianism . . . " appearing in the various numbers of the "Journal of the Presbyterian Historical Society."

Subjects of special interest have been treated as under: "When was the First Presbytery of the Presbyterian Church in the United States of America Organized?" by B. L. Agnew, ("Jour. Pres. Hist. Soc." Vol. III, No. 1); "The Beginning of the American Presbyterian Church" ("Pres. and Reformed Ch. Rev." Jan. 1896); "Scotch and Scotch-Irish in American Soil" (1878) by J. G. Craighead; "The Scotch-Irish in America; Their History, Traits, Institutions, and Influences, . . . " (1906) by John W. Dinsmore; "Early Attempted Union of Presbyterians with Dutch and German Reformed" by Professor James I. Good ("Jour. Pres. Hist. Soc." Vol. III, No. III); "Presbyterians and Quakers in Colonial Pennsylvania" by Isaac Sharpless (*ibid.* Vol. III, No. II). The contribution of Presbyterians to religious liberty in Virginia is described in "The Triumph of the Presbytery of Hanover; or The Separation of Church and State in Virginia, . . . " (1887) by Jacob H. Patton; "Virginia Presbyterianism and Religious Liberty in Colonial and Revolutionary Times" (1907, an important work with several documents) by Professor Thomas C. Johnson; "The Struggle of Protestant Dissenters for Religious Toleration in Virginia" ("J. H. U. Studies," Series, XII) by H. R. McIlwaine; and the studies of James, Thorne, and Zeller (see page 281).

For the Great Awakening, the reader is referred to page 212f. with the following important supplementary material: "The Danger of an Unconverted Ministry, Considered in a Sermon on Mark vi. 34, preached at Nottingham, Pa." (1740) by Gilbert Tennent; "A Vindication of the Brethren who were Unjustly and Illegally Cast Out of the Synod of Philadelphia, from Maintaining Principles of Anarchy in the Church" (1744) by Samuel Blair; "The Men and Times of the Reunion of 1758" ("Amer. Pres. & Theol. Review," July 1868); "The Trial of Rev. William Tennent" ("Biblical Repertory and Princeton Review" July, 1868); "The True Character of the Adopting Act" ("Amer. Pres. Rev." January, 1869); "Memorabilia of the Tennents" ("Jour. Pres. Hist. Soc." Vol. I, No. V) by D. B. K. Ludwig; "Life of the Rev. William Tennent . . ." (1843), author not specified.

"The Works of President Edwards" are accessible in a four volume New York edition (1843), reprint of an earlier (1809) Worcester edition and in a six volume Edinburgh edition (1847). The latter has material supplementary to what is embodied in the former, but not of intrinsic value to the historian. "Some Early Writings of Jonathan Edwards, A.D. 1714-1726" by Egbert C. Smith ("Proc. Amer. Antiq. Soc." New Series, Vol. X, pp. 212-247) has considerable original material.

Studies on Edwards are as follows: "Jonathan Edwards, his Character, Teaching, and Influence" ("Bibl. Sacra," October, 1861); "Jonathan Edwards" (*ibid.* April, 1869); "Jonathan Edwards" in "American Religious Leaders" (1889) by Alexander V. G. Allen; "Jonathan Edwards and the Great Awakening" ("Bibliotheca Sacra," Jan. 1898); "The Manuscripts of Jonathan Edwards" by F. B. Dexter, ("Proc. Mass. Hist. Soc." Series II, Vol. XV, pp. 2-20); "Jonathan Edwards; A Retrospect. Being the Addresses Delivered in Connection with the Unveiling of a Memorial Tablet at Northampton . . . " edited (1901) by H. N. Gardiner; "The Edwards Bicentenary at Andover" (1904) by J. W. Platner and others. His bicentenary is discussed in the "Jour. Pres. Hist. Soc." Vol. II, No. III. A useful inventory of all the periodical literature appearing in connection with this bicentennial will be found in this Jounal, pp. 169-210.

On John Witherspoon, the following works are to be commended: "John Witherspoon, Patriot, 1722-1794" (n.d.) by J. F. Dickie; "Life of John Witherspoon, D.D., With the Sermon Preached at his Funeral by John Rogers, D.D." (prefixed to his works, IV Vols. 1800-1807) by Samuel S. Smith; and "John Witherspoon" (1906) by David Walker Woods, Jr.

The Log College may be studied in Rev. Archibald Alexander's "Biographical Sketches of the Founder and the Principal Alumni of the Log College, Together with an Account of the Revivals of Religion under their Ministry" (1845); "Historical Discourses relating to the First Presbyterian Church in Newark" (1853) by Rev. Jonathan S. Stearns; "The History of the Presbytery of the Log College" (1889) by Rev. Thomas Murphy; "The Charter and By-Laws of the Trustees of Princeton University" by Rev. Elijah R. Craven; and the same author's brief article, "The Log College of Neshaminy, and Princeton University" ("Jour. Pres. Hist. Soc." Vol. I, No. IV).

The history of Princeton has been related by Rev. John MacLean in a "History of the College of New Jersey, . . . ' (II Vols. 1877), a narrative based on the minutes of the Board of Trustees. An older work, "Princeton College during the Eighteenth Century" (1872) by Samuel D. Alexander, gives biographical notes of its alumni. John De Witt in connection with the Sesquicentennial Celebration, prepared three papers on the following subjects: "The Planting of Princeton College," "Princeton College Administrations in the Eighteenth Century," and "Princeton College Administrations in the Nineteenth Century" ("Pres. & Ref. Rev." April, July, and October, 1897). Ashbel Green has a "Historical Sketch of the Origin of the College of New Jersey, With an account of the Administrations of its First Five Presidents" (1822) which comes to 1768. A concise sketch is a "History of the College of New Jersey" (1844) by W. A. Dod; still briefer, a "Historical Sketch of the College of New Jersey" (1859) by Robert Edgar. "Princeton" ("Amer. College and Univ." Series, 1914) by V. L. Collins tells in a fascinating way 'the characteristics of the life and atmosphere,' of Princeton, and the 'variety and color in its history.' "The Story of Princeton" (1917) by E. M. Norris is a popular work.

On Makemie, there is the following: "The Days of Makemie, or The Vine Planted: A.D. 1680-1708" (with an appendix, 1885) by L. P. Bowen; "A Narrative of a New and Unusual American Imprisonment of two Presbyterian Ministers, and Prosecution of Mr. Francis Makemie; one of them for Preaching One Sermon at the City of New York. By a Learner of Law and a Lover of Liberty" (1707). His "Sermon Preached at New York, January 19, 1706-7" appears in "Coll. New York Hist. Soc." Year 1870. "Records of Accomack County, Virginia, Relating to Rev. Francis Makemie" contributed by H. C. McCook, will be found in "Jour. Pres. Hist. Soc." Vol. IV, Nos. I, II, III, and IV. A "Transcript of the Entries in the Minutes of the Presbytery of Laggan, Ireland, which refer to Francis Makemie" are accessible in the same "Journal," Vol. III, No. VI. For "Some Recently Discovered Makemie Letters" contributed by Rev. Joseph B. Turner, see this "Journal," Vol. VII, No. V. Other Letters will be found in the appendix to Briggs' "Presbyterianism." The "Makemie Memorial" proceedings are fully described in the "Journal," Vol. IV, No. VIII. A carefully compiled chronological survey of his career is appended.

For missionary work among the Indians see page 526 f.

In connection with the Revolution, the following will be found serviceable: "The Chaplains and Clergy of the American Revolution" (1861) by J. T. Headley; "An Historical Discourse on Presbyterians and the Revolution" (1876) by William P. Breed; "Life and Labors of John Rosbrugh, the Clerical Martyr of the Revolution" (1880) by John G. Clyde; "A Revolutionary Hero—James Caldwell" by Harry P. Ford ("Jour. Pres. Hist. Soc." Vol. VI, No. VII); "Presbyterians and the Revolution" (ibid. Vol. V, No. III). The last article tabulates losses sustained by the churches in Philadelphia.

Concerning sources, in addition to the many documents cited above, there is the collection (1841) of William M. Engles, "Records of the Presbyterian Church in the United States of America, containing the Minutes of the Presbytery of Philadelphia from A.D. 1706 to 1716; Minutes of the Synod of Philadelphia from A.D. 1717 to 1758; Minutes of the Synod of New York, from A.D. 1745 to 1758; Minutes of the Synod of New York and Philadelphia from A.D. 1758 to 1788." A second edition (1852) like the first unfortunately had no index. Recently (1904) this defect has been remedied by Rev. W. H. Roberts who under the title "Records of the Presbyterian Church in the United States of America" republished all the documents of the Engles edition, and added the "Minutes of the General Convention for Religious Liberty, 1766-

1775" which may also be consulted with introduction by Roberts under separate cover (1904). "The Minutes of the Presbytery of New Brunswick for the Year 1739 f.", edited by George H. Ingram will be found in the "Jour. Pres. Hist. Soc." Vols. VI, No. VI, VIII, and Vol. VII, No. III, IV, V, VII. Several eighteenth century documents are incorporated in "A Collection of the Acts, Deliverances, and Testimonies of the Supreme Judicatory of the Presbyterian Church from its Origin in America to the Present time; With Notes and Documents" (2nd ed. 1855) by Samuel J. Baird. In the "Jóur. Pres. Hist. Soc. (Vols. I, II, III, and IV) there is a series of contributions giving the early records of the following churches: Neshaminey, Tinicum, Newtown, Abingdon, Norrington, Great Valley, Charlestown, West Chester, Bethel, Collegiate Presbyterian Church of Monmouth County, Fairfield, Deerfield, Woodbury, Greenwich, Pennsneck, Cape May, and First Church, Philadelphia.

DOCUMENTS

I. THE ADOPTING ACT OF 1729—SYNOD OF PHILADELPHIA

Although the Synod do not claim or pretend to any authority of Imposing our faith upon other men's consciences, but do profess our just dissatisfaction with, and abhorrence of such impositions, and do utterly disclaim all legislative power and authority in the Church, being willing to receive one another as Christ has received us to the glory of God, and admit to fellowship in sacred ordinances, all such as we have grounds to believe Christ will at last admit to the kingdom of heaven, yet we are undoubtedly obliged to take care that the faith once delivered to the saints be kept pure and uncorrupt among us, and so handed down to our posterity; and do therefore agree that all the ministers of this Synod, or that shall hereafter be admitted into this Synod, shall declare their agreement in, and approbation of, the Confession of Faith, with the Larger and Shorter Catechisms of the Assembly of Divines at Westminster, as being in all the essential and necessary articles, good forms of sound words and systems of Christian doctrine, and so also adopt the said Confession and Catechisms as the confession of our faith. And we do also agree, that all the Presbyteries within our bounds shall always take care not to admit any candidate of the ministry into the exercise of the sacred function but what declares his agreement in opinion with all the essential and necessary articles of said Confession, either by subscribing the said Confession of Faith and Catechisms, or by a verbal declaration of their assent thereto, as such minister or candidate shall think best. And in case any minister of this Synod, or any candidate for the ministry, shall have any scruple with respect to any article or articles of said Confession or Catechisms, he shall at the time of his making said declaration declare his sentiments to the Presbytery or Synod, who shall, not withstanding, admit him to the exercise of the ministry within our bounds, and to ministerial communion, if the Synod or Presbytery shall judge his scruple or mistake to be only about articles not essential and necessary in doctrine, worship, or government.

But if the Synod or Presbytery shall judge such ministers or candidates erroneous in essential and necessary articles of faith, the Synod or Presbytery shall declare them uncapable of communion with them. And the Synod do solemnly agree, that none of us will traduce or use any opprobrious terms of those that differ from us in these extra-essential and not necessary points of doctrine, but treat them with the same friendship, kindness, and brotherly love, as if they had not differed from us in such sentiments.

. . . .

All the ministers of this Synod now present, except one that declared himself not prepared, . . . after proposing all the scruples that any of them had to make against any articles and expressions in the Confession of Faith and Larger and Shorter Catechisms of the Assembly of Divines at Westminster, have unanimously agreed in the solution of those scruples, and in declaring the said Confession and Catechisms to be the confession of their faith, excepting only some clauses in the twentieth and twenty-third chapters, concerning which clauses the Synod do unanimously declare, that they do not receive those articles in any such sense as to suppose the civil magistrate hath a controlling power over Synods with respect to the exercise of their ministerial authority; or power to persecute any for their religion, or in any sense contrary to the Protestant succession to the throne of Great Britain.

Text—Engles: *Records of the Presbyterian Church*, pp. 94-95.

II. *RESOLUTIONS REGARDING CANDIDATES FOR MINISTRY, 1734—SYNOD OF PHILADELPHIA*

Mr. Gilbert Tennent having brought some overtures into the Synod with respect to the trials of candidates, both for the ministry and the Lord's Supper, that there be due care taken in examining into the evidences of the grace of God in them, as well as of their other necessary qualifications, the Synod doth unanimously agree, that as it has been our principle and practice, and as it is recommended in the directory for worship and government, to be careful in this matter, so it awfully concerns us to be most serious and solemn in the trials of both sorts of candidates above mentioned. And this Synod does therefore in the name and fear of God, exhort and obtest all our Presbyteries to take special care not to admit into the sacred office, loose, careless, and irreligious persons, but that they particularly inquire into the conversations, conduct, and behaviour of such as offer themselves to the ministry, and that they diligently examine all the candidates for the ministry in their experiences of a work of sanctifying grace in their hearts, and that they admit none to the sacred trust that are not in the eye of charity serious Christians. And the Synod does also seriously and solemnly admonish all the ministers within our bounds to make it their awful, constant, and diligent care, to approve themselves to God, to their own consciences, and to their hearers, serious, faithful stewards of the mysteries of God, and of holy and exemplary conversations. And the Synod does also exhort all the ministers within our bounds to use due care in examining those they admit to the Lord's Supper.

This admonition was approved by the whole Synod.

And the Synod does further recommend unanimously, to all our Presbyteries, to take effectual care that each of their ministers are faithful in the discharge of their awful trust. And in particular, that they frequently examine, with respect to each of their members, into their life and conversation, their diligence in their work, and their methods of discharging their ministerial calling. Particularly that each Presbytery do, at least once a year, examine into the manner of each minister's preaching, whether he insist in his ministry upon the great articles of Christianity, and in the course of his preaching recommend a crucified Saviour to his hearers as the only foundation of hope, and the absolute necessity of the omnipotent influences of the Divine grace to enable them to accept of this Saviour; whether he do in the most solemn and affecting manner he can, endeavour to convince his hearers of their lost and miserable state whilst unconverted, and put them upon the diligent use of those means necessary in order to obtaining the sanctifying influences of the Spirit of God; whether he do, and how he doth, discharge his duty towards the young people and children of his congregation, in a way of catechizing and familiar instruction; whether he do, and in what manner he doth, visit his flock and instruct them from house to house.

And the Synod hereby orders, that a copy of this minute be inserted into the books of each of our Presbyteries, and be read at every of their Presbyterial meetings, and a record of its being read minuted in said books at the beginning of every session, and that there be also an annual record in each Presbytery book of a correspondence with this minute.

And in case any minister within our bounds shall be found defective in any of the above mentioned cases, he shall be subject to the censure of the Presbytery, and if he refuse subjection to such censure, the Presbytery are hereby directed to represent his case to the next Synod. And the Synod recommends to each of the ministers within our bounds to be as much in catechetical doctrines as they in prudence may think proper.

Text—Engles: *Records of the Presbyterian Church*, pp. 110-111.

III. *EXPLANATORY ACT OF 1736—SYNOD OF PHILADELPHIA*

That the Synod do declare, that inasmuch as we understand that many persons of our persuasion, both more lately and formerly, have been offended with some expressions or distinctions in the first or preliminary act of our Synod, contained in the printed paper, relating to our receiving or adopting the Westminster Confession and Catechisms, &c: That in order to remove said offence, and all jealousies that have arisen or may arise in any of our people's minds, on occasion of said distinctions and expressions, the Synod doth declare, that the Synod have adopted and still do adhere to the Westminster Confession, Catechisms, and Directory, without the least variation or alteration, and without any regard to said distinctions. And we do further declare, that this was our meaning and true intent in our first adopting of said Confession, as may particularly appear by our adopting act which is as followeth: All the ministers of the Synod now present, (which were eighteen in number, except one that declared himself not prepared,) after proposing all the scruples any of them had to make against any articles and expressions in the Confession of Faith, and Larger and Shorter Catechisms of the Assembly of Divines at Westminster, have unanimously agreed in the solution of these scruples, and in declaring the said Confession and Catechisms to be the confession of their faith, except only some clauses in the twentieth and twenty-third chapters, concerning which clauses the Synod do unanimously declare, that they do not receive these articles in any such sense as to suppose the civil magistrate hath a controlling power over Synods with respect to the exercise of their ministerial authority, or power to persecute any for their religion, or in any sense contrary to the Protestant succession to the throne of Great Britain.

And we hope and desire, that this our Synodical declaration and explication may satisfy all our people, as to our firm attachment to our good old received doctrines contained in said confession, without the least variation or alteration, and that they will lay aside their jealousies that have been entertained through occasion of the above hinted expressions and declarations as groundless. This overture approved *nemine contradicente*.

Text—Engles: *Records of the Presbyterian Church*, pp. 126, 127.

IV. *A PROTESTATION PRESENTED TO THE SYNOD (PHILADELPHIA) JUNE 1, 1741*

Reverend Fathers and Brethren,

We, the ministers of Jesus Christ, and members of the Synod of Philadelphia, being wounded and grieved at our very hearts, at the dreadful divisions, distractions, and convulsions, which all of a sudden have seized this infant church to such a degree, that unless He, who is King in Zion, do graciously and seasonably interpose for our relief, she is in no small danger of expiring outright, and that quickly, as to the form, order, and constitution of an organized church, which hath subsisted for above these thirty years past, in a very great degree of comely order and sweet harmony, until of late.

. . . .

Reverend Fathers and Brethren, we hereby humbly and solemnly protest, in the presence of the great and eternal God, and his elect angels, as well as in the presence of all here present, and particularly to you, Reverend Brethren, in our own names, and in the names of all, both ministers and people, who shall adhere to us, as follows:

1. We protest that it is the indispensable duty of this Synod, to maintain and stand by the principles of doctrine, worship, and government, of the Church of Christ, as the same are summed up in the Confession of Faith, Catechisms, and Directory, composed by the Westminster Assembly, as being agreeable to the word of God, and which this Synod have owned, acknowledged, and adopted, as may appear by our synodical records of the years 1729, 1736, which we desire to be read publicly.

2. We protest that no person, minister, or elder, should be allowed to sit and vote in this Synod, who hath not received, adopted, or subscribed, the said Confessions, Catechisms, and Directory, as our Presbyteries respectively do, according to our last Explication of the adopting act; or who is either accused or convicted, or may be convicted, before this Synod, or any of our Presbyteries, of holding or maintaining any doctrine, or who act and persist in any practice, contrary to any of those doctrines, or rules contained in said Directory, or contrary to any of the known rights of Presbytery, or orders made or agreed to by this Synod, and which stand yet unrepealed, unless, or until he renounce such doctrine, and being found guilty, acknowledge, confess, and profess his sorrow for such sinful disorder, to the satisfaction of this Synod, or such inferior judicatory as the Synod shall appoint or empower for that purpose.

3. We protest that all our protesting brethren have at present no right to sit and vote as members of this Synod, having forfeited their right of being accounted members of it for many reasons, a few of which we shall mention afterwards.

4. We protest that, if, notwithstanding of this our protestation, these brethren be allowed to sit and vote in this Synod, without giving suitable satisfaction to the Synod, and particularly to us, who now enter this protestation, & those who adhere to us in it, that whatsoever shall be done, voted, or transacted by them, contrary to our judgment, shall be of no force or obligation to us, being done and acted by a judicatory consisting in part of members who have no authority to act with us in ecclesiastical matters.

5. We protest that, if, notwithstanding this our protestation, and contrary to the true intent and meaning of it, these protesting brethren, and such as adhere to them, or support and countenance them in their antipresbyterial practices, shall continue to act as they have done this last year, in that case we. and as many as have clearness to join with us, and maintain the rights of this judicatory, shall be accounted in nowise disorderly, but the true Presbyterian Church in this province; and they shall be looked upon as guilty of schism, and the breach of the rules of Presbyterial government, which Christ has established in his church, which we are ready at all times to demonstrate to the world.

Reverend and dear Brethren, we beseech you to hear us with patience, while we lay before you as briefly as we can, some of the reasons that move us thus to protest, and more particularly, why we protest against our protesting brethren's being allowed to sit as members of this Synod.

1. Their heterodox and anarchical principles expressed in their Apology, pages twenty-eight and thirty-nine, where they expressly deny that Presbyteries have authority to oblige their dissenting members, and that Synods should go any further, in judging of appeals or references, &c. than to give their best advice, which is plainly to divest the officers and judicatories of Christ's kingdom of all authority, (and plainly contradicts the thirty-first article of our Confession of Faith, section three, which these brethren pretend to adopt,) agreeable to which is the whole superstructure of arguments which they advance and maintain against not only our synodical acts, but also all authority to make any acts or orders that shall bind their dissenting members, throughout their whole Apology.

2. Their protesting against the Synod's act in relation to the examination of candidates, together with their proceeding to license and ordain men to the ministry of the gospel, in opposition to, and in contempt of said act of Synod.

3. Their making irregular irruptions upon the congregations to which they have no immediate relation, without order, concurrence, or allowance of the Presbyteries or ministers to which congregations belong, there by sowing the seeds of division among people, and doing what they can to alienate and fill their minds with unjust prejudices against their lawfully called pastors.

4. Their principles and practice of rash judging and condemning all who do not fall in with their measures, both ministers and people, as carnal, graceless, and enemies to the work of God, and what not, as appears in Mr. Gilbert Tennent's sermon against unconverted ministers, and his and Mr. Blair's papers of May last, which were read in open Synod; which rash judging has been the constant practice of our protesting brethren, and their irregular probationers, for above these twelve months past, in their disorderly itinerations and preaching through our congregations, by which, (alas! for

it,) most of our congregations, through weakness and credulity, are so shattered and divided, and shaken in their principles, that few or none of us can say we enjoy the comfort, or have the success among our people, which otherwise we might, and which we enjoyed heretofore.

5. Their industriously persuading people to believe that the call of God whereby he calls men to the ministry, does not consist in their being regularly ordained and set apart to that work, according to the institution and rules of the word; but in some invisible motions and workings of the Spirit, which none can be conscious or sensible of but the person himself, and with respect to which he is liable to be deceived, or play the hypocrite; that the gospel preached in truth by unconverted ministers, can be of no saving benefit to souls; and their pointing out such minsters, whom they condemn as graceless by their rash judging spirit, they effectually carry the point with the poor credulous people, who, in imitation of their example, and under their patrociny, judge their ministers to be graceless, and forsake their ministry as hurtful rather than profitable.

6. Their preaching the terrors of the law in such a manner and dialect as has no precedent in the word of God, but rather appears to be borrowed from a worse dialect; and so industriously working on the passions and affections of weak minds, as to cause them to cry out in a hideous manner, and fall down in convulsion-like fits, to the marring of the profiting both of themselves and others, who are so taken up in seeing and hearing these odd symptoms, that they cannot attend to or hear what the preacher says; and then, after all, boasting of these things as the work of God, which we are persuaded do proceed from an inferior or worse cause.

7. Their, or some of them, preaching and maintaining that all true converts are as certain of their gracious state as a person can be of what he knows by his outward senses; and are able to give a narrative of the time and manner of their conversion, or else they conclude them to be in a natural or graceless state, and that a gracious person can judge of another's gracious state otherwise than by his profession and life. That people are under no sacred tie or relation to their own pastors lawfully called, but may leave them when they please, and ought to go where they think they get most good.

For these and many other reasons, we protest, before the Eternal God, his holy angels, and you, Reverend Brethren, and before all here present, that these brethren have no right to be acknowledged as members of this judicatory of Christ, whose principles and practices are so diametrically opposite to our doctrine, and principles of government and order, which the great King of the Church hath laid down in his word.

. . . .

Reverend Fathers and Brethren, these are a part, and but a part, of our reasons why we protest as above, and which we have only hinted at, but have forborne to enlarge on them, as we might, the matter and substance of them are so well known to you all, and the whole world about us, that we judged this hint sufficient at present.

. . . .

Text—Engles: *Records of the Presbyterian Church*, pp. 157-160.

V. *THE PLAN OF UNION—SYNODS OF NEW YORK AND PHILADELPHIA, 1758*

The Synods of New York and Philadelphia, taking into serious consideration the present divided state of the Presbyterian church in this land, and being deeply sensible that the division of the church tends to weaken its interests, to dishonour religion, and consequently its glorious Author; to render government and discipline ineffectual, and finally to dissolve its very frame; and being desirous to pursue such measures as may most tend to the glory of God and the establishment and edification of his people, do judge it to be our indispensable duty to study the things that make for peace, and to endeavour the healing of that breach which has for some time subsisted amongst us, that so its hurtful consequences may not extend to posterity, that all occasion of reproach upon our society may be removed, and that we may carry on the great designs of religion to better advantage than we can do in a divided state; and since both Synods continue to profess the same principles of faith, and adhere to the same form of worship, government, and discipline, there is the greater reason to endeavour the compromising those differences, which were agitated many years ago with too great warmth and animosity, and unite in one body.

For which end, and that no jealousies or grounds of alienation may remain, and also to prevent future breaches of like nature, we agree to unite and do unite in one body, under the name of the Synod of New York and Philadelphia, on the following plan.

I. Both Synods having always approved and received the Westiminster Confession of Faith, and Larger and Shorter Catechisms, as an orthodox and excellent system of Christian doctrine, founded on the word of God, we do still receive the same as the confession of our faith, and also adhere to the plan of worship, government, and discipline, contained in the Westminster Directory, strictly enjoining it on all our members and probationers for the ministry, that they preach and teach according to the form of sound words in said Confession and Catechisms, and avoid and oppose all errors contrary thereto.

II. That when any matter is determined by a major vote, every member shall either actively concur with, or passively submit to such determination; or, if his conscience permit him to do neither, he shall, after sufficient liberty modestly to reason and remonstrate, peaceably withdraw from our communion, without attempting to make any schism. Provided always, that this shall be understood to extend only to such determinations as the body shall judge indispensable in doctrine or Presbyterian government.

III. That any member or members, for the exoneration of his or their conscience before God, have a right to protest against any act or procedure of our highest judicature, because there is no further appeal to another for redress, and to require that such protestation be recorded in their minutes. And as such a protest is a solemn appeal from the bar of said judicature, no member is liable to prosecution on the account of his protesting. Provided always, that it shall be deemed irregular and unlawful, to enter a protestation against any member of members, or to protest facts or accusations instead of proving them, unless a fair trial be refused, even by the highest judicature. And it is agreed, that protestations are only to be entered against the public acts, judgments, or determinations of the judicature with which the protester's conscience is offended.

IV. As the protestation entered in the Synod of Philadelphia, *Ann. Dom.* 1741, has been apprehended to have been approved and received by an act of said Synod, and on that account was judged a sufficient obstacle to an union; the said Synod declare, that they never judicially adopted the said protestation, nor do account it a Synodical act, but that it is to be considered as the act of those only who subscribed it;

and therefore cannot in its nature be a valid objection to the union of the two Synods, especially considering that a very great majority of both Synods have become members, since the said protestation was entered.

V. That it shall be esteemed and treated as a censurable evil, to accuse any member of heterodoxy, insufficiency, or immorality, in a calumniating manner, or otherwise than by private brotherly admonition, or by a regular process according to our known rules of judicial trial in cases of scandal. And it shall be considered in the same view, if any Presbytery appoint supplies within the bounds of another Presbytery without their concurrence, or if any member officiate in another's congregation, without asking and obtaining his consent, or the session's in case the minister be absent; yet it shall be esteemed unbrotherly for any one, in ordinary circumstances, to refuse his consent to a regular member when it is requested.

VI. That no Presbytery shall license or ordain to the work of the ministry, any candidate, until he give them competent satisfaction as to his learning, and experimental acquaintance with religion, and skill in divinity and cases of conscience, and declare his acceptance of the Westminster Confession and Catechisms as the confession of his faith, and promise subjection to the Presbyterian plan of government in the Westminster Directory.

VII The Synods declare it is their earnest desire, that a complete union may be obtained as soon as possible, and agree that the united Synod shall model the several Presbyteries in such manner as shall appear to them most expedient. Provided nevertheless, that Presbyteries, where an alteration does not appear to be for edification, continue in their present form. As to divided congregations it is agreed, that such as have settled ministers on both sides be allowed to continue as they are; that where those of one side have a settled minister, the other being vacant, may join with the settled minister, if a majority choose so to do; that when both sides are vacant they shall be at liberty to unite together.

VIII. As the late religious appearances occasioned much speculation and debate, the members of the New York Synod, in order to prevent any misapprehensions, declare their adherence to their former sentiments in favour of them, that a blessed work of God's Holy Spirit in the conversion of numbers was then carried on; and for the satisfaction of all concerned, this united Synod agree in declaring, that as all mankind are naturally dead in trespasses and sins an entire change of heart and life is necessary to make them meet for the service and enjoyment of God; that such a change can be only effected by the powerful operations of the Divine Spirit; that when sinners are made sensible of their lost condition and absolute inability to recover themselves, are enlightened in the knowledge of Christ and convinced of his ability and willingness to save, and upon gospel encouragements do choose him for their Saviour, and renouncing their own righteousness in point of merit, depend upon his imputed righteousness for their justification before God, and on his wisdom and strength for guidance and support; when upon these apprehensions and exercises their souls are comforted, notwithstanding all their past guilt, and rejoice in God through Jesus Christ, when they hate and bewail their sins of heart and life, delight in the laws of God without exception, reverently and diligently attend his ordinances, become humble and self denied, and make it the business of their lives to please and glorify God and to do good to their fellow men; this is to be acknowledged as a gracious work of God, even though it should be attended with unusual bodily commotions or some more exceptional circumstances, by means of infirmity, temptations, or remaining corruptions; and wherever religious appearances are attended with the good effects above mentioned, we desire to rejoice in and thank God for them.

But on the other hand, when persons seeming to be under a religious concern, imagine that they have visions of the human nature of Jesus Christ, or hear voices, or see external lights, or have fainting and convulsion-like fits, and on the account of these judge themselves to be truly converted, though they have not the Scriptural characters of a work of God described above, we believe such persons are under a dangerous delusion. And we testify our utter disapprobation of such a delusion, wherever it attends any religious appearances, in any church or time.

Now as both Synods are agreed in their sentiments concerning the nature of a work of grace, and declare their desire and purpose to promote it, different judgments respecting particular matters of fact, ought not to prevent their union; especially as many of the present members have entered into the ministry since the time of the aforesaid religious appearances.

Upon the whole, as the design of our union is the advancement of the Mediator's kingdom; and as the wise and faithful discharge of the ministerial function is the principal appointed mean for that glorious end, we judge, that this is a proper occasion to manifest our sincere intention, unitedly to exert ourselves to fulfil the ministry we have received of the Lord Jesus. Accordingly, we unanimously declare our serious and fixed resolution, by divine aid, to take heed to ourselves that our hearts be upright, our discourse edifying, and our lives exemplary for purity and godliness; to take heed to our doctrine, that it be not only orthodox but evangelical and spiritual, tending to awaken the secure to a suitable concern for their salvation, and to instruct and encourage sincere Christians; thus commending ourselves to every man's conscience in the sight of God; to cultivate peace and harmony among ourselves, and strengthen each other's hands in promoting the knowledge of divine truth, and diffusing the savour of piety among our people.

Finally, we earnestly recommend it to all under our care, that instead of indulging a contentious disposition, they would love each other with a pure heart fervently, as brethren who profess subjection to the same Lord, adhere to the same faith, worship, and government, and entertain the same hope of glory. And we desire that they would improve the present union for their mutual edification, combine to strengthen the common interests of religion, and go hand in hand in the path of life; which we pray the God of all grace would please to effect, for Christ's sake. Amen.

The Synod agree, that all former differences and disputes are laid aside and buried; and that no future inquiry or vote shall be proposed in this Synod concerning these things; but if any member seek a Synodical inquiry, or declaration about any of the matters of our past differences, it shall be deemed a censurable breach of this agreement, and be refused, and he be rebuked accordingly.

Text—Engles: *Records of the Presbyterian Church*, pp. 285-288.

VI. *A SCHEME FOR SUPPORTING YOUNG MEN OF PIETY AND PARTS AT LEARNING FOR THE WORK OF THE MINISTRY*

This scheme, adopted by the Synod of New York and Philadelphia May 22, 1771, probably the first attempt made by a Christian organization in America to grapple with the problem of religious leadership, foreshadows in several respects the policy of the Education Societies developed within the succeeding fifty years.

1st. That every vacant congregation in our bounds, who ask this Presbytery for supplies, do annually at the fall meeting pay into the hands of a treasurer to be chosen, the sum of two pounds.

2d. That every minister belonging to this Presbytery, pay into the hands of said treasurer, at the said time, the sum of one pound.

3d. That any gentleman willing to contribute to this pious design, may have an opportunity of subscribing to pay annually.

4th. That at every spring meeting of this Presbytery, there shall be a treasurer chosen, (a member of Presbytery) who shall keep a fair stated account of all the money received, and the disbursements, and shall pay no money without a written order, an act of the Presbytery signed by their moderator and clerk for the time being.

5th. That every member of this Presbytery may recommend any young man they think proper, who, after such an examination as shall be thought convenient, shall receive or be refused the benefit of this donation, by the major vote of this Presbytery.

6th. That after any young man is thus received, the Presbytery shall look upon themselves as the guardians of his education, and as such shall give all orders relative thereto, and in case of any difference of opinion the major vote shall always determine.

7th. That every young man thus educated, shall be looked upon as natively belonging to this Presbytery, and when introduced into the work of the ministry, shall continue at least one year preaching in the vacancies within the bounds of this Presbytery.

8th. That every young man thus educated, and afterwards not inclining to the work of the ministry, shall give a bond to some minister of this Presbytery, to the amount of all the money expended by this Presbytery in his education, payable in five years after date.

Text—Engles: *Records of the Presbyterian Church*, pp. 419-420.

CHAPTER XV

BAPTISTS IN THE COLONIAL PERIOD

Bibliography

Of general histories of American Baptists the oldest is that of David Benedict entitled "A General History of the Baptist Denomination in America and Other Parts of the World" (1813). Though this work contains much information, the arrangement is confused and the treatment has now become antiquated. "A Baptist History . . . to the Close of the Eighteenth Century" (1869) by Rev. J. M. Cramp suffers from the attempt to cover too much ground. Thomas Armitage in "A History of the Baptists" (1887) writes elegantly, and has a commanding knowledge of Baptist world history, but in dealing with a single area such as America he is compelled to generalize. In a "Short History of the Baptists" (1892, new ed. 1907) by Henry C. Vedder, six brief chapters are devoted to a popular statement of Baptist achievements in America. "A History of the Baptist Churches in the United States" ("Amer. Ch. Hist. Ser." Vol. II, 4th ed. 1902) by Professor A. H. Newman is by far the best presentation. "A Century of Baptist Achievement" (1901) edited by Professor Newman, although dealing with the nineteenth century, throws considerable light upon the late eighteenth century Baptist situation. "Elements in Baptist Development" (1913) edited by Rev. Ilsley Boone, has little historical ballast. In "The Universal Register of the Baptist Denomination in North America for the years 1790, 1791, 1792, 1793 and part of 1794," by John Asplund, much valuable data is to be found concerning the organization and distribution of the churches, their pastor, and their creeds. This old Register (1794) is indispensable for investigative purposes.

It is to sectional histories that the student must turn for really satisfactory direction.

Beginning with the New England area, there is "A History of New England with Particular Reference to the Denomination of Christians Called Baptists" (1777-96, 2nd edition with notes by D. Weston, II Vols. 1871) by Isaac Backus. With its fairmindedness and abundance of documentary material, this work is of prime importance. "A History of the Baptists in New England" (1894) by Henry S. Burrage, though brief shows the accuracy of an author working in constant touch with the sources. In "The History of the First Baptist Church of Boston (1665-1899)" Rev. Nathan E. Wood has laid under scholarly tribute the rich archives of this old church which alone of Baptist churches of America has preserved its seventeenth century records. C. B. Crane's "First Baptist, Church, Boston: Bi-Centenary Commemoration" (1865) is less complete. "A Summer Visit of Three Rhode-Islanders to the Massachusetts Bay in 1651" (1896) by Rev. H. M. King, gives an account of the experiences of Clarke, Holmes, and Crandall. John Clarke himself tells the story in "Ill Newes from New England; or a Narrative of New England's Persecution" (1652, "Coll. Mass. Hist. Soc." Series IV, Vol. II). The "Life of Henry Dunster" (1872) by J Chaplin; "History of the Dunster Family" (1876) by S. Dunster; and "The Life, Journals, Letters, . . . of the Rev. Hezekiah Smith, D.D., . . . 1735-1805" (1885) by R. A. Guild supply important material in the biographical field.

The struggle for religious liberty in New England may be approached through Backus' "History" and "A Memoir of the Life and Times of the Rev. Isaac Backus" (1859) by Alvah Hovey. On Backus, see also a complete list of books and pamphlets issued by him in the "Christian Review," March, 1849. There are also the "Life, Times, and Correspondence of James Manning" (1864) by R. A. Guild; "The Rise of Religious Liberty in America" (1902) by S. H. Cobb, and most notably, an article by H. S. Burrage entitled "The Contest for Religious Liberty in Massachusetts" ("Papers Amer. Soc. Ch. Hist." Vol. VI, pp. 149-168).

The part played by the Baptists in connection with the Revolution and amendment VI of the American Constitution may be studied in Backus' "History"; "The Life, Journals, Letters . . . of the Rev. Hezekiah Smith"; "The Baptists and the American Revolution" (2nd ed. 1876) by William Cathcart; also the monographs of Thom, James, McIlwaine and Eckenrode (see below,) and in smaller degree "The Chaplains and Clergy of the Revolution" (1861) by Joel Tyler Headley.

The rapid progress of the Baptists in New England and Virginia during the Revolutionary period is set forth by Backus in his "History"; also by John S. Barrett in "Development of the Popular Churches after the Revolution" ("Proc. Mass. Hist. Soc." Vol. XLVIII, pp. 254-268).

On Baptist History in Maine the older work is "A History of the Baptists in Maine" (1845) by Joshua Millet. The standard work is the recent (1904) "History of the Baptists in Maine" by Henry S. Burrage. Through access to associational and convention minutes and thorough mining of older monographs, the author has given an exhaustive study with documentation which will easily lead to all necessary sources.

Connecticut has little in the way of literature relating to Baptists. Besides "A Discourse delivered at the 100th Anniversary of the Organition of the First Baptist Church in North Stonington, September 20, 1843" with an appendix (1844) by A. G. Palmer; "Increase and Characteristics of Connecticut Baptists" (1887) by B. O. True; and his "Address at Centennial Anniversary of the First Baptist Church, Meriden" (Oct. 7, 1886), one must rely upon works dealing with Connecticut as a part of the larger New England basis.

With Rhode Island it is otherwise. For the Roger Williams literature the reader is referred to the bibliography on Rhode Island (page 000). To this may be added one small mono raph: "The Baptism of Roger Williams" (1897) by Rev. H. M. King.

Morgan Edwards has done good work in his "Materials for a History of the Baptists in Rhode Island" (1867, "Coll. R. I. Hist. Soc." Vol. VI, pp. 302-370). Benedict's treatment of the Rhode Island Baptists is one of the best portions of his work. The First Baptist Church of Providence is the subject of the following studies: "Historical Discourse, First Baptist Church" (1839) by W. Hague; "Historical Discourse of the First Baptist Church" (1865) by S. L. Caldwell; and his "History of the First Baptist Church" (1877); "The Mother Church (First Baptist)" (1896) by Rev. H M. King; also his "Historical Discourse, First Baptist Meeting House" (1900); and "A Historical Catalogue of the Members of the First Baptist Church in Providence, Rhode Island" (1908).

The First Baptist Church, Newport, in point of age the rival of Providence, has been treated by S. Adlam in "The First Baptist Church in Providence, not the Oldest" (1850), and by C. E. Barrows in "Historical Sketch of the First Baptist Church, Newport, Rhode Island" (1876). In connection with Newport, where he was pastor for six years, mention should be made of "The Diary of John Comer", edited with notes by C. E. Barrows and J. W Willmarth (1893, "Coll. R. I. Hist. Soc." Vol. VIII.) The "Semi-Centennial Celebration of the Rhode Island Baptist State Convention, May 12, 1875" (1875) has the usual smattering of history connected with celebration addresses.

"Brown University—Bibliography, 1756-1898" (1898) issued by the Librarian, gives a complete statement respecting the literature of this old Baptist institution. In this connection it will be sufficient to mention the scholarly work of R. A. Guild, "Life, Times, and Correspondence of James Manning" (1864) and his "History of Brown University" (1867).

In "The Sesquicentennial of Brown University, 1764-1914, A Commemoration" (1915) there are some historical addresses. "The Literary Remains of the Rev. Jonathan Maxey, D.D., second President of Brown University . . . with a Memoir of his Life" (1844) by Romeo Elton, has considerable data. The following articles by Reuben Guild are suggestive: "The Charter of Brown University" ("Baptist Quarterly" April 1875), and "The Denominational Work of President Manning" ("Baptist Review" October-December 1880, and January-March, 1881).

The Separates who in several particulars resembled the Baptists have been sympathetically presented by Rev. S. LeRoy Blake in "The Separates or Strict Congregationalists of New England" (1902). Professor Williston Walker writes an introduction, and a bibliography is added. Backus' "History of the Baptists," Trumbull's "Connecticut," and Hovey's "Memoir of . . . Isaac Backus" should be consulted.

Another group which for lack of a better connection may be referred to here, because of their evangelical zeal and simplicity, was the Sandemanians. A good interpretation by Williston Walker "The Sandemanians of New England" appears in the "Ann. Rpt. Amer. Hist. Assn.," 1901, Vol. I Sec. V. Another contribution is by H. H. Edes, "The Places of Worship of the Sandemanians in Boston" (Pub. Col. Soc. Mass., Vol. VI, pp. 109-123).

Coming to the middle states, as an introduction to the field "A History of the Baptists in the Middle States" (1898) by H. C. Vedder, will be found interesting and carefully executed. "Biographical Memoirs of the Late Rev. John Gano of Frankfort written principally by Himself" (1806) tells the story of one who itinerated throughout the middle states and elsewhere. Morgan Edwards again will be found of substantial service in his "Materials towards a History of the Baptists of Jersey"(1792), and "Materials towards a History of the Baptists in Delaware State" (1791, "Pa. Mag. of History and Biography" Vol. IX, p. 45 f. and 197 f.). To these should be added, "The Early and Later Delaware Baptists" (1880) by R. B. Cook, and more particularly "A History of Baptists in New Jersey" (1904) by T. S. Griffiths.

Virginia has been a field of special interest to Baptist historians. "A History of the Rise and Progress of the Baptists in Virginia" (1810) by Robert B. Semple, though antiquated holds a recognized place because of its accurate details. A revised edition (1894) by Rev. G. W. Beale, has annotations and supplementary matter which makes it better proportioned, clearer, and more up to date than the original. William Fristoe's "History of the Ketocton Baptist Association" (1808) fills an important place among the older works. "The Writings of the late John Leland, including some Events in his Life, written by himself, with additional Skethces" edited (1845) by Mrs. L. F. Greene is illuminating. See also an article by J. T. Smith entitled "Life and Times of the Rev. John Leland" ("The Baptist Quarterly" April 1871). "Sketches of Virginia" (Series I, 1850) by Rev. W. H. Foote, gives considerable data. "Early Baptists of Virginia" (1857) by R. B. C. Howell, is well conceived, reliable, and worthy of a place among more recent workers. "Virginia Baptist Ministers" (in 2 Series, II Vols. 3rd Edition 1860, introd. by Rev. J. B. Jeter,) by James B. Taylor, has short biographical sketches of some six score Baptist valiants. The "Life and Times of J. B. Taylor" (1872) by G. B. Taylor is particularly helpful.

The part played by Baptists in the cause of religious liberty in Virginia has been the subject of several studies. The older and less significant contributions are as follows: "The Virginia Baptist: or A View and Defence of the Christian Religion as it is Professed by the Baptists of Virginia" (1774) by David Thomas; "Struggles and Triumphs of Virginia Baptists" (a discourse, 1873) by J. L. M. Curry; also his "Establishment and Disestablishment" (1889); "The Trials and Victories of Religious Liberty in America" (A Centennial Memorial 1876) by G. S. Bailey; and "Religious Persecution in Virginia" ("Christian Review," January and April, 1858).

The recent publication of four excellent monographs leaves little more to be said upon this subject: "The Struggle of Protestant Dissenters for Religious Toleration in Virginia" ("J. H. U. Studies" Series XII) by H. R. McIlwaine; a "Documentary History of the Struggle for Religious Liberty in Virginia" ("Religious Herald," December 8, 1898, and following numbers, issued also in book form) by C. F. James; "The Struggle for Religious Freedom in Virginia: The Baptists" ("J. H. U. Studies" Series XVIII) by William Taylor Thom; and the "Separation of Church and State in Virginia" (1910) by H. J. Eckenrode. A "Comparison of Denominational Forces in the Struggle for Religious Liberty in Virginia" (D. B. Dissertation, U. of Chicago, 1904) by J. C. Zeller gives decisive significance to the Baptists. For the Presbyterian side of the case see p. 264.

Because of the prominence of Virginian Baptists in constutional struggles, it should be noted that considerable data bearing upon them will be found in the "Journals of Virginia House of Burgesses"; "Journals of Virginia Conventions, 1775-1776"; "Journals of the General Assembly of Virginia"; Hening's "Statutes at Large" and the writings of George Washington.

For Pennsylvania, Morgan Edwards did pioneer work in his "Materials towards a History of the American Baptists in XII Volumes, . . . " Vol. I (1770) of which treated of Pennsylvania. "Minutes of the Philadelphia Baptist Assocation from A.D. 1707 to A.D. 1807, being the first One Hundred Years of its Existence" (1851) edited by A. D. Gillette, is of prime significance. "The Bi-Centennial Celebration of the Founding of the First Baptist Church of the City of Philadelphia" edited (1898) by William Williams Keen tells the story of this historic church. The appendix has several quotations from Morgan Edwards, and a few notable documents. H. G. Jones has a "Historical Sketch of the Lower Dublin (or Pennepek) Baptist Church, Philadelphia" (1869). "The Early Baptists of Philadelphia" (1877) by Rev. David Spencer gives a fair summary of the period 1684-1815.

For North Carolina an introductory sketch may be found in "A History of the Baptists in North Carolina" (1901) by Rev. C. B. Williams. In the "North Carolina Baptist Historical Papers" there are several important contributions bearing upon the early history of the Baptists of the state. The most notable is that of Rev. J. D. Hufham (six papers, Vols. I, II, and III), entitled "The Baptists in North Carolina." This really gives a good history. Other articles are as follows: "The Colonial Period of North Carolina Baptist History" by Rev. N. B. Cobb (Vol. I); the "History of the Meherrin Church" by S. J. Wheeler (Vol. I); "Bear Marsh Church" by Rev. J. T. Albritton (Vol. II); "The Baptists in the Fork of the Yadkin" by J. T. Alderman (Vol. II); "Elder Shubael Stearns" by C. E. Taylor (Vol. II); "Abbotts Creek Church" by H. Sheets (Vol. III, important documents); "Early Baptist Efforts in Charlotte" by T. J. Taylor (Vol. III); "The Preparation for Baptist Work in North Carolina" by T. M. Pittman (Vol. III); "Notes from Records of Reedy Creek Church, Tar River Association" by B. P. Davis (Vol. III). In the section "Notes, Queries, Criticisms" of the various numbers of this publication, one may come upon an eagerly sought bit of documentary material. Three other important histories should be added: "A Concise History of the Kehukee Baptist Association" (1803) by Lemuel Burkitt and Jesse Reed; "A History of the Sandy Creek Baptist Association from its Organization in A.D. 1758 to A.D. 1858" (1859) by Elder G. W. Purefoy; and "A History of the Liberty Baptist Association from its Organization in 1832 to 1905" (1907) by Elder Henry Sheets. This last, though dealing with the national era, has some introductory material bearing upon the beginnings of Baptist work.

For South Carolina there is "A Discourse containing some Fragments of the History of the Baptist Church in Charleston, S. C." (1837) by B. Manly; "A History of the Charleston Association" (1811) by Furman Wood, only a small portion of which deals with colonial times; and "Two Centuries of the First Baptist Church of South Carolina, 1683-1883" (1889) by H. A. Tupper. Rev. William Screven, who directed the first Baptist group to South Carolina is treated by H. S. Burrage in "Coll. & Proc. Maine Hist. Soc." Series II, Vol. I, pp. 45-56, and Vol. V, pp. 275-284.

In the colonial era Baptists in Georgia were just emerging into existence. There is therefore little to record in the way of literature. A "History of the Georgia Baptist Association" (1838) by Jesse Mercer; "Memoirs of Elder Jesse Mercer" (1844) by C. D. Mallary; and "Georgia Baptists" (1874) by J. H. Campbell, with the more satisfactory "History of the Baptist Denomination in Georgia" compiled for the "Christian Index" (1881) is all that there is to record.

The beginnings of Baptist history in Alabama are set forth by H. Holcombe in "A History of the Rise and Progress of the Baptists in Alabama" (1840)

In conclusion it should be noted that "Baptist Councils in America" (1906) a doctoral dissertation devoted 'to a historical setting of their origin, and the principles of their development' by W. H. Allison meets every requirement in this part of the field. Credal formulas may be found in "Baptist Confessions of Faith" (1911) by W. J. McGlothlin.

DOCUMENTS

I. *THE WHIPPING OF OBADIAH HOLMES*

For preaching and baptizing in William Witter's house, denying the lawfulness of infant baptism, and persistently refusing to remove his hat during worship, Holmes was condemned to the humiliation described by himself as under:

"Not long after these troubles I came upon occasion of business into the colony of Massachusetts, with two other brethren, as brother Clarke being one of the two can inform you, where we three were apprehended, carried to (the prison at) Boston, and so to the Court, and were all sentenced. What they laid to my charge, you may here read in my sentence, upon the pronouncing of which, as I went from the bar, I expressed myself in these words:—I bless God, I am counted worthy to suffer for the name of Jesus. Whereupon John Wilson (their pastor, as they call him) struck me before the judgment-seat, and cursed me, saying, The curse of God or Jesus go with thee. So we were carried to the prison, where not long after I was deprived of my two loving friends, at whose departure the adversary stepped in, took hold of my spirit, and troubled me for the space of an hour, and then the Lord came in, and sweetly relieved me, causinge me to look to himself; so was I stayed, and refreshed in the thoughts of my God. . . .

. . . .

"And when I heard the voice of my keeper come for me, even cheerfulness did come upon me, and taking my Testament in my hand, I went along with him to the place of execution, and after common salutation here stood. There stood by also one of the magistrates, by name Increase Nowel, who for a while kept silent, and spoke not a word, and so did I, expecting the governor's presence, but he came not. But after a while Mr. Nowel bade the executioner do his office. Then I desired to speak a few words, but Mr. Nowel answered, It is not now a time to speak. Whereupon I took leave, and said, Men, brethren, fathers and countrymen, I beseech you give me leave to speak a few words, and the rather because here are many spectators to see me punished, and I am to seal with my blood, if God give me strength, that which I hold and practice in reference to the word of God, and testimony of Jesus. That which I have to say in brief is this, Although I confess I am no disputant, yet seeing I am to seal what I hold with my blood, I am ready to defend it by the Word, and to dispute that point with any that shall come forth to withstand it. Mr. Nowel answered me, now was no time to dispute. Then said I, Then I desire to give an account of the faith and order I hold, and this I desired three times, but in comes Mr. Flint, and saith to the executioner, Fellow, do thine office, for this fellow would but make a long speech to delude the people. So I being resolved to speak, told the people; That which I am to suffer is for the Word of God, and testimony of Jesus Christ. No, saith Mr. Nowel, it is for your error, and going about to seduce the people. To which I replied, Not for error, for in all the time of my imprisonment wherein I was left alone (my brethren being gone) which of all your ministers in all that time came to convince me of an error; and when upon the governor's words a motion was made for a public dispute, and upon fair terms so often renewed, and desired by hundreds, what was the reason it was not granted. Mr. Nowel told me, it was his fault that went away and would not dispute, but this the writings will clear at large. Still Mr. Flint calls to the man to do his office; so before and in the time of his pulling off my clothes I continued speaking, telling them, that I had so learned, that for all Boston I would not give my body into their hands thus to be bruised upon another account, yet upon this I would not give the hundredth part of a *wampum peaque* to free it out of their hands, and that I made as much conscience of unbuttoning one button, as I did of paying the thirty pounds in reference thereunto. I told them moreover, The Lord having manifested his love towards me, in giving me repentance towards God and faith in Jesus Christ, and so to be baptized in water by a messenger of Jesus into the name of the Father, Son and Holy Spirit, wherein I have fellowship with him in his death, burial and resurrection, I am now come to be baptized in afflictions by your hands, that so I may have further fellowship with my Lord, and am not ashamed of his sufferings, for by his stripes am I healed.

"And as the man began to lay the strokes upon my back, I said to the people, Though my flesh should fail, and my spirit should fail, yet my God would not fail. So it pleased the Lord to come in, and so to fill my heart and tongue as a vessel full, and with an audible voice I broke forth praying unto the Lord not to lay this sin to their charge; and telling the people, that now I found he did not fail me, and therefore now I should trust him forever who failed me not; for in truth, as the strokes fell upon me, I had such a spiritual manifestation of God's presence as the like thereof I never had nor felt, nor can with fleshly tongue express; and the outward pain was so removed from me, that indeed I am not able to declare it to you, it was so easy to me, that I could well bear it, yea and in a manner felt it not although it was grievous as the spectators said, the man striking with all his strength (yea spitting in his hand three times as many affirmed) with a three-corded whip, giving me therewith thirty strokes. When he had loosed me from the post, having joyfulness in my heart, and cheerfulness in my countenance, as the spectators observed, I told the magistrates, You have struck me as with roses; and said moreover, Although the Lord hath made it easy to me, yet I pray God it may not be laid to your charge.

"After this many came to me rejoicing to see the power of the Lord manifested in weak flesh; but sinful flesh takes occasion hereby to bring others in trouble, informs the magistrates hereof, and so two more are apprehended as for contempt of authority. . . ."

Text—*Clarke's Narrative*, pp. 16-23, quoted in *Backus, History of the Baptists* . . ., Vol. I, pp. 189-192.

II. *THOMAS GOULD AND THE ORGANIZATION OF THE CHARLESTOWN BAPTIST CHURCH*

Below is given a portion of Gould's account of the experiences that drove him with others to public baptism and church covenant fellowship in his home in Charlestown March 28, 1665.

"At another meeting the church required me to bring out my child to baptism. I told them I durst not do it, for I did not see any rule for it in the word of God. They brought many places of Scripture in the Old and New Testaments, as circumcision and the promise to Abraham, and that children were holy, and they were disciples. But I told them that all these places made nothing for infants' baptism. Then stood up W. D. in the church and said, *"Put him in the Court! Put him in the Court!"* But Mr. Sims answered, I pray forbear such words; but it proved so, for presently after, they put me in the Court, and put me in seven or eight Courts, whilst they looked upon me to be a member of their church. The elder pressed the church to lay me under admonition, which the church was backward to do. Afterwards I went out at the sprinkling of children, which was a great trouble to some honest hearts, and they told me of it. But I told them I could not stay, for I look upon it as no ordinance of Christ. They told me that now I had made known my judgment I might stay, for they know I did not join with them. So I stayed and sat down in my seat when they were at prayer and administering that service to infants. Then they dealt with me for my unreverent carriage. . . . One stood up and accused me, that I stopped my ears; but I denied it.

"At another meeting they asked me if I would suffer the church to fetch my child and baptize it? I answered, If they would fetch my child and do it as their own act they might do it; but when they should bring my child, I would make known to the congregation that I had no hand in it; then some in the church were against doing of it. A brother stood up and said, Brother Gould, you were once for children's baptism, why are you fallen from it? I answered, It is true, and I suppose you were once for crossing in baptism, why are you fallen from that? The man was silent. But Mr. Sims stood up in a great heat, and desired the church to take notice of it, that I compared the ordinance of Christ to the cross in baptism! This was one of the great offences they dealt with me for. After this the Deputy Governor meeting me in Boston, called me to him and said, Goodman Gould, I desire you that you would let the church baptize your child. I told him that if the church would do it upon their account they should do it, but I durst not bring out my child. So he called to Mrs. Norton of Charlestown, and prayed her to fetch Goodman Gould's child and baptize it. So she spake to them, but not rightly, informing them, she gave them to understand that I would bring out my child. They called me out again and asked me if I would bring forth my child? I told them No, I durst not do it, for I see no rule for it. One of the brethren stood up and said, If I would not let my child partake of one ordinance, it was meet I should not partake of the other, so many of the church concluded to lay me under admonition; but before they did it Mr. Sims told me, it was more according to rule for me to withdraw from the ordinance, than for them to put me by; bringing that place of Scripture, If thou bring thy gift to the altar, and there rememberest that thy brother hath aught against thee, leave there thy offering and be reconciled first to thy brother. But I told them I did not know that my brother had anything justly against me; for they had not shown me any rule of Christ that I had broken, therefore I durst not withdraw from that ordinance that I had found so much of God in; but if they would put me by, I hoped God would feed my soul another way. So they proceeded to admonition. Elder Green said, Brother Gould, you are to take notice that you are admonished for three things; the first is, that you refused to bring your child to be baptized; the second is, for your contentious words and unreverent carriage in the time of that ordinance; the third is, for a late lie you told; and therefore you are to take notice, that you are not to partake any more of the ordinance of Christ with us, till you give satisfaction for these things. But when that late lie was told I know not, except it was when the letter was found in brother Wilder's pocket. This admonition was between seven and eight years before they cast me out. After this I went to Cambridge meeting, which was as near my house as the other; upon that they put me into the Court, that I did not come to hear; but many satisfied the Court that I did come constantly to Cambridge; so they cleared me. Then the church called me to account and dealt with me for schism, that I rent from the church. I told them, I did not rend from them, for they put me away. Master Sims was very earnest for another admonition for schism, which most of the church were against; but it seems he set it down for an admonition on a bit of paper. This continued for a long time before they called me out again. In the meantime, I had some friends who came to me out of old England, who were Baptists, and desired to meet at my house of a First-day, which I granted. Of these was myself, my wife and Thomas Osburne, that were of their church. Afterwards they called me forth and asked why I kept the meeting in private on the Lord's day, and did not come to the public? My answer was, I know not what reason the church had to call me forth. They asked me if I was not a member of that church? I told them they had not acted toward me as a member, who had put me by the ordinances of Christ seven years ago; . . . they had denied me the privileges of a member. They asked me whether I looked upon admonition as an appointment of Christ? I told them, Yes, but not to lie under it above seven years, and to be put by the ordinances of Christ in the church; for the rule of Christ is first to deal with men in the first and second place, and then in the third place before the church; but the first time they ever dealt with me, they called me before the whole church. Many meetings we had about this thing, whether I was a member or not, but could come to no conclusion; for I still affirmed that their actings rendered me no member. Them Mr. Sims told the church that I was ripe for excommunication, and (he) was very earnest for it, but the church would not consent. Then I desired that we might send to other churches for their help to hear the thing betwixt us; but Master Sims made me this answer: We are a church of Christ ourselves, and you shall know that we have power to deal with you ourselves. Then said Mr. Russell, We have not gone the right way to gain this our brother, for we have dealt too harshly with him. But still Master Sims pressed the church to excommunicate me. Mr. Russell said, There were greater errors in the church in the apostles' time, and yet they did not so deal with them.

. . . .

"Now after this, considering with myself what the Lord would have me to do; not likely to join with any of the churches of New England any more, and so to be without the ordinances of Christ; in the meantime God sent out of Old England some who were Baptists; we, consulting together what to do, sought the Lord to direct us, and taking counsel of other friends who dwelt among us, who were able and godly, they gave us counsel to congregate ourselves together; and so we did, being nine of us, to walk in the order of the gospel according to the rule of Christ, yet knowing that it was a breach of the law of this country; that we had not the approbation of magistrates and ministers, for that we suffered the penalty of that law, when we were called before them. After we had been called into one or two Courts, the church understanding that we were gathered into church order, they sent three messengers from the church to me, telling me the church required me to come before them the next Lord's day. I replied, The church had nothing to do with me, for they had put me from them eight years before. . . . They told me again that if I did not come, the church would proceed against me the next Lord's day. I told them that I could not come for we were to break bread the next Lord's day. They told me that they would return my answer to the church. One of them asked if I would come the next Lord's day after? But another presently said, We have no such order from the church; so they departed. The last day of that week three loving friends coming to me of their own account, one of them was pleased to say to me, Brother Gould, though you look upon it as unjust for them to cast you out, yet there be many that are godly among them, that will act with them through ignorance, which will be a sin of them, and you are persuaded, I believe, that it is your duty to prevent any one from any sinful act, for they will cast you out for not hearing the church; now your coming will stop them from acting against you, and so keep many from that sin. Upon these words I was clearly convinced that it was my duty to go, and replied, Although I could not come the next day, yet I promised them that if I was alive and well, I would come the next Lord's day if the Lord permit. He replied, What if the church I was joined to was not willing? I told him I did not question that any one would be against it upon this ground. After I had propounded it to the church, not one was against it. I entreated these friends to make it known to the elders that I would come to them the next Lord's day after, yet, though they knew of it, they proceeded against me that day, and delivered me up to Satan for not hearing the church."

Text—Wood: *The History of the First Baptist Church of Boston*, pp. 46-51.

III. *THE BAPTISTS AND SEPARATES→BEECH WOODS CONFERENCE*

Isaac Backus gives the following account of a conference between himself, Rev. I. Hovey of Rochester, and others, November 22, 1749.

"After committing the case to God, we began the conference. And first Mr. Hovey asked what we thought of the churches generally in this land. We answered that we believed they were churches of Christ, though greatly degenerated and corrupted. He said he was of the same mind. Next he asked what we thought of the ministers. We answered that we believed many of them were ministers of Christ. He agreed with us therein. Then he asked what were the reasons of our separation, and also how far we did separate from them. We answered, that the reasons were the corruptions which had crept into the churches, and that we desired to separate from nothing but their corruptions; that although we could not join in the communion of those churches, yet if any who remained in them and gave evidence of their being saints desired it, we could freely receive them to our communion; and that we desired to join with them in anything that was right. Upon this we had much talk, but could not be of a mind. When he asked our views respecting the power of ordination, we told him that we held the power to be in the churches. He held the power of choosing (a minister) to be in the churches, but the power of ordaining to be in the ministers. Next he asked our minds concerning the knowledge of the brethren. I told him that the way I knew them, was by what came from them in word and action, and also that the rule which God has given us to know them by is a perfect rule; but as we are imperfect creatures, we may be imperfect in (applying) that as well as in other things. Here he agreed with me. Then he asked concerning visions, prophecies, etc. Herein we agreed that the Scripture is our perfect rule, and that we are not to give heed to anything contrary thereto. We then discoursed about persons' bodies being overcome; and herein we agreed that it was no certain evidence either for or against them. In the whole of our discourse we were kept very free from bitterness on both sides, and we agreed in all but two points. One is, he thought we ought not to separate, but to stay in the churches, groaning under the burdens and laboring for a reformation. The other relates to the power of ordination."

Text—Alvah Hovey: *A Memoir of the Life and Times of the Rev. Isaac Bachus, A.M.*, pp. 51-52.

IV. *THE CHARTER OF BROWN UNIVERSITY, FEBRUARY, 1764*

The denominational aspect of this institution is presented as under:

"Whereas institutions for liberal education are highly beneficial to society, by forming the rising generation to virtue, knowledge, and useful literature; and thus preserving in the community a succession of men duly qualified for discharging the offices of life with usefulness and reputation, they have therefore justly merited and received the attention and encouragement of every wise and well-regulated State: and whereas a public school or seminary, erected for that purpose within this Colony, to which the youth may freely resort for education in the vernacular and learned languages, and in the liberal arts and sciences, would be for the general advantage and honor of the government: . . .

"Now, THEREFORE, KNOW YE, That being willing to encourage and patronize such an honorable and useful institution, we, the said Governor and Company, in General Assembly convened, do, for ourselves and our successors, in and by virtue of the power and authority within the jurisdiction of this Colony, to us by the Royal Charter granted and committed, enact, grant, constitute, ordain and declare, and it is hereby enacted, granted, constituted, ordained and declared, that the Hon. Stephen Hopkins . . . or so many of them as shall, within twelve months from the date hereof, accept of this trust, and qualify themselves as hereinafter directed, and their successors, shall be forever hereafter one body corporate & politic, in fact and name, to be known in law by the name of TRUSTEES AND FELLOWS OF THE COLLEGE OR UNIVERSITY IN THE ENGLISH COLONY OF RHODE ISLAND AND PROVIDENCE PLANTATIONS, IN NEW ENGLAND, IN AMERICA; the Trustees and Fellows, at any time hereafter, giving such more particular name to the College, in honor of the greatest and most distinguished benefactor, or otherwise, as they shall think proper; . . .

"And furthermore, by the authority aforesaid, it is hereby enacted, ordained and declared, That it is now, and at all times hereafter shall continue to be, the unalterable constitution of this College or University, that the Corporation thereof shall consist of two branches, to wit: That of the Trustees, and that of the Fellowship, with distinct, separate and respective powers: And that the number of the Trustees shall and may be thirty-six; of which twenty-two shall forever be elected of the denomination called Baptists, or Antipaedobaptists; five shall forever be elected of the denomination called Friends or Quakers; four shall forever be elected of the denomination called Congregationalists, and five shall forever be elected of the denomination called Episcopalians: And that the succession in this branch shall be forever chosen and filled up from the respective denominations in this proportion, and according to these numbers; which are hereby fixed, and shall remain to perpetuity immutably the same. . . . And that the number of the Fellows, inclusive of the President (who shall always be a Fellow) shall and may be twelve; of which, eight shall be forever elected of the denomination called Baptists, or Antipaedobaptists; and the rest indifferently of any or all denominations. . . .

"And furthermore, it is declared and ordained, That the succession in both branches shall at all times hereafter be filled up and supplied according to these numbers, and this established and invariable proportion, from the respective denominations, by the separate election of both branches of this Corporation, which shall at all times sit and act by separate and distinct powers: And in general, in order to the validity and consummation of all acts, there shall be in the exercise of their respective, separate and distinct powers, the joint concurrence of the Trustees and Fellows, by their respective majorities, except in adjudging and conferring the academical degrees, which shall forever belong, exclusively, to the Fellowship, as a learned Faculty.

"And furthermore, it is constituted, that the instruction and immediate government of the College shall forever be and rest in the President and Fellows or Fellowship.

. . . .

"And, in case any President, Trustee or Fellow, shall see cause to change his religious denomination, the Corporation is hereby empowered to declare his or their place or places vacant, and may proceed to fill up it or them accordingly, as before directed, otherwise each Trustee and Fellow, not an officer of instruction, shall continue in his office during life, or until resignation. And further, in case either of the religious denominations should decline taking a part in this catholic, comprehensive and liberal institution, the Trustees and Fellows shall and may complete their number, by electing from their respective denominations, always preserving their respective proportions herein before prescribed and determined: And all elections shall be by ballot, or written suffrage: . . .

. . . .

"And furthermore, it is hereby enacted and declared That into this liberal and catholic institution shall never be admitted any religious tests: But, on the contrary all the members hereof shall forever enjoy full, free, absolute and uninterrupted liberty of conscience: And that the places of Professors, Tutors, and all other officers, the President alone excepted, shall be free and open for all denominations of Protestants: And that youth of all religious denominations shall and may be freely admitted to the equal advantages, emoluments and honors of the College or University, and shall receive a like fair, generous and equal treatment, during their residence therein, they conducting themselves peaceably, and conforming to the laws and statutes thereof. And that the public teaching shall, in general, respect the sciences; and that the sectarian differences of opinions, shall not make any part of the public and classical instruction, although all religious controversies may be studied freely, examined and explained, by the President, Professors and Tutors, in a personal, separate and distinct manner, to the youth of any or each denomination: And above all, a constant regard be paid to, and effectual care taken of, the morals of the College.

. . . .

"And furthermore, for the greater encouragement of this seminary of learning, and that the same may be amply endowed and enfranchised with the same privileges, dignities and immunities, enjoyed by the American colleges, and European universities, we do grant, enact, ordain and declare, and it is hereby granted, enacted, ordained and declared, That the College estate, the estates, persons and families of the President and Professors, for the time being, lying and being within the Colony, with the persons of the tutors and students, during their residence at the College, shall be freed and exempted from all taxes, serving on juries, and menial services: And that the persons aforesaid shall be exempted from bearing arms, impresses and military services, except in case of an invasion."

Text—Reuben Guild: *History of Brown University, with Illustrative Documents*, pp. 132-138.

V. *STRUGGLE FOR RELIGIOUS LIBERTY—NEW ENGLAND*

The Warren Association and the "Plan to Collect Grievances."

"Whereas complaints of oppressions, occasioned by a non-conformity to the religious establishment in New England, have been brought to this Association, and whereas the laws obtained for preventing and redressing such oppressions have, upon trial, been found insufficient (either through defect in the laws themselves, or iniquity in the execution thereof), and whereas humble remonstrances and petitions have not been duly regarded, but the same oppressive measures continued: This is to inform all the oppressed Baptists in New England that the Association of Warren, (in conjunction with the Western or Philadelphia Association) is determined to seek remedy for their brethren where a speedy and effectual one may be had.   In order to pursue this resolution by petition and memorial, the following gentlemen are appointed to receive well attested grievances, to be by them transmitted to the Rev. Samuel Stillman of Boston, namely, Rev. Hezekiah Smith of Haverhill, Rev. Isaac Backus of Middleborough, Mr. Richard Montague of Sunderland, Rev. Joseph Meacham of Enfield, and Rev. Thomas Whitman of Groton in Connecticut."

In pursuance of this plan, the committee published the advertisement above referred to.   It appeared in the Boston Evening Post of August 20, 1770, and was as follows:

"To the Baptists in the Province of the Massachusetts Bay, who are, or have been, oppressed in any way on a religious account.   It would be needless to tell you that you have long felt the effects of the laws by which the religion of the government in which you live is established.   Your purses have felt the burden of ministerial rates, and when these would not satisfy your enemies, your property hath been taken from you and sold for less than half its value.   These things you cannot forget.   You will therefore readily hear and attend, when you are desired to collect your cases of suffering, and have them well attested, such as, the taxes you have paid to build meetinghouses, to settle ministers and support them, with all the time, money, and labor you have lost in waiting on courts, feeing lawyers, &c., and bring or send such cases to the Baptist Association to be held at Bellingham, when measures will be resolutely adopted for obtaining redress from another quarter than that to which repeated application hath been made unsuccessfully.   Nay, complaints, however just and grievous, have been treated with indifference, and scarcely, if at all, credited.   We deem this our conduct perfectly justifiable, and hope you will pay a particular regard to this desire, and be exact in your accounts of your sufferings, and punctual in your attendance at the time and place above mentioned.

"Boston, July 31st, 1770."

Text—Backus: *History of the Baptists,* Vol. II, pp. 154-155.

Memorial at Philadelphia, October 14, 1774

At a conference attended by Isaac Backus agent of the Warren association, the Massachusetts delegates Thomas Cushing, Samuel Adams, John Adams and Robert Paine, the Mayor of Philadelphia, some Quakers, some Baptist elders, and others, President Manning read the following memorial—

"It has been said by a celebrated writer in politics, that but two things were worth contending for,—Religion and Liberty   For the latter we are at present nobly exerting ourselves through all this extensive continent; and surely no one whose bosom feels the patriot glow in behalf of civil liberty, can remain torpid to the more ennobling flame of RELIGIOUS FREEDOM.

The free exercise of private judgment, and the unalienable rights of conscience, are of too high a rank and dignity to be subjected to the decrees of councils, or the imperfect laws of fallible legislators.   The merciful Father of mankind is the alone Lord of conscience. Establishments may be enabled to confer worldly distinctions and secular importance. They may make hypocrites, but cannot create Christians. They have been reared by craft or power, but liberty never flourished perfectly under their control. That liberty, virtue, and public happiness can be supported without them, this flourishing province is a glorious testimony; and a view of it would be sufficient to invalidate all the most elaborate arguments ever adduced in support of them. Happy in the enjoyment of these undoubted rights, and conscious of their high import, every lover of mankind must be desirous, as far as opportunity offers, of extending and securing the enjoyment of these inestimable blessings.

These reflections have arisen from considering the unhappy situation of our brethren, the Baptists, in the province of Massachusetts Bay, for whom we now appear as advocates; and from the important light in which liberty in general is now beheld, we trust our representation will be effectual. The province of the Massachusetts Bay, being settled by persons who fled from civil and religious oppression, it would be natural to imagine them deeply impressed with the value of liberty, and nobly scorning a domination over conscience. But such was the complexion of the times, they fell from the unhappy state of being oppressed, to the more deplorable and ignoble one of becoming oppressors.

But these things being passed over, we intend to begin with the charter obtained at the happy restoration. . . .

. . . .

Upon this short statement of facts we would observe, that the charter must be looked upon by every impartial eye to the infringed, so soon as any law was passed for the establishment of any particular mode of worship. All Protestants are placed upon the same footing; and no law whatever could disannul so essential a part of a charter intended to communicate the blessings of a free government to his Majesty's subjects. Under the first charter, as was hinted, church-membership conferred the rights of a freeman; but by the second, the possession of property was the foundation. Therefore, how could it be supposed that the collective body of the people intended to confer any other power upon their representatives than that of making laws relative to property and the concerns of this life?

Men unite in society, according to the great Mr. Locke, 'with an intention in every one the better to preserve himself, his liberty and property. The power of the society, or Legislature constituted by them, can never be supposed to extend any further than the common good, but is obliged to secure every one's property.' To give laws, to receive obedience, to compel with the sword, belong to none but the civil magistrate and on this ground *we affirm* that the magistrate's power extends not to the establishing any articles of faith or forms of worship, by force of laws; for laws are of no force without penalties. The care of souls cannot belong to the civil magistrate, because his power consists only in outward force; but pure and saving religion consists in the inward persuasion of the mind, without which nothing can be acceptable to God.

It is a just position, and cannot be too firmly established, that we can have no property in that which another may take, when he pleases, to himself; neither can we have the proper enjoyment of our religious liberties, (which must be acknowledged to be of greater value), if held by the same unjust and capricious tenure; and this must appear to be the case when temporary laws pretend to grant relief so very inadequate.

It may now be asked—*What is the liberty desired?* The answer is; as the kingdom of Christ is not of this world, and religion is a concern between God and the soul with which no human authority can intermeddle; consistently with the principles of Christianity, and according to the dictates of Protestantism, we claim and expect the liberty of worshipping God according to our consciences, not being obliged to support a ministry we cannot attend, whilst we demean ourselves as faithful subjects. These we have an undoubted right to, as men, as Christians, and by charter as inhabitants of Massachusetts Bay."

Text—Hovey: *A Memoir of the Life and Times of the Rev. Isaac Backus*, A.M. pp. 204-210.

VI. *STRUGGLE FOR RELIGIOUS LIBERTY—VIRGINIA*

To the Honourable Peyton Randolph, Esq., and the several delegated Gentlemen, convened at Richmond, to concert Measures conducive to the Good and Well-being of this Colony and Dominion, the humble Address of the Virginia Baptists, now Associated in Cumberland, by Delegates from their several Churches:

Gentlemen of the Convention—While you are (pursuant to the important Trust reposed in you) acting as the Guardians of the Rights of your Constituents, and pointing out to them the Road to Freedom, it must needs afford you an exalted satisfaction to find your Determinations not only applauded, but cheerfully complied with by a brave and spirited people. We, however distinguished from the Body of our Countrymen by appellatives and sentiments of a religious nature, do nevertheless look upon ourselves as Members of the same Commonwealth, and, therefore, with respect to matters of a civil nature, embarked in the same common Cause.

Alarmed at the shocking Oppression which in a British Cloud hangs over our American Continent, we, as a Society and part of the distressed State, have in our Association consider'd what part might be most prudent for the Baptists to act in the present unhappy Contest. After we had determined "that in some Cases it was lawful to go to War, and also for us to make a Military resistance against Great Britain, in regard of their unjust Invasion, and tyrannical Oppression of, and repeated Hostilities against America," our people were all left to act at Discretion with respect to inlisting, without falling under the Censure of our Community. And as some have inlisted, and many more likely so to do, who will have earnest Desires for their Ministers to preach to them during the Campaign, we therefore delegate and appoint our well-beloved Brethren in the Ministry, Elijah Craig, Lewis Craig, Jeremiah Walker and John Williams, to present this address and to petition you that they may have free Liberty to preach to the Troops at convenient Times without molestation or abuse; and as we are conscious of their strong attachment to American Liberty, as well as their soundness in the principles of the Christian Religion, and great usefulness in the Work of the Ministry, we are willing they may come under your examination in any Matters you may think requisite.

We conclude with our earnest prayers to Almighty God for His Divine Blessing on your patriotic and laudable Resolves, for the good of Mankind and American Freedom, and for the success of our Armies, in Defence of our Lives, Liberties, and Properties. Amen.

Sign'd by order and in behalf of the Association the 14th of August, 1775.

SAM'L HARRIS, Moderator

JOHN WALLER, Clerk.

Text—James: *Documentary History of the Struggle for Religious Liberty in Virginia*, pp. 218-219.

"*Resolved*, That it be an instruction to the commanding officers of the regiment or troops to be raised, that they permit dissenting clergymen to celebrate divine worship and to preach to the soldiers, or exhort from time to time, as the various operations of the military service may permit, for the ease of such scrupulous consciences as may not choose to attend divine service as celebrated by the chaplain."

Text—*as above*, p. 53.

To the Honourable the Speaker and House of Delegates:
The Memorial of the Baptist Association, met at Sandy Creek, in Charlotte, the 16th day of October, 1780, in behalf of themselves and those whom they represent, humbly sheweth:
That a due Regard to the Liberty and Rights of the People is of the highest Importance to the Welfare of the State; That this heaven-born Freedom, which belongs equally to every good Citizen, is the Palladium which the Legislature is particularly intrusted with the Guardianship of, and on which the Safety and Happiness of the State depend. Your Memorialists, therefore, look upon every Law or Usage now existing among us, which does not accord with that Republican Spirit which breathes in our Constitution and Bill of Rights, to be extremely pernicious and detrimental, and that such Law or Usage should immediately be abolished.

As Religious Oppression, or the interfering with the Rights of Conscience, which God has made accountable to none but Himself, is of all Oppression the most inhuman, and insupportable, and as Partiality to any Religious Denomination is its genuine offspring, your Memorialists have with Grief observed that Religious Liberty has not made a single Advance in this Commonwealth without some Opposition. They have been much surprised to hear it said of Things indisputably right and necessary, "It is not now a proper Time to proceed to such Affairs, let us first think of defending our selves," &c., when there cannot, surely be a more suitable Time to allow ourselves the Blessings of Liberty, which we have in our own Power, than when contending with those who endeavor to tyrannize over us.

As the Completion of Religious Liberty is what, as a Religious Community, your Memorialists are particularly interested in, they would humbly call the attention of your Honourable House to a few Particulars, viz.: First, the Vestry Law, which disqualifies any person to officiate who will not subscribe to be conformable to the Doctrine and Discipline of the Church of England, by which Means Dissenters are not only precluded, but also not represented, they not having a free Voice, whose Property is nevertheless subject to be taxed by the Vestry, and whose Poor are provided for at the Discretion of those who may possibly be under the Influence of Party Motives. And what renders the said Law a greater Grievance, is, that in some Parishes so much time has elapsed since an Election, that there is scarcely one who was originally chosen by the People, the Vacancies having been filled up by the remaining Vestrymen. Secondly, the Solemnization of Marriage, concerning which it is insinuated by some, and taken for granted by others, that to render it legal it must be performed by a Church Clergyman, according to the Rites and Ceremonies of the Church of England; conformably to which Sentiment Marriage Licenses are usually worded and directed. Now, if this should in Reality be the Case, your Memorialists conceive that the ill Consequences resulting from thence, which are too obvious to need mentioning render it absolutely necessary for the Legislature to endeavour their Removal. This is an Affair of so tender a Nature, and of such Importance, that after the Restoration one of the first Matters which the British Parliament proceeded to was the Confirmation of the Marriages solemnized according to the Mode in use during the Interregnum and the Protectorate of Cromwell. And the Propriety of such a Measure in Virginia evidently appears from the vast number of Dissenters who, having Objections against the Form and Manner prescribed in the Book of Common Prayer, proceed to marry otherwise; and also that in many Places, especially over the Ridge, there are no Church Parsons to officiate. On the other Hand, if Marriages otherwise solemnized are equally valid, a Declaratory Act to that Purport appears to your Memorialists to be highly expedient, because they can see no Reason why any of the free Inhabitants of this State should be terrified by a mere Mormo from their just Rights and Privileges, or censured by others on Suspicion of their acting contrary to Law. To these Considerations your Memorialists would just beg leave to add that those who claim this Province of officiating at Marriage Solemnities as their sole Right, undertake at the same Time to be the sole Judges of what they are to receive for the same.

Your Memorialists humbly hope that your Honourable House will take effectual measures to redress these Grievances in such a Way as may manifest an equal Regard to all the good People of this Commonwealth, however diversyfied by Appellations or Religious Sentiments; and that, as it is your glory to represent a free People, you will be as forward to remove every just Cause of Offence as your Constituents are to complain of them; and in particular that you will consign to Oblivion all the Relicks of Religious Oppression, and make a public Sacrifice of Partiality at the glorious Altar of Freedom.

SAM'L HARRISS, Mod'r.

Signed by order.
JOHN WILLIAM, Clk.

Text—James: *Documentary History of the Struggle for Religious Liberty in Virginia*, pp. 219-221.

CHAPTER XVI

The Catholic Church in the Colonial Period

Bibliography

Of historians who have dealt in a comprehensive way with the colonial period, the earliest is Rev. John Gilmary Shea, who produced two works, "The Catholic Church in Colonial Days . . . 1521-1763" (1886), and the "Life and Times of the Most. Rev. John Carroll . . . embracing the History of the Catholic Church in the United States, 1763-1815" (1888). These works are incorporated as Vols. I and II of a four volume "History of the Catholic Church in the United States." In the "American Church History Series" (Vol. IX, 1893) Professor Thomas O'Gorman contributes "A History of the Roman Catholic Church in the United States." The latter work shows considerable bias, and is therefore not so satisfactory as the former.

In connection with the Jesuits, the richest mine of documentary material is to be found in "The Jesuit Relations and Allied Documents, 1610-1791 . . . " (LXXIII Vols.) edited (1896-1901) by R. G. Thwaites. The text, with a good translation on opposite pages and illuminating introductory sections, makes this an indispensable work for the investigator of American Jesuit missions.

Source material in smaller proportions may be found in O'Callaghan's " . . . Documentary History of the State of New York" (IV Vols. 1849-51); his "Jesuit Relations of Discoveries and other Occurrences in Canada and the Northern and Western States of the Union, 1632-1672" (1847); and his "Documents Relative to the Colonial History of the State of New York" (Vols. I to X, 1856-58); the "Relations des Jésuites, contenant ce qui s'est passé de plus remarquable dans les missions des pères de la Compagnie de Jésus dans la Nouvelle France" Pub. by the Canadian Government, (III Vols. 1858; "Découvertes et établissements des Français dans l'ouest et dans le sud de l'Amérique septentrionale, (1614-1754): memoires et documents originaux" by Pierre Margry, (VI Vols. 1876-86).

Of histories that deal with Jesuits missions, passing over the pioneer works of Le Clercq and Lescarbot, there is the notable "History and

General Description of New France" by Rev. P. F. X. de Charlevoix, S J. 1744, (VI Vols. trans. by J. G. Shea, 1866-71). Then follow in chronological order, "The Early Jesuit Missions in North America . . . " (1846) by W. I. Kipp; "History of the Catholic Missions among the Indian Tribes of the United States, 1529-1854" (1855) by J. G. Shea; "Cours d'histoire du Canada" (VI Vols. 1861-65) by J. B. A. Ferland; "The Jesuits in North America in the Seventeenth Century" (1867) by Francis Parkman; "Count Frontenac and New France under Louis XIV" (1877) by the same author; "Early Chapters of Cayuga History: Jesuit missions in Goi-o-gouen, 1656-1684 . . . " (1879) by Charles Hawley; also his "Early Chapters of Seneca History . . . " (1884); "Kaskaskia and its Parish Records . . . " (1881) by E. G. Mason; "History of the Discovery of the Northwest by Jean Nicolet in 1634, with a Description of his Life" (1881) by C. W. Butterfield; "Histoire du Canada depuis sa découverte jusqu'a nos jours." (IV Vols. 4th ed. 1883) by F. X. Garneau; "Histoire des Canadiens-Francais, 1608-1680; origine, histoire, religion . . . " (VIII Vols. 1882) by B. Sulte; "Isaac Jogues de la Compagnie de Jesus, premier apôtre des Iroquois" by F. Martin, translated by J. G. Shea, (1885); "Missionary Labors of Fathers Marquette, Menard and Allouez, in the Lake Superior Region" (1886) by C. Verwyst; "The Jesuits, Recollets, and the Indians" by J. G. Shea (Winsor's "Narr. and Crit. His.," Vol. IV); "Joliet, Marquette and La Salle" by J. Winsor (ibid.); "Sketch of Father Louis Andre, S. J., an Early Wisconsin Missionary" (1890?); "Pioneers of France in the New World" (25 ed. 1892), and "A Half Century of Conflict" (II Vols. 1892) by Francis Parkman; "A Typical Missionary; Rev. Sabastien Rale, the Apostle of the Abnakis" by Rev. H. C. Schuyler ("Records, Amer. Cath. Hist. Soc." Vol. XVIII, p. 121 f. and 306 f.); "The Mission of Father Rasles" by E. C. Cummings ("Coll. and Proc. Maine Hist. Soc." Series II, Vol. IV, p. 146 f., 265 f., 404 f.); "Capuchin and Jesuit Fathers at Pentagoêt" by the same author (ibid., Vol. V, p. 161 f.); "The Pioneers of New France in New England, with Contemporary Letters and Documents" (1894) by J. P. Baxter; "Les Jésuites et la Nouvelle-France au XVII siècle, d'après beaucoup de documents inédits" (III Vols. 1895-6) by Camille de Rochemonteix; "The Catholic Church in Wisconsin" (1895-98) by H. H. Heming; "Claude Jean Alloues, The Apostle of the Ottawas . . . " (1897 "Parkman Club Pubs." No. 17); "Père René Ménard, the Predecessor of Alloues and Marquette in the Lake Superior Region" (1897 "Parkman Club Pubs.," No. 11); "Missions on Chequamegon Bay" ("Coll. Wis. State Hist. Soc." Vol. XII, pp. 434-452;

Vol. XIII, pp. 397–425; *ibid*. pp. 426–440); "Early History and Condition of Wisconsin" (*ibid*. Vol. II, pp. 72–97); "Père Marquette, the Missionary Explorer" by Thomas Weadock ("Cath. Hist. Mag." Vol. IV, pp. 371–95); "Father Marquette" (1902) ·by R. G. Thwaites; "The History of the Marquette Statue presented to the Statuary Hall in the Capitol by the State of Wisconsin" ("Records and Studies," Vol. III, Part II); and "The French Régime in Wisconsin" (Coll. Wisc. State Hist. Soc. Vol. XVI, documents).

A fine portraiture of all the American Jesuit missionaries is drawn by Rev. T. J. Campbell S. J., in his "Pioneer Priests of North America 1642–1710" (III Vols. 1908–1911).

On the California missions, documents will be found in "Spanish Exploration in the Southwest, 1542–1706," ("Original Narratives of Early American History" edited, 1916, by H. E. Bolton, Ph.D.). An interpretative study of value is "The Mission as a Frontier Institution in the Spanish-American Colonies" (Amer. Hist. Rev. Vol. XXIII, No. 1). The "Diary" of Serra (translated) may be consulted in "Out West" Vols. XVI and XVII. The following histories are valuable: "History of Catholic Missions. . . " by Shea (as above); "The Spanish Conquest of America" (IV Vols. 1868) by Sir Arthur Helps; "History of California" (VII Vols. 1884-1890) by H. H. Bancroft, also his "Arizona and New Mexico" (1889); "History of California" (II Vols. 1885) by T. H. Hittel; and "The Founding of Spanish California . . . (1916) by C. E. Chapman which is especially good. Studies are as follows: "Padre Junipero Serra" (1884) by Rev. J. Adam; "Fra Junipero Serra and the Californian Mission" by Ann Judge ("Hist. Records and Studies," Vol. VII); "Spanish Institutions of the Southwest" by Frank W. Blackmar ("J. H. U. Studies" Extra Series, Vol. X, particularly valuable); "History of the Mission of San Gabriel . . . " (1896) by J. J. Bodkin; "The Franciscans in California" (1898) by Rev. Z. Engelhardt, O.S.F.; "Letters of Father Adam Gilg, S.J." by August Rupp, ("Hist. Records and Studies," Vol. VIII); "On the Trail of a Spanish Pioneer; the Diary and Itinerary of Francisco Garcés, 1775-76" (II Vols. translated 1900) by Elliot Coues; "Spanish Friars in California" ("Amer. Cath. Quar. Rev." Vol. XXVII); and "History of the Pious Fund of California" by J. T. Doyle (Papers Cal. Hist. Soc. Vol. I, Part I). The foregoing have now been outclassed by Engelhardt's "Missions and Missionaries of California (IV Vols. 1908–15).

On the missions in New Mexico and Arizona, the histories of Shea and Bancroft are valuable, Bolton's "Explorations . . . 1542–1706," and

Blackmar's "Spanish Institutions of the Southwest". "The Discovery of America" (1891) by John Fiske should not be overlooked. The "Indians of the Southwest" (1891) by A. F. Bandelier merits attention, also his "Contributions" (1890). Particularly valuable is "The Spanish Settlements within the Present Limits of the United States, 1513-1561" (1901) by Woodbury Lowery. "A Historical Sketch of the Catholic Church in New Mexico" (1888) by Rev. J. H. Defouri; "Soldiers of the Cross: Notes on the Ecclesiastical History of New Mexico, Arizona, and Colorado" (1898) by Rev. J. B. Salpointe; and "The Franciscans in Arizona" (1899) by Z. Engelhardt, are especially useful.

On the Florida mission, in addition to Charlevoix's and Shea's histories, Fiske's "Discovery of America," and Parkman's "Pioneers of France in the New World," one should consult "The Territory of Florida" (1837) by J. L. Williams; "History of Florida" (1871) by G. R. Fairbanks; "The History of St. Augustine, Florida" (1881) by W. W. Dewhurst; and notably, "The Spanish Settlements within the Present Limits of the United States. Florida, 1562-1574" (1905) by W. Lowery.

For Virginia, the only significant study is that of Martin I. J. Griffin, "Catholics in Colonial Virginia" ("Rec. Amer. Cath. Hist. Soc." Vol. XXII, pp. 84-100.).

For Maryland, in addition to what is cited on page 24, there is the following: "Bohemia Mission of St. Francis Xavier, Cecil County, Maryland" by E. I. Devitt ("Rec. Amer. Cath. Hist. Soc.," Vol. XXIV, pp. 97-139); "Letters of Father Joseph Mosly, S. J., and Some Extracts from his Diary (1757-1786)" with notes by I. E. Devitt (ibid., Vol. XVII, p. 180 f. 289 f.).

For Pennsylvania and Delaware the literature is more extensive: "History of St. Patrick's Church, Carlisle, Pennsylvania" by Rev. H. G. Ganss (ibid. Vol. VI, pp. 266-422, important); "The Catholic Church at Lancaster, Pennsylvania" by S. M. Sener, edited by Rev. T. C. Middleton (ibid. Vol. V, pp. 307-356); "Catholicity in the Three Lower Counties" by Charles Esling (ibid. Vol. I, pp. 117-157); "John and Elizabeth Tatham, 1681-1700" by Rev. T. C. Middleton (ibid. Vol. VI, pp. 61-135); "William Penn, the Friend of Catholics" by Martin I. J. Griffin (ibid. Vol. I, pp. 71-86); "Properties of the Jesuits in Pennsylvania 1730-1830" by Rev. Thomas Hughes, S. J. (ibid. Vol. XI, p. 177 f. 281 f.); "Life and Letters of Henry Van Rensselaer, Priest of the Society of Jesus" (1908) edited by E. P. Spillam.

Several church registers are to be found in the "Records" as above. Scattered references to Penn's attitude to the Roman Catholics may be located in the "Researches, Amer. Cath. Hist. Soc."

For New York, there is the "Register of the Clergy Laboring in the Archdiocese of New York from Early Missionary Times till 1885" edited by Rev. M. A. Corrigan ("Hist. Records and Studies" Vols. I to VIII); "Catholic Footsteps in Old New York, 1524–1807" (n.d.) by W. H. Bennett; "An Early Catholic Settlement" (1898) by Rev. T. C. Middleton.

For New England there is a "History of the Catholic Church in the New England States" (II Vols. 1899) by Rev. J. H. O'Donnell and others; and a "History of the Diocese of Hartford" (1900) by O'Donnell.

For developments in the West there is "A History of the Catholic Church in the Diocese of Vincennes" (1883) by H. A. Alerding; "Very Rev. Pierre Gibault, V.G., with some Newly Published Documents" by C. G. and H. F. Herbermann, ("Hist. Records and Studies," Vol. VI, Part II, pp. 130-165); "Pierre Gibault, Priest and Patriot of the Northwest in the Eighteenth Century" by Pauline L. Peyton (Prize Essay "Rec. Amer. Cath. Hist. Soc." Vol. XII, pp. 452-498); "The Records of the Parish of St. Francis Xavier at Post Vincennes, Indiana, 1747–1773" translated by Rev. E. J. P. Schmitt (*ibid*. Vol. XII); "An Account of the Progress of the Catholic Religion in the Western States of North America" (1824—"Amer. Cath. Hist. Researches" Vol. X, pp. 146-159); "Letters from the Archepiscopal Archives at Quebec," edited with notes by Abbe Lionel Lindsay ("Rec. Amer. Cath. Hist. Soc.," Vol. XX); "Prairie du Roche Church Records" translated by Rev. C. J. Eschmann, also "Kaskaskia Church Records" ("Pubs. Ill. State Hist. Library" No's. 8 and 9).

In connection with the attitude of the Roman Catholics to the Revolution, the following should be noted: "The Anti-Catholic Spirit of the Revolution" by Martin I. J. Griffin ("Amer. Cath. Hist. Researches" Vol. VI, pp. 146-178); also "Catholic Loyalists of the Revolution" by the same author (*ibid*., pp. 77-88); "George Meade, A Patriot of the Revolutionary Era" by Captain R. Meade ("Rec. Amer. Cath. Hist. Soc." Vol. III, pp. 193-220); "Thomas Fitzsimmons, Pennsylvania's Catholic Signer of the Constitution" by Martin I. J. Griffin, (*ibid*. Vol. II, pp. 43-114); "Catholics and the American Revolution" author not specified ("Amer. Cath. Hist. Researches," New Series, Vol. II, pp. 1-40).

On the question of the influence of Quebec and the Quebec Act on the Revolution there is a scholarly monograph by Victor Coffin, Ph.D.

entitled, "The Province of Quebec and the Early American Revolution" ("Bulletin, Univ. of Wisconsin, Economic, Political Science and History Series," Vol. I).

It should be added that much miscellaneous information bearing upon many topics not referred to above will be found in the "Records and Studies," "Historical Researches," "Records of the American Catholic Historical Society," the "American Catholic Quarterly Review" and the "Illinois Catholic Historical Review."

DOCUMENTS

I. *ROMAN CATHOLICISM IN MARYLAND*

See *The Jesuit Propaganda*, p. 27f.
The *Act Concerning Religion*, p. 30f.

II. *THE JESUIT IDEAL OF MISSIONARY SERVICE*

The following, from Le Jeune's "Relation" of 1635, is given as illustrative of Jesuit missionary devotion at its best:

"Three mighty thoughts console a good heart which is in the infinite forests of New France, or among the Hurons. The first is, "I am in the place where God has sent me, where he has led me as if by the hand, where he is with me, and where I seek him alone." The second is, in the words of David, "according to the measure of the pain I endure for God, his Divine consolations rejoice my soul." The third, that we never find Crosses, nails, nor thorns, in the midst of which, if we look closely, we do not find Jesus Christ. Now, can a person go wrong when he is in the company of the Son of the living God?

When I see myself surrounded by murderous waves, by infinite forests, and by a thousand dangers there comes to mind that precious saying of the martyred St. Ignace, *Nunc incipio esse Christi discipulus:* to-day I begin to be of the Company of Jesus. For what avail so many exercises, so many fervent Meditations, so many eager desires? all these are nothing but wind, if we do not put them into practice. So old France is fitted to conceive noble desires, but the New is adapted to their execution; that one desires in old France is what one does in the New.

I do not know what the country of the Hurons is, where God sends me in his infinite mercy, but I do know that I would rather go there than to an Earthly paradise, since I see that God has so ordained. Strange thing! the more Crosses I see prepared for me there, the more my heart laughs and flies thither; for what happiness to see with these eyes nothing but Savages, Crosses, and Jesus Christ. Never have I understood in my life in France what it was to distrust self entirely and to trust in God alone; I say alone, and without the presence of any creature: *Major est Deus corde nostro,* "God is greater than our hearts;" this is evident in New France, and it is an unutterable consolation that when we find nothing else we immediately encounter God, who communicates himself most richly to good hearts.

My consolation among the Hurons is that I confess every day, and then I say Mass as if I were to take the Viaticum and die that very day, and I do not think that a person can live better, nor with more satisfaction and courage, and even merit, than to live in a place where he expects every day to die, and to have the motto of St. Paul, *Quotidie morior fratres, etc.*, "I protest, brethren, that I die daily."

To convert the Savages, not so much knowledge is necessary as goodness and sound virtue. The four Elements of an Apostolic man in New France are Affability, Humility, Patience, and a generous Charity. Too ardent zeal scorches more than it warms, and ruins everything; great magnanimity and compliance are necessary to attract gradually these Savages. They do not comprehend our Theology well, but they comprehend perfectly our humility and our friendliness, and allow themselves to be won.

The Huron Nation is becoming disposed to receive the light of the Gospel, and inestimable good is to be hoped for in all those regions; but two kinds of persons are necessary to accomplish this,—those in old France, assisting by their holy prayers and their charity; the others in the New, working with great gentleness and tirelessness; on the goodness of God and on this sweet harmony depends the conversion of many thousand souls, for each one of whom Jesus Christ has shed all his precious blood.

. . . .

One of the thoughts which weigh most upon those who are so fortunate as to serve God among these forests, is their unworthiness of their Apostolic and so exalted calling, and that they have so few of the virtues worthy of a noble work. He who sees New France only through the eyes of the flesh and of nature, sees only forests and crosses; but he who looks upon these with the eyes of grace and of a noble vocation, sees only God, the virtues, and the graces; and he finds therein so many and so firm consolations, that, if I were able to buy New France by giving in exchange all the Terrestrial Paradise, I would certainly buy it. My God! how good it is to be in the place where God has placed us by his grace, truly I have found here what I had hoped for, a heart in harmony with God's heart, which seeks God alone.

. . . .

I had thought that miracles were necessary to convert these flying Savages; but I was mistaken, for the real miracles of New France are the following: To do them much good, and endure many pains; to complain to God alone; to judge oneself unworthy, and to feel one's uselessness. He who has these virtues will perform miracles greater than miracles, and will become a Saint. Indeed, it is harder to humiliate oneself deeply before God and men, and to annihilate oneself, than to raise the dead; for that needs only the word, if one has the gift of miracles, but to humiliate oneself as one ought to,—truly, that requires a man's whole life.

. . . .

One meets men so devoid of every notion of Religion, that one cannot find a name to make them understand God; we have to call him the great Captain of men, he who feeds all the world, he who lives on high. We do all we can; what obligations will they be under to those who instruct them and who try to make them know a God in order to serve him as well as they can. Here deep learning is not needed, but a profound humility, an unconquerable patience, and an Apostolic charity, to win these poor Savages, who in other respects have good common sense. And if we begin once to gain them, the fruit will be incalculable.

A thousand times the thought of saint Francois Xavier passes through our minds, and has great power over us. If the men of the world, in order to have Beaver skins, and codfish, and I know not what commodities, do not fear either the storms on the sea, or the Savages on land, or the sea, or death; how dreadful will be the confusion of God's servants for being afraid of these things, or of a few little hardships, in trying to win souls ransomed by the precious blood of Jesus Christ, and empurpled by his blood of inestimable value? On the day of judgment will not these petty traders and fishers of cod rise up to condemn us, if they take more pains to gain a piece of money than we do to help save the Savages? This thought stings our hearts so deeply that we do not feel our sufferings, or if we feel them we do not dare to complain of them.

There are many persons in France who are of no use, and have nothing to do there; they are scholars and that is all, and that is of no use in the Church of God; alas! in New France these men would be Apostles, if they would come here to use their talents; less wisdom, and more humility and zeal, would perform miracles here, and it is possible they would gain more in one year than they will do in a lifetime in France.

Experience shows us that those of the Society who come to New France should be impelled to it by a special and very forcible call; persons who are dead to themselves and to the world; men truly Apostolic, who seek God alone, and the salvation of souls, who love with real love the Cross and self-mortification; who do not spare themselves; who can endure the hardships of the sea and of the land, and who desire the conversion of a Savage more than the Empire of all Europe; who have Godlike hearts, all filled with God; who are like little John the Baptists, crying through these deserts and forests like voices from God, which summon all these poor Savages to acknowledge Jesus Christ; in fine let them be men whose sole satisfaction is in God and to whom suffering is the greatest delight. That is what experience shows us every day; but it is also true that it seems as if God shed the dew of his grace much more abundantly upon this New France than upon the old, and that the internal consolations and the Divine infusions are much stronger here, and hearts more on fire. *Novit Dominus qui sunt ejus.* But it belongs to God alone to choose those whom he will use, and whom he favors by taking them into New France, to make saints of them. Saint Francois Xavier said that there was an Island in the Orient which was quite capable of making a person lose his sight, by crying from excessive joy of the heart; I know not if our New France resembles this Island, but we know from experience that, if any one here gives himself up in earnest to God, he runs the risk of losing his sight, his life, his all, and with great joy, by dint of hard work; it belongs only to those who are here and who enjoy God to speak from experience."

Text—*Letters of 1635*, in Thwaites: *The Jesuit Relations and Allied Documents*, Vol. VIII, pp. 177-189.

III. *A DAY'S PROGRAM IN A JESUIT MISSION TO THE INDIANS*

Lalemants "Relation" of 1638-39, describing work among the Hurons, furnishes a typical illustration of how Jesuits conducted their work.

". . . Let us come to our usual occupations in these countries.

From four o'clock until eight in the morning, the time is passed in Masses and other special devotions. About eight o'clock the door of the House is opened to the Savages; in the past, this was not closed again until four o'clock in the evening,—as much to save themselves the annoyance that was otherwise apprehended,—the Savages not seeming able to understand a refusal to enter, at least in the daytime, the cabins that are in their country, which are not usually closed then to any one,—as to take opportunity to profit by this custom. For, whatever the number of barbarians that come to see you, they are so many Masters and pupils visiting you, and saving you the trouble of going to them,—Masters, I say, in the use of the language; Pupils, as regards their salvation and Christianity.

However,—the importunity of these Barbarians, lazy to the last degree, becoming unbearable, and henceforward almost profitless, since we have found the secret of their language,—we have taken the reasonable liberty of no longer admitting any except those by whom we hope to profit. It was somewhat difficult to bring this about, but God himself seems to have guided the affair so that we have fortunately come out victorious, with great comfort inside and outside our houses,—except perhaps, in the case of a few of these Barbarians, whose minds are more perverted.

Those of our Fathers who remain upon guard take turns in staying in the cabin, and especially the one who keeps the little school for children, Christians, and Cate-chumens; the others go to the Village to make the rounds and visits in their quarters, the Village being divided into as many districts as there are persons familiar with the language and consequently capable of working. But on account of the few laobrers there are now for this purpose, some of us are charged with forty cabins,—in several of which there are four or five fires, that is, eight or ten families,—which would lay out for them much more work than they could execute, if their courage did not give them strength for that, and even more.

These visits consist, first, in seeing the sick, and taking care that not one of them, child or adult, dies without Baptism or without instruction,—to attain which more easily, we give them all the temporal relief and assistance possible, and especially reme-dies and bleedings, which have very good effects. In the 2nd place, we watch to seize opportunities to instruct those who are well, and to inculcate in them especially the in-struction at the last Catechisms,—or councils, to speak according to the manner of the country,—and to prepare them for an intelligent understanding of the next ones. But, above all, we apply ourselves to discovering the soil or persons where the seed and the germ of the word of God may have taken root, in order to give our attention to them afterwards and cultivate them as Catechumens.

At four or five o'clock, according to the season, we withdraw, and the Savages who are in our cabin go away; then we have a conference, sometimes on the obstacles against and means for advancing the conversion of these peoples; sometimes on matters inci-dent to the establishment of a new Church; but generally upon the rules of the lan-guage, and the new words and idioms that we have heard. In these exercises, and in others that regard the Spiritual and the individual duties of each one, the time passes so quickly, that although it may be true that there is here a dearth of all the comforts that are found in France,—as we have only the four elements, and, besides, no more of ordinary food and covering than that necessary to keep us from dying with hunger and cold,—yet I have only heard one complaint, namely, that there is not time enough. And in fact there is not enough, by half.

Public Catechisms are held several times a week in this way: First, Sundays and Feast days are set aside for the suitable and individual instruction of our Neophytes and new Christians. In the morning, during the Mass, they are given instruction in the form of a sermon, in which we are careful to instruct them in what they ought to know, and at the same time train their minds to piety and Christian devotion. In the afternoon, after Vespers, we feed them in these beginnings with the pure word of God,— relating to them one Sunday the histories and the connection of the old Testament, with reflections upon the profit they ought to derive from them; and, the next Sunday, doing the same thing from the New,—all, that it may conform to what is written, *Haec est vita aeterna, ut cognoscant te Deum, et quem misisti Jesum Christum.*

We take one working-day of the week to give another public lesson to all alike,— be they believers or unbelievers,—which takes place thus: At the hour of Noon, a man goes calling aloud through the village, or with the bell, in the streets and public places, inviting to the council, but to the council of councils, which concerns the important matter of salvation. In a place where there is no Chapel, and where our cabin is too small, we do this as well as we can outdoors, and when the weather and season do not permit it, it is done indoors,—but then we admit only the men, reserving the women and children for the next day. The people having assembled, after the invocation of the holy Ghost we say or chant a Prayer suitable to this service, in the Huron language. After this we begin the instruction, which is sometimes interrupted by the approbation or objections of the Savages; at the end of this, we have them say a few prayers, and among others, a little one in which is included the act of contrition. After that, we engage in singing the *Credo*, the Commandments, the *Pater*, the *Ave*, and other prayers,— many or few, as we see the Savages attentive and in a condition to profit by them.

Besides this public instruction, on another day in the week we give a less general one, to which are especially invited the people that we wish to have present,—the Captains and most notable men of the Village who have been recognized as having pious tendencies and a leaning towards Christianity, and whom it is particularly important to make well understand the mysteries of our faith, and to have them duly informed of our intentions in this country through all these various meetings and preparations.

In addition to all the above, in a place where Catechumens cannot be sufficiently instructed through private talks with those who have charge of their cabins, they are assembled every evening and are together given the instruction considered most suitable, touching the things they should know before being baptized.

We are not satisfied with working in the Villages where we have residences; but feeling ourselves a little stronger, than in the past, in workers familiar with the language, we have undertaken Missions in the Villages, large and small, of the country,— especially during the Winter, which is the only time suitable for this. The Hurons take up their abode in their cabins at this season only; at all other times, they are either at war, or engaged in trading, hunting, or fishing. We shall first go all over the country which was the first to receive us, then push farther on,—and always on and on,—until we have accomplished our task, which, as we have already said, is only bounded by the setting Sun."

Text—*Lalemant's Relation of 1638-39*, in *Thwaites': The Jesuit Relations and Allied Documents*, Vol. XVI, pp. 241-249.

IV. *THE JESUIT MISSION AMONG THE FIVE NATIONS*

The following documents throw some light upon the motives that underlay this enterprise.

"I see at the South and at the West a great number of Tribes that cultivate the land and that are entirely sedentary, but have never heard of Jesus Christ; the door to all these peoples has been shut against us by the Hiroquois. In all these vast tracts there are only the Hurons, and some other neighboring Tribes, to whom we have carried the good news of the Gospel; but then we are obliged to approach them by horrible roads and long detours, and in continual danger of being boiled or roasted and then eagerly devoured by the wretched Hiroquois. We do not lose courage on account of this; we believe that God will make a light in this darkness, and that some powerful Spirit will open the door to the Gospel of Jesus Christ in these vast regions, and that old France will save the life of the New, which is going to be lost, unless it be vigorously and speedily succored; the trade of these Gentlemen, the French Colony, and the Religion which is beginning to flourish among the Savages, will be subverted, if the Hiroquois be not overcome. Fifty Hiroquois are capable of making two hundred Frenchmen leave the country,—not if they fought unflinchingly, for in that case fifty Frenchmen would rout five hundred Hiroquois, if the Dutch did not give them firearms. If these Barbarians become enraged at our Frenchmen, they will never let them sleep soundly; a Hiroquois will remain for two or three days without food behind a stump, fifty paces from your house, in order to slay the first person who shall fall into his ambush. If he be discovered, the forest serves him for an asylum; where a Frenchman would find only hindrance, a Savage will bound as lightly as a deer. What opportunity is there to take breath, in such anxieties? If we do not make friends with these people, or if they be not exterminated, we must abandon to their cruelty many good Neophytes; we must lose many beautiful hopes, and see the Demons reenter their empire."

Text—*Le Jeune's Relation of 1640-41*, in *Thwaites': The Jesuit Relations and Allied Documents* Vol. XXI, pp. 119-121.

"Add to this the fury of a Hiroquois enemy who closes the way to us; who deprives us of the necessities of life and of the help that may be sent us in a forsaken country; who kills and massacres those who come to our aid; whose insolence grows from year to year; who depopulates the country, and makes our Hurons think of giving up the trade with the French, because they find that it costs them too dear, and they prefer to do without European goods rather than to expose themselves every year, not to a death that would be endurable, but to fires and flames, for which they have a thousand times greater horror.

Now, therefore, what can we expect in the midst of a barbarous nation where we shall no longer have the necessaries of life; where they will no longer venture to send us the reinforcement of laborers that would be required here to promote the affairs of God; where all who shall remain will be abandoned to the fury of a desperate people, who will no longer be restrained from massacring us all by the fear of losing their trade with the French,—which they will find impossible to them, and which will be completely ruined, as far as they are concerned? In that case, the Christains who compose this nascent Church will then see themselves without Pastors, without Sacraments, without Sacrifice, and without the means of having recourse to those who alone are their refuge in their desolation, their support in their weakness, the sacred tie that binds them to God, and their succor against the powers of Hell.

Beyond a doubt, these are reasonable fears,—difficulties capable of arresting our minds, obstacles insurmountable to our weakness, and misfortunes that seem inevitable,—if France does not make extraordinary efforts to overthrow this enemy, who with one and the same blow destroys these Nations and the Faith that we preach to them. . . . "

Text—*Lalemant's Relation of 1644-45*, in *Thwaites: The Jesuit Relations and Allied Documents*, Vol. XXVIII, pp. 57-59.

"We have always wished for the Conversion of our enemies, even when their cruelty was directly opposed to the salvation of all these countries. Their fury laid waste the lands of the Algonquin and Huron Nations at the very time when they were beginning to form a thoroughly Christian People; they cruelly burned both pastors and flock. But at length the blood of the martyrs has made itself heard in heaven; and we see ourselves called to proclaim the Faith by those cruel Barbarians whose sole purpose in the world seemed to be to oppose it. In short, the Iroquois are pressing us to go and instruct them, and they urgently request us to build on their Lake a French settlement that shall serve them as an asylum, and be a bond of peace between them and us.

. . . .

Were it only for baptizing the Children, who are dying every day without baptism, that were an assured gain for heaven, worth more than a thousand lives. Were it only for the succor that is expected of us on the part of a Captive Church, embracing more than a thousand Christians, Huron men and women who, in their captivity, have not lost their faith, after losing country, liberty, kinsfolk, and livelihood,—we would be bound, as their guardian Angels, to go through fire and flame, that we might extend to them a helping hand and lead them to heaven. But since God gives us reason to hope for something even more conducive to his glory than all that, and since the Infidels themselves implore us to consent to make them Christians, we cannot refuse them this grace without becoming ourselves unfaithful to the grace of God.

. . . .

The site which they have assigned to us for this new settlement is on the great lake of the Iroquois, who stretch away in a southerly direction. The region toward the Northwest is the former country of the Hurons, and offers the shortest route both for spreading the faith and for carrying on trade with many very populous Nations, who have always been allied to us, and have themselves many alliances with other more distant Nations. Some of these already have the first elements of the Faith, and all are destined to receive it some day, since Jesus Christ must at last be worshipped by all the nations of the world.

We are, however, but few laborers, for so extensive a country and we lift up our hands to heaven in request for aid. Whoever loves his life as he ought to love it, and wishes to lose it in a holy cause, will find his heart's desires fulfilled in these abandoned Missions."

Text—*Mercier's Relation of 1653-54;* in *Thwaites: The Jesuit Relations and Allied Documents*, Vol. XLI, pp. 131-135.

Governor Dongan to Monsieur de Denonville

"20 June 1687.

Sir

The inclosed came to my hands last night from England with orders to have it proclaimed which has accordingly bin done, what is there agreed upon I will observe to the least title and I doubt not but your Excell: will do the same and I hope bee so kinde as not desire or seeke any correspondence with our Indians of this side of the Great lake if they doe amisse to any of your Governm^t you make it known to me you shall have all justice done and if any of your people disturbe us I will have the same recourse to you for satisfaction. as for those further nations, I suppose that to trade with them is free and common to us all until the meers and bounds bee adjusted though truly the scituation of those parts bespeakes the King of England to have a greater right to them then the French King, they lying to the southward of us just on the back of other partes of our Kings dominions and a uery great way from you. I am informed by some of our Indians that Your Excell: was pleased to desire them to meet you at Cadarague; I could hardly believe it till I had a letter from Father Lamberuille, wherein he informs me that 'tis true. I am also informed of your Fathers endevours dayly to carry away our Indians to Canada as you have already done a great many, you must pardon me if I tell you that that is not the right way to keepe fair correspondence. I have also been informed that you are told I have given to Indians orders to rob the French wherever tney could meet them, that is as false as tis true that God is in heaven, what I have done was by your own desire which was that I should suffer none of Canada to come to Albany without they had your passe in complyance wherewith I ordered, both, the Indians and the people of Albany that if they found any French or English on this side of the great lake, without either your passe or mine, they should seize them and bring them to Albany; I am now sorry that I did it since its not agreeable to you and has as I am informed hindered the comeing of a great many Beauers to this place—I shall therefore recall those orders. I am daily expecting Religious men from England which I intend to put amongst those five nations. I desire you would order Monsr de Lamberuille that soe long as he stayes amongst those people he would meddle only with the affairs belonging to his function and that those of our Indians that are turned Catholiques and live in Canada may content themselves with their being alone without endeavouring to debauch others after them, if they do and I can catch any of them I shall handle them very severely. S^r setting aside the trust my Master has reposed in me I should be as ready and willing to serve Monsr de Nonuille as any friend he has. . . .

I am—Sir. You^r most humble servant
THO. DONGAN.

S^r I send you some Oranges hearing they are a rarity in your partes and would send more, but the bearer wants conveniency of Carriage—"

Text—O'Callaghan: *Documents Relative to the Colonial History of the State of New York, Vol. 111, p. 465.*

Monsieur de Denonville's Remarks on Governor Dongan's Letter

"The Marquis de Denonville's Answer by paragraphs to M. Dongan's letter of the 22^d August 1687.
Sir,

. . . .

Since you have been informed that I wished to see the Iroquois at Cataracouy to arrange with them the causes of discontent I had on account of their violence and misbehaviour, this is telling me that it is you who prevented them coming to give me an explanation of their violence. Therefore, Sir, I have no reason to doubt but you would wish to induce me to proclaim war against them. The Revd Fathers Lamberville were justified in advising you that I had called the said Iroquois to Catarocouy as I instructed them to warn the five Nations to come there. Had you loved peace and union you would have sent thither some one on your behalf to contribute to the general peace between the nations.

If you had been better informed of the zeal of the King for the increase of the Christian and Catholic Faith, you would have been aware of the great number of Jesuit missionaries who have laboured for more than 80 years with infinite pains for the conversion of the poor savages of this country. I am astonished that you are ignorant of the number of martyrs who have spilt their blood and sacrificed their lives for the faith of Jesus Christ. I am further astonished that you should be ignorant that before Manate belonged to the King your Master—being in possession of the heretic Dutch as you are aware,—our missionaries, persecuted and martyred, found there an asylum and protection. Is it possible now, when the same country has the happiness to be under the dominion of a great King, the protector and defender of the truth of the Gospel, that you, Sir, who represent his sacred person and profess his Holy Religion should find it strange, and be scandalized that our Missionaries labour so usefully as they do for the general conversion of these poor Heathen people. You did not reflect, Sir, when you complained of it. But I have much greater cause to find it strange that people should have come last year into our missions with presents from you to debauch and dissuade our christians from continuing in the exercise of the Holy Religion, which they profess with so much edification. Pardon me if I say that this is not a right way to preserve good correspondence.

. . . .

I should think, Sir, that you ought to have awaited the decision of the differences between our masters relative to the boundaries, before dreaming of introducing religious men among the Five Nations; your charity, Sir, for the conversion of these people would have been more useful to them, and more honorable to you had you commenced by lending your protection to the missionaries they had for the advancement of religion, instead of taking pains to drive them from their missions and prevent them converting the heathen. You cannot deny, Sir, that should our missionaries leave, these poor infidels will be a long time without instruction if they must await the arrival of your religious men, and until these have learned the language. Regarding your desire that our missionaries content themselves with what Christian savages they have in Canada, you little understand, Sir, their zeal. I assure you there is not one who would not willingly be burnt alive, were he assured that he could attract by his martyrdom all the Indians to the Christian and Catholic faith. Can you censure them for this charity, and can you accuse them of debauching people when they seek only their salvation and God's glory?

I should wish you would desire to be on such good terms as that we could visit each other. I would willingly repair to the confines of your government, which are very close to Orange. Therefore you would not have much of a journey to make.

I thank you, sir, for your oranges. It was a great pity that they should have been all rotten.

I am, sir,

Your very humble and

very obedient servant,

The M. DE DENONVILLE.

Text—O'Callaghan: *Documents Relative to the Colonial History of the State of New York*, Vol. III, pp. 469-472.

V. *THE CALIFORNIA MISSION*

The extracts given below form sections of a report submitted by Fr. Paloú, Feb. 12, 1772, in answer to questions from Fr. Guardian Verger designed to secure a complete report concerning all the California Mission Stations.

Mission Purisima Concepcion de Cadegomó.

"This was founded in 1713 and endowed by the Marqués de Villapuente in the manner that has been related of the others. It was administered by the Fathers of the Company of Jesus until January, 1768. In April of said year Fr. Juan Crespi received charge of it from the College, and from that time until the 8th of December, 1771, there have been baptized thirty-nine children, one hundred and twenty children and adults have died, and fifteen couples have been married. It has no pueblos de visíta, as the Indians all live at the mission. There are forty-nine families, seven widowers, and three widows, with sixty children of both sexes, or in all one hundred and sixty-eight souls.

"The mission is distant from that of Comundú about ten leagues; from Guadalupe about thirty leagues; from the ocean it is seven leagues, and nine from the gulf. It is in twenty-six and one-half degrees north, situated on the banks of an arroyo called Cadegomó, on a beautiful spot and in a pleasant climate. It has enough land capable of cultivation upon which may be sown several fanegas of wheat, with an abundance of water from the said arroyo, though for irrigating it depends upon a very large dam built across the arroyo, and upon the floods, which when there is high water carry it away, as happened in the past year 1770, when from this the mission was put back, because they waited too long in restoring it for want of laborers; but, thanks be to God, they finished it and the mission has returned to its former condition. It has a church of stone and mud and partly of adobe roofed with tules like the dwelling.

"It has some vineyards, many fig-trees and pomegranates, and much cotton is grown to aid in clothing the Indians. Ordinarily many figs are raised, and there was a year when nine hundred arróbas were obtained. In the last year only three hundred were gathered on account of the damage done by the locusts; for the same reason not a grain of wheat or corn was harvested, when about two hundred fanégas were expected. At present seven fanégas of wheat have been sown; if they remain free from the plague the mission may harvest a good crop. It has about sixty tinájas of wine, . each holding sixty pints. It has no rancho, nor a place for one; only in the neighborhood of the mission it has twenty-eight tame but old oxen, of which only four pair are of service for work; in addition there are nineteen cows, one steer, and twelve yearling calves. There are other cattle running wild, which cannot be counted. It has thirty-seven mares, thirty-nine horses and fillies, thirty-six asses, twenty-two mules, two thousand and seventy-four head of sheep, and two hundred and eleven goats."

Mission San Ignacio

". . . The mission occupies a pleasant site on a height, whence there is a view over a broad valley with its arroyo containing enough water which is collected by means of a dam and led through ditches to the mission, where it is kept in a large reservoir of masonry. It has enough land; though in the year 1770 the flood from the arroyo carried away the soil, when it destroyed the dam, leaving the land one sandy field, there is still sufficient land left.   It has its vineyards, olives, pomegranates, fig-trees and a field of cotton from which shawls are manufactured to help clothe the Indians though the locust plague of the preceding year, as I said, laid waste everything and did the same to the vineyards and orchards by devouring everything; the Father writes me, however, that everything is again beginning to grow.   The mission has its church of adobe roofed with tules; another church building of masonry is under way, and when it is finished, it will be the best building in California.

"The mission owns eighty-seven tame and a number of wild cattle, one hundred and twelve horses, mares, and foals, twenty mules, thirty-two asses, seven hundred and twenty sheep, and two hundred and forty-three goats, though I later received a letter in which I am told that the Indians had slaughtered some sheep and had done great damage which it was impossible to prevent."

Mission Santa Gertrudis

". . . . It was governed by the Jesuit Fathers until the month of January, 1768, Fr. Diónisio Basterra received it from the College on the last of April of said year. Since then until August 1771 there have been baptised two-hundred and fifty-four children, four hundred and three children and adults were interred, and one hundred and two marriages took place, so that there are found living in the mission district three hundred and fifty-seven married couples, forty-one widowers and widows, and four hundred and thirty-three boys and girls, who in all compose the number one thousand one hundred and thirty-eight persons.   Of all these families only forty families live at the mission and one hundred and seventy-four souls, and all the rest are scattered in seven houseless rancherías which surround the mission proper in every direction, all looking for wild fruits and changing about according to the seasons.   It is not possible for all to live at the mission itself, because of the shortage of the land and of the water to irrigate it.   Nor was it less impossible to execute the order of the inspector to remove those that could be spared to the missions of Purisima and San José, because they resisted and gave us to understand that they would go over to the Gentiles.

The mission is situated in a narrow valley, so that it was necessary to clear land by means of the crow-bar in order to construct a pueblo.   It has an adobe church and dwelling which are covered with tules.   The work of building up the pueblo with huts of adobe for the Indians is finished, and it is interesting.   It has vineyards and orchards of figs, olives, pomegranates, and also some peaches.   There is little land fit for sowing and the water is scarce.   It is situated in twenty-eight degrees and a half north latitude on a spot called La Piedad, about twelve leagues from the gulf, where the shore is called San Miguél de la Peña, and it is there the launches usually stop. From the ocean it is distant about two days' travel; from Mission San Ignacio, thirty-five leagues, and from San Borja somewhat more.

It has a rancho for both large and small stock where one hundred and thirteen cattle of all kinds graze, besides one hundred and forty-two horses of all kinds, twenty-five mules, two asses with their young, one hundred and forty sheep, and four hundred and seventy goats.   There are also some wild cattle on the other coast which it is difficult to control for lack of water, because they subsist on *chuzas* which supply the absence of water.   On the last of August the Father wrote me that the mission had on hand one hundred and eighty fanégas of wheat (espinguin), twenty fanégas of barley, but no corn, because one piece of land which had a good growth was destroyed by the locusts, which also did much damage to the fruit-trees and vines."

Mission San Francisco de Borja.

. . . There have died four hundred and ninety-nine children and adults, and two hundred and seventy-three couples were married, as the Father informs me. In the whole mission district there is not one pagan left, as far as known. At the mission itself there are forty-four families and three widowers, or in all one hundred and eighty-four souls. Besides the mission proper there are five rancherías, one called San Juan with forty-six families, three widowers and seven widows, with one hundred and sixty souls; another, named San Francisco Regis, has twenty-three families, five widowers and nine widows, with ninety-two souls; a third, Nuestra Señora de Guadalupe with seventy-four families, eighteen widowers and fourteen widows, or in all two hundred and fifty-six souls; the fourth, San Ignacio, with seventy-eight families, twenty-three widowers and twenty widows, or in all three hundred and fifty-seven souls; the fifth, called Longeles, has thirty-seven families, five widowers and fourteen widows, forming a population of one hundred and five souls. All these with those at the mission number together one thousand four hundred and seventy-nine persons. These rancherías have no chapel, nor any house whatever, because the Indians move about and live where they find any wild fruit to eat; nor is it possible to gather more at the mission on account of the shortage of land and the scarcity of water, so that, even to maintain the few families mentioned, it is necessary to do the planting at two places well separated from the mission, called San Regis and El Paraiso. In the beginning of last September the Father wrote me that he had harvested about three hundred fanégas of wheat (espinguin) and eighteen fanégas of barley, upon which they were subsisting since July; but corn, though a piece of land was planted with it, they did not expect to obtain, because the locusts had devoured it

"The mission has a rancho for the large stock where it possesses five hundred head of cattle of all kinds; there are no wild cattle; in addition it owns seventeen hundred head of sheep and nine hundred and thirty goats, two hundred and fifteen horses of all kinds, forty-three mules, and three asses. It has some vineyards which the Father planted, also fig-trees, pomegranates, and much cotton from which shawls are manufactured to help clothe the Indians.

Text—Engelhardt: *The Missions and Missionaries of California*, Vol. I, pp. 431-445.

Translation of the report sent by Fray Francisco Paloú in December 1773, to the Viceroy of Mexico, with reference to the condition of the Mission of San Antonio de Padua, one of the five which had already been established in Upper California.

The Mission of San Antonio de Padua was founded on the 14th day of July, 1771, on the banks of a river bearing the same name.

A year and a half after the opening of the mission . . . it became necessary to change its location, because the water in the river bed had dried up to such an extent that there was not sufficient for the ordinary necessities of life. Consequently another site was chosen half a league farther up the same river, on the banks of a little stream called San Miguel, which even in the driest months of the year gives an abundance of water. Here is to be found today the mission, which consists of a small church built of adobles and roofed with mud, a small house of the same construction for the use of the missionary fathers, a workshop, and other small houses built of wood and mud. Besides all this, there is a barracks for the guard, a house for each of the three soldiers who are married to Indian women of the mission, and a little group of Indian huts built of sticks and reeds.

Since the founding of the mission, a hundred and fifty-eight have been baptized between old and young, of whom eight have died; fifteen of the young converts have been married and live quite contentedly on the mission premises.

The new site is now supplied with plenty of water from the neighboring stream. An irrigation ditch brings the water to a large field in the immediate vicinity of the mission, where a good sized piece of ground has already been prepared and where they are intending to sow two bushels of wheat, which is the only seed grain that they now have. In due season they hope to produce a sufficiently large crop of corn and beans to provide for the maintenance of the native Christians, and to attract the rest of the natives, who do not feel the least hesitation in accepting the faith of our Lord Jesus Christ nor in living beside the missionaries themselves, for whom they have manifested the most marked affection, providing them with wild grains, rabbits and squirrels which are not so bad for eating after all.

There is no doubt but that, once we have enough with which to feed and clothe the native converts, a large centre of population will spring up around the mission composed of those who have been brought under our influence. . .

The mission has at its disposal various stretches of pasture ground well adapted to the raising of all kinds of flocks and herds. There is also an abundance of timber of different kinds, oak, pine, and other trees which are unknown to us except that their lumber is red in color and is excellent for construction; nor is there any lack of building stone of all kinds, boulders, stone suitable for dressing, and even rock for the production of lime.

There are at present to be found at the mission thirty-eight head of cattle, four mares, one stallion, four horses, two saddle mules, and nine cargo mules provided with all necessary equipment; there are two plows with their accessories and all the tools that are needed both for the cultivation of the land and for masonry and carpentry work; over and above all this, there are thirty hogs which do well in the valley where there is a liberal supply of acorns upon which they live.

Text—*Noticias de la Nueva California escritas por el Rev. Padre Fr. Francisco Palou.*

CHAPTER XVII

METHODISM: ITS RISE AND ORGANIZATION

Bibliography

On John Wesley, the most important source of information continues to be his "Journal," the older editions (Benson, Jackson and Emory) of which have been completely outclassed by the recent work of Nehemiah Curnock assisted by experts (VIII Volumes, 1909-1916). Its voluminous critical notes, supplementary material, and copious index make this edition indispensable to every critical Wesley scholar. "The Journal of John Wesley, Popular Edition Condensed" with introduction (1903) by Rev. W. L. Watkinson is excellent as a condensation. "The Heart of John Wesley's Journal" (1903) edited by Percy L. Parker, with introduction by Hugh Price Hughes 'gives the heart of Wesley himself' and therefore is really as much a biography as a journal.

Of biographies of Wesley there are legion. The "Memoirs of the late Rev. John Wesley, A.M. . . . " (III Vols. 1791) by Rev. John Hampson, a disgruntled preacher who had severed his connection with Wesley, must be read with discrimination. The "Life of the Rev. John Wesley, M.A. . . . " (1792) by Dr. T. Coke and H. Moore, which was popular at the time of its appearance because of its literary elegance and sympathetic interpretation of its hero, will repay attention. The "Life of the Rev. John Wesley . . . " (II Vols. 1793 revised 1805) by John Whitehead, M.D., reflecting the instability of its author, is almost worthless, save in its later reprints where it has undergone substantial revision. "The Life of Wesley and the Rise and Progress of Methodism" by Robert Southey (1820, edited by Rev. C. C. Southey, A.M.; 2nd American edition with notes by the Rev. Daniel Curry, A.M., II Vols., 1847) gives a fine insight into the moral and spiritual conditions prevailing throughout England in the early eighteenth century. It fails however, to give a satisfactory interpretation of the motives of Wesley. It was on this account that Richard Watson soon after published his "Observations on Southey's Life of Wesley" in which he effectively called Southey to task for his strictures upon Wesley. Meanwhile Moore, after having

314

spent years upon further investigations, was prepared to publish his "Life of the Rev. John Wesley" (II Vols. 1824). Although this work never was popular due in part to its unnecessarily lengthy theological discussions, yet it has held a place as a standard work. Shortly after (1831) there appeared the "Life of John Wesley" by Richard Watson, who wrote in response to a demand for a brief inexpensive presentation of the facts of Wesley's life. "Wesley and Methodism" (1851) by Isaac Taylor, is concerned with the philosophy rather than the history of Methodism. Next appeared "The Life and Times of the Rev. John Wesley, A.M., Founder of the Methodists" (III Vols. 1870-73) by Rev. Luke Tyerman. Although in several respects this is not an ideal biography, yet for the purposes of the serious student it is probably the best work because of the mass of material that it contains. "John Wesley and the Evangelical Reaction of the Eighteenth Century" (1870) by Julia Wedgewood shows marked dependence upon Southey, though it takes a more appreciative attitude to Wesley. "John Wesley, his Life and his Work" (1871, translated by the author's brother) by Rev. Matthew Lelièvre is a well proportioned epitome of his life. "Memorials of the Wesley Family" (1876) by George J. Stevenson has a wealth of information which later writers have laid under contribution. "The Wesley Memorial Volume" (1880) by J. G. Clark is useful for the richness of its miscellaneous information. A comparatively recent restatement entitled "John Wesley" (1891) by J. H. Overton, A.M., is a model of abbreviated biography. "The Life of John Wesley" (new ed. 1899) by John Telford, is detailed, accurate, and well documented. Probably it is the best short history of Wesley. "John Wesley" ("Westminster Biographies" 1900) by Frank Banfield is a pocket edition of rare literary excellence. "Wesley and Methodism" (1900) by F. G. Snell, though defective in point of intellectual depth and seriousness, is informing. "Wesley and his Preachers" (1903) by G. Holden Pike is confined to the English side of Wesleyanism. "The Life of John Wesley" (1906) by C. T. Winchester is well written and entertaining though by no means thorough.

Other studies that are worthy of notice are "Wesley and his Biographers" by Rev. W. C. Hoyt ("Meth. Quart. Rev." July 1848—a scholarly bibliographical contribution); "Wesley the Catholic" by Rev. Charles Adams (*ibid.*, April, 1850); "John Wesley's Place in Church History" (1870) by R. D. Urlin; "The Relations of John Wesley and of Wesleyan Methodism to the Church of England, Investigated and Determined" ("Brit. Quart. Rev." Oct. 1871, also under separate cover); "The Churchmanship of John Wesley" (1878) by J. H. Rigg; also "The

Living Wesley" (2nd ed. 1891) by the same author. A Roman Catholic interpretation of Wesley is given by Rev. J. G. Shea in the "Amer. Cath. Quart. Review" Vol. VII. "Was John Wesley the Founder of American Methodism?" (a brief anonymous article, "Meth. Review" July-August, 1891) and "John Wesley, Christian Socialist" by W. H. Meredith ("Meth. Review" May-June, 1901) are suggestive. In the "Proceedings of the Wesley Historical Society" further suggestions may be found respecting Wesley bibliography, also in "The Roots of Methodism" (1903) by W. B. Fitzgerald (pp. 216-217), and the "Wesley Bibliography" by Rev. Richard Green.

Thomas Coke is the subject of two biographies: "The Life of the Rev. Thomas Coke, LL.D. (1817) by Samuel Drew; and the "Life of Doctor Coke" (1860) by J. W. Etheridge. "The Journal of Thomas Coke" covering the period Sept. 18, 1784 to June 3, 1785, has been edited (1896) by Rev. J. J. Tigert (reprint from the "Arminian Magazine" Philadelphia, May-August, 1789), appearing in "The Methodist Review" for September-October, 1896, also under separate cover.

Francis Asbury is known to us through his "Journals" (III Vols. 1821, and later improved edition, 1854) which are quite indispensable to a knowledge of early American Methodism; "Asbury and his Coadjutors" (II Vols. 1853) by Rev. W. C. Larrabee; "Bishop Asbury" by Rev. S. W. Coggeshall ("Meth. Quar. Rev." July 1854); "The Life and Times of Francis Asbury" (1859) by W. P. Strickland; the "Life and Work of Bishop Francis Asbury" by Rev. Asbury Lowrey, D.D. ("Papers, Amer. Soc. Ch. Hist.," Vol. VI, pp. 37-62); "Francis Asbury" (1909) by George P. Mains; "Francis Asbury; The Prophet of the Long Road" (1916) by Ezra S. Tipple; and "Francis Asbury; a Biographical Study" (1909) by H. M. Du Bose, which is especially commendable.

Bishop McKendree has been presented by Robert Paine, in "Life and Times of William McKendree" (II Vols. 1859-69). This work is rich in source material and highly illuminative of prevailing religious conditions. An abbreviated one volume edition by "H. N. M." appeared in 1880. Other biographies are those of Benjamin Fry (1852) and Bishop Du Bose (1914). The latter is notably illuminating.

Rev. Freeborn Garrettson reveals himself through an autobiography entitled " . . . Experience and Travels, . . . " published in Philadelphia, 1791. His "Journal" (reprint, English "Arminian Magazine," 1794) is regarded by Tigert as a reprint of the "Experience and Travels" (see "The Making of Methodism by Tigert, p. 119n.). The "Life of the Rev. Freeborn Garrettson: Compiled from his Printed and Manuscript Journals and other Authentic Documents" (5th ed. 1832) by Nathan Bangs, is a work of first rate importance.

Bishop Whatcoat may be studied in the "Memoirs of the Rev. Richard Whatcoat, . . . " (1828) by William Phoebus; and "The Life of Rev. Richard Whatcoat, . . . " (1852) by Benjamin St. James Fry.

Thomas Ware has left two publications: "Sketches of the Life and Travels of Rev. Thomas Ware, Written by Himself" (1839 ? revised by the editors); and "The Christmas Conference of 1784" ("Meth. Mag. and Quart. Rev.," Jan. 1832).

William Watters, one of the earliest of American itinerants, published "A Short Account of the Christian Experience and Ministerial Labors of William Watters. Drawn up by Himself" (1806).

Ezekiel Cooper a member of the Christmas Conference receives considerable attention in "Beams of Light on Early Methodism in America Chiefly Drawn from the Diary, Letters Manuscripts, Documents and Original Tracts of Rev. Ezekiel Cooper," compiled (1887) by George A. Phoebus.

Composite biographical monographs which supply much useful data are "Memoirs of Mr. Wesley's Missionaries to America, Compiled from Authentic Sources" (1843) by Rev. P. P. Sandford; "Biographical Sketches of Eminent Itinerant Ministers distinguished for the most part as Pioneers of Methodism . . . " edited (1858) by T. O. Summers; "Lives of Methodist Bishops" edited (1882) by Theodore L. Flood and John W. Hamilton; also the older work of Larrabee, "Asbury and his Coadjutors" (as above).

Historical work upon Methodism in America began with Jesse Lee in "A Short History of the Methodists in the United States of America, beginning in 1766, and Continued till 1809" (1809). As a contemporary of the period under investigation, his testimony has the weight of a source document. A "History of the Methodist Episcopal Church" (IV Vols. 1839-41) by Nathan Bangs, is a standard work of solid worth embodying a vast number of official records. It covers the period 1766 to 1840. The "History of the Rise and Progress of Methodism in America" (1859) by John Lednum, though brief, is remarkably accurate. The "History of the Methodist Episcopal Church" (IV Vols. 1864) by Abel Stevens, surpasses that of Bangs in its literary excellence, while maintaining a high standard of painstaking research. "A History of Methodists" (1884) by Bishop Holland N. McTyeire scarcely maintains the standards set by the older histories. "A History of Methodists in the United States" by Rev. J. M. Buckley ("Amer. Ch. Hist. Ser." Vol. V,

4th ed. 1900) is probably the best one volume history, being fair-minded, thorough, and highly readable. "The Methodists" (Series, "The Story of the Churches" 1903) by John Alfred Faulkner, though brief, is very satisfactory as an introductory study on the rise of Methodism.

Many facts have been unearthed in the following monographs: "Lost Chapters Recovered from the Early History of American Methodism" (1858, new ed. 1889) by Rev. J. B. Wakeley; ":Beams of Light on Early Methodism in America" (1887) by George A. Phoebus; "The Beginnings of the Wesley Movement in America, and the Establishment Therein of Methodism" (1896) by John Atkinson.

Studies devoted to local areas of Methodism are as follows: "Memorials of the Early Progress of Methodism in the Eastern States" (1850) by Abel Stevens; "Early Methodism within the bounds of the old Genesee Conference from 1788 to 1828 . . . in Northern Pennsylvania, Central and Western New York . . . " (1860) by George Peck; "Memorials of Methodism in New Jersey from the Foundation of the First Society . . . 1770 to the Completion of the first Twenty Years of its History . . ." (1860) by John Atkinson; "Reverend Enoch Mudge" ("Meth. Quart. Rev." July 1861, discusses New England Methodism in early nineteenth century); "Memorials of Methodism in Virginia, . . . " (1871, based on the manuscript Journal of the Rev. Stiff Mead, covering the period 1772-1829) by the Rev. Wm. W. Bennett; "The History of Methodism in Georgia and Florida from 1785 to 1865" (1877) by George G. Smith; "The History of Methodism in South Carolina" (1882) by Rev. Albert M. Shipp; "Sketches of the Pioneers of Methodism in North Carolina and Virginia" (1883) by Rev. M. H. Moore; "The Chronicles of St. Mark's Parish, Santee Circuit, and Williamsbury Township, South Carolina, 1731–1885" (1885) by James M. Burgess, M.D.; "Annals of New York Methodism, . . . " (1893) by Samuel A. Seaman; "Early Methodism in the Carolinas" (1897) by Rev. A. M. Chreitzberg; "Devereaux Jarratt and the Beginnings of Methodism in Virginia" by J. W. Smith ("The John P. Branch Historical Papers of Randolph–Macon College" June 1901, pp. 3-21); "History of Methodism in North Carolina from 1772 to the Present Time" (1905) by W. L. Grissom; "The Story of Hunt's Methodist Episcopal Church, Sherwood, Baltimore County, Maryland" (1910) by H. Wilson Burgan.

Periodical articles are as follows: "Early Methodism in Maryland, especially in Baltimore" ("Meth. Review" July 1856); "The First Methodist Conference West of the Alleghany Mountains" ("Quart. Rev. Meth. Epis. Ch. South" Oct. 1888); "Early Days of Methodism in the Blue Ridge Section of Virginia" (*ibid.* July 1891); "Early Methodism in Provincetown, Massachusetts" ("Meth. Review" July–August, 1906).

The educational interests of early Methodism are set forth in "Some Account of Cokesbury College" ("Meth. Quar. Review" April, 1859); "The Wesleyan University" (*ibid.* Jan. 1867); and "The Early Schools of Methodism" (1886) by A. W. Cummings.

On the institutional side of Methodism an old work is that of Robert Emory (revised and brought down to 1856 by W. P. Strickland) entitled, "History of the Discipline of the Methodist Episcopal Church." "A Digest of Methodist Law" (revised 1888) by Bishop S. M. Merrill, is a useful manual. Bishop Thomas B. Neely is the author of three monographs of substantial worth: "The Evolution of Episcopacy and Organic Methodism" (1888); "A History of the Origin and Development of the Governing Conference in Methodism" (1892); and "The Bishops and the Supervisional System of the Methodist Episcopal Church" (1912). "A Constitutional History of American Episcopal Methodism" (2nd ed. 1904) by John J. Tigert, is a masterly work, in large measure superseding all earlier work. The appendices have highly important material. "The Making of Methodism. Studies in the Genesis of Institutions" (1898) by the same author is a scholarly work especially significant for its treatment of the development of the presiding eldership and the Christmas conference. The same author's reprint with introductions of the doctrinal tracts in the disciplines, entitled, "The Doctrines of the Methodist Episcopal Church in America as Contained in the Disciplines, . . . 1788–1808, and so designated in their title pages" (II Vols. 1902) is indispensable.

A "Constitutional and Parliamentary History of the Methodist Episcopal Church" (1912) by James M. Buckley is accurate and worthy of a place beside Tigert's work.

For investigative purposes, in addition to the "Journals" already cited, there are "The Minutes of the Conference" (1773 f.) which, in spite of inacurracies in early numbers of dates and names, are of prime importance; also the "Journal of the General Conference" (1792 f.), and the "Discipline of the Methodist Episcopal Church" comprising XVI Volumes for the period 1785–1808 (for full bibliographical direction see Tigert, "Constitutional History, Appendix I). "The Methodist Magazine", the "Methodist Quarterly Review", the "Quarterly Review of the Methodist Episcopal Church South", and the "Methodist Review" will be found fertile in material bearing upon a wide range of subjects, while the "Arminian Magazine", the "London Quarterly Review", and the "Wesleyan Methodist Magazine" will give substantial returns, although in not such large proportions as the first mentioned.

DOCUMENTS

I. GENERAL RULES OF THE UNITED SOCIETIES

1. In the latter end of the year 1739, eight or ten persons came to me in London, who appeared to be deeply convinced of sin and earnestly groaning for redemption. They desired (as did two or three more the next day) that I would spend some time with them in prayer, and advise them how to flee from the wrath to come, which they saw continually hanging over their heads. That we might have more time for this great work, I appointed a day when they might all come together, which from thenceforward they did every week, namely, on Thursday, in the evening. To these, and as many more as desired to join with them (for their number increeaed daily), I gave those advices, from time to time, which I judged most needful for them; and we always concluded our meeting with prayer suited to their several necessities.

2. This was the rise of the United Society, first in London, and then in other places. Such a society is no other than "a company of men having the form and seeking the power of godliness, united in order to pray together, to receive the word of exhortation, and to watch over one another in love, that they may help each other to work out their salvation."

3. That it may the more easily be discerned whether they are indeed working out their own salvation, each society is divided into smaller companies, called *classes*, according to their respective places of abode. There are about twelve persons in every class, one of whom is styled *the leader*. It is his business (1) To see each person in his class once a week at least, in order to inquire how their souls prosper; to advise, reprove, comfort, or exhort, as occasion may require; to receive what they are willing to give toward the relief of the poor. (2) To meet the minister and stewards of the society once a week, in order to inform the minister of any that are sick, or of any that walk disorderly, and will not be reproved; to pay to the stewards what they have received of their several classes in the week preceding; and to show their account of what each person has contributed.

4. There is only one condition previously required in those who desire admission into these societies—a desire "to flee from the wrath to come, to be saved from their sins": but wherever this is really fixed in the soul it will be shown by its fruits. It is therefore expected of all who continue therein that they should continue to evidence their desire of salvation:

First, by doing no harm, by avoiding evil in every kind; especially that which is most generally practiced: such is the taking the name of God in vain; the profaning the day of the Lord, either by doing ordinary work thereon, or by buying or selling; drunkenness, buying or selling spirituous liquors, or drinking them, unless in cases of extreme necessity; fighting, quarreling, brawling; brother going to law with brother; returning evil for evil, or railing for railing; the using many words in buying or selling; the buying or selling uncustomed goods; the giving or taking things on usury, that is, unlawful interest; uncharitable or unprofitable conversation, particularly speaking evil of magistrates or of ministers; doing to others as we would not they should do unto us; doing what we know is not for the glory of God, as the "putting on of gold or costly apparel," the taking such diversions as cannot be used in the name of the Lord Jesus, the singing those songs, or reading those books, which do not tend to the knowledge or love of God; softness and needless self-indulgence; laying up treasures upon earth; borrowing without a probability of paying; or taking up goods without a probability of paying for them.

5. It is expected of all who continue in these societies that they should continue to evidence their desire of salvation:

Secondly, by doing good, by being in every kind merciful after their power; as they have opportunity, doing good of every possible sort, and as far as is possible to all men: to their bodies, of the ability which God giveth, by giving food to the hungry, by clothing the naked, by visiting or helping them that are sick or in prison; to their souls by instructing, reproving, or exhorting all that they have any intercourse with; trampling under foot that enthusiastic doctrine of devils, that "we are not to do good unless our heart be free to it"; by doing good especially to them that are of the household of faith, or groaning so to be; employing them preferably to others; buying one of another; helping each other in business, and so much the more because the world will love its own, and them only; by all possible diligence and frugality, that the gospel be not blamed; by running with patience the race that is set before them, "denying themselves, and taking up their cross daily;" submitting to bear the reproach of Christ, to be as the filth and offscouring of the world; and looking that men should "say all manner of evil of them falsely for the Lord's sake."

6. It is expected of all who desire to continue in these societies that they should continue to evidence their desire of salvation:

Thirdly, by attending upon all the ordinances of God. Such are the public worship of God; the ministry of the Word, either read or expounded; the Supper of the Lord; family and private prayer; searching the Scriptures; and fasting, or abstinence.

7. These are the general rules of our societies; all which we are taught of God to observe, even in his written word, the only rule and the sufficient rule both of our faith and practice. And all these, we know, his Spirit writes on every truly awakened heart. If there be any among us who observe them not, who habitually break any of them, let it be made known unto them who watch over that soul as they that must give an account. We will admonish him of the error of his ways; we will bear with him for a season; but then if he repent not he hath no more place among us. We have delivered our own souls.

JOHN WESLEY,
CHARLES WESLEY.

May 1, 1743.

Text—*Buckley: A History of Methodists in the United States,* (Amer. Ch. Hist. Ser. Vol. V) pp. 687-690.

II. *WESLEY, AND THE ORDINATION OF SUPERINTENDENTS FOR AMERICA*

"Bristol, September 10, 1784

"To Dr. Coke, Mr. Asbury, and our brethren in North America:

By a very uncommon train of providences many of the provinces of North America are totally disjoined from the mother country and erected into independent States. The English government has no authority over them, either civil or ecclesiastical, any more than over the states of Holland. A civil authority is exercised over them, partly by the Congress, partly by the provincial assemblies. But no one either exercises or claims any ecclesiastical authority at all. In this peculiar situation some thousands of the inhabitants of these States desire my advice, and in compliance with their desire I have drawn up a little sketch.

Lord King's account of the primitive church convinced me many years ago that bishops and presbyters are the same order, and consequently have the same right to ordain. For many years I have been importuned, from time to time, to exercise this right by ordaining part of our traveling preachers. But I have still refused; not only for peace' sake, but because I was determined as little as possible to violate the established order of the national church to which I belonged.

But the case is widely different between England and North America. Here there are bishops who have a legal jurisdiction. In America there are none, neither any parish minister. So that for some hundreds of miles together there is none either to baptize or to administer the Lord's Supper. Here therefore, my scruples are at an end; and I conceive myself at full liberty, as I violate no order and invade no man's right by appointing and sending laborers into the harvest.

I have accordingly appointed Dr. Coke and Mr. Francis Asbury to be joint superintendents over our brethren in North America; as also Richard Whatcoat and Thomas Vasey to act as elders among them, by baptizing and administering the Lord's Supper. And I have prepared a liturgy, little differing from that of the Church of England (I think the best constituted national church in the world), which I advise all the traveling preachers to use on the Lord's day in all the congregations, reading the Litany only on Wednesdays and Fridays, and praying extempore on all other days. I also advise the elders to administer the Supper of the Lord on every Lord's day.

If any one will point out a more rational and Scriptural way of feeding and guiding these poor sheep in the wilderness, I will gladly embrace it. At present I cannot see any better method than that I have taken.

It has indeed been proposed to desire the English bishops to ordain part of our preachers for America. But to this I object: 1. I desired the Bishop of London to ordain one, but could not prevail. 2. If they consented, we know the slowness of their proceedings, but the matter admits of no delay. 3. If they would ordain them now, they would expect to govern them. And how grievously would this entangle us! 4. As our American brethren are now totally disentangled, both from the state and the English hierarchy, we dare not entangle them again, either with the one or the other. They are now at full liberty simply to follow the Scriptures and the primitive church. And we judge it best that they should stand fast in that liberty wherewith God has so strangely made them free.

JOHN WESLEY."

Text—*Wesley's Works*, Vol. VII, pp. 311, 312.

III. *ASBURY'S ULTIMATUM TO THE VIRGINIANS*

Drafted at Baltimore April 24, 1780, these questions represent the basis upon which Asbury was able at the Conference at Manakintown to hold the aggressive Virginians to the original Wesleyan platform.

"*Ques.* 7. Ought not all the Assistants to see to the settling of all the preaching houses by trustees, and order the said trustees to meet once in half a year, and keep a register of their proceedings; if there are any vacancies choose new trustees for the better security of the houses, and let all the deeds be drawn in substance after that in the printed Minutes? *Ans.* Yes.

Ques. 8. Shall all the traveling preachers take a license from every Conference, importing that they are Assistants or helpers in connection with us? *Ans.* Yes.

Ques. 9. Shall Brother Asbury sign them in behalf of the Conference? *Ans.* Yes.

Ques. 10. Ought it to be strictly enjoined on all our local preachers and exhorters, that no one presume to speak in public without taking a vote every quarter (if required) and be examined by the Assistant with respect to his life, his qualification, and reception? *Ans.* Yes.

Ques. 12. Shall we continue in close connection with the Church, and press our people to a closer communion with her? *Ans.* Yes.

Ques. 13. Will this Conference grant the privilege to all the friendly clergy of the Church of England, at the request or desire of the people, to preach or administer the ordinances in our preaching houses or chapels? *Ans.* Yes.

Ques. 16. Ought not this Conference to require those traveling preachers who hold slaves to give promises to set them free? *Ans.* Yes.

Ques. 17. Does this Conference acknowledge that slavery is contrary to the laws of God, man, and nature, and hurtful to society; contrary to the dictates of conscience and pure religion, and doing that which we would not others should do to us and ours? Do we pass our disapprobation on all our friends who keep slaves, and advise their freedom? *Ans.* Yes.

Ques. 20. Does this whole Conference disapprove the step our brethren have taken in Virginia? *Ans.* Yes.

Ques. 21. Do we look upon them no longer as Methodists in connection with Mr. Wesley and us till they come back? *Ans.* Agreed.

Ques. 22. Shall brother Asbury, Garrettson, and Watters attend the Virginia Conference, and inform them of our proceedings in this, and receive their answer? *Ans.* Yes.

Ques. 23. Do we disapprove of the practice of distilling grain into liquor? Shall we disown our friends who will not renounce the practice? *Ans.* Yes.

Ques. 24. What shall the Conference do in case of brother Asbury's death or absence? *Ans.* Meet once a year, and act according to the Minutes.

Ques. 25. Ought not the Assistant to meet the colored people himself, and appoint as helpers in his absence proper white persons, and not suffer them to stay late, and meet by themselves? *Ans.* Yes.

Ques. 26. What must be the conditions of our union with our Virginia brethren? *Ans.* To suspend all their administrations for one year, and all meet together in Baltimore."

Text—Tigert: *A Constitutional History of American Episcopal Methodism,* revised edition, 1904, pp. 111-112.

IV. *THE CHRISTMAS CONFERENCE OF 1784*

The following questions from the Minutes give the structure and spirit of Methodism.

"Q. 2. What can be done in order to the future Union of the Methodists?

A. During the Life of the Rev. Mr. Wesley, we acknowledge ourselves his Sons in the Gospel, ready in Matters belonging to Church-Government, to obey his Commands

And we do engage after his Death, to do every Thing that we judge consistent with the Cause of Religion in *America* and the political Interests of these States, to preserve and promote our Union with the Methodists in *Europe*.

Q. 3. As the Ecclesiastical as well as Civil Affairs of these United States have passed through a very considerable Change by the Revolution, what Plan of Church-Government shall we hereafter pursue?

A. We will form ourselves into an Episcopal Church under the Direction of Superintendents, Elders, Deacons and Helpers, according to the Forms of Ordination annexed to our Liturgy, and the Form of Discipline set forth in these Minutes.

. . . .

Q. 23. May our Ministers or Travelling-Preachers drink spirituous Liquors?

A. By no means, unless it be *medicinally*.

Q. 24. Do not Sabbath-breaking, Evil-speaking, unprofitable Conversation, Lightness, Expensiveness or Gaiety of Apparel, and Contracting Debts without due Care to discharge them, still prevail in several Places? How may these Evils be remedied?

A. 1. Let us preach expressly on each of these Heads. 2. Read in every Society the Sermon on Evil-speaking. 3. Let the Leaders closely examine and exhort every Person to put away the accursed Thing. 4. Let the Preacher warn every Society, that none who is guilty therein can remain with us. 5. Extirpate smuggling, buying or selling encustomed Goods, out of every Society. Let none remain with us who will not totally abstain from every Kind and Degree of it. 6. Extirpate Bribery, receiving any Thing, directly or indirectly, for voting in any Election. Shew no Respect of Persons herein, but expel all that touch the accursed Thing.

Q. 26. What is the Office of a *Superintendent*?

A. To ordain *Superintendents*, *Elders* and *Deacons*; to preside as a Moderator in our Conferences; to fix the appointments of the Preachers for the several Circuits: and in the Intervals of the Conferences, to change, receive or suspend Preachers, as Necessity may require; and to receive Appeals from the Preachers and People, and decide them.

N. B. No Person shall be ordained a *Superintendent*, *Elder* or *Deacon*, without the Consent of a Majority of the Conference and the Consent and Imposition of Hands of a Superintendent; except in the Instance provided for in the 29th. Minute.

Q. 27. To whom is the *Superintendent* amenable for his Conduct?

A. To the Conference: who have Power to expel him for improper Conduct, if they see it necessary.

Q. 28. If the *Superintendent* ceases from Travelling at large among the People, shall he still exercise his Office in any Degree?

A. If he ceases from Travelling without the Consent of the Conference, he shall not thereafter exercise any ministerial Function whatsoever in our Church.

Q. 29. If by Death, Expulsion or otherwise there be no Superintendent remaining in our Church, what shall we do?

A. The Conference shall elect a Superintendent, and the Elders or any three of them shall ordain him according to our Liturgy.

Q. 30. What is the Office of an *Elder*?

A. To administer the Sacraments of Baptism and the Lord's Supper, and to perform all the other Rites prescribed by our Liturgy.

Q. 31. What is the Office of a *Deacon*?

A. To baptize in the Absence of an Elder, to assist the Elder in the Administration of the Lord's Supper, to marry, bury the Dead, and read the Liturgy to the People as prescribed, except what relates to the Administration of the Lord's Supper.

. . . .

Q. 35. How are we to proceed with those *Elders* or *Deacons* who cease from Travelling?

A. Unless they have the Permission of the Conference declared under the Hand of a Superintendent, they are on no account to exercise any of the peculiar Functions of those Offices among us. And if they do, they are to be expelled immediately.

Q. 36. What Method shall we take to prevent improper Persons from Preaching among us as Travelling-Preachers?

A. Let no Person be employed as a Travelling-Preacher, unless his Name be printed in the Minutes of the Conference preceding, or a Certificate be given him under the Hand of one or the other of the Superintendents, or, in their Absence, of three Assistants as is hereafter provided. And, for this Purpose, let the Minutes of the Conference be always printed.

. . . .

Q. 41. Are there any Directions to be given concerning the Negroes?

A. Let every Preacher, as often as possible, meet them in Class. And let the Assistant always appoint a proper *White Person* as their Leader. Let the Assistants also make a regular Return to the Conference, of the Number of Negroes in Society in their respective Circuits.

Q. 42. What Methods can we take to extirpate Slavery?

A. We are deeply conscious of the Impropriety of making new Terms of Communion for a religious Society already established, excepting on the most pressing Occasion: and such we esteem the Practice of holding our Fellow-Creatures in Slavery. We view it as contrary to the Golden Law of God on which hang all the Law and the Prophets, and the unalienable Rights of Mankind, as well as every Principle of the Revolution, to hold in the deepest Debasement, in a more abject Slavery than is perhaps to be found in any Part of the World except America, so many Souls that are all capable of the Image of God.

We therefore think it our most bounden Duty, to take immediately some effectual Method to extirpate this Abomination from among us: And for that Purpose we add the following to the Rules of our Society: viz.

1. Every Member of our Society who has Slaves in his Possession, shall within twelve Months after Notice given to him by the Assistant (which Notice the Assistants are required immediately and without any Delay to give in their respective Circuits) legally execute and record an Instrument, whereby he emancipates and sets free every Slave in his Possession who is between the Ages of Forty and Forty-five immediately, or at farthest when they arrive at the Age of Forty-five:

And every Slave who is between the Ages of Twenty-five and Forty immediately, or at the farthest at the Expiration of five years from the Date of the said Instrument:

And every Slave who is between the Ages of Twenty and Twenty-five immediately, or at farthest when they arrive at the Age of Thirty:

And every Slave under the Age of Twenty, as soon as they arrive at the Age of Twenty-five at farthest.

And every Infant born in Slavery after the above-mentioned Rules are complied with, immediately on its Birth.

2. Every Assistant shall keep a Journal, in which he shall regularly minute down the Names and Ages of all the Slaves belonging to all the Masters in his respective Circuit, and also the Date of every Instrument executed and recorded for the Manumission of the Slaves, with the Name of the Court, Book and Folio, in which the said Instruments respectively shall have been recorded; Which Journal shall be handled down in each Circuit to the succeeding Assistants.

3. In Consideration that these Rules form a new Term of Communion, every Person concerned, who will not comply with them, shall have Liberty quietly to withdraw himself from our Society within the twelve Months succeeding the Notice given as aforesaid: Otherwise the Assistant shall exclude him in the Society.

4. No Person so *voluntarily withdrawn* or so *excluded*, shall ever partake of the Supper of the Lord with the Methodists, till he complies with the above Requisitions.

5. No Person holding Slaves shall, in future, be admitted into Society or to the Lord's Supper, till he previously complies with these rules concerning Slavery.

N. B.   These Rules are to affect the Members of our Society no farther than as they are consistent with the Laws of the States in which they reside.

And respecting our Brethren in *Virginia* that are concerned, and after due Consideration of their peculiar Circumstances, we allow them *two Years* from the Notice given, to consider the expedience of compliance or Non-compliance with these Rules.

Q. 43.   What shall be done with those who buy or sell Slaves, or give them away?

A.   They are immediately to be expelled: unless they buy them on purpose to free them.

Text—Tigert: *A Constitutional History of American Episcopal Methodism*, revised edition, 1904, pp. 534-556.

V. *THE COUNCIL*

Adopted by the Conference in 1789, this instrument, was short lived, being confined to two sessions.

"1. Our bishops and presiding elders shall be the members of this Council; provided, that the members who form the Council be never fewer than nine.   And if any unavoidable circumstance prevent the attendance of a presiding elder at the Council, he shall have authority to send another elder out of his own district to represent him; but the elder so sent by the absenting elder shall have no seat in the Council without the approbation of the bishop, or bishops, and presiding elders present.   And if, after the above-mentioned provisions are complied with, any unavoidable circumstance or any contingencies reduce the number to less than nine, the bishop shall immediately summon such elders as do not preside, to complete the number.

2. These shall have authority to mature everything that they shall judge expedient: (1) To preserve the general union.   (2) To render and preserve the external form of worship similar in all our societies through the continent.   (3) To preserve the essentials of the Methodist doctrines and discipline pure and uncorrupted.   (4) To correct all abuses and disorders; and, lastly, they are authorized to mature everything they may see necessary for the good of the Church, and for the promoting and improving our colleges and plan of education.

3. Provided, nevertheless, that nothing shall be received as the resolution of the Council, unless it be assented to unanimously by the Council; and nothing so assented

to by the Council shall be binding in any district till it has been agreed upon by a majority of the Conference which is held for that district.

4. The bishops shall have authority to summon the Council to meet at such times and places as they shall judge expedient.

5. The first Council shall be held at Cokesbury, on the first day of next December."

Text—*Original pamphlet, Minutes*, 1789, pp. 12-13

VI. *THE DELEGATED GENERAL CONFERENCE*

An account of the preponderating influence of the Baltimore and Philadelphia representatives in the New York Conference, the following plan after brief debate was carried May 23, 1808.

"Ques. 2. Who shall compose the General Conference, and what are the regulations and powers belonging to it?

Ans. 1. The General Conference shall be composed of one member for every five members of each Annual Conference, to be appointed either by seniority or choice, at the discretion of such Annual Conference, yet so that such representatives shall have traveled at least four full calendar years from the time they are received on trial by an Annual Conference, and are in full connection at the time of holding the Conference.

2. The General Conference shall meet on the first day of May, in the year of our Lord 1812, in the city of New York, and thence forward on the first day of May once in four years, perpetually, in such place or places as shall be fixed on by the General Conference from time to time. But the general superintendents, with or by the advice of all the Annual Conferences, or, if there be no general superintendent, all the Annual Conferences respectively, shall have power to call a General Conference, if they judge it necessary, at any time.

3 At all times when the General Conferences meet, it shall take two-thirds of the representatives of all the Annual Conferences to make a quorum for transacting business.

4. One of the general superintendents shall preside in the General Conference; but in case no general superintendent be present, the General Conference shall choose a president *pro tempore*.

5. The General Conference shall have full powers to make rules and regulations for our Church, under the following limitations and restrictions, viz:

1. The General Conference shall not revoke, alter, or change our Articles of Religion, nor establish any new standards or rules of doctrine contrary to our present existing and established standards of doctrine.

2. They shall not allow of more than one representative for every five members of the Annual Conference, nor allow of a less number than one for every seven.

3. They shall not change or alter any part or rule of our government, so as to do away episcopacy or destroy the plan of our itinerant general superintendency.

4. They shall not revoke or change the General Rules of the United Societies.

5. They shall not do away the privileges of our ministers or preachers of trial by a committee, and of an appeal. Neither shall they do away the privileges of our members of trial before the society or by a committee, and of an appeal.

6. They shall not appropriate the produce of the Book Concern, nor of the Chartered Fund, to any purpose other than for the benefit of the traveling, supernumerary, superannuated, and worn-out preachers, their wives, widows, and children.

Provided, nevertheless, that upon the joint recommendation of all the Annual Conferences, then a majority of two-thirds of the General Conference succeeding shall suffice to alter any of the above restrictions."

Text—*Discipline of 1808*, pp. 14-16.

With the Goucher Substitute of May, 1892, as under, the plan as above became a constitution.

"The section on the General Conference in the Discipline of 1808, as adopted by the General Conference of 1808, has the nature and force of a Constitution.

That section, together with such modifications as have been adopted since that time in accordance with the provisions for amendment in that section, is the present Constitution, etc."

Text—*General Conference Journal*, Vol. XII, 1892, p. 206.

CHAPTER XVIII

The Second Awakening

Bibliography

To familiarize oneself with conditions on the frontier where this awakening was so pronounced, one does well to begin with the journal and travel literature of the period. The following arranged chronologically is reasonably complete: Francis Baily, "Journal of a Tour in Unsettled Parts of North America, 1796, 1797" (1856); F. M. Bayard, "Voyages dan l'intérieur des États-Unis à Bath, Winchester, dans la Vallée de Shenandoah . . . Pendant l'été 1797" (1798); I. Weld, "Travels in North America and Canada" (1799); Andrew Ellicott, "Journal of . . . during Part of the Year 1796, the Years 1797, 1798, and Part of the Year 1800" (1814); John Davis, "Travels of Four and One-Half Years in the United States of America during 1798, 1799, 1800, 1801, and 1802" (1803); F. A. Michaux, "Travels to the Westward of the Alleghany Mountains in the States of the Ohio, Kentucky, and Tennessee, and Return to Charlestown . . . 1802" (1805); Thaddeus M. Harris, "The Journal of a Tour into the Territory North-West of the Alleghany Mountains; Made in the Spring of the Year 1802" (1805); Josiah Espy, ". . . A Tour in Ohio, Kentucky, and Indiana Territory, . . . 1805" (1870); C. J. Schultz, "Travels in New York, Pennsylvania, Virginia, Ohio, Kentucky, Tennessee, Indiana . . . 1807, 1808" (II Vols. 1810); F. Cuming, "Sketches of a Tour to the Western Country through the states of Ohio and Kentucky, . . . 1807-1809" (1810); John Bradbury, "Travels in the Interior of America, including a Description of Upper Louisiana, together with the States of Ohio, Kentucky Indiana, and Tennessee, with the Illinois and Western Territories, in the Years 1809, 1810, and 1811" (1817); John Melish, "Travels in the United States of America, 1806, 1807, 1809–1811" (II Vols. 1812); H. B. Fearon, "Sketches of America; A Journal Through the Eastern and Western States, 1817" (1818); Estwick Evans, "A Pedestrous Tour of Four Thousand Miles Through the Western States and Territories during the Winter and Spring of 1818" (1818); Morris Birkbeck, "Notes on a Journey in America, Virginia, to the Territory of Illinois" (1817);

Thomas Hulmes, "A Journal of a Tour in the Western Counties of America; September 30, 1818–August 19, 1819" (1828); Richard Flower, "Letters from the Illinois, 1820, 1821, . . ." (1822); John Woods, "Two Years' Residence in the Settlement of the English Prairie in the Illinois Country, United States. . . . A Description of the Principal Towns, Villages, etc., with the Habits and Customs of the Backwoodsmen" (1822); James Flint, "Letters from America" (1822); Timothy Flint, "Recollections of the Last Ten Years, Passed in Occasional Residences and Journeys in the Valley of the Mississippi" (1826). The reader will find most of these works embodied in "Early Western Travels" edited by R. G. Thwaites.

As to older histories descriptive of frontier conditions, one dealing with the area as.a whole is that of George Imlay, "A Topographical Description of the Western Territory of North America, . . . " (1792). Of local histories, the following are recommended. For the Carolinas—David Ramsay, "The History of South Carolina, 1670-1808" (II Vols. 1809). See also p. 188f. For West Virginia—Samuel Kerchival, "A History of the Valley of Virginia" (1850); Joseph Doddridge, "Notes on the Settlement and Indian Wars of Western Virginia and Pennsylvania, 1763-1783. Together with a view of the state of society, and manners of the first settlers of the western country" (ed. A. Williams, 1876). For Tennessee—J. G. M. Ramsey, M.D., "The Annals of Tennessee, . . . " (1852); John Case, "Early Times in Middle Tennessee" (1857); A. W. Putnam, "History of Middle Tennessee, or Life and Times of General James Robertson" (1858); James Phelan, "History of Tennessee" (1889). For Kentucky—John Filson, "The Discovery, Settlement, and Present State of Kentucky" (1784); Humphrey Marshall, "The History of Kentucky, Including an Account of the Discovery, Settlement . . . and Present State of the Country" (1812, enlarged 1824); Mann Butler, "A History of the Commonwealth of Kentucky from its Exploration and Settlement by the Whites to the Close of the North-Western Campaign in 1813" (1834); "Pioneer Life in Kentucky—A Series of Reminiscent Letters from Daniel Drake, M.D." (1870); Z. F. Smith, "The History of Kentucky" (4th ed. 1901. This last work has an exhaustive bibliography. On Ohio and the Northwest Territory—Caleb Atwater, "A History of the State of Ohio, Natural and Civil" (1838); S. P. Hildreth, "Pioneer History . . . Ohio Valley, and the Early Settlement of the Northwest Territory" (1848—several important documents); J. Burnet, "Notes on Early Settlement of Northwest Territory" (1847); Henry Howe, "Historical Collections of Ohio"

(1847, Centennial edition, 1889); W. H. Venable, "Footprints of the Pioneers in Ohio Valley" (1888); also "Beginnings of Literary Culture in the Ohio Valley" (1891—exceptionally useful); W. C. Howell, "Recollections of Life in Ohio 1813-1840" (1895, valuable); B. A. Hinsdale, "The Old Northwest" (1888, revised ed. 1898). The last will be found good for political and legal aspects.

Mention should be made of a few recent books that set forth the significance of frontier life: John B. McMaster, "A History of the People of the United States" (1885-1892, especially Vols. III and IV); T. Roosevelt, "The Winning of the West" (IV Vols. 1889-1896); F. J. Turner, "The Significance of the Frontier in American History" ("Ann. Rpt. Amer. Hist. Assn." 1893, Sec. XVIII; also "Proc. State Hist. Soc. Wisconsin," 1893, pp. 79-112); Justin Winsor, "The Westward Movement. The Colonies and the Republic west of the Alleghanies, 1763-1798" (1897); F. J. Turner, "Rise of the New West" ("Amer. Nation Ser." Vol. XIV, 1906), and "The Frontier in American History" (1920).

Having gained an acquaintance with frontier conditions, the next type of literature to study is religious autobiography, where one finds descriptions of spiritual dearth, revival phenomena, and an estimate of the significance of the awakening: "Rev. Paul Henkel's Journal" (1806, "Ohio. Arch. & Hist. Quarterly" Vol. XXIII, No. 2); "The Life of Rev. Thomas Coke," (1817) by Samuel Drew; "Memoirs of Rev. Robert Finley . . . with Brief Sketches of some of His Contemporaries" (1819) by Isaac V. Brown; "The Journal of Rev. Francis Asbury 1771-1815" (III Vols. 1821); "Autobiography of Rev. William Hickman" (1838); "Life of Rev. Jesse Lee" (1848) by L. M. Lee; "The Biography of Elder David Purviance . . . written by himself . . . with sketch of the Great Kentucky Revival" (1848) by Elder Levi Purviance; "Recollections and Reflections of an Old Itinerant" (A series of letters, 1848,) by Rev. Henry Smith; "A Memoir of Rev. Joseph Badger, Containing an Autobiography and Selections from his Private Journal and Correspondence" (1851); "The Biography of Elder Barton W. Stone, Written by Himself, with Additions and Reflections" (1853) by Elder John Rogers, also to be found in "The Cane Ridge Meeting House" (1910) by James R. Rogers; "Life and Times of Rev. Finis Ewing" (1853) by F. R. Cossitt; "Sketches and Incidents of Rev. John Clark, by An Old Pioneer" edited (1855) by Rev. J. M. Peck; "Autobiography of Peter Cartwright the Backwoods Preacher" (1858); "Life of Rev. George Donnell" (1858) by F. C. Anderson; "Autobiography of a Pioneer, Or the Nativity, Experience, Travels, and Ministerial Labors of Rev. Jacob Young" (1860); "H. Boehm,

Reminiscences, History, and Biography of Sixty-Four Years in the Ministry" edited (1865) by J. B. Wakeley; "Autobiography of Rev. James B. Finley" edited (1867) by W. P. Strickland; "Life, Journals, and Correspondence of Rev. Manasseh Cutler, LL.D." (II Vols. 1888) by William and Julia P. Cutler; "The Autobiography of Thomas Ewing" edited by C. L. Martzolff ("Ohio Arch. & Hist. Quarterly" Vol. XXII, No. 1).

Accounts of the revival strictly contemporary, or written so sho tly after as to give them the weight of source material, are as follows: "Gospel News or a Brief Account of the Revival of Religion in Kentucky and Several Other Parts of the United States" (1801); "Increase of Piety or the Revival of Religion in the United States of America Containing Several Interesting Letters Not Before Published" (1802) by Angier March; "A Discourse Preached in Boston before the Massachusetts Baptist Missionary Society, May 25, 1803. Being their First Anniversary" by Samuel Stillman; "Sermon Before the New York Missionary Society at Their Annual Meeting, April 3, 1804. Appendix and Other Papers Relating to American Missions" (1809) by John H. Livingston; "A Sermon on the Present Revival of Religion. . . . Preached at the Opening of the Kentucky Synod" (1804) by David Rice; "The Kentucky Revival" (1808) by Richard McNemar; "Extracts of Letters Containing Some Account of the Work of God since 1800 Written by Preachers and Members of the Methodist Episcopal Church to their Bishops" (1812); "Diary of Rev. John Lyle" (Durrett Coll., Univ. of Chicago); "The Posthumous Works of James McGready" edited (II Vols. 1831) by Rev. James Smith; "An Address to the Christian Churches in Kentucky, Tennessee, and Ohio on Several Important Doctrines of Religion" (1821) by Barton W. Stone; The "New York Missionary Magazine" (1800-1803—especially valuable, containing McGready's "Narrative of the Great Revival in Logan County" and many letters describing the revivals in various parts of the United States); the "Connecticut Evangelical Magazine" (1800-1807); the "Massachusetts Baptist Missionary Magazine" (1803-10); the "Massachusetts Missionary Magazine" (1803-1808).

For the way in which the awakening a few years later affected the older colonial areas north and southeast, one should consult in addition to the magazines just mentioned, "The Life of Ashbel Green . . . begun to be written by Himself . . . (1849); "An Historical Sketch of the College of New Jersey (1859) anonymous; the "Quar. Reg. and

Jour. Amer. Educ. Soc."; and the "Autobiography, Correspondence . . . of Lyman Beecher (II Vols. 1864).   (See also pp. 364f, 420.)

Of monographs on the revival, besides McNemar's "Revival" (*supra*); there are, "Lectures on Revivals of Religion" (1833) by W. B. Sprague; "The Western Sketch-Book" (1850) by James Gallagher; "Revival Sketches and Manual" (1859) by Heman Humphrey; "The Great Revival of 1800" (1872) by William Speer; "The Great Awakening" by Isaac Smucker ("Proc. Amer. Antiq. Soc.," 1874, pp. 59-67); "The Kentucky Revival of 1799-1805, With Especial Reference to its effects upon Christianity in Ohio" by Rev. D. L. Leonard ("Papers Ohio Church Hist. Soc." Vol. V, pp. 44-71); "The Kentucky Revival and Its Influence in the Miami Valley" by J. P. MacLean, ("Pub. Ohio Arch. & Hist. Soc." Vol. XII, pp. 242-281); "The Great Revival in the West, 1797-1805" (1916) by Catharine C. Cleveland.   This is the most satisfactory treatment for the area it discusses.   An appendix has some illuminating documents, and a good bibliography is supplied.   There is also, "The Development of Religion in Kentucky, to 1830" (A. M. Dissertation, Univ. of Chicago, 1916) by Josephine P. Snapp, which is good in its interpretation of revival results.

Denominational histories have accounts more or less detailed.   So far as the Baptists are concerned, to the histories of Benedict, Burkitt and Read, Semple, and James B. Taylor (see p. 277f) there is to be added the following, the first three of which are of real significance: "History of Ten Baptist Churches" (1823) by John Taylor; "Journal of Baptists in Northwest Territory" (1840) by J. B. Jones; "History of the Miami Baptist Association from Its Organization in 1797 to a Division . . . in 1836" (1869) by A. H. Dunlevy; "History of the Baptists in the Western States East of the Mississippi" (1896) by Justin A. Smith; and "History of the Southern Baptists East of the Mississippi" (1898) by B. F. Riley.

The works on Methodism cited elsewhere (see page 316f) should be supplemented by "The Lives of Eminent Methodist Ministers" (1852) by P. D. Gorrie; "Sketches of Western Methodism" (1854) by J. B. Finley; "The History of Methodism in Kentucky" (III Vols. 1868-70) by A. H. Redford; "History of the Methodists in Tennessee" (III Vols. 1869) by J. B. McFerrin; "Memorials of Methodism in Virginia" (1871) by W. W. Bennett; "Holston Methodism" (III Vols. 1904-1908) by R. N. Price.

In connection with Presbyterianism, the following works in addition to those mentioned on p. 260f are to be noted: "Minutes of the General Assembly 1789-1820" (1847); "Outline History of the Church in the

State of Kentucky, 1783-1823. . . . Memoirs of Rev. David Rice"
(1824) by Robert H. Bishop; "History of the Presbyterian Church in the
State of Kentucky" (1847) by Rev. Robert Davidson; "Old Redstone, or
Historical Sketches of Western Presbyterianism and its Early Ministers"
(1854) by Joseph Smith; "The Plan of Union: or a History of the Pres-
byterian and Congregational Churches of the Western Reserve, with
Biographical Sketches of the Early Missionaries" (1856) by William S.
Kennedy; "History of the Presbyterian Church in Ohio" (1875) by J. B.
Fairchild; "History of Chillicothe Presbytery, 1799-1899" (1899) by
C. B. Galbreath; "Presbyterianism North of Ohio" (1890) by Rev. J. G.
Monfort.

Cumberland Presbyterianism which originated with this revival, is
referred to in the above mentioned works on Presbyterianism. A more
thorough study will require the following biographical works: "The
Life and Times of the Rev. Finis Ewing, one of the Fathers and Founders
of the Cumberland Presbyterian Church" (1853) by Rev. F. R. Cossitt,
and the "Life of Rev. Robert Donnell" (1867) by David Lowry. Of histories there are a "History of the Christian Church, Including a History
of the Cumberland Presbyterian Church" (1835) by Rev. James Smith;
"Biographical Sketches of the Early Ministers of the Cumberland Presbyterian Church" (II Vols. 1867) by Rev. Richard Beard, D.D.; "Origin
and Doctrines of the Cumberland Presbyterian Church" (1875) by Rev.
E. B. Chrisman; "Sources and Sketches of Cumberland Presbyterian
History" (in "Theological Medium," Nashville, 1877-78) by J. B. Linds-
ley, D.D.; "Old Log House, History and Defense of the Cumberland
Presbyterian Church" (1878) by Rev. T. C. Blake; "History of the Cumberland Presbyterian Church" (1888) by Rev. B. W. McDonnold. On
the doctrinal aspect of the subject, "Two Letters written by a Gentleman
to his Friend in Kentucky . . . with Some Strictures on the Apology of
the Springfield Presbytery" (1804) show the controversial issues. Rev.
A. B. Miller has a useful book entitled, "Doctrine and Genius of the Cumberland Presbyterian Church" (1892). A "Sketch of the History of the
Cumberland Presbyterian Church" ("Amer. Ch. Hist. Ser. "Vol. XI, 1894)
by Robert V. Foster is satisfactory as a condensed treatment. Several
documents have been inserted. A brief illuminating article by W. H.
Black, entitled "The Cumberland Presbyterian Church; Its Origin, Distinctive Features, and the Grounds for Preserving its Denominational
Integrity" appears in the "Journal Pres. Hist. Soc." Vol. I, No. II.

For the Disciples of Christ, in addition to McDonnold and Chrisman
there are the following biographical studies: "Biography of Barton W

Stone, Written by Himself with Additions and Reflections" (1847) by John Rogers; "Memoirs of Elder Thomas Campbell" (1861) by Alexander Campbell; "Life of John Smith" (1870) by John A. Williams; "Memoirs of Alexander Campbell" (II Vols. 1868-70) by Robert Richardson; "Life of Elder Walter Scott" (1874) by William Baxter; "Life and Letters of L..L. Pinkerton" (1876) edited by John Shackleford; "Memoirs of Isaac Errett" (II Vols. 1894) by J. S. Lamar; "Life of Aexander Campbell" (1897) by T. W. Grafton.

Historical work has been done by A. S. Hayden in a "History of the Disciples in the Western Reserve" (1875); "The Origin of the Disciples of Christ" (1889) by G. W. Longan; "History of the Disciples" by B. B. Tyler, ("Amer. Ch. Hist. Ser." Vol. XII, 1894); "Origin of the Disciples of Christ, . . . " (4th ed. 1899) by W. H. Whitsitt, D.D.; "The Reformation of the Nineteenth Century. Historical Sketches Dealing with the Rise and Progress of the Religious Movement Inaugurated by Thomas and Alexander Campbell" (1901) by J. H. Garrison; "The Early Relation and Separation of Baptist and Disciples" (1904) by Errett Gates, Ph.D.; his " . . . Disciples of Christ" (1905, in "The Story of the Churches" series); "A Comprehensive History of the Disciples of Christ, . . . " (1909) by W. T. Moore.

Of source works, there is the "Christian Baptist" (VII Vols. 1823-1830) and the "Millennial Harbinger" (XXXVI Vols. 1830-1866) edited by Alexander Campbell; his "Debate with Robert Owen" (1829), "Debate with J. B. Purcell" (1837), and "Debate with N. L. Rice" (1843); and a selection of "Historic Documents" edited (1904) by C. A. Young.

On the Shakers, an older but illuminating work (1874) is that of Charles Nordhoff "The Communistic Societies of the United States." Detailed bibliographical information is added. J. P. MacLean, has made the following significant contributions: "The Society of Shakers—Rise, Progress, and Extinction of the Society at Cleveland" ("Pub. Ohio Arch. & Hist. Soc." Vol. IX, pp. 32-116); "The Shaker Community of Warren County—Its Origin, Rise, Progress and Decline" (ibid. Vol. X, pp. 251-304); "Shaker Mission to the Shawnee Indians" (ibid. Vol. XI, pp. 215-229); "Mobbing the Shakers of Union Village" (ibid. Vol. XI, pp. 108-133); "Origin, Rise, Progress, and Decline of the Whitewater Community of Shakers, . . . " (ibid. Vol. XIII, pp. 401-443); "An Expedition Against the Shakers" by B. Seth Youngs (ibid. Vol. XXI, pp. 403-415). "A Summary View of the Millenial Church or United Society of Believers (commonly called Shakers)" by Calvin Green and Seth Y. Wells, though antiquated (1823) is informing. "Two years Experience among the Shakers" (1848) by D. R. Lamson should not be overlooked. An "Autobiography of a Shaker and Revelation of the Apocalypse" with an appendix (1869) by Frederic Evans tho designated anonymous, gives valuable inside knowledge. "Shaker Sermons, . . . " (1879) by H. L. Eads with "Shakerism, its Meaning and Message" (1904) by Anna White and Leila Taylor give the substance of Shaker theology and the social significance of this group. Miss Clara Endicott Sears has just issued (1916) "Gleanings from Old Shaker Journals." A bibliography of Shaker literature has been compiled by J. P. MacLean, and may be consulted in "Pub. Ohio Arch. and Hist. Soc." Vol. XII, pp. 282-286, also under separate cover.

Because of communistic resemblances to the Shakers, but not as connected in any way with the second awakening, reference may be made to the Separatists of Zoar who emigrated to Ohio in 1818.

On this group there are two studies: "The Separatists of Zoar" by George B. Landis, ("Ann. Rpt. Amer. Hist. Assn." 1898, Sec. X); and "The Separatist Society of Zoar" by E. O. Randall ("Pub. Ohio Arch. & Hist. Soc." Vol. VIII pp. 5-105). "The Communistic Societies of the United States" (1874) by Charles Nordhoff has a brief section.

DOCUMENTS

I. REVIVAL PHENOMENA

The Cain Ridge meeting of August, 1801, is thus described,

"I am sure the most discerning and observant pensman, or the nicest pencil, could not pourtray to your imagination, the full idea of the meeting that took place at Kain-ridge in Bourbon-county:—This meeting was published about one month generally, throughout the Presbyterian connexion as one of their annual sacraments; thither assembled the religious of every denomination, some from 100 miles distant, but more particularly the Presbyterians and Methodists, who are in full communion with each other:—lastly the Baptists, who preach with each other but do not commune. To this general assembly, I set off last Friday and arrived there on Saturday about 10 o'clock: I then began to note some of the most extraordinary particulars: I first proceeded to count the waggons containing families, with their provisions, camp equipage, &c., to the number of 147. At 11 o'clock the quantity of ground occupied by horses, waggons, etc., was about the same size as the square between Market, Chestnut, Second and Third streets of Philadelphia. . . . There was at this place a stage erected in the woods about 100 yards from the meeting-house, where were a number of Presbyterian and Methodist ministers; one of the former preaching to as many as could get near enough to hear—in the house also was another of the same denomination, preaching to a crowded audience—at the same time another large concourse of people collected about 100 yards in an east direction from the meeting-house, hearing a Methodist speaker—and about 150 yards in a fourth course from the house an assembly of black people, hearing the exhortation of the blacks, some of whom appeared deeply convicted and others converted.   The number of communicants who received tokens were 750, nor was there a sufficiency of them—(these tokens are small pieces of lead the size of a five-penny bit with the letter A or B impressed thereon and distributed by the ministers to the members of the several churches not excluding any Baptists who apply for them).   I believe there was at one time as many as 300 who exhorted on this occasion.   I noted a remarkable instance of a little girl, by the name of Barbara, about 7 years old, who was set upon a man's shoulder, agreeably to her desire to speak to the multitude, which she did until she appeared almost exhausted, and leaned back her head on her bearer.   A tender hearted old man standing close behind her, observed, "Poor thing she had better be laid down", at which she quickly turned round her head, and said, "Don't call me poor, for Christ is my brother, God my father, and I have a kingdom to inherit, therefore don't call me poor, for I am rich in the blood of the Lamb."

Text—March: *Increase of Piety*, pp. 57-58.

Referring to "the jerks," McNemar writes:

"Nothing in nature could better represent this strange and unaccountable operation than for one to goad another, alternately on every side, with a piece of red-hot iron.   The exercise commonly began in the head which would fly backward and forward, and from side to side with a quick jolt which the person would naturally labor to suppress but in vain, and the more any one labored to stay himself and be sober the more he staggered and the more rapidly his twitches increased.   He must necessarily go as he was stimulated, whether with a violent dash on the ground and bounce from place to place like a foot-ball, or hop round with head, limbs, and trunk, twitching and jolting in every direction, as if they must inevitably fly asunder. . . .   By this strange operation the human frame was commonly so transformed and disfigured, as to lose every trace of its natural appearance.   Some times the head would be twitched right and left to a half round with such velocity that not a feature could be discovered, but face appear as much behind as before, and in the quick progressive jerk, it would seem as if the person was transmuted into some other species of creature.   Head dresses were of little account among the female jerkers.   Even handkerchiefs bound tight round the head would be flirted off almost with the first twitch, and the hair put into the utmost confusion, this was a very great inconvenience to redress which the generality were shorn, though directly contrary to their confession of faith.   Such as were seized with the jerks wrested at once, not only from under their own government, but that of every one else so that it was dangerous to attempt confining them, or touching them in any manner, to whatever danger they were exposed."

Text—McNemar: *The Kentucky Revival*, pp. 61-62.

Extracts from Cummins' letter to his friend (July 7, 1802) describing the meeting in Spartanburgh, South Carolina, give a good idea of one of the week-end protracted meetings.

"The Meeting was appointed some months since by the Presbytery and commenced on Friday the 2nd instant.   The grove wherein the camp was pitched was near the waters of Tyger river, and being in a vale which lay between two hills gently inclining towards each other, was very suitably adapted to the purpose. The first day was taken up in encampment until two o'clock, when divine service commenced with a sermon by the Rev'd. Jno. B. Kennedy. He was succeeded by the Rev'd. William Williamson in an address explanatory of the nature and consequences of such meetings. The assembly was then dismissed. After some short time, service commenced again with a sermon by the Rev'd. James Gilleland; who was followed by the Rev'd. Robert Wilson in a very serious and solemn exhortation. Afterwards the evening was spent in singing and praying alternately. About sun-down, people was dismissed to their respective tents. By this time the countenances of all began to be shaded by the clouds of solemnity and to assume a very serious aspect. At ten o'clock two young men were lying speechless, motionless and sometimes to all appearance, except in the mere act of breathing, dead. Before day, five others were down; these I did not see. The whole night was employed in reading and commenting upon the word of God; and also in singing, praying and exhorting, scarcely had the light of the morning sun dawned on the people, ere they were engaged in what may be called family worship. The adjacent tents collected in groups, here and there, all round the whole line. The place of worship was early repaired to, by a numerous throng. Divine worship commenced at eight by one of the Methodist brethren, whom I do not now recollect. He was followed by the Rev'd. Shackleford, of the Baptist profession. Singing, praying, and exhorting, by the Presbyterian clergymen continued until two o'clock when an intermission of some minutes was granted, that the people might refresh themselves with water, &c. By this time, the audience became so numerous, that it was impossible for all to crowd near enough to hear one speaker; although, the ground rising about the stage theatrically, afforded aid to the voice. Hence, the assembly divided, and afterwards preaching was performed at two stages. An astonishing and solemn attention in the hearers, and an animating and energetic zeal in the speakers was now everywhere prevailing. Service commenced half after two by the Rev'd Jno. Simpson at one stage, and at the other, by the Rev'd James McElhenny, who were succeeded by the Rev. Francis Cummins. After these sermons, fervent praying, &c. were continued until and through the night in which time, many were stricken and numerous were brought to the ground.

"The next morning (i.e., the Sabbath morning) a still higher, if possible, more engaged, and interesting spirit pervaded the whole grove, singing and praying echoed from every quarter until eight o'clock, when divine service commenced again at both stages before two great and crowded assemblies. The action sermons were delivered by the Rev. Robert Wilson at one stage and the Rev. William Cummins Davis at the other. I did not hear Mr. Wilson. But Mr. Davis was one of the most popular, orthodox gospel sermons that I ever heard. No sketch exhibited in words, would be adaquate to pourtray the appearence of the audience under this discourse. Imagine to your self thousands under the sense of the great possible danger, anxious to be informed in all that related to their dearest interests, in the presence of a counsellor, who, labouring with all his efforts, should be endeavouring to point out the way to security; and you may have some faint conception of this spectacle.

"Thence ensued the administration of the Lord's Supper. To the communion sat down about four hundred persons. It was a matter of infinite satisfaction to see on this occasion the members of the Methodist and Presbyterian churches united; all owning and acknowledging the same God, the same Saviour, the same Sanctifier, and the same Heaven. We are sorry to add, that the Baptists refused to join, whether their objections were reasonably justifiable, we shall not presume to say.

"The evening exercises, although greatly interrupted by the intemperance of the weather, progressed as usual, until about dark; when there commenced one of the most sublime, awfully interesting, and glorious scenes which could possibly be exhibited on this side of eternity. The penetrating sighs and excruciating struggles of those under exercise, the grateful exultations of those brought to a sense of their guilty condition, and to a knowledge of the way to salvation, mingled with the impressions which are naturally excited by the charms of music and the solemnities of prayer on such occasions; and to all this added the nature of the scenery, the darkness of the night, and the countenances of all the spectators, speaking in terms more expressive than language, the sympathy, the hope and the fear, of their hearts; were sufficient to bow the stubborn neck of infidelity, silence the tongue of profanity, and melt the heart of cold neglect though hard as adamant.

"This scene continued through the night. Monday morning dawned big with the fate of its importance. The morning exercises were conducted as usual. About half after seven, the assembly met the ministers at the stage, and service commenced by the Rev. Moses Waddell After which ensued, singing, exhorting and a concert of prayer. At length the business closed with an address, energetic and appropriate by the Rev. Francis Cummins. In the course of this day many were stricken, numbers of whom fell.

"I cannot say, that the parting was not one of the most moving, and affecting scenes which presented itself throughout the whole. Families, who had never seen each other, until they met on the ground would pour forth the tears of sympathy, like streams of water, many friendships were formed, and many attachments contracted, which, although the persons may never meet again will never be dissolved.

. . . .

"The multitude on this occasion far exceeded anything which had come under my observation There were various conjectures of the numbers present; some allowed three, some seven, some four, some five, some six, some eight thousand. I have not been in the habit of seeing such multitudes together, and therefore do not look upon myself capable of reckoning any ways accurately on the subject. But I do candidly believe five thousand would not be a vague conjecture. The district of Spartanburgh where the meeting was held, contains not less than twelve thousand souls. Men of information who resided therein, said to one who might be travelling, the country would appear almost depopulated, and hesitated not in the least to say that at least two-thirds of the inhabitants were present. Now supposing only one-third to have attended from that district itself there would have been four thousand."

Text—*Augusta Herald*, July 28, 1802. Reprint in Cleveland's: *The Great Revival*, appendix III.

The later awakening at Yale (1812), typical of movements throughout the East, is thus described by Ashbel Green:

For nearly a year past—that is, since the commencement of the last summer session—a very large proportion of the students have attended on all the religious exercises and instructions of the College with more than ordinary seriousness; and the minds of some of them, as now appears, were ripening, through this whole period, for what has since taken place. There was nothing more apparent, however, for six weeks after the commencement of the present session, than an increase of this serious attention to the religious duties of College; an increase both of the degree of seriousness, and of the number of those in whom it was visible. Every religious service, both on secular days and on the Sabbath, was attended with a solemnity which was sensible and impressive. In this manner the revival commenced, or rather became apparent, in the second week of January without any unusual occurrence in providence;— without any alarming event, without any extraordinary preaching, without any special instruction, or other means that might be supposed peculiarly adapted to interest the mind. The divine influence seemed to descend like the silent dew of heaven; and in about four weeks there were very few individuals in the College edifice who were not deeply impressed with a sense of the importance of spiritual and eternal things. There was scarcely a room—perhaps not one—which was not a place of earnest secret devotion. For a time it appeared as if the whole of our charge was pressing into the kingdom of God; so that at length the inquiry, in regard to them, was, not who was engaged about religion? but who was not?—After this state of things had continued, without much variation, for about two months, it became manifest that a change was taking place. Some were becoming confirmed in the hopes and habits of evangelical piety; some were yet serious, thoughtful and prayerful, though perhaps not in so great a degree, or at least not so apparently, as once they had been; while some were plainly losing the impressions which they had lately felt. And such has continued to be the state of this interesting concern to the time of making this report. The result is, that there are somewhat more than forty students, in regard to whom, so far as the time elapsed will permit us to judge, favourable hopes may be entertained that they have been made the subjects of renewing grace. Perhaps there are twelve or fifteen more, who still retain such promising impressions of religion as to authorize a hope that the issue, in regard to most of them, may be favourable. And nearly the whole of the remainder show a great readiness to attend on all the social exercises of religion; not only on those which are stated and customary, but those which are occasional, and the attendance on which is entirely voluntary. Thus, of the students who are now in the College, a majority may be viewed as hopefully pious; and a large proportion of the residue appear to possess much tenderness of conscience, and show a very desirable regard to religious duties and obligations. . . . .

Four such causes appear to have had a manifest agency—

1. And chiefly, the study of the Holy Scriptures; accompanied with comments on the portion read, and a practical application of the leading truths contained in it. God has remarkably honoured and blessed his own word. Strange as it may seem, this study of the Bible has always been a favourite one among the youth of the College, not excepting the most gay and dissipated. Pains have, indeed, been taken to render it interesting; but the degree in which it has been so, has been truly surprising. . . . . .

The circumstances in which the students have lately attended on public worship have been peculiarly favourable to their religious improvement. They have worshipped, in consequence of the burning of the church in this place, in the prayer hall of the College, for more than two years past. For about eighteen months they have worshipped separately from the people of the town; and have, with the theological students, who joined them partially at first and generally of late, formed an audience or congregation by themselves. This has given an opportunity, which has been carefully improved, to choose such subjects and adopt such a manner, in preaching to them, as appeared best calculated to arrest their attention. Appropriate addresses have frequently been made, and the service has, in all respects, been conducted with a special view to their advantage and Religious edification. . . . .

3. The effect of moral discipline has been manifestly favourable to this revival. This discipline, vigorously and vigilantly maintained, has preserved the youth, generally, from those practices, habits and vicious indulgences, which counteract, dissipate, and destroy all serious and religious impressions. It has had an influence in preventing that hardness of heart and insensibility of conscience, which are the natural and usual effects of unrestrained vice. It has formed a practical testimony against the moral vileness of several things which youth are apt to consider, if not as entirely innocent, yet, as evidences of manliness and spirit. . . . .

4. The few pious youths who were members of College before the revival, were happily instrumental in promoting it. They had, for more than a year, been earnestly engaged in prayer for this event. When they perceived the general and increasing seriousness which has been noticed, several of them made an agreement to speak, privately and tenderly, to their particular friends and acquaintance, on the subject of religion. . . . .

The special means made use of to promote and cherish this revival, besides the circumstances already mentioned, were the following—A short address on the subject of religion was made, after prayers, on every Saturday evening. In preaching on the Lord's day morning, subjects were selected suited to the existing state of the College—in this particular we are deeply indebted to the theological professors, who have generally conducted the morning service. A particular reference was often made to the religious attention which had been excited among the students, in the remarks which accompanied their Bible recitations. A weekly lecture, intended for the students exclusively, was given by myself, on every Tuesday evening. A social prayer meeting was held, on every Friday evening, at which one of the theological professors commonly made an address. A family prayer meeting (as the students called it) was, every evening, held among themselves, at which a large proportion of the whole College attended. Smaller and more select associations for prayer were also formed. . . . . . I shall conclude my report on this subject with a few short remarks, offered with a view to give a correct apprehension of its nature and character.

1. It has been, so far as I am able to judge, remarkably free from extravagance and enthusiasm. I know of nothing, in regard to this revival, that I think would be called extravagant or enthusiastic, by any one who really believes in the great doctrines of the Protestant Reformation. Particular pains were early taken to guard against the evil here contemplated; and, by the divine blessing, they have been made so successful that I am not acquainted with a single incident or occurrence, indicative of intemperate feeling or conduct, that we are called to regret.

2. There has been no sectarian spirit accompanying or mingling with this revival. There are students in the College belonging to four or five different denominations of Christians. At first, there appeared to be some apprehension in the minds of those who were not Presbyterians, lest they should be drawn into a union with this denomination, if they yielded to the sentiments and feelings which began to be prevalent. But I told them, in the first address that I made to them on a Tuesday evening, that it was my fixed purpose to inculcate no doctrine or tenet that was not found in all the public orthodox creeds of Protestant Christendom—that I was indeed earnestly desirous that they should all become real practical Christians, but that I had no wish to make

a single proselyte. This, I believe, removed every apprehension—and the intimation then given has been sacredly regarded. Not a single thing has been said by myself, nor, I am persuaded, by the theological professors who have preached to them, that has had any intentional tendency toward proselytism. On the contrary every thing has been general. The great catholic doctrines of the gospel have been exclusively inculcated. It is believed that there is not an individual of the College who would, if questioned, complain that he has, in any instance, felt himself pressed with opinions which interfered with his educational creed.

3. There has been no neglect of study. A report was circulated that study was laid aside in the College to attend to religion. Nothing could be more false. Study has probably never been pursued with more diligence and success. Our pupils were informed that if, at any particular recitation, an individual should find that his mind had been so exercised as not to permit him to get his lesson, he should, on application to his teacher, be specially excused; and this indulgence has been frequently asked and granted. But not a single recitation of a class has been omitted; and every individual lesson or recitation, incidentally omitted, has been strictly required to be made up for the quarterly and semi-annual examinations.

4. There have been no compulsory exercises. Everything, beyond the stated religious instructions and duties of the College in ordinary times, has been perfectly voluntary; unless the short address, on Saturday evening after prayers, may be considered as a slight exception. No one has suffered either censure or reproach, who chose to be absent from any religious exercise or engagement which had its origin in this revival.

Text—"*The Life of Ashbel Green, V.D.M. Begun . . . by himself . . .*" pp. 619-622.

II. *THE LAST WILL AND TESTAMENT OF THE SPRING-FIELD PRESBYTERY*

The members of the Springfield Presbytery having seceded because of their anti-Calvinistic doctrines, which may be consulted in "The Apology of Springfield Presbytery," finding, however, that their name savored of a party spirit, decided to repudiate any name save that of Christian. They therefore drew up the document as under, which is fundamental in the Stone movement in Kentucky.

"For where a testament is, there must of necessity be the death of the testator; for a testament is of force after men are dead, otherwise it is of no strength at all, while the testator liveth. Thou fool, that which thou sowest is not quickened except it die. Verily, verily, I say unto you, except a corn of wheat fall into the ground, and die, it abideth alone; but if it die, it bringeth forth much fruit. Whose voice then shook the earth; but now he hath promised, saying, yet once more I shake not the earth only, but also heaven. And this word, yet once more, signifies the removing of those things that are shaken as of things that are made, that those things which cannot be shaken may remain.—Scripture.

THE PRESBYTERY OF SPRINGFIELD, sitting at Caneridge, in the County of Bourbon being through a gracious Providence in more than ordinary bodily health, growing in strength and size daily; and in perfect soundness and composure of mind; but knowing that it is appointed for all delegated bodies once to die; and considering that the life of every such body is very uncertain, do make, and ordain this our last Will and Testament, in manner and form following, viz:

Imprimis. We *will*, that this body die, be dissolved, and sink into union with the Body of Christ at large; for there is but one Body and one Spirit, even as we are called in one hope of our calling.

Item. We *will*, that our name of distinction, with its *Reverend* title, be forgotten that there be but one Lord over God's heritage, and his name One.

Item. We *will*, that our power of making laws for the government of the church, and executing them by delegated authority forever cease; that the people may have, free course to the Bible, and adopt *the law of the Spirit of life in Christ Jesus.*

Item. We *will*, that candidates for the Gospel ministry henceforth study the Holy Scriptures with fervent prayer, and obtain license from God to preach the simple Gospel, *with the Holy Ghost sent down from Heaven*, without any mixture of philosophy, vain deceit, traditions of men, or the rudiments of the world. And let none henceforth take this honour upon himself, but he that is called of God, as was Aaron.

Item. We *will*, that the church of Christ resume her native right of internal government—try her candidates for the ministry, as to their soundness in the faith, acquaintance with experimental religion, gravity and aptness to teach, and admit no other proof of their authority but Christ speaking in them. We *will*, that the Church of Christ look up to the Lord of the harvest to send forth labourers into his harvest; and that she resume her primitive right of trying those *who say they are apostles, and are not*

Item. We *will*, that each particular church, as a body, actuated by the same spirit, choose her own preacher, and support him by a free will offering, without a written *call* or *subscription*—admit members—remove offences; and never henceforth delegate her right of government to any man or set of men whatever.

Item. We *will*, that the people henceforth take the Bible as the only sure guide to heaven; and as many as are offended with other books, which stand in competition with it, may cast them into the fire if they choose; for it is better to enter into life with one book, than having many to be cast into hell.

Item. We *will*, that preachers and people, cultivate a spirit of mutual forbearance, pray more, and dispute less; and while they behold the signs of the times, look up, and confidently expect that redemption draweth nigh.

Item. We *will*, that our weak brethren, who may have been wishing to make the Presbytery of Springfield their king, and wot not what is now become of it, betake themselves to the Rock of Ages, andfollow Jesus for the future.

Item. We *will*, that the Synod of Kentucky examine every member, who may be *suspected* of having departed from the Confession of Faith, and suspend every such suspected heretic immediately; in order that the oppressed may go free, and taste the sweets of gospel liberty.

Item. We *will*, that Ja . . . . , the author of two letters lately published in Lexington, be encouraged in his zeal to destroy *partyism.* We *will*, moreover, that our past conduct may be examined into by all who may have correct information; but let foreigners beware of speaking evil of things which they know not.

Item. Finally, we *will*, that all our sister bodies read their Bibles carefully, that they may see their fate there determined, and prepare for death before it is too late.

SPRINGFIELD PRESBYTERY } L.S.
June 28th, 1804 }

JOHN DUNLAVY	)	
RICHARD M'NEMAR	)	
B. W. STONE	)	*Witnesses.*
JOHN THOMPSON	)	
DAVID PURVIANCE	)	
ROBERT MARSHALL	)	

The Witnesses' Address

We, the above named witnesses of the Last Will and Testament of the Springfield Presbytery, knowing that there will be many conjectures respecting the causes which have occasioned the dissolution of that body, think proper to testify, that from its first existence it was knit together in love, lived in peace and concord, and died a voluntary and happy death.

Their reasons for dissolving that body were the following: With deep concern they viewed the divisions, and party spirit among professing Christians, principally owing to the adoption of human creeds and forms of government. While they were united under the name of a Presbytery, they endeavoured to cultivate a spirit of love and unity with all Christians; but found it extremely difficult to suppress the idea that they themselves were a party separate from others. This difficulty increased in proportion to their success in the ministry. Jealousies were excited in the minds of other denominations; and a temptation was laid before those who were connected with the various parties, to view them in the same light. At their last meeting they undertook to prepare for the press a piece entitled Observations on Church Government, in which the world will see the beautiful simplicity of Christian church government, stripped of human inventions and lordly traditions. As they proceeded in the investigation of that subject, they soon found that there was neither precept nor example in the New Testament for such confederacies as modern Church Sessions, Presbyteries, Synods, General Assemblies, etc. Hence they concluded, that while they continued in the connection in which they then stood, they were off the foundation of the Apostles and Prophets, of which Christ himself is the chief corner stone. However just, therefore, their views of church government might have been, they would have gone out under the name and sanction of a self-constituted body.

Therefore, from a principle of love to Christians of every name, the precious cause of Jesus, and dying sinners who are kept from the Lord by the existence of sects and parties in the church, they have cheerfully consented to retire from the din and fury of conflicting parties—sink out of the view of fleshly minds, and die the death. They believe their death will be the great gain to the world. But though dead, as above, and stripped of their mortal frame, which only served to keep them too near the confines of Egyptian bondage, they yet live and speak in the land of Gospel liberty; they blow the trumpet of jubilee, and willingly devote themselves to the help of the Lord against the mighty. They will aid the brethren, by their council, when required; assist in ordaining elders, or pastors—seek the divine blessing—unite with all Christians—commune together, and strengthen each others' hands in the work of the Lord.

We design by the grace of God, to continue in the exercise of those functions, which belong to us as ministers of the gospel, confidently trusting in the Lord, that he will be with us.   We candidly acknowledge, that in some things we may err, through human infirmity; but he will correct our wanderings, and preserve his church.   Let all Christians join with us, in crying to God day and night, to remove the obstacles which stand in the way of his work, and give him no rest till he make Jerusalem a praise in the earth.   We heartily unite with our Christian brethren of every name, in thanksgiving to God for the display of his goodness in the glorious work he is carrying on in our Western country, which we hope will terminate in the universal spread of the gospel, and the unity of the church."

Text—Moore: *A Comprehensive History of the Disciples of Christ*, pp. 243-246.

III. *THOMAS CAMPBELL'S Declaration and Address.*

Written for the Christian Association of Washington (organized August 17, 1809) by Thomas Campbell.

Let none imagine that the subjoined propositions are at all intended as an overture toward a new creed or standard for the Church, or as in any wise designed to be made a term of communion, nothing can be further from our intention.   They are merely designed for opening up the way, that we may come fairly and firmly to original ground upon clear and certain premises, and take up things just as the apostles left them; that thus disentangled from the accruing embarrassments of the intervening ages, we may stand with evidence upon the same ground on which the Church stood at the beginning.   Having said so much to solicit attention and prevent mistake, we submit as follows:

Prop. 1.That the Church of Christ upon earth is essentially, intentionally, and constitutionally one; consisting of all those in every place that profess their faith in Christ and obedience to him in all things according to the Scriptures, and that manifest the same by their tempers and conduct, and of none else; as none else can be truly and properly called Christians.

(2) That although the Church of Christ upon earth must necessarily exist in particular and distinct societies, locally separate one from another, yet there ought to be no schisms, no uncharitable divisions among them.   They ought to receive each other as Christ Jesus hath also received them, to the glory of God.   And for this purpose they ought all to walk by the same rule, to mind and speak the same thing; and to be perfectly joined together in the same mind, and in the same judgment.

(3) That in order to this, nothing ought to be inculcated upon Christians as articles of faith; nor required of them as terms of communion, but what is expressly taught and enjoined upon them in the Word of God.   Nor ought anything to be admitted, as of Divine obligation, in their Church constitution and managements, but what is expressly enjoined by the authority of our Lord Jesus Christ and his apostles upon the New Testament Church; either in express terms or by approved precedent.

(4) That although the Scriptures of the Old and New Testaments are inseparably connected, making together but one perfect and entire revelation of the Divine will, for the edification and salvation of the Church, and therefore in that respect cannot be separated; yet as to what directly and properly belongs to their immediate object,

the New Testament is as perfect a constitution for the worship, discipline, and government of the New Testament Church, and as perfect a rule for the particular duties of its members, as the Old Testament was for the worship, discipline, and government of the Old Testament Church, and the particular duties of its members.

(5) That with respect to the commands and ordinances of our Lord Jesus Christ, where the Scriptures are silent as to the express time or manner of performance, if any such there be, no human authority has power to interfere, in order to supply the supposed deficiency by making laws for the Church; nor can anything more be required of Christians in such cases, but only that they so observe these commands and ordinances as will evidently answer the declared and obvious end of their institution. Much less has any human authority power to impose new commands or ordinances upon the Church, which our Lord Jesus Christ has not enjoined. Nothing ought to be received into the faith or worship of the Church, or to be made a term of communion among Christians, that is not as old as the New Testament.

(6) That although inferences and deductions from Scripture premises, when fairly inferred, may be truly called the doctrine of God's holy word, yet are they not formally binding upon the consciences of Christians farther than they perceive the connection, and evidently see that they are so; for their faith must not stand in the wisdom of men, but in the power and veracity of God. Therefore, no such deductions can be made terms of communion, but do properly belong to the after and progressive edification of the Church. Hence, it is evident that no such deductions or inferential truths ought to have any place in the Church's confession.

(7) That although doctrinal exhibitions of the great system of Divine truths, and defensive testimonies in opposition to prevailing errors, be highly expedient, and the more full and explicit they be for those purposes, the better; yet, as these must be in a great measure the effect of human reasoning, and of course must contain many inferential truths, they ought not to be made terms of Christian communion; unless we suppose, what is contrary to fact, that none have a right to the communion of the Church, but such as possess a very clear and decisive judgment, or are come to a very high degree of doctrinal information; whereas the Church from the beginning did and ever will, consist of little children and young men, as well as fathers.

(8) That as it is not necessary that persons should have a particular knowledge or distinct apprehension of all Divinely revealed truths in order to entitle them to a place in the Church; neither should they, for this purpose, be required to make a profession more extensive than their knowledge; but that, on the contrary, their having a due measure of Scriptural self-knowledge respecting their lost and perishing condition by nature and practice, and of the way of Salvation through Jesus Christ, accompanied with a profession of their faith in and obedience to him, in all things, according to his word, is all that is absolutely necessary to qualify them for admission into his Church.

(9) That all that are enabled through grace to make such a profession, and to manifest the reality of it in their tempers and conduct, should consider each other as the precious saints of God, should love each other as brethren, children of the same family and Father, temples of the same Spirit, members of the same body, subjects of the same grace, objects of the same Divine love, bought with the same price, and joint-heirs of the same inheritance. Whom God hath thus joined together no man should dare to put asunder.

(10) That division among the Christians is a horrid evil, fraught with many evils. It is anti-Christian, as it destroys the visible unity of the body of Christ; as

if he were divided against himself, excluding and excommunicating a part of himself. It is anti-Scriptural, as being strictly prohibited by his sovereign authority; a direct violation of his express command. It is anti-natural, as it excites Christians to condemn, to hate, and oppose one another, who are bound by the highest and most endearing obligations to love each other as brethren, even as Christ has loved them. In a word, it is productive of confusion and of every evil work.

(11) That (in some instances) a partial neglect of the expressly revealed will of God, and (in others) an assumed authority for making the approbation of human opinions and human inventions a term of communion, by introducing them into the constitution, faith, or worship of the Church, are, and have been, the immediate, obvious, and universally acknowledged causes of all the corruptions and divisions that ever have taken place in the Church of God.

(12) That all that is necessary to the highest state of perfection and purity of the Church upon earth is, first, that none be received as members but such as having that due measure of Scriptural self-knowledge described above, do profess their faith in Christ and obedience to Him in all things according to the Scriptures; nor, secondly, that any be retained in her communion longer than they continue to manifest the reality of their profession by their tempers and conduct. Thirdly, that her ministers, duly and Scripturally qualified, inculcate none other things than those very articles of faith and holiness expressly revealed and enjoined in the Word of God. Lastly, that in all their administrations they keep close by the observance of all Divine ordinances, after the example of the primitive Church, exhibited in the New Testament; without any additions whatsoever of human opinions or inventions of men.

(13) Lastly. That if any circumstantials indispensably necessary to the observance of Divine ordinances be not found upon the page of express revelation, such, and such only, as are absolutely necessary for this purpose should be adopted under the title of human expedients, without any pretence to a more sacred origin, so that any subsequent alteration or difference in the observance of these things might produce no contention nor division in the Church.

Text—Moore: *A Comprehensive History of the Disciples of Christ*, pp. 115-118.

IV. *THE CUMBERLAND PRESBYTERIANS*

A Circular Letter

"*Addressed to the Societies and Brethren of the Presbyterian Church recently under the care of the Council by the late Cumberland Presbytery, in which there is a correct statement of the origin, progress, and termination of the difference between the Synod of Kentucky and the former Presbytery of Cumberland.*" Russellville, Ky. Printed by Matthew Duncan, at the office of the "Farmer's Friend," 1810.

DEAR BRETHREN: The time is at last come when we must either sacrifice our religious liberties and conscience to what we judge unreasonable demands, cease our endeavors to promote the work of God among us as we have hitherto done, or constitute a Presbytery separate from the Synod of Kentucky. . . .

A number of you will easily recollect that about the close of the last century, or beginning of the present, God in a very remarkable manner began to revive his work amongst the inhabitants of this western country, the first symptoms of which appeared under the ministerial labors of the Rev. James McGready in Logan County. At the first commencement of this glorious revival, as also in its progress, the bodily affections and exercises of a number of those who were its subjects were very uncommon.   This soon caused a rumor to go abroad, and the people from every quarter *came out to see.* The consequence of which was, they not only had their curiosity satisfied, but a great number had their hearts deeply affected.   This, in the hand of God, was a blessed means of spreading the work through various parts of our country.   For a while, at first, all the ministers in our bounds seemed to participate in the glorious effusion of the Holy Spirit, and, correspondent to this, proclaimed themselves friends to the revival. But alas! it was soon after discoverable that some of them had changed their opinion, otherwise they had never been well established.   The consequence of this apparent change may easily be inferred; notwithstanding, the work still progressed.   And although the few who remained friends to the revival labored in the work of the ministry *night and day,* yet the cries of the people for more preaching were incessant; and those cries soon became so general that they were heard from many parts of an extensive frontier.   The ministers in return could only pity and pray for them; the congregations being so numerous, and in such a scattered situation, that they could not by any pos. sible endeavor supply them.

About this time a venerable father in the ministry, who was then resident in one of the upper counties of Kentucky, came down and attended a communion with some of our preachers in a vacant congregation; and he having learned the situation of our country, and the pressing demand that there was for more preaching, proposed the plan of encouraging such amongst us as appeared to be men of good talents, and who also discovered a disposition to exercise their gifts in a public way, to preach the gospel, although they might not have acquired that degree of human education which the letter of discipline requires.   This proposition was truly pleasing to our preachers, and, indeed, it found general acceptance amongst the people as soon as intimations thereof were given.   The consequence was, an uncommon spirit of prayer now seemed to prevail throughout the societies, that the great Head of the church would not only open an effectual door into the ministry, but also that he would raise up, qualify, and bring men into that sacred office, whose labors he would own and bless.   And, brethren, that God who never told *Israel to seek him in vain* evidently heard and answered the prayers of his people.   Some, whose minds had been previously impressed with the duty of calling sinners to repentance, and of bearing public testimony to the work of God and the religion of Jesus Christ, and upon whom also the eyes of the church for some time had been fixed with a degree of expectation, now made their exercise of mind on this subject known to their fathers in the ministry.   The prospect was truly pleasing to the preachers, yet they considered it expedient to act with the greatest caution; for although the step about to be taken was not unprecedented in the Presbyterian Church, yet, seeing it was out of the common track, they were well aware that some of their brethren in the ministry would oppose the measure.   However, they ventured to encourage three or four of the young men to prepare written discourses, and present them to the Transylvania Presbytery as a specimen of their abilities.   They accordingly prepared discourses, and at the next stated session of said Presbytery their case was brought before that reverend body.   They met with warm opposition, arising principally, however, from a quarter rather inimical to the revival.   But after a lengthy conversation on the subject, in which there was much altercation, a majority of the members consented and agreed that the young men might be permitted to read their discourses to an aged member alone, who should make report to the judicature.   We believe the report was favorable.   It was then directed, as well as we can recollect, that those men should prepare other discourses to be read at the next Presbytery. They accordingly prepared, and three of them attended; but as soon as the subject of their case was resumed, a warm debate ensued. At length, however, a majority of the members agreed to hear their discourses. After they were read the question was put: "Shall these men be received as candidates for the ministry?" The vote being taken, one of the three was received, and two rejected by a majority of one vote only. This circumstance much depressed the spirits of a number of the preachers who were real friends to the revival, and likewise the congregations generally, who had so earnestly desired their licensure; but more especially the spirits of those two candidates were depressed. They were men in a matrimonial state, and could not, consistently with those relative duties by which they were bound to their families, go and acquire the knowledge of all those forms of literature required by the Book of Discipline. Fain would they have returned home and solaced themselves in the enjoyment of their domestic comforts as private Christians, if they could have done so and kept a good conscience; but this they could not do; nor could they with clearness become members of any other Christian society where the ministerial door was not so strait and difficult, and consequently where they might have been at liberty to exercise their popular talents with approbation. No; they were attached to all the essential doctrines and likewise the Discipline of the Presbyterian Church. . . .

. . . In the meantime, candidates and other eminent characters who were assiduously endeavoring in one way or another to promote the work of God were encouraged by their fathers in the ministry to continue the exercise of their gifts in a way of public exhortation, which several of them did, laboring much till the next Presbytery; at which time several petitions were presented with hundreds of signatures, praying the Presbytery to license and send to their relief certain denominated persons. The subject was again taken into consideration, after which the Presbytery, who were personally acquainted with those men embraced in the petitions, knowing their piety, soundness in the faith, *aptness to teach*, etc., and taking into view the situation of the congregations and the extraordinary demand for preaching, determined to hear trial sermons from three or four of them (at the present session), to be considered as popular discourses; which accordingly were delivered and sustained by a large majority of the judicature. And after an examination on various subjects touching the ministry,which were also sustained, they were "licensed to preach the gospel within the bounds of the Transylvania Presbytery, or wherever else God in his providence might call them."

Certain members who had always been opposed to the measure entered their protest against the proceedings of the majority. But the majority were not deterred thereby from pursuing in their official capacity that method which they conscientiously believed best calculated to promote the Redeemer's kingdom in the world.

The Synod not long after this divided the Transylvania Presbytery, and formed what was called the Cumberland Presbytery; the bounds of which included all the members that attended the preceding session of the Transylvania Presbytery. Which act gave a decided majority in the new Presbytery to the promoters of the revival and those who were friendly to the licensure of the aforementioned young men; which majority ever after continued, and increased until the Presbytery were dissolved

. . . .

The members who entered their protest sent a petition to the next session of Synod, referring them to the protest, "which they thought should have operated as an appeal," in which they complained of various irregularities in the Cumberland Presbytery with respect to the licensure and ordination of men to the ministry. The Synod at that time did or said but little about the matter; but at their succeeding session they appointed a commission of Synod to meet shortly afterward in the bounds of the Cumberland Presbytery at Gasper River, and directed certain members of the commission to cite, previously to that meeting all our preachers, licentiates, candidates, and public exhorters, who generally met in obedience to the citation.

. . . .

After the commission had met, and also the accused (who were then known as the majority of the Cumberland Presbytery), the commission selected from the minutes and other sources a number of irregularities, as chargeable against the majority of the Presbytery. All of which, however, were comprised in the two following particulars, to wit: first, "the licensing unlearned men, or such as had not been examined on the learned languages, etc.; secondly, that those men who were licensed, both learned and unlearned, were only required to adopt the Confession of Faith partially—that is, as far as they believed it to agree with the Word of God."

. . . .

After much reasoning as well as positive assertion on the subject, the commission demanded of the Presbytery to give up to them all those men whom they had licensed and ordained for reexamination. The Presbytery refused, suggesting the danger of the example, and also that such a demand was without precedent. They moreover declared that they believed the Discipline of the Presbyterian Church had deposited the sole power in the several presbyteries to judge of the faith and qualifications of their own candidates for the ministry.

After the refusal of the Presbytery, the moderator of the commission proceeded to adjure the young men to submit to their authority and be reexamined; when one of them asked liberty for himself and brethren to retire and ask counsel of God before they would give an answer. This reasonable request was at first strongly opposed by one or two leading members of the commission, but at length it was granted, and the young men retired to ask counsel of Him who is all-wise. In a short time after, they returned, when they were asked individually if they would submit as above. They all (except one or two who wanted longer time to deliberate) answered in the negative, for the following reasons, to wit: first, they believed the Cumberland Presbytery, which was a regular church judicature, to be competent judges of the faith and abilities of their own candidates; secondly, that they themselves had not been charged with heresy or immorality; and if they had, the Presbytery would have been the proper judicature first to have called them to an account. Notwithstanding, the commission of Synod proceeded formally to prohibit all the men, learned and unlearned, whom the Cumberland Presbytery had licensed and ordained from preaching the gospel in the name of Presbyterians! And also cited what were called the Old Members to attend the next stated session of Synod to be examined on faith, and to answer for not having given up their young brethren to be reexamined.

. . . .

Some months after, there was a general meeting or council held at Shiloh, consisting of the ministers, elders, and representatives from vacancies which formerly composed a majority of Cumberland Presbytery. At that council it was agreed on to petition the General Assembly, and in the meantime cease our operations as a Presbytery, but continue to meet from time to time in the capacity of a council, and promote the interest of the church as well as we could, until an answer could be obtained from the Assembly. . .

.   .   .   .

The Assembly addressed a letter to the Synod informing them that what they had done "was at least of questionable regularity," and requested them to review their proceedings, and rectify what might have been done amiss. The Synod, we understood, reviewed, but confirmed all their commission had done. The council, notwithstanding, were encouraged to forward another petition. After which we were informed, by a private letter from another influential member of the Assembly, that it would be most proper for us to apply to the Synod to rescind their former order as it respected the Presbytery, and if they refused, then for the council to appeal to the Assembly, who, "no doubt, would redress their grievances" . . . But before there was an opportunity of doing so (after such conclusion), we heard, to our astonishment, that the Assembly had decided in favor of the Synod. This step at once superseded the necessity of an appeal; therefore the council generally thought it was now time to constitute into a Presbytery, and proceed to business again in that capacity. But some of the members wished to make the last effort with the Synod, who now had the business in their own hands, and the whole agreed, at the Ridge Meeting-house in August last, to propose their last terms and forward them to the Transylvania Presbytery or Synod by two commissioners to be appointed for that purpose, which was accordingly done, and the terms in substance were as follows:

"We, the preachers belonging to the council, both old and young, from a sincere desire to be in union with the general body of the Presbyterian Church, are willing to be examined on the tenets of our holy religion by the Transylvania Presbytery, Synod or a committee appointed for that purpose; taking along the idea, however, that we be received or rejected as a connected body. Also all our ministers, ordained and licentiates, retain their former authority derived from the Cumberland Presbytery. It was moreover understood, that if the Synod should require the preachers to re-adopt the Confession of Faith, it should be with the exception of fatality only."

Our commissioners were directed to go, and take a copy of the above minute, without any discretionary power whatsoever to alter the propositions in any way. And it was unanimously agreed and determined, that if the Synod would not accede to the propositions, on the fourth Tuesday in October ensuing they (the whole council) would go into a constituted state. The comissioners accordingly went to the Synod, and after their return informed us that the Synod would not consider our case as a body, but as individuals; neither would they suffer any of our preachers to make the exception to the Confession of Faith.

.   .   .   .

"In Dixon County, Tennessee State, at the Rev. Samuel McAdow's this fourth day of February, 1810.

"We, Samuel McAdow, Finis Ewing, and Samuel King, regularly ordained ministers in the Presbyterian Church, against whom no charge, either of immorality or heresy, has ever been exhibited before any of the church judicatures, having waited in vain more than four years, in the meantime petitioning the General Assembly for a redress of grievances and a restoration of our violated rights, have and do hereby agree and determine to constitute into a Presbytery, known by the name of the Cumberland Presbytery, on the following conditions, to wit: all candidates for the ministry who may hereafter be licensed by this Presbytery, and all the licentiates or probationers who may hereafter be ordained by this Presbytery, shall be required, before such licensure and ordination, to receive and adopt the Confession and Discipline of the Presbyterian Church, except the idea of fatality, that seems to be taught under the mysterious doctrine of predestination. It is to be understood, however, that such as can clearly receive the Confession without an exception shall not be required to make any. Moreover, all licentiates, before they are set apart to the whole work of the ministry (or ordained), shall be required to undergo an examination on English grammer, geography, astronomy, natural and moral philosophy, and church history. The Presbytery may also require an examination on all or any part of the above branches of literature, before licensure, if they deem it expedient."

Thus, brethren, we have, in the integrity of our hearts, endeavored to give you as correct and impartial an account of the rise and progress of the cause or causes that have brought us into our present situation, as justice to ourselves and our best recollection would admit. We have not intentionally and unjustly exposed or covered the conduct of any man or judicature. We have only aimed at giving a clear, honest view of the matter, that you might be enabled to judge for yourselves whether we have acted with propriety or impropriety. If we be in error, we are not conscious of it.

We think, brethren, precipitancy or rashness cannot be justly imputed to us in the present case. . . .

Permit us further to inform you what we do know to be an incontestable fact—that is, there are a number of ministers who are kept in the bosom of the Presbyterian Church who have deviated infinitely more from the Confession than we have done. One can boldly deny the imputation of Christ's active obedience to the sinner in justification and publish it to the world; another can deny the operation of the Holy Spirit in the work of regeneration; and yet we, who only object to the unqualified idea of eternal reprobation, cannot be indulged in that objection!

. . . .

Some have feared because of the smallness of our number. Brethren, we have yet left in the bounds of our Presbytery almost as many ministers, exclusive of candidates, as our blessed Lord chose to spread the gospel through the world. . . .

Some of you are afraid you cannot be supplied by the Presbytery. Brethren, the same almighty *Lord of the harvest* who heard your prayers on that subject ten years ago is willing to hear again. Is *the harvest* indeed *great and the laborers few?* Well, then, pray the Lord to send more laborers.

Some fear lest the Presbytery should take too much liberty in licensing and ordaining unlearned men. If by this you mean you are afraid the Presbytery (in some instances) will dispense with the dead languages, your fears are well grounded. But if you are afraid we will license and ordain without a good English education, we hope your fears are without foundation. And while we thus candidly declare our intention to receive men as candidates, without a knowledge of languages, who are men of good talents, and who appear to be evidently called of God, (believing, as we do, that there are thousands in the Presbyterian Church of such description, who would make more able, respectable, and more useful ministers of Jesus Christ than many who say they have been brought up at the feet of Gamaliel), we would nevertheless recommend it to all parents who have sons who promise fair for the ministry, to have them taught the Greek language, especially the Greek Testament. Some of us, brethren, intend to do ourselves what we here recommend, and thereby more fully convince you of our sincerity.

. . . .

SAMUEL MCADOW, *Moderator."*

Test, YOUNG EWING, *Clerk.*

Text—Foster: *A Sketch of the Cumberland Presbyterian Church,* (Amer. Ch. Hist. Series Vol. XI) pp. 272-285.

V. *THE SHAKERS*

A Brief Exposition &c.

Many erroneous opinions are entertained concerning the people generally known by the name of Shakers, which are calculated to mislead the public mind, in respect to the true character of this *Society.* Many false reports and incorrect statements have been circulated respecting our principles and practice, which have no foundation in truth. With a view to correct these erroneous opinions, and as far as in our power, to remove prejudices and false impressions, we are induced, from a sense of duty, to lay before the candid public a brief statement of facts respecting the principles, government, temporal order, and practical regulations of the Society. . . .

I. FAITH AND PRINCIPLES OF THE SOCIETY

1. A life of *innocence* and *purity,* according to the example of Jesus Christ and his first true followers; implying entire abstinence from all sensual and carnal gratifications.
2. LOVE. . . .
3. PEACE. —"Follow peace with all men," is a divine precept, hence our abstinence from war and bloodshed, from all acts of violence towards our fellow men, from all the party contentions and politics of the world, and from all the pursuits of pride and worldly ambition. "My kingdom (said Christ) is not of this world."
4. JUSTICE. . . .
5. HOLINESS. . . .
6. GOODNESS. . . .
7. TRUTH. . . .

II. OF ADMITTING MEMBERS

It must be obvious to every reasonable person, that the foregoing principles are, in many respects, very contrary to the carnal and selfish nature of fallen man, and doubtless more so than those of any other religious society. Therefore there is little danger to be apprehended of any person's being flattered or inveigled into this Society, or of joining it from any other motive than purely from the operations of faith & conscience. This of itself is the most powerful guard that can be set against the deceptions so often reported to be practised by the Society in procuring members. Indeed it precludes the possibility of such deceptions to any alarming extent. To this it may be truly added, that all reasonable precaution is used against admitting any person to membership while ignorant of our real faith and principles, or of the following *General Rules.*

1. All persons who unite with us, in any degree, must do it freely and voluntarily, according to their own faith and unbiased judgment.
2. In our testimony, both public and private, no flattery, nor any undue influence is used; but the most plain and explicit statements of our faith and principles are laid

before the inquirer; so that the whole ground may be comprehended, as far as possible by every candidate for admission.

3. No considerations of property are ever made use of, to induce any person to join us, nor to prevent any one from leaving us; because it is our faith, that no act of devotion or service that does not flow from the free and voluntary emotions of the heart, can be acceptable to God as an act of true religion.

4. No believing husband or wife is allowed, by our rules, to separate from an unbelieving partner, except by mutual agreement; unless the conduct of the unbeliever be such as to warrant a separation by the laws of the land. Nor can any husband or wife who has otherwise abandoned his or her partner, be received into communion with the Society.

5. Any person becoming a member must rectify all his wrongs, and, as fast and as far as it is in his power, discharge all just and legal claims, whether of creditors or filial heirs. Nor can any person, not conforming to this rule, long remain in union with the Society. But the Society is not responsible for the debts of any individual, except by agreement; because such responsibility would involve a principle ruinous to the institution.

6. No difference is to be made in the distribution of parental estate among the heirs, whether they belong to the society or not; but an equal partition must be made as far as may be practicable and consistent with reason and justice.

7. If an unbelieving wife separate from a believing husband, by agreement, the husband must give her a just and reasonable share of the property; and if they have children who have arrived to years of understanding sufficient to judge for themselves, and who chuse to go with their mother, they are not to be disinherited on that account. Tho the character of this institution has been much censured on this ground; yet we boldly assert that the rule above stated has never, to our knowledge, been violated by this Society.

8. Industry, temperance, and frugality are prominent features of this institution. No member who is able to labor, can be permitted to live idly upon the labors of others. All are required to be employed in some manual occupation, according to their several abilities, when not engaged in other necessary duties.

III. Manner of Government

. . . .

1. The effective basis of the government so established, and which is the support of all its institutions, is the faith, voluntary choice, union and general approbation of the members. It is an established maxim in the Society, that any member who is not reconciled to the faith, order, and government established in it, is more injurious than beneficial to it; besides the loss to himself of his own time and privilege; therefore, whenever this is found to be the case with any one, and he continues in that situation, he is advised peaceably to withdraw. As all who unite with this Society do it voluntarily, and can at any time withdraw, they are in duty bound to submit to its government. . . .

2. The first leading gift in the Society is vested in a Ministry, generally consisting of four persons, including both sexes. It belongs to the Ministry to appoint Elders and Trustees. These, in union with the Ministry, constitute the general government of the Society in all its branches, and being supported by the general union and approbation of the members, are invested with power to appoint their successors and other

subordinate officers, as occasion may require, to counsel, advise and direct in all matters, whether of a spiritual or temporal nature; to superintend the concerns of the several families, and establish all needful orders, rules, & regulations for the direc tion and protection of the several branches of the Society; but no rules can be made, nor any member assume a lead, contrary to the original faith & known principles of the Society. And nothing which respects the government, order and general arrangement of the Society, is considered as fully established, until it has received the general approbation of the Society, or of that branch of it which it more immediately concerns.

3. No creed can be framed to limit the progress of improvement. It is the faith of the society, that the operations of divine light are unlimited. All are at liberty to improve their talents and exercise their gifts, the younger being subject to the elder, and all in concert with the general lead.

4. In the order and government of the Society no corporal punishment is approved, nor any external force or violence exercised on any member. *Faith, Conscience,* or *Reason* is sufficient to influence a rational being, but where these are wanting, the necessary and proper means of restraint are not prohibited.

5. The management of temporal affairs, in families holding a united interest,as far as respects the consecrated property of the Society, is committed to Trustees. These are appointed by the Ministry and Elders; and being supported as aforesaid. are legally invested with the fee of the real estate belonging to the Society.

All the consecrated property comes under their general charge, together with the oversight of all public business, & all commercial dealings without the bounds of the community. But all the transactions of the Trustees, in the use, management, and disposal of this united interest must be done in behalf, and for the joint benefit of the Society, and not for any personal or private use or purpose whatever. And in all these things, they are strictly responsible to the general lead of the Society for the faithful performance of their duty.

It is also an established principle, that no Trustee, nor any member whatever. shall contract debts of any kind, in behalf of the Society.

IV. ORDER AND ARRANGEMENT OF THE SOCIETY

THIS community, is divided into several different branches, commonly called ïamilies. This division is generally made for the sake of convenience, and is often rendered necessary on account of local situation and occurrent circumstances; but the proper division and arrangement of the community, without respect to local situation is into three classes, or progressive degrees of order, as follows:

1. The first, or novitiate class, are those who receive our faith, and come into a degree of relation, but chuse to live in their own family order, and manage their own temporal concerns. Any who chuse, may live in that order, and be owned as brethren and sisters in the gospel, so long as they live up to its requirements.

Parents are to be kind and dutiful to each other, to shun every appearance of evil. provide for their family, bring up their children in a godly manner, use, improve, and dispose of their property wisely, and manage their affairs according to their own discretion. They may thus continue as long as it comports with their faith, their circumstances, and their spiritual improvement. But they are required to bear in mind the necessity and importance of a spiritual increase, without which they are ever exposed to fall back into the course and spirit of the world; and they can hold their connection with the Society, only so long as they continue to conform to its religious faith and principles.

Such persons are admitted to all the privileges in the Society spiritual or temporal, necessary to give them a full understanding of all that they wish to know. No control is exercised, by the Society, over their persons, property, nor children; but being members of a religious society, they are to be subject to the spiritual direction of their leaders, and may receive counsel in temporal matters, whenever they feel it necessary to apply. If at any time they desire to make a donation to any religious or charitable purpose of the Society, they are at liberty to do so; provided they be clear of debt, and their circumstances will otherwise admit of it; but after having freely made the donation, they can have no more right to reclaim it, than the members of other religious societies have to reclaim the like donations.

The education and government of children belonging to this class, is an important object. Where the number of private families is sufficient, they may establish a school, and jointly contribute to the support of it, and in this way dispose of their property for the joint benefit of their posterity; but if any have estates, they may reserve them, in whole or in part, for the benefit of their children when they become of age.

No children are ever taken under the immediate charge of the Society, except with the free consent of all parties. But few comparatively are admitted.

Those taken into the Society are treated with care and tenderness, receive a good school education, according to genius, are trained to industry and virtuous habits, restrained from vice, and at a suitable age, led into the knowledge of the Sacred Scriptures, & practically taught the divine precepts contained in them, particularly those of Jesus Christ and the Apostles.

2. The second, or junior class, is composed of persons who, not having the charge of families, and being under no embarrassments to hinder them from uniting together in community order, chuse to enjoy the benefits of that situation. These (for mutual safety) enter into a contract to devote their services, freely, to support the interest of the family of which they are members, so long as they continue in that order; stipulating, at the same time, to claim no pecuniary compensation for their services. But all the members of such families are mutually benefitted by the united interest and labors of the whole family, so long as they continue to support the order thereof; and they are amply provided for in health, sickness, and old age. These benefits are secured to them by contract.

Members of this class or order have the privilege, at their option, by contract, to give the improvement of any part or all of their property, to be freely used for the mutual benefit of the family to which they belong. The property itself may be resumed at any time, according to the contract; but no interest can be claimed for the use thereof; nor can any member of such family be employed therein for wages of any kind. Members of this order may retain the lawful ownership of all their own property as long as they think it proper, and chuse so to do, but at any time, after having sufficient experience, to be able to act deliberately and understandingly, they may, if they chuse, dedicate and devote a part or the whole, and consecrate it forever, to the support of the institution. But this is a matter of free choice, we urge no one to do so, but they are rather advised, in such cases, to consider the matter well, so as not to do it until they have a full understanding of its consequences; lest they should do it prematurely, and afterwards repent of it.

3. The third, or *Senior* class is composed of such persons as have had sufficient time and opportunity practically to prove our faith and manner of life, and are thus prepared to enter fully, freely, and voluntarily, into a united and consecrated interest. These, solemnly, covenant and agree to dedicate and devote themselves and services, with all they possess, to the service of God and the support of the gospel forever, solemnly promising never to bring debt, nor damage, claim nor demand against the Society, nor against any member thereof, for any property or service which they have thus devoted to the uses and purposes of the institution.

To enter fully into this order, is considered by the Society to be a matter of the utmost importance to the parties concerned, and therefore requires the most mature and deliberate consideration; for after having made such a dedication, according to the laws of justice and equity there can be no ground for retraction. Nor can they by those laws, recover any thing whatever which has been thus dedicated. Of this all are fully apprised before entering into the contract. Yet should any afterward withdraw, and be disappointed in their worldly prospects, the society may charitably supply their wants as a matter of grace, but not of debt, nor to support them in idleness and dissipation. No person who withdraws peaceably is sent away empty.

During a period of more than forty years, since the permanent establishment of this Society, at New–Lebanon and Watervliet, there never has been a legal claim entered, by any person, for the recovery of property brought into the Society; but all claims of that nature, if any have existed, have been amicably settled to the satisfaction of the parties concerned. Complaints and legal prosecutions have not, hitherto, come from persons who brought property into the Institution; but from those who came destitute of property, and who, generally speaking have been no benefit to the Society, in any way; but on the contrary, after having enjoyed its hospitality, and brought no small share of trouble upon the people, have had the assurance to lay claim to wages which they never earned, or property to which they never had any just nor legal claim.

No person can be received into this order until he shall have settled all just and legal claims, both of creditors and filiar heirs; so that whatever property he may possess, may be justly and truly his own. Minors cannot be admitted as covenant members of this order; yet they may be received under its immediate care and protection. And when they shall have arrived at a lawful age, if they should chuse to continue in the Society, and sign the covenant of the order, and support its principles, they are then admitted to all the privileges of members. The members of this order are all equally entitled to the benefits and privileges thereof, without any difference made on account of what any one may have contributed to the interest of the Society. All are equally entitled to their support and maintenance, and to every necessary comfort, whether in health, sickness or old age, so long as they continue to maintain the principles, and conform to the orders, rules and regulations of the institution. They therefore give their property and services for the most valuable of all temporal considerations; an ample security, during life, for every needful support, if they continue faithful to their contract and covenant, the nature of which they clearly understand before they enter into it.

. . . .

This Society [New-Lebanon] has served as a pattern for all the societies or branches of the community which have been established in various parts of the United States. In every place where the faith & testimony of the Society has been planted, the same orders and rules of government have been gradually established & maintained; so that the Society and its members are now generally known; and from the striking peculiarities which distinguish them from all other societies, no person need be deceived by imposters.

The perpetuity of the Society is the last thing to be considered, on which we offer the following remarks.

We believe it will be generally granted, that the history of the world does not furnish a single instance of any religious institution, which has stood fifty years without a visible declension of the principles of the institution in the general purity and integrity of its members. This has been generally acknowledged by the devotees of such institutions, and facts have fully verified it. But we would appeal to the candid judgment of those who have known this institution from the beginning, and have had a fair opportunity of observing the progress of its improvement, whether they have, in reality, found any declension, either in the external order and regulations of the Society, or in the purity and integrity of its members, in the general practice of the moral and christian duties; and whether they have not, on the contrary, discovered a visible and manifest increase in all these respects. . . .

Published in behalf of the Society, by

CALVIN GREEN) Committee
and   )   of
SETH Y. WELLS) Publication

New-Lebanon, March 15th, 1830.

Text—Green and Wells: *A Brief Exposition of the Established Principles, and Regulations of the United Society of Believers Called Shakers,* edited by McNemar and Spining, pp. 3-14.

VI. *THE SEPARATISTS OF ZOAR*

The Principles of Bimeler

"I. We believe and confess the Trinity of God; Father, Son and Holy Ghost.

II. The fall of Adam, and of all mankind, with the loss thereby of the likeness of God in them.

III. The return through Christ to God, our proper Father.

IV. The Holy Scriptures as the measure and guide of our lives, and the touchstone of truth and falsehood. All our other principles arise out of these, and rule our conduct in the religious, spiritual, and natural life.

V. All ceremonies are banished from among us, and we declare them useless and injurious, and this is the chief cause of our Separation.

VI. We render to no mortal, honors due to God, as to uncover the head, or to bend the knee. Also we address every one as 'thou'—*du.*

VII. We separate ourselves from all ecclesiastical connections and constitutions, because true Christian life requires no sectarianism, while set forms and ceremonies cause sectarian divisions.

VIII. Our marriages are contracted by mutual consent, and before witnesses. They are then notified to the political authority; and we reject all intervention of priests or preachers.

IX. All intercourse of the sexes, except what is necessary to the perpetuation of the species, we hold to be sinful and contrary to the order and command of God.

Complete virginity or entire cessation of sexual commerce is more commendable than marriage.

X. We can not send our children into the schools of Babylon (meaning the clerical schools of Germany), where other principles contrary to these are taught.

XI. We can not serve the state as soldiers, because a Christian can not murder his enemy, much less his friend.

XII. We regard the political government as absolutely necessary to maintain order, and to protect the good and honest and punish the wrongdoers; and no one can prove us to be untrue to the constituted authorities."

Text—*Publications Ohio Archeological and Historical Society*, Vol. VIII, pp. 13-14.

Constitution of 1832

"*In the Name of God the Father, and Jesus Christ, the Son, and the Holy Ghost, Amen.*

In order furthermore to secure to our consciences that satisfaction, proceeding from the faithful execution of those duties which the Christian religion demands, and to plant and establish the Spirit of Love as the bond of Peace and Unity for a permanent foundation of social order for ourselves and our posterity forever, we, therefore, seek and desire, in accordance to pure Christian principles, to unite our various individual interests into one common stock and conformably with the example of the Primitive Christians, all inequalities and distinctions of rank and fortune shall be abolished from amongst us, and, consequently, to live as brethren and sisters of one common family.

Pursuant to the foregoing principles and resolution, we, voluntarily, unite and bind ourselves by this joint agreement, under the name and title of Separatist Society of Zoar. And we obligate ourselves, each to the other, that we will hold to the following articles and rules, that we will observe and support the same to the best of our abilities, which from the day of the date hereof, shall be in force and virtue in law:

Article I

Regulating Elections

All elections, for the divers necessary officers of the Society, shall, agreeable with the provisions of the act of incorporation, be held on the second Tuesday of May, annually, and in accordance with the statute of the State of Ohio, be decided by ballot and majority of votes. . .

Article II

Election of Trustees and Their Duties

The Society shall elect from amongst its members three suitable persons as its Directors or Trustees, and their successors in office, who shall take charge of the joint property of all undersigned members. Said Trustees shall, as stated in the first article, be elected by majority and agreeable to the following regulations: The majority for three years; second majority for two years, and third majority for one year, and after the expiration of one year, annually one Trustee. . .

Said Trustees are hereby empowered and in duty bound to take charge of all the property, real and personal, which this Society, either now or in the future, may possess, including all property of newly acquired members, movable and immovable, of whatever name and description it may be; likewise are they authorized to receive all kinds of legacies, donations and personal claims, in fine every species of property to which any one of the members may at any time have just claim, to demand and collect the same by legal proceedings, and shall appropriate and apply the same conscientiously to the best of their knowledge and skill, in behalf and for the exclusive benefit, use and advantage of said Society. And it shall also be the duty of said Trustees, carefully to furnish each member, without respect to person, with board, clothing and dwelling and other necessaries, alike in days of sickness and of health, as good as circumstances will allow. Said Trustees shall furthermore take charge of the economical affairs of this Society, to consult over and direct all the business, and consequently to assign to each individual member its duty and work to be performed, to which at least the majority of said Trustees, if not all of them, shall be agreed. . .

. . . .

Article VI

Delivery of Property, and Duties of the Members

We, the undersigned, members second class of the Separatist Society of Zoar, declare by these presents, that all our property, of all and every description, which we either now or in future may possess, movable or immovable, or both; together with all claims, titles, rights, devise and legacies, etc., of whatever kind and name they may be, as well for our own selves, as our descendants, heirs, executors and administrators, shall be forever given up to said Society, with the express condition, that such property shall, from the date of the signature of each member, forever henceforth, consequently after the death of each respective member, be and remain the exclusive property of said Society. Also do we promise and bind ouselves, most faithfully and industriously to execute all the orders and regulations of said Trustees and their sub-trustees or agents, without opposition and murmuring; and we likewise agree to apply all our strength, good will, industry and skill, for life, to the general benefit of said Society, and to the satisfaction of its Trustees. Likewise do we promise and agree, under the same conditions and regulations, to place our children, whilst they are in a state of minority, under the directions and regulations of said Trustees, in same manner, as if they were legally bounden by lawful indenture, to them and their successors in office, until they shall have attained their proper age, as defined by the laws of this State.

Article VII

Acceptance of Members

In accepting new members, the following rule and order is to be observed: Each and every person wishing and desiring to become a member of the second class of this Society shall first of all have attained to the lawful age; that is, a male person shall be twenty-one and a female eighteen years of age; secondly, shall such person or persons have lived in, and dwelled with the Society, for the term of at least one year, and shall have been a member of the first class of this Society, (without exception, if even born and educated in the Society) and provided, that they have faithfully fulfilled the contract, previously concluded with the Trustees of this Society at their entrance into the first class. . . . .

ARTICLE VIII

Education Institute

In accordance with this article the Society shall keep or establish a general education institute for all the children in the community, at the head of which such male or female overseers shall be placed, whose qualifications shall be found best suited for said purpose. And agreeable to this proviso, all the parents of children in this Society, bind themselves by these presents, to deliver up and place their children, after having arrived at the third year of their age, or sooner, to the overseers of said institution, where such children shall receive, according to their age and faculties, appropriate education and tuition. . . .

. . . .

ARTICLE X

Contentions, Etc.

Casual contentions between two or more members, and complaints of whatever kind and description they may be, shall be brought before the Trustees and by them to be examined and settled.   But, in case one or the other party should not be satisfied with the decision of said Trustees, or should any one or more of the Trustees be envolved in such contentions, etc., then appeal may be had to the Standing Committee or Court of Appeal, whose decisions shall in all cases be final and binding; whosoever shall act contrary to this provision, and will not be satisfied with their judgment looseth and debarreth him or herself of all further enjoyments and rights of a member.

ARTICLE XI

Seceding Members

Should any member or members find cause to secede from the Society, they shall make known such their intentions to one or more of the Trustees, whose duty it shall be to notify the Society thereof, in order that if any complaints be existing against such member or members, they may betimes brought forward to said Trustees, who shall thenceforward act in respect to them agreeable to all the attending circumstances. . .

In case any seceding person should refuse to comply with the demands of the Trustees, in pursuance of the decision of the Standing Committee, the Trustees shall be authorized to prosecute such person or persons, and by course of law to bring them, or cause them to be brought to the due fulfillment of the duty or payment as aforesaid. . . . "

Text—*Publications Ohio Archeological and Historical Society*, Vol. VIII, pp. 88-95.

CHAPTER XIX

THE ERA OF ORGANIZATION

Bibliography

The awakening of interest in world evangelization throughout America is connected with the corresponding, though slightly earlier, movement in Britain. As a preliminary study it is therefore necessary to acquaint oneself with the salient facts of Carey's career and the organization of the pioneer British missionary societies. For William Carey, the following will be found sufficient: "The Story of Carey, Marshman, and Ward" (II Vols. 1859) by J. C. Marshman; "The Life of William Carey, D.D., Shoemaker and Missionary" (new ed. 1888) by George Smith; and "William Carey and Others, Serampore Letters; Being the Unpublished Correspondence of William Carey and Others with John Williams, 1800-1816" (new ed. 1898) edited by Leighton and Mornay Williams.

The Baptist Missionary Society has been well presented by F. A. Cox in his "History of the Baptist Missionary Society" (II Vols. 1842). From an extensive bibliography on the Church Missionary Society the following is selected as sufficient for the purpose in hand: "The Early History of the Church Missionary Society to A.D. 1814" (1896) by Rev. Charles Hole; "One Hundred Years: Being the Short Story of the Church Missionary Society" (1898) by Eugene Stock; and "The History of the Church Missionary Society: Its Environment, Its Men and Its Work" (III Vols. 1899) by the same author. On the London Missionary Society there is "The Story of the London Missionary Society, 1795-1895" (new ed. 1904) by Rev. C. Sylvester Thorne, and the more exhaustive ". . . History of the London Missionary Society, 1795-1895" (II Vols. 1899) by Richard Lovett, M.A. In the "Baptist Register" (first four volumes) there will be found some British missionary literature that was finding its way into American churches.

Passing to the American field proper, there are several histories that treat the subject in a general way. The earliest is "A Sketch or History of the Principal Attempts to Propagate Christianity among the Heathen" (1819) by Miron Winslow, A.M. Next came a "History of American Missions" (1834) by Rev. S. Worcester. This work was soon

362

completely outclassed by "The Origin and History of Missions, . . ."
(1832) by Rev. John Choules and Rev. Thomas Smith, continued (II
Vols. 1838-39) by John Williams. Shortly after appeared a "History
of American Missions to the Heathen from their Commencement to the
Present time" (1840) edited by Joseph Tracy. A scholarly work discussing in detail the activities of the various missionary societies but failing to
trace the circumstances out of which each of these societies arose, is that
of Rev. William Brown, M.D., "The History of the Christian Missions
of the Sixteenth, Seventeenth and Eighteenth Centuries, . . ." (3rd
ed. enlarged and improved, III Vols. 1864). In an "Outline ot the History of Protestant Missions, . . ." by Dr. Gustav Warneck (translated
from the German by Rev. Thomas Smith, 1882, later edition, 1901) brief
reference is made to features of outstanding interest in the field of American activity. "The Encyclopaedia of Missions" (1891) edited by Rev.
E. M. Bliss, has many informing articles, and an exhaustive bibliography. "A Hundred Years of Missions . . ." (1895) by D. L. Leonard
is well written, but designed only for popular purposes.

In respect of denominational histories, the Baptists are represented
by "A History of American Baptist Missions, . . ." (1849) by W. Gammell, a work of careful execution, though now antiquated; "The Story of
Baptist Missions in Foreign Lands, . . ." (centennial ed. 1892) by Rev.
G. W. Hervey, quite popular, though not superficial; and "A History of
American Baptist Missions (1900, new edition 1913) by Rev. E. F. Mer-
riam, a serviceable manual for beginners, but in no sense equal to the
demands of an exacting investigator. "The Morning Hour of American
Baptist Missions" (1907) by Albert L. Vail is a popular monograph well
written and packed with information for the busy layman, but not sufficient for the careful student of missionary institutions.

For the Methodists, there is the excellent work "Missions and
Missionary Societies of the Methodist Episcopal Church" (II Vols.
1879) by Rev. J. M. Reid, revised and extended (III Vols. 1896) by Rev.
J. P. Gracey; also an older informing but unindexed "History of the
Missions of the Methodist Episcopal Church from the Organization of
the Missionary Society to the Present Time" (1850) by Rev. W. P.
Strickland.

For the Presbyterians, there is a "Historical Sketch of the Domestic
and Foreign Missions of the Presbyterian Church of the United States"
(1838, revised and supplemented, 1868, by J. C. Lowrie) by Ashbel Green;
and the "Origin of the Board of Foreign Missions of the Presbyterian
Church, United States of America" (1879) by W. H. Howard.

Lutheran interest in evangelization appears in a "History of Lutheran Missions" (1900) by Rev. Preston A. Laury.

Turning from histories general and denominational, we pass to Samuel J. Mills who played such a significant part in the organization of American foreign missionary work. Of biographies there are the following: "Memoirs of the Rev. Samuel J. Mills" (several editions, 1820 f.) by Gardiner Spring; "Memoirs of American Missionaries formerly connected with the Society of Inquiry, Published under the direction of the Society" (1833); "A Story of One Short Life (Samuel J. Mills)" (n.d.) by Elizabeth G. Stryker; "Samuel J. Mills, Missionary Pathfinder, Pioneer, and Promoter" (1906) by Thomas C. Richards. The last is a valuable work, written in a scholarly spirit, with an exhaustive bibliography. Several histories refer to Mills, as follows: "A Biographical History of the County of Litchfield, Connecticut" (1851); "History of Torrington, Connecticut" (1878) by Rev. Samuel Orcutt; "Torringford: In connection with the Centennial of the first pastor, Rev. Samuel J. Mills" (1870); "History of the Foreign Missionary Work in Litchfield County during the present Century" (n.d.) by Mrs. G. P. and Miss L. E. Prudden; "Historical Records of the Town of Cornwall, Litchfield County, Connecticut" (1877) by T. S. Gold. Various articles concerning Mills appear in the "Massachusetts Missionary Magazine," "Evangelical Magazine," "Panoplist," "Religious Intelligencer," "Missionary Register," "Christian Spectator," "Missionary Herald," "American Quarterly Register," "American Theological Review," and "Hartford Seminary Record" (for list see "Samuel J. Mills" by Richards, as above, pp. 269-271). Especially worthy of mention is the "Origin of American Foreign Missions" by Rev. S. M. Worcester, D.D. ("Amer. Theol. Rev." November 1860.)

How the American Board of Commissioners for Foreign Missions came into being, and the record of its achievements has been set forth by William E. Strong in "The Story of the American Board: An Account of the First Hundred Years of the American Board for Foreign Missions" (1910). There is also a "Memorial Volume of the First Fifty Years of the American Board of Commissioners for Foreign Missions" (1861) by Rufus Anderson. Still older is the "History of the American Board of Commissioners for Foreign Missions" (1840, 2nd ed. 1842) by Joseph Tracy.

Adoniram Judson has been the subject of several memoirs, of which the most notable are those of J. Clement (1851), Francis Wayland (II Vols. 1853), his son Edward (1883), and W. C. Richards (1890). The careers of the three Mrs. Judson have been set forth by James D. Knowles

(1829), Emily C. Jackson (1847), Mrs. A. W. Stewart (1852), Mrs. C. L. Balfour (1854), and A. C. Kenrick (1860). Luther Rice is the subject of a memoir by James B. Taylor (1840); and Mrs. Harriet Newell, by Rev. Leonard Woods (1816). A "Memoir of George Dana Boardman, Late Missionary to Burmah" (enlarged edition 1852) by Alonzo King, with an Introductory Essay by William R. Williams fills an important place.

For the organization of the Baptist Society for Propagating the Gospel in India and Other Parts, the Philadelphia Convention of May 14, 1814, and the subsequent periodic meetings of the Triennial Convention, copious details are given in "The American Baptist Missionary Magazine," the "American Baptist Missionary Union—Fiftieth Anniversary at Philadelphia" (1865), and "Missionary Sketches; Concise History of the American Baptist Union" (1879) by S. F. Smith.

For the American Bible Society, one should consult the "Report of John F. Schermerhorn and Samuel J. Mills to the Philadelphia Bible Society" (1813); "A Correct View of that Part of the United States which lies west of the Alleghany mountains with regard to Religion and Morals" (1814) by John F. Schermerhorn and Samuel J. Mills; "Report to the Society for propagating the Gospel Among the Indians and Others in North America" by John F. Schermerhorn and Samuel J. Mills (1814, "Coll. Mass. Hist. Soc." Ser. II, Vol. II); "Report of a Missionary Tour through that part of the United States which lies west of the Alleghany mountains; performed under the direction of the Massachusetts Missionary Society, by Samuel J. Mills, and Daniel Smith" (1815). The "History of the American Bible Society" (1856) by W. P. Strickland, and the "American Bible Society, Jubilee Number" will fill in all necessary details connected with the organization of this society. "The Centennial History of the American Bible Society" (1916) by Henry Otis Dwight is a rich treasury of information.

The New York Religious Tract Society, and the New England Tract Society which later became the American Tract Society, may be studied through the contemporary religious periodicals (see below); also in "American Tract Society—First Ten Years, 1814-1823" (III Vols. also in condensed single volume).

On Williams College there are two works: the "History of Williams College" (1860) by Rev. Calvin Durfee, and "Williamstown and Williams College" (3rd ed. 1904) by Arthur L. Perry, LL.D.

Andover Theological Seminary is the subject of a "History" (1885) by Rev. Leonard Woods. "A Memorial of the Semi-Centennial Celebration of the Founding of the Theological Seminary at Andover" (1859) supplies useful information. A "Memoir of the Life and Character of Ebenezer Porter, D.D. late President of the Theological Seminary at Andover" (1836) by Lyman Matthews merits attention.

The American Education Society has not been written up in any worthy manner. Its annual "Reports" are summarized in the magazines of the period (see below). A "Memoir of the Rev. Elias Cornelius" (1833) by B. B. Edwards is the nearest approach to a history.

It was during this period of organization that many religious journals came into being. They are as follows: "The Armenian (American) Magazine" (1789, for only a few years), "The New York Missionary Magazine" (1800), "The Connecticut Evangelical Magazine" (1800-1807) becoming later (1808) "The Connecticut Evangelical Magazine and Religious Intelligencer," "The Massachusetts Missionary Magazine" (1803-8), "The Massachusetts Baptist Missionary Magazine" (1803) later becoming "The American Baptist Magazine," "The Missionary Herald" (1804), "The Panoplist" (1805), "The Churchman's Magazine" (1806), "The Methodist Magazine" (1818), "The Christian Watchman" (1819), "The Wesleyan Repository" (1821), "The Baptist Christian Secretary" (1822), "The American Missionary Register" (1820), "The Quarterly Register and Journal of the American Education Society" (1827), "The Spirit of Missions" (1836—Episcopalian). For more complete list see "Quar. Jour. Amer. Educ. Soc." Oct. 1828, p. 132. For the Unitarian magazines, see p. 392f.

These magazines will be found indispensable for annual reports of the various Missionary, Bible, Female, Mite, Cent, and Educational Societies. They also furnish reprints of representative missionary literature.

DOCUMENTS

I. THE EARLIER MISSIONARY SOCIETIES

Missionary Society of Connecticut

Organized June 19, 1796, with the following Constitution:

"The General Association of the State of Connecticut, impressed with the obligation on all the friends of Christianity to propagate a knowledge of its gracious and holy doctrines, also encouraged by the late zealous exertions for this end, in sundry Christian bodies, cannot but hope the time is near in which God will spread his truth through the earth. They also consider it a thing of great importance that some charitable assistance be extended to new Christian settlements in various parts of the United States. The salvation of these souls is precious. The happiness of the rising generation and the order and stability of civil government are most effectually advanced by the diffusion of religious and moral sentiments through the preaching of the gospel. In deep feeling of these truths, having by prayer sought the direction of God, in the fear of His great name, they have adopted the following Constitution of a Missionary Society:

Article I. This society shall be known by the name of the Missionary Society.

Article II. The General Association of the State of Connecticut shall be the said Missionary Society.

Article III. The General Association shall, annually, by ballot, appoint twelve trustees, whereof six shall be clergymen and six shall be brethren of our churches, who shall conduct the business of our society in the manner hereinafter prescribed.

Article IV. The object of this society shall be to christianize the heathen in North America, and to support and promote Christian knowledge in the new settlements, within the United States; and both shall be pursued as circumstances shall point out, and as the trustees, under the superintendence of the General Association, shall direct. . . .

BENJAMIN TRUMBULL, *Moderator*

Passed in General Association at Hebron, June 21, 1798.

Test: NATHAN PERKINS, *Scribe.*"

Text—*Publications of the Illinois State Historical Library*, No. 10. pp. 266-267.

The Massachusetts Missionary Society

Organized May 28, 1799, and introduced to the churches in the following *Address*:

"Christian Brethren,

Wishing that grace, mercy, and peace may be abundantly multiplied unto you, through the knowledge of our Lord and Savior Jesus Christ, we take the liberty to announce to you, that impelled by a deep commiseration for the unhappy fate of thousands, who are perishing through lack of those precious means of salvation which we enjoy; by a recollection of our solemn vows to devote ourselves faithfully to the good of the kingdom of our dear Redeemer; and by the imitable examples of many others, both in our own country and in Europe, who have nobly stepped forward in the cause of Zion; we, a number of ministers and people of Christ, convened in Boston, on Tuesday May the 28th, in the year of our Lord 1799, for the purpose of attending to our duty in this regard, have deemed it expedient to form into a *Society*, in order to collect and combine our efforts, for the spread of the knowledge of the glorious Gospel of Christ among the poor Heathens, and in those remote parts of our country, in which the inhabitants do not enjoy the benefit of a Christian Ministry, and Christian ordinances. . . .

To exclude all misconstruction and prejudice, we solemnly declare, that it is totally foreign from our views, to weaken the evangelical influence of any society of a similar complexion already existing; that we renounce all party objects, and utterly refuse to suffer any political interest or consideration whatever to have place in the design or operations of the Society . . .

With these considerations before your minds; with the perishing, and therefore very compassionable state of every impenitent sinner; with your own immense indebtedness to redeeming grace, your solemn covenant vows, your accountability, and your hopes in view, be intreated to cast the eye of attentive observation upon the condition of thousands and millions of our guilty race, in other countries and our own, particularly among the Heathen tribes, and on the frontiers of the United States, forming a vast line of new settlements, peculiarly embarrassed with respect to their religious interests by local circumstances; and ask, whether, when their danger is so great, when their spiritual wants are so urgent, when there is so much zeal on the part of wickedness, infidelity and atheism, counteracting the Gospel, there be not reason for us to put forth every exertion, for the spread of that precious Gospel, which is the grand charter of our eternal inheritance. . . .

In behalf of the Society,

NATHANIEL EMMONS,

President."

Text—*The Connecticut Evangelical Magazine*, Vol. I, No. 9, pp. 353-355.

II. *ANDOVER SEMINARY*

Opened Sept. 29, 1808, the following revised Laws of 1827 set forth the aims of this notable institution.

ADMISSION

Sect. I.   This Institution shall be equally open to Protestants of every denomination, for the admission of young men of requisite qualifications.

II.   Every candidate for admission into this Seminary shall, previously to his examination, produce to the Faculty satisfactory testimonials, from persons of information and respectability and reputed piety, that he possesses good natural and acquired talents; that he has been regularly educated at some respectable College or University, or has otherwise made literary acquisitions which, as preparatory to theological studies, are substantially equivalent to a liberal education, and that he sustains a fair moral character, is of a prudent and discreet deportment, and is hopefully possessed of personal piety.   He shall also exhibit to the Faculty proper testimonials of his being in full communion with some Church of Christ; in default of which, he shall subscribe a Declaration of his belief in the Christian Religion, in the following words. "I ——— ——— do solemnly declare, that I believe the Christian Religion is of divine original, and that the Scriptures of the Old and New Testaments contain a perfect rule of faith and practice.   ·

. . . .

THE FACULTY

. . . .

IV.   Every Professor in this Seminary shall be a Master of Arts, of the Protestant Reformed Religion, in communion with some Christian Church of the Congregational or Presbyterian denomination, and sustain the character of a discreet, sober, honest, learned and pious man; and shall be of sound and orthodox principles in Divinity, according to that form of sound words, or system of evangelical doctrines, drawn from the Scriptures, and denominated The Westminster Assembly's Shorter Catechism. If on the Associate Foundation, he must also be an ordained Minister of the Congregational or Presbyterian denomination, and must, previously to his inauguration, be carefully examined by the Visitors with reference to his religious principles.

V. Every person appointed or elected a Professor in this Seminary, shall, on the day of his inauguration into office, and in the presence of the Trustees, publicly make and subscribe the following Declaration.

"I believe that there is one and but one living and true God; that the word of God, contained in the Scriptures of the Old and New Testament, is the only perfect rule of faith and practice; that, agreeably to those Scriptures, God is a Spirit . . . ; that in the Godhead are three Persons . . . ; that God created man . . . ; that Adam . . . ; that God, of his mere good pleasure, from all eternity elected some to everlasting life . . . , that the only REDEEMER of the elect is the eternal SON OF GOD . . . . that the righteousness of CHRIST is the only ground of a sinner's justification . . . ; that regeneration . . . , and that a Christian Church ought to admit no person to its holy communion, before he exhibit credible evidence of his godly sincerity, that perseverance in holiness is the only method of making our calling and election sure, and that the final perseverance of saints, though it is the effect of the special operation of GOD on their hearts, necessarily implies their own watchful diligence. . . . I moreover believe that God, according to the counsel of his own will, and for his own glory, hath foreordained whatsoever comes to pass . . . ; that man has understanding and corporeal strength to do all, that GOD, requires of him; so that nothing, but the sinner's aversion to holiness, prevents his salvation . . . ; and that all the evil, which has existed, and will forever exist, in the moral system, will eventually be made to promote a most important purpose under the wise and perfect administration of that ALMIGHTY BEING, who will cause all things to work for his own glory, and thus fulfil all his pleasure.—And furthermore, I do solemnly promise that I will open and explain the Scriptures to my pupils with integrity and faithfulness; that I will maintain and inculcate the Christian faith, as expressed in the Creed by me now repeated, together with all the other doctrines and duties of our holy religion, so far as may appertain to my office, according to the best light God shall give me, and in opposition, not only to Atheists and Infidels, but to Jews, Mahometans, Arians, Pelagians, Antinomians, Arminians, Socinians, Unitarians, and Universalists, and to all other heresies and errors, ancient or modern, which may be opposed to the Gospel of Christ, or hazardous to the souls of men; that, by my instructions, counsels and example, I will endeavour to promote true piety and godliness; that I will consult the good of this Institution, and the peace of the churches of our Lord Jesus Christ, on all occasions; and that I will religiously conform to the Constitution and Laws of this Seminary, and to the Statutes of my Foundation."—Professors on the Associate Foundation will add to the promissory part of the preceding Declaration, the word "Papists" between the words "Jews" and "Mahometans," and the word "Sabellians" between the words "Socinians" and "Unitarians."

The preceding Declaration shall be repeated by every Professor in this Seminary, in the presence of the Trustees, at the expiration of every successive period of five years; and no man shall be continued as President or Professor in this Institution who shall not continue to approve himself, to the satisfaction of the Trustees, a man of sound and orthodox principles in Divinity, agreeably to the system of evangelical doctrines contained in the said Westminster Shorter Catechism, and more concisely delineated in the aforesaid Creed. Accordingly, if at any meeting regularly appointed, it should be proved to the satisfaction of a majority of the whole number of the said Trustees, that the President, or any Professor in this Institution, has taught or embraced any of the heresies or errors alluded to in the Declaration aforesaid, or should he refuse to repeat the same as required by this Article, he shall be forthwith removed from office.

. . . .

DEVOTIONAL EXERCISES

It should be regarded, by every student and Resident Licentiate in this Seminary, as an object of primary importance to grow continually in a spirit of enlightened devotion and fervent piety. . . .

I. It is expected that every student and Resident Licentiate connected with this Seminary will daily spend a portion of time, in devout meditation, reading the Scriptures with a view to a personal and practical application, and in humble and fervent prayer. The Sabbath is to be employed in religious duties, social and secret. Walking abroad for exercise, and conversation, and pursuits not adapted directly to promote personal piety, are, on this day, to be avoided. Associations for prayer and praise, and for religious conference, are proper for this day, subject to such regulations as the President may see fit to prescribe.

II. Every morning and evening, during term time, religious exercises shall be performed in the Chapel, in the following manner. . . .

. . . .

VI. Every student in this Seminary, shall constantly, punctually and seriously attend, morning and evening prayers; the public services of the Chapel on the Sabbath, and on days of fasting and of thanksgiving; and on all stated and occasional Conferences, and seasons of special devotion, appointed by the Faculty.

. . . ."

Text—Woods: *History of the Andover Theological Seminary*, pp. 285-306.

III. *THE CONSTITUTION OF THE SOCIETY OF BRETHREN*

The following, written in cipher and kept a profound secret, is the constitution of what may be regarded as the first foreign missionary society in America.

"Article I. This Society shall be distinguished by the appellation "Brethren."

Article II. The object of this Society shall be to effect in the persons of its members a mission, or missions, to the heathen.

Article III. The government of this Society shall be vested in a President, Vice-President, and Secretary, who shall be annually chosen, and shall perform the ordinary duties of their respective offices.

Article IV. The existence of this Society shall be kept secret.

Article V. The utmost care shall be exercised in admitting members. All the information shall be acquired of the character and situation of a candidate which is practicable. No person shall be admitted who is under any engagement of any kind which shall be incompatible with going on a mission to the heathen. No person shall be admitted until he express a firm belief in those distinguishing doctrines commonly denominated evangelical. No person shall be permitted to see this constitution until from personal acquaintance it is fully believed by at least two members that he is a suitable person to be admitted, and that he will sign it, and until he is laid under the following affirmation:—"You solemnly promise to keep inviolably secret the existence of this Society."

Article VI. Each member shall keep absolutely free from every engagement which, after his prayerful attention and after consultation with the Brethren, shall be deemed incompatible with the object of this Society, and shall hold himself in readiness to go on a mission when and where duty may call.

Article VII. Any member on application shall be released from this Society; and the Society shall have power to dismiss any member, when satisfied that his engagement or character, or situation render it expedient.

Article VIII. No alteration shall be made in this constitution without the concurrence of two-thirds of the members of the Society."

Text—Richards: *Samuel J. Mills, Missionary Pathfinder, Pioneer and Promoter,* pp. 35-37

IV. *THE AMERICAN BOARD OF COMMISSIONERS FOR FOREIGN MISSIONS*

Upon the advice of their Andover professors, and introduced by Dr. Spring, the four undersigned presented to the Massachusetts General Association at Bradford, June 27, 1810, the following request. Acting favorably upon the petition, the Association proceeded to organize the American Board of Commissioners for Foreign Missions.

"The undersigned, members of the Divinity College, respectfully request the attention of their Reverend Fathers, convened in the General Association at Bradford, to the following statement and inquiries:

They beg leave to state, that their minds have been long impressed with the duty and importance of personally attempting a Mission to the Heathen; that the impressions on their minds have induced a serious, and they trust a prayerful consideration of the subject in its various attitudes, particularly in relation to the probable success and the difficulties attending such an attempt; and that after examining all the information which they can obtain, they consider themselves as devoted to this work for life, whenever God in his providence shall open the way. They now offer the following inquiries on which they solicit the opinion and advice of this Association.

Whether with their present views and feelings, they ought to renounce the object of Missions as visionary or impracticable; if not, whether they ought to direct their attention to the eastern or the western world; whether they may expect patronage and support from a Missionary Society in this country, or must commit themselves to the direction of a European Society; and what preparatory measures they ought to take previous to actual engagement?

The undersigned, feeling their youth and inexperience, look up to their Fathers in the Church, and respectfully solicit their advice, direction, and prayers.

(Signed)   ADONIRAM JUDSON, JR.
        SAMUEL NOTT, JR.
        SAMUEL J. MILLS
        SAMUEL NEWELL."

Text—Richards: *Samuel J. Mills, Missionary Pathfinder, Pioneer and Promoter* pp. 72. 73.

Address to the Christian Public, November 1812

The American Board of Commissioners for Foreign Missions, at their late annual meeting, appointed the subscribers a committee to prepare and publish an address to the Christian Public, in the name and on the behalf of the Board. . . . .

The two great objects which the Board have in view, and to which they would direct the attention of their brethren, are the establishment and support of missions among the heathen, and the translation and publication of the Bible in languages spoken by unevangelized nations. That these objects are transcendently important, it would be a waste of time to prove; that they are admirably calculated to go hand in hand seems, also, undeniable. Neither the Bible without preachers, nor preachers without the Bible, will ever effect any great change among ignorant and idolatrous people. . .

The two objects, which have been mentioned are sufficiently great, extensive, and attainable, to solicit, nay to command, exertions and sacrifices from every benevolent person throughout the Christian world.

These objects are *great.* Every thing which has a direct tendency to promote the salvation of immortal souls is great beyond the power of language to express, or imagination to conceive. . . .

The objects are *extensive.* They admit, they *require,* the labors of multitudes. The glorious employment of being fellow laborers in the cause of God, is an employment in which all, who are so inclined, may at all times engage. But the support of missions, and the publication of the Scriptures, in all nations, are enterprises in which the efforts of multitudes can be united with peculiar facility. Christians in both hemispheres, and of every denomination, can direct their exertions to produce one result, — a result of the highest conceivable importance. Combined efforts, whether of a good ·or evil character, are incomparably more powerful than single efforts can be. How delightful, how enrapturing the sight, to behold good men of every rank and condition, in all parts of the world, uniting in one vast labor of love.

It is not only practicable for multitudes to unite in the great purpose of evangelizing the world; but such a union is absolutely necessary, in order to bring about this event in the shortest time. All the power and influence of the whole Christian world must be put in requisition, during the course of those beneficent labors which will precede the millennium. . . .

But the most animating consideration still remains—these objects are *attainable.* To deny the practicability and usefulness of missions, and translations of the Scriptures, would manifest a total ignorance of the subject, or a deep hostility to the progress of Christianity. Twenty years ago, objections to these extraordinary efforts might have been formed much more plausibly than at present. Happily for the world, such objections did not then stifle those beneficent attempts, which have already given the Bible to nations in the heart of Asia, in their own languages. Whether Providence shall bless the efforts of this Board, it is not in the power of man to determine. Let us wait with humility and submission. But that the objects in view will be attained, and by human instruments too, will not be doubted by those, who expect the final prevalence of true religion over error and sin. If the faith of Christians in America should be tried at the outset, it is no more than has frequently been experienced by Christians in every age. Such trials have often preceded the most signal success, and far from disheartening, should stimulate to more animated and faithful labors.

Possibly it may be thought by some, that the present times are unfavorable to the objects have described, so far as pecuniary contributions are needed; and that it would be best to defer charitable designs till our national calamities shall have been removed. We cannot yield for a moment to reasoning of this sort. It might receive many answers; a few brief hints will be sufficient.

God alone is the deliverer from public troubles, and must be regarded as such by all who have any just views of his providence. He can change scenes of national distress into scenes of joy and gratulation. He can cause light to spring up out of darkness, and educe good from evil. To him must the eyes of all be turned, who long for the happiness of mankind and the prosperity of the Church. What method so likely to secure the favor of God, as that of obeying his commandments? And it is his commandment, that the Gospel should be preached *to every creature.*

Besides, it would be adding immeasurably to all the necessary evils of war, if every charitable enterprise were to cease during its continuance. The interests of truth and beneficence would thus lose more in a short war than could be regained in a long peace. National calamities, instead of producing national repentance and reformation, would be the signal for letting loose the malignant passions, while all the charitable virtues were to lie dormant. . . . .

We are unwilling to conclude, without addressing a few words particularly, and very respectfully, to the Clergy, the reverend pastors of the American churches.

. . . .

The Board whose duty it is to superintend the first American mission to foreign parts, and to expend with fidelity such monies as may be committed to their disposal, deeply feel their responsibility. They wish for all information which can be had, relative to the subjects which will come before them. Any communications, therefore, from the Clergy, either in their individual or associated capacities, will be received with respect and thankfulness. It will be the desire and aim of the Board so to conduct their affairs, as to secure the confidence of all Christians throughout the United States, of every denomination; and they venture to hope for the countenance of all, who admit the utility of missions and translations.

Among the numerous claims upon the public liberality, you will doubtless recommend those objects as worthy of especial regard, which have a direct tendency to make men happy here, and to fit them for heaven. That all such objects may be promoted, and that they all may harmonize in producing one grand result, the universal triumph of truth and benevolence, you will not cease to labor and pray. . . . .

Let us all remember, Fathers and Brethren, that the time allotted to our earthly labors is short; that the spiritual wants of the heathen imperiously demand attention and relief; and, while urging each other and our fellow sinners to deeds of charity, let us never forget *the words of the Lord Jesus, how he said, It is more blessed to give than to receive.*

In behalf of the Board,

JEDIDIAH MORSE, }
SAMUEL WORCESTER, } *Committee.*
JEREMIAH EVARTS. }

Boston, Nov. 10, 1812.

Text—*First Ten Annual Reports of the American Board of Commissioners for Foreign Missions,* pp. 47-53.

V THE BAPTISTS AND FOREIGN MISSIONS

Judson's Changed Views on Baptism

The following letters give the circumstances under which the Baptists of America were led to organize themselves independently of Britain for foreign mission work under 'The General Missionary Convention of the Baptist Denomination in the United States of America for Foreign Missions' (May 18, 1814).

"Rev. and Dear Sir: My change of sentiments on the subject of baptism is considered by my missionary brethren as incompatible with my continuing their fellow-laborer in the mission which they contemplate on the Island of Madagascar; and it will, I presume, be considered by the Board of Commissioners as equally incompatible with my continuing their missionary. The Board will, undoubtedly, feel as unwilling to support a Baptist missionary as I feel to comply with their instructions, which particularly direct us to baptize 'credible believers with their households.'

The dissolution of my connection with the Board of Commissioners, and a separation from my dear missionary brethren, I consider most distressing consequences of my late change of sentiments, and, indeed, the most distressing events which have ever befallen me. I have now the prospect before me of going alone to some distant island, unconnected with any society at present existing, from which I might be furnished with assistant laborers or pecuniary support. Whether the Baptist churches in America will compassionate my situation, I know not. I hope, therefore, that while my friends condemn what they deem a departure from the truth, they will at least pity me and pray for me.

With the same sentiments of affection and respect as ever,
I am, sir, your friend and servant,
ADONIRAM JUDSON, JR.

Rev. Dr. Worcester, Corresponding Secretary of the American Board of Commissioners for Foreign Missions."

"Calcutta, September 1, 1812.

"Rev. Sir: I recollect that, during a short interview I had with you in Salem, I suggested the formation of a society among the Baptists in America for the support of foreign missions, in imitation of the exertions of your English brethren. Little did I then expect to be personally concerned in such an attempt.

Within a few months, I have experienced an entire change of sentiments on the subject of baptism. My doubts concerning the correctness of my former system of belief commenced during my passage from America to this country; and after many painful trials, which none can know but those who are taught to relinquish a system in which they had been educated, I settled down in the full persuasion that the immersion of a professing believer in Christ is the only Christian baptism.

Mrs. Judson is united with me in this persuasion. We have signified our views and wishes to the Baptist missionaries at Serampore, and expect to be baptized in this city next Lord's day.

A separation from my missionary brethren, and a dissolution of my connection with the Board of Commissioners seem to be necessary consequences. The mission-

aries at Serampore are exerted to the utmost of their ability in managing and supporting their extensive and complicated mission.

Under these circumstances I look to you. Alone, in this foreign heathen land, I
make my appeal to those whom, with their permission, I will call *my Baptist Brethren*
in the United States.

With the advice of the brethren at Serampore, I am contemplating a mission on
one of the eastern islands. . . .

But should I go thither, it is a most painful reflection that I must go alone, and
also uncertain of the means of support. But I will trust in God. He has frequently
enabled me to praise His divine goodness, and will never forsake those who put their
trust in Him. I am, dear sir,

Yours, in the Lord Jesus,
ADONIRAM JUDSON, JR."

(to Rev. Dr. Bolles,
    Salem, Mass.)

Text—*The Life of Adoniram Judson, by his Son, Edward Judson*, pp. 42-44.

Extract of a letter from Dr. Marshman, of Serampore, to Rev. Dr.
Baldwin, of Boston, dated September 1, 1812.

"A note which brother Judson sent to brother Carey last Saturday has occasioned
much reflection among us. In it he declares his belief that believers' baptism alone is
the doctrine of the Scriptures, and requests to be baptized in the name of the Lord
Jesus.

This unexpected circumstance seems to suggest many ideas. The change in the
young man's mind, respecting this ordinance of Christ, seems quite the effect of divine
truth operating on the mind. It began when no Baptist was near, (on board ship,)
and when he, in the conscientious discharge of his duty, was examining the subject in
order to maintain what he then deemed truth on his arrival in Bengal. And so carefully did he conceal the workings of his mind from us, on his arrival, that he scarcely
gave us a hint respecting them before he sent this note to brother Carey. This was
not indeed very difficult for him to do, as we make it a point to guard against obtruding
on missionary brethren of different sentiments any conversation relative to baptism.

This change, then, which I believe few who knew brother Judson will impute to
whim, or to any thing besides sincere conviction, seems to point out something relative to the duty of our Baptist brethren with you, as it relates to the cause of missions.
It can scarcely be expected that the Board of Commissioners will support a Baptist
missionary, who cannot, of course, comply with their instructions, and baptize *whole
households* on the parents' faith; and it is certain that the young man ought not to be
left to perish for want, merely because he loved the truth more than father or mother:
nor be compelled to give up missionary work for want of support therein. Now
though we should certainly interfere to prevent a circumstance like this happening,
particularly as we have given our Pedobaptist brother Newell, gone to the Isle of
France, an order to draw there upon us should he be in distress, yet, to say nothing of
the missionary concerns already lying on us, and constantly enlarging, it seems as
though Providence itself were raising up this young man, that you might at least partake of the zeal of our Congregational missionary brethren around you. I would
wish, then, that you would share in the glorious work, by supporting him. Let us do

whatsoever things are *becoming* and whatsoever things are *lovely*, and leave the reverse of these for others. After God has thus given you a missionary of your own nation, faith, and order, without the help or knowledge of man, let me entreat you, and Dr. Messer, and brethren Bolles and Moriarty, humbly to accept the gift.

To you I am sure I need add no more than to beg you to give my cordial love to all our brethren around you.

I may probably write you again soon, and in the mean time remain yours, in the Lord,

JOSHUA MARSHMAN. "

Text—Wayland: *Memoir of the Life and Labors of the Rev. Adoniram Judson, D.D.*, Vol. I, pp. 112-113.

Address

The General Convention of the Baptist delegates for Missionary purposes, assembled in the Meeting-House of the First Baptist Church in Philadelphia, on Wednesday, the 18th May, 1814; to their constituents, the churches of Jesus Christ, the Ministers of the Gospel, and the friends of religion in general, present their christian love and cordial wishes.

BELOVED BRETHREN AND FRIENDS.

In what manner and to what extent it has pleased the blessed God of late to direct the attention of many among us, to the interests of the Redeemer's kingdom, some of you are already sensible, and others will learn from the preceding pages. Under the smiles of a propitious Providence, a Convention has assembled in Philadelphia, consisting of delegates from parts of our union, various and remote, to devise a plan, and enter into measures, for combining the efforts of our whole denomination, in behalf of the millions upon whom the light of evangelic truth has never shone. The result of their serious and affectionate consultations, you have an opportunity of perusing.

For this glorious period the church has long and anxiously been waiting. For this thousands of the petitions of the saints have already been presented by the great Mediator before the eternal throne, and thousands more are continually ascending.

.   .   .   .

Within the last few years, it has pleased the good Spirit of our God to awaken in his churches a serious concern for the diffusion of the Saviour's cause. Numerous, and in some instances large associations of Christians have been formed for the purpose: considerable sums of money have been collected; Bibles and religious tracts are extensively and gratuitously circulating, and the hope which thousands cherish that the glory of the latter day is at hand, is as operative as it is joyous. The blessing which has succeeded the efforts of our denomination in India, demands our gratitude. In a few years, the word of life will probably be translated into all the languages of the East. The change of sentiment relative to the subject of baptism that has lately occurred in the minds of two respectable characters, who were sent out as Missionaries, by another denomination of our christian brethren, appears to have been of the Lord, and designed as a means of exciting the attention of our churches to foreign Missions. The engagedness of these worthy brethren in the work of the Lord continues. They look to us for aid, are actually under our care, and have an undoubted claim to our united and firm support. One of them is about to travel through different parts of the Union with a view of increasing the number of Missionary establishments. We anticipate with pleasure, your zealous co-operation. The brevity of life, the value of immortal souls, the obligations under which divine mercy has laid us, our past inactivity, the facility with which the great work may be effected, the excellent tendency of the spirit for foreign Missions in multiplying Missions at home, the examples of other christian persuasions, and the incalculable blessings that may follow our endeavours, form a body of motive which we hope will kindle in many of our youth an ardent desire to enter on Missionary services, and in you the holy resolution to minister of your abundance to all who shall go forth in the name of the Lord.

But, while we call your attention to the spread of evangelic truth, we would impress on your minds that many other and most important advantages may arise to the interests of Christ among us from our acting as societies and on the more extended scale of a Convention, in delightful union. The independence of the churches, we trust will ever, among us, be steadfastly maintained, but with this, as they are entirely voluntary, the holy combinations we wish for, can never interfere. Is it not a fact that our churches are ignorant of each other to a lamentable degree? But for the labours of one or two individuals, it is probable that whole Associations might have assembled in different parts of our Union without being known or knowing that others existed. We have "one Lord, one faith, one baptism," why should our ignorance of each other continue? why prevent us from uniting in one common effort for the glory of the Son of God? At the present Convention the sight of brethren who had never met each other before, and who a few months ago had never expected to meet on earth, afforded mutual and unutterable pleasure. It was as if the first interviews of heaven had been anticipated.

The efforts of the present Convention have been directed chiefly to the establishment of a foreign Mission; but, it is expected that when the general concert of their brethren, and sufficient contributions to a common fund shall furnish them with proper instruction and adequate means, the promotion of the interests of the churches at home, will enter into the deliberations of future meetings.

It is deeply to be regretted that no more attention is paid to the improvement of the minds of pious youth who are called to the gospel ministry. While this is neglected, the cause of God must suffer. Within the last fifty years, by the diffusion of knowledge and attention to liberal science the state of society has become considerably elevated. It is certainly desirable the information of the minister of the sanctuary should increase in an equal proportion. Other denominations are directing their attention with signal ardour to the instruction of their youth for this purpose. They are assisting them to peruse the sacred writings in their original languages, and supplying other aids for pulpit services, which, through the grace of the Holy Spirit, may become eminently sanctified for the general good. While we avow our belief that a refined or liberal education is not an indispensable qualification for ministerial service, let us never lose sight of its real importance, but labour to help our young men by our contributions, by the origination of education Societies, and if possible, by a general theological seminary, where some, at least, may obtain all the advantage, which learning and mature studies can afford, to qualify for acting the part of men who are set for the defence of the gospel. Improvement of this nature will contribute to roll away from the churches the reproach of neglecting to support the ministry of the word. They will be unwilling to receive for nothing that which has cost their ministers much.

Finally, brethren, "be ye steadfast, immoveable, always abounding in the work of the Lord, forasmuch as ye know that your labour is not in vain in the Lord."

RICHARD FURMAN, *President.*

Attest,

THOMAS BALDWIN, *Secretary."*

Text—*The Massachusetts Baptist Missionary Magazine,* Vol. IV, pp. 66-74.

VI. *THE "SOCIETY OF INQUIRY RESPECTING MISSIONS"*

Instituted at Andover seminary, Jan. 8, 1811, with the following as Article I of its Constitution.

Article I. . The Object of the Society shall be to devise and prosecute measures for the extension of Christianity;—and, in subserviency to this, to acquire and disseminate a knowledge of literature, morals and religion of different countries, and of the causes which operate on the moral improvement of mankind.

The letter attached, reprinted from the original that lies in the archives of Andover seminary, shows some of the interests of this Society.

Theological Seminary Andover,
Sept. 27, 1815.

The Society of Inquiry on the Subject of Missions,
to the Reverend Messrs. Hall, Newell & Nott, at Bombay

Beloved Brethren:—

At this time, when five of our number, are going forth to strengthen your hands, in the missionary work, we deem it our duty, by a friendly letter, also, to encourage your hearts. . . .

The members of this Society have not been the unmoved spectators of your example: they have not been unsolicitous about your welfare. From the time of your departure from these shores, they waited in anxiety the intelligence of your safe arrival in India. . . .

We say not this to flatter you, for it is well known, that God may choose the weakest instruments to perform his work, and that all your strength is in him; but we say it for your encouragement, and assurance, that altho your eyes should be closed in death, without having witnessed the conversion of a single heathen, your labour will not be in vain. Yet neither we, nor you can feel that enough is done, while ignorance, superstition and idolatry reign throughout so large a portion of our world.

The following we state as a summary of interesting topics, concerning which you will be able to collect ample information from the publications sent you.

The efforts and success—of Bible Societies—Domestic & Foreign Mission Societies—Tract Societies—Moral Societies—Female Cent Societies, and other charitable associations—and the lately organized Societies for the education of pious young men for the Gospel ministry. You will also obtain information of the establishment and success of the American Baptist Board of Commissioners for Foreign Missions—of the flourishing state of Colleges, revivals of religion in many of them; Princeton, Yale, Dartmouth & Williams: & the establishment of two new Colleges, Hamilton and Alleghany—of the numerous and powerful visitations of the Holy Spirit, in many towns & parishes in New England, fifty-two of which might be named in Connecticut alone; also in New Jersey & some parts of the State of New York. You will see the vast fields for missionary labour within the bounds of the United States. You will notice with pleasure the establishment of the monthly concert for prayer, that God would grant success to his work. in Christian and especially in heathen lands. You will observe the establishment of a Theological Seminary at Princeton, N. Jersey—and we might mention also a "Society of Inquiry" & that several of its members, have actually devoted themselves to the cause of foreign Missions.

In view of these things, Dear Brethren, you will with the Psalmist, & with us exclaim. "The Lord reigneth, let the earth rejoice." You will with us anticipate the time when these benevolent efforts, & this concert of prayer, shall extend thro' out the whole habitable globe, when its object shall not be the extension of the Redeemer's glory to the heathen, but its consummation in the hearts of all men.

We look for the smiles of the divine Saviour on our united exertions. We supplicate the influences of the Holy Spirit, that we all may promote the great object of evangelizing the world, while some of us, as individuals, with you, may be immediately instrumental of turning many heathen from the worship of dumb idols, to serve the living God.

Receive. beloved Brethren, our most cordial Christian salutation.

In behalf of the Society

CALVIN YALE, *Corresponding Secretary.*

VII. *THE FEMALE SOCIETIES*

The following address sets forth the spirit and activities of the various women's organizations of which the Boston Society organized in 1800, was one of the earliest and most prominent.

"Address of the Female Society, in Boston, to the Female Friends of Zion.

"Pray for the peace of Jerusalem," is the injunction of the devout psalmist; with the animating promise annexed, "they shall prosper that love her." Nor is there a duty more specially enjoined throughout the sacred scriptures than that of prayer. And the privilege is no less than the duty. Those who live much in the exercise, find "it is good for them to draw near to God." But to females the privilege is peculiarly invaluable. Though destined by the Parent of nature to fill more retired stations in life than our brethren, we are nevertheless permitted to repair to a throne of grace. (and even to unite in a social manner) to plead for the salvation of sinners, and the prosperity of Zion.

It affords us much pleasure, to hear from time to time of the constitution of Female Societies in various parts of the United States, for the purposes of prayer and of aiding Missionary exertions. And the Lord, we trust, has condescended to use these Institutions as a means of extending the triumphs of the cross.

The members of the "Boston Female Society for Missionary purposes," believing that a more extensive and particular knowledge and acquaintance with those societies of a similar nature would be promotive of the divine glory and their mutual edification, beg leave to address them through this medium.

Engaged as we professedly are, dear Sisters, in the cause of God, and the pleasing work of endeavouring to advance the spread of the gospel; we have thought it would add greatly to our happiness, could we be indulged the privilege of a correspondence with you by letter.   We think it would have a tendency to cement us together in the bonds of christian fellowship, and establish a union never to be dissolved.

We likewise think it desirable, (as far as may be convenient) that we should all hold our meetings on the same day.   The idea that many of our dear Sisters, in different places, were met at the same time, and engaged in the same delightful employment of praying down blessings on mankind, would tend to strengthen our faith, increase our union, animate our hopes, and cheer our prospects.   And we have every reason to believe, that He who has promised to be with two or three who are met in his name; and that if *two* shall *agree* in asking any thing it shall be done for them; would hear our united supplications, if presented in faith.   We therefore recommend it to you collectively, (and also to our female friends whose local situation may render it impracticable for them to meet together,) to set apart the first Monday afternoon of every month, for solemn prayer to God, for the out-pouring of his Holy Spirit; a general revival of pure and undefiled religion, and a universal spread of the gospel.—Particularly that he will send forth labourers into his harvest, and crown all Institutions, which have his glory and the good of souls for their object, with his special blessing.   Should we, beloved Sisters, engage in this solemn undertaking with our hearts rightly influenced, as the lips of eternal truth and faithfulness have promised "that they who sow in tears shall reap in joy," we feel confident it will not be long before some part of his weary heritage shall experience refreshing showers. . . .

. . . .

Though we sincerely wish to avoid an ostentatious or pharisaical spirit, we honestly confess we are not ashamed to acknowledge that we *pray*, that we meet in praying circles, and that our heart's desire and prayer to God is, that Israel may be saved.   And though we wish ever to preserve our place as females, we cannot view it inconsistent with that modesty and shamefacedness enjoined by the Apostle, thus openly to come out on the Lord's side.   We have the approbation of *good* men of different denominations; we believe angels smile on our endeavours to communicate the knowledge of salvation to those souls at whose repentance they rejoice.   God himself has disposed us to the work, and is engaged in our defence; and if He "be for us, who can be against us?"   Though we may meet the scoffs of an unthinking world, let this only increase our zeal, for more are they that are for us, than they that are for them.   And while we hear of wars and rumors of wars, and some even of the citizens of our own country are penetrating into the wilderness with the sound of the trumpet and alarm of war; be ours the pleasing privilege (through the medium of the faithful Missionary,) to resound those joyful strains which once echoed through the plains of Galilee, "Peace on earth, good will towards men." . . .

In behalf of the Society,
> Boston, Feb. 3, 1812.

MARY WEBB, *Sec'ry.*"

Text—*The Massachusetts Baptist Missionary Magazine*, Vol. III, pp. 156-157.

VIII. *THE MASSACHUSETTS BAPTIST MISSIONARY SOCIETY*—Organized September 22, 1814.

As typical of the growing appreciation among the American churches, of the need for a more highly trained ministry, the "Massachusetts Baptist Missionary Society" holds an important place. Its "Address" follows:

"ADDRESS *Of the Elders and Messengers of the* BOSTON BAPTIST ASSOCIATION, *to the Churches they Represent*

Dear Brethren,

If we compare the present state of our denomination in this land with the state it was in 50 years since, we shall see great cause of encouragement and thankfulness. We were then oppressed; we have now full liberty to worship God according to the dictates of our own consciences. We were then few in number; we have now increased to a multitude. The Lord has, indeed, done great things for us, whereof we have reason to be glad. But while we are surrounded with such tokens of his presence and favour, have we not some reason to blame ourselves for the non-improvement of those means of honouring him with which he has graciously supplied us? Much has indeed been done; but if there is reason to believe we have it in our power to do more, are we not bound to to make the attempt?

For several years past, we have been employed in missionary undertakings. These are highly important; and the success with which they have been crowned will, it is hoped, excite us to a still more vigorous prosecution of them. But is there not another object equally important which has not, as yet, engaged an equal portion of our regard? Is it not a matter of serious regret that a denomination so numerous as ours has made no adequate provision for the *education of candidates for the gospel ministry*? It will, indeed, be granted that many, without the advantage of an early education, have preached the gospel with much ability and success. Of these some have not only distinguished themselves as ministers of the word of God, but, surmounting the numerous obstacles which lay in their way, have in process of time accumulated considerable treasures of human science; while others, though never remarkable for their literary attainments, have, by their fervent piety, their knowledge of the Bible, and their assiduous attention to the duties of their sacred calling, been instrumental of great good both to the church and to the world. Such men, undoubtedly, deserve a large portion of our love and esteem; their praise is now in all the churches; and in the future world they will "shine as the brightness of the firmament, and as the stars forever and ever." But instances of this kind, it is conceived, form no weighty objection to the utility and importance of an early education. We do not admit such an objection in other cases. Many sinners have been converted to God, who, previous to their experience of that blessed change, had not been permitted to hear the Gospel clearly and faithfully preached: but we do not thence conclude that the clear and faithful preaching of the gospel is of no importance.—The truth is, the Lord is not confined to means; he can work without them; he sometimes does; but when he has put them into our hands, we are bound to employ them for his glory; and if we refuse to do so, we cannot reasonably expect to enjoy his blessing.

In this view, the case before us is a very plain one. That an early acquaintance with some of the liberal arts & sciences, and especially with sacred literature, must be

very beneficial to a gospel minister, by enlarging his mind, facilitating the communication of his ideas, and assisting him to maintain the truth against the assaults of acute
and learned adversaries, is too evident to be denied. Is it not equally evident that
in many cases, the business of procuring these advantages for pious youth whom the
Lord has endued with gifts, and called to preach the gospel, devolves on us? And have
we not much reason to hope that, should our many prayers be accompanied by suitable
exertions of this kind, the Lord of the harvest would graciously hear us and send forth a
larger supply of faithful labourers? These are greatly wanted at the present time.
Several churches belonging to this body are destitute of pastors. The like deficiency,
it is believed, is lamented by many churches belonging to our sister Associations. Besides, were all our churches well supplied, an increase of spiritual labourers would still
be needed. In many places where Baptist churches have not been planted, there is,
notwithstanding, a great call for Baptist preachers. And could we supply those places
with men of piety, and decent literary attainments, we might reasonably anticipate
the high satisfaction of witnessing the rapid progress of evangelic truth, and of seeing
the cause of our divine Master greatly advanced.

The importance of the object here contemplated will farther appear, if we consider
the great embarrassments experienced by many a pious youth whose attention has been
directed to the work of the ministry. The honour of God lies near his heart. He loves
the souls of men, and longs to be instrumental of their salvation. The ministry of reconciliation appears to him a very glorious work; and could he suppose himself in any
suitable degree qualified for it, he would immediately engage in it with all his heart.
But he realizes that it is a great and arduous work. He feels himself wholly inadequate
to it. What gifts he has are quite uncultivated. He is very ignorant; many private
christians know more than he does; and how can he appear before them in the sacred
character of a gospel minister? Had he property, he would readily sacrifice the very
last cent to procure for himself the advantages of a suitable education. But property
he has none. He makes known his situation to his friends. Of these, some attribute
his anxiety to pride, and charge him to be more humble before he undertakes to preach
the self-abasing doctrine of the cross. Others acknowledge the purity and correctness
of his views; but though favoured with a large portion of worldly wealth, it so happens
that they have nothing to spare for charitable uses. Others feel for the young man,
and would rejoice to help him; but they are so indigent, and so few in number, that
their benevolent wishes cannot be gratified. What can he do? To go forward appears
presumptuous. To stand still is painful beyond expression. To abandon the idea of
preaching, is to wound his conscience and spread an impenetrable cloud over his prospect of a happy and useful life!—Many, it is believed, have felt this distressing anxiety
for months and years. Nor is it at all improbable, that a very considerable number of
our own denomination feel it at the present time. And shall we, brethren, sit still and
suffer them to waste in unavailing grief, that precious time which ought to be employed
in the improvement and cultivation of their minds? .

In these circumstances, is it not desirable, that a Society be formed, under the
superintendence of this Association, to procure money, by subscriptions, collections,
or otherwise, in order to supply the deficiency of our Education Fund?"

Text—*The Massachusetts Baptist Missionary Magazine*, Vol. IV, pp. 118-122.

IX. *THE AMERICAN TRACT SOCIETY*

The following extracts show the spirit, aim, and program of the promoters of tract distribution:

"An Address to Christians, Recommending the Distribution of Religious Tracts.

. . . Whatever may be said as to past negligence, let it now appear that we are busied in discovering every way of access for divine truth into the human heart; and that we are resolved to employ every means we can think of as conducive to that end.

Among many others, none of which should be neglected, there is one which merits peculiar notice, and which we would earnestly recommend to the serious attention of the disciples of Jesus, as calculated to be of eminent and extensive benefit; namely

THE DISTRIBUTION OF RELIGIOUS TRACTS

. . . The advantages which may be expected to result from the distribution of Religious Tracts, are indeed so many and so great, that, where duly weighed, it is to be hoped they will have a powerful influence on the mind of every lover of Jesus and of souls. The following will be readily allowed, and carry with them their own recommendation.

It is a method *which is likely to do good*. . . . What is a Religious Tract, but a select portion of divine truth, designed and adapted to make the reader wise unto salvation?

It is *an easy way of doing good*. Every one has not the talent of talking to those he meets with, especially to strangers, on subjects of religion. . . . Here is a method by which it may be done with ease. . .

It is a *cheap way* of diffusing the knowledge of religion. The Tracts are in general small. They may be had at a very reasonable rate; and the person who will devote a small sum annually for this purpose, may convey to many hundred people in the course of a year, the knowledge of the way of salvation by a crucified Redeemer. . .

It is *not so likely to give offence* as some other methods of doing good. When we speak to a neighbor or a stranger on divine things, he is apt to consider us as assuming the place of a master, and setting up for his superior in knowledge and goodness. Pride instantly takes the alarm. . . . But when a little Tract is put into his hand, the teacher is not the giver of the book; but a third person, an absent *lettered sage*. . . .

It is *more extensive in its use*, than any other method of conveying religious knowledge which a private Christian can employ. . . . When it is considered, that a Tract given by a friend, recommends it to an attentive perusal; and when by a stranger, excites curiosity to see what it contains; and that each of these Tracts may be read not only by the person who receives it, but by four or five more who compose his household; and that it may be lent from one family to another, we may form some idea how extensively divine truth is disseminated by this means. . .

But perhaps he may inquire, 'What Tracts are most proper to be given away, and calculated to do most good, that I may procure them.' This is a question of no small importance. . . . The following qualities should be sought for and are united in a good Tract.

Pure Truth. This, flowing from the sacred fountain of the Bible, should run from beginning to end, uncontaminated with error, undisturbed with human systems; clear as crystal, like the river of life. There should be nothing in it of the *shibboleth* of a sect; nothing to recommend one denomination, or to throw odium on another; nothing of the acrimony of contending parties against those that differ from them. . .

It *should be plain.* Perspicuity here is, next to truth, the first quality of a good Tract. . .

It *should be striking.* . . . However good a Tract may be, as to purity of doctrine, and perspicuity of style, if it be not so composed as to interest the reader in a more than ordinary degree, it is in danger of being thrown aside without a perusal. . .

It *should be entertaining.* . . . A plain didactic essay on a religious subject may be read by a Christian with much pleasure; but the persons for whom these Tracts are chiefly designed, will fall asleep over it.

. . . .

It *should be full of ideas.* There are but few instances in which this quality can be dispensed with. It is but a small present, and therefore should be made as valuable as possible. Its value will rise in proportion to the number of precious truths which it contains. . . . For this purpose, truth should be compressed. The motto of every Tract should be, *Multum in parvo*; and if the foregoing qualities be attended to, there is no danger of compressing too much. . .

That small Religious Tracts possessing these qualities, must be highly valuable, and well suited to the important purpose of conveying divine instruction, will be readily acknowledged; but the difficulty is to find them.

To remove this difficulty, and to provide an abundant supply of such as have been described, that shall be always ready when called for, a Society is instituted; whose object will be to collect, compose, print, and distribute small Religious Tracts, and to dispose of them to subscribers and purchasers on the lowest terms."

Text—*Proceedings of the First Ten Years of the American Tract Society*, pp. 11-21.

X. *THE AMERICAN BIBLE SOCIETY*

Address *"To the People of the United States,* (June, 1816)

Every person of observation has remarked that the times are pregnant with great events. The political world has undergone changes stupendous, unexpected, and calculated to inspire thoughtful men with the most boding anticipations.

That there are in reserve, occurrences of deep, of lasting, and of general interest, appears to be the common sentiment. Such a sentiment has not been excited without a cause, and does not exist without an object. The cause is to be sought in that Providence, which adapts, with wonderful exactitude, means to ends; and the object is too plain to be mistaken by those who carry a sense of religion into their speculations upon the present and the future condition of our afflicted race.

An excitement, as extraordinary as it is powerful, has roused the nations to the importance of spreading the knowledge of the one living and true God, as revealed in his Son, the Mediator between God and men, Christ Jesus. This excitement is the more worthy of notice, as it has been followed by a period of philosophy falsely so called, and has gone in the track of those very schemes which, under the imposing names of reason and liberality, were attempting to seduce mankind from all which can bless the life that is, or shed a cheering radiance on the life that is to come.

. . . .

We have, indeed, the secondary praise, but still the praise, of treading in the footsteps of those who have set an example without a parallel—an example of the most unbounded benevolence and beneficence: and it cannot be to us a source of any pain, that it has been set by those who are of one blood with most of ourselves; and has been embodied in a form so noble and so Catholic, as "*The British and Foreign Bible Society.*"

The impulse which that institution, ten thousand times more glorious than all the exploits of the sword, has given to the conscience of Europe, and the slumbering hope of millions in the region and shadow of death, demonstrates to Christians of every country what they *cannot* do by insulated zeal and what they *can* do by co-operation.

In the United States we want nothing but concert to perform achievements astonishing to ourselves, dismaying to the adversaries of truth and piety; and most encouraging to every evangelical effort, on the surface of the globe.

No spectacle can be so illustrious in itself, so touching to man, or so grateful to God, as a nation pouring forth its devotion, its talent, and its treasures, for that kingdom of the Savior which is righteousness and peace.

If there be a single measure which can overrule objection, subdue opposition, and command exertion, this is the measure. . .

Under such impressions, and with such views, fathers, brethren, fellow-citizens, the *American Bible Society* has been formed. Local feelings, party prejudices, sectarian jealousies, are excluded by its very nature. Its members are leagued in that, and in that alone, which calls up every hallowed, and puts down every unhallowed, principle—the dissemination of the Scriptures in the received versions where they exist, and in the most faithful where they may be required. In such a work, whatever is dignified, kind, venerable, true, has ample scope: while sectarian littleness and rivalries can find no avenue of admission.

The only question is, whether an object of such undisputed magnitude can be best attained by a national Society, or by independent associations in friendly understanding and correspondence.

Without entering into the details of this inquiry, we may be permitted to state, in a few words, our reasons of preference to a national Society supported by local Societies and by individuals throughout our country.

Concentrated action is powerful action. The same powers, when applied by a common direction, will produce results impossible to their divided and partial exercise. A national object unites national feeling and concurrence. Unity of a great system combines energy of effect with economy of means. Accumulated intelligence interests and animates the public mind. And the Catholic efforts of a country, thus harmonzied, give her a place in the moral convention of the world; and enable her to act directly upon the universal plans of happiness which are now pervading the nations.

. . . .

In the distinct anticipation of such an urgency, one of the main objects of the *American Bible Society*, is, not merely to provide a sufficiency of well printed and accurate editions of the Scriptures; but also to furnish great districts of the American continent with well Stereotype plates, for their cheap and extensive diffusion throughout regions which are now scantily supplied, at a discouraging expense; and which, nevertheless, open a wide and prepared field for the reception of revealed truth.

Yet, let it not be supposed, that geographical or political limits are to be the limits of the *American Bible Society*. That designation is means to indicate, not the restriction of their labor, but the source of its emanation. They will embrace, with thankfulness and pleasure, every opportunity of raying out, by means of the Bible, according to their ability, the light of life and immortality, to such parts of the world, as are destitute of the blessing, and are within their reach. In this high vocation, their ambition is to be fellow workers with them who are fellow-workers with God.

. . . .

Text—*The Panoplist*, Vol. XII, pp. 269-274.

XI. THE EDUCATIONAL SOCIETIES

The following is taken from the "Address" of the Presbyterian Education Society, November 1831.

DESIGN OF EDUCATION SOCIETIES

Who will doubt that the finger of God points to Education Societies, as one of the principal means of supplying these spiritual wants. Whatever the reason may be, the fact is, that by far the greatest part of able and faithful ministers and missionaries have arisen from the middle and laboring classes of society. Their names are encircled with a halo of glory, but it was in the school of poverty that they were disciplined to great undertakings. Compelled in early life to make vigorous efforts to sustain themselves, they learned how to 'endure hardness, as good soldiers of Jesus Christ.' The worth of such men, and the need of them, in an age of enterprise and of great moral revolutions, like the present, cannot be too highly estimated. It is not the legitimate object of Education Societies to lessen the number of such men, or to impair their energies. Sooner than lead to such a result, it were well for the church and for mankind that every Education Society were blotted out of existence. The proper business of such societies is, by a wise and wholesome patronage, to increase the number of *self made men*, of men, capable of performing any service, and of enduring any hardships for Christ, to which they may be called.

ASSISTANCE BY LOANS

It does not belong to the Directors of this Society, nor of the Society with which they are so harmoniously co-operating, to speak of facts farther than they may come under their own observation. But so far as they are permitted to give their testimony, they feel constrained from a regard to the purity, the energy, and the success of the Christian ministry, to state, that the system of patronage which has been found by them best adapted to secure these important ends, is that of *loans*, made in the customary form, but without interest, until a suitable time shall have elapsed for paying, and with the further equitable provision, that, in case of *inability* to pay, arising from providential, or other good and sufficient reasons, the obligation shall be cancelled. Assistance in this way furnishes but few motives to unworthy men to apply for patronage; it leads to economy, to diligence, to personal effort, and by necessary consequence to self respect and independence; and it economizes the funds of the church, so as to render them far more useful. In proof of the soundness of these conclusions, it may be observed, that, while nearly every Education Society has commenced operations with a system of *charity* merely, experience has in a little time suggested the necessity of exchanging it for a system of *loaning;* and even in those instances where the former method has been retained, it is easy to perceive that there is a tendency to its ultimate and complete abandonment. The reports of this Society will show, that as long ago as 1821, before a union with the American Education Society was thought of, the Board felt it incumbent on them to suggest for the consideration of their Executive Committees 'whether the practice of *loaning* the sums which are advanced to beneficiaries might not, under certain modifications and restrictions, be adopted with advantage.'

AMOUNT APPROPRIATED

In this connection it is proper also to state, that taking into view the numerous facilities for self support which are afforded young men, in many places, and the aid which they frequently derive from funds belonging to the seminaries with which they are connected, the directors cannot, without unfaithfulness to those under their care, as well as to the public, recommend a larger sum, as a uniform appropriation, than that which is now made, viz. seventy-five dollars a year. To this rule, as to all others of a general nature, there are exceptions; but in the present case, they are exceptions which go to show the propriety of lessening, rather than increasing the amount appropriated; especially, since to cheapness of living, there are now added in many places, all the advantages derived from uniting labor with study.

THOROUGH EDUCATION

Another principle which is deemed of great importance is, that those who are patronized, shall aim at a *thorough* course of education for the ministry.

. No attainments in learning can indeed supply the want of a warm and active piety; and, it should be the care of Education Societies, to patronize none but those who exhibit evidence of possessing this essential qualification; nevertheless, without knowledge deep and various, even piety cannot achieve the highest success of which it is capable.   There are other principles which are regarded as having great importance in forming the character, and guarding against abuses; such as, requiring of all who receive aid from the funds, a faithful pecuniary accountability, and the exercise toward them of an affectionate pastoral care; but, upon these, the Directors forbear to dwell, since they have already been frequently made the subject of former communications

. . . .

DIRECTIONS TO THOSE WHO WISH TO APPLY FOR PATRONAGE

Chapter V.—*Of Beneficiaries*

1. No person shall be considered a candidate for assistance who has not pursued classical studies for at least three months, and who has not attained to fourteen years of age.

2. No person shall be patronized who does not furnish satisfactory evidence of promising talents, decided piety, and who is not in the way of obtaining a *thorough* classical and theological education; that is, either preparing to enter college; or a member of some regularly constituted college where a thorough classical course is pursued; or engaged in theological studies with the design of taking a regular three years' course.

3.   When a young man wishes to apply for patronage, he must pursue the following steps: *First.* He must obtain unequivocal testimonials from three or more serious and respectable persons best acquainted with him and his circumstances, (e.g.) his minister, instructor, a magistrate, or some other principal man in the vicinity, stating his age, place of residence, indigence, moral and religious character, including his

church connection, talents, previous education, and serious desire to devote his life to the Christian ministry. . . . *Secondly.* Having obtained these testimonials, the applicant must present his request for *examination and recommendation* to some Examining Committee in his neighborhood, or within the portion of the country to which he belongs. . . .

Chapter IV.—*Of Examining Committees*

2. When a candidate for patronage applies for examination, it shall be the duty of the Examining Committee, to whom the application is made, to institute a personal and faithful inquiry respecting his testimonials, his studies, his religious character, his motives in seeking an education for the Christian ministry, and his willingness to conform to the rules of the American Education Society. If, after serious and full examination, the Committee shall be satisfied that the applicant possesses the character and qualifications required of beneficiaries by the Constitution and Rules of the Society, it shall be their duty to recommend him for patronage to the Board of Directors of the Parent Society, or, of one of its Branches, if the applicant reside within the limits of a Branch Society. . . .

Text—*The Quarterly Register*, November 1831, pp. 155-158.

XII. *BAPTIST STATE CONVENTION OF SOUTH CAROLINA*—Organized December 6, 1821.

As the first State Constitution of American Baptists, this document has a significant place in the evolution of Baptist denominational organization.

"Whereas, by an address to the Baptist Associations of this State, which was circulated among the churches of their connexion during the present and past year; it was made to appear, that it would be of great advantage to the denomination to form themselves into a State Convention, which should be a bond of union, a centre of intelligence, and a means of vigorous, united exertion in the cause of God, for the promotion of truth and righteousness; that so those energies, intellectual, moral and pecuniary, which God has bestowed upon the denomination in this State, might be concentrated, and brought into vigorous, useful operation: And whereas, Delegates from the Charleston, Edgefield, and Savannah River Associations, are, in consequence of said representation, convened at Columbia at this time, to whom the proposed measure appears to be proper, interesting and important.—Therefore, we the said Delegates, (regretting indeed the failure of present co-operation on the part of the other Baptist Associations of the State, in the benevolent coalition we are forming, but indulging the hope, as well from communications received from some of them, as from the vast importance and interesting nature of the design, that, in future, such co-operation will be afforded,) do now agree upon the following outline of a plan for such union and exertion; but do designedly delay the definitive adjustment, until another meeting shall be held; that we may not be wanting in respect to our brethren, who are not represented in this body, and that we may improve the opportunity now afforded for affectionately inviting them to join in the benevolent, pious concert, whose blessed object it is to strengthen the bonds of spiritual union and intercourse, and thus to promote the glory of God our Saviour. But in prospect of this co-operation, we now agree upon the following general principles as the basis of union, and affectionately present them to the consideration of our brethren throughout the State.

1. This coalition of Associations shall be styled, "*The State Convention of the Baptist Denomination in South Carolina.*"

2. The grand objects of this Convention shall be the promotion of evangelical and useful knowledge, by means of religious education; the support of missionary service among the destitute, and the cultivation of measures promotive of the true interest of the churches of Christ in general, and of their union, love and harmony in particular.

3. This Convention shall consist of Delegates from the Associations in this State; to whom may be added representatives from other religious bodies of the Baptist connexion.

4. The Convention shall have proper officers for conducting its business.

5. The Convention shall recognize the independence and liberty of the Churches of Christ, and consequently shall not in any case arbitrarily interfere with their spiritual or secular interests. But, when requested, will be considered as under obligations to afford them any assistance which may be in their power.

6. In regard to funds which may at any time be contributed for the promotion of the general objects here contemplated, discretion in their appropriation shall be exercised by the Convention, or by a board that they may appoint for the transaction of business; but no application of monies, given for a specific object, shall be made by them or their board to any other use.

7. In what relates to education, the organization and support of a seminary of learning in this State, for the gratuitous education of indigent, pious young men for the gospel ministry, on a plan in accordance with the interests of that established by the denomination at large, in the United States, shall be considered by this body as an object of primary importance. Not but that other youth, whose education shall be paid for, may be admitted as pupils; it being distinctly understood, that the course of education and government, shall be conducted with a sacred regard to the interests of morality and religion, on principles of Christian liberality.

8. With regard to missionary service, the Convention will feel it their duty to have a special regard to its promotion, and to use their vigorous efforts to engage the most able, pious and suitable ministers of their denomination in the prosecution of this important design.

9. As duty and obligation unite to prove that religious education of children is a matter of primary importance, this Convention will feel it their duty to encourage the establishment of Sunday Schools, as well as the religious instruction of children in families.

10. This Convention proposes to embrace in its definitive plan, measures for collecting funds by means of charity sermons, societies, donations and bequests, for the purpose of carrying into effect the objects of its attention, upon those principles of liberality, zeal for God, and love to immortal souls, which the gospel inculcates.

11. The whole plan here exhibited, has been formed under a consciousness of entire dependence upon Divine Grace for success, in reference to the truth inculcated in that solemn declaration of Holy Writ, "Not by might, nor by power, but by my Spirit, saith the Lord of Hosts."

Signed by order of the Convention, this sixth day of December, A.D. 1821.

RICHARD FURMAN, *Pres.*

ABNER BLOCKER, *Sec.*"

Text—*American Baptist Magazine*, New Series, Vol. III, pp. 435-6.

CHAPTER XX

The Rise of Unitarianism and Universalism

Bibliography

UNITARIANISM

The 'Liberal Side of Puritanism' in New England has been set forth in scholarly outline by George Willis Cooke in chapter II of "Unitarianism in America" (1902). For the liberal views of Roger Williams and Ann Hutchinson, the reader is referred to bibliographies on pages 111f and 54. The Half-Way Covenant has been discriminatingly interpreted by George H. Hayes in "History of Representation and Suffrage in Massachusetts, 1620-1691" ("J. H. U. Studies" Series XII, Sec. VIII-IX). Sir Richard Saltonstall's protest against New England tyranny is referred to in "Early Settlers of Watertown" (Vol. II) by Henry Bond. William Pynchon's liberalism is reflected in his "Meritorious Price of our Redemption" (1650, for story of episode connected therewith, see "Springfield 1636-1886—History of Town and City" (1888) by Mason A. Green, p. 113).

Henry Dunster and Charles Chauncy are discussed by Josiah Quincy in "The History of Harvard University" (II Vols. 1840); the former also by J. Chaplin in a "Life of Henry Dunster" (1872). The liberal tendencies of Brattle Street Church are shown in "A History of the Church in Brattle Street . . . " (1851) by S. K. Lothrop; the "Life and Character of the late Reverend Benjamin Coleman" (1749) by E. Turell; and "The Emancipation of Massachusetts" (1886) by Brooks Adams. The rationalistic proclivites of John Wise may be seen in his "Church's Quarrel Espoused" (1710), and his "Vindication of the Government of the New England Churches" (1717). Solomon Stoddard's 'Larger Congregationalism' may be understood from "An Appeal to the Learned, being a vindication of the right of visible saints to the Lord's Supper, though they be destitute of a saving work of God's Spirit in their Hearts" (1709), also his "Doctrine of Instituted Churches" (1700). The liberal policy of Increase and Cotton Mather, and notably of Samuel Willard and John Leverett, in their administrations of Harvard, are discussed by

Quincy (as above). The controversy in Springfield over the settlement of Robert Breck is treated by Green in his "History of Springfield" (as above), also by E. H. Byington in "The Puritan in England and New England" (1896).

On the beginnings of Arminianism there is a thoughtful treatise with full bibliographical references by Professor F. A. Christie, entitled "The Beginnings of Arminianism in New England" ("Papers Amer. Soc. Ch. Hist." Series II, Vol. III, pp. 153-172). Jonathan Edwards has considerable to say of the development of Arminianism in his "Narrative of Surprising Conversions"; his "Thoughts on the Revival of Religion"; his work on the will, and in his letters. The message of Arminianism as opposed to Calvinism may be studied in "Grace Defended, in a Modest Plea for an important Truth: namely, that the offer of Salvation made to sinners comprises in it an offer of the Grace given in Regeneration" (1744) by Rev. Experience Mayhew; "The Absurdity and Blasphemy of Depreciating Moral Virtue" (1749) by Lemuel Briant; and "A Winter's Evening Conversation upon the Doctrine of Original Sin, wherein the notion of our having sinned in Adam and being on that account only liable to eternal Damnation is proved to be Unscriptural" (1757) by Samuel Webster.

Jonathan Mayhew, the 'First Outspoken Unitarian in New England' is well portrayed in the "Memoir of the Life and Writings of the Reverend Jonathan Mayhew," (1838) by Alden Bradford. His "Sermons" (pub. 1755) are important.

Charles Chauncy, the pastor for fifty years of the First Church, Boston, reveals his liberalism in his famous "Seasonable Thoughts on the State of Religion in New England" (1743), wherein he criticizes adversely the Great Awakening, and anticipates many of the points emphasized by later organized Unitarianism. His work, published in London, (1784), "The Salvation of All Men the Grand Thing aimed at in the Scheme of God: by One who wishes well to the whole human race" will repay careful reading. A complete list of the Chauncy literature has been compiled by Paul L. Ford in his "Bibliotheca Chaunciana," to which the investigator is referred.

For the silent advance of liberalism during the closing years of the eighteenth century, Thomas Belsham's "Memoirs of the Late Reverend Theophilus Lindsey M. A. . . ." (1812) is indispensable for the correspondence it embodies between the liberal group in Boston and the Unitarian ministers in London. The progress of events is succinctly told by Cooke in "Unitarianism in America" (as above).

For the controversial period of early Unitarianism, the many sermons, lectures, and addresses of Jedidiah Morse are valuable, also the sermons of W. E. Channing, notably "Unitarian Christianity" (preached in Baltimore, 1819, at Spark's ordination), and a "Half Century of the Unitarian Controversy" (1857) by George E. Ellis. In connection with this controversy, an extensive literature developed, too large to be canvassed within the limits of this bibliography. Through the services of Rev. E. H. Gillett, D.D. in "The Historical Magazine" Ser. II, Vol. IX, No. 4, the investigator will find a chronologically arranged list of books, pamphlets, sermons, and letters, covering the period 1650-1850, and exhaustive for the years 1800-1834. This is prefaced by a carefully documented history of the controversy.

For the developing organization of Unitarianism, Cooke's "Unitarianism in America" is satisfactory. An "Historical Sketch of the Unitarian Movement Since the Reformation" by J. H. Allen, D.D. ("Amer. Ch. Hist. Ser." Vol. X, 1894) may be consulted with profit. "Boston Unitarianism, 1820-1850, . . . " (1890) by O. B. Frothingham has some data. "Unitarianism: Its Origin and History" (sixteen lectures delivered in Channing Hall, Boston, 1888-1889) edited by H. G. Spaulding, has five studies on America. The exposition is lucid and historical.

The following biographies have important contributions for several phases of early Unitarianism: "Memoirs of the Rev. Noah Worcester" (1844) by Rev. H. Ware, Jr.; "Memoir of James P. Walker with Selections from his Writings" edited (1869) by Rev. T. B. Fox; "Ezra Stiles Gannett, Unitarian Minister in Boston, 1824-1871" (1875) by his son, W. C. Gannett; "William Ellery Channing, Minister of Religion" (1903) by John W. Chadwick, with extended review thereof by Edward E. Hale in the "American Journal of Theology" January, 1904; "The Life of William Ellery Channing" (1907) by his nephew, W. H. Channing; "Memoir of Jared Sparks, LL.D." by George E. Ellis ("Proc. Mass. Hist. Soc." Vol. X, pp. 211-310); and the "Life and Writings of Jared Sparks . . . " (1893) by H. B. Adams. The last is valuable for Unitarian development outside of Boston, and especially in Baltimore.

It remains to enumerate the periodicals initiated by Unitarianism: "The Monthly Anthology" (1803, literary and non-controversial); "The Christian Monitor" (1806, devotional); "The General Repository and Review" (1812, aggressive and outspoken); "The Christian Disciple" (1813, conciliatory and moderate), becoming "The Christian Examiner" (1824, more literary and theological in its interest); "The Christian Register" (1821, moderate and adapted to all classes); "Unitarian Miscellany and Christian Monitor" (1821, moderately aggressive); and the "North American Review" (1815, literary, historical, and scientific).

Appendix B in Cooke's "Unitarianism in America" has a brief history of the rise of Unitarian newspapers and magazines since 1827.

The above periodicals with "The Panoplist" (conservative in its attitude); the "Works of William Ellery Channing" (new edition with critical introduction by J. W. Chadwick, VI Vols. 1905) and the yearly reports of the Association, constitute the main sources for further investigation of nineteenth century Unitarianism.

UNIVERSALISM

To one unfamiliar with the teachings, polity, and practices of Universalism, a "Textbook of Universalism," (1845) by M. Hale Smith will be found very serviceable; also "The Columbian Congress of the Universalist Church" (1893)being papers and addresses by representative universalists.

For the European background of Universalism, there is the "Ancient History of Universalism from the Time of the Apostles to the Fifth General Council. With an Appendix tracing the Doctrine to the Reformation. With notes . . . " (1872) by Hosea Ballou; supplemented by "The Modern History of Universalism; extending from the Epoch of the Reformation to the Present time . . . " (1830 enlarged 1860) by Thomas Whittemore. A thoughtful review of these two works appears in the "Christian Examiner" Vol. VIII, pp. 220-262.

A Universalist interpretation of American history prior to John Murray's arrival in 1670 may be consulted (Vol. I, Ch. I) in "Universalism in America, A History" (1884) by Richard Eddy. Two important biographical studies of Universalist pioneers are "Rev. John Murray . . . " (1816) by his wife, and "Rev. Elhanan Winchester" (1836) by Rev. E. M. Stone. The latter should be supplemented by the preface to Winchester's work "The Universal Restoration . . . " (1794).

Representative documents of the period immediately preceding the organization of Universalism are as follows: "Two Sermons on the Nature, Extent, and Perfection of the Divine Goodness" (1763) by Jonathan Mayhew, D.D., also "A Letter of Reproof to Mr. John Cleaveland . . . " (1764) by the same writer; "Salvation for all Men illustrated and vindicated as a Scripture Doctrine . . . " (1782) by Charles Chauncy, D.D.; his "Divine Glory brought to view in the Final Salvation of all Men . . . " (1783), and "The Mystery hid from Ages and Generations . . . " (1784).

The earliest organized group of American Universalists reveals its spirit and program in "An Appeal to the Impartial Public by the Society of Christian Independents Congregating in Gloucester" (1785) written by Epes Sargent. The legal troubles of this group are canvassed by Mrs. Murray in her husband's Memoir (as above). The 'Charter of Compact' and other papers of the Oxford Association (September, 1785) may be consulted in the "Universalist Quarterly," July, 1874. 'The Articles of Faith and Plan of Church Government, composed and adopted . . . in Philadelphia May, 1790' represents the next important step in the evolution of Universalist organization.

Of histories, there are the following, arranged chronologically: "A History of the Origin and Progress of the Doctrine of Universal Salvation" (1826) by Thomas Brown; "A Brief Outline of the History of Universalism" (1833) by L. L. Sadler; "State of the Doctrine and Denomination of Universalists" by Thomas Whittemore ("Expositor and Universalist Review" Jan. 1833); "Historical Sketches and Incidents, Illustrative of the Establishment and Progress of Universalism in the State of New York" by S. R. Smith, Ser. I, 1770-1817, (1843), Ser. II, 1818-1822 (1848), Ser. III, 1823 (see "Christian Ambassador" May 31-June 14, 1856); "Dogmatic and Religious History of Universalism in America" (1848) by Hosea Ballou II ("Universalist Quarterly" Vol. V); "Early History of Universalism in New England" by John S. Barry (*ibid.* New Series, Vol. I); "Contributions to the History of Universalism" by Rev. Thomas J. Sawyer (*ibid.* New Series, Vols. VII and X); "A Century of Universalism in Philadelphia and New York . . . and elsewhere" (1872) by Abel C. Thomas; and "Fifty Notable Years. Views of the Ministry of Christian Universalism during the last half century . . . " (1882) by John G. Adams, D.D. The "Memoirs of Dr. Joseph Priestley to the Year 1795 . . . with a Continuation to the Time of his Decease . . . " (1806) is illuminating for Philadelphia in the early days. By far the best historical work has been done by Richard Eddy in his "Universalism in America. A History" (Vol. I, covering 1636-1800, 1884; Vol. II, 1801 to 1886, 1886). A satisfactory condensation of this history appears in the "American Church History Series" (Vol. X).

In addition to the above histories there are a few biographical studies that contain important historical material: "Life and Writings of Rev. Enoch M. Pingree . . . " (1850) by Rev. Henry Jewell; "Memoirs of the Life of Nathaniel Stacy . . . " (1850); "Autobiography of Rev. Abel C. Thomas . . . " (1852); "Memoir of Rev. Edward Mott

Wooley" (1855) by his daughter, Mrs. F. Gillett, assisted by Rev. A. B. Grosh; "The Early Days of Thomas Whittemore. An Autobiography; extending from A.D. 1800 to A.D. 1825" (1859); "Autobiography of the first Forty-one Years of the Life of Sylvanus Cobb, D.D. To Which is added a Memoir. By his Eldest Son, Sylvanus Cobb, Jr." (1867); "The Life-Work of Elbridge Gerry Brooks, Minister in the Universalist Church" (1881) by E. S. Brooks.

Hosea Ballou, one of the most indefatigable propagandists of Universalism, has left a literature of sermons, debates and treatises, all of which is chronologically set forth in Eddy's bibliography (see below). His "Select Works" (V Vols. 1854) contain a biography by his youngest son; notes on the parables of the New Testament; a treatise on the Atonement; lecture sermons; and select sermons. A "Life of Rev. Hosea Ballou; with accounts of his Writings, and Biographical sketches of his Seniors and Contemporaries in the Universalist Ministry" (IV Vols. 1854-55) by Thomas Whittemore, has much important material.

On Abner Kneeland it will suffice to note his "Five Words Spoken with the Understanding" (2 sermons, 1805), and "A Series of Lectures on the Doctrine of Universal Benevolence . . ." (1818). See also p. 416.

Other leaders may be studied in "Original Sermons on Various Subjects; by Living Universalist Ministers" (III Vols. "Christian Preacher" 1831–1833); and the "Universalist Pulpit . . ." (1856). In "Biographical Sketches" ("Universalist Quarterly," New Ser. Vols. VII, VIII, IX, XII, XIV, XV, XVI, XVIII, and XIX) there are studies upon Rev. Hosea Ballou, Edward Turner, George Richards, Walter Balfour, Thomas Whittemore, Hosea Ballou II, Sebastian Streeter, and Mrs. Judith Murray.

Attention should be directed to some monographs that deal with phases of Universalism: "Reflections on Revivals of Religion" (1833) by A Friend to Religion; "On Revivals and Protracted Meetings" (1837) by H. F. Ballou; "A Discourse on Revivals" (April 5, 1840) by Rev. C. C. Burr; "The lying wonders of Elder Jacob Knapp exposed and refuted" (1845) by Rev. S. B. Brittain; "The Revival of Religion" (Discourse March 21, 1858) by Rev. A. D. Mayo; "Religion and the Present Revival" (1858) by W. H. Ryder; "Address before the Universalist Anti-Slavery Convention . . . held in Lynn, Mass. November 19, 1840," by J. M. Spear; "Constitution of the New York Universalist Missionary Society" (revised, 1842); "Rise and Prevalence of UnitarianViews among the Universalists" by Hosea Ballou II ("Universalist Quarterly," Vol.V).

For further bibliographical assistance, the reader is referred to Eddy, "Universalism in America," Vol. II, pp. 485-599. This bibliography is very carefully compiled, inclusive of tracts, sermons, biographies and histories. A bibliography of periodical articles is added.

DOCUMENTS

I. *THE "MANIFESTO" OF BRATTLE STREET CHURCH*
November 17, 1699

Prepared probably by Dr. Colman, this Declaration provoked sharp controversy and was looked upon by divines such as Increase Mather, Higginson, and Noyes, as highly ominous.

"Inasmuch as God hath put it into our hearts to undertake the Building a New Meeting-House in this Town for His Publick Worship; And whereas through the gracious Smiles of Divine Providence on this our Undertaking, We now see the same Erected, and near Finished: We think it Convenient, for preventing all Misapprehensions and Jealousies, to publish our Aims and Designs herein, together with those Principles and Rules we intend by GOD's Grace to adhere unto.

We do therefore as in the Presence of GOD our Judge, and with all the Sincerity and Seriousness, which the nature of our present Engagement Commands from us, Profess and Declare both to one another, and to all the World, as follows.

I
First of all, We approve and subscribe the Confession of Faith put forth by the Assembly of Divines at Westminster.

II
We design only the true and pure Worship of GOD, according to the Rules appearing plainly to us in His Word; Conformably to the known practice of many of the Churches of the UNITED BRETHREN in London, and throughout all England.

We judge it therefore most suitable and convenient, that in our Publick Worship some part of the Holy Scripture be read by the Minister at his discretion.

In all other parts of Divine Worship as (Prayer, Singing, Preaching, Blessing the People, and Administring the Sacraments;) We conform to the ordinary practice of the Churches of Christ in this Country.

III
It is our sincere desire and intention to hold Communion with the Churches here, as true Churches; and we openly protest against all Suspicion and Jealousie to the contrary, as most Injurious to us.

IV
And although in some Circumstances we may vary from many of them, yet we joyntly profess to maintain such Order and Rules of Discipline as may preserve, as far as in us lies, Evangelical Purity and Holiness in our Communion.

V
In pursuance whereof we further Declare, that we allow of Baptism to those only who profess their Faith in Christ and Obedience to him, and to the Children of such; yet we dare not refuse it to *any* Child offered to us by *any* professed Christian, upon his engagement to see it Educated, if God give life and ability, in the Christian Religion.

But this being a Ministerial Act, We think it the Pastors Province to receive such Professions and Engagements; in whose prudence and conscience we acquiesce.

VI

As to the Sacrament of the Lords Supper, we believe that as the Ordinance is Holy, so the Partakers in it (that it may not be visibly profaned) must be persons of visible Sanctity.

VII

We judge it therefore fitting and expedient, that whoever would be admitted to partake with us in this Holy Sacrament, be accountable to the Pastor to whom it belongs to inquire into their knowledge and Spiritual State, and to require the Renewal of their Baptismal Covenant.

VIII

But we assume not to our selves to impose upon any a Publick Relation of their Experiences; however if any one think himself bound in Conscience to make such a Relation, let him do it.

For we conceive it sufficient, if the Pastor publickly declare himself satisfied in the person offered to our Communion, and seasonably Propound him.

IX

We also think our selves obliged in faithfulness to God, our own Souls, and theirs who seek our Communion, to inquire into the life and conversation of those who are so propounded, and if we have just matter of objection to prefer it against them.

X

But if no objection be made, before the time of their standing propounded is expired, it shall be esteemed a sufficient Consent and Concurrence of the Brethren, and the person propounded shall be received to our Communion.

XI

If ever any of our Communion should be so unhappy as to fall into any scandalous Sin (which God by his Grace prevent) we profess all dutiful submission to those Censures, which the Scripture directs, and the Churches here practice.

XII

Forasmuch as the same power that *Admits*, should also *Exclude*, We judge it reasonable, that the Pastor in Suspending or Excommunicating an Offender, have the consent and concurrence of the Brethren.

XIII

We apprehend that a particular Church, as such, is a Society of Christians by mutual agreement, usually meeting together for Publick Worship in the same place, and under the same Ministry, attending on the Ordinances of God there.

XIV

In every such Society, the Law of nature dictates to us, that there is implied a mutual promise and engagement of being faithful to the Relations they bear to each other, whether as private Christians, or as Pastor and Flock, so long as the Providence of God continues them in those Relations.

XV

We moreover Declare ourselves for Communion of Churches, freely allowing our Members occasionally to Communicate with other Churches of Christ, and receiving theirs occasionally to the Table of the Lord with us. And in extraordinary cases, when the Providence of God makes it needful, we conceive that any Authorized Minister of Christ, may upon our request, Administer the Sacraments unto us.

XVI

Finally, We cannot confine the right of chusing a Minister to the Male Communicants alone, but we think that every Baptized Adult Person who contributes to the Maintenance, should have a Vote in Electing.

Yet it seems but just, that persons of the greatest Piety, Gravity, Wisdom, Authority or other Endowments, should be leading and Influential to the Society in that Affair.

These are the Principles we Profess, and the Rules we purpose through the Grace of GOD, to govern our selves by; and in some of these particulars only, and in no other, do we see cause to depart from what is ordinarily Professed and Practised by the Churches of CHRIST here in *New-England*."

Text—Lothrop: *A History of the Church in Brattle Street, Boston,* pp. 20-26.

II. *JONATHAN MAYHEW'S LIBERAL VIEWS*

"What shall we say to the doctrine of God's having reprobated a great proportion of mankind; or, from eternity devoted them in his absolute decree and purpose to eternal torments, without any respect or regard to any sins of theirs as the procuring and meritorious cause of their perdition? And this, at the same time, to make manifest and glorify his JUSTICE! What can be said of this; and how shall it be reconciled with the supposition that God's tender mercies are over all his works?

I will tell you, in a very few words, what I have to say to it at present. And that is, first, that if any persons really hold such a doctrine, neither any man on earth nor angel in heaven can reconcile it with the goodness of God. And secondly, that I have not the least inclination to attempt a reconciliation of these doctrines; being persuaded that they are just as contrary as light and darkness, Christ and Belial; that one of them is most true and scriptural, joyful to man, and honorable to God; and the other most false and unscriptural, horrible to the last degree to all men of an undepraved judgment, and blasphemous against the God of heaven and earth. Neither is it possible for any man who really believes what the Scriptures teach concerning the goodness of God even to think of this other doctrine but with great indignation.

.   .   .   .

And we may, without the least presumption, conclude in general that, in the revolution of ages, something far more grand, important, and glorious than any thing which is vulgarly imagined, shall actually be the result of Christ's coming down from heaven to die on a cross, of his resurrection from the dead, and of his being crowned with glory and honor, as Lord both of the *dead* and the *living.* The word of God, and his mercy, endure forever; nor will he leave any thing which is truly his work unfinished. 'As the heavens are higher than the earth,' saith the Lord, 'so are my ways higher than your ways and my thoughts than your thoughts. My word, that goeth forth out of my mouth, shall not return unto me void, but it shall accomplish that which I please; and it shall prosper in the thing whereunto I send it.'

To conclude, then; let us all, young men and maidens, old men and children, love and honor, extol and obey the God and Father of *all,* whose tender mercies are over all his works; and who has been so gracious and bountiful to ourselves in particular. If we sincerely do thus, as becometh the children of the Highest, we shall, in due time,

partake of his goodness, in a far more glorious manner and measure than we can in the
earthly house of this tabernacle.   We shall doubtless also have a far more clear, distinct, and perfect knowledge than we can possibly have at present of what is intended
in some apparently grand and sublime, yet difficult passages in the sacred oracles,—
particularly that of John the Divine, with which I close: 'And *every creature* which is
in *heaven*, and on the *earth*, and *under the earth*, and such as are in the *sea*, and *all that
are in them*, heard I saying, Blessing, and honor, and glory, and power be unto Him
that sitteth on the throne, and unto the Lamb forever and ever (Rev. v. 13).' "

Text—*The Nature, Extent, and Perfection of the Divine Goodness*, (Sermon, Thanksgiving, 1762); quoted in Eddy: *Universalism in America*, Vol. I, pp. 93-96.

III. *ARTICLES OF ASSOCIATION OF THE INDEPEN-DENT CHURCH IN GLOUCESTER*

Suspended by the First Church because they absented themselves
from worship and ordinances, Epes Sargent and fifteen others drew up
(January 1, 1779) the following articles, which form the earliest program
of American Universalism.

"Inasmuch as it hath pleased God of his great mercy, in every age of the world, to
choose a people for himself, giving them his fear, and revealing to them his secret; and
as this Great Lord of heaven and earth, the Father of our Lord Jesus Christ, hath been
pleased to reveal to babes what he hath hid from the wise and prudent: we, the subscribers, gratefully affected with a sense of the divine goodness in thus distinguishing
us, who had nothing in us to merit his notice, think it our interest and bounden duty
to let our light shine before men, that they may see our good works, and glorify our
Father which is in heaven. As therefore it hath pleased God to make us acquainted
with the voice of the Good Shepherd, the Lord Jesus Christ, the Great Shepherd and
Bishop of souls, we cannot from henceforward follow the voice of a stranger, nor ever
give attention to such who are unacquainted with the Saviour of the world.   But
though we cannot have fellowship with them whose fellowship is not with the Father
and with his Son Jesus Christ, yet we are determined, by the grace of God, never to forsake the assembling of ourselves together, as the manner of some is, but as a Church of
Christ, meet together in his name, being persuaded, wherever or whenever two or three
are thus met together, the invisible God will be present with them.
As Christians, we acknowledge no master but Jesus Christ, and as disciples of this
divine master, we profess to follow no guide in spiritual matters but his word and
his spirit.
As dwellers in this world, though not of it, we hold ourselves bound to yield obedience to every ordinance of man, for God's sake; and we will be peaceable and obedient
subjects to the powers that are ordained of God, in all civil cases; but as subjects of
that King whose kingdom is not of this world, we cannot acknowledge the right of any
human authority to make laws for the regulating of our conscience in any spiritual matters.
Thus, as a true independent Church of Christ, looking unto Jesus the Author and
Finisher of our faith, we mutually agree to walk together in Christian fellowship,
building up each other in our most holy faith, rejoicing in the liberty wherewith Christ

hath made us free, and determining by his grace no more to be entangled by any yoke of bondage.

As disciples of the meek and lowly Jesus, we resolve, as far as in us lieth, to live peaceably with all men, yet, as believers living godly in Christ Jesus, we expect to suffer as much persecution as the laws of the country we live in will admit of. But we resolve by the grace of God none of these things shall move us to act inconsistent with our character as Christians. We will as much as possible avoid vain jangling and unnecessary disputation; and should we be reviled, endeavor in patience to possess our souls.

As an independent Church of Christ thus bound together by the cords of his love, and meeting together in his name, we mutually agree to receive as our Minister, that is, our Servant, sent to labor among us in the work of the Gospel by the great Lord of the Vineyard, our friend and Christian brother, JOHN MURRAY. This we do from a full conviction that the same God that sent the first preachers of Jesus Christ, sent him; and that the same gospel they preached we have from time to time received from him. Thus, believing him a minister of the New Testament, constantly declaring the whole counsel of God, proclaiming the same divine truth that all God's holy prophets from the beginning of the world have declared,—We cordially receive him as a Messenger from God. And as it hath pleased God to open a great and effectual door for the preaching of his Gospel by this, his servant, in sundry parts of this great continent, wherever it shall please his and our divine master to call him to preach the everlasting Gospel elsewhere, we wish him God-speed, and pray that the good-will of him that dwelt in the bush may accompany him, and make his way clear before him. But should he at any time preach any other gospel than that we have received, we will not wish him God-speed, but consider him as a stranger. And as the great Lord of the harvest has taught us to pray that he would send laborers into his harvest, and as he never taught us to pray in vain, but has assured us, every one that asketh receiveth, though he has not told us when, whenever he shall see fit to send us a messenger of glad tidings, a publisher of peace, we will with grateful hearts receive him. And as the promise of the divine presence is to any two or three that meet together in the Saviour's name, we are resolved by God's grace, whether we are blessed with the public preaching of the word or not, as often as we find convenient, to meet together to supplicate the divine favor, to praise our redeeming God, to hear his most holy word, and freely to communicate whatever God shall please to manifest to us for our mutual edification.

And that we may the more effectually show forth his praise, who hath called us out of darkness into his marvellous light, we resolve to pay a serious regard to the exhortations, admonitions, and instructions given to us by the Spirit of God in the epistles dictated to our holy apostles. We will, as far as in us lieth, do good unto all men, but especially unto them who are of the household of faith.

We will, by the grace of God, in word and in deed, endeavor to adorn the doctrine of God our Saviour. And as children of one father, as members of one head, who are united together in Christian fellowship, will, once every month, meet together to hold conference, and to deliberate on whatever may tend to our mutual profit."

Text—Eddy: *Universalism in America*, Vol. I, pp. 175-178.

IV. *CHARLES CHAUNCY'S LIBERAL VIEWS*

It is, I am verily persuaded, very much owing to the false light in which revelation has been placed, and by its very good friends too, that so many have been led to reject it. And, in truth, if the sense of revelation really was, what it has too generally been represented to be, even by Christians themselves, I see not that blame could justly be reflected on them. It is impossible that should come from God, which is unworthy of him; nor would any external evidence be sufficient to justify a man in believing him to be the author of that, which, in its own nature, is unreasonable and absurd. This, if I mistake not, is well worthy of the sober consideration of those, who profess a veneration for the BIBLE AS A DIVINE BOOK. It is a fact too evident to be denied, that the revelations of God, as contained in the writings of the Old and New Testament, have been gradually and strangely corrupted by false philosophy and vain deceit; and, perhaps, as gross absurdities, as palpably wrong and dishonourable ideas of God, have been received by believers for sacred truths, upon the foot of revelation, as were ever received by infidels upon the foot of reason, even in the darkest ages and places of Paganism. Yea, notwithstanding the light and learning of the present day, horrible absurdities, both in doctrine and worship, are still grounded on the writings even of the apostles of Jesus Christ, and by those too who profess a regard to them as wrote by inspiration of the Holy Ghost. Such are the doctrines taught in the church of Rome. More enormous falsehoods were never fathered upon the God of truth. They are indeed such an affront to the human understanding, such a defiance of common sense, as cannot but naturally and strongly tend to make men infidels. And such also, if not in so high a degree, are some of the doctrines which Protestants receive for revealed truths. Of this kind I may properly mention, upon this occasion, the doctrines of election and reprobation, of the eternity of hell torments; and of the partial design, and final effect, of the mediatory interposition of Jesus Christ. Mr. Whitton has declared it as his thought, 'that the common opinion, concerning the future torments, if it were, for certain, a real part of Christianity, would be a more insuperable objection against it, than any or all the present objections of unbelievers put together.' The same may be said, I think, with as much, if not more, truth of the doctrine of absolute reprobation, as it has been particularly explained, and warmly defended, by many Christian Divines, and of very considerable note. And the mediatory undertaking of Jesus Christ, as commonly understood, is perhaps incredible also. These, and such-like, representations of the sense of scripture, have, I doubt not, been 'stones of stumbling, and rocks of offence.' Many may have taken occasion herefrom to call that 'foolishness,' which in reality is 'the wisdom of God.' And in vain shall we hope to silence the objections of infidelity, and put a stop to its growth, till we are able to exhibit an account of the internal contents of the sacred writings, that is more honourable to the infinitely perfect Being, and more conducive to the real advantage of mankind. Such an account, it appears to me, I have given, in the foregoing work, of the revelations of scripture; an account so far from being unreasonable and absurd, that it cannot but approve itself to the human mind, as that which reflects great glory on God, and his Son Jesus, in the good it universally brings to the sons of men: And it is the more to be regarded, as it is eminently fitted to promote true piety and real virtue in the world.

If, conformably to the account we have given from the scriptures, God has so loved us as to project a scheme, which, in the final result of its prosecution, will instate us all in heavenly and immortal glory; how powerfully are we herefrom excited to yield to him the entire homage of our hearts? . . .

If Jesus Christ is the glorious person through whom God has made the promise of eternal life, and by whom, as prime minister in the kingdom of his grace, he will prepare mankind for the actual bestowment of it; how right and fit is it, that, next to God, and in subordination to him, we should make his Son, whom he has authorized to be our king and Saviour, the beloved object of our faith and hope, our submission and obedience? . . .

If God is equally the Father of us all, if we are all joint-partners in the same hope of eternal life, and shall all finally make one family, and live together as brethren in the heavenly world; how peculiarly proper is it that we should be kindly affectioned to each other, and discover that we are so by all Christian offices of goodwill and beneficence, as occasions are offered for them in providence? Should any of our race make themselves vile, as is too commonly the case, we should not be destitute, upon this account of the scripture scheme of mercy, of sufficient motives to embrace them with the tenderest affection. We might resent their folly, and in all suitable ways testify against it: But we should, at the same time, if we were ourselves good Christians, pity them under it, and do all in our power, within our proper sphere, to reclaim them from it. And should they, after all, appear to be 'vessels of wrath fitted for destruction,' instead of treating them with rancour and ill-will, we should still view them as objects of the divine mercy, and feel within ourselves a secret pleasure resulting from the thought, that they will finally be recovered from the snare of the Devil, and partake, in common with ourselves, of the temper and inheritance of God's children.

. . . From whence came evil? has been one of the grand puzzling questions in all ages of the world. We have here the most easy satisfactory answer to it. Evils and sufferings, whether present or future, in this world or another, are a disciplinary mean wisely and powerfully adapted to promote the good of the patients themselves, as well as others; they stand connected with this end in the plan of God, and will, in the last result of its operation, certainly bring it into fact. Instead therefore of being a contradiction to, they very obviously coincide with, wise and reasonable benevolence: Yea, they are a wonderful illustration of it, if it be true, as we have endeavoured to prove it to be, that they will finally issue, conformably to the original purpose of God, in an 'exceeding and eternal weight of glory.'

Text—*The Salvation of All Men* . . . Conclusion, pp. 361-367.

V. *THE STRENGTH AND POLICY OF UNITARIANS IN BOSTON, 1812*

The following is from a letter (March 21, 1812) of William Wells, Jr. of Boston, to the Rev. Thomas Belsham.

"With regard to the progress of Unitarianism, I have but little to say. Its tenets have spread very extensively in New England, but I believe there is only one church *professedly* Unitarian. The churches at Portland and Saco, of which you speak, hardly ever saw the light, and exist no longer. The Mr. Thacher who was formerly a member of Congress, and the Judge T. whom Mr. Merrick mentions, are the same. He is one of the Judges of our Supreme Court, an excellent man and most zealous Unitarian. He is now on the circuit in this town, and tells me he is obliged on Sunday to stay at home, or to hear a Calvinistic minister. He is no relation to our friend.

Most of our Boston clergy and respectable laymen (of whom we have many enlightened theologians) are Unitarian. Nor do they think it at all necessary to conceal their sentiments upon these subjects, but express them without the least hesitation when they judge it proper. I may safely say, the general habit of thinking and speaking upon this question in Boston, is Unitarian. At the same time the controversy is seldom or never introduced into the pulpit. I except the Chapel church. If publications make their appearance attacking Unitarian sentiments, they are commonly answered with spirit and ability; but the majority of those who are Unitarian are perhaps of these sentiments, without any distinct consciousness of being so. Like the first Christians, finding no sentiments but those in the N. T. and not accustomed to hear the language of the N. T. strained and warped by theological system-makers, they adopt naturally a just mode of thinking.

This state of things appears to me so favourable to the dissemination of correct sentiments, that I should perhaps regret a great degree of excitement in the public mind upon these subjects. The majority would eventually be against us. The ignorant, the violent, the ambitious, and the cunning, would carry the multitude with them in religion as they do in politics. One Dr. M., in a contest for spreading his own sentiments among the *great body* of the people, would, at least for a time, beat ten Priestleys. Not to dwell upon the consideration, that Unitarianism consists rather in *not* believing; and that it is more easy to gain proselytes to absurd opinions, than to make men zealous *in refusing* to believe, with what arms, when the οἱ πολλοί are the judges, can virtue and learning and honour contend with craft and cunning and equivocation and falsehood and intolerant zeal? Learning is worse than useless, virtue is often diffident of her own conclusions, and, at any rate, more anxious to render men good Christians, than to make them Christians of her own denomination, and that self-respect, which is the companion of virtue, disdains to meet the low cunning of her adversaries, or to flatter the low prejudices of her judges. I think then it must be assumed as an axiom, that a persevering controversy upon this question would render the multitude bigoted and persecuting Calvinists. Then come systems and catechisms in abundance. Every conceited deacon, every parishioner who has, or thinks he has, a smattering in theology, becomes the inquisitor of his pastor. In such circumstances learning and good sense have no chance. They cannot even be heard.

The violent party here have chosen to meet their opponents upon very unfavourable ground. Instead of making it a cause of orthodoxy against heresy, they have very unwisely preferred to insist upon a subscription to articles of faith. This has given great offence to many who are disposed to be in favour of their creed, and thrown them into the opposite scale. Dr. Osgood is really orthodox in sentiment, but a noble and determined supporter of the right of private judgment, and on the best possible terms with our Boston friends. This is also the case with the venerable Dr. Lathrop of West-Springfield, Mr. Palmer's friend, and many others. In short, we are now contending for the liberty of being Protestants. If we can persuade the people (and we stand upon advantageous ground) that we have the right to think upon religious subjects as our consciences and the scriptures direct, things will go on very well. Learning, good sense, and virtue will then produce their natural effects; and just modes of thinking upon subjects of this nature, as upon all others, will necessarily prevail."

Text—Belsham: *Memoirs of the Late Reverend Theophilus Lindsey*, M.A. . . . , Appendix, No. X.

VI. *CHANNING'S EXPOSITION OF UNITARIANISM*

The following excerpts from "Unitarian Christianity," a sermon preached by Channing in Baltimore, 1819, upon the occasion of Sparks' ordination, give a satisfactory statement of Unitarian belief.

There are two natural divisions under which my thoughts will be arranged. I shall endeavor to unfold, 1st, The principles which we adopt in interpreting the Scriptures. And, 2dly, Some of the doctrines which the Scriptures, so interpreted, seem to us clearly to express.

I. We regard the Scriptures as the records of God's successive revelations to mankind, and particularly of the last and most perfect revelation of his will by Jesus Christ. Whatever doctrines seem to us to be clearly taught in the Scriptures, we receive without reserve or exception. We do not, however, attach equal importance to all the books in this collection. Our religion, we believe, lies chiefly in the New Testament. . .

. . . Our leading principle in interpreting Scripture in this, that the Bible is a book written for men, in the language of men, and that its meaning is to be sought in the same manner as that of other books. We believe that God, when he speaks to the human race, conforms, if we may so say, to the established rules of speaking and writing. How else would the Scriptures avail us more than if communicated in an unknown tongue? . .

. . . We profess not to know a book which demands a more frequent exercise of reason than the Bible. In addition to the remarks now made on its infinite connections, we may observe, that its style nowhere affects the precision of science, or the accuracy of definition. Its language is singularly glowing, bold, and figurative, demanding more frequent departures from the literal sense than that of our own age and country, and consequently demanding more continual exercise of judgment. We find, too, that the different portions of this book, instead of being confined to general truths, refer perpetually to the times when they were written, to states of society, to modes of thinking, to controversies in the Church, to feelings and usages, which have passed away, and without the knowledge of which we are constantly in danger of extending to all times and places what was of temporary and local application. We find, too, that some of these books are strongly marked by the genius and character of their respective writers, that the Holy Spirit did not so guide the Apostles as to suspend the peculiarities of their minds, and that a knowledge of their feelings, and of the influences under which they were placed, is one of the preparations for understanding their writings. With these views of the Bible, we feel it our bounden duty to exercise our reason upon it perpetually; to compare, to infer, to look beyond the letter to the spirit, to seek in the nature of the subject, and the aim of the writer, his true meaning; and, in general, to make use of what is known for explaining what is difficult, and for discovering new truths. . .

We object strongly to the contemptuous manner in which human reason is often spoken of by our adversaries, because it leads, we believe, to universal skepticism. If reason be so dreadfully darkened by the fall, that its most decisive judgments on religion are unworthy of trust, then Christianity, and even natural theology, must be abandoned; for the existence and veracity of God, and the Divine original of Christianity, are conclusions of reason, and must stand or fall with it. . .

. . . The worst errors, after all, have sprung up in that church which proscribes reason, and demands from its members implicit faith. The most pernicious doctrines have been the growth of the darkest times, when the general credulity encouraged bad. men and enthusiasts to broach their dreams and inventions, and to stifle the faint remonstrances of reason by the menaces of everlasting perdition.   Say what we may, God has given us a rational nature, and will call us to account for it.   We may let it sleep, but we do so at our peril.   Revelation is addressed to us as rational beings.   We may wish, in our sloth, that God had given us a system, demanding no labor of comparing, limiting, and inferring.   But such a system would be at variance with the whole character of our present existence; and it is the part of wisdom to take revelation as it is given to us, and to interpret it by the help of the faculties which it everywhere supposes, and on which it is founded. . . .

II. Having thus stated the principles according to which we interpret Scripture I now proceed to the second great head of this discourse, which is, to state some of the views which we derive from that sacred book, particularly those which distinguish us from other Christians.

1. In the first place, we believe in the doctrine of GOD'S UNITY, or that there is one God, and one only.   To this truth we give infinite importance, and we feel ourselves bound to take heed, lest any man spoil us of it by vain philosophy.   The proposition, that there is one God, seems to us exceedingly plain.   We understand by it, that there is one being, one mind, one person, one intelligent agent, and one only, to whom underived and infinite perfection and dominion belong. . .

2. Having thus given our views of the unity of God, I proceed in the second place to observe, that we believe in the unity of Jesus Christ.   We believe that Jesus is one mind, one soul, one being, as truly one as we are, and equally distinct from the one God. We complain of the doctrine of the Trinity, that, not satisfied with making God three beings, it makes Jesus Christ two beings, and thus introduces infinite confusion into our conceptions of his character. . .

3. Having thus given our belief on two great points, namely, that there is one God, and that Jesus Christ is a being distinct from and inferior to God, I now proceed to another point on which we lay still greater stress.   We believe in the *moral perfection of God*.   We consider no part of theology so important as that which treats of God's moral character; and we value our views of Christianity chiefly as they assert his amiable and venerable attributes. . .

To give our views of God in one word, we believe in his Parental character.   We ascribe to him, not only the name, but the dispositions and principles of a father.   We believe that he has a father's concern for his creatures, a father's desire for their improvement, a father's equity in proportioning his commands to their powers, a father's joy in their progress, a father's readiness to receive the penitent, and a father's justice for the incorrigible.   We look upon this world as a place of education, in which he is training men by prosperity and adversity, by aids and obstructions, by conflicts of reason and passion, by motives to duty and temptations to sin, by a various discipline suited to free and moral beings, for union with himself, and for a sublime and ever growing virtue in heaven. . .

Now, according to the plainest principles of morality, we maintain, that a natural constitution of the mind, unfailingly disposing it to evil and to evil alone, would absolve it from guilt; that to give existence under this condition would argue unspeakable cruelty, and that to punish the sin of this unhappily constituted child with endless ruin would be a wrong unparalleled by the most merciless despotism. . .

. . . With regard to the great object which Jesus came to accomplish, there seems to be no possibility of mistake. We believe that he was sent by the Father to effect a moral or spiritual deliverance of mankind; that is, to rescue men from sin and its consequences, and to bring them to a state of everlasting purity and happiness. We believe, too, that he accomplishes this sublime purpose by a variety of methods; by his instructions respecting God's unity, parental character, and moral government, which are admirably fitted to reclaim the world from idolatry and impiety to the knowledge, love, and obedience of the Creator, by his promises of pardon to the penitent, and of Divine assistance to those who labor for progress in moral excellence; by the light which he has thrown on the path of duty; by his own spotless example, in which the loveliness and sublimity of virtue shine forth to warm and quicken, as well as guide us to perfection; by his threatenings against incorrigible guilt; by his glorious discoveries of immortality; by his sufferings and death; by that signal event, the resurrection, which powerfully bore witness to his Divine mission, and brought down to men's senses a future life; by his continual intercession, which obtains for us spiritual aid and blessings; and by the power with which he is invested, of raising the dead, judging the world, and conferring the everlasting rewards promised to the faithful. . .

. . . We regard him as a Saviour, chiefly as he is the light, physician, and guide of the dark, diseased, and wandering mind. No influence in the universe seems to us so glorious as that over the character; and no redemption so worthy of thankfulness, as the restoration of the soul to purity. Without this, pardon, were it possible, would be of little value. Why pluck the sinner from hell, if a hell be left to burn in his own breast? Why raise him to heaven, if he remain a stranger to its sanctity and love? With these impressions, we are accustomed to value the Gospel chiefly as it abounds in effectual aids, motives, excitements, to a generous and divine virtue. . . . We believe that no dispositions infused into us without our own moral activity are of the nature of virtue, and therefore we reject the doctrine of irresistible Divine influence on the human mind, moulding it into goodness, as marble is hewn into a statue. . .

Among the virtues, we give the first place to the love of God. We believe, that this principle is the true end and happiness of our being, that we were made for union with our Creator, that his infinite perfection is the only sufficient object and true resting-place for the insatiable desires and unlimited capacities of the human mind, and that without him our noblest sentiments—admiration, veneration, hope, and love—would wither and decay. We believe, too, that the love of God is not only essential to happiness, but to the strength and perfection of all the virtues; . . . We lay no stress on strong excitements. We esteem him, and him only, a pious man, who practically conforms to God's moral perfections and government; who shows his delight in God's benevolence, by loving and serving his neighbour; his delight in God's justice, by being resolutely upright; his sense of God's purity, by regulating his thoughts, imagination, and desires; and whose conversation, business, and domestic life are swayed by a regard to God's presence and authority. In all things else, men may deceive themselves. Disordered nerves may give them strange sights, and sounds, and impressions. Texts of Scripture may come to them as from heaven. Their whole souls may be moved, and their confidence in God's favor be undoubting. But in all this there is no religion.

Another important branch of virtue we believe to be love to Christ. The greatness of the work of Jesus, the spirit with which he executed it, and the sufferings which he bore for our salvation, we feel to be strong claims on our gratitude and veneration. We see in nature no beauty to be compared with the loveliness of his character, nor do we find on earth a benefactor to whom we owe an equal debt. . .

We can hardly conceive of a plainer obligation on beings of our frail and fallible nature, who are instructed in the duty of candid judgment, than to abstain from condemning men of apparent conscientiousness and sincerity, who are chargeable with no crime but that of differing from us in the interpretation of the Scriptures, and differing, too, on topics of great and acknowledged obscurity. We are astonished at the hardihood of those,who, with Christ's warnings sounding in their ears, take on them the responsibility of making creeds for his Church, and cast out professors of virtuous lives for imagined errors, for the guilt of thinking for themselves. . .

We find, that on no subject have men, and even good men, ingrafted so many strange conceits, wild theories, and fictions of fancy, as on religion; and remembering, as we do, that we ourselves are sharers of the common frailty, we dare not assume infallibility in the treatment of our fellow-Christians, or encourage in common Christians, who have little time for investigation, the habit of denouncing and condemning other denominations, perhaps more enlightened and virtuous than their own. Charity, forbearance, a delight in the virtues of different sects, a backwardness to censure and condemn—these are virtues which, however poorly practised by us, we admire and recommend, and we would rather join ourselves to the church in which they abound, than to any other communion, however elated with the belief of its own orthodoxy, however strict in guarding its creed, however burning with zeal against imagined error.

Text—*Memorable Sermons*, No. 6, American Unitarian Association Series.

VII. A PRESENT-DAY STATEMENT OF UNIVERSALIST BELIEF

The following was adopted almost unanimously in Boston, 1878:

We, the Universalist ministers of Boston and vicinity, observing the widespread agitation in the religious world with respect to the final destiny of our race, and more especially of those who die in impenitence and sin, and desirous that our views on this important subject should not be misunderstood, after much earnest thought and prayerful consideration present the following, not by any means as a full statement of our faith, but as indicating its general character:

1. We reverently and devoutly accept the Holy Scriptures as containing a revelation of the character of God and of the eternal principles of his moral government.

2. As holiness and happiness are inseparably connected, so we believe that all sin is accompanied and followed by misery, it being a fixed principle in the divine government that God renders to every man according to his works, so that 'though hand join in hand, the wicked shall not be unpunished.'

3. Guided by the express teachings of revelation, we recognize God not only as our King and Judge, but also as our gracious Father, who doth not afflict willingly nor grieve the children of men; but though he cause grief, yet will he have compassion according to the multitude of his mercies.

4. We believe that divine justice, 'born of love and limited by love,' primarily requires 'love to God with all the soul,' and to one's neighbor as one's self. Till these

requisitions are obeyed, justice administers such discipline, including both chastisement and instruction, and for as long a period, as may be necessary to secure that obedience which it ever demands. Hence it never accepts hatred for love, nor suffering for loyalty, but uniformly and forever preserves its aim.

5. We believe that the salvation Christ came to effect is salvation from sin rather than from the punishment of sin, and that he must continue his work till he has put all enemies under his feet, that is, brought them in complete subjection to his law.

6. We believe that repentance and salvation are not limited to this life. Whenever and wherever the sinner truly turns to God, salvation will be found. God is 'the same yesterday, today, and forever,' and the obedience of his children is ever welcome to him.

7. To limit the saving power of Christ to this present life seems to us like limiting the Holy One of Israel; and when we consider how many millions lived and died before Christ came, and how many since, who not only never heard his name, but were ignorant of the one living God, we shudder at the thought that his infinite love should have made no provision for their welfare, and left them to annihilation, or, what is worse, endless misery. And it is but little better with myriads born in Christian lands, whose opportunities have been so meagre that their endless damnation would be an act of such manifest injustice as to be in the highest degree inconsistent with the benevolent character of God.

8. In respect to death we believe that, however important it may be in removing manifold temptations and opening the way to a better life, and however, like other great events, it may profoundly influence man, it has no saving power. Salvation, secured in the willing mind by the agencies of divine truth, light, and love, essentially represented in Christ—whether effected here or in the future life—is salvation by Christ, and gives no warrant to the imputation to us of the 'death-and-glory' theory, alike repudiated by all.

9. Whatever differences in regard to the future may exist among us, none of us believe that the horizon of eternity will be relatively either largely or for a long time overcast by the clouds of sin and punishment, and in coming into the enjoyment of salvation, whensoever that may be, all the elements of penitence, forgiveness, and regeneration are involved. Justice and mercy will then be seen to be entirely at one, and God be all in all.

Text—Eddy: *A History of the Universalists in the United States*, (Amer. Ch. Hist. Ser. Vol. X), pp. 458-460.

CHAPTER XXI

THE EXTENSION OF THE CHURCH INTO THE MIDDLE AND FARTHER WEST

Bibliography

The "Life of David Bacon" (1876) written by his son, serves as a good introduction to the study of the awakening interest of the church in the spiritual and moral welfare of the Middle West. Three articles on "David Bacon" ("Congregational Quarterly," January, April, and July, 1876) further illumine the career of this home missionary pioneer. The pioneering work of Joseph Badger is portrayed in a "Memoir of Rev. Joseph Badger . . ." (1851) by E. G. Holland, and "Rev. Joseph Badger: The Pioneer Missionary of the Western Reserve" ("Papers, Ohio. Ch. Hist. Soc." Vol. XI, p. 522 f). Several of his letters are reprinted in the "Connecticut Magazine" (1801–1803). For the tours of Mills and Schermerhorn, valuable in indicating the religious conditions of the frontier, see page 365. The work of the American Bible Society (organized 1816) is set forth in detail in its annual reports appearing in periodicals such as the "Baptist Magazine," "Missionary Herald," "Home Missionary," "Methodist Magazine," and "Christian Review." These journals render a like service in reporting the activities of the American Tract Society, the American Education Society, and the American Sunday School Union, all of which operated effectively throughout the frontier districts.

The American Home Missionary Society, undoubtedly the most powerful christian agency in grappling with frontier problems, may be thoroughly studied in its organ, "The Home Missionary and Pastor's Journal." This is a mine of incalculable value for the investigator of frontier conditions. If one will patiently work one's way through its files, one will find almost everything sought after—statistical annual reports very carefully compiled, the distribution of ministers, their activities in Sunday school, temperance, educational and evangelistic work, the ebbs and flows of revivals, the sources of ministerial supply, the records of heroic service in lonely missionary outposts, and outstanding sermons and addresses bearing upon the claims, problems, and triumphs of home missionary work.

Another source of information almost as rich are the annual reports of the American Baptist Home Mission Society (organized 1832). - These reports, with those of local associations, show the gradual extension and consolidation of Baptist interests. For the Episcopalians, the reports of The Domestic and Foreign Missionary Society (organized 1821) will be found highly satisfactory; also the "Annual Reports on the State of the Church" appended to the "Journal of Proceedings of the Bishops, Clergy, and Laity of the Protestant Episcopal Church assembled in General Convention." For the Methodists, one should consult the reports of the Missionary Society of the Methodist Episcopal Church (organized 1819), and the Minutes of the Annual and General Conferences. These, with the "Minutes of the General Assembly of the Presbyterian Church," and "The Journals of the Lutheran Synods," form the main sources from which the history of the Protestant church of the West is to be written.

Passing from this important type of source material, another body of literature is the biographic and autobiographic. For this the student is under special indebtedness to the Methodists, who have taken pains to record the work of their pioneer itinerants and bishops. The following, while in no sense claiming to be exhaustive, gives a fair survey of the field: "Memoir of Rev. Bela Jacobs, A.M., compiled chiefly from his Letters and Journals by his Daughter . . . " (1837) by B. Sears; "Sketches of the Life and Travels of Rev. Thomas Ware . . . wri ten by Himself," revised (1839) by the editor; "The Life of the Rev. John Emory, D.D. One of the Bishops of the Methodist Episcopal Church by his eldest son" (1841); "The Life of Rev. Robert E. Roberts, One of the Bishops of the Methodist Episcopal Church" (1844) by Rev. Charles Elliott; "The Superannuate, or Anecdotes, Incidents, and Sketches of the Life and Experience of William Ryder, 'A Wornout' Preacher of the Troy Conference of the Methodist Episcopal Church" (1845); "Sketches from the Study of a Superannuated Itinerant" (1851) by Rev. E. Gavitt; "Sketches of the Life and Labors of James Quinn" (1851) by John F. Wright; "The Life of Bishop McKendree" (1852) by Benjamin Fry and the better work entitled "William McKendree, A Biographical Study" (1914) by Bishop H. M. Du Bose; "The Life of Henry D. Bascom, D.D." (1854) by Rev. M. M. Hinkle, D.D.; "Sketches of Western Methodism . . . Illustrations of Pioneer Life" by Rev. James B. Finley, edited (1854) by W. F. Strickland; "Autobiography of a Pioneer, . . . Rev. Jacob Young (1857); "Footprints of an Itinerant" (1855) by Rev. Maxwell P. Gaddis; "Sketches and Incidents of Rev. John Clark by an old Pioneer" edited (1855) by Rev. J. M. Peck; "Friendship's Offering: A Sketch of the Life of John Mason Peck, D.D." (1858) by John Reynolds; "Experience of German Methodist Preachers," (1859) collected and arranged by Rev. Adam Miller, M.D. Introduction by Charles Elliott; "Autobiography of Peter Cartwright, the Backwoods Preacher" (1859); "Fifty Years as a Presiding Elder" by Rev. Peter Cartwright edited (1871) by Rev. W. S. Hooper; two excellent articles by Monsieur Cucheval-Clavigny ("Meth. Quart. Rev." Oct. 1872, and Jan. 1873) on "Peter Cartwright and Preaching in the West"; "Rev. Peter Cartwright D.D." by M. H. Chamberlin ("Pub. Ill. St. Hist Library", No. 7); "Ten Years of Preacher Life; Chapters from an Autobiography" (1859) by Wm. Henry Milburn; also his "Pioneers, Preachers, and People of the Mississippi Valley" (1860); "Forty Years of Pioneer Life: Memoir of John Mason Peck, D.D." (1864) edited by Rufus Babcock; "Autobiography, Correspondence, . . . of Lyman Beecher, D.D." (II Vols. 1864-1865) edited by Charles Beecher; "Life and Correspondence of Theodore Parker" (II Vols. 1864) by John Weiss; "Reminiscences, Historical and Biographical, of Sixty-Four Years in the Ministry," by Rev. Henry Boehm, edited (1865) by Rev. Joseph B. Wakeley; the "Life and Letters of Leonidas L. Hamline, D.D." by Walter C. Palmer, M.D., with introductory letters by Bishops Morris, Janes, and Thomson (1866; for other works on Hamline, see a lengthy article in the "Meth. Quart. Rev." January 1881); "Personal Reminiscences of the Life and Times of Gardiner Spring, D.D." (II Vols. 1866); "A Western Pioneer: or Incidents of the Life and Times of Rev. Alfred Brunson, A.M., D.D., embracing a Period of over Seventy Years written by himself" (1872-79); "The Life and Times of George Peck, D.D. written by himself" (1874); "Thirty Years in the Itineracy" (1875) by Rev. W. G. Miller; "Life of Rev. Thomas A. Morris, D.D." (1875) by Rev. John F. Maclay; "Thomas A. Morris, D.D." ("Meth. Quart. Rev." July 1875); "The Life and Labors of Bishop Enoch Mather Marvin . . . " (1879) by Rev. T. M. Finney; "A Fruitful Life; A Narrative of the Experiences and Missionary Labors of Stephen Paxson" (1882) by B. Paxson Drury; "Autobiography of Rev. Luther Lee, D.D." (1882); "Crumbs from my Saddle Bags, . . . " (1884) by Rev. E. Gavitt; "Recollections of my Life, Fifty Years of Itineracy in the North West" (1885) by Charles Hobart; "Recollections of a Missionary in the Great West" (1900) by Cyrus T. Brady.

The four following, difficult to classify, should not be overlooked: "A Plea for the West" (1835) by Lyman Beecher; "New Guide for

Emigrants to the West . . . " (1836) by John M. Peck; "Elements of Western Character" by the same writer ("Christian Review" January, 1851); "Early Methodism in the West" by Rev. S. W. Williams ("Meth. Quart. Rev." Oct. 1871).

Turning from the literature that deals with the area as a whole to sectional studies, for Kentucky, in addition to citations on the Second Awakening (see p. 330f) there is, "An Outline of the History of the Church in the State of Kentucky during a period of Forty Years . . . with sketches of the Origin and Present State of Particular Churches" (1824) by Robert H. Bishop; "Memoirs of the Rev. Thomas Cleland, D.D., compiled from his Private Papers" by E. P. Humphrey and Thomas H. Cleland (1859); "A Brief History of the Revival of Religion in Centre College and in many of the Churches in . . . Synod of Kentucky during the Years, 1825, 1826, 1827, 1828" published by order of Transylvania Presbytery; "A History of Kentucky Baptists" (II Vols. 1885) by J. H. Spencer; "Historical Sketch of the Synod of Kentucky, 1802-1902" an address by E. W. C. Humphrey, and a "History of Ebenezer Presbytery of Kentucky" (1907) by Rev. J. P. Hendrick, D.D.

For Ohio, in addition to the references in connection with the Second Awakening (see p. 330f) there is an excellent general survey by Margaret J. Mitchell entitled, "Development of Religion in Early Ohio, 1788-1820" (A.M. Dissertation, Univ. of Chicago, 1914). Then follow "A Sketch of the Life of Rev. John Collins, late of the Ohio Conference" (1850), ascribed to Hon. John McLean; "The First Ten Years of the Protestant Episcopal Church in the Diocese of Ohio, 1818-1827" edited (1853) by W. C. French; "Ohio Congregationalism" ("Cong. Quarterly" April, 1863); "A Western Pioneer; or Incidents of the Life and Times of Rev. Alfred Brunson A. M. . . . written by Himself" (II Vols. 1872-79); "History of Western Reserve College 1826-1876" (1876) by Rev. Carroll Cutler, D.D.; "History of Presbyterianism in Ohio to the Year 1870 A.D." by Rev. William E. Moore D.D. (manuscript incomplete, Univ. of Chicago); "History of Ohio Methodism" (1898) by John M. Barker, Ph.D.; "History of the Presbyterian Church of Oxford, 1818-1825-1900" (1903) edited by Rev. T. J. Porter; "The History of Marion Presbytery" compiled (1908) by Rev. A. C. Crist; "The Presbytery of. Athens" (n.d.) by Rev. Charles B. Taylor; "Introduction of Methodism in Ohio" by Rev. I. F. King ("Pub. Ohio Arch. & Hist. Soc." Vol. X, No. 1); "Pictures of Early Methodism in Ohio" (1909) by Samuel W. Williams. "James Harris Fairchild, or Sixty-

Eight Years·with a Christian College" (1907) by Albert T. Swing throws much light upon Ohio, Oberlin College, and frontier conditions as far south as New Orleans. Considerable documentary material bearing on Congregational churches and ministers in Portage and Summit Counties will be found in the "Congregational Quarterly," July, 1861, April, and July, 1862.

The Ohio Church History Society has published the following short studies; "Early Ecclesiastical History of the Western Reserve" ("Papers, Ohio Church History Society," Vol. I, pp. 14-42); "A History of the First Religious Society in Marietta" (*ibid*. Vol. I, pp. 78-97); "Moravian Missions Upon Ohio Soil" (*ibid*. Vol. II, pp. 45-56); "Ohio Sunday School History" (*ibid*. Vol. III, pp. 1-21); "The Origin of the Disciples of Christ" (*ibid*. Vol. III, pp. 56-79); "The Story of Congregationalism on the Western Reserve (*ibid*. Vol. V, pp. 1-27); "Congregationalism in Central Ohio" (*ibid*. Vol. V, pp. 28-43); "History of Congregationalism in Ohio before 1852" (*ibid*. Vol. VII, pp. 31-55); "History of the Congregational Association of Ohio" (since 1852, *ibid*. Vol. VII, pp. 56-75); "A Century of Congregationalism in Cleveland" (*ibid*. Vol. VIII, pp. 1-45); "The History of Puritan Conference" (*ibid*. Vol. VIII, pp. 62-79); "Records of the Ecclesiastical Convention of New Connecticut" (1805-07, *ibid*. Vol. IX, pp. 1-24); "Chronological List of the Congregational Churches of Ohio" (*ibid*. Vol. IX, pp. 68-78); "History of Medina Conference" (*ibid*. Vol. XI, pp. 89-109); "A Hundred Years of Congregationalism in Upper Ohio Valley" (*ibid*. Vol. XII, pp. 12-32).

In these Papers the early history of the following churches appears: First Church, Cleveland (Vol. II, pp. 26-44); Wellington (Vol. III, pp. 27-55); First Church, Toledo (Vol. IV, pp. 17-28); Euclid Avenue, Cleveland (Vol. IV, pp. 44-57); Medina (Vol. V, pp. 72-92); Burton (Vol. VI, pp. 43-68); Columbus (Vol. VIII, pp. 45-62); Oberlin (Vol. VIII, pp. 80-109); Hudson (Vol. IX, pp. 32-41); Vine Street, Cincinnati (Vol. IX, pp. 41-57); Austinburg (Vol. X, pp. 63-79); Paddy's Run (Vol. X, pp. 79-100); Springfield (Vol. XI, pp. 51-65); Aurora (Vol. XI, pp. 66-82); Walnut Hills, Cincinnati (Vol. XII, pp. 33-46); Strongsville (Vol. XII, pp. 47-60); Geneva (Vol. XII, pp. 61-68).

For Indiana there is the following: "Life and Times of Rev. Allen Wiley, A.M." (1853) by Rev. F. C. Holliday; "Indiana Methodism; History of the Literary Institutions under the care of the Church" (1872) by the same author; "History of the Presbytery of Vincennes" (1888) by Rev. E. P. Whallen; "Indiana Methodism . . ." (1892) by Rev. J. L. Smith; "Congregationalism in Indiana" (1895) by Rev. N. A.

Hyde; "History of the Maria Creek Church" (1889) by Ben. F. Keith, M.D. (valuable for the Baptist anti-missionary movement); "The Scotch-Irish Presbyterians in Monroe County, Indiana" by James A. Woodburn ("Pub. Ind. Hist. Soc." Vol. IV, No. 8); "Indiana Methodism, 1816–1832" by Ruth Price ("Ind. Mag. of Hist." Vol. XI, No. 3); "Formation of the Christian Church in Indiana" by H. Clay Trusty (*ibid*. Vol. VI, No. 1); "Some Religious Developments in Indiana," by C. B. Coleman (*ibid*. Vol. V, No. 2); "Early History of Presbyterianism in the Whitewater Valley" by Rev. L. D. Potter (*ibid*. Vol. V, No. 1); "Plymouth Church, Indianapolis" by J. R. Roberts (*ibid*. Vol. VII, No. 1); "Early Methodist Circuits in Indiana" by W. W. Sweet (*ibid*. Vol. X, No. 4); "Franklin College, First Half Century . . . Jubilee Exercises" (1884); "Jubilee Anniversary of the First Presbyterian Church, Goshen, Indiana . . ." (1902) by Committee; "Indiana Baptist History 1798-1908" (1908) by Rev. W. T. Stott; "A History of the North Indiana Conference . . . 1844 to the Present" (1917) by H. N. Herrick and W. W. Sweet and "Circuit Rider Days in Indiana" (1916) by W. W. Sweet.

For Illinois the literature is as follows: "Sketches and Incidents of Rev. John Clark, by an old Pioneer" edited (1855) by Rev. J. M. Peck; "Memoir of John Mason Peck D.D. . . ." (1864) by Rufus Babcock and "The Prophet of the Prairies . . . John Mason Peck" (1917) by A. K. DeBlois; "Pioneer Congregational Ministers in Illinois" by G. S. F. Savage ("Jour. Ill. Hist. Soc." Vol. III, pp. 78-93); "History of Methodism in Illinois from 1793 to 1832" (1883) by Rev. James Leaton, D.D.; "Julian M. Sturtevant, An Autobiography" (1885) edited by his son, J. M. Sturtevant; "The Bishop Hill Colony. A Religious Communistic Settlement in Henry County, Illinois" by Michael A. Mikkelsen (J. H. Univ. Studies Ser. X, Sect. I); "Augustus Conant, Illinois Pioneer and Teacher" (1905) by Robert Collyer; "Life and Letters of W. A. Passavant, D.D." (1906) by G. H. Gerberding; "Church Records of Salt Creek Circuit, 1829–1833" edited by Milo Custer ("Jour. Ill. State Hist. Soc." Vol. IV, No. 1); "Early Religious Leaders and Methods in Illinois" by Rev. W. F. Short ("Pub. Ill. State Hist. Library," No. 7); "Historical Sketch of McKendree College" by President M. H. Chamberlin (*ibid*. No. 9); "Puritan Influences in the Formative Years of Illinois History" by Carrie Prudence Koford (*ibid*. No. 10); "History of the Presbyterian Church in the State of Illinois" (Vol. I, 1879) by A. T. Norton; "The Early History of Lutheranism in Illinois" ("Evang. Quart. Rev."October, 1866); "The Lutheran Church in Illinois" (*ibid*. Oct. 1873); "The Christian Church of Springfield" by Charles P. Kane ("Pub. Ill. State Hist.

Library" No. 12); "Pioneer Congregational Ministers in Illinois" by
G. S. F. Savage ("Jour. Ill. State Hist. Soc." Vol. III, No. 1); "The
Methodist Episcopal Church and Reconstruction" by W. W. Sweet,
(*ibid*. No. 20); "Fifty Years of Home Missions in Illinois" ("New Englander" July, 1876); "History of the Disciples of Christ in Illinois,
1819-1914" (1914) by N. S. Haynes; "The Pioneer School; A History of
Shurtleff College" (1900) by A. K. De Blois.

For Michigan there is literature as follows: "Protestantism in
Michigan; being a Special History of the Methodist Episcopal Church
and Incidentally of other Denominations" (1879) by E. H. Pilcher;
"Life and Labors of Elijah H. Pilcher of Michigan, fifty-nine years a
Minister of the Methodist Episcopal Church" edited (1892) by James
E. Pilcher, M.D; "The Congregational Churches of Michigan for the
first fifty years (1842–1892, addresses); "History of the Baptists in
Michigan" (1909) by M. E. D. Trowbridge and assistants; "The First
Presbyterian Church of Detroit" ("Coll. Mich. Pioneer Soc." Vol. I,
pp. 417-429); "History of the Episcopal Church in Michigan" (*ibid*. Vol.
III, pp. 213-222); "History of Methodism in Detroit" (*ibid*. Vol. III,
pp. 225-244); "History of Hillsdale College" (*ibid*. Vol. VI, pp. 137-166);
"Congregationalism in Michigan" (to 1884, *ibid*. Vol. VII, pp. 103-112);
"New England Influence in Michigan" (*ibid*. Vol. XVII, pp. 311-319).
In these "Pioneer Collections" there is much more miscellaneous
material. Most of the articles are brief and poorly worked up. Few
ecclesiastical documents have yet been published, and the historical
work does not impress one with its reliability.

Wisconsin has the following: "A Methodist Circuit Rider's Horse-
back Tour from Pennsylvania to Wisconsin, 1835" by Alfred Brunson,
D.D., the 'First Methodist Minister to set foot on soil north of the Wisconsin River' ("Coll. State Hist. Soc. of Wis." Vol. XV); "Journal of an
Episcopalian Missionary's Tour to Green Bay, 1834" by Jackson Kemper, D.D. (*ibid*. Vol. XIV); "Documents Relating to the Episcopal
Church and Mission in Green Bay, 1824-1841" edited by R.G. Thwaites
(*ibid*. Vol. XIV); "Lights and Shadows of Missionary Life; containing
Travels, Sketches, Incidents, and Missionary Efforts during nine years
spent in the region of Lake Superior" (1857) by Rev. John H. Pitezel;
"History of the Churches and Ministers Connected with the Presbyterian
and Congregational Conventions of Wisconsin, and of the Operations of
the American Home Missionary Society in the State for the Past Ten
Years" (1861) by Rev. Dexter Clary; "Pioneer Free Baptist Ministers
in Wisconsin" ("Free Will Baptist Quarterly," April, 1867); "Thirty

Years in the Itineracy" (1875) by Rev. W. G. Miller, D.D; "The Pioneer Preacher. An Autobiography" (1887) by Rev. Sherlock Bristol; "History of Methodism in Wisconsin in Four Parts" by Rev. P. S. Bennett, Part III being written (1890) by Rev. James Lawson.

Minnesota has the following: "Religious Movements in Minnesota" ("Coll. Minn. Hist. Soc." Vol. I, pp. 84-89); "Early Episcopal Churches and Missions in Minnesota" (*ibid.* Vol. X, Part I, pp. 203-231); "History of Methodism in Minnesota" (1887) by Rev. C. Hobart; "History of the First Presbyterian Church of Minneapolis, Minnesota, 1835-1910" (1910) by Rev. Albert B. Marshall, D.D.; "The History of Westminster Presbyterian Church of Minneapolis, Minnesota, and of the Celebration of its Fiftieth Anniversary, 1857–August 1907 . . . Prepared by a Committee"; "1858–1908, Synod of Minnesota. Presbyterian Church, U. S. A." (1909 historical addresses); "Congregationalism in Minnesota" (n.d.) by Rev. Archibald Hadden; "A Story of Minnesota Methodism" (1911) by Rev. W. McKinley.

For the Dakotas little seems to have been done of a constructive character. "The Baptist History of South Dakota" (1899) by T. M. Shanafelt, D.D., and "Joseph Ward of Dakota" (1913) by G. H. Durand are informing. The State Historical Societies as yet have not taken up seriously ecclesiastical phases of Dakota history.

For Iowa, the following is suggested: "Historical Sketches of Iowa Baptists" (1886) compiled by Rev. S. H. Mitchell; "The Amish Mennonites—A Sketch of their Origin and of their Settlement in Iowa" (1894) with an appendix containing their creed, by B. L. Wick;"The Quakers in Iowa" ("Annals of Iowa" Ser. III, Vol. III, pp. 263-276); "Journal of a Missionary in Jackson County, Iowa Territory, 1843–1846" (*ibid.* Vol. V, pp. 592-607); "Monona County Iowa Mormons" (*ibid.* Vol. VII, pp. 321-346); "Abner Kneeland: His Relations to Early Iowa History" (*ibid.* Vol. VI, pp. 340-364); "Whence Came the Pioneers of Iowa" (*ibid.* Vol. VII, pp. 367-379, 446-465); "Old Zion Church, Burlington, Iowa" (*ibid.* Vol. IX, pp. 524-534); "An Expedition Across Iowa in 1820; A Journal by S. W. Kearny" (*ibid.* Ser. III, Vol. X, pp. 343-371); "Journal of A. W. Harlan while Crossing the Plains in 1850" (*ibid.* Vol. XI, pp. 32-62); "Lutherans in Iowa" (*ibid.* Vol. XI, pp. 585-593); "Establishment of the Diocese of Iowa, Protestant Episcopal Church of America" (*ibid.* Vol. XI, pp. 291-303); "Early Social and Religious Experiments in Iowa" ("Iowa Hist. Record," Vol. XVI–XVIII, pp. 407-437); "Early Methodism in Northwest Iowa" (*ibid.* X–XII, pp. 296-308); "History of Presbyterianism in Iowa City" ("Iowa Jour. of Hist. and Politics" Vol. XIII, pp. 529-581); "History of the Northwest Iowa Conference,

1872–1903" (1904) by Bennett Mitchell; "History of the Iowa Annual
Conference . . . from 1833 to 1909 inclusive" (n.d.) by Edmund H.
Waring, D.D.; "Early Settlement and Growth of Western Iowa, or
Reminiscences" (1906) by Rev. John Todd; "History of the Upper
Iowa Conference . . . 1856–1906" (1907) by Stephen N. Fellows, D. D.;
"Amana, The Community of True Inspiration" (1908) by Bertha
M. H. Shambaugh, see also "The Amana Community" in "The Com-
munistic Societies of the United States (1874) by Charles Nordhoff;
"The Presbyterian Church in Iowa, 1837–1900", History Prepared by
Committee of Synod of Iowa, Joseph W. Hubbard, D. D., Chairman
(1907); "The Quakers of Iowa" by Louis T. Jones (doctoral dissertation,
1914). "The Iowa Band" (1870) by Rev. Ephraim Adams will be
found useful in the matter of Iowa Congregationalism, supplemented
by "The Pilgrims of Iowa" (1911) by Truman O. Douglas. The latter
gives classified lists of churches and pastors with dates of organizations
and inceptions.

Missouri literature is as follows: "Life and Times of Rev. William
Patton, and Annals of the Missouri Conference" (1858) by Rev. D. R.
McAnally; "Memoirs of Rev. William Jackson" (1860) by Margaret A.
Jackson; "The Early History of the Presbyterian Church in Missouri"
("Pres. Quart. Rev." July, 1861); "Memoir of Rev. Samuel B. McPheeters, D.D." (1870) by Rev. John S. Grasby; "History of Baptists in
Missouri" (1882) by R. S. Duncan; "Annals of Methodism in Missouri
. . . 1806 to 1884" (1886) by W. S. Woodard; "Historical and Biograph-
ical Sketches of the Early Churches and Pioneer Preachers of the Christian Church in Missouri" (1888) by Rev. T. P. Haley; "Fifty Years on
the Skirmish Line" (1893) by Rev. E. B. Sherwood; "Fiftieth Anniversary, Grand Avenue Presbyterian Church . . . St. Louis" (1904);
"History of the Presbyterian Church in Saline County, Missouri" (1906)
by J. L. Woodbridge; "Reminiscences of a Missionary" (1906) by Rev.
D. S. Tuttle. "Presbyterianism in the Ozarks. A History of the Work
. . . Presbyterian Church in Southwest Missouri 1834-1907 . . . "
(1909) by Rev. E. E. Stringfield; "Presbyterianism in Saline County,
Missouri" ("Mo. Hist. Review" Vol. I, pp. 267-273); "Rev. Jesse Walker, The Apostle of the Wilderness" (ibid. Vol. II, pp. 261-296); "A German Communistic Society in Missouri" (ibid. Vol. III, pp. 52-74,
99-125); "Methodist Church, Early History, in Saline County" (ibid. Vol.
VI, pp. 14-33); "History of Missouri Baptist General Association"
(ibid. Vol. VII, pp. 76-88); "Lights and Shadows of Seventy Years (1913)
by J. E. Godbey D.D.

The German Evangelical Lutheran Synod of Missouri and other States organized 1846, may be thoroughly understood by consulting "Auswanderung der saechsischen Lutheraner im Jahre 1838, ihre Niederlassung in Perry Co., Mo., und damit zusammenhaengende interessante Nachrichten . . . " (1867), Von. J. F. Koestering; the "Lebenslauf" (II Vols. 1880) of William Sihler; "Die Geschichte der Evangelisch-Lutherischen Missouri-Synode in Nordamerika, und ihre Lehrkaempfe von der saechsischen Auswanderung im Jahre 1838 an bis zum Jahre 1884," dargestellt von Christian Hochstetter, Pastor in Wolcottsville, (1885); Guentker's "Lebensbild" (1890) of C. F. W. Walther; "Doctor Carl Ferdinand Wilhelm Walther" (1917) by D. H. Steffens; Walther's "Briefe" (II Vols., 1915-16); and "Der Lutheranen" (official organ, since Sept. 1, 1844).

Kansas has the following: "Western Border Life; or what Fanny Hunter saw and heard in Kansas and Missouri" (1856); "Pioneer Days in Kansas" (1903) by Richard Cordley; "Settlements of the Friends in Kansas" ("Coll. Kansas State Hist. Soc." Vol. VII, pp. 322-361); "The Friends Establishment in Kansas Territory" (*ibid*. Vol. VIII, pp. 250-277); "Methodist Missions Among the Indian Tribes in Kansas" (*ibid*. Vol. IX, pp. 160-231); "The Methodist Episcopal Church South in Kansas 1854-1906" (*ibid*. Vol. XII, pp. 135-181); "Experiences of a Pioneer Missionary" (*ibid*. Vol. XIII, pp. 278-318, 319-344); "Memoirs of a Pioneer Missionary and Chaplain in the United States Army" (*ibid*. Vol. XIII, pp. 319-344); "Congregationalism in Kansas" ("Cong. Quarterly" July, 1876).

For Arkansas, there is a "History of Methodism in Arkansas" (1892) by Horace Jewell; "The History of Presbyterianism in Arkansas, 1828-1902" (n.d.) prepared by a Committee; and "Presbyterianism in Arkansas" ("Jour. Pres. Hist. Soc." Vol. III, pp. 57-70).

For Nebraska there is: "The Autobiography of Rev. William Hamilton" ("Trans. and Reports of the Nebr. State Hist. Soc." Vol. I, pp. 60-85); "Forty Years among the Indians and on the Eastern Borders of Nebraska" (*ibid*. Vol. II, pp. 133-166); "Congregational College History in Nebraska" (*ibid*. Vol. III, pp. 243-269); "Early Life in Nebraska" (*ibid*. Vol. V, pp. 205-240); "Extracts from the Diary of Rev. Moses Merrill, a Missionary to the Otoe Indians from 1832-1840" (*ibid*. Vol. IV, pp. 160-191); "A History of Nebraska Methodism . . . 1854-1904" (1904) by Rev. David Marquette D.D.

For the mountain and coast region, there is the following: "Journal of an Exploring Tour Beyond the Rocky Mountains, under the Direction of the A.B.C.F.M." (1838) by Rev. Samuel Parker, A.M.; "The Territories on the Pacific" ("Christian Review," October, 1850); "Oregon" ("Meth. Quarterly Review" Jan. 1850); "California" by Edwin Bryant (*ibid*. Oct. 1850); "Three Years in California" (1850) by Rev. Walter Colton; "Sixteen Months at the Gold Diggings" (1851) by Daniel B. Woods; "Seven Years Street Preaching in San Francisco, California" (1856) by Rev. William Taylor; "Wyoming, Its History, Stirring Incidents and Romantic Adventures" (1858) by George Peck, D.D.; "A History of the M. E. Church in the South West from 1844 to 1864 . . . (1865) by Rev. Charles Elliott, revised by Rev. L. M. Vernon; "The Metropolis of the Pacific" ("Meth. Quart. Rev." Jan., 1869); "Our Pacific Coast Problem" (*ibid*. Jan. 1881, see bibliography); "The Early Days of My Episcopate" (1891) by Right Rev. Wm. Ingraham Kip" D.D.; "The Relations and Results of our Early Missionary Work in Oregon" ("Meth. Quart. Rev.," May, 1893); "Missionary History of the Pacific Northwest" (1899) by Rev. H. R. Hines; "The Pioneer Preacher, An Autobiography" (1887) by Rev. Sherlock Bristol; "The Mormons" (1904) by Samuel E. Wishard, D.D., Synodical Missionary for Utah; "Dr. John McLoughlin, the Father of Oregon" (1907) by Fred V. Holman; "Addresses at the Memorial Services of Jason Lee," also "Extracts from his Journal" ("Quart. Oregon Hist. Soc.," Vol. VII, pp. 225-287); "Correspondence of the Reverend Ezra Fisher, Pioneer Missionary of the American Baptist Home Missionary Society in Indiana, Illinois, Iowa, and Oregon" (*ibid*. Vol. XVI, pp. 65-104, 227-310, 379-413); the "History of the Oregon Missions" (n.d.) by Rev. Gustanus Hines; "First Things Pertaining to Presbyterianism on the Pacific Coast" ("Quart. Oregon Hist. Soc.," Vol. XV, pp. 81-103); "My People of the Plains" by Rev. E. Talbot, D.D. (1906, has data on Wyoming and Idaho); "Reminiscences of a Missionary Bishop" (1906) by Rev. D. S. Tuttle, D.D. (gives twenty years' experience in Montana, Idaho, and Utah); "The Pioneer Work of the Presbyterian Church in Montana" (1906) edited by Rev. George Edwards, reprinted from "Contributions of the Hist. Society of Montana" Vol. VI; "Religious Progress on the Pacific Slope" (1907, addresses at semi-centennial anniversary of Pacific School of Religion, Berkeley, California—see Part II); "History of the Synod of Washington of the Presbyterian Church in the United States of America, 1835-1909" by a Committee; "Sheldon Jackson, Pathfinder and Prospector in the Rocky Mountains" (1908) by Rev. R. L. Stewart.

On the several revivals that occurred in the Middle West prior to the Civil War, the most informing accounts are those appearing in periodicals such as the "Home Missionary" and in "Annual Reports" of the various conventions and missionary societies. The following have some value: "Accounts of Religious Revivals in Many Parts of the United States from 1815 to 1818 . . . " (1819) by Joshua Bradley, A.M.; "Autobiography of Brantley York" (for revivals about 1824); "Autobiography of Elder Jacob Knapp—With an Introductory Essay by R. Jeffry" (1867); "The Religious Awakening of 1858" ("The New Englander" for 1858); "Memoirs of Rev. Charles G. Finney" written by himself, issued (1876) by J. H. Finney; "Charles Grandison Finney" (1891) by G. F. Wright; "The New York Pulpit in the Revival of 1858—A Memorial Volume of Sermons" (1858). Two related studies are suggestive: "A Stormy Epoch, 1825-1850" ("Papers, Ohio Ch. Hist. Soc." Vol. VI, pp. 1-22), and "Our Notable Decade" by D. L. Leonard ("Bibliotheca Sacra" April 1889).

The important influence exercised by the numerous colleges planted in the frontier areas has not been treated in any single monograph. The best source of information is "The American Quarterly Register and Journal" (1827 f.). This periodical has a mass of material treating of the rise of the colleges and their revivals, statistical data concerning the growth of the several religious bodies, and much literature setting forth the necessity of an educated ministry and the work of the Educational Societies.

It remains to refer to the attempts, which have been made to generalize in a historical way upon the field which has been reviewed locally. "Leavening the Nation. The Story of American Home Missions" (1902) by Joseph B. Clark, is a stirring recital of the part played by missions in national development. For the Baptists, John M. Peck has a contribution entitled "Baptists of the Mississippi Valley" ("Christian Review" October, 1852). This should be supplemented by "A History of the Baptists in the Western States East of the Mississippi" (1896) by Justin A. Smith; "A History of the Baptists in the Trans-Mississippi States" (n.d.) by Lemuel Moss; "A History of the Baptists in the Southern States East of the Mississippi" (1898) by B. F. Riley; and "A Century of Baptist Achievement" edited (1901) by A. H. Newman.

For the Presbyterians, there is the "Centennial of Home Missions in connection with the One Hundred and Fourteenth General Assembly of the Presbyterian Church in the United States of America, New York City, May 16-20, 1902" (1902), and "Presbyterian Home Missions. An Account of the Home Missions of the Presbyterian Church in the United States of America" (1902) by Sherman H. Doyle.

"Religious Progress of the Mississippi Valley" ("Christian Review" Oct. 1854) by John M. Peck gives a good survey of Presbyterianism and Congregationalism in the Western Reserve. "The Expansion of New England" (1909) by Lois K. Mathews, and "Some Activities of the Congregational Church west of the Mississippi" ("Essays in American History" dedicated to F. J. Turner, 1910) by the same writer are particularly illuminating.

On Methodism there is "The Present State, Prospects, and Responsibilities of the Methodist Episcopal Church" (1850) by Nathan Bangs, D.D., containing important statistical information; "The Centenary of American Methodism" (1865) by Abel Stevens, LL.D.; "The Centenary of American Methodism" ("Methodist Quarterly Review," April 1866); "Pages from the early History of the West and Northwest . . . Sketches of the material and religious Progress of the States of Ohio, Indiana, Illinois and Missouri, with especial Reference, to the History of Methodism" (1868) by Rev. S. R. Beggs; "Southwestern Methodism; A History of the Methodist Episcopal Church in the Southwest, from 1844 to 1864" (1865) by Rev. Charles Elliott; "Statistical History of the First Century of American Methodism—with a Summary of the Origin and Present Operations of the Denominations" (1867) by Rev. C. C. Goss; "Supplementary History of American Methodism" (1899) by Abel Stevens, covering the period 1866 to 1890.

For Lutheranism, there is "The Evangelical Lutheran Church in the United States of America" ("Evang. Quart. Rev." Jan. 1869); "The Lutheran Church Between the Potomac and the Rio Grande" (*ibid.* April 1879); "Home Mission and Church Extension Work Among Lutherans, Especially in the Great Northwest" (*ibid.* Oct. 1879), and the "Reminiscences of Deceased Lutheran Ministers" published in various numbers of this magazine between 1867 and 1870.

For the Mennonites, there is "The History of the General Conference of the Mennonites of North America" (1898) by H. P. Krehbiel, B.D.

The above histories, along with the work represented by the volumes of the "American Church History Series," constitute the small amount of historical work that has been done in this important and stimulating field.

DOCUMENTS

I. *THE PLAN OF UNION OF 1801*

Regulations adopted by the General Assembly of the Presbyterian Church in America, and by the General Association of the State of Connecticut with a view to prevent alienation and promote union and harmony, in those new settlements which are composed of inhabitants from those bodies.

1st. It is strictly enjoined· on all. their missionaries to the new settlements, to endeavor by all proper means, to promote mutual forbearance and accommodation, between those inhabitants of the new settlements who hold the Presbyterian, and those who hold the Congregational form of Church government.

2d. If in the new settlements, any Church of the Congregational order, shall settle a minister of the Presbyterian order, that Church may, if they choose, still conduct their discipline according to Congregational principles, settling their difficulties among themselves, or by a council mutually agreed upon for that purpose. But if any difficulty shall exist between the minister and the Church or any member of it, it shall be referred to the Presbytery to which the minister shall belong, provided both parties agree to it; if not, to a council consisting of an equal number of Presbyterians and Congregationalists, agreed upon by both parties.

3d. If a Presbyterian Church shall settle a minister of Congregational principles, that Church may still conduct their discipline according to Presbyterian principles; excepting that if a difficulty arise between him and his Church, or any member of it, the cause shall be tried by the Association to which the said minister shall belong, provided both parties agree to it; otherwise by a council, one half Congregationalists and the other half Presbyterians, mutually agreed on by the parties.

4th. If any congregation consist partly of those who hold the Congregational form of discipline, and partly of those who hold the Presbyterian form, we recommend to both parties, that this be no obstruction to their uniting in one church and settling a minister; and that, in this case, the Church choose a standing committee from the communicants of said church, whose business it shall be, to call to account every member of the church, who shall conduct himself inconsistently with the laws of Christianity, and to give judgment on such conduct; and if the person condemned by their judgment be a Presbyterian, he shall have liberty to appeal to the Presbytery; if a Congregationalist, he shall have liberty to appeal to the body of the male communicants of the church; in the former case, the determination of the Presbytery shall be final, unless the Church consent to a further appeal to the Synod, or to the General Assembly; and in the latter case, if the party condemned shall wish for a trial by a mutual council, the cause shall be referred to such council. And provided the said standing committee of any church shall depute one of themselves to attend the Presbytery, he may have the same right to sit and act in the Presbytery, as a ruling elder of the Presbyterian Church.

On motion, *Resolved*, That an attested copy of the above Plan be made by the stated clerk, and put into the hands of the delegates of this Assembly to the General Association, to be by them laid before that body for their consideration; and that if it should be approved by them, it go into immediate operation.

Text—Thompson: *A History of the Presbyterian Churches in the United States* (Amer. Ch. Hist. Ser. Vol. VI), 3rd edition, pp. 353-355.

II. *THE HOME MISSIONARY'S TASK*

From the "General Instructions" issued by the American Home Missionary Society, to its missionaries, one may estimate their contribution to frontier and undeveloped communities.

Although the preaching of the Gospel holds the first and highest place in the vows and responsibilities of the ministerial office, yet there are a variety of subordinate measures, which, with a view to the permanent and best effect of Gospel ordinances, require the diligent attention of every Pastor and every Missionary.   This is especially the case in congregations where, from their recent organization, or other causes, the importance of religion and of religious institutions is not generally understood and felt. The Committee of the A. H M. S. therefore request your attention to the following measures, as important to be adopted and vigorously pursued in the station assigned you.

1.   Without wishing to abridge your liberty and obligation, as a minister of Christ, to take part in the general government of the church, and as far as practicable to seek the spiritual good of the surrounding country, the Committee will expect you to confine your labours principally to the field designated in this Commission, that the people, for whose benefit the aid of this Society in your support is especially designed, may learn, from the influence of your uninterrupted efforts, suitably to appreciate the importance of a settled ministry, and that they may thus be induced and strengthened the sooner to maintain the administration of Christian ordinances without assistance from others.

2.   The visitation of families and of the sick is particularly enjoined, as second in importance only to the public preaching of the word. In the performance of these duties the Committee will expect you to visit every family within the limits of your charge, which is not under the pastoral care of some other minister; and that you will feel the importance of making your visits strictly religious and ministerial, urging upon individuals with faithfulness and affection the necessity of repentance towards God, and faith in our Lord Jesus Christ, and in families inculcating the importance of family religion.

3.   The visiting of schools, and the establishment and superintendence of sabbath schools and bible classes, are objects which claim your careful and zealous attention, and which the Committee urge upon your notice with strong solicitude. These measures, dictated by benevolence, and pursued with Christian humility and kindness, will not fail, with the blessing of God, to give you access to the best affections of the youth of your charge, and will thus secure to you the delightful and important privilege of mingling a correct and powerful moral influence in the whole system of their education.

In schools, let it be your object to encourage weekly catechetical instruction, and daily religious worship.

In the institution and conducting of sabbath schools, you will be expected to avail yourselves of the recommendation of the most approved Societies or Unions for this purpose, and in pursuance of the same, to adopt the most economical and efficient methods of instruction, and of procuring sabbath school libraries.

In your manner of conducting bible classes, reference must of course be had to the capacity and present acquirements of the individuals who compose them. Of these classes, you will be expected to be yourself the Superintendent and Teacher; and it is important that they be so organized as to extend the advantages of biblical instruction, not only to youth, but to those of more advanced life.

4.   Meetings for prayer should be held at such convenient times and places as shall afford to all the families within your charge the privilege of attending them. These meetings the Committee will expect you to encourage and promote; and particularly that you will hold the Monthly Concert for Prayer, on the evening of the

first Monday in every month. Of this it is desirable that you give previous public notice from the pulpit, and that you make it an occasion for communicating to the people, in a concise form, such missionary intelligence as you shall have received during the preceding month.

5. The Committee take a deep and lively interest in the cause of Foreign as well as of Domestic Missions, and in the objects of the Education, Bible, Tract, and Sabbath School Societies, and will expect you, by every means in your power, to promote these great enterprises of Christian benevolence. You are particularly desired to solicit the co-operation of your people, as far as they have ability, in the work of Home Missions; and where it is practicable, to form Societies or Associations auxiliary to this Society, or to the nearest County, State, Synodical, Presbyterial, or other Society connected with this.

For the purpose of supplying the destitute within the bounds of your missionary charge with bibles, tracts, and sabbath school books, you are desired to hold correspondence with each of the National Societies for these purposes, and, according to their several recommendations, to promote the formation of Societies auxiliary to the parent Institutions, or to their Branches or Auxiliaries in the State or County embracing the field of your labour. By these measures, it is believed, you will be able to procure all needed supplies of bibles, tracts, and sabbath school requisites; and having procured them, you are desired yourself, as far as is practicable, to take a leading part in their distribution.

6. The Committee regard with great pleasure and gratitude to God, the recent efforts of many churches, physicians, and leading civilians of our country, for the promotion of temperance. Among the numerous and deplorable evils resulting from the use of ardent spirits, none is more universal than that of counteracting all the means which God has appointed for the moral improvement of mankind, and the salvation of souls. You are desired, therefore, publicly and privately, to instruct the people to whom you minister, respecting the causes, symptoms, and fatal consequences of intemperance, and endeavour to persuade them to abstain from the use of intoxicating drinks.

Lastly, and particularly, it is desired, that not only 'in doctrine you be uncorrupt,' but that you 'show yourself a pattern of good works'; 'by manifestation of the truth, commending yourself to every man's conscience in the sight of God.' As an ambassador of the Prince of Peace, 'follow peace with all men'; and avoiding reflections upon other denominations of Christians, let your conversation in the world show that you have at heart, not the interests of a sect or party, but the salvation of souls, and the prosperity of the Redeemer's cause. Be eminently a man of prayer; and, as you are bound to do by the terms of your own consecration to the work of the ministry, 'preach Christ, and him crucified.' Be faithful unto death, and the fruit of your labour will be 'unto holiness, and the end everlasting life.'

Text—*The Home Missionary*, May, 1830.

III. *THE REVIVALS OF 1830*

The *recent revivals of religion*, as they have been termed, appear to have commenced in the Western part of New York, in Rochester and the surrounding region, in the autumn of 1830. During the next three or four months, the work spread rapidly, and extended itself over a considerable portion of the state. In the course of the winter, favorable appearances were observed in the city of New York, which at the opening of the spring, assumed a most cheering and decisive character.   Nearly all the evangelical churches in the city have shared in the revival, and thousands, it is hoped, have been born of God.   Whilst the work was thus pervading the city and state of New York, it made its appearance in the Western parts of Massachusetts, and in various places in Connecticut.   At the same time, the tokens of God's presence and power were displayed in some of the principal towns in Maine.   About the first of March, an unusual spirit of prayer was imparted to the churches in Boston, and it began to be apparent that the Lord was there.   From that time, the work has been in progress in Boston, and the surrounding region, and many have been made the happy subjects of renewing grace.   At the same time that the revival was thus extending itself Eastward, it was also spreading to the South and West.   Philadelphia, Charleston, the District of Columbia, Cincinnati, and various places in the Middle, Southern and Western States, have been visited, and in nearly every place to which the work has come, it is still in progress. It has been estimated by one who has paid particular attention to the subject, and has the best means of forming a judgment, that as many as a "thousand congregations in the United States have been visited within six months, to a greater or less extent, with revivals of religion; and that the whole number of conversions is probably not less than fifty thousand."   Truly this is a great and glorious work—sufficient to fill the hearts of God's people with humility and gratitude and their mouths with thanksgiving! A work, in the promotion of which holy beings on earth and in heaven have combined their influence, and have rejoiced together!

This work derives additional importance from the *situation and rank* of many of the principal places that have been visited.   It is worthy of special notice that those places have partaken most largely of the blessing which exert the greatest influence upon society.   *Cities* and *colleges* have been the scenes of the deepest interest, as if the divine Spirit would correct the streams of moral influence by purifying the fountains. The colleges which have been most favored are Yale, Amherst, Middlebury, Bowdoin, Williams, Hamilton, Jefferson, Kenyon, Union, Hampden Sydney, New-Jersey, Western Reserve, and the University of Ohio.   The whole number of students who appear to have become subjects of piety in these institutions, during the present revival, is *three hundred and twenty*.   The effects of this change will not be limited to these young men.   Hundreds and thousands will doubtless, experience in consequence of it a similar change in their characters and destiny for eternity, and a multitude which no man can number will rejoice in the result forever.

. . . .

In this work of salvation, individuals of all ranks, ages, and characters have been included.   The child of six and seven years, yet in the infant school, and the aged sinner who had passed his fourscore years in rebellion, have, in the same congregation, been brought together at the feet of Jesus, and some of all the intermediate ages.   The great and learned officers of State, and the most illiterate servants, have been found together in the same prayer meeting, on a level before the throne of God.   The man of wealth and the poor man, have united in *begging for mercy* of Him who is no respector of persons.   It is however believed that no previous revival ever took so large a proportion of the wealth and learning and influence of society as this has done.   Literary and professional man who are at the head of society, giving the tone to public sentiment, have been brought into the kingdom in far greater numbers than ever before was known.   Moral men, who have regarded themselves as approved of God on account of the purity of their lives, and the openly vicious and profane, have been alike humbled before God on account of their vileness, and the just sentence of wrath which was upon them.   In many instances the intemperate, tottering upon the verge of a drunkard's grave, have been rescued by the sovereign mercy of God, and made temperate, sober Christians.   Some of every character and condition in life have been taken, so that we need not despair of any, but should labor and pray in hope and faith for all.

In some congregations, especially in the western section of the state of New York, the work has been so general and thorough, that the whole customs of society have been changed.   Amusements and all practices of a doubtful character, the object of which is simply pleasure, have been abandoned, and far higher and purer enjoyment is found in the exercises of devotion, and engagements for the glory of God, and the salvation of men. . .

Text—*The American Baptist Magazine*, Vol. XI, pp. 276-278.

IV. *THE PLEA FOR DENOMINATIONAL CO-OPERATION*

"How often and how emphatically did our Saviour pray that his disciples might be united, and propose this as the result, 'that the world might believe that thou hast sent me.'   The conversion of the world, then, depends on the union of Christians.   As soon as the church shall flow together, the nations will flow unto her. . .

The friends of division, sometimes compare the separate movements of different denominations to those of the twelve tribes, marching in orderly procession through the wilderness.   They might rather have compared them to the journey of brethren, who are continually falling out by the way; or to the movements of allied armies, which are foolishly annoying and weakening each other, by mutual jealousies and broils, instead of uniting their whole strength against the common enemy.

. . . .

Every friend of his country, as well as every friend of religion, should therefore engage in this work.   It is most obviously our wisdom, as well as our duty, to unite in the North and East, for planting the gospel in the South and West.   The strength of the nation lies beyond the Alleghany.   The centre of dominion is fast moving in that direction.   The ruler of this country is growing up in the great valley: leave him without the gospel, and he will be a ruffian giant, who will regard neither the decencies of civilization, nor the charities of religion.   Oh, sir, it is impossible, whether we contemplate the republic, or the world, it is impossible to overrate the importance of forming the rising character of our new states on the principles of the gospel! When, then, we place ourselves on the top of the Alleghany, survey the immense valley beyond it, and consider that the character of its eighty or one hundred million inhabitants, a century hence, will depend on the direction and impulse given it now, in its forming state; must not every Christian feel disposed to forego every party consideration, and cordially unite with his fellow Christians, to furnish them those means of intellectual and moral cultivation, of which they now stand in need, and for which they are constantly sending us their importunate petitions?   And what we do, we must do quickly.   The tide of population will not wait till we have settled every metaphysical point of theology, and every canon of church government.   While we are deliberating, the mighty swell is rising higher and higher on the sides of the mountains.

. . . .

And every denomination which is a wise calculator for herself, while she obeys the stronger impulse of benevolence, will readily co-operate in the enterprise.   In this age of the world, especially in our free country, every denomination whose main energy consists in her sectarian spirit, must ultimately dwindle. "

From address of Rev. J. Van Vecten, Pastor Dutch Reformed Church, Schenectady, N. Y. at the Anniversary of the American Home Missionary Society, May, 1829. Text—*The Home Missionary*, June, 1829.

Overture for Christian Union

Submitted for the Consideration of the Evangelical Denominations in the United States (1838).

"Christian Brethren:

The undersigned respectfully address you, in the name of the Lord Jesus, on the great and cardinal interests of our common Christianity. That the blessed Saviour designed an intimate union between the different members of his mystical body, the Church, is elevated above all doubt by his own declaration, 'One is your Master, Christ, and ye are all brethren.' . . .

And what enlightened friend of Zion must not confess, that it is the divided, the fractional, the isolated, and in some measure even the hostile condition of Protestantism, which has shorn the Church of so much of her strength? . . .

The weakness of Protestantism undoubtedly lies in its divided and disjoined state, or, rather, in the principle on which its divisions are constructed. . .

Happily, the attention of the Church has been extensively arrested by the deficiences of the present Protestant organization. To say nothing of the efforts of eminent disciples of Christ in the last two centuries, leading minds of the present day, in our own and foreign lands, have had their attention fixed upon it. Not a few have spoken through the press, and there seems to be a prevailing impression that the time is at hand when something should be done in earnest to heal *the great schism*, to resist the encroachments of this Antichrist of the Protestant Churches. . .

In like manner, at the recent meeting of the General Synod of the Lutheran Church in the United States, convened in Philadelphia, the subject of Christian Union was discussed and acted on with great interest and deliberateness. Two plans were proposed, one by the Rev. Dr. Stockton of the Protestant Methodist Church and one by Rev. Dr. Schmucker, the chairman of the General Synod's committee. Whilst some features of the former were regarded with much favor, the latter plan was adopted in full, as embodied in the following resolutions:

Resolved, 1. That a committee be appointed by this body to be styled the '*Committee of Conference on Christian Union*.' . . .

4. That this committee shall consist of three ministers and two laymen, belonging to some synod or synods connected with the General Synod.

This committee, having consulted with the other subscribers, we unitedly submit to you an outline of that plan of union by which we hope the evils of schism can be gradually obviated, and the great and glorious object of Christian Union be eventually attained. . . . Attempts which terminate in new divisions are obviously premature and unwise. And we may premise as fundamental principles that the plan to be adopted must possess the following attributes: 1. It must require of no one the renunciation of any doctrine or opinion believed by him to be true, nor the profession of anything he regards as erroneous. The accession of any one denomination to this union does not imply any sanction of the peculiarities of any other. 2. It must concede to each denomination the right to retain its own organization for government, discipline, and worship, or to alter it at option.   3.   It must dissuade no one from discussing fundamentals and non-fundamentals if done in the spirit of Christian Love. 4.   The plan must be such as is applicable to all *Evangelical* *fundamentally Orthodox Churches,* and must not aim at inducing some of the denominations to relinquish their peculiar views, but must be based on the existing common ground of doctrine, and erect a superstructure of kindly feeling, and harmonious intercourse, and fraternal co-operation.   5.   Each denomination may at option adopt any part, or all the proposed features of union.

With these preliminary specifications we propose:

1.   As one object of this union is to bear witness to the truth, and as well to impress upon ourselves, as to exhibit to the world, the fundamental doctrinal unity of the Evangelical Protestant Churches, therefore, *any denomination wishing to accede to this Union, can do so by a resolution of its highest judiciary, embodying its assent to the common ground of Christian Doctrine, as exhibited, for the present, in the appended selection from the articles of the principal Protestant Confessions.* . . .

2.   Let the Supreme judicatories of the several orthodox churches resolve to open and sustain a regular ecclesiastical intercourse, by sending a delegate to the stated meetings of the highest judicatory of each such denomination, who ought to be received as advisory members, but have no vote.   This practice which already exists between some Protestant denominations has been attended by the happiest effects, and ought to be extended as far as convenient to all.

3.   Co-operation of the different associated churches in voluntary associations, local and general, should be encouraged as far as the sentiment of the respective denominations is prepared for it, under constitutions, avowing the United Apostolic Protestant Confession, and securing equal rights to all its members.   This principle is especially applicable to Bible, Tract, Sabbath School and Foreign Missionary Societies, and has already been introduced in a large portion of the Protestant denominations.

4.   The Bible should, as much as possible, be made the text-book in all theological, congregational, and Sabbath School instruction.

5.   One general Anniversary Celebration should be held at some central place, under the management of a committee of arrangements one member of which is to be selected from each confederated denomination, and after its formal accession to the union, to be appointed by its supreme judicatory. . . .

6.   Free sacramental communion ought to be occasionally practised by all whose views of duty allow it.

7.   The formal adoption of these features, or of any part of them, if the first be included, shall constitute the adopting body an integral part of the Apostolic Protestant Union.   Should any denomination wish to reserve any one of the features, except the first, for future consideration, such reservation shall not invalidate its accession to the residue. . . .

> S. S. SCHMUCKER, D.D., Prof. of Theol., Theol.
> Seminary, Gettysburg, Pa."
> and 41 other signatures representing at least
> ten leading religious bodies.

Text—Sanford: *Origin and History of the Federal Council of the Churches of Christ in America,* pp. 404-417

Weakness of Churches; its Cause and Effect

"Every denomination naturally feels that it must be strong in the centers of population; and so, without asking whether the church of Christ needs so many congregations there, we crowd our six separate enterprises, of as many rival names, into a little place where two churches would do more good than the half dozen.

The evils that result from this course are many and various.   One consequence of it is, a weakening of the unity and the moral force of the church as a whole.   Another is, the diminution of the numbers and the strength of the several local societies, so that an amount of assistance many times greater is needed, and this need is prolonged for years, when, often, its period should have been reckoned in months.   But a third consequence of this overcrowding of one portion of the missionary field is the *destitution* of other portions.   While many villages are so well supplied as to leave pastors and churches leisure to quarrel, many rural districts and young communities are almost totally neglected.   If all the preachers in the United States were evangelical men, well educated and devoted to their work, they would no more than supply the real wants of the country, upon a system of wise distribution.   On a system, then, so unfortunate as this, its destitutions are not supplied; and we hear from all quarters, the cry—send more laborers into the harvest.   Again, a fourth consequence of our denominational divisions, and another cause of destitution, is seen in the difficulty of persuading young men of enterprise to enter the ministry. . . .   There is not the least doubt that this diminution in the size of parishes is also a diminution in the attractiveness of the pastoral office.   And so, this very multitude of denominations which has increased the want of ministers, operates, in more ways than one, to diminish the supply.

But what is yet worse, it tends to *injure* the ministry.   No preacher but has felt, at times, the depressing influence of a small audience.   A large proportion of the missionaries at the West feel this at all times; and often the intellect is jaded, and the heart is wearied out, from the want of that natural stimulus which the presence of a multitude and the pressure of an important occasion alone can afford. . . .

So, churches are born weak, and are compelled to worry through a long and fretful infancy, are kept on a diet irritatingly low, and compelled to struggle, with slow and uncertain growth, toward a maturity which must come late, and may come never.

. . . .

But facts are at hand which show that the relative number of feeble churches is much larger at the West than at the East.   Of the churches in Illinois and Iowa connected with three leading denominations, the proportion that must be accounted very weak—having not more than twenty-five communicants—is almost twice as great as in the same denominations taken entire, and amounts to nearly *two fifths* of the whole number reporting.   These, again, taken with those whose membership ranges between twenty-five and fifty, make up nearly 70 *per cent.* of the whole!

With these facts before us, and in view also of the terrible prevalence of the greatest evils, and of the overwhelming preponderance which a spirit of worldliness has in affairs public and private; in view of the immensity of the work which must be accomplished before this can be considered a truly *christian* nation, is it not obvious that the cause of Christ does not call for any further subdivision.

. . . .

The exigencies of the present day call us with solemn emphasis to fling aside all prejudices of party, and to consolidate our forces upon the one great object of CHRISTIANIZING THIS AMERICAN PEOPLE. In comparison with this, it is of very little consequence whether one corner of the christian fold has more of the sheep than another; or whether we can feel that our particular position is attractive and commanding. Besides, if any part of the christian family shall be too much busied with looking out for *itself*, it may be found that the Master will not look out for them, and though they may have their reward in a great show of present numbers and influence, within two hundred years it will be evident to all, that they had clutched the shadow and lost the substance."

Text—Editorial: *Weakness of Churches, its Causes and Effects*, writer not indicated. In *The Home Missionary*, February, 1856.

V. *THE WORLD SIGNIFICANCE OF HOME MISSIONS*

How clearly Christian leaders grasped the national and international significance of home missionary work is set forth in the following:

"The relations, however, in which this country stands to the rest of the world, and the circumstances of its situation, are so peculiar, that they give rise to duties demanding our most serious consideration. As the responsibility of individuals arises in a great measure from their influence over others, so the responsibility of American Christians arises from the influence their country is destined to exert over the rest of the world. The discovery of America, and its great contemporaneous event, the discovery of the art of printing, have changed the whole course of human affairs. . . . Europe had now found her antagonist principle, necessary to the full development of her own powers. A world destined to receive her overflowing population, to be the depository of her literature and laws, to expand her liberal principles and institutions, unrestricted by the prejudices and usages of former ages; and to be the heir of her influence over the human race.

That this influence will not be diminished, but vastly increased, in passing into our hands, may be inferred with moral certainty from the peculiarities of our situation. The physical character of this country, its extent, its resources, and its facilities of communication within itself, and with the rest of the world, certainly place it on a par with Europe in all these elements of power. In other respects it has immensely the advantage. The influence of the old world has been frittered away from the fact that it never has had UNITY. It is an aggregate of nations of different usages, languages laws, religions, and modes of thinking. Besides this evil, its institutions have been such as to depress the mass of its population, and consequently to diminish its power. The fact that the little island of Great Britain, with her ten or twenty millions of inhabitants, has probably already had, and will yet have, greater influence on the human race, than all Europe besides, has resulted from her having freer institutions, a more generally enlightened population, from her protestant religion, and her peculiar local advantages. European power in passing into our hands comes to *one people*—the hundreds of millions which must one day inhabit this vast country will be one—having one language, one literature, essentially, one religion, and one common soul. This is a unity which mere political divisions, should they unhappily occur, cannot destroy

That a country thus situated must exert a dominant influence in the world is unavoidable. . . .

. . . If we are to have this controlling influence on the destinies of other nations, it is a question of unutterable importance, what is to be the nature of this influence? If this country is to be the hot-bed of infidelity and vice, then will it be the widest and most desolating curse the world has ever known; but if the Gospel is to form our character, and guide our power, we shall be a fountain of life to all nations.   The decision of this question, involving not only the temporal and eternal welfare of our own children, and of the countless millions who are to come after us, but the welfare of all the millions over whom the direct or indirect influence of this country is hereafter to extend, depends, under God, mainly on the men of this generation.   It depends on us. We live at the forming period of this great nation.   We are now in our infancy.   Now, if ever, our national character must be formed for God.   Neglect the intellectual and moral culture of an individual in youth, and you find it exceedingly difficult to mould his riper years.   His character is fixed.   The difficulty is far greater in nations, because the field of operation is so much larger, and because they must themselves be brought to engage in the work for which, under the circumstances supposed, they will have no disposition.   The population of this country is increasing with so much rapidity, there are now so many of our new settlements, and extended districts, growing up in ignorance, that the work which we have to do is appallingly great, and if neglected now, its accomplishment will be next to impossible in the generation which is to follow us.   Living, then, as we do, at this crisis of our country's history, the formation of her future character being to such an extent thrown on us, and this character being of such unutterable importance to the world, it may be questioned whether a generation ever lived on whose fidelity so much depended.

This is a responsibility which we cannot throw off.   In other countries it rests with the government to supply the means of moral and religious instruction to the people.   Here it rests with individual Christians.   Jesus Christ has here called his people to a work most gloriously difficult.   They have to support the gospel among themselves, and send it to the rising millions who must perish without it.   This constitutes the great peculiarity of our situation.   It is here to be determined whether the religion of Christ has power enough to sustain and extend itself, unaided by legislative interference.   This is an experiment on which the eyes of the world are fixed, and in the result of which, the destinies of generations are involved.

. . . .

But, sir, how is the Gospel to be brought to bear with sufficient constancy in the formation of the character of every section of our country?   The distribution of Bibles, and Tracts, and the establishment of Sunday schools, is not sufficient.   When Jesus Christ arose from the dead, and set his disciples to the great work to which he has now called us, the conversion of the world, he commanded them, "Go *preach* the Gospel."   And in making permanent provision for this object, he gave some Apostles; and some prophets; and some evangelists; and some pastors and teachers for the perfecting of the saints, and the edifying of the body of Christ.   It has pleased God by the foolishness of *preaching* to save them that believe.   Faith comest by *hearing*.   But how can they *hear* without a *preacher*.   It is then the ordinance of God, that the great object which we contemplate should be effected by the regular *preaching* of the Gospel. And the experience of every age and section of the church, proves that where there is no ministry, there is no Sabbath, and no diffused and permanent religious influence.

To establish a pastor in every neighborhood, therefore, is the only effectual means of giving the Gospel its proper and necessary influence. And this is the work of Home Missions. This is a work on whose success depends, to a great extent, the future character of this vast country; the success of our free institutions, the fate of our own children, and of the millions who are to dwell here; and the nature of our national influence over the world. If this work fail, then must the honour of religion be deeply stained; then must infidelity and superstition hold their joint reign of horror over this wide land of promise; then must our Bible societies perish, our Missionary stations be given up; and America become the curse and opprobrium of all lands. Let the churches once feel the magnitude of this subject—let them once be brought to know what a solemn thing it is to be an American Christian; how much depends on our individual exertions; to what a glorious work Jesus Christ has called us, and this cause cannot fail."

Address of Rev. Charles Hodge, Professor in Princeton Seminary at Anniversary of American Home Missionary Society, May, 1829.

Text—*The Home Missionary*, June 1, 1829.

"Meanwhile, the *immigration* from abroad is rapidly becoming a portentous fact; and whether the portent be for good or for ill, depends on the way in which we meet it. The number of foreigners arriving here in 1848, through the Atlantic ports and through Canada, is estimated at 300,000; and the causes that operate to stimulate emigration from Europe are in undiminished action. There is no rest to the bosom of the weary old world. Tossings to and fro, change without relief, war, pestilence and starvation are dissolving the ties of kindred and country, and other hundreds of thousands are about to precipitate themselves upon our shores. 'Eviction' by judicial process, and by the still more terrible mandate of famine, is rapidly transferring the question, 'What shall be done with the Irish?' from Great Britain to the United States. It cannot be too much to estimate the total immigration of 1849, as equal to 1,000 for every day throughout the year. Should our Government send out its surveyors to the frontier, to run out the boundaries of *five new states*—such as Iowa or Missouri—the foreign immigration of *this year* alone would give to every one of them a population large enough to bring it into the Union, and to elect a representative to Congress. And what shall be the next year?—and the next?

Nor do such facts as these, even, reveal the limit of our destiny, or exhaust the argument by which we are pressed on to its accomplishment. There are ulterior, and not very remote tendencies, that it is wise for us to contemplate. Out of the marvellous changes of the age, a new order of things is arising. Providence is more obviously taking the work of human progress into its own hands. An era of missions has commenced, not planned by man, nor conducted on human principles—missions, not of individuals, but of nations, offshoots from the leading races, transplanted in such masses, and with so much of the sap and vigor of their parent stocks, as to take root and gradually engross the soil. This is seen in the growing numbers and power of the British in the East, where their colonies are rapidly crowding out the original inhabitants, with their laws, social customs and languages. It is seen in the displacement of the Indians of this country by our Anglo-Saxon fathers; and in the encroachments we are now making on the Spanish race on our southwestern border. . . . What an argument is this, that our Home population—which cannot be *kept* at home—should be of such a kind, that, with themselves, they shall transfer the elements of regeneration to the countries which they enter by their traffic and control by their influence!

In this view of the enlarging sphere of American activity, may we not find some consoling explanation of the design of Providence in sending so many foreigners to our shores? As physical barriers are now so generally removed, and the whole world is coming into a condition of preparedness for receiving a christian civilization, is it not probable that a race will be raised up for this world-mission, whose character shall contain those selected elements which are most needful to make a complete missionary people? Let there be a mixture of the peculiarities of different races. For example; let the high resolve and energetic will of the Briton, which yields only to itself, with the wide and philanthropic scope of aspiration developed in our Pilgrim Fathers—form the basis of the combination. Add to this the reflection, discrimination and patience of the German mind, fruitful in the adaptation of means to ends. Let France add something, but Ireland more, of the fire of enthusiasm to quicken these elements into action. Thus would there be formed a *composite character*, more aggressive and efficient than either of the materials from which it is made up. But *where* could such a union take place? In Europe they cannot be separated from their present combinations, nor is there a space there where they could commingle. There is nowhere a common receptacle into which they can be poured, but the broad expanse of our own Mississippi Valley. For such an end as this, it has been kept in reserve for so many ages. For this, the materials are gathering, and beginning to act upon and modify each other, just as that grand movement is commencing, whose progress they will soon be wanted to assist.

In such a consideration of the uses which Providence is making of our country and our people, the duty assigned us becomes something more than merely to provide for a few hundred thousands, on the verge of the organized states. When the bearings of our work are justly considered, the distinction between Home and Foreign missions disappears. The enterprise of evangelizing this land becomes, in effect, and on a grand scale, a MISSION TO ALL MANKIND. . . .

In behalf of the Executive Committee,

MILTON BADGER,
CHARLES HALL,
Secretaries for Correspondence."

Text—*The Home Missionary*, June, 1849.

"Letters from Mr. Atkinson have been received, announcing his safe arrival at Oregon City, June 20th, 1848, and his cordial reception there, with flattering prospects of usefulness opened before him. . . . The whole territory, containing 341,463 square miles, is supposed to possess, in its natural products and resources, and in its advantages for commerce with the Pacific, the elements of a great and prosperous state. Already, some 16,000 or 18,000 people had crossed the mountains to take up their abode there, and others were rapidly coming in.

In the mean time, the late treaty with Mexico added the region of Upper California to the responsibilities of the American churches. Immediate counsels were had for an early occupation of this field also. It was foreseen, that the maritime portion of California, under the protection of a free and stable government, must attract to itself a large population; and especially, that its magnificent harbor must eventually become the *entrepot* of a commerce rivalling that of London or New York. The establishment by the United States government of a line of steamers on that coast, promised to hasten these results. Arrangements were accordingly made to send forward two pioneer missionaries, by the earliest possible conveyance. . . .

The acquisition of this territory by the United States, has already, in a single year, proved to be one of the most remarkable events of the age. This is not merely on account of the transfer of some 439,000 square miles from one government to another, but because of subsequent events, from which the most surprising social and moral results are likely to follow. The growing ascendancy of the English in China and the Asiatic Islands, simultaneously with the transfer of California to our people, completes the control of the four great coast lines of the Northern Hemisphere, by two Protestant nations, speaking the same language, and one in all the great features of their character. The bearing of this fact, coming to pass just as steam is giving ubiquity to commercial adventure, cannot but be direct and powerful on the conversion of the Pagan tribes. And the circumstances that preceded and have followed our possession of California, show that herein a great trust is committed to us by Providence, for the benefit of a new empire, about to arise in the Pacific world. God kept that coast for a people of the Pilgrim blood; he would not permit any other to be fully developed there. The Spaniard came thither a hundred years before our fathers landed at Plymouth; but though he came for treasure, his eyes were holden that he should not find it. But in the fulness of time, when a Protestant people have been brought to this continent, and are nourished up to strength by the requisite training, God commits to their possession that Western shore. But will they throw into this great enterprise such vehemence—give it such a body and soul—as the divine purpose requires? . . "

Text—*The Home Missionery*, June, 1849.

"When we begin to contemplate the instrumentalities at work for mankind's conversion, our eye rests at once on two nations, England and America. . . . These two nations, with an ultimate, but with no immediate hope of assistance from any others, have dared to venture the attempt to deliver this earth from the dominion of sin. This is their purpose—to overthrow iniquity wherever it abounds, to invade its strongest holds and most ancient citadels, and to make them fortresses of truth and righteousness. . . .

But when we think of the difficulty of reforming a single man, or a single village, when we remember how much toil and patience it requires, to accomplish a very small work upon a very few individuals, how does this undertaking of the world's conversion swell into colossal and altogether superhuman proportions! . . . And yet, it is undoubtedly the fact, that the Christians of England and America have dared to put their hand to the task of cleansing the world of its iniquity, and, though conscious of utter weakness, with the confident expectation, nevertheless, of a final triumph.

But there is another thought. Of the work performed by these two peoples, it seems apparent that the *greater part must fall to the share of America*. For America is fast becoming the larger of the two. Already in population she is nearly equal; in rate of increase she must every year show a greater and greater superiority.

The nation that is to fill the great North American valley, and to occupy these Atlantic and Pacific shores, *must* eventually surpass in magnitude any probable concentration upon the territories of Britain. In production, also, she must be superior, and the day will come when the yield of English mines and manufactories, in comparison with ours, shall be small as their harvests. America is to have a larger commerce, likewise, and must become acquainted with a larger number of the earth's richest and most active inhabitants. And upon these busy and energetic spirits her influence promises to be even proportionately greater; since she is herself more free and of freer spirit. Her magnetic touch is destined to awaken, we trust, in many millions of souls, the aspirations and capacities that have been slumbering through the long night of despotism and heathenism . . .

But in vain shall we become greater than England, if not also, better. In vain do our frontiers extend, our productions multiply, our commerce, wealth, and power increase, unless the spirit of religion keeps pace with all this growth, and rules all these elements of influence. The heathen world will be none the better for the cultivation of our boundless prairies, unless christian hands hold the plow, and christian hearts consecrate the harvests. . . . The privilege of doing the larger half of the missionary work, will not be granted us unless we secure the thorough evangelization of that 'Great West,' around whose borders the older States cling as a fringe upon a garment, and whose mines and harvests could supply the world.

But, without the assistance of the West, we cannot even sustain, in healthful growth, the work which we have already *commenced.*

. . . .
We cannot expect an interest in Foreign Missions adequate to the demands of the heathen world, unless there is an interest in Home Missions adequate to the evangelization of our own country. The two stand or fall *together.* If the West is to be left to be overrun with a wild growth of disbeliefs, and of unbeliefs, or even to be surrendered to denominations not co-operating with our work, then good by to all our dreams of converting the world—that privilege is reserved for those who will be faithful; and we shall find that the enterprise outstripped the utmost of our strength, when it absorbed the utmost of that strength into its exclusive self. No; the West is a part of the world, a part very necessary to those who wish to save the heathen—we must have the West. Within the life-time of a single generation, the contributions from that portion of our land to the American Board, must count, not by tens, but by hundreds of thousands, or its operations cannot be conducted with appropriate energy or tolerable success. Within the limits of a single generation, then, a large portion of those western States must be made to become what New England is now (and if so much, then much more) a land of churches, and schools, and charities, of pious homes and great religious enterprises. The world is to be converted *at the West.*

But again; we must not expect the growth of missions to be by a steady arithmetical ratio, just so much every year, and no more. . . . For years, our missions have to struggle with difficulties, and in darkness, like seeds in the ground, making no visible progress. But by and by, their hidden labors come to light, and then there must be a plentiful nourishment afforded them, or they wilt and die. . . . No one can tell how soon China, or even Japan, may be begging at our doors for the word of Life. . . . *How can these demands be met?* If we should be so far faithless to our own country and kindred, as to give only a feeble support to religion at home, so that throughout large regions it must maintain an ineffective war with the powers of darkness, then where is the spirit, and whence can the resources come, that shall carry on to successful results these costly foreign enterprises? Impossible! The Church must be strong throughout America, or it will never be able to push its triumphs round the world. We need the West!

And not for money alone—for *men*. At that day when God shall break down the walls, and lay open the field everywhere for the sowers of his word, and nations shall be born in a day, where shall the men be found for that pressing seed-time, and for the whitening harvests that will follow? The narrow East cannot supply them; the work is too great for our strength. But how and where shall there be strength equal to that day, if the resources of the populous West be not unlocked? There the great masses of our nation are to congregate, and there must the missionary host find recruits.

Besides,—it may be a fancy, but it may prove a truth,—is it not at the West that the American spirit is to find its freest, fullest, noblest development? May we not hope that, if the work of Home Missions is thoroughly successful, a more beautiful and liberal christian civilization shall rule there, and generations be born so *toned* in native temperament, and through the peculiar social atmosphere of that alert and vigorous race, as to furnish the most magnanimous, sympathetic, and enterprising missionaries that the Church has ever found? May we not hope that the future will, in some respects, out-do the past, and bring a breadth of energy, and a glow of out-speaking enthusiasm, and a Luther-like indomitableness of faith, in which the missionary enterprise shall renew its youth, and repeat its earlier triumphs on a larger scale?

. . . .

But how can the Church secure it? Is there any new-discovered method for turning men to God? Has this age of steam found out any new salvation for the soul? None. Preach the word! By this ancient 'foolishness of preaching,' by the sending of ministers, by the founding of churches, by the example of the good, by the power of the Holy Ghost,—thus are the multitudes of wanderers to be gathered home."

Text—*The Home Missionary*, February, 1855.

VI. *THE ALBANY CONVENTION AND THE PLAN OF UNION. 1852*

At the Albany Convention, convened Oct. 5, 1852, the first representative assembly of All-American Congregationalism, the following report on the Plan of Union was unanimously adopted.

"Whereas, The Plan of Union formed in 1801, by the General Assembly of the Presbyterian Church and the General Association of Connecticut, is understood to have been repudiated by the said Assembly before the schism in that body of 1838, though this year acknowledged as still in force by the General Assembly which met last year at Washington, D. C., and

Whereas, Many of our Presbyterian brethren, though adhering to this Plan in some of its provisions, do not, it is believed, maintain it in its integrity; especially in virtually requiring Congregational Ministers settled over Presbyterian Churches and Congregational Churches having Presbyterian Ministers, to be connected with Presbyteries; and

Whereas, Whatever mutual advantage has formerly resulted from this Plan to the two denominations, and whatever might yet result from it if acted upon impartially, its operation is now unfavorable to the spread and permanence of the Congregational polity, and even to the real harmony of these Christian communities:—

Resolved 1st, That in the judgment of this Convention it is not deemed expedient that new Congregational Churches, or Churches heretofore independent, become connected with Presbyteries.

2nd, That in the evident disuse of the said Plan, according to its original design, we deem it important, and for the purposes of union sufficient, that Congregationalists and Presbyterians exercise toward each other that spirit of love which the Gospel requires, and which their common faith is fitted to cherish; that they accord to each other the right of pre-occupancy, where but one Church can be maintained; and that, in the formation of such a Church, its ecclesiastical character and relations be determined by a majority of its members.

3rd, That is respect to those Congregational Churches which are now connected with Presbyteries,—either on the above-mentioned Plan, or on those of 1808 and 1813, between Congregational and Presbyterian bodies in the State of New York,—while we would not have them violently sever their existing relations, we counsel them to maintain vigilantly the Congregational privileges which have been guaranteed them by the Plans above-mentioned, and to see to it that while they remain connected with Presbyteries, the true intent of those original arrangements be impartially carried out."

Text—Walker: *The Creeds and Platforms of Congregationalism*, pp. 539-540.

VII. *THE PRESBYTERIANS AND THE AMERICAN HOME MISSIONARY SOCIETY*

The General Assembly of the Presbyterian Church at Buffalo, 1853, adopted the following order,

"*Resolved*, That a Committee of Conference be raised to confer with the Executive Committees of the American Home Missionary Society, and of the Philadelphia Home Missionary Society, for the purpose of ascertaining what arrangements can be made for the relief of feeble churches at the West, and in other destitute places, which may not be provided for by any existing rules of the American Home Missionary Society"—*Minutes of the Assembly*, 1853, *page* 341.

The Assembly's Committee submitted to the Executive Committee of the American Home Missionary Society, the following:

INQUIRIES

1. "Will it be consistent for them to make such an alteration in the rules of the Society, as will allow appropriations to congregations in large towns and cities?"

2. "Will they consent to make appropriations to a church or churches, in places where there is already a church aided by the Society?"

3. "Will it be consistent with the rules of the Society to assist a Missionary laboring under the direction of a Presbytery or Synod?"

To these inquiries the Executive Committee of the American Home Missionary Society made the following.

REPLY

The Executive Committee of the American Home Missionary Society have carefully considered the questions proposed to them by the Committee of the General Assembly, and in reply respectfully submit the following statement:

The *First* Inquiry is as follows: "*Will it be consistent for them to make such an alteration in the rules of the Society, as will allow appropriations to Congregations in large towns and cities?*"

The rule to which reference is made in this inquiry was adopted in the year 1844, and is as follows:

"WHEREAS, The American Home Missionary Society was originally formed, and is now patronized by the christian public, as a provision for supplying the means of grace to those who are specially destitute, and who cannot reasonably be expected to obtain the blessings of the Gospel in any other way,—and WHEREAS, In times past a few cases of Congregations in large towns have been regarded as so far extraordinary in their claims as to justify appropriations in their behalf, but recently cases thus situated are becoming so numerous as to require the adoption of a general rule, Therefore,

Resolved, That it is inexpedient for this Committee hereafter to make appropriations in aid of Congregations in this city and its vicinity, or in other similar situations, where the members may enjoy religious privileges in congregations connected with the Society, without greater inconvenience than those who live in smaller towns are subject to."

It will be observed that this rule applies to those towns and cities only, in which the means of grace already exist in connection with one or more of the denominations acting through this Society. In places, however populous, where it appears to this Committee that gospel institutions cannot be sustained by these denominations to an extent obviously needed, without missionary aid, this rule is not enforced. Exceptions are made also in favor of congregations of colored people, and those worshiping in a foreign language. But the design of the patrons of this Institution in contributing to its funds is, to send the Gospel to that portion of our population to whom it would otherwise be inaccessible. . . .

When the church accommodations of a large town or city become insufficient for its increasing population, the natural and healthful process of extension is colonization or contribution from the surrounding churches, and the local sympathy which can be enlisted in this way only, is often essential to the growth and prosperity of the assisted churches.

The attempt of this Society, therefore, to conduct City Missions of this character, would, it is believed, be regarded by its patrons with disapprobation, and would tend greatly to diminish their contributions to its funds. . . .

It should be borne in mind, also, that this department of labor is very expensive; and after satisfying the privileged claims of the towns and cities in the East, which contribute most largely to the Society's Treasury, only a small amount would probably remain, to supply the wide-spread and growing destitution of the West.

It frequently happens, moreover, in respect to this class of churches, that the necessity for their existence, and the claims to missionary support are matters of controversy between two rival denominations, both friendly to this Institution, yet both claiming the ground, and to grant or to refuse the aid sought, would render the Society a party to denominational strife.

In view of these considerations, and as the result of their experience, before and since the adoption in form of the rule in question, the Committee regard it inexpedient to undertake the work of Missions in large towns and cities, where the means of grace are already enjoyed in connection with the denominations that sustain this Society.

The *Second* Inquiry is,—*Will they consent to make appropriations to a church or churches in places where there is already a church aided by the Society?*

Most of the considerations already stated, are equally applicable to the class of cases referred to in this inquiry. Those who have convenient access to the means of grace in connection with a church sustained by this Society, are not properly considered as destitute of the Gospel, in such a sense as renders them subjects of missionary aid. Their organization into a separate church under such circumstances, is in most cases premature, resulting, as it usually does and must, in the injury and dissatisfaction of the existing church, and in the long-continued dependence of both. By assisting two churches, on the same ground, the Society would not only, in effect, be divided against itself, but would in many cases be required to appropriate double the amount to each church, or four times the amount in all that would be requisite if all were united in one church. Experience has shown, moreover, that churches of this character are apt to originate in personal or denominational difference, which the aid of the Society would have the effect to perpetuate and to increase, while the Institution itself would of course incur the censure of one or both of the parties concerned. For these reasons, the Committee believe that it would be highly injurious to the Society, and to the cause of religion in our new settlements, to encourage the multiplication of such organizations by the general pledge of missionary aid, which would be involved in an affirmative answer to this inquiry.

. . . .

The *Third* Inquiry is,—*Will it be consistent with the Rules of the Society to assist a missionary laboring under the direction of a Presbytery or Synod?*

The Committee would state, in reply to this inquiry, that the Constitution of the Society (Art. 4) makes it their duty to "appoint missionaries, and instruct them in regard to the field and manner of their labors." While, therefore, they cannot, without violating this provision, pledge assistance to missionaries in whose appointment and direction they have no voice, yet they desire in all cases to consult the views and wishes of the ecclesiastical bodies in regard to all matters pertaining to the missionary work within their bounds. Accordingly, the various Presbyteries, Associations, &c., are invited (See 27th Annual Report, p. 101) to appoint each a *Committee of Missions* from its own members, to receive applications from its churches, and suggest to the Society the proper action in each case.

These bodies are also expected to represent to the Society the condition of the destitute within their bounds, especially in places where no churches exist, and to recommend the appropriate action for their relief; and no obstacles exist to making appointments for these destitute fields, to such an extent as their necessities require and the funds of the Society allow, provided each missionary confine himself strictly to missionary labor, at definite points, within such territorial limits, not embraced in the field of another missionary, as are consistent with the greatest efficiency of his ministry.

. . . .

Text—*The Home Missionary*, November, 1855.

VIII. *THE REVIVAL OF 1856-58*

Finney, in discussing his experiences in Boston, writes,

"The next autumn we accepted an invitation to labor again in Boston. We began our labors at Park street, and the Spirit of God immediately manifested his willingness to save souls. The first sermon that I preached was directed to the searching of the church; for I always began by trying to stir up a thorough and pervading interest among professors of religion; to secure the reclaiming of those that were backslidden, and search out those that were self-deceived, and if possible bring them to Christ.

After the congregation was dismissed, and the pastor was standing with me in the pulpit, he said to me, 'Brother Finney, I wish to have you understand that I need to have this preaching as much as any member of this church. I have been very much dissatisfied with my religious state for a long time; and have sent for you on my own account, and cared for the sake of my own soul, as well as for the sake of the souls of the people.' We had at different times protracted and very interesting conversations. He seemed thoroughly to give his heart to God. And one evening at a prayer and conference meeting, as I understood, he related to the people his experience, and told them that he had been that day converted.

This of course produced a very deep impression upon the church and congregation, and upon the city quite extensively. Some of the pastors thought that it was injudicious for him to make a thing of that kind so public. But I did not regard it in that light. It manifestly was the best means he could use for the salvation of his people, and highly calculated to produce among professors of religion generally a very great searching of heart.

The work was quite extensive that winter in Boston, and many very striking cases of conversion occurred. We labored there until spring, and then thought it necessary to return to our labors at home. But it was very manifest that the work in that city was by no means done; and we left with the promise that, the Lord willing, we would return and labor there the next winter. Accordingly the next autumn we returned to Boston.

. . . .

This winter of 1857-58 will be remembered as the time when a great revival prevailed throughout all the Northern states. It swept over the land with such power, that for a time it was estimated that not less than fifty thousand conversions occurred in a single week. This revival had some very peculiarly interesting features. It was carried on to a large extent through lay influence, so much so as almost to throw the ministers into the shade. There had been a daily prayer-meeting observed in Boston for several years; and in the autumn previous to the great outburst, the daily prayer-meeting had been established in Fulton street, New York, which has been continued to this day. Indeed, daily prayer-meetings were established throughout the length and breadth of the Northern states. I recollect in one of our prayer-meetings in Boston that winter, a gentleman arose and said, 'I am from Omaha, in Nebraska. On my journey East I have found a continuous prayer-meeting all the way. We call it,' said he, 'about two thousand miles from Omaha to Boston; and here was a prayer-meeting about two thousand miles in extent.'

In Boston we had to struggle, as I have intimated, against this divisive influence, which set the religious interest a good deal back from where we had left it the spring before. However, the work continued steadily to increase, in the midst of these unfavorable conditions. It was evident that the Lord intended to make a general sweep in Boston. Finally it was suggested that a business-men's prayer-meeting should be established, at twelve o'clock, in the chapel of the Old South church, which was very central for business men. The Christian friend, whose guests we were, secured the use of the room, and advertised the meeting. But whether such a meeting would succeed in Boston at that time, was considered doubtful. However, this brother called the meeting, and to the surprise of almost everybody the place was not only crowded, but multitudes could not get in at all. This meeting was continued, day after day, with wonderful results. The place was, from the first, too strait for them, and other daily meetings were established in other parts of the city.

Mrs. Finney held ladies' meetings daily at the large vestry of Park street. These meetings became so crowded, that the ladies would fill the room, and then stand about the door on the outside, as far as they could hear on every side.

One of our daily prayer-meetings was held at Park street church, which would be full whenever it was open for prayer; and this was the case with many other meetings in different parts of the city. The population, large as it was, seemed to be moved throughout. The revival became too general to keep any account at all of the number of conversions, or to allow of any estimate being made that would approximate the truth. All classes of people were inquiring everywhere. Many of the Unitarians became greatly interested, and attended our meetings in large numbers.

This revival is of so recent date that I need not enlarge upon it, because it became almost universal throughout the Northern states. A divine influence seemed to pervade the whole land. Slavery seemed to shut it out from the South. The people there were in such a state of irritation, of vexation, and of committal to their peculiar' institution, which had come to be assailed on every side, that the Spirit of God seemed to be grieved away from them. There seemed to be no place found for him in the hearts of the Southern people at that time. It was estimated that during this revival not less than five hundred thousand souls were converted in this country.

As I have said, it was carried on very much through the instrumentality of prayer-meetings, personal visitation and conversation, by the distribution of tracts, and by the energetic efforts of the laity, men and women. Ministers nowhere opposed it that I am aware of. I believe they universally sympathized with it. But there was such a general confidence in the prevalence of prayer, that the people very extensively seemed to prefer meetings for prayer to meetings for preaching. The general impression seemed to be, 'We have had instruction until we are hardened; it is time for us to pray.' The answers to prayer were constant, and so striking as to arrest the attention of the people generally throughout the land. It was evident that in answer to prayer the windows of heaven were opened and the Spirit of God poured out like a flood. The New York Tribune at that time published several extras, filled with accounts of the progress of the revival in different parts of the United States."

Text—*Memoirs of Rev. Charles G. Finney, written by Himself*, pp. 441 444.

CHAPTER XXII

The Catholic Church in the National Period

Bibliography

Of historians who have dealt in a comprehensive way with the period under consideration, the more notable is John Gilmary Shea, who has three books which form volumes II, III and IV of his "History of the Catholic Church in the United States." They are as follows: "Life and Times of the Most Reverend John Carroll . . . embracing the History of the Catholic Church in the United States, 1763-1815" (1888); "History of the Catholic Church in the United States from the Division of the Diocese of Baltimore, 1808, and the Death of Archbishop Carroll, 1816, to the Fifth Provincial Council of Baltimore, 1843" (1890); "History of the Catholic Church in the United States from the Fifth Provincial Council of Baltimore, 1843, to the Second Plenary Council of Baltimore, 1866" (1892). In the "American Church History Series," (Vol. IX, 1893) Professor Thomas O'Gorman contributes "A History of the Roman Catholic Church in the United States." His work, while useful, does not compare with the more exhaustive treatment of Shea. "The Hierarchy of the Catholic Church in the United States" (1886) by Shea has considerable general information on this period. "Three-quarters of a Century (1807 to 1882), A Retrospect . . . " (1904) by Rev. A. J. Thebaud, S.J. edited by C. G. Herbermann has considerable data (Vol. III) relating to Roman Catholic problems and development, during the first half of the nineteenth century.

On archbishop Carroll and the organization of the hierarchy, one may profitably begin with the "Documents relative to the Adjustment of the Roman Catholic Organization in the United States to the Conditions of National Independence" contributed by Carl R. Fish ("Amer. Hist. Rev." Vol. XV, No. 4). These documents in translated form may be consulted under "Propaganda Documents" in the "Rec. Amer. Cath. His. Soc.," Vol. XXI. Much light is thrown upon Carroll in "Correspondence between the Sees of Quebec and Baltimore 1788-1847" edited with notes by Abbe Lionel Lindsay (*ibid.* Vol. XVIII); "Miscellaneous Letters to Bishop John Carroll 1784-1815" with notes by

Rev. E. I. Devitt, S.J.(*ibid*.Vol. XIX); and "Letters from the Archdiocesan Archives at Baltimore, 1787-1815" edited by Rev. E. I. Devitt, S.J. (*ibid*. Vol. XX). The following biographical studies should be consulted: "The Life and Times of Archbishop Carroll" by Bernard Campbell ("Cath. Magazine" Vols. IV and VI); "The Life of Charles Carroll of Carrollton 1737-1832, with his Correspondence and Public Papers" (II Vols. 1897) by Kate M. Rowland; "The Rev. Lawrence Graessel" by H. Herbermann, ("Hist. Rec. & Studies" Vol. VIII); and "Father Ferdinand Farmer, S.J. An Apostolic Missionary . . . " by Rev. J. F. Quick. Many of Carroll's letters are accessible in the "Amer. Cath. Hist. Rev." for the years 1897 to 1900.

On Georgetown College, it will be profitable to consult "Memorial of the First Centenary of Georgetown College, D.C., And an Account of the Centennial Celebration by a Member of the Faculty" (1891) by J. G. Shea, D.D.

On Bishop Conwell, the following is suggested: "Correspondence Between Bishop Conwell of Philadelphia and Bishop Plessis of Quebec 1821-1825" ("Rec. Amer. Cath. Hist. Soc." Vol. XXII), "Life of Bishop Conwell of Philadelphia" by Martin I. J. Griffin ("Rec. Amer. Cath. Hist. Soc." Vol. XXIV-XXVI); "Bishop Conwell of Philadelphia, and Rev. William Hogan" ("Amer. Cath. Hist. Rev. 1896)".

Trusteeism is discussed in "The Anti-Catholic Riots in Philadelphia" ("Amer. Cath. Hist. Rev." 1896); and "Evils of Trusteeism" by Rev. G. C. Treacy, S.J. ("Hist. Rec. & Studies," Vol. VIII).

Cardinal Cheverus and the school question may be studied in "Some Friendly Letters (from A.D. 1814 to 1823) from Cardinal Cheverus, First Bishop of Boston" edited by Isabel O'Reilly ("Rec. Amer. Cath. Hist. Soc." Vol. XIV.) Another series (1823-1836) may be consulted in the "Records" Vol. XV.

Bishop England's "Works" (V Volumes) are the most valuable source for a study of this significant ecclesiastic. "Letters from the Right Reverend John England D.D. to the Honorable William Gaston, LL.D." ("Rec. Amer. Cath. Hist. Soc." Vols. XVIII and XIX) are worth consulting. Many of his letters are reprinted (*ibid*. Vol. VII and VIII) among "Papers Relating to the Church in America". "St. Mary's Church, Charleston, South Carolina" (1898) by T. F. Hopkins has some information.

The Know-Nothing Movement may be understood from the following: "History of the Know-Nothing Party in Maryland" by L. F. Schmeckebier ("J. H. U. Studies" Ser. XVII, Nos. 4 and 5); "A

Know-Nothing Legislature" by G. H. Haynes (Ann. Rep. Amer. Hist. Ass. year 1896, Sec. VII); "The Causes of Know-Nothing Success in Massachusetts" by the same writer (Amer. Hist. Rev. Vol. III, No. 1); "The Origin and Progress of the American Party in Politics" (1855) by John Hancock Lee; and "Constitutional Freedom of Religion and the Revivals of Religious Intolerance" by Peter Condon ("Hist. Rec. & Studies" Vols. II, III, and IV).

Archbishop Hughes should be studied in his "Works"; also "Letters of Father John Hughes" ("Rec. Amer. Cath. Hist. Soc." Vol. XXI); his letters to Governor Seward on the school question (*ibid*. vol. XXIII); "History of the Common School System of the State of New York from its Origin in 1795 to the Present Time including the Various City and other Organizations, and the Religious Controversies of 1821, 1832, and 1840" (1871) by S. S. Randall; "The History of the Public School Society of the City of New York" (1873) by Wm. Oland Bourne; "Letters to the Rev. John Hughes . . ." (1855) by Kirwan; "Letters of Sister Saint Augustine Relative to the Burning of the Convent" contributed by Peter Condon ("Hist. Rec. and Studies" Vol. IV); "Religious Education in the Public Schools of the State and City of New York" by Arthur J. Hall (Doctoral dissertation, Univ. of Chicago, 1914).

On the extension of the Catholic Church into Kentucky and the Middle West during the first quarter of the nineteenth century, in addition to Carroll, O'Gorman, and Thebaud as above, the following will give abundant detail: "Sketches of the Early Catholic Missions of Kentucky" (1844) by M. J. Spalding; "The Centenary of Catholicity in Kentucky" (1884) by B. J. Webb; "History of the Catholic Church in the Diocese of Pittsburgh and Allegbany" (1880) by Rev. A. A. Lambing; "Letters from the Archepiscopal Archives at Baltimore" with notes by the Rev. E. I. Devitt ("Rec. Amer. Cath. Hist. Soc." Vol. XX); "Correspondence Between the Most Reverend Joseph Octavius Plessis . . . and the Reverend Joseph Flaget . . ." (*ibid*. Vol XVIII); "Letters from the Baltimore Archives" annotated by Rev. E. I. Devett (*ibid*. Vol. XIX); "Diary of Reverend Father Marie Joseph Durand" translated by Ella M. Flick (*ibid*. Vol. XXVI); "Parish Registers of Prairie du Chien, Galena . . ." translated by Isabel O'Reilly (*ibid*. Vol. XXII); "The Church in Kentucky" (letters) by Rev. S. T. Badin (*ibid*. Vol. XXIII); "Sketches of the Early Catholic Missions in Kentucky from their Commencement in 1785 to the Jubilee of 1826–27", author not specified; "The First Three Catholic Churches in Zanesville, Ohio" by R. J. J. Harkins ("Rec. Amer. Cath. Hist. Soc." Vol. XXV);

"Gethsamene, Ky. the Home of Trappist Monks" by Caroline M. Berry ("Americana" Vol. IX, pp. 496-506).

For developments in the Middle West during the second quarter of the century, the following is suggested: "The Church in Northern Ohio and in the Diocese of Cleveland from 1817 . . . to 1877" (1888) by Geo. F. Houck; "Eizbishop Johann Martin Henni, D. D. Ein Lebensbild aus der Pionier Zeit von Ohio und Wisconsin" (1888) by Rev. N. Marti O. S. B.; "Letters Concerning Some Missions of the Mississippi Valley (1818-1827)" translated by N. dos Santos, ("Rec. Amer. Cath. Hist. Soc." Vol. XIV); "Selections from the Correspondence of the Late Mark Anthony Frenay" (ibid. Vols. XIII and XIV); "Letters of Reverend P. J. De Smet, S. J. . . ." translated by J. E. Cahalan ("Hist. Rec. and Studies" Vol. V.); "Some Correspondence Relating to the Diocese of New Orleans and St. Louis, 1818-1843," with notes by Abbe Lionel Lindsay ("Rec. Amer. Cath. Hist. Soc." Vol. XIX); "The Diocese of St. Louis in Gleanings from Early Catholic Journals" communicated by Rev. J. H. O'Donnell ("Hist. Rec. and Studies" Vol. II, Part II); "Sketches of the Life, Times and Character of Right Reverend Benedict Joseph Flaget, First Bishop of Louisville" (1852) by M. J. Spalding, D. D.; "Memoirs, Historical and Edifying of a Missionary Apostolic of the Order of Saint Dominic" (1915, deals with Father S. E. Mazzuchelli, see also "Coll. State Hist. Soc. of Wisc." Vol. XIV, pp. 155-162); "Life and Labors of Rev. Frederic Baraga . . ." (1900) by P. C. Verwyst; "Documents Relating to the Catholic Church in Green Bay and the Mission of Little Chute, 1825-1840" edited by R. G. Thwaites ("Coll. State Hist. Soc. Wisc." Vol. XIV); "The Mission to the Owabache" by Jacob P. Dunn ("Pubs. Indiana Hist. Soc." Vol. III, No. IV).

On the extension of Catholicism in the West, there is literature as follows: "The Life of Rev. Charles Nerinckz . . ." (1879) by I ev. C. P. Maes; "History of the Trappist Abbey of New Millcray, Dubuque County, Iowa" (1892) by W. R. Perkins; "Life and Writings of the Right Reverend John McMullen, Bishop of Davenport, Iowa" (n.d.) by Rev. I. McGovern; "History of the Catholic Church in Iowa" (Part I, 1888) by Rev. J. F. Kemper; "Catholic Missionaries in the Early and in the Territorial Days in Iowa" by same writer ("Annals of Iowa," Series III, Vol. X, pp. 54-62); "Right Reverend Mathias Loras, D. D., First Bishop of Dubuque," by Rev. B. C. Lenehan (ibid. Vol. III, pp. 577-600); "Recollections of the First Catholic Missions in Central Missouri" by Rev. J. H. Schmidt ("Mo. Hist. Rev." Vol. V, pp. 83-93); "A Catholic University and Its Founders" by Rev. M. J. O'Connor, S. J.

("Hist. Rec. & Studies," Vol. VII); "Missions Among the Indians in Kansas" by Right Rev. J. B. Miege S. J. ("Trans. Kansas Hist. Soc." Vol. IX); "Monsignor Adrian J. Croquet Indian Missionary" compiled with notes, by the Rev. J. Van der Heyden ("Rec. Amer. Cath. Hist. Soc." Vol. XVI and XVII); "Some Correspondence Relating to the Diocese of New Orleans and St. Louis" with notes by Abbe Lionel Lindsey (*ibid*. Vol. XIX); "Doctor John McLoughlin" by Rev. T. J. Campbell, S. J. ("Hist. Rec. and Studies" Vol. VIII); "Joseph Sadoc Alemany, O. P., Archbishop of San Francisco" by Gaynor Maddox (*ibid* Vol. VIII); "The Origin of the Flathead Mission of the Rocky Mountains" by Major Edmond Mallett ("Rec. Amer. Cath. Hist. Soc." Vol. II); "The Flathead Indians" by Rev. James O'Connor (*ibid*. Vol. III); "The Jesuits in American California" by Bryan J. Clinch (*ibid*. Vol. XVII); "History of the Pious Fund of California" by J. T. Doyle ("Papers Cal. Hist. Soc." Vol. I, Part I); "Missions and Missionaries of California" (IV Vols. 1908–1915) by Rev. Z. Engelhardt, O. S. F.

The significant career of De Smet is set forth in "Western Missions and Missionaries" (1864) by Rev. Father P. J. De Smet S. J.; "Personal Letters of the Rev. P. J. De Smet, S. J." translated by J. E. Cahalan ("Rec. and Studies",Vol. IV);and most exhaustively in "Life, Letters,and Travels of Father Pierre-Jean De Smet, S. J. 1801–1873" by H. M. Chittenden, and A. T. Richardson. His "Letters and Sketches with a Narrative of a Year's Residence among the Indian Tribes of the Rocky Mountains" (1843), and "Oregon Missions and Travels over the Rocky Mountains in 1845–46" are embodied in Thwaites, "Early Western Travels, 1748–1846" (Vols. XXVII and XXIX).

For the extension of Catholicism in the South, "Catholicity in the Carolinas and Georgia; Leaves of its History, 1820–1878" (1879) by Rev. J. J. O'Connell will be found serviceable.

On the attitude of the Roman Catholics to the negroes and slavery, the following should be noted: "Mission Work among Colored Catholics" by T. F. Meehan, A. M. ("Hist. Rec. & Studies" Vol. VIII); "Are Catholics Pro-Slavery and Disloyal?" ("Brownson's Quart. Rev." July, 1863). For Bishop England's experiences in schools among the colored people, see "Rec. Amer. Cath. Hist. Soc." Vol. VIII, p. 212 f.

On the Civil War, the literature is as follows: "Some Civil War Documents, A. D. 1862–1864" ("Rec. Amer. Cath. Hist. Soc." Vol. XIV); "European Catholic Opinion on Slavery" a pastoral letter of the Bishop of Orleans, April 1862 (*ibid*. Vol. XXV); "Great Riots of New York" by J. T. Headley; "The New York Riot of 1863" ("Meth. Quart.

Rev." April, 1874); "Catholics and the Anti-Draft Riots" ("Brownson's Quart. Rev." October 1863); "Archbishop Hughes and the Draft Riots" by Thomas F. Meehan, A.M. ("Hist. Rec. & Studies," Vol. I, Part II); "Angels of the Battlefield: A History of the Labors of the Catholic Sisterhoods in the Late Civil War" (1898) by George Barton; "A Year with the Army of the Potomac. Diary of the Reverend Father Tissot, S. J., Military Chaplain" ("Hist. Rec. & Studies," Vol. III, Part I); "Some Aspects of the Negro Problem" ("Catholic World" February, 1884); "The Josephites and Their Work for Negroes" (*ibid.* April, 1890).

The issue of education in separate schools is presented in the following typical literature: "The Educational Grievances of Catholics" ("Catholic World" May, 1889); "The Trouble in the Boston Schools" (*ibid.* Jan. 1889); "Our Parochial System" ("Amer. Cath. Quart. Rev." Oct. 1892); "Catholic Education and American Institutions" (1898) by Rev. J. F. Mullary; "Professor Fisher on Sectarianism in the Common Schools" ("Amer. Cath. Review" July, 1889).

The attitude of the Catholic church to the labor question is presented in "The Labor Question" ("Amer. Cath. Quart. Rev." Oct. 1878); "Capital and Labor" (*ibid.* July 1883); "Socialism" (*ibid.* April, 1883).

On Father Hecker, there is "The Church and the Age. An Exposition of the Catholic Church in View of the Needs and Aspirations of the Present Age" (1888) by Very Rev. I. T. Hecker; the "Life of Father Isaac Hecker" (1891) by Rev. W. Elliott C.S.P.; "Father Hecker: Is He a Saint? Studies in Americanism" (1890) by Rev. Charles Maignen; "Father Hecker," (1901) by H. D. Sedgwick, Jr.; and "Modernism and the Vatican" (1911) by Adam J. Loeppert.

The interest of Roman Catholicism in European immigration is discussed in "The Society of St. Raphael and the Leo House" by Joseph Schaefer and C. G. Herbermann ("Hist. Rec. & Studies" Vol. I, Parts I and II), also "The Leo House for Immigrants . . . " by I. M. O'Reilly ("Rec. Amer. Cath. Hist. Soc." Vol. XVI).

The intercourse between the Pope and American Catholics is shown in a "Report of Mgr. Gennaro Straniero's Mission for the Presentation of the Red Biretta to Cardinal Gibbons" edited by Rev. J. J. Murphy (*ibid.* Vol. XXVI); "Monsignor Bedini's Visit to the United States. The Official Correspondence" contributed by Peter Condon ("Hist. Rec. and Studies" Vol. III, Part I); and "The First American Pilgrimage to Rome" by Rt. Rev. D. J. Keiley, D.D. (*ibid.* Vol. III, Part II).

For the official proceedings with a report in full of addresses delivered at the recent (Nov. 1908) Catholic Missionary Congress, one should consult "The First American Catholic Missionary Congress," edited by Rev. Francis C. Kelley.

On the debated question as to whether or not the Church of Rome has been holding her own in America, the following will prove of interest: "The Roman Catholic Church in the United States" ("Atlantic Monthly" Vol. LXXXIII); "The Religious Conditions in the United States" ("The Outlook" Vol. LXII); "Religious Reconstruction in the United States. The Catholic Church" ("The Outlook" Vol. LXIII). "The Decay of the Church of Rome" (3rd ed. 1911) by Joseph McCabe is particularly valuable. "The Life and Labors of Pope Leo XIII . . . " (1894) by Mgr. Charles De T'Serclaes, edited and extended by M. L. Egan, has important letters, addresses, and encyclicals.

On the outstanding leaders during the last century there are the following studies: "The Right Rev. John Du Bois, D.D. Third Bishop of New York" by C. G. Herbermann, D.D. ("Hist. Rec. & Studies" Vol. I Part II); "Cardinal McCloskey" by Rt. Rev. J. M. Farley, D.D. (*ibid.* Vol. I, Part I and II; Vol. II, Part I and II); "Catholic Historical Collections in the Life and Times of Cardinal Gibbons" (III Vols. 1895) by J. T. Reily; "Life of James Cardinal Gibbons" (1911) by A. S. Will; "A Retrospect of Fifty-Years" (II Vols. 1916) by James Cardinal Gibbons; "John Cardinal Farley, Archbishop of New York" by Rt. Rev. Mgr. P. J. Hayes, D.D. ("Hist. Rec. & Studies" Vol. VI, Part II).

In connection with the various Orders that have contributed so largely to the development of Romanism in America, the literature is as follows: "The Sulpicians in the United States" by C. G. Herbermann (*ibid.* Vols. VII and VIII); "The Establishment of the Capuchin Order in the United States" by Rev. S. G. Messmerr, D.D. (*ibid.* Vol. IV, Part I); "The Capuchins in America" by Rev. Otto Jeron, O.M. (*ibid.* Vol. V, Parts I and II); "The Foundation of the Dominican Province in the United States" by A. I. Du P. Coleman, (*ibid.* Vol. II, Parts I and II); "The Early Franciscan Missions in this Country" ("Amer. Cath. Quart. Rev." Jan. 1882); "Franciscan Tertiaries, First Established in the United States at Philadelphia" by Lydia Flintham, ("Rec. Amer. Cath. Hist. Soc." Vol. XV); "The Ursuline Nuns in America" by Mrs. Ettie M. Vogel (*ibid.* Vol. I); "A Story of Fifty Years. From the Annals of the Congregation of the Sisters of the Holy Cross" (1855-1905) no author specified; "A Southern Teaching Order; The Sisters of Mercy of Charleston, S. C. 1829-1904 by a member of the order" ("Rec. Amer. Cath. Hist. Soc." Vol. XV); "The Work of the Religious of the Sacred Heart in the United States . . . " ("Messenger of the Sacred Heart" Jan. 1901);

and "The Very Reverend Charles . . . McKenna . . . Missionary
. . . Holy Name Society" (1917) by V. F. O'Daniel.

On the various Councils that have convened in America, there is the "Concilia Provincialia Baltimori habita ab anno 1829 usque ad annum 1840 "(1842);" Concilium Plenarium totius Americae Septentrionalis Foederatae Baltimori habitum anno 1852" (1853); "Concilii Plenarii Baltimorensis II. Acta et Decreta," (1868); "Acta et Decreta Concilii Plenarii Baltimorensis. Tertii" (1886); "The Council in Baltimore" (1914) by Andreas N. Niedermayer.

DOCUMENTS

I. *PAPAL ESTABLISHMENT OF THE SEE OF BALTIMORE* (November 6, 1789)

"PIUS POPE VI.

FOR THE PERPETUAL MEMORY OF THE FACT

When from the eminence of our apostolical station, we bend our attention to the different regions of the earth, in order to fulfil, to the utmost extent of our power, the duty which our Lord has imposed upon our unworthiness of ruling and feeding his flock; our care and solicitude are particularly engaged that the faithful of Christ, who, dispersed through various provinces, are united with us by Catholic communion, may be governed by their proper pastors, and diligently instructed by them in the discipline of evangelical life and doctrine. . . . Wherefore, it having reached our ears that in the flourishing commonwealth of the Thirteen American States many faithful Christians united in communion with the chair of Peter, in which the centre of Catholic unity is fixed, and governed in their spiritual concerns by their own priests having care of souls, earnestly desire that a Bishop may be appointed over them to exercise the functions of episcopal order; to feed them more largely with the food of salutary doctrine, and to guard more carefully that portion of the Catholic flock.

We willingly embrace this opportunity which the grace of Almighty God has afforded us to provide those distant regions with the comfort and ministry of a Catholic Bishop. And that this be effected more successfully, and according to the rules of the sacred canons, We commissioned our venerable Brethren the Cardinals of the holy Roman Church, directors of the Congregation 'de propaganda fide,' to manage this business with the greatest care, and to make a report to us. It was therefore appointed by their decree, approved by us, and published the twelfth day of July of the last year, that the priests who lawfully exercise the sacred ministry and have care of souls in the United States of America, should be empowered to advise together and to determine, first, in what town the episcopal see ought to be erected, and next, who of the aforesaid priests appeared the most worthy and proper to be promoted to this important charge, whom We, for the first time only, and by special grace permitted the said priests to elect and to present to this apostolic See. In obedience to this decree the aforesaid priests exercising the care of souls in the United States of America, unanimously agreed that a bishop with ordinary jurisdiction, ought to be established in the town of Baltimore, because this town situate in Maryland, which province the greater part of the priests and of the faithful inhabit, appeared the most conveniently placed for intercourse with the other States, and because from this province Catholic religion and faith had been propagated into the others. And at the time appointed for the election, they being assembled together, the sacrifice of holy Mass, being celebrated, and the grace and assistance of the Holy Ghost being implored, the votes of all present were taken, and of twenty-six priests who were assembled twenty-four gave their votes for our beloved son, John Carroll, whom they judged the most proper to support the burden of episcopacy, and sent an authentic instrument of the whole transaction to the aforesaid Congregation of Cardinals. Now all things being materially weighed and considered in this Congregation, it was easily agreed that the interests and increase of Catholic religion would be greatly promoted if an episcopal see were erected at Baltimore, and the said John Carroll were appointed the Bishop of it. We, therefore, to whom this opinion has been reported by our beloved son, Cardinal Antonelli, Prefect of the said Congregation, having nothing more at heart than to ensure success to whatever tends to the propagation of true religion, and to the honor and increase of the Catholic Church, by the plentitude of our apostolical power, and by the tenor of these presents, do establish and erect the aforesaid town of Baltimore into an episcopal see forever, for one Bishop to be chosen by us in all future vacancies; and We, therefore, by the apostolical authority aforesaid, do allow, grant and permit to the Bishop of the said city and to his successors in all future times, to exercise episcopal power and jurisdiction, and every other episcopal function which Bishops constituted in other places are empowered to hold and enjoy in their respective churches, cities and dioceses, by right, custom, or by other means, by general privileges, graces, indults and apostolical dispensations, together with all pre-eminences, honors, immunities, graces and favors, which other Cathedral Churches, by right or custom, or in any other sort, have, hold and enjoy. We moreover decree and declare the said Episcopal see thus erected to be subject or suffragan to no Metropolitan right or jurisdiction, but to be forever subject, immediately to us and to our successors the Roman Pontiffs, and to this Apostolical See. And till another opportunity shall be presented to us of establishing other Catholic Bishops in the United States of America, and till other dispositions shall be made by this apostolical See, We declare, by our apostolical authority, all the faithful of Christ, living in Catholic communion, as well ecclesiastics as seculars, and all the clergy and people dwelling in the aforesaid United States of America, though hitherto they may have been subject to other Bishops of other dioceses, to be henceforward subject to the Bishop of Baltimore in all future times; And whereas by special grant, and for this first time only, we have allowed the priests exercising the care of souls in the United States of America, to elect a person to be appointed Bishop by us, and almost all their votes have been given to our beloved Son, John Carroll, Priest; We being otherwise certified of his faith, prudence, piety and zeal, forasmuch as by our mandate he hath during the late years directed the spiritual government of souls, do therefore by the plentitude of our authority, declare, create, appoint and constitute the said John Carroll, Bishop and Pastor of the said Church of Baltimore, granting to him the faculty of receiving the rite of consecration from any Catholic bishop holding communion with the apostolical see, assisted by two ecclesiastics, vested with some dignity, in case that two bishops cannot be had, first having taken the usual oath according to the Roman Pontifical.

And we commission the said Bishop to erect a church in the said city of Baltimore, in form of a Cathedral Church, inasmuch as the times and circumstances may allow, to institute a body of clergy deputed to divine worship, and to the service of said church, and moreover to establish an episcopal seminary, either in the same city or elsewhere, as he shall judge most expedient, to administer ecclesiastical incomes, and to execute all other things which he shall think in the Lord to be expedient for the increase of Catholic faith and the augmentation of the worship and splendor of the new erected church. . . .

Given at Rome at St. Mary Major, under the Fisherman's Ring, the 6th day of November, 1789, and in the fifteenth year of our Pontificate.

R. Card. Braschi Onesti.''

Text—Shea: *History of the Catholic Church* . . ., Vol. II, pp. 337-343.

II. *TRUSTEEISM—THE CONWELL-HOGAN CONTRO-VERSY*

Address of the Committee.

On June 21, 1821, the Trustees issued an "Address of the Committee of St. Mary's Church of Philadelphia, to their Brethren of the Roman Catholic Church Faith throughout the United States of America, on the Subject of the Reform of Sundry Abuses in the Administration of our Church Discipline '' We subjoin the luminous extract:

"As these States unfortunately have not been blessed with a second Carroll, who was a native of our country, and who, consequently, was well acquainted with our institutions, and respected them, as well as our individual rights, it becomes our duty, if we wish to preserve our religion unchanged, and free from the superstition and ignorance which has been attempted to be introduced among us, to adopt some general plan for the future management and direction of a uniform system throughout the United States; without being compelled, as heretofore, to receive, pay and obey men who are a disgrace to our religion, to us, to themselves and to those who send them. A person of respectability and literary acquirements should be selected to proceed to Rome and enter into a regular and written agreement with the Pope; the basis to be

I.   We claim the exclusive right which always belonged to the Church, of electing our own Pastors and Bishops, and when a Bishop shall be so elected by the Trustees and congregations of each State, he shall be ordained in this country and receive the Bull, or approbation from Rome as a matter of course.

II.   No priest shall be suspended by the Bishop without a trial.

III.   A priest suspended, to be tried by three or more priests of distinct States from that in which the trial takes place; there shall be a right of appeal to the Arch bishop and then a further appeal to the Court of Rome.

IV.   The priest during suspension to receive his salary until final judgment.

Should these measures meet the approbation of our fellow citizens and be adopted, we have not the least doubt but that they will be approved by the Holy Father. . . . In order to obviate the difficulty of procuring persons adequate to the task imposed on them of preaching and instructing in our religion, we would propose the establishment of a College for the express purpose of educating annually a certain number of persons to enter Holy Orders.

JOHN LEAMY, *Chairman et al.''*

Text—*Records of the American Catholic Historical Society*, Vol. XXV, pp. 169-170.

The Trustee Election Mob

"Father Jordan's account flatters neither party: "On Tuesday of Easter week, the annual election of trustees of St. Mary's Church took place. The Bishopites might as well have let it pass unnoticed; it was already determined that the Leamy-Meade party should be elected. But no, if they did not get the election, they should, at least, have the fight. Sunrise saw young men and buxom maids, who had no vote, trudging in from Germantown, Manayunk and Chester, and Darby, and even from over the waters, to do and die, for Bishop and for Church. It was on this day of days, that an aged gentleman uttered the memorable threat: 'if they do not treat the Bishop better I'll go over till Jarsay and never come back to Americay again.' But this is no joking matter, it was no comedy, it was in more respects than one a tragedy. Persons at this day (1874) can tell you how bricks were thrown from the windows of the Church upon the head of the hapless Bishopites whilst striving to vote, how young men would stand in Indian file and the backmost would ascend a cellar door, so as to give greater impetus, whilst the head of the foremost made a most convenient battering ram to butt between the kidneys of some thoughtless Hoganite, who was laughing at the funny sight of some Bishopite rendered *hors de combat* and hastening home with bloody head or crippled limb. Both parties can tell you how the iron rail swayed backwards and forwards, like a reed shaken by the wind, and at last fell with a crash, that caused a piercing shriek of anguish from many a wife and mother, kneeling in the corner of her room, with her little ones, praying for the dear ones. . . . Yes, that iron railing fell with a crash, and many a heart that beat loyally for Catholicity, for a time was stilled in anguish, and the casket of many a whole-souled Catholic was mangled and disfigured for life. And some of those, who then left the Church of their Baptism, might tell you how while Rt. Rev. Henry Conwell, D.D., and Rev. Samuel Cooper, and Rev. Terence McGirr, and Rev. Patrick Kenny, yea, and Rev. Wm. Vincent Harold, O.S.D., stood at the N. E. Corner of 4th Street and Willing's Alley, *oilstock* in hand and *pyxis* near the trembling heart, to follow the bleeding forms of the wounded into the house of Charles Johnson, Sr., and other good Samaritans: Mr. William Hogan, in concert with the delicate, lady-like daughters of rebel Catholics raised shouts of laughter that could be heard above the shrieks of the wounded; which unnatural cachinnation, thanks be to God, who can draw good out of evil, has brought more than one Protestant who heard it, into the happy folds of Christ's Church. It was truly a fearful day, still with all the odds against them, Joseph Snyder, John Carrell, Sr., Cornelius Tiers, Dennis McCready, Nicholas Stafford, William Myers, Nicholas Esling, and James Eneu, Sr., were elected trustees of St. Mary's Church, receiving 437 votes, although J. Cadwalader, Esq., decided that John Leamy, John Ashley and their party received 497. It may be true that they did, but the excess came from the votes of the occupants of those pews which had been erected after the withdrawal of the Bishop, whose consent was necessary, as President according to the charter. Unhappy day! The difficulty still remained. . . . For a short while there was peace, and Rev. William Vincent Harold acted as pastor, but the truce was of short duration, and the sacrilegious Hogan again officiated at the altar of St. Mary's."

Text—*Woodstock Letters*, Vol. III, No. 1, January, 1874

Papal Denunciation

To our Venerable Brothers, Ambrose Mareschal, Archbishop of Baltimore, and his Suffragan Bishops; to our Beloved Children, Administrators of the Temporalities of Churches, and to all the Faithful of the United States of America.

"Pius PP. VII

Venerable brothers and beloved children, Grace and Apostolical benediction. It was not without great grief we understood, that the Church of Philadelphia has been for a long time so distracted by incessant discord and dissensions, that schisms have arisen, perverse doctrines have been diffused, and that the affairs of the whole church itself are thrown into the greatest confusion. These disorders have originated principally from two causes, namely, from the senseless arrogance, and nefarious proceedings of the Priest William Hogan, and also, from an abuse of power in those who administer the temporal properties of the church. For it has reached our ears that this most abandoned Priest, Hogan, despising and subverting the laws of the church, has constituted himself judge of his own Prelate, that he has presumed to lacerate his reputation by many defamatory writings, to withdraw the faithful from their legitimate Pastor, to call a council of Bishops, for the purpose of deposing the said Prelate, daring, in his letters to that effect, like one possessed of superior power, to impart to them Apostolical benediction, and finally to intrude himself into the possession of the Cathedral Church, from which he has expelled the Bishop. Neither the complaints of the good, nor the withdrawing of his faculties nor the sentence of excommunication *justly denounced against him by his Bishop*, could deter him from pursuing the course he had commenced. On the contrary, regardless of all this, he does not blush to administer the sacraments, to perform all parochial functions, and daily to profane, by an impious and sacrilegious celebration, the most holy mysteries, rendering himself publicly guilty of the body and blood of the Lord. These are certainly execrable deeds. But what strikes, both us, and the universal church, not only with the greatest astonishment, but also with indignation, is doubtless, that this Priest, in so manifest a contempt of all law, could find many followers, supporters and defenders of his pride and contumacy, who, neglecting and despising the authority of the Bishop, would rather adhere to him, than to their lawful Pastor, from whom they have not hesitated to withdraw even the means necessary for the sustenance of life. This, indeed, is a most serious injury offered, not to the Bishop only, but to us also, and to this Apostolical See, and a sign of defection from the unity of the Catholic Church; because shamefully rejecting the Pastor given to them by the Holy See, they impiously follow a wicked man, cut off from the communion of the church, without reflecting that not those only who do evil, are to be considered and treated as guilty, but those who give their consent to them, and who are not afraid, either by themselves or the agency of others, to procure their assistance, counsel, or protection. Are they ignorant that the Holy Ghost has placed the Bishops to rule the Church of God? Whence it follows that Bishops are the shepherds of the flock of Christ: and is it not sufficiently evident from their conduct in this cause, that it is not the flock which leads the shepherd, but the shepherd the flock? Are they ignorant that the order of the Hierarchy has been so established in the Church, that priests must be subject to Bishops and Bishops to the supreme Vicar of Christ; so that the *priest* is to be judged by the *Bishop*, not the *Bishop* by the *priest*; because otherwise, the government and discipline of the whole church would be totally overturned? Are they ignorant, that it belongs not to laymen to meddle with ecclesiastical judgments, which are reserved to the Bishops, and therefore, that in the case of the priest Hogan, they should not by any means have interfered, but only have submitted to their Bishop? Finally, are they ignorant, that all the acts he sacrilegiously and daringly performs, are entirely null and void? We hope these things being duly considered with the assistance of Divine Grace, that those who have adhered to him through ignorance or error, and have been seduced by his artifices, will, the truth being now known, hasten to return to the right path, and diligently beware for the future of this impious man, lest, following him, they be made partakers of his crimes, and they escape not the just judgment of God.

There is another circumstance which affords continual cause of discord and discontent, not only in Philadelphia, but also in many other places of the United States of America: the immoderate and unlimited right, which trustees or administrators of the temporal properties of the churches assume, independently of the Bishops. Indeed unless this be circumscribed by certain regulations, it may prove an eternal source of abuse and dissensions. Trustees ought therefore to bear in mind, that the properties that have been consecrated to divine worship for the support of the church and the maintenance of its ministers, fall under the power of the church, and since the Bishops, by divine appointment, preside over their respective churches, they can not, by any means, be excluded from the care, superintendence, and disposal of these properties. Whence the holy council of Trent, Sess. 22, Cap. 9 de Ref., after having established, that the administrators for the building of every church, even of a Cathedral, and of all pious institutions, were bound every year to render to the ordinary an account of their administration; expressly ordered that although, according to the particular usages of some countries, the account of the administration was to be rendered to other persons, appointed for that purpose: nevertheless the Ordinary must be called in, together with them. If the trustees, in conformity with this decree, were to administer the temporalities of the church in union of heart and mind with the Bishop, everything would be performed peaceably and according to order.

But that trustees and laymen should arrogate to themselves the right, as it has sometimes happened in these countries, of establishing for Pastors, Priests destitute of legal faculties, and even not unfrequently bound by censures (as it appears was lately the case with regard to Hogan) and also of the removing them at their pleasure, and of bestowing the revenues upon whom they please, is a practice new and unheard of in the church. And if these things have been performed in the manner in which it has been announced to us, how could so great a subversion of laws, not only ecclesiastical but divine also, be borne with? For in that case the church would be governed not by Bishops, but by laymen, the shepherd would be subject to his flock, and laymen would usurp the power which was given by Almighty God to Bishops. But those who are desirous of remaining in the bosom of their mother, the Holy Catholic Church, and of providing for their eternal salvation, are bound religiously to observe the laws of the Universal Church, and as the civil authorities must be obeyed in those things which are temporal, so also, in those which are spiritual, must the faithful comply with the laws of the church, not confounding the spiritual with the temporal. In order then, to avoid the dissensions and disturbances which frequently arise from the unbounded power of trustees, we have provided, venerable brothers, that certain regulations and instructions concerning the choice and direction of trustees should be transmitted to you, to which, we are confident, the trustees will thoroughly conform themselves. If these be observed, all things we trust will be settled rightly, and peace and tranquillity will again flourish in these regions. To this end we first exhort in the Lord, and entreat the Pastors, whose solicitude is sufficiently known to us, that they employ their most diligent endeavors, to root out abuses and to establish ecclesiastical discipline, *being instant in season and out of season, by reproving, entreating, rebuking with all patience and doctrine.* We also admonish and exhort the trustees, and the rest of the faithful, through the bowels of our Saviour Jesus Christ, to behave towards the Pastors sent them by the Holy See, with that respect, honour, and obedience which belongs to them: to receive them as their fathers, and the directors of their souls; to lend a willing ear to their admonitions; to supply them with the subsidies necessary for their support, to harbour no other ministers of the sanctuary but those who have been approved by them; finally to embrace with pleasure and with readiness, whatever may judge conducive to establish regular order and discipline, and to rest in peace, that there may be no schisms; *that all be of one mind, having the same charity, being of one accord, agreeing in sentiment. Let nothing be done through strife, nor by vain glory, but in humility let each esteem others better than themselves.* (Phil. ii, 2, 3). And since, under the protection of your prosperous and happy government, Catholics enjoy the free exercise of their holy religion, let your faith and piety shine before all, in such a manner that you may be an example for edification, not only to the faithful, but to those also who are *without*, faithfully serving God and your country. And as we trust you will, with the assistance of divine grace, diligently and willingly perform this, we most lovingly impart to you in the Lord our Apostolical Benediction.

Given at Rome, in the Church at St. Mary Major, on the 24th day of August, Year 1822 and of our Pontificate the 23d.

(Signed,) Pius P. P. VII."

Text—*Records of the American Catholic Historical Society.* Vol. XXV, pp. 325-330.

The Two Sides of the Case

Conditions on which the Trustees and Congregation worshipping at St. Mary's Church. In this city, are willing to enter into an amicable accommodation of all their differences with the Right Rev. Bishop Conwell.

1. The Bishop to consent to acknowledge the inherent right of the Trustees of St. Mary's Church, to nominate and present to him, the names of such regular clergymen of respectability of the Roman Catholic faith, as they may please to select, for pastors of said church, and that they shall be regularly inducted and continue as pastors during good behaviour.

2. In case of any unfortunate misunderstanding, occurring in future between any one of the pastors of the said church and the Bishop, or the Trustees, it is mutually agreed that the Bishop and Trustees shall act in unison, and use every exertion in their power, to prevent the scandal which always arises from the publicity of such occurrences, adopting such mild and pacific measures as the principles and doctrine of our holy religion prescribe for an accommodation of the same; but if these should not succeed, and it should become necessary to suspend the person so offending, it is expressly agreed that he shall have a fair trial and hearing and be furnished with the charges in writing, agreeably to the rules and canons of the church, and be allowed an appeal in case of need to the Archbishop, who, in union with two Bishops from other dioceses, shall be solicited to decide on the accusation, which decision shall be binding; but subject to such other appeal as the canons of the church authorize, if the parties think proper to adopt such a course.

3. The constitution of the church having vested the Trustees with the exclusive management of its temporalities, they agree to fix, from time to time, the salaries or sums to be paid to the pastors, which shall always be done with such liberality as the funds of the church will permit, without creating debts, or subjecting the property to mortgage, and also with due regard to the necessary repairs required from time to time for the preservation of the real estate.

The Trustees agree to acknowledge Bishop Conwell as bishop of the diocese, but not as pastor of St. Mary's Church, and though they acknowledge his right to officiate at the church as often as his other duties will permit, and engage to encourage by all means in their power a good understanding, and perfect harmony in the church, and among its members, yet they do not allow that St. Mary's Church is to be considered exclusively as a Cathedral, any more than the other churches of the diocese, but agree with pleasure to furnish annually a reasonable sum, according to their means, towards the maintenance and support of a Bishop, and the dignity and respect due to his character.

5. It is proposed that the election of lay trustees, held annually, shall be placed, as regards the voters, on the same footing it always was from the incorporation of the society until the year 1813, and in strict conformity with the spirit of the charter, that is, "That no pew shall be entitled to more than two votes," by which means all future disputes and disagreements will be avoided, and it is further agreed, that the judges of elections shall be obliged to make returns of every pew by its number, together with the name of every individual voter, and that the same shall be published for the information of the congregation.

6. It is agreed that the Rev. Wm. Hogan, and the Rev. . . . . shall be and are hereby acknowledged as the pastors of St. Mary's Church. The parties to this engagement voluntarily entered into, with the sole view of putting an end to all unfortunate misunderstandings that have existed for some time past in Roman Catholic Churches of this city, solemnly pledge and bind themselves to comply with its several articles, and to unite their efforts, and exert all their influence, to allay the personal animosities which exist among the members of the Church, which from the warmth of passions, and the violence of irritated feelings of its individual members, has suffered the greatest injuries.

R. W. MEADE,
JOHN LEAMY,
ARCH'D RANDALL

Bishop Conwell answered through the medium of Mr. Meade:

"Philadelphia, July 17th, 1823.

Gentlemen,

Your letter of 21st of June was duly received, and its contents have been the subject of my most serious deliberations. . . . .

We hold it as an article of faith, that the government of the Church, the mission and appointment of its pastors, and the right to judge in cases spiritual and ecclesiastical, appertain exclusively to the hierarchy; and that these powers cannot, consistently with Catholic principles, be claimed or exercised by lay persons.

When the lay members of the Board of Trustees of St. Mary's Church, instead of confining themselves to their duty as defined in the chapter, took upon themselves the government of that church and the appointment of its pastor, when they asserted the right to exclude their Bishop from his cathedral and openly resist the highest judicial authority in the Catholic Church, they left me but one course to pursue. I am bound by my oath of consecration to resist the invasion of these rights, and maintain in the flock committed to my charge the authority and the laws thus disregarded. When, therefore, you ask me, what in my opinion are the terms upon which this unhappy affair may be terminated, as a Catholic Bishop, I can only answer, it can be done by conformity to what is the settled and established order and discipline of the Church, and, according to my judgment and conscientious belief, in no other way. This, then, is the only answer which I can give, or which you could reasonably expect me to give you, to your inquiry; and I shall be truly happy, if you should become persuaded that it points out to you the only course by which you may be reunited to your brethren in the Church.

It will afford me the highest gratification to accede to every reasonable wish of that portion of St. Mary's Church represented by you; but I have no authority to change established discipline. It is my duty to maintain and uphold the system of government prescribed by the lawful power of the Church; and I cannot be expected to violate laws which I have sworn to maintain.

The right of presentation supposes the existence of a benefice, and a benefice secures to the incumbent the full and uncontrolled enjoyment of the income of his church for life, unless he should be convicted of such offence as the canon law punishes with deprivation.

The right of patronage, and the right of meddling with the income of the church, are incompatible; yet this latter right can no more be surrendered by a Trustee, than the former can be acknowledged by a Bishop. The state of church property in this country, and the Trustee system as now constituted must always stand as an insuperable bar to the right of presentation. The Trustee system is susceptible of much improvement; and I feel persuaded that it must undergo considerable changes before it will be found to harmonize with the spirit, advance the honor, or to promote the interests and the peace, of the Catholic Church.

The first duty imposed on me, as a Bishop, is to take care that the faithful, committed to my charge, be served by pious, learned, and exemplary pastors. It shall be my study, as it is, in every way, my interest, to see that the first church in my diocese be so provided. Whilst I beg you to be assured of the sincerity of this determination, I have a right to expect from you a corresponding feeling of zealous attachment to a Church which has so many claims to your veneration and regard.

Be assured of my sincere wishes for your welfare, and believe me to be

Your faithful friend and father in God,

HENRY CONWELL,
Bishop of Philadelphia.

To R. W. Meade, John Leamy, and A. Randall, Esqrs."

Text—*Records, American Catholic Historical Society*, Vol. XXVI, pp. 145-160.

III. *THE SECULARIZATION OF THE CALIFORNIA MISSION*
The Decree of May 1st, 1834

"The Vice-President of the United Mexican States in the exercise of the Supreme Executive Power to the inhabitants of the Republic. Know ye that the Congress General has decreed as follows:

"Article 1. The government shall proceed to secularize the missions of Upper California.

Art. 2. In each of said missions a parish shall be established, served by a priest of the secular clergy, with a stipend of from $2,000 to $2,500 a year, as the government may decide.

Art. 3. These parish curates shall not recover or receive any fees for marriages, Baptisms, or under any other name. As regards fees for pomp, they shall be entitled to receive such as may be specifically named in the list to be made out for that purpose with the least possible delay by the Bishop of the Diocese, and approved by the Supreme Government.

Art. 4. To the parishes shall be given the churches with the sacred vessels, vestments, and other articles now possessed by each; and also such rooms adjoining the church as in the judgment of the government may be deemed necessary for the decent service of the parish.

Art. 5. The government shall cause a burial ground to be laid out for each parish but away from the population.

Art. 6. Five hundred dollars a year are appropriated for public worship and for the sacristan of each parish.

Art. 7. Of the buildings belonging to each mission, the most suitable shall be assigned as residence for the curate, with land not exceeding two hundred varas square; and the other buildings shall be used for a town-house, primary schools, public establishments, and workshops.

Art. 8. In order to provide promptly and effectively for the spiritual needs of both Californias, a vicar-general shall be appointed, who shall reside at the capital of Upper California but with jurisdiction over both territories; and the bishop shall confer upon him the corresponding faculties as complete as possible.

Art. 9. As a compensation the vicar-general shall receive annually $3,000, and he shall perform his duties free of charge, demanding nothing under any pretext whatsoever, not even for paper.

Art. 10. If for any reason whatever the curate of the capital or of any other parish in the territory shall act as vicar, he shall receive $1,500 in addition to his stipend as curate.

Art. 11. No custom shall be introduced which obliges the inhabitants of California to make offerings, however pious they may be, or however necessary they may be declared; neither time nor consent of the said inhabitants shall give them any force or weight whatsoever.

Art. 12. The government shall effectually care that the bishop do his part, as far as he is concerned, to carry out the objects of this law.

Art. 13. The Supreme Government shall provide for the gratuitous transportation by sea of the new curates that may be appointed as well as for their household and in addition it may give to each one for the journey by land from $400 to $800, according to the distance and the number of persons in his household which he brings along.

Art. 14. The government will pay the traveling expenses of the missionary religious leaving the missions; and in order that they may comfortably return by land to their colleges or convents, there may be allowed to each one from $200 to $300, and, at discretion, whatever may be necessary in order that those who have not sworn to support the independence, may leave the republic.

Art. 15.   The Supreme Government will meet the expenses arising under this law *out of the products of the estates, capital, and revenues at present known as the Pious fund of the California Missions.*"

Text—Engelhardt: *The Missions and Missionaries of California,* Vol. III, pp. 518-519.

Reglamento Provisional, Aug. 9, 1834.

Article 1.   The governor, in accordance with the spirit of the law of August 17th, 1833, and with his instructions received from the Supreme Government, and acting in accord with the prelates of the missionary religious, will partially convert into pueblos the missions of the territory beginning at once in this month of August, with ten missions and continuing with the rest in succession.

Art. 2.   The missionary religious will be relieved of the administration of the temporalities, and will exercise the functions of their ministry only in what pertains to spiritual matters until the formal division of the parishes is made, and the Supreme Government with the bishop provide parish priests.

Art. 3.   The territorial government will reassume the administration of the temporalities, directively, on the following basis.

Art. 4.   The Supreme Government will, by the quickest route, be requested to approve this Provisional Reglamento.

Distribution of Property and Lands.

Art. 5.   To each individual head of a family, and to all who are over twenty years of age, although they have no family, will be given from the mission lands, whether irrigable or not, a plot of land of not more than four hundred and not less than one hundred varas square: In common enough land will be assigned them to pasture their live stock.   Community lands shall be allotted to each pueblo, and at the proper time municipal lands also

Art. 6.   Among the same individuals there shall be divided in proportionate and equitable shares, according to the judgment of the governor, one-half of the live-stock, taking as a basis the latest reports on all kinds of stock as presented by the missionaries.

Art. 7.   There will also be distributed to them proportionately, one-half or less of the chattels, implements, and seeds on hand which are indispensable for cultivating the soil.

Art. 8.   All the remaining lands, buildings, goods, and property of every kind will stay in the care and under the responsibility of the mayordomo or employee, whom the governor will appoint, at the disposal of the Supreme Federal Government

Art. 9.   From the common mass of this property provision shall be made for the subsistence of the missionary Fathers, the pay of the mayordomo and other servants, for the expenses of worship, schools, and other objects of public order and propriety.

Art. 10.   The governor, inasmuch as he is charged with the control of the temporalities, will after the necessary investigation determine and regulate all the expenses which it may be needful to make as well for the execution of this plan as for the conservation and increase of the property.

Art. 11.   The missionary will choose that part of the mission buildings which suits him best for his habitation and for that of his attendants, and he shall be provided with the necessary furniture and utensils.

Art. 12.   The library, sacred vestments, church goods and furniture shall be in charge of the missionary Father under the care of the person who acts as sacristan, whom the same Father may select, and who shall be paid just wages for his labor.

Art. 13.   General inventories shall be made of all the existing property of each mission, all duly classified according to the different branches; of the account books and of all kinds of documents; of the debts and credits, of which documents and information an account shall be forwarded to the Supreme Government.

Political Government of the Pueblos.

Art. 14.   The political government of the pueblos shall be organized in entire conformity with the existing laws, the governor will give the rules suitable for the establishment of the town councils and the holding of elections.

Art. 15.   The economical government of the pueblos shall belong to the town council, but as far as regards the administration of justice in contentions, they shall be subject to the primary judges constitutionally established in the nearest places.

Art. 16.   The emancipated Indians will be obliged to take part in the indispensable community work which in the judgment of the governor may be deemed necessary for cultivating the vineyards, orchards and fields which for the present remain undistributed until the Supreme Government directs otherwise.

Art. 17.   The emancipated Indians will render to the Father the personal service necessary.

Restrictions.

Art. 18.   They cannot sell, burden nor alienate under any pretext the lands which may be given them, nor can they sell their live-stock.   The contracts made against these orders shall be of no value; the government will reclaim the property as belonging to the nation and the buyers shall lose their money.

Art. 19.   The lands, the owners of which die without heirs, shall revert to the power of the nation."

Text—Engelhardt: *The Missions and Missionaries of California*, Vol. III, pp. 523-526.

IV. THE NEW YORK SCHOOL CONTROVERSY—1840

Petition

To the Honorable the Board of Aldermen of the City of New York.

The petition of the Catholics of New York RESPECTFULLY REPRESENTS:

That your petitioners yield to no class in their performance of, and disposition to perform, all the duties of citizens.   They bear, and are willing to bear their portion of every common burden; and feel themselves entitled to a participation in every common benefit.

This participation, they regret to say, has been denied them for years back, in reference to common school education in the city of New York, except on conditions with which their conscience, and, as they believe, their duty to God, did not, and does not, leave them at liberty to comply.

The rights of conscience in this country are held by both the Constitution and universal consent, to be sacred and inviolable. No stronger evidence of this need be adduced than the fact, that one class of citizens are exempted from the duty or obligation of defending their country against any invading foe, out of delicacy and deference to the rights of conscience which forbids them to take up arms for any purpose.

Your petitioners only claim the benefit of this principle, in regard to the public education of their children. They regard the public education, which the State has provided as a common benefit, in which they are most desirous, and feel that they are entitled to participate; and therefore they pray your honorable body that they may be permitted to do so, without violating their conscience.

But your petitioners do not ask that this prayer be granted, without assigning their reasons for preferring it.

.   .   .   .

It is not deemed necessary to trouble your honorable body with a detail of the circumstances by which the monopoly of the public education of children in the city of New York, and of the funds provided for that purpose, at the expense of the State, have passed into the hands of a private corporation, styled, in its act of charter, 'The Public School Society of the City of New York.' It is composed of men of different sects or denominations. But that denomination of Friends, which is believed to have the controlling influence, both by its numbers and otherwise, holds as a *sectarian principle*, that any formal or official teaching of religion is, at best, unprofitable. And your petitioners have discovered that such of *their* children as have attended the public schools are generally, and at an early age, imbued with the same principle—that they become untractable, disobedient, and even contemptuous toward their parents— unwilling to learn any thing of religion—as if they had become illuminated, and could receive all the knowledge of religion necessary for them by instinct or inspiration. Your petitioners do not pretend to assign the cause of this change in their children; they only attest the fact as resulting from their attendance at the public schools of the Public School Society.

This Society, however, is composed of gentlemen of various sects, including even one or two Catholics. But they profess to exclude all sectarianism from their schools. If they do not exclude sectarianism, they are avowedly no more entitled to the school funds than your petitioners, or any other denomination of professing Christians. If they do as they profess, exclude sectarianism, then your petitioners contend that they exclude Christianity, and leave to the advantage of infidelity the tendencies which are given to the minds of youth by the influence of this feature and pretension of their system. If they could accomplish what they profess, other denominations would join your petitioners in remonstrating against their schools. But they do not accomplish it. Your petitioners will show your honorable body that they do admit what Catholics call sectarianism (although others may call it only religion), in a great variety of ways.

In their twenty-second report, as far back as the year 1827, they tell us, p. 14, that they 'are aware of the importance of early religious instruction,' and that none but what is 'exclusively general and scriptural in its character, should be introduced into the schools under their charge.' Here, then, is their own testimony that they did introduce and authorize 'religious instruction' in their schools. And that they solved, with the utmost composure, the difficult question on which the sects disagree by determining what kind of 'religious instruction' is 'exclusively general and scriptural in its character.'

Neither could they impart this 'early religious instruction' themselves. They must have left it to their teachers; and these, armed with official influence, could impress those 'early religious instructions' on the susceptible minds of the children, with the authority of dictators.

The Public School Society, in their report for the year 1832, p. 10, describe the effects of these 'early religious instructions,' without, perhaps intending to do so, but yet precisely as your petitioners have witnessed it in such of their children as attended those schools. 'The age at which children are usually sent to school affords a much better opportunity to mould their minds to peculiar and exclusive forms of faith, than any subsequent period of life.' In p. 11 of the same report, they protest against the injustice of supporting 'religion in any shape' by public money—as if the early religious instruction, which they themselves authorized in their schools five years before, was not 'religion in some shape,' and was not supported by public taxation. They tell us again, in more guarded language, 'The trustees are deeply impressed with the importance of imbuing the youthful mind with religious impressions, and they have endeavored to attain this object, as far as the nature of the institution will admit.' Report of 1837, p. 7.

In their thirty-third annual report, they tell us that 'they would not be understood as regarding religious impressions in early youth as unimportant. On the contrary, they desire to do all which may with propriety be done to give a right direction to the minds of the children entrusted to their care. Their schools are uniformly opened with the reading of the Scriptures, and the class-books are such as recognize and enforce the great and generally acknowledged principles of Christianity.' Page 7.

In their thirty-fourth annual report, for the year 1839, they pay a high compliment to a deceased teacher for the 'moral and religious influence exerted by her over the three hundred girls daily attending her school,' and tell us that 'it could not but have a lasting effect on many of their susceptible minds.' Page 7. And yet in all these 'early religious instructions—religious impressions, and religious influence, essentially anti-Catholic—your petitioners are to see nothing sectarian. But if, in giving the education which the State requires, they were to bring the same influences to bear on the 'susceptible minds of their *own* children, in favor, and not against their *own* religion, then this Society contends that it would be sectarian!'

Your petitioners regret there is no means of ascertaining to what extent the teachers in the schools of the Society carried out the views of their principals, on the importance of conveying 'early religious instructions' to the susceptible minds of the children. But they believe it is in their power to prove that, in some instances, the Scriptures have been explained, as well as read, to the pupils.

Even the reading of the Scriptures in those schools, your petitioners cannot regard otherwise than as sectarian; because Protestants would certainly consider as such the intention of the Catholic Scriptures, which are different from theirs: and the Catholics have the same ground to objection when the Protestant version is made use of. Your petitioners have to state further, as grounds of their conscientious objections to those schools, that many of the selections in their elementary reading-lessons contain matter prejudicial to the Catholic name and character. The term 'popery' is repeatedly found in them. This term is known and employed as one of insult and contempt toward the Catholic religion, and it passes into the minds of children with the feelings of which it is the outward expression. Both the historical and religious portions of the reading-lessons are selected from Protestant writers, whose prejudices against the Catholic religion render them unworthy of confidence in the mind of your petitioners, at least so far as their own children are concerned.

The Public School Society have heretofore denied that their books contained any thing reasonably objectionable to Catholics. Proofs of the contrary could be multiplied, but it is unnecessary, as they have recently retracted their denial, and discovered, after fifteen years' enjoyment of their monopoly, that their books do contain objectionable passages. But they allege that they have proffered repeatedly to make such corrections as the Catholic clergy might require. Your petitioners conceive that such a proposal could not be carried into effect by the Public School Society, without giving just grounds for exceptions to other denominations. Neither can they see with what consistency that Society can insist, as it has done, on the perpetuation of its monopoly when the trustees thus avow their incompetency to present unexceptionable books, without the aid of the Catholic or any other clergy. They allege, indeed, that with the best intentions they have been unable to ascertain the passages which might be offensive to Catholics. With their intentions, your petitioners cannot enter into any question. Nevertheless, they submit to your honorable body that this Society is eminently incompetent for the superintendence of public education, if they could not see that the following passage was unfit for the public schools, and especially unfit to be placed in the hands of Catholic children.

They will quote the passage as one instance, taken from 'Putnam's Sequel,' p. 296.

Huss, John, a zealous reformer from popery, who lived in Bohemia toward the close of the fourteenth, and the beginning of the fifteenth centuries. He was bold and persever in but at length, trusting to the *deceitful Catholics*, he was by them brought to trial, condemned as a heretic, and burnt at the stake.

The Public School Society may be excused for not knowing the historical inaccuracies of this passage, but surely assistance of the Catholic clergy could not have been necessary to an understanding of the word 'deceitful,' as applied to all who profess the religion of your petitioners.

For these reasons, and others of the same kind, your petitioners cannot in conscience, and conscientiously with their sense of duty to God and to their offspring, in trust the Public School Society with the office of giving 'a right direction to the minds of their children.' And yet this Society claims that office, and claims for the discharge of it the common school funds to which your petitioners, in common with other citizens, are contributors. In so far as they are contributors, they are not only deprived of any benefit in return, but their money is employed to the damage and detriment of their religion, on the minds of their own children, and of the rising generation of the community at large. The contest is between the *guaranteed* rights, civil and religious, of the citizen on the one hand, and the pretensions of the Public School Society on the other; and whilst it has been silently going on for years, your petitioners would call the attention of your honorable body to its consequences on the class for whom the benefits of public education are most essential—the children of the poor.

This class (your petitioners speak only so far as relates to their own denomination), after a brief experience of the schools of the Public School Society, naturally and deservedly withdrew all confidence from it. Hence the establishment by your petitioners of schools for the education of the poor.

The expense necessary for this was a second taxation, required not by the laws of the land, but the no less imperious demands of their conscience.

They were reduced to the alternative of seeing their children growing up in entire ignorance, or else taxing themselves anew for private schools, whilst the funds provided for education, and contributed in part by themselves,' were given over to the Public School Society, and by them employed as has been stated above.

Now your petitioners respectfully submit, that without this confidence, no body of men can discharge the duties of education as intended by the State and required by the people. The Public School Society are, and have been at all times, conscious that they had not the confidence of the poor. . . . .

Your petitioners, therefore, pray that your honorable body will be pleased to designate as among the schools entitled to participate in the common school fund, upon complying with the requirements of the law and the ordinances of the Corporation of the city, or for such other relief as to your honorable body, shall seem meet—St. Patrick's school, St. Peter's school, St. Mary's school, St. Joseph's school, St. James' school, St. Nicholas' school, Transfiguration Church school, and St. John's school.

And your petitioners further request, in the event of your honorable body's determining to hear your petitioners on the subject of their petition that such time may be appointed as may be most agreeable to your honorable body; and that a full session of your honorable board be convened for that purpose.

And your petitioners, &c.,

THOMAS O'CONNOR, Chairman.

Text—Bourne: *History of the Public School Society of the City of New York*, pp. 189-195.

Remonstrance of the Methodist Episcopal Church

"To the Honorable the Common Council of the City of New York:

The undersigned committee, appointed by the pastors of the Methodist Episcopal Church in this city, on the part of eaid pastors and churches, do MOST RESPECTFULLY REPRESENT:

. . . .

It must be manifest to the Common Council, that, if the Roman Catholic claims are granted, all the other Christian denominations will urge their claims for a similar appropriation, and that the money raised for education by a general tax will be solely applied to the purposes of proselytism, through the medium of sectarian schools. But if this were done, would it be the price of peace? or would it not throw the apple of discord into the whole Christian community, should we agree in the division of the spoils? Would each sect be satisfied with the portion allotted to it? We venture to say that the sturdy claimants who now beset the Council would not be satisfied with much less than the lion's share; and we are sure that there are other Protestant denominations beside ourselves who would not patiently submit to the exaction. But, when all the Christian sects shall be satisfied with their individual share of the public fund, what is to become of those children whose parents belong to none of these sects, and who cannot conscientiously allow them to be educated in the peculiar dogmas of any one of them? The different committees who, on a former occasion, approached your honorable body, have shown that, to provide schools for these only, would require little less than is now expended, and it requires little arithmetic to show that, when the religious sects have taken all, nothing will remain for those who have not yet been able to decide which of the Christian denominations to prefer. It must be plain to every impartial observer, that the applicants are opposed to the whole system of public school instruction; and it will be found that the uncharitable exclusiveness of their creed must ever be opposed to all public instruction which is not under the direction of their own priesthood. They may be conscientious in all this; but, though it be no new claim on their part, we cannot yet allow them to guide and control the consciences of all the rest of the community. We are sorry that the reading of the Bible in the public schools, without note or commentary, is offensive to them; but we cannot allow the Holy Scriptures to be accompanied with *their* notes and commentaries, and to be put into the hands of the children who may hereafter be the rulers and legislators of our beloved country; because, among other bad things taught in these commentaries, is to be found the lawfulness of murdering heretics, and the unqualified submission, in all matters of conscience, to the Roman Catholic Church.

But if the principle on which this application is based should be admitted, it must be carried far beyond the present purpose.

If all are to be released from taxation when they cannot conscientiously derive any benefit from the disbursement of the money collected, what will be done for the Society of Friends, and other sects who are opposed to war under all circumstances? Many of these, besides the tax paid on all foreign goods thus consumed, pay direct duties at the Custom House, which go to the payment of the army and to purchase the munitions of war. And even when the Government finds it necessary to lay direct war taxes, these conscientious sects are compelled to pay their proportion, on the ground that the public defence requires it. So, it is believed, the public interest requires the education of the whole rising generation; because it would be unsafe to commit the public liberty, and the perpetuation of our republican institutions, to those whose ignorance of their nature and value would render them careless of their preservation, or the easy dupes of artful innovators; and hence every citizen is required to contribute in proportion to his means to the public purpose of universal education.

The Roman Catholics complain that books have been introduced into the public schools which are injurious to them as a body. It is allowed, however, that the passages in these books to which such reference is made are chiefly, if not entirely, historical; and we put it to the candor of the Common Council to say, whether any history of Europe for the last ten centuries could be written which could either omit to mention the Roman Catholic Church, or mention it without recording historical facts unfavorable to that Church? We assert, that if all the historical facts in which the Church of Rome has taken a prominent part could be taken from writers of her own communion only, the incidents might be made more objectionable to the complainants than any book to which they now object.

History itself, then, must be falsified for their accommodation; and yet they complain that the system of education adopted in the public schools does not teach the sinfulness of lying: They complain that no religion is taught in these schools, and declare that any, even the worst form of Christianity, would be better than none: and yet they object to the reading of the Holy Scriptures, which are the only foundation of all true religion. Is it not plain, then, that they will not be satisfied with any thing short of the total abandonment of public school instruction, or the appropriation of such portion of the public fund as they may claim to their own sectarian purposes

But this is not all. They have been most complaisantly offered the censorship of the books to be used in the public schools. The committee to whom has been confided the management of these schools in this city offered to allow the Roman Catholic bishop to expurgate from these books any thing offensive to him.

But the offer was not accepted;—perhaps for the same reason that he declined to decide on the admissibility of a book of extracts from the Bible, which had been sanctioned by certain bishops in Ireland. An appeal, it seems, had gone to the pope on the subject, and nothing could be said or done in the matter until His Holiness had decided. The Common Council of New York will therefore find that, when they shall have conceded to the Roman Catholics of this city the selection of books for the use of the public schools, that these books must undergo the censorship of a foreign potentate. We hope the time is far distant when the citizens of this country will allow any foreign power to dictate to them in matters relating to either general or municipal law.

We cannot conclude this memorial without noticing one other ground on which the Roman Catholics, in their late appeal to their fellow-citizens, urged their sectarian claims, and excused their conscientious objections to the public schools. Their creed is dear to them, it seems, because some of their ancestors have been martyrs to their faith. This was an unfortunate allusion. Did not the Roman Catholics know that they addressed many of their fellow-citizens who could not recur to the memories of their own ancestors without being reminded of the revocation of the Edict of Nantes, the massacre of St. Bartholomew's day, the fires of Smithfield, or the crusade against the Waldenses? We would willingly cover these scenes with the mantle of charity, and hope that our Roman Catholic fellow-citizens will, in future, avoid whatever has a tendency to revive the painful remembrance.

Your memorialists had hoped that the intolerance and exclusiveness which had characterized the Roman Catholic Church in Europe had been greatly softened under the benign influences of our civil institutions. The pertinacity with which their sectarian interests are now urged has dissipated the illusion. We were content with their having excluded us, *ex cathedra*, from all claim to heaven, for we were sure they did not possess the keys, notwithstanding their confident pretension; nor did we complain that they would not allow us any participation in the benefits of purgatory, for it is a place they have made for themselves, and of which they may claim the exclusive property; but we do protest against any appropriation of the public school fund for their exclusive benefit, or for any other purposes whatever.

Assured that the Common Council will do what is right to do in the premises, we are, gentlemen, with great respect,

.Your most obedient servants,

N. BANGS,
THOMAS E. BOND,
GEORGE PECK."

Text—Bourne: *History of the Public School Society of the City of New York*, pp. 198-201.

V. *KNOW-NOTHINGISM*

The National Platform of 1855

"1. The acknowledgment of that Almighty Being who rules over the universe—who presides over the Councils of Nations—who conducts the affairs of men, and who, in every step by which we have advanced to the character of an independent Nation, has distinguished us by some token of Providential agency.

2. The cultivation and development of a sentiment of profoundly intense American feeling, of passionate attachment to our country, its history and its institutions; of admiration for the purer days of our national existence; of veneration for the heroism, that precipitated our Revolution, and of emulation of the virtue, wisdom and patriotism that framed our Constitution, and first successfully applied its provisions.

3. The maintenance of the union of these United States, as the paramount political good; or, to use the language of Washington, 'the primary object of patriotic desire.' And hence—

First—Opposition to all attempts to weaken or subvert it.

Second—Uncompromising antagonism to every principle of policy that endangers it.

Third—The advocacy of an equitable adjustment of all political differences which threaten its integrity or perpetuity.

Fourth—The suppression of all tendencies to political division, founded on 'geographical discriminations, or on the belief that there is a real difference of interests and views' between the various sections of the Union.

Fifth—The full recognition of the rights of the several States, as expressed and reserved in the Constitution, and a careful avoidance by the general government of all interference with their rights by legislative or executive action.

4. Obedience to the Constitution of these United States as the supreme law of the land, sacredly obligatory upon all its parts and members, and steadfast resistance to the spirit of innovation upon its principles, however specious the pretexts. Avowing that in all doubtful or disputed points it may only be legally ascertained and expounded by the judicial power of the United States.

First—A habit of reverential obedience to the laws, whether national, State or municipal, until they are repealed or declared unconstitutional by the proper authority.

Second—A tender and sacred regard for those acts of statesmanship which are to be contradistinguished from acts of ordinary legislation by the fact of their being of the nature of compacts and agreements; and so, to be considered a fixed and settled national policy.

5. A radical revision and modification of the laws regulating immigration, and the settlement of immigrants, offering the honest immigrant, who from love of liberty or hatred of oppression, seeks an asylum in the United States, a friendly reception and protection, but unqualifiedly condemning the transmission to our shores of felons and paupers.

6. The essential modification of the naturalization laws.

The repeal by the Legislatures of the respective States of all State laws allowing foreigners not naturalized to vote. The repeal, without retrospective operation, of all acts of Congress making grants of land to unnaturalized foreigners, and allowing them to vote in the territories.

7. Hostility to the corrupt means by which the leaders of party have hitherto forced upon us our rulers and our political creeds.

Implacable enmity against the present demoralizing system of rewards for political subserviency, and of punishments for political independence.

Disgust for the wild hunt after office which characterizes the age.

These on the other hand. On the other—

Imitation of the practice of the purer days of the Republic, and admiration of the maxim that 'office should seek the man, and not man the office,' and of the rule that the just mode of ascertaining fitness for office is the capability, the faithfulness and the honesty of the incumbent candidate.

8. Resistance to the aggressive policy and corrupting tendencies of the Roman Catholic Church in our country by the advancement to all political stations—executive, legislative, judicial or diplomatic—of those only who do not hold civil allegiance, directly or indirectly, to any foreign power, whether civil or ecclesiastical, and who are Americans by birth, education and training, thus fulfilling the maxim 'Americans only shall govern America.'

The protection of all citizens in the legal and proper exercise of their civil and religious rights and privileges; the maintenance of the right of every man to the full, unrestrained and peaceful enjoyment of his own religious opinions and worships, and a jealous resistance of all attempts by any sect, denomination, or church to obtain an ascendancy over any other in the State, by means of any special privilege or exemption, by any political combination of its members, or by a division of their civil allegiance with any foreign power, potentate or ecclesiastic.

9. The reformation of the character of our National Legislature, by elevating to that dignified and responsible position men of higher qualifications, purer morals, and more unselfish patriotism.

10. The restriction of executive patronage—especially in the matter of appointments to office—so far as it may be permitted by the Constitution, and consistent with the public good.

11. The education of the youth of our country in schools provided by the State, which schools shall be common to all, without distinction of creed or party, and free from any influence or direction of a denominational or partisan character.

And, inasmuch as Christianity, by the Constitutions of nearly all the States; by the decisions of most eminent judicial authorities, and by the consent by the people of America, is considered an element of our political system, and the Holy Bible is at once the source of Christianity and the depository and fountain of all civil and religious freedom, we oppose every attempt to exclude it from the schools thus established in the States.

12. The American party, having arisen upon the ruins, and in spite of the opposition of the Whig and Democratic parties, cannot be held in any manner responsible for the obnoxious acts or violated pledges of either. And the systematic agitation of the slavery question by those parties having elevated sectional hostility into a positive element of political power, and brought our institutions into peril, it has, therefore, become the imperative duty of the American party to interpose for the purpose of giving peace to the country and perpetuity to the Union. And as experience has shown it impossible to reconcile opinions so extreme as those which separate the disputants, and as there can be no dishonor in submitting to the laws, the National Council has deemed it the best guarantee of common justice and of future peace to abide by and maintain the existing laws upon the subject of slavery, as a final and conclusive settlement of that subject, in fact and in substance.

And, regarding it the highest duty to avow their opinions upon a subject so important in distinct and unequivocal terms, it is hereby declared as the sense of this National Council that Congress possesses no power under the Constitution to legislate upon the subject of slavery in the States, where it does or may exist, or to exclude any State from admission into the Union because its Constitution does or does not recognize the institution of slavery as a part of its social system, and expressly pretermitting any expression of opinion upon the power of Congress to establish or prohibit slavery in any territory, it is the sense of the National Council that Congress ought not to legislate upon the subject of slavery within the territory of the United States, and that any interference by Congress with slavery as it exists in the District of Columbia would be a violation of the spirit and intention of the compact by which the State of Maryland ceded the district to the United States, and a breach of the national faith.

13. The policy of the Government of the United States, in its relations with foreign governments, is to exact justice from the strongest and do justice to the weakest, restraining by all the power of the Government all its citizens from interfering with the internal concerns of nations with whom we are at peace.

14. This National Council declares that all the principles of the order shall be henceforth everywhere openly avowed, and that each member shall be at liberty to make known the existence of the order, and the fact that he himself is a member, and it recommends that there be no concealment of the places of meeting of subordinate councils."

Text—Schmeckebier: *History of the Know Nothing Party in Maryland*, Appendix A. J.H.U. Studies, Series XVII, No. 4 and 5.

VI. *THE POPE'S APPEAL TO TERMINATE THE CIVIL WAR*

"*To our Venerable Brother, John, Archbishop of New York:*

POPE PIUS IX

Venerable Brother: Health and Apostolic benediction. Among the various and most oppressive cares which weigh on us in these turbulent and perilous times, we are greatly affected by the truly lamentable state in which the Christian people of the United States of America are placed by the destructive Civil War broken out among them.

For, Venerable Brother, we cannot but be overwhelmed with the deepest sorrow while we recapitulate, with paternal feelings, the slaughter, ruin, destruction, devastation, and other innumerable and ever-to-be-deplored calamities by which the people themselves are most miserably harassed and dilacerated. Hence, we have not ceased to offer up, in the humility of our hearts, our most fervent prayers to God, that He would deliver them from so many and so great evils. And we are fully assured that you also, Venerable Brother, pray and implore, without ceasing, the Lord of Mercies to grant solid peace and prosperity to that Country. But since we, by virtue of the office of our Apostolic ministry, embrace, with the deepest sentiments of charity, all the nations of the Christian world, and though unworthy, administer here on earth the vicegerent work of Him who is the Author of Peace and the Lover of Charity, we cannot refrain from inculcating, again and again, on the minds of the people themselves, and their chief rulers, mutual charity and peace.

Wherefore we write you this letter, in which we urge you, Venerable Brother, with all the force and earnestness of our mind, to exhort, with your eminent piety and episcopal zeal, your clergy and faithful to offer up their prayers, and also apply all your study and exertion, with the people and their chief rulers, to restore forthwith the desired tranquillity and peace by which the happiness of both the Christian and the civil republic is principally maintained. Wherefore, omit nothing you can undertake and accomplish, by your wisdom, authority and exertions, as far as compatible with the nature of the holy ministry, to conciliate the minds of the combatants, pacify, reconcile and bring back the desired tranquillity and peace, by all the means that are most conducive to the best interests of the people.

Take every pains, besides, to cause the people and their chief rulers seriously to reflect on the grievous evils with which they are afflicted, and which are the result of civil war, the direst, most destructive and dismal of all the evils that could befall a people or nation. Neither omit to admonish and exhort the people and their supreme rulers, even in our name, that with conciliated minds they would embrace peace, and love each other with uninterrupted charity. For we are confident that they would comply with our paternal admonitions and hearken to our words the more willingly as of themselves they plainly and clearly understand that we are influenced by no political reasons, no earthly considerations, but impelled solely by paternal charity and peace, to exhort them to charity and peace. And study, with your surpassing wisdom, to persuade all that true prosperity, even in this life, is sought for in vain out of the true religion of Christ and its salutary doctrines. We have no hesitation, Venerable Brother, but that calling to your aid the services and assistance even of your associate bishops you would abundantly satisfy our wishes, and by your wise and prudent efforts bring a matter of such moment to a happy termination.

We wish you, moreover, to be informed that we write, in a similar manner, this very day to our Venerable Brother, John Mary [Odin], Archbishop of New Orleans, that, counseling and conferring with you, he would direct all his thought and care most earnestly to accomplish the same object.

. . . .

Dated Rome, at St. Peter's, October 18, 1862, in the seventeenth year of our Pontificate.

Pius IX, Pope."

"To the Illustrious and Honorable Jefferson Davis, President of the Confederate States of America. Richmond.

Pius IX.

Illustrious and Honorable Sir, *Greeting.*

We recently received, with all the kindness that was due to him, the Envoy sent by Your Excellency to convey to Us your letter dated the 23rd of the month of September of the present year. It was certainly a cause of no ordinary rejoicing to Us to be informed—by this gentleman and by the Letter of Your Excellency—of the lively satisfaction You experienced, and of the deep sense of gratitude You entertained towards Us, Illustrious and Honorable Sir, when You first perused Our Letters addressed to those Venerable Brothers, John, Archbishop of New York, and John, Archbishop of New Orleans, on the 18th of October of last year, in which we again and again strongly urged and exhorted those Venerable Brothers, on account of their great piety and episcopal solicitude, to make it the object of their constant efforts and of their earnest study, acting thus in Our name, to put an early end to the fatal civil war prevailing in that country, and to re-establish among the American people peace and concord, as well as feelings of mutual charity and love. It was also peculiarly gratifying to Us to hear that You, Illustrious and Honorable Sir, as well as the people whom you govern, are animated by the same desire for peace and tranquillity which We so earnestly inculcated in the Letters referred to, addressed to the said Venerable Brothers. Would to God that the other inhabitants of those regions (the Northern people), and their rulers, seriously reflecting upon the fearful and mournful nature of intestine warfare, might, in a dispassionate mood, hearken to and adopt the counsels of peace. We, on Our part, shall not cease offering up Our most fervent prayers to Almighty God, begging and supplicating Him, in His Goodness, to pour out upon all the people of America a spirit of Christian charity and peace, and to rescue them from the multitude of evils now afflicting them. We also pray the same All-clement Lord of Mercies to cause to shine upon Your Excellency the Light of His Divine Grace and to unite You and Ourselves in bonds of perfect love.

Given at Rome, at St. Peter's the 3d day of December, 1863, in the eighteenth year of our Pontificate.

Pius PP. IX."

Text—*Records of the American Catholic Historical Society*, Vol. XIV, pp. 264-271.

VII. SECOND PLENARY COUNCIL OF BALTIMORE, 1866

Pastoral Letter

"Venerable Brethren of the Clergy:
Beloved Children of the Laity:
After the lapse of more than fourteen years it has again been permitted us to assemble in Plenary Council, for the purpose of more effectually uniting our efforts for the promotion of the great object of our ministry—the advancement of the interests of the Church of God. . . .

I. Authority of Plenary Councils

The authority exercised in these councils is original, not delegated; and hence their decrees have, from the time of their promulgation, the character of ecclesiastical law for the faithful in the district or region subject to the jurisdiction of the Bishops by whom they have been enacted. . . .

II. Ecclesiastical Authority

The authority thus exercised is divine in its origin, the Holy Ghost having 'placed Bishops to rule the Church of God.' Obedience to it—whether there be question of 'the faith once delivered to the saints,' or of rules of conduct—is not submission to man but to God; and consequently imposes on the Faithful no obligation incompatible with the true dignity of man. . . .

. . . Civil society requires a supreme tribunal for the adjudication of controversies in the temporal order; and without such a tribunal no society could exist. Much more does the Society, which Christ established, require that all controveries regarding the doctrines He taught and the duties He imposed, should be determined by an authority, whose decision should be final, and which, as all are bound to obey it, must be an infallible oracle of truth. . . . .

III. Relations of the Church to the State

The enemies of the Church fail not to represent her claims as incompatible with the independence of the Civil Power, and her action as impeding the exertions of the State to promote the wellbeing of society. So far from these charges being founded in fact, the authority and influence of the Church will be found to be the most efficacious support of the temporal authority by which society is governed. . . . For the children of the Church obedience to the Civil Power is not a submission to force which may not be resisted; nor merely the compliance with a condition for peace and security; but a religious duty founded on obedience to God, by whose authority the Civil Magistrate exercises his power. This power, however, as subordinate and delegated, must always be exercised agreeably to God's Law. In prescribing anything contrary to that Law the Civil Power transcends its authority, and has no claim on the obedience of the citizen. . . . The Catholic has a guide in the Church, as a divine Institution, which enables him to discriminate between what the Law of God forbids or allows; and this authority the State is bound to recognize as supreme in its sphere—of moral, no less than dogmatic teaching. . . .

While cheerfully recognizing the fact, that hitherto the General and State Governments of our country, except in some brief intervals of excitement and delusion, have not interfered with our ecclesiastical organization or civil rights, we still have to lament that in many of the States we are not as yet permitted legally, to make those arrangements for the security of Church Property, which are in accordance with the canons and discipline of the Catholic Church.

. . . .

V.   The Sacrament of Matrimony

To that sacrament of the Church which is highest in its typical signification—the sacrament of matrimony—we feel it our duty to direct in a particular manner your attention. . . .

We recall these facts, because they most strongly express the principle of the Church in regard to matrimony, and must be regarded by every well regulated mind as among the brightest jewels of her crown. We recall them, also, in order to enforce our solemn admonition to our flocks, to give no ear to the false and degrading theories on the subject of matrimony, which are boldly put forward by the enemies of the Church. According to these theories, marriage is a mere civil contract, which the civil Power is to regulate, and from which an injured or dissatisfied party may release himself or herself by the remedy of divorce, so as to be able lawfully to contract new engagements. This is in evident contradiction with the words of Christ: 'What God has joined together, let not man put asunder.' As the guardian of God's holy Law, the Church condemns this false theory, from which would follow a successive polygamy, no less opposed to the unity and stability of Christian marriage than that simultaneous polygamy, which, to the scandal of Christendom, is found within our borders. No State law can authorize divorce, so as to permit the parties divorced to contract new engagements; and every such new engagement, contracted during the joint lives of the parties so divorced, involves the crime of adultery. We refer with pain to the scandalous multiplication of these unlawful separations, which, more than any other cause, are sapping the foundations of morality and preparing society for an entire dissolution of the basis on which it rests.

. . . .

VI.   On Books and Newspapers—The Press

The Council of Trent requires, that all books which treat of Religion should be submitted before publication to the Ordinary of the Diocese in which they are to be published, for the purpose of obtaining his sanction, so as to assure the faithful that they contain nothing contrary to faith or morals. This law is still of force; and in the former Plenary Council its observance was urged, and the Bishops were exhorted to approve of no book which had not been previously examined by themselves, or by clergymen appointed by them for that purpose, and to confine such approbation to works published in their respective dioceses. . . .

In many also of our dioceses there are published Catholic Papers, mostly of a religious character; and many of such papers bear upon them the statement that they are the 'organs' of the Bishop of the diocese in which they are published, and sometimes of other Bishops in whose dioceses they circulate. We cheerfully acknowledge the services the Catholic Press has rendered to Religion, as also the disinterestedness with which, in most instances, it has been conducted, although yielding to publishers and editors a very insufficient return for their labors. We exhort the Catholic community to extend to these publications a more liberal support, in order thay they may be enabled to become more worthy the great cause they advocate.

We remind them, that the power of the Press is one of the most striking features of modern society; and that it is our duty to avail ourselves of this mode of making known the truths of our Religion, and removing the misapprehensions which so generally prevail in regard to them. If many of these papers are not all that we would wish them to be, it will be frequently found, that the real cause of their shortcomings is the insufficient support they receive from the Catholic Public. . . .

. . . .

VII. Education of Youth

We recur to the subject of the education of youth, to which, in the former Plenary Council, we already directed your attention, for the purpose of reiterating the admonition we then gave, in regard to the establishment and support of Parochial Schools; and of renewing the expression of our conviction, that religious teaching and religious training should form part of every system of school education. Every day's experience renders it evident, that to develop the intellect and store it with knowledge, while the heart and its affections are left without the control of religious principle, sustained by religious practices, is to mistake the nature and object of education; as well as to prepare for parent and child the most bitter disappointment in the future, and for society the most disastrous results. We wish also to call attention to a prevalent error on the subject of the education of youth, from which parents of the best principles are not always exempt. Naturally desiring the advancement of their children, in determining the education they will give them, they not unfrequently consult their wishes, rather than their means, and the possible position of their children, in mature age. Education, to be good, need not necessarily be either high or ornamental, in the studies or accomplishments it embraces. These things are in themselves unobjectionable; and they may be suitable and advantageous or otherwise, according to circumstances. Prepare your children for the duties of the state or condition of life they are likely to be engaged in: do not exhaust your means in bestowing on them an education that may unfit them for these duties. This would be a sure source of disappointment and dissatisfaction, both for yourselves and for them. . . . .

VIII. Catholic Protectories and Industrial Schools

Connected with this subject of education, is the establishment of Protectories and Industrial Schools for the correction or proper training of youth, which has of late years attracted universal attention. It is a melancholy fact, and a very humiliating avowal for us to make, that a very large proportion of the idle and vicious youth of our principal cities are the children of Catholic parents. Whether from poverty or neglect, the ignorance in which so many parents are involved as to the true nature of education, and of their duties as Christian parents, or the associations which our youth so easily form with those who encourage them to disregard parental admonition; certain it is, that a large number of Catholic parents either appear to have no idea of the sanctity of the Christian family, and of the responsibility imposed on them of providing for the moral training of their offspring, or fulfil this duty in a very imperfect manner. . . . The only remedy for this great and daily augmenting evil is, to provide Catholic Protectories or Industrial Schools, to which such children may be sent; and where, under the only influence that is known to have really reached the roots of vice, the youthful culprit may cease to do evil and learn to do good. We rejoice that in some of our dioceses —would that we could say in all!—a beginning has been made in this good work; and we cannot too earnestly exhort our Venerable Brethren of the Clergy to bring this matter before their respective flocks, to endeavor to impress on Christian parents the duty of guarding their children from the evils above referred to, and to invite them to make persevering and effectual efforts for the establishment of Institutions, wherein, under the influence of religious teachers, the waywardness of youth may be corrected, and good seed planted in the soil in which, while men slept, the enemy had sowed tares.

IX. Vocations to the Priesthood

We continue to feel the want of zealous priests, in sufficient number to supply the daily increasing necessities of our dioceses. While we are gratified to know, that in some parts of our country the number of youths who offer themselves for the Ecclesiastical state is rapidly increasing, we are obliged to remark, that in the other parts, notwithstanding all the efforts and sacrifices which have been made for this object, and the extraordinary encouragements which have been held out to youthful aspirants to the ministry, in our Preparatory and Theological Seminaries, the number of such as have presented themselves and persevered in their vocations has hitherto been lamentably small. Whatever may be the cause of this unwillingness to enter the sacred ministry on the part of our youth, it cannot be attributed to any deficiency of ours in such efforts as circumstances have enabled us to make. We fear that the fault lies, in great part, with many parents, who, instead of fostering the desire, so natural to the youthful heart, of dedicating itself to the service of God's sanctuary, but too often impart to their children their own worldly-mindedness, and seek to influence their choice of a state of life, by unduly exaggerating the difficulties and dangers of the priestly calling, and painting in too glowing colors the advantages of a secular life. To such parents we would most earnestly appeal; imploring them not to interfere with the designs of God on their children, when they perceive in them a growing disposition to attach themselves to the service of the Altar. If God rewards the youthful piety of your sons by calling them to minister in His sanctuary, the highest privilege He confers on man, do not endeavor to give their thoughts another direction. Do not present to your children the priesthood in any other light than as a sublime and holy state, having indeed, most sacred duties and most serious obligations, but having also the promise of God's grace to strengthen and sustain human weakness in their fulfilment, and the divine blessing, here and hereafter, as their reward. . .

X. The Laity

We continue to have great consolation in witnessing the advance of Religion throughout the various Dioceses, as shewn in the multiplication and improved architectural character of our churches, the increase of piety in the various congregations, and the numerous conversions of so many who have sacrificed early prejudices and every consideration of their temporal interests and human feelings at the shrine of Catholic Truth. We must, however, in all candor say, that we cannot include all, or indeed the greater part of those who compose our flocks, in this testimony to fidelity and zeal. Too many of them, including not unfrequently men otherwise of blameless lives, remain for years estranged from the sacraments of the Church, although they attend the celebration of the divine Mysteries, and listen to the preaching of God's word with an earnestness and attention in themselves deserving of all praise. . .

In this connection, we consider it to be our duty to warn our people against those amusements which may easily become to them an occasion of sin, and especially against those fashionable dances, which, as at present carried on, are revolting to every feeling of delicacy and propriety, and are fraught with the greatest danger to morals. We would also warn them most solemnly against the great abuses which have sprung up in the matter of Fairs, Excursions, and Picnics, in which, as too often conducted, the name of Charity is made to cover up a multitude of sins. We forbid all Catholics from having anything to do with them, except when managed in accordance with the regulations of the Ordinary, and under the immediate supervision of their respective Pastors.

We have noticed, with the most sincere satisfaction and gratitude to God, the great increase among us of Societies and Associations, especially of those composed of young and middle-aged men, conducted in strict accordance with the principles of the Catholic Religion, and with an immediate view to their own sanctification. . .

XII. The Emancipated Slaves

We must all feel, beloved Brethren, that in some manner a new and most extensive field of charity and devotedness has been opened to us, by the emancipation of the immense slave population of the South. We could have wished, that in accordance with the action of the Catholic Church in past ages, in regard to the serfs of Europe, a more gradual system of emancipation could have been adopted, so that they might have been in some measure prepared to make a better use of their freedom, than they are likely to do now. Still the evils which must necessarily attend upon the sudden liberation of so large a multitude, with their peculiar dispositions and habits, only make the appeal to our Christian charity and zeal, presented by their forlorn condition, the more forcible and imperative.

We urge upon the Clergy and people of our charge the most generous co-operation with the plans which may be adopted by the Bishops of the Dioceses in which they are, to extend to them that Christian education and moral restraint which they so much stand in need of. Our only regret in regard to this matter is, that our means and opportunity of spreading over them the protecting and salutary influences of our Holy Religion, are so restricted.

XIII. Religious Communities

We are filled with sentiments of the deepest reverence for those holy Virgins, who, in our various religious communities, having taken counsel of St. Paul, have chosen the better part, that they may be holy 'in body and in spirit.' . . . "

Text—*Concilii Plenarii Baltimorensis II* . . . pp. 27-52.

VIII. *THIRD PLENARY COUNCIL OF BALTIMORE, 1884*

Pastoral Letter

"*Venerable Brethren of the Clergy,*
Beloved Children of the Laity;

Full eighteen years have elapsed since our predecessors were assembled in Plenary Council to promote uniformity of discipline, to provide for the exigencies of the day, to devise new means for the maintenance and diffusion of our holy religion, which should be adequate to the great increase of the Catholic population. . .

. . . .

We have no reason to fear that you, beloved brethren, are likely to be carried away by these or other false doctrines condemned by the Vatican Council, such as materialism or the denial of God's power to create, to reveal to mankind His hidden truths, to display by miracles His almighty power in this world, which is the work of His hands.   But neither can we close our eyes to the fact that teachers of skepticism and irreligion are at work in our country.   They have crept into the leading educational institutions of our non-Catholic fellow-citizens; they have (though rarely) made their appearance in the public press and even in the pulpit.   Could we rely fully on the innate good sense of the American people and on that habitual reverence for God and religion which has so far been their just pride and glory, there might seem comparatively little danger of the general diffusion of those wild theories which reject or ignore Revelation, undermine morality, and end not unfrequently by banishing God from his own creation.   But when we take into account the daily signs of growing unbelief, and see how its heralds not only seek to mould the youthful mind in our colleges and seats of learning, but are also actively working amongst the masses, we cannot but shudder at the dangers that threaten us in the future.

. . . .

. . . A Catholic finds himself at home in the United States, for the influence of his Church has constantly been exercised in behalf of individual rights and popular liberties.   And the right-minded American nowhere finds himself more at home than in the Catholic Church, for nowhere else can he breathe more freely that atmosphere of Divine truth, which alone can make him free (John viii., 32).

We repudiate with equal earnestness the assertion that we need to lay aside any of our devotedness to our Church to be true Americans, and the insinuation that we need to abate any of our love for our country's principles and institutions, to be faithful Catholics. . .

EDUCATION OF THE CLERGY

During the century of extraordinary growth now closing, the care of the Church in this country has been to send forth as rapidly as possible holy, zealous, hard-working priests, to supply the needs of the multitudes calling for the ministrations of religion. She has not on that account neglected to prepare them for their divine work by a suitable education, as her numerous and admirable seminaries testify; but the course of study was often more rapid and restricted than she desired.   At present our improved circumstances make it practicable both to lengthen and widen the course, and for this the Council has duly provided.

PASTORAL RIGHTS

. . . .

But while it is our desire to do all on our part that both justice and affection can prompt, for fully securing all proper rights and privileges to our priests, let us remind you, beloved brethren, that on your conduct must their happiness chiefly depend.   A grateful and pious flock is sure to make a happy pastor.   But if the people do not respond to their pastor's zeal, if they are cold and ungrateful and disedifying, then indeed is his lot sad and pitiable. . . . .

One generation buys or builds, another generation improves and adorns, and each generation uses and transmits for the use of others yet to come;—bishops and priests having the burden of the administration and being sacredly responsible for its faithful performance.

In the discharge of this duty it often becomes necessary to contract church debts. Where the multiplication of the Catholic population has been so rapid, rapid work had to be done in erecting churches and schools.   And if, under such circumstances, pastors had to wait till all the means were collected before beginning the work, a generation would be left without necessary spiritual aids, and might be lost to the Church and to God. .

CHRISTIAN EDUCATION

. . . .

To shut religion out of the school, and keep it for home and the Church, is, logically, to train up a generation that will consider religion good for home and the Church, but not for the practical business of real life.   But a more false and pernicious notion could not be imagined.   Religion, in order to elevate a people, should inspire their whole life and rule their relations with one another.   A life is not dwarfed, but ennobled by being lived in the presence of God.   Therefore the school, which principally gives the knowledge fitting for practical life, ought to be pre-eminently under the holy influence of religion.   From the shelter of home and school, the youth must soon go out into the busy ways of trade or traffic or professional practice.   In all these, the principles of religion should animate and direct him.   But he cannot expect to learn these principles in the work-shop, or office or the counting-room.   Therefore let him be well and thoroughly imbued with them by the joint influences of home and school, before he is launched out on the dangerous sea of life.

. . . .

Two objects therefore, dear brethren, we have in view viz., to multiply our schools and to perfect them.   We must multiply them, till every Catholic child in the land shall have the means of education within its reach.   There is still much to be done ere this is attained.   There are still hundreds of Catholic children in the United States deprived of the benefit of a Catholic school.   Pastors and parents should not rest till this defect be remedied.   No parish is complete till it has schools adequate to the needs of its children, and the pastor and people of such a parish should feel that they have not accomplished their entire duty until the want is supplied.

But then, we must also perfect our schools.   We repudiate the idea that the Catholic school need be in any respect inferior to any other school whatsoever.   And if hitherto, in some places, our people have acted on the principle that it is better to have an imperfect Catholic school than to have none at all, let them now push their praiseworthy ambition still further, and not relax their efforts till their schools be elevated to the highest educational excellence.   And we implore parents not to hasten to take their children from school, but to give them all the time and all the advantages that they have the capacity to profit by, so that, in after life, their children may 'rise up and call them blessed.'

THE CHRISTIAN HOME

. . . Christian schools sow the seed, but Christian homes must first prepare the soil, and afterwards foster the seed and bring it to maturity.

1. *Christian Marriage.*—The basis of the Christian home is Christian marriage; that is, marriage entered into according to religion, and cemented by God's blessing. So great is the importance of marriage to the temporal and eternal welfare of mankind, that, as it had God for its Founder in the Old Law, so, in the New Law, it was raised by our Divine Lord to the dignity of a sacrament of the Christian religion. . .

2. *The Indissolubility of Marriage.*—The security of the Christian home is in the indissolubility of the marriage tie. Christian marriage, once consummated, can never be dissolved save by death. Let it be well understood that even adultery, though it may justify 'separation from bed and board,' cannot loose the marriage tie, so that either of the parties may marry again during the life of the other. Nor has 'legal divorce' the slightest power, before God, to loose the bond of marriage and to make a subsequent marriage valid. 'What God hath joined together, let not man put asunder' (Matth. xix., 6). In common with all Christian believers and friends of civilization, we deplore the havoc wrought by the divorce-laws of our country. These laws are fast loosening the foundations of society.

. . . .

4. *Good Reading.*—Let the adornments of home be chaste and holy pictures, and, still more, sound, interesting and profitable books. No indelicate representation should ever be tolerated in a Christian home. Artistic merit in the work is no excuse for the danger thus presented . . .

The same remark applies equally to books and periodicals. Not only should the immoral, the vulgar, the sensational novel, the indecently illustrated newspaper and publications tending to weaken faith in the religion and the Church of Jesus Christ, be absolutely excluded from every Christian home, but the dangerously exciting and morbidly emotional, whatever, in a word, is calculated to impair or lower the tone of faith or morals in the youthful mind and heart, should be carefully banished. . . . Teach your children to take a special interest in the history of our own country. We consider the establishment of our country's independence, the shaping of its liberties and laws, as a work of special Providence, its framers 'building better than they knew,' the Almighty's hand guiding them. And if ever the glorious fabric be subverted or impaired, it will be by men forgetful of the sacrifices of the heroes that reared it, of the virtues that cemented it and of the rights on which it rests; or ready to sacrifice principle and virtue to the interests of party or self. As we desire therefore that the history of the United States should be carefully taught in all our Catholic schools, and have directed that it be specially dwelt upon in the education of ecclesiastical students in our preparatory seminaries; so also we desire that it form a favorite part of the home library and home reading. We must keep firm and solid the liberties of our country, by keeping fresh the noble memories of the past, and by sending forth continually from our Catholic homes into the arena of public life recruits of patriots and not of partisans.

5. *The Holy Scriptures.*—It can hardly be necessary for us to remind you, beloved brethren, that the most highly valued treasure of every family library, and the most

frequently and lovingly made use of, should be the Holy Scriptures. . . . We hope that no family can be found amongst us without a correct version of the Holy Scriptures. . . .

6. *The Catholic Press.*— . . . If the head of each Catholic family will recognize it as his privilege and his duty to contribute towards supporting the Catholic press, by subscribing for one or more Catholic periodicals, and keeping himself well acquainted with the information they impart, then the Catholic press will be sure to attain to its rightful development and to accomplish its destined mission. But choose a journal that is thoroughly Catholic, instructive and edifying; not one that would be, while Catholic in name and pretense, uncatholic in tone and spirit, disrespectful to constituted authority, or biting and uncharitable to Catholic brethren.

. . . .

The Lord's Day

. . . To turn the Lord's Day into a day of toil, is a blighting curse to a country; to turn it into a day of dissipation would be worse. We earnestly appeal, therefore, to all Catholics, without distinction, not only to take no part in any movement tending toward a relaxation of the observance of Sunday, but to use their influence and power as citizens to resist in the opposite direction.

There is one way of profaning the Lord's Day which is so prolific of evil results, that we consider it our duty to utter against it a special condemnation. This is the practice of selling beer or other liquors on Sunday, or of frequenting places where they are sold. This practice tends more than any other to turn the Day of the Lord into a day of dissipation, to use it as an occasion for breeding intemperance. ' While we hope that Sunday-laws on this point will not be relaxed, but even more rigidly enforced, we implore all Catholics, for the love of God and of country, never to take part in such Sunday traffic, nor to patronize nor countenance it. . . . .

And here it behooves us to remind our workingmen, the bone and sinew of the people and the specially beloved children of the Church, that if they wish to observe Sunday as they ought, they must keep away from drinking places on Saturday night. Carry your wages home to your families, where they rightfully belong. Turn a deaf ear, therefore, to every temptation; and then Sunday will be a bright day for all the family. . . . Let the exertions of our Catholic Temperance Societies meet with the hearty co-operation of pastors and people; and not only will they go far towards strangling the monstrous evil of intemperance, but they will also put a powerful check on the desecration of the Lord's Day, and on the evil influences now striving for its total profanation.

. . . .

Forbidden Societies

One of the most striking characteristics of our times is the universal tendency to band together in societies for the promotion of all sorts of purposes. This tendency is the natural outgrowth of an age of popular rights and representative institutions. It is also in accordance with the spirit of the Church, whose aim, as indicated by her name Catholic, is to unite all mankind in brotherhood. It is consonant also with the spirit of Christ, who came to break down all walls of division, and to gather all in the one family of the one heavenly Father.

But there are few good things which have not their counterfeits, and few tendencies which have not their dangers. . . . Hence it is the evident duty of every reasonable man, before allowing himself to be drawn into any society, to make sure that both its ends and its means are consistent with truth, justice and conscience.

In making such a decision, every Catholic ought to be convinced that his surest guide is the Church of Christ. . . . Thus our Holy Father Leo XIII has lately shown that the Masonic and kindred societies,—although the offspring of the ancient Guilds, which aimed at sanctifying trades and tradesmen with the blessings of religion; and although retaining, perhaps, in their 'ritual,' much that tells of the religiousness of their origin; and although in some countries still professing entire friendliness toward the Christian religion,—have nevertheless already gone so far, in many countries, as to array themselves in avowed hostility against Christianity, and against the Catholic Church as its embodiment, that they virtually aim at substituting a world-wide fraternity of their own, for the universal brotherhood of Jesus Christ, and at disseminating mere Naturalism for the supernatural revealed religion bestowed upon mankind by the Saviour of the world. . .

Whenever, therefore, the Church has spoken authoritatively with regard to any society, her decision ought to be final for every Catholic.

. . . .

There is one characteristic which is always a strong presumption against a society, and that is secrecy. . . . When, therefore, associations veil themselves in secrecy and darkness, the presumption is against them, and it rests with them to prove that there is nothing evil in them.

. . . .

CATHOLIC SOCIETIES

It is not enough for Catholics to shun bad or dangerous societies, they ought to take part in good and useful ones. If there ever was a time when merely negative goodness would not suffice, such assuredly is the age in which we live. This is pre-eminently an age of action, and what we need to-day is active virtue and energetic piety. . .

In the first place, we hope that in every parish in the land there is some sodality or confraternity to foster piety among the people. We therefore heartily endorse anew all approbations previously given to our many time-honored and cherished confraternities, such as those of the Sacred Heart of Jesus, of the Blessed Sacrament, and of the Blessed Virgin.

Next come the various associations for works of Christian zeal and charity. . . .

Then there are associations for the checking of immorality, prominent among which are our Catholic Temperance Societies. These should be encouraged and aided by all who deplore the scandal given and the spiritual ruin wrought by intemperance. . .

We likewise consider as worthy of particular encouragement associations for the promotion of healthful social union among Catholics,—and especially those whose aim is to guard our Catholic young men against dangerous influences, and to supply them with the means of innocent amusement and mental culture. It is obvious that our young men are exposed to the greatest dangers, and therefore need the most abundant helps. . .

. . . .

We also esteem as a very important element in practical Catholicity, the various forms of Catholic beneficial societies and kindred associations of Catholic working-men. . .

HOME AND FOREIGN MISSIONS

. . . .

In nearly all European countries there are Foreign Mission Colleges, and also associations of the faithful for the support of the missions by their contributions. Hitherto we have had to strain every nerve in order to carry on the missions of our own country, and we were unable to take any important part in aiding the missions abroad.   But we must beware lest our local burdens should make our zeal narrow and uncatholic.   There are hundreds of millions of souls in heathen lands to whom the light of the Gospel has not yet been carried, and their condition appeals to the charity of every Christian heart.   Among our own Indian tribes, for whom we have a special responsibility, there are still many thousands in the same darkness of heathenism, and the missions among our thousands of Catholic Indians must equally look to our charity for support.   Moreover, out of the six millions of our colored population there is a very large multitude, who stand sorely in need of Christian instruction and missionary labor; and it is evident that in the poor dioceses in which they are mostly found, it is most difficult to bestow on them the care they need, without the generous cooperation of our Catholic people in more prosperous localities.   We have therefore urged the establishment of the Society for the Propagation of the Faith in every parish in which it is not yet erected, and also ordered a collection to be made yearly in all the dioceses, for foreign missions and for the missions among our Indians and Negroes . . ."

Text—*Acta et Decreta Concilii Plenarii Baltimorensis Tertii*, pp. 68-101.

IX. *THE IMMIGRATION PROJECT OF THE SOCIETY OF SAINT RAPHAEL*

The following sections from a supplication addressed to the Pope, February, 1891, aroused the indignation of the American people, and was regarded by the Holy Father as 'neither opportune nor necessary.'

"In order that European Catholics may preserve in the country of their adoption and transmit to their children the Faith and the blessings which it procures, the undersigned have the honor of submitting to Your Holiness the conditions which experience and nature of things indicate as essential to be established in the countries of immigration.   The losses which the Church has suffered in the United States of North America amount to ten millions.

1. It will be necessary to establish in distinct parishes, congregations or missions, the groups of emigrants from each nation, in all circumstances where their number and their resources permit;

2. It will be necessary to entrust the direction of these parishes to priests belonging to the same nationality as the faithful.   The most sweet and the dearest souvenirs of the fatherland will thus at each moment be recalled, and they will love the more the Church which procures these blessings to them;

3. In the districts where emigrants from various nations have established themselves, not in sufficiently great numbers to be constituted in distinct national parishe it is desirable that a priest be chosen to direct these groups, who is acquainted with the diverse idioms of the emigrants.   This priest will be strictly required to teach the catechism and to give instruction to each group in its own language.

4. Wherever there are no Christian public schools, parochial schools should be established, and as far as possible, they should be distinct for each nationality. The program of these schools will always include instruction in the national language as well as in the language and history of the country of adoption.

5. It will be necessary to grant to the priests who devote themselves to the emigrants, all the rights, privileges, favors, etc., enjoyed by the priests of the country. This arrangement, conformable to justice, will have the result of attracting to the emigrants priests of each nationality, zealous, pious and desirous to sanctify souls.

6. It will be desirable to form and to encourage Catholic associations of diverse nature: Brotherhoods, mutual benefit and aid societies, etc. By these means Catholics will be grouped together, and they will be preserved from perverse societies, such as those of the Freemasons and other analogous societies.

7. It will be very desirable, whenever deemed possible, to permit the Catholics of each nationality to have a Bishop of their own extraction in the episcopate of the country of immigration. It seems that the organization of the Church will then be complete. Each of the immigrant peoples will be represented, and their interests, their needs, will be safeguarded in the assemblies of the Bishops, in the councils, etc."

Text—De T'Serclaes: *The Life and Labors of Pope Leo XIII*, pp. 278-279.

X. ARCHBISHOP IRELAND AND THE SCHOOL QUESTION

The Faribault-Stillwater Agreement

Archbishop Ireland so described the agreement before the hierarchy in its meeting at St. Louis, 1891.

"1. The school buildings remain the property of the parish. They are leased to the school commissioners during the school hours only—that is, from 9 A.M. to 3:45 P.M. Outside these hours they are at the sole disposal of the parish; the pastor and the Sisters who teach can hold in them such exercises as they deem proper. The lease is for one year only; at the end of the year, the archbishop may renew the lease or resume the exclusive control of the buildings.

2. The teachers must hold diplomas from the State, and the progress of the pupils is determined, as to the various branches of profane learning, by parochial examinations held in conformity with official requirements. The class rooms have been furnished and are kept by the school commission, and the Sisters receive the same salaries as are paid to the ordinary teachers.

3. During school hours, the Sisters give no religious instruction; but as they are not only Catholics, but also members of a reilgious order, they wear their religious habits, and do not alter their teachings in any respect. The schools, although under the control of the State, are, in respect to instruction, precisely what they were before the arrangement was made. The Sisters teach the catechism after school hours, in such a way that the pupils notice merely a change from one lesson to another. Besides, at 8:30 A.M., that is, before the regular school hour, the children attend mass; and on Sundays, the school buildings are at the exclusive disposition of the parish.

4. The public schools are scattered in various parts of Minnesota cities, and children are required to attend the school in the district wherein they live. Faribault and Stillwater are excepted from this rule. Catholic children can attend the schools

in question from all parts of the cities; the Protestant children living in the districts where our schools are situated may do so, but are not obliged. The result is that almost all the Catholic children of the two cities attend these schools, whereas there are very few Protestants, and the influence is almost wholly Catholic."

Text—Will: *Life of James Cardinal Gibbons*, pp. 224-225.

To remove any doubts as to whether or not, in view of Ireland's successful appeal to Rome, and Archbishop Satolli's pronouncements at New York (November 17, 1892) on educational policy, the decrees of the Third Plenary Council of Baltimore remained valid, the Pope wrote as follows:

"*To Our Beloved Son, James Gibbons, Cardinal Priest of the Holy Roman Church, Titular of St. Mary's Beyond the Tiber, Archbishop of Baltimore, and to Our Venerable Brethren, the Archbishops and Bishops of the United States of North America, Pope Leo XIII:*
Beloved Son and Venerable Brethren, Health and Apostolic Benediction!

. . . .

Now, in Our paternal solicitude for your welfare, We had, above all things, commanded the Archbishop of Lepanto to use all his endeavors and the utmost skill of his fraternal charity to extirpate all the germs of dissension bred by the too well known controversies concerning the proper instruction of Catholic youth,—a dissension which was developed by various writings published on both sides of the dispute. This command of Ours Our Venerable Brother fully obeyed, and in the month of November of last year he repaired to New York, where there had assembled with you, beloved Son, all the other Archbishops of your country, in compliance with the desire which I had communicated to them through the Sacred Congregation of the Propaganda, that, after having conferred with their suffragans, they should join counsel and deliberate concerning the best method of providing for those Catholic children who attend the public instead of the Catholic schools.

The things which you wisely decreed in that meeting were pleasing to the said Archbishop of Lepanto, who bestowed deserved praise upon your prudence, and expressed his belief that these decrees would prove most useful. This opinion We, also, with great pleasure confirm, and to yourself and to the other Prelates then assembled, We give merited praise for having thus opportunely responded to Our counsel and Our expectation. But, at the same time, Our said Venerable Brother, wishing, according to Our desire, to adjust the questions concerning the right instruction of Catholic youth, about which, as above stated, controversy was being waged and writings published with excited minds and angry feelings, laid before you certain propositions drawn by himself, touching both the theoretical principles involved in the subject and their practical application. When the meeting of the Archbishops had seriously weighed the significance and bearing of these propositions and had requested certain declarations and corrections in them,—all this the Archbishop of Lepanto gladly complied with, which, being done, the distinguished assemblage closed its sessions with a declaration of gratitude and of satisfaction with the way in which he had fulfilled the commission entrusted to him by Us. All this We find *in the minutes of the meeting, which you have been careful to send Us.*

But these propositions of Our Delegate having been inopportunely made public, minds were at once excited and controversies started afresh, which, through false interpretations and malignant imputations scattered abroad through the newspapers, grew more widespread and more serious. Then certain Prelates of your country, whether displeased with the interpretations put upon some of these propositions or fearing the injury to souls which it seemed to them might thence result, confided to Us the reason for their anxiety. And We, knowing that the salvation of souls is the supreme law to be ever assiduously borne in mind by Us, desiring, moreover, to offer you another proof of Our solicitous affection, requested that each of you should, in a private letter, fully open his mind to Us on the subject, a request which was diligently complied with by each of you. From the examination of these letters it became clear to Us that some of you found in the propositions no reason for apprehension, while to others it seemed that the propositions partially abrogated the disciplinary law concerning schools enacted by the Council of Baltimore, and they feared that the diversity of interpretations put upon them would engender sad dissension, which would prove detrimental to the Catholic schools.

After carefully weighing the matter, We are thoroughly convinced that such interpretations are quite alien from the meaning of Our Delegate, as they are assuredly far from the mind of the Apostolic See. For the principal propositions offered by him were drawn from the decrees of the Third Plenary Council of Baltimore, and especially declare that Catholic schools are to be most sedulously promoted, and that it is to be left to the judgment of the Ordinary to decide, according to the circumstances, when it is lawful and when unlawful to attend the public schools. Now, if the words of any speaker are so to be construed that the latter part of his discourse shall be understood to agree, and not to disagree, with what he had said before, it is surely unbecoming and unjust so to explain his later utterances as to make them disagree with the foregoing ones. And this is the more true since the meaning of the writer was in no wise left obscure. For while presenting his propositions to the distinguished meeting in New York , he expressly declared (*as is evident from the minutes*) his admiration for the zeal manifested by the Bishops of North America in the most wise decrees enacted by the Third Plenary Council of Baltimore for the promotion of the Catholic instruction of the young. He added, moreover, that these decrees, in so far as they contain a general rule for action, are *faithfully* to be observed, and that, although the public schools are not to be entirely condemned (since cases may occur, as the Council itself had foreseen, in which it is lawful to attend them), still every endeavor should be made to multiply Catholic schools and to bring them to perfect equipment. But in order that, in a matter of such grave importance, there may be no further room for doubt or for dissension of opinion, as We have already declared in Our letter of the 23rd of May of last year to Our venerable brethren, the Archbishop and the Bishops of the Province of New York, so W again, as far as need be, declare that the decrees the Baltimore Councils, agreeably to the directions of the Holy See, have enacted concerning parochial schools, and whatever else has been prescribed by the Roman Pontiffs, whether directly or through the Sacred Congregations, concerning the same matter are to be stedfastly observed.

. . . .

Given at Rome, from St. Peter's, on the 31st day of May, in the year 1893, the sixteenth year of Our Pontificate.

LEO XIII, POPE.

Text—De T'Serclaes: *The Life and Labors of Pope Leo XIII*, pp. 269-273.

XI. *THE PAPACY AND AMERICANISM*

The Apostolical Letter *Testem Benevolentiae* (January 22, 1899) expounds Father Hecker's program, and sets forth the Papal attitude thereto as under:

"With this opinion about natural virtue, another is intimately connected, according to which all Christian virtues are divided as it were into two classes, *passive* as they say, and *active*; and they add the former were better suited for the past times, but the latter are more in keeping with the present. It is plain what is to be thought of such division of the virtues. There is not and cannot be a virtue which is really passive. 'Virtue,' says St. Thomas, 'denotes a certain perfection of a power; but the object of a power is an act; and an act of virtue is nothing else than the good use of our free will' (I. II. a. I.); the divine grace, of course helping, if the act of virtue is supernatural. . . .

From this species of contempt of the evangelical virtues, which are wrongly called *passive*, it naturally follows that the mind is imbued little by little with a feeling of disdain for the religious life. And that this is common to the advocates of these new opinions we gather from certain expressions of theirs about the vows which religious orders pronounce. For, say they, such vows are altogether out of keeping with the spirit of our age, inasmuch as they narrow the limits of human liberty; are better adapted to weak minds than to strong ones; avail little for Christian perfection and the good of human society, and rather obstruct and interfere with it. But how false these assertions are, is evident from the usage and doctrine of the Church, which has always given the highest approval to religious life. And surely not undeservedly. For those who, not content with the common duties of the precepts, enter of their own accord upon the evangelical counsels, in obedience to a divine vocation, present themselves to Christ as His prompt and valiant soldiers. Are we to consider this a mark of weak minds? In the more perfect manner of life is it unprofitable or hurtful? Those who bind themselves by the vows of religion are so far from throwing away their liberty that they enjoy a nobler and fuller one—that, namely, *by which Christ has set us free* (Galat. iv. 31.).

. . . .

If there are any, therefore, who prefer to unite together in one society without the obligation of vows, let them do as they desire. That is not a new institution in the Church, nor is it to be disapproved. But let them beware of setting such association above religious orders; nay rather, since mankind is more prone now than heretofore to the enjoyment of pleasure, much greater esteem is to be accorded to those *who have left all things and have followed Christ*.

Lastly, not to delay too long, it is also maintained that the way and the method which Catholics have followed thus far for recalling those who differ from us is to be abandoned and another resorted to. In that matter, it suffices to advert that it is not prudent, Beloved Son, to neglect what antiquity, with its long experience, guided as it is by apostolic teaching, has stamped with its approval. From the word of God we have it that it is the office of all to labor in helping the salvation of our neighbor in the order and degree in which each one is. The faithful indeed will most usefully fulfil their duty by integrity of life, by the works of Christian charity, by instant and assiduous prayer to God. But the clergy should do so by a wise preaching of the gospel, by the decorum and splendor of the sacred ceremonies; but especially by expressing in themselves the form of doctrine which the apostles delivered to Titus and Timothy.   So that if among the different methods of preaching the word of God that sometimes seems preferable by which those who dissent from us are spoken to, not in the church but in any private and proper place, not in disputation but in amicable conference, such method is indeed not to be reprehended; provided, however, that those who are devoted to that work by the authority of the bishop be men who have first given proof of science and virtue.   For We think that there are very many among you who differ from Catholics rather through ignorance than because of any disposition of the will, who, perchance, if the truth is put before them in a familiar and friendly manner, may more easily be led to the one sheepfold of Christ.

Hence, from all that We have hitherto said, it is clear, Beloved Son, that We cannot approve the opinions which some comprise under the head of Americanism.   If, indeed, by that name be designated the characteristic qualities which reflect honor on the people of America, just as other nations have what is special to them: or if it implies the condition of your commonwealths, or the laws and customs which prevail in them, there is surely no reason why We should deem that it ought to be discarded. But if it is to be used not only to signify, but even to commend the above doctrines, there can be no doubt but that our Venerable Brethren the bishops of America would be the first to repudiate and condemn it, as being especially unjust to them and to the entire nation as well.   For it raises the suspicion that there are some among you who conceive of and desire a church in America different from that which is in the rest of the world.   One in the unity of doctrine as in the unity of government, such is the Catholic Church, and, since God has established its centre and foundation in the Chair of Peter, one which is rightly called Roman, for where Peter is there is the Church.   Wherefore he who wishes to be called by the name of Catholic ought to employ in truth the words of Jerome to Pope Damasus, 'I following none as the first except Christ am associated in communion with your Beatitude, that is, with the Chair of Peter; upon that Rock I know is built the Church; whoever gathereth not with thee scattereth (S. Ambr. in Ps. xi. 57).'"

Text—*The Great Encyclical Letters of Pope Leo XIII, Translated from Approved Sources*, pp. 440-452.

CHAPTER XXIII

Bibliography

Source material in its largest proportions will be found in the various periodicals of the Mormons, as follows: "The Evening and Morning Star" (published monthly first at Independence and later at Kirtland between June 1832 and September 1834), succeeded by the "Latter Day Saints' Messenger and Advocate" (Kirtland, 1834-1837), in turn followed by the "Elder's Journal" (published at Far West, Missouri) which continued until the removal of the colony from Missouri. "Times and Seasons," published at Nauvoo (1839-1845) is another important journal. All the above are scarce, inasmuch as Brigham Young took steps toward their repression. "The Millennial Star" published at Liverpool since 1840 is a journal rich in documentary material.

Apart from these periodicals, and the "Reports of the Annual Conference" (LXXXVI Vols.), the "Biographical Sketches of Joseph Smith and his Progenitors for many Generations" (1853) written by Lucy Smith is a reliable source, so much so that Brigham Young declared that it contained many mistakes and in consequence had it suppressed in 1858. Its second edition, censored by Young, appeared in 1880. The "History of Joseph Smith" appearing in "The Millennial Star" (Vols. XIV to XXIV) is valuable. Better however, is a "History of the Church of Jesus Christ of Latter Day Saints. Period I, History of Joseph Smith the Prophet, by Himself" with introduction and notes (V Vols., 1902-1909) by Elder B. H. Roberts. The "Autobiography" of P. P. Pratt edited (1875) by his son is another important source.

The "Reports of the Utah Commission" (1892 f.) are indispensable for facts bearing upon recent controversies.

To one entirely unacquainted with the beliefs and practices of the Latter Day Saints, the following will supply all fundamental information: "The Book of Mormon . . . translated by Joseph Smith" (divided into chapters with references, 1879) by Orson Pratt; "The Doctrine and Covenants of the Church of Jesus Christ of Latter Day Saints" (verse divisions, 3rd ed. 1891) by the same writer; the "Key to the

Science of Theology . . . " (5th ed. 1891) by P. P. Pratt; "A Series of Pamphlets on the Doctrines of the Gospel" (1891) by Elder Orson Pratt; "A Compendium of the Doctrines of the Gospel" (3rd ed. 1892) by Franklin D. Richards and James Little; "A New Witness for God" (1895) by Elder B. H. Roberts; "Mormon Doctrine, or Leaves from the Tree of Life" (2nd ed. 1897) by Charles W. Penrose; "The Story of the Book of Mormon" (2nd ed. 1898) by Elder George Reynolds; "The Articles of Faith" (lectures on leading doctrines, 1899) by James E. Talmage; "The Pearl of Great Price; a Selection from the Revelations, Translations, and Narratives of Joseph Smith" arranged (1902) by James E. Talmage; and "Scientific Aspects of Mormonism" (1904) by Nels L. Nelson, favorable to Mormonism as 'good, true and beautiful, a religion and not a sect' and philosophical rather than historical or expository.

Unfavorable estimates begin as early as 1834 in "Mormonism Unveiled" by E. D. Howe. Then follow "Mormonism and the Mormons; An Historical View of the Rise and Progress of the Sect self-styled Latter Day Saints" (1842) by Daniel P. Kidder; "The City of the Mormons, or Three Days at Nauvoo in 1842" (1842) by Henry Caswell; "The History of the Saints, or An Expose of Joe Smith and Mormonism" (1842) by John C. Bennett; "Mormonism in all Ages" (1842) by J. B. Turner; "The Mormons" (1850) by Thomas L. Kane; "Utah and the Mormons" (1854) by Benjamin G. Ferris; "Female Life among the Mormons; A Narrative of Many Years Personal Experience. By the Wife of a Mormon Elder recently from Utah" (1855) by Mrs. Maria Ward; "History of the Mormons of Salt Lake" (1856—especially good) by Lieut. J. W. Gunnison; "Mormon Wives: A Narrative of Facts Stranger than Fiction" (1856) by M. V. Fuller; "The Husband in Utah: Sights and Scenes Among the Mormons with Remarks on their Morals and Social Economy" (1857) by Austin N. Ward; "Mormonism, Its Leaders and Designs" (1857—with important inside information) by Elder John Hyde; "The City of the Saints and Across the Rocky Mountains to California" (1862—favorable to Mormons) by Richard F. Burton; "The Mormons at Home" ("The London Review" July, 1862); "The Mormon Prophet and his Harem" (1866) by Mrs. C. V. Waite; "Life Among the Mormons and a March to their Zion (1868) by an Officer of the U. S. Army"; "Mormonism; Its Rise, Progress, and Present Condition, embracing the Narrative of Mrs. M. E. V. Smith, and other Startling Facts" (1870); "Life in Utah . . ." (1870) by J. H. Beagle; "Mormonism Unveiled" (1877) by John D. Lee; "The Mormons" ("Amer. Cath. Quart. Rev." 1879); "Mormonism" ("Presbyterian Review" April,

1881); "Utah and the Mormon Problem" ("Meth. Quart. Rev." April 1882—see also bibliography); "The Utah Problem" ("Princeton Review" March, 1883); "Apples of Sodom; Story of Mormon Life" (1883); "Biography of Lorenzo Snow" (1884) by Eliza R. Snow (important); "The Mormon Question and the United States Government" ("Amer. Cath. Quart. Rev." April, 1884); "Mormonism" ("Quart. Review M. E. Church South" July, 1884); "Side Lights from Mormonism" ("Andover Review" July, 1885); "New Light on Mormonism" (1885) by Mrs. E. E. Dickenson; "The Mormon Problem, An Appeal to the American People. With an Appendix containing Four Original Stories of Mormon Life" (1886) by Rev. C. P. Lyford; "The Mormon Propaganda" ("Andover Feview" July, 1887); "Family Life Among the Mormons" ("North American Review" March, 1890); "The Prophet of Palmyra; Mormonism Fevived" (1890) by T. Gregg; "Recent Reverses of Mormonism" ("Our Day" April, 1890); "The Mormons" ("Contemporary Review" January, 1894); "Revival of the Mormon Problem" ("North American Review" April, 1899); "The Mormon Menace" (1905) being the confession of John Doyle Lee, with an introduction by Alfred H. Lewis; "Lights and Shadows of Mormonism" (1909) by J. F. Gibbs.

Although considerable historical data is contained in several of the books and articles noted above, there remain a few works that may be properly classed as histories. The earliest is, "A History of Illinois from its Commencement . . . to 1847, by Gov. T. Ford (edited by Gen. James Shields, 1854). This is good for the Illinois Mormon charter. Soon after appeared the "History of the Mormons" (1857) by S. M. Smuker. Then followed the "Origin and Progress of the Mormons" (1867) by Palmeroy Tucker, which is notably important because of the author's acquaintance with the Smiths, Harris, and Cowdry. In the "Early History of the Disciples in the Western Reserve" (1875) by Amos S. Hayden, considerable attention is given to the early movements of the Mormons. Tullidge's "History of Salt Lake City" (1886) has some important papers, although its value as a history is considerably lessened because of its having been censored by a committee of the Mormons before its publication. The "History of Utah" (1889) by H. H. Bancroft is really a Mormon production, giving the Mormon view in the text, with criticisms thereof only in notes. The "History of Utah" (1892–1898, III Vols. incomplete) by O. F. Whitney, is pro-Mormon and untrustworthy. "The Life of John Taylor, Third President of the Church of Jesus Christ of Latter Day Saints" (1892) by Elder B. H. Roberts has considerable light to throw upon the progress of the Mormon propaganda. "The Rise and Fall of Nauvoo " (1900), and "The Missouri Persecutions" (1900) both by Elder B. H. Roberts are well written stories with considerable bias. By far the best history is that of William Alexander Linn, entitled "The Story of the Mormons from the Date of their Origin to the Year 1901" (1902). This work is scientifically written, and incorporates many interesting source documents. "One Hundred Years of Mormonism. A History . . . from 1805 to 1905" (1905) by J. H. Evans, A.M. is free from much of the extravagance of Mormon literature. A dignified attempt to write the history of Mormonism from the Mormon viewpoint is that of Brigham H. Roberts entitled "History of the 'Mormon' Church" (appearing in "Americana" Vols. IV–X, 1909–1915). This has good documentation and introduces considerable source material.

"The Origin of the Book of Mormon" has been elaborately discussed in a controversy between Theodore Schroeder and Brigham H. Roberts ("Amer. Hist. Magazine" Vol. I, Nos. 4 and 6; Vol. II, Nos. 1 and 3; Vol. III, Nos. 5 and 6; and "Americana" Vol. IV, Nos. 1 and 2). This controversial literature completely overshadows the superficial work of Elder George Reynolds, "The Story of the Book of Mormon" (1888). "The Founder of Mormonism. A Psychological Study of Joseph Smith, Jr." (1902) by I. Woodbridge Riley, with an introductory preface by George T. Ladd, is a painstaking investigation, though based on some unfounded assumptions.

An economic study of Mormonism is "The Mormon Question in its Economic Aspects; a Study of Cooperation and Arbitration in Mormondom, from the Standpoint of a Wage Earner" (pamphlet 1888) by Dyer D. Lum. "Three Phases of Cooperation in the West "by Amos G. Warner, ("J. H. U. Studies" Series VI, Sec. VII–VIII) has a brief reference to the Mormons.

The following short articles deal with particular phases of early Mormon history: "The Mormon Sojourn in Ohio" ("Papers Ohio Ch. Hist. Soc." Vol. I, pp. 43-60); "The Mormon Settlements in the Missouri Valley" ("Quart. Oregon Hist. Soc." Vol. VIII, pp. 276-289); same topic ("Proc. & Coll. Neb. Hist. Soc." Series II, Vol. X, pp. 1-25); "The Mormon Trails in Iowa" ("Iowa Jour. of Hist. & Pol." Vol. XII, pp. 3-16); "Monona County Iowa Mormons" "Annals of Iowa, Series" III, Vol. VII, pp. 321-346); "The Mormon Settlements in Illinois" ("Pub. Ill. State Hist. Library" No. 11).

DOCUMENTS

I. *THE ARTICLES OF FAITH*

"1. We believe in God, the Eternal Father, and in His Son, Jesus Christ, and in the Holy Ghost.

2. We believe that men will be punished for their own sins, and not for Adam's transgression.

3. We believe that through the atonement of Christ, all mankind may be saved, by obedience to the laws and ordinances of the Gospel.

4. We believe that the first principles and ordinances of the Gospel are:—(1) Faith in the Lord Jesus Christ; (2) Repentance; (3) Baptism by immersion for the remission of sins; (4) Laying on of Hands for the Gift of the Holy Ghost.

5. We believe that a man must be called of God, by prophecy, and by the laying on of hands, by those who are in authority, to preach the Gospel and administer the ordinances thereof.

6. We believe in the same organization that existed in the Primitive Church, viz: apostles, prophets, pastors, teachers, evangelists, etc.

7. We believe in the gift of tongues, prophecy, revelation, visions, healing, interpretation of tongues, etc.

8. We believe the Bible to be the word of God, as far as it is translated correctly; we also believe the Book of Mormon to be the word of God.

9. We believe all that God has revealed, all that He does now reveal, and we believe that He will yet reveal many great and important things pertaining to the Kingdom of God.

10. We believe in the literal gathering of Isreal and in the restoration of the Ten Tribes; that Zion will be built upon this [the American] continent; that Christ will reign personally upon the earth; and, that the earth will be renewed and receive its paradisiacal glory.

11. We claim the privilege of worshipping Almighty God according to the dictates of our own conscience, and allow all men the same privilege, let them worship how, where, or what they may.

12. We believe in being subject to kings, presidents, rulers, and magistrates, in obeying, honoring, and sustaining the law.

13. We believe in being honest, true, chaste, benevolent, virtuous, and in doing good to *all men*; indeed, we may say that we follow the admonition of Paul, We believe all things, we hope all things, we have endured many things, and hope to be able to endure all things. If there is anything virtuous, lovely, or of good report or praiseworthy, we seek after these things.—JOSEPH SMITH."

Text—Smith: *The Pearl of Great Price,* pp. 102-103.

II. *MORONI'S APPEARANCE AND THE FINDING OF THE PLATES,* (September 21, 1823)

". . . after I had retired to my bed for the night, I betook myself to prayer and supplication to Almighty God for forgiveness of all my sins and follies, and also for a manifestation to me, that I might know of my state and standing before Him; for I had full confidence in obtaining a divine manifestation, as I previously had one. While I was thus in the act of calling upon God, I discovered a light appearing in my room, which continued to increase until the room was lighter than at noonday, when immediately a personage appeared at my bedside, standing in the air, for his feet did not touch the floor. He had on a loose robe of most exquisite whiteness. It was a whiteness beyond anything earthly I had ever seen; nor do I believe that any earthly thing could be made to appear so exceedingly white and brilliant. His hands were naked, and his arms, also, a little above the wrist; so, also, were his feet naked, as were his legs, a little above the ankles. His head and neck were also bare. I could discover that he had no other clothing on but this robe, as it was open, so that I could see into his bosom. Not only was his robe exceedingly white, but his whole person was glorious beyond description, and his countenance truly like lightning. The room was exceedingly light, but not so very bright as immediately around his person.

When I first looked upon him, I was afraid; but the fear soon left me. He called me by name, and said unto me that he was a messenger sent from the presence of God to me, and that his name was Moroni; that God had a work for me to do; and that my name should be had for good and evil among all nations, kindreds, and tongues, or that it should be both good and evil spoken of among all people. He said there was a book deposited, written upon gold plates, giving an account of the former inhabitants of this continent, and the source from whence they sprang. He also said that the fulness of the everlasting Gospel was contained in it, as delivered by the Savior to the ancient inhabitants; also, that there were two stones in silver bows—and these stones, fastened to a breastplate, constituted what is called the Urim and Thummim—deposited with the plates; and the possession and use of these stones were what constituted 'Seers' in ancient or former times; and that God had prepared them for the purpose of translating the book.

After telling me these things, he commenced quoting the prophecies of the Old Testament. . . .

Again, he told me, that when I got those plates of which he had spoken—for the time that they should be obtained was not yet fulfilled—I should not show them to any person; neither the breast plate with the Urim and Thummim; only to those to whom I should be commanded to show them; if I did I should be destroyed. While he was conversing with me about the plates, the vision was opened to my mind that I could see the place where the plates were deposited, and that so clearly and distinctly that I knew the place again when I visited it.

.   .   .   .

I shortly after arose from my bed, and, as usual, went to the necessary labors of the day; but in attempting to work as at other times, I found my strength so exhausted as to render me entirely unable. My father, who was laboring along with me, discovered something to be wrong with me, and told me to go home. I started with the intention of going to the house; but, in attempting to cross the fence out of the field where we were, my strength entirely failed me, and I fell helpless on the ground, and for a time was quite unconscious of anything. The first thing that I can recollect was a voice speaking unto me, calling me by name. I looked up, and beheld the same messenger standing over my head, surrounded by light as before. . . . I returned to my father in the field, and rehearsed the whole matter to him. He replied to me that it was of God, and told me to go and do as commanded by the messenger. I left the field, and went to the place where the messenger had told me the plates were deposited; and owing to the distinctness of the vision which I had had concerning it, I knew the place the instant that I arrived there.

Convenient to the village of Manchester, Ontario county, New York, stands a hill of considerable size, and the most elevated of any in the neighborhood. On the west side of this hill, not far from the top, under a stone of considerable size, lay the plates, deposited in a stone box. This stone was thick and rounding in the middle on the upper side, and thinner towards the edges, so that the middle part of it was visible above the ground, but the edge all round was covered with earth.

Having removed the earth, I obtained a lever, which I got fixed under the edge of the stone, and with a little exertion raised it up. I looked in, and there indeed did I behold the plates, the Urim and Thummim, and the breastplate, as stated by the messenger. The box in which they lay was formed by laying stones together in some kind of cement. In the bottom of the box were laid two stones crossways of the box, and on these stones lay the plates and the other things with them.

I made an attempt to take them out, but was forbidden by the messenger, and was again informed that the time for bringing them forth had not yet arrived, neither would it, until four years from that time; but he told me that I should come to that place precisely in one year from that time, and that he would there meet with me, and that I should continue to do so until the time should come for obtaining the plates. Accordingly, as I had been commanded, I went at the end of each year, and at each time I found the same messenger there, and received instruction and intelligence from him at each of our interviews, respecting what the Lord was going to do, and how and in what manner His kingdom was to be conducted in the last days.

. . . .

Text—*History of Joseph Smith, the Prophet, by Himself, . . ."* Roberts Edition, Vol. I,

III. *THE TRANSLATION AND CONFIRMATION OF THE PLATES*

"At length the time arrived for obtaining the plates, the Urim and Thummim, and the Breastplate. On the twenty-second day of September, one thousand eight hundred and twenty-seven, having gone as usual at the end of another year to the place where they were deposited, the same heavenly messenger delivered them up to me with this charge: that I should be responsible for them; that if I should let them go carelessly, or through any neglect of mine, I should be cut off; but that if I would use all my endeavors to preserve them, until he, the messenger, should call for them, they should be protected.

. . . .

Mr. Harris, having returned from this tour, left me and went home to Palmyra, arranged his affairs, and returned again to my house about the 12th of April, 1828, and commenced writing for me while I translated from the plates, which we continued until the 14th of June following, by which time he had written one hundred and sixteen pages of manuscript, on foolscap paper. Some time after Mr. Harris had begun to write for me, he began to importune me to give him liberty to carry the writings home and show them; and desired of me that I would inquire of the Lord, through the Urim and Thummim, if he might not do so. I did inquire, and the answer was that he must not. However, he was not satisfied with this answer, and desired that I should inquire again. I did so, and the answer was as before. Still he could not be contented, but insisted that I should inquire once more. After much solicitation, I again inquired of the Lord, and permission was granted him to have the writings on certain conditions; which were, that he show them only to his brother, Preserved Harris, his own wife, his father and his mother, and a Mrs. Cobb, a sister to his wife.   In accordance with this last answer, I required of him that he should bind himself in a covenant to me in the most solemn manner that he would not do otherwise than had been directed.   He did so.   He bound himself as I required of him, took the writings, and went his way.   Not withstanding, however, the great restrictions which he had been laid under, and the solemnity of the covenant which he had made with me, he did show them to others, and by stratagem they got them away from him, and they never have been recovered unto this day.

In the meantime, while Martin Harris was gone with the writings, I went to visit my father's family at Manchester.   I continued there for a short season, and then returned to my place in Pennsylvania.   Immediately after my return home, I was walking out a little distance, when, behold, the former heavenly messenger appeared and handed to me the Urim and Thummim again—for it had been taken from me in consequence of my having wearied the Lord in asking for the privilege of letting Martin Harris take the writings, which he lost by transgression—and I inquired of the Lord through it, and obtained the following:

Revelation to Joseph Smith, Jun., given July, 1828, concerning certain manuscripts of the first part of the Book of Mormon, which had been taken from the possession of Martin Harris.

1. The works, and the designs, and the purposes of God cannot be frustrated, neither can they come to nought.

. . . .

3. Remember, remember that it is not the work of God that is frustrated, but the work of men;

4. For although a man may have many revelations, and have power to do many mighty works, yet if he boasts in his own strength, and sets at nought the counsels of God, and follows after the dictates of his own will and carnal desires, he must fall and incur the vengeance of a just God upon him.

5. Behold, you have been entrusted with these things, but how strict were your commandments; and remember, also, the promises which were made to you, if you did not transgress them;

6. And behold, how oft you have transgressed the commandments and the laws of God, and have gone on in the persuasions of men;

. . . .

10. But remember God is merciful; therefore, repent of that which thou hast done which is contrary to the commandment which I gave you, and thou art still chosen, and art again called to the work;

11. Except thou do this, thou shalt be delivered up and become as other men, and have no more gift.

. . . .

After I had obtained the above revelation, both the plates and the Urim and Thummim were taken from me again; but in a few days they were returned to me, when I inquired of the Lord, and the Lord said thus unto me:

Revelation, given to Joseph Smith, Jun., informing him of the alteration of the manuscript of the fore part of the Book of Mormon

1. Now, behold, I say unto you, that because you delivered up those writings which you had power given unto you to translate by the means of the Urim and Thummim, into the hands of a wicked man, you have lost them.

. . . .

6. Behold, they have sought to destroy you, yea, even the man in whom you have trusted, has sought to destroy you.

. . . .

8. And because you have delivered the writings into his hand, behold wicked men have taken them from you:

. . . .

10. And, behold, Satan hath put it into their hearts to alter the words which you have caused to be written, or which you have translated, which have gone out of your hands.

11. And behold, I say unto you, that because they have altered the words, they read contrary from that which you translated and caused to be written;

12. And, on this wise, the devil has sought to lay a cunning plan, that he may destroy this work;

13. For he hath put it into their hearts to do this, that by lying they may say they have caught you in the words which you have pretended to translate.

14. Verily, I say unto you, that I will not suffer that Satan shall accomplish his evil design in this thing.

15. For, behold, he has put it into their hearts to get thee to tempt the Lord thy God, in asking to translate it over again;

16. And then, behold, they say and think in their hearts, We will see if God has given him power to translate; if so, He will also give him power again;

17. And if God giveth him power again, or if he translate again, or, in other words, if he bringeth forth the same words, behold, we have the same with us, and we have altered them:

18. Therefore they will not agree, and we will say that he has lied in his words, and that he has no gift, and that he has no power:

19. Therefore we will destroy him, and also the work, and we will do this that we may not be ashamed in the end, and that we may get glory of the world.

. . . .

30. Behold, I say unto you, that you shall not translate again those words which have gone forth out of your hands.

. . . .

38. And now, verily, I say unto you, that an account of those things that you have written, which have gone out of your hands, is engraven upon the plates of Nephi;

39. Yea, and you remember it was said in those writings that a more particular account was given of these things upon the plates of Nephi.

40. And now, because the account which is engraven upon the plates of Nephi is more particular concerning the things which, in my wisdom, I would bring to the knowledge of the people in this account;

41. Therefore, you shall translate the engravings which are on the plates of Nephi, down even till you come to the reign of King Benjamin, or until you come to that which you have translated, which you have retained.

42. And behold, you shall publish it as the record of Nephi, and thus I will confound those who have altered my words.

43. I will not suffer that they shall destroy my work; yea, I will show unto them that my wisdom is greater than the cunning of the devil.

44. Behold, they have only got a part or an abridgment of the account of Nephi.

45. Behold, there are many things engraven upon the plates of Nephi which do throw greater views upon my Gospel; therefore, it is wisdom in me that you should translate this first part of the engravings of Nelphi, and send forth in this work.

. . . .

On the 5th day of April, 1829, Oliver Cowdery came to my house, until which time I had never seen him.   He stated to me that having been teaching school in the neighborhood where my father resided, and my father being one of those who sent to the school, he went to board for a season at his house, and while there the family related to him the circumstance of my having received the plates, and accordingly he had come to make inquiries of me.   Two days after the arrival of Mr. Cowdery (being the 7th of April) I commenced to translate the Book of Mormon, and he began to write for me. . . .

. . . .

During the month of April I continued to translate, and he to write, with little cessation, during which time we received several revelations.   A difference of opinion arising between us about the account of John the Apostle, mentioned in the New Testament, as to whether he died or continued to live, we mutually agreed to settle it by the Urim and Thummim, and the following is the word which we received:

. . . .

Whilst continuing the work of translation, during the month of April, Oliver Cowdery became exceedingly anxious to have the power to translate bestowed upon him, and in relation to this desire the following revelations were obtained:

. . . .

'Revelation, given to Oliver Cowdery, April, 1829

1. Behold, I say unto you, my son, that because you did not translate according to that which you desired of me, and did commence again to write for my servant, Joseph Smith, Jun., even so I would that ye should continue until you have finished this record, which I have entrusted unto him:

2. And then, behold, other records have I, that I will give unto you power that you may assist to translate.

3. Be patient, my son, for it is wisdom in me, and it is not expedient that you should translate at this present time.

4. Behold, the work which you are called to do, is to write for my servant Joseph;

5. And, behold, it is because that you did not continue as you commenced, when you began to translate, that I have taken away this privilege from you.

6. Do not murmur, my son, for it is wisdom in me that I have dealt with you after this manner.

7. Behold, you have not understood; you have supposed that I would give it unto you, when you took no thought, save it was to ask me;

8. But, behold, I say unto you, that you must study it out in your mind, then you must ask me if it be right, and if it is right, I will cause that your bosom shall burn within you; therefore, you shall feel that it is right;

9. But if it be not right, you shall have no such feelings, but you shall have a stupor of thought that shall cause you to forget the thing which is wrong; therefore you cannot write that which is sacred, save it be given you from me.

. . . .

We still continued the work of translation, when, in the ensuing month (May, 1829), we on a certain day went into the woods to pray and inquire of the Lord respecting baptism for the remission of sins, that we found mentioned in the translation of the plates. While we were thus employed, praying and calling upon the Lord, a messenger from heaven descended in a cloud of light, and having laid his hands upon us, he ordained us, saying:

'Upon you my fellow servants, in the name of Messiah, I confer the Priesthood of Aaron, which holds the keys of the ministering of angels, and of the Gospel of repentance, and of baptism by immersion for the remission of sins; and this shall never be taken again from the earth, until the sons of Levi do offer again an offering unto the Lord in righteousness.'

. . . .

The messenger who visited us on this occasion, and conferred this Priesthood upon us, said that his name was John, the same that is called John the Baptist in the New Testament, and that he acted under the direction of Peter, James and John, who held the keys of the Priesthood of Melchisedek, which Priesthood he said would in due time be conferred on us, and that I should be called the first Elder of the Church, and he (Oliver Cowdery) the second. It was on the 15th day of May, 1829, that we were ordained under the hand of this messenger and baptized.

. . . .

In the course of the work of translation, we ascertained that three special witnesses were to be provided by the Lord, to whom He would grant that they should see the plates from which this work (the Book of Mormon) should be translated; and that these witnesses should bear record of the same. . . . Almost immediately after we had made this discovery, it occurred to Oliver Cowdery, David Whitmer, and the aforementioned Martin Harris (who had come to inquire after our progress in the work) that they would have me inquire of the Lord to know if they might not obtain of Him the privilege to be these three special witnesses, and finally they became so very solicitous, and urged me so much to inquire that at length I complied; and through the Urim and Thummim, I obtained of the Lord for them the following:

. . . .

Not many days after the above commandment was given, we four, viz., Martin Harris, David Whitmer, Oliver Cowdery and myself, agreed to retire into the woods, and try to obtain, by fervent and humble prayer, the fulfillment of the promises given in the above revelation—that they should have a view of the plates. We accordingly made choice of a piece of woods convenient to Mr. Whitmer's house, to which we retired, and having knelt down, we began to pray in much faith to Almighty God to bestow upon us a realization of these promises.

According to previous arrangement, I commenced by vocal prayer to our Heavenly Father, and was followed by each of the others in succession. We did not at the first trial, however, obtain any answer or manifestation of divine favor in our behalf. We again observed the same order of prayer, each calling on and praying fervently to God in rotation, but with the same result as before.

Upon this, our second failure, Martin Harris proposed that he should withdraw himself from us, believing, as he expressed himself, that his presence was the cause of our not obtaining what we wished for. He accordingly withdrew from us, and we knelt down again, and had not been many minutes engaged in prayer, when presently we beheld a light above us in the air, of exceeding brightness; and behold, an angel stood before us. In his hands he held the plates which we had been praying for these to have a view of. He turned over the leaves one by one, so that we could see them, and discern the engravings thereon distinctly. He then addressed himself to David Whitmer, and said, 'David, blessed is the Lord, and he that keeps His commandments'; when, immediately afterwards, we heard a voice from out of the bright light above us, saying, 'These plates have been revealed by the power of God, and they have been translated by the power of God. The translation of them which you have seen is correct, and I command you to bear record of what you now see and hear.'

I now left David and Oliver, and went in pursuit of Martin Harris, whom I found at a considerable distance, fervently engaged in prayer. He soon told me, however, that he had not yet prevailed with the Lord, and earnestly requested me to join him in prayer, that he also might realize the same blessings which we had just received. We accordingly joined in prayer, and ultimately obtained our desires, for before we had yet finished, the same vision was opened to our view, at least it was again opened to me, and I once more beheld and heard the same things; whilst at the same moment, Martin Harris cried out, apparently in an ecstasy of joy, 'Tis enough; 'tis enough, mine eyes have beheld; mine eyes have beheld'; and jumping up, he shouted, 'Hosanna,' blessing God, and otherwise rejoiced exceedingly.

Having thus, through the mercy of God, obtained these glorious manifestations, it now remained for these three individuals to fulfill the commandment which they had received, viz., to bear record of these things, in order to accomplish which, they drew up and subscribed the following document:

The Testimony of Three Witnesses

Be it known unto all nations, kindreds, tongues, and people unto whom this work shall come, that we, through the grace of God the Father, and our Lord Jesus Christ, have seen the plates which contain this record—which is a record of the people of Nephi, and also of the Lamanites their brethren, and also of the people of Jared who came from the tower of which hath been spoken; and we also know that they have been translated by the gift and power of God, for His voice hath declared it unto us, wherefore we know of a surety that the work is true. And we also testify that we have seen the engravings which are upon the plates, and they have been shown unto us by the power of God, and not of man; and we declare with words of soberness, that an angel of God came down from heaven, and he brought and laid before our eyes, that we beheld and saw the plates and the engravings thereon; and we know that it is by the grace of God the Father, and our Lord Jesus Christ, that we beheld and bear record that these things are true, and it is marvelous in our eyes; nevertheless, the voice of the Lord commanded us that we should bear record of it; wherefore, to be obedient unto the commandments of God, we bear testimony of these things; and we know that if we are faithful in Christ, we shall rid our garments of the blood of all men, and be found spotless before the judgment seat of Christ, and shall dwell with him eternally in the heavens. And the honor be to the Father, and to the Son, and to the Holy Ghost, which is one God. Amen.

OLIVER COWDERY,
DAVID WHITMER.
MARTIN HARRIS."

Text—*History of Joseph Smith the Prophet, by Himself*, Roberts Edition, Vol. I, pp. 18-57.

IV. *THE MARRIAGE COVENANT*

"1. Verily, thus saith the Lord unto you, my servant Joseph, that inasmuch as you have inquired of my hand, to know and understand wherein I, the Lord, justified my servants Abraham, Isaac and Jacob; as also Moses, David and Solomon, my servants, as touching the principle and doctrine of their having many wives and concubines:

. . . .

15. Therefore, if a man marry him a wife in the world, and he marry her not by me, nor by my word; and he covenant with her so long as he is in the world, and she with him, their covenant and marriage are not of force when they are dead, and when they are out of the world; therefore, they are not bound by any law when they are out of the world;

16. Therefore, when they are out of the world, they neither marry, nor are given in marriage; but are appointed angels in heaven, which angels are ministering servants, to minister for those who are worthy of a far more, and an exceeding, and an eternal weight of glory;

17. For these angels did not abide by my law, therefore they cannot be enlarged, but remain separately and singly, without exaltation, in their saved condition, to all eternity, and from henceforth are not Gods, but are angels of God, for ever and ever.

18. And again, verily I say unto you, if a man marry a wife, and make a covenant with her for time and for all eternity, if that covenant is not by me, or by my word, which is my law, and is not sealed by the Holy Spirit of promise, through him whom I have anointed and appointed unto this power—then it is not valid, neither of force when they are out of the world, because they are not joined by me, saith the Lord, neither by my word; when they are out of the world, it cannot be received there, because the angels and the Gods are appointed there, by whom they cannot pass; they cannot, therefore, inherit my glory, for my house is a house of order, saith the Lord God.

19. And again, verily I say unto you, if a man marry a wife by my word, which is my law, and by the new and everlasting covenant, and it is sealed unto them by the Holy Spirit of promise, by him who is anointed, unto whom I have appointed this power, and the keys of this Priesthood; and it shall be said unto them, ye shall come forth in the first resurrection; and if it be after the first resurrection, in the next resurrection; and shall inherit thrones, kingdoms, principalities, and powers, dominions, all heights and depths—then shall it be written in the Lamb's Book of Life, that he shall commit no murder whereby to shed innocent blood, and if ye abide in my covenant, and commit no murder whereby to shed innocent blood, it shall be done unto them in all things whatsoever my servant hath put upon them, in time, and through all eternity, and shall be of full force when they are out of the world; and they shall pass by the angels, and the Gods, which are set there, to their exaltation and glory in all things, as

hath been sealed upon their heads, which glory shall be a fullness and a continuation of the seeds for ever and ever.

. . . .

26. Verily, verily I say unto you, if a man marry a wife according to my word, and they are sealed by the Holy Spirit of promise, according to mine appointment, and he or she shall commit any sin or transgression of the new and everlasting covenant whatever, and all manner of blasphemies, and if they commit no murder, wherein they shed innocent blood—yet they shall come forth in the first resurrection, and enter into their exaltation; but they shall be destroyed in the flesh, and shall be delivered unto the buffetings of Satan unto the day of redemption, saith the Lord God.

. . . .

37. Abraham received concubines, and they bear him children, and it was accounted unto him for righteousness, because they were given unto him, and he abode in my law, as Isaac also, and Jacob did none other things than that which they were commanded; and because they did none other things than that which they were commanded, they have entered into their exaltation, according to the promises, and sit upon thrones and are not angels, but are Gods.

38. David also received many wives and concubines, as also Solomon and Moses my servants; as also many others of my servants, from the beginning of creation until this time; and in nothing did they sin, save in those things which they received not of me.

39. David's wives and concubines were given unto him, of me, by the hand of Nathan, my servant, and others of the prophets who had the keys of this power; and in none of these things did he sin against me, save in the case of Uriah and his wife; and, therefore he hath fallen from his exaltation, and received his portion; and he shall not inherit them out of this world; for I gave them to another, saith the Lord.

40. I am the Lord thy God, and I gave unto thee, my servant Joseph, an appointment, and restore all things; ask what ye will, and it shall be given unto you according to my word:

41. And as ye have asked concerning adultery—verily, verily I say unto you, if a man receiveth a wife in the new and everlasting covenant, and if she be with another man, and I have not appointed unto her by the holy anointing, she hath committed adultery, and shall be destroyed.

42. If she be not in the new and everlasting covenant, and she be with another man, she hath committed adultery;

43. And if her husband be with another woman, and he was under a vow, he hath broken his vow, and hath committed adultery,

44. And if she hath not committed adultery, but is innocent, and hath not broken her vow, and she knoweth it, and I reveal it unto you, my servant Joseph, then shall you have this power, by the power of my Holy Priesthood, to take her, and give her unto him that hath not committed adultery, but hath been faithful, for he shall be made ruler over many,

. . . .

51. Verily, I say unto you, a commandment I give unto mine handmaid, Emma Smith, your wife, whom I have given unto you, that she stay herself, and partake not of that which I commanded you to offer unto her; for I did it, saith the Lord, to prove you all, as I did Abraham; and that I might require an offering at your hand, by covenant and sacrifice;

52. And let mine handmaid, Emma Smith, receive all those that have been given to my servant Joseph, and who are virtuous and pure before me; and those who are not pure, and have said they were pure, shall be destroyed, saith the Lord God;

. . . .

54. And I command mine handmaid, Emma Smith, to abide and cleave unto my servant Joseph, and to none else. But if she will not abide this commandment, she shall be destroyed, saith the Lord; for I am the Lord thy God, and will destroy her, if she abide not in my law;

55. But if she will not abide this commandment, then shall my servant Joseph do all things for her, even as he hath said; and I will bless him and multiply him and give unto him an hundred-fold in this world, of fathers and mothers, brothers and sisters, houses and lands, wives and children, and crowns of eternal lives in the eternal worlds.

. . . .

61. And again, as pertaining to the law of the Priesthood: If any man espouse a virgin, and desire to espouse another, and the first give her consent; and if he espouse the second, and they are virgins, and have vowed to no other man, then is he justified; he cannot commit adultery with that that belongeth unto him and to no one else.

62. And if he have ten virgins given unto him by this law, he cannot commit adultery, for they belong to him, and they are given unto him, therefore is he justified.

63. But if one or either of the ten virgins, after she is espoused, shall be with another man; she has committed adultery, and shall be destroyed; for they are given unto him to multiply and replenish the earth, according to my commandment, and to fulfill the promise which was given by my Father before the foundation of the world; and for their exaltation in the eternal worlds, that they may bear the souls of men; for herein is the work of my Father continued, that he may be glorified.

64. And again, verily, verily I say unto you, if any man have a wife, who holds the keys of this power, and he teaches unto her the law of my Priesthood, as pertaining to these things, then shall she believe, and administer unto him, or she shall be destroyed, saith the Lord your God, for I will destroy her; for I will magnify my name upon all those who receive and abide in my law."

Text—*The Doctrine and Covenants of the Church of Jesus Christ of Latter-day Saints*, Sec. 132.

V. *THE NEW CHURCH*

Revelation Given Through Joseph Smith, April 1830

"1. The rise of the church of Christ in these last days, being one thousand eight hundred and thirty years since the coming of our Lord and Saviour Jesus Christ in the flesh, it being regularly organized and established agreeable to the laws of our country, by the will and commandments of God, in the fourth month, and on the sixth day of the month which is called April;

2. Which commandments were given to Joseph Smith, jun., who was called of God, and ordained an apostle of Jesus Christ, to be the first elder of this church;

3. And to Oliver Cowdery, who was also called of God, an apostle of Jesus Christ, to be the second elder of this church, and ordained under his hand;

4. And this according to the grace of our Lord and Savior Jesus Christ, to whom be all glory, both now and for ever. Amen.

. . . .

38. *The duty of the elders, priests, teachers, deacons, and members of the church of Christ.*—An apostle is an elder, and it is his calling to baptize.

39. And to ordain other elders, priests, teachers, and deacons;

40. And to administer bread and wine—the emblems of the flesh and blood of Christ.

41. And to confirm those who are baptized into the church, by the laying on of hands for the baptism of fire and the Holy Ghost, according to the scriptures;

42. And to teach, expound, exhort, baptize, and watch over the church;

43. And to confirm the church by the laying on of the hands, and the giving of the Holy Ghost,

44. And to take the lead of all meetings.

45. The elders are to conduct the meetings as they are led by the Holy Ghost, according to the commandments and revelations of God.

46. The priest's duty is to preach, teach, expound, exhort, and baptize, and administer the sacrament,

47. And visit the house of each member, and exhort them to pray vocally and in secret, and attend to all family duties;

48. And he may also ordain other priests, teachers, and deacons.

49. And he is to take the lead of meetings when there is no elder present;

50. But when there is an elder preseut, he is only to preach, teach, expound, exhort, and baptize,

51. And visit the house of each member, exhorting them to pray vocally and in secret, and attend to all family duties.

52. In all these duties the priest is to assist the elder if occasion requires.

53. The teacher's duty is to watch over the church always, and be with and strengthen them,

54. And see that there is no iniquity in the church—neither hardness with each other—neither lying, backbiting, nor evil speaking;

55. And see that the church meet together often, and also see that all the members do their duty;

56. And he is to take the lead of meetings in the absence of the elder or priest—

57. And is to be assisted always, in all his duties in the church, by the deacons, if occasion requires;

58. But neither teachers nor deacons have authority to baptize, administer the sacrament, or lay on hands:

59. They are, however, to warn, expound, exhort, and teach and invite all to come unto Christ.

60. Every elder, priest, teacher, or deacon, is to be ordained according to the gifts and callings of God unto him; and he is to be ordained by the power of the Holy Ghost, which is in the one who ordains him.

61. The several elders, composing this church of Christ are to meet in conference once in three months, or from time to time as said conferences shall direct or appoint;

62. And said conferences are to do whatever church business is necessary to be done at the time.

63. The elders are to receive their licenses from other elders, by vote of the church to which they belong, or from the conferences.

64. Each priest, teacher, or deacon, who is ordained by a priest may take a certificate from him at the time, which certificate when presented to an elder, shall entitle

him to a license, which shall authorize him to perform the duties of his calling, or he may receive it from a conference.

65. No person is to be ordained to any office in this church, where there is a regularly organized branch of the same, without the vote of that church;

66. But the presiding elders, traveling bishops, High Counselors, High Priests, and elders, may have the privilege of ordaining, where there is no branch of the church that a vote may be called.

67. Every President of the High Priesthood (or presiding elder), bishop, High Counselor, and High Priest, is to be ordained by the direction of a High Council or general conference.

68. *The duty of the members after they are received by baptism*—The elders or priests are to have a sufficient time to expound all things concerning the church of Christ to their understanding, previous to their partaking of the sacrament and being confirmed by the laying on of the hands of the elders, so that all things may be done in order.

69. And the members shall manifest before the church, and also before the elders, by a Godly walk and conversation, that they are worthy of it, that there may be works and faith agreeable to the Holy Scriptures—walking in holiness before the Lord.

70. Every member of the church of Christ having children, is to bring them unto the elders before the church, who are to lay their hands upon them in the name of Jesus Christ, and bless them in his name.

71. No one can be received into the church of Christ, unless he has arrived unto the years of accountability before God, and is capable of repentance.

72. Baptism is to be administered in the following manner unto all those who repent:—

73. The person who is called of God, and has authority from Jesus Christ to baptize, shall go down into the water with the person who has presented him or herself for baptism, and shall say, calling him or her by name—Having been commissioned of Jesus Christ, I baptize you in the name of the Father, and of the Son, and of the Holy Ghost. Amen.

74. Then shall he immerse him or her in the water, and come forth again out of the water.

75. It is expedient that the church meet together often to partake of bread and wine in the remembrance of the Lord Jesus;

. . . .

80. Any member of the church of Christ transgressing, or being overtaken in a fault, shall be dealt with as the scriptures direct.

81. It shall be the duty of the several churches composing the church of Christ, to send one or more of their teachers to attend the several conferences held by the elders of the church.

82. With a list of the names of the several members uniting themselves with the church since the last conference, or send by the hand of some priest, so that a regular list of all the names of the whole church may be kept in a book by one of the elders, whoever the other elders shall appoint from time to time;

83. And also if any have been expelled from the church, so that their names may be blotted out of the general church record of names.

84. All members removing from the church where they reside, if going to a church where they are not known, may take a letter, certifying that they are regular members and in good standing, which certificate may be signed by any elder or priest, if the

member receiving the letter is personally acquainted with the elder or priest, or it may be signed by the teachers or deacons of the church."

Text—*The Doctrine and Covenants of the Church of Jesus Christ of Latter-day Saints* . . . , Sec. 20.

VI. *REPRESSIVE LEGISLATION*

Edmunds-Tucker Law—March 3, 1887.

"SEC. 1.   That in any proceeding or examination before a grand jury, a judge, justice, or a United States commissioner, or a court, in any prosecution for bigamy, polygamy, or unlawful cohabitation, under any statute of the United States, the lawful husband or wife of the person accused shall be a competent witness, and may be called, but shall not be compelled to testify in such proceeding, examination, or prosecution without the consent of the husband or wife, as the case may be, and such witness shall not be permitted to testify as to any statement or communication made by either husband or wife to each other, during the existence of the marriage relation, deemed confidential at common law.

SEC. 2.   That in any prosecution for bigamy, polygamy, or unlawful cohabitation, under any statute of the United States, whether before a United States commissioner, justice, judge, a grand jury, or any court, an attachment for any witness may be issued by the court, judge, or commissioner, without a previous subpoena, compelling the immediate attendance of such witness, when it shall appear by oath or affirmation, to the commissioner, justice, judge, or court, as the case may be, that there is reasonable ground to believe that such witness will unlawfully fail to obey a subpoena issued and served in the usual course in such cases, and in such case the usual witness fee shall be paid to such witness so attached:

. . . .

SEC. 15.   That all laws of the legislative assembly of the Territory of Utah, or of the so-called government of the State of Deseret, creating, organizing, amending, or continuing the corporation or association called the Perpetual Emigrating Fund Company are hereby disapproved and annulled; and the said corporation, in so far as it may now have, or pretend to have, any legal existence, is hereby dissolved; and it shall not be lawful for the legislative assembly of the Territory of Utah to create, organize, or in any manner recognize any such corporation or association, or to pass any law for the purpose of or operating to accomplish the bringing of persons into the said Territory for any purpose whatsoever.

. . . .

SEC. 17.   That the acts of the legislative assembly of the Territory of Utah incorporating, continuing, or providing for the corporation known as the Church of Jesus Christ of Latter-Day Saints, and the ordinance of the so-called general assembly of the State of Deseret incorporating the Church of Jesus Christ of Latter-Day Saints, so far as the same may now have legal force and validity, are hereby disapproved and annulled, and the said corporation, in so far as it may now have, or pretend to have, any legal existence, is hereby dissolved.   That it shall be the duty of the Attorney-General of the United States to cause such proceedings to be taken in the supreme court of the Territory of Utah as shall be proper to execute the foregoing provisions of this section and to wind up the affairs of said corporation conformably to law; and in such proceedings the court shall have power, and it shall be its duty, to make such decree or decrees as shall be proper to effectuate the transfer of the title to real property now held and used by said corporation for places of worship, and parsonages connected therewith, and burial grounds, and of the description mentioned in the proviso to section thirteen of this act and in section twenty-six of this act, to the respective trustees mentioned in section twenty-six of this act, and for the purposes of this section said court shall have all the powers of a court of equity.

. . . .

SEC. 19. That hereafter the judge of probate in each county within the Territory of Utah provided for by the existing laws thereof shall be appointed by the President of the United States, by and with the advice and consent of the Senate; and so much of the laws of said Territory as provide for the election of such judge by the legislative assembly are hereby disapproved and annulled.

SEC. 20. That it shall not be lawful for any female to vote at any election hereafter held in the Territory of Utah for any public purpose whatever, and no such vote shall be received or counted or given effect in any manner whatever; and any and every act of the legislative assembly of the Territory of Utah providing for or allowing the registration or voting by females is hereby annulled.

. . . .

SEC. 24. That every male person twenty-one years of age resident in the Territory of Utah shall, as a condition precedent to his right to register or vote at any election in said Territory, take and subscribe an oath or affirmation, before the registration officer of his voting precinct that he is over twenty-one years of age, and has resided in the Territory of Utah for six months then last passed and in the precinct for one month immediately preceding the date thereof, and that he is a native-born (or naturalized, as the case may be) citizen of the United States, and further state in such oath or affirmation his full name, with his age, place of business, his status, whether single or married, and, if married, the name of his lawful wife, and that he will support the Constitution of the United States and will faithfully obey the laws thereof, and especially will obey the act of Congress approved March twenty-second, eighteen hundred and eighty-two, entitled 'An act to amend section fifty-three hundred and fifty-two of the Revised Statutes of the United States, in reference to bigamy, and for other purposes,' and will also obey this act in respect of the crimes in said act defined and forbidden, and that he will not, directly or indirectly, aid or abet, counsel or advise, any other person to commit any of said crimes. . . . No person shall be entitled to vote in any election in said Territory, or be capable of jury service, or hold any office of trust or emolument in said Territory who shall not have taken the oath or affirmation aforesaid. No person who shall have been convicted of any crime under this act, or under the act of Congress aforesaid approved March twenty-second, eighteen hundred and eighty-two, or who shall be a polygamist, or who shall associate or cohabit polygamously with persons of the other sex, shall be entitled to vote in any election in said Territory, or be capable of jury service, or to hold any office of trust or emolument in said Territory.

SEC. 25. That the office of Territorial superintendent of district schools created by the laws of Utah is hereby abolished; and it shall be the duty of the supreme court of said Territory to appoint a commissioner of schools, who shall possess and exercise all the powers and duties heretofore imposed by the laws of said Territory upon the Territorial superintendent of district schools, and who shall receive the same salary and compensation, which shall be paid out of the treasury of said Territory, and the laws of the Territory of Utah providing for the method of election and appointment of such Territorial superintendent of district schools are hereby suspended until the further action of Congress shall be had in respect thereto. The said superintendent shall have power to prohibit the use in any district school of any book of a sectarian character or otherwise unsuitable. Said superintendent shall collect and classify statistics and other information respecting the district and other schools in said Territory, showing their progress, the whole number of children of school age, the number who attend school in each year in the respective counties, the average length of time of their attendance, the number of teachers and the compensation paid to the same, the number of teachers who are Mormons, the number who are so-called gentiles, the number of children of Mormon parents and the number of children of so-called gentile parents, and their respective average attendance at school; all of which statistics and information shall be annually reported to Congress, through the governor of said Territory and the Department of the Interior.

SEC. 26. That all religious societies, sects, and congregations shall have the right to have and to hold, through trustees appointed by any court exercising probate powers in a Territory, only on the nomination of the authorities of such society, sect, or congregation, so much real property for the erection or use of houses of worship, and for such parsonages and burial grounds as shall be necessary for the convenience and use of the several congregations of such religious society, sect, or congregation.

SEC. 27. That all laws passed by the so-called State of Deseret and by the legislative assembly of the Territory of Utah for the organization of the militia thereof or for the creation of the Nauvoo Legion are hereby annulled, and declared of no effect; and the militia of Utah shall be organized and subjected in all respects to the laws of the United States regulating the militia in the Territories: *Provided, however*, That all general officers of the militia shall be appointed by the governor of the Territory, by and with the advice and consent of the council thereof. The legislative assembly of Utah shall have power to pass laws for organizing the militia thereof, subject to the approval of Congress."

Text—*Statutes at Large*, Forty-Ninth Congress, Second Session, pp. 635-641.

The Woodruff Manifesto, Sept. 25, 1890

"To Whom it May Concern:

Press dispatches having been sent for political purposes, from Salt Lake City, which have been widely published, to the effect that the Utah Commission, in their recent report to the Secretary of the Interior, allege that plural marriages are still being solemnized and that forty or more such marriages have been contracted in Utah since last June or during the past year; also that in public discourses the leaders of the Church have taught, encouraged and urged the continuance of the practice of polygamy;

I, therefore, as President of the Church of Jesus Christ of Latter-day Saints, do hereby, in the most solemn manner, declare that these charges are false. We are not teaching polygamy, or plural marriage, nor permitting any person to enter into its practice, and I deny that either forty or any other number of plural marriages have, during that period, been solemni. ed in our temples or in any other place in the Territory.

One case has been reported, in which the parties alleged that the marriage was performed in the Endowment House, in Salt Lake City, in the spring of 1889, but I have not been able to learn who performed the ceremony; whatever was done in this matter was without my knowledge. In consequence of this alleged occurrence the Endowment House was, by my instructions, taken down without delay.

Inasmuch as laws have been enacted by Congress forbidding plural marriages, which laws have been pronounced constitutional by the court of last resort, I hereby declare my intention to submit to those laws, and to use my influence with the members of the Church over which I preside to have them do likewise.

There is nothing in my teachings to the Church or in those of my associates, during the time specified, which can reasonably be construed to include or encourage polygamy, and when any Elder of the Church has used language which appeared to convey such teaching he has been promptly reproved. And I now publicly declare that my advice to the Latter-day Saints is to refrain from contracting any marriage forbidden by the law of the land.

(Signed)   WILFORD WOODRUFF
President of the Church of Jesus Christ of Latter-day Saints."
Text—*Deseret News*, Oct. 4, 1890, p. 476.

CHAPTER XXIV

The Jews

Bibliography

The first student of Jewish history in America was Judge C. P. Daly who published in the "Jewish Times" (1875c.) a series of articles on the "Settlement of the Jews in North America." This was afterwards (1893) published in book form. "Statistics of the Jews in the United States" (1880) by W. B. Hackenburg and Simon Wolf has considerable material other than statistics. Other general historical works are "Hebrews in America" (1888) by Isaac Markens; and "The Jews in America: A Short History of their Part in the Building of the Republic" (1905) by Madison C. Peters, D.D.. "The Immigrant Jew in America" (1907) by E. J. James and others, discusses the general aspects of Jewish life, its religious activities, philanthropic, economic, industrial and educational interests. It is therefore a very valuable work. "The Russian Jew in the United States" (1905), edited by C. S. Bernheimer resembles the work of James in conception but limits its investigation to New York, Philadelphia and Chicago. A short article of general character is "The German-Jewish Migration to America" by Max. J. Kohler ("Pubs. Amer. Jewish Hist. Soc." No. IX, pp. 87-105). Some useful material is incorporated in the "Two Hundred and Fiftieth Anniversary of the Settlement of the Jews in the United States. Addresses and Selected Editorial Utterances" (*ibid*. No. XIV). "Jewish Immigration to the United States from 1881 to 1910" by Samuel Joseph ("Columbia University Studies . . . in History . . . " Vol. LIV, No. 4) fills an important place.

For New York the following is available: "Phases of Jewish Life in New York before 1800" by Max. J. Kohler ("Pub. Amer. Jewish Hist. Soc." No. II, pp. 77-93; No. III, pp. 73-86); "Points in the First Chapter of New York Jewish History" by A. M. Dyer (*ibid*. No. III, pp. 41-60); "Civil Status of the Jews in Colonial New York" by Max J. Kohler (*ibid*. No. VI, pp. 81-106); "Whence Came the First Jewish Settlers of New York" by Leon Hühner (*ibid*. No. IX, pp. 75-85); "Items Relating to the History of the Jews of New York" by N. T. Phillips (*ibid*. Vol. XI, pp. 149-161); "The Early History of the Jews in New York, 1654-1664. Some New Matter on the Subject" by Samuel Oppenheim (*ibid*. Vol. XVIII, pp. 1-91—several important documents); "The Jews in New York" by R. Wheatley ("The Century" January and February, 1892).

On Pennsylvania there is "Jews in Philadelphia Previous to the Year 1800" (1883) by H. P. Rosenbach; "Jews of Philadelphia" (1894) by H. S. Morais; "Notes on the First Settlement of Jews in Pennsylvania 1655-1703" by A. S. Rosenbach ("Pubs. Amer. Jewish Hist. Soc." No. V, pp. 191-198); "The Beginnings of Russian Immigration to Pennsylvania" by Davis Sulzberger (*ibid*. No. XIX, pp. 125-150); "The Jews of New Jersey from the Earliest Times to 1850" by A. M. Friedenberg (*ibid*. Vol. XVII, pp. 33-43).

New England seems to have only three studies: "The Jews in Newport" by Max J. Kohler (*ibid*. No. VI, pp. 61-80); "The Jews in New England (Other than Rhode Island) Prior to 1800" by Leon Hühner (*ibid*., No. XI, pp. 75-99); "The Jews in Boston till 1875" by Joseph Lebowich (*ibid*., No. XII, pp. 101-112).

On Maryland there is "Some Unpublished Material Relating to Doctor Jacob Lumbrozo of Maryland" by J. H. Hollander (*ibid*., No. I, pp. 25-40); "The Civil Status of the Jews in Maryland, 1634-1776" by the same writer (*ibid*., No. II, pp. 33-44); "Unequal Religious Rights in Maryland since 1776" by B. H. Hartogensis (*ibid*., No. XXV, pp. 93-107).

On Virginia there is "The Jews of Virginia from the Earliest Times to the Close of the Eighteenth Century" (*ibid*., No. XX, pp. 85–105), by Leon Hühner and "The History of the Jews of Richmond, 1769–1917" (1917) by H. T. Ezekiel.

The Carolinas have "The Jews of South Carolina" (IV sections, 1695 to 1800) and "A History of the Congregation Beth Elohim . . . " by Rabbi B. A. Elzas (1902); "The Jews of South Carolina from the Earliest Settlement to the End of the American Revolution" by Leon Hühner (*ibid*., No. XII, pp. 39–61); "The Struggle for Religious Liberty in North Carolina, with Special Reference to the Jews" by the same writer (*ibid*., Vol. XVI, pp. 37–71).

Georgia has four studies: "The Settlement of the Jews in Georgia" by C. C. Jones (*ibid*., No. I, pp. 5-13); "The Jews of Georgia in Colonial Times" by Leon Hühner (*ibid*., No. X, pp. 65-95); "The Jews of Georgia from the Outbreak of the American Revolution to the Close of the Eighteenth Century" by the same author (*ibid*., No. XVII, pp. 89-108);

"Some Notes on the Early History of the Sheftalls of Georgia" by E. H. Abrahams (*ibid.*, No. XVII, pp. 167-186).

On the Middle and Farther West the following is recommended: "Settlement of the Jews in Texas" by Rev. Henry Cohen (*ibid.*, No. II, pp. 139-156; No. IV, pp. 9-19); "The Jewish Pioneers of the Ohio Valley" by D. Philipson (*ibid.*, No. VIII, pp. 44-57); "The Jews of Chicago" by H. Eliassof (*ibid.*, No. XI, pp. 117-130); "A History of the Jews of Mobile" by Rabbi A. G. Moses (*ibid.*, XII, pp. 113-125); "A History of the Jews of Montgomery" by the same writer (*ibid.*, No. XIII, pp. 83-88); "Jewish Beginnings in Michigan before 1850" by D. E. Heineman (*ibid.*, No. XIII, pp. 47-70); "Some Jewish Factors in the Settlement of the West" by Max J. Kohler (*ibid.*, XVI, pp. 23-35).

The attitude of the Jews to the slave issue and the Civil War appears in the following: "The Jews and the American Anti-Slavery Movement" by Max Kohler (*ibid.*, No. V, pp. 137-155; No. IX, pp. 45-56); "The American Jew as Patriot, Soldier and Citizen" (1895) by Simon Wolf; "Lincoln and the Jews" by Isaac Markens (*ibid.*, No. XVII, pp. 109-165).

Miscellaneous studies of interest are as follows: "Jews in Connection with the Colleges of the Thirteen Original States Prior to 1800" by Leon Hühner (*ibid.*, No. XIX, pp. 101-124); "The Problem of Jewish Education in America and the Bureau of Education of the Jewish Community of New York City" by Israel Friedlander ("United States Bureau of Education." Report 1913. Vol. I, Chapter XVI.); "The Jews and the American Sunday Laws" by A. M. Friedenberg (*ibid.*, No. XI, pp. 101-115); "Jewish Philanthropy; An Exposition of Principles and Methods of Jewish Social Life on the United States" (1917) by Boris D. Bogen.

Studies bearing more specifically upon the religious aspects of Jewish life are as follows: "Some Early American Zionist Projects" by Max J. Kohler (*ibid.*, No. VIII, pp. 75-118—important documents); "Phases in the History of Religious Liberty in America, with Special Reference to the Jews" by Max J. Kohler (*ibid.*, No. XI, 53-73; No. XIII, pp. 7-36); "The Congregation Shearith Israel" by N. T. Phillips (*ibid.*, No. VI, pp. 123-140); "Site of the First Synagogue of the Congregation Shearith Israel of New York" by A. M. Dyer (*ibid.*, No. VIII, pp. 25-41); "The History of the First Russian-American Jewish Congregation" by J. D. Eisenstein (*ibid.*, No. IX, pp. 63-74); Notes on the History of the Earliest German Jewish Congregation in America" by Rev. Henry Berkowitz (*ibid.*, No. IX, pp. 123-127); "The Earliest Extant Minute Books of the

Spanish and Portuguese Congregation Shearith Israel in New York, 1728-1786" edited by Committee (*ibid.*, No. XXI, pp. 1-170); The Oldest Jewish Congregation in the West" (1894) by Rabbi David Philipson.

A complete bibliography of sketches of Jewish Congregations in New York City, prepared by A. S. Freidus appears in the "Bulletin of the New York Public Library May," 1901, pp. 198-200.

For the last thirty years of American Jewish religious history one should keep in touch with the annual reports (1889 f.) of the Central Conference of American Rabbis. These contain Committee reports and discussions upon such notable topics as marriage and divorce, the Bible in the public schools, religious education in the home and church, the Sabbath question, Zionism, religious work in the universities, and social service. The appendices contain presidential addresses, historical reviews, and scholarly studies upon topics related to Jewish history.

Much documentary material on religious aspects of Jewish life will be found in the "Proceedings of the Union of American Hebrew Congregations" (Vol. I, 1873-1879; Vol. II, 1879-1895; Vol. III, 1896-1901). From the "Jewish Quarterly Review," the "American Jews Annual," the "American Hebrew," the "Menorah Monthly" and the "Menorah Journal" some gleanings may be made.

DOCUMENTS

I. ℸ *MODEL CONSTITUTION FOR CONGREGATIONS*

To give Gentiles an intelligent idea of the workings of a Jewish congregation, the following, submitted to the Central Conference of American Rabbis, July 1918, is submitted:

ARTICLE I.

Sec. 1. This congregation shall be known as.............................

ARTICLE II
Members

Sec. 1. THE UNIT OF MEMBERSHIP IN THIS CONGREGATION SHALL BE THE INDIVIDUAL.

Sec. 2. Any person of the Jewish faith..... years of age and over may be elected to membership by the Board of Trustees.

Sec. 3. A MEMBER SHALL PAY SUCH ANNUAL DUES AS SHALL BE DETERMINED BY THE DECLARATION AS TO THE AMOUNT HE OR SHE IS WILLING TO PAY SUBJECT TO THE APPROVAL OF THE BOARD OF TRUSTEES.

Sec. 4. A member shall be entitled to all the privileges of membership.

Sec. 5. The dues shall be payable................in advance.

Sec. 6. Any member who is in arrears for dues for a period of 12 months may be deprived of the rights of membership.

Sec. 7. YOUNG PEOPLE FROM THE AGE OF CONFIRMATION UP TO THE AGE OF FULL MEMBERSHIP SHALL BE ELIGIBLE TO JUNIOR MEMBERSHIP IN THE CONGREGATION. Junior members shall have no right to vote or to hold elective office.

ARTICLE III
Board of Trustees

Sec. 1. The Congregation shall annually elect a Board of Trustees to be composed of the President, the Vice-President, the Secretary, the Treasurer, and......
....................other Trustees.

Sec. 2. The Board of Trustees shall govern the affairs of this congregation, control its revenue and property, and take such action as shall in its judgment best promote the welfare thereof.

Sec. 3. ....members of the Board of Trustees shall be elected by ballot at each annual meeting of the congregation to serve for a term of ....years.

Sec. 4. The Board of Trustees shall have power to
  (a) elect members in accordance with the Constitution;
  (b) determine all dues and assessments of members of the congregation;
  (c) remit the whole or any portion of such dues according to its best judgment;
  (d) select such employees as may be necessary and fix their duties and compensation;
  (e) authorize the appropriation of not more than......................;
  (f) order a meeting of the congregation whenever it may be deemed necessary;
  (g) remove any Trustee or member of the congregation for cause, provided two-thirds of all trustees vote for such removal.

Sec. 5. The Board of Trustees shall meet at least once every month.

Sec. 6. A majority of the Board shall constitute a quorum.

ARTICLE IV
Officers

Sec. 1. The officers of this congregation shall consist of a President, a Vice-President, a Secretary and a Treasurer, elected by ballot for a term of one year, at the annual meeting of the congregation.

Sec. 2. The President shall preside at all meetings of the Congregation and Board of Trustees; shall enforce the Constitution and By-Laws; sign all official documents.

It shall be his duty also to:
  (a) decide all questions of order, subject to appeal by any member.
  (b) Sign all orders drawn on the Treasurer, which have been approved by the Board of Trustees.
  (c) Appoint such committees as may from time to time be required, except as otherwise provided.
  (d) Call a meeting of the Board of Trustees, upon receipt of a request signed by three members of the Board of Trustees. The request shall state the subject matter to be brought before the Board.
  (e) Call a special meeting of the Congregation whenever..........members in good standing shall make a written request for same, setting forth the

purpose of such meeting. On the refusal or failure of the President to act within ten (10) days after the receipt of such request, the Vice-President, or in his absence or refusal, the Treasurer shall call such meeting.

(f) Call a meeting of the Congregation or Board of Trustees, whenever, in his opinion, necessity therefor exists.

(g) Be the custodian of all valuable documents and records of the Congregation, and to deliver them at the expiration of his term to his successor in office.

(h) Appoint the representatives from the Congregation with the advice and consent of the Board of Trustees to all bodies wherein the Congregation may be entitled to representation.

(i) Appoint at the first meeting of the Board of Trustees, after the installation of officers, the Standing Committees, of each of which he is to be an *ex-officio* member.

(j) Cast the deciding vote on all questions in which there may be an equal division of votes, except in the election of officers and appeals from his decision.

(k) Make a written report to the Congregation at its annual meeting of the status of the affairs of the Congregation.

Sec. 3. The Vice-President shall, in the absence of the President, assume all the duties and responsibilities incumbent upon the President.

Sec. 4. It shall be the duty of the Secretary to

. . . .

Sec. 5. The Treasurer, in the absence of the Vice-President, shall assume all the duties and responsibilities incumbent upon the Vice-President. It shall be his duty to:

. . . .

ARTICLE V
Rabbi

Sec. 1. THE RABBI SHALL BE ELECTED AT A REGULAR MEETING OF THE CONGREGATION OR AT A SPECIAL MEETING CALLED FOR THIS PURPOSE. It shall require a majority vote of those present to elect for such salary and period of time as may be determined.

Sec. 2. He shall be an *ex-officio* member of the Board of Trustees and of the Congregation.

Sec. 3. He shall perform all duties incumbent upon, and in accord with his office.

ARTICLE VI
Seats

Sec. 1. SEATS IN THE SYNAGOG SHALL BE UNASSIGNED. IT SHALL HOWEVER BE THE DUTY OF THE BOARD OF TRUSTEES, WHENEVER REQUIRED BY SPECIAL OCCASIONS, TO MAKE A RESERVATION SUFFICIENT TO ACCOMODATE THE MEMBERSHIP; IT BEING UNDERSTOOD THAT NO SPECIFIC ASSIGNMENTS TO INDIVIDUALS SHALL BE MADE WITHIN SAID RESERVATION.

Article VII

Committees

Sec. 1. The following standing Committees shall be appointed by the President at the first meeting of the Board of Trustees after the installation of officers:

A Finance Committee consisting of......................members;

A Ritual Committee consisting of.........................members;
> The Rabbi shall by virtue of his office be chairman of this Committee

A Building Committee consisting of......................members;

A Choir Committee consisting of..........................members;
> The Rabbi shall be an ex-officio member of this Committee

A Membership Committee consisting of....................members;

A Religious School Committee consisting of................members;
> The Rabbi shall be an ex-officio member of this committee

A Cemetery Committee consisting of.....................members;

Sec. 2. It shall be the duty of the Finance Committee to pass on all dues and assessments; to make a detailed estimate of the income and current expenses for the ensuing year; to audit the accounts of the Congregation.

Sec. 3. It shall be the duty of the Ritual Committee to see that the form of worship is adhered to and to recommend to the Board of Trustees any change they may deem advisable. The Board of Trustees shall, when the projected change is of a fundamental character, submit it to a regular or special meeting of the Congregation, and it shall become a law when adopted by a majority vote of the members present. The proposed change shall be specified in the call for the regular or special meeting.

Sec. 4. It shall be the duty of the Building Committee to keep the building and property of the Congregation in good order and repair.

Sec. 5. It shall be the duty of the Choir Committee to engage the organist and the members of the choir and to supervise the music arranged for the religious services.

Sec. 6. It shall be the duty of the Committee on Membership to promote such activities as shall tend to increase the membership of the Congregation as well as the spirit of fellowship among the members.

Sec. 7. It shall be the duty of the Committee on Religious School to make all regulations necessary for the government of the School, including employment of teachers, and adoption of course of study.

Sec. 8. It shall be the duty of the Committee on Cemetery to have supervision and control of the Cemetery.

Article VIII

Meetings

Sec. 1. An annual meeting of this Congregation shall be held at such place and on such day in the month of......................as shall be designated by the Board of Trustees. At this meeting the reports of all retiring officers whose duty it is to make reports shall be submitted, and all active and honorary officers, including the rabbi, shall be elected; provided, however, that if no election be had, the meeting shall stand adjourned, to be called again for such election at a time to be designated by the Board of Trustees. Every member of the Congregation shall be notified by mail, at least five days prior to the holding of the annual meeting, or any adjournment thereof.

Sec. 2. Special meetings of the Congregation shall be called. . . . .
Sec. 3. . . . . Members of the Congregation shall constitute a
quorum.

Article IX
Amendments

Sec. 1. . . . .
Text—*Central Conference of American Rabbis,* Vol. XXVIII, pp. 86-90.

CHAPTER XXV

The Christianization of the Indian

Bibliography

The attitude of the Pilgrims and Puritans to religious work among the Indians may be seen in Bradford's "History of the Plymouth Plantation"; Robert Cushman's sermon on "The Sin and Danger of Self Love Described" (1621); The Massachusetts Bay Charter of March 4-14, 1628-29; John Winthrop's "Reasons to be Considered . . ." (see R. G. Winthrop's "Life and Letters of John Winthrop"); the Governor's "Letters" ("Records of the Governor and Company of the Massachusetts Bay in New England" Vol. I, p. 384 f.); Higginson's "A True Relation . . ." (1629, Young's "Chronicles . . ."); and John Cotton's sermon on "God's Promise to his Plantation" (1634).

On the work of John Eliot, there is "New England's First Fruits; In Respect First of the Conversion of some, Conviction of divers, Preparation of sundry Indians . . ." (1643, Sabin, No. 7); John Eliot's "The Day-Breaking if not the Sun-Rising of the Gospell with the Indians in New England" (1647, "Coll. Mass. Hist. Soc." Ser. III, Vol. IV); Thomas Shepard's "The Cleare Sunshine of the Gospell Breaking Forth upon the Indians in New-England . . ." (1648, *ibid.*); Edward Winslow's "The Glorious Progress of the Gospel Amongst the Indians in New England . . ." (1649, *ibid.*); Henry Whitfeld's "The Light appearing more and more towards the perfect Day . . ." (1651, *ibid.*); also his "Strength out of Weakness . . ." (1652, *ibid.*); Eliot and Mayhew's "Tears of Repentance: Or, A further Narrative of the Progress of the Gospel Amongst the Indians in New England . . ." (1652, *ibid.*); Eliot's "A Late and Further Manifestation of the Progress of the Gospel Among the Indians in New England . . . " (1655, *ibid.*); and his ". . . Brief Narrative of the Progress of the Gospel . . . in the year 1670" (1671). Some letters from John Eliot to Robert Boyle between 1670 and 1688 will be found in the "Coll. Mass. Hist. Soc." Series I, Vol. III. "An Account of Indian Churches in New England, in a Letter written A.D. 1673 by Rev. John Eliot of Roxbury" may be consulted in "Collections" as above, Ser. I, Vol. X. "Historical Collections of the Indians in New England . . . " (1674) by Daniel Gookin (*ibid.* Ser. I, Vol. I) shows the progress of Indian missions village by village in Massachusetts, New Plymouth, Connecticut, and Rhode Island. "The Ledger and the Record Book of the Corporation for the Propagating of the Gospel in New England. . . . 1650–1686" (Prince Soc. Publication, 1920) is informing.

The enduring character of Eliot's work during the Indian wars will be seen in Gookin's "An Historical Account of the Doings and Sufferings of the Christian Indians in New England in the Years 1675, 1676, 1677 . . ." ("Coll. Amer. Antiq. Soc." Vol. II).

Studies on Eliot are as follows: "A Life of the Renowned John Eliot" by Cotton Mather ("Magnalia" Book III, Part III); "The Historical Account of John Eliot, the First Minister of the Church in Roxbury . . . by one of the members of the Historical Society" (1800, "Coll. Mass. Hist. Soc." Ser. I, Vol. VIII); "Life of John Eliot, the Apostle to the Indians" by Convers Francis (Sparks, "American Biography," Vol. V, 1836); "Memoir of Eliot, Apostle to the North American Indians" (1842) by Martin Moore; "Life and Labors of John Eliot, the Apostle among the Indian Nations of New England" (1882) by Robert B. Caverly; "John Eliot, the Puritan Missionary to the Indians" by Ezra Hoyt Byington, ("Papers, Amer. Soc. Ch. Hist." Ser. I, Vol. VIII, pp. 111-145). Brief articles appear in the "Christian Review" (March, 1837) and the "Review of Reviews" (June, 1893). In "The Memorial History of Boston" (Vol. I, Colonial Period, Chapters VI, XII, and XVII) there are three excellent essays by G. E. Ellis, F. S. Drake, and J. Hammond Trumbull.

On the less widely known, though more significant work of the Mayhews at Nantucket and Martha's Vineyard, in addition to the Eliot literature, there is Joseph Caryl's "Of the Conversion of Five Thousand and Nine Hundred East Indians . . ." (1650); Experience Mayhew's "Indian Converts, . . . to which is added, Some Account of those English Ministers who have successively presided over the Indian Work . . . by Mr. Prince" (1727); also his "Indian Narratives . . ." (1727). The "Magnalia" (Book VI, Chap. VI) has some data. A recent (1911) appreciation of the Mayhews has been presented by Charles E. Banks in "The History of Martha's Vineyard . . ." (Vol. I, chaps. VII–IX, XIX).

The work of John Cotton, Jr. is referred to in the "Magnalia" (Book II), and Morton's "New England Memorial." The latter also gives data concerning Richard Bourne and the Marshpee Church (see also Gookin as above, Chap. VIII). On Samuel Treat the "Magnalia" (Book II) is useful, also some correspondence appearing in the "Coll. Mass. Hist. Society" Ser. I, Vol. VIII. An "Account of an Indian Visitation A.D. 1698, Copied by Rev. M. Hawley, Missionary at Marshpee" (*ibid.* Ser. I, Vol. X) gives a survey of all the Indian missions to that date.

Histories dealing with the work referred to above are as follows: William Brown, "The History of the Propagation of Christianity among the Heathen since the Reformation" (1814); Martin Moore, "A Sermon delivered at Natick, January V, MDCCCVII, . . ."; Walter Chapin, "The Missionary Gazetteer, . . ." (1825); William Biglow, "History of the Town of Natick . . ." (1830); Enoch Pratt, "A Comprehensive History, Ecclesiastical and Civil, of Eastham, Wellfleet, and Orleans, . . ." (1844); O. N. Bacon, "A History of Natick, . . ." (1856); J. S. Clark, "A Historical Sketch of the Congregational Churches in Massachusetts from 1620 to 1858" (1858). Particularly helpful are Henry M. Dexter's "Early Missionary Labors Among the Indians of Plymouth Colony" ("Sabbath at Home" Vol. II, pp. 285-397, 461-474); Edward P. Johnson's "Early Colonial Efforts for the Improvement of the Indians" (address before the Order of the Founders and Patriots of America, 1911), and "Early Missionary Work among the North American Indians" ("Papers, Amer. Soc. Ch. Hist." Ser. II, Vol. III, pp. 15-39). A good sketch of these seventeenth century Indian missions appears in "A History of Congregational Missions Among the North American Indians" by Harry T. Stock (A.M. Dissertation, Univ. of Chicago, 1917).

Passing to the eighteenth century, one should notice Joseph Baxter's "Journal of Several Visits to the Indians on the Kennebec River" (1717, with notes by Rev. Elias Nason, in "New Eng. Hist. and Geneal. Reg." Jan. 1867); and Cotton Mather's "India Christiana. A Discourse . . ." (1721).

The early (1619 f.) projects for educating the Indians in Virginia are discussed by John S. Flory in "The University of Henrico" ("Pub. South. Hist. Assn." Jan. 1903). The documents may be consulted in "Abstract Proc. Va. Comp. London, 1619-1624" ("Coll. Va. Hist. Soc." New Series, Vol. VII). The provisions for Indian instruction in William and Mary College are referred to in "The History of the College of William and Mary . . . from its Foundation, 1660, to 1874" by Lyon G. Tyler. The "Spotswood Letters" ("Coll. Va. Hist. Soc." New Series, Vols. I and II) have important information.

The interest of the S. P. G. in Indian evangelization is indicated in "Historical Notices of the Missions of the Church of England in the North American Colonies . . . from Documents of the S.P.G." (1845) by Ernest Hawkins; "An Historical Account of the Society for the Propagation of the Gospel in Foreign Parts" (1730, reprint, 1853) by David Humphreys; and "Two Hundred Years of the S.P.G., 1701-1900" (1901) by C. F. Pascoe. A few documents will be found in the "Colonial Records of the State of Georgia" edited by A. D. Candler (Vols. III, XXI, XXIV, XXV—also for S.P.C.K.), and "The Colonial Records of North Carolina" edited by W. L. Saunders (see Index, vols. XXVIII and XXX).

The efforts of the S.P.G. among the Indians of Upper New York State are discussed by W. W. Kemp in "The Support of Schools in Colonial New York, by the Society for the Propagation of the Gospel in Foreign Parts." (1913). More complete data, especially in relation to the Jesuit propaganda in New York State, is accessible in Hastings, "Ecclesiastical Records of the State of New York" (Vols. II-VI); O'Callaghan's "Documents Relative to the Colonial History of the State of New York" (Vols. IV-VIII), and his "Documentary History of the State of New York" (Vol. IV). Perry's "Historical Collections . . . " should not be overlooked, especially Vol. III, which contains correspondence relating to the "New England Society for the Propagation of Christian Knowledge among the Indians of North America."

The Stockbridge Mission may be studied in "A Letter From the Revd. Mr. Sergeant of Stockbridge, to Dr. Colman of Boston" (1743); "Historical Memoirs, Relating to the Housatunnuk Indians . . . " (1753) by Samuel Hopkins; and "A Letter from Rev. Jonathan Edwards to Hon. Thomas Hubbard, Esq. of Boston, relating to the Indian School at Stockbridge" (August 31, 1751, see "Coll. Mass. Hist. Soc." Ser. I, Vol. X). This mission, as it was in 1796, may be seen in the report of Jeremy Belknap and Jedidiah Morse to the Scottish S.P.C.K., (ibid. Ser. I, Vol. V, also "Proc. Mass. Hist. Soc." Vol. XIX, pp. 393-423). Some supplementary information will be found in "History of Madison County, State of New York" (1872) by L. K. Hammond, and "Town of Stockbridge" (1885) by E. W. B. Canning. The salient features are set forth in "Stockbridge; Past and Present; or Records of An old Mission Station" (1854) by Electa F. Jones.

The work of David Brainerd is described in his "Mirabilia Dei inter Indicos" (1746); Jonathan Edwards, "Memoirs of the Rev. David Brainerd, Missionary to the Indians on the Borders of New York, New Jersey, and Pennsylvania; chiefly taken from his own Diary" (1747, new edition by S. E. Dwight, "including his Journal, now for the First Time Incorporated with the Rest of his Diary in a Regular Chronological Order," 1822); and "Memoirs of Rev. David Brainerd" (1884) by J. M. Sherwood. John Brainerd's work appears in a "Genuine Letter from Mr. John Brainerd . . . to his Friend in England. Giving an Account of the Success of his Labours, as well as the Difficulties and Discouragements that attend his Mission among those Savages" (1753).

The Wheelock school is set forth in Eleazar Wheelock's successive narratives: "A plain and faithful Narrative . . . " (1763); "A Continuation of the Narrative . . . " (1765); "A Continuation of the Narrative . . . " (1771); "A Continuation of the Narrative . . . " (1772); same for the year 1772-3; "A Continuation of the Narrative, with a Journal of the Rev. Mr. Frisbie" (1775). Much suggestive Wheelock correspondence will be found in the "Documentary History of New York" (Vol. IV) under the section, "Papers Relating to the Six Nations."

"Memoirs of the Rev. Eleazar Wheelock . . . with a summary history of the college and School . . . " (1811) by David McClure and Elijah Parish is important.

The condition of the Indian missions throughout Massachusetts and New York at the close of the eighteenth century is presented in "A Letter from Rev. Gideon Hawley of Marshpee containing an Account of his services among the Indians of Massachusetts and New York and a Narrative of his Journey to Onohoghgwage" (July 31, 1794); also J. T. Kirkland's "Answer to Queries" (February, 1795, for both see "Coll. Mass. Hist. Soc." Ser. I, Vol. IV).

For Pennsylvania there is the "Journal of a Two Months Tour for Promoting Religion Among the Frontier Inhabitants of Pennsylvania, and Introducing Christianity Among the Indians Westward of the Alleghany Mountains" (1768) by C. B. Beattie.

For Maryland, considerable information will be found in "Early Christian Missions Among the Indians of Maryland" by R. U. Campbell ("Maryland Hist. Mag." Vol. I, pp. 293-316).

Moravian missions to the Indians have been treated in the standard work of Georg Heinrich Loskiel: "Geschichte der Mission der evangelischen Brüder unter den Indianern in Nordamerika" (1789, translated by Christian Ignatius Latrobe, 1794). Condensed statements appear in a "History of the Protestant Church of the United Brethren" (II Vols. 1825) by Rev. John Holmes; and "Historical Sketches of the Missions of the United Brethren for Propagating the Gospel Among the Heathen, from their Commencement to the year 1817" (1827). A "History of the

Moravian Brethren Among the Indians of North America . . . by a member of the Brethren's Church" (1838) is based largely on Loskiel. "The Centennial Anniversary of the Society of the United Brethren for Propagating the Gospel Among the Heathen" (1887) by Rev. E. de Schweinitz is useful as a supplement to Loskiel. The "Annual Sermons" preached under the auspices of this society embody reports of the missionaries. De Schweintz's "History of the Church known as the Unitas Fratrum . . . " (1885, 2nd ed. 1901) has condensed references. "A History of the Church Known as the Moravian Church . . . " (1900) by J. Taylor Hamilton, deals with the Indian work in a characteristically scholarly way. Zinzendorf's observations on Indian life, plans for Indian missions, narratives of journeys, and experiences among the Indians are embodied in "Memorials of the Moravian Church" (Vol. I, 1870) edited by W. C. Reichel, also in "Trans. Morav. Hist. Soc.", Vol. I. Spangenberg's "Notes on Travel to Onandaga in 1745," contributed by John W. Jordan, may be consulted in the "Pa. Mag. of Hist. and Biog." Vol. II. Bishop J. C. F. Cammerhoff's "Narrative of a Journey to Shamokin, Penna., in the Winter of 1748" edited by John W. Jordan, appears in the "Pa. Mag. of Hist. and Biog." Vol. XXIX.

"The Life and Times of David Zeisberger, the Western Pioneer and Apostle of the Indians" (1870) by Rev. Edmund de Schweinitz, is exceptionally illuminating. Miscellaneous information in connection with Zeisberger's Centennial may be consulted in "Pub. Ohio Arch. & Hist. Soc." Vol. XVIII No. 2. A "Diary of David Zeisberger's Journey to the Ohio called in Delaware the Allegene, from Sept. 20th to Nov. 10th, 1767" edited by A. B. Hulbert and W. N. Schwarze is reprinted in the same publication, Vol. XXI, No. 1. The "Diary of David Zeisberger . . . (1781-1798)" appears in translated form (II Vols. 1885) by Eugene F. Bliss. Zeisberger's "History of the North American Indians" edited by Hulbert and Schwarze may be consulted in the "Pub. Ohio Arch. & Hist. Soc." Vol. XIX, Nos. 1 & 2.

"The Narrative of the Mission of the United Brethren among the Delaware and Mohican Indians from the Commencement in the year 1740 to the close of the year 1808" by John Heckewelder, well edited (1908) by W. E. Connelley, contains his Narrative of 1792, his Journal of 1797, his Journey to Gnadenhutten, and to the Wabash. "The Rev. John Heckewelder" by Rev. W. H. Rice ("Pub. Ohio Arch. & Hist. Soc." Vol. VII, No. 3) presents the salient facts in the career of this great missionary. An older (1847) study is the "Life of John Heckewelder" by Edward Rondthaler. Complete bibliographical data on Zeisberger,

Heckewelder, and others is given by Hulbert in "Pub. Ohio Arch. & Hist. Soc." Vol. XVIII, No. 2. The political significance of Moravian missionaries is touched upon by Wallace Notestein in "The Western Indians in the Revolution" (*ibid*. Vol. XVI, No. 2).

A "History of Wachovia in North Carolina. The Unitas Fratrum or Moravian Church in North Carolina during a Century and a Half, 1752-1902" (1902) by John Henry Clewell gives exhaustive emphasis to the Indian mission of the Moravians in Carolina.

For Quaker interest in the Indians there is, in addition to such references as appear in standard Quaker histories (see page 154f.) "A Brief Sketch of the Efforts of the Religious Society of Friends to Promote the Civilization and Improvement of the Indians" (1866) by a Committee; also "A Brief Sketch of the Efforts of the Philadelphia Yearly Meeting of the Religious Society of Friends to Promote the Civilization and improvement of the Indians . . ." (1879), authorship not stated. "Friends and the Indians 1655-1917" (1917) by Rayner W. Kelsey Ph.D. covers the field in interesting scholarly fashion.

The operations of the various missionary societies among the Indians (in Connecticut, Massachusetts, New Hampshire, and elsewhere) are reported in periodicals such as the "Connecticut Evangelical Magazine," "The American Baptist Magazine," "The Panoplist," "The Panoplist and Missionary Magazine United," "Panoplist and Missionary Herald," "The Missionary Herald,." "The Home Missionary," "New York Missionary Magazine" and the "Repository of Religious Intelligence." The work of the Connecticut Society (1798 f.) in particular may be studied in its several annual reports.

The "Journal of Rev. John Taylor's Missionary Tour Through the Mohawk and Black River Counties in 1802" made at the request of the Hampshire Missionary Society is reprinted in the "Documentary History of New York" Vol. III. On Bacon's travels, see bibliography page 409; also the "Connecticut Evangelical Magazine", Vols. I, II, IV, VI. Joseph Badger's work is reported in the "Connecticut Evangelical Magazine", Vols. II, III, and VI; see also p. 409. S. J. Mills' comments on conditions among the Indians will be seen in his travel narratives, (see p. 365).

In 1817 the American Board of Commissioners for Foreign Missions began missionary work among the Indians. For detailed information on this, one may turn to the "First Ten Annual Reports of the American Board of Commissioners for Foreign Missions, With Other Documents of the Board" (1834). A "Historical Sketch of the Missions of the American Board Among the North American Indians" (1878) by S. G. Bartlett is valuable. For the interest which the several denominations revealed in sustaining important missions among the various tribes of Red men, one finds abundant information in the official annual reports of the various denominational missionary societies.

The following journals treat of missions in the middle and farther West: "A Teacher among the Senecas: Narrative of Rev. Jabez B. Hyde, 1811-1820" ("Pub. Buffalo Hist. Soc.," Vol. VI, pp. 239-275); "Journals of Rev. Thompson S. Harris, Missionary to the Senecas 1821-1828" (*ibid*. pp. 281-379"); "Documents relating to the Stockbridge Mission, 1825-1848" ("Coll. State Hist. Soc. Wisc." Vol. XV, pp. 39-204); "Protestant Missions in the Northwest" ("Coll. Minn. Hist. Soc.," Vol. VI, pp. 117-188); "Missionary Work at Red Wing, 1849-1852" (*ibid*. Vol. X, Part I, pp. 165-178); "The Oberlin Ojibway Mission" ("Papers Ohio Ch. Hist. Soc." Vol. II, pp 1-25); "Forty Years Among the Indians, and on the Eastern Borders of Nebraska" ("Trans. and Reports Nebr. State Hist. Soc." Vol. II, pp. 133-166); "Extracts from the Diary of Rev. Moses Merrill, a Missionary to the Otoe Indians, 1832-1840" (*ibid*. Vol. IV, pp. 160-191); "Missionary Life among the Pawnee" (*ibid*. Vol. XVI, pp. 268-287); "Methodist Missions among the Indian Tribes in Kansas" ("Coll. Kansas State Hist. Soc.," Vol. IX, pp. 160-231).

The following monographs will be found serviceable: "Lights and Shadows of Missionary Life" (1857) by Rev. John H. Pitezel; "Mary and I, Forty Years with the Sioux" (1880) by Stephen R. Riggs; "Ten Years of Missionary Work Among the Indians at Shokomish, Washington Territory, 1874-1884" (1886) by M. Eells; also his "History of Indian Missions on the Pacific Coast" (1882); "Two Volunteer Missionaries among the Dakotas" (1891) by S. W. Pond Jr.; "Father Eells, or the Results of Fifty-Five Years of Missionary Labors in Washington and Oregon" (1894); "Literature of the Cherokees, also Bibliography and the Story of their Genesis" (1889) by George E. Foster; "The Redemption of the Red Man; An Account of Presbyterian Missions to the North American Indians of the Present Day" (1904) by Belle M. Brain; "The Oneidas" (1907) by J. K. Bloomfield; and "Missionary Explorers Among the American Indians" (1913) by Mary Gay Humphreys.

For the bibliography of Roman Catholic Missions among the Indians, see chapters XVI & XXII.

DOCUMENTS

I. *THE JESUIT IDEAL OF MISSIONARY SERVICE*

See page 301f.

II. *A DAY'S PROGRAM IN A JESUIT MISSION TO THE INDIANS*

See page 303f.

III. *JOHN ELIOT*

"*To the Right Worshipful the Commissioners under his Majesties Great-Seal, for Propagation of the Gospel amongst the poor blind Indians in New-England.*

RIGHT WORSHIPFUL AND CHRISTIAN GENTLEMEN:

. . . .

Upon the 17th day of the 6th month, 1670, there was a Meeting at *Maktapog* near *Sandwich* in *Plimouth-Pattent*, to gather a Church among the *Indians*: There were present six of the Magistrates, and many Elders, (all of them Messengers of the Churches within that Jurisdiction) in whose presence, in a day of Fasting and Prayer, they making confession of the Truth and Grace of Jesus Christ, did in that solemn Assembly enter into Covenant, to walk together in the Faith and Order of the Gospel; and were accepted and declared to be a Church of Jesus Christ. These *Indians* being of kin to our *Massachuset-Indians* who first prayed unto God, conversed with them, and received amongst them the light and love of the Truth; they desired me to write to Mr. *Leveredge* to teach them: He accepted the Motion: and performed the Work with good success; but afterwards he left that place, and went to *Long-Island*, and there a godly Brother, named *Richard Bourne* (who purposed to remove with Mr. *Leveredge*, but hindered by Divine Providence) undertook the teaching of those *Indians*, and hath continued in the work with good success to this day; him we ordained Pastor: and one of the Indians, named Jude, should have been ordained Ruling-Elder, but being sick at that time, advice was given that he should be ordained with the first opportunity, as also a Deacon to manage the present Sabbath-day Collections, and other parts of that Office in their season. The same day also were they, and such of their Children as were present, baptized.

From them we passed over to the *Vineyard*, where many were added to the Church both men and women, and were baptized all of them, and their Children also with them; we had the Sacrament of the Lords Supper celebrated in the *Indian-Church*, and many of the *English-Church* gladly joyned with them; for which cause it was celebrated in both languages. On a day of Fasting and Prayer, Elders were ordained, two Teaching-Elders, the one to be a Preacher of the Gospel, to do the Office of a Pastor and Teacher; the other to be a Preacher of the Gospel, to do the Office of a Teacher and Pastor, as the Lord should give them ability and opportunity, Also two Ruling-Elders, with advice to ordain Deacons also, for the Service of Christ in the Church. Things were so ordered by the Lord's guidance, that a Foundation is laid for two Churches more; for first, these of the *Vineyard* dwelling at two great a distance to enjoy with comfort their Sabbath-communion in one place, Advice was given them, that after some experience of walking together in the Order and Ordinances of the

Gospel, they should issue forth into another Church; and the Officers are so chosen, that when they shall do so, both Places are furnished with a Teaching and Ruling-Elder.

Also the Teacher of the *Praying Indians* of *Nantuket*, with a Brother of his were received here, who made good Confessions of Jesus Christ; and being asked, did make report unto us that there be about ninety Families who pray unto God in that Island, so effectual is the Light of the Gospel among them. Advice was given, that some of the chief Godly People should joyn to this Church, (for they frequently converse together, though the Islands be seven leagues asunder) and after some experience of walking in the Order of the Gospel, they should issue forth into Church-estate among themselves, and have Officers ordained amongst them.

The Church of the *Vineyard* were desirous to have chosen Mr. *Mahew* to be their Pastor: but he declined it, conceiving that in his present capacity he lieth under greater advantages to stand their Friends, and do them good, to save them from the hands of such as would bereave them of their Lands, &c. but they shall alwayes have his counsel, instruction and management in all their Church-affairs, as hitherto they have had; he will die in this service of Jesus Christ. The *Praying-Indians* of both these Islands depend on him, as God's Instrument for their good. Advice also was given for the setling of Schools; every Child capable of learning, equally paying, whether he make use of it or no: Yet if any should sinfully neglect Schooling their Youth, It is a transgression liable to censure under both Orders, Civil and Ecclesiastical, the offence being against both. So we walk at *Natick*.

In as much as now we have ordained *Indian Officers* unto the Ministry of the Gospel, it is needful to add a word or two of Apology: I find it hopeless to expect *English* Officers in our *Indian* Churches; the work is full of hardship, hard labour, and chargeable also, and the *Indians* not yet capable to give considerable support and maintenance; and Men have bodies, and must live of the Gospel: And what comes from England is liable to hasard and uncertainties. On such grounds as these partly, but especially from the secret wise governance of Jesus Christ, the Lord of the Harvest, there is no appearance of hope for their souls feeding in that way: they must be trained up to be able to live of themselves in the ways of the Gospel of Christ; and through the riches of God's Grace and Love, sundry of themselves who are expert in the Scriptures, are able to teach each other: An *English* young man raw in that language, coming to teach among our Christian-*Indians*, would be much to their loss; there be of themselves such as be more able, especially being advantaged that he speaketh his own language, and knoweth their manners. Such *English* as shall hereafter teach them, must begin with a People that begin to pray unto God, (and such opportunities we have many) and then as they grow in knowledge, he will grow (if he be diligent) in ability of speech to communicate the knowledge of Christ unto them. And seeing they must have Teachers amongst themselves, they must also be taught to be Teachers: for which cause I have begun to teach them the Art of Teaching, and I find some of them very capable. And whilst I live, my purpose is, (by the grace of Christ assisting) to make it one of my chief cares and labours to teach them some of the Liberal Arts and Sciences, and the way how to analize, and lay out into particulars both the Works and Word of God; and how to communicate knowledge to others methodically and skilfully, and especially the method of Divinity. . . The Bible, and the Catechism drawn out of the Bible, are general helps to all parts and places about us, and are the ground-work of Community amongst all our *Indian*-Churches and Christians.

I find a blessing, when our Church of Natick doth send forth fit Persons unto some remoter places, to teach them the fear of the Lord. But we want maintenance for that Service; it is a chargeable matter to send a Man from his Family: The Labourer is worthy of his Hire: And when they go only to the High-wayes and Hedges, it is not to be expected that they should reward them: If they believe and obey their Message, it is enough. We are determined to send forth some (if the Lord will, and that we live) this Autumn, sundry ways. I see the best way is, *up and be doing*: In all labour there is profit; *Seek and ye shall find*. We have Christ's Example, his Promise, his Presence, his Spirit to assist; and I trust that the Lord will find a way for your encouragement.

Natick is our chief Town, where most and chief of our Rulers, and most of the church dwells; here most of our chief Courts are kept; and the Sacraments in the Church are for the most part here administred: It is (by the Divine Providence) seated well near in the center of all our praying *Indians*, though Westward the Cords of Christ's Tents are more enlarged. Here we began Civil Government in the year 1650. And here usually are kept the General-Trainings, which seven years ago looked so big that we never had one since till this year, and it was at this time but a small appearance. Here we have two Teachers, *John Speen* and *Anthony*; we have betwixt forty and fifty Communicants at the Lord's Table, when they all appear, but now, some are dead, and some decriped with age; and one under Censure, yet making towards a recovery; one died here the last Winter of the Stone, a temperate, sober, godly man, the first *Indian* that ever was known to have that disease; but now another hath the same disease: Sundry more are proposed, and in way of preparation to joyn unto the Church.

. . . .

Thus I have briefly touched some of the chiefest of our present Affairs, and commit them to your Prudence, to do with them what you please; committing your Selves, and all your weighty Affairs unto the Guidance and Blessing of the Lord, I rest.

Your Worships to serve you in the Service of our Lord *Jesus*.

JOHN ELLIOT.

Roxb. this 20th of the 7th month, 1670."

Text—*A Brief Narrative of the Progress of the Gospel . . . in the year* 1670, in *Old South Leaflets*, Vol. I, No. 21.

IV. *DAVID BRAINERD*

The following is a copy of a letter of Brainerd to Rev. Ebenezer Pemberton written November 5, 1744, describing his mission at Kaunaumeek.

"Rev. Sir,

. . . .

On March 15, 1743, I waited on the Correspondents for the Indian mission at New York; and the week following, attended their meeting at Woodbridge, in New Jersey, and was speedily dismissed by them with orders to attempt the instruction of a number of Indians in a place some miles distant from the city of Albany. And on the first

day of April following, I arrived among the Indians, at a place called by them Kaunaumeek, in the county of Albany, nearly twenty miles distant from the city eastward.

The place, as to its situation, was sufficiently lonesome and unpleasant, being
encompassed with mountains and woods; twenty miles distant from any English
inhabitants, six or seven from any Dutch; and more than two from a family that
came, some time since, from the Highlands of Scotland, and had then lived, as I
remember, about two years in this wilderness.   In this family I lodged about the space
of three months, the master of it being the only person with whom I could readily
converse in those parts, except my interpreter; others understanding very little English.

After I had spent about three months in this situation, I found my distance from
the Indians a very great disadvantage to my work among them, and very burdensome
to myself; as I was obliged to travel forward and backward almost daily on foot, having
no pasture in which I could keep my horse for that purpose.   And after all my pains,
could not be with the Indians in the evening and morning, which were usually the best
hours to find them at home, and when they could best attend my instructions.—I
therefore resolved to remove, and live with or near the Indians, that I might watch all
opportunities, when they were generally at home, and take the advantage of such
seasons for their instructions.

Accordingly, I removed soon after that; and, for some time, lived with them in
one of their *wigwams*; and, not long after, built me a small house, where I spent the
remainder of that year entirely alone; my interpreter, who was an Indian, choosing
rather to live in a wigwam among his own countrymen.—This way of living I found
attended with many difficulties, and uncomfortable circumstances, in a place where I
could get none of the necessaries and common comforts of life, (no, not so much as a
morsel of bread,) but what I brought from places fifteen and twenty miles distant,
and oftentimes was obliged, for some time together, to content myself without, for
want of an opportunity to procure the things I needed.

But although the difficulties of this solitary way of living are not the least, or most
inconsiderable, (and doubtless are, in fact, many more and greater to those who
experience, than they can readily *appear* to those who only view them at a distance,)
yet I can truly say that the burden I felt respecting my *great work* among the poor
Indians, the fear and concern that continually hung upon my spirit, lest they should
be prejudiced against Christianity, and their minds imbittered against me, and my
labours among them by means of the insinuations of some who, although they are
called *Christians*, seem to have no concern for Christ's *kingdom*, but had rather (as
their conduct plainly discovers) that the Indians should remain Heathens, that they
may with the more ease cheat, and so enrich themselves by them—were much more
pressing to me, than all the difficulties that attended the circumstances of my living.

. . . .

In my labours with them, in order to "turn them from darkness to light," I
studied what was most *plain* and *easy*, and best suited to their capacities; and endeavoured to set before them from time to time, as they were able to receive them,
the most *important* and *necessary* truths of Christianity; such as most immediately
concerned their speedy conversion to God, and such as I judged had the greatest
tendency, as means, to effect that glorious change in them.   But especially I made it
the *scope* and *drift* of all my labors, to lead them into a thorough acquaintance with
these two things.—*First*, The *sinfulness* and *misery* of the estate they were *naturally*

in; the evil of their hearts, the pollution of their natures; the heavy guilt they were under, and their exposedness to everlasting punishment. . . .—And, *secondly*, I frequently endeavoured to open to them the *fulness, all-sufficiency*, and *freeness* of that *redemption*, which the Son of God has wrought out by his obedience and sufferings, for perishing sinners; how this provision he had made, was suited to all their wants, and how he called and invited them to accept of everlasting life freely, notwithstanding all their sinfulness, inability, unworthiness, &c.

After I had been with the Indians several months, I composed sundry *forms of prayer*, adapted to their circumstances and capacities; which, with the help of my interpreter, I translated into the Indian language; and soon learned to pronounce their words, so as to pray with them in their own tongue. I also translated sundry *psalms* into their language, and soon after we were able to sing in the worship of God.

When my people had gained some acquaintance with many of the truths of Christianity, so that they were capable of receiving and understanding many others, which at first could not be taught them, by reason of their ignorance of those that were necessary to be previously known, and upon which others depended; I then gave them an *historical* account of God's dealings with his ancient professing people the Jews, some of the rites and ceremonies they were obliged to observe, as their sacrifices, &c.; and what these were designed to represent to them: as also some of the surprising *miracles* God wrought for their salvation, while they trusted in him, and sore *punishments* he sometimes brought upon them, when they forsook and sinned against him. Afterwards I proceeded to give them a relation of the birth, life, miracles, sufferings, death, and resurrection of Christ; as well as his ascension, and the wonderful effusion of the holy Spirit consequent thereupon.

And having thus endeavoured to prepare the way by such a general account of things, I next proceeded to read and *expound* to them the gospel of St. Matthew (at least the substance of it) in course, wherein they had a more distinct and particular view of what they had before some general notion.—These expositions I attended almost every *evening*, when there was any considerable number of them at home; except when I was obliged to be absent myself, in order to learn the Indian language with the Rev. Mr. Sargeant.—Besides these means of instruction, there was likewise an English *school* constantly kept by my interpreter among the Indians, which I used frequently to visit, in order to give the children and young people some proper instructions, and serious exhortations suited to their age.

The degree of *knowledge* to which some of them attained, was considerable. Many of the truths of Christianity seemed fixed in their minds, especially in some instances, so that they would speak to me of them, and ask such questions about them, as were necessary to render them more plain and clear to their understandings.—The children, also, and young people, who attended the *school*, made considerable proficiency (at least some of them) in their learning; so that had they understood the English language well, they would have been able to read somewhat readily in a *psalter*.

But that which was most of all desirable, and gave me the greatest encouragement amidst many difficulties and disconsolate hours, was, that the truths of God's word seemed, at times, to be attended with some *power* upon the hearts and consciences of the Indians. . . .

There likewise appeared a reformation in the lives and manners of the Indians.— Their idolatrous *sacrafices* (of which there was but one or two, that I know of, after my coming among them) were wholly laid aside. And their Heathenish custom of

dancing, hallooing, &c. they seemed in a considerable measure to have abandoned. And I could not but hope, that they were reformed in some measure from the sin of *drunkenness*. They likewise manifested a regard for the *Lord's day*, and not only behaved soberly themselves, but took care also to keep their *children* in order.
. . . ."

Text—Jonathan Edwards: *Memoirs of the Rev. David Brainerd* . . . , Edition 1822, pp. 168-173.

The consuming missionary passion of Brainerd finds lofty expression in the Journal entry as under, May 22, 1746.

"In the evening was in a frame somewhat remarkable. I had apprehended for some days before, that it was the design of Providence that I should *settle* among my people here, and had in my own mind begun to make provision for it, and to contrive means to hasten it; and found my heart somewhat engaged in it; hoping that I might then enjoy more agreeable circumstances of life in several respects: and yet was never fully determined, never quite pleased with the thoughts of being settled and confined to one place.   Nevertheless I seemed to have some freedom in that respect, because the congregation, with which I thought of settling, was one which God had enabled me to gather from among Pagans. For I never, since I began to preach, could feel any freedom to enter into other men's labours, and settle down in the ministry where the gospel was preached before.   I never could make that appear to be my providence. When I felt any disposition to consult my worldly ease and comfort, God has never given me any liberty in this respect, either since, or for some years before, I began to preach.   But God having succeeded my labours, and made me instrumental in gathering a church for him among these Indians, I was ready to think it might be his design to give me a quiet settlement, and a stated home of my own.   This, considering the late frequent sinking and failure of my spirits, and the need I stood in of some agreeable society, and my great desire of enjoying conveniences and opportunities for profitable studies, was not altogether disagreeable to me.   Although I still wanted to go about far and wide, in order to spread the blessed gospel among the benighted souls far remote, yet I never had been so willing to settle in any one place, for more than five years past, as I was in the preceding part of this week.   But now these thoughts seemed to be wholly dashed to pieces, not by necessity, but of choice; for it appeared to me that God's dealings towards me had fitted me for a life of solitariness and hardship, and that I had nothing to lose, nothing to do with earth, and consequently nothing to lose by a total renunciation of it.   It appeared to me just right that I should be destitute of house and home, and many of the comforts of life, which I rejoiced to see others of God's people enjoy.   At the same time, I saw so much of the excellency of Christ's kingdom and the infinite desirableness of its advancement in the world, that it swallowed up all my other thoughts, and made me willing, yea, even rejoice, to be made a *pilgrim* or *hermit* in the wilderness to my dying moment; if I might thereby promote the blessed interest of the great Redeemer.   If ever my soul presented itself to God for his service, *without any reserve of any kind*, it did so now.   The language of my thoughts and disposition now was, "*Here I am, Lord, send me; send me to the ends of the Earth; send me to the rough, the savage Pagans of the wilderness; send me from all that is called comfort in earth, or earthly comfort; send me even to death itself, if it be but in thy service, and to promote thy kingdom.*"   At the same time, I had as quick and as lively a sense of the value of worldly comforts, as I ever had; but only saw them infinitely overmatched by the worth of Christ's kingdom, and the propagation of his blessed gospel.   The quiet settlement, the certain place of abode, the tender friendship which I thought I might be likely to enjoy in consequence of such circumstances, appeared as valuable to me, considered *absolutely* and *in themselves*, as ever before; but considered *comparatively*, they appeared nothing.   Compared with the value and preciousness of an enlargement of Christ's kingdom, they vanished as stars before the rising sun.   Sure I am, that, although the comfortable accommodations of life appeared valuable and dear to me, yet I did surrender and resign myself, soul and body, to the service of God, and to the promotion of Christ's kingdom; though it should be in the loss of them all I could not *do* any other, because I could not *will* or *choose* any other.   I was *constrained*, and yet *chose*, to say, 'Farewell friends and earthly comforts, the dearest of them all, the *very dearest*, if the Lord calls for it: adieu, adieu; I will spend my life, to my latest moments, *in caves, and dens of the earth*, if the kingdom of Christ may thereby be advanced.'   I found extraordinary freedom at this time in pouring out my soul to God for his cause; and especially that his kingdom might be extended among the Indians, far remote; and I had a great and strong hope that God would do it.   I continued wrestling with God in prayer for my dear little flock here; and more especially for the Indians elsewhere; as well as for dear friends in one place and another until it was bed time, and I feared I should hinder the family, &c.   But, O, with what reluctancy did I feel myself obliged to consume time in sleep!   I longed to be as *a flame of fire,* continually glowing in the divine service, and building up Christ's kingdom, to my latest my dying moment."

Text - Jonathan Edwards: *Memories of the Rev; David Brainerd* . . ., edition 1822, pp. 311-313.

V. *THE WHEELOCK SCHOOL*

"Of the Original Design, Rise, Progress and Present State of the Indian Charity-School in Lebanon, Conn.

. . . .

The considerations first moving me to enter upon the design of educating the children of our heathen natives were such as these; viz.

The great obligations lying upon us, as God's covenant-people, who have all we have better than they in a covenant way, and consequently are under covenant-bonds to improve it in the best manner for the honour and glory of our liberal Benefactor. . . .

And there is good reason to think, that if one half which has been, for so many years past expended in building forts, manning and supporting them, had been prudently laid out in supporting faithful missionaries, and school-masters among them, the instructed and civilized party would have been a far better defence than all our expensive fortresses, and prevented the laying waste so many towns and villages: Witness the consequence of sending Mr. *Sergeant* to *Stockbridge*, which was in the very road by which they most usually came upon our people, and by which there has never been one attack made upon us since his going there; and this notwithstanding there has been, by all accounts, less appearance of the saving effects of the gospel there than in any other place, where so much has been expended for many years past.

. . . .

And the Christianizing the natives of this land is expressly mentioned in the royal charter granted to this colony, as a motive inducing His Majesty to grant that royal favour to our fathers.   And since we are risen up in their stead, and enjoy the inestimable favour granted to them, on this consideration; What can excuse our not performing to our utmost, that which was engaged by, and reasonably expected from, them? . . .

And as there were few or none who seemed so much to lay the necessity and importance of the case to heart, as to exert themselves in earnest, and lead the way therein, I was naturally put upon consideration and enquiry what methods might have the greatest probability of success; and upon the whole was fully perswaded that this, which I have been pursuing, had by far the greatest probability of any that had been proposed, viz. by the mission of their own sons in conjunction with the *English*; and that a number of girls should also be instructed in whatever should be necessary to render them fit, to perform the female part, as house-wives, school-mistresses, tayloresses, &c. and to go and be with these youth, when they shall be hundreds of miles distant from the *English* on the business of their mission: And prevent a necessity of their turning savage in their manner of living, for want of those who may do those offices for them, and by this means support the reputation of their mission, and also recommend to the savages a more rational and decent manner of living, than that which they are in. . . .   And I am more and more perswaded, that I have sufficient and unanswerable reasons to justify this plan.

As,

1. The deep rooted prejudices they have so generally imbibed against the *English*, that they are selfish, and have secret designs to incroach upon their lands, or otherwise wrong them in their interests. . . .   And it seems there is no way to avoid the bad influence and effects of these prejudices, at present, unless it be by the mission of their own sons.   And it is reasonable to suppose their jealousies are not less, since the late conquest in this land, by which they are put into our power, than they were before.

2. An *Indian* missionary may be supported with less than half the expence, that will be necessary to support an *Englishman*, who can't conform to their manner of living, and who will have no dependence upon them for any part of it.   And an *Indian* who speaks their language, it may reasonably be supposed, will be at least four times as serviceable among them, supposing he be otherwise equally qualified as one who can communicate to or receive nothing from them, but by an interpreter: He may improve all opportunities not only in public, but, 'when he sits in the house, walks by the way, when he lies down, and when he rises up:'   And speak with as much life and spirit as the nature and importance of the matter require, which is very much lost when communicated by an interpreter.

3. Indian missionaries may be supposed better to understand the tempers and customs of *Indians*, and more readily to conform to them in a thousand things than the *English* can; and in things wherein the nonconformity of the *English* may cause disgust, and be construed as the fruit of pride, and an evidence and expression of their scorn and disrespect.

4. The influence of their own sons among them will likely be much greater than of any *Englishman* whatsoever.   They will look upon such an one as one of them, his interest the same with theirs. . . .

5. The acquaintance and friendship which *Indian* boys from different and distant tribes and places, will contract and cultivate, while together at school, may, and if they are zealously affected will, be improved much for the advantage and furtherance of the design of their mission; while they send to, hear from, or visit one another, confirming the things which have been spoken.   And this without so much ceremony to introduce one another, as will be necessary in the case of *English* missionaries; and without the cumber and expence of interpreters.

6. Indian missionaries will not disdain to own English ones, who shall be associates with them, (where the *English* can be introduced) as elder brethren; nor scorn to be advised or reproved, counselled or conducted by them. . . .

7. In this school, children of different nations may, and easily will learn one another's language, and English youth may learn of them; and so save the vast expence and trouble of interpreters; and their ministry be much more acceptable and edifying to the *Indians*.

8. There is no such thing as sending *English* missionaries, or setting up and maintaining *English* schools to any good purpose, in most places among them, as their temper, state and condition have been and still are. . . .

And what are a few instances, where schools may possibly be maintained to some good purpose, compared with those tribes and nations of them, where there are no circumstances at present, but their misery and necessity, to invite us so much as to make the trial.

. . . .

9. There are very few or no interpreters, who are suitable and well-accomplished for the business, to be had.   Mr. *Occom* found great difficulty, last year in his mission on this account.   And not only the cause, but his own reputation suffered much by the unfaithfulness of the man he employed.

I suppose the interpreters now employed by the Hon. Commissioners are the best that are to be had at present.   But how many nations are there for whom there is no interpreter at all, except, it may be, some ignorant and perhaps vicious person, who has been their captive, and whom it is utterly unsafe to trust in matters of such eternal consequence.   And how shall this difficulty be remedied?   It seems it must be by one of these two ways, viz. either their children must come to us, or ours go to them. . . .

When, and as soon as the method proposed by the Rev'd Mess. *Sergeant* and *Brainerd*, can be put into execution, viz. to have lands appropriated to the use of *Indian* schools, and prudent skilful farmers, or tradesmen, to lead and instruct the boys, and mistresses to instruct the girls in such manufactures as are proper for them, at certain hours, as a diversion from their school exercises, and the children taken quite away from their parents, and the pernicious influence of *Indian* examples, there may be some good prospect of great advantage by schools among them.

. . . .

10. I have found by experience, there may be a thorough and effectual exercise of government in such a school, and as severe as shall be necessary, without opposition from, or offence taken by, any. . . .

11. We have the greatest security we can have, that when they are educated and fitted for it, they will be employed in that business.   There is no likelihood at all that they will, though ever so well qualified, get into business, either as school-masters or ministers, among the *English*. . . .

And there may also be admitted into this school, promising *English* youth of pregnant parts, and who from the best principles, and by the best motives, are inclined to devote themselves to that service; and who will naturally care for their state.

. . . .

In such a school their studies may be directed with a special view to the design of their mission. Several parts of learning, which have no great subserviency to it, and which will consume much time, may be less pursued, and others most necessary made their chief study. And they may not only learn the pagan languages, but will naturally get an understanding of their tempers, and many of their customs, which must needs be useful to missionaries. And instead of a delicate manner of living, they may by degrees, as their health will bear, enure themselves to such a way of living as will be most convenient for them to come into when on their mission.

. . . .

With these views of the case, and from such motives as have been mentioned, above eight years ago I wrote to the Reverend *John Brainerd*, missionary in *New-Jersey*, desiring him to send me two likely boys for this purpose, of the *Deleware* tribe: He accordingly sent me *John Pumshire* in the 14th, and *Jacob Woolley* in the 11th years of their age; they arrived here *December 18th*. 1754. and behaved as well as could be reasonably expected; *Pumshire* made uncommon proficiency in writing. They continued with me till they had made considerable progress in the Latin and Greek tongues; when *Pumshire* began to decline, and by the advice of physicians, I sent him back to his friends, with orders, if his health would allow it, to return with two more of that nation, whom Mr. *Brainerd* had at my desire provided for me. *Pumshire* set out on his journey, *November 14th*. 1756. and got home, but soon died. And on *April 9th*. 1757, *Joseph Woolley* and *Hezekiah Calvin* came on the horse which *Pumshire* rode.

. . . .

Sometime after those boys came, the affair appearing with an agreeable aspect, it being then a time of profound peace in this country, I represented the affair to Colonel *Elisha Williams*, Esq; late rector of *Yale-College*, and to the Rev'd Messi'rs *Samuel Moseley* of *Windham*, and *Benjamin Pomeroy* of *Hobron*, and invited them to join me; they readily accepted the invitation; and a gentleman learned in the law supposed there might be such an incorporation among ourselves as might fully answer our purpose. And Mr. *Joshua Moor*, late of *Mansfield*, deceased, appeared to give a small tenement in this place, for the foundation, use and support of a Charity-School, for the education of *Indian* youth, &c. But it pleased God to take the good Colonel from an unthankful world soon after the covenant was made and executed, and thus deprived us of the benefit of his singular learning, piety and zeal in the affair. Notwithstanding, a subscription was soon made of near £. *500* lawful money, towards a fund for the support of it at 6 per cent.

. . . .

I have had two upon my hands since *December 18th*. 1754, and four since *April*, 1757, and five since *April*, 1759, and seven since *November*, 1760, and eleven since *August 1st*. 1761, and after this manner they have increased as I could obtain those who appeared promising. And for some time I have had twenty-five devoted to school as constantly as their health will allow, and they have all along been so, excepting that in an extraordinary croud of business, I have sometimes required their assistance. . . . .

Three of this number are *English* youth, one of which is gone for a time to *New-Jersey* College, for the sake of better advantage for some parts of learning: He has made some proficiency in the Mohawk tongue: The other two are fitting for the business of missionaries. One of the *Indian* lads is *Jacob Woolley*, who is now in his last year at *New-Jersey* College, and is a good scholar; he is here by the leave and order of the President, designing to get some acquaintance with the *Mohawk* tongue. Two others are sent here by the Rev. Mr. *Brainerd*, and are designed for trades; the one for a blacksmith (a trade much wanted among the Indians) and is to go to his apprenticeship as soon as a good place is ready for him; the other is designed for a carpenter and joiner, and is to go to an apprenticeship as soon as he has learned to read and write. . . . Several of my scholars are considerably well accomplished for schoolmasters, and 7 or 8 will likely be well fitted for interpreters in a few years more. And four of this number are girls, whom I have hired women in this neighbourhood to instruct in all the arts of good housewifery, they attending the school one day in a week to be instructed in writing, &c. till they shall be fit for an apprenticeship, to be taught to make men's and women's apparel, &c. in order to accompany these boys, when they shall have occasion for such assistance in the business of their mission. . . .

. . . .

The method of conducting this school has been, and is designed to be after this manner, viz. they are obliged to be clean, and decently dressed, and be ready to attend prayers, before sunrise in the fall and winter, and at 6 o'clock in the summer. A portion of Scripture is read by several of the seniors of them: And those who are able answer a question in the *Assembly's Catechism*, and have some questions asked them upon it, and an answer expounded to them. After prayers, and a short time for their diversion, the school begins with prayer about 9, and ends at 12, and again at 2, and ends at 5 o'clock with prayer. Evening prayer is attended before the day-light is gone. Afterwards they apply to their studies, &c. They attend the publick worship, and have a pew devoted to their use, in the house of God. On Lord's-Day morning, between and after the meetings, the master, or some one whom they will submit to, is with them, inspects their behaviour, hears them read, catechises them, discourses to them, &c. And once or twice a week they hear a discourse calculated to their capacities upon the most important and interesting subjects. And in general they are orderly and governable: They appear to be as perfectly easy and contented with their situation and employment as any at a father's house. I scarcely hear a word of their going home, so much as for a visit, for years together, except it be when they first come.

. . . .

And as this school was set up when there was no scheme devised, or plan laid which this could be in opposition to; so it is not continued in opposition to any other measures which are proposed or pursued by others.

And, blessed be God that he has put it into the hearts of a number of gentlemen of ability in and near Boston, to contribute so liberally towards the furtherance of the general design. And is it not a pity that Christians of all denominations should not unite their utmost endeavours for the accomplishment of it, and especially now while the door is so widely opened for it? . . ."

Text—*Wheelock's Narrative* (1762) in *Old South Leaflets*, Vol. I, No. 22.

VI. *THE MORAVIANS*

It is impossible within brief space to select from journals and diaries a reading that adequately sets forth the manner in which the Moravians conducted their Indian missions. The following show their ideals and distinctive features.

A Candid Declaration of the Church known by the name of THE UNITAS FRATRUM, *relative to their Labour among the Heathens.* (Published 1740).

" We will not decline to give the public once more an opportunity of getting a more clear insight into the nature of our labour among the Heathen, by publishing the following concise points:

I. We never enter into controversy with any other denomination; nor do we endeavour to draw their members over to us.

II. Much less do we attempt to win over to our church any of the Heathen who are already in connexion with those of any other church;

III. Or to stand in the way of the missionaries of any other church.

IV. We are very attentive that the bond between the government and the Heathen may not in the least suffer by means of the evangelical tenets; for, should this appear unavoidable in any place, through the nature of things, we should, in that case, rather chuse to retire from thence.

V. We never attempt, by means of our missions, to obtain the least influence in civil or commercial affairs; but are contented with what we can earn by our own industry in useful employments for our support, to the satisfaction of the government.

VI. As to the rights of the sovereign and of the magistracy, we require no farther insight into them, than to know what is commanded, and what is prohibited, that we may act conformably thereunto, as loyal and obedient subjects. Least of all would we act out of any other principle, than that of being, with our whole heart, subject to all magistrates who have the rule over us, and gladly exert ourselves to the utmost to maintain the best understanding between the government and the converted Heathen; yea, to be as instrumental as possible in establishing the same good principles even among the unconverted.

VII. We carefully avoid intermeddling with any thing that can increase the wrong and prejudicial ideas, which the Heathen, savages, or slaves, have imbibed against the Christian religion.

VIII. We confess, and preach to the Heathen, *Jesus Christ, and him crucified,* as the Saviour of the world, because *there is no other name under heaven given among men, whereby we can be saved, but the name of Jesus Christ*; and we seek, as far as in us lies, to keep them ignorant of the many divisions in Christendom: but, if they happen to have been informed thereof by others, we endeavour, with great precaution, to approve ourselves impartial, speak of the several divisions with much tenderness, and to extenuate, and not exaggerate, the differences; that thus the knowledge of the mystery of Christ may be increased, and misapprehensions diminished."

Text—Crantz: *The Ancient and Modern History of the Brethren* . . . . La Trobe's translation, pp. 579-580.

Zinzendorf's Account of His Experiences Among the Indians

"'Tis also my Intention to be as brief as I can in relating what has been my Plan in the whole Affair of the Heathen, and how far Matters were carried on during my being there, since it is what we believe in general, that the Time of the Heathen is not yet come. For it is believed in our Church that the Conversion of the Jews, and of all Israel must needs go before, ere the proper Conversion of the Heathen can go forward.

And we look upon all what has been done hitherto, even by ourselves, among the Heathen, *as first Fruits only*; so that one must likewise go about the Conversion of the Heathen with great Care and Circumspection.

Therefore we directly oppose the Conversion of the Heathen Nations to the Profession of the Christian Religion; and likewise the Methods hitherto made Use of in the Conversion of both Jews and Heathens. For if Christian Princes and Divines should go so far as to convert the Heathen Nations to their Customs and Ways in our Days, they would thereby do the greatest Piece of Service to the Devil. Therefore I do not in the least believe that the Devil would oppose any one in such an Undertakeing, but wo'd rather help them as much as he co'd.

And I believe concerning those quick and wonderful Conversions of whole Nations, where all Sorts of People, good and bad are made Christians, 'tis much the same whether one calls it the Work of the Lord or the Work of the Devil.

This one finds verified to this very Day in those Nations which are well known unto us, and which have been called *Converted* these several 100 Years; the Wends, the Lettlanders, the Estlanders, for instance; great Numbers of which even to this very Day Worship Images; that it is impossible to evade it by putting the common Gloss upon this Matter and saying it is only a Relic of Heathenism. . . . . . .

Therefore it is most plain to us that the Conversion of the Heathen must be of the same Kind as the Conversion among those that are already called Christians. And that all the Souls among the Heathen whom we shall admit to Baptism, must be awakened to eternal Life by the Lord Jesus and his Spirit in like Manner as a Person in Christendom who would be Converted must first be awaken'd. And therefore have we, in the Conversion of the Heathen, entirely rejected the Method of Teaching them such Matters as they can keep in their Head, and learn by Rote, to say after one. And a Heathen by our Way of Preaching or Instructing in heavenly Things, shall not be able so much as to talk when he has not the Matter in his heart.

Therefore it is impossible that we can convert the Heathen by thousands; yea, 'tis even a Wonder to ourselves when we convert them by twentys or thirtys. And I often tremble to this Hour when I see and must believe (and 'tis not possible to do otherwise) that out of a 1000 awakened in St. Thomas within these 6 years, 300 are become United Brethren and Sisters. For the whole Nation together is but about 3000. And that the 10th Part of a Nation sho'd be wholly our Savior's is a Thing never heard of before. Undoubtedly ev'ry one of us wou'd think it a great Matter when the 10th Part of Great Brittain shuld consist of true Children of God, Brethren of the Lamb."

Text—Reichel: *Memorials of the Moravian Church*, Vol.I, pp. 115—118.

Statutes agreed upon by the Christian Indians, at Langun-toutenünk and Welhik-Tuppeek, in the month of August, 1772.

I.   We will know no other God but the one only true God, who made us and all creatures, and came into this world in order to save sinners; to Him alone we will pray.

II.   We will rest from work on the Lord's Day, and attend public service.

III.   We will honor father and mother, and when they grow old and needy we will do for them what we can.

IV.   No person shall get leave to dwell with us until our teachers have given their consent, and the helpers (native assistants) have examined him.

V. We will have nothing to do with thieves, murderers, whoremongers, adulterers, or drunkards.

VI. We will not take part in dances, sacrifices, heathenish festivals, or games.

VII. We will use no *tshapiet*, or witchcraft, when hunting.

VIII. We renounce and abhor all tricks, lies, and deceits of Satan.

IX. We will be obedient to our teachers and to the helpers who are appointed to preserve order in our meetings in the towns and fields.

X. We will not be idle, nor scold, nor beat one another, nor tell lies.

XI. Whoever injures the property of his neighbor shall make restitution.

XII. A man shall have but one wife - shall love her and provide for her and his children. A woman shall have but one husband, be obedient to him, care for her children, and be cleanly in all things.

XIII. We will not admit rum or any other intoxicating liquor into our towns. If strangers or traders bring intoxicating liquor, the helpers shall take it from them and not restore it until the owners are ready to leave the place.

XIV. No one shall contract debts with traders, or receive goods to sell for traders, unless the helpers give their consent.

XV. Whoever goes hunting, or on a journey, shall inform the minister or stewards.

XVI. Young persons shall not marry without the consent of their parents and the minister

XVII. Whenever the stewards or helpers appoint a time to make fences or to perform other work for the public good, we will assist and do as we are bid.

XVIII. Whenever corn is needed to entertain strangers, or sugar for love-feasts, we will freely contribute from our stores.

XIX. We will not go to war, and will not buy anything of warriors taken in war."

Text—De Schweinitz: *The Life and Times of David Zeisberger*, pp. 378—379.

CHAPTER XXVI

The Christianization and Emancipation of the Negro
Colonial Period to the Civil War

Bibliography

A good introductory survey is that of R. C. Reed, "A Sketch of the Religious History of the Negroes in the South" ("Papers Amer. Soc. Ch. Hist." Ser. II, Vol. IV, pp. 177-204). "The Education of the Negro Prior to 1861" (1915) by C. G. Woodson, gives a more thorough orientation. An older work (1842) by Rev. C. C. Jones, "The Religious Instruction of the Negroes in the United States" has much information well arranged.

The legislative steps taken by several of the colonies to guard against manumission as an accompaniment of conversion and baptism, are set forth succinctly by M. W. Jernegan in "Slavery and Conversion in the American Colonies" ("Amer. Hist. Rev." Vol. XXI, No. 3).

The work of the Church of England referred to in the standard Episcopalian histories (see p. 7) is more elaborately described by Frederick Dalcho in "An Historical Account of the Protestant Episcopal Church in South Carolina, from the First Settlement of the Province to the War of the Revolution . . ." (1820). On the important work of the S. P. G. one should consult "An Historical Account of the Incorporated Society for the Propagation of the Gospel in Foreign Parts" (1730, reprint 1853) by David Humphreys, D.D.; a "Classified Digest of the Records of the Society for the Propagation of the Gospel in Foreign Parts, 1701-1892, with Much Supplementary Information" (1893) by C. F. Pascoe; "The Support of Schools in Colonial New York by the Society for the Propagation of the Gospel in Foreign Parts" (1913) by W. W. Kemp; and C. F. Pascoe's "Two Hundred Years of the S.P.G., 1701-1900 . . ." (1901). Considerable correspondence of this Society appears in Perry's "Historical Collections Relating to the American Colonial Church" (IV Vols.); "The Colonial Records of North Carolina" (many vols.) edited by W. L. Saunders; "The Colonial Records of the State of Georgia" (many vols.) edited by A. D. Candler; and the "South Carolina Historical Magazine" Vols. IV and V. The annual sermons preached before the Society by outstanding clergymen of England, printed with extracts from the annual reports, are important. A complete set, with one exception, is in the Newberry Library, Chicago, in the 'E. E. Ayer Collection.' Thomas Secker's Sermon (Feb. 20, 1741) and that of William Warburton (Feb. 21, 1766) are specially important.

"The Negroes' and Indians' Advocate" (1680) by Morgan Godwyn; "Sermons Addressed to Masters and Servants" by Thomas Bacon (1743, republished by William Meade, 1805); and "A Compassionate Address to the Christian Negroes in Virginia and other British Colonies in North America" (1755c) by Benjamin Fawcett, have important data.

In ". . . Two Hundred Years; The History of the S. P. C. K. 1698-1898" by Allen and McClure (1902) information will be found concerning the effort of the Salzburger missionaries to convert the slaves. Suggestive documentary material is available in Candler's "Colonial Records of the State of Georgia", Vols. XXI-XXV. See also p. 204.

In "Letters from the Rev. Samuel Davies and others showing the State of Religion in Virginia, particularly among the Negroes, . . ." (2nd ed. 1757), light is thrown upon the colporteur activities among the negroes of the 'Society for Propagating Christian Learning.'

For Quaker interest in the negroes, an indispensable documentary manual is "A Brief Statement of the Rise and Progress of the Testimony of the Religious Society of Friends against Slavery and the Slave Trade. Published by direction of the Yearly Meeting, held in Philadelphia, in the fourth month, 1843." An excellent survey is given by Professor A. C. Thomas in "The Attitude of the Society of Friends Toward Slavery in the Seventeenth and Eighteenth Centuries, particularly in Relation to its own Members" ("Papers Amer. Soc. Ch. Hist." Vol. VIII, pp. 263-299). Less detailed, but informing general statements will be found in "Anti-Slavery in America . . . 1619-1808" ("Radcliffe College Monographs" No. 11, 1901) by Mary S. Locke, and "The Neglected Period of Anti-Slavery in America (1808-1831)" (ibid. No. 14, 1908) by Alice D. Adams. "Notes on the History of Slavery in Massachusetts . . ." (1866) by G. H. Moore, may be profitably consulted.

Coming to outstanding individual Quakers, George Fox's negro sympathy finds expression in his epistle "To Friends Beyond Seas that have Blacks and Indian Slaves" ("A Collection of many Select and Christian Epistles, . . ." 1831, Epistle 153). George Keith's "An Exhortation and Caution to Friends concerning buying or keeping of Negroes . . ." appears in "Pa. Mag. of Hist. . . ." Vol. XIII, pp. 265-270. "The Works of John Woolman, in two parts" (1775) gives all necessary data concerning the contribution of this prominent Quaker. Elihu Coleman, a Quaker preacher, has left "A Testimony against that Anti-Christian Practice of making Slaves of Men . . ." (1733). Anthony Benezet may be studied in "Observations on the inslaving, importing, and purchasing of Negroes . . with some Advice thereon . . ." (1748) and "Some Historical Account of Guinea . . . With an Inquiry into the Rise and Progress of the Slave Trade . . ." (1788). The "Memoirs of the Life of Anthony Benezet" (1817) by Roberts Vaux, is useful, also the companion volume "Memoirs of the Lives of Benjamin Lay and Ralph Sandiford" (1815).

The Pennsylvania Quakers are discussed in a "History of the Rise, Progress, and Abolition of the African Slave Trade" (1808) by Thomas Clarkson; "A History of Education in Pennsylvania . . ." (1886) by J. P. Wickersham; and notably in "The Negro in Pennsylvania" (1911) by E. P. Turner. For the Quakers in the South, the following are recommended: "John Woolman's Journal" (above); "Journal of William Ferriss" ("Friends Miscellany" Vol. XII); "The Negro in Maryland; A Study of the Institution of Slavery" by Jeffery R. Brackett; ("J. H. U. Studies" Extra Volume VI); "Southern Quakers and Slavery, A Study in Institutional History" (1896) by Stephen B. Weeks; "Slavery and Servitude in the Colony of North Carolina" by John S. Bassett ("J.H.U. Studies" Ser. XIV, Sec. IV–V, and more complete in Ser. XVII); "Slavery in the Province of South Carolina 1670–1770" by Edward McCrady ("Ann. Report, Amer. Hist. Assn." 1895, Sec. XXVIII); and "The Education of the Negro Prior to 1861" (1915) by C. G. Woodson, which has considerable information on the Virginia situation.

For New England, studies are as follows: "Slavery in Rhode Island, 1755-1776" by William D. Johnston, ("Pub. R. I. Hist. Soc.," New Ser. Vol. II); "The Early African Slave Trade in New England" by William B. Weeden ("Proc. Amer. Antiq. Soc." New Ser. Vol. V, pp. 107-128); "The Connection of Massachusetts with the Slave-Trade and with Slavery" by Charles Deane (ibid. Vol. IV, pp. 191-222); "Negro Slavery in Massachusetts" by Robert Rantoul ("Hist. Coll. Essex Institute," Vol. XXIV, Parts IV-VI, pp. 81-109). A few details may be gleaned from the "Friends Review", Vol. V; and Peterson's "History of Rhode Island" (1853).

For the Congregationalists, "Notes on the History of Slavery in Massachusetts" (1866) by G. H. Moore, will be found quite indispensable; and the "History of Slavery in Connecticut" by B. C. Steiner, ("J. H. U. Studies" Ser. XI, Sec. IX-X). The attitude to slavery of prominent clergymen such as Jonathan Edwards and Stiles is discussed by W. C. Fowler in the "Historical Status of the Negro in Connecticut" ("Hist. Mag. and Notes and Queries" 3rd Ser. Vol. III). Cotton Mather's views may be seen in his Diary, ("Coll. Mass. Hist. Soc." Ser. VII, Vol. VIII); also "Cotton Mather and His Slaves" by H. W. Haynes ("Proc. Amer. Antiq. Soc." New Series, Vol. VI, pp. 191-5). In the "Life and Death of the Rev. John Eliot . . . " (1694) Mather sets forth Eliot's views on the teaching of slaves, and incidentally reveals his own humane sentiments. "The Records of the General Association of the Colony of Connecticut, 1738-1799" (1888) give considerable data for the sentiment respecting negro baptism. The 'Rules for the Society of Negroes, 1693' are reprinted in "Proc. Amer. Antiq. Soc.," New Ser. Vol. V, pp. 419-420.

For the Presbyterians, one should consult "The Religious Instruction of the Negroes . . . " (1842) by C. C. Jones; "William and Mary College Quarterly" Vols. XI and XIII; Perry's "Historical Collections" (Virginia); "Letters from the Rev. Samuel Davies and others . . . " (above); "The Testimony and Practice of the Presbyterian Church in Reference to American Slavery . . . " (1852) by Rev. John Robinson; "A Collection of the Acts, Deliverances, and Testimonies of the Supreme Judicatory of the Presbyterian Church from its Origin in America to the Present Time" (1856) by Samuel J. Baird; and "Presbyterianism—Its Relation to the Negro" (1897) by Matthew Anderson.

George Whitefield's sanction upon slavery when humanely conducted, appears in his letters ("The Works of the Rev. George Whitefield, M.A. . . . " ed. 1771, Vol. II, pp. 90, 105, 208, and Vol. IV, p. 37). His appeal for the religious instruction of the negro may be consulted in the "New England Weekly Journal" April 29, 1740. John Wesley's views are set forth in "Thoughts upon Slavery. In the Potent Enemies of America Laid Open, Reprinted in Philadelphia with Notes, 1774." "The Gospel among the Slaves" (1893) edited by W. P. Harrison is especially good in describing early Methodist activities. Standard works setting forth the attitude of early Methodism toward the negro are as follows: "The Journal of the Reverend Francis Asbury, Bishop of the Methodist Episcopal Church from August 7, 1781, to Dec. 7, 1815" (III Vols. 1821); "The Life of the Rev. Freeborn Garrettson: compiled from his printed and manuscript journals . . . " (5th ed. 1832) by Nathan Bangs; "The History of American Slavery and Methodism from 1780 to 1849" (1849) by Rev. L. Matlack; "A History of Methodism . . . " (1884) by Holland N. McTyeire; and "A History of the Methodist Episcopal Church" (IV Vols. 1845) by Nathan Bangs. The Minutes of the Methodist Conference, 1785, embodied in Charles Elliott's "History of the Great Secession from the Methodist Episcopal Church . . . " (1854) shows the warm interest in negro education taken at that time by Methodists. All necessary documentary material for the several Conferences will be found in the "Minutes of the Methodist Conferences held in America, 1773-1813" (1813). In the supplement to "A Constitutional History of American Episcopal Methodism" (2nd ed. 1904) J. J. Tigert has embodied several valuable documents.

For the Baptists, "A Concise History of the Kehukee Baptist Association" (1803) by Burkitt and Read; with "A History of the Rise and Progress of the Baptists in Virginia" (1810) by R. B. Semple, enlarged edition (1894) by G. W. Beale; and "A General History of the Baptist Denomination in America and Other Parts of the World" (1813) by D. Benedict; supplemented by the scholarly work of W. T. Thom, "The Struggle for Religious Freedom in Virginia: The Baptists" ("J. H. U. Studies" Ser. XVIII) represent the most important material.

The work of the Moravians is referred to by L. T. Reichel in "The Early History of the Church of the United Brethren . . . 1734 to 1748" (1888); J. T. Hamilton in "A History of the Church Known as the Moravian Church . . . " (1900); Adelaide Fries in "The Moravians in Georgia" (1904); and W. S. Plumer in "Thoughts on the Religious Instruction of Negroes."

For the Salzburgers, one should consult, "The Salzburgers and their Descendants . . . " (1855) by P. A. Stroebel. Some pertinent correspondence of Bolzius may be found in "The Colonial Records of the State of. Georgia" edited by Candler, Vols. XXI-XXV. See also p. 204.

The marked deepening of interest in negro welfare during the revolutionary and early national period is ably discussed by W. E. B. Du Bois in "The Suppression of the African Slave Trade in the United States of America, 1638-1870" ("Harvard Hist. Studies" Vol. I, 1896). "Anti-Slavery in America . . . " (above) by Mary S. Locke is well worth consulting, particularly Chapter II. The following documents are of outstanding importance: "Earnest Address to my Country on Slavery" (1769) by Samuel Webster (reprint, in part "A Sketch of the History of Newbury, . . . " by Joshua Coffin, 1845); "An Address to the Inhabitants of the British Settlements on the Slavery of the Negroes in America" (1773) by Benjamin Rush; "A South Carolina Protest Against Slavery . . . " (1776) by Henry Laurens; "A Forensic Dispute on the

Legality of Enslaving the Africans, held at the public Commencement in Cambridge, New England, July 21, 1773"; "A Dialogue concerning the Slavery of the Africans . . . Dedicated to the Honorable Continental Congress" by Samuel Hopkins ("Works" Vol. II, pp. 547-594); also his "Discourse upon the Slave Trade and the Slavery of the Africans . . . May 17, 1793" ("Works" Vol. II, pp. 595-612); "The African Slave Trade" (Discourse, Sept. 9, 1790) by James Dana; "The Injustice and Impolicy of the Slave Trade, and of the Slavery of the Africans . . . a Sermon . . . Sept. 15, 1791" by Jonathan Edwards; "Slavery inconsistent with Justice and Good Policy" by Rev. David Rice (1792, speech delivered at Constitutional Convention of Kentucky); "Queries respecting the Slavery and Emancipation of Negroes in Massachusetts, proposed by Judge Tucker of Virginia, and answered by Rev. Thomas Belknap" ("Coll. Mass. Hist. Soc." Ser. I, Vol. IV, also Ser. V, Vol. III); "Negro Slavery Unjustifiable," (Discourse, 1802) by Rev. Alexander McLeod.

On the rise and extension of the abolition societies, in which the Quakers played a conspicuous rôle, "An Historical Memoir of the Pennsylvania Society . . ." (1848) by Edward Needles, is indispensable. "Anti-Slavery Opinions before the year 1800" (1872) by W. F. Poole has much data upon this and related topics. "Anti-Slavery in America . . ." (above) by Mary Locke, compresses the salient facts into a few pages. Alice D. Adams has a similar condensation for the later period in the "Neglected Period of Anti-Slavery in America" (above). For the 'American Convention of Abolition Societies' (1794–1831) the "Minutes of the Proceedings" give the most informing accounts—(For complete list see Woodson, "The Education of the Negro," pp. 415-417, or Adams, "Neglected Period" pp. 280-289.) The following biographical studies have a considerable amount of material: "Life of Ezra Stiles, D.D., LL.D. . . ." (1798) by Abiel Holmes; "Life of Ezra Stiles, President of Yale College" (1845) by James L. Kingsley (Sparks, "Library of American Biography," 2nd Ser. Vol. VI); "Memoir of the Life and Character of Samuel Hopkins" by E. A. Park (1854, "Hopkins' Works" Vol. I,); "James G. Birney, and his Times . . ." (1890) by William Birney.

For the American Colonization Society, the biographies as above are to be supplemented by those setting forth S. J. Mills (see p. 364). The "Reports," (1818–1832) give detailed information. "The American

Colonization Society 1817–1840" by E. L. Fox (Johns Hopkins Univ. Studies Ser. XXXVII, No. 3) is useful.

The attitude of the churches to negro welfare during the first four decades of the nineteenth century, is discussed in several monographs. Probably the most scholarly, though quite condensed, is "The Neglected Period of Anti-Slavery in America 1808–1831" by Alice D. Adams (above). Harrison's "Gospel Among the Slaves" is valuable, notably chapts. XII–XIV which describe the 'Gospel on the Plantation.' Two articles ("Meth. Quar. Rev.," April and July, 1881) by Daniel Dorchester, "The Relation of the Churches and Mr. Garrison to the American Anti-Slavery Movement" are recommended as a counterpart to J. G. Birney's "The American Churches, the Bulwarks of American Slavery" (1842) and "The Church as it is, or the Forlorn Hope of Slavery" (2nd ed. 1885) by Parker Pillsbury. "Slavery and Anti-Slavery" (1852) by William Goodell has much information, and in lesser degree "The History of the Anti-Slavery Cause in the State and Nation" (1886) by Rev. Austin Willey. "The History of American Slavery and Methodism from 1789 to 1849" (1849) and "The Anti-Slavery Struggle and Triumph in the Methodist Episcopal Church" (1881) by Rev. L. C Matlack, though defective in literary form and arrangement, give copious details for the Methodists and considerable information for other bodies. "The Church and Slavery" (1857) by A. Barnes, and "American States, Churches, and Slavery" (1863) by J. R. Balme, are strongly partizan.

The persistent opposition of the Quakers appears in a "History of the Separation in the Indiana Yearly Meeting of Friends which took place in the winter of 1842 and 1843, on the Anti-Slavery Question."

The 'underground railroad' is presented in "Reminiscences of Levi Coffin, reputed President of the Underground Railroad" (2nd ed. 1880); "The Underground Railroad in Ohio" ("Papers, Ohio Ch. Hist. Soc." Vol. X, pp. 31-52); "The Underground Railroad . . ." (1872) by W. Still; "History of the Underground Railroad in Chester and the Neighboring Counties of Pennsylvania" (1883) by R. C. Smedley; and "The Underground Railroad from Slavery to Freedom" (1898) by William H. Siebert.

Notable documents of the period are as follows: "An Admonitory Picture and a Solemn Warning principally addressed to professing Christians in the Southern States of North America . . ." (April 16, 1810) by Lewis Dupré; "The Book and Slavery Irreconcilable" (1816) by George Bourne; also his "Pictures of Slavery in the United States" (1818); "Exposition of the Views of the Baptists relative to the Coloured Population of the United States, in a communication to the governor of South Carolina" (1822) by Rev. Richard Furman; "A View of the Present State of the Slave Trade, Published by direction of a meeting representing the Religious Society of Friends in Pennsylvania, New-Jersey, . . ." (1824); "An Address to the People of North Carolina on the Evils of Slavery, by the Friends of Liberty and Equality" (1830); "Two letters on the subject of slavery from the presbytery of Chillicothe to the Churches under their care" (1830); "An Address to Christians of all Denominations, on the Inconsistency of Admitting Slave holders to Communion and Church Membership" (1831) by Evan Lewis; "Letters on Slavery Addressed to the Cumberland Congregation, Virginia, by John D. Paxton, their former pastor" (1833); "A Detail of a Plan for the Moral Improvement of Negroes on Plantations" (1833) by T. S. Clay; "Lectures on Slavery and its Remedy" (1834) by Amos A. Phelps; "A Catechism for Colored Persons" (1834) by C. C. Jones; "Letters on American Slavery, addressed to Mr. Thomas Rankin . . ." (1836) by John Rankin.

In the autobiographical field, the following are suggested as particularly illuminating: Asbury's "Journal"; "Recollections of the last Ten Years, a series of letters to the Rev. Joseph Flint of Salem, Mass. by T. Flint . . ." (1826); "Journal of the Life and Religious Labors of Elias Hicks, Written by himself" (5th ed. 1832); "Thirty Years' View, 1820-1850" (1854) by Thomas H. Benton; "Autobiography of Peter Cartwright, a Backwoods Preacher" (1858), edited by W. P. Strickland; "Journal of the Life and Religious Labors of John Comly" (1853) published by his children; "Memoirs of John Quincy Adams, comprising portions of his diary from 1795–1848" (1875) edited by Charles Francis Adams; "Reminiscences of Levi Coffin . . ." (2nd ed. 1880).

Travel literature will ofttimes give good returns to the investigator of this period. In this connection the following are suggested, additional to what has been cited in connection with the "Second Awakening" (see p. 329f.): "Travels through . . . the United States of America in the years 1806, 1807 and 1808" (III Vols. 1810) by John Lambert; "Letters from the South, written during an excursion in the summer of 1816 . . ." (1817) by J. K. Paulding; "Travels in New England and New York" (1821) by Timothy Dwight; "An Account of the United States of America . . ." (1823) by Isaac Holmes; "Travels Through part of the United States and Canada . . .1818 and 1819" (II Vols. 1823) by J. M. Duncan; "A Summary View of America . . ." (1824) by Isaac Candler; "The United States and Canada in 1832, 1833, and

1834" (II Vols. 1834) by C. D. Arfwedson; "Personal Narrative of Travels in Virginia . . . In the Illinois Country, 1817, 1818" by E. P. Fordham, edited (1906) by F. A. Ogg.

Of biographies that have more or less bearing upon slave conditions during this period, the following are especially recommended: "The Life of the Rev. Freeborn Garrettson . . . " (1832) by Nathan Bangs; "The Life, Travels, and Opinions of Benjamin Lundy, Compiled under the direction of his Children" (1847) by Thomas Earl; "Isaac T. Hopper; A True Life" (1853) by Lydia M. Childs; "Life and Times of Bishop Hedding, D.D. . . . " (1855) by Rev. D. W. Clark, D.D.; "The Life of William Capers . . . ; including an Autobiography" (1858) by W. M. Wightman; "The Life of Jacob Gruber" (1860) by W. P. Strickland; "The Life and Times of Nathan Bangs, D.D." (1863) by Abel Stevens; "Life and Correspondence of Theodore Parker" (II Vols. 1864) by John Weiss; "William Lloyd Garrison and His Times" (1880) by O. Johnson; "The Life of Edmund S. Janes, D.D. . . . " (1882) by H. B. Ridgeway; "Arthur and Lewis Tappan . . . " (1883 a paper) by C. W. Bowen; "John B. McFerrin, A Biography" (1889) by O. P. Fitzgerald; "The Life of Bishop Matthew Simpson . . . " (1890) by Rev. G. R. Crooks; "James G. Birney and his Times" (1890) by W. Birney; "William Lloyd Garrison, the Abolitionist" (1892) by A. H. Grimke; "William Jay and the Constitutional Movement for the Abolition of Slavery" (1893) by B. Tuckerman; "William Lloyd Garrison, 1805-1879. The Story of his Life told by his Children" (IV Vols. 1894) by F. J. and W. T. Garrison; "The Life and Times of Wendell Phillips" (1901) by G. L. Austin. "George Bourne, The Pioneer of American Anti-Slavery" ("Meth. Quar. Rev." Jan. 1887) is an important article dealing with the works of this philanthropist, and presenting a picture of slavery for the period.

For the literature bearing upon the division in the Baptist and Methodist bodies due to the slavery issue see page 578f. and 580f.

The Quaker cleavage is set forth in "A History of the Separation in Indiana Yearly Meeting of Friends; which took place in the winter of 1842 and 1843 on the Anti-Slavery Question . . . " (1855) by Walter Edgerton; and "Divisions in the Society of Friends (1869, 2nd ed. enlarged 1893) by Thomas Speakman.

The "Relation of the American Board of Commissioners for Foreign Missions to Slavery" (1861) by C. K. Whipple covers an important field. For the study of the attitude of the American Home Missionary Society to slavery, the most satisfactory source is the "Home Missionary", which from 1849 has much data.

In the years immediately preceding the War, several sermons, essays, and debates appeared, discussing the issue of slavery. The following are representative: "Bible Defence of Slavery: or the Origin, History, and Fortunes of the Negro Race . . . " (1849) by Josiah Priest, A.M.; "A Defence of the South against the Reproaches and Encroachments of the North . . . in which Slavery is shown to be an institution of God intended to form the Basis of the best Social State, and the only Safeguard to the Permanence of a Republican Government" (1850) by Rev. Iveson L. Brookes, A.M.; "God the Refuge of His People" by Whiteford Smith, D.D. (sermon, December 6, 1850); "Scriptural and Statistical Views in Favor of Slavery" (1856) by Thornton Stringfellow D.D.; "Sinfulness of American Slavery Proved from its Evil Sources; its Injustice . . . . together with Observations on Emancipation and the Duties of American Citizens in regard to Slavery," by Rev. Charles Elliott, D.D., edited (1857) by Rev. B. F. Tefft, D.D.; "The Christian Doctrine of Slavery" (1857) by Geo. D. Armstrong, D.D.; "Slavery Ordained of God" (1857) by Rev. F. A. Ross; "Ought American Slavery to be perpetuated—A Debate between Rev. W. G. Brownlow and Rev. A. Pryne" (1858); "God Against Slavery; and the Freedom and Duty of the Pulpit to Rebuke it as a Sin against God" (n.d.) by George B. Cheever, D.D.; "An Essay on Liberty and Slavery" (1857) by Albert Taylor Bledsoe, LL.D.; "The Appeal of the Religious Society of Friends to their Fellow Citizens of the United States in behalf of the Coloured Races" (1858); "American Slavery Distinguished from the Slavery of English Theorists and Justified by the Law of Nature" (1861) by Rev. Samuel Seabury, D.D.; "A Scriptural, Ecclesiastical, and Historical View of Slavery, from the Days of the Patriarch Abraham to the Nineteenth Century . . . " (5th ed. 1864) by John Henry Hopkins, D.D., Bishop of the Diocese of Vermont; "Southern Slavery in its Present Aspects, Containing a Reply to the Late Work of the Bishop of Vermont on Slavery" (1864) by Daniel R. Goodwin.

On the matter of the relation of the Bible to slavery, there appeared, in addition to Priest's "Bible Defence" and Stringfellow's "Scriptural and Statistical View" (supra), "An Inquiry into the Scriptural Views of Slavery" (1846) by Albert Barnes; "The Bible and Slavery" ("Bibliotheca Sacra," July, 1862); "Does the Bible Sustain Slavery?" ("Christian Review" Oct. 1862); "The Bible Against Slavery" (1864) by Stephen Vail, D.D.; "The Bible Against Slavery" (1864) by J. B. Dobbins.

The following are significant discussions in religious periodicals bearing upon slavery and the Union—"The Extension of Slavery" ("Christian Review" Jan. 1849); "The Churches North and South in their Relation to the Union of the States" (*ibid*. April, 1850); "Revival of the Slave Trade" ("Southern Presbyterian Review" Oct. 1859); "The Raid of John Brown and the Progress of Abolition" (*ibid*. Jan. 1860); "Reopening of the African Slave Trade" ("The New Englander" Feb. 1860).

DOCUMENTS

I. *THE PROPOSALS OF REV. MORGAN GODWYN* (1681)

Before we enter upon this Debate, to prevent all troublesome Clamors and Objections against it, upon the score of *Interest*, this Position should first be laid down, and as a Principle fixt and Eternal, and from which a true Christian cannot recede, be resolved on, (*viz*.) That no Interest how great or (otherwise) just forever, may be admitted to stand in Competition with *Christianity*. . .

And here also in this Consideration, we are especially to avoid Splitting upon this Solecism, both in Policy and Discretion, and against which, *Ecclus* hath so wisely cautioned us, ch. 37, *v*. 11. [*Not to ask Counsel for Religion of one that hath no Religion, nor of Justice of him that hath no Justice*] *nor of a Coward about Matters of War, nor of a Merchant concerning Exchange, nor of a Buyer concerning selling &c. for such will counsel for themselves, ver. 8.* So likewise for a *Christian* not to be guided or led by *Self-ended* Men, Enemies to his Profession, in these Debates and Proposals made for the Advancement of it. Such being only like to raise *Obstructions*, as hitherto they have always done; and (as lately) to render that for impossible, which has not the least difficulty in it, where a right Method is used for effecting it.

No more are we to proceed herein, by the sole Advice of Persons *unacquainted* with the true State and Condition of the places where this Settlement or Conversion is to be wrought. . .

These things being agreed on, we must then fall to consider of the People amongst whom we are to take our lot, and thereto to have an especial regard: As, whether they be *Slaves*, subject to the *English*, such as most of the *Negro's* there are; or *free People* living of themselves, either amongst, or distant from the *English*; such as most of the *Indians* on the Continent (in *Virginia*, &c.) are. Or lastly, whether this is to be performed by way of further Setling and Establishment, even amongst the *English* themselves, which also is no less necessary. . .

Now concerning the *Negro's*, whom I should think fit to be first taken in hand (as being the easiest Task, would their Owners be perswaded to consent thereto; & the most absolutely necessary, this neglect being the most scandalous, and withal, the most impossible to be defended or excused:) The first and great step will be to procure (what I but just mentioned) their *Owners consent*, as being to be supposed *averse* thereto: not altogether, as is here believed, out of *Interest* (it being already secured to them by Laws of their own;) but by reason of the trouble, and the fancied *needlessness* of the Work; and to prevent all danger from their Slaves being furnisht with knowledge, consequent, they conceive thereto. However, because they pretend the other (and something there may be in that too,) to take off that *pretence*, it will be requisite.

1. That a Law be enacted to confirm such Laws of theirs, as are or shall be here-after made to *secure their just Interest* in their Slaves; That they may thereby be continued in their present State of *Servitude*, notwithstanding their being afterward *baptised.*

2. That all *unjust* Interests, and *ungodly* Advantages arising from their Slaves *Sunday-labour* and *Polygamie* (neither of them sufferable among *Christians*) be upon severest Penalties prohibited; and this as well to the *unbaptised*, as to the rest. . .

These *pretences* being thus fairly removed, if any *Aversion* still remains (as 'tis feared there will, and that for the truest Reasons above mentioned,) they must afterwards be invited thereto by good *Sermons & Books*, Preacht and Writ upon this Subject, and by discoursing with them in *private*. As also by the Example of the *Ministers* themselves in their *Families*. And lastly, (and which will do more then all the rest) by *Encouragments* from the *Government*. . .

Another way, and which 'tis possible might prove most effectual, would be to get this impiety decryed here in *England*, where our *Planters* have an extraordinary *Ambition* to be *thought well of*, and thereby to *shame* them into *better Principles*. . .

Now for the *Planter's* late Objections against this Work, as I have heard them represented (and I believe they are the best they had), . . .

1. They object their *Negro's* want of *English*; Whereas 'tis certain that there are some thousands of them, who understand *English*, no worse than our own People. *Let them begin with those:*

2. That it would make them *less governable*; the contrary to which is experimentally known amongst their Neighbours, both *French & Spaniards* in those parts. Now 'twould be too great a blemish to the *Reformation*, to suppose that *Popery* only makes its Converts better, but *Protestancy* worse; as this Allegation being admitted, it must be granted. And to prevent any fond conceit in them of *Libertie*, (an especial Branch of the same *Article*,) if there be any such danger, let two or three of each great *Family* be first *baptised*; whereby the rest seeing them continued as they were, that Opinion would soon vanish: . . .

3. As for their pretended Aversion to Christianity, the contrary thereto is known of most of them. And tho it is to be confessed that some are more careless and indifferent (having bin taught by the *English* to be *needless for them*) yet for the *general* they are observed to be rather *ambitious* of it. Nor, I dare affirm, can any single *Instance* of such *aversion* in any one of them, be produced.

4. As to their (alike pretended) *Stupidity*, there is as little truth therein: divers of them being known and confessed by their *Owners*, to be extraordinary *Ingenious*, and even to exceed many of the *English*. And for the rest, they are much the same with other People, destitute of the means of knowledge, and wanting *Education*.

5. One thing more there remains to be added, of which, tho they may be most afraid, yet they carefully keep it to themselves, and that is the possibility of their Slaves Expectation, not of *Freedom*, but of more *merciful Vsage* from them. . .

Text -M. G. [Morgan Godwyn]: *A Supplement to the Negro's & Indian's Advocate*, pp. 5-12.

II. *BISHOP OF LONDON'S LETTERS TO MASTERS AND MISTRESSES*

The Care of the Plantations abroad being committed to the Bishop of LONDON as to Religious Affairs; I have thought it my Duty to make particular Enquiries into the State of Religion in those Parts, and to learn, among other Things, what numbers of Slaves are employ'd within the several Governments, and what Means are used for their Instruction in the Christian Faith. I find the Numbers are prodigiously great . . . ; I find there has not only been very little Progress made in the Works, but that all *Attempts* towards it have been by too many industriously discouraged and hindered; partly, by magnifying the Difficulties of the Work beyond what they really are; and partly, by mistaken Suggestions of the Change which Baptism would make in the Condition of the *Negroes*, to the Loss and Disadvantage of their Masters.

1. As to the Difficulties; it may be pleaded, That the Negroes are *grown Persons* when they come over, and that having been accustomed to the Pagan Rites and Idolatries of their own Country, they are prejudiced against all other Religions, and more particularly against the Christian, as forbidding all that Licentiousness which is usually practised among the Heathens. But if this were a good Argument against attempting the Conversion of Negroes, it would follow, that the Gospel is never to be further propagated than it is at present, and that no Endeavours are to be used for the Conversion of Heathens, at any Time, or in any Country whatsoever.

BUT a farther Difficulty is, that they are utter Strangers to our Language, and we to theirs; and the Gift of Tongues being now ceased, there is no Means left of instructing them in the Doctrines of the Christian Religion. And this, I own, is a real Difficulty, as long as it continues, and as far as it reaches. But, if I am rightly informed, many of the Negroes, who are grown Persons when they come over, do of themselves attain so much of our Language, as enables them to understand, and to be understood, in Things which concern the ordinary Business of Life; and they who can go so far of their own accord, might doubtless be carried much farther, if proper Methods and Endeavours were used to bring them to a competent Knowledge of our Language, with a pious View to the instructing them in the Doctrines of our Religion. At least, some of them, who are more capable and more serious than the rest, might be easily instructed both in our Language and Religion, and then be made use of to convey Instruction to the rest in their own Language. And this, one would hope, may be done with great Ease, wherever there is a hearty and sincere Zeal for the Work.

But whatever Difficulties there may be in instructing those who are *grown-up* before they are brought over; there are not the like Difficulties in the Case of their Children, who are born and bred in our Plantations, who have never been accustomed to Pagan Rites and Superstitions, and who may easily be train'd up, like all other Children to any Language whatsoever, and particularly to our own, if the making them good Christians be sincerely the Desire and Intention of those, who have the Property in them, and the Government over them.

But supposing the Difficulties to be much greater than I imagine; they are not such as render the Work *impossible*, so as to leave no Hope of any Degree of success; and nothing less than an *Impossibility* of doing any good at all, can warrant our giving over and laying aside all Means and Endeavours, where the Propagation of the Gospel, and the saving of Souls, are immediately concerned. - . . . .

I am loath to think so hardly of any *Christian* Master, as to suppose that he can *deliberately hinder* his Negroes from being instructed in the Christian Faith; or, which is the same Thing, that he can, upon sober and mature Consideration of the Case, finally resolve to deny them the *Means* and *opportunities* of Instruction: Much less may I believe, that he can, after he has seriously weigh'd this Matter, permit them to labour on the Lord's Day; and least of all, that he can put them under a kind of *Necessity* of labouring on that Day, to provide themselves with the *Conveniences* of Life. . . . .

If it be said, That no Time can be spared from the daily Labour and Employment of the Negroes, to instruct them in the Christian Religion; this is in Effect to say, that no Consideration of propagating the Gospel of God, or Saving the Souls of Men, is to make the *least Abatement* from the temporal Profit of the Masters. . . . .

II. But it is further pleaded, That the Instruction of Heathens in the Christian Faith, is in order to their Baptism; and that not only the *Time* to be allowed for Instructing them, would be an Abatement from the Profits of their Labour, but also that the *Baptizing* them when instructed, would destroy both the Property which the Masters have in them as Slaves bought with their Money, and the Right of selling them again at Pleasure; and that the making them Christians, only makes them less diligent, and more ungovernable. . . . . . .

To which it may be very truly reply'd, That Christianity, and the embracing of the Gospel, does not make the least Alteration in Civil Property, or in any of the Duties which belong to Civil Relations; but in all these Respects, it continues Persons just in the same State as it found them.   The Freedom which Christianity gives, is a Freedom from the Bondage of Sin and Satan, and from the Dominion of Mens Lusts and Passions and inordinate Desires; but as to their *outward* Condition, whatever that was before, whether bond or free, their being baptized, and becoming Christians, makes no manner of Change in it. . . . . . .

As to their being more ungovernable after Baptism, than before; it is certain that the Gospel every where enjoins, not only Diligence and Fidelity, but also *Obedience*, for Conscience Sake; and does not deprive Masters of any proper Methods of enforcing Obedience, where they appear to be necessary.   Humanity forbids all cruel and barbarious Treatment of our Fellow-Creatures, and will not suffer us to consider a Being that is endow'd with Reason, upon a Level with Brutes; and Christianity takes not out of the Hands of Superiors any Degrees of Strictness and Severity, that fairly appear to be necessary for the preserving Subjection and Government. . . . .

I cannot omit to suggest to you one of the best Motives that can be us'd, for disposing the Heathens to embrace Christianity; and that is, *the good Lives of Christians*. Let them see, in you and your Families, Examples of Sobriety, Temperance and Chastity, and of all the other Virtues and Graces of the Christian Life. . . . .

By these Means, you will open their Hearts to Instruction, and prepare them to receive the Truths of the Gospel, to which if you add a pious *Endeavour* and *Concern* to see them duly instructed, you may become the Instrument of saving many Souls, and will not only secure a Blessing from GOD upon all your undertakings in this World, but entitle your selves to that distinguishing Reward in the next, which will be given to all those who have been zealous in their Endeavours to promote the Salvation of Men, and enlarge the Kingdom of CHRIST.   And that you may be found in that Number at the great Day of Accounts, is the sincere Desire and earnest Prayer of

Your Faithful Friend,

EDM. 'LONDON',

May 19, 1727.

Text—Humphreys: *An Historical Account of the Incorporated Society for the Propagation of the Gospel in Foreign Parts*, pp. 257-270.

III. *COMMISSARY GARDEN'S NEGRO SCHOOL IN SOUTH CAROLINA*

Our worthy Benefactors were informed in the Abstract of the last Year, of the Reverend Mr. Commissary Garden's purchasing, at the Expence of the Society, two promising Negroe Youths, to be put to School, and to be qualified under his Care and Instruction for the Edification of their fellow Negroe Slaves; and that Mr. Garden hoped in about twelve months to give the Society an Account of a considerable Number of Young Negroe Children under their Tuition, regulated by his Direction and Inspection. These Hopes, Thro' the Blessing of God, are fulfilled; for the Society hath the great Pleasure to be informed by a Letter from *Mr. Garden*, dated *Charles-Town South Carolina, October* 10, 1743. That assisted by the voluntary Contributions of some good Christians of that Place, he had built a School-house, and the School was actually opened on *Monday* the 12th Day of *September* preceding, when several Negroe Children were sent thither for Instruction. The Number was, at the Date of his letter, about 30, and was daily increasing, insomuch that he expected soon more Children than one Master could well manage; and therefore proposes to employ both the Negroe Youths in this School, till some other Parish shall provide proper Accommodations for another School. Mr. *Garden* computes, that after the first two Years this School will annually send out 30 or 40 Children capable to read the Scriptures, and instructed in the Chief Principles of Christianity, which will amount, in the Space of 20 Years, to the Number of nigh half the Negroes of this Parish, And thus the Society hath opened a Door, (and it is to be hoped, thro' the divine Goodness, an effectual one) by which the Light of the blessed Gospel will speedily and abundantly pour in among the poor Negroes of *Carolina*, and that without the least further Charge to the Society for some Years, (that of a few Books only excepted) which the Society is most ready to furnish, and hath ordered a large Quantity of Bibles, Testaments, Common Prayer, and Spelling Books, to be sent them forthwith.

Text—*Abstract Proceedings S.P.G. 1744-45*, pp. 53-54.

IV. *THE MENNONITE PROTEST AGAINST SLAVERY*

Drawn up at Thomas Kunder's house February, 1688, and sent to the quarterly and yearly meetings of the Quakers, only to be of too great importance 'to meddle with,' this protest is, so far as is known, the first public protest against the holding of slaves in America.

"This is to ye Monthly Meeting held at Rigert Worrells. These are the reasons why we are against the traffick of mens-body as followeth: Is there any that would be done or handled at this manner? viz. to be sold or made a slave for all the time of his life? How fearfull and fainthearted are many on sea when they see a strange vessel being afraid it should be a Turck, and they should be tacken and sold for Slaves in Turckey. Now what is this better done as Turcks doe? yea rather is it worse for them, wch say they are Christians for we hear, that ye most part of such Negers are brought heither against their will & consent, and that many of them are stollen. Now tho' they are black, we cannot conceive there is more liberty to have them slaves, as it is to have other white ones. There is a saying, that we shall doe to all men, licke as we will be done our selves: macking no difference of what generation, descent, or Colour they are.   And those who steal or robb men, and those who buy or purchase them, are they not all alicke?   Here is liberty of Conscience, wch is right & reasonable, here ought to be lickewise liberty of ye body, except of evildoers, wch is another case.   But to bring men hither, or to robb and sell them against their will, we stand against.   In Europe there are many oppressed for Conscience Sacke; and here there are those oppressed wch are of a black Colour.   And we, who know that men must not commit adultery, some do commit adultery in others, separating wifes from their housbands, and giving them to others and some sell the children of those poor Creatures to other men.   Oh, doe consider well this things, you who doe it, if you would be done at this manner? and if it is done according Christianity? you surpass Holland and Germany in this thing.   This mackes an ill report in all those Countries of Europe, where they hear off, that ye Quackers doe here handel men, Licke they handel there ye Cattle, and for that reason some have no mind or inclination to come hither.   And who shall maintaine this your cause or plaid for it!   Truely we can not do so except you shall inform us better hereoff, viz. that christians have liberty to practise this things.   Pray!   What thing in the world can be done worse towarts us then if men should robb or steal us away & sell us for slaves to strange Countries, separating housband from their wife & children.   Being now this is not done at that manner we will be done at, therefore we contradict & are against this traffick of men body.   And we who profess that it is not lawfull to steal, must lickewise avoid to purchase such things as are stolen, but rather help to stop this robbing and stealing if possibel and such men ought to be delivred out of ye hands of ye Robbers and set free as well as in Europe.   Then is Pensilvania to have a good report, in stead it hath now a bad one for this sacke in other Countries.   Especially whereas ye Europeans are desirous to know in what manner ye Quackers doe rule in their Province & most of them doe loock upon us with an envious eye.   But if this is done well, what shall we say, is don evil?

If once these slaves (wch they say are so wicked and stubbern men) should joint themselves, fight for their freedom and handel their masters & mastrisses, as they did handel them before; will these masters & mistrisses tacke the sword at hand & warr against these poor slaves, licke we are able to believe, some will not refuse to doe?   Or have these negers not as much right to fight for their freedom, as you have to keep them slaves?

Now consider well this thing, if it is good or bad? and in case you find it to be good to handel these blacks at that manner, we desire & require you hereby lovingly that you may informe us herein, which at this time never was done, viz. that Christians have Liberty to do so, to the end we shall be satisfied in this point, & satisfie lickewise our good friends & acquaintances in our natif Country, to whose it is a terrour or fairfull thing that men should be handeld so in Pensilvania.

"This is was from our meeting at Germantown hold ye 18 of the 2 month 1688 to be delivered to the monthly meeting at Richard Warrels.

> GERRET HENDRICKS
> DERICK OP DE GRAEFF
> FRANCIS DANIELL PASTORIUS
> ABRAHAM OP DEN GRAEF."

Text—*The Pennsylvania-German Society Proceedings and Addresses*, Vol. IX, pp. 197-199.

V. *THE FIRST PRINTED PROTEST AGAINST SLAVERY IN AMERICA*

By George Keith, 1693

"An Exhortation & Caution to Friends Concerning Buying or Keeping of Negroes.

Seeing our Lord Jesus Christ hath tasted Death for every Man, and given himself a Ransom for all, to be testified in due time, and that his Gospel of Peace, Liberty and Redemption from Sin, Bondage and all Oppression, is freely to be preached unto all, without Exception, and that *Negroes, Blacks* and *Taunies* are a real part of Mankind, for whom Christ hath shed his precious Blood, and are capable of Salvation, as well as *White Men*; and Christ the Light of the World hath (in measure) enlightened them, and every Man that cometh into the World; and that all such who are sincere *Christians* and true Believers in Christ Jesus, and Followers of him, bear his Image, and are made conformable unto him in Love, Mercy, Goodness and Compassion, who came not to destroy men's Lives, but to save them, nor to bring any part of Mankind into outward Bondage, Slavery or Misery, nor yet to detain them, or hold them therein, but to ease and deliver the Oppressed and Distressed, and bring into Liberty both inward and outward.

Therefore we judge it was necessary that all faithful Friends should discover themselves to be true *Christians* by having the Fruits of the Spirit of Christ, which are *Love, Mercy, Goodness, and Compassion* towards all in Misery, and that suffer Oppression and severe Usage, so far as in them is possible to ease and relieve them, and set them free of their hard Bondage, whereby it may be hoped, that many of them will be gained by their beholding these good Works of sincere *Christians*, and prepared thereby, through the Preaching the Gospel of Christ, to imbrace the true Faith of Christ. And for this cause it is, as we judge, that in some places in *Europe* Negroes cannot be bought and sold for Money, or detained to be Slaves, because it suits not with the Mercy, Love & Clemency that is essential to *Christianity*, nor to the Doctrine of Christ, nor to the Liberty the Gospel calleth all men unto, to whom it is preached. And to buy Souls and Bodies of men for Money, to enslave them and their Posterity to the end of the World, we judge is a great hinderance to the spreading of the Gospel, and is occasion of much War, Violence, Cruelty and Oppression, and Theft & Robbery of the highest Nature; for commonly the Negroes that are sold to white Men, are either stollen away or robbed from their Kindred, and to buy such is the way to continue these evil Practices of Man-stealing, and transgresseth that Golden Rule and Law, *To do to others what we would have others do to us.*

Therefore, in true *Christian Love*, we earnestly recommend it to all our Friends and Brethren, Not to buy any Negroes, unless it were on purpose to set them free, and that such who have bought any, and have them at present, after some reasonable time of moderate Service they have had of them, or may have of them, that may reasonably answer to the Charge of what they have laid out, especially in keeping Negroes Children born in their House, or taken into their House, when under Age, that after a reasonable time of service to answer that Charge, they may set them at Liberty, and during the time they have them, to teach them to read, and give them a Christian Education.

Some Reasons and Causes of our Being Against Keeping of Negroes for Term of Life

First, Because it is contrary to the Principles and Practice of the *Christian Quakers* to buy Prize or stollen Goods, which we bore a faithful Testimony against in our Native Country. . .

Secondly, Because Christ commanded, saying, *All-things whatsoever ye would that men should do unto you, do ye even so to them.* . .

Thirdly, Because the Lord hath commanded, saying, *Thou shalt not deliver unto his Master the Servant that is escaped from his Master unto thee, he shall dwell with thee, even amongst you in that place which he shall chuse in one of thy Gates, where it liketh him best; thou shalt not oppress him, Deut.* 23, 15, 16. . .

Fourthly, Because the Lord hath commanded, saying, *Thou shalt not oppress an hired Servant that is poor and needy, whether he be of thy Brethren, or of the Strangers that are in thy Land within thy Gates, least he cry against thee unto the Lord, and it be sin unto thee; Thou shalt neither vex a stranger nor oppress him, for ye were strangers in the Land of* Aegypt, *Deut.* 24, 14, 15. *Exod.* 12, 21. . .

Fifthly, Because Slaves and Souls of Men are some of the *Merchandize of Babylon* by which the Merchants of the Earth are made Rich; but those Riches which they have heaped together, through the cruel Oppression of these miserable Creatures, will be a means to draw Gods Judgments upon them, therefore, *Brethren,* let us hearken to the Voice of the Lord, who saith, *Come out of* Babylon, *my People, that ye be not partakers of her Sins, and that ye receive not her Plagues; for her Sins have reached unto Heaven, and God hath remembered her Iniquities, for he that leads into Captivity shall go into Captivity,* Rev. 18. 4, 5. & 13. 10.

Given forth by our Monthly Meeting in Philadelphia, *the 13th day of the 8th Moneth,* 1693, *and recommended to all our Friends and Brethren, who are one with us in our Testimony for the Lord Jesus Christ, and to all others professing* Christianity."

Text—*The Pennsylvania Magazine of History and Biography,* Vol. XIII, pp. 265-70.

VI. *EARLY QUAKER TESTIMONIES*

The Yearly Meeting of 1758

'One of the most important religious convocations in the history of the Christian Church'—J. G. Whittier.

"After weighty consideration of the circumstances of Friends within the compass of this meeting, who have any negro or other slaves, the accounts and proposals now sent up from several quarters, and the rules of our discipline relative thereto; much time having been spent, and the sentiments of many Friends expressed, there appears an unanimous concern prevailing, to put a stop to the increase of the practice of importing, buying, selling, or keeping slaves for term of life; or purchasing them for such a number of years, as manifests that such purchasers, do only in terms, and not in fact, avoid the imputation of being keepers of slaves. This meeting very earnestly and affectionately intreats Friends, individually, to consider seriously the present circumstances of these and the adjacent provinces, which, by the permission of Divine Providence, have been visited with the desolating calamities of war and bloodshed, so that many of our fellow-subjects are now suffering in captivity; and fervently desires, that, excluding temporal considerations, or views of self-interest, we may manifest an humbling sense of these judgments, and in thankfulness for the peculiar favour extended and continued to our Friends and brethren in profession, none of whom have, as we have yet heard, been slain, nor carried into captivity, would steadily observe the injunction of our Lord and Master, 'To do unto others, as we would they should do unto us;' which it now appears to this meeting, would induce such Friends who have any slaves, to set them at Liberty,—making a Christian provision for them, according to their ages, &c.   And in order that Friends may be generally excited to the practice of this advice, some Friends here now signified to the meeting, their being so fully devoted to endeavour to render it effectual, that they are willing to visit and treat with all such Friends who have any slaves: the meeting, therefore, approves of John Woolman, John Scarborough, John Sykes and Daniel Stanton undertaking that service; and desires some elders or other faithful Friends in each quarter, to accompany and assist them therein; and that they may proceed in the wisdom of Truth, and thereby be qualified. to administer such advice as may be suitable to the circumstances of those they visit, and most effectual towards obtaining that purity, which it is evidently our duty to press after.   And if after the sense and judgment of this meeting, now given against every branch of this practice, any professing with us should persist to vindicate it, and be concerned in importing, selling, or purchasing slaves, the respective Monthly Meet ings to which they belong, should manifest their disunion with such persons, by refus- ing to permit them to sit in meetings for discipline, or to be employed in the affairs of Truth, or to receive from them any contribution towards the relief of the poor, or other services of the meeting.   But if any cases of executors, guardians, trustees or any others should happen, which may subject any such Friends to the necessity of being concerned with such slaves, and they are nevertheless willing to proceed according to the advice of the Monthly Meetings they belong to; wherever such cases happen the Monthly Meetings are left to judge of the same in the wisdom of Truth, and, if necessary, to take the advice of the Quarterly Meeting therein."

Text—*A Brief Statement* . . . Reprint,—*The Friend*, Vol. XVI, No. 51.

The Yearly Meeting of 1776

"We, the committee, appointed to take under our consideration the deeply affect- ing case of our oppressed fellow-men of the African race and others, as also the state of those who hold them in bondage, have several times met, and heard the concurring sentiments of divers other Friends, and examined the reports from the Quarterly Meet- ings, by which it appears, that much labour and care have been extended since the last year, for the convincement of such of our members who had, or yet have them in pos- session; many of whom have of late, from under hand and seal, properly discharged such as were in their possession, from a state of slavery.

Yet sorrowful it is, that many there are in membership with us, who, notwithstand- ing the labour bestowed, still continue to hold these people as slaves; under the consid- eration whereof, we are deeply affected, and united in judgment, that we are loudly called upon to a faithful obedience to the injunction of our blessed Lord, 'To do to all men as we would they should do unto us;' and to bear a full and clear testimony to these truths, that 'God is no respecter of persons,' and that 'Christ died for all men without distinction.'   Which we earnestly and affectionately intreat may be duly con- sidered in this awful and alarming dispensation, and excite to impartial justice and judgment, to black and white, rich and poor.

Under the calming influences of pure love, we do with great unanimity, give it as our sense and judgment, that Quarterly and Monthly Meetings should speedily unite in a further close labour with all such as are slave-holders, and have any right of mem- bership with us.   And where any members continue to reject the advice of their breth- ren, and refuse to execute proper instruments of writing, for releasing from a state of slavery, such as are in their power, or to whom they have any claim, whether arrived

to full age, or in their minority, and no hopes of the continuance of Friends' labour be
ing profitable to them, that Monthly Meetings after having discharged a Christian
duty to such, should testify their disunion with them.

And it appearing from the reports of the several Quarters, that there are many
difficult and complicated cases, which relate to those oppressed and much injured
people, requiring great circumspection and close attention, in order that our religious
testimony may be promoted, and that the cause of Truth may not suffer by unprofitable delays, we apprehend all such cases might well be submitted to the Quarterly
Meetings where they subsist, whose advice and judgment should be observed and
regarded; so that any member who refuses or declines complying therewith, after being
laboured with in the spirit of love and wisdom, should be testified against."

Text—*A Brief Statement* . . . Reprint,—*The Friend*, Vol. XVI, No. 52.

VII. *CONSTITUTION OF THE PENNSYLVANIA SOCIE-TY FOR PROMOTING THE ABOLITION OF SLAVERY, ETC.* 1787

'The Society for the Relief of Poor Negroes unlawfully held in Bondage',
organized April 14, 1775, but interrupted in its meetings during the
Revolution, resuscitated in 1784, and described in its Constitution as
under, became the model for the many abolition societies that sprang
up in New England and elsewhere.

"It having pleased the Creator of the world, to make of one flesh all the children
of men—it becomes them to consult and promote each other's happiness, as members
of the same family, however diversified they may be, by colour, situation, religion or
different states of society. It is more especially the duty of those persons, who profess
to maintain for themselves the rights of human nature, and who acknowledge the
obligations of Christianity, to use such means as are in their power, to extend the blessings of freedom to every part of the human race, and in a more particular manner, to
such of their fellow creatures, as are entitled to freedom by the laws and constitutions
of any of the United States, and who, notwithstanding, are detained in bondage, by
fraud or violence. From a full conviction of the truth and obligation of these principles—from a desire to diffuse them, wherever the miseries and vices of slavery exist,
and in humble confidence of the favour and support of the Father of Mankind, the
subscribers have associated themselves, under the title of the 'Pennsylvania Society for
promoting the Abolition of Slavery, and the Relief of free Negroes unlawfully held in
Bondage.'

For effecting these purposes, they have adopted the following constitution:
I. The officers of the society shall consist of a president, two vice-presidents, two
secretaries, a treasurer, twelve counsellors, (viz.: six from the city and county of
Philadelphia, and one from each of the following counties, viz.: Bucks, Montgomery,
Lancaster, York, Northampton and Delaware) an electing committee of twelve, and
a board of education of thirteen, and an acting committee of six members; all of whom,
except the last named committee, shall be chosen annually by ballot, on the last Fifth-
day called Thursday, in the month called December.

. . . .

V. The business of the counsellors shall be to explain the laws and constitutions of the states, which relate to the emancipation of slaves, and to urge their claims to freedom, when legal, before such persons or courts as are authorised to decide upon them.

. . . .

VII. The board of education shall superintend the schools established by the society, and manage the funds appropriated to their support. .

. . . .

XI. No person holding a slave shall be admitted a member of this Society.

XII. No law or regulation shall contradict any part of the constitution of the Society, nor shall any law or alteration in the constitution be made, without being proposed at a previous meeting. All questions shall be decided, where there is a division, by a majority of votes. In those cases where the Society is equally divided, the presiding officer shall have a casting vote."

Text—Needles: *An Historical Memoir of the Pennsylvania Society, for Promoting the Abolition of Slavery*, pp. 113-115.

VIII. *THE ADDRESS OF THE DELEGATES FROM THE SEVERAL SOCIETIES, FORMED IN THE DIFFERENT PARTS OF THE UNITED STATES, FOR PROMOTING THE ABOLITION OF SLAVERY, IN CONVENTION ASSEMBLED AT PHILADELPHIA, ON THE FIRST DAY OF JANUARY, 1794*

As probably the first address on the subject of slavery ever put forth by a public body in the United States, this document, drafted by a committee of which Dr. Benjamin Rush was chairman, represents the propaganda carried forward for more than a quarter century.

"FRIENDS AND FELLOW CITIZENS—United to you by the ties of citizenship, and partakers with you of the blessings of a free government, we take the liberty of addressing you upon a subject, highly interesting to the credit and prosperity of the United States.

It is the glory of our country to have originated a system of opposition to the commerce in that part of our fellow creatures who compose the nations of Africa.

Much has been done by the citizens of some of the States to abolish this disgraceful traffic, and to improve the condition of those unhappy people, whom the ignorance or the avarice of our ancestors had bequeathed to us as slaves; but the evil still continues, and our country is yet disgraced by laws and practices, which level the creature man with a part of the brute creation.

Many reasons concur in persuading us to abolish domestic slavery in our country.

It is inconsistent with the safety of the liberties of the United States.

Freedom and slavery cannot long exist together. An unlimited power over the time, labour, and posterity of our fellow-creatures, necessarily unfits men for discharging the public and private duties of citizens of a republic.

It is inconsistent with sound policy, in exposing the States which permit it, to all those evils which insurrections and the most resentful war have introduced into one of the richest islands in the West Indies.

It is unfriendly to the present exertions of the inhabitants of Europe, in favour of liberty. What people will advocate freedom, with a zeal proportioned to its blessings, while they view the purest republic in the world tolerating in its bosom a body of slaves?

In vain has the tyranny of kings been rejected, while we permit in our country a domestic despotism, which involves, in its nature, most of the vices and miseries that we have endeavoured to avoid.

It is degrading to our rank as men in the scale of being. Let us use our reason and social affections for the purposes for which they were given, or cease to boast a preeminence over animals, that are unpolluted with our crimes.

But higher motives to justice and humanity towards our fellow-creatures remain yet to be mentioned.

Domestic slavery is repugnant to the principles of Christianity. It prostrates every benevolent and just principle of action in the human heart. It is rebellion against the authority of a common FATHER. It is a practical denial of the extent and efficacy of the death of a common SAVIOUR. It is an usurpation of the prerogative of the GREAT SOVEREIGN of the Universe, who has solemnly claimed an exclusive property in the souls of men.

But if this view of the enormity of the evil of domestic slavery should not affect us, there is one consideration more which ought to alarm and impress us, especially at the present juncture.

It is a violation of a divine precept of universal justice, which has, in no instance, escaped with impunity.

The crimes of nations, as well as of individuals, are often designated in their punishments; and we conceive it to be no forced construction, of some of the calamities which now distress or impend our country, to believe that they are the measure of evils which we have meted to others.

The ravages committed upon many of our fellow-citizens by the Indians, and the depredations upon the liberty and commerce of others of the citizens of the United States, both unite in proclaiming to us, in the most forcible language, 'to loose the bands of wickedness, to break every yoke, to undo the heavy burthens, and to let the oppressed go free.'

We shall conclude this address by recommending to you,

First. To refrain immediately from that species of rapine and murder which has improperly been softened with the name of the African trade. It is Indian cruelty, and Algerine piracy, in another form.

Secondly. To form Societies in every State, for the purpose of promoting the abolition of the slave-trade, of domestic slavery, the relief of persons unlawfully held in bondage, and for the improvement of the condition of Africans, and their descendants amongst us.

The Societies which we represent, have beheld with triumph, the success of their exertions, in many instances, in favour of their African brethren; and, in full reliance upon the continuance of divine support and direction, they humbly hope, their labours will never cease, while there exists a single slave in the United States."

Text—Needles: *An Historical Memoir of the Pennsylvania Society, for Promoting the Abolition of Slavery*, pp. 50-52.

IX. *THE GENESIS OF THE AMERICAN COLONIZATION SOCIETY*

"To all who are desirous to promote the kingdom of Christ on earth, in the salvation of sinners, the following narrative and proposal are offered, to excite and solicit their charity and prayers.

There are two colored men, members of the First Congregational Church in Newport, on Rhode Island, named *Bristol Yamma*, and *John Quamine*, who were hopefully converted some years ago, and have from that time sustained a good character as Christians, and have made good proficiency in Christian knowledge. . .

These persons, thus acquainted with Christianity, and apparently devoted to the service of Christ, are about thirty years old; have good natural abilities; are apt, steady, and judicious, and speak their native language—the language of a numerous, potent nation in Guinea, to which they both belong. They are not only *willing*, but *very desirous* to quit all worldly prospects, and risk their lives in attempting to open a door for the propagation of Christianity among their poor, ignorant, perishing heathen brethren.

The concurrence of all these things has led to set on foot a proposal to send them to Africa, to preach the gospel there, if, upon trial, they shall appear in any good measure qualified for this business. In order to this, they must be put to school, and taught to read and write better than they now can, and be instructed more fully in divinity, &c. And if, upon trial, they appear to make good proficiency, and shall be thought by competent judges to be fit for such a mission, it is not doubted that money may be procured sufficient to carry the design into execution.

.   .   .   .

And it is humbly proposed to those who are convinced of the iniquity of the *slave trade*, and are sensible of the great inhumanity and cruelty of enslaving so many thousands of our fellow-men every year, with all the dreadful and horrid attendants, and are ready to bear testimony against it in all proper ways, and do their utmost to put a stop to it, whether they have not a good opportunity of doing this, by cheerfully contributing according to their ability, to promote the mission proposed; and whether this is not the best compensation we are able to make the poor Africans, for the injuries they are constantly receiving by this unrighteous practice and all its attendants.

.   .   .   .

EZRA STILES,
SAMUEL HOPKINS.

Newport, Rhode Island, August 31, 1773."

Text—*The Works of Samuel Hopkins, D.D.*, Vol. I, pp. 131-132.

Mr. Hopkins thus wrote to Moses Brown:

"April 29, 1784. There has been a proposal on foot for some time, that a number of blacks should return to Africa, and settle there; that a number, who have been under the most serious impressions of religion, should lead the way, and when they are fixed there, should improve all opportunities to teach the Africans the doctrines and duties of Christianity, both by precept and example. In order to this, a number who shall be thought best qualified for this business, must *first* be sent to Africa, to treat with some of the nations there, and request of them lands, proper and sufficient for them and as many as shall go with them to settle upon. It is presumed land would be freely given. And it is thought, that such a settlement would not only be for the benefit of those who shall return to their native country, but it would be the most likely and powerful means of putting a stop to the slave trade, as well as of increasing Christian knowledge among those heathens. . . . I communicate these hints of a plan to you, that I may know how far you approve of it, and whether you think it practicable. And if you do, whether you, in conjunction with some of your able friends, would advance any thing considerable to promote such a design. It has been said by some, and doubtless by many, 'There are a number of men who have large estates, much of which they have gotten by the slave trade, who now profess to be convinced they have done wrong in having any hand in that trade, and manifest great zeal against it, and are great enemies of slavery. Let them show their repentance by their *works*; by giving up a considerable part of their estates to liberate the Africans and promote their good. Let them do this, and we will believe them sincere and honest men, but not before,' "

Text—*The Works of Samuel Hopkins, D.D.*, Vol. I. p. 139.

After his discourse at Providence, May 17, 1793, he outlines more clearly his project.

"There are a considerable number of free blacks in New England, and in other parts of the United States, some of whom are industrious, and of a good moral character; and some of them appear to be truly pious, who are desirous to remove to Africa, and settle there. They who are religious would be glad to unite as Christian brethren, and move to Africa, having one instructor, or more, and cultivate the land which they may obtain there, and maintain the practice of Christianity in the sight of their now heathen brethren; and endeavor to instruct and civilize them, and spread the knowledge of the gospel among them.

In order to effect this in the best manner, a vessel must be procured, and proper sailors provided, to go to Africa, with a number of persons, both white and black, perhaps, who shall be thought equal to the business, to search that country, and find a place where a settlement may be made with the consent of the inhabitants there; the land being given by them, or purchased of them, and so as best to answer the ends proposed. If such a place can be found, as no doubt it may, they must return, and the blacks must be collected who are willing to go and settle there, and form themselves into a civil society, by agreeing in a constitution and a code of laws, by which they will be regulated.

And they must be furnished with every thing necessary and proper to transport and settle them there, in a safe and comfortable manner; with shipping and provisions, till they can procure them in Africa, by their own labor, and with instruments and utensils necessary to cultivate the land, build houses, &c.; and have all the protection and assistance they will need, while settling, and when settled there. And, if necessary, a number of white people must go with them; one or more, to superintend their affairs, and others to survey and lay out their lands, build mills and houses, &c. But these must not think of settling there for life; and the blacks are to be left to themselves, when they shall be able to conduct their own affairs, and need no further assistance, and be left a free, independent people.

This appears to be the best and only plan to put the blacks among us in the most agreeable situation for themselves, and to render them most useful to their brethren in Africa, by civilizing them, and teaching them how to cultivate their lands, and spreading the knowledge of the Christian religion among them. The whites are so habituated, by education and custom, to look upon and treat the blacks as an inferior class of beings, and they are sunk so low by their situation, and the treatment they receive from us, that they never can be raised to an equality with the whites, and enjoy all the liberty and rights to which they have a just claim; or have all the encouragements and motives to make improvements of every kind, which are desirable. But, if they were removed to Africa, this evil would cease, and they would enjoy all desirable equality and liberty, and live in a climate which is peculiarly suited to their constitution. And they would be under advantages to set an example of industry, and the best manner of cultivating the land, of civil life, of morality and religion, which would tend to gain the attention of the inhabitants of that country, and persuade them to receive instruction, and embrace the gospel.

. . . This will gradually draw off all the blacks in New England, and even in the Middle and Southern States, as fast as they can be set free, by which this nation will be delivered from that which, in the view of every discerning man, is a great calamity, and inconsistent with the good of society; and is now really a great injury to most of the white inhabitants, especially in the Southern States.

. . . .

That such a plan is practicable, is evident from the experiment which has lately been made in forming a settlement of blacks at Sierra Leone. Above a thousand blacks were transported from Nova Scotia to that place last year; who, by the assistance of a small number of whites, and supplies from England, have formed a town and plantation, which, by the latest accounts, is now in a flourishing condition. . . .

Are there not, then, motives sufficient to induce the Legislature of this nation to enter upon and prosecute this design? to form a plan, and execute it, as wisdom shall direct? And is there not reason to think that it would meet with general approbation? But if this cannot be, may not this be effected by the societies in these States, who are formed with a design to promote the best good of the Africans? . . ."

Text—*The Works of Samuel Hopkins, D.D.,* Vol. I, pp. 145-146.

X. *METHODIST DELIVERANCES*

Conference of 1780

Quest. 16. *Ought not this Conference to require those travelling preachers who hold slaves to give promises to set them free?*

Yes.

Quest. 17. *Does this Conference acknowledge that slavery is contrary to the laws of God, man, and nature, and hurtful to society; contrary to the dictates of conscience and*

pure religion, and doing that which we would not others should do to us and ours? Do we pass our disapprobation on all our friends who keep slaves, and advise their freedom?
Yes.

Conference of 1783

Quest. 10. *What shall be done with our local preachers who hold slaves contrary to the laws which authorize their freedom in any of the United States?*

We will try them another year. In the mean time let every assistant deal faithfully and plainly with every one, and report to the next Conference. It may then be necessary to suspend them.

Conference of 1784

Quest. 12. *What shall we do with our friends that will buy and sell slaves?*

If they buy with no other design than to hold them as slaves, and have been previously warned, they shall be expelled, and permitted to sell on no consideration.

Quest. 13. *What shall we do with our local preachers who will not emancipate their slaves in the states where the laws admit it?*

Try those in Virginia another year, and suspend the preachers in Maryland, Delaware, Pennsylvania, and New-Jersey.

Text—*Minutes of the Annual Conferences of the Methodist Episcopal Church,* Vol. I, pp. 12, 18, and 20

The Christmas Conference of 1784.

See Page 323f.

Conferences of 1796 and 1800

Sections 2 and 3 were incorporated in 1800.

"Quest. What regulations shall be made for the extirpation of the crying evil of African slavery?

Ans. 1. We declare that we are more than ever convinced of the great evil of African slavery, which still exists in these United States, and do most earnestly recommend to the Yearly Conferences, Quarterly Meetings, and to those who have the oversight of Districts and Circuits, to be exceedingly cautious what persons they admit to official stations in our church; and in the case of future admission to official stations, to require such security of those who hold slaves, for the emancipation of them, immediately, or gradually, as the laws of the States respectively, and the circumstances of the case will admit; and we do fully authorize all the Yearly Conferences to make whatever regulations they judge proper, in the present case, respecting the admission of persons to official stations in our church.

2. When any travelling preacher becomes an owner of a slave, or slaves, *by any means,* he shall forfeit his ministerial character in our church, unless he executes, if it be practicable, a legal emancipation of such slaves, conformably to the laws of the State in which he lives.

3. No slaveholder shall be received into society till the preacher who has the oversight of the Circuit, has spoken to him freely and faithfully upon the subject of slavery.

4. Every member of the society who sells a slave, shall immediately, after full proof, be excluded from the society; and if any member of our society purchases a slave, the ensuing Quarterly Meeting shall determine on the number of years in which the slave so purchased would work out the price of his purchase. And the person so purchasing, shall immediately after such determination, execute a legal instrument for

the manumission of such slave at the expiration of the term determined by the Quarterly Meeting. And in default of his executing such instrument of manumission, or on his refusal to submit his case to the judgment of the Quarterly Meeting, such member shall be excluded from the society. Provided also, that in the case of a female slave, it shall be inserted in the aforesaid instrument of manumission, that all her children who shall be born during the years of her servitude, shall be free at the following times, namely:— every female child at the age of *twenty-one*, and every male child at the age of *twenty-five*. Nevertheless, if the member of our society, executing the said instrument of manumission, judge it proper, he may fix the times of manumission of the female slaves before-mentioned, at an earlier age than that which is prescribed above.

5. The preachers and other members of our society, are requested to consider the subject of negro slavery with *deep attention*; and that they *impart to the General Conference*, through the medium of the yearly conferences, *or otherwise, any important thoughts upon the subject*, that the Conference may have full light in order to take further steps toward the eradicating this ENORMOUS EVIL from that part of the Church of God to which they are connnected.

6. The Annual Conferences are directed to draw up addresses for the gradual emancipation of the slaves, to the legislatures of those States in which no general laws have been passed for that purpose. These addresses shall urge, in the most respectful, but pointed manner, the necessity of a law for the gradual emancipation of the slaves; proper committees shall be appointed by the Annual Conferences, out of the most respectable of our friends, for the conducting of the business; and the presiding elders, elders, deacons, and travelling preachers, shall procure as many proper signatures as possible to the addresses, and give all the assistance in their power, in every respect to aid the committees, and to further this blessed undertaking. LET THIS BE CONTINUED FROM YEAR TO YEAR TILL THE DESIRED END BE ACCOMPLISHED."

Text—Matlack: *The History of American Slavery and Methodism* . . . , pp. 19-20.

XI. *BAPTIST DELIVERANCES*

General Committee of Baptists, Richmond, Virginia, August, 1789

"*Resolved*, That slavery is a violent deprivation of the rights of nature and inconsistent with a republican government, and therefore recommend it to our brethren to make use of every legal measure to extirpate this horrid evil from the land; and pray Almighty God that our honorable Legislature may have it in their power to proclaim the great Jubilee, consistent with the principles of good policy."

Text—Semple: *A History of the Rise and Progress of the Baptists in Virginia*, p. 105.

Philadelphia Baptist Association, October, 1789

"Agreeably to a recommendation in the letter from the church at Baltimore, this Association declare their high approbation of the several societies formed in the United States and Europe, for the gradual abolition of the slavery of the Africans, and for guarding against their being detained or sent off as slaves, after having obtained their liberty; and do hereby recommend to the churches we represent to form similar societies, to become members thereof, and exert themselves to obtain this important object."

Text—Gillette: *Minutes of the Philadelphia Baptist Association, from* A.D. *1707, to* A.D. *1807*, p. 247.

XII. *PRESBYTERIAN DELIVERANCES*

The Synod of New York and Philadelphia, May 28, 1787

The Synod taking into consideration the overture concerning slavery, transmitted by the committee of overtures last Saturday, came to the following judgment:

The Synod of New York and Philadelphia do highly approve of the general principles in favour of universal liberty, that prevail in America, and the interest which many of the states have taken in promoting the abolition of slavery; yet, inasmuch as men introduced from a servile state to a participation of all the privileges of civil society, without a proper education, and without previous habits of industry, may be, in many respects, dangerous to the community, therefore they earnestly recommend it to all the members belonging to their communion, to give those persons who are at present held in servitude, such good education as to prepare them for the better enjoyment of freedom; and they moreover recommend that masters, wherever they find servants disposed to make a just improvement of the privilege, would give them a *peculium*, or grant them sufficient time and sufficient means of procuring their own liberty at a moderate rate, that thereby, they may be brought into society with those habits of industry that may render them useful citizens; and, finally, they recommend it to all their people to use the most prudent measures, consistent with the interest and the state of civil society, in the counties where they live, to procure eventually the final abolition of slavery in America.

Text—Engles: *Records of the Presbyterian Church*, p. 540.

Resolution of Presbyterian General Assembly, 1818
(adopted unanimously)

The General Assembly of the Presbyterian Church, having taken into consideration the subject of slavery, think proper to make known their sentiments upon it to the churches and people under their care. We consider the voluntary enslaving of one part of the human race by another, as a gross violation of the most precious and sacred rights of human nature; as utterly inconsistent with the law of God, which requires us to love our neighbor as ourselves; and as totally irreconcilable with the spirit and principles of the Gospel of Christ, which enjoins that 'all things whatsoever ye would that men should do to you, do ye even so to them.' Slavery creates a paradox in the moral system; it exhibits rational, accountable, and immortal beings in such circumstances as scarcely to leave them the power of moral action. It exhibits them as dependent upon the will of others, whether they shall receive religious instruction; whether they shall know and worship the true God; whether they shall enjoy the ordinances of the Gospel; whether they shall perform the duties and cherish the endearments of husbands and wives, parents and children, neighbors and friends; whether they shall preserve their chastity and purity, or regard the dictates of justice and humanity. Such are some of the consequences of slavery-consequences not imaginary-but which connect themselves with its very existence. . .

We rejoice that the Church to which we belong commenced as early as any other in this country the good work of endeavoring to put an end to slavery, and that in the same work many of its preachers have ever since been, and now are, among the most active, vigorous and efficient laborers. We do indeed tenderly sympathize with those portions of our Church and our country where the evil of slavery has been entailed upon them; where a *great* and the *most virtuous part* of the community abhor slavery, and wish

its extermination as sincerely as any others; but where the number of slaves, their ignorance, and their vicious habits generally, render an immediate and universal emancipation inconsistent alike with the safety and happiness of the master and the slave.
With those who are thus circumstanced, we repeat, we tenderly sympathize. At the
same time, we earnestly exhort them to continue, and if possible, to increase their exertions to effect a total abolition of slavery.   We exhort them to suffer no greater delay
to take place in this most interesting concern than a regard to the public welfare truly
and indispensably demands. . . .

Having thus expressed our views of slavery, and of the duty indispensably incumbent on all christians to labor for its complete extinction, . . .

1. We recommend to all our people to patronize and encourage the society lately
formed for colonizing in Africa, the land of their ancestors, the free people of color in
our country. We hope that much good may result from the plans and efforts of this
society. . . .

2. We recommend to all the members of our religious denomination, not only to
permit, but to facilitate and encourage the instruction of their slaves in the principles
and duties of the christian religion, by granting them the liberty to attend upon the
preaching of the Gospel, when they have the opportunity; by favoring the instruction
of them in Sabbath schools, wherever those schools can be formed, and by giving them
all proper advantages for acquiring the knowledge of their duty both to God and·
man. . . .

3. We enjoin it on all church sessions and Presbyteries under the care of this
Assembly to discountenance, and as far as possible, to prevent all cruelty, of whatever kind, in the treatment of slaves; especially the cruelty of separating husband and
wife, parents and children, and that which consists in selling slaves to those who will
either themselves deprive these unhappy people of the blessings of the Gospel, or who
will transport them to places where the Gospel is not proclaimed, or where it is forbidden to slaves to attend upon its institutions. The manifest violation or disregard
of the injunction here given, in its true spirit and intention, ought to be considered
as just ground for the discipline and censures of the church.   And if it shall ever happen that a christian professor in our communion shall sell a slave, who is also in communion and good standing in our Church, contrary to his or her will and inclination, it
ought immediately to claim the particular attention of the proper church judicatories;
and unless there be such peculiar circumstances attending the case as can but seldom
happen, it ought to be followed without delay by a suspension of the offender from all
the privileges of the church, till he repent and make all the reparation in his power to
the injured party.

Text—Robinson: *The Testimony and Practice of the Presbyterian Church
in Reference to American Slavery*, pp. 23-29.

Resolution of Presbyerian General Assembly, 1845
(adopted by vote of 168 to 113)

The question which is now unhappily agitating and dividing other branches of
the Church, and which is pressed upon the attention of the Assembly by one of the
three classes of the memorialists just named, is, *whether the holding of slaves is, under all
circumstances, a heinous sin, calling for the discipline of the Church.*

The Church of Christ is a spiritual body, whose jurisdiction extends only to the
religious faith and moral conduct of her members.   She cannot legislate where Christ

has not legislated, nor make terms of membership which he has not made. The question, therefore, which this Assembly is called upon to decide is this: Do the Scriptures teach that the holding of slaves, without regard to circumstances, is a sin, the renunciation of which should be made the condition of membership in the Church of Christ?

It is impossible to answer this question in the affirmative without contradicting some of the plainest declarations of the word of God. That slavery existed in the days of Christ and his Apostles is an admitted fact. That they did not denounce the relation itself as sinful, as inconsistent with christianity; that slave-holders were admitted to membership in the Churches organized by the Apostles, that whilst they were required to treat their slaves with kindness and as rational, accountable, immortal beings, and, if christians, as brethren in the Lord, they were not commanded to emancipate them; that slaves were required to be 'obedient to their masters according to the flesh, with fear and trembling, with singleness of heart as unto Christ,' are facts which meet the eye of every reader of the New Testament. This Assembly cannot, therefore denounce the holding of slaves as necessarily a heinous and scandalous sin, calculated to bring upon the Church the curse of God, without charging the Apostles of Christ with conniving at such sin, introducing into the Church such sinners, and thus bringing upon them the curse of the Almighty.

In so saying, however, the Assembly are not to be understood as denying that there is evil connected with slavery. Much less do they approve those defective and oppressive laws by which, in some of the States, it is regulated. Nor would they by any means countenance the traffic in slaves for the sake of gain; the separation of husbands and wives, parents and children, for the sake of 'filthy lucre,' or for the convenience of the master; or cruel treatment of slaves in any respect. . .

Nor is this assembly to be understood as countenancing the idea that masters may regard their servants as *mere property*, and not as human beings, rational, accountable, immortal. The Scriptures prescribe not only the duties of servants, but also of masters, warning the latter to discharge those duties 'knowing that their Master is in heaven, neither is their respect of persons with him.'

. . . .

As to the extent of the evils involved in slavery, and the best methods of removing them, various opinions prevail, and neither the Scriptures nor our constitution authorize this body to prescribe any particular course to be pursued by the churches, under our care. . .

In view of the above stated principles and facts,

Resolved, 1st, That the General Assembly of the Presbyterian Church in the United States was originally organized, and has since continued to be the bond of union in the Church, upon the conceded principle that the existence of domestic slavery, under the circumstances in which it is found in the Southern portion of the country, is no bar to christian communion.

2d, That the petitions that ask the Assembly to make *the holding of slaves in itself* a matter of discipline, do virtually require this judicatory to dissolve itself, and abandon the organization under which, by the Divine blessings, it has so long prospered. The tendency is evidently to separate the northern from the southern portion of the Church, a result which every good citizen must deplore as tending to the dissolution of the union of our beloved country, and which every enlightened christian will oppose as bringing about a ruinous and unnecessary schism between brethren who maintain a common faith.

Text—Robinson: *Testimony and Practice of the Presbyterian Church in Reference to American Slavery*, pp. 35-39.

Resolution of the General Assembly New School, 1850

Resolved,   1st, That we deeply deplore the working of the whole system of American slavery, interwoven as it is with the policy of the slave-holding States, and with the social and domestic life of their citizens; and regarding it, as in former years we have explicitly stated, to be fraught with serious injury to the civil, political, intellectual, and moral interests of society, and leading to much sin, we declare it to be in all cases, where the laws of the State, the obligations of guardianship, and the demands of humanity, do not render it *unavoidable,* an offence in the proper sense of that term, as used in our Book of Discipline, chap. 1, sec. 3.

2. *Resolved,* That while we regard all cases in which the holding of slaves is sinful, a matter for the exercise of such discipline as falls within the proper jurisdiction of the inferior church courts or sessions; yet, as our constitution declares, 'the exercise of discipline in such a manner as to edify the Church, requires not only   much of the spirit of piety, but also much prudence and discretion,' and, therefore, 'it becomes the rulers of the Church to take into view all the circumstances which may give a different character to conduct, and render it more or less offensive, and which may of course require a very different mode of proceeding in similar cases, at different times, for the attainment of the same end.'   Book of Dis. chap. 1, sec. 5.

. . . .

In this spirit we repeat our former testimonies; and while on the one hand we beseech the churches more immediately brought into contact with the evils of slavery, to watch and guard most carefully against the admission and retention in their fellowship of unworthy members, if there are any, and to endeavor to preserve and promote their purity; on the other hand, we earnestly entreat that those who feel afflicted by the dreadful and atrocious evils of slavery, existing in the States where human beings are by law declared and held as chattels, and bought and sold as merchandise, would carefully guard against being embittered towards such of their brethren as may be surrounded, embarrassed, and often frustrated in their good desires and designs, by a stern force of law they cannot control; and that they would extend to them their prayers and sympathies, and fraternal co-operation for the prosperity of the Church, and the best interests of humanity.

Text—Robinson: *The Testimony and Practice of the Presbyterian Church in Reference to American Slavery*, pp. 226-229.

XIII. *THE SLAVERY ISSUE AMONG THE INDIANA QUAKERS*

A Declaration

" 'We feel ourselves called upon, by the circumstances in which we are placed, in justice to ourselves, to the Society of Friends throughout the world, to the cause of truth and righteousness in the earth, and by a just regard to the feelings of the community at large, to make a public declaration of the causes by which we have been driven into our present position. . . .

But after much good had been effected, through the agency of these institutions (Anti-Slavery Societies), a combination of adverse circumstances conspired to change the current of feeling. The hand of cruel avarice became afresh nerved to its unholy grasp by the prospect of extensive gain, through the facilities offered by the invention of the cotton gin. This prospect and desire of gain was not confined to those immediately engaged in holding slaves, but extended with lamentable effect to many of those in the Free states inclined to enter into mercantile or manufacturing operations. This class included a number of the most wealthy and influential in the Society of Friends, in the middle and eastern states, and the natural and consequent intercourse between them and the slave-holders of the south, had a direct tendency to leaven them into the same lordly, pompous, and intolerant feeling. This circumstance, taken in connection with that of the formation and active operation of the Colonization Society, instituted mainly by slave-holders, and purposely for the removal of the 'free people of color' from the country, and in order that none of the despised class might enjoy liberty among us, almost sealed the fate of genuine Anti-Slavery feeling in the Society. Those associations, instituted for the purpose of creating this feeling, were suffered to go down, and the energies and resources of the people prostituted to that of sending out of the country those who already enjoyed personal freedom, instead of their being applied to the alleviation of the distresses of the bondman. In short, the cold hand of apathy, and the still more withering influence of an inveterate prejudice, spread almost a universal gloom around the cause of African freedom. There were still, however, those in different parts of the country who bore a decided testimony against the spirit of the times. In 1832, a resuscitation of the Anti-Slavery cause commenced in one of the eastern states. . .

Here, it is worthy of remark, that ever since the issuing of the advices repudiating the Colonization scheme, there were some of our prominent members open advocates of that institution, who appeared to have been fired with indignation at the expression of such sentiments, evidently entertaining a settled purpose to prostrate the Anti-Slavery cause and its advocates in the Society, if ever a favorable opportunity should present. And now as this cause progressed, the main body of its enemies who had heretofore entertained but little apprehension of its success, and who had remained apparently in almost a state of indifference in regard to the subject, through the alarm taken and communicated by those of kindred spirits in the east, and by discovering the project so gratifying to their prejudices (the Colonization scheme,) to sink in public estimation, in consequence of the Anti-Slavery movement, together through the instrumentality of the individuals above referred to, suddenly became aroused to action, and inspired with a determination to arrest its onward course. Hence, no time was lost at this favorable moment, in taking occasion from the circumstances in which we were placed by the Advices referred to, to cry out 'insubordination,' 'want of proper subordination to the authority of the church,' etc. Advice in regard to joining with others, from year to year grew more and more positive, gradually, however, becoming divested of the mask under which it was at first covered, and approximating as time advanced, and as the Anti-Slavery cause prospered, to the full development of that Pro-Slavery spirit which has so sorrowfully found its way into the bosom of Society, and which the following exhibition of facts and circumstances will serve more fully to illustrate. . .

In 1841, the opposition becoming more emboldened, it was again repeated, and confined to A. S. Societies altogether; and even the use of our meeting-houses was refused to such societies for their accommodation in the transaction of their business.

At our last Yearly Meeting, in addition to this, not only those who had joined in these associations, but also such as had not, but yet could not for conscience' sake denounce others therefor, were by special act of the Meeting, deprived of any privilege in regard to the transaction of any of its important business, and subordinate meetings were advised to pursue the same course of conduct down to the most remote and inferior branches; and that ostensibly on account of their being opposed to the advice and travail of the body; while at the same time, some who were the most forward in endeavoring to enforce submission to *this* advice, were of those who were actively engaged in mixed associations of a different character, and in supporting, both directly and indirectly, the Colonization scheme, which, as we have already shown, the Yearly Meeting not only advised against, but declared to be unjust and oppressive. . .

Being aware, upon reflection, that the consumption of the proceeds of slavery was the very thing which had reduced this people to a situation, demanding the appointment of such a committee, many Friends, members of this committee, deemed it important, in order to carry out its object, as well as the spirit and design of the Discipline above cited, that Friends should endeavor to avoid the use of such articles. Accordingly, one branch of the committee forwarded a report to its general meeting, treating the subject at some length, showing the impropriety and inconsistency of Friends sustaining a market for such productions. But when it was read in that body, it was spurned, it was rejected with manifest bitterness and contempt, and the subject prohibited being introduced again into the committee upon the allegation that it was foreign to its object. Supposing that the subject demanded a serious examination, at least, in some departments of Society, one of the Quarterly meetings, in its reports, forwarded a proposition or request to our last Yearly Meeting, to take into consideration, whether the use of such products was not a support to Slavery and the Slave Trade, and whether they were not essentially prize goods: but when it came before that body, it refused to take any action whatever upon the subject.

Near the commencement of our last Yearly Meeting, a rule was adopted, that no person who stood in opposition to the advice and travail of the body, should be appointed on any important business in the meeting; but it was evidently intended to be applied exclusively to those favorable to the Anti-Slavery enterprise.

Thus it is evident, so far as an extensive tissue of facts and circumstances can establish, and so far as the fruit of a tree can manifest its character, that the influence by which the Yearly Meeting is now governed is Pro-Slavery, and that unsoundness lies at the bottom of the opposition with which we have been assailed. Various, however, are the grounds of this opposition with different individuals, and much too complicated to be fully described in our limits. But that which we doubt not is occupied by the greater number, is plainly alluded to in the following extract from the Epistle of Advice of 1841: 'Thus maintaining our peaceable and Christian principles in unbroken harmony, we shall, we believe, be enabled, as way opens, more availingly to plead the cause of this much-injured race of our fellow-men, *and retain the place and influence which, as a Society, we have heretofore had with the rulers of the land.*'

The rulers of our land being such as have been chosen by a Pro-Slavery community, are consequently opposed to the Anti-Slavery cause. They hate it—they despise it. Hence it is rightly judged impossible to retain a place and influence with such men, and hold any connection therewith—it is, indeed, too unpopular.

In accordance with the sweeping system of virtual disownment, to which we have referred, eight members of the Meeting for Sufferings were reported to the Yearly

Meeting as unfit for the station, under the vague charge of disqualification. And the committee continued, to make further report, if other obnoxious members should be found. It should constantly be borne in mind that the professed cause of the adoption of these proscriptive measures, was that of some Friends going contrary to the advice and travail of the body; and surely a disregard of the general code of discipline should not be considered of less importance. . .

Ministers and Elders who do not abandon the Anti-Slavery societies, or turn their hand against such as do not, or, in other words, unite with the 'advice and travail of the body,' are by special direction, to be removed from their stations. Agreeably to the course adopted and most strenuously adhered to by the Yearly Meeting, these committees have endeavored to prohibit any examination of the subject, except on their own side. They have invariably manifested a disposition in meetings, not to hear the reasons we would advance in our behalf. In short, like the poor victims for which we plead, we are not permitted to plead for ourselves. . .

' . . . is it better for us to suffer ourselves to be separately disowned, and scattered abroad, to be deprived of the comforts, consolations and preserving influence of church fellowship, or to avail ourselves of our indisputable right to form a religious society in which we can enjoy these privileges? The answer to this inquiry, we apprehend, must be obvious to every sober and reflecting person who has any confidence in the usefulness of religious society. Consequently we have deemed it our duty to adopt the latter alternative. . .

We wish not to be understood as denying that there is any Anti-Slavery feeling among the members of the Yearly Meeting, from which we have now seceded; on the contrary we doubt not but that many of them are desirous to promote immediate and unconditional emancipation, and are only restrained from active labors in the cause by the proscriptive measures of the 'Body' so called; measures which have been brought about chiefly by the agency of those individuals who, we believe, are too anxious to 'retain a place and influence with the rulers of the land.' Our opposers have argued for, and some who have appeared to be strong Abolitionists, seem to have adopted, the doctrine, that it is the duty of members to yield obedience to the authority of the Yearly Meeting even when its requisitions are contrary to their own convictions of what is right. Such we conceive to be in a very precarious situation, and in danger of quenching the spirit, in order to obey the body. . . .

With entire consciousness of our innocence and the justice of our cause, we. in humble confidence in the protection of the God of the oppressed, submit that cause to Him who judgeth righteously."

Text—Edgerton: *A History of the Separation in Indiana Yearly Meeting of Friends*, pp. 74-92.

XIV. *THE BAPTIST DIVISION ON THE ISSUE OF SLAVERY*

See page 589f.

XV. *THE METHODIST DIVISION OCCASIONED BY THE ISSUE OF SLAVERY*

See page 594f.

XVI. *THE MISSIONARY ON THE PLANTATION*

"Memory carries me back to the time when, early in the morning, through heat and cold, sunshine and rain, I used to see a plantation missionary set out in his buggy and go to preach the gospel to the slaves on the surrounding plantations; and my joy would be full as I would be invited to take my seat in the buggy and go with the missionary on his rounds. . . .

When we reached the plantation gate, the cry would be heard on all sides, 'Preacher's comin'! preacher's comin'!' and from every side we could see the little negroes gathering. At least twenty of the grinning, ebony-faced little creatures would spring forward to open the gate for us and to escort the preacher's buggy up to the 'catechising place.' Others of the larger children would hurry to deposit the little brothers and sisters they were nursing with the old 'maumas' at the hospital; while others, again, impressed with a sense of the decorum of the occasion, would go through the ceremony of hand and face washing ere presenting themselves before the preacher.

At last silence and perfect order reigned. A line would be drawn under the shade of some spreading old oak and the catechising begin. The class was rarely under fifty in number, ranging in age from the toddling wee thing of three and four to boys and girls of fourteen and fifteen, clad generally in the most *airy* of garments. I cannot now recall one instance of bad conduct, nor do I remember once having seen one of the class deprived of the handshake from the preacher, an honor most highly prized by them all, and never denied except in cases of extreme naughtiness.

The preacher would then carry them through Capers's Catechism, the Creed, and Commandments, give them a little—very little talk, then sing a simple hymn, and afterward, with bared head, kneel upon the ground, and, with all these slave children clustering around him, together they would repeat: 'Our Father who art in heaven.'

Since that time I have seen God worshiped in many ways. I have knelt with the multitude in the grandeur of a great cathedral, where the 'dim religious Light' came softly stealing through the pictured glass and the rich-toned organ melted the heart to thoughts of prayer. I have listened to the gospel in the midst of a crowd of gray-uniformed men, whose next orders might be a summons to death. I have heard the words of truth proclaimed on the top of a lofty mountain, where we seemed 'to see God in every cloud, and hear him in the wind.' I have mingled with the throng around the holy altar in the midst of a widespreading forest, where every breeze that swept by seemed to say: 'The groves were God's first temples.' I have sat in the rustic church amid the humble country worshipers, sunburned with toil and hardened with care, when I have said to myself: 'God is here worshiped in spirit and in truth.' Yet now as I look back, it seems to me I have never been in circumstances so pleasing to God and his holy angels, or seen worship so welcome to them as when I saw that man of God teaching the little negro slaves to say: 'Our Father.'

The catechism lesson being over, the preacher would inquire for the sick. If any were very sick or too old to leave their cabins, he would be taken to them to minister of spiritual things, and sometimes, though, little child as I was, I knew it not, I was very near the gate of heaven. Often I have seen the missionary's face radiant with the light of the throne as he came from these ministrations beside the bed of the dying Christian slave.

As we were leaving a pleasing scene would occur, pleasing to me at least, for then the old 'maumas' would come from their cabins with two or three eggs apiece, or the children with old birds' nests, sassafras roots, blackberries, and other simple treasures, to show their love of the missionary by these humble offerings to his little daughter. These scenes would recur at one plantation and another until the whole of a long summer morning would be exhausted, and so would pass the week away.

When Sunday morning would come, the grown negroes, who were at work in the fields during the week days, would assemble for preaching in neat, clean garments. Sometimes this would be in an upper room over the ginhouse, nicely arranged with pulpit and benches, or again in a pleasant little church built by the liberal and pious slave owners.   Long before we reached the plantations gates we could hear the untutored voices of the assembled worshipers in songs of praise.   Then would follow the simple service of the Methodist ritual and a sermon gloriously beautiful in its gospel simplicity, followed by the repeating of the Commandments and Creed by the whole congregation, occasionally by the administration of the holy communion, and very often a marriage and baptism."

Text—Isabel D. Martin: *Recollections of a Plantation Missionary's Daughter*, quoted in Harrison, *The Gospel Among the Slaves*, pp. 276-278.

XVII. *THE SCRIPTURAL DEFENSE OF SLAVERY*

Slave-holding does not appear in any catalogue of sins or disciplinable offences given us in the New Testament.

This fact, which none will call in question, is presumptive proof that neither Christ nor his Apostles regarded slave-holding as a sin or an 'offence.' That we may give to this presumption its proper weight, we must take account of such facts as the following:

§ 2. First.   The Catalogues of Sins and Disciplinable Offences, given us in the New Testament, are numerous, and in some instances, extended and minute.
. . . .

§ 3. Second.   All the books of the New Testament were written in slave-holding states, and were originally addressed to persons and churches in slave-holding states: One of them—the epistle to Philemon—is addressed to a slave-holder. . . . .

§ 4. Third.   The condition of slaves in Judea, in our Lord's day, was no better than it now is in our Southern states, whilst in all other countries it was greatly worse. .

§ 5. Fourth.   Slavery, and the relations which it establishes are frequently spoken of, and yet more frequently referred to by Christ and his Apostles. . . . .

§ 7. II. The Apostles Received Slave-Holders into the Christian Church, and Continued them therein, without giving any intimation either at the time of their Reception, or Afterwards, that Slave-Holding was a Sin before God, or to be accounted an offence by the Church.   Proof.—*Eph. VI. 9, Col. IV.* 1, I *Tim. VI.* 2, *Philemon I. 2.* . . .

§ 8. Paul sent back a Fugitive Slave, after the Slave's hopeful Conversion, to his Christian Master again, and assigns as his reason for so doing that Master's right to the services of his Slave.   Proof.—*Philemon*, 10-19.

§ 9. The Apostles repeatedly enjoin the relative Duties of Masters and Slaves, and enforce their Injunctions upon both alike, as Christian Men, by Christian Motives; uniformly treating the Evils which they sought to correct as incidental Evils, and not part and parcel of slavery itself.   Proof.—*Eph. VI.* 5-9; *Col. III.* 22-25, *IV.* 1; 1 *Tim. VI.* 1, 2; *Titus II.* 9, 10; 1 *Pet. II.* 18, 19."

. . . .

§10. Paul declares that his Doctrine respecting the Duties of Slaves and Masters is wholesome doctrine, according to Godliness and the Doctrine of the Lord Jesus Christ. Proof.—1 *Tim. VI.* 1-3. . .

§11. Paul treats the Distinctions which Slavery creates as Matters of very little Importance in so far as the Interests of the Christian Life are Concerned. Proof.—*Gal. III.* 28; 1 *Cor. XII.* 13; *Col. III.* 11; 1 *Cor. VII.* 20, 21. . .

§12. Paul directs the Christian Minister to teach this Doctrine respecting the Duties of Slaves and Masters in the Church, and prohibits the teaching of any Doctrine at variance with it under most solemn Sanctions. Proof.—I *Tim.* VI. 3-5; *Titus,* II. 9, 10, 15. . .

Slavery, in the Bible sense of the term, is a Condition of Mutual Rights and Obligations. The rights of the master, and the corresponding obligations of the slave, are to obedience and service. . .

The Rights of the Slave and the Corresponding Obligations of the Master are, to 'that which is just and equal'. . .

The Scriptural theory respecting the origin of Slavery, may be stated, in brief, thus:—The effect of sin, i.e., disobedience to God's laws, upon both individuals and nations, is *degradation.* A people under this influence, continued through many generations, sink so low in the scale of intelligence and morality as to become incapable of safe and righteous self-government. When, by God's appointment, slavery comes upon them—an appointment at once punitive and remedial; a punishment for sin actually committed, and at the same time a means of saving the sinning people from that utter extermination which must otherwise be their doom, and gradually raising them from the degradation into which they have sunk. . .

Where sin has been persisted in for a time by any people, then comes the *second degree* of slavery, i.e., subjection to despotic government. The deep foundations of despotism in Europe are laid in the degradation of the people. Overturn those despotisms a thousand times, and you cannot make the people free, unless you can first raise them in the scale of intellectual and moral being. Where sin has been persisted in for many generations, and a people have become deeply degraded, then comes the *third degree* of slavery, i.e., personal slavery. Uniformly the people who have been reduced to slavery, have been those degraded by the long-continued operation of sin in just this way.

Text—Armstrong: *The Christian Doctrine of Slavery,* pp. 9-112.

XVIII. *GOD'S WAY WITH SLAVERY*

"Where God has appointed a *work* for his Church, he has generally appointed the *way* also in which that work is to be done. And where this is the case, the Church is as much bound to respect the one appointment as the other. . .

In the case of a race of men in slavery, the *work* which God has appointed his Church—as we learn it, both from the example and the precepts of inspired men—is to labor to secure in them a Christian life on earth and meetness for his heavenly kingdom. . .

In what *way* is this work to be done? We answer, By preaching the same Gospel of God's grace alike to the master and the slave; and when there is credible evidence given that this Gospel has been received in faith, to admit them, master and slave, into the same Church—the Church of the Lord Jesus Christ, in which 'there is neither bond nor free'—and to seat them at the same table of the Lord, that drinking of the same cup, and eating of the same loaf, they may witness to the world their communion in the body and blood of the same Savior. And having received them into the same Church, to teach them the duties belonging to their several 'callings' out of the same Bible, and subject them to the discipline prescribed by the same law, the law of Christ. And this, the teaching of the Church, is to be addressed not to her members only, but to the world at large; and her discipline of her members is to be exercised not in secret, but before the world, that the light which God has given her may appear unto all men. This is just *the way* in which Christ and his Apostles dealt with slavery. The instructions they have given us in their life and in their writings prohibit any other.

In this way must the Church labor to make 'good masters and good slaves, just as she labors to make 'good husbands, good wives, good parents, good children, good rulers, good subjects'. With the ultimate effect of this upon the civil and political condition of the slave the Church has nothing directly to do. If the ultimate effect of it be the emancipation of the slave—we say— in God's name, 'let it come.' 'If it be of God, we *cannot*'—and we *would not* if we could—'overthrow it, lest haply we be found even to fight against God.' If the ultimate effect be the perpetuation of slavery divested of its incidental evils—a slavery in which the master shall be required, by the laws of man as well as that of God, 'to give unto the slave that which is just and equal,' and the slave to render to the master a cheerful obedience and hearty service—we say, let slavery continue. It may be, that such a slavery, regulating the relations of capital and labor, though implying some deprivation of personal liberty, will prove a better defense of the poor against the oppression of the rich, than the too great freedom in which capital is placed in many of the free States of Europe at the present day. . .

To this way of dealing with slavery, thus clearly pointed out in God's word, does God in his providence 'shut us up,' for years to come. None but the sciolist in political philosophy can regard the problem of emancipation—even granting that this were the aim which the Christian citizen should have immediately in view—as a problem of easy solution. . .

Is slavery to continue? We want the best of Christian masters and the best of Christian slaves, that it may prove a blessing to both the one and the other. Is ultimate emancipation before us? We want the best of Christian masters to devise and carry out the scheme by which it shall be effected, and the best of Christian slaves, that their emancipation may be an enfranchisement indeed. And this is just what the Bible plan of dealing with slavery aims at. The *future* may be hidden from view in 'the clouds and darkness' with which God oft veils his purposes; but there is light—heaven's light—upon the *present*. And it is with the *present alone* we have immediately to do."

Text—Armstrong: *The Christian Doctrine of Slavery*, pp. 131-136.

XIX. *THE SECESSION OF THE SOUTHERN PRESBY-TERIANS ON THE ISSUE OF SLAVERY*

See page 607f.

CHAPTER XXVII

The Disruption of the Churches

Bibliography

I. THE QUAKERS

Elias Hicks reveals himself in the "Journal of the Life and Religious Labors of Elias Hicks. Written by Himself" (5th ed. 1832). His Letters are valuable in elucidating his doctrinal views. "The Life and Labours of Elias Hicks" (1910) by Henry W. Wilbur is a faithful representation based on sermons, journals and letters. For the course of events connected with the separation, the "Journal of the Life and Religious Labors of John Comly" (1853) published by his children is indispensible, the appendix to which contains important documents. The legal case that arose in connection with the Crosswicks School Fund is reported by J. J. Foster in "The Quaker Trial, Shotwell versus Hendrickson . . ." (II Vols. 1831). This report throws much light upon the teaching of Hicks, also upon the influences that contributed to the cleavage. Judge Drake's Ruling on this case, useful for its succinct statement of the historical background, may be consulted in the "Report of Cases decided in the Court of Chancery of the State of New Jersey" Vol. I, sec. edition, 1800, pp. 578-685. "A Full Report of the Case of Stacy Decow . . .vs. Thomas L. Shotwell, decided . . . 1833. Taken down in Shorthand . . ." (1834) is accessible. "The Friend", Vols. I and II has much material on this controversy. The story is told in detail by standard Quaker writers (see p. 154f), especially Janney and Jones. "Divisions in the Society of Friends" (1869 enlarged 1893) by Thomas Speakman is valuable.

II. THE PRESBYTERIANS

For Hopkinsinianism and the controversies awakened in the second decade of the nineteenth century, one should consult "A Contrast between Calvinism and Hopkinsinianism" (1811) by Ezra Stiles Ely; his "History of the Ecclesiastical Proceedings Relative to the Third Presbyterian Church in Philadelphia, the Rev. E. S. Ely, and the Judicatories of the

Church with which they are Connected" (1814); "A Plea for Sacramental Communion upon Catholic Principles" (1816) by John M. Mason; and "The Triangle: A Series of Numbers upon Three Theological Points Enforced from Various Pulpits in the City of New York" (1816) by S. Whelpley.

The Barnes incident may be studied in the following: "A Report of the Debates in the Presbytery of Philadelphia, at a Special Meeting held in the City of Philadelphia on the 30th of November, and Continued on the First and Second of December, 1830" (1830); "The Way of Salvation: A Sermon . . . Together with Mr. Barnes' Defense of the Sermon, Read before the Synod of Philadelphia . . ." (1836) by Albert Barnes; "Letters to Presbyterians on the Present Crisis in the Presbyterian Church in the United States" (1833) by Samuel Miller; "A Correct Narrative of the Trial of the Rev. Albert Barnes" (1835) by W. L. McCalla; "The Vindication, containing a History of the Trial of the Rev. Albert Barnes . . ." (1836) by George Junkin; "Trial of the Rev. Albert Barnes before the Synod of Philadelphia . . . as reported for the *New York Observer* by Arthur J. Stansbury" (1836); "The Life of Ashbel Green, V.D.M., begun to be Written by Himself in his Eighty-Second Year . . ." (1849) by Joseph H. Jones.

The views and experience of George Duffield are set forth in "Spiritual Life; or Regeneration Illustrated in a Series of Disquisitions Relative to its Author, Subject, Nature, Means" (1832) by George Duffield; and "The Principles of Presbyterian Discipline Unfolded and Illustrated in the Protests and Appeals of Rev. George Duffield, Entered during the Process in the Presbytery of Carlisle" (1835).

The Lyman Beecher incident has literature as follows: "The Trial and Acquittal of Lyman Beecher, D.D., before the Presbytery of Cincinnati on the Charge of Heresy" (1835); "Views in Theology" (1836) by Lyman Beecher; "The Plea in the Case of Lyman Beecher, D.D. before the Synod of Cincinnati" (1837) by J. L. Wilson; "Memoir of the Rev. Elijah P. Lovejoy . . ." (1838) by Joseph C. and Owen Lovejoy; "Narrative of the Riots at Alton in Connection with the Death of Rev. Elijah P. Lovejoy" (1838) by Edward Beecher; "Autobiography, Correspondence, . . . of Lyman Beecher, D.D." (II Vols. 1866) by Charles Beecher.

On the several incidents referred to above, autobiography and biography has considerable light. The following are recommended: "A Memoir of the Rev. John M. Rice, D.D. . . ." (1835) by William Maxwell; "A Sketch of the Life of Professor James Richards, D.D., of

Auburn Theological Seminary" (1846) by S. H. Gridley; "Memoirs of John M. Mason, D.D., S.T.P., With Portions of his Correspondence" (1856) by Jacob Van Vechten; "Forty Years Familiar Letters, constituting with the Notes a Memoir of his Life" (II Vols. 1860) by James W. Alexander (ed. by John Hall, D.D.); "The Life of Samuel Miller, D.D., . . . Second Professor in the Theological Seminary of the Presbyterian Church in Princeton, New Jersey" (II Vols. 1869) by Samuel Miller; "Personal Reminiscences of the Life and Times of Gardiner Spring" (II Vols. 1866); and "The Life of James Addison Alexander, D.D., Professor in the Theological Seminary at Princeton, New Jersey" (II Vols. 1870) by Henry C. Alexander.

The several histories of Princeton College should also be consulted, (see p. 265).

Of histories there are the following: "Facts and Observations concerning the Organization of Churches in the Three Synods of Western New York and the Western Reserve" (1837) by James Wood; "The Catastrophe of the Presbyterian Church in 1837, including a Full History of the Recent Theological Controversies in New England" (1838) by Zebulon Crocker; "Report of the Presbyterian Church Case . . ." (1839) by Samuel Miller, Jr.; "Review of the Controversy in the Presbyterian Church showing the Points of Difference and Causes of Division" (1840) by a Member of the Synod of West Tennessee; "The Old and New Schools" (n.d.) by Rev M. L. Rice; "Differences Between Old and New School Presbyterians" (1848) by Rev. Lewis Cheeseman; "History of the Division of the Presbyterian Church of the United States of America" (1852) by a Committee of the Synod of New York and New Jersey; "Historical Contributions relating to the Founders, Principles, and Acts of the Presbyterian Church. With Special Reference to the Division of 1837–1838"—See "Essays and Discourses" (1861) by C. Van Rensselaer; and "A History of the New School and of the Questions Involved in the Disruption of the Presbyterian Church in 1838" (1868) by Samuel J. Baird.

III. THE BAPTISTS

A good starting point is "Limitations of Human Responsibility" (1838) in which Francis L. Wayland discussed the limits within which efforts to remove slavery were to be restricted.

"Domestic Slavery Considered as a Scriptural Institution: in a Correspondence between the Rev. Richard Fuller of Beaufort, S.C. and the Rev. Francis Wayland of Providence, R. I." (1845) is a work of prime importance. "A Review of the 'Correspondence' of Messrs. Fuller and Wayland" (1847) by C. P. Grosvenor, defends the abolitionists from the criticisms of Wayland and Fuller.

For the reports of the Baptist Anti-Slavery Conventions, the Triennial Conventions of 1841 and 1844, and the Addresses of Boards to the Baptist constituency, one should consult the official minutes of the respective organizations, the "Baptist Missionary Magazine" (1841–1845), the "Liberator" (1840–1845), the "Northwestern Baptist" (1844), the "Religious Herald" (1841–1846), and Niles "Register" (1838–1846).

Biographies necessary to a mastery of this controversy are as follows: "Some Account of the Life of Spencer Houghton Cone" (1856) by Edward and Spencer W. Cone; "A Memoir of the Life and Labors of Francis Wayland, D.D., LL.D., Late President of Brown University, including Selections from his Personal Reminiscences and Correspondence" (II Vols. 1868) by his sons, Francis and H. L. Wayland; "Life of Dr. Richard Fuller" (1879) by J. H. Cuthbert; "Life of J. B. Jeter, D.D." (1887) by William B. Hatcher; "Francis Wayland" (1891) by James O. Murray; and a "Memoir of J. P. Boyce" (1893) by J. A. Broadus.

Quite important are "William Lloyd Garrison, The Story of His Life Told by His Children" (IV Vols. 1885–9) by F. J. and W. P. Garrison; "James G. Birney and His Times" (1890) by William Birney; and "The Life and Times of Wendell Phillips" (1901) by G. L. Austin.

References of more or less bearing will be found in "American Churches, The Bulwarks of American Slavery" (1842) by James G. Birney; "A Second Visit to the United States of North America" (II Vols. 1849) by Charles Lyell; "Slavery and Anti-Slavery" (1852) by William Goodell; "Miscellaneous Writings on Slavery" (1853) by William Jay; "Some Recollections of the Anti-Slavery Conflict" (1869) by S. J. May; "The Anti-Slavery Struggle and Triumph in the Methodist Episcopal Church" (1881) by L. C. Matlack; "Acts of the Anti-Slavery Apostles" (1883) by Parker Pillsbury; and "The Church as it is, or the Forlorn Hope of Slavery" (II Vols. 1885) by the same writer; "The History of the Anti-Slavery Cause in State and Nation" (1886) by Austin Willey; "William Jay and the Constitutional Movement for the Abolition of Slavery" (1894) by B. Tuckerman.

Of histories, probably the best is "Baptists and Slavery, 1840–1845" (Ph. M. dissertation, Univ. of Chicago, 1910) by Mary B. Putnam. The writer has made a close study of the newspaper literature. Condensed statements appear in "The Baptists" (1903) by H. C. Vedder; "A History of the Baptists in the Southern States East of the Mississippi"

(1898) by B. F. Riley; "A History of the Baptist Church in the United States" ("Amer. Ch. Hist. Series" Vol. II, 4th ed. 1902) by A. H. Newman; and his "Century of Baptist Achievement" (1901).

Two notable magazine articles appear in the "Christian Review" (Dec. 1845 and May 1846) entitled, "The Division of the Baptist General Convention, Minutes of the Southern Baptist Convention Held at Augusta, May 1845," and "An Examination of the Review of the Minutes of the Southern Baptist Convention held at Augusta, May, 1845."

IV. THE METHODISTS

For the secession, and organization of the Methodist Protestant Church, and the course of events to 1842, there is a "History of the Methodist Protestant Church" (1843) by James R. Williams. Though antiquated, this work contains important documents which supplemented with the "Journals" and "Minutes" of the period give all necessary source material. A recent but rhetorical contribution is a "History of Methodist Reform . . . with Special Reference to the Methodist Protestant Church" (II Vols. 1898) by Edward J. Drinkhouse, M.D., D.D. The standard histories of Methodism (see p. 317f.) should be consulted.

For the more serious disruption between the Methodists of the North and South, documentary material is to be found in the "Journals of the General Conferences of the Methodist Episcopal Church" (Vols. I, II, and III); and the "Journals of the General Conferences of the Methodist Episcopal Church South" (Vol. I). Most of this material is incorporated in the highly useful "History of the Organization of the Methodist Episcopal Church South, Comprehending all the Official Proceedings of the General Conference, the Southern Annual Conferences, and the General Conventions, with such other Matters as are necessary to a Right Understanding of the Case" (1845) compiled and published by the editors and publishers of the *Southwestern Christian Advocate* for the M. E. Church South. "Debates of the General Conference of 1844" by L. C. Matlack and L. M. Lee fill an important place. "The Methodist Church Property Case" (report of suit heard before Court, May, 1851) by R. Sutton is a *multum in parvo* for the investigator.

The following magazine contributions are thorough and contain considerable source material: "The General Conference of 1844" ("Meth. Quar. Review" April, 1870); "The General Conference of 1844" (*ibid.*

April, 1871); "The General Conference of 1844" (*ibid.* Jan. 1876); "The Disruption of Methodism" (*ibid.* April, 1876).

"An Essay on Church Polity; Comprehending an Outline of the Controversy on Ecclesiastical Government, and a Vindication of the Ecclesiastical System of the M. E. Church" (1847) by Rev. Abel Stevens, and "The Constitutional Powers of the General Conference, with Especial Application to the Subject of Slave Holding" (1856) by Bishop W. L. Harriss, are good for constitutional aspects of the controversy.

Of histories, in addition to those that cover this chapter as part of the entire field of American Methodism (see p. 317f.), there are the following: "History of the Methodist Episcopal Church South" (1845) anonymous; a "History of the Great Secession . . . " (1854) by Charles Elliott (particularly valuable because of its copious source material); "History of the Organization of the Methodist Episcopal Church South" (1871) by A. H. Redford; "The Disruption of the Methodist Episcopal Church, 1844–1846" (1875) by Edward H. Myers (showing an irenical spirit as part of a movement to bring together the churches of the North and South); "The Methodist Episcopal Churches North and South" (1872) by an anonymous Southern bishop (a pamphlet marred by bitter prejudice); "An Appeal to the Records in Vindication of the Policy and Proceedings of the Methodist Episcopal Church in Relation to the South . . ." (1876) by E. Fuller; "A History of Methodism" (1884) by Holland N. McTyeire ('Not a history of southern Methodism, but of Methodism from a Southern point of view'); and a "History of the Methodist Episcopal Church South" ("Amer. Ch. Hist. Series" Vol. XI, 1894) by Gross Alexander.

Of biographies in addition to those referred to elsewhere (see p. 316, and 410f.) there are "The Life and Letters of James Osgood Andrews" (1882) by George C. Smith; "Life of Henry Bidleman Bascom, D.D." (1854) by Rev. M. M. Henkle; "Life of William Capers, D.D. . . ." (1858) by W. M. Wightman, D.D.; "Life of Orange Scott" (1847) by L. C. Matlack; "Life and Letters of Stephen Olin" (II Vols. 1853); and "The Life and Labors of Enoch Mather Marvin . . ." (1879) by T. M. Finney.

The following studies on various phases of the struggle should not be overlooked: "History of the Old Baltimore Conference . . . to 1857" (1907) by James E. Armstrong; "Methodism and Slavery . . ." (1845) by H. B. Bascom; "Brief Appeal to Public Opinion, . . . affecting the Rights and Interests of the Methodist Episcopal Church South" (1848, with many documents) by H. B. Bascom and others; Matlack's two works "The History of American Slavery and Methodism from 1780 to 1849" (1849), and "The Anti-Slavery Struggle and Triumph in the Methodist Episcopal Church" (1881).

The secession of the Wesleyan Connection has received attention as a phase of the larger conflict between the North and South in much of the literature cited above. Matlack's ". . . History of American Slavery and Methodism from 1780 to 1849" (part II) entitled "History of the Wesleyan Methodist Connection of America" (1849) will be found particularly serviceable.

For the critical period between the disruption and the civil war, there is literature as follows: "A South Side View of Slavery" (1854) by Nehemiah Adams, D.D.; "Progress Considered with Particular Reference to the Methodist Episcopal Church South" (1855) by Rev. Wm. J. Sassrett; "The Annals of Southern Methodism" (3 annual volumes 1855, 56 & 57) by Charles F. Deems; "America and American Methodism" (1857) by Rev. T. B. Sargent and Rev. John Hannah; "The Methodist Episcopal Church and Slavery" (1857) by Daniel DeVinné; "The Impending Crisis of the South, How to Meet it" (1857) by Hinton R. Helper; "Border Methodism and Border Slavery; Being a Statement and Review of the Action of the Philadelphia Annual Conference Concerning Slavery at its Late Session at Easton, Pennsylvania" (1858) by Rev. J. M. McCarker; "A Vindication of Border Methodism" (1858) by Rev. Samuel Huffman, with introduction by Rev. J. L. Conklin; "Slavery in the Methodist Episcopal Church" (1859) by Elias Bowen; "The Constitutional Powers of the General Conference. With a Special Application to the Subject of Slave Holding" (above); and "Methodism, Suggestions Appropriate to its Present Condition" ("Meth. Quar. Review" Jan. 1860).

"The Methodist Episcopal Church and the Civil War" (1912) by W. W. Sweet is illuminating.

DOCUMENTS

I. *EPISTLE FROM THE YEARLY MEETING OF FRIENDS*

Held in Philadelphia, by adjournment, from the 12th of the fourth month to the 17th of the same, inclusive, 1830.

To the yearly meeting of friends held in London.

Dear Friends:—

On looking over the annals of our religious society, it is pleasing to perceive that for more than one hundred and forty years the Yearly Meeting of London and that of Pennsylvania preserved the most cordial relations. During this time an affectionate interchange of their views and sentiments was maintained, to their mutual edification and comfort, binding them more firmly together in the bonds of gospel fellowship. Greatly desiring to preserve such an intercourse uninterrupted, this meeting, in the fourth month, 1828, addressed to you an affectionate epistle, in which we adverted to the division which had taken place in the Yearly Meeting of Philadelphia, and stated our views of the causes which had led to that event. We did this in the hope that by making you acquainted with our case as we understood it ourselves, you might be preserved from any improper bias, and be induced to suspend your decision on the subject, until time and a further investigation of circumstances might enable you to form an impartial judgment. By your answer to this friendly effort for the preservation of harmony between us, we perceive, that on the *ex parte* evidence of a committee, acting as the representatives of a small minority of Friends in this section of our country, you have pronounced us 'separatists,' and have declared it the judgment of your meeting, 'neither to read, nor accept the communication' we sent you!

. . . .

We are aware, dear friends, that our opponents have pronounced us infidels and deists! They have said we have departed from the Christian faith, and renounced the religion of our worthy predecessors in the Truth. Nothing is easier than to make such charges as these; but, in the present case, we are happily assured that nothing is harder than to prove them. We are not sensible of any dereliction on our part from the principles laid down by our blessed Lord. The history of the birth, life, acts, death, and resurrection of the holy Jesus, as in the volume of the book it is written of him, we reverently believe. 'We are not ashamed of the gospel of Christ, because it is the power of God unto salvation to all them that believe.' Neither do we hesitate to acknowledge the divinity of its author; because we know from living experience that he is the *power* of God and the *wisdom* of God; that, under the present glorious dispensation, he is the *one* holy principle of Divine *life* and *light*—the unlimited *word* of grace and truth, which only can build us up in the true faith, and give us an inheritance among all those who are sanctified.

Neither are we sensible of any departure from the faith or principles of our primitive Friends. We are not ignorant that on some points of a speculative nature, they had different views, and expressed themselves diversely; but notwithstanding this was the case, such were the aboundings of the love of God and of one another, that these differences did not interrupt the excellent harmony that existed among them. In the fundamental principle of the Christian faith, '*the light of Christ within, as God's gift for man's salvation*,' and which, as William Penn delcares, 'is as the root of the goodly tree of doctrines, which grew and branched out from it,' *they were all united.* And in that which united them we are united with them; believing in the *same fundamental principle*, and in all *the blessed doctrines* which grow from it as their root, both as they are laid down in the Scriptures of Truth, and in their writings; desiring above all things the growth and advancement of this principle in ourselves, and in the world at large. .

. . . .

The charges brought against *us* by our opposers, to injure and invalidate our character as a Christian people, are the same that were preferred against our primitive Friends; and, we apprehend, upon the same grounds . . . We do not believe that the dissensions which have appeared among us, had their origin so much in differences of opinion on doctrinal points, as in a disposition, apparent in some, to exercise an oppressive authority in the church. These, in our meetings for discipline, although a small minority of the whole, assumed the power to direct a course of measures, painful to the feelings and contrary to the deliberate judgment of their brethren. Thus the few usurped a power over the many, subversive of our established order, and destructive to the peace and harmony of society. After long and patient forbearance, in the hope that our opposing brethren might see the impropriety of such a course, the great body of the Yearly Meeting saw no way to regain a state of tranquillity, but by a *disconnection* with those who had produced, and were promoting such disorders among us.

. . . .

Signed by direction, and on behalf of said meeting, by

JOHN COMLY,
Clerk to the Men's Meeting
LUCRETIA MOTT,
Clerk to the Women's Meeting.

Text—*Journal of the Life and Religious Labours of John Comly, published by his children*, pp. 638-641.

II. *THE WESTERN MEMORIAL*

The following excerpts from a lengthy document set forth the grievances of the Old School Party. It was signed by about 18 ministers and 99 elders.

"*To the Moderator and Members of the General Assembly of the Presbyterian Church in the United States, to meet in the city of Philadelphia, on the 15th of May, 1834.*

"*Reverend Fathers and Brethren*—We, the subscribers, Ministers and Elders of the Presbyterian Church, respectfully present to you this our *memorial*, praying you to take into your most serious consideration, the subjects to which it asks your attention.

It would be inconsistent with the opinion which we entertain of the intelligence of your reverend body, to offer any proof of what is too lamentably notorious, that from sundry causes, our once united and harmonious Church, for some time past, has been afflicted with alienations, strifes, and divisions. . . .

Plainly as the path is marked out in our excellent Constitution, it is with grief that we feel constrained to say, that for some years past a policy of an evasive character has distinguished many of the proceedings of the General Assemblies, as also a number of inferior judicatories, wherein they have, apparently at least, sought to avoid a prompt discharge of their constitutional duties, and have substituted a course of procedure unknown and repugnant to the prescribed order of our form of government. . . .

We feel alarmed at the evidences which press upon us, of the prevalence of unsoundness in doctrine, and laxity in discipline; and we view it as an aggravating consideration, that the General Assembly, the constitutional guardian of the Church's purity, even when a knowledge of such evils has been brought before it, in an orderly manner, has, within a few years past, either directly or indirectly refused to apply the constitutional remedy. . . .

That we may not be misunderstood, we premise here our free admission, that some of the measures about to be complained of, were adopted at the time with the best intentions, and if the results could have been foreseen by the authors of those measures, they would never have been carried into effect.

I. We believe this to have been particularly the case with regard to the 'Plan of Union' with Congregational churches, adopted in 1801. A careful comparison of that Plan with the Constitution of our Church, will make it evident, that the General Assembly of 1801, in adopting it, assumed power nowhere assigned to them in the constitution. . . .

II. Closely connected with the influence of Congregational prepossession and principles introduced gradually into our Church, we regard the existence of a sentiment now avowed by numbers who bear the Presbyterian name, that every man in professing to receive and adopt our ecclesiastical formularies, has a right to put thereon his *own construction*, without being responsible for the construction, or the character of his explanations. They who hold this principle, practise accordingly; and thus an unnatural mixture of conflicting elements is brought into the bosom of the Church, unfavourable alike to its purity and peace.

III. We next notice another course of unconstitutional proceedings, which adds to the evils that now afflict us. We refer to the practice of Presbyteries in ordaining men, *sine titulo*, to preach and administer the ordinances of the gospel, in other parts of the Presbyterian Church, where Presbyteries already exist, and are ready to perform their constitutional functions, as the necessities of the churches under their care require. There is also just ground to suspect, that in many cases of such ordination, it is done to suit the convenience of men who are not prepared to pass through the constitutional ordeal when applied by those Presbyteries, within whose bounds they expect to labour, either on account of their lack of ministerial furniture, or because they do not cordially receive, either our Creed, or Form of Government: hence, they prefer to receive licensure and ordination in such Presbyteries as are known, or supposed to be, not particular on these points. . . .

IV. We also ascribe to the principles of Independency, introduced through the medium of the compact already noticed, another departure of the General Assembly, from the due discharge of its own constitutional duties, *first*, in conniving at an irresponsible, voluntary association in assuming to a great extent, the management of domestic missions within the Presbyterian Church; and *secondly*, in that when the General Assembly had become convinced of the duty of giving increased energy to the exercise of their appropriate functions, in this matter, they nevertheless not merely connived at the continued exercise of the powers which the American Home Missionary Society had usurped, but actually *encouraged* them by a *recommendation*, in 1829—a measure which, at the time, deceived many Presbyterians, as to the nature of that institution, inducing a belief that its operations and influences were compatible both with the constitution and interests of the Presbyterian Church.

. . . .

V. We now proceed to show, that these relaxing principles, which are undermining the beauty and order of our Zion, have developed themselves in the proceedings of the General Assembly, and we may add, of inferior courts also, when called upon to decide on points of doctrine. That we may not be tedious, we shall confine ourselves to one case, which occurred in the proceedings of the General Assembly.

In order to understand the real nature and influence of these relaxing principles, the operations of which we are attempting to illustrate, let the proceedings of the

Assembly, in 1831, in the Barnes' case, be contrasted with the proceedings of former Assemblies, in the cases of Mr. Balch, in 1798, and of Mr. Davis, in 1810. . . .

VI.   In connection with these tokens of the prevalence of a relaxing and corrupting influence in the Presbyterian Church, we complain of a course of procedure, in church courts, commenced and sanctioned by the General Assembly, which has a tendency to render all the principles of our constitution nugatory, and the government of the Church no better than a spiritual anarchy. . . .

VII.   We solemnly remonstrate against the act of the General Assembly, in 1832, for dividing the Presbytery of Philadelphia. Aside from the principle upon which they separated the Ministers and Churches, we consider that act, under the circumstances in which it was passed, as a gross violation of the constitution, being an evident usurpation of a power vested exclusively in the Synod. . . .

VIII.   In the last place, we remonstrate and testify against the following errors, which are held and taught within the Presbyterian Church, and which the General Assembly are constitutionally competent to suppress, by warnings, recommendations and injunctions to the Churches, Presbyteries and Synods under their care, and by faithfully and constitutionally deciding on cases brought before them by reference, complaint or appeal.

1. That Adam was not the covenant head, or federal representative of his posterity, and sustained no other relation to them than that which subsists between every parent and his offspring. . . .

2. That we have nothing to do with the first sin of Adam more than with the sin of any other parent; and that it is not imputed to his posterity. . .

3. That infants have no moral character—that they are neither sinful nor holy. . .

4. That all sin consists exclusively in voluntary acts or exercises, and consequently that there is no innate, inherent or derived corruption in the souls of fallen men. . .

5. That man in his fallen state, is possessed of entire ability to do whatever God requires him to do, independently of any new power or ability imparted to him by the gracious operations of the Holy Spirit. . .

6. That regeneration is essentially a voluntary change, which the soul is active in producing; and that the Holy Spirit acts only mediately in the way of moral suasion, by the presentation of motives. . .

7. That Christ did not become the legal substitute of sinners—did not pay the debt of his people, or endure the penalty of the law in their behalf. . .

8. That the Atonement is merely an exhibition of the wrath of God against sin—an expedient for enabling God to forgive sin, consistently with the welfare of the universe—of itself, not securing the salvation of any one, and not satisfying divine justice. . .

9. That the Atonement is general, made for all men alike, as much for the non-elect as for the elect. . .

The spirit manifested, and the acts passed, in former days, by the superior judicatory of the Presbyterian Church, not only warrant us to believe that your reverend body has the requisite power, but also to call upon you for the exercise of that power, for the suppression of these, and other errors, that are held, preached and published by Ministers of our denomination. . . "

Text—Baird: *A Collection of the Acts, Deliverances . . . of the Presbyterian Church . . .* , pp. 659-667.

III. *PASTORAL LETTER TO THE CHURCHES UNDER THE CARE OF THE GENERAL ASSEMBLY*

"*Dear Brethren*—As the doings of the present General Assembly have been of an unusual character, and such as may produce important consequences, we think it proper to lay an abstract of our decisions and the reasons of them before the Churches under our care. Discerning men have perceived for a number of years, that the affairs of our beloved Church were hastening to a crisis; and when the members of the present Assembly came together, the state of parties was such as to make it manifest that a division of the Church was the most desirable object that could be effected. What are called the Old-school and New-school parties are already separated in fact; in almost every part of our country where those parties exist, they have less ministerial or Christian communion with one another than either of those parties have with Christians of other denominations; and they are so equally balanced in point of power that for years past it has been uncertain, until the General Assembly was fully organized, which of those parties would predominate in that body.

. . . .

So fully was this Assembly convinced, that a separation of the parties was the only cure for the evils under which we labour, that a committee was appointed by common consent, composed of equal numbers from the different sides of the house, to adjust if possible the terms of an amicable division of the Church into two separate and independent denominations. This joint committee agreed upon the principles of the division, but could not agree upon the form. It was admitted on all hands, that the Old-school party should retain the name and the funds of the Church, and especially all the funds and property connected with the Theological Seminaries at Princeton and Pittsburgh. But on the mode of separation the committee could not agree. The New-school party would consent to no other plan than that of referring it to the Presbyteries, in order to have the division made by the next General Assembly. To this plan the other party thought there were insuperable objections. It was believed that, our Presbyteries being so widely dispersed, the returns from them would be uncertain; that many things might occur to defeat the arrangement; and that, as the probable result, the parties would come to the next Assembly, with more determination to contend for the power and government of the whole Church than on any former occasion.

On reviewing the causes from which our troubles have arisen, another plan presented itself to the view of the majority, which appeared better calculated to effect, in a peaceable manner, that division of the Church which all seemed to consider as a matter of indispensable necessity. The contentions which distract the Church evidently arose from the Plan of Union formed in 1801, between the General Assembly and the Association of Connecticut. This Plan was indeed projected and brought into operation by some of the wisest and best men the Presbyterian Church has ever known, and it evidently originated from the purest and most benevolent motives. It has, however, been disastrous in its effects. We mean no disrespect to the Congregationalists of New England, as such; indeed there is no denomination of Christians beyond the pale of our own Church whom we esteem and love more sincerely; and yet we believe that the attempt, by this Plan of Union, to bring Congregationalists and Presbyterians into the same denomination, has been the principal cause of those dissensions which now distract and rend the Church to pieces.

We allude to these circumstances merely for the purpose of explaining the only remedy which appears applicable to our present troubles. The Plan of Union adopted in 1801, was evidently unconstitutional in its nature, and of a tendency to subvert the institutions and distinctive character of the Presbyterian Church; and such being the fact, it was certainly the duty of the present Assembly to abrogate said Plan, and to declare it void from the beginning. From this act of abrogation, and from the declaration that it was void from the beginning, it would necessarily follow, that the Churches, Presbyteries, and Synods formed under said Plan, were of course not to be considered as parts of the Presbyterian Church. From this view of the subject it appears, that the *separation*, so necessary for the well being of the Presbyterian Church, exists already, and that we have nothing to do but to act on the facts of the case and secure our tranquillity.

. . . .

Having traced thus far the unconstitutional and pernicious tendency of this *act*, it only remains to say, that when this act is abrogated by the proper authority, as a matter of course everything which arose under its influence and training, is abrogated with it. This we presume is the ground on which all the jurisprudence of our country stands, and upon which all our political courts and legislatures act. It has indeed been said, that when an unconstitutional law forms a contract, the abrogation of the law cannot set the contract aside, as this would suppose that a person might take the advantage of his own wrong to relieve himself from a just obligation. But to this it may be answered, that an unconstitutional law can give rise to no binding contract. The unconstitutionality supposes that the organ of government is granting what it has no right to grant, and therefore no obligation can be imposed. But in the present case, the *act in question* goes to the subversion of the Presbyterian Church, and therefore any contract which could arise under it, calculated to destroy that Church, would be of such an immoral tendency as could impose no obligation. It is one of the first principles of morals, that an unlawful contract is not to be fulfilled.

It then appears plain to us, that, by the abrogation of the act of 1801, the Synods of the Western Reserve, Utica, Genesee, and Geneva, are independent bodies, standing on their own ground, and free to choose their future connections, and that thus far a separation exists between us and them, which may greatly conduce to the peace and comfort of both parties. . . . In our present connection, there is no hope of peace. The controversy threatens to become more fierce, more extensive, and more destructive of all the vital principles of religion, the longer we continue together. Indeed, the great motives for all the measures of separation to which we have resorted on the present occasion, are the peace, prosperity, and holiness of our beloved Church; and these objects, we believe, can never be obtained until this separation is effected.

Our brethren of the minority seemed to consider it as an insult, when we urged the fact, that the abrogation of an unconstitutional law left us as distinct and separate bodies; we intended no insult; the ground we took and the language we used implied none; we only said that they were separate from us, and we from them; if this implied disgrace on them, it implied the same on ourselves; we wished both parties to consider themselves as on equal ground; and as to the unconstitutional law from which all our misapprehensions had arisen, we were willing that the greater blame should lie on us. In fact, our wish was and is to part as brethren, and as in certain important points of doctrine and Church order we cannot agree, let each party take the word of God as their rule of faith and practice, and pursue their course as those who must give account to the great Shepherd and Bishop of their souls.

. . . .

DAVID ELLIOTT, *Moderator*
JOHN M'DOWELL, *Stated Clerk.*

Philadelphia, June 8th, 1837."

Text—Baird: *A Collection of the Acts, Deliverances . . . of the Presbyterian Church . . ."* pp. 743-747.

IV. *LETTER OF THE ALABAMA BAPTIST STATE CONVENTION TO THE BOARD OF MANAGERS OF THE BAPTIST GENERAL CONVENTION*

"November 25, 1844

Rev. Daniel Sharp, President of the Board of Managers of the Baptist General Convention.

DEAR BROTHER:—Agreeably to the appointment of 'The Baptist State Convention of Alabama,' we transmit to you the following Preamble and Resolutions, and request you to lay them before your Board. We shall wait your reply.

PREAMBLE AND RESOLUTIONS

WHEREAS, The holding of property in African negro slaves has for some years excited discussion, as a question of morals, between different portions of the Baptist denomination united in benevolent enterprise; and by a large portion of our brethren is now imputed to the slaveholders in these Southern and Southwestern States, as a sin, at once grievous, palpable, and disqualifying:—

1. *Resolved,* By the Convention of the Baptist Denomination in the State of Alabama, that when one party to a voluntary compact between Christian brethren is not willing to acknowledge the entire social equality with the other, as to all the privileges and benefits of the union, nor even to refrain from impeachment and annoyance, united efforts between such parties, even in the sacred cause of Christian benevolence, cease to be agreeable, useful, or proper.

2. *Resolved,* That our duty requires us, at this crisis, to demand from the proper authorities in all those bodies to whose funds we have contributed, or with whom we have in any way been connected, the distinct, explicit avowal that slave-holders are eligible, and entitled, equally with non-slaveholders, to all the privileges and immunities of their several unions; and especially to receive any agency, mission, or other appointment, which may fall within the scope of their operations or duties.

3. *Resolved,* That to prevent a gradual departure from the principles of church independence, and the assumption, by Societies, Boards, or Committees, of the inalienable rights of the churches, as well as to prevent the recurrence of difficulties in future, this Convention do hold, that in all those Conventions, Societies, or Boards, of which we may be a constituent part, whenever the competency or fitness of an individual to receive an appointment, is under discussion, if any question arises affecting his morals, or his standing in fellowship as a Christian, such question should not be disposed of to

the grief of the party, without ultimate appeal to the particular church of which such individual is a member,—as being the only body on earth authorized by the scriptures, or competent, to consider and decide this class of cases.

4. *Resolved*, That the President and Secretary of this body be a Committee to transmit copies of this preamble and these resolutions to those bodies for whose treasuries any of the funds, now in hand, or hereafter to be received, may be designed,—and to call their attention expressly to our *second resolution*:—that, should any responses be received, the President of this Convention shall call together the officers and directors hereof, by a notice in the Alabama Baptist, inserted at least thirty days previous to the time of meeting;—that a majority of these persons, or eight in number, shall be a quorum for business; and the quorum assembled, or a majority of them, shall decide whether the said moneys, or any portion of them, shall be forwarded to the bodies for whom they were designed, or be held until the next meeting of this body, subject to be re-claimed or re-appropriated by the donors severally.

5. *Resolved*, That the Treasurer of this body be, and he is hereby instructed, not to pay any money, intended to be applied without the limits of this State, except at the written order of the President of this Convention, with the concurrence of the board of officers before mentioned; and this body, profoundly sensible of the vast issues dependent on the principles herein advanced, will await, in prayerful expectation, the responses of our non-slaveholding brethren.

6. *Resolved*, That the Secretary of this Convention, as far as practicable, transmit at least one copy of these Minutes, when published, to the presiding officer of each Baptist State Convention, or General Association, in the slaveholding States.

JESSE HARTWELL,
President of the Alabama Baptist State Convention.

M. P. Jewett, *Record. Sec.*"

Text—*The Baptist Missionary Magazine*, Vol. XXV, pp. 220-221.

Reply of the Acting Board

"*Boston, December 17, 1844.*

DEAR SIR:—We have received from you a copy of a Preamble and Resolutions, which were passed by the 'Baptist State Convention of Alabama.' And as there is a 'demand' for distinct and explicit answers from our Board, to the inquiries and propositions which you have been pleased to make, we have given to them our deliberate and candid attention.

Before proceeding to answer them, allow us to express our profound regret that they were addressed to us. They were not necessary. We have never, as a Board, either done, or omitted to do, any thing which requires the explanations and avowals that your Resolutions 'demand.' They also place us in the new and trying position of being compelled to answer hypothetical questions, and to discuss principles; or of seeming to be evasive and timid, and not daring to give you the information and satisfaction which you desire. If, therefore, in answering with entire frankness your inquiries and demands, we should express opinions which may be unsatisfactory or displeasing to you, our plea must be, that a necessity was laid upon us. We had no other alternative, without being wanting, apparently, in that manly openness which ought to characterize the correspondence of Christian brethren.

In your first Resolution, you say 'that when one party to a voluntary compact between Christian brethren is not willing to acknowledge the entire social equality with the other, as to all the privileges and benefits of the union, nor even to refrain from impeachment and annoyance, united efforts between such parties, even in the sacred cause of Christian benevolence, cease to be agreeable, useful, or proper.' In these sentiments we entirely coincide. As a Board, we have the highest consciousness, that it has always been our aim to act in accordance therewith. We have never called in question your social equality as to all the privileges and benefits of the Foreign Mission-ary Union. Nor have we ever employed our official influence in impeaching or annoy-ing you. Should we ever do this, 'our united efforts,' as you justly say, would 'cease to be agreeable, useful, or proper.'

In your second Resolution, you 'demand the distinct and explicit avowal, that slaveholders are eligible and entitled to all the privileges and immunities of their several unions, and especially to receive any agency, mission, or other appointment, which may fall within the scope of their operations and duties.'

"We need not say, that slaveholders, as well as non-slaveholders, are unquestion-ably entitled to all the privileges and immunities which the Constitution of the Bap-tist General Convention permits, and grants to its members. We would not deprive either of any of the immunities of the mutual contract. In regard, however, to any agency, mission, or other appointment, no slaveholder or non-slaveholder, however large his subscriptions to foreign missions, or those of the church with which he is connected, is on that account entitled to be appointed to an agency or a mission. The appointing power, for wise and good reasons, has been confided to the 'Acting Board,' they holding themselves accountable to the Convention for the discreet and faithful discharge of this trust.

Should you say, 'the above remarks are not sufficiently explicit; we wish dis-tinctly to know, whether the Board would or would not appoint a slaveholder as a missionary;'—before directly replying, we would say, that in the thirty years in which the Board has existed, no slaveholder, to our knowledge, has applied to be a missionary. And, as we send out no domestics or servants, such an event as a missionary taking slaves with him, were it morally right, could not, in accordance with all our past arrangements or present plans, possibly occur. If, however, any one should offer himself as a missionary, having slaves, and should insist on retaining them as his property, we could not appoint him. One thing is certain, we can never be a party to any arrangement which would imply approbation of slavery.

In your third Resolution you say, that, 'whenever the competency or fitness of an individual to receive an appointment is under discussion, if any question arises affect-ing his morals, or his standing in fellowship as a Christian, such question should not be disposed of to the grief of the party without ultimate appeal to the particular church of which such an individual is a member —as being the only body on earth authorized by the scriptures, or competent, to consider and decide this class of cases.'

In regard to our Board, there is no point on which we are more unanimously agreed, than that of the independence of churches. We disclaim all and every pre-tention to interfere with the discipline of any church. We disfellowhip no one. Nev-theless, were a person to offer himself as a candidate for missionary service, although commended by his church as in good standing, we should feel it our duty to open our eyes on any facts to the disadvantage of his moral and religious character, which might come under our observation. And while we should not feel that it was our province to excommunicate, or discipline a candidate of doubtful character, yet we should be un-worthy of our trust, if we did not, although he were a member of a church, reject his application. It is for the Board to determine on the prudential, moral, religious, and theological fitness of each one who offers himself as a missionary; it is for the church of which such an one is a member, to decide whether he be a fit person to belong to their body.

The other Resolutions which were passed in your recent Convention, regard more your own action than ours. They, therefore, call for no remarks from us. We should have been gratified, in the present impoverished and embarrassed state of our treasury, if the brethren in Alabama, confiding in the integrity and discretion of the Acting Board, could unhesitatingly have transmitted to us their funds. We have sent out missionaries, and enlarged our operations, in the expectation that, so long as we acted in conformity with the rules and spirit under which we were appointed, we should be sustained both by the East and the West, the North and the South. If in this just expectation we are to be disappointed, we shall experience unutterable regret.

We have, with all frankness, but with entire kindness and respect, defined our position. If our brethren in Alabama, with this exposition of our principles and feelings, can cooperate with us, we shall be happy to receive their aid. If they cannot, painful to us as will be their withdrawal, yet we shall submit to it, as neither sought nor caused by us.

There are sentiments avowed in this communication, which, although held temperately and kindly, and with all due esteem and Christian regard for the brethren addressed, are, nevertheless, dearer to us than any pecuniary aid whatever.

> We remain yours truly,
> In behalf of the Board,
> DANIEL SHARP, *President.*

Baron Stow, *Rec. Sec.*

Rev. Jesse Hartwell, *President of Alabama Baptist State Convention.*"

Text—*The Baptist Missionary Magazine*, Vol. XXV, pp. 220-223.

V. *METHODIST PROTESTANT CHURCH: ARTICLES OF ASSOCIATION*

PREAMBLE

WHEREAS, the friends of a fair and equal representation in the government of the Methodist Episcopal Church, when they have insisted on the necessity of a modification in the polity of the Church, which should recognize the fundamental principle, the only safeguard to the liberties of the people, and when they have submitted respectful petitions and memorials to the General Conference, praying for the admission of the principle, have been met in a manner which has encouraged and prepared the friends of absolute power, to request and urge them to withdraw from the fellowship of the Church, and to threaten them with excommunication if they should refuse to comply:—
And WHEREAS, many of our highly esteemed and useful members in the Church, by an unjustifiable violence, have been excluded from the fellowship of their brethren, and have been thereby compelled for the time being, to form themselves into religious fraternities, for the purposes of christian fellowship.

. . . And WHEREAS, the late decisions of the Baltimore and the Ohio Annual Conferences, as also the ultimate proceedings and report of the General Conference, in relation to this subject, have placed every friend of representation in the Methodist Episcopal Church, in such a situation that their opponents have it completely in their power to compel them to renounce their principles, or be excluded from the fellowship of their brethren: And WHEREAS, the ministers favourable to the principles of representation, in sundry places, are no longer admitted to ordination, or to occupy the pulpits in the Methodist Episcopal Church, to the great greivance of many:— . . . Therefore, we, the delegates of the friends of a REPRESENTATIVE FORM OF GOVERNMENT in the Methodist Episcopal Church, elected and appointed by them to meet in convention in the city of Baltimore, in November 1828, . . . do therefore adopt the following Articles of Association for the government of such Societies as shall agree thereto, under the appellation of ASSOCIATED METHODIST CHURCHES.

ARTICLES OF ASSOCIATION
To be observed until the next Convention

Article I. The articles of religion, general rules, means of grace, moral discipline, rites and ceremonies of the Methodist Episcopal Church, are hereby declared to be the rules of faith and practice for those societies which may unite in this Association; and the mode of administering the same is hereby adopted, except when contravened by some other article.

Article II. Each society, or Church, shall have the sole power to admit serious persons into full membership, and to regulate its own temporal concerns, in accordance with these articles. The stewards to be elected by the male members, over the age of twenty-one years, and the leaders by the respective classes.

Article III. The right of property is declared to be vested in the respective societies, or Churches, who shall elect trustees for the purpose of holding the same for their benefit.

Article IV. The trial of members shall be conducted according to the 7th section, 2d chapter of the Discipline of the Methodist Episcopal Church; Provided, however, that nothing therein contained shall be so construed as to deprive an accused member of the right to challenge; and provided further, that the accused shall have a right to appeal from the decision of the committee, to the next Quarterly Conference; and no member of that conference who shall have set on any case as a committee man, shall be permitted to vote on the appeal.

Article V. There shall be a Quarterly Conference in each station and circuit, composed of all the ordained and licensed preachers and exhorters, belonging thereto, and of all the stewards and leaders. The preacher in charge shall be the president of the conference. The conference shall elect its own secretary. The business of the Quarterly Conference shall be, first, to inquire into the official and religious character of all its members; Secondly, to license exhorters and suitable persons to preach the Gospel, and to recommend to the Annual Conference, preachers for ordination, or to travel. They shall also hear and decide upon appeals from committees.

Article VI. There shall be in each State, as soon as may be, one, or not exceeding two, Annual Conferences, to be composed of all the ordained ministers, and an equal number of lay delegates; but until such time, conferences may be formed when it shall be most convenient. The lay delegates to the Annual Conferences shall be chosen by the licensed preachers, and lay male members over the age of twenty-one years, at the quarterly meetings next preceding the sitting of the Annual Conferences.

Article VII. Each Annual Conference shall elect a president and secretary.

Article VIII. Each Annual Conference shall provide the mode of stationing its own preachers.

Article IX. It shall be the duty of the presidents of the Annual Conferences, to travel through their respective bounds, to fill vacancies, and to make such changes in the circuits, or stations, as may be deemed absolutely necessary. The president shall have the right of the pulpit in whatever place he may be, but shall not supercede the prerogatives of the minister in charge.

Article X. Each Annual Conference shall have power to make such rules and regulations for its own government, and the government of the stations and circuits within its bounds, as may be necessary for the promotion of the spiritual interests of the community; Provided, nevertheless, that no rule shall be binding on the preachers or people, which shall contravene the provisions of these articles.

Article XI. Each Annual Conference shall have power to receive into the itinerancy, and to ordain, such preachers as may be recommended to that body by the Quarterly Conference. The president, assisted by two or more elders, shall perform the ordination. .

Text—Williams: *History of the Methodist Protestant Church*, pp. 282-285.

VI. *METHODIST BISHOPS AND ABOLITION AGITATION*

Address of Bishops Hedding and Emory

To the Ministers and Preachers of the Methodist Episcopal Church, within the New England and New Hampshire Annual Conferences, September 10, 1835

DEAR BRETHREN:—Grace to you, and peace from God, our Father, and the Lord Jesus Christ.

We have marked with deep solicitude the painful excitement which, in some parts of your section of our charge, has been producing disturbance on the subject of the immediate abolishment of slavery in the slaveholding states. We are happy, at the same time, to be able to say, that having now, between us, attended the northern and eastern conferences, as far as the Troy, inclusive, we have found no such excitement, of any moment, within any of them except yours; and even within yours we know that a large and highly-respectable portion of yourselves, with, we are inclined to think, a majority of our members and friends, greatly disapprove and deplore the existing agitations on this question. That a large majority of our preachers and people within those of the non-slaveholding States generally, to which our recent visitations, have extended, are decidedly opposed to the modern measures of immediate abolitionists we are well assured; and believing, as we do, that these measures have already been productive of pernicious results, and tend to the production of others yet more disastrous, both in the Church and in the social and political relations of the country, we deem it our duty to address to you a pastoral letter on the subject.

Enjoying as we do, in common with all our fellow-citizens, the protection of the Constitution of the United States, and the inestimable blessings resulting from the general union of the states under its happy auspices, are we not bound, in conscience and honor, while we accept the benefit on one hand, to maintain on the other, in good faith, that fundamental principle of the original compact of union by which each state reserves to itself, and has guaranteed to it by all the rest, the exclusive control of its internal and domestic affairs; and for which, consequently, the citizens of other states are no more responsible than for the domestic regulations under any foreign government? Can we, indeed, taking human nature and the established laws of intercourse between states and nations as they are, reasonably suppose that the peace of the country, or even of the world, can be preserved on any other principle?

That a deep political game is involved in the present agitation of this question, there are evidences too strong to be resisted. Will you take it amiss, then, if we warn you against being drawn into that vortex, or suffering yourselves to be made the instruments of drawing others in?

The question of slavery, itself, it is not our purpose here to discuss; nor is there any occasion for it. The sentiment of our Church on this subject is well known. Our object is rather to confine ourselves to the practical considerations which press upon us in the present crisis, and which, we presume, can not fail to arrest the attention of the humane, the pious, and the reflecting of all parties. . . .

There is one other important practical bearing of the question which greatly affects us, and on which humanity itself demands of you the most serious reflection. We allude to the interests of the colored population themselves, both bond and free. That many well-meaning persons are totally misled on this point, we are entirely confident. One of us has traveled through every slaveholding state in the Union, except one; and the other through nearly all. We have conversed freely and extensively with intelligent men of all parties; and have narrowly observed the progress and bearings of the modern agitations on this subject; and on a review of the whole, we are compelled to express our deliberate conviction that nothing has ever occurred so seriously tending to obstruct and retard, if not absolutely to defeat the cause of emancipation itself; to bring upon the slaves increased rigor of treatment and privation of privileges; to overwhelm the multitudes of free colored people in the slaveholding states with persecution, and banishment; to involve the friends of gradual emancipation within those states in injurious and dangerous suspicions; and, above all, to embarrass all our efforts, as well as by the regular ministry as by missionary means, to gain access to and to promote the salvation of both the slaveholders and their slaves.

. . . .

That the New Testament Scriptures, or the preaching or practice of our Lord or his apostles, were ever intended to justify the condition of slavery, we do not believe. Yet are we as well satisfied that the present course of immediate abolitionists is equally foreign from the practical examples furnished us by those high and sacred authorities, and in circumstances less difficult than ours. . . .

We entreat, therefore, that none of you will take part in such measures, or in any others calculated to inflame the public mind with angry passion, and to stir up civil or ecclesiastical strife and disunion, in violation of our solemn vows. And if any will persist in so doing, whether from the pulpit or otherwise, we earnestly recommend to our members and friends every-where, by all lawful and Christian means, to discountenance them in such a course. The presiding elders, especially, we earnestly exhort to discountenance such practices, both by their counsel and example. And if any, of whatever class, go beyond their own bounds, or leave their proper appointments, whether under the pretext of agencies or otherwise, to agitate other societies or communities on this subject, we advise the preachers, the trustees, and the official and other members to manifest their disapprobation, and to refuse the use of their pulpits and houses for such purposes. Let us leave off contention before it be meddled with, and maintain and set forward, as much as lieth in us, quietness, peace and love, among all Christian people, and especially among those committed to our charge.

. . . .

In conclusion, permit us, beloved brethren, to cherish a confidence in the Lord touching you, that ye both do and will do the things which we entreat you.

May we be mutually guided by that wisdom that cometh from above; and the Lord direct our hearts into the love of God, and into the patient waiting for Christ.

ELIJAH HEDDING,

J. EMORY.

Text—Elliott: *History of the Great Secession*, Document 18, pp. 898-899.

VII. *THE CONFERENCE ISSUE*

Bishop Waugh's Letter of June 8, 1837

To T. Merritt, I. Bonney, J. A. Merrill, and others:—

DEAR BRETHREN:—Last evening I received a communication signed by you, and upward of sixty other members of the New England conference of the Methodist Episcopal Church, in which you inform me that you have in your possession a large number of memorials on the subject of slavery—similar to the one shown me by the Rev. J. A. Merrill—which you wish the privilege of presenting to the conference. You also proceed to say, 'We respectfully ask it, as our right as a conference, to appoint a committee to consider and report on the said memorials, as also the right to act in a conference capacity on any report from such committee,' and you close by asking me to inform you 'whether you are to expect any opposition from me as the president of the conference, against any action of the conference in the premises above stated.'

In reply to your communication, I respectfully and affectionately say to you, that, as far as may be consistent with my obligations to the General conference of the Methodist Episcopal Church, it will afford me pleasure to abstain from any course in which conflict or disagreement would be likely to rise on any subject which may come before the conference. I can not, however, admit the doctrine which you have set up in your communication, when you say that it is your RIGHT to appoint a committee to report on said memorial, and also to act on any report from such committee. I can not admit this unqualified and unlimited doctrine of right, because I know of no instrument, or organization, or established usage, which gives such a right to an annual conference. Annual conferences owe their existence to the General conference, and can not have organization without the action of that body in fixing the bodies thereof. The General conference determines not only the locations and bounds of an annual conference, but defines the business to which its action extends. It will not be pretended by any one that an annual conference is a legislative body. Its functions are judicial and executive. Whence, then, the right claimed to receive memorials on the subject of slavery, to refer them to a committee, and to act on any report which may be made by such committee? Has any conference, but the General conference, jurisdiction over the subject of slavery? I believe not. It is, indeed, admitted that those conferences within whose bounds slavery exists can, and ought, to take such cognizance of the subject as they are empowered and directed to do by the General conference; but what executive act can be performed by an annual conference on the subject of slavery, in whose bounds it has no existence? But the doctrine set up can not be admitted because of its destructive tendency. If an annual conference can extend its jurisdiction over questions other than those which are judicial and executive, then it may introduce and prosecute measures which may arraign, censure, or condemn the very body which gives it existence. It may appoint a committee to investigate and report on any of our doctrines, either favorably or unfavorably. It may take under its revision the very Discipline itself, and by report sanction or condemn it. Such a doctrine is too absurd and subversive of order to be admitted. But even if it were true that the right existed, would there be EXPEDIENCY in its exercise on the subject of slavery and abolition at the present time? Will you, brethren, hazard the unity of the Methodist Episcopal Church, destroy and break down her onward march, by agitating those fearfully-exciting topics, and that too, in opposition to the solemn decision, and deliberate conclusion of the General Conference? . . .

I beg you, dear brethren, to pause and consider before you proceed. I am not the apologist of slavery; I have, long since, settled my opinions against it. I would that it were obliterated from the earth; but, in view of the terrible consequences which are likely to follow the agitation of those exciting topics, at the present, I can not consent to be participant, in any sense or degree, in those measures which are advocated by modern abolitionists. I am, nevertheless, earnestly desirous to avoid any collision with so large and respectable a portion of the New England conference as have signed the communication named in this reply. For all of you brethren, I cherish the most kind and affectionate regard. Some of you are my intimate friends, in whose society I have spent many pleasant moments. You must know that I can have no motives of personal or selfish nature in the course which I pursue on this unhappy subject. I have deliberated and prayed; I have counseled and advised; and have, tremblingly, yet firmly arrived at the following conclusions, and I now offer you the alternative. Before, however, I proceed to state them, I beg you to understand the ground on which the first proposition is predicated. It is offered as a conciliatory measure, and is distinctly declared to be without intention or design to have it understood that the New England conference, as such, is committed, by this peace-offering, to the cause of modern abolition.

First, I will not oppose the reading of the memorials alluded to in the conference, nor will I object to putting the question to a motion to refer them to a committee to consider and report thereon: provided you will agree to two things, which are so reasonable in themselves, that I flatter myself they will readily meet your concurrence. These are, First, That, in your report you will confine your action on the question of slavery to a respectful petition, or memorial, to the General Conference of 1840; and, secondly, That you will agree not to publish your report to either the civil or religious community, so as to increase or keep up an excitement upon the subject.

But if you like not this course, nor agree to it, then I must say that, on a motion to refer the memorial to a committee, I shall deem it my duty, for reasons which I will assign at the time, to refuse to put the motion to the vote, and time and eternity must disclose the true doctrine of responsibility for the consequences resulting.

Affectionately yours,

B. WAUGH.

Text—Elliott: *History of the Great Secession*, Document 26, pp. 922, 923.

Report of the Methodist Anti-Slavery Convention—Lynn: October 25, 1837

"The committee to whom was referred the subject of conference rights, beg leave to report:

. . . .

If we understand this subject, the rights claimed by some of our annual conferences, and of which they think they have been unjustly deprived, are such as involve moral obligations—obligations imposed upon them by what our Discipline pronounces a 'great evil,' and an evil which exists in the Church of which we are members. The cries of suffering humanity, and of those perishing for lack of knowledge, urge us on to the performance of those duties which some of our presidents have prohibited.

. . . .

The ground assumed by two of our bishops, is, that they are not obliged to put any questions to the vote, in an annual conference, except such as is specified in the Discipline; and that an annual conference is not obliged to do any other business. It is admitted that an annual conference can not force its president to put any question to the vote, whether specified in the Discipline or not; neither can the president force the conference to do any business, more or less. But it appears to your committee that both the nature and fitness of things, requires annual conferences to do all the business, which, in their judgment the interests of the Church demand; provided they do not conflict with the provisions of the charter. The conference, we think should be the judge—providing it keeps within the provisions of the charter—as to what business the interests of the Church require to be done.

. . . .

To suppose that one man can be under a moral obligation to prevent a hundred others from performing what they conscientiously believe to be a Christian duty, is absurd. And to suppose the conscience of a president is the standard by which the consciences of the whole body are to be tested, is equally absurd. The president has a conscience as well as the members; and if he can not conscientiously perform the duties of the chair, he can resign his office. But while he fills the chair, has he any right to make his conscientious scruples a pretext for laying heavy burdens on the consciences of hundreds of ministers and thousands of Church members? The conference does what it does, on moral subjects, under a sense of moral obligation. The president puts these matters to the vote, not because HE believes the measure judicious or injudicious, but because HE IS THE PRESIDENT. He has not been appointed to that office to do certain things, and nothing else; but to put to the vote any business the conference may wish to act upon, providing it keep within the provisions of the constitution. And if it be contrary to the Discipline to express an opinion on the evils of slavery, let it be shown. If, therefore, an annual conference feels itself religiously bound to oppose any sin, and especially such sins as the Discipline acknowledges to be moral evils, the president can have no right to prevent such expression of opinion; and to do so, is to establish a principle dangerous as a precedent, and oppressive in its nature and tendency."

Text—Elliott: *History of the Great Secession*, Document 29, pp. 939-942.

VIII. *A PLAN OF PACIFICATION.—NEW ENGLAND CONFERENCE, June 6, 1838*

Common Ground

Whereas, The Methodist Episcopal Church in the North has been and is still greatly excited on the subject of American Slavery, and the means which should be used for its removal from the Church—and

Whereas, We deem it of vital importance that the peace of the Church should be secured, in order to her prosperity—

And, Whereas it is recognized as a cardinal virtue in religion by our blessed Lord, that his followers should be 'Peace Makers,' and love one another—and which are even given as tests of discipleship—

Therefore, the undersigned, ministers of said Church, after mutual consultation, have agreed to adopt the following Principles and Measures for the purposes above named.

Principles

We believe that the system of American Slavery is a great moral evil: and that the relations springing from this, which bind an innocent race to perpetual bondage to others against their wish, are sinful: although we concede that the master who sustains this relation, is not, in every case, necessarily guilty.

Measures

We agree that, in any action we may be disposed to take on this or any other subject, we will . . .

1. Never attack an officer, clergyman, or private member of the Church in a public journal or lecture, or publicly arraign the official acts of any church officer: but all such difficulties shall be adjusted according to the Discipline of our Church. Provided, however, that this shall not prevent the courteous investigation of principles and opinions.

2. We agree that we will not countenance any brother in leaving his proper work to lecture upon this or any other subject, without the sanction of the proper authorities of the Church.

3. No paper shall be established ostensibly for the purpose above stated by our aid or sanction, or shall be countenanced by us, which claims to be controlled by any Wesleyan or Methodist societies, or having appellations attached to them peculiar to our Church.

4. We agree that no societies or conventions claiming the character specified in section 3d, shall receive our approbation or aid. Our conviction is that, in the present state of affairs, the peace of the Church claims at our hands that organizations of this character should not exist.

5. We hold that our ministers and private members are at liberty (nor shall it be regarded as an offence for them thus to do) to connect themselves as they may choose with any Anti-Slavery Society independent of the Church; provided, however, that our action in such cases shall not contravene the principles of this agreement.

6. It shall not be regarded as an offence—but considered just—that prayer be offered in public by us for the master and his slave, or for the abolishment of the system. But we recommend that the apostolic language be used, as far as may be, in such devotions.

7. Our preachers have liberty not only to read our rules once a quarter to the societies, and once a year to the whole congregation, but to explain at these seasons any part of our Discipline.

8. We hold that our people have the right of petitioning the General Conference through the yearly conferences or otherwise, upon this or any subject with which *they have to do.*

9. Nevertheless, in all circumstances relating to the above, we recommend to our preachersand people to exercise 'the wisdom of the serpent and the harmlessness of the dove.'

Text—Matlack: *The History of American Slavery and Methodism* . . . , pp. 182-184.

IX. *THE WESLEYAN METHODIST CHURCH PASTORAL ADDRESS*

Of the Convention assembled at Utica, N.Y., May 31, 1843, for the purpose of organizing the Wesleyan Methodist Church.

"To the Members and Friends of the same:

BELOVED BRETHREN AND FRIENDS:—The Convention having accomplished the object for which it assembled, we deem it proper, before we retire to our respective fields of labor, to address you on the subject of its happy issue, and the duties and prospects that lie before us. . .

We can do no less than congratulate you, brethren, on the organization of a Christian community, free from the above-named objectionable features, while it retains all that is valuable in Methodism, all that most of us ever loved, in view of which we joined the M. E. Church, and for the sake of which many of us spent the ardor of our youth and the strength of our manhood to build her up. Did we leave behind the valuable features of Wesleyan Methodism, we should think we were making a sacrifice indeed, but such is not the case; we retain all that is essential to it, all that is peculiar to the whole family of Wesleyan Methodists in Europe and America, while we have thrown off those peculiarities which distinguish the M. E. Church from the other portions of the Wesleyan family.

The most important changes which we have made, consist in our repudiation of all connection with Slavery and slaveholders, and our rejection of the prerogative system of Episcopacy, and in these it cannot be pretended that we have sacrificed any essential part of Wesleyan Methodism. That our divorce from Slavery and slaveholders cannot be considered a sacrifice of Wesleyanism is plain, since its founder said, that 'Slavery is the sum of all villainies,' and that 'all men-buyers' (slaveholders) 'are exactly on a level with men-stealers.' Nor can it be contended that Episcopacy is any part of Wesleyan Methodism, for it forms no part of the economy of the Wesleyan Connection in Europe and Canada, but is peculiar to the Methodist E. Church in this country. . .

We must expect to meet with opposition, endure reproach, and make sacrifices, but these we can cheerfully bear, in the cause of God, justice, mercy and humanity. . .

But, brethren, we deem it proper to caution you against indulging in an improper spirit towards those from whom you may receive wrong treatment. . . . You must expect to be misrepresented, and have your motives impugned; those who remain in the M. E. Church cannot be expected to appreciate your reasons for secession; . . . Not only so, but the history of the past shows that the members of any religious community are wont to feel less friendship for seceders from their own communion, and their general policy is apt to be more bitter and persecuting towards such, than towards other branches of the Church, who are much further removed from their common views. We do not now say why this is so, nor do we say that it is right, but only advert to it as a fact, which sheds some light on the treatment which we shall all, probably, receive from many of our former associates, with whom we have taken sweet counsel in days gone by. . .

Your enlightened Christian benevolence will so direct you, as to render it unnecessary for us to say much, by way of giving specific direction; yet you will suffer us to advert to a few leading objects, worthy of the best efforts of every Christian. Your first efforts are, of course, due to the maintainance of the ministrations of truth in your own neighborhood. . .

In connection with the above, we would call your attention to the cause of Sabbath-schools. Too much importance cannot be attached to the religious instruction of the children and youth under our care; it will do more to banish infidelity, to dry up the fountains of vice, to brighten the prospects of the future church, and to lay the foundation for a more glorious era in the history of Christianity, than any other one branch of moral effort.

We also trust you will not be wanting in your efforts to support the cause of Missions, and we are happy to say that measures are already in progress to give you an opportunity to show your zeal in this enterprise, as you will be more particularly informed through another channel. Many have had their benevolence restrained in this branch of moral effort for want of a channel through which to direct their liberality, unpolluted by slavery; and as this obstacle is now removed, we doubt not principal and interest will soon be forthcoming.

The cause of the bleeding slave, you will never forget; nor will you overlook the cause of Temperance, which has already done so much for the restoration of the degraded, and to make the wretched happy. In a word, we desire that every member of the Wesleyan Connection should not only be a zealous advocate of every branch of moral reform, but co-workers, even in the front rank, battling side by side with those who contend with the Lord's enemies.

But above all, brethren, we exhort you to make holiness your motto. It is holiness of heart and life that will arm you against every assault, that will give you moral power to oppose the evils and corruption in the world, against which we have lifted up a standard. . .

LUTHER LEE, Chairman,
G. PEGLER, J. WATSON, M. SWIFT, R. BENNETT.

Utica, N. Y., June 8, 1843.''

Text—Matlack: The History of American Slavery and Methodism . . . and History of the Wesleyan Methodist Connection . . . in Two Parts . . . , pp. 338-344.

X. BISHOP ANDREW'S CASE

"A. Griffith and J. Davis offered the following preamble and resolution, which were read and debated;—

'WHEREAS, The Rev. James O. Andrew, one of the Bishops of the M. E. Church, has become connected with slavery, as communicated in his statement in his reply to the inquiry of the Committee on the Episcopacy, which reply is embodied in their report, No. 3, offered yesterday: and WHEREAS it has been, from the origin of said Church, a settled policy and the invariable usage to elect no person to the office of Bishop who was embarrassed with this 'great evil,' as under such circumstance it would be impossible for a bishop to exercise the functions and perform the duties assigned to a general Superintendent with acceptance, in that large portion of his charge in which slavery does not exist; and WHEREAS Bishop Andrew was himself nominated by our brethren of the slaveholding states, and elected by the General Conference of 1832, as a candidate who, though living in the midst of a slave-holding population, was nevertheless free from all personal connection with slavery; and WHEREAS, this is, of all periods in our history as a Church, the one least favourable to such an innovation upon the practice and usage of Methodism as to confide a part of the itinerant general superintendency to a slaveholder: therefore,

Resolved, That the Rev. James O. Andrew be, and he is hereby affectionately requested to resign his office as one of the Bishops of the Methodist Episcopal Church.'

. . . .

Bishop Waugh, in behalf of the Bishops, presented the following communication, which was read by himself, and also by the Secretary:—

'*To the General Conference of the Methodist E. Church.*

REV. AND DEAR BRETHREN:—The undersigned respectfully and affectionately offer to your calm consideration the result of their consultation this afternoon in regard to the unpleasant and very delicate question which has been so long and so earnestly debated before your body. . . . At this painful crisis they have unanimously concurred in the propriety of recommending the postponement of further action in the case of Bishop Andrew until the ensuing General Conference. It does not enter into the design of the undersigned to argue the propriety of their recommendation, otherwise strong and valid reasons might be adduced in its support. They cannot but think that if the embarrassment of Bishop Andrew should not cease before that time, the next General Conference, representing the pastors, ministers, and people of the several Annual Conferences, after all the facts in the case shall have passed in review before them, will be better qualified than the present General Conference can be to adjudicate the case wisely and discreetly. Until the cessation of the embarrassment, or the expiration of the interval between the present and the ensuing General Conference, the undersigned believe that such a division of the work of the general superintendency might be made without any infraction of a constitutional principle, as would fully employ Bishop Andrew in those sections of the church in which his presence and services would be welcome and cordial. If the course pursued on this occasion by the undersigned be deemed a novel one, they persuade themselves that their justification, in view of all candid and peace-loving persons, will be found in their strong desire to prevent disunion, and to promote harmony in the church.

Very respectfully and affectionately submitted,

JOSHUA SOULE,
ELIJAH HEDDING,
B. WAUGH,
T. A. MORRIS.

Thursday afternoon, May 30, 1844.'

. . . .

'WHEREAS, The Discipline of our church forbids the doing anything calculated to destroy our itinerant general superintendency, and WHEREAS Bishop Andrew has become connnected with slavery by marriage and otherwise, and this act having drawn after it circumstances which, in the estimation of the General Conference, will greatly embarrass the exercise of his office as an itinerant general Superintendent, if not in some places entirely prevent it; therefore,

Resolved, That it is the sense of this General Conference that he desist from the exercise of his office so long as this impediment remains.'

. . . .

To the General Conference

Bishop Soule presented the following communication:—

'To the General Conference.

REV. AND DEAR BRETHREN:—As the case of Bishop Andrew unavoidably involves the future action of the Superintendents, which, in their judgment, in the present position of the Bishop, they have no discretion to decide upon; they respectfully request of this General Conference official instruction, in answer to the following questions:—

1. Shall Bishop Andrew's name remain as it now stands in the Minutes, Hymn-books and Discipline, or shall it be struck off of these official records?

2. How shall the Bishop obtain his support? As provided for in the form of Discipline, or in some other way?

3. What work if any, may the Bishop perform; and how shall he be appointed to the work?

> JOSHUA SOULE,
> ELIJAH HEDDING,
> BEVERLY WAUGH,
> THOMAS A. MORRIS.'

J. T. Mitchell offered the following resolutions, in reply to the several inquiries of the Superintendents:—

'1. *Resolved*, As the sense of this Conference, that Bishop Andrew's name stand in the Minutes, Hymn-book and Discipline, as formerly.

2. *Resolved*, That the rule in relation to the support of a Bishop, and his family, applies to Bishop Andrew.

3. *Resolved*, That whether in any, and if any, in what work, Bishop Andrew be employed, is to be determined by his own decision and action, in relation to the previous action of this Conference in his case."

Text—*Journals of the General Conference* . . . Vol. II, pp. 63, 64, 75, 83, 84, 117, 118.

CHAPTER XXVIII

The Churches and the Civil War

Bibliography

The following volumes give some idea of what the pulpit was saying during the War: "Fast Day Sermons or The Pulpit on the State of the Country" (1861); "Our Country: Its Trial and Its Triumph"—A Series of Discourses suggested by the Varying Events of the War for the Union" (1865) by George Peck; "National Sermons: Sermons, Speeches and Letters on Slavery and Its War; from the Passage of the Fugitive Slave Bill to the Election of President Grant" (1869) by Gilbert Haven. A lengthy editorial article discussing the latter appears in the "Methodist Quarterly Review," April, 1870.

While the war was in progress the periodicals discussed various aspects of this crisis. It is in this literature that the student will find significant material for investigating the attitude of the church to the war, and the influence of church forces upon its fortunes. The articles are as follows: "State of the Country—Question at Issue" ("Evang. Rev."Oct. 1, 1861) "The State of the Country" ("Pres. Quar. Rev." July, 1861); "The National Crisis" ("Christian Rev." July, 1861); "The Moral Aspects of the Present Struggle" ("Amer. Theol. Rev." Oct. 1861); "The Lessons of our National Conflict" ("New Englander, Oct. 1861); "Our Country, Its Peril, Its Deliverance" ("Danville Quar. Rev." March, 1861); "Liberty and Slavery" ("Free-Will Bapt. Quar." April, 1861); "Christianity and the War" ("Univ. Quar. and Gen. Rev." Oct. 1861); "The National Question" ("Merc'burg Rev." July, 1861); "Our National Crisis" ("Evang. Rev." July, 1861); "The Great Rebellion Traced to Its Source" ("Unit. Pres. Quar. Rev." July, 1861); "The State of the Country" ("So. Pres. Rev." Jan. 1861); "The Pulpit and the Crisis" ("New Englander" Jan. 1861); "The American Quarterly Church Review, and our National Crisis" ("Amer. Quar. Ch. Rev." April, 1861); "The Study of the Prophetic Scriptures, Especially a Duty at the Present Time" ("Theol. and Lit. Jour." April, 1861); "The Princeton Review on the State of the Country" ("So. Pres. Rev." April, 1861); "A Vindication of Secession of

604

the South" (*ibid.* April, 1861); "The Lessons Taught by the late Extraordinary Political Events and the Catastrophe to which they are Tending" ("Theol. and Lit. Jour." April, 1861); "Is Cotton King and the American Constitution at the Present Crisis" ("Nat'l Review" Oct. 1861); "Slavery and the War" ("Brownson's Quar. Rev." Oct. 1861).

"Slavery and the Slave Trade" ("Bibl. Rep. and Prince. Rev." July, 1862); "The American Crisis" ("Meth. Quar. Rev." Oct. 1862); "The National Crisis" ("Amer. Theol. Rev." Oct. 1862); "The State and Slavery" ("Bibl. Sacra" Oct. 1862); "Our Duty as a Nation" ("New Englander" Jan. 1862); "The Wars of the Lord" (*ibid.* Jan. 1862); "The War for the Union" ("Pres. Quar. Rev." Jan. 1862); "The War and Slavery" ("Freewill Bapt. Quar." April, 1862); "The Secession Conspiracy in Kentucky and its Overthrow" ("Danville Rev." March, 1862); "A Providential View of War" ("Univ. Quar." July, 1862); "The Test Hour of Popular Liberty and Republican Government" ("New Englander," April, 1862); "The Two Rebellions—An Analogy of Faith" ("Pres. Quar. Rev." Oct. 1862); "A Review of the Reasons Assigned for the Rebellion" ("Univ. Quar." April, 1862); "Negro Slavery and the Civil War" ("Danville Rev." Dec. 1862); "State Rebellion, State Suicide, and Emancipation and Colonization" ("Brownson's Rev." April, 1862); "Emancipation" ("New Englander," Oct. 1862).

"The Moral and Religious Value of our National Union" ("Bibl. Sacra" Jan. 1863); "The War" ("Bibl. Rep. and Prince. Rev." Jan. 1863); "The Proclamation of Freedom" ("Freewill Bapt. Quar." Jan. 1863); "Loyalty and Disloyalty, Interpreting the Constitution" ("New Englander" April, 1863).

"The Loyalty Demanded by the Present Crisis" ("Danville Rev.," March, 1864); "Disloyalty in the Church" (*ibid.*); "The Logic and the End of the Rebellion" ("Univ. Quar." Jan. 1864); "The Union, the Constitution, and Slavery" ("Amer. Quar. Ch. Rev." Jan. 1864).

"The Rights of the Nation and the Duty of Congress" ("New Englander" Oct. 1865); "Ought Treason Against the Government of the United States to be Punished?" (*ibid.*); "Christianity and the War Power" ("Meth. Quar. Rev." April, 1865); "The Great Election" (*ibid.*); "Slavery and Christianity" ("Amer. Pres. & Theol. Rev." Oct. 1865).

The following present the opinions of different wings of the American Church: "Lectures on Slavery" (1860), also "Our Country and the Church" (1861) by N. L. Rice, D.D.; "The National Controversy: Or The Voice of the Fathers upon the State of the Country" (1861) by J. C.

Stiles; "Slavery and the War, A Historical Essay" (1863) by Rev. Henry Darling.

The present European conflagration lends interest to the literature that discussed the rightfulness of war. The following are to be noted, though some antedate the rebellion: "Wickedness of War" ("Christian Rev." June, 1838); "Can War Under any Circumstances be justified on the principles of the Christian Religion?" (*ibid.*, Sept. 1847); "Objection to the Present War Policy of the Nation" (*ibid.*, May, 1849); "Christianity and War" (*ibid.*, Oct. 1861); "Arbitration as a Substitute for War" ("Pres. Quar. and Princ. Rev." April, 1874); "A Review—Life of William Ladd, The Apostle of Peace" by Jacob S. Willets, abridged (1875) from a memoir by John Hemmenway.

"The Church and the Rebellion" (appendix to "The Political History of the United States of America during the Great Rebellion," sec. edition 1865), by Edward McPherson, gives the deliverances of the northern churches in the war; the action of the churches in the Insurrectionary States; the orders of the Secretary of War respecting the Southern houses of worship; the 'Baltimore,' 'McPheeters,' and 'Anderson' cases; and other documentary material.

The contribution made by the churches in sending men to the front, and the consequences thereof upon church activity, notably in the weaker missionary churches, are abundantly presented in journals such as "The Home Missionary," also in the official records of the various church organizations. "The Women of the Northwest during the War" ("New Englander," Oct. 1868) will repay reading.

A suggestive sermon by Beecher setting forth the decisive influence of home missionary effort in connection with the response of the Northwest to the call for soldiers appears in "The Home Missionary" 1863-64, pp. 110 f.

The benevolent activities of the churches in seeking to ameliorate war distress are set forth as under: "The Philanthropic Results of the War in America—Collected from Official and other Authentic Sources by an American Citizen" (1864); "Philanthropy in War Time" ("Meth. Quar. Rev." Jan. 1865); The official "Annual Reports" of the Christian Commission; "The United States Christian Commission" ("Evang. Quar. Rev.," April, 1865); "A Memorial Record of the New York Branch of the United States Christian Commission, compiled under direction of the Executive Committee" (1866); "Annals of the United States Christian Commission" (1868) by Rev. Lemuel Moss. Also see article in the "Baptist Quarterly," Vol. II, pp. 194-227.

"A Narrative of the Great Revival which Prevailed in the Southern Armies During the Late Civil War . . . " (1877) by W. W. Bennett, D.D., sets forth a slight recompense received by the Church in this time of stress.

Two notable recent studies are "The Cleavage between Eastern and Western Virginia," by Chas. H. Ambler ("Amer. Hist. Rev." Vol. XV, No. 4), and "The Fight for the Northwest, 1860," by W. E. Dodd (*ibid.*, Vol. XVI, No. 4). The latter gives the pro-slavery attitude of the churches, especially the Presbyterian, Methodist, Baptist, and Congregationalist.

"The Methodist Episcopal Church and the Civil War," 1912), W. W. Sweet skillfully treats a delicate subject, also "The Lutheran Church and the Civil War" (1920) by C. W. Heathcote.

DOCUMENTS

1. *THE SECESSION OF THE PRESBYTERIAN CHURCH IN THE CONFEDERATE STATES OF AMERICA*

The General Assembly of the Presbyterian Church in the Confederate States of America, to all the Churches of Jesus Christ throughout the earth, greeting: Grace, mercy, and peace be multiplied unto you!

"Dearly beloved brethren: It is probably known to you that the Presbyteries and Synods in the Confederate States, which were formerly in connection with the General Assembly of the Presbyterian Church in the United States of America, have renounced the jurisdiction of that body; and dissolved the ties which bound them ecclesiastically with their brethren of the North. This act of separation left them without any formal union among themselves. But as they were one in faith and order, and still adhered to their old standards, measures were promptly adopted for giving expression to their unity, by the organization of a Supreme Court, upon the model of the one whose authority they had just relinquished. Commissioners, duly appointed, from all the Presbyteries of these Confederate States, met accordingly, in the city of Augusta, on the fourth day of December, in the year of our Lord one thousand eight hundred and sixty-one, and then and there proceeded to constitute the General Assembly of the Presbyterian Church in the Confederate States of America. . . . In thus taking its place among sister churches of this and other countries, it seems proper that it should set forth the causes which have impelled it to separate from the Church of the North, and to indicate a general view of the course which it feels it incumbent upon it to pursue in the new circumstances in which it is placed.

. . . .

1. In the first place, the course of the last Assembly, at Philadalphia, conclusively shows that if we should remain together, the political questions which divide us as citizens, will be obtruded on our Church Courts, and discussed by Christian ministers and elders with all the acrimony, bitterness, and rancor, with which such questions are usually discussed by men of the world. Our Assembly would present a mournful spectacle of strife and debate. Commissioners from the Northern would

meet with Commissioners from the Southern Confederacy, to wrangle over the questions which have split them into two confederacies, and involved them in furious and bloody war. . . .

The only conceivable condition, therefore, upon which the Church of the North and the South could remain together as one body, with any prospect of success, is the rigorous exclusion of the questions and passions of the forum from its halls of debate. This is what always ought to be done. The provinces of Church and State are perfectly distinct, and the one has no right to usurp the jurisdiction of the other. The State is a natural institute, founded in the constitution of man as moral and social and designed to realize the idea of justice. It is the society of rights. The Church is a supernatural institute, founded in the facts of redemption, and is designed to realize the idea of grace. . . . When the State makes wicked laws, contradicting the eternal principles of rectitude, the Church is at liberty to testify against them and humbly to petition that they may be repealed. In like manner, if the Church becomes seditious and a disturber of the peace, the State has a right to abate the nuisance. In ordinary cases, however, there is not likely to be a collision. Among a Christian people, there is little difference of opinion as to the radical distinctions of right and wrong. The only serious danger is where moral duty is conditioned upon a political question. Under the pretext of inculcating duty, the Church may usurp the power to determine the question which conditions it, and that is precisely what she is debarred from doing. .

Had these principles been steadily maintained by the Assembly at Philadelphia, it is possible that the ecclesiastical separation of the North and the South might have been deferred for years to come. . . .

2. Though the immediate occasion of separation was the course of the General Assembly at Philadelphia in relation to the Federal Government and the war, yet there is another ground on which the independent organization of the Southern Church can be amply and scripturally maintained. The unity of the Church does not require a formal bond of union among all the congregations of believers throughout the earth. . .

Churches may be perfectly at one in every principle of faith and order, and yet geographically distinct, and mutually independent. As the unity of the human race is not disturbed by its division into countries and nations, so the unity of the spiritual seed of Christ is neither broken nor impaired by separation and division into various Church constitutions. . . .

If it is desirable that each nation should contain a separate and an independent Church, the Presbyteries of these Confederate States need no apology for bowing to the decree of Providence, which, in withdrawing their country from the government of the United States, has, at the same time, determined that they should withdraw from the Church of their fathers. It is not that they have ceased to love it—not that they have abjured its ancient principles, or forgotten its glorious history. It is to give these same principles a richer, freer, fuller development among ourselves than they possibly could receive under foreign culture. It is precisely because we love that Church as it was, and that Church as it should be, that we have resolved, as far as in us lies, to realize its grand idea in the country, and under the Government where God has cast our lot. With the supreme control of ecclesiastical affairs in our hands, we may be able, in some competent measure, to consummate this result. In subjection to a foreign power, we could no more accomplish it than the Church in the United States could have been developed in dependence upon the Presbyterian Church of Scotland. The difficulty there would have been, not the distance of Edinburgh from

New York, Philadelphia, or Charleston, but the difference in the manners, habits, customs, and ways of thinking, the social, civil, and political institutions of the people. These same difficulties exist in relation to the Confederate and United States, and render it eminently proper that the Church in each should be as separate and independent as the Governments.

In addition to this, there is one difference which so radically and fundamentally distinguishes the North and the South, that it is becoming every day more and more apparent that the religious, as well as the secular, interests of both will be more effectually promoted by a complete and lasting separation. The antagonism of Northern and Southern sentiment on the subject of slavery lies at the root of all the difficulties which have resulted in the dismemberment of the Federal Union, and involved us in the horrors of an unnatural war. The Presbyterian Church in the United States has been enabled by Divine grace to pursue, for the most part, an eminently conservative, because a thoroughly scriptural, policy in relation to this delicate question. It has planted itself upon the Word of God, and utterly refused to make slaveholding a sin, or non-slaveholding a term of communion. But though both sections are agreed as to this general principle, it is not to be disguised that the North exercises a deep and settled antipathy to slavery itself, while the South is equally zealous in its defence. Recent events can have no other effect than to confirm the antipathy on the one hand and strengthen the attachment on the other. The Northern section of the Church stands in the awkward predicament of maintaining, in one breath, that slavery is an evil which ought to be abolished, and of asserting in the next, that it is not a sin to be visited by exclusion from communion of the saints. The consequence is, that it plays partly into the hands of abolitionists and partly into the hands of slaveholders, and weakens its influence with both. It occupies the position of a prevaricating witness whom neither party will trust. It would be better, therefore, for the moral power of the Northern section of the Church to get entirely quit of the subject. At the same time, it is intuitively obvious that the Southern section of the Church, while even partially under the control of those who are hostile to slavery, can never have free and unimpeded access to the slave population. Its ministers and elders will always be liable to some degree of suspicion. . . .

In the first place, we would have it distinctly understood that, in our ecclesiastical capacity, we are neither the friends nor the foes of slavery; that is to say, we have no commission either to propagate or abolish it. The policy of its existence or non-existence is a question which exclusively belongs to the State. We have no right, as a Church, to enjoin it as a duty, or to condemn it as a sin. Our business is with the duties which spring from the relation; the duties of the masters on the one hand, and of their slaves on the other. . . . Is slavery, then, a sin?

In answering this question, as a Church, let it be distinctly borne in mind that the only rule of judgment is the written word of God. . . . Do the Scriptures directly or indirectly condemn slavery as a sin? If they do not, the dispute is ended, for the Church, without forfeiting her character, dares not go beyond them.

Now, we venture to assert that if men had drawn their conclusions upon this subject only from the Bible, it would no more have entered into any human head to denounce slavery as a sin, than to denounce monarchy, aristocracy, or poverty. The truth is, men have listened to what they falsely considered as primitive intuitions, or as necessary deductions from primitive cognitions, and then have gone to the Bible to confirm the crotchets of their vain philosophy. They have gone there determined to find a particular result, and the consequence is, that they leave with having made, instead of having interpreted, Scripture. Slavery is no new thing. It has not only existed for ages in the world, but it has existed, under every dispensation of the covenant of grace, in the Church of God. . . .

. . . We have assumed no new attitude. We stand exactly where the Church of God has always stood—from Abraham to Moses, from Moses to Christ, from Christ to the Reformers, and from the Reformers to ourselves. We stand upon the foundation of the Prophets and Apostles, Jesus Christ himself being the chief cornerstone. Shall we be excluded from the fellowship of our brethren in other lands, because we dare not depart from the charter of our faith? . . . We feel that the souls of our slaves are a solemn trust, and we shall strive to present them faultless and complete before the presence of God.

Indeed, as we contemplate their condition in the Southern States, and contrast it with that of their fathers before them, and that of their brethren in the present day in their native land, we cannot but accept it as a gracious Providence that they have been brought in such numbers to our shores, and redeemed from the bondage of barbarism and sin. Slavery to them has certainly been overruled for the greatest good. It has been a link in the wondrous chain of Providence, through which many sons and daughters have been made heirs of the heavenly inheritance. The Providential result is, of course, no justification, if the thing is intrinsically wrong; but it is certainly a matter of devout thanksgiving, and no obscure intimation of the will and purpose of God, and of the consequent duty of the Church. . . .

As to the endless declamation about human rights, we have only to say that human rights are not a fixed, but a fluctuating quantity. Their sum is not the same in any two nations on the globe. The rights of Englishmen are one thing, the rights of Frenchmen another. There is a minimum without which a man cannot be responsible; there is a maximum which expresses the highest degree of civilization and of Christian culture. The education of the species consists in its ascent along this line. . . . Before slavery can be charged with doing him injustice, it must be shown that the minimum which falls to his lot at the bottom of the line is out of proportion to his capacity and culture—a thing which can never be done by abstract speculation. The truth is, the education of the human race for liberty and virtue, is a vast Providential scheme, and God assigns to every man, by a wise and holy decree, the precise place he is to occupy in the great moral school of humanity. . . .

. . . Whatever is universal is natural. We are willing that slavery should be tried by this standard. We are willing to abide by the testimony of the race, and if man, as man, has everywhere condemned it—if all human laws have prohibited it as crime—if it stands in the same category with malice, murder, and theft; then we are willing, in the name of humanity, to renounce it, and to renounce it forever. But what if the overwhelming majority of mankind have approved it? what if philosophers and statesmen have justified it, and the laws of all nations acknowledged it? what then becomes of these luminous intuitions? They are an *ignis fatuus*, mistaken for a star. . .

The ends which we propose to accomplish as a Church are the same as those which are proposed by every other Church. To proclaim God's truth as a witness to the nations; to gather his elect from the four corners of the earth, and through the Word, Ministers, and Ordinances, to train them for eternal life, is the great business of His people. The only thing that will be at all peculiar to us, is the manner in which we shall attempt to discharge our duty. In almost every department of labor, except the pastoral care of congregations, it has been usual for the Church to resort to societies more or less closely connected with itself, and yet, logically and really distinct. It is our purpose to rely upon the regular organs of our government and executive agencies directly and immediately responsible to them. We wish to make the Church, not merely a superintendent, but an agent. We wish to develop the idea that the congregation of believers, as visibly organized, is the very society or corporation which is divinely called to do the work of the Lord. We shall, therefore, endeavor to do what has never yet been adequately done—bring out the energies of our Presbyterian system of government. From the Session to the Assembly we shall strive to enlist all our courts, as courts, in every department of Christian effort. We are not ashamed to confess that we are intensely Presbyterian. We embrace all other denominations in the arms of Christian fellowship and love, but our own scheme of government we humbly believe to be according to the pattern shown in the Mount, and by God's grace, we propose to put its efficiency to the test. . . .

(Signed)   B. M. PALMER, *Moderator*,
JNO. N. WADDEL, *Stated Clerk*,
JOSEPH R. WILSON, *Permanent Clerk*,
D. McNEILL TURNER, *Temporary Clerk*.

Text—McPherson: *The Political History of the United States of America During the Great Rebellion*, pp. 509-512.

II. ADDRESS TO CHRISTIANS THROUGHOUT THE WORLD, BY THE CLERGY OF THE CONFEDERATE STATES OF AMERICA

This document, signed by representatives of the Baptist, Disciples, Methodist Episcopal, Methodist Protestant, Protestant Episcopal, Presbyterian, United Synod, Associate Reformed, Cumberland Presbyterian, Lutheran, and German Reformed Churches, originated in a conference of ministers that convened in Richmond, Virginia.

"CHRISTIAN BRETHREN:—In the name of our Holy Christianity, we address you in this form, respecting matters of great interest to us, which we believe deeply concern the cause of our Blessed Master, and to which we invoke your serious attention.

We speak not in the spirit of controversy, not by political inspiration, but as the servants of the Most High God, we speak the 'truth in love,' concerning things which make for peace. . . .

We submit for your consideration as the first point of our testimony and ground of protest,—

That the war waged against our people, in principle and in fact, proposes to achieve that which, in the nature of the case, it is impossible to accomplish by violence. The war proposes the restoration of the *Union*.

We can rationally suppose a war for conquest, or to expel an invader, or to compel respect for stipulations of peace and international intercourse which have been violated; but how measures of violence can reunite independent States, restore their broken fellowship, re-establish equality of representatives' rights, or coerce a people to brotherly kindness, unity, and devotion to each other, is utterly beyond our conception. . . .

Christian brethren, could the hand of violence win you to desire fellowship with a people while it destroyed your peace, polluted your sanctuaries, invaded the sacred precincts of your homes, robbed you of your property, slaughtered your noble sons, clothed your daughters in grief, filled your land with sorrow, and employed its utmost strength to reduce your country to the degradation of a subjugated province? Would it not rather animate you to prefer death—honorable death—the patriot's alternative, the Christian's martyrdom? . . .

No attempt has been made to overthrow the Government of the United States, unless by the fanatical party which now administers its affairs. The South never entertained such an idea. If that Government fall for lack of Southern support, let men discriminate between the downfall of an oppression when the oppressed have escaped, and a wanton effort to break up good government. So Pharoah fell, but not by the hand of Israel. . . .

The war is forced upon us. We have always desired peace. After a conflict of opinions between the North and the South in Church and State, of more than thirty years, growing more bitter and painful daily, we withdraw from them to secure peace—they send troops to compel us into re-union! Our proposition was peaceable separation, saying 'We are *actually* divided, our *nominal* union is only a platform of strife.' The answer is a call for *seventy-five thousand* troops, to force submssion to a Government whose character, in the judgment of the South, had been sacrificed to sectionalism. . . .

The second general point which we submit for your Christian consideration is,—

The separation of the Southern States is universally regarded by our people as final, and the formation of the Confederate States' Government as a fixed fact, promising in no respect, a restoration of the former Union.

Politically and ecclesiastically, the line has been drawn between North and South. It has been done distinctly, deliberately, finally, and in most solemn form. The Confederacy claims to possess all the conditions and essential characteristics of an independent Government. Our institutions, habits, tastes, pursuits, and religion, suggest no wish for reconstruction of the Union. We regard the Confederacy, in the wise providence of the Almighty, as the result of causes which render its independent existence a moral and political necessity, and its final and future independence of the United States not a matter that admits of the slightest doubt.

Among all the indefensible acts growing out of the inexcusable war waged against us, we will refer to one especially, in regard to which, for obvious reasons, we would speak, and as becometh us, plainly and earnestly:—*The recent proclamation of the President of the United States, seeking the emancipation of the slaves of the South, is, in our judgment, a suitable occasion for solemn protest on the part of the people of God throughout the world.*

First, upon the hypothesis that the proclamation could be carried out in its design, we have no language to describe the bloody tragedy that would appal humanity. Christian sensibilities recoil from the vision of a struggle that would inevitably lead to the slaughter of tens of thousands of poor deluded insurrectionists! Suppose their owners suffered; in the nature of things the slaves would suffer infinitely more. Make it absolutely necessary for the public safety that the slaves be slaughtered, and he who should write the history of that event would record the darkest chapter of human woe yet written.

But, *secondly*, suppose the proclamation—as indeed we esteem it in the South— a mere political document, devised to win favor among the most fanatical of the Northern people, uttering nothing that has not already been attempted, practically, but in vain, by the United States; suppose it to be worth no more than the paper upon which its bold iniquity is traced, nevertheless it is the avowal of a principle, the declaration of a wish, the deliberate attempt of the chief magistrate of a nation to do that which, as a measure of war, must be repugnant to civilisation, and which *we* calmly denounce as worthy of universal reprobation, and against which Christians in the name of humanity and religion ought to protest. . .

Let philanthropists observe, even according to its own terms, this measure is in no proper sense an act of mercy to the slave, but of malice toward the master. It provides for freeing *only the slaves of those who fight* against the United States. The effort is not to relieve that Government of slavery, where the philanthropy has full opportunity for displaying its generosity, and the power to exercise it in respect to slavery, if it exists at all, can be indulged; but the effort is simply to invoke slavery as an agent against the South, reckless of the consequences to the slaves themselves. . .

. . . .

We submit further: *That the war against the Confederate States has achieved no good result, and we find nothing in the present state of the struggle that gives promise of the United States accomplishing any good by its continuance.* . . . Nothing is therefore conquered—no part of the country is subdued; the civil jurisdiction of the United States, the real test of their success, *has not been established by any force of arms.* Where such civil jurisdiction exists at all along the border, it had existed all the while, was not obtained by force, and is not the fruit of conquest. The fact is admitted by our enemies themselves. . .

The only change of opinion among our people since the beginning of the war, that is of material importance to the final issue, has been the change from all lingering attachment to the former Union, to a more sacred and reliable devotion to the Confederate Government. The sentiments of the people are not alterable in any other respects by force of arms. If the whole country were occupied by United States' troops, it would merely exhibit a military despotism, against which the people would struggle in perpetual revolutionary effort, while any Southrons remained alive. Extermination of the inhabitants could alone realise civil possession of their soil. Subjugation is, therefore, clearly impossible. Is extermination desired by Christians?

The moral and religious interests of the South ought to be appreciated by Christians of all nations.

These interests have realised certainly no benefit from the war. We are aware that, in respect to the moral aspects of the question of slavery, we differ from those who conceive of emancipation as a measure of benevolence, and on that account we suffer much reproach which we are conscious of not deserving. With all the facts of the system of slavery in its practical operations before us, 'as eye-witnesses and ministers of the Word, having had perfect understanding of all things' on this subject of which we speak, we may surely claim respect for our opinions and statements. Most of us have grown up from childhood among the slaves; all of us have preached to and taught them the word of life; have administered to them the ordinances of the Christian Church; sincerely love them as souls for whom Christ died; we go among them freely, and know them in health and sickness, in labor and rest, from infancy to old age.   We are familiar with their physical and moral condition, and alive to all their interests; and we testify in the sight of God, that the relation of master and slave among us, however we may deplore abuses in this, as in other relations of mankind, is not incompatible with our holy Christianity, and that the presence of the Africans of our land is an occasion of gratitude on their behalf before God; seeing that thereby Divine Providence has brought them where missionaries of the Cross may freely proclaim to them the word of salvation, and the work is not interrupted by agitating fanaticism.   The South has done more than any people on earth for the Christianization of the African race.   The condition of slaves here is not wretched, as northern fictions would have men believe, but prosperous and happy, and would have been yet more so but for the mistaken zeal of the Abolitionists.   Can emancipation obtain for them a better portion?   The practicable plan for benefiting the African race must be the Providential plan—the Scriptural plan.   We adopt that plan in the South; and while the State should seek by wholesome legislation to regard the interests of master and slave, we, as ministers, would preach the word to both as we are commanded of God.   This war has not benefited the slaves.   Those who have been encouraged or compelled to leave their masters have gone, and we aver can go, to no state of society that offers them any better things than they have at home, eiher in respect to their temporal or eternal welfare.   We regard Abolitionism as an interference with the plans of Divine Providence.   It has not the signs of the Lord's blessing. . .

The Christians of the South, we claim, are pious, intelligent, and liberal.   Their pastoral and missionary works have points of peculiar interest.   There are hundreds of thousands here, both white and colored, who are not strangers to the blood that bought them.   We rejoice that the great Head of the Church has not despised us.   We desire as much as in us lieth to live peaceably with all men, and though reviled, to revile not again.

Much harm has been done to the religious enterprises of the Church, by the war; we will not tire you by enumerating particulars.   We thank God for the patient faith and fortitude of our people during these days of trial.

Our soldiers were before the war our fellow-citizens, and many of them are of the household of faith, who have carried to the camp so much of the leaven of Christianity, that, amid all the demoralizing influences of army life, the good work of salvation has gone forward there.

Our President, some of our most influential statesmen, our commanding general, and an unusual proportion of the principal generals, as well as scores of other officers, are prominent, and we believe consistent members of the Church.   Thousands of our soldiers are men of prayer.   We regard our success in the war as due to Divine mercy, and our Government and people have recognized the hand of God in the formal and humble celebration of His goodness.   We have no fear in regard to the future.   If the war continue for years, we believe God's grace sufficient for us.

In conclusion, we ask for ourselves, our churches, our country, the devout prayers of all God's people—'the will of the Lord be done!'

.   .   .   .

'Charity beareth all things, believeth all things, hopeth all things, endureth all things.' We desire to 'follow after charity'; and 'as many as walk according to this rule, peace be on them, and mercy, and upon the Israel of God.'

Signatures to the Address."

Text—McPherson: *The Political History of the United States of America During the Great Rebellion*, Appendix, pp. 517-520.

III. *MILITARY ORDERS RESPECTING DISLOYAL SOUTHERN CHURCHES*

An order similar to the following was issued placing Baptist, United Presbyterian, Presbyterian and United Brethren churches under leaders whose loyalty was ass ured.

"War Department, Adjutant General's Office,
Washington, November 30, 1863.

To the Generals commanding the Departments of the Missouri, the Tennessee, and the Gulf, and all Generals and officers commanding armies, detachments, and posts, and all officers in the service of the United States in the above mentioned Departments:

You are hereby directed to place at the disposal of Rev. Bishop Ames all houses of worship belonging to the Methodist Episcopal Church South in which a loyal minister, who has been appointed by a loyal Bishop of said church, does not now officiate.

It is a matter of great importance to the Government, in its efforts to restore tranquility to the community and peace to the nation, that Christian ministers should, by example and precept, support and foster the loyal sentiment of the people.

Bishop Ames enjoys the entire confidence of this Department, and no doubt is entertained that all ministers who may be appointed by him will be entirely loyal. You are expected to give him all the aid, countenance, and support practicable in the execution of his important mission.

You are also authorized and directed to furnish Bishop Ames and his clerk with transportation and subsistence when it can be done without prejudice to the service, and will afford them courtesy, assistance and protection.

By order of the Secretary of War:

E. D. TOWNSEND
Assistant Adjutant General."

Text—McPherson: *The Political History of the United States of America During the Great Rebellion*, appendix p. 521.

Enforcement and Consequences of the Order

In accordance with the Government plan concerning the churches of the South, the Board of Missions of the Methodist Episcopal Church have sent the Rev. J. P. Newman, D.D., to New Orleans, to take charge of all the churches of that powerful denomination there. A very large audience, composed of some of the most influential citizens, assembled on the evening of the 23d inst., at the Carondelet street Church, to extend to the reverend gentleman a cordial welcome.

On being introduced by the chairman, Dr. Newman said:

'There were three reasons for sending a minister from New York to New Orleans:

1. It was in harmony with the theory of labor as held by the Methodist Church. There is no such Church as the Methodist Church North. Ours is the Methodist Episcopal Church. We are not sectional. We acknowledge no geographical limits less than the world itself. Every minister of our church may say with its founder, "The world is my parish and Heaven is my home." (Applause.) In the separation of 1844 our church relinquished no right to labor in the South, but since has claimed, as before, and still claims, to send her ministers to the equator and to the poles, and all latitudes between. We reject the sentiment that we are encroaching upon the rights of others. If the theory that we are sectional be true, what right have we to send ministers to Europe, to Scandinavia, Bulgaria and Constantinople? This movement, then, is in strict harmony with our system of labor.

2. It is required by the present state of the country. Thousands of our citizens have followed in the track of our victorious armies, "to build the old wastes, and raise up the former desolations and repair the waste cities," and the church had been recreant to her trust had she not provided them with the ministry of the Word. We have too long trusted our Northern men who have taken up their residence South to the exclusive influence of Southern teaching; but that day is past, and the Church now declares that she will not trust these thousands of her sons and daughters to—(the words of the speaker were here lost in a storm of applause.) Whatever mountains they may climb, into whatever valleys they may descend, on whatever plains they may spread themselves, or whatever seas they may cross, she claims the right to follow them with her ministers of truth and peace. (Applause.)

3. This movement was justified by the present disorganized and destitute condition of the Southern churches. Their former ministers had either fled or been silenced, or imprisoned, or banished, and it had become the solemn duty of the Mother Church to send shepherds to these deserted and scattered flocks. A shepherd should never leave his flock though all of Uncle Sam's guns were turned against him. (Applause.)

. . . .

These are the reasons which influenced the Missionary Board to recommend to the Bishops to make this provision for the spiritual wants of this section of our country.

But we find ourselves met on the threshold by two embarrassments, of which I have heard since my arrival in New Orleans:

1. The question of property confronts us. We are denounced as church robbers; are charged with having robbed the people of the South of their church property.

My answer is: The right of church property has never been disturbed, as far as we are concerned.

The General Government has seen fit to seize these churches, but it has not conveyed their title to us. There has been no passing of deeds. We do not own an inch either of this or any other church in the South. The Secretary of War wrote to the General commanding this Department to place at the disposal of Bishop Ames the Methodist churches for the use of the loyal ministers. If there has been any robbery the accusation lies against the General Government. But the General Government has committed no robbery. It was aware that these churches were occupied (so far as they were occupied at all) by congregations united by disloyal sympathies and by teachers disposed to inculcate treason. It knew that if they were placed under the care of the Methodist Church they would be occupied by no ministers but would be loyal to the Government, and that they would be likely to gather around them loyal hearers.

(Applause.) So much then for property. He did not want to hear another word about the robbery of church property while he was in New Orleans.

2. Another embarrassment is the charge that the Methodist Church is a political church, and, therefore, should not be tolerated in the South.

Let us analyze this charge. Does it mean that it is united to the State like the Church of England? Have we not recently heard the disclaimer of our President, that he does not "run the churches?"

. . . Does it mean that our church is loyal to the General Government? If this be the meaning, I shall admit the charge. We hold and teach that loyalty is a religious duty, as truly obligatory as prayer itself. The twenty-third article of the Discipline is equally binding on the clergy and the laity, and constitutes us a confessedly loyal church. Nor is it optional with the minister whether he inculcated loyal sentiments or not, for how shall a man be saved unless he be loyal?

Does it mean that we are opposed to the doctrine of State sovereignty, Secession and Rebellion? I accept the definition. From the Sabbath-school scholar to the minister, from the exhorter to the bishop, our whole membership reprobate these doctrines.

Does it mean that our ministers denounce political corruptions? I accept the definition. . . ' "

Text—*The True Delta*, March 23, 1864, quoted in McPherson, *The Political History of the United States of America During the Great Rebellion*, Appendix, p. 523.

IV. *THE QUAKER PETITION*

"To the President, Senate and House of Representatives of the United States:
This Memorial of the Representative Committee, or Meeting for Sufferings of the Religious Society of Friends, of Pennsylvania, New Jersey, Deleware, and adjacent parts of Maryland, respectfully showeth, that

We respect, honor and love this Government, which we believe Divine Wisdom has placed over us, and because of this, we desire that it may, in no particular, be found striving against God, or persecuting His children, however humble in position or numbers they may be.

Under the present law of Congress, every able-bodied citizen within certain ages, in time of war, is liable to be called upon by the Government to bear arms in its defence.

We represent a people who cannot comply with this law without disobeying the command of God to them.

Neither can they furnish a substitute or pay any equivalent or fine imposed for exemption from military service, because in so doing, they feel that they would implicate themselves in a violation of their conscientious scruples in this respect.

We hold, that the doctrine that human governments are ordained of God, does not imply the infallibility of those who administer them, and gives them no right to require us to violate our allegiance to the Almighty, who is sovereign Lord of conscience, and whose right it is to rule and reign in the hearts of His children.

For more than two hundred years our Society has held the doctrine, that all wars and fighting were forbidden to them, as followers of Christ—differing in this respect from nearly all other associations of men claiming the Christian name.

For asserting and maintaining this, and other testimonies of the 'Truth as it is in Jesus' they were brought under cruel persecution, enduring the despoiling of their estates, incarceration in prisons and loathsome dungeons, and death.

Through this long season of darkness, their dependence was upon Divine Power, under which, their patient suffering and earnest remonstrance obtained in some degree the favor of those in authority.

For the free enjoyment of civil and religious liberty, they came to this land, to seek amongst the so-called savages of the wilderness, immunities and privileges denied them at the hands of a professed Christian nation. Here William Penn and his friends planted their infant colony, and proved the efficacy of the principle of Peace. The conflict of arms was unknown, and history bears no record of strife between the Indian and the Friend.

We their descendants, now approach you, not alone with a view to shield ourselves from suffering, but under a sense of duty to God, to assert the sacred rights of conscience, to raise the standard of the Prince of Peace before the nation, and in His name to ask you to so modify the law, that it shall not require those who administer it, to bring under persecution innocent men for obeying His commands—'Ye are my friends if ye do whatsoever I command you.'—'Whether it be right in the sight of God to hearken unto you more than unto God, judge ye.'

In thus defining our position, we enter not into judgment or condemnation of those who differ from us. We appreciate the difficulties that surround those upon whom rests the responsibility of guiding the nation through the awful perils of civil war.

We appeal to you under a sense of suffering—afflictions and mourning surround us, and sorrow hath filled our hearts.

Many of our young men, overcome by the spirit of war, have rushed into the conflict, where some of them have found an early death; some have purchased their release from the draft by the payment of money; others have remained steadfast to their faith in the hour of trial, thereby subjecting themselves to the penalty for desertion. Trusting in the mercy of our Heavenly Father, we desire that He may so touch your hearts and understandings with His wisdom, that you may grant our petition.

Signed by the direction, and on behalf ot the Committee.

SAMUEL PARRY, *Clerk.*

Philadelphia, 1st mo. 22d, 1864."

Text—McPherson: *The Political History of the United States of America During the Great Rebellion*, Appendix, pp. 503-4.

V. *THE CHRISTIAN COMMISSION; ITS PRINCIPLES*

I. CATHOLICITY

.   .   .   .

II. NATIONALITY

The Church of Christ of various names united in behalf of the men of every State gone to the war—a new thing under the sun!

These principles in combination, guarantee freedom from sectional favoritism in distribution or sectarian influence in teaching, and give breadth of resource for supply at home and power of equalization in application to those in the field. By their action, ministers and others are enlisted from different denominations, stores gathered from all the people, and publications secured from the religious press, and all are sent where and when they are needed, without flooding one part to the neglect of another, whilst the defenders of the nation from every State and of every denominational preference are cared for without partiality.

III. VOLUNTARINESS

This is not new. . .

It is, however, new and wonderful in this new example, embracing all the members of the Commission and its numerous branches, with their chief executive officers, offices and storerooms, the regulated freedom of 20,000 miles of railway, 20,000 miles of telegraph, and of all Government vessels, the services of more than fifteen hundred Christian ministers and laymen, and a large part of the immense supplies distributed, all on the principle, *freely received, freely given.*

IV. COMBINATION OF BENEFITS FOR BODY AND SOUL

The ardent followers of John Wesley, who sought and won trophies on so many fields a hundred years ago, preached the Gospel with remarkable results in the army of Great Britain. Their aim was for the soul alone.

The English Florence Nightingale—name sweeter than the enchanting nightsong of her own English namesake—in her aim combined bodily relief with religious benefits. Yet although her name is national, and her fame universal, her work was individual. . . .

The Christian Commission alone, and the first since the world began, is a national agency, embracing man as mortal yet immortal, in plans of beneficence for all parts of an immense army and navy actively engaged in war.

V. RELIANCE UPON UNPAID DELEGATES

The system adopted eighteen hundred years ago by our Lord Jesus Christ was in principle the same. He selected and sent forth *men* full of faith and the Holy Ghost, men so loving the world as to be willing to leave their homes and go without fee or reward to bear the glad tidings of a Saviour to the lost, and carrying with them their relief for the sick and the suffering in the Divine power of miracles for all maladies.

But in a national organization, and in application to a vast army and navy engaged in active hostilities, this principle is new. . .

VI. PERSONAL DISTRIBUTION WITH PERSONAL MINISTRATIONS

Stores given—*never if the soldier is under the surgeon's care without his consent and counsel, but always if possible directly from the delegate to the soldier,* and always adding such personal service to the value of the gift as may be needed.

Is the gift a shirt, drawers and socks for the soldier wounded or sick? Wash him first, and then put them on!

Is it a bed? make it up in order and tenderly place him on it!

Is it only a blanket? wrap him in it!

Is it some delicacy for the sick, or coffee or soup for the worn or the wounded, or a meal for the hungry wayfarer? Prepare it nicely and serve it! The reward will come when in heaven the table shall be spread, and the King of kings shall come forth and serve you.

Enhance the value of both gifts and services by kind words to the soldier as *a man*, not a machine; as a man *beloved* for his heroic devotion to the Union, not despised as mere hireling food for powder and shot. Set his heart all aglow with thoughts of the loving ones at home, who send the gifts and send the delegates to give them, and who wait for tidings and pray for the soldiers, and long for the time when, the war ended, peace restored, the Union saved, liberty achieved, republican government rescued and guaranteed, the soldiers shall be welcomed back again, and the unsullied, coming forth like pure gold from the crucible, shall be loved and trusted as long as they live, and honored long after they are dead as the heroes who helped to save the nation!

Then when good gifts and kind words and deeds have made their impress, and the soldier exclaims, 'Well, this *is* religion!' and says, 'Tell me all about it, *how I can* become a real Christian?' then tell him of Jesus, his love, his sacrifice for sin, his power to save, his abundant grace, his readiness to pardon, his perfect righteousness, all, all the sinner's own by simple faith, and induce him to accept of the unspeakable gift, and let the news of a sinner saved ascend on angel wing to give new joy in the presence of God above, and let it go home to fill the waiting, longing hearts of loving ones with glad surprise, and there also waken the inquiry for the way of life, and bring others to repentance.

Then go stand in the chapel-tent, with its red, white, and blue flag afloat above it, . . . crowded inside and around by men who have learned to reverence religion from such fruits, and there proclaim the Gospel of peace to these men of war, preach Jesus and eternal life to these bronzed, battle-scarred heroes of many hairbreadth escapes, who know that there is but a step between them and death, and oh how they listen! How their breasts heave and tears course their cheeks!

VII. CO-OPERATION

1. With Chaplains.—The chaplaincy is the governmental provision for the Christian care and culture of the army and navy. It is right and worthy of a Christian nation. . .

. . . To meet the deficiency of chaplain service as far as possible by its delegate system, and to aid the tried and noble men who, through all perils, hindrances, and hardships, still remain to serve God and our country to the end of the war by supplying them with Scriptures, Hymns and Psalms, and the best issues of the religious press in every form, fresh, frequent, and copious as possible, is both wise, patriotic, and Christian.

The idea, however, that this work of supplementing and supplying the chaplaincy, is or ought to be the main work of the Christian Commission, is extremely contracted, and would reduce the sphere of the Commission from that of a great national, religious, and relief agency between the people, the church, the home, the press, on the one hand, and the army and navy on the other, to that of little more than a mere receiving and distributing agency between publishing establishments and chaplains. With these facts in view, co-operation with chaplains has been a steadfast principle with the Commission form the first. Help has never been sought in vain within the boundaries of our objects and means by any chaplain; nor will it ever be.

VIII. RESPECT FOR AUTHORITIES

. . . In each military department, general hospital, permanent camp and separate post or station, the consent and counsel of those in command have been sought and obtained at the threshold.

Delegates are strictly enjoined, in the prosecution of their religious duties, to offer every possible assistance to chaplains, but never to intrude uninvited upon their proper domain.   And in their work of ministering to the health and comfort of those under medical treatment and care, to do nothing without instructions from the surgeons in charge, and in all great emergencies on the battle-ground, or in the field hospital, or at points where the wounded are to be fed and cared for, during their removal from the front, always to report themselves to the medical director or surgeon in charge, and place themselves under his instructions for just that service which will most effectually aid him in the work of relieving and saving our wounded heroes. . . "

Text—*Second Annual Report (1863) United States Christian Commission*, pp. 15-21.

The Christian Commission at Work

James Cole, Field Agent for the armies in Eastern Virginia reports as follows for the year 1864.

"It was resolved, in beginning the winter's work, to reach in a thorough and effective manner, every regiment, battery, and squadron in the army, giving to each a regular supply of good religious reading, comprising Bibles, Testaments, Soldiers' Hymn Books, religious papers, of all denominations and from all sections of the country, tracts and books, expressly prepared for this circulation; and also, by establishing 'stations,' each provided with a comfortable chapel-tent, to give to every man an opportunity of hearing the preaching of the Word. . .

From these stations, and from these chapels, an influence, more powerful than any human tongue can tell, went forth   At every station of the Commission, and in very many of the Brigade chapels, meetings for the worship of God were held *each night*—besides meetings for the study of the Bible, which, in some stations, were held daily; and at all, the presence of the Divine Spirit was manifest, in the conviction and conversion of men.

The 'stations' of the Commission were all, with the exception of those in the villages, constructed upon the same plan.   The large chapel tent, beautifully proportioned, of white canvas, with an arched awning over its broad door, and the white chapel-flag floating above it, was the crowning feature of the station.   Within, besides the closely arranged seats, was a table to be used in the day-time, as a counter for books, and papers, and as a writing table for such soldiers as might desire to use it.   Sometimes a 'bunk' was placed in one corner for the use of the delegates, or any visitors who might there chance to spend the night.   Besides this tent, was one wall-tent, and sometimes two, small, but well floored, and well arranged, and used for kitchen, dining-room, and lodging.

Three delegates were usually at each station—one of them, at least, being a clergyman.   The cooking for the station was sometimes done by a detailed soldier, but more frequently by the delegates themselves, each taking his turn.

The work performed at the station, is of quite a varied nature.   Early in the morning, two of the delegates taking an armful of papers and books, go to some regiment or battery in their field, perhaps a mile distant, and distribute these to the soldiers they meet, seeking out the sick, if there be any, and giving an invitation for all to come to the evening meeting, or making an appointment for an open-air meeting. By personal conversation they exhort the soldiers, with whom they come in contact, to live holy lives, appealing to their better nature against the various forms of sin which assail them. At the tent the Bible-class is held; in some cases, forty or fifty soldiers attending. In the course of the day, many visitors come to the station; chaplains, to get reading for their men, or some delicacy for a sick man; officers, for a copy of their home paper, or a book from the library; soldiers, for reading, or perhaps a towel, or 'house-wife,' or perhaps with anxious minds, desiring to talk with the man of God about the way of salvation.

So the day passes—each hour filled with busy work, which, although not recorded on earthly tablets, leaves an impress for eternity.

As the evening hour approaches, the soldiers from all directions may be seen flocking to the chapel. Here a soldier, who, all alone, is turning his feet toward the tabernacle, there, a group of eight or ten from a distant camp.

The tent is soon filled; every seat, and every foot of standing-room occupied. The service begins; the old time-honored hymn is followed by the earnest prayer, the tearful exhortation; the anxious ones rise amid their fellows, asking prayers, that they too might receive eternal life. Yes, in that lowly tabernacle, in the midst of camps, and of warlike men, is found a sweet foretaste of the coming heaven! . . .

In such labors as these the months passed quickly. The warm days of spring came again. . .

It was decided to organize the entire force of the Christian Commission for the active campaign into *sections*, each being in charge of an experienced agent, and being as far as possible, complete in itself. . .

Joining the flying hospitals of each corps during the days of the 'Wilderness' battles, each section was vigorously at work. . .

"Working by day, marching by night, exposed to rain and cold and danger, cooking food for the famishing, binding the wounds of the suffering, cheering with Christian consolation the despondent and the dying, doing a thousand acts of kindness, as soon forgotten as performed, these delegates and agents of the Commission staid at their posts through all those days of fighting and marching, which at length brought the army of the Potomac and the army of the James together, on either side of the Appomattox, before the strong works of Petersburg. . .

. . . .

An interesting feature of the work, this winter, is that among the colored soldiers. Schools, as well as religious meetings, are to be held for these, and the *Primer* and *First Reader* must precede the *Testament*. Arrangements have been made to organize schools throughout the colored corps, and teachers are already on the ground.

The 'tabernacles, which are sent us by churches at the North, are worthy of notice. These are beautiful large tents, capable of holding four or five hundred persons. These, bearing the names given by the donors, are occupied as chapels, and a constant communication is kept up between the home Church and the army tabernacle. . .

Truly yours,

J. A. COLE."

Text—*Third Annual Report (1864) United States Christian Commission*, pp. 66-78.

VI. *HOME MISSIONS AND NATIONAL UNITY*

"With this record we close the labors of a most eventful year. It has been distinguished throughout by peculiar embarrassments and trials; yet it has been crowned with the signal favor and loving kindness of God. We have been permitted, at some former Anniversaries, to report a larger number of laborers sustained, of churches gathered, of sanctuaries built, and of souls converted; but we have witnessed, during the past year, some fruits of this enterprise which have never been disclosed before, and which no patriot or Christian can contemplate without rejoicing and praise. While that portion of the country which has repelled the overtures, and persecuted the messengers of this Society, has been swept into the vortex of rebellion, the States which have been the theater of its most successful labors, have been preeminent for their patriotism and their devotion to the cause of truth and right. Since it commenced its operations, the Northwestern States have received about nine tenths of their entire population. Coming from different portions of our own country, and from various foreign lands; trained under diverse forms of government, of social order, and of religious faith, they seemed to be elements of national weakness and danger, rather than of strength and safety. But the hour of our great trial has come, and the energy, the resources, the unity, the patriotic devotion displayed by these youthful States, attest the value and success of the agencies by which their institutions have been planted, and their character has been formed. The churches which this and kindred Societies have planted have been the schools, the ministers they have sustained have been the educators of those brave and patriotic men who have poured out their blood so freely on the battle fields of freedom and the Union. Many a missionary, with words of cheer and tears of joy, has dismissed to his country's service nearly every one of those on whom he had mainly depended for cooperation in his labors, and for pecuniary support. Many a missionary church has, today, a larger membership in the camp and the field than it has at home. . .

In behalf of the Executive Committee,

MILTON BADGER,
DAVID B. COE,
DANIEL P. NOYES,
Secretaries for Correspondence."

Text—*The Home Missionary,* July, 1862.

"This extraordinary crisis has given us a most deeply interesting view of the value of the Home Missionary work as it has already been advanced. We diffuse the Gospel—especially carrying it to new settlements, and communities rising into life. We have turned our eyes with deepest interest to that vast missionary field opening in the immense regions of the West, and especially so because we have seen accumulating there, with wonderful rapidity, all the elements of national power and greatness.

Now we may justly claim that nineteen-twentieths of all the Gospel influences that have been sent to these vast regions have been sent by Home Missionary labors. . . .

By all this, a moral atmosphere has been created, most healthful to the growth of all patriotic principles and emotions. Thus, undesignedly, and yet most surely, there has been going on a most important preparation for that great convulsion that is now shaking the land. 'Every school house sermon,' says a Western writer, 'for these many years, has been a lesson preparatory to the struggle of today. Every town, village, or country edifice that has been raised by Home Missions has been a fortress for free institutions. Here has the Constitution been sure of brave defenders. If the American Home Missionary Society had dated its origin thirty years later than it did, the Government could hardly have reckoned, as it now can, on the loyalty of its right-hand power, the Valley of the Mississippi.

We claim, as one of the blessed results of our Home Missionary work, and as a most striking proof of its value, that it has so enlightened the men of the great West, that not less than two hundred thousand of them are now fighting the battles of their country. But for such Gospel light as has been thrown upon their minds, such patriotic emotions would not have been theirs, and the country, in its perils, would not have nad them for its defenders. We have sown bountifully, and now bountifully are we reaping.

. . . . ''

Text—*The Home Missionary*, August, 1862.

"Had the work of Home Missions been prosecuted throughout the South as thoroughly and as successfully as it has been at the North and Northwest, it is morally certain that this rebellion would not have occurred. And had the work been hindered or neglected in the North or Northwest, and those portions of the country been suffered to remain till this day as destitute of Gospel institutions as they would have been if no more of this kind of labor had been performed in them than has been in the South, it is morally certain that, when this rebellion came, the nation could have made no successful stand against it."

Text—*The Home Missionary*, December, 1862.

"Who does not know that the loyalty of the West, which along with the East has gone down against the South as did the hordes of Northern Europe, has been produced to a large extent by the sturdy influence of the pioneer missionaries? Every where patriotic, every where rallying the people and using their pulpits for recruiting stations, they have but reaped the fruit of their former teachings in the enlistment-rolls that have often taken away their sons and the strength of their temporal support. By responses to a recent circular, we learn that the Congregational churches of Illinois have sent to the war one in *eight* of their male members; Wisconsin, one in *nine*; Minnesota, one in *seven*; Iowa, one in *five*; making in all several Ironside regiments. All this, besides their influence upon enlistment in the community generally. And now, as the war sickens our heart by hope deferred, they are foremost in inspiriting the people, in ministering moral and sanitary succor to the braves of the army, and in sustaining the hands of the Government.

If you would trace the practical effect of this evangelizing enterprise, you will find that the seam along which our Government has cracked asunder, was the Southern line of our general Home Missionary operations. These labors were not welcomed, nor scarcely allowed at the South. Never over fifty of the regiment of a thousand missionaries were employed there, and these were rejected as soon as the Society, seven years ago, laid down the rule of "no more slaveholders in the missionary churches.' And yet the Society is ready to re-enter the field as soon as ponderous war shall have battered down the walls with which Southern barbarism has encircled itself.

. . . . ''

Text—*The Home Missionary*, August, 1863.

". . . We owe our preparation for great patience and endurance, in behalf of future generations, under God, to the fidelity of those christian ministers who, in the Western States, from the beginning of those States, preached a Gospel that was a Gospel for the poor and for the poorest, for the weak and for the weakest, for the oppressed and against the oppressor. We reap the benefit of their fidelity; for it is true, as has been said, that you may almost mark the line of rebellion by the line of the American Home Missionaries. Where they labored most, there is the strength of patriotism; but where they were not found, there slavery and ignorance and the want of patriotism, which is treason, have been found. It is the Gospel that has saved the West and the Northwest to this nation. It is to the power of the Lord Jesus Christ, through the ministration of his word, at the hand of his servants, that we owe the perpetuation of this government in all our Western and Northwestern Territory.

. . . .

. . . if any thing is demonstrated, it is that the Puritan idea of carrying emancipation with religion is the true idea. There has been a development of the Puritan spirit in many directions. It is a peculiarity of Puritan preaching that it is second to no other in religious enthusiasm and devotional sentiment. It tends to institution. It inaugurates, wherever it goes, means of education. We have had it shown that without education there can not be patriotism, and there can not be union. The fact is, that New England is patriotic because she has had intelligence, while Tennessee has been wanting in patriotism because she has lacked intelligence. Make yourself familiar with the condition of these two regions, and you will find it to be so. The statistical tables will tell the story. Those States that have the most men who can not read and write are the most stubbornly rebellious, while those States that have the most men who can read and write cling the most tenaciously to the Union. All that we have had by which to save the country has been religion and popular intelligence; and we have come near losing half of our territory simply because the mases of the people at the South have lived in such profound ignorance. . . ."

Text—*The Home Missionary*, September, 1863.

CHAPTER XXIX

Since the Civil War

Bibliography

For the reunion of the Episcopalian forces immediately after the War, documentary material is found in the "Journals of the Proceedings" of the various State and General Conventions. The story is told by standard writers, such as Perry, McConnell, and Tiffany (see p. 7).

For the unsuccessful attempt on the part of the Southern and Old School Presbyterians to unite, source material is available in the "Minutes of the General Assembly of the Presbyterian Church in the United States"; "The Distinctive Principles of the Presbyterian Church in the United States as set forth in its Formal Declarations and illustrated by extracts from the minutes of its General Assembly"; "Minutes of the General Assembly, Old School" (1861 f.), and the "Minutes of General Assembly, New School" (1855 f.). The "History of the Southern Presbyterian Church" by Thomas C. Johnson, D.D. ("Amer. Ch. Hist. Ser." Vol. XI, 1900) presents the situation with a strong Southern bias.

In connection with the reunion of the Old and New School Presbyterians the literature is more extensive. The documentary material is found in the "Minutes" of the several Assemblies of the two bodies: "The Presbyterian Union Convention, held in Philadelphia November 6, 1867; Minutes and Phonographic Report" (1868); "Proceedings of Presbyterian Reunion at Pittsburgh, November 12, 1869" (1869); and "Presbyterian Reunion; A Memorial Volume, 1837-1871" (1871). Historical works are as follows: "The General Assembly of 1866" (1867) by H. A. Boardman; "Reunion of the Old and New School Presbyterian Churches" (1867) by Charles Hodge; "Reunion of the Presbyterian Churches" (1867) by Henry B. Smith; "A History of the New School, and of the Questions Involved in the Disruption of the Presbyterian Church in 1838" (1868) by S. J. Baird (valuable.—See below). The following contributions appear in the religious periodicals: "The Presbyterian General Assemblies" ("Amer. Theol. Rev." July, 1862); "Principles of Church Union; and the Reunion of Old and New School Presbyterians" ("Bibl.

Rep. and Princ. Rev.," April, 1865); "Presbyterian Reunion" ("Amer. Pres. and Theol. Rev.," Oct. 1868); "Presbyterian Union Convention" ("Merc'burg Rev.," Jan. 1868); "Historical Sketch of the Reunion" ("Amer. Pres. Rev." July, 1869); "Proceedings of the Late Assemblies on Reunion," also "Exposition and Defence of the Basis of Reunion," and "The New Basis of Union" ("Princ. Rev." July, 1869); "Presbyterian Division and Reunion," also "The Philadelphia Presbyterian Union Convention" ("Amer. Pres. and Theol. Rev." Jan. 1868); "Presbyterian Reunion" ("Bibl. Rep. and Princ. Rev.," Jan. 1868); "Doctor Baird's History of the New School" ("Amer. Pres. Rev.," Jan. 1869); "The Presbyterian Disruption of 1838—A Review of Dr. S. J. Baird's History of the New School" ("New Englander" Jan. 1869); "Baird's History of the New School" ("Princ. Rev.," Jan. 1869); "Smaller Bodies of American Presbyterians" (*ibid.*, Oct. 1869).

In the literature that follows, it will become clear why it was that the Methodists of the South and North were unable to unite: "Methodism and the War" ("Meth. Quar. Rev." July, 1863); "Methodist Churches North and South" (*ibid.* Oct. 1865, excellent); "The Two Methodisms, North and South" (*ibid.* April, 1866); "The Second General Conference" (*ibid.* July 1866); "The New York East Conference, and the Southern General Conference" (*ibid.* July 1866, good); "Our Present and Past Relations to Slavery" (*ibid.* April 1868, historically valuable); "The Episcopal Correspondence on Church Reunion" (*ibid.* July 1869, good); "Did the 'Church South' Secede?" (*ibid.* April, 1870); "The Present Crisis" ("South. Rev." Jan. 1873); "The Methodist Episcopal Church in the Southern States" ("Meth. Quar. Rev." Jan. 1872); "Our Work at the South" (*ibid.* Jan. 1874); "Educational Work of the Methodist Episcopal Church in the South" (*ibid.* May, 1886); "The Methodist Episcopal Church in the South" (*ibid.* March, 1888); "The Two Methodisms" (*ibid.* Sept. 1888); "The Methodist Episcopal Church in the South" (*ibid.* Jan. 1890, significant); "The Methodist Episcopal Church in the South" (*ibid.* May, 1896); "Preparatory Education from the Southern Standpoint" ("Quar. Rev. M. E. Church South" July, 1891, significant for the union of recent date).

"An Appeal to Facts. A Reply to Dr. Godbey's Defense of Southern Methodism" (1890) by B. Fry, D.D. should be read along with "The Organic Union of American' Methodism" (1892) by Bishop Merrill.

For the documents bearing upon the breakdown of the negotiations looking toward union, in addition to the "Minutes of the Conferences," the student will find everything he needs in "Formal Fraternity. Proceedings of the General Conferences of the Methodist Episcopal Church and of the Methodist Episcopal Church South in 1872, 1874, and 1876, and of the Joint Commission of the two Churches on Fraternal Relations at Cape May, New Jersey, August 16-23, 1876" (1877).

The recent attempts of the Methodists of the North and South to get together are set forth in the Reports of the Committee of Fraternity embodied in the "Journals"; "American Methodism—Its Divisions and Unification" (1915) by Bishop T. B. Neely; "A Working Conference on the Union of American Methodism" (report of meeting, Feb. 15-17, 1916 at Harris Hall, Evanston, Illinois); the "Proceedings of the Joint Commission on Unification . . . held at Baltimore Dec. 28, 1916, to Jan. 2, 1917"; and "Proceedings" of the meeting held at Savannah, Georgia, Jan. 23, 1918.

In connection with lay representation, adopted in 1872, the following is the representative literature: "Analysis of the Principles of Church Government; Particularly that of the Methodist Episcopal Church" (1852) by Rev. M. M. Hinkle; "Lay Representation in the General Court of the Church proven to be Unscriptural, Unreasonable, and Contrary to Sound Policy" (1863) by William Barnes; "Lay Representation in the Methodist Episcopal Church, Its Justice and Expediency" (1864) by Gilbert Haven; "Lay Delegation in the Methodist Episcopal Church Calmly Considered. Its Injustice and Impracticability" (a pamphlet 1867) by James Porter, D.D.

From the literature that follows, the student may see what issues have exercised the Methodists during the last forty years: "Proposed New Articles of Religion" ("Meth. Quar. Rev." April, 1872); "The Presiding Eldership" (*ibid.* Jan. 1875); "Should Presiding Elders be Elected?" (*ibid.* April, 1876, see also April and October 1879); "Ecumenical Methodism" (*ibid.* Oct. 1880); "The Methodist Ecumenical Conference"(*ibid.* Jan. 1882); "An Inside View of the Great Methodist Ecumenical Conference of 1881" ("Amer. Meth. Epis. Ch. Rev." July 1884); "The Itinerant Ministry of the Methodist Episcopal Church" ("Meth. Quar. Rev." Jan. and April, 1880); "Our Methodist Local Preachers" (*ibid.* April, 1882); "The Solidarity of Methodism" (*ibid.* Oct. 1883,—contains important data respecting pastorless churches of all denominations, and discusses the superiority of itinerancy); "The Removal of the Time Limit" (*ibid.* May, 1894); "The Time Restriction in the Methodist Itinerancy" (*ibid.* March, 1888); "Principles of Church Government, with Special Application to a Polity of Episcopal Methodism and a

Plan for the Reorganization of the General Conference into Two Distinct, Separate and Concurrent Houses" (1888) by Wm. H. Perrine, D.D. . . ."; "The Two House Plan" ("Meth. Rev." March, 1891—contains documents); "The Ground of Woman's Eligibility" (*ibid*. May, 1891); "The Eligibility of Women not a Scriptural Question" (*ibid*. March, 1891); "The Real, Judicial Declaration of 1888" (*ibid*. Jan. 1896); "That Pseudo-Judicial Declaration of 1888 . . .": (*ibid*. Jan. 1896); "The Life Tenure of the Methodist Episcopacy" (*ibid*. Jan. 1892); "Methodist Episcopacy in Transition ' (*ibid*. Sept. 1895); "The Inadvisability of Districting Bishops" (*ibid*. March, 1896).

For Methodism of the last forty years a good interpretation from the southern standpoint is given by Bishop Du Bose in "A History of Methodism" (1916). "The Bishops and the Supervisional System of the Methodist Episcopal Church" (1912) by Bishop Neely elaborately discusses a living issue.

The spiritual and intellectual interests of the negro have been a subject of great concern to the churches during the period under consideration. The best documentary material on this subject are the annual reports of the Freedmen's Societies. · There is also valuable material in the reports of the missionary societies of the various churches. "Negro Education, A Study of the Private and Higher Schools for Colored People in the United States" (II Vols. 1917 Bulletin 1916, No. 33. Department of the Interior) is encyclopaedic in its range of information. "Documentary History of Reconstruction" (Vol. II, 1907) by W. L. Fleming has some readings. In addition the following will be found useful: "The Future of the Colored Race in America" ("Pres. Rev." July, 1862); "The Negro Problem Solved; Africa as She Was, and Is and Shall Be" by Hollis Reid (1864—advocates voluntary colonization); "Relations of the Colored People to the Methodist Episcopal Church South" ("Meth. Quar. Rev." July, 1866—good); "The Africo-American" (*ibid*. April 1868—very informing); "The Religious Future of the Negro" ("Church Quar." April, 1874); "The Freedmen" ("Meth. Quar. Rev." July, 1877—especially valuable for bibliography and historical data); "Education Among the Freedmen" (*ibid*. Jan. 1878); "Our Southern Field" (*ibid*. April, 1878—good); "Religious Education of the Colored People of the South" ("New Englander" Sept. 1878); "The Education of Freedmen" ("N. Amer. Rev." June and July, 1879), by Harriet Beecher Stowe; "Southern Methodism and Colored Missions" ("Quar. Rev. M. E. Church South" Oct. 1880); "Education in the South" ("Luth. Quar." April, 1882); "The African in the United States" ("Meth.

Quar. Rev." April, 1883—suggests colonization as solution); "Educational Problems in the South" ("Quar. Rev. M. E. Church South" Oct. 1883); "Educational Work in the South" (1883) by Rev. R. S. Rust, D.D.; "The Problem of our African Population" ("Meth. Quar. Rev." Jan. 1884); "The Race Problem in the South" ("Quar. Rev. M. E. Church South" April, 1889); "The Southern Church and the Negro" ("Cumb. Pres. Rev." April, 1889); "Notes on the Progress of the Coloured People in Maryland since the War" by J. R. Brackett, Ph.D. ("J.H.U. Studies," Ser. VIII); "The Colored Man in the Methodist Episcopal Church" by Rev. L. M. Hagood, M.D. (1890—some valuable documents); "Problem of Education in the Southern States" ("Meth. Rev." Jan. 1892—much valuable data); "Our Church in her Relation to the Negro" ("Meth. Rev." Sept. 1894—very informing); "Reminiscences of Thirty-Years Labor in the South" (1895) by C. H. Corey; "Apology for the Higher Education of the Negro" (*ibid.* Sept. 1897). "Tuskegee, Its Story and its Work" (1900) by M. B. Thrasher; "From Servitude to Service" (1905—gives lectures on the history and work at Howard, Berea, Tuskegee, Hampton, Atlanta and Fish); "Tuskegee. Its People: Their Ideals and Achievements" (1905) by B. T. Washington. See also Papers and Discussions in "Proc. Baptist Congress" years 1890 and 1902; and more notably the "Publications of Atlanta University."

It is during the last fifty years that the American churches have been aroused to the relation of the Gospel to social ills. In this connection the following articles and monographs will prove illuminating: "The Prison Association of New York" ("Meth. Quar. Rev." Jan. 1864); "Prisons and Reformatories" ("Bib. Rep. and Princ. Rev." Jan. 1868); "The Reformation of Criminals" ("Meth. Quar. Rev." July, 1868); "Prevention and Reform of Juvenile Crime" (*ibid.* Oct. 1872—gives beginnings of this work); "The Dangerous Classes and their Treatment" (*ibid.* July, 1873); "The Relation of the Church to Crime" ("Christian Quar." July, 1873); "Social Reform and the Church" ("Univ. Quar." April, 1879); "Relations of Politics and Christianity" ("Meth. Quar. Rev." July, 1879); "Christianity and Wages" ("New Englander," July, 1882); "Christianity and Social Science" ("Jour. Christian Phil." Jan. 1883); "The Church Lyceum, Its Organization and Management" (1883) by Rev. T. B. Neely—(see also editorial review in "Meth. Quar. Rev." Oct. 1883); "The Labor Question" ("Church Rev." July, 1886); "The Clergy and the Labor Question" ("New Princ. Rev." July, 1886); "Christ and the Labor Movement" ("Quar. Rev. Evang. Luth. Ch." July, 1890);

"The Church in Modern Society" (1890) by Julius H. Ward; "Synods and Senates" ("Quar. Rev. M. E. Church South" Jan. 1891—discusses the duty of the church in denouncing bad legislation, corrupt elections, etc.); "Sociological Christianity a Necessity" ("Meth. Rev." May, 1891); "Regeneration as a Force in Reform Movements" (*ibid.* Nov. 1891, and Nov. 1892—significant); "Church's Tribute to Vice" ("Quar. Rev. U. B. in Christ" Oct. 1891—pleads for Christian principles in the political arena); "Socialism and Christianity and Social Reforms" ("Pres. and Ref. Rev." Jan. 1892); "The Study of Social Science in Theological Seminaries" ("Christian Thought" April, 1892); "Applications of our National Principles" ("Bapt. Quar. Rev." Oct. 1892); "The Ethical Aim of Christianity" ("Luth. Quar." Oct. 1892—notable); "The New Era, or the Coming Kingdom" (1893) by Rev. Josiah Strong; "Civic Christianity" ("Luth. Quar." Jan. 1893); "Improved Homes for Wage Earners" ("Bibl. Sacra" July, 1897); "What are the Functions of the Church?" ("Meth. Rev." July, 1893—a plea for the institutional church); "The Social Teaching of Jesus" (1897) by Shailer Mathews; "Christianity and the Social State" (1898) by G. C. Lorimer; "The Place of the Pulpit in Modern Life and Thought" ("Bibl. Sacra" July, 1898); "The Value of the Study of Political Economy to the Christian Minister" ("Meth. Rev." Sept. 1898); "The Christian Conception of Wealth" ("Bibl. Sacra" April, 1899); "Religious Movements for Social Betterment" (1900) by Josiah Strong; "Jesus Christ and the Social Question" (1900) by Francis G. Peabody; "Laboratory and Pulpit, The Relation of Biology to the Preacher and His Message" (1901) by William L. Poteat; "The Duty of the Church in Relation to the Labor Movement" ("Amer. Jour. Theol." Oct. 1901); "The Church and Popular Education" by H. B. Adams, ("J. H. U. Studies" ser. XVIII); "The Church and Society, A New Alignment for a New Ideal" ("Meth. Rev." Jan. 1901); "Democracy and Social Ethics" (1902) by Jane Adams; "Social Salvation" by Washington Gladden, (1902, Beecher Lectures, Yale University); "Christianity and Socialism" (1904) by Washington Gladden; "The Social Message of the Modern Pulpit" (1906, Yale Lectures,) by Charles R. Brown; "Christianity and the Social Crisis" (1907) by Walter Rauschenbusch; "Social Aspects of Religious Institutions" (1908) by Edwin L. Earp; "Jesus Christ and the Civilization of Today" (1908) by Joseph Alexander Leighton; "The Church and the Changing Order" (1908) by Shailer Mathews; "The Christian Ministry and the Social Order" (1908, Yale Lectures) edited by C. S. MacFarland; "The Approach to the Social Question" (1909) by F. G.

Peabody; "Social Ministry. An Introduction to the Study and Practice of Social Service. Edited for the Methodist Federation for Social Service" (1910) by H. F. Ward; "Christianity and Social Questions" (1911) by W. Cunningham; "Socialism from the Christian Standpoint" (1912) by Father Bernard Vaughan, S.J.; "Spiritual Culture and Social Service" (1912) by C. S. MacFarland; "Christianizing the Social Order" (1912) by Walter Rauschenbusch; "Social Creed of the Churches" (1912) edited by H. F. Ward; "The Church and Social Reforms" (1913) by James R. Howerton; "Christianity and Politics" by Wm. Cunningham (1914, Lowell Lectures); "The Function of the Church in Modern Society" ("Amer. Jour. Theol." Jan. 1914); "Social Evangelism" (1915) by H. F. Ward. Important papers and discussions appear in "Proc. Baptist Congress" Years 1883, 1892, 1899, 1906, 1907 and 1909; and "Minutes of the National Council of the Congregational Churches" for meetings 1905 and since.

With this awakened social interest, the church has been stimulated to a deepening concern for temperance reform, the literature of which is as follows: "The Temperance Reform" ("Meth. Quar. Rev." July, 1873—good for historical data); "Relations of the Methodist Episcopal Church to the Cause of Temperance" (*ibid.* Oct. 1876); "Do the Scriptures Prohibit the Use of Alcoholic Beverages?" ("Bibl. Sacra" July, 1880, see also for the same type of argument, "Meth. Quar. Rev." all numbers, 1882); "A Restatement of the Temperance Problem" ("Univ. Quar." April, 1881); "Is Total Abstinence True Temperance?" ("Pres. Rev." April, 1882); "Christian Citizenship with Reference to the Liquor Traffic" ("Christian Quar. Rev." April, 1882); "Methodism and the Temperance Reformation" (1882) by Rev. Henry Wheeler; "Prohibition and Temperance" ("Quar. Rev. M. E. Church South," April, 1883); "The Liquor Problem in All Ages" by Daniel Dorchester 1884—a good book bringing the subject to date of composition, and confined almost exclusively to America); "Some Plain Words on Prohibition" ("The New Princ. Rev." Sept. 1887); "What More Can be Done by Law on the Cause of Temperance?" ("Andover Rev." June, 1889); "A Scheme of the Devil" ("Quar. Rev. U. B. in Christ" Oct. 1890—criticizes high license. See also Jan. 1895); "The Duties of Church Members in the Temperance Reform" ("Our Day" June, 1893); "Immoral Use and Sale of Intoxicants" ("Cath. World," Oct. 1894).

The rise of our larger cities has awakened the churches to their distinctive religious and moral problems. These are discussed as under: "City Missions" ("Christian Review" Oct. 1854—note bibliography);

"New York City a Field For Church Work" ("Amer. Quar. Ch. Rev." July, 1864); "Our Work in Cities—the Chicago Church" ("Freewill Baptist Quar." Jan. 1867); "The Pauperism of our Cities, its Character, Condition, Causes and Relief" ("Pres. Quar. and Princ. Rev." April, 1874); "Our Home Mission Work in Cities" ("Quar. Rev. Ev. Luth. Ch." Oct. 1876); "City Methodism" ("Meth. Quar. Rev." Jan. 1878); "Modern Cities and their Religious Problems" (1886) by S. L. Loomis; "City Evangelization" ("Meth. Rev." March, 1887, also Sept. 1888); "The Problem of the Modern City Church" ("Andover Rev." Dec. 1889); "City Missions and Social Problems" ("Meth. Rev." March, 1893); "The Church and the City" (*ibid.* Jan. 1894—valuable for relative strength of Protestant and Catholic work in the cities); "Redemption of the Slums" (*ibid.* March, 1895); "The Twentieth Century City" (n.d.) by Josiah Strong; "The Church in the City" (1915) by F. D. Leete.

The Chinese problem was first seriously approached by Rev. O. Gibson, A.M. in "The Chinese in America" (1877). An informing article with bibliography is "Some Phases of the Chinese Problem" ("Meth. Quar. Rev." April, 1878). An earlier contribution is "The Chinese Problem" ("Evang. Quar. Rev." Jan. 1870).

The secularization of the Sabbath has been discussed as follows: "Rational Sunday Observance" ("N. Amer. Rev." Dec. 1880); "The Teaching of our Lord Regarding the Sabbath, and Its Bearing on Christian Work" ("Pres. Rev." Jan. 1883); "The Sabbath for Man . . . " (1885) by Rev. Wilbur F. Crafts; "The Sunday Question" ("New Princ. Rev." July, 1886); "Our Rest Day, Its Origin, History, and Claims, With Special Reference to Present Day Needs" (1890) by Thomas Hamilton, D.D.; "Man's Inheritance in the Sabbath" ("Christian Thought" Oct. 1890). See also "Proc. Baptist Congress" Years 1886 & 1889.

The increasing appreciation of the value of the Sunday-school, and of religious education among the young, is a subject around which an extensive bibliography centers—"The History of Sunday Schools and of Religious Education from the Earliest Times" (1847) by Lewis G. Pray; "Forty Years Experience in Sunday Schools" (1860) by Stephen H. Tyng, D.D.; "Sabbath Schools, Their Origin and Progress" ("Unit. Pres. Quar. Rev." Oct. 1861); "The Sunday School" ("Meth. Quar. Rev." April, 1869); "The Growth of the Sunday School Idea in the Methodist Episcopal Church" (*ibid.* July, 1871); "Sunday Schools and their Importance in Missionary Work" ("Theol. Medium" Jan. 1873);

"Sunday Schools and their Importance in Missionary Work" ("Christian Quar." Jan. 1873); "The Sunday School Movement in its Relation to the Cause of Educational Religion" ("Merc'burg Rev." Jan. 1873); "The Sunday School in its Relation to the Church" (*ibid.* July, 1873); "The Sunday School, Its Past and Present" ("Pres. Quar. and Princ. Rev." July, 1873); "The Training of the Young of the Church" ("Meth. Quar. Rev." Oct. 1873); "The Religious Education of Children" ("Christian Quar." April, 1875); "Our Sunday School Literature" ("Meth. Quar. Rev." April, 1876); "Is the Modern Sunday School Method a Success?" (*ibid.* April, 1876); "The Care of the Young of the Church" ("Quar. Rev. Ev. Luth. Ch." July, 1876); "The Scope of Effective Sunday School Instruction" ("Bapt. Quar." Oct. 1877); "Thorough Personal Preparation in Sunday School Work" ("New Englander" Sept. 1878); "Shall the Church Rely on Revivalism or on Christian Nurture?" (*ibid.* Nov. 1879); "The Church School and its Officers" (1886), "The Modern Sunday School" (1887), and "The Church School and Normal Guide" (1889) all by Rev. J. H. Vincent; "The American Sunday School" ("Pres. Rev." April, 1889); "Should the General Convention Set Forth A Course of Study for the Sunday School?" ("Church Rev." Oct. 1899); "The Sabbath School as a Factor in Religious Training" ("Quar. Rev. Evang. Luth. Ch." April, 1890); "The Modern Sunday School" ("Meth. Rev." Jan. 1891); "The Sunday School, Its Place and its Purpose in the Church" ("Quar. Rev. M. E. Ch. South" Jan. 1893); "The Sabbath School Movement of Today" ("Pres. and Ref. Rev." April, 1894); "The Religion of Childhood" ("Meth. Rev." July, 1900).

From the extensive historical and scientific literature of the last twenty years, the following is selected as the most significant: "The Training of Children in Religion" (1901) by G. Hodges; "Sunday School Movements in America" (1901) by M. C. Brown; "Modern Methods in Sunday School Work," (1903) by G. W. Mead; "The Pedagogical Bible School" (1903) by S. B. Haslett; "Principles and Ideals for the Sunday School" (1903) by E. D. Burton; "The Childs Religious Life (1903) by W. G. Koons; "The Sunday School in the Development of the American Church" (1904) by O. S. Michael; "The Evolution of the Sunday School", (1911) by H. F. Cope; "Efficiency in the Sunday School" (1912) by the same author: "The Minister and the Boy" (1912) by Allan Hoben; "The Boy and the Sunday School . . . " (1913) by J. L. Alexander; "Worship in the Sunday School" (1913) by H. Hartshorne; "The Religious Development of the Child" (1913) by R. W. Weaver;

"The Sunday School under Scientific Management" (1914) by E. J. Denner; The Church School (1914) by W. S. Athearn; "Graded Social Service for the Sunday School" (1914) by N. S. Hutchins; "The Sunday-School Building and its Equipment" (1914) by H. F. Evans; "Religious Education in the Family" (1915) by H. F. Cope; "How to conduct a Sunday School" (1915) by M. Lawrence; "Character through Recreation" (1915) by H. P. Young; "Recreation and the Church" (1917) by H. W. Gates; "The Boy Scout Movement Applied by the Church" (1915) by Richardson and Loomis; "The Church and the People's Play" (1915) by H. A. Atkinson; "The Modern Sunday School and its Present Day Task" (1916) by H. F. Cope; "Religious Training in the School, and Home" (1917) by Sneath, Hodges and Tweedy; "A Social Theory of Religious Education" (1917) by G. A. Coe; "Christian Nurture" (1917) by H. Bushnell; "The Sunday School Movement 1780-1917, and the American Sunday School Union . . . " (1917) by E. W. Rice; "Religious Education in the Church" (1918) by H. F. Cope. "The Sunday School and the Teens" and "The Teens and the Rural Sunday School" edited (1913-14) by J. L. Alexander discusses the problems of adolescence. The Reports of the Religious Educational Association are rich in scientific material. "Religious Education" the magazine of this Association contains much relating to principles and methods of religious education.

On revivalism there is the following: " Revivals "("Evang.Quar. Rev." April, 1868); "The Influence of Revivals on the State of Religion" (*ibid.* Jan. 1870); "Revivals of Religion—How to Make them Productive of Permanent Good" ("New Englander" Jan. 1874); "Modern Revivalism," also "Evangelists, Their Office and Work" ("Christ. Quar." Jan. 1876); "Revivals and the Ordinary Working Conditions of the Churches" ("Congr. Quar." Jan. 1876); "The Revivals of the Century" ("Pres. Quar. and Princ. Rev." Oct. 1876); "Strictures on Revivals of Religion" ("Bibl. Sacra" April, 1877); "Recent Evangelistic Movements" ("New Englander" Jan. 1879); "Do We Need an Ethical Revival?" (*ibid.* Sept. 1880); "The Coming Revival, Its Characteristics," also "Signs of Its Coming" ("Homil. Rev." Jan. and Feb. 1897).

On Moody's work, there is "The American Evangelists, D.L. Moody and Ira L. Sankey, in Great Britain and Ireland" (1875) by John Hall; "D. L. Moody and his Work" (1875) by Rev. W. H. Daniels; "The Life of Dwight L. Moody" (1900) by William R. Moody. "The Moody Revival of the Seventies" (A.M. Dissertation, Univ. of Chicago, 1915) by V. F.

Schwalm is a satisfactory treatment which contains an exhaustive bibliography, including newspaper material.

In connection with Young People's work, there is "Young People's Christian Societies"("Quar. Rev. U.B. in Christ" July, 1890);"The Christian Endeavor Movement" ("Pres. Quar." April, 1891); "Opportunities and Perils of the Epworth League" ("Meth. Rev." May, 1894); "Young People's Societies and Our Church" ("Pres. Quar." July, 1895); "Christian Endeavor and the General Assembly" ("Pres. and Ref. Rev." Oct. 1896) and a "History of the Baptist Young Peoples Union of America (1913) by J. W. Conley. A doctoral dissertation by Rev. F. O. Erb entitled "Development of the Young People's Movement" (Univ. of Chicago, 1916) gives an exhaustive survey of the rise of the various young people's organizations. A good bibliography is appended.

The emergence of women into the public activities of the church has a literature as follows: "Woman's Place in Religious Meetings" ("Congr. Rev." Jan. 1868); "Silence of Women in the Churches" (*ibid.*); "Woman's Place in Assemblies for Public Worship" ("Pres. Quar. and Princ. Rev." Jan. 1873); "Women in the Church" ("Quar. Rev. Evang. Luth. Ch." April, 1874); "May a Woman Speak in a Promiscuous Religious Assembly?" ("Congr. Quar." April, 1874); "Woman's Right to Public Forms of Usefulness in the Church" ("New Englander" April, 1877); "Silence of Women in the Churches" ("Meth. Quar. Rev." April, 1878—see also appended bibliography); "Women Keeping Silence in Churches" ("Bibl. Sacra" Jan. 1878); "Women and Missions" ("Meth. Rev." Sept. 1886—good for early history of Women's Boards); "Woman's Position and Work in the Church" ("Pres. Rev." April, 1889); "Woman's Work in the Modern Church" ("Christian Thought" Oct. 1890). See also literature dealing with women's right to representation in the Methodist Conferences, p. 629.

Efficiency in church work is discussed in "Characteristics of an Efficient Church" ("Freewill Bapt. Quar." Jan. 1864); "Organization for Efficient Work" ("Meth. Quar. Rev." Oct. 1873); "The Problem of our Church Benevolences" (*ibid.* Jan. 1882 and April, 1883—valuable); "The Church's Future" ("Luth. Quar. Rev." July, 1882); "How to Develope and Direct the Benevolences of the Church" (*ibid.* Jan. 1883); "Religious Problem of the Country Town" ("Andover Rev." 1885, several papers in successive numbers); "The Ideal Church" ("The Forum" April, 1886); "Methods of Church Work, Religious, Social, and Financial" (1887) by Rev. Sylvanus Stall; "The Problem of a Second Service on Sunday" ("Andover Rev." March, 1889); "The Country

Church" ("Bibl. Sacra" April, 1890); "Country Missions" ("Pres. and Ref. Rev." Oct. 1891); "Modern Methods in Church Work. The Gospel Renaissance" (1897, later ed. 1901) by Rev. Geo. W. Mead; "The Sunday Night Service" (1902) by Wm. F. Sheridan; "Training the Church of the Future" (1902 Auburn Seminary Lectures,) by Francis E. Clark; "Missionary Reorganization" ("Meth. Rev." March, 1905); "What our Country Churches Need" (*ibid.* July, 1907); "Country Life and the Country School" (1912) by Mabel Carney; "Shall Churches Increase their Efficiency by Scientific Methods?" ("Amer. Jour. Theol." Jan. 1915); "Vocational Efficiency and the Theological Curriculum" (*ibid.* April, 1915); "Practical Theology and Ministerial Efficiency" (*ibid.* July, 1915); "Systematic Theology and Ministerial Efficiency" (*ibid.* Oct. 1915); "The Contribution of Critical Scholarship to Ministerial Efficiency" (*ibid.* Jan. 1916).

The question of the Bible in the schools is treated in the following: "The Church and the School" ("Merc'burg Rev." Jan. 1869); "The Bible in the Common Schools" (*ibid.* Jan. 1870; see also "Theological Medium" Jan. 1870); "Romanism and the Common Schools" ("Meth. Quar." Rev. April, 1870); "Recent Publications on the School Question" ("Bibl. Rep. and Princ. Rev." April, 1870); "The Bible in the Public Schools" ("Christian Quar." April, 1870); "The Bible and the State" ("Baptist Quar." July, 1871); "What Does the Bible Represent in the American Common Schools" ("Univ. Quar." July, 1874); "Shall we Retain the Bible in our Common Schools?" (*ibid.* April, 1877); "Shall State Education be Exclusively Secular?" ("Meth. Quar. Rev." April, 1880); "The Church, the State and the School" ("N. Amer. Rev." Sept. 1881); "Are Our Public Schools Godless?" ("Pres. Rev." Jan. 1889); "Public Instruction in Religion" ("Andover Rev." Jan. 1889); "Perils of the Public Schools" ("Our Day" Feb. 1889); "Religious Instruction in the Public Schools" ("Andover Rev." June, 1889); "The Bible and the Public Schools" ("Bibl. Sacra" July, 1889); "Romanism Versus the Public School System" (1889) by Daniel Dorchester; "The Great Conspiracy against our American Public Schools" (1891, addresses) by Rev. R. Harcourt; "Romanism and the Public Schools" ("Pres. Quar. South" Oct. 1892); "The Roman Catholic Church and the Public Schools" ("Quar. Rev. U. B. in Christ" June, 1893). See also Papers and Discussions in "Proc. Baptist Congress," Years 1886 & 1906.

For Roman Catholic literature of the subject see page 447.

The following articles reflect Protestant reactions upon events at Rome: "Romanism in the United States" ("Meth. Quar. Rev." Oct.

1868); "The Secret of Roman Catholic Success" ("Christian Quar."
Jan. 1869); "The Temporal Power of the Pope" ("Bibl. Repert. and
Princ. Rev." Jan. 1871); "Papal Infallibility" ("Quar. Rev. Evang.
Luth. Ch." Oct. 1871); "Papal Infallibility" ("Bapt. Quar." Jan. 1874);
"The Roman Question," "First Dogmatic Decree on the Church of
Christ, published in the Fourth Session of the Holy Ecumenical Council
of the Vatican," and "The Old Catholic Movement" ("Merc'burg Rev."
April, 1873); "Leo XIII and the Social Question" ("N. Amer. Rev."
Aug. 1895); "Phases in the Pontificate of Leo XIII" ("Meth. Rev."
Nov. 1895); "Pope Leo XIII on the Validity of Anglican Orders"
("Pres. Quar." July, 1897); "Romanism in the United States; The
Proper Attitude Toward It." ("Quar. Rev. U. B. in Christ" Jan. 1894).

For the Briggs Case, the "Minutes of the General Assembly of the
Presbyterian Church" will be found rich in documentary material, espec-
cially for the year 1893. "The Case Against Professor Briggs" (1893)
by Charles Augustus Briggs has the documents—three parts under separate covers. "The Trial of Dr. Briggs before the General Assembly.
A Calm Review of the Case by a Stranger who attended all the Sessions
of the Court" (1893) is respectful but critical. The article, "The General
Assembly of the Presbyterian Church in the United States of America"
in the "Presbyterian and Reformed Review" (July, 1893) has a good
review of the situation. "Another Decade in the History of the Union
Theological Seminary" (1889) by G. L. Prentiss reviews some aspects
of this conflict (see Part II). The "Andover Review" Nov. 1891, has
a report of the Committee that prosecuted Professor Briggs. The following articles should also be consulted: "The Relation of the Church
to Modern Scientific Thought" ("Andover Rev." July, 1891); "The
Higher Criticism" ("Luth. Quar " July, 1893). The Briggs literature
is cited in the "Methodist Review" Sept. 1891, p. 838.

Especially valuable as a condensed statement of the more recent
phases of the Union Seminary issue is the "Report" of the Committee of
the General Assembly on Union Theological Seminary, submitted May 25,
1915 (see "Minutes of the General Assembly . . ." New Series Vol.
XV, pp. 129-167).

The earlier heresy case of David Swing is exhaustingly set forth in
"The Trial of the Rev. David Swing" (1874) edited by a Committee of
the Presbytery.

"The Andover Case" is treated in the following: "The American
Board and the Late Boston Council" ("New England and Yale Rev."
Dec. 1888); "The American Board at Springfield" (*ibid.* Dec. 1889);

"Is it Domination or Dependence?" ("Andover Rev." Nov. 1889); "The American Board and Recent Discussions" ("Bibl. Sacra" April, 1890); "Boston Monday Lectures" ("Our Day" March, 1890). Documentary material on this controversy is accessible in the "Annual Reports" of the A.B.C.F.M. The background may be mastered by consulting many articles bearing upon the issue of the New Theology that appeared in the leading periodicals during the decade preceding this case.

The World Parliament of Religions is reported by Rev. John Henry Barrows in "The World's Parliament of Religions" (II Vols. 1893), and W. R. Houghton (editor-in-chief) in "The Parliament of Religions and Religious Congresses at the World's Columbian Exposition" (1893). Articles appear in the "Missionary Review of the World" Dec. 1894 and the "Methodist Review" Jan. 1894.

The Student Volunteer Movement is treated in "The Twenty-fifth Anniversary of the Student Volunteer Movement" (1911, addresses). The "Reports" of the International Conventions (1891 and quadrennially since 1894) with their historical addresses and bibliographical apparatus constitute a substantial library for the student of present-day missions. "Reports of the Conferences of Foreign Mission Boards . . . " are valuable, also the "Report" of the Ecumenical Missionary Conference in New York, 1900.

In connection with Christian Science, one needs to begin with the works of Mrs. Eddy: "Christian Healing" (1896); "Church Healing and the People's Idea of God" (1909); "Christian Science vs. Pantheism and Other Messages to the Mother Church" (1909); "A Complete Concordance to Science and Health, with Key to the Scriptures" (1911); "Miscellaneous Writings, 1883-1896" (1910). "The Life of Mary Baker Eddy" has been set forth (1907) by Sibyl Wilbur. "The Christian Science Journal" (1882 f.) has scattered items of historical value. Two brief polemical studies are "A Short Method with Christian Science" (1902) by Albert G. Lawson, and "The Christian Science Cult" (1902) by J. J. Taylor. The following will be found of value: "Christian Science and the New Church" ("New Jerus. Mag." March, 1889); "Christian Science or Mind Cure" ("Pres. and Ref. Rev." Jan. 1890); "Faith Healing, Christian Science, and Kindred Phenomena" (1892) by Rev. J. M. Buckley; "Facts and Fallacies of Christian Science" (1894) by Rev. A. W. Patten; "Christian Science" ("New Church Rev." Jan. 1896); "Christian Science and Its Problem" (1898) by J. H. Bates; "Christian Science—The Truths of Spiritual Healing and their Contribution to the Growth of Orthodoxy" (1898) by R. H. Newton; "Christian Science Examined" (1899) by Henry Varley; "The Absurd Paradox of Christian Science" ("N. Amer. Rev." July, 1901); "The Religious Significance of the Psycho-Therapeutic Movement" ("Amer. Jour. Theol." Oct. 1910).

The Dowie movement is canvassed in "John Alexander Dowie and the Christian Catholic Church in Zion" (1906) by Rolvix Harlan, with an introductory preface by Franklin Johnson.

One of the most important movements connected with recent American Christianity, has been Church Union and Federation: "Denominationalism not Sectarianism" ("Amer. Theol. Rev." May, 1860); "Ecclesiastical Organizations and Foreign Missions" ("Amer. Pres. Theol. Rev." Oct. 1864); "The Union of Christians—How can it be Accomplished?" also "The Union Movement, What will Come of it" (both in "Christian Quar." Jan. 1869); "Church Union" ("Merc'burg Rev." July, 1869); "Union in the Lutheran Church" ("Evang. Quar. Rev." April, 1871); "Disciples and Baptists—Will they Unite?" ("Christian Quar." July, 1871); "The Basis of Christian Union" (*ibid*. April, 1873); "The Unity of the Church" and "The Relations of the Church of England to the Other Protestant Churches" ("New Englander" Jan. 1874); "The Organic Unity of the Church" ("Pres. Quar. and Princ. Rev." Oct. 1876); "The True Grounds of Christian Union" ("Bapt. Quar." July, 1873); "The Organic Reunion of Churches" ("Bibl. Sacra" April, 1878); "Pan-Presbyterian Council" ("Meth. Quar. Rev." Jan. 1881); "Organic Union—Disruption and Fraternity" ("Quar. Rev. M. E. Ch. South" Oct. 1881); "Fraternity, Another View" (*ibid*. Jan. 1882); "American Lutherans and Their Divisions" ("Meth. Quar. Rev." July, 1882); "The American Congress of Churches" (Proceedings of the Cleveland Meeting, published under the direction of the Executive Committee, 1886); "Church Unity"—Lectures delivered in Union Theological Seminary, winter of 1896, by C. W. Shields, E. B. Andrews, J. F. Hurst, H. C. Potter, and A. H. Bradford; "Is Christian Union to be Organized?" ("Andover Rev." July, 1886); "Cooperation in Foreign Missions" ("Pres. Rev." July, 1887); "Obstacles to Christian Unity" ("Church Rev." Nov. 1887); "Church Union and Anglican Ordination" ("Meth. Quar. Rev." Jan. 1888); "Is Protestant Unity Possible?" ("Andover Rev." March, 1888); "Christian Unity and the Historic Episcopate" ("Pres. Rev." July, 1888); "Unity Better than Union" ("Southern Meth. Rev." Nov. 1888); "Scheme for Church Reunion" ("New Princ. Rev." Nov. 1888); "The Historic Episcopate" ("Quar. Rev. Evang. Luth. Ch." July, 1890, and Jan. 1891); "The Union for which Jesus

Prays" ("Pres. Quar." Jan. 1891); "The Peace of the Church, A Review" ("Unit. Rev." Sept. 1891); "The Peace of the Church" (1892) by Wm. R. Huntington; "A Suppressed Chapter of Recent Church History" ("Meth. Rev." July, 1893); "The Lambeth Ultimatum" ("Pres. Quar." Oct. 1894); "The Historic Episcopate; an Essay on the Four Articles of Church Unity, Proposed by the American House of Bishops and the Lambeth Conference" (n.d.) by Rev. C. W. Shields; "The Question of Unity" (1894) edited by A. H. Bradford, D.D.; "The Historic Episcopate, A Story of Anglican Claims and Methodist Orders" (1897) by R. J. Cooke, D.D.; "Christian Unity, or the Kingdom of Heaven" by Thomas Davidson ("Papers, Amer. Soc. Ch. Hist." Vol. IV, pp. 55-78); "Should the Denominational Distinctions of Christian Lands be Perpetuated on Mission Fields?" ("Amer. Jour. Theol." April, 1907); "The Inter-Church Conference on Federation" ("Meth. Rev." Sept. 1905;) Papers and Discussions in "Proc. Baptist Congress" Years 1887, 1890, 1907, 1908, 1911; "Church Federation Proceedings of the Inter-Church Conference . . . Mar. 15-21, 1905" edited (1906) by Elias B. Sanford, D.D.; "The Federal Council of Churches of Christ in America. Report of the First Quadrennial Session . . . 1908" (1909) edited by E. B. Sanford; "Christian Reunion; A Plan for the Restoration of the Ecclesia of God" (1909) by Frank Spence; "Church Unity" (1909) by C. A. Briggs; "Christian Unity at Work. Reports and Addresses of the Convention of the Federal Council of the Churches of Christ in America" (1912) edited by C. S. MacFarland; "The Message of the Disciples of Christ for the Union of the Church" (1913) by Peter Ainslee; "The New Interdenominationalism" ("Amer. Jour. Theol." Oct. 1916). "The Churches of the Federal Council" (1916) by C. S. MacFarland; "Origin and History of the Federal Council of the Churches of Christ in America" (1916) by E. B. Sanford; "The Library of Christian Cooperation. Proceedings and Reports of the Federal Council for the Quadrennium 1913-1916" (VI Vols. 1917) edited by C. S. MacFarland.

Interpretative of all the movements of the last half century are two scholarly historical addresses: "The Progress of Theological Thought during the Past Fifty Years" by Arther C. McGiffert, ("Amer. Jour Theol." July, 1916), and "Religious Advance in Fifty Years" by William H. P. Faunce (*ibid.*).

I. *THE BURIAL HILL DECLARATION OF FAITH; AND THE STATEMENT OF PRINCIPLES OF POLITY*, 1865

At a National Convention assembled in Boston, June 1865, to receive reports on polity and doctrine prepared by Committees appointed at a preliminary conference that had met in New York, the preceding autumn, serious differences developed respecting a Calvinistic paragraph. Happly at Burial Hill to which the Assembly proceeded while in the heat of debate, all contention subsided, and a hastily written statement completed only as the train rolled Plymouth-ward was adopted almost unanimously. Revised slightly, it was adopted June 23, without opposition.

While these debates respecting creed were in progress, discussion had arisen on the report of the committee dealing with polity. A twenty-seven page statement was finally, unanimously set aside for the brief statement given below:

"*Standing by the rock where the Pilgrims set foot upon these shores, upon the spot where they worshipped God, and among the graves of the early generations, we, Elders and Messengers of the Congregational churches of the United States in National Council assembled,—like them acknowledging no rule of faith but the word of God,—do now declare our adherence to the faith and order of the apostolic and primitive churches held by our fathers, and substantially as embodied in the confessions and platforms which our Synods of 1648 and 1680 set forth or reaffirmed. We declare that the experience of the nearly two and a half centuries which have elapsed since the memorable day when our sires founded here a Christian Commonwealth, with all the development of new forms of error since their times, has only deepened our confidence in the faith and polity of these fathers.* We bless God for the inheritance of these doctrines. We invoke the help of the Divine Redeemer, that, through the presence of the promised Comforter, He will enable us to transmit them in purity to our children.

In the times that are before us as a nation, times at once of duty and danger, we rest all our hope in the gospel of the Son of God. It was the grand peculiarity of our Puritan Fathers, that they held this gospel, not merely as the ground of their personal salvation, but as declaring the worth of man by the incarnation and sacrifice of the Son of God; and therefore applied its principles to elevate society, to regulate education, to civilize humanity, to purify law, to reform the Church and State, and to assert and defend liberty; in short, to mould and redeem, by its all transforming energy, every thing that belongs to man in his individual and social relations.

It was the faith of our fathers that gave us this free land in which we dwell. It is by this faith only that we can transmit to our children a free and happy, because a Christian, Commonwealth.

We hold it to be the distinctive excellence of our Congregational system, that it exalts that which is more, above that which is less, important, and by the simplicity of its organization, facilitates, in communities where the population is limited, the union of all true believers in one Christian Church; and that the division of such communities into several weak and jealous societies, holding the same common faith, is a sin against the body of Christ, and at once the shame and the scandal of Christendom.

We rejoice that, through the influence of our free system of apostolic order, we can hold fellowship with all who acknowledge Christ; and act efficiently in the work of restoring unity to the divided Church, and of bringing back harmony and peace among all 'who love our Lord Jesus Christ in sincerity.'

Thus recognizing the unity of the Church of Christ in all the world, and knowing that we are but one branch of Christ's people, while adhering to our own peculiar faith and order, we extend to all believers the hand of Christian fellowship, upon the basis of those great fundamental truths in which all Christians should agree. With them we confess our faith in God, the Father, the Son, and the Holy Ghost, the only living and true God; in Jesus Christ, the incarnate word, who is exalted to be our Redeemer and King; and in the Holy Comforter, who is present in the Church to regenerate and sanctify the soul.

With the whole Church, we confess the common sinfulness and ruin of our race, and acknowledge that it is only through the work accomplished by the life and expiatory death of Christ that believers in him are justified before God, receive the remission of sins, and through the presence and grace of the Holy Comforter are delivered from the power of sin, and perfected in holiness.

We believe also in the organized and visible Church, in the ministry of the Word, in the sacraments of Baptism and the Lord's Supper, in the resurrection of the body, and in the final judgment, the issues of which are eternal life and everlasting punishment.

We receive these truths on the testimony of God, given through the apostles and prophets, and in the life, the miracles, the death, the resurrection, of his Son, our Divine Redeemer—a testimony preserved for the Church in the Old and New Testaments, which were composed by holy men as they were moved by the Holy Ghost.

Affirming now our belief that those that thus hold 'one faith, one Lord, one baptism,' together constitute one Catholic Church, the several households of which, though called by different names, are the one body of Christ; and that these members of his body are sacredly bound to keep 'the unity of the spirit in the bond of peace,' *we declare that we will cooperate with all who will hold these truths. With them we will* carry the gospel into every part of this land, *and with them we will go into all the world, and 'preach the gospel to every creature.'* May He to whom 'all power is given in heaven and earth' fulfill the promise which is all our hope: 'Lo, I am with you alway, even to the end of the world.' Amen."

Text—*Congregational Quarterly*, Vol. X, pp. 377-378.

II. *STATEMENT OF CONGREGATIONAL PRINCIPLES*

"*Resolved*, That this Council recognizes as distinctive of the Congregational polity . . .

First, The principle that the local or Congregational church derives its power and authority directly from Christ, and is not subject to any ecclesiastical government exterior or superior to itself.

Second, That every local or Congregational church is bound to observe the duties of mutual respect and charity which are included in the communion of churches one with another; and that every church which refuses to give an account of its proceedings, when kindly and orderly desired to do so by neighboring churches, violates the law of Christ.

Third, That the ministry of the gospel by members of the churches who have been duly called and set apart to that work implies in itself no power of government, and that ministers of the gospel not elected to office in any church are not a hierarchy, nor are they invested with any official power in or over the churches."

Text—*Debates and Proceedings of the National Council of Congregational Churches Held at Boston, Mass., June 14-24, 1865*, pp. 463-464.

III. *THE EVANGELICAL ALLIANCE.*

Statement issued at the organization of the American branch of the Evangelical Alliance, January, 1867.

"*Resolved,* That in forming an Evangelical Alliance for the United States, in co-operative union with other Branches of the Alliance, we have no intention or desire to give rise to a new denomination or sect; nor to effect an amalgamation of Churches, except in the way of facilitating personal Christian intercourse and a mutual good understanding; nor to interfere in any way whatever with the internal affairs of the various denominations; but simply to bring individual Christians into closer fellowship and co-operation, on the basis of the spiritual union which already exists in the vital relation of CHRIST to the members of his body in all ages and countries.

Resolved, That, in the same spirit, we propose no new creed; but, taking broad, historical and evangelical catholic ground, we solemnly re-affirm and profess our faith in all the doctrines of the inspired Word of GOD, and in the *consensus* of doctrines as held by all true Christians from the beginning. And we do more especially affirm our belief in the *Divine-human person* and *atoning work of our* LORD *and* SAVIOUR JESUS CHRIST, as the only and sufficient source of salvation, as the heart and soul of Christianity, and as the centre of all true Christian union and fellowship.

Resolved, That, with this explanation, and in the spirit of a just Christian liberality in regard to the minor differences of theological schools and religious denominations, we also adopt, as a summary of the *consensus* of the various Evangelical Confessions of Faith, the Articles and Explanatory Statement set forth and agreed on by the Evangelical Alliance at its formation in London, 1846, and approved by the separate European organizations; which articles are as follows:

1. The divine inspiration, authority, and sufficiency of the Holy Scriptures.

2. The right and duty of private judgment in the interpretation of the Holy Scriptures.

3. The Unity of the Godhead, and the Trinity of the Persons therein.

4. The utter depravity of human nature in consequence of the Fall.

5. The incarnation of the SON of GOD, his work of atonement for the sins of mankind and his mediatorial intercession and reign.

6. The justification of the sinner by faith alone.

7. The work of the HOLY SPIRIT in the conversion and sanctification of the sinner.

8. The immortality of the soul, the resurrection of the body, the judgment of the world by our LORD JESUS CHRIST, with the eternal blessedness of the righteous, and the eternal punishment of the wicked.

9. The divine institution of the Christian ministry, and the obligation and perpetuity of the ordinances of Baptism and the LORD'S Supper.

It being, however, distinctly declared that this brief summary is not to be regarded in any formal or ecclesiastical sense as a creed or confession, nor the adoption of it as involving an assumption of the right authoritatively to define the limits of Christian brotherhood, but simply as an indication of the class of persons whom it is desirable to embrace within the Alliance."

Text—*Evangelical Alliance, Proceedings, Essays, Addresses, 1873,* p. 760.

IV. *PLAN OF REUNION OF THE PRESBYTERIAN CHURCH IN THE UNITED STATES OF AMERICA*

Adopted by the Assemblies, New York, May 27, 1869, and ratified in Joint Assembly, Pittsburgh, Pennsylvania, November 12, 1869.

"Believing that the interests of the Redeemer's kingdom would be promoted by the healing of our divisions, and that the two bodies bearing the same name, having the same Constitution, and each recognizing the other as a sound and orthodox body according to the principles of the Confession common to both, cannot be justified by any but the most imperative reasons in maintaining separate and, in some respects, rival organizations; we are now clearly of the opinion that the reunion of those bodies ought, as soon as the necessary steps can be taken, to be accomplished, upon the Basis hereinafter set forth:

1. The Presbyterian Churches in the United States of America, namely, that whose General Assembly convened in the Brick Church in the city of New York, on the 20th day of May, 1869, and that whose General Assembly met in the Church of the Covenant in the said city, on the same day, shall be re-united as one Church, under the name and style of the Presbyterian Church in the United States of America, possessing all the legal and corporate rights and powers pertaining to the Church previous to the division in 1838, and all the legal and corporate rights and powers which the separate Churches now possess.

2. The reunion shall be effected on the doctrinal and ecclesiastical basis of our common Standards; the Scriptures of the Old and New Testaments shall be acknowledged to be the inspired word of God, and the only infallible rule of faith and practice; the Confession of Faith shall continue to be sincerely received and adopted as containing the system of doctrine taught in the Holy Scriptures; and the Government and Discipline of the Presbyterian Church in the United States shall be approved as containing the principles and rules of our polity.

3. Each of the said Assemblies shall submit the foregoing Basis to its Presbyteries which shall be required to meet on or before the 15th day of October, 1869, to express their approval or disapproval of the same. . . .

If the two General Assemblies shall then find and declare that the above-named Basis of Reunion has been approved by two-thirds of the Presbyteries connected with each branch of the Church, then the same shall be of binding force, and the two Assemblies shall take action accordingly.

5. The said General Assemblies shall then and there make provision for the meeting of the General Assembly of the united Church on the third Thursday of May, 1870. The Moderators of the two present Assemblies shall jointly preside at the said Assembly of 1870 until another Moderator be chosen. The Moderator of the Assembly now sitting at the Brick Church aforesaid, shall, if present, put all votes, and decide questions of order; and the Moderator of the other Assembly shall, if present, preach the opening Sermon; and the Stated Clerks of the present Assemblies shall act as Stated Clerks of the Assembly of the united Church until a Stated Clerk or Clerks shall have been chosen thereby; and no Commissioner shall have a right to vote or deliberate in said Assembly until his name shall have been enrolled by the said Clerks, and his commission examined and filed among the papers of the Assembly.

6. Each Presbytery of the separate Churches shall be entitled to the same representation in the Assembly of the united Church in 1870 as it is entitled to in the Assembly with which it is now connected."

Concurrent Declarations of the General Assemblies of 1869.

"As there are matters pertaining to the interests of the Church, when it shall have become re-united, which will manifestly require adjustment on the coming together of two bodies which have so long acted separately, and concerning some of which matters it is highly desirable that there should be a previous good understanding, the two Assemblies agree to adopt the following declarations, not as articles of compact or covenant, but as in their judgment proper and equitable arrangements, to wit:

1. All the ministers and churches embraced in the two bodies should be admitted to the same standing in the united body, which they may have held in their respective connections, up to the consummation of the union.

2. Imperfectly organized churches are counselled and expected to become thoroughly Presbyterian, as early within the period of five years as may be permitted by the highest interests to be consulted; and no other such churches shall be hereafter received.

3. The boundaries of the several Presbyteries and Synods should be adjusted by the General Assembly of the united Church.

4. The official records of the two branches of the Church for the period of separation should be preserved and held as making up one history of the Church; and no rule or precedent which does not stand approved by both the bodies, should be of any authority until re-established in the united body, except in so far as such rule or precedent may affect the rights of property founded thereon.

5. The corporate rights now held by the two General Assemblies, and by their Boards and Committees, should, as far as practicable, be consolidated, and applied for their several objects, as defined by law.

6. There should be one set of Committees or Boards for Home and Foreign Missions, and the other religious enterprises of the Church; which the churches should be encouraged to sustain, though free to cast their contributions into other channels if they desire to do so.

7. As soon as practicable after the union shall have been effected, the General Assembly should reconstruct and consolidate the several Permanent Committees and Boards which now belong to the two Assemblies, so as to represent, as far as possible with impartiality, the views and wishes of the two bodies constituting the united Church.

8. The publications of the Board of Publication and of the Publication Committee should continue to be issued as at present, leaving it to the Board of Publication of the United Church to revise these issues and perfect a catalogue for the united Church, so as to exclude invidious references to past controversies.

9. In order to a uniform system of ecclesiastical supervision, those Theological Seminaries that are now under Assembly control, may, if their Boards of Direction so elect, be transferred to the watch and care of one or more of the adjacent Synods; and the other Seminaries are advised to introduce, as far as may be, into their Constitutions, the principle of Synodical or Assembly supervision; in which case they shall be entitled to an official recognition and approbation on the part of the General Assembly.

10. It should be regarded as the duty of all our judicatories, ministers, and people in the united Church, to study the things which make for peace, and to guard against all needless and offensive references to the causes that have divided us; and in order to avoid the revival of past issues by the continuance of any usage in either branch of the Church, that has grown out of former conflicts, it is earnestly recommended to the lower judicatories of the Church that they conform their practice in relation to all such usages, as far as is consistent with their convictions of duty, to the general custom of the Church prior to the controversies that resulted in the separation."

Text—*Minutes of the General Assembly of the Presbyterian Church in the United States of America*, Vol. XVIII, pp. 914-16.

V. THE CONSTITUTION OF THE NATIONAL COUNCIL AND OBERLIN DECLARATION

At the Pilgrim Memorial Convention which met in Chicago April 27, 1870, a resolution was passed recommending the conferences and associations "to unite in measures for instituting on the principle of fellowship, excluding 'ecclesiastical authority, a permanent National Conference." Pursuant to the call of a preliminary committee, a Council met at Oberlin, Ohio, Nov. 15, 1871, attended by 276 delegates representing 25 states and territories. A Constitution and Declaration on the Unity of the Church as such was adopted.

THE CONSTITUTION.

"The Congregational churches of the United States, by elders and messengers assembled, do now associate themselves in National Council:

To express and foster their substantial unity in doctrine, polity, and work; and

To consult upon the common interests of all the churches, their duties in the work of evangelization, the united development of their resources, and their relations to all parts of the kingdom of Christ.

They agree in belief that the Holy Scriptures are the sufficient and only infallible rule of religious faith and practice; their interpretation thereof being in substantial accordance with the great doctrines of the Christian faith, commonly called evangelical, held in our churches from the early times, and sufficiently set forth by former General Councils.

They agree in the belief that the right of government resides in local churches, or congregations of believers, who are responsible directly to the Lord Jesus Christ, the One Head of the church universal and of all particular churches; but that all churches, being in communion one with another as parts of Christ's catholic church, have mutual duties subsisting in the obligations of fellowship.

The churches, therefore, while establishing this National Council for the furtherance of the common interests and work of all the churches, do maintain the Scriptural and inalienable right of each church to self-government and administration; and this National Council shall never exercise legislative or judicial authority, nor consent to act as a council of reference.

And for the convenience of orderly consultation, they establish the following Rules:

I. *Sessions.*—The churches will meet in National Council every third year. They shall also be convened in special session whenever any five of the general State organizations shall so request.

II. *Representation.*—The churches shall be represented, at each session, by delegates, either ministers or laymen, appointed in number and manner as follows:—

1. The churches, assembled in their local organizations, appoint one delegate for every ten churches in their respective organizations, and one for a fraction of ten greater than one-half, it being understood that whenever the churches of any State are directly united in a general organization, they may, at their option, appoint the delegates in such body, instead of in local organizations, but in the above ratio of churches so united.

2. In addition to the above, the churches united in State organization appoint by such body one delegate, and one for each ten thousand communicants in their fellowship, and one for a major fraction thereof:—

3. It being recommended that the number of delegates be, in all cases, divided between ministers and laymen, as nearly equally as is practicable.

4. Such Congregational general societies for Christian work, and the faculties of such theological seminaries, as may be recognized by this Council, may be represented by one delegate each, such representatives having the right of discussion only.

. . . . , ...

DECLARATION ON THE UNITY OF THE CHURCH

The members of the National Council, representing the Congregational churches of the United States, avail themselves of this opportunity to renew their previous declarations of faith in the unity of the church of God.

While affirming the liberty of our churches, as taught in the New Testament, and inherited by us from our fathers, and from martyrs and confessors of foregoing ages, we adhere to this liberty all the more as affording the ground and hope of a more visible unity in time to come. We desire and purpose to cooperate with all the churches of our Lord Jesus Christ.

In the expression of the same catholic sentiments solemnly avowed by the Council of 1865, on the Burial Hill at Plymouth, we wish, at this new epoch of our history, to remove, so far as in us lies, all causes of suspicion and alienation, and to promote the growing unity of council and of effort among the followers of Christ. To us, as to our brethren, 'There is one body and one spirit, even as we are called in one hope of our calling.'

As little as did our fathers in their days, do we in ours, make a pretension to be the only churches of Christ. We find ourselves consulting and acting together under the distinctive name of Congregationalists, because, in the present condition of our common Christianity, we have felt ourselves called to ascertain and do our own appropriate part of the work of Christ's church among men.

We especially desire, in prosecuting the common work of evangelizing our own land and the world, to observe the common and sacred law, that in the wide field of the world's evangelization, we do our work in friendly cooperation with all those who love and serve our common Lord.

We believe in 'the holy catholic church.' It is our prayer and endeavor, that the unity of the church may be more and more apparent, and that the prayer of our Lord for his disciples may be speedily and completely answered, and all be one; that by consequence of this Christian unity in love, the world may believe in Christ as sent of the Father to save the world."

Text—*Minutes of the National Council . . . Held in Oberlin, 1871,* pp. 29-32, 63-67.

VI. *LAY DELEGATION IN THE GENERAL CONFERENCE OF THE METHODIST EPISCOPAL CHURCH*

After an agitation extending thro several Conferences, the following was passed May 1, 1872 by a vote of 252 to 36.

Answer 1. The General Conference shall be composed of ministerial and lay delegates. The ministerial delegates shall consist of one member for every thirty members of each Annual Conference, to be appointed by seniority or choice, at the discretion of such Annual Conference, yet so that such representatives shall have travelled at least four full calendar years from the time that they were received on trial by an Annual Conference, and are in full connection at the time of holding the Conference.

The lay delegates shall consist of two laymen for each Annual Conference, except such Conferences as have but one ministerial delegate, which Conferences shall be entitled to one lay delegate each.

The lay delegates shall be chosen by an Electoral Conference of laymen, which shall assemble for the purpose on the third day of the session of the Annual Conference, at the place of its meeting, at its session immediately preceding the General Conference.

The Electoral Conference shall be composed of one layman from each circuit or station within the bounds of the Annual Conference, and, on assembling, the Electoral Conference shall organize by electing a chairman and secretary of their own number: such layman to be chosen by the last Quarterly Conference preceding the time of its assembling: *Provided,* that no layman shall be chosen a delegate either to the Electoral Conference or to the General Conference who shall be under twenty-five years of age, or who shall not have been a member of the Church in full connection for the five consecutive years preceding the elections.

Text—*Journal of the General Conference . . . 1872,* p. 46.

VII. *THE CAPE MAY RESOLUTIONS*

"The Commissioners adopted, without a dissentient voice, the following
DECLARATION AND BASIS OF FRATERNITY
Status of the Methodist Episcopal Church, and of the Methodist Episcopal Church,
South, and their Coordinate Relation as Legitimate Branches
of Episcopal Methodism

Each of said Churches is a legitimate Branch of Episcopal Methodism in the United States, having a common origin in the Methodist Episcopal Church organized in 1784; and since the organization of the Methodist Episcopal Church, South, was consummated in 1845 by the voluntary exercise of the right of the Southern Annual Conferences, ministers, and members, to adhere to that Communion, it has been an Evangelical Church, reared on scriptural foundations, and her ministers and members with those of the Methodist Episcopal Church, have constituted one Methodist family, though in distinct ecclesiastical connections.

It was next incumbent on us to consider the questions concerning conflicting claims to Church Property, and some special cases that could not conveniently be referred to the operation of a general rule. . .

We have considered the papers in all cases that have been brought to our notice. These arose in the following States: Virginia, West Virginia, Maryland, Tennessee, Louisiana, North Carolina, and South Carolina. In respect of some of these cases we have given particular directions; but for all other cases the Joint Commission unanimously adopted the following

RULES FOR THE ADJUSTMENT OF ADVERSE CLAIMS TO CHURCH PROPERTY.

Rule I. In cases not adjudicated by the Joint Commission, any Society of either Church, constituted according to its Discipline, now occupying the Church Property, shall remain in possession thereof; provided that where there is now, in the same place, a Society of more members attached to the other Church, and which has hitherto claimed the use of the property, the latter shall be entitled to possession.

Rule II. Forasmuch as we have no power to annul decisions respecting Church Property made by the State Courts, the Joint Commission ordain in respect thereof,—

1. In cases in which such a decision has been made, or in which there exists an agreement, the same shall be carried out in good faith.

2. In communities where there are two Societies, one belonging to the Methodist Episcopal Church, and the other to the Methodist Episcopal Church, South, which have adversely claimed the Church Property, it is recommended that, without delay, they amicably compose their differences irrespective of the strict legal title, and settle the same according to Christian principles, the equities of the particular case, and, so far as practicable, according to the principle of the aforegoing Rule.

But if such settlement cannot be speedily made, then the question shall be referred for an equitable decision to three Arbitrators, one to be chosen by each claimant from their respective Societies, and the two thus chosen shall select a third person not connected with either of said Churches; and the decision of any two of them shall be final.

3. In communities in which there is but one Society, Rule I shall be faithfully observed in the interest of peace and fraternity.

Rule III. Whenever necessary to carry the aforegoing Rules into effect, the legal title to the Church property shall be accordingly transferred.

Rule IV. These Rules shall take effect immediately.

In order to further promote the peaceful results contemplated by this Joint Commission, and to remove as far as may be all occasion, and especially to forestall all further occasion, for hostility between the two Churches, we recommend to members of both, as a wise rule of settlement where property is in contest, and one or both are weak, that they compose their differences by uniting in the same communion; and in all cases, that the ministers and members recognize each other in all relations of fraternity, and as possessed of ecclesiastical rights and the privileges of equal dignity and validity. They should each receive from the other ministers and members in good standing with the same alacrity and credit as if coming from their own Church, and, without interference with each other's institutions or missions, they should, nevertheless, co-operate in all Christian enterprises.

It is not to be supposed, in respect of some matters of mere opinion, that all ministers and members in either Church will be in accord; but we trust and believe that a spirit of fellowship and mutual regard will pervade the reconciled ranks of the entire ministry and membership of both Churches. We believe, also, that their supreme allegiance to the cause of the Great Master will triumph over all variation of personal sentiments, and will so exalt the claims of brotherly affection, that from this auspicious hour a new epoch in Methodism will begin its brighter history, so that we shall know no unfraternal Methodism in the United States, or even in the wide world. . . .

We cannot restrain the expression of our united congratulations to both of the great Churches whose Commissions we have executed, in uniting between them the broken cords of affectionate and brotherly fraternization. Henceforth they may hail each other as from the auxiliary ranks of one great army. The only differences they will foster will be those friendly rivalries that spring from earnest endeavors to further to the utmost the triumphs of the gospel of peace. Whatever progress is made by the one Church or by the other will occasion general joy. They will rejoice in each other's success as a common good; and, amid the thousand glorious memories of Methodism, they will go forward devoted to their one work of spreading Scriptural holiness over these lands. . . .

Now unto Him that is able to keep us from falling, and to present us faultless before the presence of his glory with exceeding joy; to the only-wise God, our Savior, be glory and majesty, dominion and power, both now and ever. Amen.

In the bonds of the Gospel of peace,

Your brethren and servants,

MORRIS D'C. CRAWFORD,   EDWARD H. MYERS,
Commissioners of M. E. Church   *Commissioners of M. E. Church South.*
Cape May, N. J., August 23, 1876."

Text—*Formal Fraternity. Proceedings of the General Conferences . . . 1872, 1874, 1876 . . .* , pp. 78-83.

VIII. *THE COMMISSION CREED OF 1883*

The doctrinal formulations of 1865 and 1871 proving too general for the local churches, the Ohio Association memorialized the National Council in May 1880 to prepare a "formula that shall not be mainly a reaffirmation of former confessions, but that shall state in precise terms in our living tongue the doctrines which we hold today." The Council, in harmony with this request, appointed a commission of twenty-five which, Dec. 19, 1883, presented the statement as under signed by twenty-two of their number.

Statement of Doctrine

I. We believe in one God, the Father Almighty, Maker of heaven and earth, and of all things visible and invisible;

And in Jesus Christ, His only Son, our Lord, who is one substance with the Father; by whom all things were made;

And in the Holy Spirit, the Lord and Giver of life, who is sent from the Father and Son, and who together with the Father and Son is worshipped and glorified.

II. We believe that the providence of God, by which he executes his eternal purposes in the government of the world, is in and over all events; yet so that the freedom and responsibility of man are not impaired, and sin is the act of the creature alone.

III. We believe that man was made in the image of God, that he might know, love, and obey God, and enjoy him forever; that our first parents by disobedience fell under the righteous condemnation of God; and that all men are so alienated from God that there is no salvation from the guilt and power of sin except through God's redeeming grace.

IV. We believe that God would have all men return to him; that to this end he has made himself known, not only through the works of nature, the course of his providence, and the consciences of men, but also through supernatural revelations made especially to a chosen people, and above all, when the fullness of time was come, through Jesus Christ his Son.

V. We believe that the Scriptures of the Old and New Testaments are the records of God's revelation of himself in the work of redemption; that they were written by men under the special guidance of the Holy Spirit; that they are able to make wise unto salvation; and that they constitute the authoritative standard by which religious teaching and human conduct are to be regulated and judged.

VI. We believe that the love of God to sinful men has found its highest expression in the redemptive work of his Son, who became man, uniting his divine nature with our human nature in one person; who was tempted like other men, yet without sin; who by his humiliation, his holy obedience, his sufferings, his death on the cross, and his resurrection, became a perfect Redeemer; whose sacrifice of himself for the sins of the world declares the righteousness of God, and is the sole and sufficient ground of forgiveness and of reconciliation with him.

VII. We believe that Jesus Christ, after he had risen from the dead, ascended into heaven, where, as the one mediator between God and man, he carries forward his work of saving men; that he sends the Holy Spirit to convict them of sin, and to lead them to repentance and faith; and that those who through renewing grace turn to righteousness, and trust in Jesus Christ as their Redeemer, receive for his sake the forgiveness of their sins, and are made the children of God.

VIII. We believe that those who are thus regenerated and justified, grow in sanctified character through fellowship with Christ, the indwelling of the Holy Spirit, and obedience to the truth; that a holy life is the fruit and evidence of saving faith; and that the believer's hope of continuance in such a life is in the preserving grace of God.

IX. We believe that Jesus Christ came to establish among men the kingdom of God, the reign of truth and love, righteousness and peace; that to Jesus Christ, the Head of his kingdom, Christians are directly responsible in faith and conduct; and that to him all have immediate access without mediatorial or priestly intervention.

X. We believe that the Church of Christ, invisible and spiritual, comprises all true believers, whose duty it is to associate themselves in churches, for the maintenance of worship, for the promotion of spiritual growth and fellowship, and for the conversion of men; that these churches, under the guidance of the Holy Scriptures and in fellowship with one another, may determine—each for itself—their organization, statements of belief, and forms of worship, may appoint and set apart their own ministers, and should co-operate in the work which Christ has committed to them for the furtherance of the gospel throughout the world.

XI. We believe in the observance of the Lord's Day, as a day of holy rest and worship; in the ministry of the word; and in the two sacraments, which Christ has appointed for his church, Baptism, to be administered to believers and their children, as a sign of cleansing from sin, of union to Christ, and of the impartation of the Holy Spirit; and the Lord's Supper, as a symbol of his atoning death, a seal of its efficacy, and a means whereby he confirms and strengthens the spiritual union and communion of believers with himself.

XII. We believe in the ultimate prevalence of the kingdom of Christ over all the earth; in the glorious appearing of the great God and our Saviour Jesus Christ; in the resurrection of the dead; and in a final judgment, the issues of which are everlasting punishment and everlasting life.

Text—Walker: *The Creeds and Platforms of Congregationalism*, pp. 580-581.

IX. *A SUMMARY OF CHRISTIAN SCIENCE BELIEF*

I. God is infinite, the only Life, substance, Spirit, or Soul, the only intelligence of the universe, including man. Eye hath neither seen God nor His image and likeness. Neither God nor the perfect man can be discerned by the material senses. The individuality of Spirit, or the infinite, is unknown, and thus a knowledge of it is left either to human conjecture or to the revelation of divine Science.

II. God is what the Scriptures declare Him to be, Life, Truth, Love. Spirit is divine Principle, and divine Principle is Love, and Love is Mind, and Mind is not both good and bad, for God is Mind; therefore there is in reality one Mind only, because there is one God.

III. The notion that both evil and good are real is a delusion of material sense, which Science annihilates. Evil is nothing, no thing, mind, nor power. As manifested by mankind it stands for a lie, nothing claiming to be something,—for lust, dishonesty, selfishness, envy, hypocrisy, slander, hate, theft, adultery, murder, dementia, insanity, inanity, devil, hell, with all the etceteras that word includes.

IV. God is divine Life, and Life is no more confined to the forms which reflect it than substance is in its shadow. If life were in mortal man or material things, it would be subject to their limitations and would end in death. Life is Mind, the creator reflected in His creations. If He dwelt within what He creates, God would not be reflected but absorbed, and the Science of being would be forever lost through a mortal sense, which falsely testifies to a beginning and an end.

V. The Scriptures imply that God is All-in-all. From this it follows that nothing possesses reality nor existence except the divine Mind and His ideas. The Scriptures also declare that God is Spirit. Therefore in Spirit all is harmony, and there can be no discord; all is Life, and there is no death. Everything in God's universe expresses Him.

VI. God is individual, incorporeal. He is divine Principle, Love, the universal cause, the only creator, and there is no other self-existence. He is all-inclusive, and is reflected by all that is real and eternal and by nothing else. He fills all space, and it is impossible to conceive of such omnipresence and individuality except as infinite Spirit or Mind. Hence all is Spirit and spiritual.

VII. Life, Truth, and Love constitute the triune Person called God,—that is, the triply divine Principle, Love. They represent a trinity in unity, three in one,—the same in essence, though multiform in office: God the Father-Mother; Christ th spiritual idea of sonship; divine Science or the Holy Comforter. These three express in divine Science the threefold, essential nature of the infinite. They also indicate the divine Principle of scientific being, the intelligent relation of God to man and the universe.

VIII.   Father-Mother is the name for Deity, which indicates His tender relationship to His spiritual creation. . . . . . .

IX.   Jesus was born of Mary. Christ is the true idea voicing good, the divine message from God to men speaking to the human consciousness. The Christ is incorporeal, spiritual,—yea, the divine image and likeness, dispelling the illusions of the senses; the Way, the Truth, and the Life, healing the sick and casting out evils, destroying sin, disease, and death. . . . . . .

X.   Jesus demonstrated Christ; he proved that Christ is the divine idea of God—the Holy Ghost, or Comforter, revealing the divine Principle, Love, and leading into all truth . . . .

XIII.   The advent of Jesus of Nazareth marked the first century of the Christian era, but the Christ is without beginning of years or end of days. . . .

XV.   The invisible Christ was imperceptible to the so-called personal senses whereas Jesus appeared as a bodily existence. This dual personality of the unseen and the seen, the spiritual and material, the eternal Christ and the corporeal Jesus manifest in flesh, continued until the Master's ascension, when the human, material concept, or Jesus, disappeared, while the spiritual self, or Christ, continues to exist in the eternal order of divine Science, taking away the sins of the world, as the Christ has always done, even before the human Jesus was incarnate to mortal eyes. . . . . . .

XX.   Mind is the divine Principle, Love, and can produce nothing unlike the eternal Father-Mother, God. Reality is spiritual, harmonious, immutable, immortal, divine, eternal. Nothing unspiritual can be real, harmonious, or eternal. Sin, sickness, and mortality are the suppositional antipodes of Spirit, and must be contradictions of reality.

XXI.   The Ego is deathless and limitless, for limits would imply and impose ignorance. Mind is the I AM, or infinity. Mind never enters the finite. Intelligence never passes into non-intelligence, or matter. Good never enters into evil, the unlimited into the limited, the eternal into the temporal, nor the immortal into mortality. The divine Ego, or individuality, is reflected in all spiritual individuality from the infinitesimal to the infinite.

XXV. . . .For true happiness, man must harmonize with his Principle, divine Love; the Son must be in accord with the Father, in conformity with Christ. According to divine Science, man is in a degree as perfect as the Mind that forms him. The truth of being makes man harmonious and immortal, while error is mortal and discordant.

XXVI.   Christian Science demonstrates that none but the pure in heart can see God, as the gospel teaches. In proportion to his purity is man perfect; and perfection is the order of celestial being which demonstrates Life in Christ, Life's spiritual ideal. . .

XXX.   The destruction of sin is the divine method of pardon. Divine Life destroys death, Truth destroys error, and Love destroys hate. Being destroyed, sin needs no other form of forgiveness. Does not God's pardon, destroying any one sin, prophesy and involve the final destruction of all sin?

XXXI. Since God is All, there is no room for His unlikeness. God, Spirit, alone created all, and called it good. Therefore evil, being contrary to good, is unreal, and cannot be the product of God. . . .

XXXII. As the mythology of pagan Rome has yielded to a more spiritual idea of Deity, so will our material theories yield to spiritual ideas, until the finite gives place to the infinite, sickness to health, sin to holiness, and God's kingdom comes 'in earth, as it is in heaven.' The basis of all health, sinlessness, and immortality, is the great fact that God is the only Mind; and this Mind must be not merely believed, but it must be understood. To get rid of sin through Science, is to divest sin of any supposed mind or reality, and never to admit that sin can have intelligence or power, pain or pleasure. You conquer error by denying its verity. Our various theories will never lose their imaginary power for good or evil, until we lose our faith in them and make life its own proof of harmony and God.

Text—Mary Baker Eddy: "*Science and Health with Key to the Scriptures.*" (1917) pp. 330-340.

X. THE LAMBETH ARTICLES

DECLARATION OF THE HOUSE OF BISHOPS OF THE PROTESTANT EPISCOPAL CHURCH, ADOPTED OCTOBER 20, 1886.

WHEREAS, In the year 1853, in response to a Memorial signed by many Presbyters of this Church, praying that steps might be taken to heal the unhappy divisions of Christendom, and to more fully develop the catholic idea of the Church of Christ, the Bishops of this Church, in Council assembled, did appoint a Commission of Bishops empowered to confer with the several Christian bodies in our land who were desirous of promoting godly union and concord among all who loved the Lord Jesus Christ in sincerity and truth; and,

WHEREAS, This Commission, in conformity with the terms of its appointment, did formally set forth and advocate sundry suggestions and recommendations intended to accomplish the great end in view; and,

WHEREAS, In the year 1880, the Bishops of the American Church, assembled in Council, moved by the appeals from Christians in foreign countries, who were struggling to free themselves from the usurpations of the Bishop of Rome, set forth a Declaration to the effect that in virtue of the solidarity of the Catholic Episcopate in which we have part, it was the right and duty of the Episcopates of all national Churches, holding the primitive Faith and Order, and of the several Bishops of the same, to protect in the holding of that Faith and the recovering of that Order those who have been wrongfully deprived of both, and this without demanding a rigid uniformity or the sacrifice of their national traditions of worship and discipline, or of their rightful autonomy; and,

WHEREAS, Many of the faithful in Christ Jesus among us are praying with renewed and increasing earnestness that some measures may be adopted at this time for the reunion of the sundered parts of Christendom:

Now, therefore, In pursuance of the action taken in 1853 for the healing of the divisions among Christians in our own land, and in 1880 for the protection and encouragement of those who had withdrawn from the Roman Obedience; we, Bishops of the Protestant Episcopal Church in the United States of America, in Council assembled, as Bishops in the Church of God, do hereby solemnly declare to all whom it may conern.

and especially to our fellow-Christians of the different Communions in this land, who, in their several spheres, have contended for the religion of Christ:

1. Our earnest desire that the Saviour's prayer 'that we all may be one' may, in its deepest and truest sense, be speedily fulfilled.

2. That we believe that all who have been duly baptized with water in the Name of the Father, and of the Son, and of the Holy Ghost, are members of the Holy Catholic Church.

3. That in all things of human ordering or human choice relating to modes of worship and discipline, or to traditional customs, this Church is ready in the spirit of love and humility to forego all preferences of her own.

4. That this Church does not seek to absorb other Communions, but rather, cooperating with them on the basis of a common Faith and Order, to discountenance schism, to heal the wounds of the Body of Christ, and to promote the charity which is the chief of Christian graces and the visible manifestation of Christ to the world.

But, furthermore, We do hereby affirm that the Christian unity, now so earnestly desired by the memorialists, can be restored only by the return of all Christian Communions to the principles of unity exemplified by the undivided Catholic Church during the first ages of its existence, which principles we believe to be the substantial Deposit of Christian Faith and Order committed by Christ and His Apostles to the Church unto the end of the world, and therefore incapable of compromise or surrender by those who have been ordained to be its Stewards and Trustees, for the common and equal benefit of all men.

As inherent parts of this sacred Deposit, and, therefore, as essential to the restoration of unity among the divided branches of Christendom, we account the following, to wit:

1. The Holy Scriptures of the Old and New Testament as the Revealed Word of God;

II. The Nicene Creed as the sufficient statement of the Christian Faith;

III. The Two Sacraments—Baptism and the Supper of the Lord—ministered with unfailing use of Christ's words of institution, and of the elements ordained by Him.

IV. The Historic Episcopate, locally adapted in the methods of its administration to the varying needs of the nations and peoples called of God into the unity of His Church;

Furthermore, Deeply grieved by the sad divisions which afflict the Christian Church in our own land, we hereby declare our desire and readiness, so soon as there shall be any authorized response to this declaration, to enter into brotherly conference with all or any Christian bodies seeking the restoration of the organic unity of the Church, with a view to the earnest study of the conditions under which so priceless a blessing might happily be brought to pass.

A true and official copy.

Attest:

HERMAN C. DUNCAN, *Secretary of Commission.*

Text—*Minutes of the General Assembly of the Presbyterian Church in the United States of America,* New Series, Vol. X, (1887), pp. 154-155.

XI. *THE ANDOVER CASE*

The following is the copy of Mr. A's reply to Secretary Alden concerning clause 11 in a statement of doctrine submitted to candidates for the foreign field, and the reply of the clerk.

"To the Prudential Committee A.B.C.F.M.:

GENTLEMEN,—I hold the hypothesis of future probation of those who have not the gospel. Since the gospel is for every man, we may hope that every man may have the gospel. Perhaps my position may be made more evident without long discussion by stating briefly some of the main reasons I have for holding this hypothesis.

I. Because this hypothesis is not without support in Scripture, and is confirmed by what we may reasonably expect God will do for men in view of the revelation of himself made in Jesus Christ.

II. Because I do not find this hypothesis in contradiction to any of the teachings of Scripture; nor to the doctrines of the early symbols of the faith, for example, the Apostles' Creed or the Nicene Creed; nor to any of the doctrines commonly held and taught in our churches.

III. May I add as additional reasons:—

1. This hypothesis has not for me 'cut the nerve of missions.' On the contrary, my present conception of the love and grace of Christ for every man has given me a larger zeal and a more-in-earnest purpose to carry such a Savior to those who do not know him.

2. This hypothesis does not conflict with scriptural views of the importance of the present life. The view of Scripture is, as I understand it, that the present life furnishes the most favorable opportunity for hearing the gospel on account of the danger of sinful habit, and to those who have enjoyed this most favorable opportunity it is the only opportunity.

Note.—It is practically unnecessary to define what men have had sufficient light to enable them to accept Christ or to condemn them for not accepting Christ, for it goes without saying that an unconverted man who knows enough to have any interest in that question knows enough to accept Christ.

3. This hypothesis puts no limit upon the mighty triumph of Christ for men save man's resisting will. It regards Christ as truly Victor over sin and death; as 'he who hath the keys of hell and death.'

Further statement I am willing to make, provided this does not put my position plainly before you.

Respectfully."

Clerk of Committee to Mr. A.

"February 9, 1887.

Your statement, received upon the 3rd instant., with your application for missionary appointment, and testimonials in part, was presented to the Prudential Committee yesterday afternoon, and the expression around the table from members of the Committee and executive officers was unanimous on the following points:—

1. A hearty recognition of the frankness and manliness of your clear utterance of your own conscientious convictions upon the subject referred to.

2. Regret that your views upon this subject had changed from those under which you were educated and which you formerly entertained—the views which have been commonly held by our Evangelical Churches.

3. The earnest desire and hope that your views upon this subject may be so modified that the great longing of your heart for missionary work abroad under the care of the American Board may be met.

4. The only action which the Committee feels itself authorized, under the instructions of the Board, to take is expressed in the following minute:—

" 'In view of the declaration of Mr. A. in his written statement that he holds 'the hypothesis of future probation for those who have not the gospel,'—this declaration, being accompanied with his reasons for holding this hypothesis,—it was unanimously agreed that in accordance with the instructions received from the Board at its last Annual Meeting, the Committee has no option but to 'decline to appoint the candidate so long as he holds these views.' " . . . .

I remain, respectfully and truly yours."

The attitude of those who criticized the action of the Prudential Committee is expressed in a minority report signed by Prof. G. P. Fisher and Pres. H. M. Buckham.

". . .We have to add that, in our judgment, the Secretary fails to justify his practice of submitting creeds, composed by himself or by others, to the candidates for missionary service, for their guidance and instruction in doctrine. The creeds in question are such as have had no general recognition. We are persuaded that in taking this course the Home Secretary has transcended his proper function. Some of his correspondents professed to accept these confessions as a formulation of their belief, and no doubt all regarded them as the Secretary's standard of orthodoxy by which their acceptance or rejection as candidates would probably be determined. On the whole we cannot avoid the impression that an attempt has been made to use the Board as a makeweight in a theological controversy and to draw it into the fires of a debate from which it should have endeavored to stand aloof.

Passing gladly from the personal questions to which our attention has been compelled, we desire to speak briefly on the general principles applicable to the appointment of missionaries to go out under the auspices of the Board. A fundamental principle, to be constantly kept in mind, is that this Society is not a synod. It is not a body empowered by the Congregational churches to define orthodoxy for them. Its missionaries are to hold the evangelical faith, but the Board must take other means of ascertaining the soundness of candidates than by framing creeds on all, or any one, of the great departments of theology. That is a work which must be done, if it is done at all, by ecclesiastical assemblies, authorized by the churches to undertake so difficult and responsible a work. The American Board is a great central organized agency for carrying forward the work of foreign missions, mainly, if not exclusively, for the Congregational churches. Because of this exalted position and influence, it is the more strictly bound to remember that it is not a representative body—a body chosen of the churches —and to guard against every transgression of its proper limits of prerogative. If it should be misled into the performance of work, such, for example, as pertains to a general assembly in the Presbyterian Church, we should have what is equivalent to a central authority, enunciating definitions of doctrine, with the effect of attaching a stigma to dissent; and yet that central authority would not be a body of representatives, but a self-perpetuating close corporation chartered by a State. It seems clear, therefore, that the Board, under its present constitution, should refrain from sending to the Prudential Committee specific doctrinal instructions either on one side or the other of existing doctrinal controversies.

It follows that we do not approve of the proposal, in whatever form it may be made, to direct the Committee to refuse all candidates for the missionary work who are favorably inclined to other views respecting the heathen that die without having known of the gospel, than those to which the recently rejected candidates have been required to subscribe. In our judgment the decision of the Prudential Committee should be made in the case of each individual by itself and in view of the sum total of his characteristics and of all the circumstances properly bearing on the decision of the question.

Before closing these observations we desire to add two remarks. In the first place it appears to us that candidates for appointment as missionaries, especially where questions of peculiar difficulty arise, should meet the Prudential Committee face to face, instead of the present system, under which the Committee act solely on data furnished them by intermediates. Secondly, we cannot but think that, when highly important questions relating to theological doctrine or to the right policy to be adopted in the conduct of the missionary work are in debate, the Prudential Committee should not be made up exclusively of adherents to one of the differing parties. Duty and expediency alike dictate that there should be a fair representation in the Committee of both sides. We believe that a greater degree of harmony among the supporters of the Board and of confidence in the Executive Officers would be the result, and that no serious evil would ensue from an arrangement so natural and so obviously fair.

When Congregationalists have spoken as a denomination they have manifested a catholic evangelical spirit. The Boston National Council in 1865, after setting forth the fundamental truths of the gospel, thus speaks: 'We declare that we will cooperate with all who hold these truths. With them we will carry the gospel into every part of this land, and with them will go into all the world, and " 'preach the gospel of every creature.' " From this catholic evangelical spirit let there be no 'new departure'! It is in this spirit that we recommend the passage of the following resolutions:—

1. The Board reaffirms the position that neither this Board nor its Prudential Committee is in any sense a theological court, to settle doctrinal points of belief.

2. The Board also specially approves and commends the statement of the manual for missionary candidates, that 'It is a glorious fact that the points which constitute emphatically the message of missionaries to the heathen are those in which all evangelical bodies mainly agree.' And it would have its missionaries always remember that they are sent to preach and teach these essential truths of Christianity.

3. The missionaries of this Board shall have the same right of private judgment in the interpretation of God's Word, and the same freedom of thought and of speech as are enjoyed by their ministerial brethren in this country. In the exercise of their rights they should have constant and careful regard to the work of their associates and to the harmony and effectiveness of the missions in which they labor.

4. All persons, otherwise well qualified, are to be regarded as acceptable candidates for missionary appointment, who heartily receive the fundamental truths of the gospel held in common by the churches sustaining the Board and ascertained by their actual usages."

Text—*Seventy-seventh Annual Report of the A. B. C. F. M.*, pp. 23, 24 and xix, xx.

XII. *THE CASE OF PROFESSOR BRIGGS AND UNION THEOLOGICAL SEMINARY*

Memorial of the Directors of Union Theological Seminary, May 16, 1870.

"WHEREAS, In the recent negotiations for re-uniting the two branches of the Presbyterian Church, great importance was attached to some uniform system of ecclesiastical supervision over the several Theological Seminaries of the denomination; and

WHEREAS, The Directors of the Union Theological Seminary in New York—an institution founded before the disruption of the Presbyterian Church, belonging exclusively to neither of its branches, and administered upon its own independent charter—are desirous of doing all in their power to establish confidence and harmony throughout the whole Church, in respect to the education of its members; and

WHEREAS, It has appeared to many, and especially to those who took an active part in founding the Union Theological Seminary, that there are many disadvantages, infelicities, not to say, at times, perils, in the election of Professors of those Seminaries, directly and immediately by the General Assembly itself—a body so large, in session for so short a time, and composed of members to so great an extent resident at a distance from the Seminaries themselves, and therefore personally unacquainted with many things which pertain to their true interest and usefulness; therefore, be it

Resolved, That the Board of Directors of the Union Theological Seminary, in the city of New-York, being all of them ministers or members of the Presbyterian Church, do hereby memorialize the General Assembly to the following effect, viz.: That the General Assembly may be pleased to adopt it as a rule and plan, in the exercise of the proprietorship and control over the several Theological Seminaries, that, so far as the election of Professors is concerned, the Assembly will commit the same to their respective Boards of Directors, on the following terms and conditions:

First, That the Board of Directors of each Theological Seminary shall be authorized to appoint all Professors for the same.

Second, That all such appointments shall be reported to the General Assembly, and no such appointment of Professor shall be considered as a complete election, if disapproved by a majority vote of the Assembly.

And further be it resolved, That the Board of Directors of the Union Theological Seminary of the city of New-York, persuaded that the plan proposed in the Memorial will meet the cordial approval of the patrons, donors, and friends of all these Seminaries, and contribute to the peace and prosperity of the Church, do hereby agree, if the said plan shall be adopted by the General Assembly, that they will agree to conform to the same, the Union Seminary in New York being, in this respect, on the same ground with other Theological Seminaries of the Presbyterian Church. The Assembly complied with this request."

Text—*Minutes of the General Assembly of the Presbyterian Church in the United States of America*, New Series, Vol. I, (1870), pp. 148-149.

THE THEOLOGICAL ISSUE

Committee on Judgment

"Your Committee to whom was entrusted the duty of formulating an explanatory minute of this Assembly on the doctrinal points involved in the appeal of the Committee of Prosecution from the judgement of the Presbytery of New York, in the case of the Presbyterian Church in the United States of America *vs.* the Rev. Charles A. Briggs, D.D., report as follows:

1. We find that the doctrine of the errancy of the Scripture as it came from them to whom, and through whom, God originally communicated His revelation, is in conflict with the statements of the Holy Scripture itself, which assert that 'all Scripture' or 'every Scripture' is given by 'Inspiration of God' (2 Tim. iii. 16); 'That the prophecy came not of old by the will of man, but holy men of God spake as they were moved by the Holy Ghost' (2 Peter i, 12), and also that the statements of the Standards of the Church which assert that 'the Holy Scriptures of the Old and New Testaments are the Word of God.' (Larger Catechism, Question 3), 'Of Infallible Truth' and 'Divine Authority' (Conf. of Faith, Chap. i, Sec. v.)

2. That we find in this case involved the questions of the sufficiency of the human reason and of the Church, as authorized guides in the matter of salvation. Your Committee recommend that this General Assembly declare that the reason and the Church are not to be regarded as fountains of divine authority; that they are unreliable and fallible, and whilst they may, and no doubt are, channels or media through which the Holy Spirit may reach and influence for good the human soul, they are never to be relied upon as sufficient in themselves, and aside from Holy Scripture, to lead the soul to a saving knowledge of God. To teach that they are sufficient is most dangerous, and contrary to the Word of God and our Standards, and our ministers and church members are solemnly warned against such teachings.

3. We find involved in this case a speculation in regard to the process of the soul's sanctification after death, which in the judgment of this Assembly is a dangerous hypothesis, in direct conflict with the plain teaching of the divine Word and the utterance of the Standards of our Church. These Standards distinctly declare that 'the souls of believers are at their death made perfect in holiness, and do immediately pass into glory, while their bodies being still united to Christ do rest in their graves till the Resurrection.' (Shorter Catechism, Question 37; 2 Cor. v. 8; Phil. i. 23; John xvii. 24)"

The Protest:

"The undersigned enter respectful and earnest protest against the action of this Assembly, which declares the inerrancy of the original autographs of Scripture to be the faith of the Church. We protest against this action.

1. Because it is insisting upon a certain theory of inspiration, when our Standards have hitherto only emphasized the fact of inspiration. So far as the original manuscript came from God, undoubtedly it was without error. But we have no means of determining how far God controlled the penmen in transcribing from documents in matters purely circumstantial.

2. Because it is dogmatizing on a matter of which, necessarily, we can have no positive knowledge.

3. Because it is insisting upon an interpretation of our Standards which they never have borne, and which, on their face, is impossible. No man in subscribing to his belief in the Scriptures as the Word of God, and the only infallible rule of faith and practice, has his mind on the original autographs.

4. Because it is setting up an imaginary Bible as a test of orthodoxy. If an inerrant original Bible is vital to faith, we cannot escape the conclusion that an inerrant present Bible is vital to faith.

5. Because it is disparaging the Bible we have, and endangering its authority under the pressure of a prevalent hostile criticism. It seems like flying for shelter to an original autograph, when the Bible we have in our hands today is our impregnable defense.

Believing these present Scriptures to be 'The very Word of God' and 'immediately inspired by God,' 'kept pure in all ages' and 'our only infallible rule of faith and practice,' notwithstanding some apparent discrepancies in matters purely circumstantial, we earnestly protest against the imposing of this new interpretation of our Standards upon the Church, to bind men's consciences by enforced subscription to its terms"—(The above was subscribed by 83 signatures).

Text—*Minutes of the General Assembly of the Presbyterian Church in the United States of America*, New Series, Vol. XVI (1893) pp. 165-168.

Report of the Standing Committee on Theological Seminaries, June 1, 1893.

"From Union Seminary we have received the usual Report. The Board of Directors have sent a special communication which is as follows:

'The Board of Directors of the Union Theological Seminary in the city of New York addressed a memorial to the General Assembly of the Presbyterian Church in the United States of America, which met at Portland, May 19, 1892. In that paper we stated, with the utmost courtesy, some of the practical reasons which render it necessary, in our judgment, that the veto power conceded to the General Assembly in 1870 should no longer reside in that body. The memorial concluded with this language: 'There are other and weighty considerations which we have preferred not to urge. While there exists the undoubted right of either party to the agreement of 1870 to act alone in its abrogation, yet this memorial is submitted with the earnest hope that your reverend body may cordially concur with us in annulling the arrangement of 1870, thus restoring Union Seminary to its former relations to the General Assembly." The hope thus expressed was disappointed. With no official notice whatever of the reasons assigned by us, the answer to our memorial was: 'That the Assembly declines to be a party to the breaking of the compact with Union Theological Seminary.' In view of this action of the late General Assembly, we are constrained now to urge those considerations which we had preferred to reserve. They are constitutional and legal.

1. *The Constitutional Considerations.*—There is no provision whatever in our charter or Constitution for 'the principle of Synodical or Assembly supervision.' The Committees on Reunion and both Assemblies in 1869 recognized this important fact, and advised the introduction of that principle into our Constitution. Upon this advice no action was taken. The Constitution was not changed. Therefore the Seminary could not rightfully give, and the Assembly could not rightfully receive or exercise, the veto power under our existing charter and Constitution.

2. *The Legal Considerations.*—Since the action of the General Assembly at Portland, our Board has obtained the best legal advice as to the points at issue between the Seminary and the Assembly. This advice leaves us no room to doubt that, under the laws of the State of New York, the attempted agreement of 1870 was beyond the powers of the Board of Directors of the Seminary. We 'cannot abdicate any of our official duties in whole or in part.'

Therefore, as the sole Directors of Union Seminary, we are compelled by the practical considerations presented in our memorial, and by constitutional and legal considerations, to maintain our rights and to fulfill our chartered obligations, which can be neither surrendered nor shared. In this action we regret deeply that we have been refused that concurrence of the Assembly which we respectfully asked, and which would have done much towards softening the past and relieving the present. Obliged to act alone for the protection of the institution committed to our care, and actuated by sincere regard for the highest interests both of Union Seminary and of the Church we love, we do now

1. *Resolve*, That the resolution passed May 16, 1870, adopting the memorial to the General Assembly of the Presbyterian Church in the United States of America, which provided that all appointments of professors 'shall be reported to the General Assembly, and no such appointment of professor shall be considered as a complete election if disapproved by a majority vote of the Assembly,' be, and the same is, hereby rescinded.

2. *Resolve*, That the said arrangement between the Union Theological Seminary in the city of New York and the General Assembly of the Presbyterian Church in the United States of America be, and the same is, hereby terminated; thus reinstating the relations between the Seminary and the General Assembly as they existed prior to May, 1870.

3. *Resolve*, That official notice of the action be duly given to the General Assembly, and also to the public, with the assurance of the undiminished loyalty of Union Seminary to the doctrine and government of the Presbyterian Church in the United States of America, to which the Directors and Faculty are personally bound by their official vow, and of our earnest desire for the restoration of our former relations to the General Assembly.

CHARLES BUTLER, President.
E. M. KINGSLEY, Recorder.'

. . . .

For twenty-one years the most cordial relations existed between Union Theological Seminary and the General Assembly. In the discharge of what seemed its plain but most painful duty, the General Assembly at Detroit declared its disapproval of the appointment of Professor Briggs to the Chair of Biblical Theology. The Board of Directors, instead of removing Dr. Briggs, or at least requiring him to desist from teaching in the Seminary until the question at issue between the Assembly and the Seminary as to the full and proper meaning of the compact had been decided, resolved to continue Dr. Briggs in the Chair which the Assembly had declared he ought not to occupy. This action was the more questionable, because the Assembly appointed a Committee of fifteen 'to confer with the Directors of the Union Theological Seminary in regard to the relation of the said Seminary to the General Assembly.'

This conference resulted in practical failure to remove the misunderstanding, and it was so reported to the Assembly of 1892, meeting in Portland. That Assembly appointed five arbitrators to meet a like number selected by the Directors of Union Seminary, with power to select five others, to determine the interpretation of the compact, viz., as to the transfer of a professor. The Stated Clerk of the Assembly notified the Directors of the Seminary on July 16, 1892, that the Assembly had appointed such a Committee of Arbitration. On the 4th of August, Dr. T. Ralston Smith, Chairman of the Committee, addressed a similar communication to the Directors. To this letter the Recorder of the Board responded that the Board could not take any action before the middle of October. On the 15th of October, the Board of Directors met and resolved to terminate the compact. This action was taken nearly three months after the Board had been officially informed of the appointment of a Committee of Arbitration, and before any opportunity was given to the Committee of the General Assembly to present their case. This extraordinary action of the Board of Directors is inexplicable to the Assembly. The high character of the gentlemen composing the Board fully warranted the expectation that so fair a proposition as that of arbitration would not be treated in such a way. While there remained to the Assembly the hope that by conference or arbitration the difficulty that had arisen would be removed, the Assembly did not think it best to discuss the points raised by the Directors of Union Seminary in attempted justification of their action. But now the Assembly takes issue with the statement made in the memorial presented to the Portland Assembly that 'there exists the undoubted right of either party to the agreement of 1870 to act alone in its abrogation.' No such right is expressed in the agreement, and, in the nature of things, no agreement where valuable interests are involved, not to say valuable considerations are given and received, can in good morals be abrogated by one party to the agreement without the consent and against the expressed desire of the other party. . . . Whatever force the constitutional and legal objections may have, to the making and continuance of such a compact by the Directors, there was an easy and simple way to remove them if the Directors so desired. The Legislature of the State of New York would doubtless have amended the charter if the Directors had requested it.

Because, then, of the strange and unwarranted action of the Directors in retaining Dr. Briggs after his appointment had been disapproved by the Assembly; and because of the refusal by the Directors to arbitrate the single point in dispute between the Assembly and the Board; and because of the attempt by the Board and on its own motion and against the expressed desire of the Assembly to abrogate the compact of 1870, the Assembly disavows all responsibility for the teaching of Union Seminary, and declines to receive any report from its Board until satisfactory relations are established. The Assembly, however, cherishes the hope, and will cordially welcome any effort to bring Union Seminary into such a relationship with itself, as will enable the Assembly to commend the institution again to students for the ministry.

Your Committee would further recommend that the Board of Education be enjoined to give aid to such students only as may be in attendance upon seminaries approved by the Assembly.

Your Committee would also recommend that the reelection of the Rev. Charles A Briggs, D.D., by the Presbytery of Newark, as a Director of the German Theological Seminary, at Bloomfield, N. J., be disapproved by this Assembly.

. . . .

JOHN DIXON, *Chairman.*"

Text—*Minutes of the General Assembly of the Presbyterian Church in the United States of America,* New Series, Vol. XVI (1893) pp. 156-161.

XIII. *FEDERATION NEGOTIATIONS AMONG THE PRESBYTERIANS*

To the Synods and General Assemblies of the Reformed Churches in the United States holding the Presbyterian System:

DEAR BRETHREN:—The General Assembly of the Presbyterian Church in the United States of America, at its meeting at Saratoga, N.Y., in May, 1890, expressed a desire for a Federation of the Christian Churches of the land, and instructed us as a Committee to make this desire known to other Churches.

We, therefore, beg to call your attention to the subject, and to indicate briefly the general idea which is in our mind.

A partial illustration of the benefit of such a Federation already exists in the Evangelical Alliance.

The annual meetings of the Alliance have been productive of great good in bringing closer together prominent and influential ministers and members of the different denominations; in showing the fundamental and essential agreement of the Evangelical bodies; in the moral influence on the community at large of such a christian union; in the valuable contributions to the literature of the Church and to the discussion of great religious, moral and social questions which they have made; and, as it is hoped, in educationally preparing the way for a closer and still more practical and effective union.

The Alliance is composed of individuals simply. It does not officially represent organizations by commissioned delegates. It is voluntary, and can do nothing but seek to mould public opinion on the great questions that are discussed at its meetings. An organization with a closer organic connection with the Churches, and, therefore, vested with some measure of power, seems to be needed.

It seems to us that it would be wise and right for the Christian Churches of the land to form a Federal Union, in which there should be no renunciation by the different Churches of their peculiarities or independent organization, and no interference with their doctrines, government, worship or internal affairs, but by which specific powers should be delegated to a Federal Council for the concentration of the influence of all upon such phases of Christian effort as might meet the approval of all.

Some of the measures which would come within the scope of such a Federation are:

1. United work for the reclamation of the Christless masses in the large cities, towns and old rural settlements.

2. The conduct of the home missionary work of the different denominations in the new settlements of the country, in such a way as to remove denominational friction and prevent the multiplication of weak and antagonistic organizations where unnecessary; the prosecution of the foreign missionary work by the different denominations on the same principle of comity; different Churches cultivating particular fields so as to avoid unseemly strife before the heathen.

3. The National Council of such a Federation could be potential in its influence on the community at large. It could educate and strengthen the public conscience with Scriptural views on marriage and divorce, the Sabbath, temperance, education, and other moral and social questions.

It certainly seems to us worth while to attempt, so to bring together all the Evangelical Churches, that, in their necessary separate denominational work, they shall not harmfully clash with each other, and that they may, in a great degree, unite in the work which none can separately prosecute with vigor and success. And in this aspect of the matter should be particularly emphasized the influence which the Churches of the land should exert upon its citizens for the preservation of their religious inheritances and the maintenance of their fundamental principles.

This proposition is first addressed to the Synods and Assemblies of the Reformed Churches holding the Presbyterian system, with a view to securing their cooperation in extending a similar proposition to the other Evangelical Churches of our country.

May we, dear brethren, ask you to take this into consideration, and if, in its general idea, it commend itself to your judgment, appoint a Committee to confer with us and with similar Committees that may be appointed by other Churches to consider and report upon it.

Fraternally yours,

JOSEPH T. SMITH, D.D., *Chairman.*

Baltimore, April 23, 1891.

Text—*Minutes of the General Assembly of the Presbyterian Church in the United States of America.* New Series, Vol. XIV (1891) pp. 206-207.

Plan of Federation.

The following is the Plan of Federation which the Committees of the Associate Reformed Synod of the South, the Cumberland Presbyterian General Assembly, the Synod of the (Dutch) Reformed Church in America, the Synod of the (German) Reformed Church in the United States, the Synod of the Reformed Presbyterian Church, General Synod of the Reformed Presbyterian Church, United Presbyterian General Assembly, and the General Assembly of the Presbyterian Church in the United States of America, at their meeting in Philadelphia (1894) agreed to recommend to their appointing bodies for adoption:

For the glory of God, and for the greater unity and advancement of the Church of which the Lord Jesus Christ is the Head, the Reformed Churches in the United States holding the Presbyterian System, adopt the following articles of Federal Union:

1. Every denomination entering into this union shall retain its distinct individuality, as well as every power, jurisdiction and right which is not by this constitution expressly delegated to the body hereby constituted.

2. The acts, proceedings and records of the duly constituted authorities of each of the denominations shall be received in all the other denominations, and in the Federal Council, as of full credit and with proper respect.

3. For the prosecution of work that can be better done in union than separately, an Ecclesiastical Assembly is hereby constituted, which shall be known by the name and style of The Federal Council of the Reformed Churches in the United States of America holding the Presbyterian System.

4. The Federal Council shall consist of four ministers and four elders from each of the constituent denominations, who shall be chosen, with alternates, under the direction of their respective supreme judicatories, in such manner as those judicatories shall respectively determine.

5. The Federal Council shall promote the cooperation of the federated denominations in their home and foreign missionary work, and shall keep watch on current religious, moral and social movements, and take such action as may concentrate the influence of all the Churches in the maintenance of the truth that our nation is a Protestant Christian nation, and of all that is therein involved.

6. The Federal Council may advise and recommend in all matters pertaining to the general welfare of the kingdom of Christ, but shall not exercise authority, except such as is conferred upon it by this instrument, or such as may be conferred upon it by the federated bodies. It shall not interfere with the creed, worship or government of the federated denominations. In the conduct of its meetings it shall respect their conscientious views. All matters of discipline shall be left to the exclusive and final judgment of the ecclesiastical authorities of the denominations in which the same may arise.

7. The Federal Council shall have the power of opening and maintaining a friendly correspondence with the highest assemblies of other religious denominations for the purpose of promoting union and concert of action in general or common interests.

8. All differences which may arise among the federated bodies, or any of them, in regard to matters within the jurisdiction of the Federal Council, shall be determiued by such executive agencies as may be created by the Federal Council, with the right of appeal to the Federal Council for final adjudication.

9. The officers of the Federal Council shall be a President, Vice-President, Clerk and Treasurer.

10. The Federal Council shall meet annually, and on its own adjournment, at such time and place as may be determined. Special meetings may be called by a unanimous vote of the officers of the Council on thirty days' notice.

11. The expenses of the Council shall be met by a contigent fund to be provided by a *pro rata* apportionment on the basis of the number of communicants in each denomination; and the expenses of the delegates to the Council shall be paid from this fund.

12. Amendments to these articles may be proposed by the Federal Council or by any of the supreme judicatories of the Churches in the Federation; but the approval of all those judicatories shall be necessary for their adoption.

Text *Minutes of the General Assembly of the Presbyterian Church in the United States of America,* New Series, Vol XVII, (1894), pp. 164-165.

XIV. *THE ORGANIC LAW OF THE METHODIST EPISCOPAL CHURCH.*—Adopted 1800.

THE GENERAL CONFERENCE

ARTICLE I.—*How Composed*

The General Conference shall be composed of ministerial and lay delegates, to be chosen as hereinafter provided.

ARTICLE II.—*Ministerial Delegates*

1. Each Annual Conference shall be entitled to at least one ministerial delegate. The General Conference shall not allow more than one ministerial delegate for every fourteen members of an Annual Conference, nor less than one for every forty-five; but for a fraction of two thirds or more of the number fixed by the General Conference as the ratio of representation an Annual Conference shall be entitled to an additional delegate.

2. The ministerial delegates shall be elected by ballot by the members of the Annual Conference, at its session immediately preceding the General Conference. Such delegates shall be elders, at least twenty-five years of age, and shall have been members of an Annual Conference four successive years, and at the time of their election and at the time of the session of the General Conference shall be members of the Annual Conference which elected them. An Annual Conference may elect reserve delegates, not exceeding three in number, and not exceeding the number of its delegates.

3. No minister shall be counted twice in the same year in the basis for the election of delegates to the General Conference, nor vote in such election where he is not counted, not vote in two Conferences in the same year on a constitutional question.

ARTICLE III.—*Lay Delegates*

1. A Lay Electoral Conference shall be constituted quadrennially, or whenever duly called by the General Conference, within the bounds of each Annual Conference, for the purpose of electing lay delegates to the General Conference, and for the purpose of voting on constitutional changes. It shall be composed of lay members, one from each pastoral charge within its bounds, chosen by the lay members of the charge over twenty-one years of age, in such manner as the General Conference may determine. Each pastoral charge shall also elect in the same manner one reserve delegate. Members not less than twenty-one years of age, and holding membership in the pastoral charges electing them, are eligible to membership in the Lay Electoral Conference.

2. The Lay Electoral Conference shall assemble at the seat of the Annual Conference on the first Friday of the session immediately preceding the General Conference, unless the General Conference shall provide otherwise.

3. The Lay Electoral Conference shall organize by electing a president and secretary, shall adopt its own rules of order, and shall be the judge of the election returns and qualifications of its own members.

4. Each Lay Electoral Conference shall be entitled to elect as many delegates to the General Conference as there are ministerial delegates from the Annual Conference. A Lay Electoral Conference may elect reserve delegates, not exceeding three in number, and not exceeding the number of its delegates. These elections shall be by ballot.

5. Lay members twenty-five years of age or over, holding membership in pastoral charges within the bounds of the Lay Electoral Conference, and having been lay members of the Church five years next preceding, shall be eligible to election to the General Conference. Delegates-elect who cease to be members of the Church within the bounds of the Lay Electoral Conference by which they were elected shall not be entitled to seats in the General Conference.

. . . .

ARTICLE VI.—*Presiding Officers*

1. The General Conference shall elect by ballot from among the travelling elders as many General Superintendents as it may deem necessary.

2. The General Superintendents shall preside in the General Conference in such order as they may determine; but if no General Superintendent be present, the General Conference shall elect one of its members to preside *pro tempore*.

3. The presiding officer of the General Conference shall decide questions of order, subject to an appeal to the General Conference; but questions of law shall be decided by the General Conference.

ARTICLE VII.—*Organization*

When the time for opening the General Conference arrives the presiding officer shall take the chair, and direct the secretary of the preceding General Conference, or in his absence one of his assistants, to call the roll of the delegates-elect. Those who have been duly returned shall be recognized as members, their certificates of election being *prima facie* evidence of their right to membership; *provided*, however, that in case of a challenge of any person thus enrolled, such challenge being signed by at least six delegates from the territory of as many different Annual Conferences, three such delegates being ministers, and three laymen, the person so challenged shall not participate in the proceedings of the General Conference, except to speak on his own case, until the question of his right shall have been decided. The General Conference shall be the judge of the election returns and qualifications of its own members.

Article VIII.—*Quorum*

When the General Conference is in session it shall require the presence of two thirds of the whole number of delegates to constitute a quorum for the transaction of business; but a less number may take a recess or adjourn from day to day in order to secure a quorum, and at the final session may approve the Journal, order the record of the roll call, and adjourn *sine die*.

Article IX.—*Voting*

The ministerial and lay delegates shall deliberate together as one body. They shall also vote together as one body with the following exception: A separate vote shall be taken on any question when requested by one third of either order of delegates present and voting. In all cases of separate voting it shall require the concurrence of the two orders to adopt the proposed measure; except that for changes of the constitution a vote of two thirds of the General Conference shall be sufficient, as provided in Article XI.

Article X.—*Powers and Restrictions*

The General Conference shall have full power to make rules and regulations for the Church under the following limitations and restrictions, namely:

1. The General Conference shall not revoke, alter, nor change our Articles of Religion, nor establish any new standards or rules of doctrine contrary to our present existing and established standards of doctrine.

2. The General Conference shall not organize nor authorize the organization of an Annual Conference with less than twenty-five members.

3. The General Conference shall not change nor alter any part or rule of our government so as to do away Episcopacy, nor destroy the plan of our itinerant General Superintendency; but may elect a Missionary Bishop or Superintendent for any of our foreign missions, limiting his episcopal jurisdiction to the same respectively.

4. The General Conference shall not revoke nor change the General Rules of our Church.

5. The General Conference shall not deprive our ministers of the right of trial by the Annual Conference, or by a select number thereof, nor of an appeal; nor shall it deprive our members of the right of trial by a committee of members of our Church nor of an appeal.

6. The General Conference shall not appropriate the produce of the Book Concern, nor of the Chartered Fund, to any purpose other than for the benefit of the travelling, supernumerary, and superannuated preachers, their wives, widows and children.

Text— *Journal of the General Conference. . . 1900* pp. 417-420.

XV. *THE FEDERAL COUNCIL OF THE CHURCHES OF CHRIST IN AMERICA.*

I. The Constitution

Plan of Federation Recommended by The Interchurch Conference of 1905, Adopted by the National Assemblies of Constituent Bodies, 1906-1908, Ratified by the Council at Philadelphia, December 2-8, 1908, and Amended at Chicago, December 4-9, 1912.

Preamble

WHEREAS, In the providence of God, the time has come when it seems fitting more fully to manifest the essential oneness of the Christian Churches of America, in Jesus

Christ as their Divine Lord and Saviour, and to promote the spirit of fellowship, service and cooperation among them, the delegates to the Interchurch Conference on Federation, assembled in New York City, do hereby recommend the following Plan of Federation to the Christian bodies represented in this Conference for their approval:

PLAN OF FEDERATION

1. For the prosecution of work that can be better done in union than in separation a Council is hereby established whose name shall be the Federal Council of the Churches of Christ in America.

2. The following Christian bodies shall be entitled to representation in this Federal Council on their approval of the purpose and plan of the organization:

[Here follow the names of thirty-three Protestant Bodies]

3. The object of this Federal Council shall be—

I. To express the fellowship and catholic unity of the Christian Church.

II. To bring the Christian bodies of America into united service for Christ and the world.

III. To encourage devotional fellowship and mutual counsel concerning the spiritual life and religious activities of the churches.

IV. To secure a larger combined influence for the churches of Christ in all matters affecting the moral and social condition of the people, so as to promote the application of the law of Christ in every relation of human life.

V. To assist in the organization of local branches of the Federal Council to promote its aims in their communities.

4. This Federal Council shall have no authority over the constituent bodies adhering to it; but its province shall be limited to the expression of its counsel and the recommending of a course of action in matters of common interest to the churches, local councils and individual Christians.

It has no authority to draw up a common creed or form of government or of worship or in any way to limit the full autonomy of the Christian bodies adhering to it.

5. Members of this Federal Council shall be appointed as follows: Each of the Christian bodies adhering to this Federal Council shall be entitled to four members, and shall be further entitled to one member for every 50,000 of its communicants or major fraction thereof.

6. Any action to be taken by this Federal Council shall be by the general vote of its members. But in case one third of the members present and voting request it, the vote shall be by the bodies represented, the members of each body voting separately; and action shall require the vote, not only of a majority of the members voting, but also of the bodies represented.

. . . .

II. BY-LAWS OF THE COUNCIL

. . . .

8. The following Commissions subject to the Executive Committee shall be appointed to serve until their successors are elected and shall report at least annually to the Executive Committee and as much oftener as the Executive Committee may require.

. . . . . .

A Commission on State and Local Federations, to consist of fifteen members appointed by the Executive Committee of the Council. This Commission shall advise with State and Local Federations, disseminate information respecting them, and arrange for future conferences of representatives of these Federations, especially in connection with the sessions of the Federal Council. It shall carry on its work subject to the Executive Committee.

The Commissions other than the Commission on State and Local Federations shall consist of at least twenty-five members, three fifths of whom must be members of the Council. . . . .

These Commissions shall be as follows:

(a) A Commission of Foreign Missions, to which shall be referred all matters relating to the administration of missions in the foreign field.

(b) A Commission on Home Missions, to which shall be referred all matters relating to the administration of missions in the home field.

(c) A Commission on the Church and Religious Education, to which shall be referred all matters relating to moral and religious education.

(d) A Commission on The Church and Social Service, to cooperate with similar church organizations in the study of social conditions and to secure a more natural relationship between working men and the Church.

(e) A Commission on Family Life, to which shall be referred all matters relating to marriage and divorce and the development of family life.

(f) A Commission on Sunday Observance, to which shall be referred all matters relating to a better observance of the Lord's Day.

(g) A Commission on Temperance, to which shall be referred all matters relating to the suppression of the drink traffic.

(h) A Commission on Peace and Arbitration, to which shall be referred all matters relating to peace and international relations.

(i) A Commission on Evangelism, to which shall be referred all matters connected with the promotion of the spirit of evangelism and evangelistic work in this country.

. . . .

Text—*Federal Council Year Book, 1915,* pp. 15-22.

XVI. *THE REUNION OF THE CUMBERLAND PRESBY-TERIAN AND THE PRESBYTERIAN CHURCH IN THE UNITED STATES OF AMERICA*

Joint Report on Union

"The Committee on Church Cooperation and Union of the Presbyterian Church in the United States of America and the Committee on Fraternity and Union of the Cumberland Presbyterian Church, after a free and full interchange of views, with continued supplications for Divine guidance, earnestly recommend to their respective General Assemblies for their consideration, and, if they deem proper, for their adoption, the accompanying papers, viz.:

I. Plan of Reunion and Union of the Two Churches.

We believe that the union of Christian Churches of substantially similar faith and polity would be to the glory of God, the good of mankind, and the strengthening of Christian testimony at home and abroad.

We believe that the manifest providential developments and leadings in the two Churches since their separation, together with present conditions of agreement and fellowship, have been and are such as to justify their reunion.

Therefore we cordially recommend to our respective General Assemblies, that the reunion of the Presbyterian Church in the United States of America and the Cumberland Presbyterian Church be accomplished as soon as the necessary steps can be taken, upon the basis hereinafter set forth.

1. The Presbyterian Church in the United States of America, whose General Assembly met in the Immanuel Church, Los Angeles, California, May 21, 1903, and the Cumberland Presbyterian Church, whose General Assembly met in the First Cumberland Presbyterian Church, Nashville, Tennessee, May 21, 1903, shall be united as one Church, under the name and style of THE PRESBYTERIAN CHURCH IN THE UNITED STATES OF AMERICA, possessing all the legal and corporate rights and powers which the separate Churches now possess.

2. The union shall be effected on the doctrinal basis of the Confession of Faith of the Presbyterian Church in the United States of America, as revised in 1903, and of its other doctrinal and ecclesiastical Standards; and the Scriptures of the Old and New Testaments shall be acknowledged as the inspired Word of God, the only infallible rule of faith and practice.

. . . .

II. Concurrent Declarations.

As there are matters pertaining to the interests of the Church which will manifestly require adjustment when the reunion shall have been accomplished, and concerning which it is highly desirable that there shall be a previous good understanding, the two Assemblies agree to adopt the following Concurrent Declarations, as in their judgment proper and equitable arrangements and agreements:

1. In adopting the Confession of Faith of the Presbyterian Church in the United States of America, as revised in 1903, as a Basis of Union, it is mutually recognized that such agreement now exists between the systems of doctrine contained in the Confessions of Faith of the two Churches as to warrant this union—a union honoring alike to both. Mutual acknowledgment also is made of the teaching and defense of essential evangelical doctrine held in common by these Churches, and of the divine favor and blessing that have made this common faith and service effectual.

It is also recognized that liberty of belief exists by virtue of the provisions of the Declaratory Statement, which is part of the Confession of Faith of the Presbyterian Church in the United States of America, and which states that 'the ordination vow of ministers, ruling elders and deacons, as set forth in the Form of Government, requires the reception and adoption of the Confession of Faith only as containing the system of doctrine taught in the Holy Scriptures.' This liberty is specifically secured by the Declaratory Statement, as to Chapter III and Chapter X Section 3 of the Confession of Faith. It is recognized, also, that the doctrinal deliverance contained in the Brief Statement of the Reformed Faith, adopted in 1902 by the General Assembly of the Presbyterian Church in the United States of America, 'for a better understanding of our doctrinal beliefs,' reveals a doctrinal agreement favorable to reunion.

2. All the ministers and churches included in the two denominations shall be admitted to the same standing in the united Church which they may have held in their respective connections up to the consummation of the reunion.

•

3. The boundaries of the several Presbyteries and Synods shall be adjusted by the General Assembly of the United Church.

4. The official records of the two Churches during the period of separation shall be preserved and held as making up the history of the one Church.

5. As soon as practicable after the union shall have been effected the General Assembly shall reconstruct and consolidate the several permanent Committees and Boards which now belong to the two Assemblies, so as to represent with impartiality the views and wishes of the two bodies constituting the reunited Church.

6. The institutions of learning, together with the endowment and other property, real and personal, owned by them, which are now under the control of the Cumberland Presbyterian Church, shall remain in charge of and be controlled by the Boards of Trustees, or other managers respectively, now in charge of such institutions, endowment and property, or by their successors similarly appointed or elected; and no greater control of such institutions, their property or affairs, shall be exercised by the General Assembly, or other ecclesiastical court or body, or the reunited Church, than is now exercised by the General assembly, or other ecclesiastical court or body, of the Cumberland Presbyterian Church. Provided, that the governing Board of any of said institutions of learning shall be at liberty to enter into such special arrangement or agreement with the ecclesiastical body controlling it as may enable said institution to preserve its integrity and maintain its present policy. And also provided, that nothing in this declaration shall affect the relationship or control of any of the institutions of learning now connected with the General Assembly, or other ecclesiastical court or body, of the Presbyterian Church in the United States of America.

7. The corporate rights now held by the two General Assemblies and by their Boards and Committees shall be consolidated and applied for their several objects as defined and permitted by law.

8. It should be regarded as the duty of all our judicatories, ministers and people to study the things which make for peace, to guard against all needless and offensive references to the causes which have divided us, and to avoid the revival of past issues."

Text—*Minutes of the General Assembly of the Presbyterian Church, in the United States of America,* New Series, Vol. IV, No. 2 (1904), pp. 135-138.

XVII. *THE COUNCIL OF THE REFORMED CHURCHES IN AMERICA HOLDING THE PRESBYTERIAN SYSTEM*

Articles of Agreement

"The Reformed Churches in America holding the Presbyterian System, desiring to evince and develop their spiritual unity and to promote closer relations and more effective administrative cooperation among these Churches, hereby adopt the following Articles of Agreement in furtherance of these purposes:

1. For the prosecution of work that can be done better unitedly than separately an Ecclesiastical Council is hereby established, which shall be known by the name and style of 'The Council of the Reformed Churches in America holding the Presbyterian System.'

2. The Council shall consist of at least four representatives, ministers or ruling elders, from each of the constituent Churches, for each one hundred thousand communicants or fraction thereof up to three hundred thousand; and where a Church has more than three hundred thousand communicants, then four representatives, ministers or elders, for

each additional two hundred thousand communicants or fraction thereof. These persons shall be chosen with their alternates under the direction of their respective supreme judicatories, in such manner as those judicatories shall respectively determine.

3. Every Church entering into this Agreement retains its distinct individuality, its own creed, government and worship, as well as every power, jurisdiction and right, which is not by these Articles expressly and exclusively delegated to the body hereby constituted.

4. The Council shall exercise only such powers as are conferred upon it by these Articles, or such as may hereafter be conferred upon it by the constituent Churches. It shall not interfere with the creed, worship or government of the Churches, and, in particular, all matters of discipline shall be left to the exclusive and final judgment of the ecclesiastical authorities of the Churches concerned. All acts of the Council affecting the interests of any of the constituent Churches shall have only advisory authority, except in matters covered by Articles 6 and 7.

5. The Council shall promote the cooperation of the Constituent Churches in their Foreign Missionary work, and also in their general work in the United States of America, in connection with Home Missions, Work among the Colored People, Church Erection, Sabbath-schools, Publication and Education. The Council may also advise and recommend in other matters pertaining to the general welfare of the kingdom of Christ.

6. The Council shall have power to deal with questions which may arise between the constituent Churches, in regard to matters within the jurisdiction of the Council, which the constituted agencies of the Churches concerned have been unable to settle, and which may be brought to the attention of the Council by the supreme judicatories of the parties thereto; and such differences shall thereupon be determined by the Council or by such agencies as it may appoint. If determined by an agency, such as a Committee or Commission, there shall be the right of appeal to the Council for final decision. The representatives in the Council, of Churches which are parties to questions at issue, shall be excluded from voting upon such questions. Every final decision shall be transmitted by the Council to the supreme judicatories of the Churches concerned, which shall take such steps as are necessary to carry the decision into effect.

7. The Council shall have power to deal with any other matters of interest common to any two or more of the constituent Churches, which may be referred to it by the supreme judicatories of the Churches concerned for its action, with such authority in the premises and under such conditions as may be agreed upon by the Churches which make the reference. It may also initiate movements having cooperation in view, subject to the approval of the Churches concerned.

8. The Council shall have power to open and maintain a friendly correspondence with the Presbyterian and other Evangelical Churches for the purpose of promoting concert of action in matters of common interest; but nothing in this Article shall be construed as affecting the present rights of correspondence of the constituent Churches.

9. The Council shall give full faith and credit to the acts, proceedings and records of the duly constituted authorities of the several constituent Churches.

. . . .

15. After this Council shall have been constituted, any Church holding the Reformed Faith and Presbyterian Polity may be received into the Council by a majority of the representatives of the Churches, voting by the unit rule, and upon its adoption of the Articles of Agreement.

16. Any Church in the Council may withdraw therefrom on notice officially given, and on its observance of the same constitutional steps as were followed in its adoption of these Articles.

. . . .

18. These Articles of Agreement shall go into effect when any two or more Churches shall adopt the same by proper action, and elect their representatives in the manner herein provided.

The above Articles were adopted at Charlotte, N. C., March 16, 1906 by the Committees on Closer Relations of the Reformed Presbyterian Church (General Synod), the Reformed Church in America, the Presbyterian Church in the United States of America, the United Presbyterian Church, the Presbyterian Church in the United States, the Reformed Church in the United States, and the Associate Reformed Presbyterian Church.

J. PRESTON SEARLE, *Chairman,*
WM. H. ROBERTS, *Secretary."*

Text—*Minutes of the General Assembly of the Presbyterian Church in the United States of America,* New Series, Vol. VI, No. 2, (1906), pp. 127-130.

XVIII. *THE GENESIS OF THE LAYMEN'S MISSIONARY MOVEMENT*

The following resolutions were adopted at a conference held in Fifth Avenue Presbyterian Church, New York City, Nov. 15th, 1906, after an address delivered by J. Campbell White, secretary of the Men's Movement of the United Presbyterian Church.

"WHEREAS, in the marvellous providence of God the one hundredth anniversary of the beginnings of the American Foreign Missionary Movement finds the doors of every nation open to the gospel message, and

WHEREAS, the machinery of the missionary boards, women's boards, student and young people's missionary movements is highly and efficiently organized, and

WHEREAS, the greatly increased participation of the present generation of responsible Christian business and professional men is essential to the widest and most productive use of the existing missionary agencies, and is equally vital to the growth of the spiritual life at home, and

WHEREAS, in the management of large business and political responsibilities, such men have been greatly used and honored, and

WHEREAS, in but few of the denominations have aggressive movements to interest men in missions been undertaken—

Therefore, be it resolved, that this gathering of laymen, called together for prayer and conference on the occasion of the centennial anniversary of the Haystack Prayer-meeting, designate a committee of twenty-five or more representative laymen to consult with the secretaries of the missionary boards of all the denominations in the United States and Canada, if possible, at their annual gathering in January, with reference to the following vitally important propositions:

1. To project a campaign of education among laymen to be conducted under the direction of the various boards.

2. To devise a comprehensive plan (in conjunction with said board secretaries) looking to the sending of the message of the Gospel to the entire non-Christian world during the next twenty-five years.

3. To endeavor to form, through the various boards, a Centennial Commission of Laymen, fifty or more in number, to visit as early as possible, the mission fields and report their findings to the church at home."

Text—*The Missionery Review of the World*, January, 1907, pp. 19, 20.

XIX. *THE EPISCOPALIANS AND A WORLD CONFERENCE ON UNION*

At the General Convention in 1910 of the Protestant Episcopal Church in the United States of America, held in Cincinnati, the following report was presented to the House of Clerical and Lay Deputies and unanimously adopted.

"The Joint Committee to which was referred the following resolution:

'*Resolved*, The House of Bishops concurring, That a Joint Committee, consisting of seven Bishops, seven Presbyters and seven Laymen, be appointed to take under advisement the promotion by this Church of a Conference following the general method of the World Missionary Conference, to be participated in by representatives of all Christian bodies throughout the world which accept our Lord Jesus Christ as God and Savior, for the consideration of questions pertaining to the Faith and Order of the Church of Christ, and that said Committee, if it deem such a Conference feasible, shall report to this Convention;'

have considered the same, and submit the following report, and recommend the immediate consideration and passage of the resolution appended to the report.

Your Committee is of one mind. We believe that the time has now arrived when representatives of the whole family of Christ, led by the Holy Spirit, may be willing to come together for the consideration of questions of Faith and Order. We believe, further, that all Christian Communions are in accord with us in our desire to lay aside self-will, and to put on the mind which is in Christ Jesus our Lord. We would heed this call of the Spirit of God in all lowliness, and with singleness of purpose. We would place ourselves by the side of our fellow Christians, looking not only on our own things, but also on the things of others, convinced that our one hope of mutual understanding is in taking personal counsel together in the spirit of love and forbearance. It is our conviction that such a Conference for the purpose of study and discussion, without power to legislate or to adopt resolutions, is the next step toward unity.

With grief for our aloofness in the past, and for other faults of pride and self-sufficiency, which make for schism; with loyalty to the truth as we see it, and with respect for the convictions of those who differ from us; holding the belief that the beginnings of unity are to be found in the clear statement and full consideration of those things in which we differ, as well as of those things in which we are at one, we respectfully submit the following resolution:

WHEREAS, There is today among all Christian people a growing desire for the fulfillment of Our Lord's prayer that all His disciples may be one; that the world may believe that God has sent Him:

Resolved, The House of Bishops concurring, That a Joint Commission be appointed to bring about a Conference for the consideration of questions touching Faith and Order, and that all Christian Communions throughout the world which confess our Lord Jesus Christ as God and Savior be asked to unite with us in arranging for and conducting such a Conference. The Commission shall consist of seven Bishops appointed by the Chairman of the House of Bishops, and seven Presbyters and seven Laymen, appointed by the President of the House of Deputies, and shall have power to add to its number and to fill any vacancies occurring before the next General Convention."

On·October 19, 1910, the above resolution was adopted unanimously by both the House of Bishops and the House of Clerical and Lay Deputies."

Text—*Minutes of the General Assembly of the Presbyterian Church in the United States of America*, New Series. Vol. XI, No. 3, (1911), pp. 231-232.

XX. *EPISCOPAL SUPERVISION IN THE METHODIST EPISCOPAL CHURCH*

Adopted May 20, 1912.

"WHEREAS, It is clear that the fixing of the official residences of the Bishops by the General Conference was intended to secure more direct spiritual and inspirational leadership in the Conferences adjacent to such residences; and,

WHEREAS, It is evident that this purpose fails to be realized under a system which takes from the resident Bishop all definite responsibility and right of leadership in such Conferences; and,

WHEREAS, It is evident from the large number of memorials received that there is dissatisfaction among our preachers and people under the present method, and a widespread demand for some modification; therefore,

Resolved, 1. That we recommend that in the intervals of the Annual Conference sessions each resident Bishop shall be held responsible for the administration of the spiritual and temporal interests of the Church in those Conferences adjacent to his residence, the decision as to which Conferences are adjacent to a particular residence being left to the Board of Bishops. To make this provision effective, we recommend that thirty days after the adjournment of an Annual Conference the presidency of the Conference shall pass to the Bishop resident in the group of which it forms a part, and shall remain so until thirty days before the next ensuing Annual Conference.

Resolved, 2. That in order to secure detailed and comprehensive knowledge of the activities, achievements, and needs of the entire Connection, each Bishop is hereby requested to make a quadrennially written report of his administration of the group over which he exercises residential supervision; such reports to be presented to the General Conference and printed in the General Conference Handbook and Journal.

Resolved, 3. That for the purpose of securing more economical and efficient presidential administration we earnestly recommend to the Board of Bishops to arrange our American Connection into at least four divisions; and we urgently request the Board of Bishops to assign the Annual Conferences within the division of which his residential Conferences form a part to each Bishop for presidential administration.

Resolved, 4. That the recommendations of the General Conference of 1908, printed as ¶ 47, § 3 of the Appendix to the Book of Discipline of 1908, be withdrawn. Adopted, May 20."

Text—Journal of the General Conference, 1912. pp. 529-530.

XXI. *THE TRUCE OF GOD*

"New York, N.Y., March 21, 1914

To our Christian Brethren in every land,
GREETING:

We, the Advisory Committee, representatives by appointment of many Churches in the United States, have become associated with the Commission of the Protestant Episcopal Church in the preparation of a World Conference on questions of Faith and Order as a first step towards unity. We believe in the one people of God throughout the world. We believe that now is a critically hopeful time for the world to become Christian. We believe that the present world problems of Christianity call for a World Conference of Christians.

This proposal has already received the approval and cooperation of a large number of Christian Churches; approaches are being made to others as rapidly as possible; so that we hope that ere long its world-wide representative character will be established beyond peradventure. In the work of preparation for its convening, we have no authority or desire to enter into a discussion of the important questions which the Conference itself will meet to consider. It is our immediate concern to take whatever measures may be advisable to secure the best possible presentation to the Conference of the matters to be considered. In so doing we cannot, however, remain indifferent to present conditions which may either promote or tend to thwart the purposes and hopes which the approaching World Conference should fulfill.

At the present moment some of these inportant issues have suddenly become matters of renewed controversy. From the mission field the long outstanding problem of Christian unity has been brought by the providence of God and set directly in the way before all Christian Communions. It cannot longer be passed by. The great interests which Christian people of every name have most at heart call for its solution. But solution cannot be secured by surrender. It must be preceded by conference. Before conference there must be truce. The love of Christ for the world constrains us to ask you to join with us and with His disciples of every name in proclaiming among the Churches throughout Christendom a Truce of God. Let the questions that have troubled us be fairly and clearly stated. Let scholars, Catholic and Protestant, give freely to the people whatever light from their historical studies they can throw over these subjects. More than that, it is of essential importance for us to seek to understand what in the religious experience of others, are the things of real value which they would not lose, and which should be conserved in the one household of faith. We pray also that each Christian Communion may avoid, so far as possible, any controversial declaration of its own position in relation to others, but rather that all things be said and done as if in preparation for the coming together of faithful disciples from every nation and tongue, to implore a fresh outpouring of God's Holy Spirit.

Before all indifference, doubt and misgivings, we would hold up the belief that the Lord's prayer for the oneness of His disciples was intended to be fulfilled; and that it ought not to be impossible in the comprehension of the Church, as it is practicable in the State, for men of various temperaments and divergent convictions to dwell together on agreed principles of unity. We would, therefore, urge all who hold positions of leadership or authority in the Church to labor without ceasing to work out in this generation, by mutual recognitions and possible readjustments, a practical basis of unity in liberty, in order, in truth, in power and in peace, To this end we ask your prayers.

By order of the Advisory Committee of the Commissions on the World Conference on Faith and Order.

WILLIAM T. MANNING, *Chairman,*

ROBERT H. GARDINER, *Secretary.*"

Text—*Minutes of the General Assembly of the Presbyterian Church in the United States of America,* New Series, Vol. XIV (1914), pp. 37-38.

XXII. *CONSTITUTION OF THE NORTHERN BAPTIST CONVENTION*

DECLARATION

The Northern Baptist Convention, Incorporated June 1910, held its first assembly in Chicago in May of the same year. The constitution as under embodies amendments to 1917.

The Northern Baptist Convention declares its belief in the independence of the local church, and in the purely advisory nature of all denominational organizations composed of representatives of churches. It believes also that, in view of the growth of the Baptist denomination and its extension throughout our country, there is need for an organization to serve the common interests of the entire denomination as State and district organizations serve their respective constituencies.

BY LAWS

ARTICLE I

Membership

SECTION I. The Convention shall be composed of accredited delegates appointed as follows:

(a) Any Baptist church in the United States may appoint one delegate, and one additional delegate for every one hundred members.

(b) Any Baptist State Convention may appoint ten delegates, and one additional delegate for every ten District Associations included in it, above the first ten.

SEC. 2. Accredited officers and members of Boards of Managers of cooperating organizations shall be delegates *ex officio.*

The accredited officers and members of the Boards of Managers of the Woman's Missionary Societies auxiliary to or cooperating with the American Baptist Home Mission Society or the American Baptist Foreign Mission Society shall be delegates *ex officio.*

Officers and members of committees of the Convention during their terms of service shall be delegates *ex officio.*

ARTICLE II

Officers

. . . .

ARTICLE III
Meetings

. . . .

ARTICLE IV
Committees

SECTION 1. (a) There shall be an Executive Committee elected by ballot, and composed of the officers and former presidents of the Convention, and thirty others, of whom at least fifteen shall be laymen. Of the thirty first elected, ten shall serve for three years, ten for two years, and ten for one year; and thereafter there shall be elected annually ten to serve for three years. Vacancies caused by the death, resignation, or refusal to act of any of the thirty may be filled by the remaining members of the Committee.

(b) No one, other than an officer or a former President of the Convention, shall be eligible to membership in the Executive Committee after service thereon for six consecutive years, until the expiration of one year after the termination of such service.

. . . .

(d) No appeals for money shall be made and no collections shall be taken at the meetings of the Convention which have not been approved by the Executive Committee.

SEC. 2. (a) There shall be a Finance Committee of nine, a majority of whom shall be laymen.

(b) It shall be the duty of this Committee to prepare and present to the Convention at each annual meeting a budget based on the budgets submitted by the Executive Committee and by the cooperating organizations.

(c) In case of an emergency arising between the annual meetings of the Convention, the committee, by the majority vote of all its members, may approve the incurring of indebtedness by a cooperating organization. Should such approval be given, the committee shall report its action with the reasons therefor to the Convention at its next annual meeting.

SEC. 3. (a) There shall be an Apportionment Committee appointed at each annual meeting. It shall be composed of a representative from each of the following bodies: The Executive Committee of the Convention, the Board of Education, each of the cooperating organizations, a city church, a rural church, and a State Apportionment Committee, together with a District Secretary of a cooperating organization and an executive officer of a State Convention.

(b) It shall be the duty of this committee:

1. To divide among the States represented in the Convention the respective amounts to be raised as specified in the budget approved by the Convention, and to communicate to the Apportionment Committee of each State the amount apportioned to it;

2. To appoint an Apportionment Committee for any State where no such committee is appointed;

3. To employ such agents and methods and to take such other action to carry the apportionment into effect as to it may seem wise;

4. To divide ratably among the beneficiaries of the budget the expenses incurred in the performance of the duties of the committee.

. . . .

SEC. 10. There shall be a Law Committee consisting of six persons. It shall be the duty of this committee to consider and report upon all matters referred to it by the Convention or the Executive Committee.

SEC. 11. There shall be a Committee on City Missions consisting of nine persons. It shall be the duty of this Committee to study questions related to cooperation between City Mission organizations and State Conventions, and the cooperating organizations of the Northern Baptist Convention, and also all other general questions related to City Mission work throughout the country.

SEC. 12. There shall be a Committee on Baptist Brotherhood consisting of twelve persons. It shall be the duty of this Committee to further the organization of men in Baptist churches for study, fellowship, and service, and to consider all questions related thereto.

SEC. 13. There shall be a Committee on State Conventions consisting of nine persons. It shall be the duty of this Committee to review the work of the State Conventions that are affiliating organizations and to consider all questions concerning such Conventions and their relation to the Northern Baptist Convention.

SEC. 14. There shall be a Committee on Social Service consisting of twelve persons. It shall be the duty of this Committee to study social conditions and needs, to ascertain the activities of Baptist churches in the field of social service, to organize and enlist Baptists in practical and definite lines of Community Service in city and country, to cooperate with similar agencies of other religious bodies, and from time to time to report its findings and recommendations through the religious press.

SEC. 15. There shall be a Committee on Religious Education consisting of nine persons. It shall be the duty of this Committee to study the educational needs of the local church, and in cooperation with the American Baptist Publication Society to prepare educational courses for the promotion of the intelligent growth of the church, and for its symmetrical development in its varied relations to the community, to the outspread of Christianity, and to the world at large.

SEC. 16. There shall be a Committee on Young People's Work consisting of nine persons. It shall be the duty of this Committee, in cooperation with the American Baptist Publication Society, to superintend the organization of young people's work, and to foster inspirational and educational activities in connection therewith.

SEC. 17. There shall be a Committee on Evangelism consisting of nine persons. It shall be the duty of this Committee to study the subject of Evangelism with a view to discover and suggest the most effective means for promoting it, and in cooperation with the American Baptist Home Mission Society to disseminate evangelistic literature, and in all other practical ways to encourage and promote personal evangelism, organized evangelism in the local church, and cooperative evangelism among the churches.

SEC. 18. There shall be a Committee on the Coordination of Baptist Bodies Using Foreign Languages consisting of eighteen persons. It shall be the duty of this Committee to study and report on the best methods for coordinating Baptist bodies using foreign languages with one another and also with other Baptist bodies, and also to report such other facts and such statistics related to the work of the Committee as to it may seem proper.

. . . .

ARTICLE V

Cooperating Organizations

SECTION 1. On its application and the approval of the Convention by a two-thirds vote, any general denominational missionary, educational, or philanthropic organization, whose constituency resides in the States represented in the Convention, may become a cooperating organization.

SEC. 2. A cooperating organization must agree:

(a) To insert in its by-laws a provision that all accredited delegates to each annual meeting of the Northern Baptist Convention shall be annual members of the organization;

(b) To regulate its expenditures in accordance with a budget to be annually approved by the Convention;

(c) To solicit funds only on the approval of the Convention, or on the approval of the Finance Committee given between the annual meetings of the Convention as provided by Article IV, Section 2, Subdivision (c);

(d) To incur no indebtedness without the previous approval of the Convention, or of the Finance Committee as provided by Article IV, Section 2, Subdivision (c);

(e) To submit its books and accounts to the inspection of the Finance Committee; to prepare its budgets and to make its financial reports in such form as that Committee shall request.

SEC. 3. The Convention, through its Executive and Finance Committees, will aid in raising funds needed to carry on the work of each cooperating organization.

SEC. 4. Cooperation between the Convention and a cooperating organization shall be terminated on the expiration of a year after written notice of a desire to terminate cooperation shall have been given by one to the other.

ARTICLE VI

Boards

SECTION 1. (a) There shall be a Board of Education, to be composed of twenty-one persons, to be appointed by the Executive Committee. Of the twenty-one first appointed, seven shall serve for three years, seven shall serve for two years, and seven shall serve for one year, and thereafter seven shall be appointed annually by the Executive Committee to serve for three years. Vacancies caused by the death, resignation, or refusal to act of any of the twenty-one may be filled by the Executive Committee.

(b) It shall be the duty of this Board to develop the educational convictions of our churches, to make a comprehensive study of our educational problems, and to foster such denominational institutions and denominational ministries in other schools of learning as the Board may approve.

. . . .

ARTICLE VII

Affiliating Organizations

SECTION 1. On its application and the approval of the Convention any Baptist State Convention in any State represented in the Convention may become an affiliating organization.

SEC. 2. An affiliating organization should agree:

(a) To adopt the following statement of its objects:

To promote in the State of . . . . the preaching of the Gospel, ministerial and general education, the establishment, maintenance, and assistance of Baptist churches and Bible schools, and the care of worthy pastors, their wives or widows, and their dependent children.

To give expression to the opinions of its constituency upon moral, religious, and denominational matters, to promote denominational unity and efficiency in efforts for the evangelization of the world, to support earnestly the work of cooperating organizations of the Northern Baptist Convention, and by affiliation with that Convention to promote its plans and work.

(b) To provide for the promotion of these objects by thorough and efficient organization.

(c) To appoint an Apportionment Committee whose duty it shall be to receive from the Apportionment Committee of the Northern Baptist Convention the statement of the amount apportioned by the latter to the State, to add to that amount the sum adopted by the State Convention for all other objects, and to apportion the aggregate amount equitably among the churches of the State and to notify each church of the amount apportioned to it. District Secretaries of the organizations cooperating with the Northern Baptist Convention and the State Secretary shall be advisory members of the State Apportionment Committee.

(d) To employ such agents and methods and to take such other action to carry the apportionment into effect as to it may seem wise.

. . . .

Article IX

Amendments

These By-laws may be amended at any annual meeting of the Convention, either on the recommendation of the Executive Committee, given at a previous session of the Convention at which such amendment is submitted, or after written notice of the proposed amendment, given at a previous annual meeting and signed by at least twenty-five delegates, representing not less than five States.

Text—*Annual of the Northern Baptist Convention, 1917*, pp. 9-15.

The following modifications of the By-laws· were approved at the Denver Convention, May 1919.

Sec. 3. (a) There shall be a General Board of Promotion, to consist of: (1) The president of the Northern Baptist Convention; (2) four members of the executive committee of the Northern Baptist Convention, elected by said committee; (3) an administrative officer and three members of the board of managers of each co-operating organization; (4) an administrative officer and three members of the Ministers and Missionaries Benefit Board; (5) an administrative officer and three members of the Board of Education; (6) two representatives of each affiliating organization to be elected by the affiliating organization, one of the two to be an administrative officer of the organization and the other a member of a Baptist church (pastor, layman or woman) in the territory of said affiliating organization; (7) one representative of each standard city mission society recognized as such by the Northern Baptist Convention, to be elected by the city mission society represented; and (8) twenty-four members at large, to be elected by the Convention.

. . . .

(g) The board shall appoint standing committees as follows: A Finance Committee; an Apportionment Committee; all Administrative Committee; such other committees as it shall find necessary.

(h) The Finance Committee shall consist of nine persons, a majority of whom shall be laymen.

(i) The Apportionment Committee shall consist of a representative of each of the following bodies: The executive committee of the Convention, the Ministers and Missionaries Benefit Board, the Board of Education, the board of managers of each of the co-operating organizations, a city church, a rural church, and a State apportionment committee, together with an administrative officer of a State convention.

(j) The Administrative Committee shall consist of the following members of the board: An administrative officer and a member of the board of managers of each of the co-operating organizations; an administrative officer and a member of the Ministers and Missionaries Benefit Board; an administrative officer and a member of the Board of Education; an administrative officer of one affiliating organization and a lay representative of one affiiliating organization; six other members of the board, of whom not less than two shall be pastors and not less than two shall be women.

(k) Of the members first elected to the Finance and Apportionment Committees respectively, one-third shall serve till the close of the next annual meeting of the board, one-third to the close of the second annual meeting of the board and one-third to the close of the third annual meeting, and thereafter there shall be elected annually one-third of the number of the members to serve for three years. The members of the Administrative Committee shall be elected at the first meeting of the board to serve till the close of the next annual meeting, and thereafter the committee shall be elected annually to serve to the close of the next annual meeting; except that of the six members last named under subsection (j) two shall serve till the close of the third annual meeting, two to the close of the second annual meeting, and two to the close of the first annual meeting, and thereafter two shall be elected at each annual meeting to serve for three years.

(1) It shall be the duty of the executive secretary at least three months before the annual meeting of the board to request the board of managers of each of the co-operating organizations, the managers of the Ministers and Missionaries Benefit Board, and the Board of Education to send to him for the use of the General Board of Promotion, not less than one month before the annual meeting, reports of their activities of the preceding fiscal year, a proposed budget of receipts and expenditures for the fiscal year next ensuing, and other information respecting their plans for said year, likely to be useful to the board in its annual meeting. These reports and budgets, together with the reports of the standing committees of the board, hereinafter provided for, shall be submitted to the board at its annual meeting. On the basis of them the Board shall approve a combined budget for the Convention and its co-operating organizations for the next ensuing fiscal year, designate the amount to be apportioned to the States represented in the Convention, to be in turn apportioned to the churches, divide this amount equitably among the States, and report to the apportionment committee of each State the amount apportioned to that State.

(m) It shall also be the duty of the executive secretary, not less than three months before the annual meeting of the board, to request from the affiliating organizations and standard city mission societies reports of their activities, proposed budgets for the next ensuing fiscal year, and other information concerning their plans. The respective State conventions shall be requested also to make recommendations respecting moneys proposed or necessary to be raised by or for the denominational educational institutions in their respective States, and concerning any other special financial campaigns that are in contemplation. It shall be competent for the board to express its judgment respecting the wisdom and adequacy of these budgets and campaigns.

(n) In voting on any matter in the General Board of Promotion or the Administrative Committee the vote shall be taken by the individual members thereof in attendance and entitled to vote, each such person being entitled to one vote; but if requested by one-third of those present a tentative vote shall be taken on the subject under discussion, in which the vote shall be representative in the following proportions:

Representative of the Northern Baptist Convention, three votes; representative of the American Baptist Foreign Mission Society, two votes; representative of the American Baptist Home Mission Society, two votes; representative of the Woman's American Baptist Foreign Mission Society, two votes; representative of the Woman's American Baptist Home Mission Society, two votes; representative of the American Baptist Publication Society, two votes; representative of the Ministers and Missionaries Benefit Board, one vote; representative of the Board of Education, one vote; representative of the City Mission Societies, one vote; representative of the affiliating organizations, five votes; the delegates at large, one vote.

If on the taking of such tentative votes two-thirds or more shall vote on one side, the tentative vote shall stand as the vote of the body, if on the tentative vote neither side shall receive two-thirds vote the final vote shall be taken by the individuals present in the customary manner.

(o) The board shall send a memorandum of its actions to the boards of managers of the several co-operating organizations, to the Ministers and Missionaries Benefit Board, and the Board of Education, to the State conventions affiliating with the Northern Baptist Convention, to the State Boards of Promotion, and to the standard city mission societies. It shall also make a full report to the Northern BaptistConvention at its next meeting.

(p) It shall be the duty of the Finance Committee—

1. To consider the budgets submitted to the General Board of Promotion as provided in section (1) above, and to prepare and present to the General Board of Promotion at its annual meeting a combined budget of the Convention and its co-operating organizations, also to make advisory recommendations, respecting the budgets of the affiliating organizations and standard city mission societies.

2. To appoint an auditor to examine the books and audit the accounts of the Convention and its boards, and agents of the Ministers and Missionaries Benefit Board, and of the co-operating organizations, to receive the auditor's reports and transmit them to the General Board of Promotion.

3. In case of emergency arising between the annual meetings of the Convention, to consider any requests which may come from a co-operating organization, from the Ministers and Missionaries Benefit Board, or from a board of the Convention, to incur indebtedness or to solicit funds in excess of the budget approved by the Convention. The committee shall have authority by majority vote of all its members to approve the incurring of such indebtedness or the solicitation of such funds. Should such approval be given, the committee shall report its action, with reasons therefor, to the

General Board of Promotion, which shall in turn include report of such action in its report to the Convention at its next annual meeting.

(q) It shall be the duty of the Apportionment Committee—

1. At the annual meeting of the General Board of Promotion to recommend to the board a distribution among the several States represented in the Convention of the total amount to be raised on apportionment to the churches, as specified in the budget approved by the board.

2. To appoint an apportionment committee for any State in which provision for the appointment of such committee is not made by the State Convention.

(r) The Administrative Committee shall, subject to such regulations as the Convention may from time to time adopt, have the management of all the financial affairs of the Convention, appoint its own meetings, and adopt such regulations as to it may seem proper, including those for the control and disposition of the real and personal property of the Convention and the sale, leasing or mortgaging thereof, provided such regulations are not inconsistent with the act of incorporation or by-laws of the Convention. All transactions respecting the receipt and disposal of real estate or securities shall be reported to the General Board of Promotion at its next meeting.

(s) It shall be the duty of the Administrative Committee under the authority and instruction of the General Board of Promotion:

1. To disseminate among the constituency of the Convention information concerning the work of the Convention, its boards, the Ministers and Missionaries Benefit Board, and the co-operating organizations, and in all legitimate ways to develop a spirit of beneficence among the constituency.

2. To devise and execute ways and means of raising the money necessary for the prosecution of the work of all the organizations named in the paragraph next preceding.

3. In the prosecution of these ends to work in close conference with these organizations, and with the organizations affiliating with the Convention, seeking the co-operation of all these bodies and availing themselves of the services of the officers of the co-operating organizations who are in close touch with their boards in presenting the work of these organizations to the denomination.

4. To appoint such subcommittees and officers and to create such departments as it may find necessary, and to direct their work and that of all the secretaries and other salaried officers of the General Board of Promotion.

5. To prepare a budget of receipts and expenditures for the Northern Baptist Convention and to present the same to the Finance Committee one month before the annual meeting of the board.

6. To direct the treasurer as to the distribution of such moneys and property as may come into his hands, in conformity with conditions imposed by the donors and with the budget approved by the Convention.

7. To give notice of all its meetings to its own members and to the chairmen and all administrative officers of the boards of managers of the co-operating organizations, of the Ministers and Missionaries Benefit Board, and the boards of the Convention, and to give to such persons, not members of the committee, a seat and the privileges of the floor, but without the right to vote.

8. To submit a report of all its activities to the General Board of Promotion at its annual meeting.

. . . .

Text—*The Watchman-Examiner*, April 3, 1919.

XXIII. *CONSTITUTION OF THE UNITED LUTHERAN CHURCH IN AMERICA*

The first convention of the above body assembled in The Hippodrome, New York, Nov. 17, 1918.

PREAMBLE

In the Name of the Father, and of the Son, and of the Holy Spirit. Amen.

Having been called by the Gospel and made partakers of the grace of God, and, by faith, members of our Lord and Saviour Jesus Christ, and, through Him, of one another,

We, members of Evangelical Lutheran congregations in America, associated in Evangelical Lutheran Synods, recognizing our duty as people of God to make the inner unity which we have with one another manifest in the common confession, defense and maintenance of our faith, and in united efforts for the extension of the Kingdom of God at home and abroad; realizing the vastness of the field that God has assigned us for our labors in this Western world, and the greatness of the resources within our beloved Church which are only feebly employed for this purpose; conscious of our need of mutual assistance and encouragement; and relying upon the promise of the divine Word that He who hath begun this work will perfect it until the day of Christ Jesus,

Hereby unite, and now invite and until such end be attained continue to invite all Evangelical Lutheran congregations and synods in America, one with us in the faith, to unite with us, upon the terms of this Constitution, in one general organization, to be known as THE UNITED LUTHERAN CHURCH IN AMERICA.

ARTICLE I

Name

The name and title of the body organized under this Constitution shall be THE UNITED LUTHERAN CHURCH IN AMERICA.

ARTICLE II

Doctrinal Basis

Section 1. The United Lutheran Church in America receives and holds the canonical Scriptures of the Old and New Testaments as the inspired Word of God, and as the only infallible rule and standard of faith and practice, according to which all doctrines and teachers are to be judged.

Section 2. The United Lutheran Church in America accepts the three ecumenical creeds: namely, the Apostles', the Nicene, and the Athanasian, as important testimonies drawn from the Holy Scriptures, and rejects all errors which they condemn.

Section 3. The United Lutheran Church in America receives and holds the Unaltered Augsburg Confession as a correct exhibition of the faith and doctrine of the Evangelical Lutheran Church, founded upon the Word of God; and acknowledges all churches that sincerely hold and faithfully confess the doctrines of the Unaltered Augsburg Confession to be entitled to the name of Evangelical Lutheran.

Section 4. The United Lutheran Church in America recognizes the Apology of the Augsburg Confession, the Smalkald Articles, the Large and Small Catechisms of Luther, and the Formula of Concord, as in the harmony of one and the same pure Scriptural faith.

Article III

Principles of Organization

In accordance with the foregoing Doctrinal Basis, The United Lutheran Church in America sets forth and declares the following principles as fundamental to its organization:

Section 1. All power in the Church belongs primarily and exclusively to our Lord and Saviour Jesus Christ, the Head of the Church. This power is not delegated to any man or body of men.

Section 2. All just power exercised by the Church has been committed to her for the furtherance of the Gospel through the Word and sacraments, and is conditioned by this end and pertains to her as the servant of Jesus Christ. The Church, therefore, has no power to bind the conscience except as she teaches what her Lord teaches and faithfully commands what He has charged her to command.

Section 3. Congregations are the primary bodies through which power committed by Christ to the Church is normally exercised.

Section 4. In addition to the pastors of Churches, who are *ex officio* representatives of their congregations the people have the right to choose representatives from their own number to act for them under such constitutional limitations as the congregations may approve.

Section 5. The representatives of congregations convened in Synod and acting in accordance with their Constitution are, for the ends defined in it representatively the congregations themselves, and have the right to call and set apart ministers for the common work of all the congregations; whose representatives they thereby become, and as such also members of the Synod.

Section 6. Congregations representatively constituting the various Synods may elect delegates through those Synods to represent them in a general body, all decisions of which, when made in accordance with the Constitution, bind so far as the terms of mutual agreement make them binding, those congregations and Synods which consent to be represented in the general body.

Section 7. In the formation and administration of a general body, the Synods may know and deal with each other only as Synods. In all such cases, the official record is to be accepted as evidence of the doctrinal position of each Synod and of the principles for which alone the other Synods are responsible by connection with it.

Article IV

Membership

Section 1. The United Lutheran Church in America at its organization shall consist of the congregations that compose the Evangelical Lutheran Synods which have been in connection with the General Synod of the Evangelical Lutheran Church in the United States of America, the General Council of the Lutheran Church in North America, or the United Synod of the Evangelical Lutheran Church in the South, and which accept this Constitution with its Doctrinal Basis as set forth in Article II.

Section 2. Any Evangelical Lutheran Synod applying for admission which has accepted this Constitution with its Doctrinal Basis as set forth in Article II, and whose Constitution has been approved by the Executive Board, may be received into membership by a majority vote at any regular Convention.

Article V
Delegates

Section 1. Each Synod connected with The United Lutheran Church in America shall be entitled to representation at its Conventions by one ordained minister and one layman for every ten pastoral charges, or major fraction thereof, on its roll; provided, however, that each Synod shall be entitled to at least one ministerial and one lay delegate; and provided further that the delegates elected by the Synods to the last conventions of the general bodies to which they respectively belong held prior to the first convention hereunder, shall be and they are in the adoption hereof chosen by their respective Synods as their duly elected delegates' to said first convention hereunder, irrespective of the basis of representation upon which they were chosen. The ratio of representation may be changed at any regular Convention of The United Lutheran Church in America by a two-thirds vote, provided that notice of the proposed change has been given at the preceding regular Convention.

Section 2. Each Synod shall choose its delegates in such manner as it may deem proper. The delegates from each Synod shall elect one of their own number as chairman unless the Synod itself has designated the chairman.

Article VI
Objects

The objects of The United Lutheran Church in America are:

Section 1. To preserve and extend the pure teaching of the Gospel and the right administration of the sacraments. (Eph. 4:5, 6; The Augsburg Confession, Article VII).

Section 2. To conserve the unity of the true faith (Eph. 4: 3-16; I Cor. 1:10), to guard against any departure therefrom (Rom. 16:17), and to strengthen the Church in faith and confession.

Section 3. To express outwardly the spiritual unity of Lutheran congregations and synods, to cultivate co-operation among all Lutherans in the promotion of the general interests of the Church, to seek the unification of all Lutherans in one orthodox faith, and thus to develop and unfold the specific Lutheran principle and practice and make their strength effective.

Section 4. To awaken, coordinate and effectively direct the energies of the Church in such operations as the following:

(a). The training of ministers and teachers to be witnesses of the Word.

(b). The extension of the kingdom of God by Home, Foreign and Inner Missions.

(c). The proper regulation of the human externals of worship, that the same, in character and administration, may be in keeping with the New Testament and the liberty of the Church, and may edify the Body of Christ.

(d). The appointment of editorial committees or editors of Church papers and Sunday School literature.

(e). The preparation and publication of such literature as shall promote the dissemination of knowledge as to the doctrines, practice, progress, and needs of the Lutheran Church.

(f). The creation, organization and development, through Boards and Committees, of agencies to carry on all departments of work.

Section 5. To lay apportionments, and to solicit and disburse the funds necessary for these and other purposes defined in this Constitution.

Section 6. To foster and develop the work of Synods, to exercise a general supervision of the Church, and on appeal of Synods to give counsel and to adjudicate questions of doctrine, worship and discipline.

Section 7. To enter into relations with other bodies in the unity of the faith and to exchange official delegates with them.

. . . .

ARTICLE VIII
Powers

Section 1. *As to External Relations.* The United Lutheran Church in America shall have power to form and dissolve relations with other general bodies, organizations and movements. To secure uniform and consistent practice no Synod, Conference or Board, or any official representative thereof, shall have power of independent affiliation with general organizations and movements.

Section 2. *As to Internal Relations.* The United Lutheran Church in America shall have power to deal with internal matters that affect all its constituent Synods or the activities of The United Lutheran Church as a whole, except that when the operation of such power takes place within the domain of any of the Synods their consent and co-operation must first be secured.

Section 3. *As to Intersynodical Dealings.* The United Lutheran Church in America shall have power to address and counsel its constituent Synods for the promotion of intersynodical harmony. Any question of interpretation of law, rights, or principle, that comes within its jurisdiction, or any proper cases referred to it on appeal of a Synod, shall be determined by a Commission of Adjudication hereinafter provided for.

Section 4. *As to Individual Synods and Specific Cases.* If Synods have had due and legal opportunity to be represented in the Conventions of The United Lutheran Church in America, they are bound by all resolutions that have been passed in accordance with this Constitution. But each Synod retains every power, right and jurisdiction in its own internal affairs not expressly delegated to The United Lutheran Church in America.

Section 5. *As to Doctrine and Conscience.* All matters of doctrine and conscience shall be decided according to the Word of God alone. If, on grounds of doctrine or conscience, the question be raised as to the binding character of any action, the said question shall be referred to the Commission of Adjudication. Under no circumstances shall the right of a minority be disregarded or the right to record an individual protest on the ground of conscience be refused.

Section 6. *As to the Maintenance of Principle and Practice.* The United Lutheran Church in America shall protect and enforce its Doctrinal Basis, secure pure preaching of the Word of God and the right administration of the sacraments in all its Synods and congregations. It shall also have the right, where it deems that loyalty to the Word of God requires it, to advise and admonish concerning association and affiliation with non-ecclesiastical and other organizations whose principles or practices appear to be inconsistent with full loyalty to the Christian Church, but the Synods alone shall have the power of discipline.

Section 7. *As to Books of Devotion and Instruction, etc.* The United Lutheran Church in America shall provide books of devotion and instruction, such as Liturgies,

Hymn Books and Catechisms, and no Synod without its sanction shall publish or recommend books of this kind other than those provided by the general body.

Section 8. *As to Work and Administration.* The United Lutheran Church in America shall have the power to engage in the work described under "Objects" (see Article VI), to create and regulate Boards and Committees, to determine budgets, and to lay apportionments.

Section 9. The executive power of The United Lutheran Church in America shall be vested in the officers of the general body, in an Executive Board, and in various other Boards for special purposes, subject to this Constitution and the Conventions of the general body.

. . . .

ARTICLE XII
Commission of Adjudication

Section 1. A Commission of Adjudication shall be established to which shall be referred, for interpretation and decision, all disputed questions of doctrine and practice, and this Commission shall constitute a court for the decision of all questions of principle or action arising within The United Lutheran Church in America, and which have been properly referred to it by resolution or by appeal of any of the Synods.

Section 2. This Commission of Adjudication shall consist of nine members, six ministers and three laymen, learned in the doctrine, the law and the practice of the Church. All of the members of this Commission shall be elected at the first Convention of The United Lutheran Church in America, two ministers and one layman for a period of six years, two ministers and one layman for a period of four years, and two ministers and one layman for a period of two years. As their terms expire their successors shall be elected at each Convention for a term of six years.

Section 3. The Commission shall elect its own officers, and shall meet at least semi-annually for the transaction of business. When it holds meetings, or renders decisions, due notice of the time and place of meeting shall be given by its secretary to all persons interested, and a standing notice of the time and place of its regular meetings shall be published in the Church papers.

Section 4. The consent of at least six members shall always be necessary for a decision.

Section 5. The commission shall render a written report of all its actions and decisions to the next regular Convention, but the right of appeal from its decisions shall always be recognized.

Text—*Constitution and By-Laws of the United Lutheran Church in America,* pp. 3-14.

ARTICLE XIV
Synods

. . . .

Section 1. No Synod in connection with The United Lutheran Church in America shall alter its geographical boundaries without the permission of the general body.

Section 2. Synods shall give advice to their ministers and congregations concerning doctrine, life and administration, and shall exercise such disciplinary measures as may be necessary.

Section 3. The Presidents of Synods shall exercise an oversight of the pastors and congregations composing their respective Synods, and shall be charged with the duty of carrying out the rules and regulations adopted by the Synods. When requested by the Executive Board they shall appear before it to represent their Synods. They may also make suggestions to the Executive Board, or seek its advice, with respect to the conditions and work in their Synods.

Section 4. Should any Synod in connection with The United Lutheran Church in America desire to continue its established lines of works for reasons satisfactory to the general body, such privilege may be granted.

XXIV. THE INTERCHURCH WORLD MOVEMENT OF NORTH AMERICA

Findings of the Cleveland Conference

These findings were prepared by a committee of twenty-one appointed by the Cleveland Conference. While obviously not attempting to outline plans, these paragraphs present a general conception of the scope and possibilities of the Movement.

We are impressed with the providential character of the steps and events leading up to this meeting at Cleveland. We reverently recognize what we believe to be the leadings of the Divine Spirit in this Interchurch World Movement.

We believe that the magnitude and the urgency of the present duty of the Christian church to carry the gospel to all men and to all life, call for the greatest possible measure of effective cooperation among the churches.

We are convinced that the spirit of life and of common service which is now abroad among the churches needs for its expression and for its use such an instrumentality as the Interchurch World Movement provides.

We welcome this Movement as providentially presenting to the evangelical churches and organizations of America an unprecedented opportunity for co-operative effort to serve the whole world unitedly, effectively, and in the Spirit of Christ.

It seems to us to be of extraordinary significance that it should come into being at a time when the cataclysm of the world war has prepared the minds of men for religious impressions, thrown down the barriers to missionary advance and created an atmosphere favorable to the review and readjustment of industrial, social and international relations, in accordance with the teachings of Christ.

We commend the proposed method of basing the program of action upon facts to be ascertained by means of comprehensive and careful surveys. We understand that these surveys will not only cover those fields commonly classified as "missionary" but will include all evangelistic effort; the religious nurture of children; the enlistment and special preparation of youth for life service; the educational system of the churches at home and abroad—general, theological, vocational and professional; philanthropic institutions—hospitals, orphanages, asylums and child-welfare agencies; the means for the support of the ministry in retirement, as well as in active service; and the contribution of the church to the solution of the definite social and industrial problems of the new day of readjustment and reconstruction.

We believe that upon such a foundation of established fact the churches and organizations with which we are severally connected can unitedly appeal to the Protestant constituency of America in support of a program large enough and wise enough and practical enough to command the prayers, the money and the dedication of life sufficient to man, equip and spiritually energize the Movement, whose aim is nothing less than to make the Divine Christ ruler of the hearts and lives of all men.

We are persuaded that close and trustful cooperation in such a movement will weaken no true and worthy loyalty to denominational duty but will require the fullest contribution which each body can make in the line of its own distinctive responsibility.

To meet the natural and proper inquiries of our churches as to the character and purpose of the Movement we deem it wise to state: that the Interchurch World Movement is a coöperative effort of the missionary, educational and other benevolent agencies of the evangelical churches of United States and Canada to secure the necessary resources of men and money and power required for these tasks; that it is a spiritual undertaking of survey, education, and inspiration; that it is an instrumentality of coöperation and coördination of administrative agencies, designed to serve and not to supplant them.

It is this positive character of the Movement that we desire to exalt. At the same time, to prevent misapprehension, we affirm our definite understanding that this is not an ecclesiastical movement nor an effort at organic church union. It will not disturb the autonomy or interfere with the administration of any church or board. Neither will it undertake to administer or to expend funds for any purpose beyond its own proper administrative expenses. It has a definite and temporary mission. It will not duplicate or conflict with other denominational agencies. It does not assume responsibility or authority in questions of church or missionary policy, recognizing that these belong to the coöperating agencies and organizations. And we disclaim all statements, by whomsoever made, contrary to this declaration of principles.

We believe that the churches need not fear to trust to the fullest extent such a coöperative effort created by their own agencies and responsible to their control.

In this endeavor unitedly to survey their common task and together to enlist the resources of its accomplishment, we see an opportunity for all our churches to bring to bear upon the needs of our nation and of the world the full measure of their Christian conviction and devotion, with no compromise of our denominational trusts and distinctive principles and no confusion of our individual responsibilities. This Movement makes possible our unreserved coöperation in an effort where each body gives itself to the common service and in accord with our Lord's promise, finds itself again enriched in the common life and strengthened with new power.

Text—Leaflet: *Findings of the Cleveland Conference.*

What It Is

The main features of the plan are five in number:

1. A United Study of the World Field. County by county in this country and district by district in foreign lands, it is proposed that the exact facts be discovered to the end that the needs of each community and region may be appraised and the whole task of the church put in clear light and due proportion.

2. A United Budget. On the basis of the world survey it is proposed that a joint budget be made, every item of which shall approve itself to the judgment of the several mission boards, so far as it relates to the work of each board, and have the approval of a strong interdenominational committee aided by experts in the various fields covered, this committee to review and harmonize the details. While this budget will be for one year, it will take account of needs for five years.

3. A United Cultivation of the Home Church. In order to bring the facts contained in the surveys to the attention of the people and to widen their vision and deepen their interest there will be a nation-wide field campaign and special attention will be given in the whole Movement to missionary information, Bible study, religious education, stewardship, life service and the deepening of the prayer life of the church.

4. A United Financial Appeal. During a given number of days at some period in 1920 is proposed that the 50,000,000 people constituting the Protestant constituency of America be asked, community by community, to underwrite the united budget for the year ahead, payment of pledges to be made week by week through customary church channels. There will be a united treasury to care for undesignated gifts. Many have asked what the total of the anticipated united budget will be. Not even an estimate can now be made. Only when the world survey is completed, with its painstaking examination of every section of the field and its balancing of obligations, can a figure be named.

5. A United Program of Work. It is proposed that this plan shall carry the steadily growing co-operation of recent years in the mission field on to the point of the most complete co-ordination which the conditions of our separate organizations permit. Funds secured will be expended with detailed regard to the requirements of fraternal co-operation.

It is proposed that the whole broad field of missions be covered, including home and foreign missions in all their branches, Christian education in all its aspects and Sunday school interests of every type. Interdenominational agencies of the types above indicated are included to the end that there may be close co-operation between all forces.

Text—Leaflet: *What It Is.*

. . . .

XXV. *THE BAPTISTS AND ORGANIC CHURCH UNION*

The following statement and report received enthusiastic endorsement at the Convention in Denver, May 1919.

A Statement of the Baptist Position on Organic Church Union

Whereas, the Northern Baptist Convention has been invited to send delegates to a council looking toward organic union of the Protestant denominations.

Be It Resolved, that the Northern Baptist Convention, while maintaining fraternal relations with evangelical denominations in extending the influence of the gospel of Jesus Christ, does not believe that organic union with other denominations is possible. It, therefore, declines to send delegates to the proposed council. In declining the invitation, however, Christian courtesy demands that the Northern Baptist Convention should state its position as to organic church union with other Christian denominations. This we make not with any desire to pose as judge of our Christian brethren, but in the interest of mutual understanding.

The Baptist denomination is a collection of independent democratic churches. None of these churches recognizes any ecclesiastical authority superior to itself. They are grouped in associations, state conventions and a national convention, but none of these groups has any control over a local church, beyond that which lies in common faith, practice and service. The denomination, in so far as it has unity, is a federation of independent democracies. In the nature of the case, therefore, anything like organic church union of the Baptist churches with other denominations is impossible. There is no centralized body that could deliver the Baptist churches to any merger or corporate unity. If Baptist churches do not have organic unity among themselves, they obviously cannot have organic unity with other denominations. By the very nature of our organization, we are estopped from seeking organic union with other denominations.

This situation does not arise from any desire on the part of the Baptists to withhold themselves from fellowship with other Christian bodies in the pursuance of Christian work. Nor does it arise from any desire to impose upon them our own convictions. We grant to others all rights that we claim for ourselves. But the liberty of conscience and the independence of the churches which characterizes our position are involved in our fundamental conception as to the nature of the church and of its relation to the religious life.

We believe in the complete competency of the individual to come directly into saving relationship with God. We hold that a church is a local community of those who have consciously committed themselves to Jesus Christ. The only church universal is, in our belief, spiritual fellowship of individual souls with God. We do not believe in any form of sacerdotalism or sacramentalism among Christians who are all equally priests of the Most High. We reject ecclesiastical orders and hold that all believers are on a spiritual equality. With us, ordination is only a formal recognition on the part some local church that one of its members is judged worthy to serve as a pastor. The fact that such appointment is generally recognized in all our churches is simply a testimony to denominational good faith. But we cannot modify these convictions for the sake of establishing a corporate unity with other denominations. Any compromise at this point would be an abandonment of structural beliefs.

We heartily believe in the necessity of combined impact of Christian forces upon the evil of the world. Such impact, however, does not depend for its efficiency upon organic union of the churches. For ourselves, we are convinced that our fundamental conception of the church, the nature of our organization, the democracy which is the very basis of our denominational life, make any organic union with groups of Christians holding opposite views unwise and impossible.

Report of the Commission on Faith and Order

In the year 1910, the Protestant Episcopal Church in America requested the various Protestant denominations to appoint commissions to unite with it in calling and arranging for a world conference to discuss the questions of Christian faith and order. All the larger and more conspicuous denominations of the Christian church in America have appointed the desired commissions. These were called in a general meeting in New York City three years ago, but the exigencies of the late war delayed the prosecuting of their main purpose. Prior to the war, the Episcopal commission enlisted the interest of the Established Church of England and the Free churches of Great Britain.

Your commission has had a number of informal conferences with representatives of the Episcopal Church. Its hope is that in a world conference we may arrive at some basis of faith and order upon which the divided Christian denominations may become united into one church of God and present a uniform witness of the gospel of the world. The Episcopal Church has a distinct connotation in the words "faith" and "order."

By "faith" it means some statement of belief, which may express the common experience of all Christians. It considers that such a statement has become sufficiently concrete and clear in the Nicene and Apostle's Creed. By the word "order" it means the nature, character, validity and function of the ministry in the church. Here also it is convinced that the divine order consists in the threefold office of deacons, priests and bishops, who receive their ordination through an historic episcopate. For it the sacraments are only valid when administered by a priesthood thus regularly ordained.

Since the cessation of war hostilities, the Episcopal commission has sent a deputation abroad to interview the heads of the Roman Catholic and Greek Orthodox churches, in the hope that they may also join in a world conference on the aforenamed issues.

From the meetings thus far held it has become evident to your commission that the Episcopal commission urges the necessity of Episcopal ordination as a primal necessity to validate the exercise of the ministry in the church. It proposes, however, a concession to the non-Episcopal clergy who may be willing to accept Episcopal ordination at the hands of Episcopal bishops. Ministers of other denominations seeking such ordination shall not be required to accept the Episcopal *theory*, but only the *fact* of the episcopate. It differentiates these terms, meaning by "theory" the doctrine of an unbroken historic succession of the ministry traceable to the apostles; whereas by the word "fact" it means that the Episcopal form of government has historically indicated itself as desirable and efficient. In thus accepting the fact without the theory, it hopes that the non-Episcopal churches, especially the ministers, may without the sacrifice of any vital principle see their way clear to act upon the ground of expediency, and so meet what is to the Episcopal communion a matter of conscience. Your commission has been unequivocal in its reply to these propositions. We have said to the Episcopal commission with utmost candor that the trend of our views and attitude is in the opposite direction from its, and that our convictions concerning ordinances, sacraments and ministry of the church are at such variance with its conceptions that we are convinced that its above named overtures would not elicit the interest, much less a serious consideration, on the part of our Baptist people. On these grounds there is nothing to hope for in the direction of church union.

One year ago, the General Assembly of Presbyterian Churches in the United States of America appointed a special committee to invite other committees representing the Protestant evangelical churches of the North to confer with it upon the proposition looking toward organic church union. The first meeting of these several committees was held in the city of Philadelphia in December, 1918. Some eighteen denominations were represented and the delegates numbered 1800. As our convention had no opportunity of appointing a special committee, the executive committee of the convention requested your commission on faith and order to represent the convention at this gathering. Several committees stated in formal manner the history and present attitude of their churches toward any movement in the direction of church union. Your commission was explicit in saying that it could not commit the denomination to any action, nor could it even reflect the sentiment of our many independent churches on such a subject. We ventured, however, to say that we desired to discover the leadings of the spirit of God and be found co-operating with all who are seeking to serve our generation according to the will of God. This general meeting appointed an ad interim committee, advising it to arrange for and call a national council to consider the question of organic church union, and to present some tentative plan upon which the discussion might proceed. Sub-committees are now working upon such plans and are expecting to call the council in November of this year, or early in 1920. They are petitioning the national denominational bodies, meeting during the spring or autumn, to appoint official delegates to attend such a council.

It is too early to premise or anticipate the propositions that may be laid before the national council. It is not designed to supersede any present organization of church co-operation such as the Federal Council of Churches, or to forestall any proposed movement such as the Interchurch World Movement. The desire is to co-operate with' all such agencies and, if possible, supply some element of united service in which every movement is only a part. It has become evident to us that organic church union, in the sense of common merging of all denominations into one general body, is neither possible, desirable nor expedient.

In the proposition so far considered, there has been a generous and sympathetic feeling for one another's convictions and an attempt to understand our several differences. There is no disposition to ask any church to discredit its past history, to reject its own traditions, or to forego its requirements for church membership or order of service.

Your commission desires to bear witness that in these meetings a most gracious and Christian attitude has been manifested. So far from our commission having to argue for and insist on the peculiar tenets which divided us from others, the delegates who differed from us not only sought intelligently to understand the grounds of such differences, but actually championed a just consideration of those things which are matters of honest conviction and conscience with us.

We expressed to the ad interim committee our belief that the churches of the Northern Baptist Convention welcome every manifestation of the leading of the spirit of God toward better relations between all Christian churches. They cannot, however, accept or consider any basis of union which implies the irregularity of their ministry, long blessed of God, and which is inconsistent with the priesthood of all believers and God's right to call any or whom he will into his service, or which may be based upon any other than the evangelical conception of the teaching of our Lord and his apostles.

Text—*The Standard*, May 31, 1919.

XXVI. *THE COLORADO HOME MISSIONS COUNCIL AND LEAGUE OF CHURCHES*

The Colorado Home Missions Council organized as a direct result of the Neglected Field Survey in 1910 adopted three years later the following Statement of Principles and Constitution. Subsequently it evolved a League of Churches as set forth below.

Colorado Home Missions Council

The signatory members of this Council believing in a practical demonstration and realization of our Lord's petition in John 17:21—"That they all may be one; as thou, Father, art in me, and I in thee, that they also may be one in us: that the world may believe that thou hast sent me."—agree on the following:

Statement of Principles

1. A community being served by one or more evangelical denominations should not be entered by any other denomination through its official agencies without conference with the denomination or denominations on the field.

2. A feeble church should be revived, if possible, rather than a new one established to become its rival.

3. The preference of a community should always be respected by denominational committees, missionary committees, individual workers, and other agencies.

4. Those denominations having churches nearest at hand, should, other things being equal, be recognized as in the most advantageous position to encourage and aid a new enterprise in their vicinity. This is to be so interpreted as to preserve the balance between efficiency and economy of administration.

5. Temporary suspension of church work by any denomination occupying a field should not be considered sufficient warrant in itself for entrance into that field by another denomination.

6. When it is clearly evident that a community is over-churched, the principle of affiliating the weaker church or churches, and of consolidating the entire Christian population in fewer and stronger churches, should be encouraged.

7. All cases of friction between different denominations or churches of different denominations shall be referred to the Executive Committee. It shall have power to constitute an Advisory Committee for such cases under Article 5 of the Constitution.

8. All questions of interpretation of foregoing statement shall be referred for decision to the Executive Committee.

Constitution

ARTICLE I—NAME

This organization shall be called the COLORADO HOME MISSIONS COUNCIL, Auxiliary to the National Home Missions Council.

ARTICLE II—OBJECT

Section 1—The object of the Council shall be the promotion of effective co-operation among the churches and Christian workers of Colorado, that their sense of unity be manifested; that the evangelization of every community may be more systematically accomplished; that a means may be found for expressing the united Christian sentiment of the State in regard to moral issues, that the various Christian and benevolent activities of the State may be more completely co-ordinated; and that other appropriate ends may be secured.

Section 2—It shall be its object to promote co-operation in the organization and maintenance of evangelical churches in Colorado; to prevent waste of resources and effort in small communities; and to stimulate missionary work in the destitute regions.

ARTICLE III—ANNUAL AND QUARTERLY MEETINGS

. . . .

ARTICLE IV—OFFICERS

. . . .

ARTICLE V—EXECUTIVE COMMITTEE

. . . .

Section 2—It shall be the duty of the Executive Committee to recommend to the Council for its action such rules and regulations as shall be necessary to make effective the work of the Council and to make annual report of the Council to each affiliating denomination and agency.

Section 3—It shall be the duty of the Executive Committee to act on matters arising under Statement of Principles Number 7, as follows:

(a) Direct the interested parties to make an earnest effort to settle differences through their Home Mission or general field representative or superintendent.

(b) Failing in this, petition the Secretary of the Council, who shall proceed as per Article 7 of the Statement of Principles, when the Executive Committee shall name an Advisory Committee of three or five connected with denominations other than the parties concerned. This Advisory Committee shall hear the testimony on both sides, carefully weigh the same, and give a written decision to the parties concerned, and to the Secretary of the Council for record. Provided, however, that notice of time and place at least one month in advance of hearing shall have been given the local parties interested, each of which shall have the privilege of being represented by Counsel, consisting of two persons agreeable to the Advisory Committee.

(c) In cases of controversy three methods or procedure are to be undertaken by the Executive Committee:

(1) The matter shall first be taken to the state officials of the denomination in question:

(2) If this fails, the Executive Committee shall take the matter directly to the officers of the National Society of the offending denomination;

(3) And if this fails, a campaign of education on comity may be undertaken by the Executive Committee in the local community affected.

Section 4—Working agreement. Where a new church organization is contemplated in a community where a church of another denomination already exists, the Field Worker of the denomination proposing the new church is expected to first advise the Executive Committee of the Home Missions Council and secure its consent for the organization of the proposed new church. Any refusal upon the part of the Executive Committee of the Council to grant such consent may be appealed to a vote of the Home Missions Council.

ARTICLE VI—DEPARTMENTS

Section 1—Department of City and County Organization.

A Commission of three members shall be elected by the Council at its annual meeting whose duty it shall be to promote the organization of City and County or District Church Councils, which shall be auxiliaries to the Colorado Home Missions Council.

Section 2—Department of Field Work.

A Commission of three members shall be elected by the Council at its Annual meeting whose duty it shall be:

(a) To investigate by survey or other means fields which in their judgment afford opportunity for constructive evangelization.

(b) To make a full report of such findings at a regular or called meeting of the Council together with definite recommendations as to the line of procedure that in their judgment may be indicated.

(c) Upon the receipt of such reports and recommendations, it shall be the duty of the Council to give due consideration to the case in hand, and the commission shall be intrusted and empowered with the introduction and application of such plans as may be agreed upon by a two-thirds vote of the members present at any meeting in which the recommendations of this Commission shall be received and considered.

Section 3—Department of Union, Federated and Community Churches.

A Commission of three members of the Council shall be elected whose duty it shall be to co-operate with all union, federated, or community churches, not identified with any denomination, in such a way as to help them realize their greatest usefulness.

(a) It shall be the duty of this commission to get in touch with all such churches and report conditions prevailing in the work of these churches.

(b) Representatives of this commission shall visit these churches with a view to lending helpful co-operation.

(c) This Commission shall urge all such churches to contribute to missionary causes.

(d) This Committee should suggest to these churches that they contribute to the Colorado Home Missions Council money for home missions purposes, this money to be spent in such ways as the Council may advise.

ARTICLE VII—AMENDMENTS

By-Laws

1. Members. The members of the Council shall consist of the Field Workers and Chairman of Home Missions Committees of all affiliating evangelical denominations and the State field workers of the following interdenominational organizations: The Young Men's Christian Association, the Colorado Sunday School Association, and the American Sunday School Union, together with two delegates from each city, county, or district church council, and a lay member named from each denomination by its state organization or delegation in the Missions Council.

District and Local Organizations

1. The Home Missions Council invites the organization of local and district Councils to further its interests throughout the state.

Such Councils should make surveys of unchurched districts and make recommendations to the Home Missions Council;

Should hear any complaints arising from over-churching in their respective districts and decide such cases, with right of appeal to the Missions Council;

Should give publicity to the principles of the Council and in every way extend the influence of these principles;

Should in all cities and locations act as a church federation to carry out all the common purposes of the churches.

2. Such organizations should be based on the principles already accepted by the Council:

Should appoint officers and a Committee to see to the effective carrying out of these principles in their locality;

Should include members of all denominations working in conjunction with the Council, as comity must rest on assured equity.

Where the organization is a district organization it may appoint local committees to represent it in the towns and centers of the district.

3. The Council suggests the following proposed Home Missions Council districts, centers and territory:

....

Statement

The Colorado Home Missions Council presents the following articles to the various denominational church bodies of Colorado, for consideration and adoption. The wide spread and growing desire of the people of the towns and villages, and suburban sections of the state for some plan of local religious co-operation must be met sympathetically. The strength and wisdom of denominationalism in this arrangement is given to the initiation, propagation and supervision of a work that challenges the unselfish interest and support of a United Church. The plan proposed provides for the incorporation of a League of Churches in accord with the following suggested provisions.

Suggested Articles of Incorporation

1. The corporate name of this Association shall be "The League of Churches of Colorado."
2. The particular business and objects for which this Association is formed shall be
   (a) The encouragement and fostering of the religious life of certain communities within the State of Colorado.
   (b) The incorporation shall have full powers to own or lease property within the state, both real and personal.
3. The number of directors shall be not less than six.
4. The directors for the first year shall be:

Suggested By-Laws

ARTICLE 1. MEMBERSHIP

Sec. 1. The membership of the League shall consist of one delegate from each religious body having a membership of ten thousand or less, two delegates from bodies of more than ten thousand but less than twenty thousand, and three delegates from bodies of twenty thousand or more within the state of Colorado which shall, by proper action of its Conference, Convention, Association or other authorized State body approve the purposes of the incorporation and elect its delegates according to the provisions of the incorporation's by-laws.

Sec. 2. All churches under the direction or supervision of the League shall be organized into a working State Association which shall in turn, be entitled to two delegates in the membership of the league.

ARTICLE 2. PURPOSES

Sec. 1. The League shall assume fostering direction over the organized religious life of any community within the State of Colorado which shall, by a vote of two-thirds of its church membership, express a desire for a larger church program and request such a relationship.

Sec. 2. It may organize non-denominational churches in any communities within the state not being served at the time by effective church organization.

Sec. 3. In all local church organizations organized and fostered by the League, the requirements for church membership shall be determined by the local church.

Sec. 1.   The local Community Church shall be required by the League to make regular offerings for Missions and other designated agencies for the extension of the work of the Kingdom of Jesus Christ.

Sec. 2.   The funds given for Home Missions by the churches, under the direction and supervision of the League, shall be expended for the extension of the work of the League and may be appropriated to any Home Missions projects designated by a majority vote of the Board of Directors.

Sec. 3.   The Board of Directors, after requesting submission of suitable suggestions from the Board of Foreign Missions of each of the denominations represented in the League, shall designate the projects on the foreign mission field to which the foreign missionary offerings of the churches under the supervision of the League shall be appropriated for the ensuing calendar year, and the Directors shall specify the amount to be appropriated to each project.

Text—Pamphlets: *The Colorado Home Missions Council;* and *Proposed League of Churches of Colorado.*

XXVII.   *EPISCOPALIAN-CONGREGATIONALIST NEGO-TIATIONS TOWARD UNION*

The following statement sets forth the negotiations between Episcopalians and Congregationalists.

Proposals for An Approach Towards Unity

The undersigned, members of the Protestant Episcopal Church and of Congregational Churches, without any official sanction and purely on our private initiative, have conferred with each other, partly by correspondence and partly by meeting, with a view to discover a method by which a practical approach towards making clear and evident the visible unity of believers in our Lord according to his will, might be made. For there can be no question that such is our Lord's will. The Church itself, in the midst of its divisions, bears convincing witness to it. "There is one Body and one Spirit, one Lord, one Faith, one Baptism." There has never been, there can never be, more than one Body or one Baptism. On this we are agreed. There is one fellowship of the Baptized, made one by grace, and in every case by the self-same grace. And the unity given and symbolized by Baptism is in its very nature visible.

We are agreed that it is our Lord's purpose that believers in Him should be one visible society. Into such a society, which we recognize as the Holy Catholic Church, they are initiated by Baptism; whereby they are admitted to fellowship with Him and with one another. The unity which is essential to his Church's effective witness and work in the world must express and maintain this fellowship. It cannot be fully realized without community of worship, faith, and order, including common participation in the Lord's Supper. Such unity would be compatible with a rich diversity in life and worship.

We have not discussed the origin of the episcopate historically or its authority doctrinally; but we agree to acknowledge that the recognized position of the episcopate in the greater part of Christendom as the normal nucleus of the Church's ministry and as the organ of the unity and continuity of the Church is such that the members of the episcopal Churches ought not to be expected to abandon it in assenting to any basis of reunion.

We also agree to acknowledge that Christian Churches not accepting the episcopal order have been used by the Holy Spirit in his work of enlightening the world, converting sinners, and perfecting saints. They came into being through reactions from grave abuses in the Church at the time of their origin, and were led in response to fresh apprehensions of divine truth to give expression to certain necessary and permanent types of Christian experience, aspiration and fellowship, and to secure rights of Christian people which had been neglected or denied.

No Christian community is involved in the necessity of disowning its past; but it should bring its own distinctive contribution not only to the common life of the Church, but also to its methods of organization. Many customs and institutions which have been developed in separate communities may be preserved within the larger unity. What we desire to see is not grudging concession, but a willing acceptance of the treasures of each for the common enrichment of the united Church.

To give full effect to these principles in relation to the Churches to which we respectively belong requires some form of corporate union between them. We greatly desire such corporate union. We also are conscious of the difficulties in the way of bringing it about, including the necessity for corporate action, even with complete good will on both sides. In this situation we believe that a practical approach toward eventual union may be made by the establishment of intercommunion in particular instances. It is evident to us that corporate union between bodies whose members have become so related will thereby be facilitated. Mutual understanding and sympathy will strongly reinforce the desire to be united in a common faith and order, and will make clearer how the respective contributions of each community can best be made available to all.

We recognize as a fact, without discussing whether it is based upon sound foundations, that in the episcopal Churches an apprehension exists that if episcopally conferred orders were added to the authority which non-episcopal ministers have received from their own communions, such orders might not be received and used in all cases in the sense or with the intention with which they are conferred. Upon this point there ought to be no room for doubt. The sense or intention in which any particular order of the ministry is conferred or accepted is the sense or intention in which it is held in the Universal Church. In conferring or in accepting such ordination neither the bishop ordaining nor the minister ordained should be understood to impugn thereby the efficacy of the minister's previous ministry.

The like principle applies to the ministration of sacraments. The minister acts not merely as the representative of the particular congregation then present, but in a larger sense he represents the Church Universal; and his intention and meaning should be our Lord's intention and meaning as delivered to and held by the Catholic Church. To this end such sacramental matter and form should be used as shall exhibit the intention of the Church.

When communion has been established between the ordaining bishop of the Episcopal Church and the ordained minister of another communion, appropriate measures ought to be devised to maintain it by participating in the sacrament of the Lord's Supper and by mutual counsel and co-operation.

We are not unmindful that occasions may arise when it might become necessary to take cognizance of supposed error of faith or of conduct, and suitable provision ought to be made for such cases.

In view of the limitations imposed by the law and practice of the Episcopal Church upon its bishops with regard to ordination, and the necessity of obtaining the approval of the General Convention of the Episcopal Church to the project we have devised, a form of canonical sanction has been prepared which is appended as a schedule to this statement. We who are members of the Episcopal Church are prepared to recommend its enactment. We who are members of Congregational Churches regard it as a wise basis upon which in the interests of Church unity, and without sacrifice on either side, the supplementary ordination herein contemplated might be accepted.

It is our conviction that such procedure as we here outline is in accordance, as far as it goes, with our Lord's purposes for his Church; and our fond hope is that it would contribute to heal the Church's divisions. In the mission field it might prove of great value in uniting the work. In small communities it might put an end to the familiar scandal of more churches than the spiritual needs of the people require. In the army and navy, chaplains so ordained could minister acceptably to the adherents of Christian bodies who feel compunctions about the regularity of a non-episcopal ministry. In all places an example of a practical approach to Christian unity, with the recognition of diversities in organization and in worship, would be held up before the world. The will to unity would be strengthened, prejudices would be weakened, and the way would become open in the light of experience to bring about a more complete organic unity of Christian Churches.

While this plan is the result of conference in which members of only one denomination of non-episcopal Churches have taken part, it is comprehensive enough to include in its scope ministers of all other non-episcopal communions; and we earnestly invite their sympathetic consideration and concurrence.

New York, March 12, 1919.

BOYD VINCENT,
Bishop of Southern Ohio

PHILIP M. RHINELANDER,
Bishop of Pennsylvania

WILLIAM H. DAY,
Moderator of Congregational National Council

HUBERT C. HERRING,
Sec. of National Council

. . . .

SCHEDULE
Form of Proposed Canon

I. In case any minister who has not received episcopal ordination shall desire to be ordained by a Bishop of this Church to the Diaconate and to the Priesthood without giving up or denying his membership or his ministry in the Communion to which he belongs, the Bishop of the Diocese or Missionary District in which he lives, with the advice and consent of the Standing Committee or the Council of Advice, may confirm and ordain him.

II. The minister desiring to be so ordained shall satisfy the Bishop that he has resided in the United States at least one year; that he has been duly baptized with water in the name of the Trinity; that he holds the historic faith of the Church as contained in the Apostles' Creed and the Nicene Creed; that there is no sufficient objection on grounds physical, mental, moral or spiritual; and that the ecclesiastical authority to which he is subject in the Communion to which he belongs consents to such ordination.

III. At the time of his ordination the person to be ordained shall subscribe and make in the presence of the Bishop a declaration that he believes the Holy Scriptures of the Old and New Testaments to be the Word of God and to contain all things necessary to salvation; that in the ministration of Baptism he will unfailingly baptize with water in the name of the Father and of the Son and of the Holy Ghost; and (if he is being ordained to the Priesthood) that in the celebration of the Holy Communion he will invariably use the elements of bread and wine, and will include in the service the words and acts of our Lord in the institution of the Sacrament, the Lord's Prayer, and (unless one of these Creeds has been used in the service immediately preceding the celebration of the Holy Communion) the Apostles, or the Nicene Creed as the symbol of the faith of the Holy Catholic Church; that when thereto invited by the Bishop of this Church having jurisdiction in the place where he lives, he will (unless unavoidably prevented) meet with such Bishop for Communion and for counsel and co-operation; and that he will hold himself answerable to the Bishop of this Church having jurisdiction in the place where he lives, or if there be no such Bishop, to the Presiding Bishop of this Church, in case he be called in question with respect to error of faith or of conduct.

IV. In case a person so ordained be charged with error of faith or of conduct he shall have reasonable notice of the charge and reasonable opportunity to be heard, and the procedure shall be similar to the procedure in the case of a clergyman of this Church charged with the like offense. The sentence shall always be pronounced by the Bishop and shall be such as a clergyman of this Church would be liable to. It shall be certified to the ecclesiastical authority to which the defendant is responsible in any other Communion. If he shall have been tried before a tribunal of the Communion in which he has exercised his ministry, the judgment of such tribunal proceeding in the due exercise of its jurisdiction shall be taken as conclusive evidence of facts thereby adjudged.

V. A minister so ordained may officiate in a Diocese or Missionary District of this Church when licensed by the ecclesiastical authority thereof, but he shall not become the Rector or a minister of any parish or congregation of this Church until he shall have subscribed and made to the Ordinary a declaration in writing whereby he shall solemnly engage to conform to the doctrine, discipline and worship of this Church. Upon his making such declaration and being duly elected Rector or minister of a parish or congregation of this Church, and complying with the canons of this Church and of the Diocese or Missionary District in that behalf, he shall become for all purposes a Minister of this Church.

At the Convention in October 1919 the Episcopalians ratified this Concordat in the following resolution:

1. That the General Convention recognizes with profound gratitude to Almighty God the earnest desire of these representative members of Congregational Churches and of this Church to find a way by which the first step toward eventual Church Unity may be taken, and especially the irenic attitude of those who are not in communion with this Church, but who have indicated their desire to enter into certain relations with it for the furtherance of that unity for which we together pray.

2. That as a step toward the accomplishment of so great a purpose, this Church declares its willingness *to initiate action that may make it possible*[1] to enact legislation

---

[1] Words italicized were added by the House of Bishops.

such as shall permit the ordination as Deacons and as Priests of Ministers in other Christian bodies, who accept the Holy Scriptures as the revealed word of God, the Nicene Creed as a sufficient statement of the Christian faith, and the Sacraments of Baptism and the Supper of the Lord, under conditions which are stated in the afore-mentioned Proposals for an Approach Toward Unity, whenever evidence shall be laid by any applicant Minister before the Bishop of this Church having jurisdiction in the place in which such minister resides, of his acceptance of the principles set forth in these Proposals.

We, however, direct the Joint Commission to be constituted that in proposing such legislation the following points shall be carefully considered:

Text—Pamphlet: *Proposals for An Approach Towards Unity.*

XXVIII. *THE UNITED CHURCHES OF CHRIST IN AMERICA*

The following Constitution with slight verbal changes was adopted at the Interdenominational Council on Organic Union which met in Philadelphia Feb. 3–6, 1920. The comments and recommendations of the Ad Interim Committee are attached.

PREAMBLE

WHEREAS: we desire to share, as a common heritage, the faith of the Evangelical churches, which has, from time to time, found expression in great historic statements; and

Whereas: we all share belief in God our Father; in Jesus Christ, his only Son, our Saviour; in the Holy Spirit, our Guide and Comforter; in the Holy Catholic Church, through which God's eternal purpose of salvation is both to be proclaimed and realized; in the Scriptures of the Old and New Testaments as containing God's revealed will, and in the life eternal; and

WHEREAS: having the same spirit and owning the same Lord, we none the less recognize diversity of gifts and ministrations for whose exercise due freedom must always be afforded in forms of worship and in modes of operation:

PLAN

Now, we the churches hereto assenting as hereinafter provided in Article VI do hereby agree to associate ourselves in a visible body to be known as the "United Churches of Christ in America," for the furtherance of the redemptive work of Christ in the world. This body shall exercise in behalf of the constituent churches the functions delegated to it by this instrument, or by subsequent action of the constituent churches, which shall retain the full freedom at present enjoyed by them in all matters not so delegated.

Accordingly, the churches hereto assenting and hereafter thus associated in such visible body do mutually covenant and agree as follows:

I. *Complete autonomy in purely denominational affairs.*

In the interest of the freedom of each and of the coöperation of all, each constituent church reserves the right to retain its creedal statements, its form of government in the conduct of its own affairs, and its particular mode of worship:

In taking this step, we look forward with confident hope to that complete unity toward which we believe the Spirit of God is leading us. Once we shall have coöperated wholeheartedly, in such visible body, in the holy activities of the work of the church, we are persuaded that our differences will be minimized and our union become more vital and effectual.

II. *The Council.* (Its Constitution.)

The United Churches of Christ in America shall act through a Council or through such Executive and Judicial Commissions, or Administrative Boards, working *ad interim*, as such Council may from time to time appoint and ordain.

The Council shall convene in 19— and every second year thereafter. It may also be convened at any time in such manner as its own rules may prescribe. The Council shall be a representative body.

Each constituent church shall be entitled to representation therein by an equal number of ministers and of laymen.

The basis of representation shall be: two ministers and two laymen for the first one hundred thousand or fraction thereof of its communicants; and two ministers and two laymen for each additional one hundred thousand or major fraction thereof.

III. *The Council.* (Its Working.)

The Council shall adopt and promulgate its own rules of procedure and order. It shall define the functions of its own officers, prescribe the mode of their selection and their compensation, if any. It shall provide for its budget of expense by equitable apportionment of the same among the constituent churches through their supreme governing or advisory bodies.

IV. *Relation of Council and Constituent Churches.*

The supreme governing or advisory bodies of the constituent churches shall effectuate the decisions of the Council by general or specific deliverance or other mandate whenever it may be required by the law of a particular state, or the charter of a particular Board, or other ecclesiastical corporation; but, except as limited by this Plan, shall continue the exercise of their several powers and functions as the same exist under the denominational constitution.

The Council shall give full faith and credit to the authenticated acts and records of the several governing or advisory bodies of the constituent churches.

V. *Specific Functions of the Council.*

In order to prevent overlapping, friction, competition or waste in the work of the existing denominational boards or administrative agencies, and to further the efficiency of that degree of coöperation which they have already achieved in their work at home and abroad:

(*a*) The Council shall harmonize and unify the work of the United Churches.

(*b*) It shall direct such consolidation of their missionary activities as well as of particular churches in over-churched areas as is consonant with the law of the land or of the particular denomination affected. Such consolidation may be progressively achieved, as by the uniting of the boards or churches of any two or more constituent denominations, or may be accelerated, delayed, or dispensed with, as the interests of the United Churches may demand.

(*c*) If and when any two or more constituent churches, by their supreme governing or advisory bodies, submit to the Council for its arbitrament any matter of mutual concern, not hereby already covered, the Council shall consider and pass upon such matter so submitted.

The Council shall undertake inspirational and educational leadership of such sort and measure as may be decided upon by the constituent churches from time to time in the fields of Evangelism, Social Service, Religious Education, or the like.

VI. The assent of each constituent church to this Plan shall be certified from its supreme governing or advisory body by the appropriate officers thereof to the Chairman of the Ad Interim Committee, which shall have power to convene the Council as soon as the assent of at least six denominations shall have been so certified.

Your Ad Interim Committee submitting this draft of a plan would respectfully emphasize the following features thereof:

(a) That it is in the nature of a federal union in that the constituent churches coöperate in the furtherance of Christ's redemptive work in the world through an independent body by which their various joint activities are mediated.

(b) That it is an organic union in that it has the vital principle of growth and development; that the Council has definite functions and duties, and that these functions and duties may from time to time be developed in like manner as the functions of our federal government in the United States of America may from time to time, by Constitutional Amendment, be modified or enlarged.

Among the papers that are submitted with this report subject to the orders of Council are the successive reports of the Sub-Committee on Plan, recording the inadvisability of attempting to achieve by one step what may more orderly and surely be accomplished by several steps, and in particular the following from the third report of such Sub-Committee (see page 15 of "Paper E."). "In order to progress, the first step must be taken in the right direction . . . the plan of federal union (that is, by uniting the churches through the mediation of a Council that shall have real powers of review and control and unify the work of all the communions participating), will have this result: That, after it shall have been in operation for a term of years, the importance of divisive names and creeds and methods will pass more and more into the dim background of the past, and acquire, even in the particular denomination itself, a merely -historical value, and that the churches then will be ready for and will demand a more complete union; so that what was the *United Churches* of Christ in America can become the *United Church* of Christ in America, a real ecclesiastical entity, with ecclesiastical powers, holding and administering ecclesiastical property and funds of such united church.

Accordingly this Committee has submitted but one plan with its recommendation, but there appear in the Blue Book (Pages —), submitted with this report, among the other plans considered by your Ad Interim Committee, documents embodying plans of such complete united church, with more specific articulations of powers and functions, which can be preserved for the consideration of the Council at some future time when it may be deemed expedient to take a further step in the direction of organic union.

We respectfully submit that the form of union at present commended for the consideration of the Council does not interject into its deliberation any disputatious topic, any question of the validity of orders or of the modes and subjects of baptism or of the formulation of a specific or comprehensive creed. But that we contemplate a preliminary period of coöperating in this union that shall fulfill the hope and longing expressed by the Conference (see p. 25, "Paper A"), "That the evangelical churches may give themselves with a new faith and ardor to the proclamation of the Gospel, which is the only hope of our stricken world, and to all those ministries of Christian love and leading for the community, the nation and the nations, by which they shall reveal to men the mind of Christ and hasten the coming of his Kingdom."

We call to the notice of the Council that the taking of this first step toward unity will not call for a present report on any legal questions since denominational autonomy is continued and no property rights impaired.

Recommendations

First. We recommend that the foregoing plan be placed upon the docket of the Council for its consideration and action.

Second. We recommend that, in contemplation of the fact that in the various groups of churches belonging to the same denomination mergers or unions may from time to time occur by appropriate ecclesiastical action and resulting in the creation of new or consolidated denominations: the Council should establish a commission to be known as "The Commission on Group Union of Constituent Bodies," for the purpose of conferring with any communion about to merge or consolidate, with a view if possible to the unification of the constitutions of such consolidating churches in order to simplify the progress of all the churches toward the ultimate adoption of a constitution for the United Church of Christ in America.

Third. We recommend that the Council consider, and if deemed advisable, make provision for its relationship to such independent, unattached, or so-called union or community churches which shall hold to the faith commonly held in the Council as shall in time effectually relate them in this movement for the organic union of the evangelical churches of America.

Fourth. We recommend that the attention of the constituent churches be called to the fact that the assent called by Article VI of the Plan should be secured in conformity with the constitution of each constituent church.

The constitution of the *United Church of America* referred to in the foregoing document as the ultimate of this union movement, is as follows:

ARTICLE I. NAME

The name of this body shall be the United Church of America.

ARTICLE II. MEMBERSHIP

It shall consist of all denominations and local churches which accept this Constitution and are admitted to membership by the National Conference of the United Church.

ARTICLE III. FAITH

The United Church recognizes in the historic creeds of the evangelical communions varying expressions of their common Christian faith. It shares their belief in God the Father, Infinite in wisdom, goodness and love; and in Jesus Christ, his Son, our Lord and Saviour, who for us and our salvation lived and died and rose again and liveth evermore; in the Holy Spirit, who taketh of the things of Christ and revealeth them to us, renewing, comforting, and inspiring the souls of men; in the Holy Scriptures by which the will of God is revealed; in the Church, the living body of Christ; and in life eternal beyond the grave. It accords its members both as groups and as individuals in all lesser matters that broad liberty wherewith Christ has set us free.

Each local church belonging to the United Church will have authority over the following matters:—

(a) The control of property held by it. See (n) below.

(b) The terms of admission of members on confession of faith.

(c) The times and modes of administering the Sacraments, save as limited by (j) and (k) below.

(d) The initiative in the settling or dismissal of a pastor. See Article V (e) below.

(e) The forms of worship used.

(f) The discipline of members save as limited by V (f) below.

(g) The causes to which it shall contribute and the amounts to be given for the same.

In the interest of fraternity, order and union of effort, each church becoming a member of the United Church agrees to the following:—

(h) It will receive into its membership, without other condition, any person bearing a certificate of dismission from any church of the United Church.

(i) It will maintain the stated observance of the sacraments of baptism and the Lord's Supper in the use of the words and acts prescribed in the New Testament.

(j) It will make careful and fraternal provision for administering baptism by immersion to those who desire that form.

(k) It will make provision for administration of infant baptism either statedly or (if baptism of adults only be its regular mode) at the request of parents, a neighboring pastor being asked to officiate if needful.

(l) It will recognize the authority of the District Council in whose territory it is located on the matters and within the limits described below.

(m) It will participate through statedly chosen delegates in the meetings of its District Council.

(n) It will make definite legal provision for the reversion of its property to the Synod of its State, if it shall cease to exist as a church and for a decision by a Board of Appraisers (see below) as to the respective equities of itself and the United Church in its property in case it withdraws from the United Church.

Local churches belonging to the United Church shall be grouped geographically into District Councils of such size as shall appear expedient. Each church shall be represented in the Council by its pastor and one delegate, with an additional delegate for each 100 members or major fraction thereof.

The powers and duties of the District Council shall be as follows:—

(a) To pass upon applications for ordination to the ministry and to ordain the candidates accepted.

(b) To pass upon applications for acceptance made by ministers of other communions and, in case of those received, to require reordination if deemed desirable. All ministers received under this section or under (a) above become ministers of the United Church, their membership being thenceforth not in a local church, but in a District Council, by which they may be transferred to other Councils. In the case of communions initially joining to form the United Church in case of any communion thereafter accepted as a body, all ministers become *ipso facto* ministers of the United Church.

(c) To have oversight of the ministers enrolled in its membership with power of discipline or expulsion under conditions prescribed by the National Conference.

(d) To have oversight of the churches enrolled in its membership calling their attention to any failure to meet obligations assumed under this constitution and with power to terminate the membership of any church persistently refusing to meet those obligations.

(e) To receive from the churches within its bounds nominations to vacant pulpits and to pass upon the same. Approval of such nomination shall be requisite for the establishment of the pastoral relation whether in the form of temporary supply or of installation. The National Conference shall present the details under which this relationship shall be conducted.

(f) To hear and pass upon appeals from decisions of local churches.

(g) To collect from each church in its membership an annual sum not exceeding 25 cents per member, the same to be known as "Council Dues." With the amount thus collected the Council shall meet its own expenses and its share of the administrative expenses of the State Synod and the National Conference.

(h) To serve the churches in its membership on all the lines of practical church life as opportunity may offer.

(i) To share in the general life and work of the United Church under plans adopted by the National Conference.

(j) To conform in its organization, times of meeting and procedure to the general plan prescribed by the National Conference.

ARTICLE VI. THE STATE SYNOD

The churches in each state (contiguous states being grouped or single states being divided if circumstances suggest) shall form a State Synod. It shall consist of five delegates from each District Council and five additional delegates for each 25 churches or major fraction thereof in such Council. Its duties shall be as follows:

(a) To have charge of such missionary work within its bounds as may be assigned it under the general plan adopted by the National Conference. This duty includes the educational and Sunday school field as well as the church field.

(b) To have charge of the promotion of beneficence within its bounds.

(c) To support the Bishop or Bishops chosen by it in the prosecution of his or their duties.

(d) To form a legal incorporation to receive, hold and administer property given or bequeathed, also church properties reverting under Article IV (n) above.

(e) To make provision under general plans adopted by the National Conference for appraisal and division of church properties under Article IV (n) above.

(f) To promote relations of fellowship and to give inspirational leadership among the churches composing it.

(g) To hear and pass upon appeals from decisions of District Councils, such appeals being limited to questions on which the Council has original jurisdiction.

The central authority in the United Church shall be vested in the National Conference. It shall meet annually and shall be composed of two delegates chosen by each Synod, with two additional for such number of churches in each Synod as shall make the Conference membership not less than 500 nor more than 1000 at any time.

The duties and powers of the National Conference shall be as follows:—

(a) To receive and pass upon applications for membership in the United Church, whether by local churches or denominational bodies. Assignment of churches thus received to District Councils shall be made by the Conference or delegated by it to the Synod.

(b) To organize, control and conduct all missionary operations of the United Church. In the discharge of this duty it will assign such functions and authority to Synods and Councils as it deems expedient.

(c) To maintain and direct such Commissions, Committees or officials in the fields of evangelism, social service, etc., as may seem needful to give due leadership to the thought and work of the churches. It may require the appointment of corresponding committees in Synods and Councils.

(d) To maintain a national office for collection and dissemination of statistical and other information and for rendering assistance to committees of the Conference not having other executive service at their disposal.

(e) To represent the United Church in relations with other religious bodies and with the civil authorities where needful.

(f) To make regulations for the orderly and uniform operation of the provisions of this Constitution as related to Synods and Councils.

(g) To provide for all matters of common concern not reserved by this Constitution to Synods, Councils or local churches.

(h) To allocate to the Councils the raising of such annual sums as are required for the maintenance of its national office, payment of expenses of delegates to its meetings, etc.

(i) To hear and pass upon appeals from Synods, such appeals being limited to matters in which the Synod has original jurisdiction.

(j) To provide for such officials of oversight in the Synods as may prove expedient.

ARTICLE VIII. AMENDMENTS

This Constitution may be amended by a majority vote of two General Conferences, provided that in the intervening period the proposed amendment receives the approval of two-thirds of the District Councils.

Text—Pamphlet: *Reports and Plans for the Interchurch Council on Organic Union.*

XXIX. RELIGIOUS EDUCATION IN THE MODERN CHURCH

The following program, issued 1915, by the Baptists is representative of what many progressive churches in several denominations are endeavoring to carry through.

A. INTRODUCTION

I. The task of every church is (a) to provide means of worship, (b) to evangelize the community in which it exists, (c) to educate its members and its young people especially, (d) to organize them for service.

II. Religious education must be carried on with (a) a definite purpose to cultivate the religious nature so as to get a response to spiritual forces, and an adoption of a high standard of personal Christian life; (b) thorough organization by means of the Sunday-school, the young people's society, and men's and womens's organizations; (c) efficient instruction by means of graded courses and trained teachers.

III. The purpose of education can be achieved by (a) an appeal to the emotions through forms of worship and a study of human life; (b) an appeal to the intellect through Bible study and Christian history and doctrine; (c) an appeal to the will through training in right habits and character study.

IV. Thorough organization can be secured by (a) definite organization of each study group in the church; (b) cooperation of the various groups in the church to prevent omissions or duplications; (c) grading the Sunday-school, and giving it proper superintendence.

V. Efficient instruction can be obtained by (a) making the teacher's effort worth while through the adoption of a good curriculum, occasional tests of the pupils, and a policy of religious promotion; (b) encouraging and providing for teacher-training.

B. ORGANIZATION

I. THE COMMITTEE ON RELIGIOUS EDUCATION.

1. Its *members:* Pastor (who shall be chairman), superintendent of the Sunday-school, a representative of the men's organization, a representative of the women's societies, a representative of the young people's societies, and a representative of the Social Service Committee—these last four to be selected for educational qualifications.

2. Its *duties:* (a) To serve as a church cabinet on all work in religious education; (b) to unify and coordinate work in Sunday-school, young people's society, and men's and women's organizations, and to provide a unified program of religious education in the church; (c) to pass upon courses of study and standards of graduation and promotion; (d) to determine teaching qualifications, and appoint, on the superintendent's recommendation, all teachers in the educational work; (e) to promote the interest of the church in religious education and secure adequate support for this work.

3. Its *organization:* The pastor and superintendent are members by virtue of their respective offices. Other members are elected at the annual church meeting to serve one year. The committee may organize itself into subcommittees on courses of study, cooperation of organizations, worship, recreation, and community service.

4. Its *meetings:* These should be held monthly, or at the call of the pastor, the superintendent, or any three members.

II. THE SUNDAY-SCHOOL.

1. Its *purpose:* To develop efficient character by means of definite, organized, and carefully selected instruction in the Bible and in the religious life. It deals particularly with youth. It is 'the school of the church,' meeting on Sunday for class study.

2. Its *officers:* In a church of this size the leadership of the pastor in all religious education must be kept in mind.

    a. The Superintendent.
    b. The Assistant Superintendent, . . .
    c. The Secretary, . . .
    d. The Treasurer, . . .
    e. The Librarian, . . .
    f. The Director of Music, . . .

NOTE. All these officers are chosen annually by the church on nomination of the Committee on Religious Education.

g. The School Cabinet of all the above officers, together with all teachers. This body should meet once a month to consider the progress of the school and to advise together on problems as they arise.

3. Its *classification:* All pupils are grouped in classes:

a. Beginners', all pupils under six years of age.

b. Primary, all pupils of six, seven, and eight years of age.

c. Junior, all pupils of nine, ten, eleven, and twelve years of age.

d. Intermediate, all pupils of thirteen, fourteen, fifteen, and sixteen years of age.

e. Senior, all pupils of seventeen, eighteen, nineteen, and twenty years of age.

f. Advanced, all pupils over twenty years of age.

NOTE. If it seems advisable on account of sex or numbers to divide these classes, let each division be lettered A, B, C, etc. In very small schools the first two and the last two may be united.

g. Training, all pupils over sixteen preparing to teach or work in school.

h. Home Department, including all persons unable to attend the sessions of the school who may be enrolled for regular study of the lesson at home.

III. Other educational departments of the church may properly organize themselves and arrange their educational courses at their own discretion, but in coöperation with the Committee on Religious Education.

C. COURSES OF STUDY

I. THE SUNDAY-SCHOOL.

The Graded Series of the International Lessons is well adapted for general use, and contains the following subjects of study:

1. *Beginners' Course.* Aim: To lead the little child to the Father.

a. First year. The loving care of God and the love of children in return.

b. Second year. God's protection and help, and children as helpers.

2. *Primary Course.* Aim: To lead the child to know the heavenly Father, and to inspire within him a desire to live as God's child.

a. First year. God's power, love, and care, and the child's response.

b. Second year. Jesus the Saviour, and the helpers of Jesus doing his will.

c. Third year. Stories of Jesus and other Bible characters who did God's will.

3. *Junior Course.* Aim: To awaken interest in the Bible, to present high ideals, to deepen personal responsibility, and show what it means to be a Christian.

a. First year. Stories of the Old Testament and parables of Jesus.

b. Second year. Bible stories from the Old and New Testaments.

c. Third year. Old Testament tales, with four temperance lessons, and an introduction to the New Testament.

d. Fourth year. Mark's Gospel and studies in the Acts, with missionary stories and five lessons on the structure and contents of the Bible.

4. *Intermediate Course.* Aim: To call out good impulses and habits of right living through acquaintance with the noble characters of history; especially those of the Hebrews, Jesus himself, and missionaries.

a. First year. Old Testament biography, and a few lessons on American religious pioneers.

b. Second year. Jesus the leader of men, followed by two parallel courses—one on New Testament characters, the other on the lives of later Christian leaders, particularly Alexander Mackay, the missionary.

c. Third year. The life of Jesus, followed by a quarter's lessons on his teachings or, as a parallel course, the life of David Livingstone.

d. Fourth year. Studies in Christian living: the Bible, principles of the Christian life, and the church as the organization of the Christian life.

5. *Senior Course.*

a First year. Aim: To teach the meaning of Christian life and how the pupil may relate himself to it. Subjects: The World as a Field of Service; Social Problems of Youth; Ruth; and James.

b. Second year. Aim: To stimulate interest in the religion of the Old Testament, and to relate its lessons to present life. Subjects: The Life and Literature of the Hebrew People.

c. Third year. Aim: To awaken appreciation of the New Testament for itself and as a guide to Christian conduct. Subjects: The Beginnings of Christianity, with a Special Study of the Apostolic Church as a Brotherhood.

d. Fourth year. The Bible and social living.

Advanced Courses suitable for adults are in course of preparation.

For schools fitted to do advanced work there are admirable courses published by Scribner's—Completely Graded Series—and by the University of Chicago—Constructive Bible Studies. These include Bible study, Christian and missionary history, social duties, and the work of the modern church. They are based on the same principles of instruction, and should be examined before a choice of lesson helps is made.

If the International Uniform Lessons are used, there should be supplementary exercises or lessons in missions and social service.

II. THE YOUNG PEOPLE.

The Christian Culture Courses of the Young People's Department of the American Baptist Publication Society and the Young People's Commission of the Northern Baptist Convention are intended to give training for Christian service, and should be correlated with the work of the Sunday school.

1. *Junior Department.*

a. Bible Readers' and Sacred Literature Courses. 1914-1915. Truths for which the Baptist church stands, as illustrated in biography, followed by vacation studies.

b. Conquest Missionary Course. 1914-1915. Hero stories of Christian pioneers, followed by vacation studies.

2. *Senior Department.*

a. Bible Readers' Course. A systematic course of Bible reading.

b. Sacred Literature Course. 1914-1915. "The Church a Field of Service," by C. H. Rust.

c. Conquest Missionary Course. 1914-1915. Monthly studies in the general missionary enterprises of the denomination.

3. *Advanced Courses.*

a. Bible Readers' Course. Ancestry of the English Bible.

b. Sacred Literature Course. "Why is Christianity True?" by E. Y. Mullins, D.D., LL.D.

c. Conquest Missionary Course. History of missions.

There are also optional courses on Baptist principles and history and on practical efficiency.

III. Adults.

Most evangelical denominations and their missionary boards are now united in their plans for mission study, and there is great gain in using the program upon which they have agreed.

The material available includes programs, data for sermons, mission-study courses, stereopticon lectures, etc.

1914-1915. The Social Force of Christian Missions.

a. On foreign missions. Faunce, "The Social Aspects of Foreign Missions"; Labaree, "The Child in the Midst."

b. On home missions. Douglass, "The New Home Missions"; Bennett, "Missionary Women and the Social Question."

c. On both. Mathews, "The Individual and the Social Gospel."

Proposed subjects for:

1915-1916. The Church and the Nations.

1916-1917. The Two Americas.

1917-1918. The Missionary Force of Modern Christendom.

2. *Studies in Social Service*, for adult classes, brotherhoods, and social study groups.

The responsibilities of the Christian in the community are being considered seriously in various church organizations and in men's classes in the Sunday-school, and courses of study on the principles and methods of social service are suggested by the Social Service and Religious Education Commissions of the Northern Baptist Convention in Folder No. 3 of the Social Service Commission. Among these are: Social Ethics of the Old Testament, Social Ideals of Christ, The Modern Social Awakening, Principles of Social Service, Social Institutions, Social Duties, Social Problems, and Social Activity. Other useful courses are those published as "Studies in the Gospel of the Kingdom" by the American Institute of Social Service, New York. Valuable books for reading and study are: Sears, "Redemption of the City"; Fiske, "The Challenge of the Country"; Tupper, "Foreign-born Neighbors."

DIAGRAM

	SUNDAY-SCHOOL	YOUNG PEOPLE	ADULTS
Bible.	Graded lessons.	Bible Readers' and Sacred Literature Courses.	Organized Bible classes.
Missions.	In graded lessons or supplementary.	Conquest Missionary Courses.	United missionary courses.
Social Service.	In graded lessons or supplementary.	Studies in principles and activity.	Studies in principles and activity.

D. The Training of Teachers

There is as much reason for the thorough preparation of Sunday-school teachers as of public-school teachers, and it is the custom in the best schools to maintain a teacher-training department. A two years' course of study in *a.* The Bible as suited to the Sunday-school workers' needs;

b. The study of the pupil in the varied stages of his growing life;

c. The work and methods of the teacher;

d. The Sunday-school, and its organization and management, is specified as a minimum requirement in teacher-training by the Sunday-school Council (interdenominational), and is urged by the Educational Department of the American Baptist Publication Society, which gives a certificate on its completion.

Beyond this it is helpful if teachers will read missionary literature, the history of Christianity, and Christian ethics. Every school should own a small set of books for the use of this department, such as Athearn, "The Church School"; Faris, "The Sunday-school at Work"; McElfresh, "The Training of Sunday-school Teachers and Officers."

E. Methods of Administration

The success of a program for religious education depends much on the practical methods in use. The Northern Baptist Convention has adopted a model Standard of Efficiency for Baptist Sunday-schools, prepared by the Commission on Religious Education (Folder No 2), which is distributed free of charge by the American Baptist Publication Society. The Society gives special recognition to schools that maintain this model Standard. Among the points emphasized are:

1. *Grading and Promotion.*

Every church should have organized instruction for children, young people, and adults. In the Sunday-school classes should be arranged and courses graded so that a pupil may be promoted after suitable tests from one class to another with public recognition by means of graduation exercises. In young people's societies and adult organizations Bible study, missions and social service should each have its place, with regular courses of standard value, and when a series of courses is completed and young people have arrived at a suitable age they should graduate from their own society into an adult group.

2. *Organized Classes.*

There are advantages in organizing adult and senior classes in the Sunday-school for activities as well as study. They should have their regular officers and occasional business sessions, but remain closely affiliated with the other educational departments.

3. *Membership and Attendance.*

A regular plan should be adopted for adding new members to the educational classes and for keeping up the attendance. A cradle roll and a Home Department of the Sunday-school have proved useful devices for connecting the school and the home. Special days, such as Rally Day, Children's Day, and Promotion Day arouse interest and give recognition to special phases of the Sunday-school.

4. *Teachers' Meetings.*

These are useful for keeping up the standards, exchanging ideas, and finding ways of cooperation. They may properly include the members of the training class, and should be led by its teacher or by the superintendent or pastor.

5. *Activities.*

The aim of every Bible-school should be to train for service. Education must find expression in action. The young members of the school may be organized as Boy Scouts or Camp Fire Girls; the older young people as a community club for social welfare. Adult organizations should find ways of putting into practice the principles and information that they acquire in their periods of study. The ultimate object of all departments of the Christian church is to transform society into a kingdom of God on earth ruled by the spirit of love and helpfulness.

Text—Bulletin (Revised): *A Program of Religious Education in the Small Church.*

XXX. *THE CHURCH AND SOCIAL SERVICE*

The following is taken from the report of a Commission of the Federal Council of the Churches on the Church and Social Service.

1. *Unemployment.* We urge upon our churches that they first do the things nearest at hand; that they help their young people to their first employment, and that they watch over their early industrial experiences, to safeguard their welfare and to better them, and that they give constant attention to the unemployed in their own congregations.

2. *Housing.* The problem of housing, stated briefly, is to secure for the masses of the nation, particularly those who live in tenements, good homes for their families at reasonable rental, with sufficient sunlight, breathing-space, and pure air, and with protection against fire, disease, and vice. . . . The churches may act directly upon the problem: first, upon owners of tenements who are members of churches; secondly, upon homes which the churches are working to uplift. However, the primary matter is to secure proper legislation governing the construction of houses and tenements, to provide for thorough and constant inspection, and to see to the enforcement of house codes.

3. *Recreation.* The importance of the leisure time of the people and the function of recreation in social well-being is increasingly apparent. The universal tendency to reduce hours of labor makes it incumbent upon communities, including churches, to help people who are released from toil to a beneficial use of their leisure hours. . . . To secure wholesome and abundant recreation for all ages, to assist in coordinating the recreational agencies of a community to this end, to enlarge the churches as neighborhood centers, to attack and to aid in purging vicious commercialized recreation and vicious private organizations, is not only of extreme importance, but is also to work together with God.

4. *Commercialized Vice.* Nothing lies more clearly within the proper field of churches than the diminution of personal immorality and the cultivation of personal purity. Men, particularly young men, must be frankly and frequently told that the prime responsibility for personal impurity rests with them. . . .

It is a constant function of the churches to seek for the fallen, to succor them, and to bring them back into purity of life. But the social evil has wider implications. It is related to bad housing, unfortunate home surroundings, inadequate and unprotected public recreation, and particularly to low wages. . . An arduous work of education, involving churches, schools, Christian Associations, parents, physicians, social agencies, and public authorities, is to be developed. The church must tirelessly urge this effort upon a reluctant public, and it must endeavor to see that a human and redemptive spirit animates all that is undertaken.

5. *Prison Reform.* The nation is entering a new day in prison reform, involving honor systems, self-government, labor colonies, road-work, farm industrial prisons, employment of county-jail prisoners, separation of youth from hardened offenders, the probation system, preventive work in place of the dreadful penal system of the

past. The great significance of this reform is that it represents the application by the state of the principle of redemption to these unfortunate men and women. The churches, and the people of the churches individually, should study prison reform, should be patient during the experimental stage of the new method, and should rally everywhere to the support of the movement. Prison Sunday should be observed in some effective manner, and representatives from reformatories, farm colonies, and prison reform associations, should be brought before the brotherhoods of the churches.

Radical changes have also taken place in the methods of dealing with children who have to be brought before judges and magistrates. Churches should heartily support the establishment of children's courts and their conduct along these lines. Church-members should be made familiar with the procedure, and many of them can aid the courts as volunteer probation officers and in other ways. The churches should study the prisons and jails in their community and should insist upon the proper segregation of prisoners. They should visit all prisoners, forming personal acquaintance with them, and finding them employment on their release. Beyond all, they should study the causes of delinquency and crime, and should initiate and encourage all preventive measures.

6. *The Equal Status of Women.* No movement of modern times or of any time is greater or more vital to the welfare of society than the struggle of women the world over for freedom and for equality of opportunity and status with men.

We urge the importance of training our boys to be good husbands and fathers as carefully as girls are trained for wifehood and motherhood. The same laws of chastity are binding upon each, and the two must live together in marriage upon a basis of intelligence, mutual considerateness, and justice. We urge that the churches lend their aid to the women; that they use their utmost endeavors to protect the home and to safeguard those women, particularly those girls, who go out from it into industry; that they stand for the principles of equality of recompense where there is equal service, and for full freedom of entrance into the world's work; that they reenforce the spirit of chivalry toward women under these changed conditions.

INDUSTRIAL CONDITIONS

The task of securing Christian standards in industry must be pushed to completion by the churches and other allied forces. In particular, there is most urgent need to relieve large groups of toilers in both agriculture and industry from the physical and moral consequences of inadequate income and the exhaustion of fatigue.

1. *Overwork.* Exhaustive investigations conclusively demonstrate that overwork impairs health, intelligence, morality, and religion. . . Science has demonstrated that fatigue lowers the resistance power both of the body to disease and of the moral nature to the contagion of evil. Therefore overwork is a foe to the spiritual life, and the churches must help to destroy it.

2. *A Living Wage.* The Federal Council has declared for a living wage as a minimum in every industry. The results of the lack of a living wage must be reckoned in social terms. Low wages mean bad housing, under-nourishment, limited intellectual opportunity, and the breakdown of the family circle through forcing its members into industry. Individually the church constantly faces these starved and weakened lives. .

It is our bounden duty to declare to the industrial leaders of the nation that no urgency of industrial competition in the economic warfare that looms in sight as a consequence of the present European struggle can possibly justify the economic exploitation of the immigrant. In our strength we are the keepers of our brothers. We cannot live off their lives.

3. *Unequal Distribution of Wealth.* Out of many of the very industries that pay inadequate wages great fortunes are being built. . . . Against such injustice the Christian conscience must protest, for it means poverty, bitter struggle, loss of opportunity, and social unrest. The church must find a way to remove them. The measures that are now being used to this end are trade agreements between employers and organized workers, the minimum wage, profit-sharing, cooperative ownership and management. We urge upon the members of our churches as employers, investors, or wage-earners, to do everything that lies in their power to initiate and promote measures and movements that make for the realization of the standard of a living wage as a minimum in every industry, the highest wage that each industry can afford, and the most equitable division of the product of industry that can be devised.

4. *Industrial Disputes.* The industrial question is at bottom a question of human relations. The present industrial system, with its rapid extension of corporate ownership and management, has separated owners and employers into two groups and depersonalized their relations. The churches stand for "adequate means of conciliation and arbitration in industrial disputes." Therefore it is the duty of the churches to urge that society constitute judicial processes for violence in the settlement of industrial disputes. It is the higher duty of the church to permeate the industrial world with the spirit of conciliation and to press for the adoption of such methods of conciliation as will prevent industrial disputes from developing into industrial warfare.

5. *Industrial Democracy.* Notwithstanding the improvement in conditions of industry in the last four years, during the same period the nation has witnessed some extremely bitter and wide-spread industrial struggles. These have raised, not only the question of industrial conditions, but also the deeper issue of industrial relations.

The first method of realizing democracy in industry is through collective bargaining. This principle is agreed to in the report of the employers' section of the Federal Commission on Industrial Relations. To those employers and workers, however, who reject this method, the churches must point out that they are under moral obligation to discover some other form of collective bargaining that will make more for the good of their industry and of society at large.

The church itself is a large employer. In its capacity as employer and landlord, through its publishing interests, educational institutions, denominational boards, and other business agencies, the church has the opportunity to give a practical demonstration of Christian standards. It should lead and not merely keep pace with the best practices of modern business in matters of hours and wages, in provision for sickness and old age, in developing the principle of cooperation. .

Christian democracy applied to industry means the development of cooperative relations to the fullest possible extent. The church should therefore clearly teach the principle of the fullest possible cooperative control and ownership of industry and the natural resources upon which industry depends, in order that men may be spurred to develop the methods that shall express this principle.

When all who participate in industry shall become cooperators with each other and coworkers with God in the service of humanity, using the materials which he has provided for the common good, and not for selfish advantage, then will industry become a religious experience developing mutual service and sacrifice, the expression in economic terms of the fatherhood of God and the brotherhood of man.

6. *Stewardship of Property.* We call upon our members to interpret and apply the principle of stewardship to the whole of their incomes and property, both as to acquisition and use, and always in relation to the needs and rights of others. We insist that the stewardship of property carries with it the obligation to supervise and moralize all property, and to consecrate its use to public welfare.

Text—*Annual of the Northern Baptist Convention,* 1917. pp. 270-274.

FINIS

INDEX

723